WITHDRAWN

The Geological Society of America
Memoir 176

Basin and Range Extensional Tectonics Near the Latitude of Las Vegas, Nevada

Edited by

Brian P. Wernicke
Department of Earth and Planetary Sciences
Harvard University
Cambridge, Massachusetts 02138

1990

Published by The Geological Society of America, Inc.
3300 Penrose Place, P.O. Box 9140, Boulder, Colorado 80301

GSA Books Science Editor Richard A. Hoppin.

Printed in U.S.A.

This volume is designated Publication No. 0180 of the
International Lithosphere Program.

Library of Congress Cataloging-in-Publication Data

Basin and range extensional tectonics near the latitude of Las Vegas,
    Nevada / edited by Brian P. Wernicke.
        p.   cm. — (Memoir / Geological Society of America ; 176)
    Includes bibliographical references and index.
    ISBN 0-8137-1176-2
    1. Geology, Structural—Nevada—Las Vegas Region.   I. Wernicke,
Brian P., 1958–   .   II. Geological Society of America.
III. Series: Memoir (Geological Society of America) ; 176.
QE627.5.N3B37   1990
551.8'09793'135—dc20   90-21415
                                                                 CIP

10   9   8   7   6   5   4   3   2

Contents

Foreword

In the last decade, there has been an explosion of interest in Basin and Range extensional tectonics, due largely to the recognition that it provides a rare, well exposed view into the workings of large-magnitude intracontinental extension. Despite the large amount of work done in the province over this time, many studies remain outside of the refereed literature and are not easily accessible, particularly to those interested in the Basin and Range who do not regularly attend regional meetings. This volume is a collection of studies of extensional tectonic features of the Basin and Range province near Las Vegas, Nevada, resulting from a symposium at the 1988 Cordilleran Section Meeting of the Geological Society of America in Las Vegas.

The Basin and Range province has traditionally been divided into northern and southern parts. To the north the province is wide (700 to 800 km) and lies at an average elevation of about 2,000 m above sea level, while to the south it is narrower (350 to 500 km) and at lower average elevation, generally within about 1,000 m above sea level. The transition zone lies at about latitude 37°N, just north of Las Vegas. The Las Vegas area is particularly well suited to studying extensional tectonism because it shares the low average elevation (and hence rainfall) characteristic of the southern Basin and Range and, in addition, contains the thick miogeoclinal stratigraphy largely restricted to the north. The result is some of the most spectacular exposures of extensional structure in the world (particularly in carbonates), many of which are amenable to precise reconstruction because they involve the relatively straightforward miogeoclinal section. While similar to the rest of the province in that Cenozoic extension has been accommodated on normal fault systems, the Las Vegas area is somewhat atypical in that major synrift strike-slip faults (e.g., Garlock, Death Valley, and Las Vegas Valley fault systems) are ubiquitous.

The ordering of chapters in the volume is largely geographic, progressing from cratonic areas in the east to miogeoclinal areas in the west. The following overview of the volume reflects several groupings of topical emphasis of the chapters, which are largely independent of geography.

Severinghaus and Atwater present a provocative analysis of the kinematics and thermal state of subducting lithosphere beneath the North American plate that may have significant bearing on the cause of Basin and Range extension. They suggest that the distance a subducting slab is able to remain coherent beneath a continent (and hence influence tectonism) is strongly dependent on the age of the subducting plate, especially when the plate is young. Thus old, rapidly subducting plates (e.g., as in Laramide time) are more likely to influence tectonism in the overriding plate than young, relatively slowly subducting plates (e.g., as in Neogene time near the latitude of Las Vegas).

Chapters by Faulds and others, Duebendorfer and others, and Rowland and others address varied aspects of the highly extended region of the upper Colorado River trough, where extension is developed largely within cratonic North America east of the Cordilleran miogeocline. Faulds and others present a detailed treatment of an extensional accommodation zone. They observe that major strike-slip faults (which one might expect given the high angle between the extension direction and the accommodation zone) are absent, and that torsional flexure of individual fault blocks across the boundary seems to predominate. These kinematics are found difficult to reconcile with the concept of two oppositely dipping master detachment surfaces beneath the fault blocks of the respective domains. Duebendorfer and others document the northernmost exposure of sub-detachment, mylonitic crystalline rocks in the Colorado River trough. They suggest that the mylonites and overlying Saddle Island detachment are components of a major west-rooted detachment system that underlies much of the Lake Mead area. Rowland and others document a variety of aspects of Paleozoic and Tertiary sedimentary rocks of the nearby Frenchman Mountain structural block, and find that it was translated some 80 km west-southwest away from the Colorado Plateau in Miocene time, implying a similar magnitude of extension for the upper Colorado River trough as a whole.

Farther west in the miogeocline, east-vergent Mesozoic thrust faults are prevalent, and often are intimately associated with normal faults. Chapters by Axen and others, Bartley and Gleason, and Cemen and Wright focus on problems of identifying and distinguishing normal faults and thrusts. Axen and others studied a zone where intense normal faulting is superimposed on the frontal ramp zone of the easternmost Mesozoic thrust, and find normal faults that both reactivate and cut discordantly across pre-existing thrusts. They find that normal faulting typically results in severe, clast-rotated brecciation of rocks adjacent to the faults, while such breccias are far less common adjacent to thrust faults. Farther west in the thick miogeocline, Cemen and Wright present two examples of normal faults in the Funeral Mountains near Death Valley that reactivated Mesozoic thrust faults. Along strike of the miogeocline to the north in the Grant and Quinn Canyon ranges, Bartley and Gleason document two new thrust faults, both of which are subtly expressed owing to normal faults which have largely excised the original thrust contacts. The excision resulted in older-on-younger stratigraphic juxtaposition across faults which did not have a history of thrust offset.

Chapters by Jayko and Guth provide overviews and new geologic mapping of two adjacent areas northwest of Las Vegas which heretofore have been studied mainly in reconnaissance. They emphasize a variety of issues, including relations between thrusts and normal faults, the nature of the basal Tertiary unconformity, timing of extensional events and interactions between extensional structures and strike-slip faults.

The relations between magmatic activity and extensional tectonism are the subject of chapters by Turner and Glazner, Taylor, Coleman and Walker, and Carr. Turner and Glazner report on the structure and volcanic history of the Castle Mountains to the south of Las Vegas. Miocene magmatism in the area evolved from intermediate to bimodal then back to intermediate composition, with the bimodal magmatism coeval with normal faulting. Taylor studied a region of strongly extended Oligocene volcanic rocks in the Pahroc Range to the north of Las Vegas. She notes that while the area has had a long history of extension from at least early Oligocene to Quaternary time, the most voluminous magmatism in the area occurred at a time of relative tectonic quiescence. Coleman and Walker present a detailed petrographic and isotopic study of Miocene–Pliocene volcanic rocks from the Death Valley region, which were erupted during major extensional tectonism from sources just west of the locus of extension. Volcanism progressed from entirely basaltic in the early stages of magmatism to basalt-andesite-rhyolite later on. They present evidence for extensive contamination of magmas, probably by the lower crustal material. Carr synthesizes geological and geophysical evidence in the Nevada Test Site area, concluding that major middle Miocene silicic magmatism occurred in an extensional pull-apart zone corresponding to a right-step in the northwest-trending Walker Lane belt.

Carr's synthesis of the Nevada Test Site and environs is complemented by Scott's analysis of the tectonic setting of the Yucca Mountain area, a proposed site for a civilian high-level radioactive waste repository lying just west of the Test Site. Scott's conclusions differ in detail from those of Carr, placing less emphasis on a genetic link between extensional structures and magmatic activity.

Chapters by Michel-Noël and others, Spencer, Serpa, Labotka, Hodges and others, and McKenna and Hodges use a broad range of techniques to address problems of structural styles and mechanisms of normal faulting, at a variety of scales. In an area of synvolcanic extensional tectonism northwest of Las Vegas near Caliente, Nevada, Michel-Noël and others studied slip directions of numerous faults at a variety of scales. The older event of Miocene age was the more intense of the two, with a southeasterly extension direction. The younger event, occurring less than 10 Ma ago (largely reactivating faults of the older event) was directed WNW, suggesting a clockwise rotation of the extension direction through time as documented elsewhere in the Basin and Range. Spencer investigates the geology of the Avawatz Mountains near the southern terminus of Death Valley, concluding that Miocene extension in the area was followed by roughly orthogonal compressional tectonism of Plio–Quaternary age, apparently the product of the intersection of the conjugate Garlock and southern Death Valley fault zones. Using deep seismic reflection images, Serpa contrasts the reflective character of the upper crust in the Mojave Desert area with that of the Death Valley region. She finds that throughgoing, low-angle reflections are common in the upper crust in the Mojave, but that in the Death Valley region upper crustal reflections are moderately to steeply dipping. While both areas contain highly reflective deep crust, a band of particularly bright reflections rises from Moho depths beneath the Mojave to mid-crustal depths beneath Death Valley, apparently defining the top of a deep-crustal dome, inferred to be related to magmatic processes.

Labotka combines thematic mapper imagery and detailed mapping to analyze the unroofing history of the Panamint Range west of Death Valley, focusing on relationships between emplacement of major breccia sheets and faulting and uplift. Hodges and others and McKenna and Hodges describe the unroofing history of the same range based on mapping a transect just north of the area studied by Labotka, documenting the multistage evolution of a system of normal faults, the younger of which served as the lower boundary to an upper Miocene growth fault basin.

Relations between sedimentation, regional stratigraphy and extensional tectonism are emphasized in chapters by Snow and White, Stewart and Diamond, and Marzolf. Snow and White use the details of stratigraphic pinchouts and local facies relations in synrift deposits to constrain the rotation history of a major rollover structure in the northernmost Panamint Range, apparently related to motion on the younger of the fault systems studied by Hodges and others. Stewart and Diamond analyze depositional patterns in a Miocene basin in the Walker Lane belt, which appears to be unrelated to fault systems responsible for the current configuration of basins and ranges in the area. They conclude that the shifting patterns of deposition indicate a reorganization of tectonic controls on sedimentation in latest or post-Miocene time. Marzolf analyzes regional patterns of early Mesozoic sedimentation to provide a template for Cenozoic extension and to better understand processes responsible for the Mesozoic basins.

I would like to acknowledge the fine efforts on the part of both authors and reviewers in bringing this volume to fruition in a relatively short time. Thanks go to Dick Hoppin, G.S.A. books editor, and to Lee Gladish and the editorial staff at G.S.A. for their help in ensuring high standards of presentation, which is especially difficult for volumes with a large number of oversized figures. Most importantly, I thank Carolyn White for her tireless efforts in the time-consuming task of managing the manuscript flow and correspondence with authors and reviewers.

This Memoir is designated Publication No. 0180 of the International Lithosphere Program, under the auspices of Working Group 3, Intraplate Phenomena, of the Interunion Commission on the Lithosphere.

Brian Wernicke

Dedication

This volume honors two great pioneers in continental extensional tectonics, Lauren A. Wright and Bennie W. Troxel. Their work was instrumental in the recognition of shallowly-dipping normal faults as fundamental to extensional tectonism, a recognition which began with a handful of detailed mapping projects conducted in well-exposed areas of the Basin and Range in the 1960s and early 1970s. These little-recognized studies foreshadowed an explosion of research over the past decade in continental extensional tectonism which has had profound influence on concepts of continental dynamics, on par with the discovery of large-scale overthrusts in western Europe more than a century ago. Wright and Troxel's mapping in one of these areas, encompassing the type area of the Amargosa chaos in the southern Death Valley region, stands out as one of the earliest studies documenting the existence of low-angle normal faults and ascribing their origin to the accommodation of crustal extension.

The spectacularly exposed chaos was so named by Levi F. Noble because of its unusual structural complexity, consisting of an intricate mosaic of brittlely deformed lenses of rock bounded by low-angle faults. Owing to inadequate topographic base maps and an incomplete knowledge of the stratigraphic succession, Noble was only able to describe the chaos in reconnaissance in his classic paper published in the Geological Society of America *Bulletin* in 1941. At his urging, Wright and Troxel began systematic stratigraphic and structural work in the chaos. With newly refined stratigraphy and field mapping at 1:10,000 scale, they documented that nearly all of the faults in the chaos were normal (many of them plainly listric), that a number of them cut deeply into the crystalline basement, and that the largest block in the chaos was an intact, rotated normal fault block with the chaotic deformation developed mainly on its underside. These observations were difficult to reconcile with an origin by gravity gliding or overthrust faulting, as earlier proposed by a number of writers based on Noble's descriptions. Rather, Wright and Troxel proposed that the chaos represented the downward coalescence of a system of closely spaced, listric normal faults that accommodated regional crustal extension in late Cenozoic time, perhaps representing an example of the eroded roots of Basin and Range structure. This was a controversial interpretation when proposed

Bennie W. Troxel and Lauren A. Wright

in the late 1960s, as it conflicted with nearly a century of doctrine on the origin of Basin and Range structure. Today, this explanation for the chaos is widely accepted, and represents a class of models routinely applied to normal fault systems worldwide.

The contributions of Wright and Troxel are by no means limited to the decoding of the chaos. They established the stratigraphy and depositional environments of the Proterozoic Pahrump Group and overlying strata in the Death Valley region, which was crucial to deciphering the chaos, and a major contribution to understanding Proterozoic sedimentation and tectonics in the Cordillera. They recognized the extensional origin of the Death Valley turtleback surfaces, publishing a diagram in 1974 representative of numerous sections drawn five to ten years later depicting the evolution of Cordilleran metamorphic core complexes. Wright's interpretation of the abundance of strike-slip faults in addition to normal faults at the latitude of Las Vegas as indicative of a constrictional stress state was well ahead of its time.

Painstaking mapping in the Funeral Mountains, working out the volcanic stratigraphy of the central Death Valley volcanic field, and the recognition of the eastward migration of major normal faulting across the Death Valley region, are among their more recent contributions that have inspired the rush of activity by geologists now working in the region, many of whom are contributors to this volume.

It is the rare geologist who can lay claim to having made fundamental contributions to a field of such broad significance so far ahead of the pack. Still rarer is the subset of those dedicated to teaching. Perhaps Wright and Troxel's most important contribution is the example, both personal and professional, they have set for a generation of students and professionals working in the Death Valley region. Their openness with unpublished data, emphasis on observation, extraordinary knowledge of the geology of the region and infectious collegiality have set high scientific and ethical standards for those who follow them. More inspiring still, they have parlayed their "retirement" into a full-time assault on problems of Death Valley geology, challenging the minds (and legs) of scores of geologists who have followed in their path. They are valued critics whose leadership and example ensure many decades of discoveries in Basin and Range geology, many of which we have yet to even dream about.

PARTIAL BIBLIOGRAPHY OF LAUREN A. WRIGHT AND BENNIE W. TROXEL

Noble, L. F., and Wright, L. A., 1954, Geology of the central and southern Death Valley region, California, *in* Jahns, R. H., ed., Geology of southern California: California Division of Mines Bulletin 170, Chapter II, p. 143–160.

Wright, L. A., and Troxel, B. W., 1966, Strata of late Precambrian–Cambrian age, Death Valley region, California–Nevada: American Association of Petroleum Geologists Bulletin, v. 50, p. 846–857.

Hill, M. L., and Troxel, B. W., 1966, Tectonics of the Death Valley region, California: Geological Society of America Bulletin, v. 77, p. 435–438.

Wright, L. A., and Troxel, B. W., 1967, Limitations on right-lateral, strike-slip displacement, Death Valley and Furnace Creek fault zone, California: Geological Society of America Bulletin, v. 78, p. 933–950.

Troxel, B. W., 1967, Sedimentary rocks of late Precambrian and Cambrian age in the southern Salt Spring Hills, southeastern Death Valley, California: California Division of Mines and Geology Special Report 92, p. 33–41.

Wright, L. A., 1968, Talc deposits of the southern Death Valley–Kingston Range region, California: California Division of Mines and Geology Special Report 95, 79 p.

Wright, L. A., and Troxel, B. W., 1969, Chaos structure and Basin and Range normal faults; Evidence for a genetic relationship: Geological Society of America Abstracts with Programs for 1969, Part 7, p. 242.

Wright, L. A. and Troxel, B. W., 1973, Shallow fault interpretation of Basin and Range structure, southwestern Great Basin, *in* de Jong, K. A. and Scholten, R., eds., Gravity and tectonics: John Wiley and Sons, New York, p. 397–407.

Wright, L. A., Otton, J. K., and Troxel, B. W., 1974, Turtleback surfaces of Death Valley viewed as phenomena of extensional tectonics: Geology, v. 2, p. 53–54.

Wright, L. A., 1974, Geology of the southeast quarter of the Tecopa quadrangle, Inyo County, California: California Division of Mines and Geology Map Sheet 20 (1:24,000).

Troxel, B. W., 1974, Geologic guide to the Death Valley region, California and Nevada, *in* Guidebook, Death Valley region, California and Nevada: Death Valley Publishing Company, Shoshone, California, p. 2–16.

Wright, L. A., Troxel, B. W., Williams, E. G., Roberts, M. T., and Diehl, P. E., 1976, Precambrian sedimentary environments of the Death Valley region, eastern California: California Division of Mines and Geology Special Report 106, p. 7–15.

Wright, L. A., 1976, Late Cenozoic fault patterns and stress fields in the Great Basin and westward displacement of the Sierra Nevada block: Geology, v. 4, p. 489–494.

Wright, L. A., Troxel, B. W., Burchfiel, B. C., Chapman, R., and Labotka, T. C., 1981, Geologic cross section from the Sierra Nevada to the Las Vegas Valley, eastern California to southern Nevada: Geological Society of America Map and Chart Series MC-28M (1:250,000).

Wright, L. A., and Troxel, B. W., 1984, Geology of the northern half of the Confidence Hills 15′ quadrangle, Death Valley region, eastern California: The area of the Amargosa chaos: California Division of Mines and Geology Map Sheet 34 (1:24,000).

Wright, L. A., Drake, R. E. and Troxel, B. W., 1984, Evidence for the westward migration of severe Cenozoic extension, southeastern Great Basin, California: Geological Society of America Abstracts with Programs, v. 16, p. 701.

Troxel, B. W., and Wright, L.A., 1987, Tertiary extensional features, Death Valley region, eastern California, *in* Hill, M. L., ed., Decade of North American geology centennial field guide, Volume 1: Geological Society of America, Boulder, p. 121–132.

Troxel, B. W., and Wright, L. A., 1989, Geological map of the central and northern Funeral Mountains and adjacent areas, Death Valley region, southern California: U.S. Geological Survey Open File Report 89–348 (1:48,000).

Geological Society of America
Memoir 176
1990

Chapter 1

Cenozoic geometry and thermal state of the subducting slabs beneath western North America

Jeff Severinghaus and Tanya Atwater
Department of Geological Sciences, University of California, Santa Barbara, California 93106

ABSTRACT

We have reconstructed the isochron pattern of the Farallon and Vancouver plates in order to predict the thermal state and geometry of subducting slabs beneath western North America during the Cenozoic. Slabs do not last indefinitely; they warm up by conduction when bathed in the asthenosphere. As they warm up, they lose the ability to have earthquakes. Studies of modern subduction zones show that slabs become aseismic after a duration approximately equal to one-tenth their age upon subduction. Combined with a mathematical heat conduction model, these studies give us confidence that the thermal state of a slab can be characterized if we know the time since subduction and the age upon subduction. We reconstruct isochrons on subducted plates using the magnetic anomalies recorded in the Pacific plate, assuming symmetrical spreading and taking into account propagating rifts. Using the improved global plate reconstructions of Stock and Molnar (1988), we position the reconstructed plates with respect to North America to obtain maps of time since subduction and age upon subduction. The result is a series of maps of the slab geometry and approximate thermal condition at six times during the Cenozoic. With these maps we examine postulated relations between the presence and condition of the underlying slab and the occurrence of volcanism and tectonism in the overlying plate. We find that the very long flat slab proposed to have caused the Laramide Orogeny could have easily reached Colorado because of its fast average subduction rate and moderate age upon subduction, and because of the tendency for shallowly dipping slabs to last longer because they heat up more gradually while passing beneath the overriding plate. We find that the eastern edge of the proposed late Cenozoic "slab window" never existed, because of the young age of the slab. Instead, a region of effectively no slab gradually developed as early as 35 Ma, and it was farther inland than the proposed "slab window." Lacking an eastern edge, the "slab window" is better described as a "slab gap." The southern boundary of the gap is diffuse, and its location is poorly constrained, whereas the northern edge is sharp and has clear, predictable geologic manifestations.

INTRODUCTION

Subduction has dominated the Mesozoic and Cenozoic geologic history of the western United States. During much of Jurassic and Cretaceous time, geologic manifestations (e.g., Franciscan formation, Sierra Nevada batholiths, Sevier thrust belt) suggest that subduction was occurring in a rather typical steep, fast subduction zone. By contrast, the geologic records of subduction from late Cretaceous and Cenozoic times suggest some relatively unusual events, as follows. Starting in the late Cretaceous, the cessation of the Sierran magmatic belt and the occurrence, far inland, of magmatism and the Laramide Orogeny have been attributed to a shallowly dipping slab (e.g., Coney and Reynolds, 1977; Cross, 1986; Bird, 1984, 1988). A Cenozoic westward

Severinghaus, J., and Atwater, T., 1990, Cenozoic geometry and thermal state of the subducting slabs beneath western North America, *in* Wernicke, B. P., ed., Basin and Range extensional tectonics near the latitude of Las Vegas, Nevada: Boulder, Colorado, Geological Society of America Memoir 176.

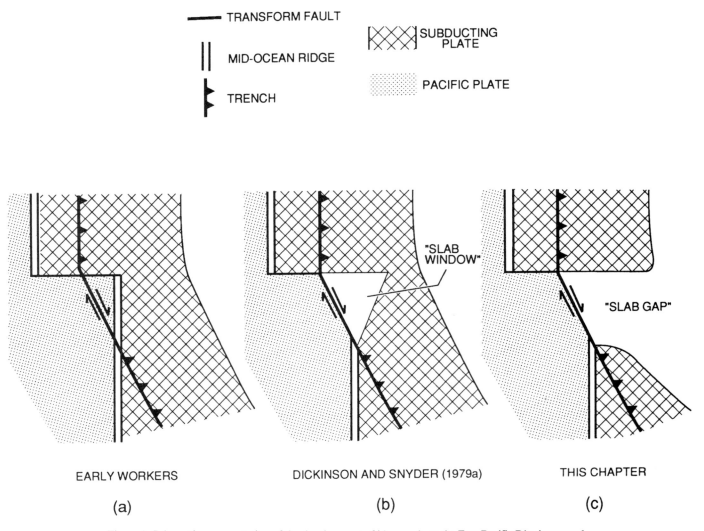

Figure 1. Schematic representation of the development of ideas on how the East Pacific Rise interacted with North America.

migration of arc magmatism seen at some latitudes has been attributed to the resteepening or disintegration of this postulated flat slab (e.g., Coney and Reynolds, 1977; Cross and Pilger, 1978).

Starting in the mid Cenozoic, the time-transgressive cessation of arc magmatism has been attributed to the replacement of the subduction system by the San Andreas boundary (e.g., Atwater, 1970; Dickinson and Snyder, 1979b). The exceptionally low seismicity and short slab length of the present-day Cascadia subduction zone has been attributed to the unusual youth of the subducting slab and the slow subduction rate (e.g., Sugi and Uyeda, 1984). All of these events and many more can be related at least partially to the slabs that were being subducted beneath North America. Thus, we undertook a project to map the geometries and thermal states of these slabs for a number of Cenozoic time steps. In this paper we present the resulting maps and discuss their implications and uncertainties.

Our primary interest concerned the mid- to late Cenozoic

transition in regimes, during which the subduction system was gradually replaced by the San Andreas boundary. This occurred as the East Pacific Rise encountered the trench at the margin of North America (e.g., Atwater, 1970, 1989). The nature and geometry of this transition and its imprint on the geologic record have been the subject of a number of studies and speculations.

Some early workers supposed that the East Pacific Rise merely slipped beneath the North American plate, maintaining its precollision geometry and continuing to spread unabated as it had under the ocean (Fig. 1a). This idea is incompatible with our modern understanding of oceanic spreading systems, which except in the vicinity of hot spots, are basically passive features where asthenosphere fills in the space between diverging lithospheric plates and cools to form new lithosphere. The creation and growth of the cold oceanic lithosphere from the hot asthenosphere depends critically on the efficient removal of heat by cold seawater. If plates diverge beneath the thermal blanket of a continental plate rather than beneath seawater, the asthenosphere filling the space will cool only extremely slowly so that no additional lithosphere will be accreted to the slabs and no coherent spreading center can be maintained.

Dickinson and Snyder (1979a) pointed out this effect and postulated that a triangular slab-free region, a "slab window," developed and grew beneath the rim of North America during the late Cenozoic (Fig. 1b). They constructed the approximate geometry of such a window for several time steps. Numerous geologic events have been attributed to the development of this slab-free region, including the cessation of arc volcanism, the evolution of the San Andreas system and its related basins, the onset of major Basin and Range extension, and the regional uplift of the Sierra Nevada and Colorado plateau (e.g., Crough and Thompson, 1977; Dickinson and Snyder, 1979a; Glazner and Supplee, 1982). Thus, the timing, geometry and nature of the slab-free region is of considerable interest to the geological community.

In this chapter, we modify and enlarge upon the slab window concept. In particular, we question the implicit assumption made by Dickinson and Snyder (1979a) that lithosphere, once formed on the sea floor, acts indefinitely as a coherent, strong slab. We assert, rather, that the duration of a slab after subduction depends critically on its age when it entered the subduction zone. In particular, young lithosphere is thin and hot, so that after subduction it will heat up and equilibrate with the asthenosphere rather quickly. In the case of the postulated slab window, the slab that would have formed its eastern edge was very young, hot, and weak when it was subducted and so would not have persisted as a coherent slab for any length of time. Indeed, it appears that this portion of the slab was fragmented before the ridge even arrived at the trench, i.e., before the window even began to form. Therefore, we conclude that a "slab gap" developed (Fig. 1c), rather than a slab window, and that it appeared earlier and farther inland than the postulated window. By a slab gap we mean a region of no slab, bordered on the north and south by coherent slabs.

Two distinct lines of evidence lead us to this conclusion. First, we present evidence from the sea-floor spreading record that the slab has been broken in this region since the early Cenozoic and that it further fragmented into several small pieces as the ridge approached the trench. The sea-floor spreading record also indicates that the larger plates to the north and south acted independently, showing that their connection had been broken. Second, we use a combination of heat conduction theory, slab seismicity observations, and plate reconstructions to model and map the thermal condition of the slabs.

Our maps of the thermal states of the slabs also contain information of interest for discussions of the Laramide flat slab scenario. Our simple thermal models show that the early Cenozoic slab was much longer and cooler than those for later times. Because of this, we conclude that the slab could have easily reached Colorado during Laramide time, contrary to the opinions of some workers that the slab would have been too hot and weak (e.g., Molnar and others, 1979). We also examine the Paleogene

transition from a long, cool slab to a short, warm one as it may relate to the end of the Laramide.

We present this study in this volume to provide a larger plate tectonic context for the more local events described. Of course, we also suspect that many tectonic events of hill and mountain-range scale may ultimately be ascribed to specific plate tectonic events. Broad regions of plate interiors are primarily affected by subduction and slab-related plate events such as those examined here. In particular, the mid-Cenozoic geologic record in the region including southern Nevada and Utah, Arizona, and southeastern California should record the warming and shortening (and steepening or disintegration?) of the slab and the arrival and passage of the Mendocino slab gap edge. Although the uncertainties in the plate locations and in the continental deformation reconstructions are still too great to allow specific correlations between plate motion events and local geologic events, this study is a step in that direction.

OBSERVATIONS FROM THE SEA-FLOOR SPREADING RECORD

We made a new compilation and interpretation of the magnetic anomaly data in the North Pacific (Atwater and Severinghaus, 1989). Figure 2 shows selected isochrons from the northeast Pacific portion of these maps. These isochron patterns include three distinct indications that the subducting Farallon plate was broken throughout much of the Cenozoic.

Magnetic isochrons formed during late Cretaceous and earliest Cenozoic time are consistent with the existence of one huge, rigid Farallon plate moving to the east-northeast with respect to the Pacific plate (Rosa and Molnar, 1988). As the East Pacific Rise approached the Americas, this plate slowly narrowed, and a narrow neck developed south of the Mendocino and Pioneer fracture zones. At about 55 Ma (chron 24), the relative motion direction of the plate segment north of this neck changed to east while the segment to the south continued moving to the east-northeast with respect to the Pacific plate. Menard (1978) noted this change and named the new northern plate the Vancouver plate. Rosa and Molnar (1988) found poles of rotation for the Vancouver and Farallon plates relative to the Pacific plate, showing that these plates were indeed moving as separate bodies and that they were converging upon one another at a slow rate.

Atwater and Severinghaus (1987) and Atwater (unpublished) show that the boundary between the two plates lay midway between the Pioneer and Murray fracture zones after 45 Ma. The trace of the Pacific-Vancouver-Farallon triple junction can be seen on Figure 2 as a curving, toothlike pattern of offsets in the 45 to 30 Ma isochrons (anomalies 19–10) near 37°N, between the Pioneer and Murray fracture zones. This zigzag trace indicates that the triple junction migrated north and south many times, requiring the boundary between the Farallon and Vancouver plates to also move, which would suggest that these subducting plates were broadly sheared in the vicinity of their common plate boundary. For the purposes of this chapter, these data show that

sheared and buckled lithosphere was being delivered to the subduction zone in the slab gap region long before the gap appeared.

The fragmentation of the subducting plates became more
severe abruptly at 30 Ma, halfway through anomaly 10. This
change is documented by the magnetic anomaly data offshore of
San Francisco, presented in Figure 3a. Our isochron interpretation, shown in Figure 3b, is modified after Lonsdale (1990). A
sudden change from fast, eastward motion to slow, southeastward
motion away from the Pacific plate is documented by the northeast trend and close spacing of the anomalies younger than 10.

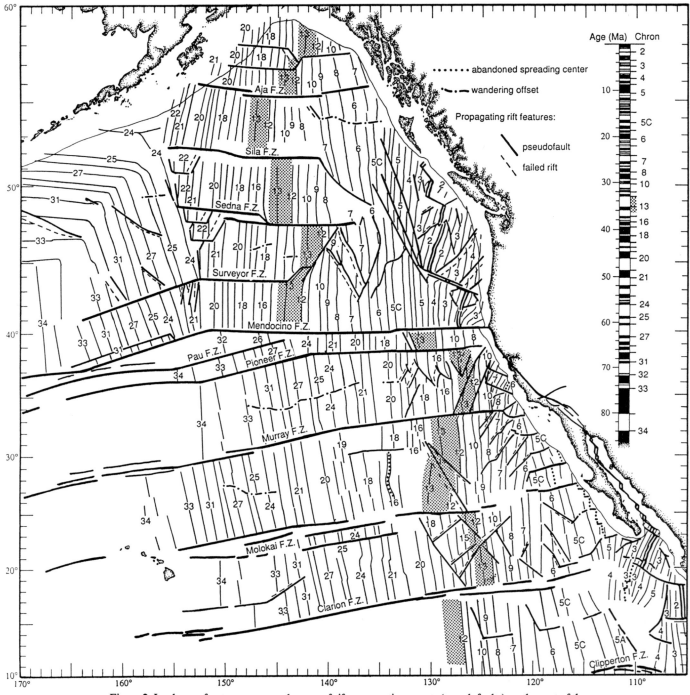

Figure 2. Isochrons, fracture zones, and traces of rift propagation events (pseudofaults) on the part of the
Pacific plate used to reconstruct the Farallon and Vancouver plates, from Atwater and Severinghaus
(1989). Sea floor formed at around 35 Ma has been shaded to demonstrate the early Cenozoic shape of
the East Pacific rise. Magnetic chron numbers are labeled. They can be translated to dates (Ma) using the
time scale shown, from Berggren and others (1985). The complete digital data set used in this study is
presented in Appendix II.

The rates and directions indicate that two small plates, here called the Monterey and Arguello plates, broke free of the fast-subducting Farallon plate to the south. We note in passing that the small Monterey and Arguello plates are highly analogous to the modern situation near Vancouver Island where the Explorer plate has broken free of the Juan de Fuca plate and slowed in the last 4 m.y. (Hyndman and others, 1979).

About 19 Ma, just after anomaly 6, Pacific-Monterey spreading is interpreted to have ceased altogether, the last remnant of the Monterey plate being incorporated into the Pacific plate (Lonsdale, 1990). The defunct ridge crest is marked by dotted lines in Figures 2 and 3b near 35.5°N. It never even reached the subduction zone.

In contrast to the plate segments between the Pioneer and Murray fracture zones, the segment north of the Pioneer fracture zone did not slow as it approached the trench. Rather, this segment continued to move with the Vancouver plate away from the Pacific plate at about 120 mm/yr whole rate (Fig. 3b). It would appear that this narrow slice of young slab was firmly attached across the Mendocino fracture zone to the fast-moving plate to the north. It is the only segment that would have had the potential to develop a "slab window" with even a short-lived eastern edge,

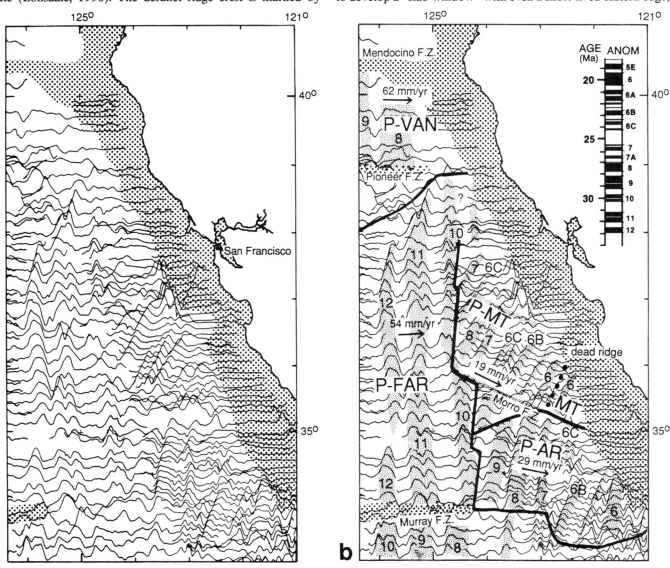

Figure 3. (a) Magnetic anomaly profiles offshore of San Francisco after Atwater and Severinghaus (1987). Systematic survey from Theberge (1971). (b) Isochron interpretation of magnetic anomalies in (a). Heavy lines delineate areas of the Pacific plate sea floor that were created by spreading between various plate pairs: P-VAN = Pacific-Vancouver spreading, P-FAR = Pacific-Farallon spreading, P-MT = Pacific-Monterey spreading, P-AR = Pacific-Arguello spreading. The Vancouver, Farallon, and Arguello plates have been entirely subducted in this area. A small fragment of the Monterey plate (MT) remains embedded in the Pacific plate southeast of the dotted line marked "dead ridge." Half-spreading rates and directions are shown by arrows. Changes in rates and trends at chron 10 (30 Ma) indicate that the slab fragmented at this time. Time scale is from Berggren and others (1985).

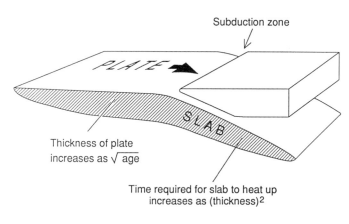

Thickness of plate
increases as √age

Time required for slab to heat up
increases as (thickness)²

. Slab warming time should be directly
.. proportional to slab age upon entry

Figure 4. Results of simple heat conduction theory. Ocean floor lithosphere cools and thickens away from the mid-ocean ridge as a function of the square root of its age (Parker and Oldenburg, 1973). Subducting oceanic lithospheric warms and thins in a time proportional to its thickness squared (McKenzie, 1969, 1970). Therefore, the warming time of the slab is proportional to its age when it is subducted (see also Appendix I and Molnar and others, 1979).

since only this segment remained coherent right up to the ridge-trench encounter. This sector sharply contrasts with the one immediately to the south, in which the slab came to pieces and spreading slowed long before the ridge-trench encounter.

A third observation demonstrating the lack of coherence of the slab to the east of the window comes from descriptions of the motions of the major plates since 30 Ma. We noted above that the northern (Vancouver) and southern (Farallon) plates moved somewhat differently starting about 55 Ma, but this difference was small and their spreading directions were quite steady. Starting about 30 Ma, the Vancouver plate became quite erratic in its motions, spreading away from the Pacific about highly variable poles both to the north and south of the plate (Wilson, 1988). It is as though this plate were finally cut adrift from the larger system. The reaction of the spreading systems to this variable plate motion can be seen in the many propagating rifts that appear in the isochrons in Figure 2 starting about 30 Ma (anomaly 10).

The southern (Farallon) plate also became more erratic in its motions coming forward in time, although this is surely due in part to the Cocos-Nazca breakup at about 25 Ma and to later fragmentation of a number of additional pieces as the plate narrowed. In our slab reconstructions, we found that if we assumed that slabs remained intact indefinitely, this pivoting would require a large overlap of the two slabs and rapid sideways movement of slab through the mantle. The observed pivoting reinforces our conviction that slabs have finite lives and, in particular, that these post–30 Ma slabs did not extend far inland because of their youth.

Starting about 14 Ma, the portion of the subducting plate off Baja California broke free of the larger plate to the south and

changed direction and rate, then apparently stopped spreading about 12.5 Ma (Lonsdale, 1990). Again, the spreading center stalled before it reached the subduction zone. This pattern of ridges stalling before they reach the subduction zone leads us to believe that very young, hot slabs resist subduction, due to their lack of negative buoyancy.

DESCRIBING THE THERMAL STATE OF A SLAB: THE PARAMETER *S*

Our goal is to map the approximate geometry and extent of the subducting slabs beneath North America during the Cenozoic. To do this we must devise some method to locate the point at which a slab becomes so warm that it no longer acts as a coherent body or, alternatively, the point at which it becomes incapable of inducing tectonism and volcanism in the overriding plate. In this section we define a parameter S to serve as a measure of the thermal state of a subducting slab, and we relate it to thermal models and observational data for modern slabs. We then attempt to find the value of S that corresponds to the point where, for practical purposes, the slab assimilates with the asthenosphere. Unfortunately, the latter assignment has proven to be extremely difficult. We will conclude that the assimilation point is probably about $S = 3$ or 5, but it could be as much as $S = 10$ for medium and short slabs. Fortunately, the changes in the conditions of the slabs caused by the approach of the East Pacific rise to North America are so dramatic that the implications for slab geometry are very similar no matter which of these values of S one chooses.

Mathematical models have been constructed to describe the thermal states of lithospheric plates from their creation at spreading centers to their destruction in subduction zones. As they move away from spreading centers, they cool and their thickness increases at a rate proportional to the square root of age (Parker and Oldenburg, 1973). After subduction into the asthenosphere, they heat up as the square of their thickness upon subduction (McKenzie, 1969, 1970). When these two results are combined, they predict that the time required for a slab to warm up after being subducted is approximately proportional to its age upon subduction (Molnar and others, 1979). These relations are illustrated schematically in Figure 4, and the relevant mathematical formulation and results are presented in Appendix I.

A second way to examine the thermal state of subducting slabs—an observational method—is to examine the distribution of earthquakes occurring within their cores. The dipping planes of earthquakes at most modern subduction zones are seen to have a definite lower bound, called the "seismic cutoff." The ability to store the stress required to trigger earthquakes reflects the strength of the slab, which in turn is primarily a function of its temperature (Chen and Molnar, 1983). Thus, the position of the seismic cutoff is one observable measure of the thermal state of modern subducting slabs. Molnar and others (1979) made a compilation of the lengths of seismic slabs in modern subduction zones and showed that the time required for the slabs to become aseismic is proportional to their age upon subduction, in agreement with the mathematical models, and that it is approximately equal to one-tenth their age upon subduction (Fig. 5a). In a similar study, Jarrard (1986) confirmed the linearity of the relation, although he found a somewhat greater slope, as much as 15 rather than 10, depending on various assumptions (Fig. 5b). We adopt 10 for the sake of computational simplicity.

Following these theoretical and empirical relationships, we define the parameter S. At each point on the slab, S equals the time since subduction divided by one-tenth of the age of that point at the time it was subducted. We thus arbitrarily set $S = 1$ at the seismic cutoff (it would be about $S = 0.7$ if the regression preferred by Jarrard were adopted). We then map contours of the values of S for various times in the past, given the age upon entry and the time since entry, both of which we obtain from plate reconstructions. The equation we use in our calculations is

$$S = \frac{10T}{(A-T-C)} \tag{1}$$

where A is the age of the magnetic anomaly (DNAG timescale; Berggren and others, 1985; Kent and Gradstein, 1985), T is the time since subduction, and C is the age of the particular map being constructed.

A weakness in McKenzie's (1969, 1970) mathematical description of the slab is the assumption that the top of the subducting slab is always immersed in hot asthenosphere. In fact, the tops of the slabs spend a time beneath the relatively cool overriding plate before they enter the asthenosphere. Thus, the warming of the slab will be slower at first than predicted (Jarrard, 1986), and a lag will be introduced. This lag time will be variable, depending on the dip of the slab, the amount of frictional heating generated between the plates, and the thermal structure of the overriding plate. In the observational data, the lag time manifests itself as a nonzero intercept in the correlations of Jarrard (1986) (Fig. 5b) and causes slabs with shallow dips to appear above the line in the correlation of Molnar and others (1979) (Fig. 5a).

We approximate the lag by adding 200 km to the lengths of all slabs. We chose this as an average of estimates of the lag, which range from the intercept of 303 km in Jarrard's (1986) regression (Fig. 5b) to an intercept of 100 to 150 km suggested by Figure 11 in Sugi and Uyeda (1984). The latter is a recompilation of the data of Molnar and others (1979) with a reexamination of the shortest slabs. The uncertainty introduced by this lag correction (about ±100 km) is probably not greater than the other uncertainties except in the case of the early Cenozoic, when the slab is thought to have been flat and in contact with the overriding plate as far east as the Rockies (Coney and Reynolds, 1977). In this case, 200 km is certainly an underestimate of the lag effect and, as a result, all the S values in Figure 8, below, are too high.

We note that McKenzie's (1969, 1970) mathematical formulation of slab heating used here is quite simple. A number of more complete and complex mathematical models have been developed, but we feel that these refinements would add complexity without improving our results. Most of the refinements to the mathematical formulation concern interactions with the overriding plate or the effects of phase changes, and both of these

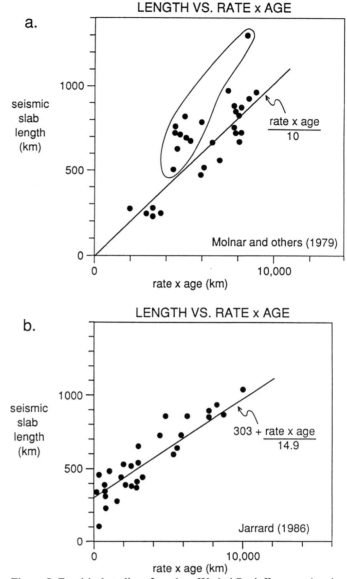

Figure 5. Empirical studies of modern Wadati-Benioff zones, showing relations among seismic slab length, subduction rate, and age on entry. (a) Plot of down-dip length of modern seismic zones versus convergence rate times age of the subducting lithosphere at the trench, from Molnar and others (1979). Slabs with dip less than 30° are circled. The tendency for these low-dip slabs to be several hundred kilometers longer than predicted (i.e., to lie above the line) can be explained if slabs warm up more slowly while passing beneath the overriding lithosphere. (b) Same relation with some new data and slightly different methods: Age is an estimate of the slab age at the seismic cutoff extrapolated from the age gradient near the trench, and back-arc spreading is not included in convergence rates, from Jarrard (1986). Line is the author's preferred regression of selected points.

groups of effects are quite sensitive to slab dip. Our ignorance of slab paleodip and also our present inability to choose the proper S value within a factor of two, as described next, render such refinements unrealistic.

HOW LONG DO SLABS LAST AFTER BEING SUBDUCTED?

Our interest in this chapter is to map the ancient extent of coherent subducting slabs beneath North America. We emphasize that the seismic cutoff, $S = 1$, is merely one measure of the thermal state of the slab and that the slab certainly can last beyond that point. Unfortunately, how much farther a slab persists beyond the seismic cutoff is not well known, even for present-day subduction zones.

Slab duration can be conceptualized in several different ways; it can be a measure of (1) how long slabs remain capable of inducing arc volcanism and tectonism, (2) how long they are detectable as a mantle seismic velocity anomaly (high velocity suggests the presence of cold material), or (3) how long they last as a coherent body before they disaggregate. Although the first question is the most interesting from a geological standpoint, the latter two are more approachable. We examine the latter two questions and presume that slabs will become incapable of inducing tectonism and volcanism well before they disaggregate or become seismically undetectable.

Modern old, cold lithosphere subducting at fast rates often extends as a seismic slab to a length of 1,000 km or more and a depth of nearly 680 km in the earth. Seismic velocity anomalies are reported beneath some of these slabs, extending a few hundred kilometers farther down (Creager and Jordan, 1986). These anomalous regions can be interpreted to be the aseismic extensions of the slabs into the lower mantle and, as such, would suggest that the slab is still present and detectable to perhaps $S = 1.5$. However, these long, deep slabs may not be relevant to our study since they encounter the 680-km discontinuity, a horizon in the mantle believed to represent a large increase in viscosity (Hager, 1986) and hence a profound impediment to the passage of slabs, if they pass through at all.

More relevant modern examples are those subduction zones with slower rates and/or younger lithosphere. Relatively well-studied examples are the medium- and short-length slabs at the Aleutian and Cascadia subduction zones, respectively. Analysis of seismic P and PcP wave velocity anomalies beneath the Aleutian arc indicates that the slab extends at least down to 600 km depth, with some indications that it may continue to 1,000 km (Boyd and Creager, 1987, and personal communication, 1988). The seismic cutoff occurs here at about 250 to 300 km, so we conclude that the slab still exists and is detectable as a velocity anomaly to about $S = 3$ to 5.

The Cascadia subduction zone is the best studied example of a modern short slab, but unfortunately, it presents some important difficulties that limit its usefulness to our study. The subducting lithosphere is young and the subduction rate is slow, so that the calculated S contours occur relatively near to the trench, predicting a short slab. However, in this case, the lag in heating during contact with the overriding plate introduces a very large uncertainty, as large as the length of the slab itself. Furthermore, the subduction is mostly aseismic, so that the location of $S = 1$ is

not easily established in the field. The Cascade volcanoes do demonstrate that arc volcanism can occur over aseismic slabs, but because of the uncertainty in the lag correction we cannot determine the value of S beneath the arc. The one part of this slab that may be helpful to us is the section passing beneath Puget Sound. Here some earthquakes do occur in a dipping plane, reaching to about 100 km depth (Weaver and Baker, 1988). A region of slightly high seismic velocity extends downward with about 65° dip from that point and is detectable to about 400 km (Michaelson and Weaver, 1986; Rasmussen and others, 1987). If we place $S = 1$ at the last earthquakes and adjust our calculated S values accordingly, we calculate a tenuous S value of about 7 for the slab at 400 km.

These observations of the various slab lengths, although they are quite variable, do give us independent confirmation that the slabs extend beyond the seismic zones, beyond $S = 1$. Furthermore, since seismic velocities are quite sensitive to temperature variations, the fact that the slabs are not presently detectable beyond about $S = 5$ or 7 leads us to believe that they are approaching mantle temperatures by that time.

Another way to predict slab duration is to study the results of mathematical thermal models and try to estimate the temperature at which the slab would be too hot to continue to act coherently. The oceanic lithosphere is often described as a quasi-rigid plate underlain by a viscous "thermal boundary layer" (Parsons and McKenzie, 1978). The temperature at the boundary between these two regimes is generally taken to be about 0.75 of the asthenosphere temperatures, or about 975°C (Parsons and McKenzie, 1978). We may, by analogy, suppose that when the cold core of the slab warms beyond this temperature it will no longer hold together as a coherent body.

Olivine flow laws derived from laboratory studies (Goetze, 1978), when extrapolated to strain rates appropriate to this problem (3×10^{-15} s^{-1}), predict that olivine begins to flow significantly in this temperature range (975°C) and hence are in general agreement with the temperature assumed for the thermal boundary layer (Chen and Molnar, 1983). By way of comparison, the temperature at the seismic cutoff is estimated to be significantly lower, between 600 and 800°C (Molnar and others, 1979; Wortel, 1982).

As seen in Appendix I, Figure A3, slab core temperatures of 975°C occur at about $S = 3$ to 4. A strong slab probably does not persist beyond about this point. The core of the slab reaches a temperature of 0.97 of asthenosphere temperature at $S = 10$, i.e., it is nearly indistinguishable from the asthenosphere.

Because of the great uncertainty in actual slab duration, we show contours as far as $S = 10$, but we do not in fact believe that strong slabs extend beyond about $S = 3$. Fortunately, the changes in slab thermal state through the Cenozoic are so striking that the particular choice of S value for slab assimilation makes little difference to the conclusions.

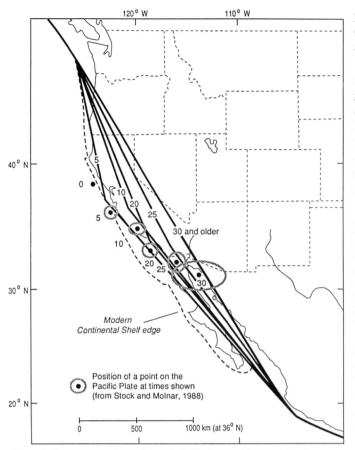

Figure 6. Reconstructed continental shelf-edge positions used as input to the thermal model. These were generated by assuming that the coast of North America distended as if pinned to the Pacific plate at the Mendocino fracture zone and with pivot points at the mouth of the Columbia River and Gulf of California. Pacific plate positions and uncertainties with respect to a fixed North America are shown by a sea-floor test point, calculated from global circuits by Stock and Molnar (1988) for the times listed (times in Ma). This distension is generally consistent with other reconstructions (e.g., Frei, 1986) and is assumed to reflect the combined effects of Basin-and-Range extension and deformation in California.

RECONSTRUCTIONS OF THE EDGE OF NORTH AMERICA

In order to map the thermal state of slabs, we must know the approximate location of the edge of North America through the Cenozoic. In particular, we need to account for changes in trench position due to Basin-and-Range extension and strike-slip deformation. To approximate this, we make the assumption that a test point on the Pacific plate just south of the Pioneer fracture zone was the same distance from the continental shelf edge at 30 Ma that it is today (see Fig. 6 for location of this point). We then allow the coastline to distend, coming forward in time, as if it were two chords pinned to stable North America at the mouth of the Columbia River and the mouth of the Gulf of California, and

pinned to the Pacific plate near the Mendocino Triple Junction (Fig. 6). In essence, we use the global circuit to predict the timing and amount of continental deformation.

One justification for the assumption that the test point was no farther from the continent at 30 Ma than it is today is that the global plate circuit, if correct, requires 340 ± 200 km of Basin-and-Range extension along an azimuth of S60°W or 500 ± 250 km along N70°W (Stock and Molnar, 1988). This is already near the upper limit permitted by geologic constraints (Wernicke and others, 1988). If the trench were some distance farther east of the test point than it is today, even more Basin-and-Range extension must have occurred, which we find geologically unpalatable.

Although obviously an oversimplification, this reconstruction of the continental edge is compatible with reconstructions based on a combination of geologic constraints from the Basin and Range province and paleomagnetic reconstructions that combine rigid body rotation of the Oregon and Washington Coast Ranges with no rotation of the Sierra Nevada (Frei, 1986). Note that this approach results, coincidentally, in a straight coastline before the ridge-trench encounter at 30 Ma.

We recognize that this reconstruction is an approximation and note that errors in our assumed trench positions will introduce errors in our calculated slab thermal conditions. The location of the trench determines the ridge-trench distance and, therefore, the amount of time the lithosphere can cool before entering the trench. However, this uncertainty is small compared to our uncertainty in assigning the lag time due to the overriding plate, so we do not treat it further.

CONSTRUCTION OF MAPS OF THE SLAB THERMAL STATE

Figure 7 shows an example, at 20 Ma, of the steps in the method used to map the inferred thermal state of the slab. Using an interactive graphics computer, we found rotation poles for many short steps in the spreading history of the magnetic anomalies on the Pacific plate. We then used these rotations and their combinations to reconstruct isochrons on the Farallon and Vancouver plates, assuming symmetrical spreading and taking into account the propagating rifts (Fig. 7a). Next, we positioned these plates with respect to North America using the Pacific–North America global circuit of Stock and Molnar (1988) and using a deformed rim of North America, as described in the previous section. From these reconstructions we created a map of time since subduction (Fig. 7b) and a map of age upon entry (Fig. 7c). The ratio of these two parameters, multiplied by ten, yielded the final product, a map of the inferred thermal state of the slabs beneath North America 20 m.y. ago, presented as contours of S in Figure 11, below.

The positions of the contours of S, mapped in this way and presented in Figures 8 through 13, are subject to some significant uncertainties. Since some of these uncertainties are quantifiable and some are quite subjective, we have not attempted a rigorous analysis of the total uncertainties. Rather, we show components of the uncertainties that can be quantified and have simply described the rest. On our maps we include the global circuit error ellipses of Stock and Molnar for Pacific–North America positions and a subjective slab-length error resulting from this global circuit uncertainty plus our estimate of Pacific-Farallon uncertainties. In Figure 8 alone, the slab-length error includes all additional sources of error, since these are especially large for this particular reconstruction.

THERMAL STATE OF THE SLAB THROUGH TIME

Figures 8 through 13 show the inferred thermal state of the slabs from 50 Ma through the present. Contours for $S = 1, 2, 3, 5$, and 10 are shown. Note that we have not corrected the locations of the contours for slab dip. For a 45° slab dip, the contours should be moved coastward about 30 percent. Since the dip is suspected to be highly variable, sometimes very shallow, and since the importance of the contours lies not in their absolute locations but rather in their striking order-of-magnitude variations through time, we chose not to include this factor.

State boundaries are shown in Figures 8 through 13 for reference, with Basin and Range extension and strike-slip deformation approximately removed back to 30 Ma. Total deformation is made to fit our assumption for the position of the trench, while the distribution of deformation is guided by geologic constraints.

50-Ma reconstruction

Figure 8 shows contours of S in the slab at 50 Ma, toward the end of the Laramide Orogeny. We have little information about the age of the crust formed during the Cretaceous Quiet Period, between magnetic anomalies 34 (84 Ma) and M0 (118 Ma). This reconstruction was made assuming steady symmetrical spreading during the Quiet Period on the ridge segment south of the Murray fracture zone. Crustal ages were interpolated linearly between 84 and 118 Ma on all ridge segments. Also, this reconstruction was made on a flat Earth, unlike the other reconstructions, which were done on a sphere.

The large uncertainty introduced by these assumptions turns out to have little effect on our overall conclusions. The slab age was probably between 40 and 60 m.y. upon entry, giving a seismic cutoff ($S = 1$) between 4 and 6 m.y. after entry. Using the average subduction rate of 120 ± 20 mm/yr between 70 and 50 Ma (Stock and Molnar, 1988) and adding the 200 km lag, the seismic slab length would have been between 600 and 1100 km. Although this length is uncertain by a factor of two, it is much longer than those calculated for the later Cenozoic.

Note that the $S = 2$ contour is near Denver, Colorado, meaning that the slab has been subducted about twice as long as necessary to become aseismic. Note also that if the slab were flat and in direct contact with the overlying lithosphere of the North

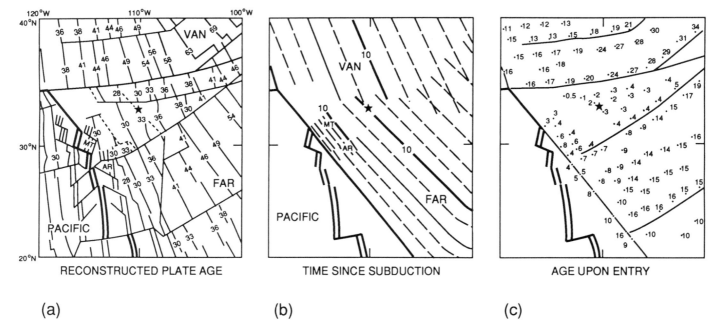

(a)   (b)   (c)

Figure 7. Examples from reconstruction for 20 Ma, showing method used to construct contours of S in the slab. (a) Map of reconstructed isochrons on Farallon (FAR), Vancouver (VAN), Monterey (MT), and Arguello (AR) plates. Ages (Ma) of magnetic anomalies from DNAG timescale (Berggren and others, 1985). (b) Map of time since subduction, showing trench positions on the slabs at intervals of 2 m.y. Solid lines are independent determinations; dashed lines are interpolations. (c) Map of age upon entry, made by subtracting values in (b) and reconstruction age (20 Ma) from (a). S values are calculated by dividing values in (b) by those in (c), times 10. For example, the star is located on the reconstructed anomaly 12, age 33 Ma. It has been subducted for 10 m.y. at the time of this 20-Ma reconstruction, so it was 3 m.y. old when subducted. Thus, its predicted thermal state is $S = 33$, meaning that it has been subducted 33 times longer than necessary to become aseismic.

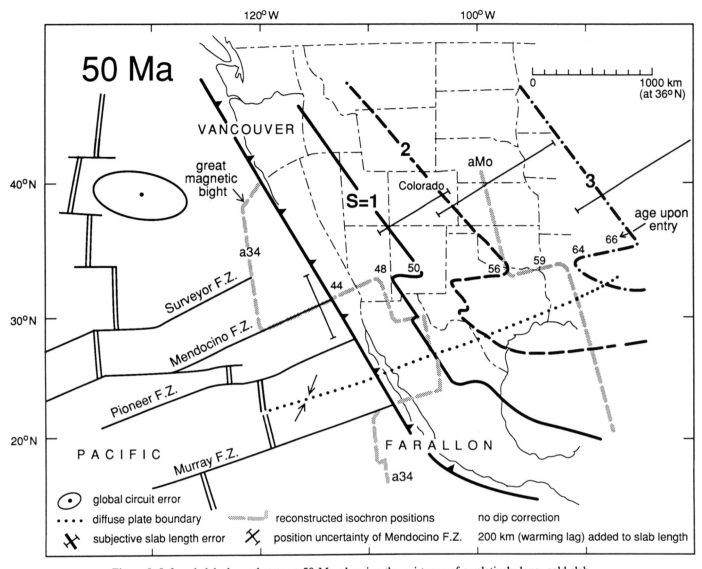

Figure 8. Inferred slab thermal state at 50 Ma, showing the existence of a relatively long, cold slab during the Laramide Orogeny. Large, heavy numbers indicate values of *S*; light numbers show age on entry (Ma). Pacific plate position with respect to North America with uncertainty (ellipse) is taken from the global circuit reconstruction of Stock and Molnar (1988). Gray lines show positions of the reconstructed aM0 and a34 isochrons. Because of ambiguities in the spreading history during the Cretaceous quiet period, a34 is the eastern limit of well-known crustal age. Dotted line shows approximate position of the Vancouver-Farallon plate boundary, and arrows on this boundary show relative motion across it. We conclude that the flat slab hypothesis cannot be ruled out on the basis that the slab would have been too young and hot to reach beneath Colorado; in fact, it could have easily extended this far.

American plate, as is often asserted, it would have been heated mostly from below, so that the equation for *S* seriously underestimates the seismic slab length.

We portray our best estimate of the summed uncertainties in the "subjective slab length error" bars shown in Figure 8. Because of the many uncertainties in this particular reconstruction, the actual values of *S* are poorly known. The primary value lies in its striking contrast to the much shorter slabs of the later Cenozoic.

35-Ma Reconstruction

Figure 9 shows contours of *S* in the slab at 35 Ma. The slab has significantly shortened everywhere. If the early Cenozoic flat slab scenario is adopted, this shortening of the slab is probably recorded by the mid-Cenozoic westward sweep of magmatism reported in many areas (e.g., Coney and Reynolds, 1977; Cross and Pilger, 1978; Cross, 1986). The nearly simultaneous matur-

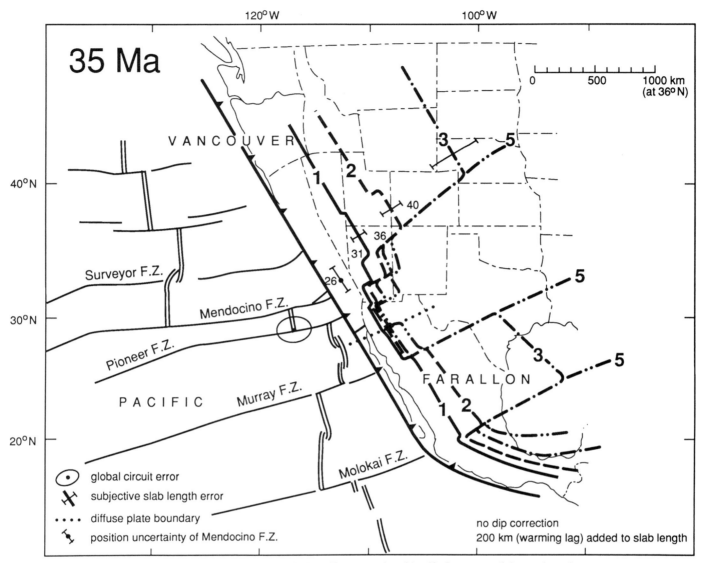

Figure 9. Inferred slab thermal state at 35 Ma. Heavy numbers identify *S* contours; light numbers show age on entry (Ma). *S* contours approach the trench from the east as the ridge approaches the trench from the west, creating a symmetrical hourglass shape. Except for the short slabs near the coast, the slab sector between the Pioneer and Murray fracture zones is already hot and weak enough that it is best described as a "slab gap."

ing of a long portion of the slab suggests that this shortening event may not necessarily have taken place as an orderly steepening and "roll back" of the slab, as is often imagined, but rather that it disintegrated piecemeal over a large region, as depicted in Figure 10 of Cross and Pilger (1978), for example.

At 35 Ma the slab is already extremely short between the Pioneer and Murray fracture zones, the future site of the slab-free region, reaching *S* = 5 and 10 within a few hundred kilometers of the coast. We infer that except for the near-coast region where the young slab persists, this section of the slab has been reassimilated into the asthenosphere, leaving a "slab gap" between northern Mexico and New Mexico. Note that this is 15 to 20 m.y. earlier than the time when the "slab window" as proposed by Dickinson

and Snyder (1979a) would have grown to significant size; subduction is still occurring all along the western margin of North America at this time.

30-Ma Reconstruction

Figure 10 shows contours of *S* in the slab at 30 Ma. At this time, the slab segment between the Murray and Pioneer fracture zones broke free of the Farallon plate to the south. Presumably, it had become so thin and warm that it was no longer strong enough to remain rigidly attached to and moving with the Farallon plate, and its own slab no longer supplied enough negative buoyancy to maintain fast subduction.

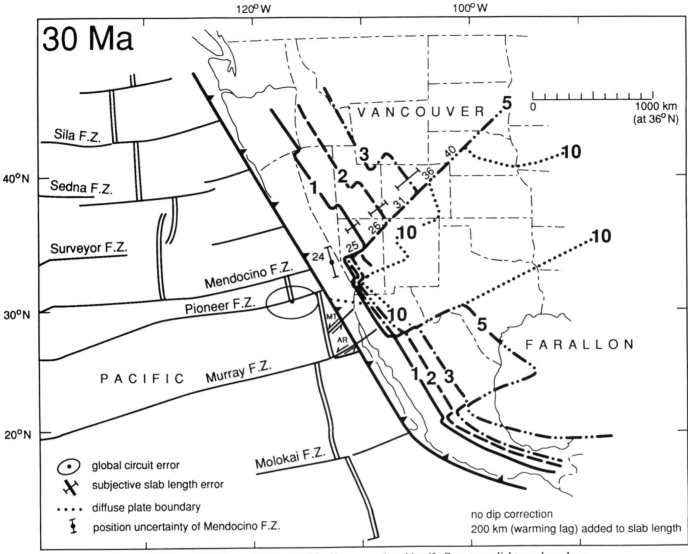

Figure 10. Inferred slab thermal state at 30 Ma. Heavy numbers identify S contours; light numbers show age on entry (Ma). Almost all of the slab between the Pioneer and Murray fracture zones shows values of S greater than 10. The Farallon Slab broke at this time, forming the Monterey (MT) and Arguello (AR) plates. Small plate boundaries are drawn assuming they are strike-slip boundaries, by analogy to the present-day Nootka fault separating the Explorer and Juan de Fuca plates.

The strike slip faults drawn between the newly formed Monterey and Arguello plates and the Farallon plate are speculative. We use the analogy, mentioned above, of the modern Explorer plate. This small plate broke free of its parental Juan de Fuca plate along the Nootka fault, a strike-slip fault oriented in the direction of relative plate motion (Hyndman and others, 1979). Thus we draw our new plate boundaries parallel to the directions of relative motion between the various plates.

It is interesting to speculate on the geometry of the subterranean breaks in the slab that led to the birth of the Arguello and Monterey plates. Although the exact geometry cannot be resolved, we argue that the strike-slip faults mentioned above would be likely to extend down through the slab to the deep,

plastic regions of this very short slab. Thus, our bias is that the entire slabs of these plates slowed with the plates, with primarily strike-slip breaks between them.

Another alternative is that the small plates may have separated from their slabs along trench-parallel breaks of extensional nature. Relatively buoyant basalt undergoes a phase change to much denser eclogite at depths estimated from 40 to 80 km (Ringwood and Green, 1966; Pennington, 1983). Eclogite is more dense than ordinary mantle and is thought to be an important factor in the slab-pull force to which plate motion is attributed. Because buoyant basalt resists subduction while eclogite drives it, the basalt-eclogite transition would be a likely place for a slab to break free of the plate it is pulling. If such a break

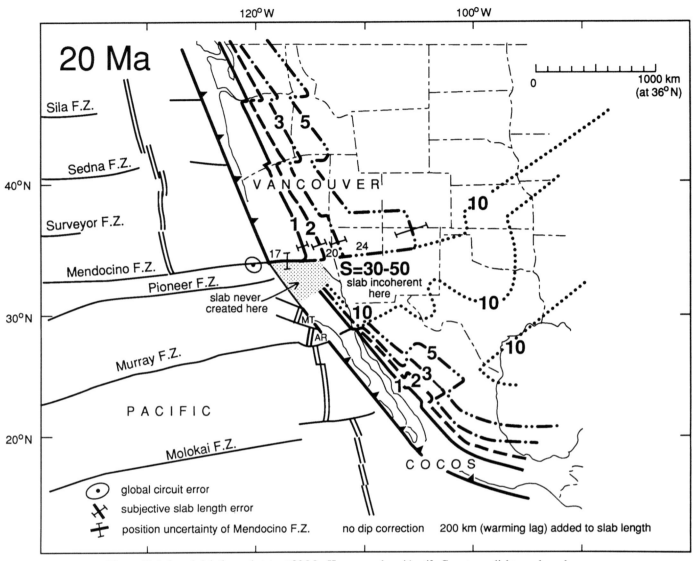

Figure 11. Inferred slab thermal state at 20 Ma. Heavy numbers identify *S* contours; light numbers show age on entry (Ma). In the Mendocino-Murray corridor, the MT and AR slabs are extremely short, and to their north no slab was ever formed (the slab window concept). The entire region of slab to the east of the emerging slab-free region has been subducted 30 to 50 times longer than necessary to become aseismic; i.e., it is probably indistinguishable from the asthenosphere.

occurred, asthenosphere would have upwelled to fill the break in the separating slab, with the possible consequence of voluminous, "dry," basaltic volcanism. In contrast, if the entire slab slowed, as described above, such a pulse of volcanism would not be expected.

20-Ma Reconstruction

By 20 Ma (Fig. 11), the slab just south of the subducted Mendocino fracture zone would have been subducted 30 to 50 times longer than necessary to become aseismic, and therefore we infer that it was indistinguishable from asthenosphere. Note that to the north of the subducted Mendocino fracture zone the slab

persisted, whereas to the south it was gone. This slab–no slab edge coincides with the northern edge of Dickinson and Snyder's (1979a) proposed slab window, but it extends indefinitely to the east.

10-Ma and present-day reconstructions

The East Pacific Rise stopped spreading offshore of a large part of Baja California about 12 Ma, significantly lengthening the Pacific–North America boundary, as seen in the 10-Ma reconstruction (Fig. 12). We assume that subduction of this plate segment also stopped at this time. *S* values in Figure 13 were calculated assuming that the slab stopped moving but continued

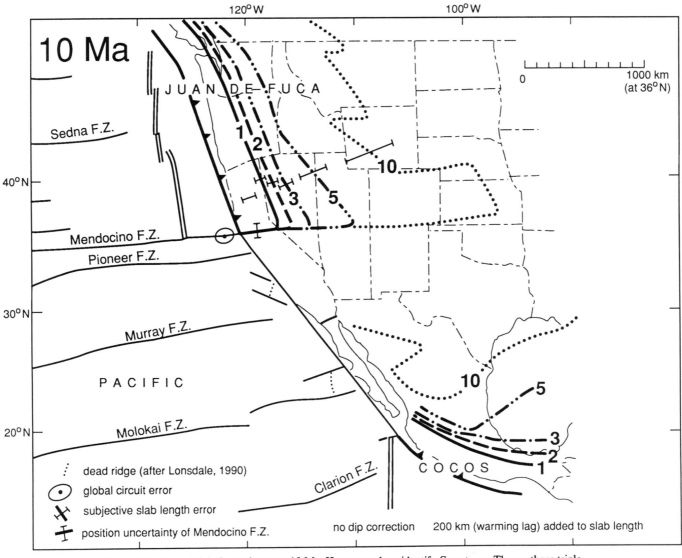

Figure 12. Inferred slab thermal state at 10 Ma. Heavy numbers identify *S* contours. The southern triple junction jumped south at 12 Ma, shutting off subduction along most of Baja California. Cocos slab beneath this section is assumed to have broken free of the main Cocos plate to the south and hence is positioned arbitrarily, but *S* values are so high that its location is not important.

to warm in situ. We include them merely to emphasize the extremely high *S* values that developed in the eastern and southern margins of the idealized "slab window"; the position of the slab is a moot point because it probably did not exist.

DISCUSSION

Figure 14 shows our interpretation of the approximate geometry of the slabs as the East Pacific Rise approached the trench off North America during the Cenozoic. For this figure, we show the *S* = 2 contour as the end of the slab, but we could equally well choose *S* = 3, shown dashed. With the addition of

slab dip, these positions might correspond more closely to *S* = 3–5. In Figure 15, we summarize the evolution of slab geometry during the Cenozoic in a single picture, to emphasize changes through time.

A distinction needs to be made between the slab window concept, which describes a region where a slab was never formed, and the slab gap as described in this chapter, which includes regions of no slab originating both from nonformation and from thermal equilibration with the asthenosphere. A slab is not formed when spreading between two lithospheric plates occurs beneath a third plate rather than beneath water. It is the differing thermal character of the overlying medium—cold water versus a lithospheric plate—that distinguishes normal sea-floor spreading

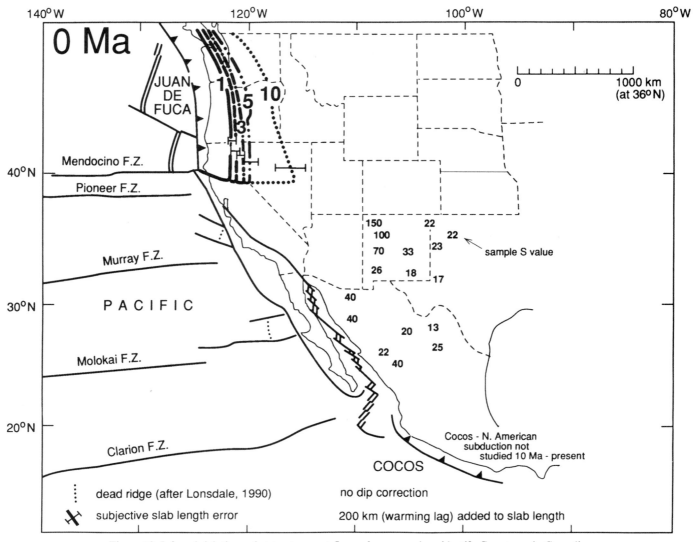

Figure 13. Inferred slab thermal state at present. Large, heavy numbers identify *S* contours in Cascadia (Juan de Fuca) slab. Smaller numbers are representative *S* values, not contoured. Position of slab with these values is arbitrary; values shown only to emphasize the extreme nature of the thermal parameters. Note small predicted size of Cascadia slab, consistent with observations that this slab lacks a well-developed Wadati-Benioff zone.

from formation of a slab window. Thus, the slab window does not include areas where a slab was overlain by water even for a short time before being subducted.

The thermal state of a very young slab is not very different from that of a slab window. In one important respect, however, the slab is different: no matter how young, it will be topped by hydrothermally altered basalts and thus will be capable of delivering water to the asthenosphere where it may induce arc volcanism (A. F. Glazner, written communication, 1988). This fact bears on the question of when arc volcanism would be expected to cease as subduction slows and stops.

As segments of the East Pacific rise arrived at the rim of North America, triple junctions were established at the two ends of the Pacific–North America plate boundary (San Andreas sys-

tem) and moved apart as that boundary grew in length. The passage of these triple junctions should mark the cessation of subduction and arc magmatism, leaving a migrating "arc switch-off" in the geologic record (Christiansen and Lipman, 1972; Dickinson and Snyder, 1979a).

This is a good model for the northern, Mendocino triple junction since it corresponds to a straight, strong slab edge with a large thermal contrast and a true asthenospheric window edge. The southern triple junction, on the other hand, corresponds to a ragged, broken edge with vanishingly small thermal contrast and includes slowly subducting pieces and stalled slab fragments. Furthermore, because of uncertainties in the reconstructions of the plate positions and of the deformation of North America, the timing and position of the final cessation of subduction at the

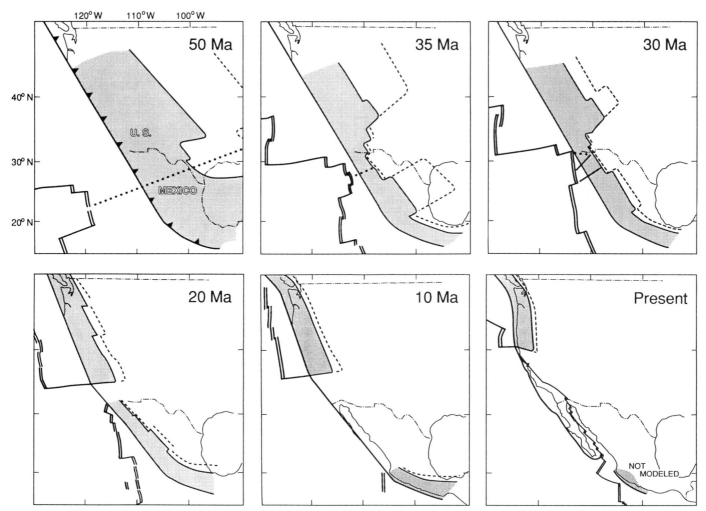

Figure 14. Probable geometry of the slab beneath North America at six time steps through the Cenozoic. Slab area with *S* value less than 2 is stippled. *S* = 3 contours shown dashed. Dotted lines show approximate locations of diffuse Vancouver-Farallon plate boundary. Note that the Laramide slab was relatively long. It shortened dramatically throughout the Cenozoic as the East Pacific Rise approached the trench. The development of a San Andreas transform was anticipated by and accompanied by a widening "slab gap." The transition, during the Paleogene, from a long cool slab to a short warm one happened rather quickly, suggesting that the long, flat slab may have disintegrated and fallen away in pieces.

southern triple junction are poorly known. The age of the youngest Pacific plate sea floor offshore gives us an upper bound for this switch-off age (Atwater, 1970, 1989), but we cannot preclude later slow subduction. California may have "overridden" the Pacific Plate by some unknown amount, covering up the anomalies that would give the true switch-off age.

We conclude that the position of the southern arc switch-off through time is poorly constrained by plate kinematic models. We hope, rather, that it will be established from the careful characterization and dating of continental magmatic rocks and that these may, in turn, help us determine the plate histories and interactions.

Note that the northern edge of the slab-free region is the only edge with a large thermal contrast, owing to the age differ-

ence across the Mendocino fracture zone (Figs. 10 through 13). We believe that this edge is the only well-defined edge of the slab gap and may be the only edge that has had observable geologic consequences for the North American continent. Thus our findings support postulated relations between the passage of this northern edge and geologic events such as a migrating arc switch-off (e.g., Snyder and others, 1976; Cross and Pilger, 1978; Glazner and Supplee, 1982), the uplift of the Colorado plateau and Sierra Nevada (Crough and Thompson, 1977), and, perhaps, the onset of major extensional episodes in the southern Basin and Range (e.g., Dickinson, 1981). In the California coast ranges, uplift patterns, lithosphere structure, and heat flow anomalies can likewise be attributed to this thermal edge and its migration (e.g., Lachenbruch and Sass, 1980; Zandt and Furlong, 1982).

Severinghaus and Atwater

CONCLUSIONS

The shrinkage of the slab beneath western North America during the Cenozoic is a predictable consequence of the approach of the ridge to the trench. We have roughly quantified the shape and thermal condition of the waning slabs by constructing contour maps of the thermal condition of the slab core, shown in some detail in Figures 8 through 13 and in summary in Figures 14 and 15. The positions of the particular thermal contours on our maps are quite uncertain. We believe that their primary value lies in their relative positions in space and their striking order-of-magnitude changes through time. Our conclusions, below, are all based on variations that are much greater than any that could be caused by the uncertainties.

During the time of the Laramide orogeny the slab was relatively long and cold, so the hypothesis that a flat slab extended intact as far inland as Colorado seems viable. Indeed, if the slab was flat or shallow dipping, it would have been even longer than shown on Figures 8, 14, and 15 because of our underestimate of the lag time arising from extended contact with the overriding plate.

During the mid-Cenozoic, the length of cold slab shortened significantly and rapidly everywhere. This is caused by a combination of decreasing age upon entry and a slowing in the subduction rate. If the early Cenozoic flat-slab scenario is adopted, this shortening of the slab is probably related to the mid-Cenozoic westward sweep of magmatism reported in many areas. Two small plates called the Monterey and Arguello plates broke free of the Farallon plate at 30 Ma, slowed, and underwent a clockwise change in spreading direction, indicating that the slab must have broken at this time.

If the idealized "slab window" hypothesis were correct, the slab that would have formed the eastern flank of this region was roughly 1 to 5 m.y. old when it was subducted, meaning that by 20 Ma, it would have been subducted 30 to 50 times longer than necessary to become aseismic ($S = 30$ to 50). We conclude that slab in this thermal state is indistinguishable from the asthenosphere. At 10 Ma and at present, the eastern flank is even hotter ($S = 70$ to 150). Thus, we conclude that the proposed slab window is better described as a "slab gap," a region of no slab flanked by coherent slabs to the north and south.

The slab gap developed gradually through the early and mid-Cenozoic, centered beneath northern Mexico. The gap first developed from the east, as a marked shortening in this portion of the slab. Subduction continued at the coast but with a disrupted and increasingly short-lived slab. Starting at 30 Ma, this short slab fragmented, and part of the slab gap began to be a region where slab was never formed (the "window" concept). The north-south widening of the slab gap continued to the present in concert with the evolution of the San Andreas transform regime on the North American margin. During the evolution of the gap, the entire pattern was drifting northwestward, as well, beneath North America.

The position and timing of the south-migrating edge of the

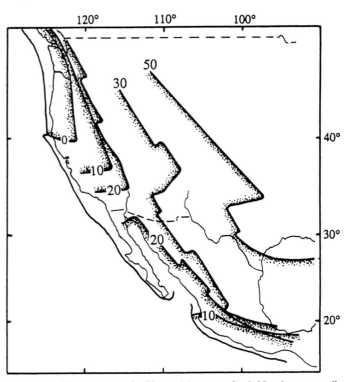

Figure 15. Slab geometry in Figure 14 summarized. Numbers are millions of years before present.

slab gap throughout much of its history is indeterminate because of an ambiguity in the timing of cessation of subduction. The northern edge of the slab gap, defined by the Mendocino fracture zone, is probably the only margin of the no-slab region that may have had observable geologic consequences that can be related to the kinematically predicted position of the slab edge through time.

ACKNOWLEDGMENTS

We thank Joann Stock and Peter Molnar for providing global circuit data before publication, Peter Lonsdale for providing tectonic interpretations of offshore California and Baja California before publication, and Douglas Wilson for providing data on northeast Pacific fracture zones before publication. We thank Chris Scotese, Cathy Mayes, Lisa Gahagan, Larry Lawver, and John Sclater of the Paleo-Oceanographic Mapping Project at the University of Texas in Austin for helping us to digitize our magnetic anomaly interpretations and providing use of the Evans and Sutherland graphics computer. Cathy Mayes and Lisa Gahagan deserve special recognition for their generous assistance in making the reconstructions. David Crouch helped produce the figures. Partial funding for this project was provided by a University of California Academic Senate Research Grant. The paper benefited greatly from reviews by Joann Stock, Douglas Wilson, Suzanne Carbotte, and an anonymous reviewer.

APPENDIX 1: THEORETICAL CALCULATIONS OF THE THERMAL STATE OF THE SLAB

We have displayed the thermal state of subducting slabs by mapping contours of S and have noted that $S = 1$ corresponds approximately to the location of the seismic cutoff in modern slabs. We here explore the relationship between S and temperatures in the core of the slab.

McKenzie (1969, 1970) derived an equation for the potential temperature within a subducting slab (potential temperature is the temperature rock would have if raised to the surface). He assumed that the slab began with a thickness, h, and a constant potential temperature gradient from the temperature of seawater, $\theta = 273°K$ (0°C), at the top of the slab to that of the asthenosphere, $\theta = \theta_a$, at the bottom. Upon subduction, the slab is bathed in asthenosphere at $\theta = \theta_a$. It warms up by heat flowing in through both surfaces.

Using the coordinate system shown in Figure A1, the equation for potential temperature (in °K), modified from McKenzie (1970), is

$$\theta\,(x,z) = \theta_a + 2\,(\theta_a - 273) \sum_{n=1}^{\infty} \frac{(-1)^n}{n\pi} \exp\left[\frac{Rx}{h}\left(1 - \sqrt{1 + \frac{n^2\pi^2}{R^2}}\,\right)\right] \sin\frac{n\pi z}{h} \qquad (1)$$

where R is the thermal Reynolds number, $R \equiv \dfrac{\rho C_p vh}{2k}$, and θ_a is the potential temperature of the asthenosphere, $\theta_a \sim 1473°K$, or 1200°C, and where h is the slab thickness in cm, v is the subduction speed in cm/sec, ρ is the density, $\rho \sim 3.35$ g/cm^3, C_p is the heat capacity, $C_p \sim 10^7$ erg/(g°C), and k is the thermal conductivity, k $\sim 3 \times 10^5$ erg/(cm°C sec).

Some of these parameters, in turn, can be combined as K, the thermal diffusivity.

$$K = \frac{k}{\rho Cp}, \quad K \sim 9 \times 10^{-3}\ cm^2/sec \qquad (2)$$

and

$$R = \frac{vh}{2K}. \qquad (3)$$

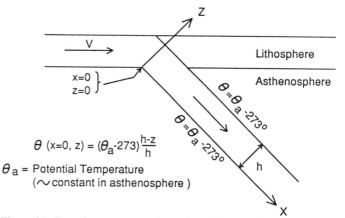

$$\theta\,(x=0, z) = (\theta_a - 273)\frac{h-z}{h}$$

θ_a = Potential Temperature ($\sim$ constant in asthenosphere)

Figure A1. Coordinate system and some boundary conditions used in the calculation of the thermal state of a subducting slab, modified from McKenzie (1970).

The square root term in the exponential in equation (1) can be expressed as a binomial series, and since $R \gg \pi$, we keep only the first two terms.

Substituting these and equation (3) into equation (1), we get

$$\theta\,(x,z) = \theta_a + 2\,(\theta_a - 273) \sum_{n=1}^{\infty} \frac{(-1)^n}{n\pi} \exp\left[-\frac{n^2\pi^2 Kx}{vh^2}\right] \sin\frac{n\pi z}{h}. \qquad (4)$$

We would like to explore this expression in relation to our parameter S, in which

$$S = \frac{\text{time since subduction} \times 10}{\text{age upon subduction}}$$

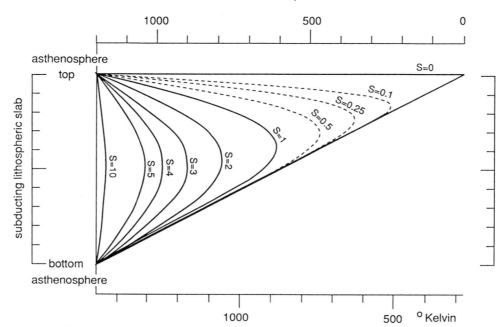

Figure A2. Cross-slab profiles of potential temperature calculated for various values of the parameter S.

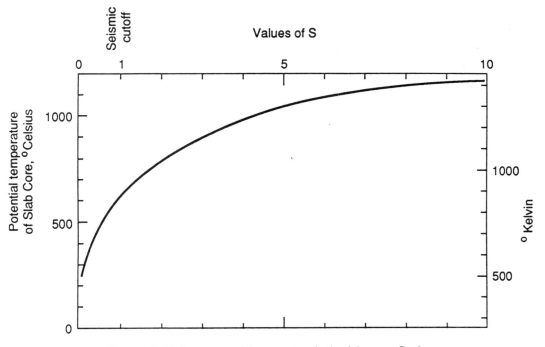

Figure A3. Minimum potential temperature in the slab versus *S* value.

The thickness of an oceanic plate, h, has been shown to be approximately proportional to the square root of its age, or $h(km) = 9.4t^{1/2}$ (m.y.) for plates less than about 100 m.y. old (Parker and Oldenburg, 1973; Parsons and Sclater, 1977), or $t(sec) = 35.65h^2$ (cm).

For a constant subduction velocity, the time since subduction is equal to x/v. Thus,

$$S = \frac{x}{Cvh^2} \qquad (5)$$

where $C = 3.56$. Note that for a constant plate age and subduction velocity, S is simply proportional to distance down slab.

Substituting (5) in (4), we have:

$$\theta (x,z) = \theta_a + 2 (\theta_a - 273) \sum_{n=1}^{\infty} \frac{(-1)^n}{n\pi} \exp\left[-Cn^2\pi^2KS\right] \sin \frac{n\pi z}{h} \qquad (6)$$

Figure A2 presents cross-slab profiles of potential temperature calculated from equation (6) at points down the slab corresponding to

various values of *S*. The slab was assumed to start out with the temperature profile labeled $S = 0$. The calculated curves show that the cold top of the slab heats quickly at first as heat flows across the steep thermal gradient there. By the time the slab has been subducted for the duration corresponding to $S = 1$, the coldest core of the slab is found well below the top surface and has heated to more than half of θ_a, the asthenosphere potential temperature. Heating during subsequent steps is much slower because of the reduced gradients.

Figure A3 shows minimum potential temperature, i.e., the potential temperature of the cold core of the slab, for increasing values of *S*. For our purposes, we would like to know the value of *S* at which the slab becomes so hot that it is too weak to continue to act as a rigid plate. We do not know at what temperature this slab failure will occur, but we note that by the time the slab has reached $S = 3$, its coldest core has reached 77 percent of θ_a. At $S = 6$, its core is 90 percent of θ_a, and it is practically indistinguishable from the asthenosphere.

REFERENCES CITED

Atwater, T. M., 1970, Implications of plate tectonics for the Cenozoic tectonic evolution of western North America: Geological Society of America Bulletin, v. 81, p. 3518–3536.
—— , 1989, Plate tectonic history of the northeast Pacific and western North America, *in* Winterer, E. L., Hussong, D. M., and Decker, R. W., eds., The Eastern Pacific Ocean and Hawaii: Boulder, Colorado, Geological Society of America, The Geology of North America, v. N, p. 21–72.
Atwater, T. M., and Severinghaus, J., 1987, Propagating rifts, overlapping spreading centers, and duelling propagators in the northeast Pacific magnetic anomaly record: EOS Transactions of the American Geophysical Union, v. 68, p. 1493.
—— , 1989, Tectonic maps of the northeast Pacific, *in* Winterer, E. L., Hussong,

D. M., and Decker, R. W., eds., The Eastern Pacific Ocean and Hawaii: Boulder, Colorado, Geological Society of America, The Geology of North America, v. N, p. 15–20.
Berggren, W. A., Kent, D. V., Flynn, J. J., and van Couvering, J. A., 1985, Cenozoic geochronology: Geological Society of America Bulletin, v. 96, p. 1407–1418.
Bird, P., 1984, Laramide crustal thickening event in the Rocky mountain foreland and Great Plains: Tectonics, v. 3, p. 741–758.
—— , 1988, Formation of the Rocky Mountains, western United States; A continuum computer model: Science, v. 239, p. 1501–1507.
Boyd, T. A., and Creager, K. C., 1987, Kinematic flow model of the Aleutian Slab: EOS Transactions of the American Geophysical Union, v. 68, p. 1500.

Appendix II. Data set used to make the reconstructions shown in Figures 7 through 15. Each cross is a data point representing a ship crossing of a magnetic anomaly. Available in digital form from the Paleo-Oceanographic Mapping Project, Institute for Geophysics, University of Texas at Austin.

Chen, W. P., and Molnar, P., 1983, Focal depths of intracontinental and intra-plate earthquakes and their implications for the thermal and mechanical properties of the lithosphere: Journal of Geophysical Research, v. 88, p. 4183–4214.

Christiansen, R. L., and Lipman, P. W., 1972, Cenozoic volcanism and plate tectonic evolution of the western United States; Part 2, Late Cenozoic: Proceedings of the Royal Society of London, v. 271, p. 249–284.

Coney, P. J., and Reynolds, S. J., 1977, Cordilleran Benioff zones: Nature, v. 270, p. 403–406.

Creager, K. C., and Jordan, T. H., 1986, Slab penetration into the lower mantle beneath the Mariana and other island arcs of the northwest Pacific: Journal of Geophysical Research, v. 91, p. 3573–3589.

Cross, T. A., 1986, Tectonic controls of foreland basin subsidence and Laramide style deformation, western United States: International Association of Sedimentologists Special Publication 8, p. 15–39.

Cross, T. A., and Pilger, R. H., Jr., 1978, Constraints on absolute motion and plate interaction inferred from Cenozoic igneous activity in the western United States: American Journal of Science, v. 278, p. 865–902.

Crough, T. S., and Thompson, G. A., 1977, Upper mantle origin of Sierra Nevada uplift: Geology, v. 5, p. 396–399.

Dickinson, W. R., 1981, Plate tectonic evolution of the southern Cordillera, *in* Dickinson, W. R., and Payne, W. D., eds., Relations of tectonics to ore bodies in the southern Cordillera: Arizona Geological Society Digest, v. 14, p. 113–135.

Dickinson, W. R., and Snyder, W. S., 1979a, Geometry of subducted slabs related to San Andreas Transform: Journal of Geology, v. 87, p. 609–627.

—— , 1979b, Geometry of triple junctions related to San Andreas transform: Journal of Geophysical Research, v. 84, p. 561–572.

Frei, L. S., 1986, Additional paleomagnetic results from the Sierra Nevada; Further constraints on Basin and Range extension and northward displacement in the western United States: Geological Society of America Bulletin, v. 97, p. 840–849.

Glazner, A. F., and Supplee, J. A., 1982, Migration of Tertiary volcanism in the southwestern United States and subduction of the Mendocino fracture zone: Earth and Planetary Science Letters, v. 60, p. 429–436.

Goetze, C., 1978, The mechanism of creep in olivine: Philosophical Transactions of the Royal Society of London, series A, v. 288, p. 99–119.

Hager, B. H., 1986, The layered mantle; To be or not to be? Yes!: EOS Transactions of the American Geophysical Union, v. 67, p. 1257.

Hyndman, R. D., Riddihough, R. P., and Herzer, R., 1979, The Nootka Fault Zone; A new plate boundary off western Canada: Geophysical Journal of the Royal Astronomical Society of London, v. 58, p. 667–683.

Jarrard, R. D., 1986, Relations among subduction parameters: Reviews of Geophysics, v. 24, p. 217–284.

Kent, D. V., and Gradstein, F. M., 1985, A Cretaceous and Jurassic geochronology: Geological Society of America Bulletin, v. 96, p. 1419–1427.

Lachenbruch, A. H., and Sass, J. H., 1980, Flow and energetics of the San Andreas fault zone: Journal of Geophysical Research, v. 85, p. 6185–6223.

Lonsdale, P., 1990, Structural patterns of the Pacific floor offshore of Peninsular California, *in* Dauphin, J., ed., Gulf and Peninsula Provinces of the Californias: American Association of Petroleum Geologists Memoir 47 (in press).

McKenzie, D. P., 1969, Speculations on the consequences and causes of plate motions: Geophysical Journal of the Royal Astronomical Society of London, v. 18, p. 1–32.

—— , 1970, Temperature and potential temperature beneath island arcs: Tectonophysics, v. 10, p. 357–366.

Menard, H. W., 1978, Fragmentation of the Farallon plate by pivoting subduction: Journal of Geology, v. 86, p. 99–110.

Michaelson, C. A. and Weaver, C. S., 1986, Upper mantle structure from teleseismic P wave arrivals in Washington and northern Oregon: Journal of Geophysical Research, v. 91, p. 2077–2094.

Molnar, P., Freedman, D., and Shih, J.S.F., 1979, Lengths of intermediate and deep seismic zones and temperatures in downgoing slabs of lithosphere: Geophysical Journal of the Royal Astronomical Society of London, v. 56, p. 41–54.

Parker, R. L., and Oldenburg, D. W., 1973, Thermal models of ocean ridges: Nature Physical Science, v. 242, p. 137–139.

Parsons, B., and McKenzie, D., 1978, Mantle convection and the thermal structure of the plates: Journal of Geophysical Research, v. 83, p. 4485–4496.

Parsons, B., and Sclater, J. G., 1977, An analysis of the variation of ocean floor bathymetry and heat flow with age: Journal of Geophysical Research, v. 82, p. 803–827.

Pennington, W. D., 1983, Role of shallow phase changes in the subduction of oceanic crust: Science, v. 220, p. 1045–1047.

Rasmussen, J. R., Humphreys, E., and Dueker, K. G., 1987, P-wave velocity structure of the upper mantle beneath Washington and northern Oregon: EOS Transactions of the American Geophysical Union, v. 68, p. 1379.

Ringwood, A. E., and Green, D. H., 1966, An experimental investigation of the gabbro-eclogite transformation and some geophysical implications: Tectonophysics, v. 3, p. 383–427.

Rosa, J.W.C., and Molnar, P., 1988, Uncertainties in reconstructions of the Pacific, Farallon, Vancouver, and Kula plates and constraints on the rigidity of the Pacific and Farallon (and Vancouver) plates between 72 and 35 Ma: Journal of Geophysical Research, v. 93, p. 2997–3008.

Snyder, W. S., Dickinson, W. R., and Silberman, M. L., 1976, Tectonic implications of space-time patterns of Cenozoic magmatism in the western United States: Earth and Planetary Science Letters, v. 32, p. 91–106.

Stock, J., and Molnar, P., 1988, Uncertainties and implications of the Late Cretaceous and Tertiary position of North America relative to the Farallon, Kula, and Pacific plates: Tectonics, v. 7, p. 1339–1384.

Sugi, N., and Uyeda, S., 1984, Subduction of young oceanic plates: Bulletin de la Société de France, v. 26, p. 245–254.

Theberge, A. E., Jr., 1971, Magnetic survey off southern California and Baja California: Rockwell, Maryland, National Oceanic and Atmospheric Administration Marine Geophysics Group Operational Data Report NOS DR-12, 10 p.

Weaver, C. S. and Baker, G. E., 1988, Geometry of the Juan de Fuca plate beneath Washington and northern Oregon from seismicity: Bulletin of the Seismological Society of America, v. 78, p. 264–275.

Wernicke, B. P., Axen, G. J., and Snow, J. K., 1988, Basin and Range extensional tectonics at the latitude of Las Vegas, Nevada: Geological Society of America Bulletin, v. 100, p. 1738–1757.

Wilson, D. S., 1988, Tectonic history of the Juan de Fuca Ridge over the last 40 million years: Journal of Geophysical Research, v. 93, p. 11863–11876.

Wortel, R., 1982, Seismicity and rheology of subducted slabs: Nature, v. 296, p. 553–556.

Zandt, G., and Furlong, K. P., 1982, Evolution and thickness of the lithosphere beneath coastal California: Geology, v. 10, p. 376–381.

MANUSCRIPT ACCEPTED BY THE SOCIETY AUGUST 21, 1989

Geological Society of America
Memoir 176
1990

Chapter 2

Miocene volcanism, folding, and faulting in the Castle Mountains, southern Nevada and eastern California

Ryan D. Turner and Allen F. Glazner
Department of Geology, CB# 3315, University of North Carolina, Chapel Hill, North Carolina 27599

ABSTRACT

Field, geochemical, and geochronological studies in the Castle Mountains constrain the timing and nature of magmatism, folding, and normal faulting related to Miocene crustal extension in the northern Colorado River trough. Volcanism began at approximately 18 Ma; it evolved from initial production of intermediate-composition lavas to bimodal basalt-rhyolite volcanism and returned to intermediate-composition volcanism after 12.8 Ma. Although these transitions in volcanic style are not sharply defined, the bimodal assemblage apparently was erupted during active extension by normal faulting. Linear compositional trends, disequilibrium textures, and elevated $^{87}Sr/^{86}Sr$ ratios in silicic rocks indicate that the spectrum of compositions observed in the volcanic rocks was produced by magma mixing accompanied by minor crystal fractionation. These compositional and textural features are similar to those seen in other extension-related magmatic suites of the southwestern United States.

Rocks in the Castle Mountains are folded into a northeast-trending anticline and are cut by east-dipping low-angle normal faults and high-angle strike- and oblique-slip faults. High-angle faults generally cut low-angle faults. The different fault sets may be part of a continuum in which early high-angle faults are rotated to low dips by younger high-angle faults. The anticline involves both Precambrian basement rocks and Tertiary cover. K-Ar dates on the youngest folded unit and on rhyolite plugs, which apparently were intruded during the latest stages of folding, indicate that folding occurred about 13 Ma.

INTRODUCTION

The Castle Mountains straddle the California-Nevada border approximately 100 km south of Las Vegas, Nevada (Fig. 1). They lie in the northern Colorado River trough, a region that was profoundly affected by crustal extension in the late Oligocene and Miocene (e.g., Davis and others, 1980; Frost and Martin, 1982; Spencer, 1985). Rocks in the Castle Mountains are cut by low-angle normal faults, but displacement on these faults is small (<1 km), and the range was not extended as severely as neighboring ranges such as the Whipple Mountains (Davis and others, 1980) and the Eldorado Mountains (Anderson, 1971).

In the Castle Mountains, Miocene rocks and Proterozoic basement are folded into a large, southwest-plunging anticline (hereafter called the Castle anticline). Folds occur in other ex-

tended parts of the Colorado River trough (e.g., Spencer, 1984), but the mechanism or mechanisms by which these structures of diverse orientation form in an extensional environment is not well understood (e.g., Spencer, 1985; Holt and others, 1986).

This chapter documents the stratigraphy of the Castle Mountains and the chronologic development of the Castle anticline and associated structures. A heterogeneous suite of volcanic flow and pyroclastic rocks and associated intrusions was erupted from 18.0 to 12.8 Ma. These rocks were folded into a southwest-plunging anticline and were later cut by small-displacement, east-dipping, low-angle normal faults and by high-angle, northeast-trending, strike- and oblique-slip faults. Volcanism and deformation in the Castle Mountains were part of a northward-moving belt of volcanism and faulting that moved up the Colorado River trough during the Miocene (Glazner and Bartley, 1984). Faulting

Turner, R. D., and Glazner, A. F., 1990, Miocene volcanism, folding, and faulting in the Castle Mountains, southern Nevada and eastern California, *in* Wernicke, B. P., ed., Basin and Range extensional tectonics near the latitude of Las Vegas, Nevada: Boulder, Colorado, Geological Society of America Memoir 176.

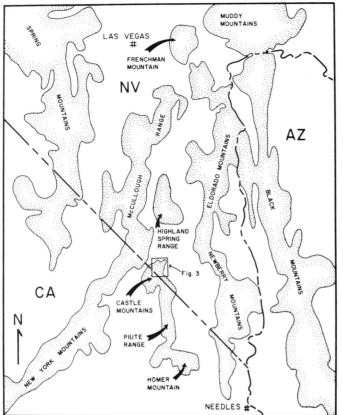

Figure 1. Map showing the location of the Castle Mountains.

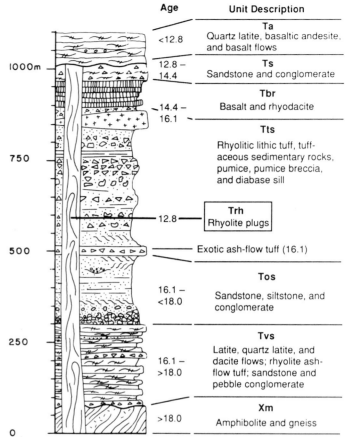

Figure 2. Stratigraphic column for the Castle Mountains. Includes all stratigraphic units shown on the geologic map (Fig. 3). Undivided rhyolite and sedimentary rocks unit (Tu) is not shown. Age constraints derived from K-Ar dating are indicated.

in the Castle Mountains is temporally, and probably genetically, related to well-documented extensional terranes to the east in the Colorado River trough region.

GEOLOGY OF THE CASTLE MOUNTAINS

Previous Work

The first published description of the geology of the Castle Mountains was Hewett's (1956) reconnaissance (1:125,000 scale) study of the Ivanpah quadrangle. Later studies include regional geologic mapping by Bingler and Bonham (1973) and a detailed map and descriptions of the geology of the western Castle Mountains by Medall (1964). The Tertiary stratigraphy of the surrounding region was first characterized by Longwell (1963) and later refined by Anderson (1971). Spencer (1985) discussed the fold in the Castle Mountains in a regional synthesis of Miocene low-angle normal faulting and dike emplacement in the northern Colorado River trough.

Stratigraphy

The Castle Mountains comprise a sequence of Miocene volcanic and sedimentary rocks that nonconformably overlies Prot-

erozoic basement (Fig. 2). The volcanic rocks range in composition from basalt to rhyolite and include flows, flow breccias, ash-flow tuffs, lithic tuffs, and air-fall tuffs. Rhyolitic to basaltic dikes locally intrude other units in the northeastern Castle Mountains. Sedimentary rocks include arkosic and volcaniclastic siltstone, sandstone, and conglomerate. Figure 2, Appendix 1, and Turner (1985 and U.S. Geological Survey MF map, in preparation) provide stratigraphic relations and detailed lithologic descriptions.

The Proterozoic basement consists of amphibolite and gneiss. Well-developed compositional layering in the metamorphic rocks is subhorizontal to vertical and is apparently folded about several different axes. Wasserburg and Lanphere (1965) included these rocks in their 1600- to 1800-Ma "Mojave Complex."

The contact of Miocene over Proterozoic rocks is a nonconformity with limited relief. Miocene rocks at the base of the section are andesitic flows and flow breccia plus interbedded rhyolite ash-flow tuff and arkosic and volcaniclastic sedimentary rocks. Varicolored lacustrine and fluvial sedimentary rocks are

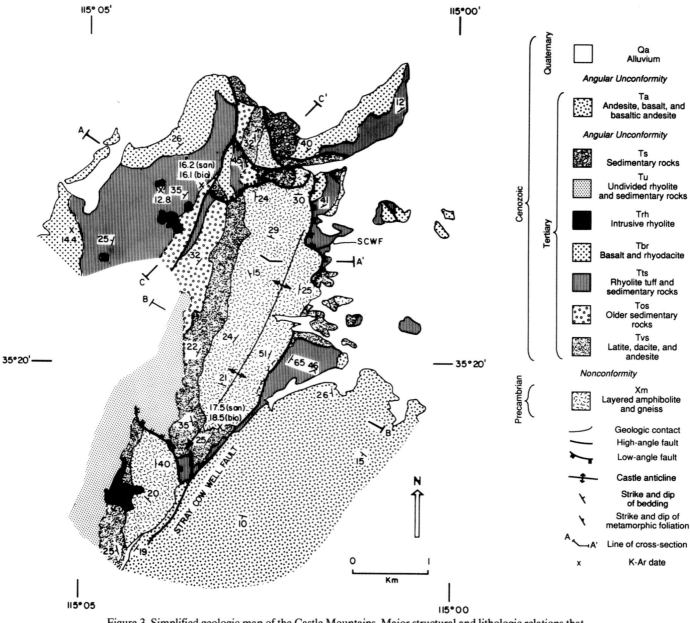

Figure 3. Simplified geologic map of the Castle Mountains. Major structural and lithologic relations that define the geologic evolution of the area include (1) the Castle anticline, (2) intrusive rhyolite that cuts the folded rocks, (3) east-dipping low-angle normal faults and strike-slip faults, and (4) gently dipping flows (Ta) of the Piute Range, which lies to the south. SCWF = possible northern, low-angle segment of the Stray Cow Well fault.

common in the middle of the section and occur with rhyolite ash-flow tuff, lithic air-fall tuff, and pumice and pumice breccia. Basaltic and andesitic flows and flow breccias, rhyodacite ash-flow tuffs, and younger fine- and coarse-grained sedimentary rocks occupy the top of the Miocene section. Rhyolite plugs, domes, and apophyses intrude the entire section.

Lateral variability of volcanic and sedimentary units and one major unconformity in the Miocene section complicate the stratigraphy. Fluvial and lacustrine sedimentary rocks (unit Tos

and the lower part of unit Tts), which abound in the northern Castle Mountains, pinch out to the south and east. Basal volcanic and sedimentary rocks (unit Tvs) also appear to pinch out to the northeast, where unit Tts rests directly on Proterozoic basement. An angular unconformity within the Tertiary sequence is exposed in the southern portion of the area, where andesitic volcanic rocks of unit Ta depositionally overlap both a low-angle normal fault and highly tilted lithic tuffs of unit Tts (Fig. 3; Fig. 4, cross section B-B'). Steep dips of unit Tts in the east-central part of the area

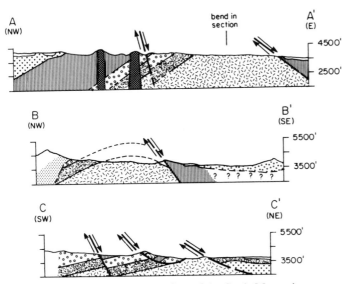

Figure 4. Geologic cross sections of the Castle Mountains.

may be a result of fault drag along the northeast-trending Stray Cow Well fault (Fig. 3).

Volcanism and sedimentation in the Castle Mountains occurred between 18 and 12 Ma, based on the K-Ar dates given in Table 1 and Spencer (1985). Biotite and sanidine from a rhyolite ash-flow tuff collected at the base of the section yielded dates of 18.5 ± 0.5 and 17.5 ± 0.4 Ma, respectively. Another biotite-sanidine pair from a rhyolite crystal tuff at the base of unit Tts yielded dates of 16.1 ± 0.4 Ma (biotite) and 16.2 ± 0.4 Ma (sanidine). A rhyodacite tuff near the top of the section was dated at 14.4 ± 0.2 Ma (biotite). Rhyolite plugs that intrude tilted volcanic and sedimentary rocks in the northwestern portion of the mapped area were dated at 12.8 ± 0.2 Ma (sanidine).

Geochemistry and textures of the volcanic rocks

Major-element, trace-element, and $^{87}Sr/^{86}Sr$ analyses of volcanic rocks from the Castle Mountains (Table 2) indicate that magma mixing and assimilation played a major role in producing the observed spectrum of compositions. Three lines of evidence support magma mixing: (1) major-element compositional trends, (2) a positive correlation between $^{87}Sr/^{86}Sr$ and SiO_2, and (3) disequilibrium-phenocryst textures in many rocks. These relations are displayed in Figures 5, 6, and 7.

Analyzed volcanic rocks range from slightly alkalic basalts ($\approx\frac{1}{2}$ wt % normative nepheline) to high-silica rhyolites. Although alteration has affected the chemistry of the rocks to an unknown extent, trends displayed by petrographically fresh volcanic rocks in the Castle Mountains mimic those shown by the Pliocene-Pleistocene Coso volcanic field (Novak and Bacon, 1986) and by rocks from the Miocene Mojave volcanic belt (Glazner, 1990). With the exception of MgO and Al_2O_3, plots of most major-element oxides against SiO_2 are roughly linear (Fig. 5). Also

plotted on Figure 5 is the average of 36 high-silica rhyolites from the Coso volcanic field (Bacon and others, 1981), which lies 250 km northwest of the Castle Mountains. The Coso average rhyolite plots on the trends exhibited by the Castle Mountains rocks for most oxides, indicating that it is a suitable major-element analog for the silicic mixing component.

Mixing/fractional crystallization calculations indicate that nonlinearity of the MgO and Al_2O_3 versus SiO_2 trends can be accounted for by mixing between slightly alkalic basalt and rhyolite, combined with minor fractionation of olivine and augite. Specifically, addition of Coso-like rhyolite combined with removal of magnesian olivine and augite in the weight proportions 8:1:1 reproduces observed trends, within error, for all oxides up to approximately 60 wt % SiO_2. For compositions more silicic than approximately 60 wt % SiO_2, the chemical variations can be explained by magma mixing without significant crystal fractionation. Details of the calculations are given in Glazner (1990).

Trace-element trends are roughly linear for some elements but show a high degree of scatter for others. This scatter probably occurs largely because major elements and trace elements are decoupled during magma mixing; that is, silicic anatectic melts of broadly similar major-element composition can have vastly different trace-element compositions depending on the degree of partial melting, the composition of the source rock, and other factors. Alteration may also contribute to the scatter.

Magma mixing or assimilation is also indicated by the observed variation of $^{87}Sr/^{86}Sr$ with SiO_2. Measured $^{87}Sr/^{86}Sr$ values increase from 0.705 to 0.706 in basalts to 0.709 to 0.716 in rhyolites (Fig. 6). Calculated initial $^{87}Sr/^{86}Sr$ values, assuming an age of 15 Ma, range from 0.705 to 0.706 in basalts to 0.708 to 0.710 in andesites, dacites, and rhyolites. However, one rhyolite yielded an impossibly low calculated initial $^{87}Sr/^{86}Sr$ ratio (0.678), presumably because alteration has affected its Rb/Sr ratio. Leaching of Sr from (or addition of Rb to) volcanic glass

TABLE 1. K-Ar AGE DETERMINATIONS

Sample	62T	62T	178T	178T
Unit	Tts	Tts	Tvs	Tvs
Latitude (°N)	35.3653	35.3653	35.3203	35.3203
Longitude (°W)	115.0561	115.0561	115.0550	115.0550
Material	san	bio	san	bio
K_2O, wt%	8.82	8.68	9.37	8.66
$^{40}Ar^*$, 10^{-10} mol/g	2.06631	2.02179	2.36518	2.32116
%$^{40}Ar^*$	58.24	72.43	50.70	65.70
Age, Ma	16.2	16.1	17.5	18.5
$\pm\sigma$	0.4	0.4	0.4	0.5

$^*{}^{40}Ar$ = radiogenic argon; bio = biotite; san = sanidine.
Decay constants from Dalrymple (1979).
Analyses by J. Nakata, P. Klock; mineral separations by D. Sorg; at U.S. Geological Survey laboratories.

TABLE 2. MAJOR-ELEMENT, TRACE-ELEMENT, AND ^{87}Sr/^{86}Sr ANALYSES OF SELECTED SAMPLES FROM THE CASTLE MOUNTAINS

Unit	Td	Td	Tvs	Tvs	Tvs	Tts	Tbr	Tbr	Trh	Trh	Tvs	Tu	Tu	Ta	Ta
Sample	151B-T	183-T	11-T	19-H	8-H	62-T	139-T	122-T	137-T	140-T	40-T	24-H	71-T	351-T	353-T
SiO$_2$	61.8	77.2	52.8	52.7	61.2	70.4	47.5	48.7	71.9	68.1	52.1	74.9	74.9	65.4	58.9
TiO$_2$	1.02	0.08	1.15	1.15	0.65	0.31	1.64	1.44	0.3	0.37	1.23	0.11	0.09	0.81	0.88
Al$_2$O$_3$	16.3	11.9	15.8	16.0	15.3	13.9	16.8	16.1	14.2	14.7	16.6	11.8	12.7	16.7	17.3
FeO^t	4.48	0.74	6.34	6.23	3.70	1.52	9.17	8.68	1.60	1.84	7.24	0.81	1.63	4.27	4.37
MnO	0.04	0.03	0.07	0.06	0.04	0.04	0.16	0.14	0.05	0.05	0.13	0.03	0.04	0.06	0.08
MgO	1.33	0.10	4.13	3.50	2.31	0.53	7.31	8.31	0.45	0.58	5.23	0.16	0.16	1.07	0.48
CaO	4.46	0.58	6.99	6.35	4.54	1.12	10.40	9.06	1.21	1.60	8.24	0.86	0.73	4.22	5.28
Na$_2$O	3.71	3.49	3.61	3.92	3.70	3.44	3.19	3.50	3.84	3.98	3.38	3.53	3.66	4.15	4.29
K$_2$O	3.84	4.56	4.30	3.87	2.68	6.56	0.65	1.16	4.92	4.68	1.72	4.66	4.94	3.70	4.06
P$_2$O$_5$	0.42		1.06	1.08	0.32	0.10	0.26	0.56	0.08	0.10	0.31		0.00	0.26	0.27
H$_2$O$^+$	0.90	0.35	0.49	1.27	2.48	0.68	1.97	0.96	0.43	2.36			0.32		
H$_2$O$^-$	0.75	0.19	0.55	1.47	1.78	0.01	0.61	0.41	0.33	0.64			0.16		
CO$_2$	0.13	0.31	0.10	1.26	0.27	0.19	0.18	0.20	0.24	0.16			0.04		
Total	99.2	99.5	97.4	98.9	99.0	98.8	99.8	99.2	99.6	99.2	96.2	96.9	99.4	100.6	95.9
Rb	129	224	47	88	81	200	31	55	175	145	45	165	175	88	100
Sr	862	17	2401	2298	1148	127	453	913	157	203	552	5	3	512	531
Y	9	36	32	17	3	30	33	21	16	26	29	29	30	23	31
Zr	300	125	534	437	258	314	165	186	237	272	191	181	175	355	357
Ba	1132	0	2451	2230	1333	433	272	571	474	680			91	1270	1335
^{87}Sr/^{86}Sr		0.71624	0.70976	0.70990	0.70990	0.70990	0.70584	0.70526	0.70899		0.70729		0.71403	0.70817	0.70846

Oxides in wt%, trace elements in parts per million by weight.

Major-element oxide analyses for all samples except two analyses of unit Ta by U.S. Geological Survey laboratories, Menlo Park, California. Analysts: J. Baker, A. Bartel, G. Mason, S. Neil, H. Neiman, J. Ryder, J. Taggart, and J. S. Wahlberg. All trace-element analyses and major-element analyses of unit Ta by x-ray fluorescence by R. D. Turner at the University of North Carolina at Chapel Hill. Sr-isotope analyses by R. D. Turner and A. F. Glazner at the University of North Carolina at Chapel Hill.

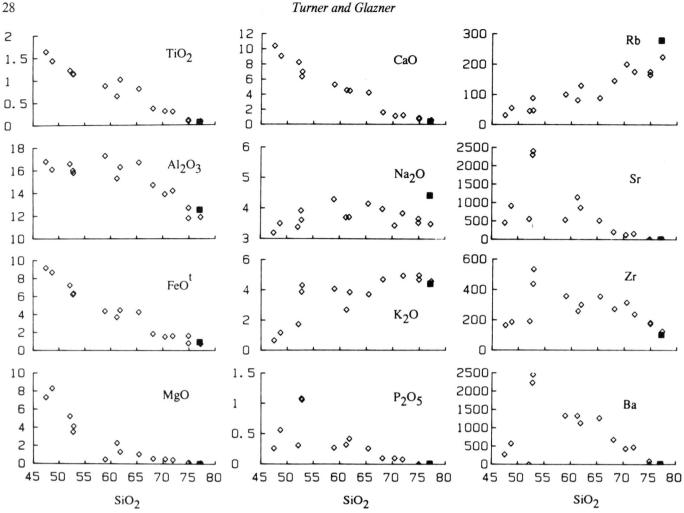

Figure 5. Variation diagrams of major-element oxides and trace elements versus SiO_2. Note the crude linearity of many trends. Oxides in wt %; trace elements in parts per million by weight. Filled squares give the mean composition of high-silica rhyolite from the Coso volcanic field (Bacon and others, 1981); note that most of the compositional variability of the suite can be explained by mixing of high-silica rhyolite with basalt.

would not affect the measured $^{87}Sr/^{86}Sr$ value but would increase the Rb/Sr ratio, leading to a lower calculated initial $^{87}Sr/^{86}Sr$ ratio. Therefore, these calculated initial ratios are suspect and may be too low, especially in the rhyolites.

Disequilibrium phenocryst textures (Fig. 7) include augite-rimmed quartz and reverse-zoned, dusty plagioclase in intermediate rocks. Rounded quartz grains with augite rims and rhyolitic glass inclusions are common in volcanic rocks of the Mojave Desert. They are apparently incompletely digested remnants of melted granitic rocks (Mies and Glazner, 1987; compare Eichelberger, 1978). Novak and Bacon (1986) and Glazner (1990) discuss the textures of other mixed-magma, extension-related volcanic rocks from the Mojave Desert and adjacent areas.

Structural geology

Folds. Bedding attitudes and the trace of the Miocene-Proterozoic contact define a broad, open anticline. Bedded Miocene volcanic and sedimentary rocks that flank Proterozoic basement dip to the northwest and southeast, and the basal Miocene contact forms a U-shaped map pattern (Fig. 3). Tertiary rocks in the southern McCullough Mountains dip to the southeast at approximately 20° (Hewett, 1956), suggesting that a syncline of equivalent dimensions underlies the valley between the two ranges.

Because bedded rocks on the northwest and southeast limbs dip on average about 30° and 45°, respectively, the Castle anticline is asymmetric (Figs. 3, 4, 8). This geometry may have been modified by a northeast-trending high-angle fault that separates much of the southeast limb of the anticline from rocks to the northwest. In its present state, the half-wavelength of the Castle anticline is at least 5 km, and the fold amplitude is at least 750 m (the minimum amplitude illustrated in cross section B-B', Fig. 4). These estimates are necessarily minima because only one fold axis and portions of the fold limbs are exposed in the Castle Mountains. The axial plane of the Castle anticline is oriented N36°E, 80°NW.

Faults. Faults exposed in the Castle Mountains dip to the northeast, east, and southeast at both high and low angles. Low-angle faults generally dip to the east or northeast at 25 to 40°, whereas high-angle faults generally dip to the southeast at 65 to 90°.

Map relations suggest that the high-angle faults cut the low-angle faults. For example, in the northern portion of the area, two low-angle faults are clearly cut by a northeast-trending high-angle fault (Fig. 3), and the southernmost low-angle fault is depositionally overlain by flows of unit Ta, which are in turn cut by the northeast-trending, high-angle segment of the Stray Cow Well fault. The entire set of faults may represent a continuum in which early high-angle faults are cut by later high-angle faults and rotated to low dips (e.g., Proffett, 1977). Map relations give no indication that high-angle faults feed into throughgoing low-angle faults, although the Stray Cow Well fault appears to shallow in dip as it swings north (Fig. 3). Alternatively, the Stray Cow Well fault may actually be two faults: an older, north-trending, low-angle fault to the north that was cut by a younger, northeast-trending, high-angle fault.

Slickenside striations are rare, but those observed record a consistent pattern of relative movement. Moderately plunging striations were observed on two exposed surfaces of the northeast-trending high-angle faults. In contrast, only down-dip striations were observed on the poorly exposed low-angle faults.

Separation of stratigraphic marker horizons plus a faulted fold axis indicates that throw on the low-angle normal faults is less than 5 km. In the southern Castle Mountains, the gently southwest-plunging Castle anticline is offset by a low-angle fault (Fig. 3). The intersection of the fold's axial plane with the nonconformity can be regarded as a piercing point in the fault plane, and its offset gives an estimate of displacement of approximately 0.5 km.

Because rocks above and below the low-angle faults are lithologically and stratigraphically identical, it is unlikely that

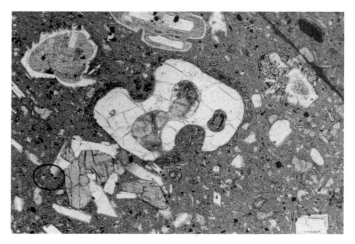

Figure 7. Photomicrograph of andesite dike showing disequilibrium textures that are common in andesites and dacites from the Castle Mountains. Width of field approximately 4 mm. The rounded central grain is a quartz xenocryst that contains blebs of brown rhyolite glass and is surrounded by a thin corona of green augite. Plagioclase in this rock generally has a clear core (An_{32}), a dusty intermediate region, and a thin, clear rim that is more calcic (An_{55}) than the core.

they have moved far relative to each other. In addition, lithic air-fall tuffs of unit Tts, which are clearly of local origin (based on the large size of lithic fragments and the common occurrence of bomb sags), are common in the upper plate. These rocks have probably not moved more than approximately 5 km from their source area in the heart of the Castle Mountains to the southwest. Similar relations suggest that displacement of the high-angle faults is probably not more than 3 or 4 km. These relations indicate that the Castle Mountains have only experienced moderate east-directed extension.

Timing constraints. The age of folding in the Castle Mountains is apparently constrained by rhyolite plugs that intrude the northwest flank of the Castle anticline. Jane Nielson (personal communication, 1983) observed that the plugs are emplaced in rocks that are tilted 20 to 40° to the northwest, yet are themselves nearly vertical, and thus apparently intruded a previously tilted section. If this accurately records the relative sequence of events, then dates on the youngest tilted unit (14.4 Ma) and on the unrotated rhyolite plugs (12.8 Ma) bracket the timing of folding.

The orientation of flow foliation at the chilled margins of three rhyolite plugs indicates that a distinct angular discordance does exist between the plugs and the bedded rocks in the northwest limb of the anticline (Fig. 8). These data show that the mean cylinder axis for all three plugs is approximately vertical, whereas bedding dips 33° to the northwest. Thus, if the plugs were intruded vertically, then most of the tilting occurred before intrusion. K-Ar analysis of sanidine from one rhyolite plug (unit Trh) yielded an age of 12.8 ± 0.2 Ma, and biotite from a rhyodacite ash-flow tuff at the top of the folded section was dated at 14.4 ±

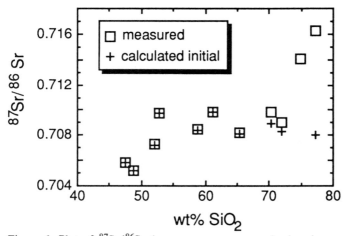

Figure 6. Plot of $^{87}Sr/^{86}Sr$ (open squares—measured; plus signs—calculated initial) versus SiO_2 for 10 samples. Calculated initial values are suspect owing to alteration, especially for the rhyolites. The general increase of $^{87}Sr/^{86}Sr$ with SiO_2 is consistent with contamination by radiogenic crustal rocks.

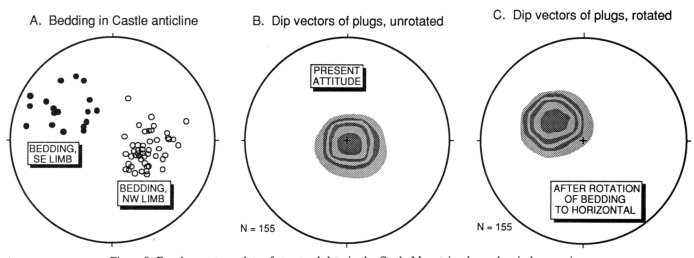

Figure 8. Equal-area stereoplots of structural data in the Castle Mountains, lower-hemisphere projection. A. 61 poles to bedding from the Castle anticline. The mean pole to bedding in the northwest limb plunges 57° to S54°E. B. Contour diagram (using the method of Kamb, 1959) of 155 dip vectors of flow foliation at the margins of three rhyolite plugs that intrude the northwest flank of the Castle anticline. For perfect, vertical cylinders, the points would all plot at the center of the diagram. These data define the rhyolite plugs as near-vertical cylinders that have intruded bedded rocks tilted an average of 33° to the northwest. The mean dip vector plunges 85° to S27°E with a 95 percent confidence interval of 2°; thus, the plugs are essentially vertical. Contour interval 6σ; outermost shaded contour interval is 6–12σ. C. The same dip vectors as plotted in B, rotated 33° about a horizontal axis oriented N36°E, in order to make bedding on the northwest flank of the anticline horizontal. Rotation of dip vectors away from the vertical supports the interpretation that most folding occurred before intrusion of the plugs. Same contour intervals as B.

0.2 Ma (Spencer, 1985). These dates suggest that most folding in the Castle Mountains occurred between 14.4 Ma and 12.8 Ma.

DISCUSSION

Nature of volcanism

Middle Miocene volcanism in the Castle Mountains is similar to extension-related volcanism in surrounding areas. Glazner (1990) showed that volcanism in the Mojave Desert can be divided into two age belts: a southern belt, approximately 20 m.y. old, which runs through the central Mojave Desert from the town of Mojave eastward through Barstow and the Whipple Mountains, and a northern belt, about 15 m.y. old, at the latitude of the Garlock fault. The Castle Mountains are part of the northern belt. In each of these belts, intense but brief episodes of Miocene volcanism occurred after an early Tertiary hiatus, and volcanism was coincident (within a few million years) with significant crustal extension. Abundant evidence for magma mixing indicates that these volcanic episodes resulted from large-scale intrusion of the crust by basaltic magma. Silicic rocks are largely recycled crust, and intermediate rocks are mixtures of mantle-derived basalt and recycled crust, with or without crystal fractionation.

Although the causes and mechanisms of extension and magmatism are not well understood, it is clear that extension and magmatism in the corridor south of Las Vegas were temporally related to the tectonics of the continental margin. Glazner and

Bartley (1984) showed that volcanism and extension coincided in time (given the errors in plate reconstructions) with passage of the Mendocino triple junction past a given area. Following Ingersoll (1982), they related this correspondence to the unstable configuration of the triple junction. At the latitude of the Castle Mountains, subduction ceased approximately 17 ± 1 Ma (Glazner and Bartley, 1984; Stock and Molnar, 1988).

Data from the Castle Mountains support a link between active tectonics and magmatism. There is a subtle but distinct transition from early intermediate volcanism (unit Tvs) to bimodal volcanism (units Tts and Tbr) and then back to intermediate volcanism (unit Ta). Arguments presented above (for example, overlapping of a low-angle fault by unit Ta) indicate that units Tts and Tbr were erupted during or slightly before active normal faulting. Similar arguments can be made for the southeastern Cady Mountains (100 km southwest of the Castle Mountains), where bimodal volcanism interbedded with coarse clastic deposits is sandwiched between periods of intermediate volcanism (Glazner, 1988).

These subtle transitions may reflect the influence of strain rate on magma mixing. Several authors (e.g., Eichelberger, 1978; Hildreth, 1981; Bacon, 1982) have argued that active extension favors eruption of basalt, because faulting provides pathways to the surface and shortens the residence time of a magma in the crust. However, Glazner and Ussler (1989) showed that synextensional rocks are dominantly intermediate in character and that basalts are generally erupted well after extension has ceased. This is true for the Castle Mountains area, where the regional transition to dominantly basaltic volcanism occurred well after both subduction and extension had ceased (e.g., Anderson and others, 1972; Dohrenwend and others, 1984). Data from the Castle Mountains indicate the possibility that both models are correct; active extension may shift otherwise intermediate volcanism to more basaltic compositions.

Origin of the Castle anticline

Although broad warps in detachment surfaces of the northern Colorado River trough are common (e.g., Spencer, 1985), folds such as the Castle anticline are rare. Folding in the Castle Mountains occurred during crustal extension in the Colorado River trough and thus may be related to the extension process. Possible origins for the fold include (1) folding during isostatic warping of detachment surfaces, (2) normal or reverse drag along normal faults, (3) drag along strike-slip faults, and (4) regional shortening. These alternatives are discussed below.

1. Isostatic warping. Spencer (1985) related formation of the Castle anticline and a reverse fault in the Dead Mountains to compressional forces produced by concave-upward isostatic flexure of lower-plate rocks. By mapping a Miocene dike swarm exposed at nearby Homer Mountain (Fig. 9), Spencer inferred a maximum compressive stress orientation of N80°W ± 10° around 15 Ma. This is discordant by 27° to the maximum compressive stress orientation implied by the Castle anticline (N53°W) at 12.8 to 14.4 Ma. However, given the uncertainties in both these estimates and the rapid temporal changes in stress orientation in the southwestern United States during the Miocene (e.g., Best, 1988), this discrepancy may not preclude an isostatic origin for the Castle anticline.

2. Normal or reverse drag along an unidentified normal fault. If the Castle Mountains are underlain by a large-displacement, listric normal fault, then the Castle anticline could have formed by reverse drag (e.g., Hamblin, 1965). This hypothesis is confounded by the absence of identified faults that could be responsible for dragging the section.

3. Drag related to strike-slip faulting. Well-documented examples of extension-related strike-slip faults, such as the Garlock fault (Davis and Burchfiel, 1973) and those in the Lake Mead region (Anderson, 1971; Bohannon, 1979, 1983; Weber and Smith, 1987; Ron and others, 1986), indicate the importance of strike-slip faulting in crustal extension. Additionally, extension-related structures located to the north of the Castle Mountains are consistently younger than those to the south (Fig. 9; Glazner and Bartley, 1984). Because extension occurred at different times in different areas, structures that accommodate differential crustal extension seem to be required. Thus, the Castle anticline could be a drag fold related to strike-slip faulting at the margin of an extended terrane. As with the normal fault hypothesis, no candidate faults for this mechanism have been identified.

4. Regional north-south shortening. Wright (1976), Glazner and Bartley (1984), and Wernicke and others (1988)

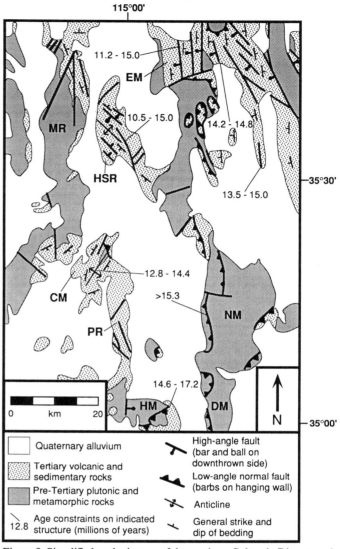

Figure 9. Simplified geologic map of the northern Colorado River trough area, showing timing constraints on structures related to crustal extension in the region. Mountain ranges are: CM—Castle Mountains; DM—Dead Mountains; EM—Eldorado Mountains; HM—Homer Mountain; HSR—Highland Spring Range; MR—McCullough Range; NM—Newberry Mountains; PR—Piute Range. Timing constraints from Anderson and others (1972), Davis (1984), Spencer (1985), and this chapter.

proposed, on the basis of regional strain considerations, that eastern California has undergone significant north-south shortening in the Neogene. Recent field work in the Mojave Desert (Bartley and others, 1990) has identified numerous folds and reverse faults that accommodate this shortening, and Glazner and others (1989) and Fletcher and Bartley (1990) showed that strain in footwall mylonites of the Waterman Hills detachment fault, near Barstow, is constrictional. Folding in the Castle Mountains could be related to these events.

Relation to adjacent areas

Structures in the Castle Mountains formed at roughly the same time as prominent extension-related structures in the northern Colorado River trough. Figure 9 shows some of the major extensional structures in this region and gives timing constraints for their formation. Most of these structures formed between 10.6 and 17.2 Ma and are coincident with low- and high-angle faulting and folding in the Castle Mountains.

Anderson (1971) documented extreme crustal extension in the region pictured in Figure 9, and Spencer (1985) inferred that the area contains a distended aggregate of upper-plate rocks that is separated from a structurally coherent lower plate by a low-angle fault system. To the south and east of the Castle Mountains, Spencer recognized an east-dipping low-angle fault system that is exposed in the Piute Wash hills and the Homer, Newberry, and Dead Mountains. According to Spencer, the faults exposed at Homer Mountain and the Piute Wash hills represent a breakaway that separates a broad areas of low-angle normal faulting in the Colorado River trough from an unextended area to the west. This breakaway fault projects northward toward the Castle Mountains. In contrast, Anderson (1971) and Weber and Smith (1987) describe a low-angle normal fault system that dips west under the Eldorado Mountains and presumably is rooted under the Highland Spring Range and McCullough Mountains. The structural and temporal relations between the inferred east-dipping and west-dipping systems, and their relation to the Castle Mountains, are not well known. The east-dipping, low-angle normal faults exposed in the Castle Mountains may represent the northward extension, or a splay of the northward extension, of the east-dipping breakaway fault described by Spencer.

CONCLUSIONS

1. Volcanism in the Castle Mountains began with eruption of intermediate-composition and minor silicic lavas near 18.0 Ma, was followed by deposition of an ash-flow tuff at 16.1 Ma, changed to production of bimodal basaltic and rhyolitic flows and intrusions that lasted until 12.8 Ma, and culminated with deposition of primarily intermediate-composition lavas sometime after 12.8 Ma. Eruption of the bimodal assemblage apparently coincided with extension by normal faulting.

2. The spectrum of compositions observed in volcanic rocks from the Castle Mountains was apparently produced by mixing of basalts with silicic melts derived from the basement and by basement assimilation, coupled with minor crystal fractionation.

3. Bedded rocks in the Castle Mountains were folded into a northeast-trending anticline and were cut by east-dipping low-angle normal faults and high-angle strike-slip faults. Rhyolite plugs that intrude the northwest flank of the Castle anticline appear to have been emplaced late in the folding episode. Dates of 12.8 ± 0.4 Ma from a rhyolite plug and 14.4 ± 0.4 Ma from an ash-flow tuff at the top of the folded section indicate that folding occurred near 12.8 ± 0.4 Ma but may be as old as 14.4 ± 0.4 Ma.

4. Low-angle normal faults and strike-slip faults formed at the same time as similar structures related to crustal extension in nearby ranges of the Colorado River trough.

ACKNOWLEDGMENTS

Supported by National Science foundation grant EAR 82-19032 to A.F.G. and by grants to R.D.T. from Sigma Xi and from the McCarthy fund of the University of North Carolina Department of Geology. This research would never have begun without the encouragement and support of Jane Nielson and Jon Spencer. We thank R. Ernest Anderson, Brian Wernicke, Phil Gans, and Jon Spencer for constructive criticism of the manuscript, and Jane Nielson, John Bartley, J. Robert Butler, Eugene Smith, and Peter Weigand for comments on earlier versions. Field assistance was cheerfully and ably provided by Jackie Huntoon. The U.S. Geological Survey provided analytical and field support.

APPENDIX 1: LITHOLOGIC DESCRIPTIONS OF UNITS IN THE CASTLE MOUNTAINS

Metamorphic rocks (Xm)

Very light-gray to black gneiss that is compositionally layered on a 1- to 5-m scale. Predominant lithologies include coarse-grained amphibolite and quartzofeldspathic gneiss with garnet, muscovite, biotite, hornblende, and sillimanite. Coexistence of garnet-biotite gneiss with biotite-sillimanite gneiss indicate that these rocks equilibrated at upper amphibolite facies conditions (Turner, 1981, p. 209). Leucocratic granitic pegmatite dikes of unknown age locally intrude the older metamorphic rocks.

Basal volcanic and sedimentary rocks (Tvs)

Dark-gray, grayish-green, and brownish-gray andesite, basaltic andesite, and dacite flows and flow breccias with minor interbedded light-pink to buff rhyolite ash-flow tuff and gray to brownish-gray volcaniclastic and arkosic sedimentary rocks. The rhyolite ash-flow tuff is 2 to 3 m thick and is discontinuously found at the base of the section. Similar tuffs occur as thin lenses interbedded with other volcanic and sedimentary rocks throughout the unit. Basaltic andesite to dacite flows and flow breccias occur from the base of the unit to the top. Coarse- to fine-grained sandstone and conglomerate are interbedded with volcanic lithologies near the top of the unit. Flow rocks contain phenocrysts of augite, hornblende, biotite, phlogopite, apatite, plagioclase, and quartz in a groundmass of plagioclase microlites with intergranular, intersertal, hyalopilitic, or pilotaxitic texture. Resorbed quartz xenocrysts armored by microcrystalline mantles of clinopyroxene occur in the intermediate-composition flow rocks. Rhyolite ash-flow tuff contains quartz, sanidine, and biotite phenocrysts in a devitrified matrix of rhyolite ash. Interbedded sedimentary rocks are fine- to coarse-grained sandstone and conglomerate that contains clasts of volcanic rocks of intermediate composition and high-grade metamorphic rocks. Biotite and sanidine from a rhyolite tuff at the base of the section yielded dates of 18.5 ± 0.5 and 17.5 ± 0.4 Ma respectively (Table 1, samples 178T (bio) and 178T (san).

Older sedimentary rocks (Tos)

Light-gray, grayish-yellow, pale greenish-yellow, and light-red volcaniclastic and arkosic siltstone, sandstone, and conglomerate. A basal conglomerate contains cobble- to boulder-sized clasts of volcanic and high-grade metamorphic rocks. Overlying the conglomerate are varicolored lake sediments and fine- to medium-grained fluvial deposits. Lake sediments are chiefly siltstone and mudstone interbedded with minor limestone, arkosic sandstone, and water-laid tuff. Cross-bedded and channel-scoured sandstone and pebble conglomerate occur at the top of the unit.

Rhyolite tuffs and sedimentary rocks (Tts)

Poorly welded light-tan crystal ash-flow tuff and lithic tuff, medium- to light-gray pumice and pumice breccia, and yellowish-gray tuffaceous sedimentary rocks. The 3- to 4-m-thick crystal ash-flow tuff lies at the base of the unit and is overlain by fine- to coarse-grained tuffaceous sedimentary rocks. Well-bedded lithic tuff, pumice, and pumice breccia predominate at the top of the unit. The upper part of the unit is locally intruded by a diabase sill. The basal tuff contains phenocrysts of sanidine, plagioclase, biotite, hornblende, augite, zircon, and quartz in a devitrified ashy matrix. Tuffaceous sedimentary rocks show varying degrees of rounding, sorting, and cross-stratification and include buff to gray volcaniclastic siltstone, fine- to medium-grained sandstone, and pebble to cobble conglomerate. The lithic tuff is planar-bedded and contains a heterogeneous assemblage of lithologies, including pink flow-banded rhyolite, gray pumice, and yellow-tan crystal tuff. The pumice and pumice breccia is aphyric. Concordant K-Ar dates on biotite (16.1 ± 0.4 Ma) and sanidine (16.2 ± 0.4 Ma) indicate that the basal crystal tuff was deposited about 16.1 Ma (Table 1, sample 62T).

Bingler and Bonham (1973) correlated this basal tuff with the tuff of Bridge Spring of Anderson (1971). However, concordant K-Ar dates of 16.1 ± 0.4 Ma (biotite) and 16.2 ± 0.4 Ma (sanidine) on the basal tuff may be significantly different from the 14.9 ± 0.6 Ma (biotite) and 14.8 ± 0.5 Ma (sanidine) dates that Anderson and others (1972) determined on the tuff of Bridge Spring in the Eldorado Mountains (ages corrected using the constants of Dalrymple, 1979). Differences in composition may also be significant. The ash-flow tuff in the Castle Mountains (sample 62T, Table 2) is higher in SiO_2, K_2O, and Sr and lower in Al_2O_3, TiO_2, and MgO than the tuff of Bridge Spring exposed in the Eldorado Mountains (data for comparison from Anderson, 1978, and E. I. Smith, written communication, 1986). Consequently, whereas the phenocryst mineralogies and stratigraphic positions of the tuffs are similar, their emplacement ages and chemistries may be different. Therefore correlation of the tuff in the Castle Mountains with the tuff of Bridge Spring is probably not valid.

Dike rocks (Td)

Black to gray-green basalt and andesite plus light-pink to buff rhyolite. Basalt and andesite dikes contain moderate amounts of olivine, clinopyroxene, hornblende, and plagioclase phenocrysts in a groundmass of tachylite and plagioclase microlites. One andesite dike contains xenocrystic quartz with augite rims (Table 2, sample 151B-T; Fig. 7). Rhyolite dikes contain sanidine, quartz, and biotite phenocrysts in a matrix of devitrified glass.

Basalt and rhyodacite (Tbr)

Black to dark-red basalt flows and flow breccias are overlain by gray-brown rhyodacite crystal tuff with a well-defined 3- to 6-m-thick black basal vitrophyre. Basalt is commonly vesicular and bears phenocrysts of olivine, augite, plagioclase, and minor apatite and xenocrystic, augite-rimmed quartz in a pilotaxic groundmass of tachylite and plagioclase microlites. The rhyodacite tuff contains phenocrysts of sanidine, biotite, augite, and hornblende in a recrystallized matrix. A eutaxitic texture that is evident in hand sample is often contorted into meter-scale isoclinal folds that resemble flow banding. Biotite from the rhyodacite yielded a K-Ar date of 14.4 ± 0.2 Ma (Spencer, 1985; Turner and others, 1983).

Rhyolite of Hart Peak (Trh)

Light pink to red-brown flow-banded rhyolite plugs, domes, and sills. Sparse phenocrysts of sanidine, biotite, and rare quartz and clinopyroxene rest in a groundmass of devitrified rhyolite glass with abundant spherulites. Spherulites are often evident in hand specimen. Sanidine from one of the plugs yielded a K-Ar date of 12.8 ± 0.2 Ma (Spencer, 1985; Turner and others, 1983).

Undivided rhyolite and sedimentary rocks (Tu)

Red-brown to pink rhyolite flows, light-tan to buff rhyolite tuff and tuffaceous sedimentary rocks, and buff to gray sandstone, siltstone, and conglomerate that are intruded by a complex mosaic of rhyolite plugs and apophyses. Volcanic and sedimentary rocks are from units Tos and Tts, and the intrusive rhyolite correlates directly with unit Trh.

Sedimentary rocks (Ts)

Consolidated stream sands, gravels, and fanglomerate with minor interbedded dark-red to black basalt flows and flow breccias. Clast lithologies are identical to older volcanic and basement rocks in the mapped area and include basalt to rhyolite and gneiss. Sedimentary structures include planar- and cross-stratification in finer-grained rocks and massive chaotic bedding in coarse-grained conglomerate. Minor basalt is vesicular and contains phenocrysts of plagioclase, olivine, and clinopyroxene in a matrix of tachylite and plagioclase microlites.

Andesitic volcanic rocks (Ta)

Dark-red, gray, or black andesite, basaltic andesite, and rare basalt flows and flow breccias that contain minor interbedded light-tan to buff rhyolite lithic tuff and tuffaceous sedimentary rocks. Flow rocks are highly to sparsely porphyritic andesite and basaltic andesite bearing phenocrysts of plagioclase, augite, hornblende, phlogopite, and apatite. Subordinate basalt contains phenocrysts of plagioclase, olivine, and augite. A pilotaxitic matrix of plagioclase microlites is common to all flow rocks, and augite-rimmed quartz xenocrysts were noted in some thin sections. Minor lithic tuff and tuffaceous sedimentary rocks are identical to those in unit Tts.

REFERENCES CITED

Anderson, R. E., 1971, Thin skin distension in Tertiary rocks of southeastern Nevada: Geological Society of America Bulletin, v. 82, p. 43–58.
—— , 1978, Chemistry of Tertiary volcanic rocks in the Eldorado Mountains, Clark County, Nevada, and comparisons with rocks from some nearby areas: U.S. Geological Survey Journal of Research, v. 6, p. 409–424.
Anderson, R. E., Longwell, C. R., Armstrong, R. L., and Marvin, R. F., 1972, Significance of K-Ar ages of Tertiary rocks from the Lake Mead region, Nevada–Arizona: Geological Society of America Bulletin, v. 83, p. 273–288.
Bacon, C. R., 1982, Time-predictable bimodal volcanism in the Coso Range, California: Geology, v. 10, p. 65–69.
Bacon, C. R., Macdonald, R., Smith, R. L., and Baedecker, P. A.,1981, Pleistocene high-silica rhyolites of the Coso volcanic field, Inyo County, California: Journal of Geophysical Research, v. 86, p. 10223–10241.
Bartley, J. M., Glazner, A. F., and Schermer, E. R., 1990, North-south contraction of the Mojave block and strike-slip tectonics in southern California: Science, v. 248, p. 1398–1401.
Best, M. G., 1988, Early Miocene change in direction of least principal stress, southwestern United States; Conflicting inferences from dikes and metamorphic core-detachment fault terranes: Tectonics, v. 7, p. 249–259.
Bingler, E. C., and Bonham, H. F., 1973, Reconnaissance geologic map of the McCullough Range and adjacent areas, Clark County, Nevada: Nevada Bureau of Mines and Geology Map 45, scale 1:125,000.
Bohannon, R. G., 1979, Strike-slip faults of the Lake Mead region of southern Nevada, in Armentrout, J. M., Cole, M. R., and Terbest, H., Jr., eds., Cenozoic paleogeography of the western United States: Society of Economic Paleontologists and Mineralogists Pacific Coast Paleogeography Symposium 3, p. 129–140.

—— , 1983, Geologic map, tectonic map, and structure sections of the Muddy and northern Black Mountains, Clark County, Nevada: U.S. Geological Survey Miscellaneous Investigations Map I-1406, scale 1:62,500.
Dalrymple, G. B., 1979, Critical tables for conversion of K-Ar ages from old to new constants: Geology, v. 7, p. 558–560.
Davis, G. A., and Burchfiel, B. C., 1973, Garlock fault: An intracontinental transform structure, southern California: Geological Society of America Bulletin, v. 84, p. 1407–1422.
Davis, G. A., Anderson, J. L., Frost, E. G., and Shackelford, T. J., 1980, Mylonitization and detachment faulting in the Whipple–Buckskin–Rawhide Mountains terrane, southeastern Califronia and western Arizona, in Crittenden, M. D., Jr., Coney, P. J., and Davis, G. H., Cordilleran metamorphic core complexes: Geological Society of America Memoir 153, p. 79–129.
Davis, S. O., 1984, Structural geology of the central part of the Highland Spring Range, Clark County, Nevada [M.S. thesis]: Los Angeles, University of Southern California, 190 p.
Dohrenwend, J. C., McFadden, L. D., Turrin, B. D., and Wells, S. G., 1984, K-Ar dating of the Cima volcanic field, eastern Mojave Desert, California; Late Cenozoic volcanic history and landscape evolution: Geology, 12, p. 163–167.
Eichelberger, J. C., 1978, Andesitic volcanism and crustal evolution: Nature, v. 275, p. 21–27.
Fletcher, J. M., and Bartley, J. M., 1990, Constrictional strain in the footwall of the central Mojave metamorphic core complex, California: Geological Society of America Abstracts with Programs, v. 22, p. 23.
Frost, E. G., and Martin, D. L., 1982, Mesozoic–Cenozoic tectonic evolution of the Colorado River region, California, Arizona, and Nevada: San Diego, California, Cordilleran Publishers, 608 p.
Glazner, A. F., 1988, Stratigraphy, structure, and potassic alteration of Miocene volcanic rocks in the Sleeping Beauty area, central Mojave Desert, California: Geological Society of America Bulletin, v. 100, p. 424–435.
—— , 1990, Recycling of continental crust in Miocene volcanic rocks from the Mojave block, southern California, in Anderson, J. L., ed., The nature and origin of Cordilleran magmatism: Geological Society of America Memoir 174, p. 147–168.
Glazner, A. F., and Bartley, J. M., 1984, Timing and tectonic setting of Tertiary low-angle normal faulting and associated magmatism in the southwestern United States: Tectonics, v. 3, p. 385–396.
Glazner, A. F., and Ussler, W. III, 1989, Crustal extension, crustal density, and the evolution of Cenozoic magmatism in the Basin and Range of the western United States: Journal of Geophysical Research, v. 94, p. 7952–7960.
Glazner, A. F., Bartley, J. M., and Walker, J. D., 1989, Magnitude and significance of Miocene crustal extension in the central Mojave Desert, California: Geology, v. 17, p. 50–53.
Hamblin, W. K., 1965, Origin of "reverse drag" on the downthrown side of normal faults: Geological Society of America Bulletin, v. 76, p. 1145–1164.
Hewett, D. F., 1956, Geology and mineral resources of the Ivanpah Quadrangle, California and Nevada: U.S. Geological Survey Professional Paper 275, 172 p.
Hildreth, W., 1981, Gradients in silicic magma chambers; Implications for lithospheric magmatism: Journal of Geophysical Research, v. 86, p. 10153–10192.
Holt, W. E., Chase, C. G., and Wallace, T. C., 1986, Crustal structure from three-dimensional gravity modeling of a metamorphic core complex; A model for uplift, Santa Catalina–Rincon mountains, Arizona: Geology, v. 14, p. 927–930.
Ingersoll, R. V., 1982, Triple-junction instability as cause for late Cenozoic extension and fragmentation of the western United States: Geology, v. 10, p. 621–624.
Kamb, W. B., 1959, Ice petrofabric observations from the Blue Glacier, Washington, in relation to theory and experiment: Journal of Geophysical Research, v. 64, p. 1891–1909.
Longwell, C. R., 1963, Reconnaissance geology between Lake Mead and Davis

Dam, Arizona and Nevada: U.S. Geological Survey Professional Paper 374–E, 51 p.

Medall, S. E., 1964, Geology of the Castle Mountains, California [M.S. thesis]: Los Angeles, University of Southern California, 107 p.

Mies, J. W., and Glazner, A. F., 1987, Quartz xenocrysts with rhyolite glass inclusions in andesite as evidence of assimilated granite [abs.]: EOS Transactions of the American Geophysical Union, v. 68, p. 434–435.

Novak, S. W., and Bacon, C. R., 1986, Pliocene volcanic rocks of the Coso Range, Inyo County, California: U.S. Geological Survey Professional Paper, v. 1383, 44 p.

Proffett, J. M., Jr., 1977, Cenozoic geology of the Yerington district, Nevada, and implications for the nature and origin of Basin and Range faulting: Geological Society of America Bulletin, v. 88, p. 247–266.

Ron, H., Aydin, A., and Nur, A., 1986, Strike-slip faulting and block rotation in the Lake Mead fault system: Geology, v. 14, p. 1020–1023.

Spencer, J. E., 1984, Role of tectonic denudation in uplift and warping of low-angle normal faults: Geology, v. 12, p. 95–98.

—— , 1985, Miocene low-angle normal faulting and dike emplacement, Homer Mountain and surrounding areas, southeastern California and southernmost Nevada: Geological Society of America Bulletin, v. 96, p. 1140–1155.

Stock, J. M., and Molnar, P., 1988, Uncertainties and implications of the Late Cretaceous and Tertiary position of North America relative to the Farallon, Kula, and Pacific plates: Tectonics, v. 7, p. 1339–1384.

Turner, F. J., 1981, Metamorphic petrology; Mineralogical, field, and tectonic aspects: New York, McGraw-Hill, 524 p.

Turner, R. D., 1985, Miocene folding and faulting of an evolving volcanic center in the Castle Mountains, southeastern California and southern Nevada [M.S. thesis]: University of North Carolina at Chapel Hill, 56 p.

Turner, R. D., Huntoon, J. E., and Spencer, J. E., 1983, Miocene volcanism, sedimentation, and folding in the northeastern Castle Mountains, California and Nevada: Geological Society of America Abstracts with Programs, v. 15, p. 433.

Wasserburg, G. J., and Lanphere, M. A., 1965, Age determinations in the Precambrian of Arizona and Nevada: Geological Society of America Bulletin, v. 76, p. 735–758.

Weber, M. E., and Smith, E. I., 1987, Structural and geochemical constraints on the reassembly of disrupted mid-Miocene volcanoes in the Lake Mead–Eldorado Valley area of southern Nevada: Geology, v. 15, p. 553–556.

Wernicke, B., Axen, G. J., and Snow, J. K., 1988, Basin and Range extensional tectonics at the latitude of Las Vegas, Nevada: Geological Society of America Bulletin, v. 100, p. 1738–1757.

Wright, L. A., 1976, Late Cenozoic fault patterns and stress fields in the Great Basin and westward displacement of the Sierra Nevada block: Geology, v. 4, p. 489–494.

MANUSCRIPT ACCEPTED BY THE SOCIETY AUGUST 21, 1989

Geological Society of America
Memoir 176
1990

Chapter 3

Structural development of a major extensional accommodation zone in the Basin and Range Province, northwestern Arizona and southern Nevada; Implications for kinematic models of continental extension

James E. Faulds*, John W. Geissman, and Chris K. Mawer
Department of Geology, University of New Mexico, Albuquerque, New Mexico 87131

ABSTRACT

Extensional accommodation zones, or tilt-block domain boundaries, facilitate reversals in the dominant tilt direction of fault blocks and possibly inversions in the dip of regional detachment systems in rifted continental crust. The amount and direction of movement of the footwall (lower plate) and hanging wall (upper plate) of the detachment terrane dictate the deformational style along accommodation zones. Various models of extension can potentially be evaluated by defining modes of deformation along accommodation zones.

A 40-km-long, east-west–trending, middle Miocene accommodation zone bisects the central Black Mountains, northwestern Arizona, and southern Eldorado Mountains, southern Nevada. The Black and Eldorado Mountains lie within the northern Colorado River extensional corridor, a 50- to 100-km-wide region of severely extended crust. The generally sublinear, 5- to 10-km-wide accommodation zone separates more than 5,000 km^2 of east-tilted fault blocks to the north from 25,000 km^2 of dominantly west-tilted fault blocks to the south. The zone may also mark the join between regionally extensive, oppositely dipping detachment systems.

Transversely oriented segments (i.e., perpendicular to strike of tilted blocks) of the accommodation zone in the upper-plate rocks correspond to areas of intermeshing conjugate normal faults. East- and west-dipping normal faults dominate the west- and east-tilted domains, respectively, whereas east- and west-dipping faults are equally common in the axial part of the zone. Some of the major normal faults in the west- and east-tilted domains terminate in drag folds within the axial part of the zone. Fault-block tilting on either side of the accommodation zone commonly exceeds 60°. Tilting decreases progressively toward the axis of the zone, where transversely oriented, oblique-slip normal faults accommodate scissors-like torsional offset between gently tilted (10 to 35°) individual fault blocks of opposing polarity. Concomitant with the decrease in tilting, fault spacing decreases, and average fault dip increases. Fault blocks within the zone were periodically tilted in opposite directions during the same episode of extension. Minor amounts of open to tight folding characterize along-strike segments (i.e., parallel to strike of tilted blocks) of the accommodation zone.

*Present address: Department of Geoscience, University of Nevada, Las Vegas, Nevada 89154

Faulds, J. E., Geissman, J. W., and Mawer, C. K., 1990, Structural development of a major extensional accommodation zone in the Basin and Range Province, northwestern Arizona and southern Nevada; Implications for kinematic models of continental extension, *in* Wernicke, B. P., ed., Basin and Range extensional tectonics near the latitude of Las Vegas, Nevada: Boulder, Colorado, Geological Society of America Memoir 176.

The lack of strike-slip faulting along transversely oriented segments and only minor amounts of compression on along-strike segments of the accommodation zone indicate little relative movement between opposing tilt-block domains. The transversely oriented, oblique-slip normal faults in the zone facilitated torsional offset, associated with differential tilting, rather than transport of upper-plate rocks away from the tilt direction. Similar structures may account for interpretations of accommodation zones in the upper-plate rocks of passive continental margins as strike-slip faults, which supposedly accommodated diametrical lateral transport of opposing tilt-block domains.

Lower-plate rocks of the detachment terrane do not crop out along the accommodation zone. Paleomagnetic data and geologic relations indicate that large crystalline terranes in the southern Eldorado and central Black Mountains correspond to structurally deep levels of highly tilted fault blocks. The sublinear trace of the accommodation zone in the upper-plate rocks may represent, however, a surface manifestation of strike-slip faulting in lower-plate rocks beneath oppositely dipping detachment faults. The axis of a 10-mGal isostatic residual gravity high, which closely corresponds to surface exposures of probable lower-plate rocks farther south in the west-tilted domain, is offset 19 km in a right-lateral sense approximately 7 km north of the zone. Strike-slip offset does not occur, however, along the hypothetical projection of the zone into relatively unextended regions, where potential lower-plate rocks of one domain are juxtaposed against upper-plate rocks of the adjacent domain.

The lack of strike-slip faulting between the upper-plate rocks of opposing tilt-block domains as well as between possible lower- and upper-plate rocks of adjacent domains in the unextended regions is difficult to reconcile with kinematic models of rifted continental crust, which involve two diverging, essentially rigid crustal slabs separated by a major detachment fault. A model that may account for the lack of strike-slip faulting depicts the opposing tilt-block domains as two sets of dominoes rotating about horizontal axes (i.e., tilting). The rotational axis of one block in each domain is fixed in an arbitrary reference frame. The blocks containing the "fixed" axis of rotation undergo pure rotation, whereas the other blocks experience both translation and rotation. If the location of the "fixed" axis of rotation and magnitude of extension do not change across an accommodation zone, only torsional strain would characterize the entire zone. Relative to an inferred north-trending, "fixed" rotational axis that remained intact across the accommodation zone in the northern Colorado River extensional corridor, blocks to the east were translated eastward and blocks to the west moved westward. If the axis of "fixed" rotation coincided with the axis of the extensional corridor, the model may partly account for opposing senses of strike-slip motion along the Lake Mead and Las Vegas Valley shear zones, both of which appear to terminate near the northern end of the axis of the corridor.

INTRODUCTION

Rifted continental crust is characterized by structural asymmetry, as evidenced by the predominance of tilted fault blocks and half-grabens in most extended terranes, including passive continental margins (Bally and Oldow, 1984; Etheridge and others, 1988), the Basin and Range province of the western United States (Anderson, 1971; Armstrong, 1972; Stewart, 1980; Anderson and others, 1983), and the East African rift system (Gregory, 1921; Bosworth and others, 1986; Rosendahl and others, 1986; Rosendahl, 1987). Block-tilting and attendant displacement on planar and listric normal faults facilitate stretching in the brittle upper crust. Block-tilting in the upper crust must be accommodated at some depth by gently dipping zones of detachment or décollement into which the superjacent normal faults sole (And-

erson, 1971; Proffett, 1977; Wernicke, 1981, 1985; Wernicke and Burchfiel, 1982; Smith and Bruhn, 1984). The term *detachment fault* is used here to describe a subregionally extensive, gently dipping normal fault that formed at a low angle and accommodated significant displacement (Reynolds and Spencer, 1985). Extension of continental crust is likely facilitated by many kilometers of normal displacement along detachment faults. The detachment faults may penetrate most of the crust (Allmendinger and others, 1983; Reynolds and Spencer, 1985; Kaufman and others, 1986) and perhaps the entire lithosphere (Wernicke, 1981, 1985). The hanging walls, or upper plates, of major detachment faults are generally dominated by one conjugate fault type and are thus uniformly tilted in one direction over large regions (Fig. 1).

Areas of unidirectional tilting, or "tilt-block domains," may

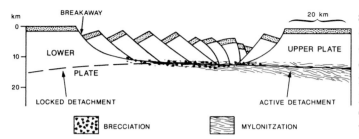

Figure 1. Cross section of hypothetical detachment terrane. Shallow-level planar and listric normal faults, which sole into gently dipping detachment zones, accommodate block tilting and the associated development of half-graben. The tilted fault blocks generally dip toward both the breakaway zone and presumed transport direction of lower-plate rocks.

reflect the geometry and movement direction of the underlying detachment faults. The displacement on block-bounding normal faults is usually sympathetic with that on the major detachment fault. Layering in the tilted blocks generally dips toward both the breakaway fault and the presumed transport direction of lower-plate rocks of the detachment terrane (Fig. 1). Large tilt-block domains commonly represent distension above one detachment fault or several faults that dip regionally in the same direction (Bosworth and others, 1986; Lister and others, 1986a). Thus, periodic reversals in the polarity of tilt-block domains, which occur along the length of most rifts, may record inversions in the asymmetry of the subjacent system of detachment faults.

Symmetrically opposed detachment systems may correspond to conjugate low-angle shear zones, as suggested by Ramsay (1980) and Kligfield and others (1984). During the early stages of rifting, opposing detachment systems may be coevally active. The mechanical inefficiency of opposing detachment systems repeatedly offsetting each other should eventually lead to the locking of one system (Fig. 1). Reversals in tilt asymmetry may be related to the manner in which competing, opposed detachments propagate laterally and eventually interfere with one another (Bosworth, 1985).

A mechanical relation may exist between sense of shear on the detachment fault and preferred conjugate fault type in the upper plate which in turn, will govern the dominant tilt direction. Mandl (1987) documented that faults in an extended brittle overburden tend to dip antithetically to the direction of creep flow in ductile substrata. He attributed this characteristic to a behavior of frictional-plastic materials known in soil mechanics as noncoaxiality. Noncoaxiality implies that in perfectly isotropic material under general loading conditions, the principal axes of strain rate (or incremental strains) and stress do not coincide (Drescher, 1976; Mandl, 1987, 1988). Assuming that regional horizontal extension of the substrata brings the brittle overburden into the active limit state, the smallest principal strain rate (extension counted as negative) will be approximately horizontal. Thus, the maximum shear rate will act along planes inclined at ±45° to the horizontal. In addition, as a result of shear stress along a detachment surface, σ_1 immediately above the detachment may be

slightly deflected from the vertical and become inclined in a down-dip direction with respect to the detachment. Consequently, conjugate slip planes sympathetic to the detachment lie closer to a plane of maximum shearing rate (Fig. 2) and are thus favored for development. The parallel normal faults in the upper plate of the detachment may also function as large-scale R_1 Riedel shears to the detachment. However, R_1 Riedel shear fractures generally develop at an angle of 10 to 20° to the sliding surface (Logan and others, 1979), which is probably significantly less than the original angle between the detachment surface and the parallel normal faults in the detachment hanging wall.

Whether linked to noncoaxiality or R_1 Riedel shears, the development of faults sympathetic to the major detachment is favored in the detachment hanging wall. This suggests that the direction of block tilting will generally face toward the direction of relative transport of the detachment footwall, or lower plate, as commonly portrayed (Fig. 1). This model for the development of upper-plate normal faults assumes that the faults nucleate near the base of the brittle upper plate at the detachment interface and propagate toward the Earth's surface. Focal depths and fault-plane solutions from normal-faulting earthquakes in continental crust appear to support this premise (Jackson, 1987).

Major tilt-block domain boundaries probably do reflect reversals in both the dip direction and sense of shear of regional

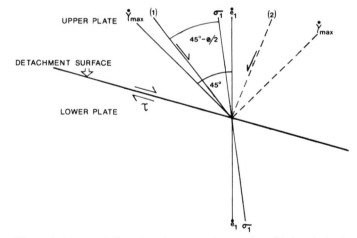

Figure 2. Noncoaxiality of strain rate and stress in a frictional plastic material as a possible explanation of the preferential development of one conjugate fault type (after Mandl, 1987). Stress, strain rate, and Coulomb-type faults shown immediately above a dipping detachment surface. Conjugate faults (1) and (2) in the upper plate are brought to the active limit state by extension in the lower plate. The direction of maximum shear rate $\dot\gamma_{max}$ is, by definition, at 45° to the direction of greatest shortening rate $\dot e_1$. The Coulomb slip direction makes an angle of 45° − $\phi/2$ (ϕ is the angle of internal friction) with the direction of greatest compressive normal stress σ_1. As a result of motion along the detachment, σ_1 may be slightly deflected from vertical immediately above the detachment surface and become inclined in a down-dip direction with respect to the detachment. If normal faults in the upper plates of detachment terranes nucleate at the detachment interface, conjugate slip planes sympathetic with the detachment (1) lie closer to a plane of maximum shear rate and are thus favored for development. One conjugate fault type becomes dominant in the upper plate, which leads to the development of regionally extensive tilt-block domains.

detachment systems, but this does not necessarily imply that tilt direction is a reliable indicator of the actual transport direction of detachment hanging walls. Wernicke and Burchfiel (1982) and Walker and others (1986) advised caution in relating the attitude of tilting to either the movement direction of upper-plate rocks or overall extension direction. Seismic reflection data from the Sevier Desert area of central Utah (McDonald, 1976) were interpreted by Wernicke and Burchfiel (1982) to indicate that parts of the upper plate of a detachment may remain untilted, whereas other parts may be tilted in opposite directions. Preexisting anisotropies and local space problems may induce small areas of anomalous tilting in large tilt-block domains. Moreover, the kinematic significance of tilt direction depends on the overall kinematic evolution of rifted continental crust, which has not been clearly deciphered.

Tilt-block domain boundaries, which facilitate along-strike reversals in the sense of rift asymmetry, have been referred to as "accommodation" zones (Reynolds, 1984; Bosworth, 1985; Rosendahl and others, 1986; Bosworth and others, 1986) or "transfer" zones (Gibbs, 1984). Accommodation zones have been observed in most continental rifts, including passive continental margins (Bally, 1982; Lister and others, 1986a; Etheridge and others, 1988), the Basin and Range province of the western United States (Stewart, 1980), Rio Grande rift (Chapin and others, 1978), North Sea area (Gibbs, 1984), Aegean Sea (Mariolakos and Stiros, 1987), and East African rift system (Moustafa, 1976; Reynolds, 1984; Reynolds and Rosendahl, 1984; Rosendahl and others, 1986; Bosworth and others, 1986; Rosendahl, 1987; Ebinger and others, 1987; Coffield and Schamel, 1989). Because accommodation zones may coordinate reversals in both the dominant tilt direction of upper-plate fault blocks and dip of regional detachment systems, the geometry and kinematics of such zones may place important constraints on the overall kinematic evolution of rifted continental crust.

This chapter describes the geologic field relations, geometry, and kinematics of a well-exposed, 40-km-long accommodation zone in the highly extended terrane of the central Black Mountains, northwestern Arizona, and adjacent southern Eldorado Mountains, southern Nevada (Figs. 3 and 4). The possible implications of the deformational style exhibited along this zone in regard to the overall kinematic evolution of rifted continental crust are then considered.

Previous work on accommodation zones

Regional tilt-block domains and intervening accommodation zones have been widely recognized in rifted continental crust (Rehrig and Heidrick, 1976; Moustafa, 1976; Chapin, 1978; Chapin and others, 1978; Stewart and Johannesen, 1979; Stewart, 1980; Bally, 1982). Despite many recent significant contributions addressing continental rifting, the nature of accommodation zones remains controversial and poorly understood (Chapin and others, 1978; Stewart, 1980; Chamberlin, 1983; Dokka, 1983; Dokka and Baksi, 1986; Gibbs, 1984; Bally and Oldow, 1984; Etheridge and others, 1985; Bosworth, 1985,

1986, 1987; Bosworth and others, 1986; Lister and others, 1986a, b; Rosendahl and others, 1986; Rosendahl, 1987; Ebinger and others, 1987; Coffield, 1987; Faulds and others, 1987a, 1988a, b; Dunkelman and others, 1988; Versfelt and Rosendahl, 1989; Coffield and Schamel, 1989).

Lister and others (1986a, b) concluded that accommodation zones on passive continental margins are dominated by a few discrete, essentially strike-slip faults that parallel the direction of maximum extension and are orthogonal to normal faults. In contrast, many workers have shown that accommodation zones in the East African rift system generally cross rift trends at oblique angles and are dominated by complex, oblique-slip fault systems (Reynolds, 1984; Reynolds and Rosendahl, 1984; Bosworth, 1985, 1986; Bosworth and others, 1986; Rosendahl and others, 1986; Rosendahl, 1987; Ebinger and others, 1987; Dunkelman and others, 1988). Accommodation zones in the East African rift system commonly (1) trend 30 to 60° from the longitudinal axis of the rift (e.g., Reynolds, 1984), (2) link arcuate traces of major normal fault systems that bound half-grabens of opposing polarity (Reynolds, 1984; Rosendahl, 1987; Ebinger and others, 1987), and (3) appear to accommodate a significant component of strike-slip displacement (Bosworth and others, 1986; Rosendahl, 1987; Ebinger and others, 1987).

Lister and others (1986b) noted that some of the discrepancies between observations of accommodation zones on passive continental margins and the East African rift system may result from different amounts of extension. In regions of relatively minor extension, as in the East African rift system, distributed faulting throughout the rock mass could accommodate along-strike variations in normal fault geometry, and the geometric requirement for compatibility between fault motions need not be strictly obeyed. As extension increases (e.g., passive margins analyzed by Lister and others, 1986a), broad accommodation zones may become increasingly dominated by a few strike-slip faults, which are generally orthogonal to the normal faults unless the movement on the normal faults is significantly oblique. In either case, the presumed strike-slip displacement along the zones has generally been related to the transport of upper-plate rocks away from their tilt direction (Bosworth and others, 1986; Rosendahl, 1987) (Fig. 5a).

Chapin and others (1978) interpreted an accommodation zone in the Rio Grande rift as an incipient transform fault connecting en echelon axes of extension. The apparent lack of strike-slip displacement along this zone was attributed to its early stage of development. Diffuse zones of en echelon oblique-slip faults, with trends that diverge 15 to 30° from the extension direction, may characterize surface expressions of incipient transform faults (Barberi and Varet, 1977). Because Chapin and others (1978) did not use tilt direction as a criterion for vergence, the inferred sense of strike-slip displacement along some accommodation zones is opposite that predicted by models in which upper-plate rocks are transported away from the tilt direction (Fig. 5a, b).

Discrete strike-slip displacement along accommodation zones, although implicit in the aforementioned models, has not

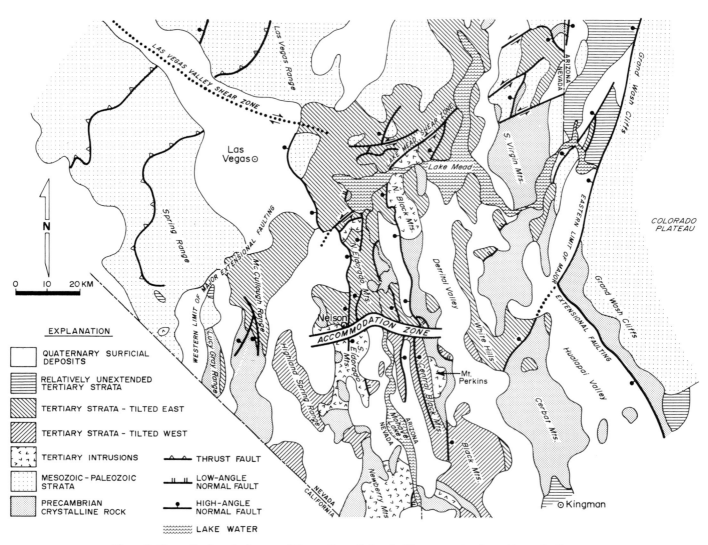

Figure 3. Generalized geologic map of the northern Colorado River extensional corridor and adjacent regions. Note accommodation zone in the central part of the map. Data from Wilson and others (1969), Anderson (1977, 1978), Longwell and others (1965), Volborth (1973), and Faulds (unpublished mapping). Faults are dotted where inferred or concealed.

been well documented. The studies by Bosworth and others (1986), Lister and others (1986a, b), and Chapin and others (1978) did not present concrete evidence of strike-slip offset. Where detailed studies have been performed, only scissors-like, torsional offset on high-angle, transversely oriented faults has been observed along accommodation zones (Chapin, 1978; Chamberlin, 1983; Mariolakos and Stiros, 1987; Coffield and Schamel, 1989). Chapin (1978) concluded that near-surface strain along accommodation zones in the Rio Grande rift was relieved primarily by scissors-like torque and a complex inter-meshing of normal faults of opposing dip rather than strike-slip faulting.

Accommodation zones within the Basin and Range province have been little studied. Stewart and Johannesen (1979) compiled regional tilt patterns of the province. Slemmons (1967) and Stewart (1980) noted, on the basis of reconnaissance efforts,

that accommodation zones in the Basin and Range province commonly have three characteristics: an absence of major tilted blocks, changes in the density and pattern of young faults, and permutations in topographic grain.

Much of the controversy concerning the geometric and kinematic characteristics of accommodation zones stems from the lack of subaerial exposures of the zones in most continental rift settings, which has generally stymied attempts at detailed studies. Most of the previous descriptions of accommodation zones are largely based on seismic reflection data as well as considerable conjecture. Detailed mapping of accommodation zones has been restricted to moderately extended continental lithosphere (e.g., Rio Grande rift, Chapin and others, 1978), where such zones may not be completely developed. To our knowledge, comprehensive investigations of subaerially exposed accommodation zones have previously not been conducted in highly extended terranes.

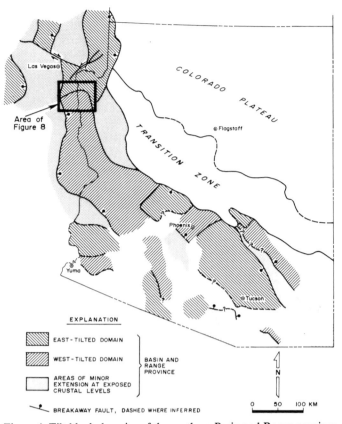

EXPLANATION

EAST-TILTED DOMAIN

WEST-TILTED DOMAIN

BASIN AND RANGE PROVINCE

AREAS OF MINOR EXTENSION AT EXPOSED CRUSTAL LEVELS

BREAKAWAY FAULT, DASHED WHERE INFERRED

0   50   100 KM

Figure 4. Tilt-block domains of the southern Basin and Range province (modified from Spencer and Reynolds, 1986). The accommodation zone in the Black and Eldorado Mountains lies within the blocked-out area (upper left).

Critical questions regarding accommodation zones remain unanswered. Do the zones facilitate significant strike-slip displacement at any crustal level? If characterized by strike-slip movement, do the zones correspond to discrete strike-slip faults that parallel the overall extension direction or to broad zones of oblique wrench-style tectonism that cross rift trends at oblique angles? Do the zones represent incipient transform faults separating en echelon axes of extension or instead reflect inversion of subjacent detachment systems? Do the zones accommodate transport of upper-plate fault blocks away from their tilt direction?

We refer to tilt-block domain boundaries as accommodation zones rather than transfer zones because (1) strike-slip movement—as opposed to reversals in rift asymmetry—formed a critical part of Gibbs's (1984) description of "transfer" zones, (2) tilt-block domain boundary was implicit in many recent accounts of "accommodation" zones (e.g., Reynolds, 1984; Bosworth, 1986; Bosworth and others, 1986; Rosendahl, 1987; Faulds and others, 1987a, 1988a, b, c; Coffield and Schamel, 1989), and (3) strike-slip displacement has not been firmly substantiated along tilt-block domain boundaries. The term *accommodation zone* probably originated in the petroleum industry, where it was in common usage by the early 1980s (W. Bosworth,

personal communication, 1989). Although tilt-block domain boundary was not intrinsic in the original usage of *accommodation zone* (Bosworth, 1985), we use *accommodation zone* and *tilt-block domain boundary* synonymously, in accord with common practice.

Unlike areas studied previously, the central Black and southern Eldorado Mountains offer exceptional exposures of a major accommodation zone in highly extended continental crust, thus permitting detailed geometric and kinematic analyses. The 1.5 km of topographic relief and exposures of a 10-km-thick section of tilted crust permit a thorough investigation of this 40-km-long accommodation zone. Fewer problems associated with the incipient development of major structures arise in the highly extended terrane of the northern Colorado River extensional corridor, where block-tilting commonly exceeds 60° and locally surpasses 90°, than in less extended terranes such as the East African and Rio Grande rift systems.

Significance of accommodation zones

A key element of accommodation zones is that their deformational style is dictated by the amount and direction of movement of the upper and lower plates of the detachment terrane (Faulds and others, 1987a). Various models of extension can potentially be evaluated by defining the modes of deformation along a zone, especially if both upper- and lower-plate rocks crop out along the zone.

For example, major strike-slip displacement between the lower plates of opposing tilt-block domains, if contemporaneous with extension, would demonstrate that accommodation zones facilitate reversal in the regional dip direction of major detachment faults and that lower-plate rocks of the detachment terrane are at least partly drawn out from upper-plate rocks in accordance with the models of Lucchitta and Suneson (1981a, b) and Wernicke (1981, 1985). Confinement of strike-slip displacement to areas in which lower-plate rocks of one domain are juxtaposed with upper- or lower-plate rocks of an adjacent domain (Fig. 6a) would indicate little relative movement between the opposing tilt-block domains in the upper plate. If strike-slip displacement also occurs between the upper-plate rocks of adjacent domains, documentation of its slip sense will determine whether upper-plate rocks are generally transported away from their tilt direction. If the accommodation zone facilitated movement in opposing directions of both upper- and lower-plate rocks, the sense of strike-slip displacement in the lower plate would be opposite that in the upper plate, and lateral offset may cease where lower- and upper-plate rocks of adjacent domains are juxtaposed (Fig. 6b).

In contrast, several possible scenarios (Fig. 6c) would result in little, if any, strike-slip displacement along accommodation zones. These scenarios include (1) lateral transport in similar directions on either side of the zone of only the lower plate, (2) diametrical movement between the upper and lower plate of the detachment but in similar directions on either side of the zone,

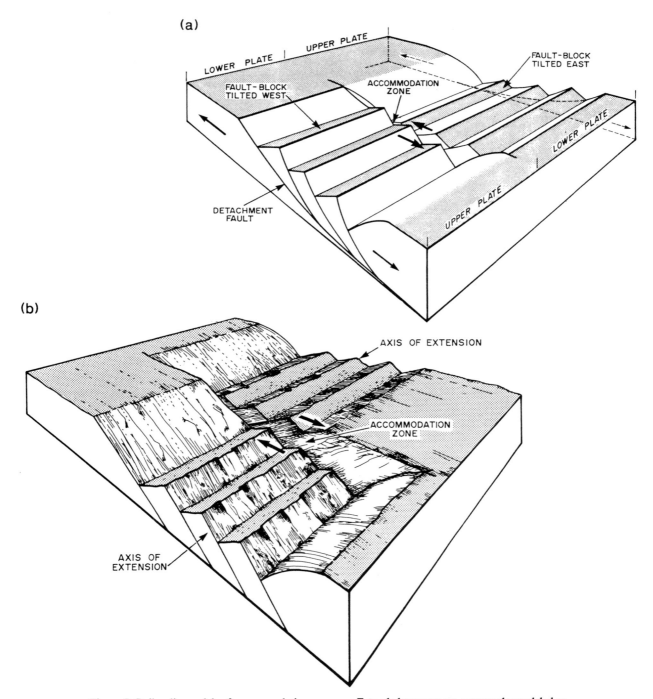

Figure 5. Strike-slip models of accommodation zones. a. Extended terranes are commonly modeled as two diverging, essentially rigid crustal slabs separated by a major detachment fault. Fault blocks in the upper plate are commonly assumed to be transported away from their tilt direction. Because they accommodate diametrical lateral transport of both upper- and lower-plate rocks, accommodation zones in this model correspond to major strike-slip fault zones. b. Chapin and others (1978) concluded that some accommodation zones are incipient transform faults that separate en echelon axes of extension. Tilt direction was not used as criterion for vergence. The Chapin and others (1978) model would predict dextral displacement along the above accommodation zone (as would be predicted for oceanic transform faults).

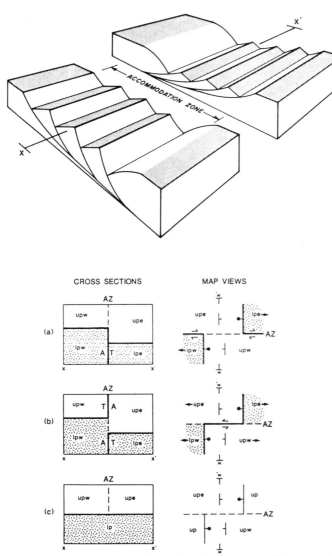

Figure 6. Possible modes of deformation along accommodation zones. In cross sections and map views: AZ = accommodation zone; upw = upper plate, west-tilted domain; upe = upper plate, east-tilted domain; lpe = lower plate, east-tilted domain; lpw = lower plate, west-tilted domain; up = untilted upper plate; lp = lower plate. A = movement away from plane of cross setion; T = movement toward plane of cross section. a. Lower plate pulled out from under relatively stationary upper plate. Strike-slip offset along the accommodation zone is confined to areas in which the lower plate of one domain is juxtaposed against either the upper or lower plate of the adjacent domain. b. Both upper and lower plates of the detachment terrane are translated significant lateral distances in opposite directions. Strike-slip offset along the accommodation zone occurs where (1) upper plates of opposing tilt-block domains are juxtaposed or (2) lower plates of adjacent domains are juxtaposed. The sense of strike-slip motion between the upper plates of opposing domains is opposite that between lower plates (sinistral vs. dextral displacement in this diagram). A vertical section of crust along parts of the accommodation zone may exhibit opposing senses of strike-slip motion at shallow and deep structural levels as well as negligible offset in the intervening sliver of crust in which the upper plate of one domain is juxtaposed against the lower plate of an adjacent domain. c. Several scenarios, as described in text, may produce little if any strike-slip displacement along the accommodation zone. In these cases, the detachment geometry may not change across the accommodation zone.

and (3) diverging lateral movement within the upper-plate rocks about discrete axes of extension whereby an entire vertical section of crust remains fixed in a specified reference frame, perhaps as parts of a brittle upper plate deform more or less in situ above a lower plate dominated by pure shear (e.g., Miller and others, 1983). In these cases, the accommodation zone may not facilitate inversion in the dip of regional detachment systems (i.e., a horizontal detachment fault may underlie both tilt-block domains) but may simply accommodate interaction between laterally propagating conjugate normal faults in the upper plate.

Whether associated with a pure-shear or simple-shear model of continental extension, the above accommodation zone models entail relatively simple kinematic behavior of upper- and lower-plate rocks of the detachment terrane. Such models may not, however, adequately depict the kinematic evolution of rifted continental crust.

The geometry and kinematics of accommodation zones may also be relevant to other types of transversely oriented (i.e., roughly orthogonal to rift trend) structures in rifted continental crust. Transverse structures accommodate along-strike (i.e., parallel to rift trend) variations in the structural and temporal evolution of continental rifts. Transverse zones commonly separate regions of differing, but not necessarily opposing, tilt and strike parallel to or slightly oblique from the extension direction (Stewart, 1980; Effimoff and Pinezich, 1981; Anderson and others, 1983; Gibbs, 1984). Like accommodation zones, many transverse zones are characterized by an absence of major tilted fault blocks and exhibit changes in both fault patterns and topographic grain (Stewart, 1980). Some transverse structures, such as the Las Vegas Valley shear zone and Garlock fault, have clearly accommodated significant strike-slip displacement and have therefore been likened to intracontinental transform faults separating regions of differential extension (Fleck, 1970; Davis and Burchfiel, 1973; Liggett and Childs, 1977; Bohannon, 1979; Guth, 1981). In many cases, however, transverse zones are not associated with discrete or identified structural features (Stewart, 1980; Zuber and others, 1986). Some transverse zones may accommodate little more than scissors-like displacement, if upper-plate rocks in at least part of an extended terrane deform more or less in situ. The kinematic history of adjacent extensional domains will determine the style of deformation along individual transverse zones. Insights into the kinematics of extended terranes gained from investigations of accommodation zones should contribute to the understanding of all types of transverse structures. Transverse structures may yield information regarding the kinematic evolution of rifted continental crust as instructive as that provided by transform faults for oceanic crust.

Because accommodation zones constitute fundamental structures in rifted continental crust, they represent potential targets for hydrocarbon exploration. Several large oil fields are associated with accommodation zones in the Gulf of Suez, Egypt (Moustafa, 1976; Coffield and Smale, 1987). Gibbs (1984) noted that various complexities make transversely oriented structures, such as accommodation zones, difficult to interpret on seismic sections. Thus, the potential for features within accommodation zones to act as reservoir seals or structural traps may be unrecognized. Resolution of the geometric and kinematic characteristics of subaerially exposed accommodation zones may clarify interpretation of seismic sections across such zones and ultimately improve methods of hydrocarbon evaluation of both passive continental margins and rift basins in continental interiors.

GEOLOGIC SETTING OF THE BLACK AND ELDORADO MOUNTAINS

The Black and Eldorado Mountains straddle the Colorado River in northwestern Arizona and southernmost Nevada, respectively. These north-trending ranges lie within the central portion of a 50- to 100-km-wide corridor of moderately to severely extended crust, bordered by the relatively unextended Spring Range to the west and the western edge of the Colorado Plateau to the east (Fig. 3). This extended region is here referred to as the northern Colorado River extensional corridor (cf. Howard and John, 1987). The northern Colorado River extensional corridor incorporates both the east- and west-tilted domains up to 50 km north and south, respectively, of the accommodation zone in the Black and Eldorado Mountains, whereas the Colorado River extensional corridor of Howard and John (1987) specifically included only the west-tilted domain south of the accommodation zone. The northern Colorado River extensional corridor terminates on the north against the left-lateral, northeast-trending Lake Mead and right-lateral, northwest-trending Las Vegas Valley shear zones.

In northwestern Arizona, highly extended parts of the Basin and Range province lie unusually close to the virtually undeformed Colorado Plateau. Flat-lying Paleozoic strata crop out along the western edge of the Colorado Plateau (Grand Wash Cliffs) only 50 km east of a highly extended terrane in the northern Colorado River extensional corridor, where low-angle normal faults are widespread, and Tertiary strata are commonly tilted in excess of 60° (Longwell, 1945; Anderson, 1971; Theodore and others, 1982; Lucchitta and Young, 1986; Myers and others, 1986; Faulds and others, 1988b).

Tertiary volcanic and sedimentary strata in the northern Colorado River extensional corridor accumulated on a surface of low relief cut primarily into Proterozoic gneisses. Paleozoic and Mesozoic strata are generally missing. By contrast, thick sections of Paleozoic strata are preserved north of the northern Colorado River extensional corridor and in the relatively unextended terranes on either side of the corridor. The Proterozoic basement is significantly dilated, particularly in the southern Eldorado Mountains (Fig. 3), by late Cretaceous to middle Miocene, silicic to intermediate plutons and felsic and mafic dike swarms. The distended Tertiary strata, which range from late Oligocene to middle Miocene in age (Anderson and others, 1972), consist of intermediate lavas and flow breccia, flow-banded rhyolites, bedded tuff, minor ash-flow tuff, conglomerate, and basalt (Fig. 7). The aggregate thickness of the Tertiary section commonly exceeds 3 km.

Early to middle Miocene extension (Anderson, 1971; Anderson and others, 1972) fragmented the region into a complex mosaic of tilted fault blocks. The average strike of layering in the tilted fault blocks and extension lineations in mylonites of probable Tertiary age indicate an east-west to west-southwest–east-northeast extension direction within the northern Colorado River extensional corridor. The region is laced with abundant, relatively planar normal faults, ranging in dip from 0 to 90°. Relatively planar fault geometries are indicated by little differential tilt between most hanging walls and footwalls and the apparent lack of major roll-over anticlines. The intricate arrays of fault blocks are probably floored by complex low-angle zones of detachment into which the numerous shingling normal faults merge (Anderson, 1971). Tilting and distension above the detachment faults produced numerous half-graben, which served as major depocenters for much of the Tertiary section.

A major east-west–trending, middle Miocene accommodation zone bisects the northern Colorado River extensional corridor, separating more than 5,000 km^2 of east-tilted fault blocks to the north from 25,000 km^2 of dominantly west-tilted fault blocks to the south (Figs. 3 and 8). The trend of the accommodation zone parallels the probable extension direction. Despite considerable work on Tertiary extension in the Colorado River extensional corridor (e.g., Anderson, 1971; Frost and Martin, 1982), the accommodation zone in the central Black and southern Eldorado Mountains has received little attention. This reversal in block-tilting was first recognized by Longwell (1963). Spencer and Reynolds (1989) speculated that the accommodation zone might correspond to a strike-slip fault zone between lower-plate rocks of the opposing tilt-block domains. Our detailed investigations have focused on the immediate vicinity of the accommodation zone. Reconnaissance work was conducted, however, in the Black and Eldorado Mountains up to 40 km north and south of the accommodation zone.

Other types of tilt-block domain boundaries do exist in the northern Colorado River extensional corridor. For example, conjugate and antithetic normal faults accommodate local areas of opposing tilt within the larger tilt-block domains. In these cases, the trend of the domain boundaries parallels the strike of the normal faults. In addition, because west-tilting directly adjacent to the unextended Colorado Plateau would have created serious space problems at depth, most of the fault blocks in the mildly extended terrane near the plateau are tilted gently to the east. Consequently, a broad north- to northwest-trending tilt-block domain boundary, which marks the eastern margin of the west-tilted domain, is located approximately 35 km west of the margin of the Colorado Plateau. The north- to northwest-trending tilt-block domain boundaries are much less significant than the east-west–trending accommodation zone in the central Black and southern Eldorado Mountains, which separates large, highly extended regions of unidirectional tilting and may be related to the geometry of subjacent detachment faults.

Although low-angle normal faults abound in the central Black and southern Eldorado Mountains, clear-cut detachment

	THICKNESS	LITHOLOGY
QTs	0–500+ m	Late Miocene to Quaternary, gently–tilted to flat–lying pebble to cobble conglomerate, primarily of fanglomerate origin.
Tb	0–600 m	Olivine–pyroxene basalt and basaltic andesite flows; correlative with upper part of Mt. Davis Volcanics of Anderson (1977, 1978); range from 14.3 +/− 0.3 to 13.1 +/− 0.3 Ma.
Tg, Tgl	0–1,000 m	Poorly sorted, pebble to cobble conglomerate, largely of fanglomerate origin; locally contains clasts of crystalline rock, including mylonitized and mineralized rock; monolithologic breccias of probable landslide origin locally occur near base of section (Tgl).
Tts, Tr	0–500 m	Syntectonic tuffaceous sedimentary rocks, volcaniclastic conglomerates, and thin pyroclastic flows (Tts); intercalated rhyolite flows (Tr); thickest in large growth–fault basins; 16.4 +/− 0.4 Ma tuff near base of section and overlain by 14.1 +/− 0.4 Ma basalt flow in west–tilted domain; probably correlative with lower part of Mt. Davis Volcanics.
Tra	0–15 m	Rhyolitic tuff (15.9 +/− 0.4 Ma) containing phenocrysts of sanidine, plagioclase, and biotite; rare in central Black Mountains; possibly correlative with Tuff of Bridge Spring of Anderson (1971).
Tba	320–600 m	Pyroxene–olivine basaltic andesite flows and volcanic breccia; thin beds of tuffaceous sedimentary rock locally intercalated; correlative with upper part of Patsy Mine Volcanics of Anderson (1977, 1978).
Tvbr	125–450 m	Massive matrix–supported volcanic breccia, conglomerate, and sandstone; lesser basaltic andesite flows and sills; probably correlative with middle part of Patsy Mine Volcanics.
Td	0–80 m	Hornblende–biotite dacite flows and subordinate breccia.
Tv	400–700 m	Complex section of intercalated hornblende andesite flows, basaltic andesite flows, dacite/rhyodacite flows, and volcanic breccia; characterized by laterally discontinuous units; may be partly correlative with lower part of Patsy Mine Volcanics.
Trt	0–10 m	Rhyolitic tuff (also noted by Anderson [1977] in northern Eldorado Mountains).
Ta	0–45 m	Pre–volcanic arkosic conglomerate and sandstone.
KTi		Late Cretaceous/Tertiary intrusions, including a 73.3 +/− 1.5 Ma granite, early to middle Miocene granodiorite plutons, and mafic to felsic dike swarms of probable Miocene age.
p€u	6,000+ m	Proterozoic gneisses of variable composition and amphibolite; mylonite of probable Proterozoic age; weakly foliated granodiorite of unknown age.

Figure 7. Stratigraphic column of the central Black Mountains.

faults have not been identified. However, a major west-dipping, low-angle normal fault zone and attendant mylonites in the east-tilted domain of the central Black Mountains may correspond to a detachment fault. Although apparently complicated by later structures, this low-angle normal fault zone may connect with a west-dipping, low-angle normal fault zone exposed 45 km to the north-northwest on Saddle Island, which Weber and Smith (1987) and Duebendorfer and others (1988, and this volume) have described as a major detachment fault. The large crystalline terrane of Wilson Ridge in the northern Black Mountains, which lies in the footwall of the Saddle Island low-angle normal fault zone, may belong to the lower plate of the detachment terrane (Weber and Smith, 1987; Smith and others, 1987). In addition, an east-dipping, low-angle normal fault zone on the east flank of the southern Eldorado Mountains may represent the northward continuation of potential detachment faults described by Mathis (1982) in the Newberry Mountains (Fig. 3). As suggested by the preponderance of Tertiary crystalline rocks, the southern Eldorado Mountains may also largely comprise lower-plate rocks of the detachment terrane. Thus, the accommodation zone in the

central Black and southern Eldorado Mountains may mark the join between two opposing detachment systems.

However, the major low-angle normal faults in this region, even those with attendant mylonite zones, do not necessarily represent original, shallowly dipping detachments, nor do the footwalls of these low-angle normal faults necessarily correspond to the lower plate of the detachment terrane. The large crystalline terranes in the northern Colorado River extensional corridor may instead belong to the deep structural levels of steeply tilted fault blocks. Accordingly, perhaps many of the major low-angle normal fault zones in this region nucleated at moderate to high angles and were later rotated about north-south–trending, subhorizontal axes during block tilting to their present low-angle attitudes (e.g., Ransome, 1909; Morton and Black, 1975; Proffett, 1977; Chamberlin, 1978, 1983; Wernicke and Burchfiel, 1982; Davis, 1983, 1987). Major low-angle normal faults within the central Black and southern Eldorado Mountains are generally restricted to steeply tilted terranes.

Tilting of crystalline terranes is a first-order problem that must be addressed in all extended regions before accurate restorations can be attempted. Determining the magnitude of tilting of crystalline terranes is especially critical to understanding the kinematics of accommodation zones, as the style of deformation along these zones may differ in the upper- and lower-plate rocks of the detachment terrane. Paleomagnetic data from several crystalline lithologies have been acquired to evaluate the magnitude of tilting of large crystalline terranes in the northern Colorado River extensional corridor (Faulds and others, 1988d). Preliminary results of paleomagnetic studies are reported below. Further details are presented in Faulds and others (in preparation). Paleomagnetic methodology and interpretation of the data are briefly described in Appendix A.

Interestingly, a 10-mGal isostatic residual gravity high (Simpson and others, 1986) closely coincides with the exposed lower plate of the detachment terrane, or core complexes (cf. Crittenden and others, 1980), in the west-tilted domain. This anomaly extends northward into the southern Eldorado Mountains, where it terminates approximately 7 km north of the accommodation zone. A major north-trending, isostatic residual gravity high in the Wilson Ridge area also ends abruptly 2 to 7 km north of the accommodation zone (Fig. 9). Simpson and others (1986) attributed the belt of gravity highs to either mafic intrusive bodies or higher than normal densities of Precambrian rocks, some of which may have been elevated from middle or

lower crustal depths during uplift of core complexes (cf. Anderson and others, 1988). Although the origin of the anomaly has not been resolved, its pattern may imply that lower-plate rocks are exposed or lie close to the surface in the northern Colorado River extensional corridor and that the distribution of lower-plate rocks changes across the accommodation zone. Neither significant heat flow anomalies nor gradients have been observed along the accommodation zone (J. Sass, written communication, 1988).

West-tilted domain

The west-tilted domain (Fig. 4) encompasses more than 25,000 km² of highly distended upper-plate rocks, well-exposed detachment faults, and tectonically denuded, commonly mylonitized, lower-plate rocks in Arizona, Nevada, and California (Davis and others, 1980; Lucchitta and Suneson, 1981a; Howard and others, 1982; Spencer, 1985; Howard and John, 1987; John, 1987; Spencer and Reynolds, 1989). In the northern Colorado River extensional corridor, the west-tilted domain is situated between the McCullough Range to the west and the gently east-tilted Cerbat Mountains and southern White Hills to the east (Fig. 3). East-dipping, north-northwest– to north-northeast–trending normal faults dominate the west-tilted domain. The strike of layering generally ranges from N25°E to N15°W.

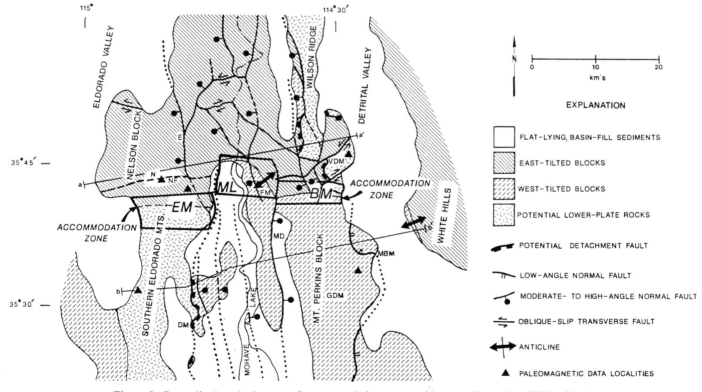

Figure 8. Generalized geologic map of accommodation zone and surrounding region. **BM** = Black Mountains segment of accommodation zone; **ML** = Mohave Lake segment; **EM** = Eldorado Mountains segment; DM = Dupont Mountain fault; MD = Mt. Davis fault; GDM = Golden Door Mine area; MBM = Mockingbird Mine fault; VDM = Van Deemen Mine fault; FM = Fire Mountain anticline; NF = Nelson fault; N = Nelson; E = Eldorado fault. Cross-section lines pertain to Figure 12. Faults dashed where inferred, dotted where concealed.

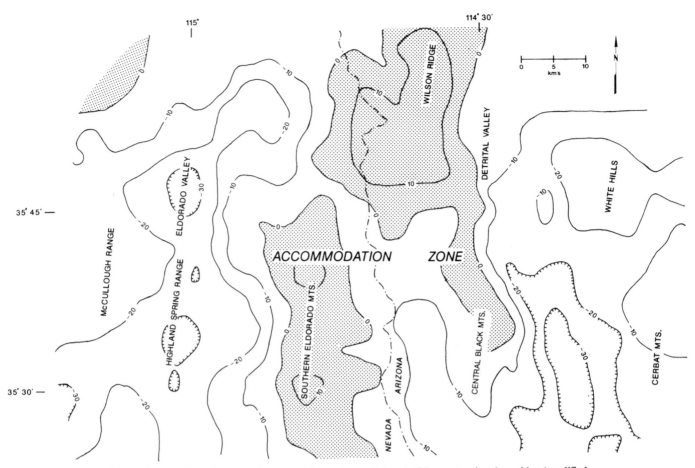

Figure 9. Isostatic residual gravity map of the northern Colorado River extensional corridor (modified from Mariano and others, 1986). Contour interval is 10 mGal. Hachured contours indicate closed gravity lows. Values greater than 0 mGal are shaded. Anomalies on isostatic residual gravity maps primarily reflect lateral density variations in the middle to upper crust (Mariano and others, 1986). Note apparent right-lateral offset of the positive gravity anomaly 2 to 7 km north of the accommodation zone. This gravity high extends southward into a belt of metamorphic core complexes (Simpson and others, 1986).

Spencer and Reynolds (1989) divided the west-tilted domain into an uplifted central belt of lower-plate rocks, which includes the Newberry and southern Eldorado Mountains (Fig. 3), and two outer belts of upper-plate rocks. Areas in the eastern outer belt, such as the central and southern Black Mountains, correspond to a wedge of fault blocks resting above an east-dipping system of detachment faults that projects beneath the Colorado Plateau. The presumed lower-plate rocks in the southern Eldorado and Newberry Mountains may have been drawn out from under the distending upper plate of the central and southern Black Mountains and the adjacent, relatively unextended region to the east. Alternatively, the central and southern Black Mountains may have been translated eastward from an original position over the southern Eldorado and Newberry Mountains. Fault blocks in the western outer belt, such as the Highland Spring Range, may lie within a detached, synformal keel of upper-plate rocks situated above a master detachment fault, which may project over the southern Eldorado Mountains

(Spencer, 1985; Spencer and Reynolds, 1989). However, the western outer belt may also include tilted fault blocks above low-angle normal faults that continue beneath the central belt of presumed lower plate. The location of a major breakaway fault has not been clearly defined for the west-tilted domain.

East-dipping, relatively planar normal faults dissect the west-tilted domain into a series of imbricate fault blocks, which can be modeled as a rotated set of dominoes. Maximum tilts of Tertiary strata increase eastward from approximately 65° in the southern Eldorado Mountains to more than 90° (i.e., slightly overturned) in the central Black Mountains.

A major east-dipping, low-angle normal fault on the east flank of the southern Eldorado Mountains, here referred to as the Dupont Mountain fault, may correspond to a major detachment fault (Figs. 3 and 8). This low-angle normal fault is best exposed 12 km south of the accommodation zone, where it dips 17° east (Fig. 10). A system of east-dipping, low-angle normal faults on the east flank of the Newberry Mountains (Mathis, 1982) may represent the southward continuation of the Dupont Mountain fault. A 30-m-thick zone of epidotized and chloritized breccia and isolated pods of mylonite mark the trace of the Dupont Mountain fault. The footwall of the fault contains the large crystalline terrane of the southern Eldorado Mountains, which is dominated by intermediate to felsic intrusions of probable Miocene age. The preponderance of Tertiary intrusions in the southern Eldorado Mountains contrasts with fairly isolated exposures of Tertiary plutons and dike swarms in the crystalline basement farther to the east. Several relatively narrow fault blocks, composed primarily of west-tilted Tertiary strata, constitute the immediate hanging wall of the Dupont Mountain fault. The contrast in structural level across the Dupont Mountain fault is indicative of a major detachment fault.

Geologic relations and preliminary paleomagnetic data suggest, however, that the crystalline terrane of the southern Eldorado Mountains is significantly tilted. Reconnaissance mapping by Longwell and others (1965) and Volborth (1973) showed a depositional contact between west-tilted Tertiary strata and crystalline basement in the southwestern part of the southern Eldorado Mountains. In addition, paleomagnetic data obtained from hypabyssal dike swarms, of probable Miocene age, on the west flank of the range (Fig. 8) imply 45 to 60° of west-tilting when compared to expected Miocene directions (Fig. 11a). Because dike emplacement may have occurred during block tilting, the magnitude of tilting inferred from paleomagnetic data is a minimum for the southern Eldorado Mountains. In contrast to the hypabyssal dike swarms on the west flank of the range, coarser-grained plutonic rocks dominate the east side, which further supports the premise of significant west-tilting. Plutonic rocks from the northern part of the range, on the other hand, yield magnetization data suggestive of significant east-tilting (Fig. 11d, e). We therefore propose that the crystalline terrane of the southern Eldorado Mountains corresponds to structurally deep levels of highly tilted fault blocks rather than to the footwall of a major detachment fault. Accordingly, the Dupont Mountain fault probably nucleated at a high angle and was in turn rotated to its present low-angle attitude by domino-like block tilting. The isostatic residual gravity high (Fig. 9) may indicate, however, that lower-plate rocks are bowed upward beneath the southern Eldorado Mountains. The width of the steeply tilted crystalline terrane in the southern Eldorado Mountains suggests that the Dupont Mountain fault accommodated a minimum of 9 km of normal separation, assuming a relatively planar fault geometry (Fig. 12b).

A large west-tilted fault block, here referred to as the Mt. Perkins block, dominates the west-tilted domain of the central Black Mountains (Figs. 8 and 12b). The Mt. Perkins block extends approximately 30 km south of the accommodation zone. Geologic field relations and paleomagnetic data demonstrate that a 10-km-thick section of crust is exposed on end in the Mt. Perkins block a few kilometers south of the cross section in Figure 12b. Thus, the original depth of the detachment along the eastern margin of the central Black Mountains exceeded 10 km. Relatively minor, moderately to steeply east-dipping normal

Figure 10. Dupont Mountain fault, looking northeast. The Dupont Mountain fault at mid-slope dips 17° to the east. Basaltic andesites and conglomerates in the hanging wall dip 65° westward. The conglomerates contain clasts of Proterozoic gneisses. The Dupont Mountain fault is characterized by 10 to 30 m of epidotized and chloritized breccia and by isolated pods of mylonite. Footwall rocks consist of Miocene (?) intrusions and Proterozoic gneisses.

faults, which generally accommodate offsets of less than 1 km, fragment much of the Mt. Perkins block. Space problems created near the base of the fault block by block tilting may have induced many of the minor faults. Unlike the major block-bounding faults, the minor east-dipping normal faults did not significantly affect the distribution of Tertiary volcanic and sedimentary strata.

The western part of the Mt. Perkins block consists of a large growth-fault basin in which stratal tilts progressively decrease up-section, from 90° in middle Miocene tuffaceous sedimentary rocks, volcaniclastic conglomerates, and pyroclastic flows, to 25° in middle Miocene basalts, and finally to less than 5° in late Miocene(?) fanglomerates (Figs. 12b and 13). The syntectonic deposits thin significantly eastward within the Mt. Perkins growth-fault basin. For example, the thickness of the middle Miocene tuffaceous rocks decreases from more than 500 m to less than 30 m from west to east across the northern part of the growth-fault basin. The east-dipping normal fault along the western margin of the Mt. Perkins block, here referred to as the Mt. Davis fault (Fig. 8), probably accommodated more than 4 km of normal separation. The apparent listric geometry of the Mt. Davis fault (Fig. 12b) is probably not primary but rather the result of high-angle propagation of the fault through the syntectonic deposits synchronous with progressive rotation of deeper increments of the fault to gentler dips.

Two major source areas contributed detritus to the half-graben basins of the west-tilted domain between the southern Eldorado Mountains crystalline terrane and the Mt. Perkins area. Steeply tilted conglomerates intercalated in the volcanic section in the immediate hanging wall of the Dupont Mountain fault commonly contain clasts of crystalline material in contrast to the

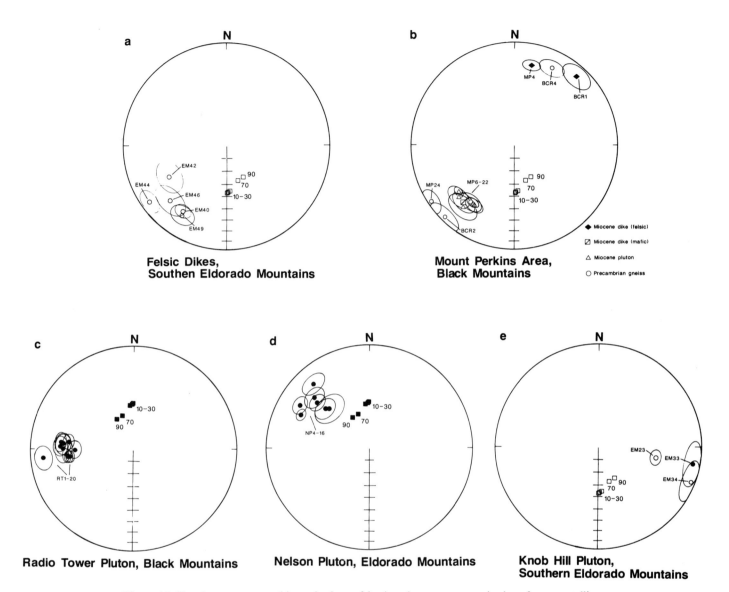

Figure 11. Equal-area stereographic projections of in-situ, site mean magnetizations from crystalline rocks in the northern Colorado River extensional corridor. Solid symbols are projections on lower hemisphere; open symbols, upper hemisphere. The projected cone of 95% confidence for each site mean is shown (see Table A1 for statistics). Poles for 10, 20, 30, 70, and 90 Ma are depicted as squares. a. Magnetizations from felsic dikes, of probable Miocene age, on the western flank of the southern Eldorado Mountains due west of the exposed trace of the Dupont Mountain fault. These data suggest 45° to 60° of west-tilting when compared to the Miocene pole direction. b. Magnetization directions from several crystalline lithologies in the Mt. Perkins block indicate 50 to 90° of west-tilting. c. Magnetization directions from a 73.3 Ma quartz monzonite pluton in the footwall of the Van Deemen Mine fault, central Black Mountains, suggest approximately 60° of east-tilting. d. Magnetizations from the Miocene Nelson pluton in the Eldorado Mountains imply 50° of east-tilting. e. Magnetization directions from a Miocene pluton in the southern Eldorado Mountains, which may be part of the 15.7 Ma Knob Hill pluton of Anderson and others (1972), indicate at least 60° of east-tilting.

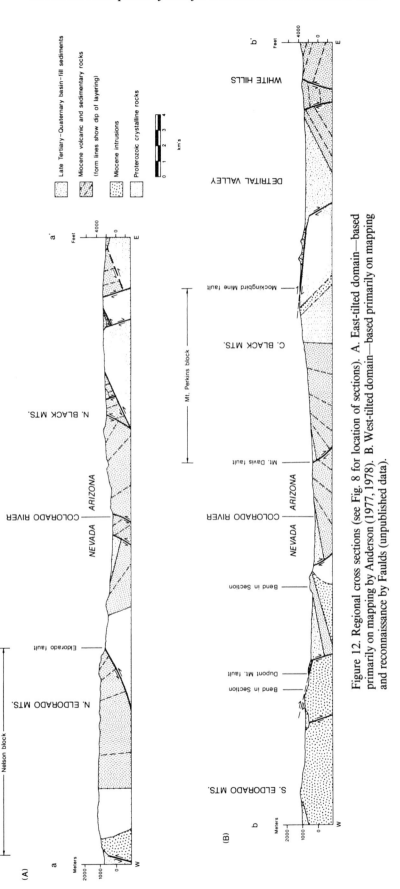

Figure 12. Regional cross sections (see Fig. 8 for location of sections). A. East-tilted domain—based primarily on mapping by Anderson (1977, 1978). B. West-tilted domain—based primarily on mapping and reconnaissance by Faulds (unpublished data).

Figure 13. Looking north at syntectonic strata in Mt. Perkins growth-fault basin. Basaltic andesite flows, which are probably correlative with the upper member of the Patsy Mine Volcanics of Anderson (1978), make up the gray rocks at lower right. The depositional contact between the conspicuous white tuffaceous rocks and basaltic andesite flows is vertical to slightly overturned to the east. West-tilting progressively decreases upward in the 450-m-thick section of tuffaceous rocks from 90° at the base to approximately 50° at the upper contact with the gray basalt flows (upper left). A thin pyroclastic flow near the base of the sequence of tuffaceous rocks yielded a K-Ar age (biotite) of 16.4 ± 0.4 Ma, whereas the basal basalt flow gave a 14.1 ± 0.4 Ma K-Ar age. Tilting continues to decrease up-section in the basalts to approximately 25° in the capping flow, which yielded a 14.3 ± 0.4 Ma K-Ar age (M. Shafiqullah, written communication, 1988). Both the tuffaceous sedimentary rocks and overlying basalt flows likely correlate with members of the middle Miocene Mt. Davis Volcanics of Anderson (1978).

to between 16.4 ± 0.4 Ma and 14.3 ± 0.4 Ma, respectively. In addition, a 13.1 ± 0.3 Ma date from a gently west-tilted (15°) basalt flow located 5 km east of the trace of the Dupont Mountain fault suggests that extension in the west-tilted domain continued until at least 13.1 Ma. On the basis of K-Ar isotopic age determinations and differential tilting, Anderson and others (1972) constrained the age of major extension in the east-tilted domain of the northern Eldorado and northern Black Mountains to middle Miocene time, roughly between 15 and 13 Ma. K-Ar dates (M. Shafiqullah, personal communication, 1989) from growth-fault deposits within a small half-graben bracket approximately 75 percent of the east-tilting in the central Black Mountains between 15.9 ± 0.4 Ma and 13.7 ± 0.3 Ma. Although extension may have begun slightly earlier in the west-tilted domain, the K-Ar dates indicate that most of the extension in the west- and east-tilted domains was contemporaneous. Coeval episodes of major extension in the west- and east-tilted domains demonstrate that the accommodation zone in the central Black and southern Eldorado Mountains did not coordinate temporal changes in deformation, but indeed accommodated simultaneous block tilting in opposite directions and possibly interaction between opposing detachment systems.

The portion of the Tertiary section within the Mt. Perkins block that predates significant tilting consists of, in ascending order, (1) a basal arkosic sandstone; (2) thin rhyolite tuff; (3) a complex unit of intercalated hornblende andesite flows, pyroxene-olivine basaltic andesite flows, and volcanic breccia; and (4) a thick sequence of pyroxene-olivine basaltic andesite flows (Fig. 7). With the exception of the hornblende andesites, these lithologies closely resemble the Patsy Mine Volcanics described by Anderson (1977, 1978) in areas to the north. Most notably, a thin rhyolite tuff, similar to that exposed near the base of the Tertiary section in the Mt. Perkins block, is also present near the base of the Tertiary section in the east-tilted domain of the northern Eldorado Mountains. In both cases, the tuff generally rests on a prevolcanic arkosic sandstone. Thus, the age of volcanism appears to differ little across the accommodation zone. Slight changes in lithologies across the region may simply represent lateral variations in a coeval volcanic pile. The apparent contemporaneity of volcanism in the vicinity of the accommodation zone allows regional correlations of both lithologic units and deformational episodes, which are critical to understanding the nature of the zone.

The eastern part of the Mt. Perkins block consists entirely of crystalline rock, including middle Miocene felsic and mafic dike swarms, a 16.8 ± 0.4 Ma (M. Shafiqullah, written communication, 1989) granodiorite pluton, and Proterozoic gneisses. In contrast to the southern Eldorado Mountains, Proterozoic gneisses predominate in the crystalline basement of the Mt. Perkins block. The 30-km-long, north-trending, steeply dipping contact between Tertiary strata and Proterozoic crystalline rock in the central part of the Mt. Perkins block is generally not a fault, as previously reported by Longwell (1963), but instead corresponds to a nonconformity, which is locally overturned to the east.

volcaniclastic conglomerates in all but the base of the section in the Mt. Perkins block. In addition, the thick sequence of tuffaceous rocks in the Mt. Perkins growth-fault basin appears to be missing in the array of narrow fault blocks between the southern Eldorado Mountains crystalline terrane and Mohave Lake. The crystalline clasts in the immediate hanging wall of the Dupont Mountain fault were probably derived from the upthrown eastern edge of a west-tilted fault block in the southern Eldorado Mountains, which further suggests that the crystalline terrane of the southern Eldorado Mountains corresponds to the structurally deep level of a highly tilted fault block. Debris shed from the crystalline terrane may have prevented deposition of the tuffaceous rocks found farther to the east. The tuffaceous rocks and volcaniclastic conglomerates within the Mt. Perkins growth-fault basin were probably derived primarily from local volcanic centers.

Stratigraphic relations, discordant tilts, and K-Ar dates indicate that the major episode of extension in the vicinity of the accommodation zone occurred during middle Miocene time. K-Ar isotopic age determinations (M. Shafiqullah, written communication, 1988) from a pyroclastic flow tilted 85° and a basalt flow tilted approximately 25° constrain more than 70 percent of the west-tilting within the Mt. Perkins growth-fault basin

Similar to the disparate tilts of Tertiary strata within the growth-fault basin, a significant discordance in the amount of tilting is also recognized, by means of paleomagnetic data, in the crystalline basement of the Mt. Perkins block. Well-defined magnetization directions have been isolated in sites from the crystalline basement of the Mt. Perkins block and compared to expected Miocene directions for tectonic inferences (Faulds and Geissman, 1986; Faulds and others, 1987b). Sites collected from the 16.8-Ma granodiorite pluton, Proterozoic gneisses within 1 km of the pluton, and a middle Miocene felsic dike swarm all yield data suggesting 40 to 50° of west tilting (Fig. 11b). The gneisses within 1 km of the margin of the pluton may have been remagnetized during pluton emplacement. In contrast, paleomagnetic data characteristic of Proterozoic gneisses more than 1 km from the margin of the pluton suggest 70 to 90° of west tilting. Although magnetization acquisition in the surrounding Proterozoic rocks probably predates that in the pluton, we suggest that the dominant magnetization in the Proterozoic gneisses more than 1 km from the pluton margin is a viscous partial thermoremanent magnetization of probable Tertiary age, as evidenced by axes of tilting similar to that of the pluton. The inferred N15°W axis of tilting of the crystalline rocks closely coincides with the average strike of layering in the Tertiary volcanic and sedimentary strata.

The apparent 20 to 50° of discordance in the amount of Miocene tilting between the Proterozoic gneisses and the 16.8-Ma pluton is similar to the angular discordance in the amount of tilting developed within the sequence of middle Miocene tuffaceous rocks, which accumulated in the growth-fault basin on the western side of the Mt. Perkins block. Tilting within these tuffaceous rocks is rarely less than the inferred amount of tilting within the granodiorite pluton and felsic dike swarm. The granodiorite pluton and felsic dike swarm may be syntectonic intrusions emplaced contemporaneously with deposition of the middle Miocene tuffaceous sequence. This tuffaceous sequence represents the only major pulse of felsic volcanism recorded in the Tertiary section of the Mt. Perkins block. However, the 16.8-Ma K-Ar date suggests that emplacement of the pluton predated the onset of extension. The paleomagnetically deduced discordance in the magnitude of tilting between the pluton and Proterozoic gneisses may instead indicate that magnetization acquisition in the pluton occurred shortly after its emplacement during tilting and tectonic denudation, which induced rapid cooling.

The remanent magnetization in the Proterozoic metamorphic rocks was also probably acquired during relatively rapid cooling in response to Tertiary uplift and tectonic denudation. Any preexisting remanent magnetization in the Proterozoic rocks was unblocked or overprinted during prolonged burial and/or magmatism during Miocene(?) time. A secondary remanent magnetization, of uplift origin (e.g., Pullaiah and others, 1975), is assumed to have been acquired at a later time. In the Mt. Perkins block, geologic constraints permit an independent check of interpretations based on paleomagnetic data. For example, because the basal part of the Tertiary section is tilted on end and rests in depositional contact on crystalline basement, the Proterozoic

Figure 14. Looking south at the gently east-dipping (7°) Mockingbird Mine fault on the northeast flank of Mt. Perkins. The fault is commonly marked by 10 to 20 m of chloritized breccia. Miocene strata in the hanging wall of the fault dip approximately 65° to the west. The footwall within view is dominated by Proterozoic gneisses and metagabbro. However, 4.5 km to the west of the fault trace, Tertiary strata rest in depositional contact with the Proterozoic gneisses. The Proterozoic/Tertiary nonconformity stands near vertical. The Mockingbird Mine fault accommodated more than 5.5 km of normal separation.

gneisses in the Mt. Perkins block must also have been tilted 90° during Miocene time, as echoed by the paleomagnetic data.

Restoration of the Mt. Perkins block places the middle Miocene tuffaceous rocks above the felsic dike swarm, which in turn would directly overlie the pluton. Thus, a genetic relation may exist between these three lithologic groups. We speculate that a volcanic center may be centered in the vicinity of the Golden Door Mine (Fig. 8), where the felsic dike swarm invades the lower part of the Tertiary section and relatively thick ash-flow tuffs make up much of the sequence of tuffaceous rocks. The bulk of the pluton and thickest part of the felsic dike swarm lie directly east and down section of the Golden Door Mine area. Thus, part of the steeply tilted Mt. Perkins block may expose a cross section of a Miocene volcano, including the plutonic roots, hypabyssal dike swarm at intermediate levels, and surficial volcanic complex.

A major east-dipping, low-angle (5 to 10°) normal fault, here named the Mockingbird Mine fault, bounds the Mt. Perkins block on the east (Figs. 8 and 14). The Mockingbird Mine fault probably nucleated at a relatively high angle and was in turn rotated to its present low-angle attitude by block-tilting, as evidenced by similar amounts of tilting within its hanging wall and footwall. West-tilting of Tertiary strata exceeds 60° in the hanging wall of the fault. The nonconformity between Tertiary strata and Proterozoic gneisses stands near vertical in the footwall of the fault, 4 to 8 km west of its exposed trace. A tentative correlation of Tertiary units between the hanging wall and footwall suggests a minimum of 5.5 km of normal separation along the Mockingbird Mine fault.

Approximately 35 km west of the Grand Wash Cliffs, the

west-tilted domain terminates eastward in an open north-northwest–trending anticline, the width of which (i.e., distance between inflection points on a folded surface) exceeds 5 km. The anticline appears to consist of a complex array of fault blocks, which are bounded by normal faults that accommodate a gradual roll-over in the tilt direction. Tilts in the vicinity of the anticline do not exceed 35°. The anticline is generally buried beneath Detrital Valley but does surface in the southwesternmost part of the White Hills (Fig. 8) and in the central Black Mountains, 35 km south of the east-west–trending accommodation zone. The northern Cerbat Mountains and adjacent Hualapai Valley correspond to a large, gently east-tilted fault block and attendant half-graben, respectively (Lucchitta, 1966).

East-tilted domain

The east-tilted domain incorporates more than 5,000 km^2 of highly distended, primarily upper-plate rocks in the northern Colorado River extensional corridor (Anderson, 1971, 1977, 1978; Anderson and others, 1972; Bohannon, 1984; Weber and Smith, 1987). If continued beyond the left-lateral Lake Mead and right-lateral Las Vegas Valley shear zones, the east-tilted domain would include more than 20,000 km^2 of northwestern Arizona, southern Nevada, and the Death Valley region of California. In the northern Colorado River extensional corridor, the east-tilted domain is situated between the western edge of the Colorado Plateau on the east, where flat-lying Paleozoic strata crop out at the Grand Wash Cliffs, and the Spring Range on the west (Fig. 3). The strike of layering in the east-tilted domain generally ranges from north-south to N25°W. Anderson (1977, 1978) mapped much of the east-tilted domain in the northern Black and northern Eldorado Mountains.

The east-tilted domain of the Black and Eldorado Mountains is essentially a mirror image of the west-tilted domain. In contrast to the predominant east-dipping normal faults in the west-tilted domain, west-dipping, north-northwest–trending normal faults bound imbricate fault blocks in the east-tilted domain. Accordingly, the vergence of major normal faults in the brittle upper crust of the east-tilted domain is exactly opposite that in the west-tilted domain. In addition, major features of the detachment terrane, including breakaway faults and potential exposures of lower-plate rocks, occur in opposite locations in the east-tilted domain relative to such features in the west-tilted domain (Fig. 8).

The east-tilted domain may be divided into a central belt of potential lower-plate rocks and two outer belts of upper-plate rocks. The western outer belt, which includes the northern Eldorado Mountains, may correspond to a wedge of fault blocks in the upper plate of a west-dipping system of detachment faults that project beneath the northern McCullough and Spring Ranges (Wernicke, 1985; Weber and Smith, 1987). The presumed lower plate of the detachment in the Wilson Ridge area of the northern Black Mountains was translated eastward relative to the northern Eldorado Mountains. The east-tilted blocks between the Grand

Figure 15. Looking north at the gently (5°) west-dipping Van Deemen Mine fault immediately north of the accommodation zone. The Van Deemen Mine fault in this area is marked by a 10- to 40-m-thick zone of mylonite. The thickest package of mylonite occupies a 300-m-wide, east-northeast–trending band immediately north of and subparallel to a major transverse structure. Gold mineralization occurs along the Van Deemen Mine fault in cataclastically overprinted zones within the band of mylonite (Drobeck and others, 1988). Footwall rocks within view consist of weakly foliated granodiorite of unknown age and Proterozoic gneisses and amphibolite. Miocene volcanic and sedimentary rocks within the hanging wall dip, on average, 60° eastward. The Van Deemen Mine fault locally accommodated at least 5 km of normal separation in middle Miocene time.

Wash Cliffs and Wilson Ridge area also probably rest above a west-dipping detachment fault, which may project above the Wilson Ridge crystalline terrane. The relation between the west-dipping, low-angle normal faults beneath the eastern and western outer belts of upper-plate rocks is complicated by a late episode of high-angle normal faulting in the Wilson Ridge area (Eschner and Smith, 1988). The breakaway fault for the east-tilted domain is likely buried beneath recent alluvium immediately west of the Grand Wash Cliffs.

A major, west-dipping, low-angle (5 to 10°) normal fault, here referred to as the Van Deemen Mine fault, bounds the crystalline terrane of the central Black Mountains on the west, immediately north of the accommodation zone (Fig. 15). The crystalline rocks in the footwall of the Van Deemen Mine fault appear to continue northward into the Wilson Ridge area (Fig. 8). The Van Deemen Mine fault may link up with major west-dipping, low-angle normal faults exposed on the northern flank of the Wilson Ridge crystalline terrane and at Saddle Island. The low-angle normal faults in the Lake Mead region may correspond to disrupted fragments of an originally continuous, west-dipping detachment fault (Weber and Smith, 1987; Smith and others, 1987; Duebendorfer and others, 1988, and this volume).

Mylonites are present along the low-angle normal fault zones in both the Van Deemen Mine and Saddle Island areas. The average extension lineation in the mylonitic rocks trends east-west (Fig. 16a). Cataclastic deformation overprints the mylonitic fabric. The low-angle normal fault at Saddle Island accommodated approximately 20 km of down-to-the-west normal separation (Duebendorfer and others, this volume). Normal separation along the Van Deemen Mine fault is constrained to a minimum of 5 km but may be much greater.

The crystalline terrane in the east-tilted domain of the central and northern Black Mountains consists of late Cretaceous to middle Miocene intrusions and Proterozoic gneisses. The intrusions, which include silicic to intermediate plutons and intermediate to mafic dike swarms, are concentrated in the northern and southern parts of the crystalline terrane. The northern part of the terrane is dominated by a large composite, middle Miocene pluton (Anderson and others, 1972; Feuerbach and Smith, 1986; Weber and Smith, 1987). A 73.3 ± 1.5 Ma (M. Shafiqullah, personal communication, 1989) quartz monzonite pluton and abundant mafic dikes of probable Miocene age crop out in the southern part of the crystalline terrane just north of the accommodation zone (Fig. 17). Intervening areas are largely composed of Proterozoic gneisses (Anderson, 1978).

As with the southern Eldorado Mountains in the west-tilted domain, the fundamental question concerning the crystalline terrane of the central and northern Black Mountains is whether it corresponds to the lower plate of a major detachment fault or to a structurally deep level of a highly tilted fault block. A well-defined magnetization obtained from the 73.3-Ma quartz monzonite pluton in the probable footwall of the Van Deemen Mine fault implies approximately 60° of east-tilting about a N30°W axis (Fig. 11c). Tertiary strata within the immediate hanging wall of the Van Deemen Mine fault display an average attitude of N10°W, 60°E. Similar tilts of the hanging wall and apparent footwall of the Van Deemen Mine fault suggest that the Van Deemen Mine fault nucleated at a relatively high angle and was in turn rotated to its present low-angle orientation by domino-like block rotations. Accordingly, the crystalline terrane in the east-tilted domain of at least the central Black Mountains probably does not correspond to the lower plate of the detachment terrane but rather to a deep structural level of a highly tilted fault block. Major transverse structures in the Van Deemen Mine area presumably accommodated oblique-slip torsional offset associated with differential tilting rather than strike-slip offset related to the withdrawal of lower-plate rocks of the detachment terrane out from under upper-plate rocks. In addition, some of the transverse structures may also correspond to lateral ramps in the Van Deemen Mine fault, as evidenced by their gently dipping segments.

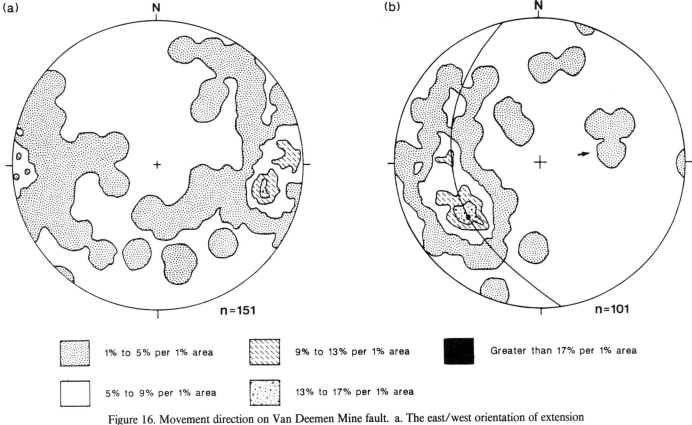

Figure 16. Movement direction on Van Deemen Mine fault. a. The east/west orientation of extension lineations closely corresponds to the apparent extension direction in Miocene time. b. Attitudes of Tertiary strata in the immediate hanging wall of the fault define a great circle with a pole of 58->N82°E. Folding of Tertiary strata in the immediate hanging wall of the fault appears to be related to corrugations, or megamullions, in the fault surface. These data suggest an east/west to east-northeast/west-southwest movement direction on the Van Deemen Mine fault.

Although it probably nucleated at a high angle, the Van Deemen Mine low-angle normal fault exhibits many characteristics of detachment faults. At least one major fault in the steeply tilted Tertiary section soles into the Van Deemen Mine fault. In addition, corrugations, or megamullions, in the fault surface significantly affected the attitude of Tertiary strata in the hanging wall. A stereographic projection of poles to layering in the hanging wall of the Van Deemen Mine fault defines a great circle, the N80°E-trending axis of which (Fig. 16b) is similar to the probable direction of transport along the fault.

The magnitude of tilting of the northern Black Mountains crystalline terrane (Wilson Ridge) is debatable. Anderson (1978) mapped a small exposure of steeply (80°) east-tilted Tertiary volcanic rock in depositional contact with Proterozoic gneisses along the east flank of the southern part of Wilson Ridge. In contrast, detailed geologic mapping and petrologic characteristics (Feuerbach, 1986; Naumann, 1987) as well as preliminary paleomagnetic data indicate that the bulk of the middle Miocene composite pluton in the northern part of the crystalline terrane is not significantly tilted. Assigning the Wilson Ridge area to the lower plate of the detachment terrane implies that a major detachment fault cut the crystalline terrane between the Wilson Ridge and Van Deemen Mine areas. Such a structure has not been observed. However, the critical area has not been mapped in sufficient detail to locate such a fault. The 10-mGal isostatic residual gravity high in the Wilson Ridge area (Fig. 9) may indicate that lower-plate rocks lie at or relatively close to the surface.

A large, steeply tilted fault block, here referred to as the Nelson block, dominates the east-tilted domain of the northern Eldorado Mountains (Figs. 8 and 12a). The east-tilted Nelson block is essentially a mirror image of the west-tilted Mt. Perkins block, as demonstrated by similarities in size, morphology, and internal distribution of lithologies. As in the Mt. Perkins block, an approximately 10-km-thick section of crust is exposed on end in the Nelson block, which implies a minimum original depth of 10 km for a detachment along the western margin of the northern Eldorado Mountains. A large growth-fault basin (Anderson, 1971, 1977), within which thick sequences of syntectonic strata accumulated, occupies the eastern part of the Nelson structural block. Tilting within the growth-fault basin decreases upward from 90 to 10° in middle Miocene syntectonic strata. The west-dipping Eldorado fault of Anderson (1977) accommodated up to 9 km of normal separation along the eastern margin of the Nelson block and attendant growth-fault basin (Fig. 12a). The north-northwest–trending nonconformity between Tertiary strata and Proterozoic gneisses is commonly overturned to the west within the Nelson block. Minor west-dipping normal faults fragment the Nelson block into numerous smaller blocks. The northern part of the Nelson block probably lies buried beneath Eldorado Valley, an area that may be disrupted by the southwestern terminus of the Lake Mead fault zone (Anderson, 1973).

A major east-west–trending transverse structure, here referred to as the Nelson fault, bounds the Nelson block on the

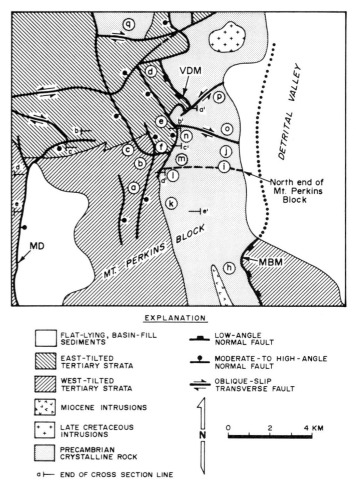

EXPLANATION

FLAT-LYING, BASIN-FILL SEDIMENTS

EAST-TILTED TERTIARY STRATA

WEST-TILTED TERTIARY STRATA

MIOCENE INTRUSIONS

LATE CRETACEOUS INTRUSIONS

PRECAMBRIAN CRYSTALLINE ROCK

◦⊢ END OF CROSS SECTION LINE

LOW-ANGLE NORMAL FAULT

MODERATE- TO HIGH-ANGLE NORMAL FAULT

OBLIQUE-SLIP TRANSVERSE FAULT

0   2   4 KM

N

Figure 17. Black Mountains segment of accommodation zone. VDM = Van Deemen Mine fault; MD = Mount Davis fault; MBM = Mockingbird Mine fault. This transversely oriented segment of the accommodation zone corresponds to a 5-km-wide belt of intermeshing conjugate normal faults in middle part of figure. Note that major east-dipping normal faults in the west-tilted domain (e.g., MBM and MD) and major west-dipping normal faults in the east-tilted domain (e.g., VDM) die out across the accommodation zone. Encircled letters refer to equal-area stereoplots of poles to layering (Fig. 18). Cross-section lines pertain to Figure 19. Faults are dashed where inferred, dotted where concealed.

south (Fig. 8). Both Hansen (1962) and Anderson (1971) noted 6.1 km of left-lateral separation of the Tertiary/Proterozoic nonconformity along this structure. As in much of the Nelson block, the basal part of the Tertiary section south of the Nelson fault is overturned to the west. The lack of change in the attitude of layering across the Nelson fault suggests that the fault is unrelated to the accommodation zone. Some transverse structures, such as the Nelson fault, may correspond to inflation faults (e.g., Shride, 1967) that served to accommodate differential intrusion. The Nelson fault essentially separates the large plutonic complex of the southern Eldorado Mountains from the Nelson block, where Miocene intrusions are relatively sparse. Much of the apparent left-lateral separation along the Nelson fault may actually equate with up-to-the-south vertical displacement resulting from the inflationary effects of the plutonic complex.

A large granodiorite pluton, of probable middle Miocene age, is emplaced into lower parts of the east-tilted Tertiary section along the Nelson fault. Anderson (1971) concluded that most of the displacement along the Nelson fault accompanied or preceded the emplacement of the pluton. The pluton yields well-defined magnetization data suggesting approximately 50° of east tilting (Fig. 11d), which is distinctly less than the amount of tilting in the surrounding country rock. Thus, magnetization acquisition in the pluton probably occurred during major extension and block tilting. Paleomagnetic data obtained from an intermediate-composition pluton of probable Miocene age 2.6 km south of the southernmost exposure of east-tilted Tertiary strata indicate at least 60° of east-tilting (Fig. 11e). These data, combined with those obtained from the west-tilted domain, constrain the location of the accommodation zone in the "tilted" crystalline terrane of the southern Eldorado Mountains to an east-west–trending belt situated 6 to 11 km south of Nelson.

A well-defined western limit to the east-tilted domain, such as the anticline on the eastern margin of the west-tilted domain, has not been observed. The east-tilted domain of the northern Colorado River extensional corridor continues westward at least as far as the northern McCullough Range (Fig. 3).

Although the composite stratigraphic column in the east-tilted domain differs little from that in the west-tilted domain, significant variations in the distribution and composition of syntectonic middle Miocene strata do occur between the two tilt-block domains. For example, the large size of the Nelson and Mt. Perkins fault blocks promoted accumulation of unusually thick syntectonic strata in the attendant growth-fault basins, resulting in an asymmetric distribution of syntectonic strata near the accommodation zone. More than 1,000 m of tuffaceous rocks, volcaniclastic conglomerates, and basalt flows deposited in the Mt. Perkins growth-fault basin thin appreciably northward across the accommodation zone as the large west-tilted Mt. Perkins block gives way to several relatively narrow east-tilted fault blocks. Because the middle Miocene tuffaceous rocks record the onset of major extension in the large growth-fault basins of both the west- and east-tilted domains, they represent an important marker. These tuffaceous rocks are generally thin or absent in the array of narrow fault blocks in both the southern part of the east-tilted domain immediately west of the crystalline terrane of the central Black Mountains and in the northern part of the west-tilted domain immediately east of the southern Eldorado Mountains. Major landslide deposits of volcanic and crystalline rock occur at the same stratigraphic interval as the tuffaceous rocks in the array of narrow fault blocks north of the accommodation zone in the central Black Mountains. The landslide deposits conformably overlie either basaltic andesite flows of the Patsy Mine Volcanics or a thin veneer of tuffaceous rock deposited on the basaltic andesites. Fanglomerates resting on the landslide deposits commonly contain abundant clasts of crystalline rock. Clasts of crys-

talline rock are also abundant in steeply tilted fanglomerates in the hanging wall of the Dupont Mountain fault immediately east of the southern Eldorado Mountains crystalline terrane. Excluding the basal arkosic conglomerate, conglomerates in the large growth-fault basins in both the east- and west-tilted domains generally contain volcanic clasts.

The abundance of crystalline material in the landslide deposits and fanglomerates indicates that extensive crystalline source terranes were exposed essentially at the onset of major extension and block tilting. The landslide deposits in the central Black Mountains conformably overlie more than 1.5 km of Tertiary volcanic and sedimentary strata. The crystalline source area in the central Black Mountains probably corresponded to the upthrown western edge of the east-tilted fault block that makes up the footwall of the Van Deemen Mine fault. Similarly, the upthrown eastern part of a major west-tilted fault block in the southern Eldorado Mountains was presumably the source area for clasts of crystalline material in the hanging wall of the Dupont Mountain fault. The landslide deposits of crystalline material and conglomerates laden with clasts of crystalline rock, both of which occur near the base of the syntectonic section, provide further evidence that the crystalline terrane of the central Black Mountains represents structurally deep levels of highly tilted fault blocks, as opposed to the lower plate of the detachment terrane. Significant tectonic denudation and isostatic rise of lower-plate rocks to the surface presumably does not occur in the early stages of an extensional orogeny.

Sections of volcanic and volcaniclastic rock, exceeding 1.5 km in thickness and in close proximity to crystalline source terranes, suggest that early Miocene strata were deposited in large grabens or half-grabens prior to the inception of major extension. Initial stages of extension in the northern Colorado River extensional corridor may have begun during early Miocene time, coincident with the outbreak of volcanism. During early stages of extension, graben subsidence probably did not keep pace with constructive volcanic processes, preventing a major influx of detritus from nearby horsts (or upthrown margins of fault blocks). A thin volcanic cover may have mantled the horsts at this time. With the onset of major extension and block tilting, rapidly subsiding half-grabens became regional depocenters. Where early-stage normal faults were reactivated during the major phase of extension, the upthrown margins of the original horsts were quickly tectonically denuded and crystalline material was shed into the developing half-grabens.

GEOMETRY AND KINEMATICS OF THE ACCOMMODATION ZONE

The east-west–trending, 40-km-long accommodation zone in the central Black and southern Eldorado Mountains consists of five distinct segments. From east to west, these are here referred to as the Grand Wash Cliffs, Black Mountains, Mohave Lake, Eldorado Mountains, and McCullough Range segments. The Grand Wash Cliffs and McCullough Range segments do not correspond to tilt-block domain boundaries but rather to the hypothetical eastern and western projections of the accommodation zone, respectively. Although not part of the accommodation zone proper, these areas are included because of their possible relevance to the kinematic history of the highly extended region. The geometry and kinematics of the segments are described prior to integrating all five into an assessment of the kinematic evolution of the entire accommodation zone and surrounding tilt-block domains.

Grand Wash Cliffs and McCullough Range segments

The hypothetical eastern and western extensions of the accommodation zone are commonly characterized by major changes in topographic grain, geometry of fault blocks, and exposed structural level. The accommodation zone terminates eastward approximately 35 km west of the Grand Wash Cliffs, where the west-tilted domain ends in the north-northwest–trending anticline. The Grand Wash Cliffs segment corresponds to the hypothetical projection of the accommodation zone east of the anticline. The large, gently tilted Cerbat Mountains fault block (Fig. 3), which includes the deep half-graben of Hualapai Valley, gives way northward in the vicinity of the eastward projection of the accommodation zone to several narrower, moderately tilted fault blocks, some of which are bounded by low-angle normal faults (Theodore and others, 1982; Myers and others, 1986). This may indicate a shallower detachment level north of the projected zone. In addition, a major inflection in the trend of the Grand Wash Cliffs occurs along the projected zone (Fig. 3). East of the Grand Wash Cliffs, no obvious topographic or surficial structural features delineate the projection of the accommodation zone. However, a significant N85°E-trending discontinuity in residual aeromagnetic contours (Sauck and Sumner, 1970) roughly corresponds to the eastward projection of the accommodation zone to nearly the longitude of Flagstaff, Arizona.

The westward projection of the accommodation zone, the McCullough Range segment, is marked by the northern edge of the Highland Spring Range, a southward trend toward deeper structural levels in both the McCullough and Lucy Gray Ranges (Fig. 3), and a northward trend toward significantly higher elevation in the Spring Range. Farther west, the left-lateral Garlock fault lies on trend with the accommodation zone. Although the Garlock fault and the accommodation zone are not linked by Tertiary or Mesozoic fault zones, the location and coincidental trend of these two structures may reflect an inherent, east-west–trending zone of crustal weakness.

The deformational style along the hypothetical eastern and western projections of the accommodation zone may place some constraints on the kinematic evolution of the region during Miocene extension. If the accommodation zone facilitates a dip reversal in regional detachment systems, a simple shear model of continental extension would predict a change from detachment footwall to detachment hanging wall along the projected accommodation zone in the relatively unextended regions on either side of the northern Colorado River extensional corridor (Figs. 5a and 6a). The lack of strike-slip faulting in these areas indicates little relative movement between the potential lower-plate rocks of one tilt-block domain and the upper-plate rocks of the adjacent opposing domain, at least within the unextended regions.

Black Mountains segment

The Black Mountains segment incorporates a well-exposed, 12-km-long portion of the accommodation zone in the central Black Mountains (Figs. 8 and 17). The entire Black Mountains segment was mapped at scales of 1:12,000 and 1:6,000. Late Miocene to Quaternary basin-fill deposits in Detrital Valley obscure the accommodation zone east of the Black Mountains segment. The western part of the segment consists of tilted Tertiary volcanic and sedimentary strata in depositional and tectonic contact with Proterozoic and Cretaceous/Tertiary crystalline rock, whereas the eastern part is composed entirely of crystalline rock.

The Black Mountains segment of the accommodation zone is characterized by an east-west–trending, 5-km-wide, sublinear zone of variably tilted narrow fault blocks. Fault-block tilting on either side of the zone commonly exceeds 60°. Tilting decreases progressively toward the axis of the zone (Figs. 18a through f and 19a through e), where minor transverse faults accommodate torsional strain between gently tilted (20 to 35°) fault blocks of opposing polarity. Major strike-slip faulting does not occur along the accommodation zone. The margins of the zone are essentially defined by diffuse zones of en echelon, oblique-slip transverse faults that facilitate the southward decrease in tilting in the east-tilted domain and the northward decline in tilting in the west-tilted domain. Concomitant with the decrease in tilting, fault spacing decreases, and average fault dip increases (Fig. 19a through e).

The Black Mountains segment of the accommodation zone corresponds to a zone of intermeshing conjugate normal faults rather than a strike-slip fault zone. In contrast to the predominance of one conjugate fault type in both the east- and west-tilted domains, east- and west-dipping faults are about equally common in the axial part of the zone. As evidenced by the lack of consistent cross-cutting relations between conjugate fault types, motion along east- and west-dipping faults was essentially coeval within the accommodation zone. Fault blocks within the zone were probably periodically tilted in opposite directions during middle Miocene extension. The direction of tilting at any particular interval was controlled by the active conjugate fault type. Horsefield (1980) demonstrated experimentally that crossing conjugate fault sets can operate more or less simultaneously, at least for small displacements. Contemporaneous movement on the east- and west-dipping faults within the zone is compatible with the presumed synchroneity of major extension in the east- and west-tilted domains, as deduced by means of K-Ar isotopic dating and structural and stratigraphic relations outside the accommodation zone. Because of the periodic reversals in tilt direction, estimates of extension based only on the dips of normal faults and magnitude of tilting (e.g., Wernicke and Burchfiel, 1982) would yield very misleading results within the accommodation zone.

Major normal faults entering the accommodation zone from both the east- and west-tilted domains generally die out within the zone before reaching steeply tilted parts of the adjacent domain. In some cases, the faults terminate in drag folds. In addition, some of the major normal faults curve into major transverse structures that accommodate the differential tilting along the margins of the accommodation zone. For example, an east-west–trending splay of the Mt. Davis fault facilitates approximately 40° of differential tilting within the east-tilted domain along the northern margin of the accommodation zone (Fig. 17).

Major low-angle normal faults grade laterally into more steeply dipping normal faults near the margins of the accommodation zone. The dip of the Van Deemen Mine fault appears to increase progressively southward as it crosses the accommodation zone and enters into the west-tilted domain (Fig. 17). This relation lends credence to the interpretation, based primarily on paleomagnetic data, that the gently dipping segment of the Van Deemen Mine fault originally formed at a relatively high angle and was then rotated to its present low-angle attitude by domino-like block rotation. Within the axial part of the accommodation zone, where relatively minor tilting has occurred, the west-dipping Van Deemen Mine fault retains a presumably primary, moderate to steep dip. In the west-tilted domain, however, the west-dipping Van Deemen Mine fault was probably rotated to steeper dips during block tilting. Moreover, within a span of 1.5 km, displacement on this apparently continuous, west-dipping normal fault zone decreases from at least 5 km in the steeply east-tilted domain immediately north of the accommodation zone to less than 10 m in the steeply west-tilted domain. Similarly, the gently east-dipping Mockingbird Mine fault probably coalesces near the southern margin of the accommodation zone with an inferred east-dipping, high-angle normal fault, which bounds Detrital Valley on the west and may continue several kilometers north of the accommodation zone (Fig. 17). Major low-angle normal faults in the central Black Mountains appear to be confined to the steeply tilted parts of the east- and west-tilted domains.

The precise location of the axis of the accommodation zone, which corresponds to the actual boundary between east- and west-tilted fault blocks, varies considerably because it is contingent on the relative proximity of major east- and west-dipping normal faults. Where major west-dipping normal faults, such as the Van Deemen Mine fault, cross the accommodation zone, east-tilted fault blocks predominate, and the axis of the zone steps southward (and vice versa; Fig. 17). The west-tilted domain may step northward in the vicinity of Detrital Valley, where the east-dipping Mockingbird Mine fault crosses the accommodation zone. Normal faults or minor open folds (Fig. 19c) generally mark the along-strike (i.e., parallel to strike of normal faults) boundaries between oppositely tilted parts of the Black Mountains segment.

Because of the gentler tilts of fault blocks and more closely spaced faults, the Black Mountains segment of the accommodation zone exhibits relatively minor topographic and structural relief as compared with the steeply tilted parts of the east- and west-tilted domains. Larger and deeper half-grabens permitted accumulation of thicker syntectonic deposits in the highly tilted terranes (compare Fig. 19c, e). The syntectonic middle Miocene tuffaceous rocks in the west-tilted domain and contemporaneous landslide deposits in the east-tilted domain thin appreciably near the margins of the accommodation zone.

The crystalline terrane in the eastern part of the Black Mountains segment and surrounding areas was mapped in order to determine whether (1) the foliation attitudes of Proterozoic gneisses mimic the nearly 180° reversal in tilt direction observed in Tertiary strata, and (2) the accommodation zone formed along an inherent zone of weakness developed during Proterozoic or Mesozoic time. Proterozoic lithologies include various compositions of quartzo-feldspathic gneisses, amphibolite, and weakly foliated granodiorite, tonalite, and metagabbro. Miocene(?) dikes of variable composition dilate much of the Proterozoic basement.

In the west-tilted domain, foliation attitudes in the Proterozoic rocks appear to reflect the progressive southward increase in the amount of tilt between the axis of the accommodation zone and the Mt. Perkins block. The moderately east-dipping to near-vertical, north-northeast–trending foliation along the axial part of the accommodation zone generally gives way southward to a gently to moderately west-dipping foliation, which is consistent with significant west-tilting (Figs. 17 and 18h, j). Although this general trend remains intact, foliation attitudes in the west-tilted domain locally change significantly across a north-trending structural zone of probable Proterozoic age along which mylonites are locally developed and weakly foliated granodiorite is emplaced (Figs. 17 and 18i, j, k through m).

Although less pronounced than in the west-tilted domain, foliation patterns in the crystalline terrane of the east-tilted domain are generally compatible with east-tilting. The moderately east-dipping to near-vertical, north-northeast–trending foliation along the axial part of the accommodation zone gives way northward to moderately to steeply west-dipping, north-trending foliations (Figs. 17 and 18j, n, o). Near the northern edge of the accommodation zone, however, the foliation attitudes become more diffuse. Here, the crystalline lithologies appear to be warped into a major west-northwest–plunging fold (Fig. 18p).

If the moderately to steeply dipping, north-northeast–striking Proterozoic foliation (e.g., Fig. 18j) was consistent across the region prior to Miocene extension, 90° of block tilting in opposite directions would produce similar foliation attitudes in steeply tilted parts of the opposing tilt-block domains. Proterozoic gneisses in the Willow Beach area of the east-tilted domain, 30 km north of the accommodation zone, exhibit attitudes similar to those in the steeply west-tilted Mt. Perkins block (compare Figs. 18h, q). However, the amount of tilting of the crystalline basement in the Willow Beach area is poorly constrained. Nevertheless, the possibility that the Proterozoic section in much of the

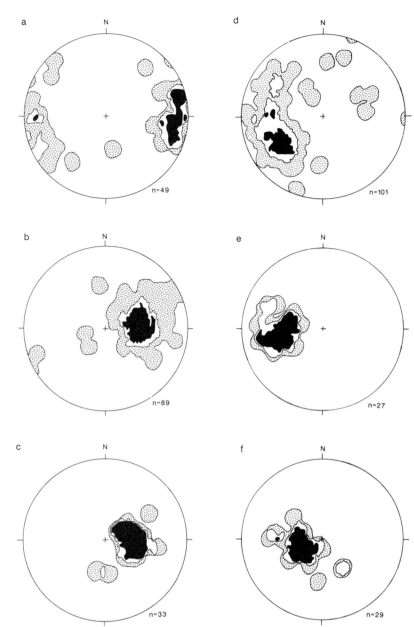

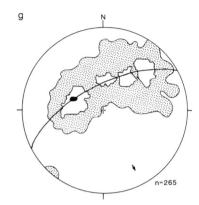

Figure 18. Equal-area stereoplots of poles to bedding and layering in Tertiary strata and poles to foliation in Proterozoic rocks, central Black Mountains. See Figure 17 for location of stereoplots. a through g—Tertiary strata; WTD = west-tilted domain; ETD = east-tilted domain. Data include all Tertiary strata except gently tilted basalt flows and fanglomerates in uppermost part of section. a. More than 2.0 km from axis of accommodation zone—WTD; b. 0.5 to 2.0 km from axis of zone—WTD; c. Less than 0.5 km from axis—WTD; d. More than 2.0 km from axis—ETD; e. 0.5 to 2.0 km from axis—ETD; f. Less than 0.5 km from axis—ETD; g. Fire Mountain anticline on along-strike segment of accommodation zone. The great circle defines a fold axis with an orientation of 24° → S62°E. h. through q—Proterozoic gneisses; WTD = west-tilted domain; ETD = east-tilted domain; h. Mt. Perkins area, 10 km south of accommodation zone; 3 km south of southern edge of map—WTD; i. East-west-trending Proterozoic shear zone approximately 0.7 to 1.7 km south of axis of accommodation zone, WTD; j. Within 0.5 km north and south of axis of zone; k. More than 2.0 km south of axis, WTD; l. 1.0 to 2.0 km south of axis, WTD; m. Within 0.5 km south and north of axis, WTD; n. 0.5 to 2.0 km north of axis, ETD; o. 0.5 to 2.0 km north of axis, ETD; p. 2.0 to 3.5 km north of axis in footwall of Van Deemen Mine fault, ETD; q. Willow Beach area, approximately 25 km north of accommodation zone, 17 km north of northern edge of map, ETD.

east-tilted domain is inverted relative to that in the west-tilted domain must be considered in petrological and structural investigations of these rocks in the northern Colorado River extensional corridor.

The reversal in tilt direction across the accommodation zone may also be reflected in the attitudes of Miocene(?) dikes that cut the crystalline basement. East-dipping dikes predominate in the west-tilted domain, whereas west-dipping dikes characterize the east-tilted domain. In contrast, dikes within the axial part of the accommodation zone generally exhibit subvertical dips. The reversal in the dominant dip direction of the dikes could be attributed entirely to differential tilting. However, preexisting anisotropies in the crystalline basement, including foliation planes and minor faults, may have controlled dike attitudes in some areas. The west-dipping dikes in the east-tilted domain and the

subvertical dikes in the axial part of the accommodation zone are nearly concordant with Proterozoic foliation. The east-dipping dikes in the west-tilted domain, however, crosscut the foliation. Some of the east-dipping dikes in the west-tilted Mt. Perkins block yield remanent magnetization directions that indicate significant west tilting (Fig. 11b).

A 1-km-wide, east-west–trending zone of discordant Proterozoic foliation and attendant mylonite in the eastern part of the crystalline terrane, 0.7 km south of the axis of the accommodation zone, may correspond to a major Proterozoic shear zone, suggesting perhaps that the southern edge of the accommodation zone developed along an inherent crustal weakness. The strike of Proterozoic foliation swings abruptly from north-northeast to east-west along the margins of the shear zone (Figs. 17 and 18i, j). In addition, an east-west–trending, steeply south-dipping mylo-

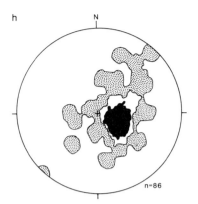

h

n=86

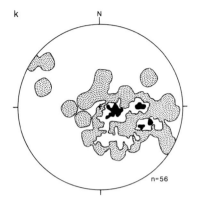

k

n=56

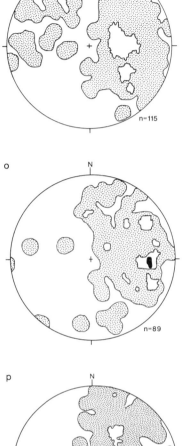

n

n=115

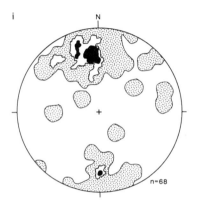

i

n=68

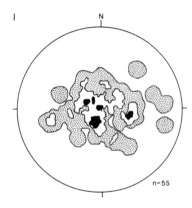

l

n=55

o

n=89

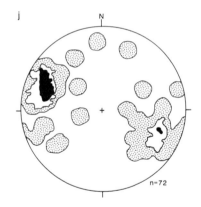

j

n=72

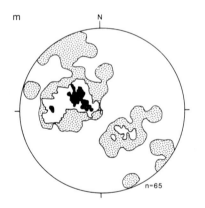

m

n=65

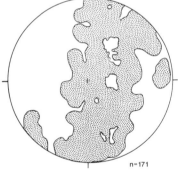

p

n=171

1% to 5% per 1% area

5% to 9% per 1% area

Greater than 9% per 1% area

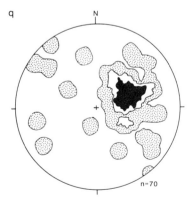

q

n=70

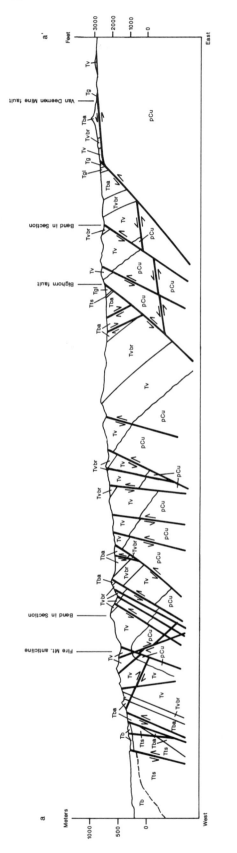

(a)

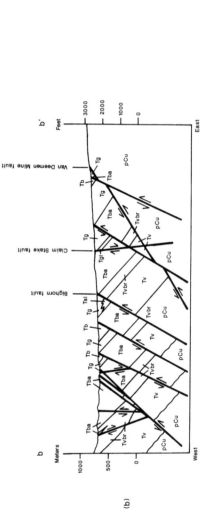

(b)

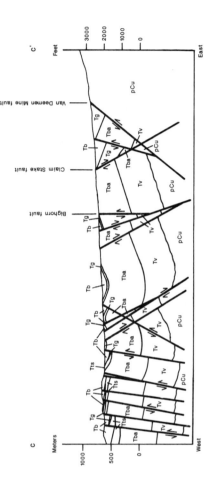

(c)

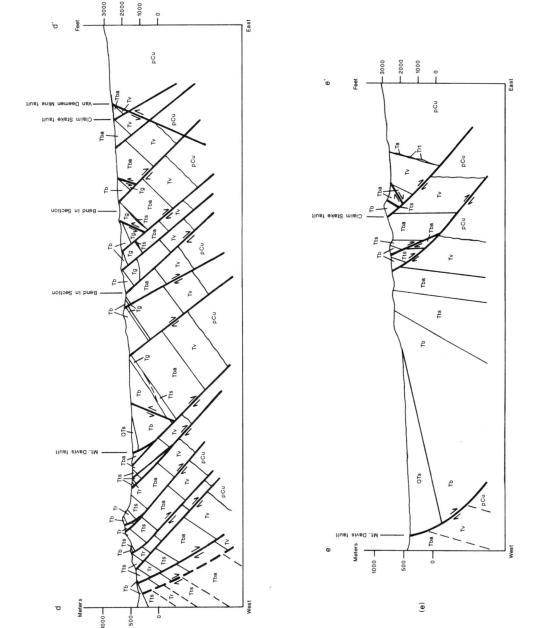

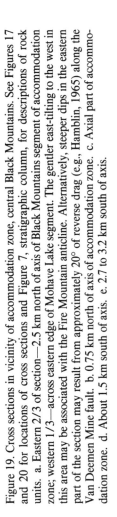

Figure 19. Cross sections in vicinity of accommodation zone, central Black Mountains. See Figures 17 and 20 for locations of cross sections and Figure 7, stratigraphic column, for descriptions of rock units. a. Eastern 2/3 of section—2.5 km north of axis of Black Mountains segment of accommodation zone; western 1/3—across eastern edge of Mohave Lake segment. The gentler east-tilting to the west in this area may be associated with the Fire Mountain anticline. Alternatively, steeper dips in the eastern part of the section may result from approximately 20° of reverse drag (e.g., Hamblin, 1965) along the Van Deemen Mine fault. b. 0.75 km north of axis of accommodation zone. c. Axial part of accommodation zone. d. About 1.5 km south of axis. e. 2.7 to 3.2 km south of axis.

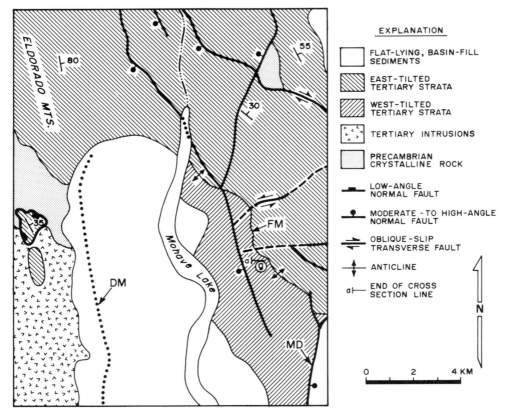

Figure 20. Mohave Lake segment of accommodation zone. DM = Dupont Mountain fault; MD = Mount Davis fault; FM = Fire Mountain anticline. Faults are dashed where inferred, dotted where concealed. The west-tilted domain steps northward in the Mohave Lake area. An open to tight anticline marks the eastern boundary of the Mohave Lake segment. The encircled letter refers to an equal-area stereoplot of poles to layering (Fig. 18). The cross-section line pertains to Figure 19.

nite zone locally marks the northern edge of the shear zone. Much of the 1-km-wide shear zone consists of weakly foliated granodiorite, tonalite, and metagabbro. These lithologies may represent syntectonic Proterozoic intrusions, as they exhibit an east-west–trending foliation in the vicinity of the shear zone and cut both the surrounding gneisses and mylonites within the shear zone. The east-west–trending shear zone projects into the diffuse zone of transverse structures that accommodates differential tilting of Tertiary strata at the southern edge of the accommodation zone. Approximately 2 km east of the Proterozoic/Tertiary nonconformity, however, the shear zone terminates against a west-dipping, north-trending structure, which separates the weakly foliated plutonic rocks to the east from strongly foliated Proterozoic gneisses to the west. Nevertheless, the location of the east-west–trending shear zone suggests that the southern edge of the accommodation zone and northern edge of the Mt. Perkins block were partly controlled by a preexisting Proterozoic structure.

In summary, the Black Mountains segment of the accommodation zone corresponds to a zone of intermeshing conjugate normal faults rather than a strike-slip fault zone. The lack of strike-slip faulting in the upper-plate rocks of the central Black Mountains indicates little relative movement between opposing tilt-block domains. Paleomagnetic data and geologic relations suggest that footwall rocks of the detachment terrane are not exposed in the central Black Mountains.

Mohave Lake segment

The Mohave Lake segment includes an 11-km-long portion of the accommodation zone centered on Mohave Lake. Highly tilted and folded Tertiary strata are well exposed in the eastern part of the segment, whereas the western part is largely concealed by late Miocene to Quaternary, flat-lying to very gently tilted basin-fill sedimentary rocks. Detailed mapping (1:12,000) was limited to the eastern part of the Mohave Lake segment.

The Mohave Lake segment of the accommodation zone encompasses a large northward extension of the west-tilted domain (Figs. 8 and 20). The eastern part of the Mohave Lake segment consists of a major south-southeast–plunging, north-northwest–trending anticline (Figs. 18g and 20), here referred to as the Fire Mountain anticline. The open to tight anticline exhibits a width of at least 2.5 km (Fig. 19a). The anticline terminates to the south at the junction between the Mt. Davis fault and the east-west–trending axis of the Black Mountains segment of the accommodation zone. However, a gradual transition from the characteristic north-striking layering of the region to northwest-striking layering on the southwest limb of the fold begins approximately 2 km south of the actual southern tip of the anticline. Closely spaced normal faults, associated with a horsetailing effect at the northern terminus of the Mt. Davis fault, fragment the southern part of the anticline into a complex array of very narrow fault blocks. The Fire Mountain anticline terminates northward near the northern edge of the west-tilted domain. The northern and western edges of the Mohave Lake segment are largely obscured by relatively undeformed late Miocene to Quaternary strata. The northern edge probably corresponds to a narrow zone of intermeshing conjugate normal faults similar to that in the Black Mountains segment. An east-dipping normal fault, which may represent the northern continuation of the Dupont Mountain fault, probably bounds the Mohave Lake segment on the west.

The northern lobe of the west-tilted domain in the Mohave Lake area probably results from the continuation of the Dupont Mountain fault well beyond the typical northern limit of major east-dipping normal faults. As evidenced by the northward extent of gently west-tilted to flat-lying, late Miocene to Quaternary basin-fill sedimentary rocks, the east-dipping Dupont Mountain fault extends approximately 8 km north of the axial part of the Eldorado Mountains and Black Mountains segments of the accommodation zone (Figs. 8 and 20). The unusual northward extent of this east-dipping normal fault may simply be a function of its large magnitude of offset on the east flank of the southern Eldorado Mountains. Although decreasing appreciably to the north, displacement along the Dupont Mountain fault and related east-dipping normal faults in the Mohave Lake area was sufficient to accommodate significant west-tilting in an area sandwiched between east-tilted blocks. Some of these normal faults dip eastward as gently as 30°, only 1.1 km west of the hingeline of the Fire Mountain anticline (Figs. 19a and 21). Stratal dips on the southwest limb of the southern part of the anticline commonly approach 70°. West-tilting appears to decrease toward the north concomitant with the decrease in offset along the Dupont Mountain fault. Tilting in the east-tilted domain decreases significantly westward between the Van Deemen Mine area and Fire Mountain anticline (Figs. 17, 19a, and 20). East-tilting rarely exceeds 45° on the east limb of the Fire Mountain anticline.

Space problems created by orthogonal-to-strike (i.e., perpendicular to strike of normal faults) variations in the direction of block tilting probably account for development of the Fire Mountain anticline during major extension. The synchroneity of folding and major middle Miocene extension is evidenced by stratigraphic relations at Fire Mountain, where a flat-lying 13.4-Ma basalt flow (Anderson and others, 1972; corrected using new constants [Dalrymple, 1979]) rests unconformably on middle Miocene tuffaceous sedimentary rocks on the southwest limb of the anticline. The middle Miocene tuffaceous sedimentary rocks at Fire Mountain correlate with syntectonic strata bracketed between 16.4 and 14.3 Ma in the Mt. Perkins growth-fault basin 5 km to the south of the southern tip of the anticline. Tilting of adjacent fault blocks in opposite directions will likely produce

Figure 21. East-dipping, low-angle (30°) normal fault on west flank of Fire Mountain, looking north. This fault accommodated approximately 1 km of normal separation, only 1.1 km west of the hingeline of the Fire Mountain anticline. The middle Miocene tuffaceous sedimentary rocks (white) in the hanging wall are juxtaposed against early to middle Miocene basaltic andesite flows. Strata dip approximately 65° west.

local areas of compression at some structural level. West-northwest–east-northeast directed compression, resulting from the orthogonal-to-strike reversal in block tilting, probably generated the north-northwest–trending Fire Mountain anticline. The regionally extensive north-northwest–trending anticline that bounds the west-tilted domain on the northeast is probably analogous to the Fire Mountain anticline.

The Mohave Lake segment essentially represents a westward continuation of the zone of intermeshing conjugate normal faults that constitutes the Black Mountains segment. The west-tilted domain steps northward in the Mohave Lake area in association with the northward extension of the east-dipping Dupont Mountain fault just as the east-tilted domain steps southward in the central Black Mountains as a result of the southward continuation of the west-dipping Van Deemen Mine fault. The lack of major thrusting and folding along the Mohave Lake segment of the accommodation zone further indicates that the fault blocks in one tilt-block domain are not transported significant lateral distances down the dip of the detachment relative to fault blocks in an opposing domain (Fig. 22).

Eldorado Mountains segment

The Eldorado Mountains segment is a 12-km-long, east-west–trending portion of the accommodation zone in the southern Eldorado Mountains (Fig. 23). The Eldorado Mountains segment consists entirely of crystalline rock, including Proterozoic gneisses and intermediate to silicic plutons of probable Miocene age. The absence of Tertiary strata precludes determination of the specific location and nature of the accommodation zone in the southern Eldorado Mountains by geologic mapping. Reconnaissance work and paleomagnetic studies, however, have defined the

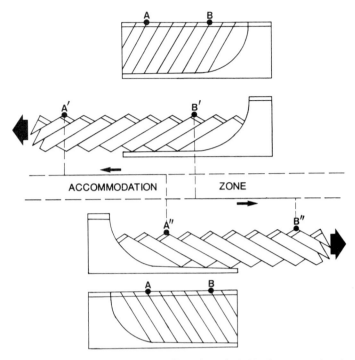

Figure 22. Imbricate fault blocks. If imbricate fault blocks are translated significant lateral distances down the dip of the detachment (relative to the breakaway zone) and away from their tilt direction, significant strike-slip faulting should characterize transversely-oriented accommodation zones. Note offset of points A and B. In addition, major compression would probably distinguish some along-strike and obliquely oriented segments of accommodation zones.

approximate location and probable nature of this segment of the accommodation zone. Flat-lying, basin-fill sedimentary rocks in Eldorado Valley conceal the accommodation zone west of the Eldorado Mountains segment.

Paleomagnetic data collected from plutonic rocks and hypabyssal dike swarms of probable Miocene age help to constrain the location of the accommodation zone in the southern Eldorado Mountains to within a 5-km-wide, east-west– to east-northeast–trending belt, the axis of which lies approximately 8 km south of Nelson, Nevada (Fig. 23). Remanent magnetization data obtained from the Miocene(?) intrusions indicate that most of the crystalline terrane of the southern Eldorado Mountains is significantly tilted. East tilting immediately north of the zone (e.g., Nelson area) approaches 70°, whereas west tilting south of the zone (e.g., west of trace of Dupont Mountain fault) exceeds 55° (Fig. 11a, e). The southernmost possible edge of the accommodation zone in the southern Eldorado Mountains is defined by the location of west-tilted fault blocks in the hanging wall of the Dupont Mountain fault. Footwall rocks of the detachment terrane probably do not crop out in the vicinity of the Eldorado Mountains segment of the accommodation zone. The large crystalline terrane of the southern Eldorado Mountains appears to be the product of the fortuitous juxtaposition of deep structural levels of oppositely tilted fault blocks.

As in the Black Mountains segment, a zone of intermeshing conjugate normal faults probably facilitates the reversal in block tilting in the Eldorado Mountains segment of the accommodation zone. No evidence of significant strike-slip faulting was observed in the vicinity of the Eldorado Mountains segment.

Kinematic evolution

The entire accommodation zone in the Black and Eldorado Mountains may be described as a zone of intermeshing conjugate normal faults. The east- and west-tilted domains intersect in a dovetail-like manner as a result of the alternating influence of west- and east-dipping, conjugate normal faults. Where major west-dipping normal faults die out across the zone, the east-tilted domain advances southward, as in the central Black Mountains. In contrast, the west-tilted domain steps northward where major east-dipping normal faults predominate, as in the Mohave Lake area. Most of the conjugate normal faults terminate within a 5- to 10-km-wide, east-west–trending belt. The style of deformation along the accommodation zone in the highly extended terrane of the northern Colorado River extensional corridor is similar to that described by Chapin (1978) for accommodation zones in the less extended terrane of the Rio Grande rift.

The lack of significant strike-slip faulting along the east-west–trending segments of the zone and only minor amounts of folding along north-northwest–trending portions indicate little relative movement between the east- and west-tilted domains. Major oblique-slip transverse faults within the accommodation zone facilitated scissors-like torsional strain, associated with differential tilting, rather than transport of detachment hanging walls away from the tilt direction. Such structures may account for interpretations of accommodation zones in the upper-plate rocks of passive continental margins as major strike-slip fault zones (e.g., Lister and others, 1986a). However, because of a lack of exposure, interpretations of accommodation zones on passive continental margins have been based primarily on seismic reflection data, with limited direct observation.

The predominantly sublinear trace of the transversely oriented accommodation zone in the upper-plate rocks of the Black and Eldorado Mountains may represent a surface manifestation of strike-slip faulting in lower-plate rocks beneath oppositely dipping detachment faults. Interestingly, the axis of the positive gravity anomaly is offset approximately 19 km in a right-lateral sense 2 to 7 km north of the accommodation zone (Fig. 9). In a simple-shear model of continental extension, right-lateral displacement would be expected between the footwalls of the presumed west-dipping detachment to the north and east-dipping detachment to the south.

If the accommodation zone in the Black and Eldorado Mountains facilitated a dip reversal in regional detachment systems, the style of deformation along the zone implies that upper plates of detachment terranes are not transported en masse for great lateral distances down the dip of the detachment relative to the breakaway fault. As concluded by Lucchitta and Suneson

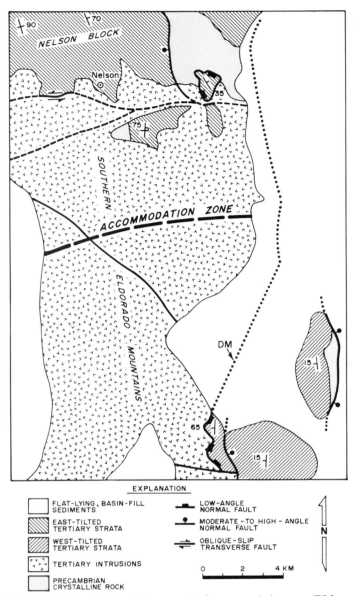

EXPLANATION

☐	FLAT-LYING, BASIN-FILL SEDIMENTS	▬▬	LOW-ANGLE NORMAL FAULT
▨	EAST-TILTED TERTIARY STRATA	▬●▬	MODERATE-TO HIGH-ANGLE NORMAL FAULT
▧	WEST-TILTED TERTIARY STRATA	⇌	OBLIQUE-SLIP TRANSVERSE FAULT
✶	TERTIARY INTRUSIONS		
☐	PRECAMBRIAN CRYSTALLINE ROCK		0 2 4 KM

Figure 23. Eldorado Mountains segment of accommodation zone. DM = Dupont Mountain fault. Faults are dashed where inferred, dotted where concealed. Paleomagnetic data and geologic relationships indicate that the crystalline terrane of the southern Eldorado Mountains corresponds to deep structural levels of oppositely tilted fault blocks. Like the Black Mountains segment, the Eldorado Mountains segment of the accommodation zone probably represents an area of intermeshing conjugate normal faults. The location of the accommodation zone in the southern Eldorado Mountains is partly constrained by paleomagnetic data, which suggest significant tilting of Miocene intrusions (Fig. 12a, e).

(1981a) on the basis of deformation observed along the northeastern margin of the Basin and Range province in west-central Arizona, detachment hanging walls do not behave as allochthonous gravity glides (e.g., Shackelford, 1980). Arrays of imbricate fault blocks in detachment hanging walls cannot consistently collapse either toward or away from the breakaway fault without

producing significant strike-slip faulting along transversely oriented parts of an accommodation zone (Fig. 22) and major compression at along-strike segments of a zone. Furthermore, in the case of the accommodation zone in the northern Colorado River extensional corridor, a model involving significant lateral transport of only the lower-plate rocks (Fig. 6a) fails to account for the lack of strike-slip faulting in areas such as the Colorado Plateau, where the presumed lower plate of one domain is juxtaposed against the upper plate of an adjacent domain. Relative to a specified reference frame, parts of an individual detachment hanging wall may instead move in opposite directions about a "fixed" axis.

Alternatively, there may be no change in detachment geometry across the accommodation zone in the northern Colorado River extensional corridor. Some accommodation zones simply may not facilitate reversals in the dip of regional detachment systems. The reversal in tilt direction in the northern Colorado River extensional corridor may be entirely an upper-plate phenomenon. Thus, the tilted fault blocks in both the east- and west-tilted domains may have been transported in the same direction during middle Miocene extension, resulting in little relative movement between the opposing tilt-block domains. Perhaps the left-lateral Lake Mead and right-lateral Las Vegas Valley shear zones actually accommodated the dip reversal in detachment faults within this region. Such a scenario seems unlikely, however, in light of (1) the probable mechanical relation between dip direction of normal faults in a detachment hanging wall and sense of shear on the detachment (Fig. 2), and (2) both the sublinear trend and narrow width of the 40-km-long accommodation zone.

Whatever the case, the style of deformation along the accommodation zone in the Black and Eldorado Mountains demonstrates that at least some transversely oriented accommodation zones are not major strike-slip fault zones. Because differential tilting must be accommodated, however, major oblique-slip transverse faults characterize accommodation zones that correspond to zones of intermeshing conjugate normal faults. Complex belts of oblique-slip faulting have been recognized along other accommodation zones, especially those that trend obliquely to the extension direction (e.g., Bosworth and others, 1986; Rosendahl, 1987). However, the style of oblique-slip faulting observed along the transversely oriented accommodation zone in the northern Colorado River extensional corridor differs significantly from that described in earlier models of obliquely trending accommodation zones. For example, the sense and regional consistency of oblique-slip motion presumed along individual obliquely trending accommodation zones in the East African rift system (e.g., Bosworth and others, 1986; Rosendahl, 1987) implied lateral transport of upper-plate fault blocks away from their tilt direction. In these cases, diametrical lateral transport of opposing tilt-block domains parallel to the extension direction induced oblique-slip motion along obliquely-trending accommodation zones. In contrast, the accommodation zone in the Black and Eldorado Mountains approximately parallels the extension direction and yet is also characterized by oblique-slip motion. The orientation of slip vectors varies considerably along this zone, because oblique-slip faulting facilitated scissors-like motion, induced by differential tilting, rather than diametrical lateral transport of the opposing tilt-block domains.

If the accommodation zone in the northern Colorado River extensional corridor does accommodate a dip reversal in regional detachment systems, then the kinematic evolution of rifted continental crust may be more complex than the commonly assumed relative diametrical lateral transport of upper and lower plates of a detachment terrane. A kinematic model satisfying the conditions obvserved in the northern Colorado River extensional corridor is developed in the following section.

DISCUSSION

The deformational style along the accommodation zone in the northern Colorado River extensional corridor may provide some constraints on kinematic models of continental rifting. With the exception of a pure-shear model, the aforementioned models (Fig. 6) cannot explain the lack of strike-slip faulting both along the accommodation zone and between the potential lower- and upper-plate rocks of adjacent domains in the relatively unextended terrane on either side of the extensional corridor (i.e., Grand Wash Cliffs and McCullough Range segments). The upper crust in this region cannot be modeled as two diverging, essentially rigid crustal slabs separated by a major detachment fault. A kinematic model is developed that satisfies the observed field relations. This model can operate within either a pure-shear or simple-shear framework of continental extension.

A model that accounts for the lack of strike-slip faulting depicts the opposing tilt-block domains as two sets of dominoes rotating about horizontal axes (i.e., tilting). The rotational axis of one block in each domain is "fixed" in an arbitrary reference frame (Fig. 24). The blocks containing the "fixed" rotational axis undergo pure rotation, whereas other blocks experience both translation and rotation. The "fixed" axis could be situated anywhere in the tilt-block array. If the position of the "fixed" axis of rotation and the amount of extension do not change across the accommodation zone, only scissors-like, torsional strain should occur along the entire zone. Relative to the "fixed" rotational axis, blocks to the east, including the Colorado Plateau, are translated eastward and those to the west move westward. The chosen reference frame in the proposed model need not be associated with any physical entity, such as an axis of extension. The rotational axis may be stationary or may actually migrate laterally in an absolute reference frame. The model simply furnishes a convenient way of portraying complex arrays of shifting fault blocks in three dimensions and can be applied equally well to a pure-shear or simple-shear framework of continental extension.

Several intriguing potential relations are recognized, however, if the "fixed" axis of crustal tilting is ascribed to a particular geological feature. For example, if the "fixed" axis of rotation roughly coincides with the axis of the northern Colorado River extensional corridor, the model may account for the opposing senses of strike-slip motion along the Lake Mead and Las Vegas Valley shear zones, both of which appear to terminate as discrete strike-slip faults near the northern end of the axial part of the extensional corridor. Within the limits of available age data, major extension in the northern Colorado River region coincided with major activity along both the Lake Mead and Las Vegas Valley shear zones (Bohannon, 1984). Relative eastward transport of fault blocks to the east of the "fixed" rotational and corridor axes may have induced sinistral offset along the Lake Mead fault zone, whereas relative westward movement of blocks west of the axes may have been accommodated by dextral displacement along the Las Vegas Valley shear zone. A direct correlation between the magnitude of offset along the shear zones and distance from the axis of the extensional corridor may be obscured, however, by the complex kinematic evolution of the extended region north of the shear zones (e.g., Anderson, 1973; Guth, 1981; Bohannon, 1984), which possibly includes other "fixed" axes of rotation.

If applicable to other regions, a coincidence between the "fixed" axis of rotation and apparent axis of extension in highly extended terranes, such as the Colorado River extensional corridor, may imply that continental crust at the macroscopic scale extends primarily in a pure-shear fashion. The style of deformation along the accommodation zone is compatible with a bulk pure-shear model of continental extension. In addition, our proposed kinematic model implies an important component of upper crustal "spreading" about discrete axes, perhaps suggesting that highly extended regions lie directly above areas of divergent flow in the asthenosphere. Thus, the left-lateral Lake Mead and right-lateral Las Vegas Valley shear zones may both correspond to intracontinental transform faults separating en echelon axes of extension (e.g., Fleck, 1970; Liggett and Childs, 1977; Bohannon, 1984).

In a pure-shear regime, the lateral propagation of normal faults away from major transform faults may be as critical to the stretching of the brittle upper crust as the upward propagation of normal faults from a detachment surface. For example, west-dipping normal faults and subsequent east tilting in the upper crust may have been favored in the northernmost part of the northern Colorado River extensional corridor because they are kinematically more compatible with oblique sinistral, down-to-the-north normal slip along the northeast-trending Lake Mead fault zone (e.g., Anderson, 1973). Unlike east-dipping normal faults, west-dipping normal faults and strands of the Lake Mead fault zone can intersect in common, west-plunging movement vectors. Much of the strike-slip faulting along the Lake Mead fault zone appears to be translated into displacement on west-dipping normal faults in the east-tilted domain (Anderson, 1973). West-dipping normal faults associated with the Lake Mead fault zone may have propagated southward until encountering an east-dipping set of normal faults propagating northward, thus producing the zone of intermeshing conjugate normal faults along the accommodation zone. The age of major extension does young northward in the west-tilted domain, from early Miocene (22 to

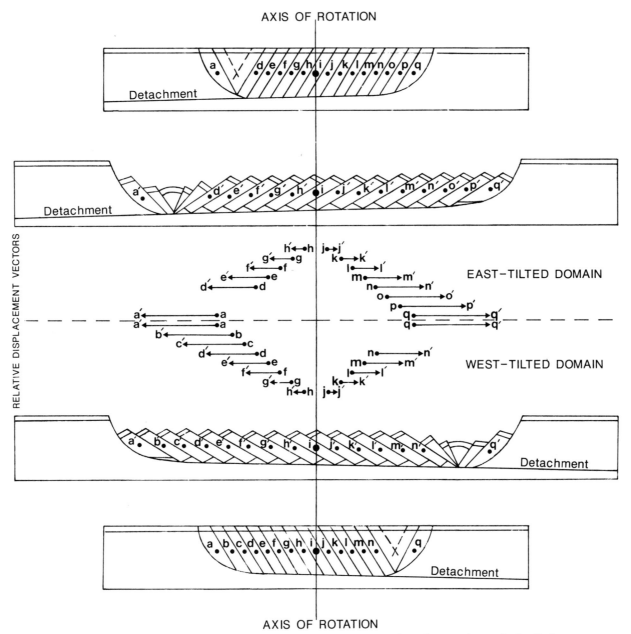

Figure 24. "Fixed" axis of rotation model for the kinematic evolution of upper-plate rocks in rifted continental crust. Displacement vectors for each fault block relative to the "fixed" axis of rotation are shown at center. See text for further explanation. Note that small amounts of right-lateral offset would characterize the accommodation zone at shallow structural levels (i.e., in those areas that lie above a subhorizontal line that is parallel to the sections and projects through the axis of rotation). In contrast, left-lateral displacement would distinguish deep structural levels (i.e., below such a line). As a result of variations in (1) exposed structural level, (2) tilting, and (3) size of fault blocks, torsional strain would probably typify the majority of the accommodation zone.

17 Ma) in the vicinity of the Whipple Mountains (Howard and John, 1987) to middle Miocene (16.4 to 13 Ma) in the northern Colorado River extensional corridor, suggesting that east-dipping normal faults in the brittle upper crust of the west-tilted domain propagated northward. A southward sweep in deformation has not been documented in the east-tilted domain.

The above scenario, involving a bulk pure-shear framework of continental extension, is difficult to reconcile, however, with the abrupt reversal in conjugate fault type across the accommodation zone. Moreover, a pure-shear model of continental extension contradicts the substantial evidence for large-scale, uniform-sense simple shear on regionally extensive, northeast-dipping detachment systems in the west-tilted domain, 60 to 150 km south of the accommodation zone (e.g., Davis and others, 1980; Spencer, 1985; Reynolds and Spencer, 1985; Howard and John, 1987; John, 1987).

In a bulk simple-shear framework of continental extension, the location of the "fixed" axis of rotation in our proposed model may be related to instabilities created by both the relative movement of the detachment hanging wall away from the break-away fault and antiformal welts of lower-plate rocks. Fault blocks between the breakaway fault and "fixed" axis of rotation may collapse toward the breakaway in order to fill a developing void between the hanging wall and footwall of the detachment terrane, whereas fault blocks on the opposite side of the "fixed" rotational axis may persistently move away from the breakaway fault. The position of isostatically induced uplifts (Spencer, 1984) of lower-plate rocks may also partly control the locations of the "fixed" rotational axes. Maximum isostatic adjustment would probably occur in areas of greatest extension. Thus, axes of "fixed" rotation may generally coincide with axes of extension. As in a pure-shear framework, if the location of the "fixed" axis of rotation and amount of extension do not change across the accommodation zone, only scissors-like torsional strain would develop along the zone. In the northern Colorado River extensional corridor, diametrical lateral transport of the lower-plate rocks of the opposing tilt-block domains requires right-lateral offset along the accommodation zone beneath the opposing detachment surfaces (Fig. 6a), which may be expressed by the apparent right-lateral offset of the isostatic residual gravity high (Fig. 9).

In both bulk pure-shear and bulk simple-shear models of continental lithospheric extension, a significant change in location of the "fixed" rotational axis across an accommodation zone would induce strike-slip faulting along the zone. Thus, some accommodation zones may indeed correspond to strike-slip fault zones.

On the basis of the characteristic deformational style, transversely oriented accommodation zones may be subdivided into torsional and strike-slip types. The kinematic evolution of opposing tilt-block domains, which may ultimately depend on the distribution of "fixed" rotational axes, dictates the deformational style along the zones. Torsional accommodation zones, which correspond to areas of intermeshing conjugate normal faults, evolve in regions where "fixed" rotational axes are continuous across the zone. The accommodation zone in the Black and Eldorado Mountains is an example of a torsional accommodation zone. If the distribution of "fixed" rotational axes changes across the zone, a strike-slip accommodation zone develops.

The style of deformation along accommodation zones may change with time in response to lateral migration of rotational axes. In a simple-shear regime, the distance between rising bodies of lower-plate rocks in opposing tilt-block domains may change during extension. If these uplifted belts of lower-plate rocks influence the position of "fixed" rotational axes in the upper-plate rocks, some torsional accommodation zones may evolve into

strike-slip accommodation zones (or vice versa). Lateral migration of rotational axes may produce complex strain patterns along any transverse structure that coordinates changes in the distribution of the axes.

In addition to placing possible constraints on the kinematic evolution of rifted continental crust, the style of deformation along the accommodation zone in the northern Colorado River extensional corridor may also influence hydrocarbon exploration along torsional accommodation zones on passive continental margins and in rift basins in continental interiors (e.g., Moustafa, 1976; Coffield and Smale, 1987). Several types of structural traps may characterize torsional accommodation zones, including (1) folds parallel with along-strike segments of the zone (e.g., Fire Mountain anticline), (2) drag folds developed at the termini of major normal faults, and (3) various fault traps associated with both oblique-slip transverse faults and intersecting conjugate normal faults. The style of deformation may differ significantly between individual segments of an accommodation zone as a result of variations in the trend of segments and exposed structural level. This, in turn, may greatly affect the nature of structural traps for hydrocarbons. Thinner accumulations of syntectonic strata within the narrower and shallower half-graben of torsional accommodation zones, which may be expressed as regional basement highs on seismic lines (e.g., Reynolds, 1984; Rosendahl, 1987), may also control the distribution of hydrocarbon deposits.

Before any major conclusions can be drawn from the geometry and kinematics of the accommodation zone in the Black and Eldorado Mountains, it must first be determined whether the style of deformation along the zone is typical of accommodation zones. We stress that our proposed kinematic model invoking upper crustal spreading about "fixed" rotational axes simply represents a convenient way to portray the kinematic evolution of tilt-block domains. The model can account for the lack of strike-slip faulting along major accommodation zones in both bulk pure-shear and simple-shear frameworks of continental extension. Although we speculate on the physical significance of the "fixed" rotational axes, there may be none. Furthermore, the "fixed" axis of rotation in the northern Colorado River extensional corridor has not yet been located.

A unifying model of the kinematic evolution of rifted continental crust awaits many additional detailed studies of accommodation zones and other types of transverse structures. Locating exposures of lower-plate rocks along a transversely oriented accommodation zone is especially critical to developing such a model. As we have documented for the southern Eldorado Mountains, however, large crystalline terranes do not necessarily belong to the lower plate of the detachment terrane. The integration of geophysical data with surficial studies of major transverse structures also holds great potential. For example, geophysical modeling may help to determine if "fixed" rotational axes correspond to specific physical entities, such as axes of extension or uplifted belts of lower-plate rocks. This, in turn, may be of fundamental importance in defining the relative significance of macroscopic pure and simple shear in the attenuation of continental crust. Before the significance of transverse structures on the kinematic evolution of rifted continental crust is better understood, kinematic modeling must be conducted cautiously. Terms such as allochthon and autochthon should be used sparingly. In addition, assumptions concerning the style of deformation along major transverse structures should not be based solely on simplistic kinematic models and/or interpretation of seismic lines. The observation that some accommodation zones correspond to zones of intermeshing conjugate normal faults and yet may also facilitate dip reversals in regional detachment systems may be critical to obtaining a better understanding of the kinematic evolution of rifted continental crust.

ACKNOWLEDGMENTS

Supported by a Kelley-Silver Graduate Student Fellowship, National Science Foundation Grant EAR-8721264, the Fischer-Watt Mining Company, and Arizona Star Resource Corporation and by grants from the Geological Society of America and Sigma Xi. We thank Eugene Smith, Jon Spencer, Ernie Anderson, Bud Hillemeyer, Sue Beard, Peter Drobeck, and Ernie Duebendorfer for fruitful discussions. We also thank the personnel at the Laboratory of Isotope Geochemistry, University of Arizona, for the K-Ar dates. Helpful reviews were provided by William Bosworth and an anonymous reviewer.

APPENDIX A: PALEOMAGNETIC INVESTIGATIONS AND DATA INTERPRETATIONS

We sampled Late Cretaceous to middle Miocene intermediate to silicic plutons, mafic and felsic dike swarms, regionally metamorphosed Proterozoic rocks near young intrusions, and Miocene volcanic rocks for paleomagnetic investigations. We used a portable field drill with nonmagnetic diamond drill bits to collect samples and prepared samples for measurement using nonmagnetic saw blades. A more extensive discussion of the paleomagnetic studies can be found in Faulds and others (in preparation).

Progressive alternating field (AF) and thermal demagnetization treatments were applied to isolate well-defined magnetizations. Orthogonal demagnetization diagrams (Zijderveld, 1967) were inspected to assess the relative intensity and directions of all remanent magnetization (RM) components in each specimen. In such diagrams (Fig. A1), the endpoint of the magnetization vector, over a series of demagnetization steps, is simultaneously projected onto both the horizontal plane (geographic coordinates, solid symbols) and the vertical plane (geographic coordinates, open symbols). Collinear trends of horizontal and vertical projections usually signify removal of a single component of magnetization over the commensurate range of demagnetization treatment. Curvilinear traces defined by a series of demagnetization steps imply removal of at least two components of magnetization over the corresponding demagnetization interval. Paleomagnetic data, including site mean directions and associated statistics, are given in Table A1.

AF and thermal demagnetization treatment (Fig. A1a, b, respectively) isolated two components of magnetization in a granodiorite pluton in the Eldorado Mountains near Nelson, Nevada. Initially, a magnetization of northerly declination and moderate positive inclination was removed. At higher peak inductions or laboratory unblocking temperatures (T_{lub}), a magnetization of shallow positive inclination and west-northwesterly declination was isolated. The first-removed magnetization is probably viscous in origin (i.e., acquired during the Brunhes normal polarity chron over the past ca. 730,000 yr). The next-removed magnetization was acquired during intrusion and cooling of the pluton in a normal polarity field. Presumably, this magnetization was originally of northerly declination and moderate positive inclination, but 50 to 60° of east tilting resulted in the present in situ magnetization direction. Abundant fine-grained, single- and/or pseudo-single domain low-Ti titanomagnetite in the Nelson pluton is critical to the preservation of this well-defined thermal remanent magnetization (TRM) of middle Miocene age.

Not all intrusions in the study area contain magnetic phases of appropriate sizes and shapes to consistently yield a well-defined or geologically stable TRM. For example, only three sites from the Knob Hill pluton in the southern Eldorado Mountains contain sufficient fine-grained titanomagnetite of relatively high coercivity and T_{lub} to yield a well-defined TRM. The TRM direction (east-southeast declination, shallow negative inclination) can be readily explained by 60 to 90° of east tilting of a reverse polarity magnetization of middle Miocene age (Fig. 1Ac). All other sites from this area, unfortunately, are characterized by abundant, coarse multidomain titanomagnetite, as evidenced by the very low peak inductions required to remove much of the magnetization (Fig. A1d). The principal magnetization removed in the low-coercivity phases exhibits a northerly declination and moderate positive inclination. Magnetizations remaining, but not fully isolated, at higher peak inductions in AF demagnetization generally display more easterly declinations and shallow positive or negative inclinations (Fig. A1e). The TRM is poorly defined because abundant coarse-grained, multidomain titanomagnetite allowed significant acquisition of a magnetization of viscous origin. The TRM in these cases can be crudely defined using remagnetization circle analysis (e.g., Bailey and Halls, 1984).

The 73.3-Ma quartz monzonite pluton in the probable footwall of the Van Deemen Mine fault also exhibits two demagnetization responses. As evidenced by T_{lub} in excess of 600°C, hematite is the dominant magnetic carrier in most samples (Fig. A1f). The magnetization residing in hematite displays a westerly declination and moderate positive inclination, suggesting approximately 60° of east tilting. This magnetization presumably originated prior to east tilting during late Cretaceous alteration and mineralization of the pluton. The few samples in which magnetization resides partially in magnetite yield magnetizations of probable viscous origin.

Some granodiorite dikes emplaced in Proterozoic gneisses in the southern Eldorado Mountains yield well-defined magnetizations of southwest declination and shallow negative inclination (Fig. A1g). Relatively high coercivities and T_{lub} indicate that this magnetization resides in fine-grained titanomagnetite. Significant west-tilting of a middle Miocene, reverse polarity magnetization probably accounts for the in-situ directions. In many cases, however, the magnetization in the granodiorite dikes resides in coarse-grained multidomain titanomagnetite, which precludes removal of a well-defined TRM.

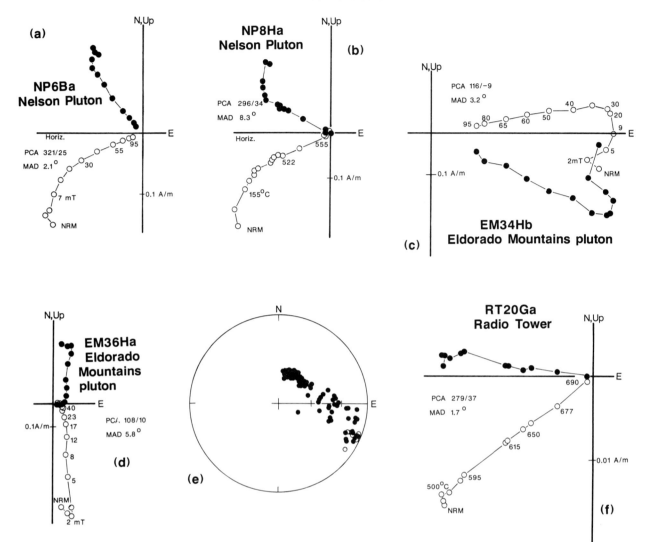

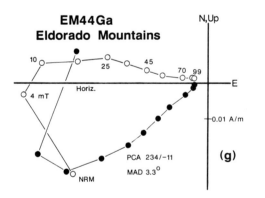

Figure A1. Orthogonal demagnetization diagrams (a-d, f-g) showing behavior of individual specimens of crystalline rock during alternating field (AF) and thermal demagnetization. Solid symbols are projections of the magnetization vector on the horizontal plane; open symbols, the vertical plane. Peak demagnetizing fields are given in milliTesla (1 mT = 10 oe) and temperatures in degrees Celsius. In each orthogonal demagnetization diagram, the direction of the magnetization component, characteristic of an individual site and/or lithology, is isolated over a range of demagnetization steps, using principal component analysis (PCA). The associated mean angular deviation (MAD) is also given. a. AF demagnetization, Nelson pluton, central Eldorado Mountains, site NP6. b. Thermal demagnetization, Nelson pluton, central Eldorado Mountains, site NP8. c. AF demagnetization, Knob Hill pluton, southern Eldorado Mountains, site EM34. d. AF demagnetization, Knob Hill pluton, southern Eldorado Mountains, site EM36. e. Equal-angle stereoplot of individual demagnetization measurements from individual specimens, Knob Hill pluton, southern Eldorado Mountains. f. Thermal demagnetization, Radio Tower pluton, footwall of gently west-dipping Van Deemen Mine fault, central Black Mountains, site RT20. g. AF demagnetization of felsic dike, southern Eldorado Mountains, site EM44.

TABLE A1. PALEOMAGNETIC DATA, IN SITU, BLACK AND ELDORADO MOUNTAINS, ARIZONA AND NEVADA

Locality Site	Lithology	N/N_0	Decl.	Inc.	a_{95}	k
SOUTHERN ELDORADO MOUNTAINS						
EM40	Felsic dike	7/7	213.9	-25.5	5.6	117.8
EM42	Felsic dike	5/6	241.5	-37.2	11.7	43.9
EM44	Felsic dike	5/7	234.5	-8.3	7.5	104.8
EM46	Felsic dike	4/6	226.2	-25.3	13.5	47.3
EM49	Felsic dike	7/9	212.6	-22.9	8.4	52.4
MT. PERKINS BLOCK						
BCR1	Felsic dike	5/5	41.9	13.1	11.2	31.0
MP4	Felsic dike	8/8	9.3	23.3	7.7	41.2
MP6	Mafic dike	6/6	222.3	-28.0	7.5	80.0
MP7	Granodiorite pluton	7/7	216.5	-32.7	2.6	548.0
MP9	Granodiorite pluton	6/6	213.6	-32.0	4.9	188.0
MP12	Granodiorite pluton	6/8	220.1	-24.9	11.3	36.0
MP17	Granodiorite pluton	6/6	229.9	-31.2	3.0	491.0
MP18	Granodiorite pluton	6/7	227.0	-28.4	7.8	53.1
BCR2	Proterozoic gneiss	7/8	224.5	-4.8	10.1	27.6
BCR4	Proterozoic gneiss	8/8	26.0	-18.6	8.0	38.1
MP22	Proterozoic gneiss	6/6	217.5	-31.6	7.1	64.9
MP24	Proterozoic gneiss	7/8	235.8	-4.6	8.1	42.4
RADIO TOWER PLUTON, CENTRAL BLACK MOUNTAINS						
RT1	Quartz monzonite	6/7	270.4	32.8	7.0	91.0
RT2	Quartz monzonite	7/7	266.0	34.5	1.9	992.9
RT4	Quartz monzonite	6/7	277.8	31.1	4.9	188.7
RT6	Quartz monzonite	5/5	264.3	15.2	8.2	88.7
RT15	Quartz monzonite	8/10	263.2	37.7	3.8	214.2
RT16	Quartz monzonite	6/7	263.6	37.4	4.1	266.4
RT17	Quartz monzonite	6/7	275.4	32.7	6.7	100.6
RT18	Quartz monzonite	7/8	271.9	30.9	6.6	85.2
RT19	Quartz monzonite	6/9	269.2	42.4	6.1	120.4
RT20	Quartz monzonite	7/8	276.3	37.0	5.2	131.2
NELSON PLUTON, CENTRAL ELDORADO MOUNTAINS						
NP4	Granodiorite	9/9	315.0	45.1	11.9	19.7
NP6	Granodiorite	8/8	319.1	20.2	7.2	60.1
NP8	Granodiorite	9/9	295.9	27.9	4.1	160.5
NP11	Granodiorite	8/8	312.8	43.4	7.4	57.7
NP14	Granodiorite	8/8	301.8	23.2	6.2	82.0
NP15	Granodiorite	5/5	312.7	29.1	8.2	87.7
NP16	Granodiorite	8/8	311.0	34.1	5.9	87.8
KNOB HILL PLUTON, SOUTHERN ELDORADO MOUNTAINS						
EM23	Granodiorite	8/9	101.2	-42.1	5.0	123.0
EM33	Granodiorite	8/8	100.5	8.7	9.9	32.4
EM34	Granodiorite	7/7	111.7	-3.5	11.0	31.3

REFERENCES CITED

Allmendinger, R. W., Sharp, J. W., Von Tish, D., Serpa, L., Brown, L., Kaufman, S., Oliver, J., and Smith, R. B., 1983, Cenozoic and Mesozoic structure of the eastern Basin and Range from COCORP seismic reflection data: Geology, v. 11, p. 532–536.

Anderson, J. L., Barth, A. P., and Young, E. D., 1988, Mid-crustal Cretaceous roots of Cordilleran metamorphic core complexes: Geology, v. 16, p. 366–369.

Anderson, R. E., 1971, Thin skin distension in Tertiary rocks of southeastern Nevada: Geological Society of America Bulletin, v. 82, p. 43–58.

——, 1973, Large magnitude late Tertiary strike-slip faulting north of Lake Mead, Nevada: U.S. Geological Survey Professional Paepr 794, 18 p.

——, 1977, Geologic mpa of the Boulder City 15-minute Quadrangle, Clark County, Nevada: U.S. Geological Survey Geologic Quadrangle Map GQ–1395, scale 1:62,500.

——— , 1978, Geologic map of the Black Canyon 15-minute Quadrangle, Mohave County, Arizona, and Clark County, Nevada: U.S. Geological Survey Geologic Quadrangle Map GQ–1394, scale 1:62,500.

Anderson, R. E., Longwell, C. R., Armstrong, R. L., and Marvin, R. F., 1972, Significance of K-Ar ages of Tertiary rocks from the Lake Mead region, Nevada-Arizona: Geological Society of America Bulletin, v. 83, p. 273–288.

Anderson, R. E., Zoback, M. L., and Thompson, G. A., 1983, Implication of selected subsurface data on the structural form and evolution of some basins in the northern Basin and Range province, Nevada and Utah: Geological Society of America Bulletin, v. 94, p. 1055–1072.

Armstrong, R. L., 1972, Low-angle (denudation) faults, hinterland of the Sevier orogenic belt, eastern Nevada and western Utah: Geological Society of America Bulletin, v. 83, p. 1729–1754.

Bailey, M. E., and Halls, H. C., 1984, Estimate of confidence in paleomagnetic directions derived from mixed remagnetization circle and direct observational data: Journal of Geophysics, v. 54, p. 174–182.

Bally, A. W., 1982, Musings over sedimentary basin evolution: Royal Society of London Philosophical Transactions, v. A305, p. 325–328.

Bally, A. W., and Oldow, J. S., 1984, Plate tectonics, structural styles, and the evolution of sedimentary basins; American Association of Petroleum Geologists short course notes: Houston, American Association of Petroleum Geologists, 238 p.

Barberi, F., and Varet, J., 1977, Volcanism of Afar; Small-scale plate tectonic implications: Geological Society of America Bulletin, v. 88, p. 1251–1266.

Bohannon, R. G., 1979, Strike-slip faults of the Lake Mead region of southern Nevada, *in* Armentrout, J. M., Cole, M. R., and Terbest, H., eds., Cenozoic paleogeography of the western United States, Pacific Coast Paleogeography Symposium 3: Pacific Section, Society of Economic Paleontologists and Mineralogists, p. 129–139.

——— , 1984, Nonmarine sedimentary rocks of Tertiary age in the Lake Mead region, southeastern Nevada and northwestern Arizona: U.S. Geological Survey Professional Paper 1259, 72 p.

Bosworth, W., 1985, Geometry of propagating continental rifts: Nature, v. 316, p. 625–627.

——— , 1986, Comment *on* Detachment faulting and the evolution of passive continental margins: Geology, v. 14, p. 890–891.

——— , 1987, Off-axis volcanism in the Gregory rift, east Africa; Implications for models of continental rifting: Geology, v. 15, p. 397–400.

Bosworth, W., Lambiase, J., and Keisler, R., 1986, A new look at Gregory's rift; The structural style of continental rifting: EOS Transactions of the American Geophysical Union, v. 67, p. 577–583.

Chamberlin, R. M., 1978, Structural development of the Lemitar Mountains, an intrarift tilted fault block uplift, central New Mexico [abs.], *in* Proceedings, International Symposium on the Rio Grande Rift, Santa Fe, New Mexico: Los Alamos Scientific Laboratory Conference Proceedings LA–7487–C, p. 22–24.

——— , 1983, Cenozoic domino-style crustal extension in the Lemitar Mountains, New Mexico; A summary: New Mexico Geological Society Guidebook, 34th Field Conference, Socorro Region II, p. 111–118.

Chapin, C. E., 1978, Evolution of the Rio Grande rift; Comparisons between segments and the role of transverse structures [abs.], *in* Proceedings, International Symposium on the Rio Grande Rift, Santa Fe, New Mexico: Los Alamos Scientific Laboratory Conference Proceedings LA–7487–C, p. 24–27.

Chapin, C. E., Chamberlin, R. M., Osburn, G. R., White, D. L., and Sanford, A. R., 1978, Exploration framework of the Socorro geothermal area, *in* Field guide to selected cauldrons and mining districts of the Datil–Mogollon volcanic field: New Mexico Geological Society Special Publication 7, p. 114–129.

Coffield, D. Q., 1987, Surface expression and internal structure of an accommodation zone, Gulf of Suez, Egypt [abs.]: American Association of Petroleum Geologists Bulletin, v. 71, no. 5, p. 540.

Coffield, D. Q., and Schamel, S., 1989, Surface expression of an accommodation zone within the Gulf of Suez rift, Egypt: Geology, v. 17, p. 76–79.

Coffield, D. Q., and Smale, J. L., 1987, Structural geometry and synrift sedimentation in an accommodation zone, Gulf of Suez, Egypt: Oil and Gas Journal, Dec. 21, p. 56–59.

Crittenden, M. D., Coney, P. J., and Davis, G. H., eds., 1980, Cordilleran metamorphic core complexes: Geological Society of America Memoir 153, 490 p.

Dalrymple, G. B., 1979, Critical tables for conversion of K-Ar ages from old to new constants: Geology, v. 7, p. 558–560.

Davis, G. A., and Burchfiel, B. C., 1973, Garlock fault; An intracontinental transform structure, southern California: Geological Society of America Bulletin, v. 84, p. 1407–1422.

Davis, G. A., Anderson, J. L., Frost, E. G., and Shackelford, T. J., 1980, Mylonitization and detachment faulting in the Whipple–Buckskin–Rawhide Mountains terrane, southeastern California and western Arizona, *in* Crittenden, M. D., Jr., Coney, P. J., and Davis, G. H., eds., Cordilleran metamorphic core complexes: Geological Society of America Memoir 153, p. 79–129.

Davis, G. H., 1983, Shear-zone model for the origin of metamorphic core complexes: Geology, v. 11, p. 342–347.

——— , 1987, A shear-zone model for the structural evolution of metamorphic core complexes in southeastern Arizona, *in* Coward, M. P., Dewey, J. F., and Hancock, P. L., eds., Continental extensional tectonics: Geological Society of London Special Publication 28, p. 247–266.

Dokka, R. K., 1983, Displacements on late Cenozoic strike-slip faults of the central Mojave Desert, California: Geology, v. 11, p. 305–308.

Dokka, R. K., and Baksi, A. K., 1986, Structure and sedimentation along the lateral boundaries of a detachment fault terrane, central Mojave extensional complex, California: Geological Society of America Abstracts with Programs, v. 18, p. 102.

Drescher, A., 1976, An experimental investigation of flow rules for granular materials using optically sensitive glass particles: Geotechnique, v. 26, p. 591–601.

Drobeck, P. A., and 8 others, 1988, Gold deposits of the Las Vegas region, *in* Weide, D. L., and Faber, M. L., eds., This extended land, geological journeys in the southern Basin and Range: Geological Society of America Cordilleran Section Field Trip Guidebook, p. 65–86.

Duebendorfer, E. M., Sewall, A. J., and Smith, E. I., 1988, Kinematic interpretation of lower-plate mylonites, Saddle Island detachment complex, Lake Mead, Nevada: Geological Society of America Abstracts with Programs, v. 20, p. 157.

Dunkelman, T. J., Karson, J. A., and Rosendahl, B. R., 1988, Structural style of the Turkana rift, Kenya: Geology, v. 16, p. 258–261.

Ebinger, C. J., Rosendahl, B. R., and Reynolds, D. J., 1987, Tectonic model of the Malawi rift, Africa: Tectonophysics, v. 141, p. 215–235.

Effimoff, I., and Pinezich, A. R., 1981, Tertiary structural development of selected valleys based on seismic data; Basin and Range province, northeastern Nevada: Royal Society of London Philosophical Transactions, ser. A, v. 300, p. 435–442.

Eschner, E., and Smith, E. I., 1988, Geometry of mid-Tertiary normal faults in the Arch Mountain area of the northern Black Mountains, Mohave County, northwest Arizona: Geological Society of America Abstracts with Programs, v. 20, p. 159.

Etheridge, M. A., Branson, J. C., and Stuart-Smith, P. G., 1985, Extensional basin-forming structures in Bass Strait and their importance for hydrocarbon exploration: Australian Petroleum Exploration Association Journal, v. 25, p. 344–361.

Etheridge, M. A., Symonds, P. A., and Powell, T. G., 1988, Application of the detachment model for continental extension to hydrocarbon exploration in extensional basins: Australian Petroleum Exploration Association Journal, v. 28, p. 167–187.

Faulds, J. E., and Geissman, J. W., 1986, Paleomagnetic evidence of tilted basement, central part of the Black Mountains, northwestern Arizona [abs.]: EOS Transactions of the American Geophysical Union, v. 67, p. 1226.

Faulds, J. E., Mawer, C. K., and Geissman, J. W., 1987a, Possible modes of deformation along "accommodation zones" in rifted continental crust: Geological Society of America Abstracts with Programs, v. 19, p. 659–660.

Faulds, J. E., Geissman, J. W., and Mawer, C. K., 1987b, Anisotropy of magnetic susceptibility data from the Mt. Perkins pluton, central Black Mountains, Arizona; Implications for evaluation of extension directions [abs.]: EOS Transactions of the American Geophysical Union, v. 68, p. 1251.

Faulds, J. E., Mawer, C. K., and Geissman, J. W., 1988a, Geometry and kinematics of a major accommodation zone in the highly extended upper-plate rocks of the northern Colorado River trough, northwestern Arizona and southern Nevada: Geological Society of America Abstracts with Programs, v. 20, p. 159.

Faulds, J. E., Hillemeyer, F. L., and Smith, E. I., 1988b, Geometry and kinematics of a Miocene "accommodation zone" in the central Black and southern Eldorado Mountains, Arizona and Nevada, *in* Weide, D. L., and Faber, M. L., eds., This extended land, geological journeys in the southern Basin and Range: Geological Society of America Cordilleran Section Field Trip Guidebook, p. 293–310.

Faulds, J. E., Geissman, J. W., and Mawer, C. K., 1988c, Implications of the style of deformation along a major accommodation zone on kinematic models of rifted continental crust: Geological Society of America Abstracts with Programs, v. 20, p. A108–A109.

——, 1988d, Paleomagnetic evidence of large-magnitude tilting of crystalline terranes in the northern Colorado River extensional corridor, northwestern Arizona and southern Nevada [abs.]: EOS Transactions of the American Geophysical Union, v. 69, p. 1163–1164.

Feuerbach, D. L., 1986, Geology of the Wilson Ridge pluton; A mid-Miocene quartz monzonite intrusion in the northern Black Mountains, Mohave County, Arizona, and Clark County, Nevada [M.S. thesis]: Las Vegas, University of Nevada, 79 p.

Feuerbach, D. L., and Smith, E. I., 1986, The mid-Miocene Wilson Ridge pluton; A subvolcanic intrusion in the Lake Mead region, Arizona and Nevada [abs.]: EOS Transactions of the American Geophysical Union, v. 67, p. 1262.

Fleck, R. J., 1970, Age and possible origin of the Las Vegas Valley shear zone, Clark and Nye Counties, Nevada: Geological Society of America Abstracts with Programs, v. 2, p. 333.

Frost, E. G., and Martin, D. L., eds., 1982, Mesozoic–Cenozoic tectonic evolution of the Colorado River region, California, Arizona, and Nevada: San Diego, California, Cordilleran Publishers, 608 p.

Gibbs, A. D., 1984, Structural evolution of extensional basin margins: Geological Society of London Journal, v. 141, p. 609–620.

Gregory, J. W., 1921, The rift valleys and geology of east Africa: London, Seeley, Service and Co., 479 p.

Guth, P. L., 1981, Tertiary extension north of the Las Vegas Valley shear zone, Sheep and Desert Ranges, Clark County, Nevada: Geological Society of America Bulletin, v. 92, p. 763–771.

Hamblin, W. K., 1965, Origin of "reverse-drag" on the downthrown side of normal faults: Geological Society of America Bulletin, v. 76, p. 1145–1164.

Hansen, S. M., 1962, The geology of the Eldorado mining district, Clark County, Nevada [Ph.D. thesis]: Columbia, University of Missouri, 328 p.

Horsefield, W. T., 1980, Contemporaneous movement along conjugate normal faults: Journal of Structural Geology, v. 2, p. 305–310.

Howard, K. A., and John, B. E., 1987, Crustal extension along a rooted system of imbricate low-angle faults; Colorado River extensional corridor, California and Arizona, *in* Coward, M. P., Dewey, J. F., and Hancock, P. L., eds., Continental extensional tectonics: Geological Society of London Special Publication 28, p. 299–311.

Howard, K. A., Goodge, J. W., and John, B. E., 1982, Detached crystalline rocks of the Mojave, Buck, and Bill Williams Mountains, western Arizona, *in* Frost, E. G., and Martin, D. L., eds., Mesozoic–Cenozoic tectonic evolution of the Colorado River region, California, Arizona, and Nevada: San Diego, California, Cordilleran Publishers, p. 377–392.

Jackson, J. A., 1987, Active normal faulting and crustal extension, *in* Coward, M. P., Dewey, J. F., and Hancock, P. L., eds., Continental extensional tectonics: Geological Society of London Special Publication 28, p. 3–17.

John, B. E., 1987, Geometry and evolution of a mid-crustal extensional fault system; Chemehuevi Mountains, southeastern California, *in* Coward, M. P., Dewey, J. F., and Hancock, P. L., eds., Continental extensional tectonics: Geological Society of London Special Publication 28, p. 313–336.

Kaufman, S., and 7 others, 1986, The COCORP Arizona transect [abs.]: EOS Transactions of the American Geophysical Union, v. 67, p. 1102.

Kligfield, R., Crespi, J., Naruk, S., and Davis, G. H., 1984, Displacement and strain patterns of extensional orogens: Tectonics, v. 3, p. 577–609.

Liggett, M. A., and Childs, J. F., 1977, An application of satellite imagery to mineral exploration: U.S. Geological Survey Professional Paper 1015, p. 253–270.

Lister, G. S., Etheridge, M. A., and Symonds, P. A., 1986a, Detachment faulting and the evolution of passive continental margins: Geology, v. 14, p. 246–250.

——, 1986b, Reply *to* Discussion *of* Detachment faulting and the evolution of passive continental margins: Geology, v. 14, p. 891–892.

Logan, J. M., Friedman, M., Higgs, N. G., Dengo, C., and Shimamoto, T., 1979, Experimental studies of simulated gouge and their application to studies of natural fault zones: U.S. Geological Survey Open-File Report 79–1239, p. 305–343.

Longwell, C. R., 1945, Low-angle normal faults in the Basin and Range province: EOS Transactions of the American Geophysical Union, v. 26, pt. 1, p. 107–118.

——, 1963, Reconnaissance geology between Lake Mead and Davis Dam, Arizona-Nevada: U.S. Geological Survey Professional Paper 374–E, 51 p.

Longwell, C. R., Pampeyan, E. H., Bowyer, B., and Roberts, R. J., 1965, Geology and mineral deposits of Clark County, Nevada: Nevada Bureau of Mines and Geology Bulletin 62, 218 p.

Lucchitta, I., 1966, Cenozoic geology of the upper Lake Mead area adjacent to the Grand Wash Cliffs, Arizona [Ph.D. thesis]: University Park, Pennsylvania State University, 218 p.

Lucchitta, I., and Suneson, N., 1981a, Comment *on* Tertiary tectonic denudations of a Mesozoic–early Tertiary (?) gneiss complex, Rawhide Mountains, western Arizona: Geology, v. 9, p. 50–52.

——, 1981b, Observations and speculations regarding the relations and origins of mylonitic gneiss and associated detachment faults near the Colorado Plateau boundary in western Arizona, *in* Howard, K. A., Carr, M. D., and Miller, D. M., eds., Tectonic framework of the Mojave and Sonoran Deserts, California and Arizona: U.S. Geological Survey Open-File Report 81–503, p. 107–109.

Lucchitta, I., and Young, R. A., 1986, Structure and geomorphic character of western Colorado Plateau in the Grand Canyon–Lake Mead region, *in* Nations, J. D., Conway, C. M., and Swann, G. A., eds., Geology of central and northern Arizona: Geological Society of America, Rocky Mountain Section Guidebook: Flagstaff, Northern Arizona University, p. 159–176.

Mandl, G., 1987, Tectonic deformation by rotating parallel faults; The "bookshelf" mechanism: Tectonophysics, v. 141, p. 277–316.

——, 1988, Mechanics of tectonic faulting: Amsterdam, Netherlands, Elsevier Science Publishing Company, 407 p.

Mariano, J., Helferty, M. G., and Gage, T. B., 1986, Bouguer and isostatic residual gravity map of the Colorado River region, Kingman Quadrangle: U.S. Geological Survey Open-File Report 86–347, scale 1:250,000 and 1:750,000.

Mariolakos, I., and Stiros, S. C., 1987, Quaternary deformation of the Isthmus and Gulf of Corinthos (Greece): Geology, v. 15, p. 225–228.

Mathis, R. S., 1982, Mid-Tertiary detachment faulting in the southeastern Newberry Mountains, Clark County, Nevada, *in* Frost, E. G., and Martin, D. L., eds., Mesozoic–Cenozoic tectonic evolution of the Colorado River region, California, Arizona, and Nevada: San Diego, California, Cordilleran Publishers, p. 326–340.

McDonald, R. E., 1976, Tertiary tectonics and sedimentary rocks along the transition, Basin and Range province to plateau and thrust belt province, *in* Hill, J. G., ed., Symposium on geology of the Cordilleran Hingeline: Denver, Colorado, Rocky Mountain Association of Geologists, p. 281–318.

Miller, E. L., Gans, P. B., and Garing, J., 1983, The Snake Range décollement; An exhumed mid-Tertiary ductile-brittle transition: Tectonics, v. 2, p. 239–263.

Morton, W. H., and Black, R., 1975, Crustal attenuation in Afar, *in* Pilger, A., and Roster, A., eds., Afar depression of Ethiopia: Inter-Union Commission on Geodynamics, Stuttgart, Germany, E. Schweizerbartische Verlagsbuchhandlung, p. 55–65.

Moustafa, A. M., 1976, Block faulting in the Gulf of Suez: 5th Egyptian General Petroleum Organization Exploration Seminar, Cairo: Cairo, DeMinex-Cairo, 19 p.

Myers, I. A., Smith, E. I., and Wyman, R. V., 1986, Control of gold mineralization at the Cyclopic Mine, Gold Basin district, Mohave County, Arizona: Economic Geology, v. 81, 1553–1557.

Naumann, T. R., 1987, Geology of the central Boulder Canyon Quadrangle, Clark County, Nevada [M.S. thesis]: Las Vegas, University of Nevada, 68 p.

Proffett, J. M., Jr., 1977, Cenozoic geology of the Yerington district, Nevada, and implications for the nature and origin of Basin and Range faulting: Geological Society of America Bulletin, v. 88, p. 247–266.

Pullaiah, G., Irving, E., Buchan, K. L., and Dunlop, D. J., 1975, Magnetization changes caused by burial and uplift: Earth and Planetary Science Letters, v. 28, p. 133–143.

Ramsay, J. G., 1980, Shear zone geometry; A review: Journal of Structural Geology, v. 2, p. 83–99.

Ransome, F. L., 1909, The geology and ore deposits of Goldfield, Nevada: U.S. Geological Survey Professional Paper 66, 258 p.

Rehrig, W. A., and Heidrick, T. L., 1976, Regional tectonic stress during the Laramide and late Tertiary intrusive periods, Basin and Range province, Arizona: Arizona Geological Society Digest, v. 10, p. 205–228.

Reynolds, D. J., 1984, Structural and dimensional repetition in continental rifts [M.S. thesis]: Durham, North Carolina, 175 p.

Reynolds, D. J., and Rosendahl, B. R., 1984, Tectonic expressions of continental rifting [abs.]: EOS Transactions of the American Geophysical Union, v. 65, p. 1116.

Reynolds, S. J., and Spencer, J. E., 1985, Evidence for large-scale transport on the Bullard detachment fault, west-central Arizona: Geology, v. 13, p. 353–356.

Rosendahl, B. R., 1987, Architecture of continental rifts with special reference to East Africa: Annual Reviews of Earth and Planetary Science Letters, v. 15, p. 445–503.

Rosendahl, B. R., and 7 others, 1986, Structural expressions of rifting; Lessons from Lake Tanganyika, Africa, *in* Frostick, L. E., Renaut, R. W., Reid, I., and Tiercelin, J. J., eds., Sedimentation in the African rifts: Geological Society of London Special Publication 25, p. 29–44.

Sauck, W. A., and Sumner, J. S., 1970, Residual aeromagnetic map of Arizona: Tucson, University of Arizona.

Shackelford, T. J., 1980, Tertiary tectonic denudation of a Mesozoic–early Tertiary (?) gneiss complex, Rawhide Mountains, western Arizona: Geology, v. 8, p. 190–194.

Shride, A. F., 1967, Younger Precambrian geology in southern Arizona: U.S. Geological Survey Professional Paper 566, 89 p.

Simpson, R. W., Gage, T. B., and Bracken, R. E., 1986, Aeromagnetic and isostatic gravity maps of the Crossman Peak wilderness study area, Mohave County, Arizona: U.S. Geological Survey Miscellaneous Field Studies Map MF–1602–B, scale 1:48,000.

Slemmons, D. B., 1967, Pliocene and Quaternary crustal movements of the Basin and Range province, USA, *in* Sea level changes and crustal movements of the Pacific: 11th Pacific Science Congress, Tokyo, 1966, Symposium 19: Osaka City University, Journal of Geosciences, v. 10, article 1, p. 91–103.

Smith, E. I., Eschner, E., Feuerbach, D. L., Naumann, T. R., and Sewall, A., 1987, Mid-Tertiary extension in the eastern Basin and Range province,

Nevada and Arizona; The Las Vegas Valley–Detrital Wash transect: Geological Society of America Abstracts with Programs, v. 19, p. 848–849.

Smith, R. B., and Bruhn, R. L., 1984, Intraplate extensional tectonics of the eastern Basin-Range; Inferences on structural style from seismic reflection data, regional tectonics, and thermal-mechanical models of brittle-ductile deformation: Journal of Geophysical Research, v. 89, p. 5733–5762.

Spencer, J. E., 1984, Role of tectonic denudation in uplift and warping of low-angle normal faults: Geology, v. 12, p. 95–98.

—— , 1985, Miocene low-angle normal faulting and dike emplacement, Homer Mountain and surrounding areas, southeastern California and southernmost Nevada: Geological Society of America Bulletin, v. 96, p. 1140–1155.

Spencer, J. E., and Reynolds, S. J., 1986, Some aspects of the middle Tertiary tectonics of Arizona and southeastern California: Arizona Geological Society Digest, v. 16, p. 102–107.

—— , 1989, Middle Tertiary tectonics of Arizona and adjacent areas, *in* Jenney, J. P., and Reynolds, S. J., eds., Geologic evolution of Arizona: Arizona Geological Society Digest, v. 17, pp. 539–574.

Stewart, J. H., 1980, Regional tilt patterns of late Cenozoic basin-range fault blocks, western United States: Geological Society of America Bulletin, v. 91, p. 460–464.

Stewart, J. H., and Johannesen, D. C., 1979, Map showing regional tilt patterns of late Cenozoic Basin-Range fault blocks in western United States: U.S. Geological Survey Open-File Report 79–1134, scale 1:2,500,000.

Theodore, T. G., Blair, W. N., and Nash, J. T., 1982, Preliminary report on the geology and gold mineralization of the Gold Basin–Lost Basin mining districts, Mohave County, Arizona: U.S. Geological Survey Open-File Report 82–1052, 322 p.

Versfelt, J., and Rosendahl, B. R., 1989, Relationships between pre-rift structure and rift architecture in Lakes Tanganyika and Malawi, East Africa: Nature, v. 337, p. 354–357.

Volborth, A., 1973, Geology of the granite complex of the Eldorado, Newberry, and northern Dead Mountains, Clark County, Nevada: Nevada Bureau of Mines and Geology Bulletin 80, 40 p.

Walker, J. D., Hodges, K. V., and Wernicke, B. P., 1986, The relation of tilt geometry to extension direction: Geological Society of America Abstracts with Programs, v. 18, p. 194.

Weber, M. E., and Smith, E. I., 1987, Structural and geochemical constraints on the reassembly of disrupted mid-Miocene volcanoes in the Lake Mead–Eldorado Valley area of southern Nevada: Geology, v. 15, p. 553–556.

Wernicke, B., 1981, Low-angle faults in the Basin and Range province; Nappe tectonics in an extending orogen: Nature, v. 291, p. 645–648.

—— , 1985, Uniform-sense normal simple shear of the continental lithosphere: Canadian Journal of Earth Sciences, v. 22, p. 108–125.

Wernicke, B., and Burchfiel, B. C., 1982, Modes of extensional tectonics: Journal of Structural Geology, v. 4, p. 105–115.

Wilson, E. D., Moore, R. T., and Cooper, J. R., 1969, Geologic map of Arizona: Tucson, Arizona Bureau of Mines and U.S. Geological Survey Map, scale 1:500,000.

Zijderveld, J.D.A., 1967, A. C. demagnetization of rocks; Analysis of results, *in* Collinson, D. W., Creer, K. M., and Runcorn, S. K., eds., Methods in paleomagnetism: Amsterdam, Elsevier, p. 254–286.

Zuber, M. T., Parmentier, E. M., and Fletcher, R. C., 1986, Extension of continental lithosphere; A model for two scales of Basin and Range deformation: Journal of Geophysical Research, v. 91, p. 4826–4838.

MANUSCRIPT ACCEPTED BY THE SOCIETY AUGUST 21, 1989

Geological Society of America
Memoir 176
1990

Chapter 4

The Saddle Island detachment; An evolving shear zone in the Lake Mead area, Nevada

Ernest M. Duebendorfer, Angela J. Sewall, and Eugene I. Smith
Department of Geoscience, University of Nevada, Las Vegas, Nevada 89154

ABSTRACT

The Saddle Island detachment fault is a major, and possibly the dominant, structural feature in the Lake Mead area, Nevada. Exposures on Saddle Island contain many of the characteristic elements of metamorphic core complexes of the Colorado River trough detachment terrane, including lower-plate mylonitic rocks, a detachment fault marked by chloritic phyllonite and microbreccia, and a brittlely deformed upper plate. The Saddle Island detachment is regionally important because it is the only well-documented exposure in the Lake Mead region of a deep-level, crystalline lower plate. The upper plate of the detachment is divided into three lithologically distinct, lens-shaped domains bounded by low-angle normal faults. The domains are lithologically heterogeneous and contain Precambrian crystalline rocks, lower Paleozoic sedimentary rocks, sedimentary rocks of the Tertiary Horse Spring Formation, and Tertiary intrusive rocks.

The lower plate of the detachment consists principally of variably mylonitized Precambrian amphibolite and quartzofeldspathic gneiss. Subhorizontal mylonitic foliation broadly parallels the detachment. Contacts between variably mylonitized rock are typically low-angle chlorite phyllonite fault zones. The lens-like character of lithologic packages in the lower plate resembles large-scale structure within the upper plate.

Kinematic analysis indicates top-to-the-west shear for mylonites and all low-angle faults within the complex. Systematic changes in retrograde mineralogy that accompany textural changes in fault rocks suggest that structures associated with the detachment represent a continuum of deformation at progressively lower temperatures (i.e., shallower crustal levels). The similarity in orientation and inferred shear sense of all fault zones suggests that they developed during a single deformational event. These geologic relations are best explained by single-stage deformation associated with an evolving, crustal-scale, normal-sense-displacement simple-shear zone.

Regional geochemical correlations allow reconstruction of structurally disrupted mid-Miocene volcanic-plutonic complexes in the Lake Mead area. The sense of movement required for restoration of these complexes is compatible with kinematic indicators within the Saddle Island detachment zone. These combined data suggest 20 km of westward translation of upper-plate rocks along the detachment. The inferred 20-km displacement along the detachment argues against *in situ* crustal extension (pure-shear models).

Available age data suggest that the Saddle Island detachment is younger than 13.5 Ma; the major period of movement along the detachment must have occurred prior to deposition of the Muddy Creek Formation (5 to 9 Ma).

Low-angle faults exposed east of Saddle Island between Lake Mead and Detrital

Duebendorfer, E. M., Sewall, A. J., and Smith, E. I., 1990, The Saddle Island detachment; An evolving shear zone in the Lake Mead area, Nevada, *in* Wernicke, B. P., ed., Basin and Range extensional tectonics near the latitude of Las Vegas, Nevada: Boulder, Colorado, Geological Society of America Memoir 176.

Wash may be correlative with the Saddle Island detachment. The lack of mylonitic
fabric in lower-plate rocks to the east can be explained by the eastward-shallowing of
the regional detachment structure.

INTRODUCTION

Saddle Island is a small, north-trending horst (Longwell, 1936) located on the western shore of Lake Mead in Clark County, Nevada (Fig. 1). Exposed within the Saddle Island horst is a mid-Miocene detachment fault (Smith, 1982) that formed during mid-Tertiary crustal extension in the Lake Mead area and, regionally, within the southern Great Basin (Coney, 1980; Armstrong, 1982; Eaton, 1982). The Saddle Island detachment is important because it provides the only well-documented exposure in the Lake Mead region of a deep-level, crystalline lower plate.

Two distinct structural domains that exhibit opposing senses vergence occur within the southern Basin and Range (Wust, 1986) (Fig. 2). A 5-km-wide accommodation zone in the central Black Mountains and southern Eldorado Mountains separates the domains of opposite vergence (Faulds and others, 1987, 1988, this volume). The domain north of the accommodation zone includes part of the Eldorado Range (Anderson, 1971), northern Black Mountains (Feuerbach, 1986; Smith and others, 1987b), and the Lake Mead and Mormon Mountains–Tule Springs Hills areas (Wernicke and others, 1985; Smith and others, 1987a). Detachment structures in this region record east-west extension with upper-plate tectonic transport to the west. The area south of the accommodation zone in western Arizona and along the Colorado River trough underwent northeast-southwest extension along east-northeast–vergent detachment-related structures (Frost and Martin, 1982; Spencer, 1984, 1985). Kinematically, the west-vergent Saddle Island detachment fault is similar to the detachment terrane north of the Colorado River trough (Choukroune and Smith, 1985; Smith and others, 1987b). However, the rocks and structures associated with the Saddle Island detachment closely resemble features observed in metamorphic core complexes in Arizona and the Colorado River trough (Fig. 2), as discussed below.

K-Ar biotite dates on lower-plate mylonitic rocks indicate a northward-younging progression of detachment faulting ranging from 20 to 30 Ma in south-central Arizona (Crittenden and others, 1980) to 14.5 to 30 Ma in the Colorado River trough (Davis and others, 1982; Spencer, 1985). The younger-to-the-north trend extends into the Lake Mead region where a K-Ar biotite date of 13.4 ± 0.3 Ma from a lamprophyre dike constrains major movement on the Saddle Island detachment to post–13.4 Ma. This date is consistent with major extensional faulting in the Eldorado (Anderson and others, 1972) and northern Black Mountains (13.5 to 15 Ma) (Anderson and others, 1972). To the north in the Mormon Mountain area, extension is at least as young as 8.5 Ma (Wernicke and others, 1985).

UPPER PLATE

Introduction

The upper plate of the Saddle Island detachment is lithologically heterogeneous, consisting of Precambrian crystalline rocks, Paleozoic and Tertiary sedimentary units, and Tertiary intrusive rocks (Fig. 3; Plate 1, in pocket inside back cover). In general, cross-cutting relations on the east side of the island indicate that upper-plate rocks were extended along low-angle faults and then subsequently down-dropped to the northeast along northwest-striking, moderate- to high-angle normal faults.

The upper plate can be divided into three lens-shaped lithologic domains that are bounded by low-angle normal fault zones (Figs. 3, 4). Domain 2 is the structurally lowest; the relation between domains 1 and 3 is unclear. Domain 1 contains Lower Cambrian Tapeats Sandstone and Pioche (Bright Angel) Shale, Tertiary fanglomerate, and mid-Miocene intrusive rocks. This domain is bounded below by the Moon Cove fault (Plate 1; Figs. 3, 4). Domain 2 is bounded below by the detachment fault and consists of Precambrian crystalline rock that is highly intruded by hypabyssal dacite and diorite. Domain 3 contains Precambrian crystalline rock intruded by dacite dikes and is bounded below by a lensoidal low-angle fault. Precambrian rock in domains 2 and 3 is amphibolite, quartzofeldspathic gneiss, mica schist, quartz monzonite, and pegmatite. All units and domain boundaries are cut by Tertiary mafic dikes.

Upper-plate rocks are pervasively, but variably, altered to epidote, clinozoisite, chlorite, and calcite. Sodium enrichment (to 10 percent Na_2O) and potassium depletion (0.48 to 0.63 percent K_2O) accompanied the alteration (Sewall, 1988).

General structural characteristics

Contoured fault-orientation diagrams (Fig. 5) show three distinct fault sets within the upper plate. Cross-cutting relations reveal that these sets represent three generations of faulting. From oldest to youngest these sets are (1) N75°W striking, south-southwest dipping, (2) N30°E striking, northwest dipping, and (3) N10°W striking, west and east dipping. Low-angle structures are within the second group. Normal displacement is indicated for all faults, and top-to-the-west transport direction is inferred for low-angle faults (Choukroune and Smith, 1985; Smith and others, 1987a, b). Smith (1982) documented similar age relations of faulting to the west of Saddle Island in the Fault Basin area of the eastern River Mountains (Fig. 1). This area is inferred to lie in the upper plate of the Saddle Island detachment (Weber and Smith, 1987; Sewall, 1988).

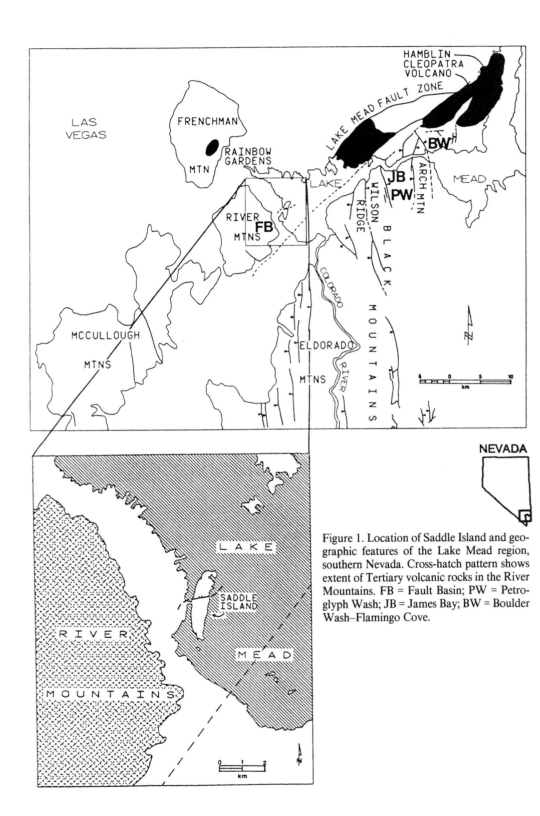

Figure 1. Location of Saddle Island and geographic features of the Lake Mead region, southern Nevada. Cross-hatch pattern shows extent of Tertiary volcanic rocks in the River Mountains. FB = Fault Basin; PW = Petroglyph Wash; JB = James Bay; BW = Boulder Wash–Flamingo Cove.

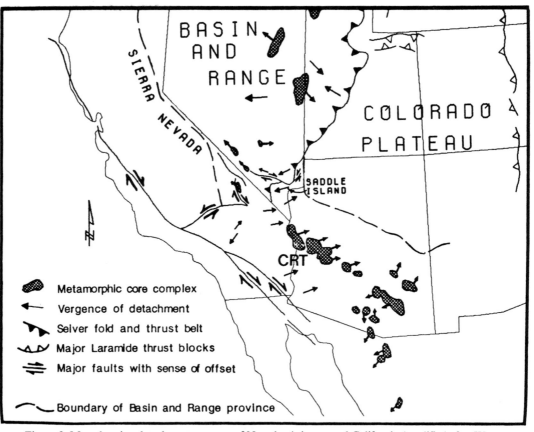

Figure 2. Map showing detachment terranes of Nevada, Arizona, and California (modified after Wust, 1986). CRT = Colorado River trough.

East-striking, moderate- to high-angle faults are marked by 10 to 30-cm wide zones of breccia and mineralization and contain striae that plunge approximately 65°S. Striae on low-angle fault surfaces exposed on the north side of the island (domain 1) plunge gently northwest, west, and southwest.

The upper plate is brecciated for 80 m above the detachment fault. Just above the breccia zone, high- and low-angle fault surfaces strike subparallel to the detachment and may merge at depth with the detachment surface.

General lithology

Domain 1. Lower Cambrian Tapeats Sandstone and Pioche Shale (Bright Angel equivalent) crop out south of Moon Cove within domain 1 (Fig. 3; Plate 1). The basal arkosic facies of the Tapeats (Hardy, 1986) is not present at Saddle Island. The lack of a basal facies and the abrupt truncation of bedding in the Tapeats (N25°W, 85°NE) suggest that the sedimentary units are bounded below by the low-angle Moon Cove fault. The transitional upper contact between the Tapeats and the Pioche is preserved, but the original contact relation between the Pioche and an overlying conglomerate is obscured by Tertiary intrusive rocks. Carbonate-clast conglomerate overlies the Lower Cambrian section and Precambrian rocks south and west of Moon

Cove, respectively. This conglomerate is a 450-m-thick fanglomerate deposit that consists of five facies (Sewall and Smith, 1986, 1988; Sewall, 1988). From base to top they are (1) coarse, clast-supported, carbonate-clast conglomerate, (2) porphyritic dacite flows, (3) subarkosic siltstone, (4) matrix-supported pebble conglomerate, and (5) a Precambrian granitic megabreccia block. Sewall and Smith (1988) and Sewall (1988) correlated the fanglomerate on Saddle Island with the Miocene Horse Spring Formation.

Domain 2. Domain 2 contains Precambrian amphibolite, quartz-feldspar gneiss, mica schist, quartz monzonite, pegmatite, mid-Miocene hypabyssal dacite, and diorite of unknown age. Precambrian foliation generally strikes northwest and dips moderately to steeply northeast (Plate I). The diorite on the east side of domain 2 (Plate I) is mineralogically similar to mid-Miocene(?) diorite and monzodiorite at Wilson Ridge (Feuerbach, 1986) and Arch Mountain (Eschner, personal communication, 1986) (Fig. 1). The upper plate on Saddle Island and the Wilson Ridge–Arch Mountain area are the only known localities of diorite in the Lake Mead region.

Domain 3. Precambrian crystalline rock of domain 3 is similar in lithology to that of domain 2; however, domain 3 contains abundant Precambrian pegmatite and few mid-Miocene intrusive rocks. Foliation in domain 3 commonly strikes north-

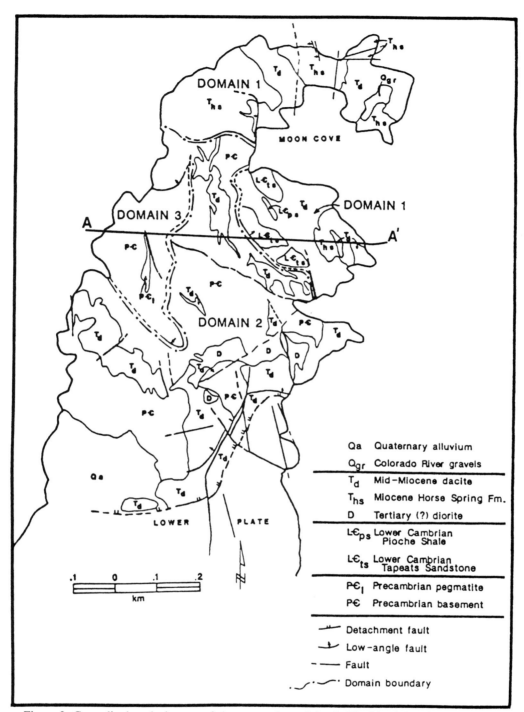

Figure 3. Generalized geologic map of the upper plate of the Saddle Island detachment showing principal lithological units. A-A′ indicates line of cross section shown in Figure 4.

east and dips variably southeast, in contrast to the northwest trends of domain 2 (Plate I). The lack of intrusive rock in domain 3 and discordance in the orientation of Precambrian foliation between domains 2 and 3 suggest that these domains represent separate fault blocks.

Domain boundaries. Domain 1 is bounded below by a brecciated, anastomosing low-angle normal fault zone—the

Moon Cove fault (Plate I, Figs. 3, 4). The fault zone contains fractured acicular barite in a matrix of fine-grained hematite and manganese oxide. South of Moon Cove, the fault strikes northeast, dips gently southeast, and juxtaposes Lower Cambrian Tapeats Sandstone over Precambrian rocks. Subhorizontal fault striae trend N45°E. The Moon Cove fault ramps up section to the north-northwest and eliminates Lower Cambrian units from do-

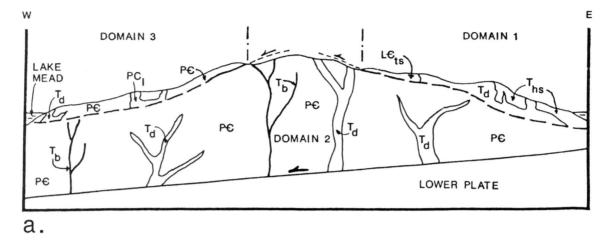

a.

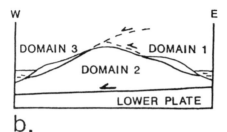

b.

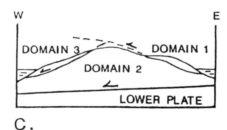

c.

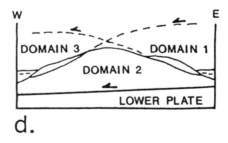

d.

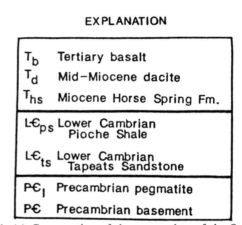

EXPLANATION

T_b	Tertiary basalt
T_d	Mid-Miocene dacite
T_{hs}	Miocene Horse Spring Fm.
$L\mathcal{C}_{ps}$	Lower Cambrian Pioche Shale
$L\mathcal{C}_{ts}$	Lower Cambrian Tapeats Sandstone
$P\mathcal{C}_l$	Precambrian pegmatite
$P\mathcal{C}$	Precambrian basement

Figure 4. (a) Cross section of the upper plate of the Saddle Island detachment (A-A'). Three schematic diagrams (b, c, d) show possible structural relations between domains of the upper plate.

main 1 on the west side of Moon Cove. At this locality, the fault strikes west-northwest, dips moderately to the northeast, and places Miocene Horse Spring Formation against Precambrian rocks. Domain 2, the structurally lowest lithologic package of the upper plate, is bounded below by the Saddle Island fault. On the basis of lithologic and structural differences between domains 2 and 3 (discussed above), we infer that domain 3 is bounded below by a low-angle fault.

The structural order of domains 1 and 3 is unclear due to equivocal field relations. Projection of the lensoidal fault zones in the upper plate of the detachment suggests that either the lower boundary fault for domain 3 forms the upper boundary fault for domain 1, or the Moon Cove fault (the lower boundary of domain 1) projects above domain 3 (Fig. 4a). Three interpretations for the relative ages are possible: (1) the Moon Cove fault of domain 1 could be truncated by the lower boundary fault of domain 3 (Fig. 4b), (2) the lower boundary fault of domain 3 is truncated by the Moon Cove fault (Fig. 4c), or (3) both faults formed at the same time and represent one zone of brittle deformation (Fig. 4d).

Minor dacite intrusions cut the low-angle bounding faults of domains 1 and 3. No intrusive rock cuts the detachment fault, which serves as the boundary for domain 2. This suggests that the low-angle bounding faults of domains 1 and 3 may have formed slightly before the detachment and may have been transported

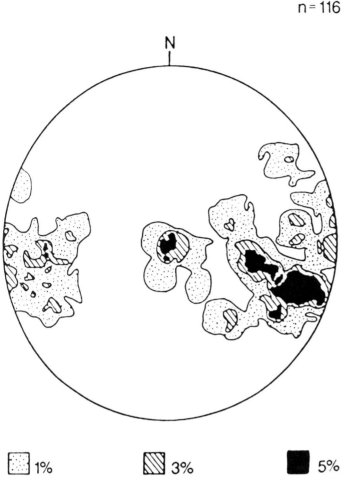

n = 116

1%   3%   5%

Figure 5. Lower hemisphere equal area projection of poles to faults in upper plate of Saddle Island detachment. Contour interval 1–3–5 percent per 1 percent area; n = 116.

Figure 6. Photograph showing chlorite phyllonite (CP) zone near detachment surface (heavy black line). UP = upper plate; LP = lower plate; thin black line marks approximate position of transitional contact between chlorite phyllonite and lower-plate mylonites. Phyllonite zone approximately 25 m thick at this locality.

farther west within the upper plate of the Saddle Island fault. This is also consistent with the structural position of the low-angle bounding faults relative to the detachment.

DETACHMENT FAULT

The detachment fault that separates upper- from lower-plate rocks on Saddle Island consists of a 2-m-thick microbreccia ledge underlain by a 30-m-thick chlorite phyllonite zone (Fig. 6).

A gray-green to black microbreccia lies directly beneath the brecciated dacite of the upper plate. Mineralogically, it is dominated by quartz, feldspar, and iron oxide. In thin section, angular and fractured quartz and feldspar grains are set in a matrix of very fine-grained comminuted material, suggesting that microcracking was the dominant deformation mechanism. This rock is best classified as an ultracataclasite using the terminology of Sibson (1977).

The chlorite phyllonite zone is developed principally from nonmylonitic amphibolite of the lower plate. Macroscopic foliation of the phyllonite is defined by the alignment of green biotite and chlorite. Grain-size reduction of quartz and feldspar occurred by microfracturing. This suggests that the chlorite phyllonite developed principally by brittle deformation mechanisms, perhaps assisted by grain-boundary sliding of phyllosilicates and finely comminuted material.

A nonpenetrative chlorite-fiber lineation is developed locally on the phyllonitic foliation surfaces. This lineation is spatially associated with and parallel to hematite-stained fault striae. The difference in character between the two linear features may reflect a change in temperature, fluid pressure and composition, strain rate, or differential response of phyllosilicate-rich versus phyllosilicate-poor rocks during deformation.

LOWER PLATE

Introduction

The lower plate of the Saddle Island detachment consists of variably mylonitized Precambrian amphibolite, quartzofeldspathic gneiss, and pegmatite (Fig. 7). The degree of mylonitization increases structurally upward in the lower plate (Fig. 8). Amphibolite is divided into three map units: nonmylonitic rock and protomylonite, mylonite, and ultramylonite (Plate I; Fig. 7). Quartzofeldspathic gneiss is generally mylonitic and is not subdivided further. Contacts between variably mylonitized rocks are typically low-angle, 1- to 3-m-thick chlorite phyllonite fault zones similar in character to the detachment zone. Contacts are unfaulted in some areas and appear to reflect sharp strain gradients.

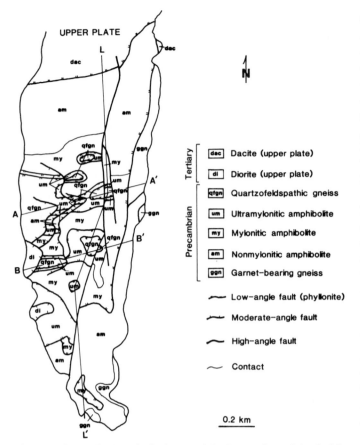

Figure 7. Generalized geological map of the lower plate of the Saddle Island detachment showing principal lithologic units. A-A', B-B', L-L' indicate lines of cross sections shown in Figure 8.

Lithology

Amphibolite. Nonfoliated amphibolite is the dominant rock type at the deepest levels of exposure in the lower plate. It is uniformly medium grained and exhibits relict hypidiomorphic-granular texture (Fig. 9A). Brown hornblende and plagioclase (An_{50-60}) are the dominant primary phases. Hornblende is locally retrograded, in the absence of a deformational fabric, to aggregates of brown biotite and epidote; subhedral plagioclase is variably saussuritized. Mineralogy, major-element chemistry, and relict igneous texture suggest a gabbro protolith.

Nonfoliated amphibolite grades into protomylonite and mylonite with increasing strain (Fig. 9B). Mylonitic amphibolites exhibit macroscopic S-C fabrics and a well-developed, penetrative mineral lineation. Grain-size reduction is macroscopically obvious only in samples approaching ultramylonite but is microscopically evident as the dynamic recrystallization of hornblende and plagioclase to finer-grained aggregates. In some mylonites, grain-size reduction is accompanied by very little retrogression. This suggests that deformation occurred under conditions of moderately high temperature, low a_{H_2O}, or both.

Mineralogical changes associated with mylonitization are summarized in Table 1. Generally, hornblende and plagioclase are replaced by aggregates of brown-green biotite, actinolite, epidote, sphene, and apatite with increasing strain. The replacement of hornblende by biotite rather than actinolite may be a function of potassium availability. Retrograde biotite and actinolite are aligned parallel to the mylonitic foliation and define the lineation, suggesting synkinematic recrystallization of these phases. Aggregates of retrograde chlorite locally cut the mylonitic foliation at a low angle. The above relations suggest a continuum of deformation and retrogression at progressively lower temperatures and increasing a_{H_2O}.

Ultramylonitic amphibolite exhibits alternating dark- and light-colored bands (Fig. 9C). Dark bands consist of biotite, epidote, and minor actinolite, chlorite, and sphene; light bands are dominated by quartz, plagioclase, and muscovite. This mineralogy suggests tectonic mixing of lithologies, perhaps by extreme transposition of original amphibolite-quartzofeldspathic gneiss contacts, during mylonitization.

Quartzofeldspathic gneiss. Variably mylonitized quartzofeldspathic gneiss occurs at the structurally highest levels in the lower plate. Where weakly deformed, it is coarse grained to pegmatitic. Contacts between gneiss and amphibolite are generally low-angle faults; original contact relations are unclear. The occurrence of 1- to 3-m-thick concordant layers of similar felsic material within amphibolite suggests that the quartzofeldspathic gneiss represents sills.

The gneiss is dominated by quartz and plagioclase, with subordinate muscovite, biotite, and epidote. Potassium feldspar was not observed, although its former presence may be indicated by muscovite. Modal composition suggests a tonalite or granodiorite protolith. Mylonitic quartzofeldspathic gneiss is strongly overprinted by cataclasis, perhaps reflecting proximity to the detachment zone (now eroded) (Fig. 8).

Garnet-bearing gneiss. A garnet-bearing, biotite quartzofeldspathic gneiss occurs in the lower plate along the east side of Saddle Island. The gneiss is generally mylonitized but locally exhibits little or no deformational fabric. In weakly deformed areas, garnet composes 10 to 50 percent of the rock and is localized in discrete bands. Subhedral microcline and plagioclase suggest an igneous protolith. Contact relations with adjacent amphibolite suggest that the gneiss may have originally been intruded as dikes.

Dikes and sills. At least three generations of dikes and sills are present in the lower plate. From oldest to youngest these are (1) quartz-feldspar pegmatite sills, (2) mafic dikes, and (3) muscovite-bearing pegmatites. Quartz-feldspar pegmatites clearly intrude amphibolite and show effects of both ductile and brittle deformation. These are interpreted as prekinematic with respect to development of the mylonitic fabric. Mafic dikes typically are intruded along low-angle chlorite phyllonite zones but locally cut them at a low angle. The dikes are in turn sheared and cut by later high-angle faults. We suggest that the mafic dikes were emplaced during the late stages of development of the chlorite phyllonite zones. Muscovite-bearing pegmatites crosscut

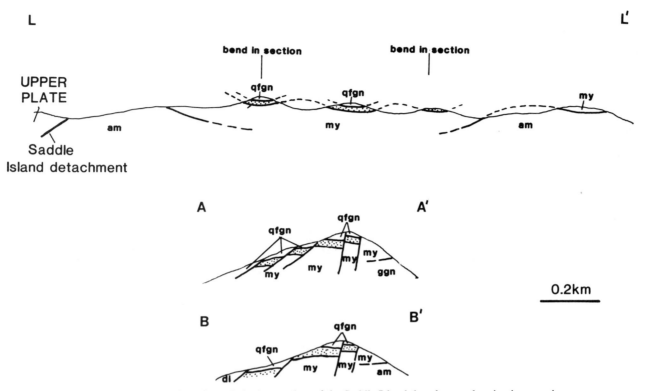

Figure 8. Cross sections through the lower plate of the Saddle Island detachment showing increase in degree of mylonitization structurally upward in lower plate. Individual packages of mylonitic rock are generally bounded by low-angle chlorite phyllonite zones. High-angle faults omitted from section L-L' for clarity. Symbols as in Figure 7 except ultramylonitic amphibolite shown in stippled pattern for emphasis.

mylonitic foliation and, locally, phyllonitic fabric. They are in turn cut by brittle high-angle faults and may be broadly contemporaneous with the mafic dikes.

Structure

Low-angle ductile and brittle shear zones and moderate- to high-angle brittle faults are present in the lower plate of the detachment. Fault rocks include mylonite, schist, phyllonite, cataclasite, and breccia. Principal structural features include subhorizontal mylonitic foliation, low-angle schistose and phyllonitic foliation, moderate-angle brittle faults, and high-angle brittle faults. In general, high-angle structures crosscut low-angle structures, with normal displacement evident along all faults. The suite of structures exposed in the lower plate of the Saddle Island detachment indicates a wide range in intensity and conditions of deformation.

Low-angle faults: Mylonite zones. A penetrative, subhorizontal mylonitic foliation and mineral lineation are well developed in rocks of the lower plate (Fig. 10A, B). The mylonite-ultramylonite zone is at least 100 m thick; the presence of numerous postmylonite low-angle faults suggests a greater original thickness. Where contacts between variably mylonitized rock are not faults, strain gradients are sharp; the transition from non-

mylonitized rock to ultramylonite occurs over a distance of a few centimeters.

Mesoscopic, intrafolial folds are developed locally in ultramylonite. A Hansen (1971) plot of fold-hinge-line orientations (Fig. 10C) shows considerable scatter, with hinge lines distributed within the plane of foliation. We interpret these data to indicate that fold hinges rotated into the finite elongation direction during progressive shearing. Rotation of fold axes into the elongation direction has been well documented from shear zones worldwide (Bryant and Reed, 1969; Sanderson, 1973; Escher and Watterson, 1974; Williams and Zwart, 1977; many others). Folds verge to the west, northwest, or southwest; slip-line analysis suggests west-directed tectonic transport (Fig. 10C). Sheath folds recognized at a few localities exhibit closure to the west, which further corroborates this interpretation.

Grain-size reduction is accomplished by dynamic recrystallization of quartz and plastic and brittle deformation in plagioclase and ferromagnesian phases. Quartz occurs as ribbons (X:Z > 50:1) that exhibit internal microtextures ranging from deformation bands, to subgrains, to completely annealed new grains. This range of microtextures in a single thin section indicates a complex, protracted deformation history of shearing, recovery, recrystallization, and further shearing.

Plagioclase microstructures include internal domains of

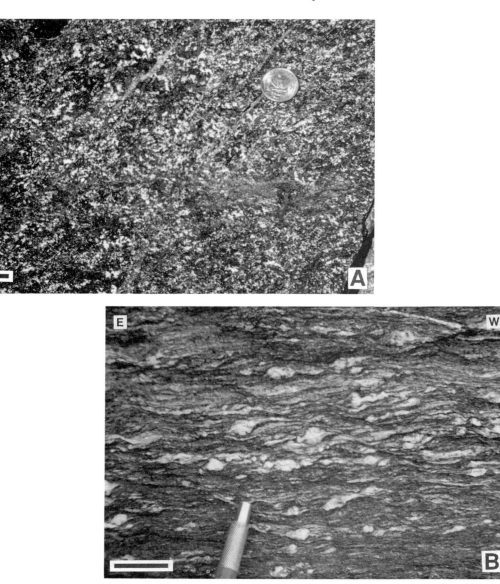

Figure 9. Field photographs of amphibolite. A: Nonmylonitic amphibolite. B: Mylonitic amphibolite. Note dextral
asymmetry of plagioclase-aggregate porphyroclasts. Vertical outcrop surface. E and W indicate east and west, respectively. C: Ultramylonitic amphibolite. Note folding of
mylonitic foliation. Vertical outcrop surface. E and W indicate east and west, respectively. Scale bar is 20 mm in all
three photographs.

**TABLE 1. MINERALOGICAL AND MICROSTRUCTURAL CHANGES ACCOMPANYING
MYLONITIZATION IN PRINCIPAL LOWER-LATE LITHOLOGIES***

Lithology	Mafic Mineralogy	Plagioclase	Quartz
Nonmylonitic amphibolite	hornblende—brown and green biotite (rare)—brown	undeformed	undeformed
Protomylonitic amphibolite	hornblende—blue-green actinolite—retrograde after hornblende biotite—brown	internally misoriented domains	annealed ribbons
Mylonitic amphibolite	hornblende (rare)—brown with blue-green rims actinolite—retrograde after hornblende biotite—green-brown chlorite—retrograde after biotite and actinolite	internally misoriented domains; minor microfracturing	annealed ribbons; unrecovered/unre-crystallized ribbons
Biotite schist	actinolite—randomly oriented pseudomorphs of horn-blende biotite—green-brown; define schistosity chlorite—retrograde after biotite and actinolite	mostly microfractured	unrecovered ribbons
Chlorite phyllonite	biotite—green chlorite	microfractured	microfractured

*Due to mixed character of the ultramylonite protolith, ultramylonite is not included.

slightly misoriented sectors, "bulge" features (Jensen and Starkey, 1985) at grain boundaries, and aggregates of finely recrystallized material along host margins. Plagioclase is locally microfractured. The misoriented sectors appear to be analogous to subgrains in strained quartz. Grain-boundary bulging has been interpreted as an important mechanism of recrystallization in feldspars (Jensen and Starkey, 1985). The aggregates of finely recrystallized feld-spar along host margins are similar to those described by Tullis and Yund (1985). The microstructures described above are char-acteristic of crystal-plastic deformation and synkinematic recrys-tallization and suggest moderately high temperatures during at least the early stages of mylonitization. Evidence for both brittle and plastic deformation is present in individual samples. This indicates either variation in strain rate at constant temperature, deformation under highly variable thermal conditions, or later brittle overprinting of an early fabric produced by crystal-plastic deformation.

Macroscopic kinematic indicators, best developed in the my-lonitic amphibolite, include S-C fabrics and asymmetric porphy-roclasts. These show overwhelmingly top-to-the-west shear sense (Sewall, 1988). This interpretation is corroborated by micro-scopic analysis of asymmetric and antithetically faulted porphy-roclasts, muscovite fish, oblique foliations in recrystallized quartz aggregates, and S-C relations in quartzofeldspathic gneiss and ultramylonite (Simpson and Schmid, 1983; Lister and Snoke, 1984). Top-to-the-west shear is indicated in more than 90 percent of the samples examined (Figs. 11A, B, C). This departs from the interpretation of Choukroune and Smith (1985).

Quartz-rich domains in two samples of mylonitic quartzo-feldspathic gneiss were selected for quartz fabric analysis. The samples exhibit a strong crystallographic preferred orientation of quartz *c*-axes (Fig. 12). The asymmetry of the single girdle fabric with respect to the foliation indicates a top-to-the-west shear sense, and its monoclinic symmetry suggests a noncoaxial strain history (Lister and Price, 1978; Lister and Williams, 1979; Simp-son and Schmid, 1983; many others). Maximum concentrations

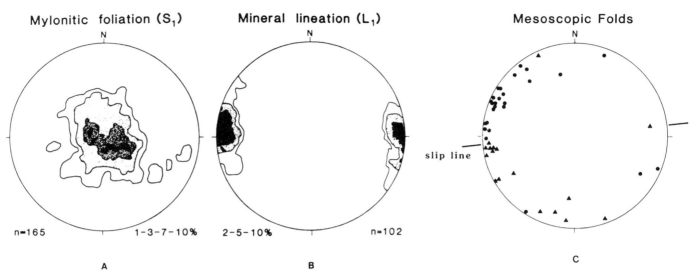

Mylonitic foliation (S₁)   Mineral lineation (L₁)   Mesoscopic Folds

n=165   1-3-7-10%   2-5-10%   n=102

A   B   C

Figure 10. Structural data from lower-plate mylonites. A: Lower hemisphere equal area projection of mylonitic foliation. Contour interval 1–3–5–7–10 percent per 1 percent area. B: Lower hemisphere equal area projection of mylonitic lineation. Contour interval 2–5–10 percent per 1 percent area. C: Lower hemisphere equal area projection of mesoscopic folds. Triangles denote clockwise sense of fold asymmetry: circles denote counterclockwise sense of fold asymmetry. Inferred slip direction indicated by heavy line (after Hansen, 1971).

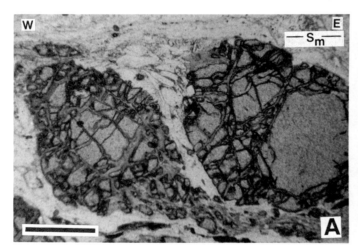

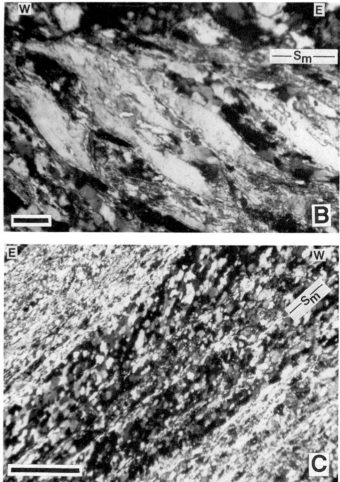

Figure 11. Microscopic kinematic indicators. S_m = mylonitic foliation, and E and W represent east and west, respectively, in all photomicrographs. Top-to-the-west–directed shear is indicated in all photomicrographs. A: Asymmetric and antithetically faulted garnet porphyroclast. Scale bar = 1.0 mm. B: Muscovite "fish." Scale bar = 0.2 mm. C: Oblique foliations in dynamically recrystallized quartz aggregates. Scale bar = 1.0 mm.

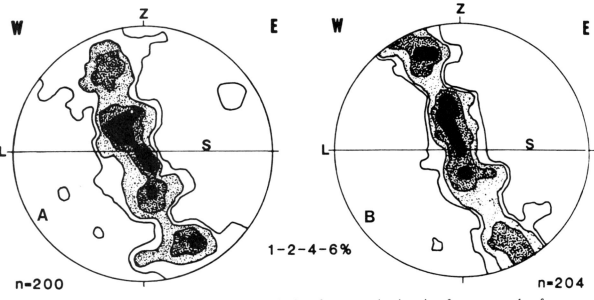

Figure 12. Lower hemisphere equal area projection of quartz *c*-axis orientations from two samples of quartzofeldspathic gneiss. Finite strain reference frame defined by mylonitic foliation (S = XY plane) and lineation (L = X direction). Z indicates foliation normal. Contour interval 1–2–4–6 percent per 1 percent area.

of *c*-axes near the inferred Y strain axis (near the center of the plots) indicate that intracrystalline plastic deformation was accomplished by prismatic <*a*> and rhomb <*a*> slip systems (Bouchez and others, 1983). These slip systems have been shown to become dominant over basal <*a*> slip at either low strain rates or at minimum temperatures corresponding to the greenschist-amphibolite facies transition (Wilson, 1975; White, 1976; Bouchez, 1977). This inference regarding thermal conditions of deformation is in accord with the deformational microtextures developed in plagioclase.

Low-angle faults: Biotite schist zones. One- to ten-meter-thick zones of biotite schist occur locally in zones between chlorite phyllonite and mylonite. The schistosity of the unit clearly overprints mylonitic foliation and is inferred to represent a deformation fabric. The schist contains biotite, actinolite, plagioclase, and minor quartz. Replacement of hornblende by actinolite and biotite suggests an amphibolite protolith. Plagioclase is generally deformed by microcracking, whereas quartz occurs as ribbons, indicating strain accommodation by intracrystalline plastic deformation mechanisms. Textural and mineralogical criteria suggest that the biotite schist developed at temperature conditions intermediate between the chlorite phyllonite and mylonite (Table 1). Microscopic kinematic indicators, including S-C fabrics and mica "fish" (Lister and Snoke, 1984), are consistent with the top-to-the-west sense of shear recorded in the mylonites.

Low-angle faults: Chlorite phyllonite zones. Low-angle chlorite phyllonite zones within the lower plate (Fig. 13A) range from a few centimeters to 5 m thick and commonly mark the low-angle boundary between variably mylonitized rock packages. Where the chlorite phyllonite zones cut individual lithologic

packages, they are anastomosing and isolate lenses of lower-plate rock (Choukroune and Smith, 1985). Mylonitic foliation is only slightly rotated where cut by the chlorite phyllonite zones. This suggests that the phyllonite zones nucleated at low angles relative to the earlier mylonitic foliation and argues against rotation of the phyllonite zones from a steeper original dip. The mineralogical and deformational character of this rock is similar to that of chlorite phyllonite zones developed immediately beneath the detachment fault.

Low-angle faults: Discussion. The similarity in orientation and inferred shear sense of the mylonite, biotite schist, and chlorite phyllonite zones suggests that these fault rocks developed during a single deformational event. Systematic changes in mineralogy that accompany textural changes (Table 1) suggest that the mylonite-schist-phyllonite sequence represents a continuum of deformation at progressively lower temperatures and, by inference, shallower crustal levels.

Moderate-angle faults. Moderately (20 to 50°) west-dipping, down-to-the-west normal faults are well developed only in the west-central part of the island (Plate I). Faults are planar or slightly listric at the level of exposure, but displaced units are not conspicuously rotated, suggesting an overall planar fault geometry. Fault surfaces are marked by zones of carbonate- and hematite-cemented breccia 1 to 50 cm thick and by west-plunging fault striae that indicate almost pure dip-slip movement. Moderate-angle faults cut both low-angle mylonitic foliation and chlorite phyllonite zones (Fig. 8, 14). The faults displace the structurally high quartzofeldspathic gneiss down to the west in a stair-step fashion. Each individual fault has no more than 10 to 20 m of stratigraphic separation; cumulatively, however, the

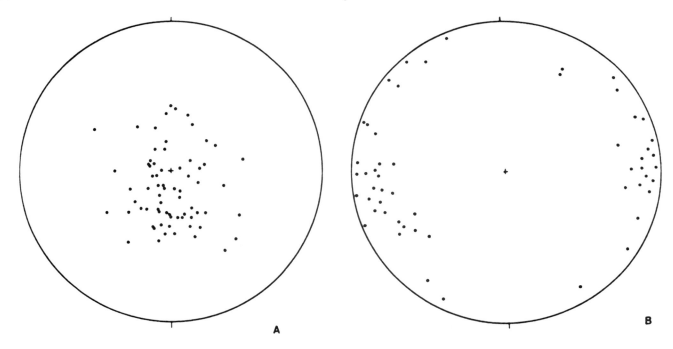

Figure 13. Structural data from chlorite phyllonite. A: Lower hemisphere equal area projection of poles
to chlorite phyllonite foliation; n = 70. B: Lower hemisphere equal area projection of fault striae and
mineral fibers developed on chlorite phyllonite surfaces; n = 54.

quartzofeldspathic gneiss is displaced 150 m over a horizontal
distance of less than 400 m.

High-angle faults. High-angle faults cut all other structures
on the island. They trend generally north-south, dip steeply west
or, less commonly, east, and are characterized by normal separation. They overlap in terms of degree of dip with the moderate-
angle faults but are clearly younger. High-angle fault surfaces are
marked by gouge zones 1 to 50 cm thick; fault striae were not
observed. High-angle faults mapped in both the upper and lower
plates are on strike with one another, and minor deflections in the
poorly exposed chloritic microbreccia in the detachment zone
suggest that these faults may be continuous across the
detachment.

REGIONAL CORRELATION

An understanding of the distribution of volcanic and plutonic rocks is central to any tectonic reconstruction of the Lake
Mead region. Detailed petrographic studies and major, trace, and
rare-earth element (REE) analyses of volcanic and plutonic rocks
in the Lake Mead region allow regional correlation. Similarities
in relatively immobile trace and rare-earth element distributions
allow correlation of volcanic rocks in the McCullough and Eldorado Ranges with the Boulder City and Nelson plutons (Smith
and others, 1986). The Boulder City pluton and rocks in the
McCullough and Eldorado Ranges exhibit high Ta concentrations (Fig. 15A) and a positive correlation between total REE
and SiO_2 (Fig. 15B). In contrast, volcanic rocks in the River

Mountains, Hoover Dam area, and Boulder Wash (Fig. 15B)
correlate chemically with the Wilson Ridge pluton (Smith, 1982,
1984; Mills, 1985; Feuerbach, 1986; Naumann, 1987; Sewall,
1988; Eschner, 1989). These rocks are characterized by low Ta
and a negative correlation between total REE concentration and
SiO_2 content. Chemical similarities between the Wilson Ridge
pluton and the River Mountain stock, a small quartz monzonite
intrusion in the vent area of the River Mountains volcano, further
strengthen the correlation (Smith, 1982; Weber and Smith,
1987). Trace and rare earth element analyses of hypabyssal dacite
from the upper plate of the Saddle Island detachment indicate a
chemical similarity to rocks of the Wilson Ridge pluton and
associated volcanic centers in the River Mountains and Hoover
Dam area (Sewall, 1988).

Based on the geochemical data summarized and cited above,
Weber and Smith (1987) proposed the existence of two coeval,
mid-Miocene compound stratovolcanoes and their associated
subjacent plutonic complexes in the south Lake Mead area. These
are the River Mountains–Hoover Dam–Boulder Wash volcanoes
and associated Wilson Ridge pluton and the McCullough-
Eldorado volcanoes and Boulder City and Nelson plutons
(Fig. 16). Any viable tectonic reconstruction of the Lake Mead–
Eldorado Valley area must honor these geochemical correlations.
As pointed out by Weber and Smith (1987), restoration of these
two volcanic centers to a position above or adjacent to their
inferred plutonic roots requires elimination of approximately
20 km of west-directed slip on combined low-angle normal and
strike-slip faults. The presence of hypabyssal dacite and diorite in

the upper plate of the Saddle Island detachment strongly suggests that the volcanic centers were displaced from their subjacent plutons by movement along low-angle faults (Weber and Smith, 1987; Sewall, 1988). The sense of movement required for this displacement is compatible with kinematic indicators within the Saddle Island detachment zone (Choukroune and Smith, 1985; Sewall, 1988; Duebendorfer and others, 1988).

AGE OF FAULTING

Principal movement along the Saddle Island detachment fault must postdate the emplacement of the Wilson Ridge pluton and associated volcanic rock suites. Existing age data are limited. Two samples of the Wilson Ridge pluton yielded K-Ar biotite dates of 15.1 and 13.6 Ma (K-Ar biotite, Anderson and others, 1972). Two felsic volcanic rocks in the River Mountains have each been dated at 13.2 Ma (K-Ar biotite; Anderson and others, 1972). The geochemically similar tuff of Hoover Dam was dated at 14.3 Ma (K-Ar biotite; Smith and others, 1990), and a dacite flow in the Boulder Wash area yielded a date of 14.2 Ma (K-Ar biotite, Thompson, 1985). A lamprophyre dike in the eastern River Mountains yielded a date of 13.4 Ma (K-Ar biotite; Sewall and Smith, 1986).

These data indicate that the Saddle Island detachment is younger than about 13.5 Ma. The upper age limit for movement is poorly constrained. The unconformable relation between the tilted River Mountains volcanics and the Muddy Creek Formation indicates that the major period of movement along the detachment must predate deposition of the Muddy Creek Formation (5 to 9 Ma).

Figure 14. Photograph showing offset of mylonitic packages by moderate-angle normal fault (heavy black line). View is to the north. Symbols: qfgn = mylonitic quartzofeldspathic gneiss, um = ultramylonitic amphibolite, my = mylonitic amphibolite. Thin black lines approximate the position of 1- to 3-m-thick, chlorite phyllonite zones that bound these packages. Compare with cross sections A-A′ and B-B′ (Fig. 8). View is approximately 150 m across.

KINEMATIC MODEL

Any model proposed to explain the varied structures and deformational fabrics exposed on Saddle Island must explain the following observations.

1. Brittlely extended surficial rocks are juxtaposed against

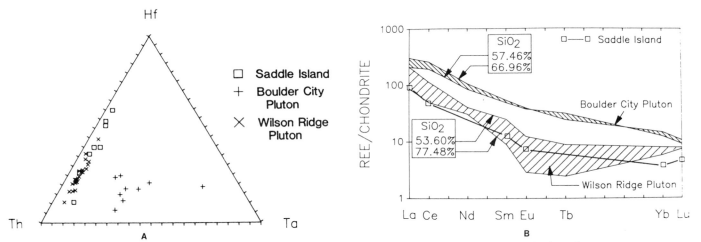

Figure 15. A. Hf-Ta-Th plot for volcanic and plutonic rocks in the Lake Mead area. Samples from the upper plate of the Saddle Island detachment (boxes) have a low Ta concentration and plot within and adjacent to the field of Wilson Ridge pluton samples. B. Chondrite-normalized rare-earth element (REE) distributions for volcanic and plutonic rocks in the Lake Mead area. Ruled areas define envelopes of chondrite-normalized REE values for Boulder City pluton (top) and Wilson Ridge pluton (bottom) for range of SiO_2 values indicated in large boxes. The REE abundance of a hypabyssal dacite from the upper plate of the Saddle Island detachment (connected small boxes) coincides closely with chondrite-normalized REE values for the Wilson Ridge pluton.

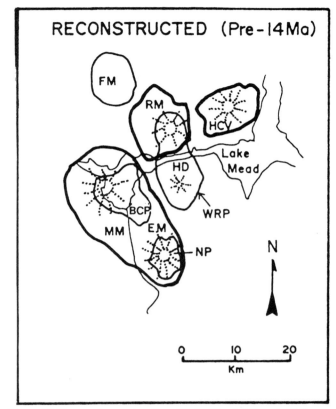

Figure 16. Proposed reconstruction of Lake Mead–Eldorado Valley area prior to mid-Miocene extension (after Weber and Smith, 1987). FM = Frenchman Mountain, RM = River Mountains, HCV = Hamblin-Cleopatra Volcano; MM = McCullough Mountains; EM = Eldorado Mountains; BCP = Boulder City pluton; NP = Nelson pluton; HD = Hoover Dam volcanic rocks; WRP = Wilson Ridge pluton.

ductilely deformed, amphibolite-grade metamorphic rocks along a 30-m-thick, low-angle, chlorite phyllonite zone.

2. Faults that separate lithologically distinct domains in the upper plate or structurally distinct domains in the lower plate are generally low angle (<20°) and anastomosing.

3. Rocks of the upper plate of the Saddle Island detachment have been correlated on the basis of petrography and major-element, trace-element, and REE geochemistry with rocks in the River Mountains and on Wilson Ridge.

4. Where kinematic data are available, all structures except the latest high-angle faults show either top-to-the-west or down-to-the-west displacement. Some high-angle faults in the upper plate of the Saddle Island detachment and in the River Mountains show down-to-the-east separation.

5. A structural sequence is observed in which brittle high-angle structures progressively overprint more ductile low-angle structures.

We suggest that the geologic relations described above are best explained by single-stage deformation along an evolving, crustal-scale, normal-sense displacement zone of simple shear (Fig. 17) (Wernicke, 1981; Wernicke and others, 1985; Spencer,

1984, 1985; Reynolds, 1985; Davis and others, 1986). The kinematic compatibility between structures formed at widely different crustal levels implies a continuum of deformation that is most easily explained by a single protracted deformational event that elevated lower-plate rocks to progressively shallower crustal levels. Quartz fabrics suggest a noncoaxial deformation path, at least locally, during mylonite development. The inferred 20-km displacement along the Saddle Island detachment argues against a model of in situ crustal extension along a subhorizontal shear zone corresponding with the "brittle-ductile" transition (e.g., Miller and others, 1983).

We argue that the rocks now exposed in the lower plate of the Saddle Island detachment originated and were deformed at moderately deep crustal levels. These rocks were drawn upward to progressively shallower crustal levels and overprinted by successively more brittle deformation. The *continuum* of retrograde assemblages and deformational fabrics argues against simple overprinting of a high-temperature fabric by a later, unrelated low-temperature event.

REGIONAL SIGNIFICANCE OF THE SADDLE ISLAND DETACHMENT

Low-angle structures preserved in north-trending horsts and grabens have been mapped east of Saddle Island (Mills, 1985; Feuerbach, 1986; Naumann, 1987; Smith and others, 1987b; Sewall, 1988; Eschner, 1989). Smith and others (1987b) suggested that the low-angle faults may be related to the Saddle Island detachment.

A geological transect from Las Vegas Valley to Detrital Wash (Smith and others, 1987b) shows that the north-trending horsts and grabens are the major structural features east of Saddle Island and south of the Lake Mead fault zone (Fig. 18). The faults that bound these blocks terminate against strike-slip faults of the Lake Mead fault zone. Isolated klippen of steeply dipping Paleozoic and Tertiary(?) sedimentary rocks and Tertiary plutonic rocks crop out within the horst and graben terrane. The klippen are bounded below by low-angle faults that place Precambrian, Paleozoic, or Tertiary rocks over Precambrian basement and/or Tertiary plutonic rocks. These areas are described below.

Petroglyph Wash klippen

Within the north-trending Gilbert Canyon–Petroglyph Wash graben (Figs. 18, 19) are two klippen bounded below by a low-angle normal fault, the Petroglyph Wash fault. This fault places steeply dipping Paleozoic rocks in its hanging wall on Precambrian crystalline basement and highly altered, brecciated rocks of the Wilson Ridge pluton.

The northern klippe is composed entirely of the Mississippian Monte Cristo Formation. The southern klippe is divided into two structural domains by a low-angle fault that lies above the Petroglyph Wash fault. The upper domain contains Monte Cristo Formation that dips moderately southwest; the lower domain

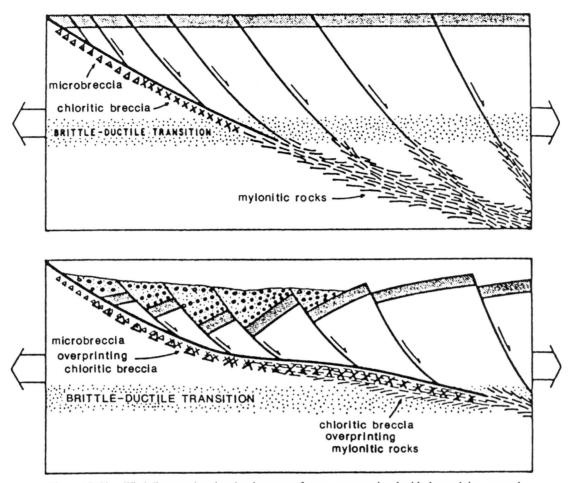

Figure 17. Simplified diagram showing development of structures associated with the evolving, normal-displacement shear zone model (modified after Reynolds, 1985).

contains Cambrian Tapeats quartzite, Bright Angel (Pioche) Shale, and Lyndon Limestone that is locally overturned 60 to 70° southwest. Both the Petroglyph Wash fault and the structurally higher low-angle fault strike north-northwest and dip about 25° to the east. Striae on the Petroglyph Wash fault trend S30°E. Drag folds within the Lyndon Limestone suggest westward motion of the upper domain. Low-angle faults associated with this system are commonly truncated by high-angle normal faults, and the western boundary of the klippe is a high-angle normal fault (Fig. 19).

Klippen are juxtaposed on Precambrian hornblende gneiss and megacrystic granite along a brittle, low-angle fault. Granitic rocks of the Wilson Ridge pluton, also present beneath the klippen, are intensely brecciated and display intense ferric and argillic alteration.

At the Cohenour Mine, 2 km southeast of the Petroglyph Wash klippen, fault-bounded wedges that contain steeply dipping Paleozoic rocks—including Tapeats quartzite, Bright Angel (Pioche) Shale, and Bonanza King Formation and conglomerate—as well as sandstone and siltstone of Tertiary age(?), are intruded by dikes related to the Wilson Ridge pluton (Eschner, 1989). A block of granite megabreccia occurs within the Tertiary (?) section. This sequence is lithologically similar to sedimentary rocks in the upper plate of the Saddle Island detachment that have been correlated with the Miocene Horse Spring Formation (Sewall, 1988; Sewall and Smith, 1988; Eschner, 1989). The nature of the basal contact of this klippe(?) is not clear.

Boulder Wash–Flamingo Cove

In the Boulder Wash–Flamingo Cove area just north of Boulder Canyon (Fig. 1), a low-angle fault zone is exposed within a triangular horst (Naumann, 1987). The zone consists of east-striking, north-dipping low-angle faults that juxtapose plates of Precambrian, Paleozoic, and Tertiary rocks. At Boulder Wash, the basal low-angle fault places Cambrian Bonanza King Formation (dipping 70° north) on Precambrian gneiss. At Flamingo Cove, at least two low-angle faults bound plates of Tapeats quartzite, Bright Angel (Pioche) Shale, and Bonanza King Formation. Low-angle faults are cut by high-angle faults. At Flamingo Cove, Bonanza King Formation in the hanging wall of a low-angle fault is offset by at least 20 down-to-the-west high-angle faults. No one fault has a displacement of more than 10 m, but total displacement is about 200 m.

Arch Mountain

The summit of Arch Mountain is capped by a klippe of Precambrian gneiss intruded by monzodiorite and quartz monzonite of the Tertiary Wilson Ridge pluton (Eschner and Smith, 1988, Eschner, 1989). A low-angle fault (the Arch Mountain fault) separates the klippe from Wilson Ridge quartz monzonite in the lower plate. The lower plate contains numerous west-dipping, low-angle faults that are coplanar with the Arch Mountain fault. Offset mafic dikes indicate top-to-the-west displacement along these lower-plate faults (Eschner, 1989). Low-angle normal faults are cut and rotated by high-angle normal faults that bound the Arch Mountain horst (Fig. 18) (Eschner, 1989).

James Bay

A subhorizontal set of basalt and lamprophyre dikes intrudes hypabyssal quartz monzonite of the Wilson Ridge pluton at James Bay (Fig. 18) (Feuerbach, 1986). Dike emplacement appears to have been controlled by a set of low-angle faults. Dikes strike north to northwest and dip gently to the west. Many of the dikes are sheared along their margins, which suggests that faulting continued after dike emplacement.

Do the klippen represent the eastward continuation of the Saddle Island Detachment?

There are many similarities between features in the upper plate of the Saddle Island detachment and many of the klippen. These include:

1. Rock types in the upper plates of the klippen are similar to those identified at Saddle Island. Steeply dipping Paleozoic rocks occur in the Petroglyph Wash, Cohenour Mine, and Boulder Wash–Flamingo Cove klippen. The Tertiary(?) conglomerate present at the Cohenour Mine may correlate with the Horse Spring Formation that occurs in the upper plate of the Saddle Island detachment. Both the rocks of the klippen and rocks in the upper plate of the Saddle Island detachment are commonly cut by quartz monzonite dikes of the Wilson Ridge pluton.

2. Klippen in the Petroglyph Wash area and on Arch Mountain are displaced to the west. The sense of movement of the other klippen is unknown.

3. In all areas, low-angle faults that bound the klippen are cut by north- or northwest-trending high-angle normal faults.

Based on these similarities, we speculate that the klippen may represent the eastward extension of the Saddle Island detachment, as first proposed by Smith and others (1987b). In the Arch Mountain–Wilson Ridge area, the postulated eastward extension of the Saddle Island fault places upper-plate rocks on *brittlely deformed* Precambrian basement and brecciated Wilson Ridge pluton. To the west, the fault places upper-plate rocks on *mylonitic* Precambrian basement. The lack of detachment-related mylonitic fabric in rocks exposed beneath the klippen can be explained by eastward shallowing of the detachment structure. This change in deformational style of lower-plate rock from east to west is consistent with models of evolving, crustal-scale shear zones described by Spencer (1984, 1985), Reynolds (1985), Wernicke and others (1985), and Davis and others (1986). These models suggest that in the direction of dip of the detachment, upper-plate rocks should be superimposed on progressively deeper-level, lower-plate rocks.

Both the upper and lower plates of the Saddle Island detachment are cut by numerous north- to northwest-trending high-angle normal faults. These faults may be related to a deeper and younger detachment structure; however, no exposure of this inferred fault has been located.

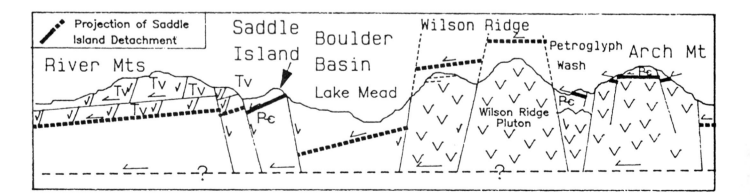

Figure 18. Transect from Las Vegas (west) to Detrital Valley (east) showing horst and graben structure south of Lake Mead. Saddle Island detachment and possible eastern extensions shown in heavy solid and broken line, respectively (after Smith and others, 1987b).

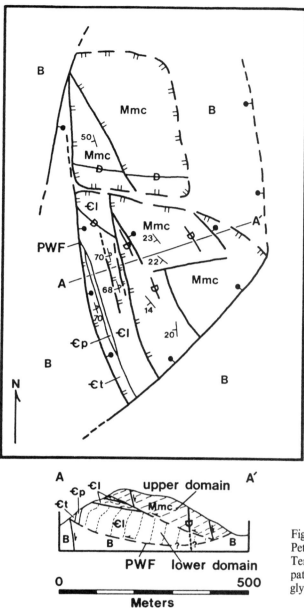

EXPLANATION

Upper Plate

Mmc Monte Cristo Formation
Bedding shown in section only.

$\in$l Lyndon Limestone

$\in$p Pioche Shale

$\in$t Tapeats Sandstone

Lower Plate

B Precambrian gneiss and schist intruded by Tertiary Wilson Ridge pluton.

Fault (ball on downthrown side, dashed where approximately located)

Low-angle normal fault (bars point toward upper plate)

Dike

Contact

23 Strike and dip of bedding

70 Strike and dip of overturned bedding

Figure 19. Geologic map and cross section of the Petroglyph Wash area (see Fig. 1 for location). Tv = Tertiary volcanic rocks: p$\in$ = Precambrian rocks: V pattern = Tertiary plutonic rocks. PWF = Petroglyph Wash fault (after Feuerbach, 1986).

Igneous activity related to the emplacement of the Wilson Ridge pluton appears to have essentially terminated before the onset of detachment faulting. Brittle deformation of the pluton indicates that it was entirely crystallized and "cold" at the time of deformation. Individual Wilson Ridge intrusions (except for dikes at James Bay) are roughly plug shaped or cylindrical, not sheet-like or dike-like, as would be expected if intrusion occurred during regional deformation. Mid-Tertiary intrusions do not cut the detachment surface, but a small volume of intrusive rock in both the upper and lower plates either intrudes or cuts low-angle faults. Many of these dikes are sheared. Therefore, minor igneous activity related to emplacement of the Wilson Ridge pluton may have occurred during and after the formation of the Saddle Island structure.

ACKNOWLEDGMENTS

The regional interpretation presented in this paper was based in part on the work and suggestions of Ed Eschner, Dan Feuerbach, and Terry Naumann. We gratefully acknowledge their contributions to this paper. Comments by Stephen J. Reynolds and an anonymous reviewer substantially improved the manuscript. Ed Thomas and Charlynn Jeffrey assisted with the drafting. Access to the island was granted by the Southern Nevada Water System and Basic Management, Inc. We also thank the Lake Mead National Recreation Area for their cooperation in issuing rock sample collecting permits.

This research was supported in part by American Chemical Society Petroleum Research Fund grant #ACS-PRF 20611-GB2 and by a grant from the University Research Council of the University of Nevada, Las Vegas. We thank the staff of the Phoenix Memorial Laboratory, University of Michigan, for completing the REE analyses. Support by the Department of Energy to the Phoenix Memorial Laboratory through the University Research Reactor Assistance Program and Reactor Facility Cost Sharing Program provided funding for these analyses.

REFERENCES CITED

Anderson, R. E., 1971, Thin skin distension in Tertiary rocks of southeastern Nevada: Geological Society of America Bulletin, v. 82, p. 42–58.

Anderson, R. E., Longwell, C. R., Armstrong, R. L., and Marvin, R. F., 1972, Significance of K-Ar ages of Tertiary rocks from the Lake Mead region, Nevada-Arizona: Geological Society of America Bulletin, v. 83, p. 273–287.

Armstrong, R. L., 1982, Cordilleran metamorphic core complexes; From Arizona to southern Canada: Annual Review of Earth and Planetary Sciences, v. 10, p. 129–154.

Bouchez, J., 1977, Plastic deformation of quartzites at low temperatures in an area of natural strain gradient: Tectonophysics, v. 39, p. 25–50.

Bouchez, J. L., Lister, G. S., and Nicholas, A., 1983, Fabric asymmetry and shear sense in movement zones: Geologische Rundschau, v. 72, p. 401–419.

Bryant, B., and Reed, J. C., 1969, Significance of lineation and minor folds near major thrust faults in the southern Appalachians and the British and Norwegian Caledonides: Geological Magazine, v. 106, p. 412–429.

Choukroune, P., and Smith, E. I., 1985, Detachment faulting and its relationship to older structural events on Saddle Island, River Mountains, Clark County, Nevada: Geology, v. 13, p. 421–424.

Coney, P. J., 1980, Cordilleran metamorphic core complexes; An overview *in* Crittenden, M. D., Jr., Coney, P. J., and Davis, G. H., eds., Cordilleran metamorphic core complexes: Geological Society of America Memoir 153, p. 7–31.

Crittenden, M. D., Jr., Coney, P. J., and Davis, G. H., eds., 1980, Cordilleran metamorphic core complexes: Geological Society of America Memoir 153, 490 p.

Davis, G. A., Anderson, J. L., Martin, D. L., Frost, E. G., and Armstrong, R. L., 1982, Geologic and geochronologic relations in the lower plate of the Whipple detachment fault, Whipple Mountains, southeastern California; A progress report, *in* Frost, E. G., and Martin, D. L., eds., Mesozoic and Cenozoic tectonic evolution of the Colorado River region, California, Arizona, Nevada: San Diego, California, Cordilleran Publishing, p. 408–432.

Davis, G. A., Lister, G. S., and Reynolds, S. J., 1986, Structural evolution of the Whipple and South Mountains shear zones, southwestern United States: Geology, v. 14, p. 7–10.

Duebendorfer, E. M., Sewall, A. J., and Smith, E. I., 1988, Kinematic interpretation of lower-plate mylonites, Saddle Island detachment complex, Lake Mead, Nevada: Geological Society of America Abstracts with Programs, v. 20, p. 157.

Eaton, G. P., 1982, The Basin and Range Province; Origin and tectonic significance: Annual Review of Earth and Planetary Sciences, v. 10, p. 409–440.

Escher, A., and Watterson, J., 1974, Stretching fabrics, folds, and crustal shortening: Tectonophysics, v. 22, p. 223–231.

Eschner, E., 1989, The geology and structural significance of the Arch Mountain area, northwestern Mohave County, Arizona [M.S. thesis]: Las Vegas, University of Nevada, 105 p.

Eschner, E., and Smith, E. I., 1988, Geometry of mid-Tertiary normal faults in the Arch Mountain area of the northern Black Mountains, Mohave County, northwest Arizona: Geological Society of America Abstracts with Programs, v. 20, p. 159.

Faulds, J. E., Mawer, C. K., and Geissman, J. W., 1987, Possible modes of deformation along "accommodation zones" in rifted continental crust: Geo-logical Society of America Abstracts with Programs, v. 19, p. 659.

Faulds, J. E., Hillemeyer, F. L., and Smith, E. I., 1988, Geometry and kinematics of a Miocene "accommodation zone" in the central Black and southern Eldorado Mountains, Arizona and Nevada, *in* Weide, D. L., and Faber, M. L., eds., This extended land; Geological Society of America Field Trip Guidebook, Cordilleran Section Meeting, Las Vegas, Nevada: University of Nevada at Las Vegas Department of Geoscience Special Publication 2, p. 293–310.

Feuerbach, D. L., 1986, Geology of the Wilson Ridge pluton; A mid-Miocene quartz monzonite intrusion in the northern Black Mountains, Mohave County, Arizona and Clark County, Nevada [M.S. thesis]: Las Vegas, University of Nevada, 79 p.

Frost, E. G., and Martin, D. L., eds., 1982, Mesozoic–Cenozoic tectonic evolution of the Colorado River region, California, Arizona, and Nevada (Anderson-Hamilton Volume): San Diego, California, Cordilleran Publishers, 608 p.

Hansen, E., 1971, Strain facies: London, George, Allen and Unwin Ltd., 207 p.

Hardy, J. K., 1986, Stratigraphy and depositional environments of lower and middle Cambrian strata in the Lake Mead region, southern Nevada and northwestern Arizona [M.S. thesis]: Las Vegas, University of Nevada, 309 p.

Jensen, L. N., and Starkey, J., 1985, Plagioclase microfabrics in a ductile shear zone from the Jotun Nappe, Norway: Journal of Structural Geology, v. 7, p. 527–539.

Lister, G. S., and Price, G. P., 1978, Fabric development in a quartz-feldspar mylonite: Tectonophysics, v. 49, p. 37–78.

Lister, G. S., and Snoke, A. W., 1984, S-C mylonites: Journal of Structural Geology, v. 6, p. 617–638.

Lister, G. S., and Williams, P. F., 1979, Fabric development in shear zones; Theoretical controls and observed phenomenon: Journal of Structural Geology, v. 1, p. 283–297.

Longwell, C. R., 1936, Geology of the Boulder Reservoir floor, Arizona–Nevada: Geological Society of America Bulletin, v. 47, p. 1393–1476.

Miller, E. L., Gans, P. B., and Garing, J., 1983, The Snake Range décollement; An exhumed mid-Tertiary ductile-brittle transition: Tectonics, v. 2, p. 239–263.

Mills, J. G., 1985, The geology and geochemistry of volcanic and plutonic rocks in the Hoover Dam 7½' Quadrangle, Clark County, Nevada and Mohave County, Arizona [M.S. thesis]: Las Vegas, University of Nevada, 119 p.

Naumann, T. R., 1987, Geology of the central Boulder Canyon Quadrangle, Clark County, Nevada [M.S. thesis]: Las Vegas, University of Nevada, 68 p.

Reynolds, S. J., 1985, Geology of the South Mountains, central Arizona: Arizona Bureau of Geology and Mineral Technology Bulletin 195, 61 p.

Sanderson, D. J., 1973, The development of fold axes oblique to the regional trend: Tectonophysics, v. 16, p. 55–70.

Sewall, A., 1988, Structure and geochemistry of the upper plate of the Saddle Island detachment, Lake Mead, Nevada [M.S. thesis]: Las Vegas, University of Nevada, 84 p.

Sewall, A. J., and Smith, E. I., 1986, The Saddle Island detachment fault, Lake Mead, Nevada; Upper plate geology and regional significance: Geological Society of America Abstracts with Programs, v. 18, p. 182.

——, 1988, Regional correlation and significance of a Tertiary fanglomerate in the upper plate of the Saddle Island detachment, Lake Mead, Nevada: Geological Society of America Abstracts with Programs, v. 20, p. 230.

Sibson, R. H., 1977, Fault rocks and fault mechanisms: Journal of the Geological Society of London, v. 133, p. 191–213.

Simpson, C., and Schmid, S. M., 1983, An evaluation of criteria to determine the sense of movement in sheared rocks: Geological Society of America Bulletin, v. 94, p. 1281–1288.

Smith, E. I., 1982, Geology and geochemistry of the volcanic rocks in the River Mountains, Clark County, Nevada, and comparisons with volcanic rocks in nearby areas, *in* Frost, E. G., and Martin, D. L., eds., Mesozoic–Cenozoic tectonic evolution of the Colorado River region, California, Arizona and Nevada: San Diego, California, Cordilleran Publishers, p. 41–54.

——, 1984, Geological map of the Boulder Beach Quadrangle, Nevada: Nevada Bureau of Mines and Geology Map 81, scale 1:24,000.

Smith, E. I., Schmidt, C. S., and Weber, M. E., 1986, Mid-Tertiary volcanic rocks of the McCullough Range, Clark County, Nevada: Geological Society of America Abstracts with Programs, v. 18, p. 187.

Smith, E. I., Anderson, R. E., Bohannon, R. G., and Axen, G., 1987a, Miocene extension, volcanism, and sedimentation in the eastern Basin and Range province, southern Nevada, *in* Davis, G. H., and Vanden Dolder, E. M., eds., Geologic diversity of Arizona and its margins; Excursions to choice areas; Geological Society of America 100th Annual Meeting Guidebook: Golden, Colorado School of Mines, p. 383–397.

Smith, E. I., Eschner, E., Feuerbach, D. L., Naumann, T. R., and Sewall, A., 1987b, Mid-Tertiary extension in the eastern Basin and Range province, Nevada and Arizona; The Las Vegas Valley–Detrital Wash transect: Geological Society of America Abstracts with Programs, v. 19, p. 848–849.

Smith, E. I., Feuerbach, D. L., Naumann, T. R., and Mills, J. G., 1990, Mid-Miocene volcanic and plutonic rocks in the Lake Mead area of Nevada and Arizona; Production of intermediate igneous rocks in an extensional environment, *in* Anderson, J. L., ed., Nature and origin of Cordilleran magmatism: Geological Society of America Memoir 174 (in press).

Spencer, J. E., 1984, Role of tectonic denudation in warping and uplift of low-angle normal faults: Geology, v. 12, p. 95–98.

—— , 1985, Miocene low-angle normal faulting and dike emplacement, Homer Mountains and surrounding areas, southeastern California and southernmost Nevada: Geological Society of America Bulletin, v. 96, p. 1140–1155.

Thompson, K. G., 1985, Stratigraphy and petrology of the Hamblin–Cleopatra volcano, Clark County, Nevada [M.S. thesis]: Austin, University of Texas, 306 p.

Tullis, J., and Yund, R. A., 1985, Dynamic recrystallization of feldspar; A mechanism for ductile shear zone formation: Geology, v. 13, p. 238–241.

Weber, M. E., and Smith, E. I., 1987, Structural and geochemical constraints on the reassembly mid-Tertiary volcanoes in the Lake Mead area of southern Nevada: Geology, v. 15, p. 553–556.

Wernicke, B., 1981, Low-angle normal faults in the Basin and Range province; Nappe tectonics in an extending orogen: Nature, v. 291, p. 645–648.

Wernicke, B., Walker, J. D., and Beaufait, M. S., 1985, Structural discordance between Neogene detachments and frontal Sevier thrusts, central Mormon Mountains, southern Nevada: Tectonics, v. 4, p. 213–246.

White, S. A., 1976, The effects of strain on the microstructures, fabrics, and deformation mechanisms in quartzites: Philosophical Transactions of the Royal Society of London, series A, v. 283, p. 69–86.

Williams, P. F., and Swart, H. J., 1977, A model for the development of the Seve-Koli Caledonian Nappe Complex, *in* Saxena, S. K., and Bhattacharji, S., eds., Energetics of geological processes: New York, Springer-Verlag, p. 170–187.

Wilson, C.J.L., 1975, Preferred orientation in quartz ribbon mylonites: Geological Society of America Bulletin, v. 86, p. 968–974.

Wust, S. L., 1986, Regional correlation of extension directions in Cordilleran metamorphic core complexes: Geology, v. 14, p. 828–830.

MANUSCRIPT ACCEPTED BY THE SOCIETY AUGUST 21, 1989

Geological Society of America
Memoir 176
1990

Chapter 5

Sedimentologic and stratigraphic constraints on the Neogene translation and rotation of the Frenchman Mountain structural block, Clark County, Nevada

Stephen M. Rowland, Joseph R. Parolini*, Edward Eschner*, Alonzo J. McAllister
Department of Geoscience, University of Nevada, Las Vegas, Nevada 89154
Jonathan A. Rice
Department of Geology, University of Nebraska, Lincoln, Nebraska 68508

ABSTRACT

The Frenchman Mountain structural block lies near the intersection of a right-lateral strike-slip fault, a left-lateral strike-slip fault, and a regionally significant low-angle normal fault. It has commonly been presumed that this block was translated several tens of kilometers northwestward or southwestward during Basin and Range extension, but the details of this translation have not been rigorously examined. Although it is not yet possible to reconstruct the detailed histories of the individual faults that were involved in the translation of the Frenchman Mountain block, the determination of the net translational and rotational history of this block can be used to evaluate the relative importance of various types of faulting during extension of the Lake Mead region.

The Frenchman Mountain block contains a thick section of Paleozoic, Mesozoic, and Miocene strata, including the syntectonic Miocene Horse Spring Formation. Comparisons of clast compositions in the breccias of the Thumb Member of the Horse Spring Formation with various areas of exposed Precambrian basement indicate that the Gold Butte granite complex, 65 km to the east, is the only viable presently exposed source area for these breccias.

Sedimentology of the Thumb Member indicates that this unit was deposited in proximal and medial alluvial fan settings. Channel orientation and facies relations indicate a transport direction of N60W ± 30°. Two-meter clasts and the presence of distinctly channelized, matrix-supported breccia indicate that these sediments were deposited no farther than 5 km from their source. Large blocks up to 100 m long and 20 m thick in southern Rainbow Gardens were translated no farther than a few hundred meters. We conclude that the pre-extension position of the Frenchman Mountain block was probably on the western or northwestern margin of the Gold Butte granite complex, directly adjacent to the Gold Butte fault. This reconstruction requires that a fault exists on the southern boundary of Rainbow Gardens roughly beneath Las Vegas Wash.

Pennsylvanian eolian cross-bed orientations at Frenchman Mountain are identical

---

*Present address: Lockheed Engineering and Science Co., 1050 E. Flamingo Road, Las Vegas, Nevada 89119.

Rowland, S. M., Parolini, J. R., Eschner, E., McAllister, A. J., and Rice, J. A., 1990, Sedimentologic and stratigraphic constraints on the Neogene translation and rotation of the Frenchman Mountain structural block, Clark County, Nevada, *in* Wernicke, B. P., ed., Basin and Range extensional tectonics near the latitude of Las Vegas, Nevada: Boulder, Colorado, Geological Society of America Memoir 176.

to those in the Gold Butte area. This suggests that no significant tectonic rotation accompanied the westward translation of the Frenchman Mountain block.

As an independent test of Frenchman Mountain's preextension position we have compared the thicknesses and facies of Cambrian and Devonian strata in the Frenchman Mountain block with those in the eastern Lake Mead region. These Paleozoic data indicate a preextension position in the northeastern part of the Lake Mead area, thus supporting the interpretation that the block originally lay adjacent to the Gold Butte granite complex.

Considering all available Paleozoic and Miocene sedimentologic and stratigraphic data, and assuming that the Gold Butte granite complex itself experienced about 10 km of westward translation, our restoration vector for the Frenchman Mountain block relative to the Colorado Plateau has a magnitude of 80 ± 8 km and a bearing of N80E ± 5°.

The documentation of 80 ± 8 km of translation and associated stratal tilting, with no significant tectonic rotation, indicates that detachment faulting has been the dominant Neogene deformational process in the Lake Mead region.

INTRODUCTION

The Frenchman Mountain structural block lies along the eastern margin of Las Vegas Valley (Figs. 1, 2). It consists of east-dipping Paleozoic, Mesozoic, and Miocene strata and underlying Precambrian crystalline basement (Longwell and others, 1965; Rowland, 1987). Because of evidence discussed below, it has become well accepted that this structural block experienced significant Cenozoic translation during Basin and Range extension (Anderson, 1973; Bohannon, 1984; Longwell, 1974; Wernicke and others, 1988). However, the magnitude and direction of this translation have been disputed. The kinematic history of this particular block is of special interest because it lies near the intersection of the Las Vegas Valley shear zone and the Lake Mead fault system (Fig. 2), the histories and interactions of which are not well understood. The Frenchman Mountain block also probably lies in the upper plate of a detachment fault exposed on Saddle Island (Fig. 2), and the detailed relation between this detachment fault and the strike-slip faults is not understood. Thus, determining the kinematic history of the Frenchman Mountain structural block is an important step in reconstructing the tectonic history of southern Nevada. Furthermore, for the purpose of kinematic analysis, the Frenchman Mountain block contains abundant and diverse rock units that can be compared with correlative units in other displaced blocks and on the unextended Colorado Plateau.

Longwell (1971, 1974) was the first to propose that Frenchman Mountain experienced significant Cenozoic displacement. He described rapakivi-granite megabreccias in the area called Rainbow Gardens, in the eastern portion of the Frenchman Mountain structural block (Fig. 2). The breccia-bearing beds are now included in the Thumb Member of the Horse Spring Formation (Bohannon, 1984).

Longwell (1951) originally described the Thumb Member breccias in a paper concerned with sedimentation downslope from major normal faults. Attempting to explain the lack of an obvious nearby source for the breccias, Longwell suggested that a former highland of Precambrian basement might now lie concealed beneath extensive Tertiary volcanic rocks to the south of the Frenchman Mountain. Twenty years later he revised his interpretation, concluding that the source was the Gold Butte granite complex 65 km to the east (Longwell, 1971, 1974). As shown in Figure 2, Longwell's 1974 interpretation involved the following events. (1) The Thumb Member megabreccias were eroded from the Gold Butte granite complex and transported south across a postulated southeastern extension of the Las Vegas Valley shear zone. (2) After deposition, right-lateral strike-slip faulting on this postulated fault translated these deposits to the northwest. (3) Subsequent left-lateral strike-slip faulting of the Lake Mead fault system offset the Las Vegas Valley shear zone and moved Frenchman Mountain to its present position.

Longwell's structural interpretation was not supported by Anderson (1973), who concluded that no southeastern extension of the Las Vegas Valley shear zone exists in the region proposed by Longwell. Contrary to Longwell, Anderson concluded that the source of the breccias was probably to the south and that Frenchman Mountain's original position was probably about 56 to 64 km to the east-northeast of its present position. Additional mapping by Bohannon (1979, 1983) supported the interpretations of Anderson. Bohannon (1984) concluded that Frenchman's Mountain's preextension position was north of the town of Overton, about 65 km northeast of its present position; it was translated to its present position by left-lateral strike-slip faulting of the Lake Mead fault system (Fig. 2).

It is implicit in Longwell's model that: (1) the Las Vegas Valley shear zone originally extended as far east as the Gold Butte area, (2) right-lateral strike-slip faulting was important in the Lake Mead region during the initial stage of extension, and (3) the left-lateral strike-slip faulting of the Lake Mead fault zone is superimposed on this right-lateral system. The Anderson-Bohannon model, on the other hand, includes no important component of right-lateral strike-slip faulting in the Lake Mead area.

Figure 1. Oblique aerial photograph of Frenchman Mountain looking northeast. Las Vegas Valley is on the left, and northern Rainbow Gardens is on the far right. A detailed stratigraphic column of Cambrian through Devonian strata is provided in Plate 1. 1—base of Cambrian section where Tapeats Sandstone lies on Precambrian crystalline basement; 2—base of Bonanza King (= Muav) Formation; 3—top of Papoose Lake Member of Bonanza King Formation (top of Muav 2 of this chapter); 4—base of Muav 6 of this chapter; 5—base of Sultan Formation; 6—base of Crystal Pass Limestone, which here is completely dolomitized; 7—base of Dawn Member of Monte Cristo Formation; 8—base of Pennsylvanian Callville Limestone; 9—base of dark, desert-varnish–coated, eolian cross-bedded beds in Callville Limestone.

Both Anderson (1973) and Bohannon (1984) considered normal faults in the Lake Mead region to be genetically related to strike-slip faults.

A new development has been the recognition of detachment faulting in the Lake Mead region (Choukroune and Smith, 1985; Weber and Smith, 1987; Smith and others, 1987; Eschner and Smith, 1988; Sewall and Smith, 1988; Duebendorfer and others, this volume). The relative importance of detachment faulting versus strike-slip faulting in the Lake Mead area has become a contentious issue. Ron and others (1986) concluded that strike-slip faulting was the dominant late Neogene deformational process along the Lake Mead fault system (see also Nur and others, 1987), whereas Guth and Smith (1987) consider strike-slip faulting to be associated with, but subordinate to, regional detachment faulting.

The purpose of this chapter is to reconstruct as precisely as possible the translational and rotational history of the French-

man Mountain structural block. We are concerned here with the Frenchman Mountain block as a unit, not with differential motion on separate fault blocks within this unit. Although it is not yet possible to completely reconstruct the detailed history of Neogene faulting in southern Nevada, by reconstructing the kinematic history of one important block we will evaluate the relative importance of strike-slip versus normal faulting in the Lake Mead region.

SOURCE OF THE THUMB MEMBER BRECCIAS

The Horse Spring Formation is a sequence of Miocene nonmarine siliciclastic and carbonate sediments that occurs in the Rainbow Gardens area of the Frenchman Mountain block (Figs. 2, 3) and throughout the Lake Mead region. These sediments are interpreted to have been deposited in basins created by Basin and Range extension (Bohannon, 1984; Salyards and Shoemaker,

1987). The entire Horse Spring Formation is more than 2,000 m thick and was divided by Bohannon (1984) into four members. The Thumb Member is the thickest (about 850 m in the Rainbow Gardens area) and consists of a basal conglomerate overlain by interbedded sandstone and breccia (Fig. 4).

The breccias of the Thumb Member in the Rainbow Gardens area have figured prominently in discussions of Frenchman Mountain's tectonic history. Longwell (1971, 1974), Anderson (1973), and Bohannon (1984) all presumed that the source of the breccias was the Gold Butte granite complex (Fig. 2). Schmitt (1984) challenged the view that this was the only possible source area. He interpreted the breccias to be debris flows that were deposited on the proximal part of an alluvial fan, and he pointed to a reported discovery of rapakivi granite on Saddle Island, a few kilometers south of Rainbow Gardens (Fig. 2). This, together with an inferred north-flowing paleocurrent, led Schmitt to reject the necessity of a distant source area; the source area might be very close but partially or completely buried. This interpretation by Schmitt is virtually identical to Longwell's (1951) original interpretation. Schmitt and Rice (1988) then suggested that the source of the breccias was the northern Black Mountains (see Fig. 6), uplifted along the Lake Mead fault system.

To more rigorously evaluate the significance of the Thumb Member breccias, we have compared the clast composition of these breccias with the lithologies exposed in significant candidate source areas in the Lake Mead region. We identified five candidate source areas: (1) the Frenchman Mountain basement complex, (2) Saddle Island, (3) the Eldorado-Newberry Mountains, (4) the northern Black Mountains, and (5) the Gold Butte granite complex. (See Fig. 6, which shows the locations of these areas

and summarizes the lithologies present as well as those in the breccias of the Rainbow Gardens area.) First we will describe the Thumb Member breccias, and then we will examine the possible source areas.

Clast composition of the Thumb Member breccias

The base of the Thumb Member is defined by a prominent, ridge-forming conglomerate in which sedimentary clasts are common and plutonic and metamorphic clasts are rare (Fig. 4). Above this basal conglomerate are several lenticular bodies of matrix-supported breccia interbedded with red sandstone. In sharp contrast to the basal conglomerate, the breccia clasts at most localities consist exclusively of plutonic and metamorphic rocks (Fig. 4).

Parolini (1986) conducted a detailed sedimentological study of the breccias in the Rainbow Gardens area at the numbered sites shown in Figure 3. He interpreted the breccias to be debris-flow deposits in an alluvial fan sequence, as Schmitt (1984) had previously suggested. Based on clast composition and relative position, Parolini identified five distinct stratigraphic intervals within the Thumb Member in which breccias occur. These are lithofacies A through E in Figure 4. Distribution of clast compositions within a single lithofacies can be quite variable from one locality to another. Figure 4 summarizes the stratigraphic position and composite composition of clasts within each lithofacies.

Based on hand-specimen identification, twenty-seven distinct plutonic and metamorphic rock types were recognized in the breccias (Table 1). The "R" numbers (for Rainbow Gardens) listed for each rock type in Table 1 will be used throughout the

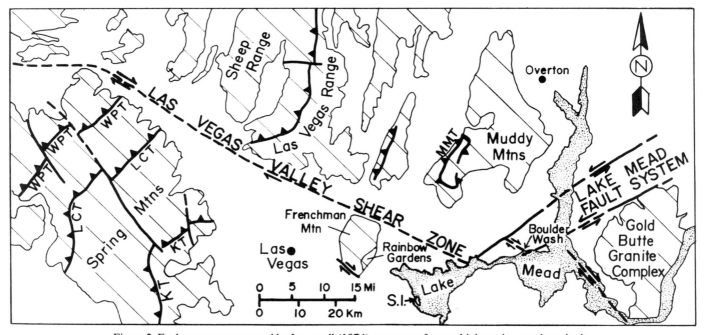

Figure 2. Fault geometry proposed by Longwell (1974) to account for rapakivi-granite megabreccias in Rainbow Gardens. LCT = Lee Canyon Thrust. MMT = Muddy Mountains Thrust. SI = Saddle Island. WPT = Wheeler Pass Thrust.

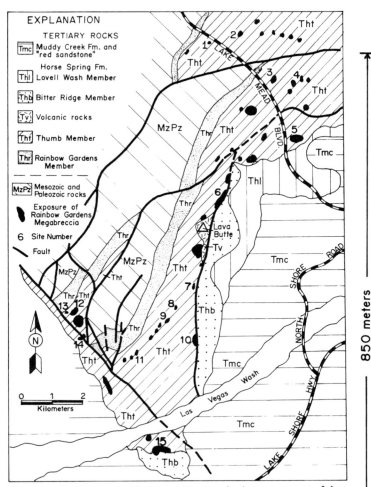

Figure 3. Geologic map of Rainbow Gardens in the eastern part of the Frenchman Mountain structural block. After Bohannon (1984), Brenner-Tourtelot (1979), and Parolini (1986). Numbered sites are those investigated by Parolini (1986). A field guide to site 3 is provided by Salyards and Shoemaker (1987).

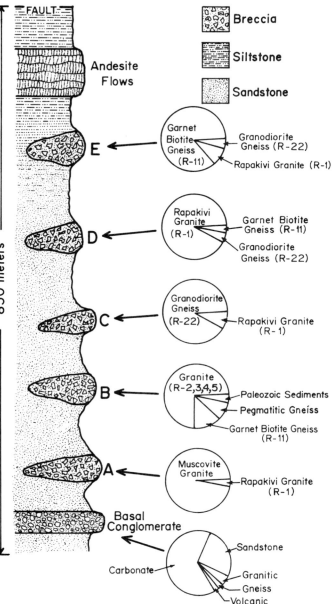

Figure 4. Generalized stratigraphic column of the Thumb Member of the Horse Spring Formation in the Rainbow Gardens area, showing clast composition of breccia and conglomerate beds. Letters A through E identify the five lithofacies of breccia described by Parolini (1986). "R" numbers refer to lithologies listed in Table 1. Circular histograms of the five breccia intervals are composites of all sites studied by Parolini. Not all breccia lithofacies are exposed at any one locality, and the relative position of each lithofacies in the column is diagrammatic. Clast composition in the basal conglomerate is from Bohannon (1984, Fig. 10, locality 7). The total thickness of the Thumb Member is at least 850 m, but everywhere its top is faulted (Bohannon, 1984).

following discussion of provenance. Modal analyses were done on thin sections and slabs of the most common rock types (Fig. 5).

The preliminary work of Longwell (1974) and Bohannon (1984) incorrectly indicated that in the Rainbow Gardens area the Thumb Member breccia clasts are all rapakivi granite. As shown in Figure 4, this is clearly not the case. Many lithologies occur in varying abundances at different sites and different stratigraphic levels. For example, breccias at site 1 (Fig. 3), which is one of the most accessible, consist of 81 percent rapakivi granite and 19 percent granodiorite gneiss. These are in lithofacies D, which is the only lithofacies that contains abundant rapakivi granite (Fig. 4); the locality sampled by Bohannon (1984, Fig. 10, his locality 8) is probably in this lithofacies. Site 3, a short distance away from site 1 (Fig. 3), is in lithofacies B, a unit that contains no rapakivi granite at all (Fig. 4).

Let us now examine each of the five possible source areas and compare the exposed lithologies with the clasts in the Thumb Member breccias (Fig. 6).

TABLE 1. LITHOLOGIES IDENTIFIED IN THE THUMB MEMBER BRECCIAS IN THE RAINBOW GARDENS AREA

Reference Number	Lithology
R-1	Biotite perthite rapakivi granite
R-2	Alkali gneissoid granite
R-3	Gneissoid granite
R-4	Muscovite granite
R-5	Aplite
R-6	Biotite hornblende schist
R-7	Biotite schist
R-8	Hornblende schist
R-9	Chlorite schist
R-10	Mica schist
R-11	Garnet biotite gneiss
R-12	Monzodiorite
R-13	Tonalite
R-14	Microcline perthite alkali granite gneiss
R-15	Leucocratic granite gneiss
R-16	Quartz diorite (low garnet) gneiss
R-17	Granophyric alkali granite gneiss
R-18	Hornblende quartz diorite gneiss
R-19	Biotite hornblende tonalite gneiss
R-20	Alkali granite gneiss
R-21	Quartz diorite (high garnet) gneiss
R-22	Granodiorite gneiss
R-23	Leucocratic garnet biotite gneiss
R-24	Alkali syenite gneiss
R-25	Porphyritic granite gneiss
R-26	Alkali granite gneiss (low garnet)
R-27	Amphibolite

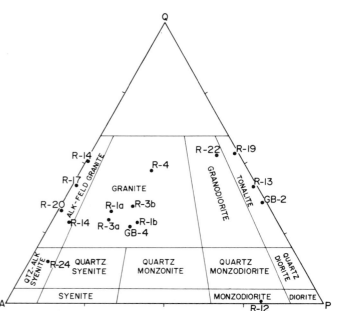

Figure 5. Modal analysis of several lithologies within the Thumb Member ("R" samples) and two samples from the Gold Butte granite complex ("GB" samples). Terminology follows Streckeisen (1976).

Frenchman Mountain

The basement complex of the Frenchman Mountain block consists of gray mica schist and pink migmatite exposed at the western foot of Frenchman Mountain (Figs. 1, 6) (Longwell and others, 1965; Rowland, 1987). Although the Frenchman Mountain rocks could not themselves have been a source of clasts in the Thumb Member (because they were buried beneath several thousand meters of nearly flat-lying Paleozoic and Mesozoic sediments), this same basement complex could conceivably have been exposed in other structural blocks. However, these lithologies were not recognized in the Thumb Member breccias.

Saddle Island

Precambrian amphibolite, chlorite schist, muscovite pegmatite dikes, porphyritic quartz monzonite, red granite, and leucogranite are exposed on Saddle Island on the western edge of Lake Mead (Fig. 6) (Smith, 1984; Choukroune and Smith, 1985; Sewall, 1988; Sewall and Smith, 1988; Duebendorfer and others, this volume). The amphibolite and quartz monzonite poorly match the similar rock types found in the Thumb Member brec-

cias. Pegmatite dikes on Saddle Island resemble an alkali granite lithology in the Thumb Member breccias (R-17), although the Saddle Island rocks are richer in muscovite.

Schmitt (1984) referred to a "discovery of nearby rapakivi granite outcrops on Saddle Island," which he used to support his argument that the Gold Butte granite complex may not be the source of the Thumb Member breccias. However, recent mapping by Sewall (1988) failed to reveal the presence of rapakivi granite on Saddle Island. What had at first appeared to be rapakivi granite turned out to be fractured granite megabreccia blocks in the upper plate of the Saddle Island detachment fault. These granite blocks are part of a 450-m-thick sequence of conglomerate, dacite, siltstone, matrix-supported pebble conglomerate, and megabreccia (Sewall, 1988). Sewall and Smith (1988) and Sewall (1988) correlate this sequence in part with the Thumb Member. The Saddle Island dacite may be related to the Lava Butte dacite of the Rainbow Gardens area.

Sewall (1988) made lithologic and geochemical comparisons between the volcanic rocks in the upper plate of the Saddle Island detachment and those at various volcanic centers in the Lake Mead region. She concluded that the Saddle Island hypabyssal rocks are genetically related to the Wilson Ridge Pluton some 20 km to the east (Fig. 6) and that they were displaced to their present position by movement on the Saddle Island detachment.

Saddle Island, therefore, can no longer be considered to represent a possible source for the Thumb Member breccias. Rather, the upper plate of the Saddle Island detachment itself contains Thumb Member breccias. The Frenchman Mountain

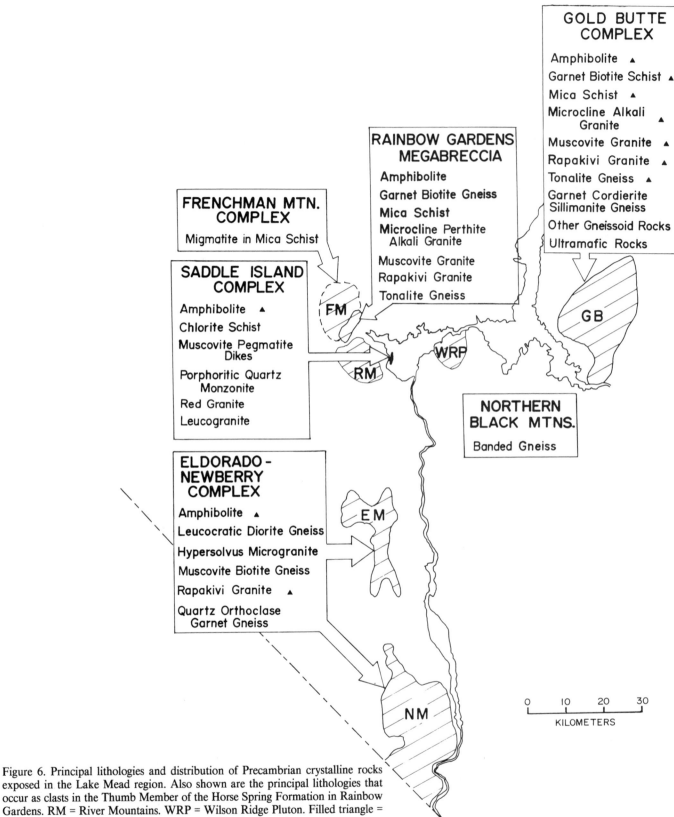

Figure 6. Principal lithologies and distribution of Precambrian crystalline rocks exposed in the Lake Mead region. Also shown are the principal lithologies that occur as clasts in the Thumb Member of the Horse Spring Formation in Rainbow Gardens. RM = River Mountains. WRP = Wilson Ridge Pluton. Filled triangle = lithologies represented by clasts in the Thumb Member breccias.

structural block probably also lies within the upper plate of the Saddle Island detachment and thus probably experienced the same 20 km of westward translation as inferred for the upper plate rocks of Saddle Island.

Newberry-Eldorado Mountains

The Eldorado and Newberry Mountains in southern Clark County contain amphibolite, rapakivi granite, hypersolvus micro-granite, and several varieties of gneiss (Fig. 6) (Volborth, 1973; Mathis, 1982; this study). A muscovite granite gneiss reported by Volborth (1973) failed to match the muscovite granite (R-4) from the Rainbow Gardens breccias because of the presence of accessory biotite in the Newberry-Eldorado rock. A diorite gneiss that occurs in the Eldorado-Newberry complex is signifi-cantly more leucocratic and less foliated than the diorite gneiss (R-16) in the Thumb Member breccias. Amphibolites are reported by Volborth (1973), but no samples were available for a detailed comparison with the amphibolite (R-27) of the Thumb Member.

With the exception of rapakivi granite, and possibly am-phibolite, the lithologies in the Eldorado-Newberry Mountains do not closely match those within the Thumb Member breccias of Rainbow Gardens (Fig. 6).

Reconnaissance mapping by Mathis (1982) indicates that much of the Newberry and Eldorado Mountains, along with several other nearby ranges, are part of an originally continuous detachment terrane. Rapakivi granite occurs in the Newberry Mountains in both the upper and lower plate, but in the lower plate it is mostly fine grained (Mathis, 1982). Coarse, crystalline rapakivi granite, such as the clasts that occur in the Thumb Member breccias, occurs in the upper plate. Mathis interpreted movement of the upper plate to have been northeastward. This would place its preextension position to the southwest, greatly reducing the viability of this area as a potential source.

Northern Black Mountains

Schmitt and Rice (1988) have suggested that the Precam-brian terrain of the northern Black Mountains (Fig. 6) was the source of the Thumb Member breccias and conglomerates. Longwell and others (1965, Plate 1) showed a few small patches of Precambrian rocks adjacent to Boulder Canyon on the north side of Lake Mead, and on the south side, Feuerbach (1986) mapped some small roof pendants of biotite-almadine gneiss, chlorite schist, and biotite schist within the Miocene Wilson Ridge Pluton. Recent mapping of the area east of the Wilson Ridge Pluton by Eschner (1989) indicates that the dominant lithology is banded gneiss (Fig. 6). Rapakivi granite is not known to occur in the northern Black Mountains, and in general the range of lithologies present in the Thumb Member breccias does not occur. Although the extensive volcanic deposits on the north shore of Lake Mead could conceal a much larger Precambrian terrain that was exposed in the Miocene, the modern exposures cannot be used to argue in favor of this area as the source.

Gold Butte

Volborth (1962) mapped and described the major rock types of the Gold Butte granite complex. A generalized version of his map is presented in Figure 7. For the purposes of this study we used Volborth's descriptions, supplemented with a few rock sam-ples from the Gold Butte area.

Rapakivi granite is abundant in the Gold Butte granite com-plex (Fig. 7). Modal analysis of one Gold Butte sample (GB-4) shows that it is more similar to one of the Thumb Member samples of rapakivi granite (R-1b) than is another Thumb Member sample (R-1a) (Fig. 5).

A wide variety of gneisses, schists, and gneissoid granites is also exposed in the Gold Butte complex (Fig. 7). One of the most common rock types is a garnet-biotite gneiss (Volborth, 1962). Analysis of hand samples, coupled with Volborth's description, indicates that this Gold Butte gneiss matches lithology R-11 (Table 1). This garnet-biotite gneiss is common in the Thumb Member breccias, especially in lithofacies B and E (Fig. 4).

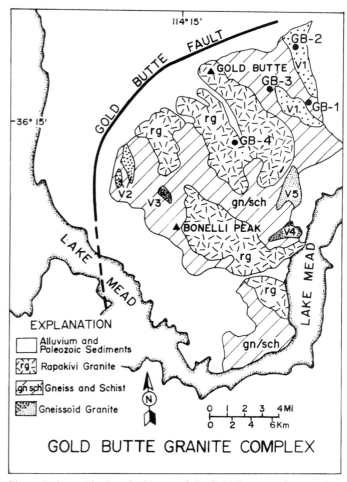

Figure 7. Generalized geologic map of the Gold Butte granite complex. After Volborth (1962). Location of Gold Butte fault is after Bohannon (1984, Plate 1A). GB1 through 4 = samples collected and examined during this study. V1 through 5 = petrographically distinct gneissoid granites described by Volborth (1962).

Volborth (1962) described several types of petrographically distinct gneissoid granites (designated V1 through V5 on Fig. 7). Analysis of a sample of rock type V1 collected from Mica Peak nera the Gold Butte town site (sample GB-2, Fig. 7) revealed that this rock type matches lithology R-19 from the Thumb Member, a biotite and hornblende-bearing tonalite (Fig. 5 and Table 1).

Volborth's (1962) mineralogic description of gray muscovite granite (rock type V2) from Twin Springs Wash in the western part of the Gold Butte granite complex (Fig. 7) closely matches that of lithology R-4 (Table 1, Fig. 5). This pink muscovite granite is the most abundant component of lithofacies A and is found in minor amounts throughout the Thumb Member breccias. Both R-4 and V2 are rich in muscovite and contain no accessory minerals.

No gneissoid granites from the Thumb Member breccias exactly match rock types V3, V4, and V5 as described by Volborth (1962). Conversely, some granites and gneissoid granite lithologies from the Thumb Member breccias (e.g., R-2, R-3, R-15, R-17, R-20, R-24, and R-25) have no known exact counterpart in the Gold Butte complex. Also, some of the melanocratic gneisses that occur as clasts in the Thumb Member breccias have not been confirmed to occur in the Gold Butte complex. Because Volborth (1962) apparently did not distinguish between the various subcategories of melanocratic biotite gneisses, it is likely that the six melanocratic gneisses identified in the Thumb Member breccias (R-11, R-13, R-16, R-29, R-21, and R-22) are mineralogic varieties of the Gold Butte garnet-biotite gneiss, which matches Thumb Member breccia lithology R-11, discussed above. Leighton (1967) mapped a 2.6-km^2 area 1.6 km east of Gold Butte and reported that the gneissic complex there contains migmatites, granulites, and quartzose rocks with complete transition between them. This statement also aptly describes the range of gneissic rocks that occurs in the Thumb Member breccias.

Volborth (1962) reported several types of ultramafic rocks in the Gold Butte area, although they are not volumetrically important. No ultramafic clasts have been identified in the Thumb Member breccias.

Fission-track dates from Rainbow Gardens and Gold Butte

Parolini and others (1981) determined fission-track ages of zircons and apatites from a rapakivi granite clast in the Thumb Member in the Rainbow Gardens area and also from a sample collected near the Gold Butte town site. The apatites from the Thumb Member sample yielded a date of about 11 Ma, compared to about 27 Ma for the Gold Butte sample. Parolini and others (1981) interpreted the anomalously young Thumb Member date to have resulted from the annealing of tracks during late Miocene volcanism in southern Nevada.

The zircon dates from the Thumb Member are also different from those of Gold Butte, and they are not as easily dismissed as the apatite dates. Zircons from the Gold Butte sample were determined to date from about 85 Ma, the same age that Volborth

(1962) reported. This date presumably records the most recent tectonism experienced by these Proterozoic granites. The Thumb Member sample, however, yielded a fission-track age of about 46 Ma. This disparity must be considered evidence against the hypothesis that the Gold Butte granite complex was the source of the Thumb Member breccias, but the reliability and significance of these fission-track ages cannot be satisfactorily evaluated without more data. Also, the zircons in the Thumb Member apparently contained a higher uranium content because the tracks were very dense and tended to overlap one another.

Parolini and others (1981) suggested that the two discordant zircon fission track dates represent two different episodes of uplift of the Precambrian granites. If this is so, then the granite source area of the Thumb Member breccia was uplifted much more recently than was the presently exposed Gold Butte granite complex. A detailed study of zircon fission track ages throughout the Gold Butte complex and at different horizons within the Thumb Member would likely shed light on this problem.

Conclusions concerning provenance

As summarized in Figure 6, the Gold Butte granite complex is the only presently exposed area of crystalline basement within the Lake Mead region where the lithologies closely match those in the Thumb Member breccias. The evidence strongly suggests that the Gold Butte granite complex was the source area for the breccias of the Thumb Member, as originally proposed by Longwell (1971, 1974) and supported by Anderson (1973) and Bohannon (1979, 1984). The apparently discordant zircon fission track ages from the two areas may indicate that the details of the relation between them are more complex than previous workers imagined; without additional dates the significance of the existing ones cannot be determined.

DIRECTION AND DISTANCE OF TRANSPORT OF THE THUMB MEMBER BRECCIAS

We turn now to the question of the distance and direction that the Thumb Member breccias traveled from their source. In the southern Rainbow Gardens area these breccias typically occur in discrete channels, whereas north of Lava Butte (Fig. 3) the breccias are not channelized and are more widely dispersed. Parolini (1986) interpreted the transition from channelized to nonchannelized breccias to represent the transition from proximal to medial fan environments. The proximal fan is dominated by channel-form processes, whereas the medial fan is below the point at which incised streams flow out onto the surface of the fan (Bull, 1977).

A good example of channelized breccia occurs at site 7 (Fig. 3), where lithofacies B (Fig. 4) occurs in a distinct channel (Fig. 8). This breccia-filled channel is over 15 m deep and 35 m wide, and it is fortuitously exposed on both sides of a small hill (Fig. 9). The two exposed faces are 117 m apart, and the southeastern end is 8 m lower than the northwestern end. The entire

Figure 8. Breccia-filled channel in the Thumb Member of the Horse Spring Formation, Rainbow Gardens site 7 (lithofacies B). A. Northwestern exposure. Note person for scale on lower right margin of channel. Channel is at least 15 m deep and 35 m wide. B. Close-up of "A" showing matrix-supported fabric. C. Large granitic clast in southeastern exposure of same channel. Boy is approximately 1 m tall; clast is approximately 2 m in diameter.

Miocene section dips to the east-southeast. Based on the interpretations of Bohannon (1984) and Parolini (1986) that some of the Thumb Member sediments were deposited subaqueously, we assume that the beds into which the site 7 channel eroded were deposited horizontally, or nearly so. When the section is restored to such a presumed untilted position the channel plunges N60°W.

On the large fans in Death Valley, proximal fan channels are consistently oriented within about 30° of the fan axis (Hunt and Mabey, 1966, Plate 2). The orientation of the site 7 channel, therefore, indicates a direction of transport of N60°W ± 30° for the Thumb Member in the Rainbow Gardens area, i.e., northwestward or westward. This does not take into account possible rotation about a vertical axis of the Frenchman Mountain block, which is addressed below.

There is also a south to north decrease in clast size within the breccias. Clasts in the site 7 channel are up to 2 m in diameter (Fig. 8C). A few kilometers away in northern Rainbow Gardens,

where the breccias are not channelized, the largest clasts are an order of magnitude smaller. The largest clasts known from the Thumb Member are huge blocks of shattered gneiss up to 100 m long and 20 m thick in lithofacies E. Significantly, these large blocks are exposed at site 15, at the extreme southern end of Rainbow Gardens (Fig. 3).

The south to north transition from proximal to medial fan environments is recorded in the finer-grained sediments of the Thumb Member as well as in the breccias. Bohannon (1984, Plate 1F) mapped an "alluvial facies" in southern Rainbow Gardens and a "fine-grained facies" in northern Rainbow Gardens.

On the largest fans in the Death Valley area (e.g., the Warm Spring Canyon fan), the transition from proximal to medial fan environments occurs no farther than 5 km from the apex of the fan (Hunt and Mabey, 1966, Plate 2), but meter-size clasts are not known to travel that far. For example, in the 1917 debris flow on

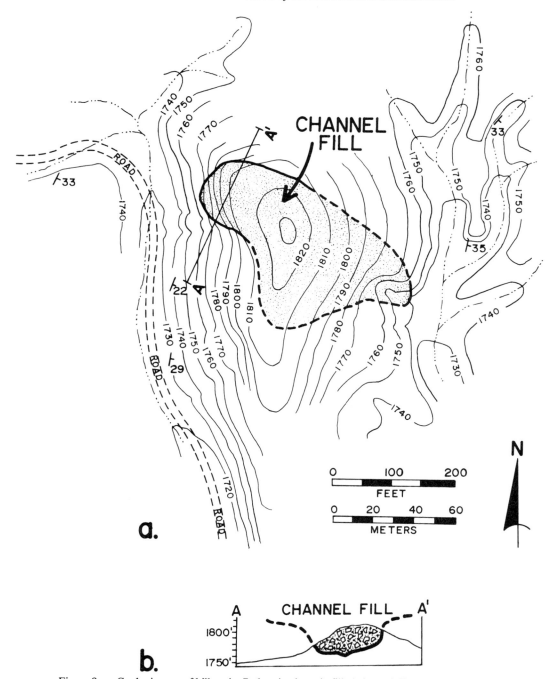

Figure 9. a. Geologic map of hill at site 7, showing breccia-filled channel. Topographic base from plane table and alidade at 1 inch = 100 feet, original scale, by R. Dover, I., Goldstein, K. Nall, and L. Whipple. Contour interval is 10 feet. b. Cross section of channel.

the Surprise Canyon alluvial fan in Panamint Valley, California, hundreds of large blocks were transported up to 1 km from the fan apex, and finer-grained material was transported up to 3 km, including one block that is comparable in size to the Thumb Member block shown in Figure 8C (Johnson, 1970). Based on a comparison with fans in the Death Valley area, we propose 5 km as the maximum distance of transport for the channelized breccias of southern Rainbow Gardens. The 100-m block exposed at

the southern end of Rainbow Gardens could not have traveled more than a few hundred meters from its source without disintegrating.

Bohannon (1984) presented a paleogeologic reconstruction during Thumb Member deposition in which he placed the Rainbow Gardens area approximately 25 km from the Gold Butte granite complex, which he considered to be the source. He placed other Thumb Member breccias even farther from their presumed source, about 45 km. Although some debris flows have been documented to have traveled several tens of kilometers from their source, such far-traveled deposits do not exhibit the abrupt facies changes downslope that are seen in the Thumb Member. For example, the Enos Creek–Owl Creek detachment mass in northwestern Wyoming traveled at least 45 km from its source (Brown and Love, 1987), and the Shasta Valley debris avalanche traveled at least 43 km beyond the base of Mount Shasta (Crandell and others, 1984). These consist of broad, lumpy sheets of breccia, rather than discrete channels entrenched in fine-grained sediments as is the case in the Thumb Member. Nor do these far-traveled debris flows contain 100-m-size blocks such as those in the Thumb Member.

There are no documented examples of meter-size, channelized matrix-supported breccias being transported more than 3 km from their source, although 5 km is conceivable based on the occurrence of proximal facies on some fans in Death Valley; such deposits are routinely deposited within 1 km of their source. We conclude that the channelized Thumb Member breccias of southern Rainbow Gardens were emplaced no farther than 5 km from their source and probably closer than 3 km. The southern end of Rainbow Gardens, where even larger blocks occur, was no farther than a few hundred meters from exposed bedrock.

The orientation of the site 7 channel, together with facies changes in the Thumb Member, indicates that the direction of transport was N60°W ± 30°.

TECTONIC ROTATION OF THE FRENCHMAN MOUNTAIN BLOCK

Considerable rotation about a vertical axis has been demonstrated in some blocks within the Lake Mead region. Using paleomagnetism, Ron and others (1986) measured 29 ± 8.5° of counterclockwise rotation for blocks of the Hamblin-Cleopatra volcano. Burdette and Marzolf (1986) using Mesozoic paleocurrent orientations, inferred approximately 130° of clockwise rotation for the Lovell Wash block.

Because of the presence of both strike-slip and normal faults in the Lake Mead region it is very possible that some blocks have rotated on inclined fault surfaces. As reviewed by MacDonald (1980), the result of such rotation cannot be assumed to have occurred about a vertical axis; therefore it is appropriately called apparent tectonic rotation rather than tectonic rotation.

In the following discussion we consider only possible rotation of the main Frenchman Mountain block (Fig. 1).

Paleomagnetic evidence

Gillett (1979, 1982) conducted a paleomagnetic study of the Cambrian strata at Frenchman Mountain. Although none of the magnetization was determined to be primary, within a red-brown sandstone interval of the Bright Angel Shale (Plate 1, in pocket inside back cover) he detected a hematite-borne magnetization that he suggested might be Paleozoic. The dip-corrected paleo-

magnetic poles for this red-brown sandstone at Frenchman Mountain are quite different from those derived from presumably age-equivalent strata in the Grand Canyon. The differences are primarily in declination, which means that they could be the product of rotation about a vertical axis. Gillett (1982) concluded that the difference in Paleozoic paleomagnetism between Frenchman Mountain and the Colorado Plateau could be caused by about 39° of post-Paleozoic clockwise rotation of the Frenchman Mountain block.

Gillett (1982) also reported data from Tramp Ridge, about 75 km to the east-northeast of Frenchman Mountain near Gold Butte (Fig. 10). There the paleomagnetism recorded in the same red-brown sandstone suggested that the Tramp Ridge section had rotated 30° clockwise relative to the Colorado Plateau.

Evidence from paleocurrent orientations

To test Gillett's suggestions that the Frenchman Mountain block (as well as the Tramp Ridge block) experienced a considerable amount of clockwise rotation, we measured the paleocurrent patterns recorded in eolian cross-bedded sandstones of the Pennsylvanian Callville Limestone (= Manakacha Formation of McKee, 1982). Paleocurrent orientations should be applicable to this problem if the regional direction is consistent and well documented, and eolian paleocurrents in general are more consistent than subaqueous ones.

McKee (1982) measured cross-bed orientations in the Manakacha Formation throughout the Grand Canyon region and established a regional southward paleocurrent. Although McKee interpreted these cross-bedded sandstones to be subaqueous in origin, Rice and Loope (1987) have described a suite of characteristics that diagnose them as eolian.

We measured the attitudes of foreset beds at six locations, three of which are tilted blocks in the Basin and Range Province and three of which are on the unextended Colorado Plateau. We measured at least twenty foreset attitudes at each locality, rotated each attitude to remove regional tilt, and then determined the resultant direction of dip on the rotated foreset. The resultant current roses are plotted on Figure 10.

Although the paleocurrent patterns of the three Basin and Range localities appear to be bimodal, this is probably an artifact of dip correction. Many of the foresets preserved in the Callville Limestone are only a few degrees steeper than bedding, whereas the regional dips on the three Basin and Range blocks are 30° or greater. In the process of removing the stratal tilt, some foresets were probably rotated past horizontal to a dip direction 180° from their original dip direction, resulting in a pseudo-bimodal current rose. This problem is especially prominent at Frenchman Mountain, where the current rose has a conspicuous, presumably false, northwestern petal (Fig. 10).

The paleocurrent direction at Toroweap Point is SSW, which is within the range of McKee's data for the Grand Canyon area generally. Toward the western margin of the Colorado Plateau, at Hidden Canyon and Pigeon Canyon, the paleocurrents

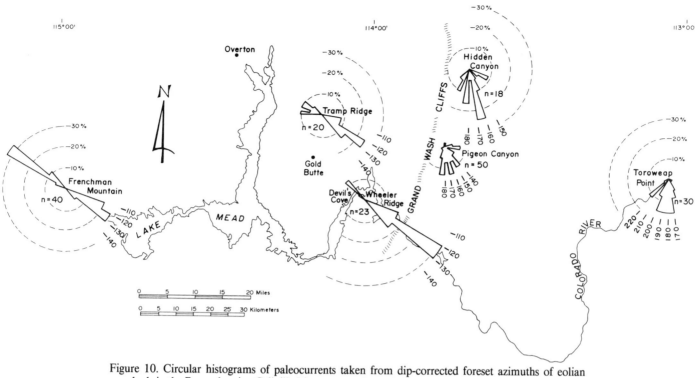

Figure 10. Circular histograms of paleocurrents taken from dip-corrected foreset azimuths of eolian crossbeds in the Pennsylvanian Callville Limestone and correlative strata on the Colorado Plateau. The bimodal pattern at Frenchman Mountain, Tramp Ridge, and Wheeler Ridge is interpreted to be an artifact of dip correction.

rotate slightly to the SSE (Fig. 10), whereas all three of the Basin and Range localities have a paleocurrent direction of approximately S55°E. Typically the wind direction over large sand seas is constant, although it may change near coastlines (J. E. Marzolf, personal communication, 1989). The fact that all three of the widely spaced Basin and Range sections show identical paleocurrent directions suggests that the shift from SSE to SE is not due to apparent tectonic rotation. Our interpretation is that this trend toward more southeastward paleocurrents in progressively western sections represents a shift in Pennsylvanian wind direction and not tectonic rotation.

Conclusions concerning apparent tectonic rotation

The Pennsylvanian eolian paleocurrent data clearly do not support Gillett's suggestion that Frenchman Mountain and Tramp Ridge rotated clockwise. The paleomagnetism that Gillett detected in the Cambrian red-brown sandstone is therefore probably not Paleozoic.

The paleocurrent data permit but do not require up to 45° of counterclockwise apparent tectonic rotation of the Frenchman Mountain block as well as the Tramp Ridge and Wheeler Ridge blocks. If such rotation did occur it affected all three of the Basin and Range blocks examined and is therefore not a result of Frenchman Mountain's westward translation. Thus, the data indicate that the Frenchman Mountain block did not experience a significant amount of tectonic rotation during translation.

FACIES AND THICKNESS TRENDS OF PALEOZOIC STRATA

As an independent test of the preextension position of the Frenchman Mountain block, we have used thickness and facies trends of Paleozoic strata. Both Anderson (1973) and Bohannon (1979) referred to a general similarity between some of the Paleozoic sections of the Lake Mead area and those in the South Virgin Mountains, thus providing evidence of large lateral displacement on the Lake Mead fault system. Detailed comparisons of Paleozoic rocks throughout the Lake Mead region have not been reported, however. The lower Paleozoic is especially suitable for such comparisons because there is a great thickness of rocks and an adequate number of stratigraphic markers. At Frenchman Mountain, for example, the Cambrian is over 800 m thick and is disconformably overlain by about 200 m of Devonian (Rowland, 1987). We present here the results of a preliminary study in which lower Paleozoic stratigraphy is used to constrain the preextension position of the Frenchman Mountain block. In a similar way, Marzolf (1987, this volume) has used lower Mesozoic strata to reconstruct the preextension position of various blocks in the Lake Mead region, including Frenchman Mountain.

In order to use lower Paleozoic stratigraphy to constrain Frenchman Mountain's preextension position, we have measured sections at Frenchman Mountain and at six localities in the eastern part of the Lake Mead region and western Colorado Plateau,

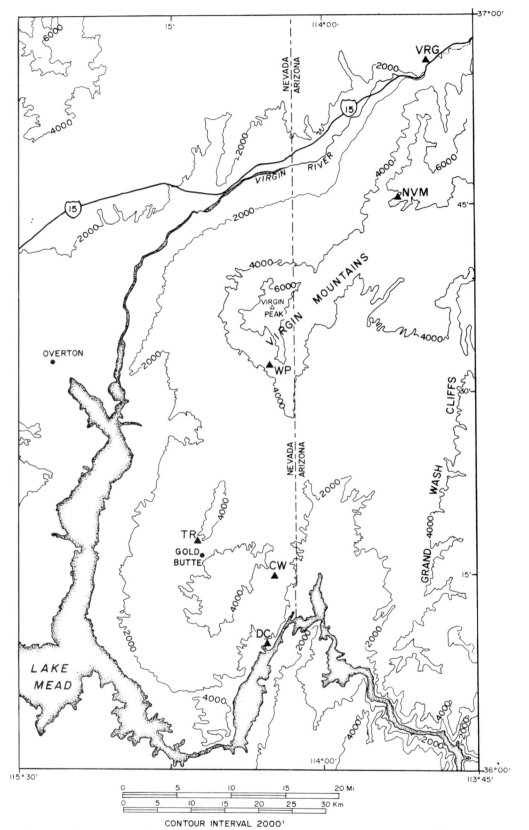

CONTOUR INTERVAL 2000'

Figure 11. Location map showing positions of six measured sections in the eastern Lake Mead region. VRG—Virgin River Gorge; NVM—North Virgin Mountains; WP—Whitney Pass; TR—Tramp Ridge; CW—Connoly Wash; DC—Devil's Cove.

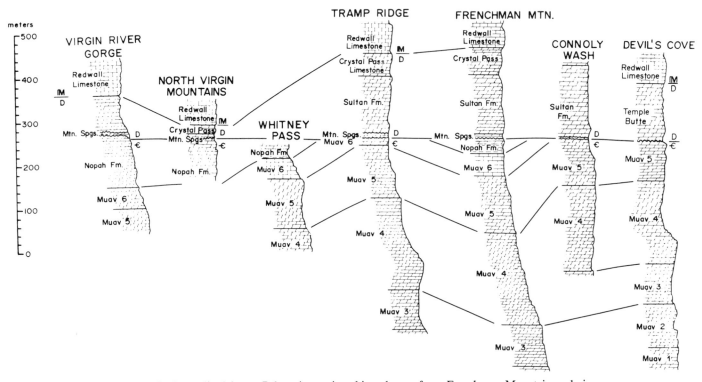

Figure 12. Generalized lower Paleozoic stratigraphic columns from Frenchman Mountain and six localities in the eastern Lake Mead region. Detailed stratigraphic sections of Frenchman Mountain and Tramp Ridge are provided in Plate 1. Locations of the eastern Lake Mead sections are shown on Figure 11.

from Devil's Cove on the south to Virgin River Gorge on the north (Fig. 11). We avoided sections that were involved in Mesozoic thrusting. Plate 1 shows the lower Paleozoic section at Frenchman Mountain and Tramp Ridge, and Figure 12 compares all seven sections. Thicknesses are listed in Table 2.

Stratigraphic nomenclature

There is considerable variation in stratigraphic terminology in the lower Paleozoic of southern Nevada. Historically, geologists working in the Basin and Range Province have developed a separate stratigraphic nomenclature from those working on the Colorado Plateau, even though in some cases the units are very similar. In this study we are most interested in correlating units at Frenchman Mountain with those adjacent to the Colorado Plateau, so wherever practical we have chosen to use Colorado Plateau nomenclature.

Cambrian. The basal Cambrian unit at Frenchman Mountain is the Tapeats Sandstone, which lies unconformably on Precambrian crystalline basement. Overlying the Tapeats is a shaly interval with conspicuous sandstone and limestone beds (Plate 1). The common practice in southern Nevada is to use Basin and Range terminology for these units (Pioche Shale, Lyndon Limestone, Chisholm Shale) as shown on Plate 1. Together these correlate to the Bright Angel Shale of the Colorado Plateau.

The remainder of the Cambrian at Frenchman Mountain is 663 m of predominantly limestone and dolomite. This carbonate interval is most commonly assigned to the Bonanza King and Nopah Formations. Gans (1974) subdivided the Bonanza King and Nopah Formations in southern Nevada and eastern California into several informal units. These units were defined in miogeoclinal sections, however; in cratonal sections such as Frenchman Mountain, the facies and thicknesses are significantly different. Farther east toward the Colorado Plateau, most of Gans's Cambrian subdivisions are unrecognizable.

In keeping with our preference for Colorado Plateau stratigraphic nomenclature, we have assigned 630 m of Cambrian carbonate at Frenchman Mountain to the Muav Formation instead of to the Bonanza King Formation. McKee and Resser (1945) defined several members of the Muav in the Grand Canyon, but many of these members cannot be distinguished in the western part of the Grand Canyon or in the Lake Mead region. To facilitate correlation and palinspastic reconstruction, we have subdivided the Muav of the Lake Mead region into six informal units (Plate 1, Fig. 12).

Overlying the Muav in some sections are additional Cambrian dolomites that we assign to the Nopah Formation. The base of the Nopah is the bottom of the recessive Dunderberg Shale Member.

There has been some confusion about the thicknesses of

**TABLE 2. THICKNESSES OF LOWER PALEOZOIC UNITS AT FRENCHMAN MOUNTAIN
AND SIX LOCALITIES IN THE EASTERN LAKE MEAD AND WESTERN
COLORADO PLATEAU AREA**

	Virgin River Gorge	North Virgin Mountains	Whitney Pass	Tramp Ridge	Frenchman Mountain	Connoly Wash	Devil's Cove
Anchor	26*	NM	NM	NM	NM	NM	NM
Dawn	48	50	NM	62	50	NM	58
Crystal Pass limestone	23	19	?	51	60	NM	NP
Sultan Mountain	62	NP	?	124	134	162	133
Springs	6	9	?	12	9	3	1
Total Dev.	91	28	?	186	203	?	134
Nopah	119	?	NM	NP	33	NP	NP
Muav-6	49	?	46	15	52	NP	NP
Muav-5	NM	?	111	119	126	303†	89
Muav-4	NM	?	NM	212	214	----	191
Muav-3	NM	?	?	88	92	NM	90
Muav-2	NM	?	?	88	96	NM	102
Muav-1	NM	?	?	49	50	NM	47
Total Muav	NM	?	?	570	630	NM	519

*Measurement from Steed (1980).
†Muav-4 and Muav-5 measured together.
NP = not present; NM = present but not measured
? = unable to determine or presence not confirmed.

both the Bonanza King and Nopah Formations at Frenchman Mountain. The Bonanza King Formation is normally subdivided into two easily recognized members: a lower Papoose Lake Member and an upper Banded Mountain Member. Gans (1974) did not measure the Papoose Lake Member at Frenchman Mountain, but he estimated the thickness to be 450 m. Our measurements indicate that this estimate is over triple the actual thickness; on Plate 1 the Papoose Lake Member corresponds to Muav 1 and Muav 2, which together are 146 m thick.

Gans (1970) reported the Banded Mountain Member of the Bonanza King Formation to be 321 m thick at Frenchman Mountain. The Banded Mountain Member corresponds to our Muav 3 through Muav 6, which total 484 m. Thus the total thickness of Bonanza King equivalent strata at Frenchman Mountain is 630 m, rather than the approximately 770 m indicated by Gans (1970, 1974). Contrary to Gans's estimates, the Papoose Lake Member composes less than 25 percent of this total.

Gans (1974) used the base of the Dunderberg Shale to define the top of the Bonanza King, but he was unable to find the Dunderberg Shale at Frenchman Mountain. Sundberg (1979) conducted a detailed study of the lower part of the Nopah Formation in southern Nevada and eastern California and located the Dunderberg Shale well above the horizon at which Gans (1970, 1974) placed the top of the Bonanza King. According to our

measurements, the total Nopah Formation at Frenchman Mountain is only 33 m thick, rather than the 494 m reported by Gans (1970). The thickness of the Nopah Formation turns out to be a very sensitive indicator of preextension position, as discussed below. Gans's incorrect thicknesses were incorporated by Burchfiel and others (1974, Fig. 2) into a frequently duplicated diagram showing thicknesses across the Spring Mountains and onto the craton at Frenchman Mountain.

Devonian. Paraconformably overlying the Cambrian dolomites at Frenchman Mountain is the Mountain Springs Formation. This is a Lower Ordovician to Middle(?) Devonian dolomite that Gans (1974) defined from exposures in the Spring Mountains. On the basis of age-diagnostic conodonts, Miller and Zilinsky (1981) identified two stratigraphic hiatuses in the Mountain Springs Formation. One hiatus is in the Ordovician, and the other is Silurian through Lower Devonian. The Mountain Springs Formation thus consists of three unconformity-bounded intervals (informally referred to as "a," "b," and "c"), the youngest of which is Lower Devonian or possibly lower Middle Devonian in age (unit 4 of Miller and Zilinsky, 1981).

On the basis of lithologic similarity and stratigraphic position, George Zilinsky (unpublished) has correlated this uppermost interval (the "c" member) of the Mountain Springs Formation to Frenchman Mountain and Tramp Ridge (Plate 1).

During this study we have further extended the occurrence of this unit to Virgin River Gorge, the North Virgin Mountains, Connoly Wash, and Devil's Cove (Figs. 11, 12).

Overlying the Mountain Springs Formation at Frenchman Mountain and other localities is an interval of very dark gray, cliff-forming, stromatoporoid-bearing dolomites that we assign to the Sultan Formation. At some localities (e.g., Frenchman Mountain and Tramp Ridge) the Sultan is in turn overlain by finely laminated, light gray dolomite or limestone assignable to the Crystal Pass Limestone; at other localities (e.g., Connoly Wash) this Crystal Pass facies is not present, and the correlative strata are placed in the Sultan (Fig. 12).

Southward from Tramp Ridge, the Sultan becomes lighter in color and less resistant to erosion. In the Devil's Cove section this interval has been transformed into a ledgy slope of medium gray dolomite without obvious stromatoporoids. This less resistant, ledgy facies is characteristic of the Temple Butte Limestone in the western Grand Canyon, so at Devil's Cove we assign these rocks to the Temple Butte (Fig. 12).

Mississippian. The Mississippian Redwall Limestone (= Monte Cristo Limestone) conformably overlies the Devonian throughout the Lake Mead area. It is not always a simple matter to consistently pick the Devonian-Mississippian contact, partly as a result of selective dolomitization in the Crystal Pass Limestone and in the lower Redwall Limestone. Throughout this study, wherever possible, we have used the base of the distinctive Thunder Springs Member of the Redwall (= Anchor Member of the Monte Cristo) as the top of our measured section.

Palinspastic significance of Paleozoic strata

The regional thickness trend for lower Paleozoic rocks in southern Nevada and eastern California is one of northwestward thickening (Stewart and Poole, 1974), presumably perpendicular to the continental margin. As a first approximation of thickness trends in the Cambrian and Devonian of the Lake Mead region we have used the isopach maps of Stewart and Poole (1974). Although Stewart and Poole did not take into account Tertiary crustal extension in the construction of their isopach maps, neither did they include the compressional effects of folding and telescoping on minor thrusts. In view of recent work on the magnitude of extension at the latitude of Las Vegas (e.g., Wernicke and others, 1988), it is likely that the Paleozoic isopachs originally trended more north-south than is indicated by Stewart and Poole (1974).

Cambrian. Based on the sections measured in this study, the Middle and Upper Cambrian strata of the Lake Mead region follow the pattern of westward and northwestward thickening indicated by Stewart and Poole (1974, Fig. 10), although we do not have enough east-west control to firmly establish the precise orientation of the isopachs. As shown on Figure 12, the Cambrian-Devonian erosion surface occurs progressively lower in the Cambrian toward the south. For example, the Nopah Formation is 119 m thick at Virgin River Gorge, whereas 75 km

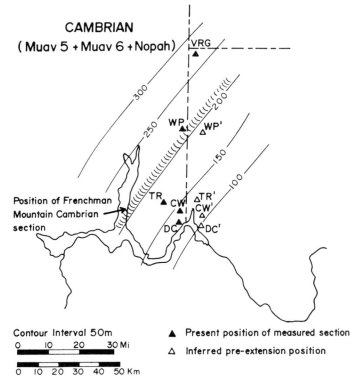

Figure 13. Reconstructed preextension isopach map of Muav 5, Muav, 6, and Nopah Formation, showing band along which the Frenchman Mountain section is inferred to have been located prior to Neogene extension. Regional thickness trend is from Stewart and Poole (1974). Thicknesses at localities shown are listed in Table 2. Spacing of isopachs is constrained by thickness and position of Virgin River Gorge section and thickness and inferred preextension position of Devil's Cove section. See caption of Figure 11 for explanation of abbreviations.

to the south, at Tramp Ridge, the Nopah was completely eroded away. In general the members of the Muav retain their thicknesses from one section to the next, but there is a southward increase in the amount of section lost off the top to erosion. Thus, Muav 6 is 46 m at Whitney Pass and almost the same thickness (49 m) at Virgin River Gorge, because the member is complete at both localities. But at Tramp Ridge, only 15 m of Muav 6 remains, and farther south there is none at all.

To locate Frenchman Mountain's preextension position relative to the Colorado Plateau we have constructed a preliminary isopach map of the Nopah Formation together with the two youngest units of the Muav (Muav 5 and Muav 6) (Fig. 13). For the purpose of preparing this map we have assumed that the isopachs are parallel and more or less straight and that the Whitney Pass, Tramp Ridge, Connoly Wash, and Devil's Cove sections have all been translated some distance to the west during Basin and Range extension. Wernicke and Axen (1988) recently examined the nature and magnitude of extension in the south Virgin Mountains, concluding that the fault block that contains the Devil's Cove section was translated up to 10 km westward relative to the Colorado Plateau. Thus on Figure 13 we have

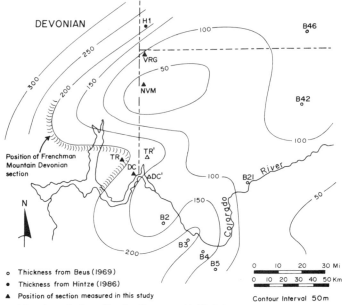

Figure 14. Reconstructed preextension isopach map of Devonian units, showing band along which the Frenchman Mountain section is inferred to have been located prior to Neogene extension. Regional thickness trends are from Stewart and Poole (1974). Thicknesses at control points are listed in Table 3.

restored the Devil's Cove section 10 km to the east prior to drawing isopachs.

The resultant isopach map (Fig. 13) is therefore constrained by (1) the position and thickness of the Virgin River Gorge section at the north end, (2) the thickness and restored position of the Devil's Cove section at the south end, and (3) the assumption that the isopachs are oriented northeast-southwest. The inferred preextension positions of the other localities in Figure 13 were dictated by the isopach map and the assumption that they were translated westward or west-northwestward by movement on normal faults.

The Cambrian isopachs, as restored in Figure 13, indicate that the Cambrian section thickens at a rate of about 3.3 m per km to the northwest. Because the individual Muav units do not, in general, thicken to the northwest, this northwestward thickening is interpreted to be primarily a product of greater post-Nopah–pre-Devonian erosion toward the southeast.

At Frenchman Mountain the Nopah, Muav 6, and Muav 5 total 211 m (Plate 1). As shown in Figure 13, this indicates a preextension position somewhere on a northeast-southwest line in the eastern Lake Mead area. If the preextension isopachs were oriented more north-south than shown in Figure 13, then Frenchman Mountain's inferred position would be farther east.

Devonian. Figure 14 is an isopach map of Devonian strata in the Lake Mead region and the western Colorado Plateau. The locations of sections measured in this study have been restored to the same presumed preextension positions as on Figure 13. The

North Virgin Mountains section is presumed not to have moved. In addition to our own measurements (Table 2), Figure 14 is based on thicknesses reported by Beus (1969) and Hintze (1986) (Table 3) and the regional patterns of Stewart and Poole (1974, Fig. 13).

Our preliminary study shows a northward thinning of Devonian strata from Tramp Ridge (186 m) to the North Virgin Mountains (28 m) (Figs. 12 and 14). Northward from the North Virgin Mountains the Devonian thickens rapidly to 91 m at Virgin River Gorge (Table 2) and over 200 m in the Beaver Dam Mountains of southwestern Utah (Table 3; Hintze, 1986).

These data require the Devonian isopachs to be oriented approximately east-west in the region between Lake Mead and the North Virgin Mountains, with an area of minimum thickness in the northwestern corner of Arizona and a wedge of thickened Devonian directly over Lake Mead (Fig. 14). This Devonian isopach pattern is in basic agreement with Stewart and Poole (1974, Fig. 13), who show a positive thickness anomaly over Lake Mead and a southwest-northeast trough of thinning in the northwestern corner of Arizona.

Beus (1969, Fig. 4) presented a Devonian isopach map for northwestern Arizona in which he shows the same basic trends as our Figure 14. However, Beus's positive thickness anomaly is centered on eastern Lake Mead, whereas ours is centered 20 km farther north near Gold Butte. The source of this discrepancy between our map and Beus's is the interpretation of certain strata in the eastern Lake Mead area. In Beus's Iceberg Ridge section, which is only about 2 km from our Devil's Cove section, he includes within the Devonian a thick interval of thinly bedded dolomite (Beus, 1969, Fig. 3), resulting in a total Devonian thickness of 393 m. Our work throughout the Lake Mead region indicates that this thinly bedded dolomite interval is actually Cambrian and that the Devonian in the Devil's Cove–Iceberg Ridge area is only 133 m thick.

TABLE 3. DEVONIAN THICKNESSES USED FOR CONTROL ON FIGURE 14

Symbol	Thickness (m)	Locality	Reference
H1	207	Beaver Dam Mts.	Hintze, 1986
VRG	91	Virgin River Gorge	This study
NVM	28	North Virgin Mts.	This study
TR	186	Tramp Ridge	This study
DC	134	Devil's Cove	This study
B2	140+	Grand Wash Cliffs	Beus, 1969
B3	226	Meriwitica Canyon	Beus, 1969
B4	163	Bridge Canyon	Beus, 1969
B5	127	Peach Springs	Beus, 1969
B21	88	Whitmore Wash	Beus, 1969
B42	142 (well)	Valen Oil #1	Beus, 1969
B46	113 (well)	McDermott #1	Beus, 1969

The positive Devonian thickness anomaly in the Lake Mead region and the negative anomaly in the North Virgin Mountains are presumed to be due to post-Sultan–pre-Redwall differential erosion. An unconformity occurs at the base of the Mississippian Redwall Limestone throughout the Grand Canyon (McKee, 1976) and presumably in the Lake Mead region as well, but it is usually not obvious in the outcrop. The base of the Redwall is thus not always conspicuous. Steed (1980), for example, shows the Whitmore Wash Member of the Redwall to be 20.7 m thick at Virgin River Gorge, underlain by 27 m of Devonian dolomite. Our work suggests that this 27 m of dolomite is probably a dolomitized interval of Redwall. So our Devonian thickness at Virgin River Gorge is 27 m thinner than Steed's.

The Devonian at Frenchman Mountain is 203 m thick (Table 2, Plate 1). Its preextension position, therefore, was somewhere near the 200-m isopach (Fig. 14).

Comparisons between Frenchman Mountain and Tramp Ridge

Of the lower Paleozoic sections examined in this study, the one that is most similar to Frenchman Mountain is Tramp Ridge. As shown in detail on Plate 1, the thicknesses and characteristics of the Cambrian units at Frenchman Mountain are very similar to those at Tramp Ridge. For example, large thrombolites were observed to occur in the Lyndon Limestone at only two localities—Frenchman Mountain and Tramp Ridge (Plate 1). The most significant difference between the two Cambrian sections is that at Tramp Ridge the Nopah Formation and much of Muav 6 were eroded away prior to deposition of the Devonian strata.

The Frenchman Mountain Devonian section, as in the Cambrian, is somewhat thicker than the Devonian interval at Tramp Ridge (Table 2). At both localities the lower portion of the Sultan Formation consists of very dark gray, cliff-forming, pitted dolomites with conspicuous fossil stromatoporoids. At Frenchman Mountain the Sultan is a cliff former throughout, whereas at Tramp Ridge the upper portion is ledgy. Although the Crystal Pass is identifiable at both localities, at Tramp Ridge it is mostly limestone, and at Frenchman Mountain it is all dolomite (Plate 1); dolomitization can be very localized in the Paleozoic of southern Nevada, and the significance of the differences cannot be determined without looking at other nearby sections.

Conclusions based on lower Paleozoic stratigraphy

Figure 15 combines the inferences of Figures 13 and 14 concerning the preextension position of the Frenchman Mountain block based on Cambrian and Devonian thickness data. The resultant preferred preextension position relative to the Colorado Plateau is approximately 8 km northwest of Gold Butte, where the Cambrian and Devonian bands intersect on Figure 15. Due to uncertainties of regional isopach orientation prior to Basin and Range extension, as well as uncertainties of the preextension

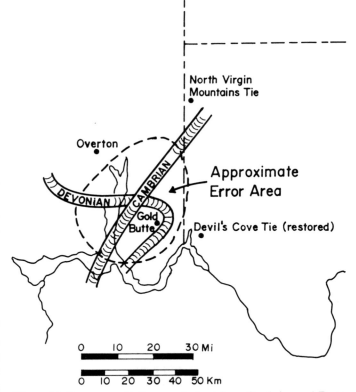

Figure 15. Summary of inferences derived from Cambrian and Devonian isopach data (Figs. 13, 14). Preferred preextension position of Frenchman Mountain section, based on lower Paleozoic stratigraphic thicknesses, is a few kilometers northwest of Gold Butte. Due to uncertainties of preextension isopach pattern, the data permit a preextension position within the dashed error area. The error area is constrained on the northeast by the North Virgin Mountains section, on the east by the unextended Colorado Plateau, and on the southeast by the restored position of the Devil's Cove section.

position of some of the measured sections, we identify a possible error area as shown on Figure 15. This error area is constrained on the north by data from the North Virgin Mountains, which we assume have not experienced significant Basin and Range extension. On the east the constraint is the edge of the Colorado Plateau itself, along with the restored position of the Devil's Cove section. The error area is constrained on the western margin only by the generalized isopach maps of Stewart and Poole (1974).

Based only on the Cambrian and Devonian stratigraphic data, the distance of net horizontal translation of the Frenchman Mountain block is conservatively constrained by the error box in Figure 15 to be 63 ± 20 km (Fig. 16); the restoration vector extends N73°E ± 12° from the block's present position (Fig. 16).

KINEMATIC CONCLUSIONS AND DISCUSSION

Based on the sedimentology of the Thumb Member of the Horse Spring Formation, we conclude that during deposition of that member the Frenchman Mountain block was directly adja-

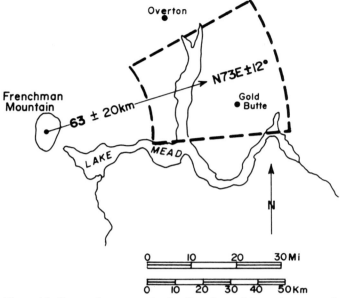

Figure 16. Restoration vector for the Frenchman Mountain structural block based exclusively on Paleozoic stratigraphic data.

cent to exposures of the Gold Butte granite complex. Although the presently exposed extent of this complex may be somewhat different than in the Miocene, the coarseness of some of the Thumb Member breccias and the wide variety of clast compositions present indicate a large, high-relief source area that would probably remain at least partially exposed today, after 13 to 17 m.y. The simplest explanation permitted by the data is that Rainbow Gardens lay adjacent to the Gold Butte fault (Fig. 7). Implicit in this reconstruction is the existence of a fault on the southeastern margin of Rainbow Gardens, roughly beneath Las Vegas Wash.

The Thumb Member breccias were deposited in proximal and medial fan settings no farther than 5 km from their source. The direction of transport was N60°W ± 30°. The preextension position, therefore, was probably on the western or northwestern margin of the Gold Butte granite complex.

Based on the presence of identical Pennsylvanian eolian paleocurrent directions at Frenchman Mountain, Tramp Ridge, and Wheeler Ridge, we conclude that the westward translation of the Frenchman Mountain block from the Gold Butte area was not accompanied by significant tectonic rotation.

An independent line of evidence that further supports the conclusion that the Frenchman Mountain block was translated from the Gold Butte area concerns the matching of distinctive stratigraphic relations between Rainbow Gardens and Horse Spring Wash, which is directly northeast of Gold Butte. In the Frenchman Mountain block, successively younger Mesozoic units occur beneath the Miocene Horse Spring Formation from south to north (Bohannon, 1979, 1984) as follows: in southern Rainbow Gardens the Horse Spring Formation lies directly on lower Triassic strata (Moenkopi Formation), in central Rainbow Gardens it lies on upper Triassic strata (Moenave-Kayenta equi-

valents), and in northern Rainbow Gardens it lies on Jurassic strata (Aztec Sandstone). The only other place in the Lake Mead region where these stratigraphic relations occur is in Horse Spring Wash (Bohannon, 1979). Bohannon (1979) used this evidence to propose that the Frenchman Mountain/Rainbow Gardens rocks originally lay adjacent to the Horse Spring Wash area, although he later (Bohannon, 1984) revised this interpretation and restored the Frenchman Mountain block to a position 40 km northeast of Horse Spring Wash. Our reconstruction is in basic agreement with Bohannon's earlier interpretation.

Combining the Paleozoic results (Fig. 16) with the interpretation that the Frenchman Mountain block was directly adjacent to the western or northwestern margin of the presently exposed Gold Butte granite complex, we conclude that the Frenchman Mountain block's preextension position relative to the Gold Butte granite complex was quite close to the Gold Butte town site. Because the Gold Butte granite complex itself has moved about 10 km westward (Wernicke and Axen, 1988; Wernicke and others, 1988), we conclude that the preextension position of Frenchman Mountain was in the southeastern quarter of the error area of Figure 16. Our resultant restoration vector (Fig. 17) for the Frenchman Mountain block, based on all available evidence, has a magnitude of 80 ± 8 km and a bearing of N80°E ± 5°. Our reconstruction is very similar to that of Wernicke and others (1988), who used a restoration vector of N70°E ± 10°, 60 to 90 km for Frenchman Mountain.

TIME CONSTRAINTS

Age of the Horse Spring Formation and overlying strata

An important time constraint on the kinematic history of the Frenchman Mountain block is the age of the Horse Spring Formation, because at least some of this unit was deposited during extension. The basal Rainbow Gardens Member has not been directly dated, but it is thought to be no older than 20 Ma (Bohannon, 1984). The Thumb Member ranges in age from 17.2 to 13.5 Ma, based on fission track dates of zircons recovered from airfall tuffs within that member (Bohannon, 1984). The Thumb Member debris-flow deposits discussed in this chapter were deposited during that interval. Thus we conclude that the Frenchman Mountain block was located adjacent to the Gold Butte granite complex between 13.5 and 17.2 Ma.

The youngest two members of the Horse Spring Formation are the Bitter Ridge Limestone (13.5 to about 13.0 Ma) and the Lovell Wash Member (13.0 to 11.9 Ma). These are overlain by an unnamed red sandstone (11.9 to 10.6 Ma), which is in turn overlain by the relatively undeformed Muddy Creek Formation. The Muddy Creek Formation is not well dated, but it contains an 8-Ma basalt and is capped by the 5.9-Ma Fortification Basalt (Bohannon, 1984)

Age of tilting of the Frenchman Mountain block

Within the Frenchman Mountain block the Rainbow Gardens and Thumb Members of the Horse Spring Formation

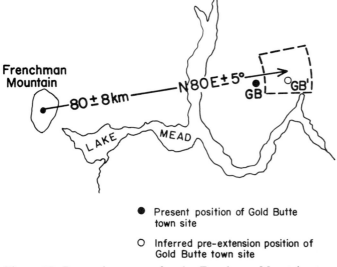

Figure 17. Restoration vector for the Frenchman Mountain structural block based on a combination of sedimentological data from the Horse Spring Formation and Paleozoic stratigraphic data. Scale approximately same as Figure 16.

dip 30° to 50° to the east, which is within a few degrees of being parallel to the underlying Paleozoic and Mesozoic beds (Longwell, unpublished; Bohannon, 1984). The younger two members of the Horse Spring Formation dip slightly less, and the overlying unnamed red sandstone dips significantly less. As pointed out by Bohannon (1984, p. 60), this indicates that significant stratal rotation did not occur until after deposition of the Thumb Member. Most of the tilting occurred after deposition of the entire Horse Spring Formation (about 12 Ma) and before deposition of the Muddy Creek Formation (8 Ma).

Age and significance of the River Mountains stratovolcano

Immediately southeast of the Frenchman Mountain block (Fig. 6) is the 13.5-Ma River Mountains andesitic stratovolcano (Smith, 1982, 1984; Weber and Smith, 1987). Geochemical studies indicate that the River Mountains volcano is comagmatic with the Wilson Ridge Pluton, approximately 20 km to the east (Fig. 6) (Weber and Smith, 1987; Sewall, 1988). The River Mountains lie in the upper plate of the Saddle Island detachment (Duebendorfer and others, this volume), which is thought to have decapitated the Wilson Ridge Pluton and translated the River Mountains to their present position (Sewall, 1988; Smith and others, 1987; Weber and Smith, 1987). Major movement on the Saddle Island detachment is interpreted to have occurred after the emplacement of a lamprophyre dike dated at 13.4 Ma (Duebendorfer and others, this volume; Weber and Smith, 1987).

The history of the relation between the Frenchman Mountain block and the River Mountains is not completely clear. Both blocks display eastward stratal rotation on west-dipping normal faults (Bell and Smith, 1980; Longwell, unpublished), which probably developed during westward translation of the upper plate of the Saddle Island detachment. Bohannon (1979) originally mapped a branch of the Lake Mead fault system between these two blocks, and Bell and Smith (1980) inferred that a major fault zone parallels Las Vegas Wash. However, Bohannon (1984) later concluded that there was no such branch of the Lake Mead fault system in that area. This latter view is supported by E. I. Smith on the basis of similar Thumb Member lithologies on both sides of Las Vegas Wash (Bell and Smith, 1980). Smith asserts that if a fault exists between Rainbow Gardens and the River Mountains it must predate deposition of the Thumb Member (E. I. Smith, personal communication, 1988). This is not compatible with our conclusion that Rainbow Gardens lay directly adjacent to the Gold Butte granite complex during Thumb Member deposition, requiring a fault to have existed directly adjacent to Rainbow Gardens at that time.

Our data suggest that sometime *after* Thumb Member deposition the Frenchman Mountain block was translated away from the Gold Butte granite complex, presumably to a position adjacent to the nascent River Mountains volcano. This translation, which was accompanied by only a few degrees of stratal tilting, was probably the result of movement on a fault that is now buried beneath Las Vegas Wash. If Bohannon (1984) is correct that there is no branch of the Lake Mead fault system between Frenchman Mountain and the River Mountains, then our inferred fault must predate the Lake Mead fault system. The history of the relation between the Frenchman Mountain structural block and the River Mountains block is a key to reconstructing the detailed fault history of the Lake Mead region.

TECTONIC IMPLICATIONS FOR THE LAKE MEAD REGION

Although it is not yet possible to precisely determine which faults were responsible for the westward translation of the Frenchman Mountain block, the foregoing analysis can be used to test various tectonic models and to indicate the relative importance of various types of faults in the general Neogene deformational history of the Lake Mead region.

Right-slip versus left-slip faulting

The azimuth of our restoration vector for the Frenchman Mountain block, N80°E ± 5°, is compatible with a large magnitude of left slip on the Lake Mead fault system, as proposed by Anderson (1973) and Bohannon (1979, 1984). However, the restoration vector is not compatible with Bohannon's (1984) palinspastic model in which the Frenchman Mountain block is restored to a position north of Overton, Nevada.

Our restoration implies that the Miocene basin in which the Horse Spring Formation was deposited was much smaller than suggested by Bohannon (1984) and that the present exposures of the Horse Spring Formation represent a much larger percentage of the original Miocene basinal deposits than has previously been thought.

Although our restoration does not support all the details of Longwell's (1974) interpretation of Frenchman Mountain's translational history (Fig. 2), it does not preclude a component of right-slip faulting during the early stages of extension in the Lake Mead region, as Longwell proposed. If the Las Vegas Valley shear zone is confined to the upper plate of a detachment fault, most of its eastern portions may have been lost to erosion. The erosional remnant of the upper plate of a detachment fault has in fact been mapped and described in the area east of the Wilson Ridge Pluton (Fig. 6) by Eschner (1989).

Normal faulting in the South Virgin Mountains

If our inferred restoration of the Frenchman Mountain block to a position adjacent to the Gold Butte granite complex is correct, then there must have been major normal faulting in that area during Thumb Member deposition. Uplift of the Gold Butte granite complex is required to account for the inferred high-relief setting and to expose the wide variety of lithologies represented by clasts in the Thumb Member breccias. Such uplift could have been due to isostatic footwall uplift accompanying tectonic denudation (Wernicke and Axen, 1988). This would require an earlier episode of tectonic unloading off the top of the Gold Butte granite complex.

Relative importance of strike-slip versus normal faulting in the Lake Mead region

Bohannon (1984) concluded that normal faulting, listric normal faulting, stratal tilting, and strike-slip faulting in the Lake Mead region were all genetically related and occurred after or during the late stages of Thumb Member deposition. Anderson (1973) specifically mentioned Frenchman Mountain and the River Mountains as outstanding examples of the close genetic relation between normal and strike-slip faulting. The relative importance of these two types of faults is not always clear, however.

Ron and others (1986) addressed the question of the relative importance of strike-slip versus normal faulting in the Lake Mead region, using the principle that the amount, sense, and orientation of the axes of block rotation provide definitive evidence of the relative roles of these two types of faults. The paleomagnetic study of block rotation in the Lake Mead fault system by Ron and others (1986) showed insignificant structural tilt and significant counterclockwise rotation about a vertical axis. This result

led them to conclude that strike-slip faulting was the dominant late Neogene deformational process in the Lake Mead fault system and that tilting in response to normal faulting was of secondary importance.

Some features of the Frenchman Mountain block, on the other hand, suggest that normal faulting has played a major role in this block's structural history. One such feature is a change in dip through time in the Horse Spring Formation: the younger members of the Horse Spring Formation dip slightly less than the older members (Bohannon, 1984). Thus, stratal rotation was occurring during deposition of the Horse Spring Formation, indicating that this unit was, at least in part, filling basins that were produced by listric normal faulting.

Another feature suggesting that normal faulting played an important role in the structural history of the Frenchman Mountain block is the geometry of the faults within the block. High-angle normal faults strike north-south and northeast-southwest (Fig. 3), roughly perpendicular to the direction of translation; rotation of blocks has been to the east, opposite to the direction of translation. This is precisely the geometry and sense of rotation that has been documented in the upper plate of low-angle normal faults (detachment faults) (Wernicke and others, 1984; Davis and Lister, 1988).

Most important is the evidence presented in this Chapter that the Frenchman Mountain structural block was translated 80 ± 8 km with 30° to 50° of stratal rotation but no significant rotation about a vertical axis. Using the criteria of Ron and others (1986), this *requires* a dominant role for low-angle normal faults. Detachment faulting is the most plausible mechanism for translating this block this far without significant tectonic rotation. We concur with Guth and Smith (1987) that detachment faulting has been the primary Neogene deformational process in the Lake Mead region.

ACKNOWLEDGMENTS

We thank Gary Axen and an anonymous reviewer for helpful reviews. We have also benefited from discussions with Sue Beard, Bob Bohannon, Joan Fryxell, Steve Gillett, John Marzolf, Gene Smith, and Tim Wallin. We gratefully acknowledge financial support from the University of Nevada, Las Vegas, Graduate Student Association to Eschner, McAllister, Parolini, and Rice. Eschner thanks David Huntley and Eric Frost of San Diego State University for originally stimulating his interest in Frenchman Mountain. Mark Hug helped measure the Devil's Cove section. Gold Butte samples were collected by Jack Glynn. The figures were cheerfully drafted by Nate Stout.

REFERENCES CITED

Anderson, R. E., 1973, Large-magnitude late Tertiary strike-slip faulting north of Lake Mead, Nevada: U.S. Geological Survey Professional Paper 794, 18 p.

Bell, J. W., and Smith, E. I., 1980, Geologic map of the Henderson Quadrangle, Nevada: Nevada Bureau of Mines and Geology Map 67, scale 1:24,000.

Beus, S. S., 1969, Devonian stratigraphy in northwestern Arizona, *in* Geology and natural history of the Grand Canyon region: Four Corners Geological Society Guidebook, p. 127–133.

Bohannon, R. G., 1979, Strike-slip faults of the Lake Mead region of southern Nevada, *in* Armentrout, J. M., Cole, M. R., and TerBest, H., eds., Cenozoic paleogeography of the western United States: Pacific Section, Society of Economic Paleontologists and Mineralogists Pacific Coast Paleogeography Symposium 3, p. 129–139.

—— , 1983, Geologic map, tectonic map, and structure sections of the Muddy and northern Black Mountains, Clark County, Nevada: U.S. Geological Survey Miscellaneous Investigations Map I–1406, scale 1:62,500.

—— , 1984, Nonmarine sedimentary rocks of Tertiary age in the Lake Mead region, southeastern Nevada and northwestern Arizona: U.S. Geological Survey Professional Paper 1259, 72 p.

Brenner-Tourtelot, E. L., 1979, Geologic map of the lithium-bearing rocks in parts of the Frenchman Mountain and Henderson quadrangles, Clark County, Nevada: U.S. Geological Survey Miscellaneous Field Studies Map MF–1079, scale 1:24,000.

Brown, T. M., and Love, J. D., 1987, The Rhodes allochthon of the Enos Creek–Owl Creek debris-avalanche, northwestern Wyoming, *in* Beus, S. S., ed., Rocky Mountain Section of the Geological Society of America: Boulder, Colorado, Geological Society of America Centennial Field Guide, v. 2, p. 179–182.

Bull, W. B., 1977, The alluvial fan environment: Progress in Physical Geography, v. 1, p. 222–270.

Burchfiel, B. C., Fleck, R. J., Secor, D. T., Vincelette, R. R., and Davis, G. A., 1974, Geology of the Spring Mountains, Nevada: Geological Society of America Bulletin, v. 85, p. 1013–1022.

Burdette, D. J., and Marzolf, J. E., 1986, Sedimentology of Moenave–Kayenta strata in southern Nevada; Early Mesozoic depositional environments and implications for Cenozoic tectonics: Geological Society of America Abstracts with Programs, v. 18, p. 344.

Choukroune, P., Smith, E. I., 1985, Detachment faulting and its relationship to older structural events on Saddle Island, River Mountains, Clark County, Nevada: Geology, v. 13, p. 421–424.

Crandell, D. R., Miller, C. D., Glicken, H. X., Christiansen, R. L., and Newhall, C. G., 1984, Catastrophic debris avalanche from ancestral Mount Shasta volcano, California: Geology, v. 12, p. 143–146.

Davis, G. A., and Lister, G. S., 1988, Detachment faulting in continental extension; Perspectives from the southwestern U.S. Cordillera, *in* Clark, S. P., Burchfiel, B. C., and Suppe, J., eds., Processes in continental deformation: Geological Society of America Special Paper 218, p. 133–160.

Eschner, E., 1989, The geology and structural significance of the Arch Mountain area, northwestern Mohave County, Arizona [M.S. thesis]: Las Vegas, University of Nevada, 105 p.

Eschner, E., and Smith, E. I., 1988, Geometry of mid-Tertiary normal faults in the Arch Mountain area of the northern Black Mountains, Mohave County, northwest Arizona: Geological Society of America Abstracts with Programs, v. 20, p. 159.

Feuerbach, D. L., 1986, Geology of the Wilson Ridge pluton; A mid-Miocene quartz monzonite intrusion in the northern Black Mountains, Mohave County, Arizona and Clark County, Nevada [M.S. thesis]: Las Vegas, University of Nevada, 79 p.

Gans, W. T., 1970, The detailed stratigraphy of the Goodsprings Dolomite, southeastern Nevada-California [Ph.D. thesis]: Houston, Texas, Rice University, 174 p.

—— , 1974, Correlation and redefinition of the Goodsprings Dolomite, southern California and eastern Nevada: Geological Society of America Bulletin, v. 85, p. 189–200.

Gillett, S., 1979, Possibly rotated Cambrian paleomagnetic pole from Frenchman Mountain, Nevada: Geological Society of American Abstracts with Programs, v. 11, p. 432.

—— , 1982, Remagnetized cratonic Cambrian strata from southern Nevada: Journal of Geophysical Research, v. 87, p. 7097–7112.

Guth, P. L., and Smith, E. I., 1987, Comment *on* Strike-slip faulting and block rotation in the Lake Mead fault system: Geology, v. 15, p. 579–580.

Hintze, L. F., 1986, Stratigraphy and structure of the Beaver Dam Mountains, southwestern Utah: Utah Geological Association Publication 15, p. 1–36.

Hunt, C. B., and Mabey, D. R., 1966, Stratigraphy and structure, Death Valley, California: U.S. Geological Survey Professional Paper 494–A, 162 p.

Johnson, A. M., 1970, Physical processes in geology: San Francisco, California, Freeman, Cooper and Co., 577 p.

Leighton, F. B., 1967, Gold Butte vermiculite deposits, Clark County, Nevada: Nevada Bureau of Mines Report 16.

Longwell, C. R., 1951, Megabreccia developed downslope from large faults (Arizona-Nevada): American Journal of Science, v. 249, p. 343–355.

—— , 1971, Measure of lateral movement on Las Vegas shear zone, Nevada: Geological Society of America Abstracts with Programs, v. 3, p. 152.

—— , 1974, Measure and date of movement on Las Vegas Valley shear zone, Clark County, Nevada: Geological Society of America Bulletin, v. 85, p. 985–990.

Longwell, C. R., Pampeyan, E. H., Bower, B., and Roberts, R. J., 1965, Geology and mineral deposits of Clark County, Nevada: Nevada Bureau of Mines Bulletin 62, 218 p.

MacDonald, W. D., 1980, Net tectonic rotation, apparent tectonic rotation, and the structural tilt correction in paleomagnetic studies: Journal of Geophysical Research, v. 85, p. 3659–3669.

Marzolf, J. E., 1987, Lower Mesozoic facies in southern Nevada; Implications for Cenozoic extension: Geological Society of America Abstracts with Programs, v. 19, p. 429.

Mathis, R. S., 1982, Mid-Tertiary detachment faulting in the southeastern Newberry Mountains, Clark County, Nevada, *in* Frost, E. G., and Martin, D. L., eds., Mesozoic–Cenozoic tectonic evolution of the Colorado River region, California, Arizona, and Nevada: San Diego, California, Cordilleran Publishers, p. 327–340.

McKee, E. D., 1976, The Paleozoic rocks of Grand Canyon, *in* Breed, W. J., and Roat, E., eds., Geology of the Grand Canyon: Museum of Northern Arizona/Grand Canyon Natural History Association, p. 41–64.

—— , 1982, The Supai Group of Grand Canyon: U.S. Geological Survey Professional Paper 1173, 504 p.

McKee, E. D., and Resser, C. E., 1945, Cambrian history of the Grand Canyon region: Carnegie Institute of Washington Publication 563, 232 p.

Miller, R. H., and Zilinsky, G. A., 1981, Lower Ordovician through Lower Devonian cratonic margin rocks of the southern Great Basin: Geological Society of America Bulletin, Part 1, v. 92, p. 255–261.

Nur, A., Ron, H., and Aydin, A., 1987, Reply *to* Comment *on* Strike-slip faulting and block rotation in the Lake Mead fault system: Geology, v. 15, p. 580.

Parolini, J. R., 1986, Debris flows within a Miocene alluvial fan, Lake Mead region, Clark County, Nevada [M.S. thesis]: Las Vegas, University of Nevada, 120 p.

Parolini, J. R., Smith, E. I., and Wilbanks, J. R., 1981, Fission track dating of rapakivi granite in the Rainbow Gardens and in the South Virgin Mountains, Clark County, Nevada: Isochron/West, no. 30 (April 1981), p. 9–10.

Rice, J. A., and Loope, D. B., 1987, Pennsylvanian eolian limestones, western Grand Canyon and southern Nevada: Geological Society of America Abstracts with Programs, v. 19, p. 818.

Ron, H., Aydin, A., and Nur, A., 1986, Strike-slip faulting and block rotation in the Lake Mead fault system: Geology, v. 14, p. 1020–1023.

Rowland, S. M., 1987, Paleozoic stratigraphy of Frenchman Mountain, Clark County, Nevada, *in* Hill, M., ed., Cordilleran Section of the Geological Society of America: Boulder, Colorado, Geological Society of America Centennial Field Guide, v. 1, p. 53–56.

Salyards, S. L., and Shoemaker, E. M., 1987, Landslides and debris-flow deposits in the Thumb Member of the Miocene Horse Spring Formation on the east side of Frenchman Mountain, Nevada; A measure of basin-range extension, *in* Hill, M., ed., Cordilleran Section of the Geological Society of America: Boulder, Colorado, Geological Society of America Centennial Field Guide, v. 1, p. 49–51.

Schmitt, J. G., 1984, Alluvial fan deposition and tectonic significance of megabreccias in the Miocene Horse Spring Formation, Rainbow Gardens, southern Nevada: Geological Society of America Abstracts with Programs, v. 16, p. 647.

Schmitt, J. G., and Rice, J. A., 1988, Sedimentology and provenance of Miocene Horse Spring Formation conglomerates; Implications for estimates of motion along the Lake Mead fault system, Nevada: Geological Society of America Abstracts with Programs, v. 20, p. 228.

Sewall, A. J., 1988, Structure and geochemistry of the upper plate of the Saddle Island detachment, Lake Mead, Nevada [M.S. thesis]: Las Vegas, University of Nevada, 84 p.

Sewall, A. J., and Smith, E. I., 1988, Regional correlation and significance of a Tertiary fanglomerate in the upper plate of the Saddle Island detachment, Lake Mead, Nevada: Geological Society of America Abstracts with Programs, v. 20, p. 230.

Smith, E. I., 1982, Geology and geochemistry of the volcanic rocks in the River Mountains, Clark County, Nevada, and comparisons with volcanic rocks in nearby areas, *in* Frost, E. G. and Martin, D. L., eds., Mesozoic-Cenozoic tectonic evolution of the Colorado River region, California, Arizona, and Nevada: San Diego, California, Cordilleran Publishers, p. 41–54.

—— , 1984, Geologic map of the Boulder Beach Quadrangle, Nevada: Nevada Bureau of Mines and Geology Map 81, scale 1:24,000.

Smith, E. I., Eschner, E., Feuerbach, D. L., Naumann, T. R., and Sewall, A. J., 1987, Mid-Tertiary extension in the eastern Basin and Range Province, Nevada and Arizona; The Las Vegas Valley–Detrital Wash transect: Geological Society of America Abstracts with Programs, v. 19, p. 848–849.

Steed, D. A., 1980, Geology of the Virgin River Gorge, northwest Arizona: Provo, Utah, Brigham Young University Geology Studies, v. 27, p. 96–115.

Stewart, J. H., and Poole, F. G., 1974, Lower Paleozoic and uppermost Precambrian Cordilleran miogeocline, Great Basin, western United States, *in* Dickinson, W. R., Tectonics and sedimentation: Society of Economic Paleontologists and Mineralogists Special Publication 22, p. 28–57.

Streckeisen, A. L., 1976, To each plutonic rock its proper name: Earth Science Reviews, v. 12, p. 1–33.

Sundberg, F. A., 1979, Upper Cambrian paleobiology and depositional environments of the lower Nopah Formation, California and Nevada [M.S. thesis]: San Diego, California, San Diego State University, 183 p.

Volborth, A., 1962, Rapakivi-type granite in the Precambrian complex of Gold Butte, Clark County, Nevada: Geological Society of America Bulletin, v. 73, p. 813–832.

—— , 1973, Geology of the granite complex of the Eldorado, Newberry, and northern Dead Mountains, Clark County, Nevada: Nevada Bureau of Mines and Geology Bulletin 80.

Weber, M. E., and Smith, E. I., 1987, Structural and geochemical constraints on the reassembly of disrupted mid-Miocene volcanoes in the Lake Mead–Eldorado Valley area of southern Nevada: Geology, v. 15, p. 553–556.

Wernicke, B., and Axen, G. J., 1988, On the role of isostasy in the evolution of normal fault systems: Geology, v. 16, p. 848–851.

Wernicke, B., Guth, P. L., and Axen, G. J., 1984, Tertiary extensional tectonics in the Sevier thrust belt of southern Nevada, *in* Lintz, J., Jr., ed., Western geological excursions; Geological Society of America annual meeting guidebook, volume 4, field trip 19: Reno, University of Nevada, p. 473–510.

Wernicke, B., Axen, G. J., and Snow, J. K., 1988, Basin and Range extensional tectonics at the latitude of Las Vegas, Nevada: Geological Society of America Bulletin, v. 100, p. 1738–1757.

Manuscript Accepted by the Society August 21, 1989

Geological Society of America
Memoir 176
1990

Chapter 6

Mesozoic and Cenozoic tectonics of the Sevier thrust belt in the Virgin River Valley area, southern Nevada

Gary J. Axen and Brian P. Wernicke
Department of Earth and Planetary Sciences, Harvard University, Cambridge, Massachusetts 02138
Michael F. Skelly
Department of Geology, Northern Arizona University, Flagstaff, Arizona 86011
Wanda J. Taylor
Department of Geology and Geophysics, University of Utah, Salt Lake City, Utah 84112

ABSTRACT

The frontal portion of the Cordilleran thrust belt at latitude 37°N is characterized by a major, east-directed décollement-style thrust system developed within Paleozoic and Mesozoic strata intermediate in thickness between the craton to the east and the Cordilleran miogeocline to the west. Large-magnitude Neogene extension dismembered the thrust system, resulting in unusually complete exposures of it, both along and across strike, and providing an ideal setting in which to study the influence of older thrust structure on extensional faults. A shallow thrust flat was reactivated as a low-angle normal fault over a large area, but the thrust ramp was not. Due to structural duplication by the thrust system, Tertiary normal faults commonly place older rocks on younger, having excised or reactivated thrusts. The hanging walls of large normal faults are commonly brecciated for 10 to 100 m above the fault, whereas thrusts caused little disruption via brecciation, even within centimeters of the fault plane. This criterion was found to be more useful than stratigraphic juxtaposition for distinguishing thrust faults from normal faults.

Detailed mapping has allowed identification and correlation both along and across strike of the following Mesozoic structural sequence: (1) autochthonous crystalline basement and depositionally overlying Phanerozoic cover (bottom), (2) subregionally developed duplexes torn from footwall ramps, (3) a regional décollement thrust that generally carries Middle Cambrian dolostone in its hanging wall, (4) an internally imbricated duplex composed of Middle and Upper Cambrian strata, and (5) an overlying roof thrust that detached at the same horizon as level (4) and carried a comparatively undisrupted sequence as young as Mississippian-Permian. The previously identified Glendale, Mormon, and Tule Springs thrusts are herein correlated and correspond to the thrust at the base of (3). The 50-km-long Weiser syncline (Longwell, 1949) formed as an inclined footwall syncline and was rotated into its recumbent attitude during Tertiary extension.

Extension in the central Mormon Mountains–East Mormon Mountains–Tule Springs Hills transect was controlled by two major west-dipping detachment faults: the older and structurally higher Mormon Peak detachment and the younger, structurally lower Tule Springs detachment. The Mormon Peak detachment cut gradually (5 to 25°) down to the west in its initial trajectory from structurally high levels of the Tule Springs

Axen, G. J., Wernicke, B. P., Skelly, M. F., and Taylor, W. J., 1990, Mesozoic and Cenozoic tectonics of the Sevier thrust belt in the Virgin River Valley area, southern Nevada, *in* Wernicke, B. P., ed., Basin and Range extensional tectonics near the latitude of Las Vegas, Nevada: Boulder, Colorado, Geological Society of America Memoir 176.

thrust plate in the east to autochthonous crystalline basement in the west. By contrast, the Tule Springs detachment followed the Jurassic footwall flat of the Tule Springs thrust in the Tule Springs Hills, then ramped downward through the Mesozoic autochthon into crystalline basement, probably flattening again at depth beneath the Mormon Mountains. Much of the uplift and eastward tilting of the East Mormon Mountains was probably caused by isostatic response to differential tectonic unloading in this extensional ramp zone. The entire Mormon Mountains–Tule Springs Hills area was translated westward, with only minor internal disruption, on the younger Castle Cliff detachment exposed along the edge of the Colorado Plateau to the east. The Mormon Peak detachment postdates ca. 14-Ma ignimbrites, the Tule Springs detachment probably predates the deposition of much or all of the Miocene-Pliocene Muddy Creek Formation, and the Castle Cliff detachment was active during Muddy Creek and more recent time.

A broad east- to east-northeast–trending zone of Tertiary dextral normal oblique-slip faulting and oroflexure in the southern Mormon and East Mormon Mountains (the Moapa Peak shear zone) was active synchronously with detachment faulting. East-west–trending faults that separate differentially extended blocks to the north and south make up the north margin of the shear zone. Gravity, magnetic, and seismic reflection data suggest that the southern boundary is a south-southeast–facing bedrock scarp that forms the north edge of the Mormon Mesa basin. We interpret this scarp as the north edge of a scoop-shaped fault. The shear zone is apparently a transfer structure between areas of differential extension in the east-central and southern Mormon Mountains and southern East Mormon Mountains.

The youngest faults in the area are steep, east- and west-dipping faults in and adjacent to the East Mormon Mountains and Tule Springs Hills. They may be related to movement on the Castle Cliff detachment. Locally, these faults cut Plio-Quaternary(?) pediment gravels, and they are associated with opening the Tule Desert basin and the basin east of the East Mormon Mountains.

INTRODUCTION

The Mesozoic Cordilleran thrust and fold belt of the eastern Great Basin (Sevier orogenic belt) has been strongly disrupted by Cenozoic extension along most of its length (Armstrong, 1968, 1972). In southern Nevada, understanding of the Sevier belt is based primarily on the geology of three range blocks that are relatively undisrupted internally by Neogene extension (Figs. 1 and 2): the Muddy–North Muddy Mountains block, the Las Vegas Range–Sheep Range block, and the Spring Mountains block (e.g., Longwell, 1949; Longwell and others, 1965; Burchfiel and others, 1974; Guth, 1981; Bohannon, 1983a, b). In other ranges the thrust belt is more difficult to understand, largely due to greater complexity of Late Tertiary structures.

Although these three blocks constrain the overall structural style of the Sevier belt in southern Nevada, aspects of the regional architecture of the thrust belt remain enigmatic. The gradual acceptance of major Tertiary crustal mobility in the southern Great Basin (e.g., Anderson, 1971, 1973; Longwell, 1974; Guth, 1981; Wernicke and others, 1982, 1984, 1985; Bohannon, 1984) indicated caution in correlating thrusts between isolated range blocks and suggested that some faults emplacing older rocks on younger be interpreted as normal faults rather than thrusts. Such faults may form either by normal motion along an older thrust plane (thrust reactivation) or by emplacement of the hanging wall

of a thrust onto its footwall along a normal fault discordant to the thrust (thrust excisement). Within the North Muddy Mountains there has been disagreement as to which structural blocks composed Sevier autochthon versus thrust plate. Longwell (1949, 1962; Longwell and others, 1965) argued that the North Muddy Mountains lie above a thrust that he correlated with the Muddy Mountain thrust and that was down-dropped to the north during the Mesozoic along the Arrowhead fault, which separates Paleozoic of the Muddy Mountains from Mesozoic strata in the North Muddy Mountains (Fig. 2). In this view, the Glendale thrust (Fig. 2) is structurally higher than the Muddy Mountain thrust. Bohannon (1983a, b) favored the interpretation that most of the North Muddy Mountains are autochthonous, because of similar Mesozoic facies in the North Muddy Mountains and on the adjacent Colorado Plateau and because of the unlikelihood that rocks as young as Jurassic in age would be preserved in the hanging wall of a major frontal thrust. Bohannon allowed that rocks above the relatively minor Summit–Willow Tank thrust system are probably allochthonous and suggested that those thrusts might connect to the North Buffington fault to the west in the subsurface and die out to the north into the Weiser syncline (Fig. 2). He correlated the Muddy Mountain and Glendale thrusts.

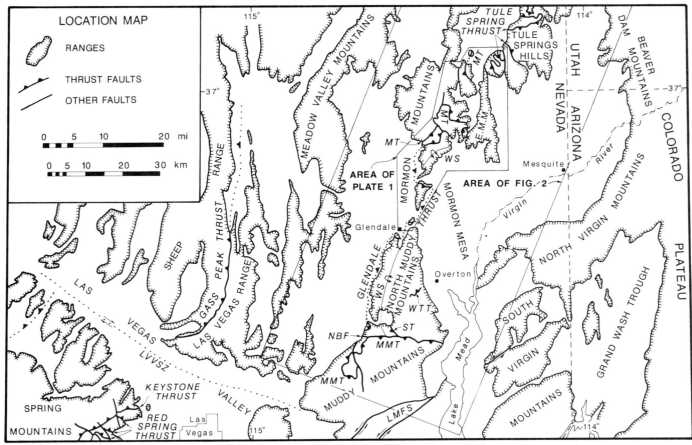

Figure 1. Location map of the southern Great Basin and adjacent Colorado Plateau, showing major thrusts and other faults. EMM, East Mormon Mountains; LMFS, Lake Mead fault system; LVVSZ, Las Vegas Valley shear zone; MMT, Muddy Mountain thrust; MT, Mormon thrust; NBF, North Buffington fault; ST, Summit thrust; WS, Weiser syncline; WTT, Willow Tank thrust.

Axen (1984) and Wernicke and others (1984, 1985) suggested that the North Muddy Mountains are allochthonous, lying above a thrust correlative with the Contact–Red Spring thrust in the Spring Mountains (Fig. 1; Longwell, 1926; Hewett, 1931; Davis, 1973; Carr, 1983). Detailed mapping in the central Mormon Mountains and reconnaissance in the southern Mormon Mountains (Wernicke, 1981; Wernicke and others, 1984, 1985) suggested that the Weiser syncline in the southern Mormon Mountains was underlain by the Mormon thrust. Because the syncline can be traced into the North Muddy Mountains, that range was regarded as allochthonous also. These authors followed Bohannon's correlation of the Glendale and Muddy Mountain thrusts and correlated the Mormon and Tule Springs thrust, following Tschanz and Pampeyen (1970) and Olmore (1971).

New detailed mapping from the southern and eastern Mormon Mountains and western Tule Springs Hills indicates that the Tule Springs, Mormon, and Glendale thrusts are all correlative (Skelly and Axen, 1988) and have been severely dismembered by Tertiary extensional tectonism. Below we describe the structural relations and essential stratigraphic nomenclature in the western

Tule Springs Hills–eastern Mormon Mountains transect and then present an integrated tectonic history of the region.

STRATIGRAPHIC NOMENCLATURE

Most of the stratigraphic nomenclature used in this report is standard for this region (Fig. 3). However, understanding the structural relations has proven to be impossible without mapping thin subunits (typically <150 m) of the Cambrian to Ordovician sequence. In particular, mapping subunits of the Middle Cambrian Bonanza King and Upper Cambrian Nopah formations has proven to be invaluable. In the ensuing discussions we use formal member/formation designations if possible, and if not, we use "map unit" when referring to designations on Plate 1 and "subunit" when referring to more detailed stratigraphy. For example, note that within the Banded Mountain Member of the Bonanza King Formation, map unit b1 comprises subunits €bb1 and €bb2.

Stratigraphic and lithologic descriptions are given in Wernicke (1982), Skelly (1987), Hintze (1986), and Olmore (1971), but here we make several revisions. Olmore (1971) considered the strata of the East Mormon Mountains to be allochthonous and everywhere separated from the crystalline basement by a thrust fault. For this reason, he inferred that the basal sandstone, which he referred to as Prospect Mountain Quartzite (a miogeoclinal unit mapped farther northwest), was everywhere tectonically thinned from initial thicknesses much in excess of those in the East Mormon Mountains. Our detailed and reconnaissance

mapping indicates that the basal sandstone is depositional on the basement in a number of places in the East Mormon Mountains and is not significantly thinned in many exposures. This unit is therefore correlated with the Tapeats Sandstone, a cratonal unit mapped on the Colorado Plateau. Olmore (1971) did not subdivide the carbonate sequence beneath the Mississippian in the eastern Mormon Mountains and western Tule Springs Hills or beneath the Ordovician in the East Mormon Mountains.

Wernicke (1982; Wernicke and others, 1985) defined most of the lithologic units that we currently map in the Cambrian-Ordovician section, although lack of fossil age constraints caused several units to be misnamed in those publications. In particular, the silty interval at the base of the Pogonip Group (Fig. 3) was believed to be the Dunderburg Shale Member of the Nopah Formation. Subsequent work (Skelly, 1987) has clarified this and shown that the Dunderburg is represented by a thin sequence of silty dolostones within subunit €bb4 as originally defined by Wernicke (1982). Therefore, subunit €bb4 as used here is restricted to strata below that sequence. Wernicke's (1982) subunit €bb5 is equivalent to our lower Nopah Formation, subunit €n1. Rocks previously mapped as Nopah Formation are included in our Pogonip Group (subunit Op1), and his Pogonip map unit is the same as our subunit Op2. His map unit Ou (upper Ordovician, undifferentiated) contains our map unit Oe, and in the thrust sheet includes fine-grained nonfossiliferous dolostone that may correlate with the Silurian Laketown Dolomite.

Limestone mapped as the lower Papoose Lake Member of the Bonanza King (€bp1) by Taylor (1984) actually belongs to subunit €bb2, which is normally a dolostone.

DESCRIPTIVE STRUCTURAL GEOLOGY

Mesozoic compressional structures in the area under consideration are commonly cut and rotated by Tertiary extensional structures. The two ages of structures are distinguished by cross-cutting relations, age of deformed strata, and structural style. Strata adjacent to thrust faults tend to be relatively undeformed, with sedimentary bedding well preserved near the contact. In contrast, thick zones of clast-rotated breccia are found adjacent to extensional structures (particularly in carbonate rocks), often destroying bedding characteristics of strata within a few to a few tens of meters of the contact. The normal faults typically cut both hanging- and footwall strata at significant angles, whereas thrust faults are generally subparallel to strata in their hanging walls and are commonly associated with folds at a variety of scales. The thrusts usually have a restricted range of hanging-wall stratigraphy directly adjacent to the fault (Fig. 3; Burchfiel and others, 1982). Because extension overprinted a thin-skinned thrust belt, an older-over-younger age relation across a fault is not sufficient to distinguish whether it is a thrust or low-angle normal fault. In this section we describe the geometry and timing of key Mesozoic and Tertiary structures. Below, we first describe the geometry of Mesozoic and Cenozoic structures, then describe how structural markers of Mesozoic age constrain Cenozoic offsets. We then

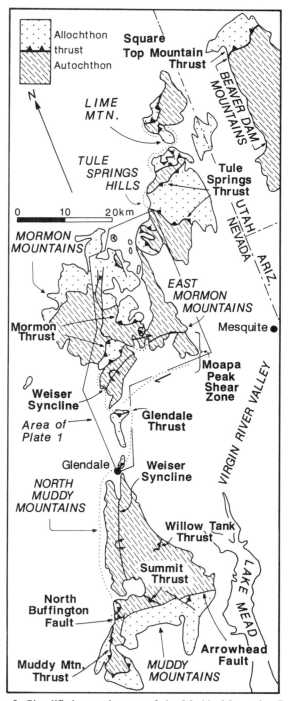

Figure 2. Simplified tectonic map of the Muddy Mountains–Beaver Dam Mountains area, showing upper and lower plates of major thrusts on a base of pre-Tertiary outcrop.

present an overall synthesis of the Mesozoic structures, including their relations with those to the south in the North Muddy and Muddy Mountains.

Mesozoic structures

The Mesozoic thrust system is dominated by an east-vergent, large-displacement décollement thrust, the hanging wall of which is detached in Middle Cambrian dolostone of the Bonanza King Formation (Fig. 3). The autochthon contains the Weiser syncline (Longwell, 1949), which is exposed for 60 km along strike in the North Muddy and southern Mormon Mountains (Fig. 2). In the central Mormon Mountains and Tule Springs Hills (Fig. 4), the footwall consists of a flat in Mississippian limestone, a ramp, and an upper flat in Jurassic red beds. A ramp from Middle Cambrian to Mississippian is required farther west in the subsurface, and a south-facing lateral ramp may have existed between the central and southern Mormon Mountains (see below). Parautochthonous thrust slivers, torn from footwall ramps and commonly folded, are present in the Mormon Mountains and Tule Springs Hills (Fig. 4). The base of the thrust allochthon is typically composed of an imbricate thrust duplex of as much as 20 to 30 repetitions of west-facing Middle and Upper Cambrian dolostone (Fig. 4). This imbricate thrust duplex forms a key structural marker for establishing thrust correlations along strike. An overlying roof thrust separates the imbricate thrusts from higher Middle Cambrian to Permo-Carboniferous strata.

Weiser syncline. The Weiser syncline (Longwell, 1949) dominates the structure of the North Muddy and southern Mormon Mountains (Fig. 2) and is delineated by a resistant ridge of overturned Kaibab limestone, which except for a short interruption in the southern Mormon Mountains, is exposed continuously for a distance of nearly 60 km along strike. Its continuity between the two ranges provides an important constraint on possible thrust correlations and Tertiary reconstructions. In the North Muddy Mountains it is north-trending, east-vergent, recumbent, and isoclinal (Longwell, 1949; Fig. 5) and ends abruptly in the south against the steeply north-dipping North Buffington fault of Bohannon (1983a; Fig. 2). Rocks of the overturned limb range in age from Middle Cambrian to Triassic, with the latter thrust eastward over upright Jurassic to Triassic strata along the Summit thrust in the southern part of the North Muddy Mountains

Figure 3. Schematic stratigraphic column, eastern Mormon Mountains–Tule Springs Hills area. Designations along the left edge are those shown on Plate 1, and the right side shows members and subunits mapped in the field, many of which are lumped together on Plate 1. Relative thicknesses are only approximate, as thickness changes occur across thrusts. Most thrusts in the region detached in the uppermost Papoose Lake or lower Banded Mountain Member of the Bonanza King Formation. The Mississippian footwall flat in the Mormon Mountains is within the Bullion or Yellow Pine Members of the Monte Cristo Formation, and the Jurassic footwall flat in the Tule Springs Hills is at the top of the Middle Member of the Kayenta Formation.

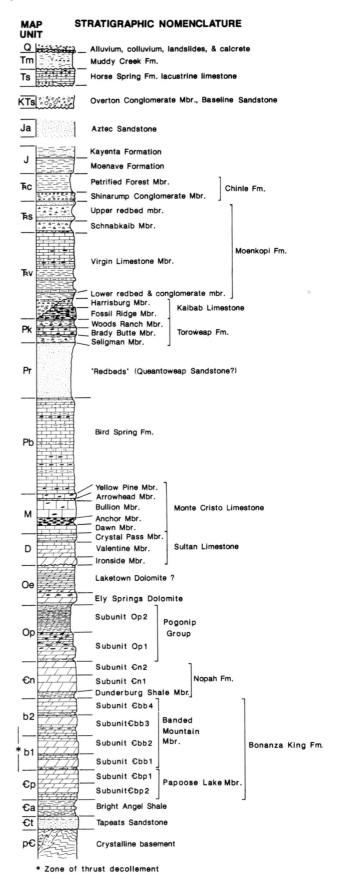

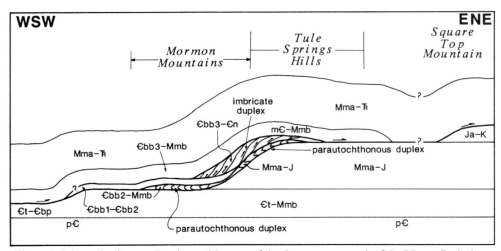

Figure 4. Schematic diagram showing architecture of the thrust system north of the Moapa Peak shear zone and age range of strata in each structural component. Mma, Mmb: Anchor and Bullion members of the Monte Cristo Formation (respectively); other unit designations as in Figure 3.

(Longwell, 1949; Fig. 2). Northward, the overturned limb is erosionally beveled by the synorogenic Overton conglomerate member of the Cretaceous–Early Tertiary Baseline Sandstone, which in turn is disconformably overlain by Miocene beds (Longwell, 1949; Bohannon, 1983b).

The syncline is concealed by a large klippe of the Glendale thrust in the southernmost Mormon Mountains but reappears to the north at Moapa Peak (Figs. 2 and 6; Plate 1, in pocket inside back cover), where it plunges gently to the southwest, apparently rotated about 40° clockwise from its trend in the North Muddy Mountains (Fig. 5). The structurally lowest exposures of the Weiser syncline are northwest of Moapa Peak, where upright Cambrian rocks of the lower limb crop out on the south flank of the Mormon Mountains structural dome (Plate 1; Skelly, 1987), which is defined by autochthonous strata and underlying basement and is roughly centered on the subcircular topography of the Mormon Mountains (Wernicke and others, 1985). The nature of the northward termination of the Weiser syncline is enigmatic at present, largely due to complex Tertiary deformation north of Moapa Peak, and is addressed below. No equivalent or correlative structure is exposed to the north.

Glendale thrust plate. Along most of its length, the Weiser syncline is flanked on the west or overlain structurally by erosional remnants of the Glendale thrust plate. The oldest footwall rocks that are clearly in stratigraphic continuity with the Weiser syncline are Middle Cambrian north of the Buffington window in the Muddy Mountains (Longwell, 1949; Bohannon, 1983a) and Upper Cambrian north of Moapa Peak (Plate 1; Skelly, 1987). In addition, Middle Cambrian strata are the lowest rocks carried by the Glendale thrust. These relations indicate that the Glendale thrust probably rode on a Middle Cambrian décollement for all or most of its length west of the Weiser syncline.

From Glendale northward, the Glendale plate is composed of a series of imbricate thrust slices of Middle Cambrian Bonanza King Formation and/or Upper Cambrian Nopah Formation

(Skelly, 1987; Plate 1; Fig. 7). Similar imbrications are present in the Glendale and Muddy Mountain thrust plates in the northwest Muddy Mountains (Bohannon, 1983a). Northwest of Moapa Peak, 20 or more thrust slices are present (Plate 1), composed of subunits Єbb3 and Єbb4 of the Banded Mountain Member of the Bonanza King Formation and subunit Єn1 of the Nopah Formation (map units b2 and Єn). The imbricate stack is underlain by a gently south-dipping fault that is parallel to subunit Єbb2 in its footwall (Fig. 8; Plate 1). The hanging wall of this fault is commonly highly brecciated, and younger-over-older relations are ubiquitous, although no more than a single subunit is omitted. We interpret this fault as a floor thrust to the imbricate duplex, which has been modified as a low-angle normal fault. We suggest reactivation rather than excisement because the fault is parallel to beds in subunit Єbb2 in the footwall, as would be expected for a floor thrust, and the oldest strata in the imbrications belong strati-

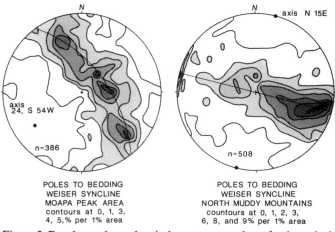

Figure 5. Equal area, lower hemisphere stereonet plots of poles to bedding in the Weiser syncline, showing 40 degrees of apparent clockwise rotation of the axis of the Weiser syncline between the North Muddy Mountains and Moapa Peak in the southern Mormon Mountains.

Figure 6. Oblique aerial photograph looking approximately southwest down the axis of the Weiser syncline. Moapa Peak is just out of the view on the right.

graphically just above the youngest beds below the fault. Fault striae and other indicators suggest latest movement in a northeast-southwest direction (R. E. Anderson, written communication, 1987). Erosion or tectonic denudation have removed any overlying roof thrust in the southern Mormon Mountains.

As with the Weiser syncline (see above), erosion of the Mormon Mountains dome has exposed lower structural levels of the Glendale thrust in the north than in the south. Exposures of the Glendale thrust along the west side of the North Muddy Mountains dip moderately west, whereas the more easterly exposures are typically subhorizontal (Longwell, 1949). Just north of Glendale the thrust is nearly flat lying (Longwell, 1949; Bohannon, 1983b; Skelly, 1987). Along strike only 1 km to the south, footwall strata are disconformably overlain by Miocene strata dipping about 20° east (Bohannon, 1983b; Smith and others, 1987). Similarly, north of Candy Peak (Fig. 7) the thrust is overlapped by Tertiary limestone dipping 20 to 30° east (Skelly, 1987; Plate 1). There, the thrust surface is not exposed, but the thrust cuts upsection eastward in its footwall, through overturned Jurassic Moenave and Kayenta Formations and Aztec Sandstone. Restoration of the Tertiary strata to horizontal imparts a west dip to the thrust at both locations, which combined with stratigraphically high footwall position, indicates that the thrust is exposed near the top of its ramp near Glendale.

On the southwest side of Moapa Peak, the thrust plate overrides overturned Mississippian and Devonian strata, and in exposures northwest of Moapa Peak the footwall is composed of upright Cambrian strata of the Nopah Formation in stratigraphic continuity with the lower limb of the Weiser syncline (Skelly, 1987; Plate 1; Fig. 9a). Near Moapa Peak the Glendale thrust is apparently exposed near the base of the ramp.

Mormon thrust plate. The Mormon thrust in the central Mormon Mountains is exposed on a footwall flat in the Bullion Member of the Mississippian Monte Cristo Limestone, from which it climbs eastward across Carboniferous beds and onto strata as high as Permian red beds, forming the base of a major ramp (Tschanz and Pampeyan, 1970; Wernicke and others, 1985; Plate 1; Fig. 4). Due to eastward rotation by Neogene normal faults, exposures of the thrust flat now dip east, and exposures of the ramp are subhorizontal to gently east dipping.

Throughout much of the central Mormon Mountains, parautochthonous duplex slices are sandwiched between the Mormon thrust plate and the underlying Mississippian footwall flat (Wernicke and others, 1985; Plate 1). These parautochthonous strata range in age from Cambrian to Mississippian and were probably torn from a Cambrian-Mississippian ramp farther west (Wernicke and others, 1985; Taylor, 1984; Ellis, 1984). In the easternmost exposures, rocks of the duplex system were transported up the base of the higher ramp, onto rocks as young as the Bird Spring Formation (Fig. 3; Plate 1). Strata of the parautochthonous duplexes are typically east facing or contorted into northwest-trending, overturned to isoclinal folds cut by minor thrusts.

Detailed (1:12,000 scale) geologic mapping of the Mormon

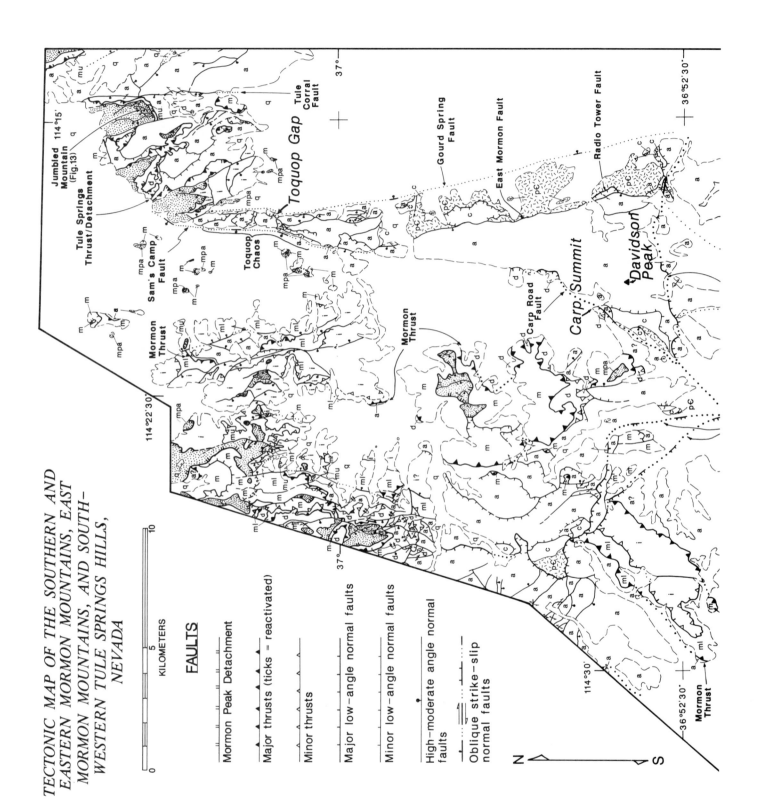

TECTONIC MAP OF THE SOUTHERN AND
EASTERN MORMON MOUNTAINS, EAST
MORMON MOUNTAINS, AND SOUTH-
WESTERN TULE SPRINGS HILLS,
NEVADA

FAULTS

Mormon Peak Detachment

Major thrusts (ticks = reactivated)

Minor thrusts

Major low-angle normal faults

Minor low-angle normal faults

High-moderate angle normal
faults

Oblique strike-slip
normal faults

KILOMETERS

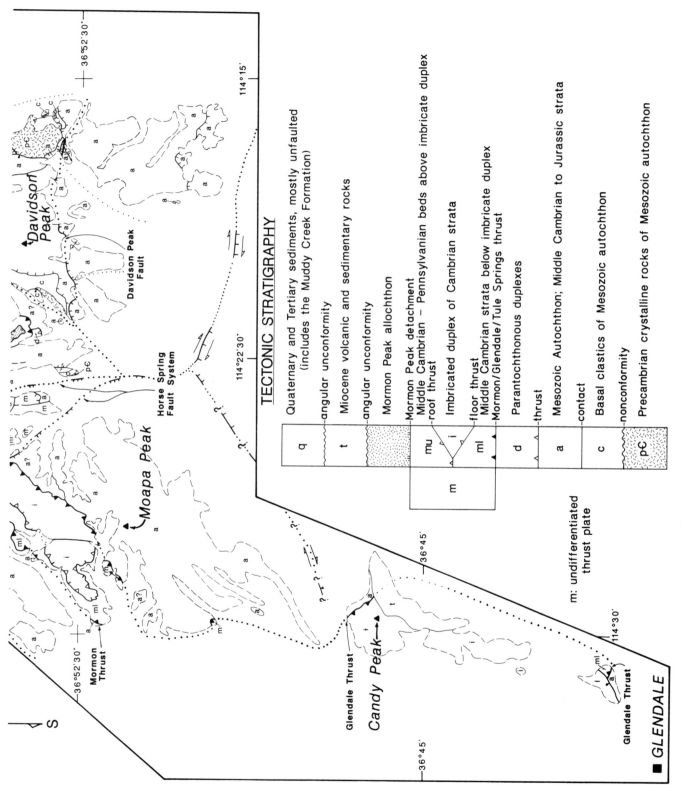

TECTONIC STRATIGRAPHY

q	Quaternary and Tertiary sediments, mostly unfaulted (includes the Muddy Creek Formation)
∿ t	angular unconformity
	Miocene volcanic and sedimentary rocks
∿	angular unconformity
	Mormon Peak allochthon
mu	Mormon Peak detachment
	Middle Cambrian – Pennsylvanian beds above imbricate duplex
i	roof thrust
	Imbricated duplex of Cambrian strata
ml	floor thrust
	Middle Cambrian strata below imbricate duplex
	Mormon/Glendale/Tule Springs thrust
d	Parantochthonous duplexes
	thrust
a	Mesozoic Autochthon; Middle Cambrian to Jurassic strata
	contact
c	Basal clastics of Mesozoic autochthon
∿ pC	nonconformity
	Precambrian crystalline rocks of Mesozoic autochthon

m: undifferentiated thrust plate

Figure 7. Simplified tectonic map of the area of Plate 1.

Figure 8. View to northeast of the (reactivated?) floor thrust (FT) and overlying imbricate thrusts northwest of Moapa Peak. Unit designations as on Figure 3.

thrust plate in the northeastern Mormon Mountains (summarized on Plate 1) has revealed the following structural sequence. The base of the Mormon plate comprises subunits €bb1, €bb2, and €bb3 of the Banded Mountain Member of the Bonanza King Formation (Fig. 3), which are structurally relatively simple, containing only a few minor thrusts. Overlying this is an internally imbricated structural package composed of subunits €bb3, €bb4, and lower Nopah Formation (Fig. 10). This imbricate duplex (Fig. 4) is floored by a thrust running on a footwall décollement high in subunit €bb2 or in subunit €bb3 (Fig. 11). The imbricate duplex is bounded above by a thrust with a hanging-wall décollement in subunit €bb3 (Fig. 12). Generally, strata preserved above the roof thrust in the Mormon Mountains are only as high as subunit €bb4 or the lowest Nopah Formation and are truncated above by the Mormon Peak detachment (Fig. 12).

The westward continuation of the roof and floor thrusts of the imbricate duplex is poorly understood due to discontinuous exposure and extensional overprinting by the Mormon Peak detachment, which cuts through the Mormon thrust and into autochthonous or parautochthonous strata within a few kilometers of the west edge of Plate 1 (Taylor, 1984; Ellis, 1984). However, in the northwest corner of Plate 1 the roof thrust can be traced west (in section 33, T10S, R68E) to a position (in section 32) where it is the only mapped thrust within the Banded Mountain Member, which there is continuous down to subunit €bb1. There the thrust is parallel to both hanging-wall and footwall strata and neither repeats nor excises significant amounts of strata, which suggests that the roof and floor thrusts merge westward into a décollement.

Tule Springs thrust plate. Structure of the Tule Springs Hills is dominated by an older-over-younger fault that places rocks as old as subunit €bb3 of the Banded Mountain Member of the Bonanza King Formation above the Triassic Chinle Formation and Jurassic Moenave and Kayenta Formations (Tschanz and Pampeyan, 1970; Smith and others, 1987; Plate 1).

Throughout most of the Tule Springs Hills (east of Plate 1) the fault is parallel to the underlying Middle Member of the Kayenta Formation (see Hintze, 1986, for a description of this unit). The hanging wall is highly extended internally by planar and listric normal faults that end at or merge with the flat fault plane. By contrast, the lower plate is not extended (Smith and others, 1987; Axen, unpublished mapping). For these reasons, the Tule Springs thrust is interpreted as a high-level thrust flat that was reactivated as a west-directed low-angle normal fault (Wernicke and others, 1984; Smith and others, 1987). This reactivated fault is labeled "Tule Springs thrust" on all figures and on Plate 1 but will be referred to as the Tule Springs detachment when extensional movement is being discussed.

In the western Tule Springs Hills the thrust is apparently preserved at the top of a ramp, cutting upsection to the east in its footwall through Triassic and Jurassic units (Plate 1). Throughout this area, a small-amplitude overturned footwall syncline is preserved, although it could not be shown everywhere on Plate 1. Figures 13 and 14 show the east end of the syncline, at the extreme top of the ramp, where the Middle Member of the Kayenta is folded. Farther west the overturned syncline folds Shinarump Conglomerate. The amplitude of this fold is only several tens of meters, but it is present in >1,000 m of section across several kilometers of outcrop, everywhere adjacent to the thrust. No folds or thrusts have been observed structurally below it. Therefore, we interpret it as a fold formed below the thrust at the top of the ramp and use it as an indicator of proximity to the original thrust surface, before reactivation.

Gently west-dipping normal faults splay downward from the Tule Springs detachment in the western Tule Springs Hills (Plate 1; Fig. 7) and cut the footwall, rotating autochthonous strata eastward and dismembering the overturned syncline discussed above. These faults mark the western edge of unextended footwall of the Tule Springs thrust.

The base of the upper plate of the Tule Springs thrust in the

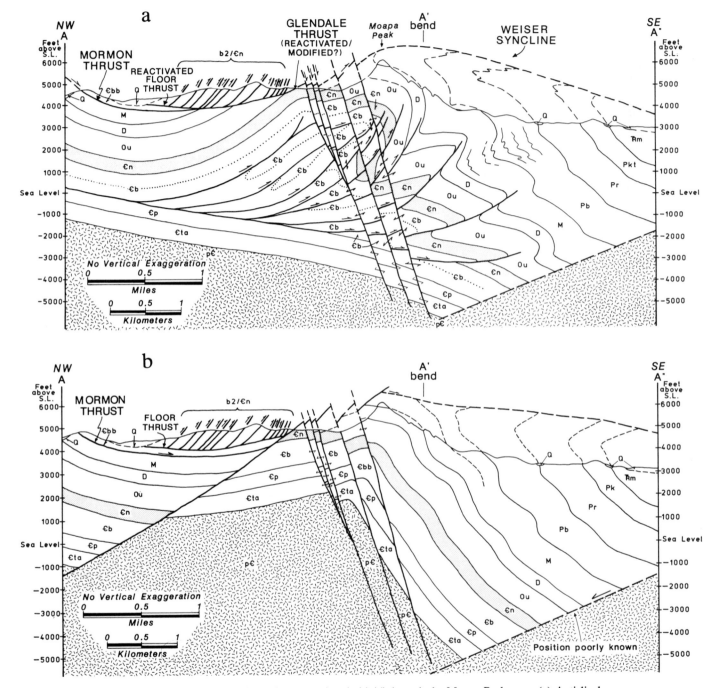

Figure 9. Alternative versions of cross section A-A′-A″ through the Moapa Peak area. (a) Anticlinal culmination northwest of Moapa Peak is interpreted as a triangle zone at the tip of a blind thrust system. (b) The anticlinal culmination interpreted as a basement-cored structure modified by a normal fault. Units as on Plate 1, except Єta, Tapeats Sandstone and Bright Angel Shale, undivided.

Figure 10. Oblique aerial view to the north-northwest of the imbricate thrust duplex (center foreground) in the northeastern Mormon Mountains. Light-colored bands are subunit €bb3 and dark-colored bands are subunit €bb4 of the Bonanza King Formation (Fig. 3).

Figure 11. Imbricate thrusts above the floor thrust (arrows) in the northeastern Mormon Mountains. Dots show the €bbs3 (light)/€bb4 (dark) contact. View is to the north-northeast.

western Tule Springs Hills is composed of several imbricate thrust slices of subunits €bb3 and €bb4 of the Banded Mountain Member of the Bonanza King Formation (Smith and others, 1987; Plate 1; Fig. 4). Generally this imbricate stack is no thicker vertically than three or four thrust slices, although three or four times that number may be present across strike. These imbricates are overlain by a roof thrust detached in subunit €bb3 of the Banded Mountain Member of the Bonanza King Formation. Northeast of the area shown on Plate 1, the roof thrust merges

with the Tule Springs thrust, forming the eastern pinchout of the imbricate duplex. The roof thrust carries a section from the oldest strata seen in the imbricate zone to as young as the Bird Spring Formation. Units 1 and 2 of the Banded Mountain Member, found below imbricate slices in the eastern Mormon Mountains, are not present in the Tule Springs Hills, where the imbricates rest directly on Mesozoic strata. Therefore, the entire amount of thrust shortening in the Tule Springs Hills may feed westward into the floor and roof thrusts of the imbricate duplex in the

Figure 12. View of a part of the imbricate thrust duplex in the northeastern Mormon Mountains, showing the floor and roof thrust and Mississippian rocks (M) above the structurally higher Mormon Peak detachment (double tick marks). Labels 3 and 4 refer to subunits €bb3 and €bb4 in the Banded Mountain Member of the Bonanza King Formation.

Mormon Mountains, rather than into the basal Mormon thrust itself (Fig. 4).

Tertiary structures

The North Muddy and southern Mormon Mountains are only mildly deformed internally by extension-related structures (Longwell, 1949; Bohannon, 1983b; Skelly, 1987; Plate 1) even though they were translated approximately 45 to 65 km west-

southwest from the Colorado Plateau (e.g., Wernicke and others, 1988, 1989; Anderson, 1973; Bohannon, 1983a) and tilted eastward (Bohannon, 1983b). In contrast, the central Mormon Mountains, East Mormon Mountains, and Tule Springs Hills were highly extended internally in Neogene time, primarily by deformation associated with movement on the Mormon Peak and Tule Springs detachments (Wernicke and others, 1984, 1985; Smith and others, 1987). The Moapa Peak shear zone intervenes between the southern and central Mormon Mountains,

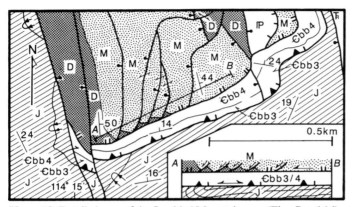

Figure 13. Detailed map of the Jumbled Mountain area (Figs. 7 and 16). The Mormon Peak detachment is shown with double ticks, the Tule Springs thrust/detachment with teeth and ticks, low-angle normal faults with single ticks, and high-angle normal faults with bar-and-ball symbols. Note that the imbricate thrust duplex is absent here, although it is present to the east (Smith and others, 1987), suggesting that this part of the Tule Springs thrust plate was translated off of the imbricate duplex by local reactivation of the roof thrust. J, Jurassic Moenave and Kayenta formations; ͞Ŧ, Triassic Moenkopi Formation; ℙ, Mississippian-Permian Bird Spring Formation; M, Mississippian Monte Cristo Formation; D, Devonian Sultan Formation; Єbb3 and Єbb4, subunits of the Cambrian Bonanza King Formation.

composing a broad east-northeast-trending to east-trending zone of right-oblique normal faults and oroflexure (Olmore, 1971; Plate 1). To date, the Moapa Peak shear zone has been described only in general terms, and its relations to detachments to the north and Tertiary features to the south have been enigmatic.

In this section we describe current knowledge of specific Tertiary structures exposed in the Mormon Mountains, East Mormon Mountains, and Tule Springs Hills. In the following section, we integrate these observations with geophysical results to constrain a kinematic model of Tertiary extensional tectonics of the area. We rely heavily on mapping by Olmore (1971) in the East Mormon Mountains, where several large normal faults and associated structures are exposed (Plate 1).

East Mormon Mountains. Olmore (1971) mapped a south-dipping fault along the southern end of the East Mormon Mountains, which we refer to as the Davidson Peak fault (Fig. 7; Plate 1). It separates the topographically high Davidson Peak block to the north, which is a relatively undisrupted, east-tilted block of Cambrian through Pennsylvanian strata and underlying basement, from low-lying ridges to the south composed of Paleozoic and Triassic strata. The Ordovician of the northern block is thicker than that south of the fault, with younger Ordovician units present below a sub–Middle Devonian unconformity on the north (Wernicke, 1982). These relations suggest right-lateral juxtaposition of facies with more miogeoclinal affinities to the north against facies with more cratonal affinities to the south (Wernicke and others, 1984). Because the Davidson Peak block is stratigraphically continuous down to the basal Phanerozoic nonconformity, and because none of the thrusts in the region carry

crystalline basement, we consider the Davidson Peak block as part of the Mesozoic autochthon. The regional disconformity of Tertiary on autochthonous strata of the Colorado Plateau (e.g., Bohannon, 1984; Wernicke and Axen, 1988), the younger-over-older juxtaposition across the fault, and the steep eastward tilt and repetition of fault blocks south of the fault suggest a Tertiary age for the Davidson Peak fault (Wernicke and others, 1984).

East of Davidson Peak, Olmore (1971) mapped a younger-on-older low-angle fault contact between Upper Paleozoic strata and Proterozoic basement that he named the East Mormon fault (Plate 1). Although it is clearly low angle near the radio towers east of Davidson Peak, most of the length of the East Mormon fault as mapped by Olmore is actually a younger high-angle (40 to 50°) fault (Wernicke and others, 1984, Stop 2.2; Plate 1). We refer to the low-angle fault as the Radio Tower fault and restrict the name East Mormon fault to the younger high-angle structure. The relative age of the East Mormon and Davidson Peak faults is unclear. Traced northward, the East Mormon fault gradually crosses to the west side of the East Mormon Mountains, where it either merges with or is cut by the Sam's Camp Fault, the range-bounding fault that cuts Pliocene(?) gravels south of Toquop Gap (Fig. 7; Plate 1).

South of Toquop Gap, gently west-dipping faults place Upper Paleozoic on Middle Cambrian (Olmore, 1971; Plate 1). These faults share a common footwall with the Radio Tower fault and like that fault are in the footwall of the East Mormon fault. They are interpreted to be correlative with the Radio Tower fault. The Radio Tower fault system as a whole apparently loses displacement to the north, where it merges with a zone of brittle structural attenuation by low-angle faults that we refer to here as the Toquop chaos (Plate 1; Fig. 7; see Noble, 1941, for definition of *chaos*). To the south the Radio Tower fault may merge with the Davidson Peak fault, where a chaos zone juxtaposes Kaibab Limestone (in the highest fault slice) over basement (Plate 1).

The East Mormon Mountains are bounded on the east by the steeply east-dipping Gourd Spring fault (Olmore, 1971; Plate 1). The Gourd Spring fault has relatively minor displacement at its north end between the East Mormon Mountains and Tule Springs Hills, juxtaposing the lowest parts of the Tule Springs thrust plate against Upper Paleozoic rocks of the autochthon in the East Mormon Mountains and cutting low-angle faults of the Toquop chaos. Small-displacement, steeply to moderately west-dipping faults that cut all other structures in the bedrock are exposed in the western Tule Springs Hills and form a complex of downdropped keystone blocks east of the Gourd Spring fault (Plate 1). To the south, the Gourd Spring fault is interpreted to become the range-bounding fault and may have been important in the opening of the basin east of the East Mormon Mountains and south of the Tule Springs Hills. The Gourd Spring fault was probably active into Plio-Quaternary(?) time (Olmore, 1971) and is younger than the low-angle faults within the range.

Between the Mormon and East Mormon Mountains, a major fault system largely concealed by alluvium juxtaposes rocks of the Mormon thrust plate or the underlying parautoch-

Figure 14. Photo of the south face of Jumbled Mountain (Fig. 13), showing a small overturned fold (dots) in Jurassic beds at the top of the thrust ramp, and the Tule Springs thrust/detachment (teeth and ticks) below subhorizontal but brecciated strata of subunits €bb3 (light) and €bb4 (dark). East-dipping Devonian (light) and Mississippian (dark) limestones lie above subunit €bb4 on the Mormon Peak detachment (double ticks). The easternmost Devonian beds are near the center of the cliff.

thonous duplex against crystalline basement of the thrust autochthon. Near Carp Summit (Fig. 7; Plate 1), Olmore (1971) mapped several gently west-dipping faults in this zone, the largest of which he called the Carp Road fault. Although the Carp Road fault itself is not exposed, it is inferred to be subparallel to the other low-angle faults at Carp Summit, and to the Radio Tower fault, and to have formed prior to formation of the relatively minor high-angle faults such as the East Mormon fault.

The crystalline basement in the footwall of the Carp Road fault terminates to the south against the Davidson Peak fault (Fig. 7; Plate 1), the hanging wall of which is composed of autochthonous Cambrian through Permian strata. Directly west of these hanging-wall rocks, across the southward projection of the Carp Road fault, are autochthonous Cambrian through Mississippian strata (Plate 1). It is very unlikely that displacement of the magnitude seen at Carp Summit is present between these autochthonous outcrops. Therefore, the Carp Road fault probably bends to the east and merges with the Davidson Peak fault, which has comparable stratigraphic throw. The ridge that runs southwest from Davidson Peak to this bend is probably a highly eroded "turtleback" structure (e.g., Wright and others, 1974), formed by tectonic denudation of an antiformal culmination in the footwall of the Davidson Peak–Carp Road fault system.

Mormon Mountains. North of Moapa Peak, the Mormon thrust and the imbricate thrust stack in the Glendale plate are truncated by a steeply to moderately south-southwest–dipping fault zone, the Horse Spring fault of Wernicke and others (1985; Plate 1; Fig. 7). Followed northwestward, the Horse Spring fault bends abruptly to a northerly strike, dipping gently westward and exposing crystalline basement in the footwall (Fig. 15), in a

geometry similar to the Davidson Peak–Carp Road fault system. Farther north it loses displacement, splaying into several small-displacement faults (Wernicke and others, 1984, 1985). At the bend it has about 3 km of down-to-the-west dip slip (Wernicke and others, 1985). This relation implies a large component of right-lateral slip on the west-northwest–trending portion of the fault zone. The northeastern strand of the Horse Spring fault zone (Fig. 7) underlies outcrops that contain a low-angle normal fault that places Cambrian strata of the Mormon thrust plate above autochthonous strata from high in the Bird Spring Formation (the Permian part, Skelly, 1987; Plate 1), indicating extensional modification of the central or upper part of the thrust ramp. In the footwall of the Horse Spring fault zone there, the Mormon thrust is exposed at the very base of its Mississippian-to-Jurassic ramp. This relation also suggests right-oblique normal slip on the northeast strand of the Horse Spring fault zone, which carried a sliver of Permian Bird Spring Formation strata from high on the ramp southwestward to a position at the base of the ramp (see the section on Tertiary kinematic history).

A series of moderately and gently west-dipping normal faults is found in the east-central Mormon Mountains, east and north of the Horse Spring fault (Plate 1, Figs. 7, 16–18; the "eastern imbricate normal fault belt" of Wernicke and others, 1985). These faults have rotated domino-style to the east, causing eastward rotation of strata and older low-angle structures such as the Mormon thrust and Mormon Peak detachment. The domino-style faults lose displacement northward in a manner similar to that of the Horse Spring fault.

The Horse Spring fault is a boundary between differentially tilted strata, with relatively flat-lying strata in its hanging wall and

Figure 15. Aerial oblique view to the north-northwest of the Horse Spring fault system (HSF) where it changes from northwesterly to northerly strike and exposes crystalline basement of the autochthon in a deeply eroded turtleback-style structure. pЄ, crystalline basement; mЄ, Bonanza King Formation; Єc, Cambrian carbonates; Pz, Ordovician to Pennsylvanian strata; MT, Mormon thrust; GT, Glendale thrust; i, imbricate thrust duplex; FT, floor thrust.

strongly east-tilted beds in its footwall (Wernicke and others, 1985; Plate 1; Fig. 18). To restore this geometry, the Horse Spring fault must be drawn as a concave-down fault that bounds the top of the domino-style fault set and allowed it to rotate east relative to the rocks to the west (Wernicke and others, 1985; Fig. 18).

The most important Tertiary structure in the Mormon Mountains is the Mormon Peak detachment (Wernicke and others, 1984, 1985), which originally had a gentle west dip (5 to 25°) and has 15 to 20 km of normal offset. From the Tule Springs Hills on the east to the western Mormon Mountains, the Mormon Peak detachment cuts gradually down to the west in its footwall, from structurally high levels within the Tule Springs thrust plate, downward through the imbricate thrust zone, parautochthonous duplexes, the Mormon thrust, autochthonous Paleozoic strata, and finally into crystalline basement rocks on the west side of the Mormon Mountains (Wernicke and others, 1984, 1985; Smith and others, 1987). In the northern Mormon Mountains the Mormon Peak detachment cuts Tertiary volcanic rocks (Ellis, 1984; Ellis and others, 1985; Shawe and others, 1988). These strata contain rhyolitic, sanidine-rich tuffs, assigned to the 12- to 15-Ma Kane Wash volcanic suite (Ekren and others, 1977). No evidence exists suggesting movement on the Mormon Peak detachment prior to deposition of the older Kane Wash units, although local landslide masses and conglomerates derived from strata as old as Late Cambrian are intercalated in the Kane Wash in the Mormon Mountains and may indicate formation of fault scarps associated with early motion on the detachment. The Mormon Peak detachment is the oldest extensional structure in the area and is offset by the "eastern imbricate normal faults," the East Mormon, Gourd Spring, and related faults, so that all of the faults described above are probably younger than mid-Miocene.

East of Candy Peak (Fig. 7; Plate 1) in the southern Mormon Mountains, the Glendale thrust is overlapped by light-colored lacustrine limestone correlative with the Miocene Rainbow Gardens Member of the Horse Spring Formation (Bohannon, 1984; Skelly, 1987; Plate 1). To the south, near Glendale, identical lacustrine beds contain intercalated tuffs dated between 19.6 ± 0.8 and 21.3 ± 0.4 Ma by K/Ar and fission track methods (Anderson and others, 1972; Shafiquillah and others, 1980; Bohannon, 1984). The Miocene(?) strata at Candy Peak are folded about gently east-plunging axes (Skelly, 1987; Plate 1). To the west of the unconformity, the imbricate thrust zone in the upper plate of the Glendale thrust is also folded but by a west-plunging fold with larger amplitude and wavelength: the Candy Peak syncline of Skelly (1987; Plate 1). These east-west–trending folds thus formed in Miocene or more recent time; the different plunges reflect the angular unconformity that existed prior to folding.

Tule Springs Hills. Klippen of the Mormon Peak detachment are exposed in the western Tule Springs Hills (Plate 1; Figs. 7 and 14). These remnants contain mainly Mississippian-Devonian strata and rest in fault contact on Cambrian rocks of the Tule Springs thrust plate (Figs. 13 and 14), similar to relations

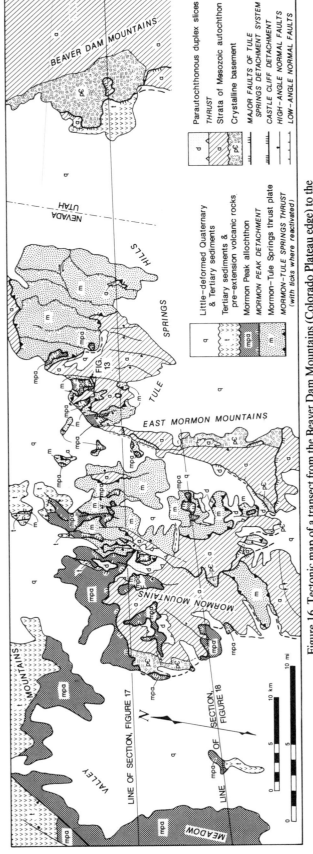

Figure 16. Tectonic map of a transect from the Beaver Dam Mountains (Colorado Plateau edge) to the Meadow Valley Mountains, showing the locations of sections in Figures 17 and 18. The cross sections show geology in the Meadow Valley Mountains that is west of this figure.

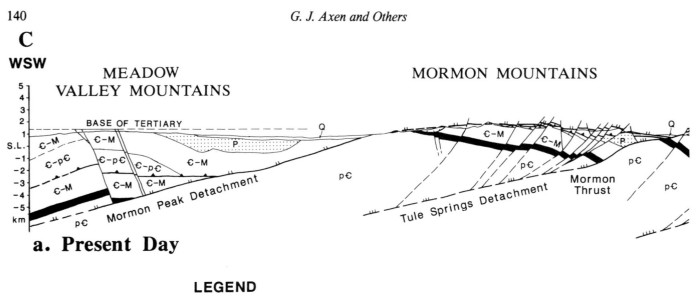

a. Present Day

LEGEND

LITHOLOGIC KEY

Q / Q-T	Quaternary – Tertiary sediments and volcanic rocks
Mz	Mesozoic strata
P	Pennsylvanian – Permian strata
€-M	Cambrian – Mississippian carbonate rocks
■	Cambrian clastic rocks (Mesozoic autochthon only)
€-p€	Cambrian – Precambrian clastic rocks (Mesozoic allochthon only)
p€	Precambrian crystalline basement (Mesozoic autochthon only)

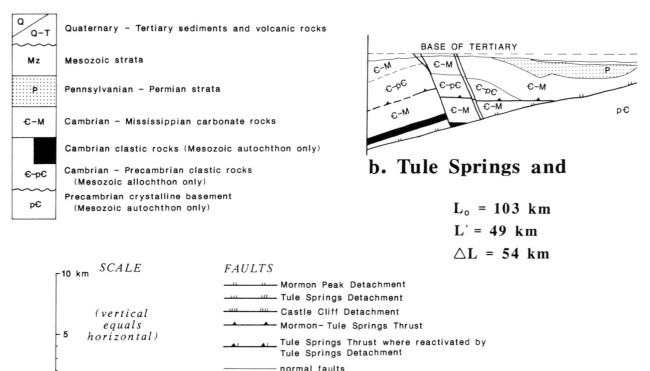

b. Tule Springs and

L_o = 103 km

L' = 49 km

$\triangle L$ = 54 km

SCALE

10 km

5

(vertical equals horizontal)

5   10 km

FAULTS

⊢—⊥—⊣	Mormon Peak Detachment
⊢—⊥—⊣	Tule Springs Detachment
⊢—⊥—⊣	Castle Cliff Detachment
▲—▲	Mormon– Tule Springs Thrust
▲—▲	Tule Springs Thrust where reactivated by Tule Springs Detachment
———	normal faults

Figure 17. Present-day and restored cross sections C-C′ from the Beaver Dam Mountains to the Meadow Valley Mountains (see Figure 16 and Plate 1 for location). See Wernicke and others (1985) and Tschanz and Pampeyan (1970) for bedrock geology west of that on Plate 1. Bedrock geology to the east from Axen (unpublished mapping in Tule Springs Hills) and Hintze (1986).

throughout the eastern Mormon Mountains and in isolated exposures in the valley between the Mormon and East Mormon Mountains (Plate 1). In the eastern Tule Springs Hills, the thrust plate is stratigraphically continuous up to the Mississippian-Permian Bird Spring Formation (Axen, unpublished mapping). These relations indicate that the Mormon Peak detachment surfaced in the central Tule Springs Hills (Smith and others, 1987).

The Tule Springs detachment breakaway zone probably lies east of the Tule Springs Hills, because even the easternmost exposures of the thrust plate are internally extended. Preliminary cross sections drawn through the Tule Springs Hills indicate 5 to 10 km of extension within the Tule Springs thrust plate (Axen, unpublished data). The detachment followed the Tule Springs thrust flat above Jurassic rocks for about 15 km (see discussion of the Tule

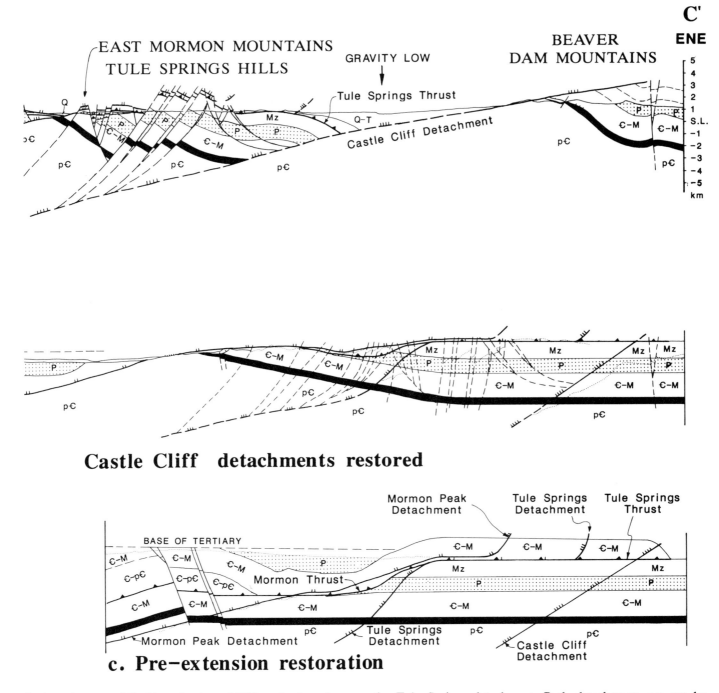

Castle Cliff detachments restored

c. Pre−extension restoration

Springs thrust, and Smith and others, 1987) and splays downward into the footwall of the thrust in the western Tule Springs Hills (Figs. 7 and 17; Plate 1), dismembering the small footwall syncline described above.

The Mormon Peak detachment in the western Tule Springs Hills is cut by several faults in the hanging wall of the Tule Springs detachment, some of which are truncated by the Tule Springs detachment. In other places the Mormon Peak detachment is tilted east and truncated by the Tule Springs detachment. Some of these are shown west of Jumbled Mountain (Fig. 7; Plate 1). Therefore the Mormon Peak detachment is older than

the Tule Springs detachment. Both detachments are cut by steeper normal faults in the Tule Springs Hills, such as the Tule Corral fault, and faults in the extreme western part of the range, which are associated with the Gourd Spring fault (Fig. 7; Plate 1).

TERTIARY KINEMATIC HISTORY

Although internal disruption of the thrust belt by Neogene structures is greatest in the Mormon Mountains, East Mormon Mountains, and Tule Springs Hills, the more continuous exposure in this area allows a more complete understanding of the exten-

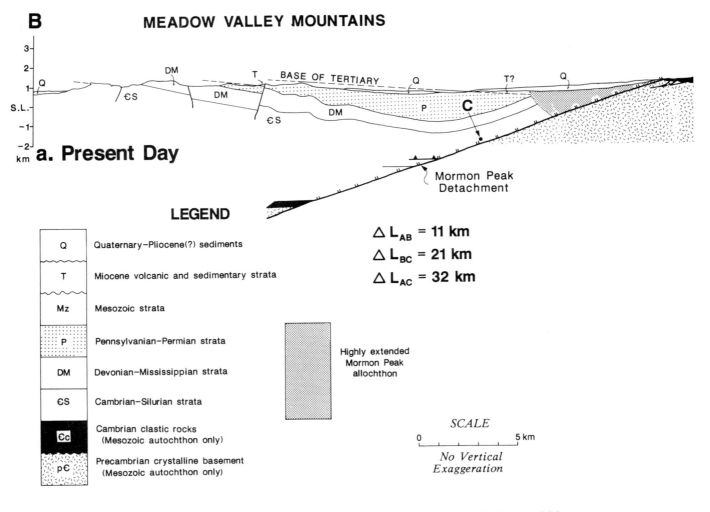

Figure 18. Present-day and palinspastically restored cross section B-B′ through the central Mormon Mountains and East Mormon Mountains. See Figure 16 and Plate 1 for section location and Wernicke and others (1985) and Tschanz and Pampeyan (1970) for bedrock geology west of that shown on Plate 1. Fault symbols as on Figure 17. Horizontal extension (ΔL) is measured between points A, B, and C.

sional and compressional architecture than is possible in ranges farther south that are relatively unextended internally. We briefly review the existing kinematic model for extension in the northern part of the area, then develop the relations of the model to structures farther south, with emphasis on a more specific definition of the Moapa Peak shear zone.

The northern transect

Restoration of the Gourd Spring fault and related faults in the westernmost Tule Springs Hills aligns the splays below the Tule Springs detachment with the low-angle normal faults in the Toquop chaos. This suggests that the Tule Springs detachment and the Toquop chaos are related. Above we indicated that the Radio Tower fault merges northward with the Toquop chaos, so that the Tule Springs detachment, Toquop chaos, and Radio Tower fault are all related kinematically. In such a restoration the

Tule Springs detachment projects above the Toquop chaos (e.g., Fig. 17a), but there is no fault with an equivalent amount of displacement (5 to 10 km, see above) exposed in the eastern Mormon Mountains. The only fault system that has a compatible amount of displacement is the Carp Road fault zone, which juxtaposes strata in the parautochthonous duplex against the lowest strata of the autochthon along the west edge of the East Mormon Mountains. For this reason we interpret the Carp Road fault, the Radio Tower fault, and the Tule Springs detachment as strands of the same detachment system, such that in the southern East Mormon Mountains there are two major splays to the detachment system: the Carp Road and Radio Tower faults (compare Figs. 17 and 18).

These correlations are supported by relations with the Mormon Peak detachment in the eastern Mormon Mountains. There the detachment is tilted to the east by a domino-style fault set (the "eastern imbricate normal fault belt" of Wernicke and

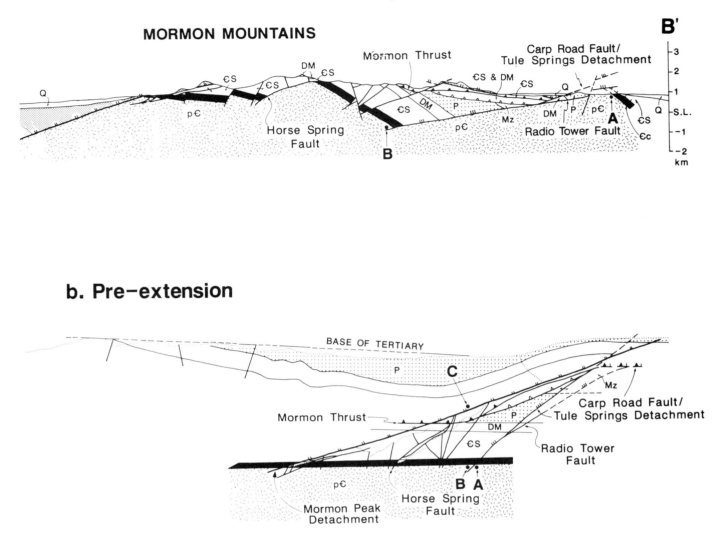

others, 1985), in a manner similar to the deformational pattern in the hanging wall of the Tule Springs detachment in the western Tule Springs Hills. The domino-style faults and east-tilted strata, Mormon Peak detachment, and thrusts are observed only in the area east and north of the Horse Spring fault and west of the Carp Road fault–Tule Springs detachment system. They are interpreted as being restricted to the hanging wall of the Tule Springs detachment and indicating an initially listric geometry of the Carp Road fault–Tule Springs detachment system at depth, so as to provide a relatively shallow basal detachment for the imbricate normal faults (e.g., Figs. 17 and 18).

This interpretation, if correct, requires that the Tule Springs detachment ramped down to the west along the west side of the East Mormon Mountains, because the Carp Road fault zone and Toquop chaos cut across autochthonous strata at moderate angles (Figs. 17 and 18). This ramping is probably responsible for the structural complexity of the Toquop chaos. The differential unloading caused by several kilometers of displacement in the ramp zone of the detachment is believed to have been responsible for

the tilting and uplift of the East Mormon Mountains, in a fashion similar to that proposed for the flexure in the Beaver Dam Mountains by Wernicke and Axen (1988; see also Spencer, 1984; Wernicke, 1985). As in that area, no fault east of the upflexed footwall of the detachment system is large enough to accommodate the differential rotation between the East Mormon Mountains and the flat-lying autochthonous strata below the central Tule Springs Hills.

Therefore, the Tule Springs detachment–Carp Road fault system is interpreted to have a flat-ramp-flat geometry. The Carp Road fault clearly carries the Mormon thrust in its hanging wall, and no evidence exists that the Mormon thrust has been reactivated as a normal fault as was the Tule Springs thrust. In fact, the Mormon thrust, including the base of the thrust ramp, is one of the structures that clearly have been rotated east by the domino-style fault set (see discussion above and Figs. 17 and 18). Therefore, the ramp in the Tule Springs detachment system splayed downward from the reactivated thrust plane near the top of the thrust ramp and cut into the autochthon at a steeper dip than the thrust (Figs. 17c and 18b). This example contrasts with the common interpretation of listric normal faults in which they follow thrust ramps down onto thrust flats (e.g, Royse and others, 1975).

To the south, the Horse Spring fault changes from its north-south trend to a south-southeast trend (see above), forming the southern boundary of the domino-style normal fault set and defining the northern boundary of the Moapa Peak shear zone in the Mormon Mountains (see below). A large amount of extension need not have occurred south of the Horse Spring fault, although the amount accommodated by reactivation of the floor thrust of the imbricate duplex northwest of Moapa Peak is unconstrained. If that amount is small, then the area south of the Horse Spring fault is not significantly extended internally, and the cumulative displacement of the domino-style faults must be added to that of the Horse Spring fault, causing it to gain right separation southeastward. This is consistent with the northward loss of displacement on the domino-style faults and Horse Spring fault.

The Carp Road fault (Olmore, 1971; Plate 1) underlies the domino-style fault set and is interpreted to be a major splay of the Tule Springs detachment on the west side of the East Mormon Mountains (Fig. 18). To the south, the Carp Road fault merges with the Davidson Peak fault (see above), indicating that the Tule Springs detachment and the Davidson Peak fault were in part active synchronously.

Moapa Peak shear zone

The Moapa Peak shear zone of Olmore (1971) is a broad, complex zone of right-lateral shear that runs from south of Davidson Peak west-southwest toward Moapa Peak (Fig. 7). Olmore interpreted it as a Mesozoic transfer zone that accommodated more thrust displacement to the north. Because of the involvement of autochthonous strata and crystalline basement, which are not carried in any thrusts in the region, Wernicke and

others (1984) suggested that it is a Neogene structure related to extension.

Definition. The Moapa Peak shear zone can be more precisely defined now that detailed maps of bedrock exposures, reflection seismic data, and gravity data are available. Figure 19 is a schematic block diagram showing our interpretation of the Moapa Peak shear zone as a zone of dextral oblique normal faulting and oroflexure that transfers extensional displacement in the central Mormon and East Mormon Mountains to the basin east of Moapa Peak and the southern Mormon Mountains.

The principal exposed faults of the shear zone are the Davidson Peak fault and the northwest-trending strands of the Horse Spring fault system (Fig. 20). The Moapa Peak shear zone probably caused clockwise rotation of the Weiser syncline at Moapa Peak relative to the North Muddy Mountains (Figs. 2 and 5) and apparent right-lateral drag of folds mapped by Olmore (1971) southeast of Davidson Peak (Plate 1; Fig. 20). The thrust ramp is also deflected clockwise about 80° between the central Mormon Mountains and Moapa Peak (Fig. 20).

The Davidson Peak fault is the northern boundary of the shear zone in the East Mormon Mountains, as originally defined by Olmore (1971). We consider the northwest-striking portion of the Horse Spring fault to be the northern boundary in the Mormon Mountains. Crystalline basement is exposed in four blocks north of those faults but never to the south (although it is probably present at shallow depth south of the Davidson Peak fault), indicating structural uplift of the area north of the Moapa Peak shear zone relative to the south, in addition to the topographic relief.

No large extensional structure disrupts bedrock continuity in the Mormon Mountains west of the Horse Spring fault, although several small variably oriented normal faults are present. An unknown amount of extension is accommodated on the reactivated(?) floor thrust below the imbricate duplex northwest of Moapa Peak, but it need not be large (Plate 1). It appears, therefore, that the northern boundary of the shear zone does not continue through the range to the west but instead loses displacement westward and northward. This is part of the basis of our interpretation of the Moapa Peak shear zone as a transfer zone.

Offset. Displacement across the Moapa Peak shear zone is constrained principally by offset of a piercing line formed by the base of the thrust ramp (Fig. 20). The elevation of that line differs by less than 1 km across the Horse Spring fault system, so that map separation can be used to draw inferences about lateral separations. North of the Horse Spring fault the line is well constrained at its northern and southern ends by exposures of the depositional contact between autochthonous Monte Cristo and Bird Spring formations in the footwall of the Mormon thrust. Between strands of the Horse Spring fault the thrust has been excised by a low-angle normal fault, which places allochthonous Upper Cambrian beds on autochthonous Permian strata stratigraphically high in the Bird Spring Formation (Skelly, 1987). Therefore, that segment of the thrust system must have originally

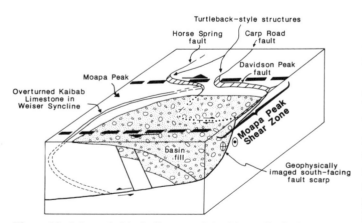

Figure 19. Schematic block diagram of the Moapa Peak shear zone, showing important exposed and subsurface structures. Large arrows show relative displacement across the zone; small arrows on front face and ellipses with cross (away) and dot (toward) show relative displacements across the basin-bounding fault.

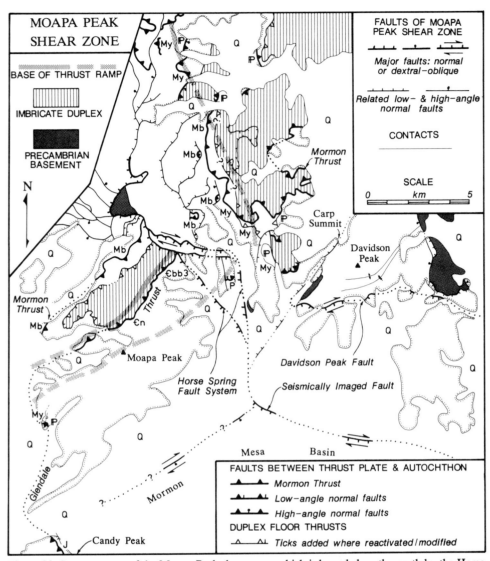

Figure 20. Structure map of the Moapa Peak shear zone, which is bounded on the north by the Horse Spring and Davidson Peak faults. Note that the Moapa Peak and Davidson Peak blocks are more coherent structurally than areas to the north and south, respectively, so that the shear zone acts as a transfer structure between areas that were extending differentially. Note that crystalline basement is exposed only north of the shear zone. The southern boundary is interpreted as the seismically imaged fault. Mesozoic markers offset across the Horse Spring fault system include the imbricate thrust duplex and the base of the thrust ramp. Footwall units of the thrust are designated as on Figure 3, except for Mb and My, the Bullion and Yellow Pine members of the Monte Cristo Formation; ℙ, Mississippian-Pennsylvanian part of the Bird Spring Formation; P, Permian Bird Spring Formation (upper part).

lain east of the base of the ramp by 1 to 2 km, depending on the ramp dip and thickness of the Mississippian-Pennsylvanian part of the Bird Spring.

Two positions for the base of the ramp are shown south of the Horse Spring fault, corresponding to the two interpretations shown in Figure 9 (we prefer that in Figure 9a for reasons discussed below). The western line corresponds to the interpretation shown in Figure 9a and is consistent with the observation in the northern transect that the imbricate duplex developed adjacent to the thrust ramp. Because the exact position at which the thrust

flattens onto Mississippian strata westward is indeterminate, the line is drawn adjacent to the eastern thrust trace. The eastern line is consistent with Figure 9b and was drawn along the present outcrop trace of upright Mississippian beds in the lower limb of the Weiser syncline or along the western trace of the axial surface of that fold, because the overturning would only occur east of the ramp base in this interpretation. These constructions both place the base of the ramp at the easternmost feasible location for each case. The lines on Figure 20 marking the base of the thrust ramp have been constructed to minimize offsets across the Horse Spring fault.

The northern strand of the Horse Spring fault offsets the ramp base in a right-lateral sense by a minimum of 1 km; 2 to 3 km probably is more appropriate, as the Permian beds south of the strand originated above and east of the ramp base. The eastern piercing line south of the Horse Spring fault system presently aligns with the ramp line between strands of the system. However, this creates an odd geometry across the southern strand of the Horse Spring fault, as it juxtaposes Mississippian or older strata from the base of the ramp or lower *above* Permian from higher up the ramp, requiring reverse separation on a normal fault. If the ramp line between fault strands is shifted west, in keeping with the low probability that Permian strata belong at the base of the ramp, then the southern strand has left-lateral separation, opposite of the right-lateral separation across the northern strand. This, and evidence discussed below, suggests that the base of the ramp is farther west, beneath the imbricate duplex.

The western ramp line south of the Horse Spring fault system is displaced 3 km right-laterally from the line between strands of that system, and the displacement could be up to 5 km if the base of the ramp is close to the Mormon thrust trace (Fig. 20). Thus, a minimum of 1 km and up to 8 km of right lateral separation of the base of the thrust ramp occurred across the Horse Spring fault zone. For reasons given above, 4 to 6 km is the most reasonable estimate.

This is in general agreement with offset of the imbricate duplex by the Horse Spring fault system, which clearly truncates the imbricate duplex northwest of Moapa Peak (Plate 1). Internal structure of the Mormon thrust plate has not yet been mapped west of Carp Summit, but unpublished field observations suggest that the thrust sheet is composed largely of imbrications in the exposures northwest and southwest of Carp Summit. In these blocks, Wernicke and others (1985) mapped very irregular dip patterns, a few minor thrusts, and large areas underlain by subunit €bb4 in the thrust plate northwest of Carp Summit. To the north, the imbricate duplex is present, dominated by north-trending thrusts, subparallel to the ramp line in Figure 20. We believe that future mapping will show that the imbricate duplex continues to the south to the outlier of the thrust sheet southwest of Carp Summit, which has been shown as part of the imbricate duplex on Figure 20. The outlier is 6 to 7 km east of the north end of the imbricate duplex northwest of Moapa Peak, giving a separation in good agreement with the estimate of right-lateral displacement of the thrust ramp.

Restoration of the offset ramp and duplex zone does not account for the apparent rotation of the Weiser syncline and overlying imbricate zone to its present trend of about N50°E (Fig. 5). Another 5 to 10 km of eastward restoration of the Glendale–North Muddy Mountains area relative to the central Mormon Mountains is necessary to reorient these features to approximately north-south trends (Wernicke and others, 1984; Skelly, 1987). A total of 6 to 18 km of right-lateral faulting and bending in the Moapa Peak shear zone between the central and southernmost Mormon Mountains is indicated; our best estimate is about 10 to 15 km. The Candy Peak area is roughly in the core

of this oroflexure, and the folds in Miocene limestone and the underlying thrust plate there (Plate 1) could be due to north-south shortening in the core region (Axen and Skelly, 1984).

Subsurface geology. Geophysical data in the Virgin Valley southeast of the area of Plate 1 are critical to understanding the geometry of the Moapa Peak shear zone and its southern boundary (Fig. 19). Gravity lows (Kane and others, 1979; Shawe and others, 1988) indicate that the Virgin River Valley is divided into two subsurface basins, below Mormon Mesa and Mesquite (Fig. 1), which are referred to as the Mormon Mesa and Mesquite basins. South of the East Mormon Mountains, gravity and magnetic surveys indicate the presence of a south-facing bedrock scarp buried beneath less dense and less magnetic sediments and possibly volcanic rocks of the Mormon Mesa basin (Kane and others, 1979; Figs. 4 and 5 of Shawe and others, 1988). This scarp is interpreted to be due to a fault of Tertiary age and has been imaged on proprietary reflection seismic lines purchased by the U.S. Geological Survey (R. G. Bohannon, oral communication, 1988).

The near-surface trace of the seismically imaged fault is about 8 km north of Interstate Highway 15 on a north-trending seismic line shot along the road over Carp Summit. On that line, the fault flattens southward. Gravity data suggest an east-northeast trend there, parallel to the regional extension direction, but the gravity gradient curves to the south, so that an antithetic(?) strand of the fault probably projects west toward the gap in bedrock exposure north of Candy Peak (Plate 1, Fig. 20). The geophysical data indicate a large fault displacement, probably emplacing Tertiary sediments and volcanics on crystalline basement. This is much larger than what the geologic relations across the gap indicate, so we infer that the main fault bends north and connects with the Horse Spring fault (Fig. 20). North of the gap, overturned Kaibab Limestone dips moderately to the northwest, and to the south, overturned southwest-dipping strata of the Jurassic Moenave and Kayenta Formations are found roughly where expected by extrapolation of the section southeastward from the Kaibab (Plate 1). Although some displacement is clearly possible, slip in excess of about 1 km misaligns the syncline with its continuation south of Glendale (Fig. 2). The gap is probably underlain by intervening unfaulted Triassic beds of the Moenkopi and Chinle Formations. Therefore, we suggest that the antithetic fault that trends toward the gap either loses displacement to the west (analogous to the Horse Spring fault) or bends to a southerly trend east of Candy Peak. In the former case, the change in strike of the overturned strata could have been caused by drag on the fault. The small east-trending folds in Miocene strata and the upper plate of the Glendale thrust around Candy Peak (Plate 1) could be due to local north-south compression in the hanging wall of a southeast-dipping, listric, right-lateral oblique normal fault that trends toward the gap. We suggest that the buried scarp is the southern boundary of the Moapa Peak shear zone, because it coincides with the southern limit of apparent disruption of the Weiser syncline, which continues southward to the Muddy Mountains without significant interruption for more than 40 km.

Timing relations. Several structural relations suggest that the Moapa Peak shear zone was active synchronously with the Tule Springs detachment system. The Horse Spring fault is the northern boundary of the Moapa Peak shear zone but is also coeval with domino-style faults in the hanging wall of the Tule Springs detachment–Carp Road fault system. The Carp Road and Radio Tower faults apparently merge with the Davidson Peak fault, which is part of the northern boundary of the Moapa Peak shear zone. However, displacement on the southern boundary of the shear zone, the seismically imaged tear fault, apparently functioned to open the Mormon Mesa basin, which is partially filled with Muddy Creek Formation. The Tule Springs detachment was probably active prior to deposition of Muddy Creek rocks in the Mesquite basin (Smith and others, 1987). Thus, some displacement on the Moapa Peak shear zone postdated cessation of activity on the Tule Springs detachment but was roughly synchronous with displacement on the Castle Cliff detachment, which was probably active in Muddy Creek time (Smith and others, 1987).

THRUST CORRELATIONS AND MESOZOIC GEOMETRY

Imbricate duplex of the Mormon thrust plate

Identification of the distinctive zone of imbricate thrusts (Fig. 4) allows for confident correlation of the Glendale, Mormon, and Tule Springs thrusts (Skelly and Axen, 1988). Several facts about the imbricate zone suggest that it is a continuous structural feature rather than several local zones. Most important is the consistent stratigraphy in the imbrications, which are always composed of lower Nopah Formation (subunit €n1) and/or subunits €bb3 and €bb4 of the Banded Mountain Member of the Bonanza King Formation. Older rocks of the Banded Mountain Member are commonly present below the imbricate thrust zone (Plate 1) and are only locally imbricated. This is indicative of another distinctive trait: The imbricate duplex originated in the hanging wall of the thrust and was left behind, rather than having been cut from a footwall ramp and transported forward, as is common in thin-skinned thrust belts (e.g., Boyer and Elliott, 1982; and the way in which the parautochthonous duplexes were emplaced). Also, the imbricates are everywhere present adjacent to a major footwall ramp, with few of the imbricates transported over the ramp onto the footwall décollement in Jurassic strata. Northwest of Moapa Peak the eastern imbricate thrusts and enclosed stratigraphy are steeper than those to the west, precluding development of the stack from west to east in a "typical" imbricate fan style, causing steepening of more westerly imbricates by rotation above lower thrusts (Boyer and Elliott, 1982). Skelly (1987) interpreted the imbricates north of Moapa Peak as having formed from east to west, functioning to decrease the dip of the roof fault through time and leaving most of the imbricate sheets below the top of the ramp, consistent with the observation that few imbricates are present on

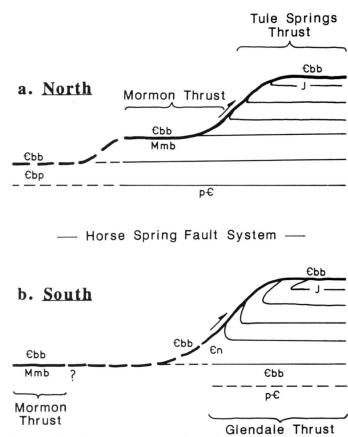

Figure 21. Schematic diagram showing differences between the thrust system footwall architecture north and south of the Horse Spring fault. Mmb, Bullion Member of the Mississippian Monte Cristo Formation; €bb and €bp, Banded Mountain and Papoose Lake members (respectively) of the Bonanza King Formation; other units as on Figure 3.

the Jurassic flat in the Tule Springs Hills (Smith and others, 1987).

In the central and northeastern Mormon Mountains and western Tule Springs Hills the imbricate stack is overlain by a roof thrust that detached at the same stratigraphic position as the imbricate thrusts. This is in turn overlain by the Mormon Peak detachment, forming a distinctive structural stack over a large part of the map area. Therefore, the correlation of the Tule Springs and Mormon thrusts is considered very strong.

Northern termination of the Weiser syncline. Although the structural style within the thrust sheet in the central Mormon Mountains is similar to that in the thrust sheet northwest of Moapa Peak, they have contrasting structural styles in their footwalls. The proposed correlation of the Mormon and Glendale thrusts requires explanation of two problematic observations (Fig. 21): (1) no structure equivalent to the Weiser syncline exists beneath the Mormon or Tule Spring thrusts north of the Moapa Peak shear zone; and (2) northwest of Moapa Peak, where the Mormon and Glendale thrusts are in closest proximity, the Mormon thrust lies on a Mississippian footwall flat, but directly to the

east the northernmost exposure of the Glendale thrust lies above
Ordovician and Upper Cambrian strata of the lower limb of the
Weiser syncline (Plate 1). If these thrusts are correlative, either
southeastward stratigraphic downcutting in the thrust footwall or
Tertiary modification of the thrust system is required northwest of
Moapa Peak.

Because no structure equivalent to the Weiser syncline exists
to the north, where the autochthon is well exposed across strike,
we infer that a mirror-image analog to the North Buffington fault
in the Muddy Mountains (Fig. 2) existed north of Moapa Peak
(Skelly and Axen, 1988; Fig. 22). The North Buffington fault dips
steeply northward and juxtaposes upright autochthonous strata to
the south against overturned autochthonous strata of the Weiser
syncline to the north (Bohannon, 1983a, b; Fig. 22c). We suggest
that the Weiser syncline never existed south of the North Buffington fault or north of its proposed equivalent north of Moapa Peak
(Fig. 22). Neither of these faults need have rooted into the crust;
rather, we view them as dying out eastward into unfolded rocks
adjacent to the lower limb and dying out downward in Cambrian
rocks, which are the stratigraphically lowest rocks affected by the
Weiser syncline and the Glendale thrust. The Weiser syncline is
thus a typical footwall syncline, which terminated to the north
and south against lateral tear faults. Footwall cross-strike faults,
abruptly ending footwall synclines, and other lower plate complexities are also common below the correlative Keystone thrust
exposed near Las Vegas in the Spring Mountains (Burchfiel and
others, 1974; Davis, 1973; Carr, 1983; Axen, 1984).

This interpretation may seem inconsistent with the presently
recumbent attitude of the axial surface of the Weiser syncline in
the North Muddy Mountains, but there the fold is overlain with
angular unconformity by moderately east-tilted Cretaceous to
Miocene strata (Longwell, 1949; Bohannon, 1983b). When these
strata are returned to horizontal, the axial surface dips moderately
west, as would be expected for a footwall syncline formed next to
a ramp. Similarly, when the Tertiary beds at Candy Peak (Plate
1; Fig. 7) are restored to horizontal, the currently flat thrust there
becomes west-dipping. However, the angular relation between the
Tertiary strata at Candy Peak and the axial surface of the
Weiser syncline at Moapa Peak is obscured by the possibility of
differential rotations between Candy Peak and Moapa Peak.

Subsurface geometry in the Moapa Peak area. Northwest of Moapa Peak, the northwest side of the imbricate duplex
is underlain by the floor thrust (which has been reactivated),
below which are strata of subunits €bb1 and €bb2 underlain by
the Mormon thrust and structurally lower Mississippian rocks.
On its southeast side, the imbricate thrust stack rests directly on
upright Upper Cambrian strata in the lower limb of the Weiser
syncline, on a fault interpreted as the Glendale thrust, although it
may have been modified or reactivated during the Tertiary (Figs.
9 and 21). This relation suggests an unusual situation where the
thrust apparently cuts downsection in its footwall in the direction
of transport. The apparent discrepancy between the footwall
stratigraphic levels of the Mormon and Glendale thrusts
northwest of Moapa Peak can be explained in at least five ways:

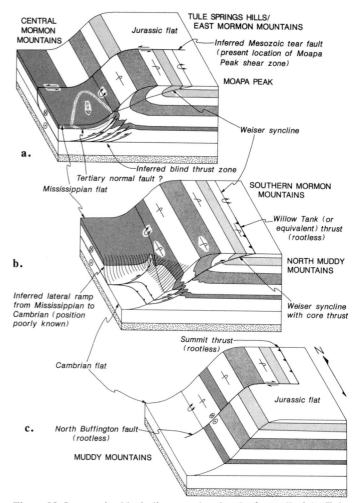

Figure 22. Interpretive block diagrams showing the footwall of the Tule
Springs–Mormon–Glendale–Muddy Mountain thrust before modification by extension. The northern block (a) has been rotated approximately 40° anticlockwise, restoring the thrust ramp and Weiser syncline
to the northerly trends observed to the north and south, respectively. The
site of the inferred lateral tear fault against which the syncline is thought
to have ended to the north is now occupied by the Moapa Peak shear
zone. If the scoop-shaped block above the normal fault (dotted) is removed, such that the imbricate thrust duplex replaces it, the observed
geometry northwest of Moapa Peak is generated. The central block (b)
shows the lateral ramp from Mississippian to Middle Cambrian west of
the syncline, and small thrusts interpreted to be rooted into the core of
the syncline are shown in the central and southern (c) blocks. The North
Buffington fault, against which the Weiser syncline ends to the south, is
interpreted as a mirror-image analog of the inferred tear fault shown in
(a).

(1) by the presence of south- or southeast-facing lateral ramp(s) in
the footwall, (2) by the presence of a blind thrust (system?) in the
footwall and formation of a triangle zone and an antiformal
culmination immediately northwest of Moapa Peak, which was
subsequently beheaded by the Glendale thrust (Fig. 9a), (3) by
Tertiary modification of the Glendale thrust associated with reactivation of the floor thrust to the imbricate duplex, (4) by a

down-to-the-northwest normal fault northwest of Moapa Peak (Fig. 9b), or (5) allochthoneity of the Weiser syncline above the Mormon thrust (e.g., Wernicke and others, 1984). Below we discuss the relative merits and drawbacks of these alternatives.

At present, the data are not sufficient to definitely exclude any of the first four, and they are not mutually exclusive. Correlation of the Mormon and Glendale thrusts requires that the Weiser syncline be autochthonous, in keeping with strong stratigraphic arguments made by Bohannon (1983b) for the North Muddy Mountains occupying an autochthonous position in the Mesozoic.

Any tenable explanation must be consistent with the following observations. The Mormon thrust northwest of Moapa Peak is in a footwall flat on the Bullion Member of the Mississippian Monte Cristo Formation and a hanging-wall flat in subunits €bb1 and €bb2 of the Bonanza King Formation, which are in turn overlain by the imbricate duplex, the floor thrust of which has been reactivated, leaving southwest-trending lineations on the fault surface (R. E. Anderson, written communication, 1987). The east side of the imbricate duplex is juxtaposed above upright Middle and Upper Cambrian strata of the lower limb of the Weiser syncline northwest of Moapa Peak (Fig. 9a) by the Glendale thrust, although it too may have been reactivated or modified along with the floor thrust of the imbricate duplex. Strata older than the Bullion Member of the Monte Cristo Formation (which forms the footwall flat of the Mormon thrust) are folded by the Weiser syncline.

We favor a combination of the first three hypotheses, which allows for consistency with these constraints. In order to explain both the Mississippian footwall flat and the presence of older strata in the steep to overturned part of the Weiser syncline to the east, we infer that a minor blind thrust system cores the anticlinal culmination northwest of Moapa Peak (Figs. 9a and 22a). This thrust system probably ended to the north against the same lateral fault that terminated the Weiser syncline (left face and top of Fig. 22a). This allows for deformation of pre-Mississippian strata in the Weiser syncline, without having structural downcutting to the east by the Mormon-Glendale thrust (front face of Fig. 22a). West of the Weiser syncline the footwall tear would only need to have been as long as the Mississippian footwall flat in the Mormon Mountains is wide, a distance of about 5 km presently, although it may have been wider in the Mesozoic.

Removal of the scoop-shaped block outlined with dots on Figure 22a leads to a footwall geometry as portrayed in Figure 9a. Slickensides on the reactivated or excised floor fault of the imbricate duplex northwest of Moapa Peak trend southwest, parallel to the thrust ramp, and top-to-the-southwest movement on such a scoop, which cut downsection to the southwest, could have juxtaposed the imbricate duplex against the upright lower limb of the Weiser syncline. Alternatively, the thrust may have cut down stratigraphic section in its direction of transport, while still climbing structurally, beheading the anticline caused by the blind thrust system and leading directly to the geometry of Figure 9a.

Strata as old as the Bonanza King Formation are steeply dipping to overturned in the extreme southwest outcrops of the Weiser syncline in the Muddy Mountains, adjacent to the North Buffington fault (Bohannon, 1983a), suggesting that the ramp there cuts directly down to that stratigraphic level, without the intervening Mississippian footwall flat seen in the Mormon Mountains. This requires another lateral ramp in the footwall, between the Mississippian flat to the north and the Cambrian décollement to the south (Fig. 22b). Such a lateral ramp must have been southwest of the outcrops of the Mormon thrust northwest of Moapa Peak, but otherwise its position is poorly constrained.

Current map data (Plate 1; Skelly, 1987) are inconsistent with the presence of a large northwest-dipping normal fault northwest of Moapa Peak (Fig. 9b). However, the rocks there are so badly brecciated and dolomitized that we feel this hypothesis should be checked by future mapping and geophysical surveys. If such a normal fault exists, it relieves any need for stratigraphic downcutting by the thrust in its direction of transport, a phenomenon that is not commonly documented (e.g., Price, 1981), introducing an autochthonous basement-cored anticline with amplitude of 2 to 3 km (Fig. 9b). Gravity data northwest of Moapa Peak show a high centered roughly on the antiformal culmination there (Shawe and others, 1988), which may indicate dense basement in the core but does not require it. A magnetic trough is present there (Shawe and others, 1988), suggesting noncrystalline rocks in the core. The principal merits of this possibility are that it requires the least complicated thrust geometry and provides a structural explanation for the topographic relief of Moapa Peak. However, Figure 9b is misleading in regard to the former, because overturned to steeply dipping Ordovician to Mississippian beds are present along strike out of the line of section.

Correlations with areas to the north. In the northern Tule Springs Hills, Tschanz and Pampeyen (1970) show a plate of Pennsylvanian-Permian strata resting above the Mesozoic autochthon. Farther north, at Lime Mountain (Fig. 2) and in the adjacent Clover Mountains, there is a thrust plate of Cambrian and younger beds above Mesozoic strata. The plate of Pennsylvanian-Permian beds might be interpreted as a parautochthonous thrust sheet below the Tule Springs thrust and its correlative at Lime Mountain. However, reconnaissance indicates that thin slivers of Cambrian strata are present beneath much of the Pennsylvanian-Permian allochthon, suggesting that lower and middle Paleozoic strata once formed the base of the overthrust sheet. Therefore, we view the intervening terrain between the central Tule Springs Hills and Lime Mountains as an area where reactivation of the Tule Springs thrust caused removal of nearly all of the middle and lower Paleozoic of the thrust sheet, rather than as an area where remnants of a parautochthonous thrust sheet are preserved below the Tule Springs thrust.

The easternmost thrust exposure in the region is at Square Top Mountain in the northern Beaver Dam Mountains (Fig. 2). There, east-tilted Pennsylvanian-Permian beds overlie autochthonous Jurassic and Cretaceous strata. The hanging-wall strata are Callville Limestone, Pakoon Dolomite, and the Queanto-weap Sandstone (Hintze, 1986), units that are generally associated with the Mesozoic autochthon, as they are typically exposed on the Colorado Plateau. Therefore, the Square Top Mountain thrust may represent a parautochthonous slice. Alternatively, it may be interpreted as the frontal part of the Tule Springs thrust plate. Footwall geometry in the Mormon Mountains and Tule Springs Hills (Fig. 4) requires an offset counterpart in the hanging wall of the Tule Springs thrust, including a hanging-wall ramp from Middle Cambrian to Mississippian, a Mississippian flat, and another hanging-wall ramp from Mississippian to Jurassic. All of these upper plate elements must occur east of the Tule Springs Hills (where the hanging wall is in a Middle Cambrian flat), assuming that they were not eroded during or after thrusting. Our regional reconstruction (Fig. 17) places the Tule Springs Hills adjacent to the Beaver Dam Mountains, suggesting that much of the eastern part of the Tule Springs thrust sheet would have overlain the Beaver Dam Mountains, particularly if the thrust plate at Square Top Mountain is a preserved portion of the main thrust allochthon.

DISCUSSION AND CONCLUSIONS

In the eastern Mormon Mountains–Tule Springs Hills area the geometric and structural details of, and interactions between, large-magnitude extensional fault systems and the frontal thrust system of the Sevier Orogen can be examined directly. Relatively small amounts of Tertiary-Quaternary cover allow particularly good observations of these systems in the vicinity of a major footwall ramp in the thrust system where it rises from Mississippian to Jurassic strata, a stratigraphic thickness of about 3.5 km. Two major Tertiary detachment systems (Mormon Peak and Tule Springs) overprint the thrust system, exposing it at various levels.

Thrust system

Recognition of distinctive structural elements in the Glendale, Mormon, and Tule Springs thrust systems, along with reconstruction of Tertiary faults in balanced cross sections, indicates that these thrusts are correlative. They may also be correlative with the thrust at Square Top Mountain in the northern Beaver Dam Mountains.

The Mesozoic thrust system in the study area is composed of the following four elements, from top to bottom (Fig. 4): (1) a thrust sheet composed of Pennsylvanian to Middle Cambrian carbonates underlain by a roof thrust, below which is found (2) an internally imbricated duplex composed of Middle and Upper Cambrian strata derived from near the base of the thrust sheet, underlain by the Mormon–Glendale–Tule Springs thrust and by (3) parautochthonous duplex slices of Cambrian to Triassic strata, and (4) an autochthon composed of Lower Cambrian to Jurassic strata nonconformably overlying Precambrian crystal-

line rocks. The parautochthonous duplexes were apparently torn from the currently exposed Mississippian to Jurassic footwall ramp or from an inferred Middle Cambrian to Mississippian ramp in the subsurface to the west. South of the Moapa Peak shear zone the autochthon was deformed by a large footwall syncline, the Weiser syncline, and the thrust system apparently ramped directly from Cambrian to Jurassic levels. The syncline preserved in the Meadow Valley Mountains to the west (Figs. 17 and 18; Tschanz and Pampeyan, 1970) is interpreted as a ramp syncline that formed adjacent to the Mississippian to Jurassic ramp and that was offset to its present location by the Mormon Peak detachment in Neogene time.

Extensional structures and their relations to the thrust system

The Tule Springs detachment system reactivated the Jurassic footwall flat of the thrust but cut into the Mesozoic autochthon and down into crystalline basement a short distance east of the thrust ramp. To the west, the Tule Springs detachment carried the entire structural sequence, from the Mesozoic autochthon and its overlying thrust plate to the structurally highest Mormon Peak detachment. These structural markers have all been tilted to the east in an imbricately normal-faulted rollover or reverse drag structure in the eastern Mormon Mountains (Fig. 17), from which we infer that the Tule Springs detachment flattens at depth. Therefore, the Tule Springs detachment system may have initially had a flat-ramp-flat geometry.

Normal slip on the flat of the Tule Springs detachment in the Tule Springs Hills could not have initiated at a depth greater than the preserved stratigraphic thickness of the thrust sheet (subunit €bb3 to the Bird Spring Formation), a depth of no more than 4 to 5 km. Latest movement would have occurred at much shallower depths, probably 1 to 2 km. If the surface of the Earth is taken as a principal stress plane (e.g., Anderson, 1951), such that the maximum principal compressive stress was subvertical (as would be expected in an extending terrain), then either the Tule Springs detachment was active at a high angle to the maximum principal stress, or stress rotations occurred at very shallow depths.

The Mormon Peak detachment apparently broke away in the central Tule Springs Hills. Easternmost klippen are composed of middle to upper Paleozoic strata that rest on the lower Nopah Formation or uppermost Bonanza King Formation (subunit €bb4), but just a few kilometers to the east the entire Paleozoic section is present in the footwall. Traced westward, the Mormon Peak detachment remains near the Nopah–Bonanza King contact above the roof thrust to a point a few kilometers west of the base of the thrust ramp. There it cuts across the Mormon thrust, downward through strata of the Mesozoic autochthon, and into autochthonous basement in the westernmost Mormon Mountains (Wernicke and others, 1984, 1985). In the western Tule Springs Hills and eastern Mormon Mountains the Mormon Peak detachment is consistently located near the contact between Nopah and Bonanza King Formations in its footwall, indicating some stratigraphic control near the major thrust ramp.

Because the Tule Springs thrust/detachment lies above a footwall flat in strata of the Mesozoic autochthon in the Tule Springs Hills, we can estimate its initial dip there fairly accurately. Where basal Tertiary strata overlie autochthonous strata throughout southern Nevada, northwestern Arizona, and southwestern Utah, they are disconformable on beds no older than Jurassic, even in areas directly adjacent to the thrust front (e.g., Wernicke and Axen, 1988). Further, in unextended portions of the frontal part of the Cordilleran foreland thrust belt—as in the Canadian Rockies, Idaho, and Wyoming—the autochthonous strata dip about 3 to 8° toward the orogen (e.g., Price, 1981; Royse and others, 1975). Therefore, the Tule Springs detachment almost certainly had an initial dip of less than 10° in the Tule Springs Hills, over an area of at least 190 km^2, or 16 km in the direction of transport.

The initial dip of the Mormon Peak detachment can be calculated similarly, with only the assumption that beds of the Mesozoic autochthon dipped gently westward. In its westernmost exposures the angle between the detachment and the Tapeats Sandstone is about 17°, suggesting an initial dip of 20 to 25° (Wernicke and others, 1985). Restoration of local (Wernicke and others, 1985) and regional balanced cross sections (Figs. 17 and 18) agrees well with this number. In the western Tule Springs Hills, the Mormon Peak detachment is subparallel to the Tule Springs thrust over significant areas above the Jurassic flat (e.g., Figs. 13 and 14), so it had an initial dip there that was also less than 10°. Note that in the restored sections (Figs. 17c and 18b), the angle between flat-lying pre-extension ignimbrites and the basal clastic beds is <5°, supporting the assumption of an initially gently west-dipping autochthon.

The regional restorations incorporated additional constraints, which are independent of the assumption of a shallowly dipping autochthon. Flat-lying, Miocene pre-extension ignimbrites in the Meadow Valley Mountains (Tschanz and Pampeyan, 1970; Ekren and others, 1977) overlap tilted Pennsylvanian-Triassic strata from the east limb of the ramp syncline. These strata dip about 35° west and must have been oriented approximately parallel to the thrust ramp exposed in the eastern Mormon Mountains, which makes an angle of about 20° with the detachment, giving an initial dip of the detachment of about 15° relative to the Tertiary ash flows (Figs. 17 and 18).

Reactivation of thrust faults by normal faults has been suggested frequently, especially for listric normal faults (e.g., Royse and others, 1975). In the Mormon Mountains-Tule Springs Hills area we have unequivocal evidence that large normal faults cut obliquely across thrust structure. Commonly, normal faults in such sections are shown merging with thrust ramps and flattening into thrust flats. However, in the Tule Springs Hills we observe the opposite relation: The Tule Springs detachment followed the thrust flat but did not reactivate the ramp.

Magnitudes of extension and compression

Our cross-section reconstruction (Fig. 17) indicates that about 54 km of extension has occurred between the Beaver Dam and Meadow Valley Mountains. The reconstruction is well constrained in the Mormon Mountains-Tule Springs Hills area; the largest source of error is the geometry beneath the northern Virgin River Valley. In that reconstruction, about 23 km of extension was accommodated on the Mormon Peak detachment, about 7 km on the Tule Springs detachment, and the remaining 24 km on the Castle Cliffs detachment. These displacements for the Tule Springs and Mormon Peak detachments are in good agreement with those from a reconstructed section farther south (Fig. 18). The width of exposure of the Tule Springs detachment in the northern Tule Springs Hills, where the entire Cambrian to Mississippian section has essentially been removed, is about 10 km in the direction of transport. This requires at least that much horizontal transport on the detachment there, also in agreement with our reconstructions. Most of the error in the extension estimate, which we believe is no more than 10 km, is introduced beneath the northern Virgin River Valley, where extensional structures are covered.

The Mesozoic overlap of the Mormon-Tule Springs thrust system measured in Figure 17c is 28 km, measured from the westernmost exposures of Banded Mountain Member strata in the footwall in the western Mormon Mountains to the east edge of the exposed thrust sheet in the Tule Springs Hills. An additional 5 to 8 km of overlap is necessary if the thrust at Square Top Mountain in the northern Beaver Dam Mountains is correlative. Significant additional shortening is required by the imbricate thrust duplex.

Significance for future studies

Within the transect we see both compressional and extensional low-angle faults. Because thrusting occurred first, older-over-younger relations are fairly common along extensional faults. We feel that this situation is very common in the Sevier thrust belt and is probably common in most compressional orogens, because even active convergent mountain belts, such as the Himalaya and the Andes, are currently undergoing extension synchronously with convergence (e.g., Burchfiel and Royden, 1985; Dalmayrac and Molnar, 1981; Moore and Wernicke, 1988). Rather than relying entirely on age relations across low-angle faults, we have also utilized structural style within the hanging walls to differentiate between thrust and normal faults. In particular, we find relatively little clast-rotated breccia adjacent to thrusts but find it common along normal faults, especially where developed in dolostone. Extensional structures are also very common in the hanging walls of normal faults and can be observed to merge with or be truncated at the basal fault. We feel that less reliance on stratigraphic juxtaposition and more on structural style will greatly aid interpretation of the structural history of most orogens by avoiding the interpretation of low-angle normal faults as thrusts and vice versa.

ACKNOWLEDGMENTS

This research was supported by National Science Foundation grants EAR 86-17869 and EAR 84-51181 awarded to B. P. Wernicke, along with grants from Shell Development Company awarded to B. P. Wernicke and G. J. Axen, a grant from the Northern Arizona University Organized Research Fund awarded to G. J. Axen, and a grant from Chevron Oil Company awarded to M. F. Skelly. We appreciate careful reviews by R. E. Anderson, C. J. Ando, and R. G. Bohannon, which greatly improved the manuscript.

REFERENCES CITED

Anderson, E. M., 1951, The dynamics of faulting: Edinburgh, Oliver and Boyd, 206 p.

Anderson, R. E., 1971, Thin-skin distension in Tertiary rocks of southwestern Nevada: Geological Society of America Bulletin, v. 82, p. 43–58.

—— , 1973, Large-magnitude late Tertiary strike-slip faulting north of Lake Mead, Nevada: U.S. Geological Survey Professional Paper 794, 18 p.

Anderson, R. E., Longwell, C. R., Armstrong, R. L., and Marvin, R. F., 1972, Significance of K-Ar ages of Tertiary rocks from the Lake Mead region, Nevada–Arizona: Geological Society of America Bulletin, v. 83, p. 273–288.

Armstrong, R. L., 1968, Sevier orogenic belt in Nevada and Utah: Geological Society of America Bulletin, v. 79, p. 429–458.

—— , 1972, Low-angle (denudational) faults, hinterland of the Sevier orogenic belt, eastern Nevada and western Utah: Geological Society of America Bulletin, v. 83, p. 1729–1754.

Axen, G. J., 1984, Thrusts in the eastern Spring Mountains, Nevada; Geometry and mechanical implications: Geological Society of America Bulletin, v. 95, p. 1202–1207.

Axen, G. J., and Skelly, M. F., 1984, Folding and low-angle faulting of Mesozoic and Tertiary age, Moapa Peak–Glendale area, southern Nevada: Geological Society of America Abstracts with Programs, v. 16, p. 434.

Bohannon, R. G., 1983a, Geologic map, tectonic map, and structure sections of the Muddy and northern Black Mountains, Clark County, Nevada: U.S. Geological Survey Miscellaneous Investigations Map I–1406, scale 1:62,500.

—— , 1983b, Mesozoic and Cenozoic tectonic development of the Muddy, North Muddy, and northern Black Mountains, Clark County, Nevada *in* Miller, D. M., Todd, V. R., and Howard, K. A., eds., Tectonic and stratigraphic studies in the eastern Grant Basin: Geological Society of America Memoir, v. 157, p. 125–148.

—— , 1984, Nonmarine sedimentary rocks of Tertiary age in the Lake Mead region, southeastern Nevada and northwestern Arizona: U.S. Geological Survey Professional Paper 1259, 72 p.

Boyer, S. E., and Elliott, D., 1982, Thrust systems: American Association of Petroleum Geologists Bulletin, v. 66, p. 1196–1230.

Burchfiel, B. C., and Royden, L. H., 1985, North-south extension within the convergent Himalayan region: Geology, v. 13, p. 679–682.

Burchfiel, B. C., Fleck, R. J., Secor, D. T., Vincelette, R. R., and Davis, G. A., 1974, Geology of the Spring Mountains, Nevada: Geological Society of America Bulletin, v. 85, p. 1013–1023.

Burchfiel, B. C., Wernicke, B. P., Willemin, J. H., Axen, G. J., and Cameron, C. S., 1982, A new style of décollement thrusting: Nature, v. 300, no. 5892, p. 513–515.

Carr, M. D., 1983, Geometry and structural history of the Mesozoic thrust belt in the Goodsprings District, southern Spring Mountains, Nevada: Geological Society of America Bulletin, v. 94, p. 1185–1198.

Dalmayrac, B., and Molnar, P., 1981, Parallel thrust and normal faulting in Peru and constraints on the state of stress: Earth and Planetary Science Letters, v. 55, p. 473–481.

Davis, G. A., 1973, Relations between the Keystone and Red Spring thrust faults, eastern Spring Mountains, Nevada: Geological Society of America Bulletin, v. 84, p. 3709–3716.

Ekren, E. B., Orkild, P. P., Sargent, K. A., and Dixon, G. L., 1977, Geologic map of Tertiary rocks, Lincoln County, Nevada: U.S. Geological Survey Miscellaneous Investigations Map I–1041, scale 1:250,000.

Ellis, B. J., 1984, Thin-skinned extension superposed on frontal Sevier thrust faults, Mormon Mountains, Nevada [M.S. thesis]: Syracuse, New York, Syracuse University, 87 p.

Ellis, B. J., Taylor, W. J., and Wernicke, B. P., 1985, Structural sequence in the northern Mormon Mountains, southern Nevada: Geological Society of America Abstracts with Programs, v. 17, p. 354.

Guth, P. L., 1981, Tertiary extension north of the Las Vegas Valley shear zone, Sheep and Desert Ranges, Clark County, Nevada: Geological Society of America Bulletin, v. 92, p. 763–771.

Hewett, D. F., 1931, Geology and ore deposits of the Goodsprings Quadrangle, Nevada: U.S. Geological Survey Professional Paper 162, 172 p.

Hintze, L. F., 1986, Stratigraphy and structure of the Beaver Dam Mountains, southwestern Utah: Utah Geological Association Publication 15, p. 1–36.

Kane, M. F., Healey, D. L., Peterson, D. L., Kaufmann, H. E., and Reidy, D., 1979, Bouguer gravity map of Nevada, Las Vegas sheet: Nevada Bureau of Mines and Geology Map 61, scale 1:250,000.

Longwell, C. R., 1926, Structural studies in southern Nevada and western Arizona: Geological Society of America Bulletin, v. 37, p. 551–558.

—— , 1949, Structure of the Northern Muddy Mountains area, Nevada: Geological Society of America Bulletin, v. 60, p. 923–968.

—— , 1962, Restudy of the Arrowhead fault, Muddy Mountains, Nevada: U.S. Geological Survey Professional Paper 450–D, p. D82–D85.

—— , 1974, Measure and rate of movement on Las Vegas Valley shear zone, Clark County, Nevada: Geological Society of America Bulletin, v. 85, p. 985–990.

Longwell, C. R., Pampeyan, E. H., Bowyer, B., and Roberts, R. J., 1965, Geology and mineral deposits of Clark County, Nevada: Nevada Bureau of Mines Bulletin, v. 62, 218 p.

Moore, A., and Wernicke, B. P., 1988, Extensional deformation on the southern Peruvian Altiplano: EOS Transactions of the American Geophysical Union, v. 69, no. 16, p. 466.

Noble, L. F., 1941, Structural features of the Virgin Spring area, Death Valley, California: Geological Society of America Bulletin, v. 52, p. 941–1000.

Olmore, S. D., 1971, Style and evolution of thrusts in the region of the Mormon Mountains, Nevada [Ph.D. thesis]: Salt Lake City, University of Utah, 213 p.

Price, R. A., 1981, The Cordilleran foreland thrust and fold belt in the southern Canadian Rocky Mountains, *in* McClay, K., and Price, N. J., eds., Thrust and nappe tectonics: Geological Society of London Special Publication 9, p. 427–448.

Royse, F., Jr., Warner, M. A., and Reese, D. L., 1975, Thrust belt structural geometry and related stratigraphic problems; Wyoming–Idaho–northern Utah: Rocky Mountain Association of Geologists 1975 Symposium, p. 41–54.

Shafiquillah, M., Damon, P. E., Lynch, D. J., Reynolds, S. J., Rehrig, W. A., and Raymond, R. H., 1980, K-Ar geochronology and geologic history of southwestern Arizona and adjacent areas: Arizona Geological Survey Digest, v. 12, p. 201–260.

Shawe, D. R., Blank, H. R., Jr., Wernicke, B., Axen, G. J., Barton, H. N., and

Gordon, W. D., 1988, Mineral resources of the Mormon Mountains Wilderness Study Area, Lincoln County, Nevada: U.S. Geological Survey Bulletin 1729, 18 p.

Skelly, M. F., 1987, The geology of the Moapa Peak area, southern Mormon Mountains, Clark and Lincoln Counties, Nevada [M.S. thesis]: Flagstaff, Northern Arizona University, 150 p.

Skelly, M. F., and Axen, G. J., 1988, Thrust correlation and Tertiary disruption within the Sevier thrust belt, Muddy Mountain–Tule Springs Hills area, southern Nevada: Geological Society of America Abstracts with Programs, v. 20, p. 232.

Smith, E. I., Anderson, R. E., Bohannon, R. G., and Axen, G. J., 1987, Miocene extension, volcanism, and sedimentation in the eastern Basin and Range province, southern Nevada, *in* Davis, G. H., and VanderDolder, E. M., eds., Geologic diversity of Arizona and its margins; Excursions to choice areas: Arizona Bureau of Geology and Mineral Technology, Geological Branch Special Paper 5, p. 383–397.

Spencer, J. E., 1984, Role of tectonic denudation in warping and uplift of low-angle normal faults: Geology, v. 12, p. 95–98.

Taylor, W. J., 1984, Superposition of thin-skinned normal faulting on Sevier Orogenic Belt thrusts, northern Mormon Mountains, Lincoln County, Nevada [M.S. thesis]: Syracuse, New York, Syracuse University, 80 p.

Tschanz, C. M., and Pampeyan, E. H., 1970, Geology and mineral deposits of Lincoln County, Nevada: Nevada Bureau of Mines and Geology Bulletin 73, 187 p.

Wernicke, B., 1981, Geology of the Mormon Mountains, Lincoln and Clark Counties, Nevada: Geological Society of America Abstracts with Programs, v. 13, p. 113–114.

——, 1982, Processes of extensional tectonics [Ph.D. thesis]: Cambridge, Massachusetts Institute of Technology, 170 p.

——, 1985, Uniform-sense normal simple shear of the continental lithosphere: Canadian Journal of Earth Sciences, v. 22, p. 108–125.

Wernicke, B., and Axen, G. J., 1988, On the role of isostasy in the evolution of normal fault systems: Geology, v. 16, p. 848–851.

Wernicke, B., Spencer, J. E., Burchfiel, B. C., and Guth, P. L., 1982, Magnitude of crustal extension in the southern Great Basin: Geology, v. 10, p. 499–502.

Wernicke, B., Guth, P. L., and Axen, G. J., 1984, Tertiary extension in the Sevier orogenic belt, southern Nevada, *in* Lintz, J. P., ed., Western geological excursions, volume 4: Reno, Nevada, MacKay School of Mines, p. 473–510.

Wernicke, B., Walker, J. D., and Beaufait, M. S., 1985, Structural discordance between Neogene detachments and frontal Sevier thrusts, central Mormon Mountains, southern Nevada: Tectonics, v. 4, p. 213–246.

Wernicke, B., Axen, G. J., and Snow, J. K., 1988, Basin and Range extensional tectonics at the latitude of Las Vegas, Nevada: Geological Society of America Bulletin, v. 100, p. 1738–1757.

Wernicke, B. P., and 6 others, 1989, Extensional tectonics in the Basin and Range Province between the southern Sierra Nevada and the Colorado Plateau; 28th International Geological Congress Field Trip Guidebook T138: American Geophysical Union, 80 p.

Wright, L. A., Otton, J. K., and Troxel, B. W., 1974, Turtleback surfaces of Death Valley viewed as phenomena of extension: Geology, v. 2, p. 53–54.

MANUSCRIPT ACCEPTED BY THE SOCIETY AUGUST 21, 1989

Geological Society of America
Memoir 176
1990

Chapter 7

Fault kinematics and estimates of strain partitioning of a Neogene extensional fault system in southeastern Nevada

G. Michel-Noël
Département de Géotectonique, Université Pierre et Marie Curie, 75230 Paris CEDEX 05 France
R. Ernest Anderson
U.S. Geological Survey, Box 25046, Denver Federal Center, Denver, Colorado 80225
Jacques Angelier
Département de Géotectonique, Université Pierre et Marie Curie, 75230 Paris CEDEX 05 France

ABSTRACT

Study of more than 1,000 strike-slip and dip-slip faults in Miocene rocks along a 10-km segment of Rainbow Canyon reveals a well-constrained paleoextension direction of 235°, representing a main stage of syndepositional extensional deformation. This direction is consistent with northeast-southwest extension computed or estimated over a large part of the Basin and Range for main-phase extension. It can be computed from separated or combined subsets of strike-slip and dip-slip faults and is independent of fault size or geographic subarea. The deformation is characterized by synfaulting deposition of volcanic and sedimentary sequences that thicken toward predominantly northwest-striking block-boundary growth faults resulting in fan-shaped patterns in northeast-southwest cross section. Concave-upward faults are common, and fault-to-bedding angles in vertical sections containing the extension direction average about 90°. The coefficient of extension at stratigraphically median levels is 1.9 (90 percent), 10 to 20 percent of which is associated with block-interior displacements on sub–map-scale faults. Though the deformation is primarily synvolcanic, it is interpreted to be more closely associated with regional extension and low-angle normal faulting than with volcano-tectonic processes.

The study provides evidence for a young stage of west-northwest extensional deformation that primarily utilized existing faults in combined strike-slip, oblique-slip, and dip-slip modes and accounted for less than 5 percent of the total observed deformation. Extension directions are less well constrained than for the early deformation owing to smaller sample sizes. As with the early deformation, those computed from subsets of strike-slip and dip-slip faults are similar to one another (average 290°). The young deformation occurred following a 55° clockwise rotation of σ_3 sometime in the last 10 m.y.

The mixture of dip-slip and strike-slip faulting during each of the deformations is interpreted as resulting from vertical and horizontal constriction normal to the extension direction, rather than from alternations of paleostress conditions. An estimated 10 to 30 percent of the total brittle strain is associated with the strike-slip faulting. This study provides strong verification that our understanding of deformation intensity is highly dependent on the scale of investigation, depth of exposure, and knowledge of slip-sense characteristics.

Michel-Noël, G., Anderson, R. E., and Angelier, J., 1990, Fault kinematics and estimates of strain partitioning of a Neogene extensional fault system in southeastern Nevada, *in* Wernicke, B. P., ed., Basin and Range extensional tectonics near the latitude of Las Vegas, Nevada: Boulder, Colorado, Geological Society of America Memoir 176.

INTRODUCTION

In this chapter, we present the results of a detailed investigation of fault distribution, size, orientation, and slip direction and sense from a small area of exceptionally well exposed Miocene rocks along northern Rainbow Canyon south of Caliente, Nevada (Figs. 1 and 2). The purpose of the study is to improve understanding of the kinematics of brittle deformation and the temporal and genetic relations between previously reported complexly interrelated systems of strike-slip and dip-slip faults at major and minor scales. The results allow understanding of the partitioning of strain with respect to (1) regional map-scale versus detailed map-scale versus sub–map-scale faulting, (2) strike-slip versus dip-slip faulting, and (3) early and late episodes of kinematically distinct faulting. The results also add to our knowledge of the directional aspects of Neogene paleostress history.

Northern Rainbow Canyon is located in the eastern part of the Basin and Range province within an enormous late Cenozoic, volcano-tectonic-caldron complex (Fig. 1)—the Caliente caldron complex of Ekren and others (1977). The structural grain of extensional features in the area trends northwest to westnorthwest as it does throughout much of the caldron complex (Ekren and others, 1977; Figs. 1 and 2). This trend is anomalous compared to the northerly trending structural grain of surrounding ranges (Fig. 1B). The canyon was cut by the south-flowing Meadow Valley Wash, a permanent stream that is part of the Colorado River system. As a result, Rainbow Canyon provides an opportunity to obtain uninterrupted cross-sectional views of structural relations and to gather abundant slip data on interrelated systems of strike-slip, dip-slip, and low-angle detachment faults.

Bowman (1985) established the local stratigraphic framework and provided us with a geologic strip map and several cross sections of the Rainbow Canyon area. Most rocks in the caldron complex are Miocene in age. The volcanism ended with basaltic eruptions about 12 to 8.5 Ma. Bowman (1985) described an outstanding stratigraphic record of syntectonic sedimentation, including accumulation of clastic and volcanic strata. The deformation is primarily extensional, with the main normal faults striking northwest. This pattern suggests, and the fault-slip data analysis confirms, that the least-compressive horizontal stress axis (σ_3) was oriented northeast-southwest during the main deformation.

STRATIGRAPHY

The Neogene stratigraphic framework of the northern Rainbow Canyon area was first studied by Ekren and others (1977). They mapped andesitic lavas of Oligocene age, overlain by ashflow tuffs with interstratified bedded tuffs and tuffaceous sedimentary rocks of Miocene age. They divided the tuffs and sedimentary rocks into three map units. The lower is mainly the Hiko Tuff. The upper two are (1) bedded tuffs and related sediments, and (2) rhyolitic ash-flow tuffs of predominantly peralkaline composition. All these volcanic and sedimentary rocks are overlain by basin-fill sediments that are as old as late Miocene. Bowman (1985) subsequently subdivided the Hiko Tuff into upper and lower parts and made a detailed subdivision of the rocks above the Hiko; these rocks, excluding the basin-fill sediments, he collectively referred to as the tuff of Rainbow Canyon (Fig. 3). Because almost all the structural data reported herein were collected from the tuff of Rainbow Canyon, as mapped by Bowman (1985), we describe only that part of the stratigraphic section in some detail.

The tuff of Rainbow Canyon (Fig. 3) includes ash-flow tuffs, ash-fall tuffs, lacustrine and fluvial sedimentary rocks, and debris-flow deposits. The volcanic rocks are part of a stratigraphically complex sequence of locally derived, areally restricted, and generally small-volume eruptions that include abundant rhyolite lava flows east and southeast of northern Rainbow Canyon. Though specific volcanic sources have not been identified, these rocks may have erupted from either the Caliente caldron complex (Ekren and others, 1977) or the Kane Springs Wash volcanic center 40 km to the southwest (Noble, 1968; Novak, 1983). Faulting that occurred during the eruptions produced locally restricted highlands on which many of the volcanic rocks were not deposited or from which they were rapidly stripped by erosion. Erosion during synvolcanic faulting produced clastic debris that accumulated as sediments or debris flows in the same restricted fault-block depocenters as the volcanic rocks.

This combined volcanic and clastic-sediment accumulation resulted in an extremely complex stratigraphic assemblage with common lateral lithologic variations (Bowman, 1985). Although this assemblage has limited potential for long-range correlations, some of the ash-flow tuffs are distinctive enough to be correlated throughout northern Rainbow Canyon. Bowman (1985) assigned a stratigraphic ranking of 1 through 5 (from base to top) to these tuffs but did not map them separately. The stratigraphic positions of his units one through four are shown in Figure 3.

STRUCTURE

Our studies in the northern Rainbow Canyon area indicate that faulting on northwest trends was active during eruption of the 17- to 19-Ma Hiko Tuff and all younger volcanic units, including 10-Ma basalts. The canyon cuts transversely across a series of fault blocks (Fig. 2) that are tilted mostly northeast in the northeast part and southwest in the southwest part. Figure 4 shows a cross section controlled by surface observations with an average physiographic relief of 250 m. The two tilt domains are separated at a keystone graben—the Sawmill graben—within which bedding is approximately horizontal (Figs. 2, 4). Although there are local exceptions to the tilt directions, the general pattern induces the appearance of a gentle anticline centered on Sawmill graben (Fig. 4). In several structural blocks, mainly northeast of Sawmill graben, synfaulting deposition has produced stratigraphic sequences that thicken toward the faults, resulting in fan-shaped depositional patterns in cross sections (Figs. 4A, 4C, 5). Stratal dips in these growth-fault assemblages increase

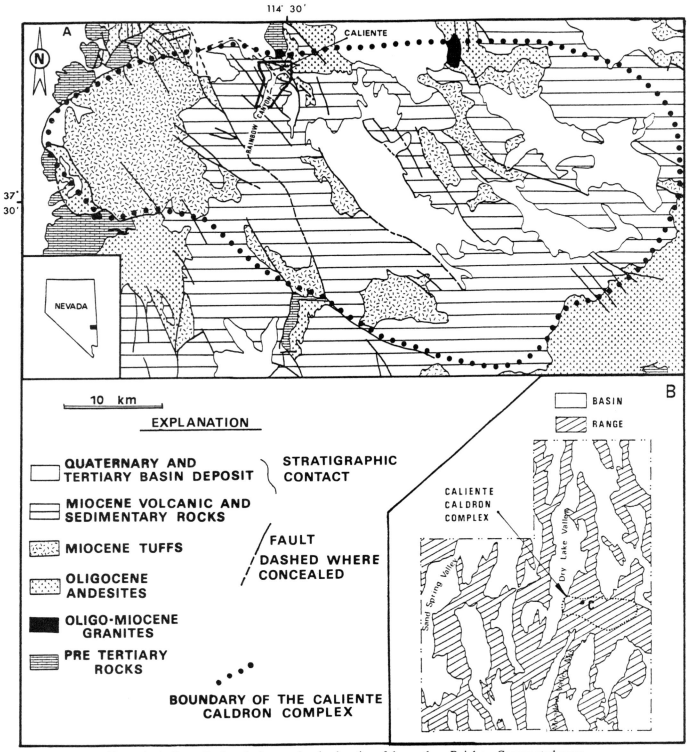

Figure 1. A, Generalized geologic map showing location of the northern Rainbow Canyon study area (enclosed by heavy line) relative to the distribution of major rock units, faults, and the boundary of the Caliente caldron complex (from Ekren and others, 1977); inset shows location of map within Nevada. B, Map of Lincoln County showing the distribution of basins and ranges and the location of the Caliente caldron complex (C for Caliente).

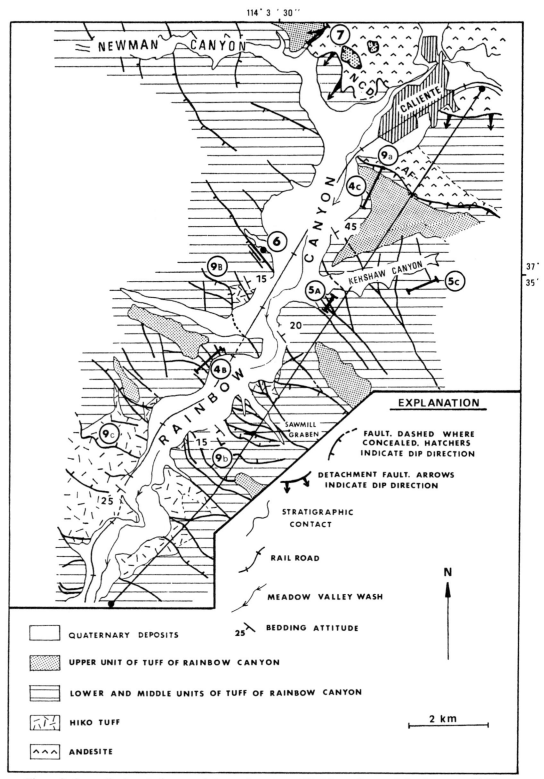

Figure 2. Generalized geologic map of the northern part of Rainbow Canyon (after Bowman, 1985). Circled numbers and letters mark locations of cross sections, photographed sites, or data-collection sites shown on other figures. Line between dots is trace of cross section on Figure 4A. NCD, Newman Canyon detachment fault; AF, Acaro fault.

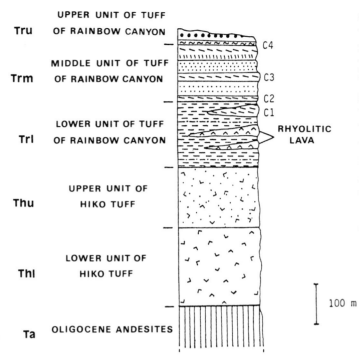

Tru	UPPER UNIT OF TUFF OF RAINBOW CANYON	
Trm	MIDDLE UNIT OF TUFF OF RAINBOW CANYON	
Trl	LOWER UNIT OF TUFF OF RAINBOW CANYON	
Thu	UPPER UNIT OF HIKO TUFF	
Thl	LOWER UNIT OF HIKO TUFF	
Ta	OLIGOCENE ANDESITES	

Figure 3. Stratigraphic column for the northern Rainbow Canyon area. Ta: andesite of Caliente. C1, C2, C3, C4: welded ash-flow tuff units (nomenclature of Bowman, 1985).

downward as much as 50° and possibly more at depth, providing valuable deformational records. For example, Figure 5 shows a fan-shaped section located south of the entrance to Kershaw Canyon on the east side of Rainbow Canyon (site 5a in Fig. 2). Below the tuff labeled C2, the thickness of the sediments does not vary greatly; between C2 and C3, it increases to the north; and between C3 and C4, the fan shape is well developed, indicating that the displacement on the bounding fault (located a short distance to the north of the view) increased during deposition of those rocks. In addition to the large-displacement block-bounding growth faults, many small-displacement faults within the blocks show synsedimentary deformation by displacements that decrease upward. Many are capped by postfault strata (Fig. 6). The stratigraphic position of the capping horizon varies from fault to fault, producing an ideal structural situation for evaluating age-dependent variations in fault-slip characteristics.

The Newman Canyon detachment fault is a structure of major importance in the northern Rainbow Canyon area. Bowman (1985) first named and described it and a similar coextensive structure to the east of it that he called the Caliente fault. We refer to both structures as the Newman Canyon detachment fault. This major detachment fault is observable at the surface in several exposures east and west of Caliente (Fig. 2). Bowman (1985) states that the fault exhibits variable attitude and sense of slip and cuts out 0.7 to 1.8 km of strata. It is the only fault in northern Rainbow Canyon that places the upper tuff of Rainbow Canyon against pre-Hiko volcanic rocks. In general, the Newman Canyon detachment fault strikes west-northwest and dips 25 to 35°

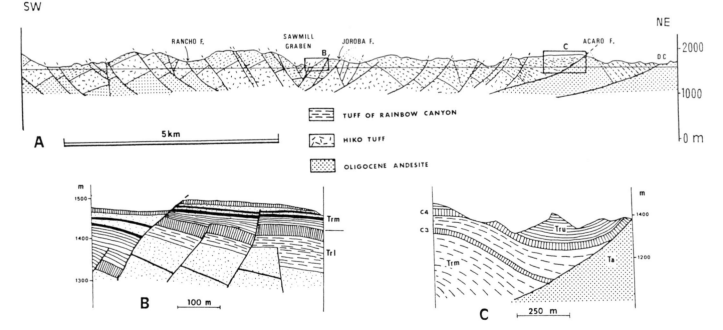

Figure 4. Cross sections. A: Schematic section along Rainbow Canyon (approximate location between large dots in Fig. 2) prepared from data in Bowman (1985) augmented by data gathered in this study. Subhorizontal line marks the approximate level of Meadow Valley Wash. B and C: Detailed sections of growth-fault assemblages. Same abbreviations for stratigraphic units as on Figure 3. Patterns illustrate stratigraphic correlations and within-block and across-fault thickness variations; they do not depict lithologic entities.

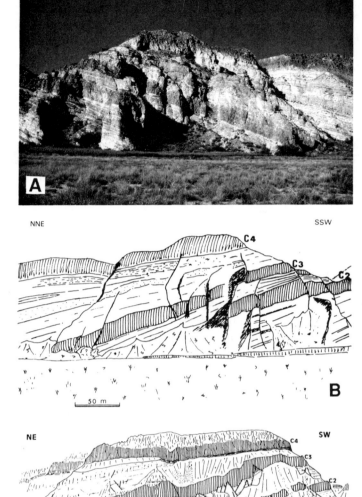

Figure 5. Illustrations of growth-fault stratigraphic fanning in the hanging-wall block of the Acaro fault. A and B are photograph and sketch of a section located south of the Kershaw Canyon (5A in Fig. 2). C is sketch of a section located in Kershaw Canyon (5C in Fig. 2). Note the surface traces of beds in the right foreground that dip as steeply as 47° below C2; beds on skyline above C4 dip about 5°. Vertically ruled strata are ash-flow tuffs with labels corresponding to those on Figure 3.

southward, with a rather sinuous trace (Fig. 2) that results, in part, from northeast-southwest corrugations. Not only does it have the largest stratigraphic separation and the shallowest dip of major faults in the area, but rocks in its hanging wall show the most intense brittle attenuation (Fig. 7) and in its footwall the most intense small-scale shearing and brecciation of any fault we observed.

Fault and bedding geometry

The many excellent exposures of major and minor faults in Rainbow Canyon enable examination of fault geometry in detail and collection of large sets of measurements that are representative of the total fault deformation. Our results are summarized in Figure 8, which shows the strikes (8a), dip directions (8b), and dips (8c) of about 1,100 fault planes. For our statistical analysis, we used 1,215 measurements. The numerical discrepancy arises because we measured some of the large fault planes two or more times. This discrepancy does not affect the general aspect of the illustrations or our computations.

The diagrams in Figure 8 show that a majority of the faults strike northwest-southeast (300 to 335°) and mainly dip southwest. The preference for southwest dip directions likely occurs because outcrop conditions resulted in most of the measurements coming from the tilt domain northeast of the Sawmill graben keystone block.

Fault-dip magnitudes are uniformly distributed between 60 and 90° (Fig. 8c). Most faults with dips between 80 and 90° are strike-slip faults (about 70 to 80 percent based on rake of striae), although some are antithetic normal faults that have been tilted during block rotation.

Exposures of faults across canyon walls 150 to 200 m high (as much as 400 m as fault traces are followed into highlands adjacent to the canyon) provide an opportunity to study the variation of fault dip with depth in order to determine if large normal faults are curved. Figure 9 shows that fault dip may increase, decrease, or remain constant over the observable depth range. This figure documents the existence of three categories of fault geometry, previously noted by Bowman (1985): concave upward listric fault, planar fault, and concave downward listric fault, respectively.

As illustrated in cross section (Fig. 4), planar faults are common mainly south of Sawmill graben, concave upward listric faults are common throughout the area, and concave downward faults are sparse. The predominance of concave-upward faults probably reflects the presence, at a relatively shallow depth, of a subhorizontal to gently dipping zone of extensional accommodation into which these faults merge. Downdip projection of the Newman Canyon detachment fault makes it a logical candidate for participation in such accommodation.

Where it is possible to follow a fault along strike for a long distance, some have listric and planar portions. Whereas hanging-wall strata above the listric portions show large amounts of tilting, little or no tilting is seen along the planar portions of such faults. Therefore, different magnitudes of tilting may occur along a single fault. Growth-fault packages produced by these irregular faults have a complex geometry (Bowman, 1985, Fig. 40). Evidence of irregular dip along major normal faults in sedimentary basins has been found using geophysical profiles in other regions, such as along the Sevier Desert detachment in the Basin and Range province (Allmendinger and others, 1983) and in the southern North Sea Basin (Blundel and Reston, 1987). According

Figure 6. Photograph and sketch of a minor syndepositional fault (F). Compass shows scale. The light-colored tuff caps the offset in the gray-red volcaniclastic sediments in the right lower part of the view. Note that the thickness of the light-colored tuff at left is three times that at right. Tuff unit C_4 is subhorizontal and unfaulted above light-colored tuff. Location shown (upper part of view) on Figure 2.

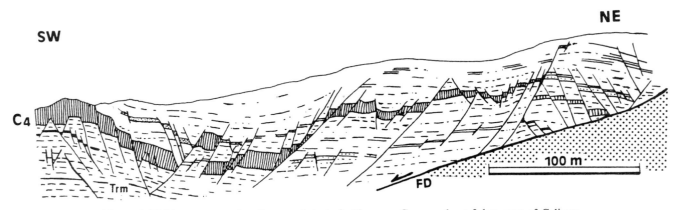

Figure 7. Field panorama of well-exposed strata in Newman Canyon about 3 km west of Caliente (location on Fig. 2) showing, in cross section, the intense fault-related attenuation seen above the Newman Canyon detachment fault. Patterns are added only to show stratigraphic throw and thickness variations of easily identifiable intervals. FD, detachment fault; other symbols as on Figure 3.

to these authors, irregular faults represent the development of secondary shears to accommodate lateral displacement along a horizontal detachment.

Rose diagrams shown in Figures 8e, f, and g depict the stratal attitudes in the same way as Figures 8a, b, and c do for fault attitudes (strike, dip direction, and dip magnitude, respectively). Stratal strikes are parallel to most faults, but they dip in the opposite direction. Because the average dip of the normal faults is about 60 to 80° and those of bedding are 15 to 30° in the opposite direction, the average angle between faults and strati-

graphic layers is close to 90°. There are many exceptions to this relation (Fig. 4). Average 90° bedding-to-fault angles have been observed in other areas of extensional deformation in the Basin and Range province (Anderson, 1971; Fryxell and others, 1987), and this geometry has been interpreted in terms of vertical tension cracks reactivated as faults during faulting-tilting processes associated with large-magnitude extension (Angelier and Colletta, 1982).

It is clear from the general geometric and cross-sectional relations that extensional deformation plays a major role in shap-

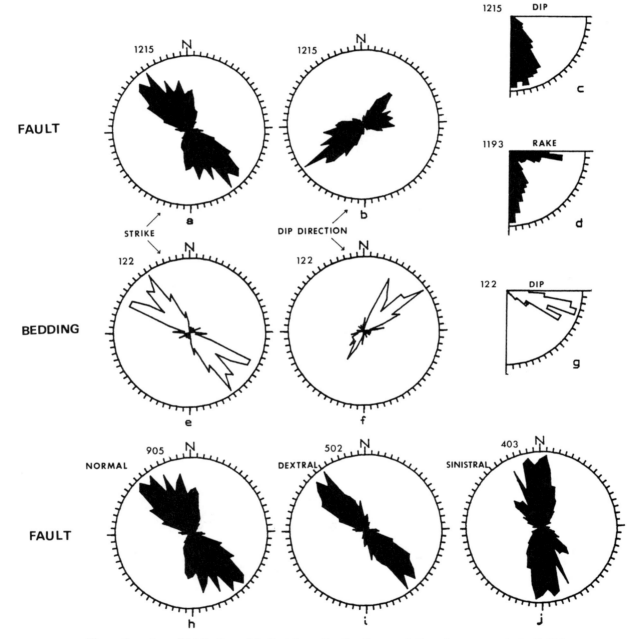

Figure 8. a, b, c: Distribution of fault strikes, dip directions, and dip values, respectively (1,215 measurements on about 1,100 fault planes). 8d: Distribution of rake angles for 1,193 fault surfaces. e, f, g: Distribution of bedding strikes, dip directions, and dip values for 122 bedding attitudes. h, i, j: Distribution of strikes of faults with normal, dextral, and sinistral components, respectively.

ing the structure of this study area. We wish, however, to increase our understanding of the role of strike-slip faulting in the deformation. To do this, we consider the direction, sense, and magnitude of fault slip in conjunction with the geometry of faulting.

Fault-slip data

Approximately 1,200 fault-slip measurements were made at about 25 localities in the Rainbow Canyon area. Each measurement includes the strike and dip of the fault, the rake of striae, and the sense of slip. Methods and criteria used to determine the sense of slip and to rank the quality of the determination are explained in Angelier and others (1985).

Dip-slip and strike-slip faults dominate, which is indicated by the bimodal distribution of rake angles (Fig. 8d). A sector of minimum rake frequency from 20 to 60° clearly separates strike-slip from dip-slip motions. The minimum is at a rake of 44°, which we use to separate the data into dip-slip and strike-slip subsamples. Dip-slip and strike-slip faults are about equally abundant, and it is important to note that both kinds of faults have roughly similar strikes. This is shown qualitatively by the strong similarity in fault-strike distribution between all faults (Fig. 8a) and dip-slip faults (Fig. 8h). Many fault surfaces in and adjacent to the Rainbow Canyon area contain both dip-slip and strike-slip striae. As will be discussed later, a common direction of extension indicates that strike-slip and dip-slip faulting are different aspects of the same deformation utilizing the same faults or faults with similar attitudes.

Slip-sense determinations showing reverse-slip faulting are very sparse in the dip-slip subsample, as is predictable for an extensional faulting regime. In the strike-slip subsample, sinistral-slip and dextral-slip faults are both very common, and each type tends to occupy separate azimuthal sectors (Figs. 8i and j), suggesting a conjugate relation.

It is difficult to graphically present fault attitude and slip data for large numbers of individual faults without making very large illustrations. In order to reduce sample size to values suitable for illustration and machine processing, the data from the Rainbow Canyon area are divided into five subsamples according to geographic areas with relatively homogeneous bedding attitude. Each subsample has about 200 measurements, and the same scheme of subdividing is used for all computations we report and discuss. Fault attitude and slip-sense distributions are similar for all subsamples, so we arbitrarily chose for illustration purposes the area between Kershaw Canyon and Sawmill graben (Figs. 2, 10). The data distributions for dip-slip faults are shown in Figures 10a and c; those for strike-slip faults are shown in Figures 10b and d. It is now necessary to discuss the relative chronology of mixed-mode faulting in order to explain the distinction between early and late phases of deformation represented by the second-stage data subdivision shown in Figure 10.

Because the Rainbow Canyon area exposes many growth-fault assemblages, relative age of faulting can be assigned on the basis of whether or not strata that are cut by one fault extend

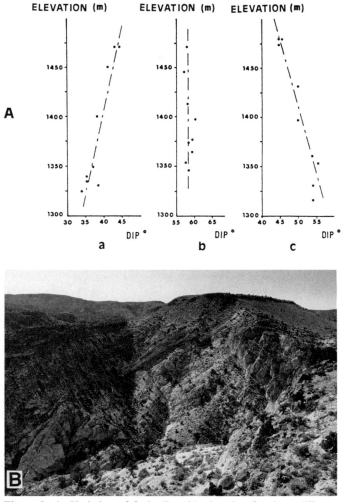

Figure 9. A: Variation of fault dip with elevation for three different faults located on Figure 2 (lower-case letters). (a) Concave upward listric fault (dip increases with elevation), (b) planar fault (constant dip), and (c) concave downward listric fault (dip decreases with increasing elevation). B: Photograph of a concave downward listric fault (see Fig. 2 for location, upper-case letter).

across another (older) fault with no offset (Figs. 4, 5, 6, and 7). Also, many fault planes contain more than one set of striations, and it is commonly possible to determine their relative ages by analysis of their superpositioning. Fault intersections also contain information regarding relative age. Unambiguous, relative-age determinations were made for 45 faults at sites distributed throughout the northern Rainbow Canyon area. These data provide a basis for evaluating whether or not the total fault-slip data sample contains an orderly deformational history reflecting contrasting deformational kinematics. Because we wish to make a general evaluation of relative age that applies to the entire area, but the field-determined relative ages apply only to individual faults or to outcrops of intersecting or nearby faults, we must first make a data subdivision and subsequently test for nonrandom distribution of relative ages among the subdivided parts.

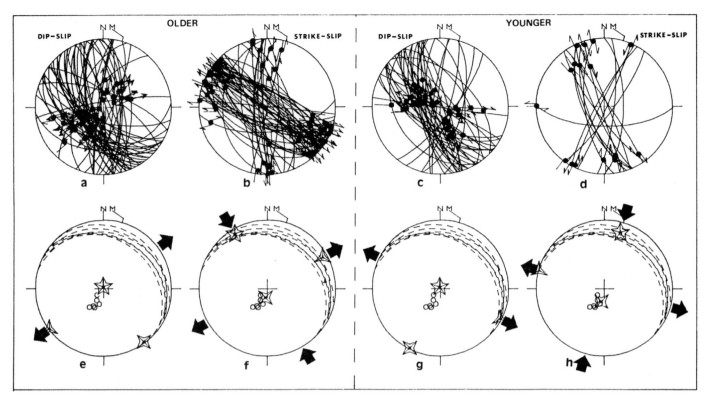

Figure 10. Lower-hemisphere Schmidt projections showing data distributions and computational results for about 200 faults and six bedding attitudes from the area between Kershaw-Ryan State Park and Sawmill graben. N = geographic north; M = magnetic north. Upper row contains projections of fault planes (lines) and striae (dots). Lower row contains projections of bedding planes (dashed lines), poles to bedding (open circles), computed paleostress axes (three-, four-, and five-pointed stars are minimum, intermediate, and maximum compressive stress axes), and azimuthal orientations of least compressive (outward heavy arrows) and maximum compressive (inward heavy arrows) paleostress components. Stereographic plots a and b include dip-slip and strike-slip subsets, respectively, for the main (early) stage of deformation. Stereographic plots c and d include the same for a later stage of deformation. Stereographic plots e, f, g, and h correspond to the subsets directly above them. In the upper-row projections, the arrows attached to the dots show the slip sense—double arrows for sinistral and dextral, single arrows for normal (centrifugal) and reverse (centripetal). The better known the sense of motion, the more complete the head of the arrow.

Machine processing of each of the five geographically determined data subsamples shows uneven distributions of striae. This can be seen as separate clusters of striae for dip slip (Figs. 10a and c) and strike slip (Figs. 10b and d). After the separation by machine processing, we looked at the distribution of relative-age determinations within the resultant data sets. The data represented by Figures 10a and b contain the older relative-age-dated striae and Figures 10c and d the younger. This qualitative evaluation suggests an early stage of northeast-southwest extension and a later stage of northwest-southeast extension. For the early stage, the associated strike-slip motions are generally younger than the dip-slip motions, as indicated by strike-slip striae overprinting dip-slip striae in 90 percent of the observations.

Two features tend to substantiate the validity of the relative-ages subdivision. First, dip-slip faulting in the early stage is characterized by high rake angles (almost pure dip slip), whereas in the late episode it is conspicuously oblique, suggesting that early-formed systems of faults had been reactivated in a stress field of different orientation. Similar relations are seen in data gathered from the other subareas. The second feature that supports different ages of deformation pertains to a dramatic reduction in the average angles of discordance between theoretical and measured maximum shear stress after the age subdivision is made. Such reductions in discordance reflect improvement in the quality of the computational results and thus point to a preferred solution, as will be discussed in the section dealing with paleostress determinations.

Large-displacement faults

Displacement magnitude was measured or estimated for about 1,100 faults. Fault-magnitude frequencies are skewed toward the small values, with most in the 0.1- to 2-m range. For the entire data set, only about 5 percent of the measured faults have displacements greater than 10 m. These large-displacement faults, their striae, and slip sense exhibit distributions and frequencies of

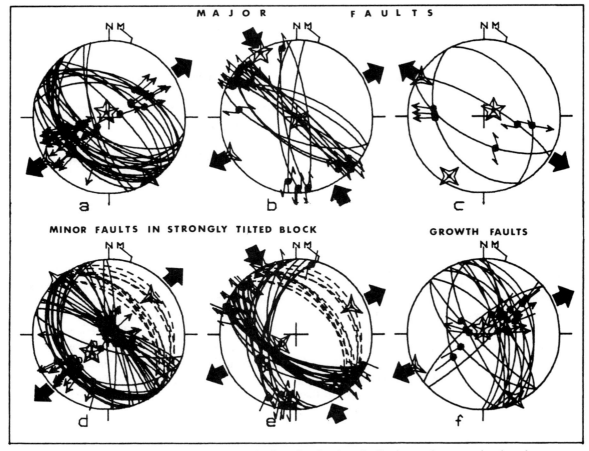

Figure 11. Lower-hemisphere Schmidt projections showing data distributions and computational results for major faults (upper row), for minor faults within a strongly tilted block (d and e of lower row), and for growth faults (f). Same symbols as on Figure 10.

dip-slip and strike-slip types very similar to those of complete samples (compare Figs. 10a, b, c, and d with Figs. 11a, b, and c). In fact, there tends to be less dispersion of fault attitude among the large faults. Despite this minor difference, faults of all scales appear to record the same deformational events.

Tilting of faults and beds

Stratal dips in northern Rainbow Canyon range from 0 to about 60°. Within one very well-exposed block bounded by large-displacement faults, many small-displacement faults cut rocks with an average stratal dip of about 55°. Plots of these fault and bedding attitudes (Figs. 11d, e) show that the faults have been tilted with the beds, because the tilted bedding plane is perpendicular to one symmetry axis of the conjugate fault sets and contains the two other axes. This is especially apparent for the strike-slip faults (Fig. 11e), the dextral and sinistral members of which intersect near the cluster of poles to bedding. It is also apparent for the dip-slip faults (Fig. 10d), the two members of which intersect in the bedding plane and make similar angles with it. Though it is clear that these faults formed when the beds had

gentle dips, it is not known whether the faults continued to be active during the tilting.

In general, the widespread occurrence of growth-fault assemblages, together with abundant evidence that faults of all sizes record the same deformational history, suggests simultaneous faulting and tilting over the full range of fault size. A plot of faults and fault-slip data gathered from growth faults (Fig. 11f) shows a higher degree of attitude and kinematic coherence with faults from areas of gentle to moderate tilting (Fig. 10) than with areas of steep tilting (Figs. 11d, e). Together, these relations suggest that faulting and moderate strata tilting occurred simultaneously but that in areas of steep tilting the small-scale faults remained passive during a significant part of the late-stage tilting.

Paleostress determinations

A qualitative assessment of the geologic map and cross sections (Figs. 1, 2, and 4) in conjunction with the fault orientation and slip-sense data presented in Figures 8, 10, and 11 indicates that the Miocene rocks in the Rainbow Canyon area were subjected to a major stage of northeast-southwest extension and to a later, less intense stage of west-northwest extension. In order to quantify the kinematics of these deformational stages, we compute for each of the five geographic subsamples sets of limited paleostress tensors using the methods described by Angelier (1984). Stress-axis orientations for a typical set are illustrated in Figures 10e, f, g, and h. Included are computations for strike-slip and dip-slip subsets for both the "early" (Figs. 10e, f) and "late" (Figs. 10g, h) deformational stages.

The computed stress-axis orientations are extremely consistent for all geographic subsamples, indicating kinematically uniform deformation. Also, the least compressive stress (σ_3) has remarkably similar orientations for dip-slip and strike-slip subsets representing the separate deformations. The average σ_3 orientations for the separate deformational stages are 235° and 290°, suggesting a 55° clockwise rotation of σ_3 with time. By virtue of close agreement with mapped field relations and much greater sample size, the orientation representing the early deformation (235°) is much more tightly constrained than the late one (290°). It is consitent with northeast-southwest Miocene extension directions known or inferred for a very large part of the southern Nevada, southwestern and western Arizona, and western New Mexico portions of the Basin and Range (Zoback and others, 1981; Angelier and others, 1985).

Not all fault-slip measurements were used in the computations. As part of the computation, the program determines the angle between the theoretical maximum shear stress and the measured striation for each fault plane in the sample. Before computing the tensor, we excluded all faults for which this angle is greater than 45°. The proportion of excluded faults does not exceed 5 percent for any of the subsets representing any of the geographic subsamples. Substantive changes in computed stress-axis orientations would not result if these faults were included in the computations.

Computations were performed for dip-slip and strike-slip subsets for each of the five geographic subsamples *before* making the subdivision into "early" and "late" subsets. The average angle between the theoretical maximum shear stress and the measured striations for those computations is 35 to 45°, in contrast to an average angle of 12 to 17° *after* the data are divided into "early" and "late" subsets. This dramatic improvement in the quality of the computational results tends to validate subdividing the data into separate and distinct deformational episodes, as noted in the subsection on fault-slip data.

Stress-axis orientations computed for large-displacement faults (Figs. 11a, b, c) are essentially the same as for subsamples dominated by small-displacement faults (the geographic subsamples that are represented in Fig. 10). The rotations from their "normal" vertical and horizontal positions respectively of σ_1 and σ_3 for dip-slip and strike-slip subsets representing strongly tilted rocks (Figs. 11d and e) reflect tilting of the faults rather than rotation of the paleostress axes. This strongly supports our interpretation, stated above, based on less rigorous evidence, that small-scale faults contained within strongly tilted blocks remained passive during much of the tilting. The azimuthal component of σ_3 for steeply tilted blocks is similar to that of other "early" main-phase deformation (Figs. 10e, f), indicating uniformity of horizontal-axis rotations. Stress-axis orientations from important growth faults also parallel the azimuths of the main-phase orientations (Fig. 11f).

Strain partitioning according to deformational event, faulting mode, and fault size

Throughout the text, we acknowledge that the "early" deformation, which is characterized mainly by northeast-southwest extension, represents the main stage of deformation. This is obvious from the control it exerts on the structural fabric and synfaulting sedimentation patterns of the area (Bowman, 1985). There is no obvious widespread set of structures along Rainbow Canyon that formed during the later deformational stage. For the most part, that deformation utilized existing faults in oblique-slip motions. Note that oblique striae plotted on Figure 11c overprinted much more conspicuous dip-slip striae related to the northeast-southwest extension.

In-progress geological studies being conducted to the east of Rainbow Canyon show the presence of weakly developed joints and faults that formed during the "late" stage. There, as in Rainbow Canyon, the magnitude of deformation appears small compared with the "early" stage. Because the major faults (Figs. 11a, b, c), the tilting processes (Figs. 11d, e), and the syndepositional faulting (Fig. 11f) are systematically associated with northeast-southwest extension, and because the motions related to the west-northwest–east-southeast extension are relatively weak, we estimate that less than 5 percent of the total Neogene brittle strain occurred during the "late" deformation.

Dip-slip and strike-slip faulting occurred during "early" and "late" stages, and we would like to know how strain is partitioned between these two faulting modes. Because the opportunity to measure or estimate displacement magnitude is much greater for dip-slip faults (which displace stratigraphic markers at a high angle to their trace on the fault) than for strike-slip faults (the slip lines of which commonly form low angles with bedding traces on fault planes), it is difficult to quantify this aspect of strain partitioning. On some faults, strike-slip striae are as common as dip-slip striae, and penetrative fabrics internal to fault-zone gouge indicate equally common long-term strike-slip and dip-slip motions. Although these faults show that strike-slip deformation is important locally, only two faults with proven strike-slip displacement greater than 20 m are recognized. More importantly, there appear to be no strike-slip displacements as large as the dip-slip displacements on the major block-bounding faults or the Newman Canyon detachment fault. Balanced against the obvious evidence for major extension as noted above, we estimate that 10 to 30 percent of the total brittle strain is accomplished by strike-slip faulting, with a preference for the low side of the estimate.

We believe that our large sample of dip-slip faults is representative of slip-magnitude frequencies for that faulting mode. Because small-displacement faults are much more common than

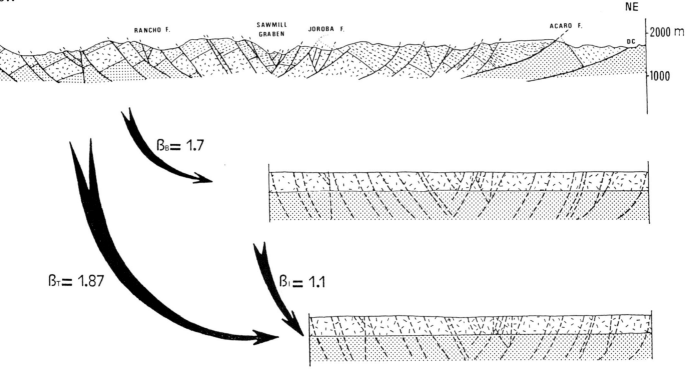

Figure 12. Two-stage palinspastic reconstruction of cross section shown on Figure 4. In the first stage, displacements on the block-bounding faults are restored resulting in a coefficient of extension (β_B) of 1.7. In the second stage, block-interior deformation (not illustrated here, but described in Fig. 13) is restored using a separately determined average coefficient of extension (β_I) of 1.1. The total coefficient of extension is the product $\beta_B \times \beta_I = 1.87$.

large-displacement faults, we wish to understand what proportion of the total strain they represent. Determining extensional strain associated with the large block-bounding faults is somewhat complicated by synfaulting sedimentation and compaction. Using geometrical reconstruction and in some cases the methods outlined by Wernicke and Burchfiel (1982), Gibbs (1983), and Davison (1986), we reconstruct the section shown in Figure 4 at the level of the Hiko Tuff and obtain an average extension factor close to 70 percent (Fig. 12).

Determination of extensional strain associated with small-scale faulting internal to the map-scale blocks (Fig. 13) is complicated by strain-magnitude variations associated with (1) stratigraphic position within growth-fault assemblages, (2) distance from major block-boundary faults, and (3) distance from the Newman Canyon detachment fault. We disregard the latter complication because it reflects a unique condition that would bias estimates toward high-extension values. To understand the other complications, a separate study was made to obtain representative coefficients of extension associated with faults of centimeter-to-meter displacements by sampling displacement magnitudes at various stratigraphic levels and distances from block-bounding faults. Coefficients of extension vary by an order of magnitude from 30 to 3 percent between the faulted boundary and interior of some blocks and can decrease to almost 0 percent in the

youngest strata of some growth-fault assemblages. We estimate that 10 percent is a reasonable average value for the coefficient of extension due to block-interior faulting in the middle part of the stratigraphic section (top of the Hiko Tuff). It may be as high as 20 percent in the lower part and may be much higher in *structurally* low positions near subhorizontal accommodation zones.

Amount and age of extension

The total amount of northeast-southwest extension at stratigraphically intermediate levels in the Rainbow Canyon area is given by the product of the coefficients of block-boundary and block-interior extension (1.7 and 1.1, respectively). The product, 1.87 or approximately 90 percent, is, of course, not an estimate of the total deformation. Such an estimate also would include (1) a significant contribution from strike-slip faulting and (2) an unknown but potentially large amount of deformation associated with volcanotectonic evolution of calderas from which the Hiko (Ekren and others, 1977) and possibly older (Rowley and Siders, 1988) ash-flow tuffs erupted.

The Hiko Tuff, from which the 90 percent extension is estimated, dates from approximately 14 Ma on the basis of unpublished K/Ar ages (H. Mehnert, written communication, 1987). Evidence for extensional deformation, kinematically con-

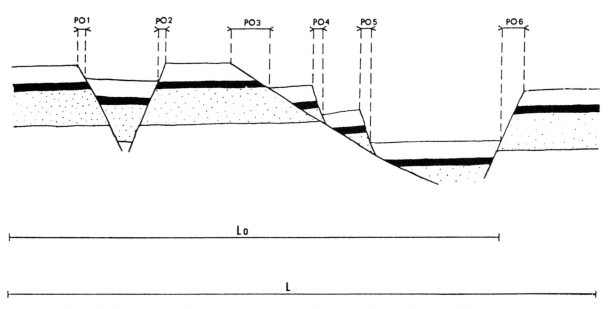

Figure 13. Cross-sectional sketch showing the convention used in determining the coefficient of internal extension (β_I). $\beta_I = L/LO$ with $LO = L - (PO1 + PO2 + \cdots + POn)$. PO = component of offset measured parallel to bedding.

sistent with this main phase of extension, can be found at the highest stratigraphic levels exposed in the canyon walls in rocks estimated to be about 12 m.y. old. Also, studies in progress directly east of Rainbow Canyon indicate that deformation consistent with a northeast-southwest σ_3 orientation continued during and after extrusion of basalts, the ages of which are about 10 Ma, on the basis of K/Ar analyses (H. Mehnert, written communication, 1987). Thus, the age of the indicated clockwise shift in extensional kinematics is younger than about 10 Ma, but its true age is not know.

SUMMARY AND DISCUSSION

Detailed structural studies of faulted and tilted Miocene volcanic and sedimentary rocks in the northern part of the Caliente caldron complex of Ekren and others (1977) suggest two kinematically distinct stages of deformation, each characterized by dip-slip and strike-slip faulting.

The first stage was of large magnitude. It is characterized by synfaulting deposition of volcanic and sedimentary sequences that thicken toward predominantly northwest-striking block-boundary growth faults, resulting in fan-shaped depositional patterns in northeast-southwest cross section. Concave-upward faults are common, and fault-to-bedding angles in vertical sections containing the extension direction average about 90°. Only about 5 percent of about 1,100 faults, for which the displacement magnitude was measured or estimated, have displacements more than 10 m.

Comprehensive fault-slip studies indicate remarkable kinematic coherence of extension direction over the full range of fault size, tilt magnitude, and faulting mode. Dip-slip and strike-slip faults yield similar azimuths of σ_3 (average 235°) on the basis of

numerous fault-slip inversions of large data samples. Dextral faults are more common than sinistral faults, but each type tends to have different strikes (Figs. 10b, d), suggesting quasi-conjugate shearing mechanically and kinematically linked to the dip-slip faulting.

The total coefficient of extension at stratigraphically median levels is 1.9 (about 90 percent). About 10 to 20 percent of this is identified as interior faulting. Important additional deformation is associated with the strike-slip faulting. We estimate that 10 to 30 percent of the total brittle strain is represented by strike-slip faulting, although accurate measurements or reliable estimates of displacement magnitudes on strike-slip faults are sparse. Also, unpublished mapping directly east of Rainbow Canyon shows that stratigraphically lower levels than those studied probably embrace additional Neogene deformation, in part volcanotectonic in origin, of significant magnitude.

The mixture of dip-slip and strike-slip faults in each of the relative-age categories may represent a permutation between intermediate- and maximum-compressive stress axes. Such permutations have been interpreted from other bimodal rake distributions and may represent a change in the paleostress regime (Angelier and Bergerat, 1983; Zoback, 1989). The change need only be a small one because the direction of extension, representing the major aspect of deformation, is the same for normal as well as strike-slip faulting. For a relatively small data set from the Hempel Wash area, Nevada, Frizzell and Zoback (1987) suggest that there is no need to infer separate and distinct deformational episodes responding to a change in paleostress to explain the bimodal rake distribution they observed. Indeed, the strike-slip faulting may reflect brittle constriction normal to the extension direction. Such constriction may be a mechanical requirement in regimes where the depth of extensional faulting is controlled by subhorizontal zones of structural accommodation. The dip-slip and strike-slip faults are seen as integral parts of the extensional and complimentary constrictional shape change of a depth-limited slab or slabs of upper crustal rocks similar to that reported by Brun and others (1985) from analogue modeling and by Hill (1982) from playing with his child's blocks.

Evidence for a second subordinate stage of kinematically contrasting deformation is seen throughout the study area and in a contiguous area currently under study to the east. In the Rainbow Canyon area, few new faults appear to have formed during this phase. Reactivation of existing faults in oblique slip is common, although dip-slip and strike-slip motions are also common. As with the first deformation, there is strong kinematic coherence of extension directions (average 290°) computed from subsets of strike-slip and dip-slip faults. Unlike the first deformation, we estimate less than 5 percent extension and only nominal magnitudes of strike-slip displacement.

Although the second phase is not a major deformational event, it provides another example of polyphase deformation resulting from apparent clockwise (55°) rotation of least compressive stress similar to that reported from other places in the Basin and Range (Anderson and Ekren, 1977; Zoback and Thompson, 1978; Zoback and others, 1981; Angelier and others, 1985). There is growing interest as to whether, in areas where strike-slip faulting is common, such rotations result from vertical-axis rotations of the rocks (Garfunkel, 1974; Ron and others, 1984; Ron and others, 1986) or the stress field. On the basis of exposures in the Rainbow Canyon area, the second phase of deformation appears to be of insufficient magnitude to have produced vertical-axis counterclockwise rock rotations of more than a degree or so. Larger, young rotations could only have occurred if the entire area had been rotated on structures that lay beyond its boundaries and at unexposed subjacent levels. Because no such structures have been identified, we conclude that any significant vertical-axis block rotations must have been an integral part of the main phase of deformation and must have developed synchronously with the horizontal-axis rock rotations that are so dramatically frozen into the geologic record in the form of growth-fault assemblages. The general absence of progressive variations in stratal and fault strikes as required analogues to the progressive variations in stratal and fault dips in the Rainbow Canyon area argues against a major synchronous component of counterclockwise vertical-axis block rotation, as does the consistency of computed σ_3 orientations and the quasi-conjugate aspect of the strike-slip faulting. Also, fault-slip studies in basin-fill strata in the Mesquite Basin, Nevada, 80 km southeast of Rainbow Canyon, indicate clockwise rotations of σ_3 similar in magnitude and orientation to those of the Rainbow Canyon area but in a geologic setting where counterclockwise rock rotations are unlikely, taking into account the structure and size of the basin and the continuity of the outcrops (Michel-Noël, 1988).

This study provides strong verification that our understand-

ing of deformation intensity is highly dependent on the scale of investigation, depth of exposure, and slip-sense determinations. On the basis of fault spacing, apparent offset, stratal attitudes, and formation contacts shown on the geologic map of Lincoln County (Ekren and others, 1977, scale 1:250,000), extension of less than 10 percent is indicated for the upper plate of the Newman Canyon detachment in the Rainbow Canyon area. Our study indicates about 90 percent, and 10 to 20 percent of that would have been missed had not a detailed study of block-interior deformation been made.

Had the erosional event that cut Rainbow Canyon and its tributary canyons not occurred, no amount of detailed study of the exposed bedrock would likely have produced evidence for more than about 10 percent extension, and we would have little, if any, knowledge of strike-slip faulting. Had Rainbow Canyon been cut somewhat deeper, we would probably have access to evidence in Neogene rocks for additional significant extensional deformation, some associated with earlier volcanotectonic activity (Rowley and Siders, 1988).

Major low-angle normal faults or detachment faults such as the Newman Canyon detachment fault play important roles in the distribution of extensional strain in the vertical rock column. Deformation in the hanging wall of the Newman Canyon detachment shows a downward-increasing "strain stratigraphy" associated with the synsedimentary faulting and is probably a maximum at the detachment. Whether or not footwalls to detachments are internally strained or rotated and uplifted coeval with extension in the hanging wall must be uniquely determined for each detachment. Unpublished geologic mapping of the area directly north and east of Caliente indicates strong internal extensional strain and moderate horizontal-axis rotation of its footwall, consistent with Bowman's (1985) observation that footwall rocks are more highly sheared than hanging-wall rocks. From this we infer that both blocks were active relative to some far-field unstrained point. Although the subsurface geometry of the detachment south of Caliente is not known, we suspect that the distribution of the major growth-fault stratigraphic packages, as well as the dip reversal at the Sawmill graben, is a function of ramp-flat detachment geometry. Such features have been shown by analogue modeling of extensional fault systems (Vendeville and others, 1987; Brun and others, 1987) to develop over ramps in the basal detachment.

ACKNOWLEDGMENTS

We thank Pete Rowley for providing us with unpublished geologic information about the area and Richard Allmendinger, Ernie Duebendorfer, Virgil Frizzell, Pete Rowley, and Bob Scott for helpful reviews, and Eleanor M. Omdahl and Tammy Carlson for expert assistance in preparation and proofing of the manuscript. The participation of Michel-Noël and Angelier was supported by the Centre National de la Recherche Scientifique, France.

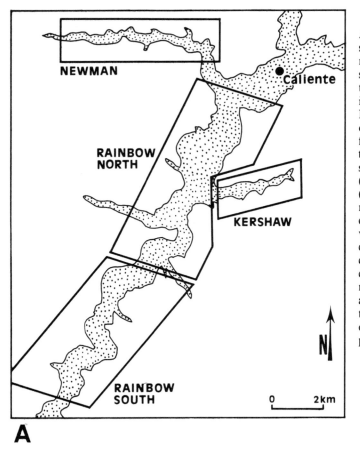

A

Appendix 1. Location map and lower-hemisphere Schmidt projections showing data distributions and computational results for data that are not illustrated in the main body of the accompanying report. Map 1A shows the location of the subareas. Sufficient data were gathered from the Rainbow North subarea to allow for two subsets—one is presented in the main body of the report, and the other is presented here (Rainbow North 1). Figures 1B, 1C, 1D, and 1E show the stereographic projections of data (Schmidt, lower hemisphere) from the subareas (see Appendix 3 for tabulated data), and the following description applies to each of them: The upper row contains projections of fault planes (lines) and striae (dots). The lower row contains projections of bedding planes (dashed lines), poles to bedding (open circles), computed paleostress axes (three-, four-, and five-pointed stars are minimum, intermediate, and maximum compressive stress axes) and azimuthal orientations of least compressive (outward heavy arrows) and maximum compressive (inward heavy arrows) paleostress components. Figures 1a and b include dip-slip and strike-slip subsets, respectively, for the main (early) stage of deformation. Figures 1c and d include the same for a later stage of deformation (see text for details). In the upper-row projections, the arrows attached to the dots show the slip sense: double arrows for sinistral and dextral, single arrows for normal (centrifugal) and reverse (centripetal). The better known the sense of motion, the more complete the head of the arrow. For Appendix 1C, the circled stars in the lower-row projections are weighted stress axes.

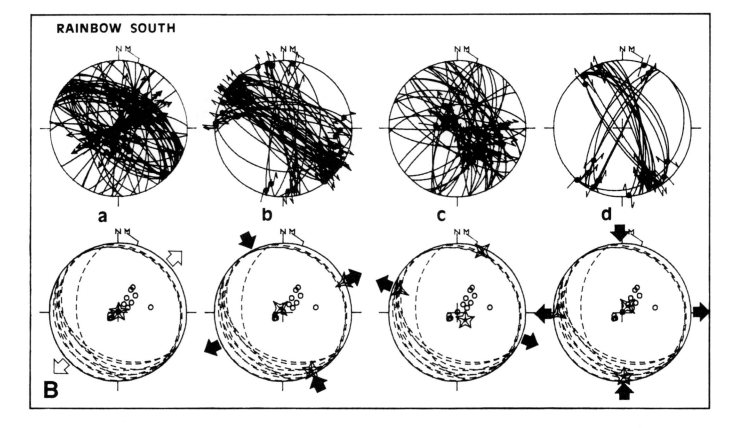

B

RAINBOW NORTH 1

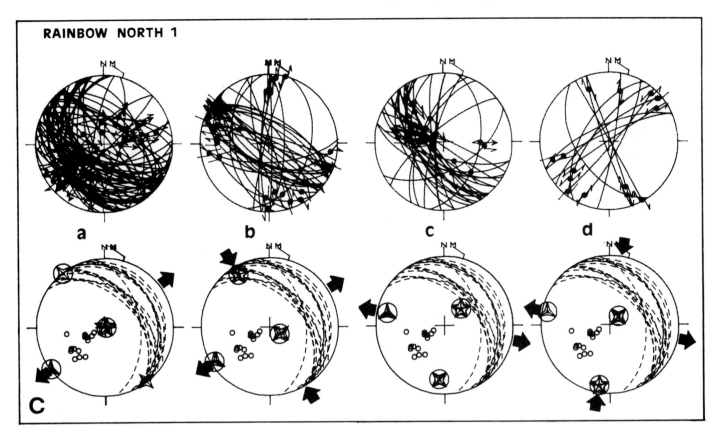

KERSHAW

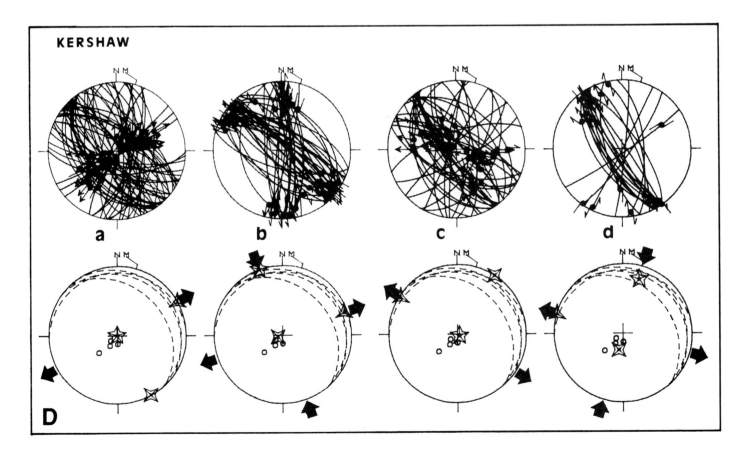

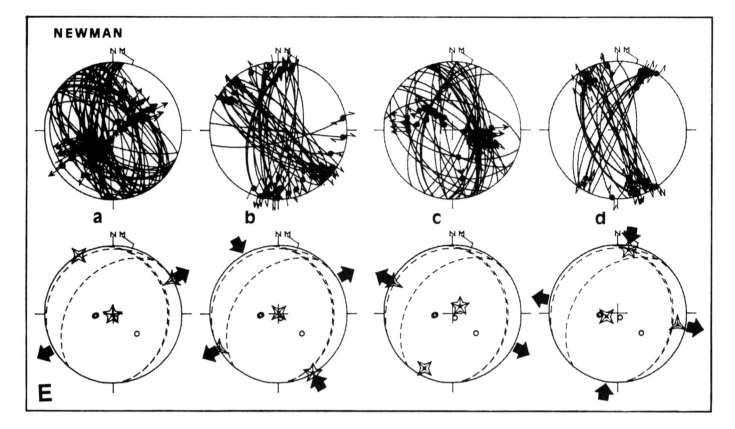

Appendix 2. Maps and lower-hemisphere Schmidt projections showing the data distributions, computed stress axes, and sample-area locations for various data subsets. Symbols in Schmidt projections are the same as in Appendix 1. Figure 2A illustrates dip-slip data for the early (NE-SW) extensional deformation. Figure 2B illustrates strike-slip data for the early (NE-SW) deformation. Figure 2C illustrates dip-slip data for the late (ESE-WNW) extensional deformation. Figure 2D illustrates strike-slip data for the late (ESE-WNW) deformation. Figure 2E illustrates data for syndepositional faults.

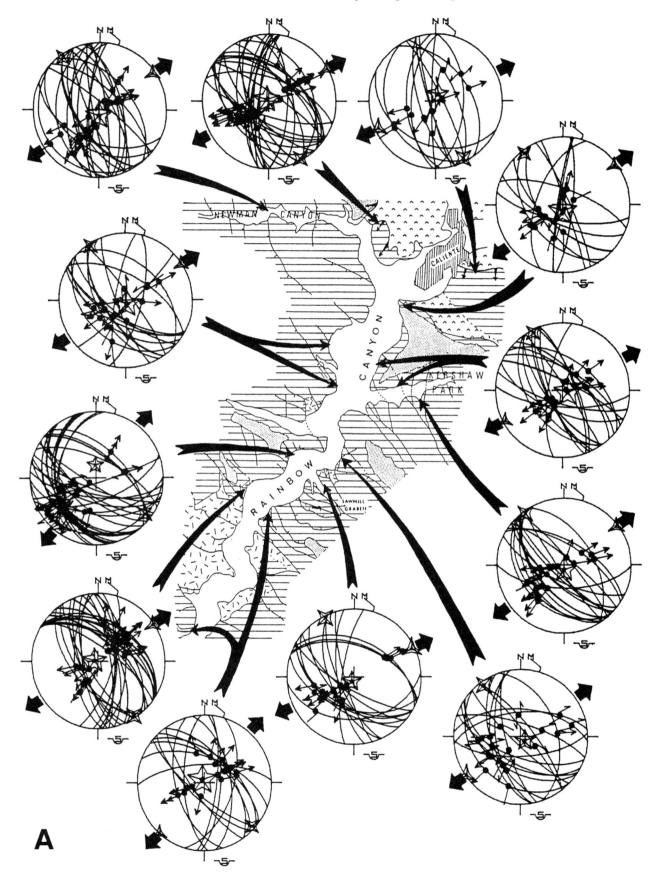

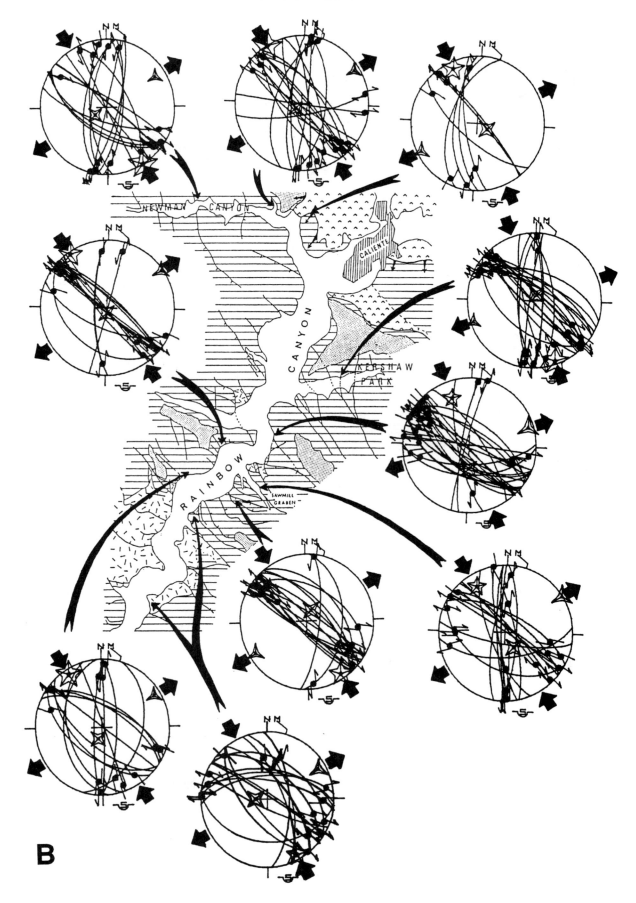

B

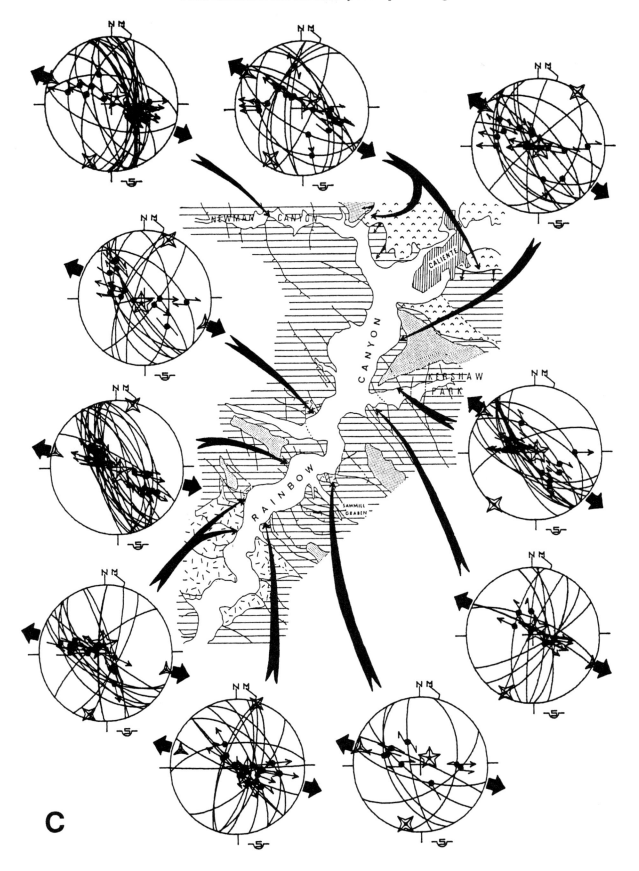

C

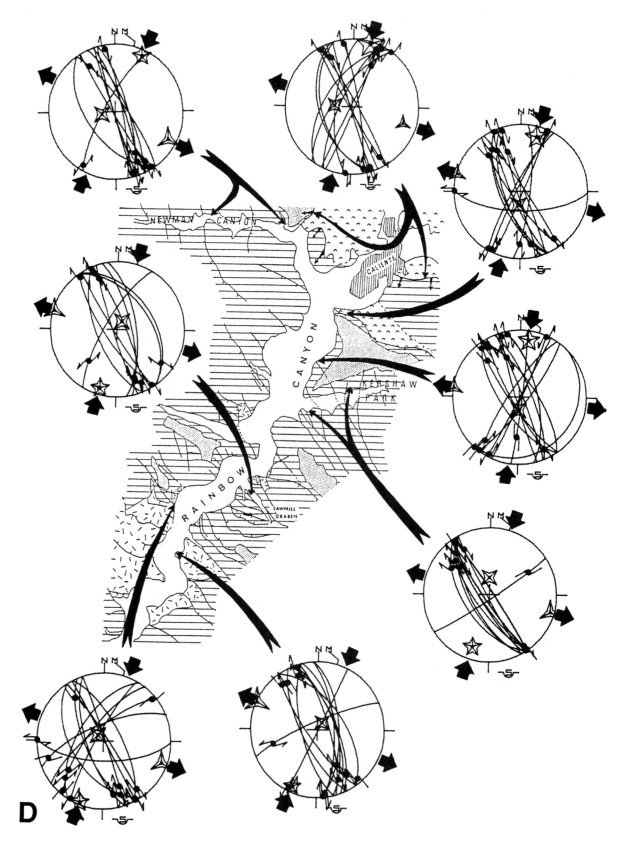

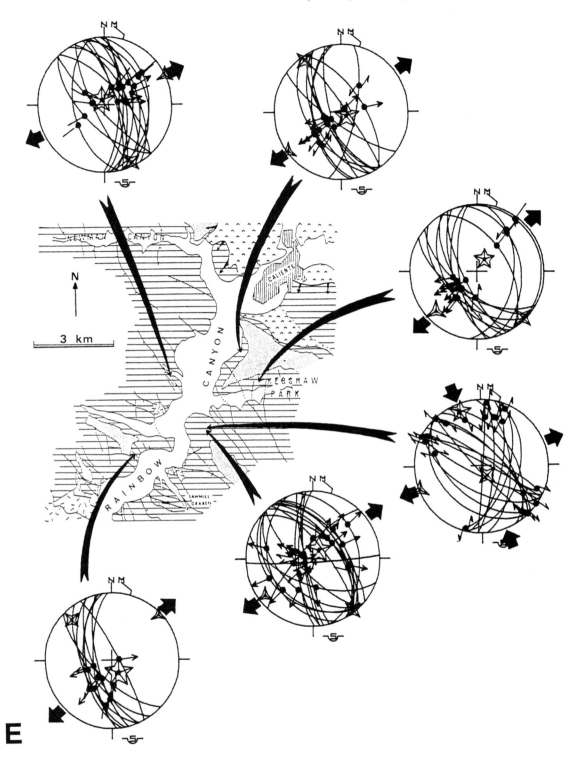

A			RAINBOW SOUTH		RAINBOW NORTH 1		RAINBOW NORTH 2		KERSHAW		NEWMAN	
			trend	plunge	trend	plunge	trend	plunge	trend	plunge	trend	plunge
TOTAL POPULATION		Sig1	159	78	351	79	164	78	53	87	237	87
		Sig2	6	11	143	10	342	12	192	2	350	1
		Sig3	275	5	234	5	72	0	283	2	80	3
OLDER EVENT	Dip-slip	Sig1	65	89	335	88	345	88	307	89	220	89
		Sig2	320	0	143	2	141	2	151	1	330	1
		Sig3	230	1	233	0	231	1	61	0	60	1
	Strike-slip	Sig1	154	6	329	13	329	8	340	0	150	1
		Sig2	328	84	120	75	192	79	250	84	26	89
		Sig3	64	1	237	7	60	7	70	6	240	1
YOUNGER EVENT	Dip-slip	Sig1	131	77	46	63	345	88	123	87	46	78
		Sig2	22	4	186	21	205	1	33	0	207	12
		Sig3	292	12	282	16	115	1	303	3	298	4
	Strike-slip	Sig1	178	8	190	10	16	17	17	20	10	6
		Sig2	40	80	50	77	192	73	194	70	253	76
		Sig3	269	7	282	8	286	1	287	1	101	12

B			RAINBOW SOUTH	RAINBOW NORTH 1	RAINBOW NORTH 2	KERSHAW	NEWMAN
TOTAL POPULATION		Nb	190	153	172	188	179
		Phi	0.37	0.62	0.79	0.12	0.30
		Ang	41°	38°	36°	41°	36°
		Coh	66%	69%	67%	62%	66%
OLDER EVENT	Dip-slip	Nb	61	66	55	65	64
		Phi	0.01	0.42	0.06	0.06	0.22
		Ang	11°	16°	14°	11°	12°
		Coh	100%	100%	100%	100%	100%
	Strike-slip	Nb	56	37	64	51	44
		Phi	0.34	0.18	0.42	0.25	0.13
		Ang	16°	17°	13°	15°	13°
		Coh	100%	100%	100%	100%	100%
YOUNGER EVENT	Dip-slip	Nb	42	30	39	40	41
		Phi	0.06	0.56	0.08	0.21	0.24
		Ang	13°	13°	17°	15°	11°
		Coh	100%	100%	100%	100%	100%
	Strike-slip	Nb	23	14	13	21	30
		Phi	0.24	0.35	0.36	0.71	0.29
		Ang	14°	16°	15°	15°	14°
		Coh	100%	100%	100%	100%	100%

Appendix 3. Tabulations of computed stress axes and stress-axis parameters. Figure 3A shows stress axes for each of the four subareas shown in Appendix 1A, as well as for the data presented in the main body of the report (Rainbow North 2); Sig1, Sig2, and Sig3 are the maximum, intermediate, and least compressive stress axes, respectively. Figure 3B shows stress-axis parameters including Nb, number of measurements; Phi, $\frac{\sigma_2 - \sigma_3}{\sigma_1 - \sigma_3}$; Ang, mean angle between the theoretical and computed maximum shear stress; Coh, percentage of faults with a value of "Ang" less than 45°.

A

A			NON WEIGHTED		WEIGHTED	
TOTAL POPULATION		Sig1	351	79	344	84
		Sig2	143	10	153	6
		Sig3	234	5	243	1
OLDER EVENT	Dip-slip	Sig1	335	88	85	88
		Sig2	143	2	323	1
		Sig3	233	0	233	2
	Strike-slip	Sig1	329	13	329	14
		Sig2	120	75	125	75
		Sig3	237	7	238	6
YOUNGER EVENT	Dip-slip	Sig1	46	63	45	62
		Sig2	186	21	186	23
		Sig3	282	16	283	16
	Strike-slip	Sig1	190	10	190	12
		Sig2	50	77	46	75
		Sig3	282	8	282	8

B

B			NON WEIGHTED	WEIGHTED
TOTAL POPULATION		Nb	153	215
		Phi	0.62	0.41
		Ang	38°	32°
		Coh	69%	74%
OLDER EVENT	Dip-slip	Nb	66	106
		Phi	0.42	0.33
		Ang	16°	15°
		Coh	100%	99%
	Strike-slip	Nb	37	49
		Phi	0.18	0.18
		Ang	17°	14°
		Coh	100%	100%
YOUNGER EVENT	Dip-slip	Nb	30	37
		Phi	0.56	0.59
		Ang	13°	12°
		Coh	100%	100%
	Strike-slip	Nb	14	18
		Phi	0.35	0.36
		Ang	16°	14°
		Coh	100%	100%

Appendix 4. Tabulations showing comparison between stress-axis orientations (4A) and stress-axis parameters (4B) computed for unweighted and weighted data from the North 1 sample area (see Appendix 1 for location and Appendix 3 for explanation).

REFERENCES CITED

Allmendinger, R. W., and 7 others, 1983, Cenozoic and Mesozoic structure of the eastern Basin and Range province, Utah, from COCORP seismic-reflection data: Geology, v. 11, p. 532–536.

Anderson, R. E., 1971, Thin-skin distension in Tertiary rocks of southeastern Nevada: Geological Society of America Bulletin, v. 82, p. 43–58.

—— , 1973, Large magnitude late Tertiary strike-slip faulting north of Lake Mead, Nevada. U.S. Geological Survey Professional Paper 794, 18 p.

Anderson, R. E., and Ekren, E. B., 1977, Comment on Late Cenozoic fault patterns and stress fields in the Great Basin and westward displacement of the Sierra Nevada block: Geology, v. 5, p. 388–389.

Angelier, J., 1984, Tectonic analysis of fault slip data sets: Journal of Geophysical Research, v. 89, p. 5835–5848.

Angelier, J., and Bergerat, F., 1983, Systemes de constrained et extension intracontinentale: Bulletin des Centres de Recherches Exploration-Production Elf-Aquitaine, v. 7, p. 137–147.

Angelier, J., and Colletta, B., 1982, Tension fractures and extensional tectonics: Nature, v. 301, no. 5895, p. 49–51.

Angelier, J., Colletta, B., and Anderson, R. E., 1985, Neogene paleostress changes in the Basin and Range; A case study at Hoover Dam, Nevada-Arizona: Geological Society of America Bulletin, v. 96, p. 347–361.

Blundell, D. J., and Reston, T. J., 1987, Geometry of sedimentary basin bounding faults through the crust: Terra Cognita, v. 7, nos. 2-3, p. 197.

Bowman, S. A., 1985, Miocene extension and volcanism in the Caliente Caldera Complex, Lincoln County, Nevada [M.S. thesis]: Golden, Colorado School of Mines, 143 p.

Brun, J. P., Choukroune, P., and Faugeres, E., 1985, Les discontinuites significatives de l'amincissement crustal; Application aux marges passive: Bulletin de la Societe Geologique de France (8), I, no. 1, p. 139–144.

Brun, J. P., Allemand, P., and Ballard, J. F., 1987, Mechanics of crustal extension; A small-scale approach: Geological Society of America Abstracts with Programs, v. 19, p. 603–604.

Davison, I., 1986, Listric normal fault profile; Calculation using bed length balance and fault displacement: Journal of Structural Geology, v. 8, no. 2, p. 209–210.

Ekren, E. B., Orkild, P. P., Sargent, K. A., and Dixon, G. L., 1977, Geologic map of Tertiary rocks, Lincoln County, Nevada: U.S. Geological Survey Miscellaneous Investigations Series Map, I-1041, scale 1:250,000.

Frizzell, V. A., and Zoback, M. L., 1987, Stress orientation determined from fault-slip data in Hempel Wash area, Nevada, and its relation to contemporary regional stress field: Tectonics, v. 6, no. 2, p. 89–98.

Fryxell, J. E., Stimac, J. A., and Reynolds, S. J., 1987, Superimposed domino-style normal faults in a Tertiary bimodal volcanic complex, Wickenburg Mountains and vicinity, central Arizona: Geological Society of America Abstracts with Programs, v. 19, no. 7, p. 670.

Garfunkel, Z., 1974, Model for the late Cenozoic tectonic history of the Mojave Desert, California, and for its relation to adjacent regions: Geological Society of America Bulletin, v. 85, p. 1931–1944.

Gibbs, A. D., 1983, Balanced cross section construction from seismic sections in areas of extensional tectonics: Journal of Structural Geology, v. 5, no. 2, p. 153–160.

Hill, D. P., 1982, Contemporary block tectonics; California and Nevada: Journal of Geophysical Research, v. 87, p. 5433–5450.

Michel-Noël, G., 1988, Mécanismes et évolution de l'extension intracontinentale des Basin and Range, et développement tectonique des bassins sédimentaires: Thèse de Doctorat, Université Paris 6, Mémoires des Sciences de la Terre 88-42, 215 p.

Noble, D. C., 1968, Kane Spring Wash volcanic center, Lincoln County, Nevada, *in* Eckel, E. B., ed., Nevada Test Site, Geological Society of America Memoir 110, p. 109–116.

Novak, W., 1983, Timing of rhyolite-trachyte volcanism at the Kane Springs Wash volcanic center, southeastern Nevada: Geological Society of America Abstracts with Programs, v. 15, p. 280.

Ron, H., Freund, R., Garfunkel, Z., and Nur, A., 1984, Block rotation by strike slip faulting; Structural and paleomagnetic evidence: Journal of Geophysical Research, v. 89, p. 6256–6270.

Ron, H., Aydin, A., and Nur, A., 1986, Strike-slip faulting and block rotation in the Lake Mead fault system: Geology, v. 14, p. 1020–1023.

Rowley, P. D., and Siders, M. A., 1988, Miocene calderas of the Caliente caldera complex, Nevada-Utah: EOS Transactions of the American Geophysical Union, v. 69, no. 44, p. 1508.

Vendeville, B., Cobbold, P., Davy, P., Brun, J. P., and Choukroune, P., 1987, Physical models of extensional tectonics at various scales, *in* Coward, M. P.,

Dewey, J. F., and Hancock, P. L., eds., Continental extensional tectonics: Geological Society of London Special Publication 28, p. 95–107.

Wernicke, B., and Burchfiel, B. C., 1982, Modes of extensional tectonics: Journal of Structural Geology, v. 4, no. 2, p. 105–115.

Zoback, M. L., 1989, State of stress and modern deformation of the northern Basin and Range province: Journal of Geophysical Research (in press).

Zoback, M. L., and Thompson, G., 1978, Basin and Range rifting in northern Nevada; Clues from a mid-Miocene rift and its subsequence offsets: Geology, v. 6, p. 111–116.

Zoback, M. L., Anderson, R. E., and Thompson, G. A., 1981, Cainozoic evolution of the state of stress and style of tectonism of the Basin and Range Province of the western United States, *in* Vine, F. J., and Smith, A. G., organizers, Extensional tectonics associated with convergent plate boundaries: Royal Society of London Proceedings, p. 189–216.

Manuscript Accepted by the Society August 21, 1989

Geological Society of America
Memoir 176
1990

Chapter 8

Spatial and temporal relations of Cenozoic volcanism and extension in the North Pahroc and Seaman Ranges, eastern Nevada

Wanda J. Taylor*
Department of Geology and Geophysics, University of Utah, Salt Lake City, Utah 84112

ABSTRACT

Data from the North Pahroc and Seaman Ranges, Nevada, constrain the timing of extension and volcanism as well as faulting characteristics. These ranges record four separate episodes of normal faulting over a period of more than 31 m.y.: (1) prevolcanic normal faults older than 31 Ma; (2) small separation, synvolcanic faults that were active between 30 and 27 Ma; (3) faults that are bracketed between 18.8 Ma and the Quaternary but that, based on stratigraphic evidence, probably were active around 15 Ma; and (4) Pliocene-Quaternary faults that control modern basin-range topography. The hypothesized breakaway for the prevolcanic extensional system, the Seaman breakaway, appears to underlie the southern White River Valley. The Miocene faults in the North Pahroc Range may be upper-plate faults to the west-dipping Highland detachment, exposed east of the North Pahroc Range. These two major extensional systems were active in this area at different times, defining two overlapping regions of different ages of major crustal extension.

INTRODUCTION

Extension and volcanism in the Great Basin are linked on a province-wide scale, but no detailed genetic relation has been established. The temporal and spatial relations of normal faulting and volcanism may constrain (1) the role of the mantle in the initiation of extension and (2) the genetic link between extension and volcanism. Considerable disagreement exists regarding whether the style of extension changed through time in the northern Basin and Range and whether temporal and compositional relations of volcanism can be linked to structural style changes. It has been suggested that Quaternary range-bounding faults are generally high-angle and represent a different style of extension from mid-Tertiary metamorphic core complexes (e.g., Coney, 1980; Coney and Harms, 1984). Such an interpretation implies a fundamental change in tectonic style through time.

In this study the characteristics of normal faulting were determined, and the relation between extension and volcanism was examined. Fault geometries as related to the manner in which

extension is accommodated, the age of extensional phases, changes in structural style through time, and the continuity of extension were all considered.

The dominantly volcanic Tertiary section in the North Pahroc and Seaman Ranges (Fig. 1) is one of the longest and most complete in the Basin and Range. Therefore, it provides a good means by which to examine Tertiary structures and their mutual age relations. The length and completeness of the Tertiary record is due to the overlapping in this area of units exposed predominantly to the east, west, or south.

UPPER PALEOZOIC SEDIMENTARY ROCKS

Devonian through Permian rocks exposed in the North Pahroc and eastern Seaman Ranges include the Devonian Guilmette Formation (Nolan, 1935), Devonian West Range Limestone (Westgate and Knopf, 1932), Mississippian Joana Limestone (Spencer, 1917), Mississippian Scotty Wash Quartzite (Westgate and Knopf, 1932), Pennsylvanian Ely Limestone (Lawson, 1906), and the Permian Arcturus Formation. Each of these formations is unconformably overlain by Tertiary rocks in the North Pahroc Range.

*Present address: Department of Geology, University of Minnesota–Duluth, Duluth, Minnesota 55812.

Taylor, W. J., 1990, Spatial and temporal relations of Cenozoic volcanism and extension in the North Pahroc and Seaman Ranges, eastern Nevada, *in* Wernicke, B. P., ed., Basin and Range extensional tectonics near the latitude of Las Vegas, Nevada: Boulder, Colorado, Geological Society of America Memoir 176.

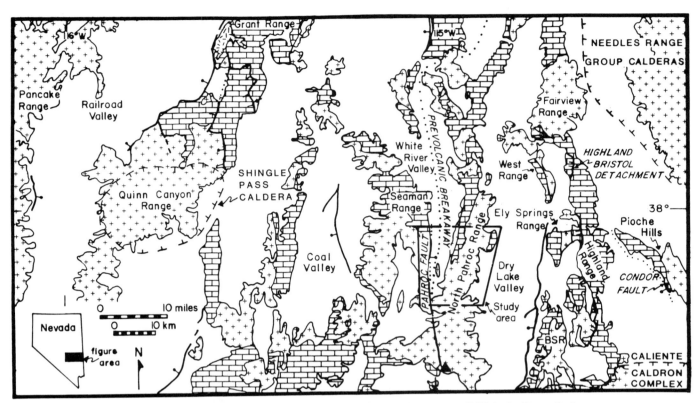

Figure 1. Map showing place names and locations of selected structures. BSR is the Burnt Springs Range. Triangle in southern North Pahroc Range is located at Pahroc Spring. "Prevolcanic breakaway" is the hypothesized Seaman breakaway. Block pattern represents Paleozoic rocks, plus pattern represents Tertiary rocks, and lack of pattern represents Quaternary deposits.

The interval between the Guilmette Formation and the Joana Limestone was mapped as the West Range Limestone, but Tschanz and Pampeyan (1970) called this interval the Pilot Shale (Spencer, 1917). I have chosen to use the newer name West Range Limestone (Westgate and Knopf, 1932) because the rock more closely resembles the rock at the type section of the West Range Limestone than that at the type section of the Pilot Shale, except perhaps for the top 10 m in the eastern Seaman Range.

Only float from the upper part of the Mississippian Chainman Shale (Spencer, 1917) is present in the area. However, cross-section restorations require the presence of the entire Chainman Shale between the Joana Limestone and Scotty Wash Quartzite. The Chainman Shale may be poorly exposed because it lies at the base of a paleotopographic low. Irregular, channeled topography is suggested by the map pattern of the sub-Tertiary unconformity, particularly in the northeasternmost hills in the study area (Plate 1). This paleovalley is suggested by the steeply dipping buttress unconformity of Tertiary rocks against Joana Limestone on the east and a more gently dipping and nonplanar unconformity of Tertiary rocks on Scotty Wash Quartzite on the west. The deepest part of the large paleovalley is located at the expected position of the Chainman Shale. The paleovalley is now filled with Tertiary tuffs, conglomerates, and lava flows.

TERTIARY ROCKS

Ash-flow tuffs dominate the Tertiary section, but sedimentary rocks and lava flows also are present (Fig. 2). The tuffs were erupted from several vent areas. The Oligocene Needles Range Group erupted from a set of nested and overlapping calderas (Best and Grant, 1987) east of the study area (Fig. 1). Some tuffs exposed in the area were erupted from the Oligocene Central Nevada Caldera Complex (U.S. Geological Survey, 1970), located 100 km northwest of the study area. An Oligocene caldera in the Quinn Canyon Range is the source of the Shingle Pass Tuff (Sargent and Houser, 1970). Miocene tuffs were erupted from the Caliente Caldron Complex southeast of the study area (Fig. 1; Ekren and others, 1977). The overlap of units from different age vents created a Tertiary section in the study area that represents a relatively complete record and long time period (31 to 18.8 Ma) for the region. Chemical changes up section in the North Pahroc and Seaman Ranges do not reflect changes within one magma chamber because the volcanic rocks were erupted from different vents that are widely separated from each other in space and time.

Many of the Tertiary units in the area correlate with regionally widespread formations. Formations not previously recognized in the study area include the Cottonwood Wash Tuff, Wah

Wah Springs Formation, Lund Formation, and the Monotony Tuff (Best and others, 1973; Ekren and others, 1971). The Cottonwood Wash Tuff, Wah Wah Springs Formation, and Lund Formation are formations within the Needles Range Group (Best and Grant, 1987).

Two angular unconformities are present within the Tertiary section, one above the tuff of Red Top and one below the Monotony Tuff (Fig. 2; Plate 1). A disconformity with some topographic relief along its surface lies below the Leach Canyon Tuff.

The main criteria used for tuff identification were modal percent phenocrysts, type of pumice, type of lithic fragments, and internal vertical stratigraphy (cf. Hildreth and Mahood, 1985). Color was not a distinctive characteristic of a particular unit; rather light colored tuffs are poorly welded, and the darkest colored tuffs are most welded. Some tuffs appear similar; in these cases, minor phenocryst phases, especially mafic phases, and vertical variations within the unit were most useful for identification. Vertical variations in amount and type of lithic clasts, phenocrysts, and degree of compaction and welding also were used to determine position within some units, which helped to estimate fault separations.

A complete definition of the Tertiary stratigraphy was required to map the structures in the North Pahroc and Seaman Ranges (see Fig. 2 for formation names). However, only the locally distributed Pahroc sequence is described below because the regionally distributed units have been described previously (e.g., Mackin, 1960; Cook, 1965; Williams, 1967; Ekren and others, 1971; Best and others, 1973).

Pahroc sequence

Cook (1965) defined the informal "Pahrock sequence" as a group of relatively thin ash-flow tuffs between the Needles Range Formation and the Leach Canyon Tuff, including the Petroglyph Cliff Ignimbrite and the Shingle Pass ignimbrite. The Petroglyph Cliff and Shingle Pass ignimbrites are herein called the Petroglyph Cliff tuff and the Shingle Pass Tuff. Because of a new definition of the Needles Range Group (Best and others, 1973) and new correlations made in this study, the Pahrock sequence as defined by Cook (1965) includes the Lund Formation (a Needles Range Group tuff) and the Monotony Tuff, both of which are regionally widespread formations. I restrict the informal term *Pahrock sequence* to exclude these regional units. I also change the spelling to *Pahroc* to conform to present U.S. Geological Survey base maps. The restricted Pahroc sequence (Table 1) contains units above the tuff of Hamilton Spring (new informal name) up to the base of the Leach Canyon Tuff. The Shingle Pass Tuff is included because of its compositional similarity to other Pahroc sequence units, but the compositionally different Petroglyph Cliff tuff is not.

Cook (1965) described only the Petroglyph Cliff tuff and the Shingle Pass Tuff when he defined the Pahrock sequence. Brief descriptions follow of all units of the redefined Pahroc sequence

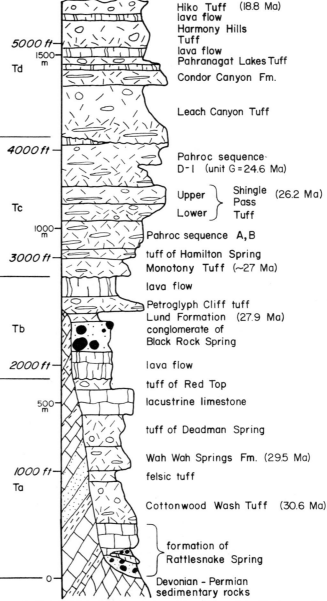

Figure 2. Simplified composite stratigraphic column of the Tertiary rocks exposed in the North Pahroc Range. Tuffs are designated by random dashed pattern. Greater dash density indicates a greater degree of welding. Pumice lapilli and fiamme are suggested by open subcircular shapes and ovals in tuffs. Unlabeled lava flows are shown by the same pattern as the labeled lava flows. Conventional patterns are used for sedimentary rocks. Clasts in conglomerate are dark subcircular shapes. Intra-Tertiary unconformities are represented by wavy lines. Unconformity-bounded packages of Tertiary rocks as designated on the left side of the column are used in other figures. Ages are from Taylor and others (1989), Best and Grant (1987), and Armstrong (1970).

in the study area. In many units the percentage of phenocrysts varies vertically because of differences in the degree of welding and laterally with differences in transport distance.

All of the restricted Pahroc sequence units except the Shingle Pass Tuff have a local distribution. Most of the Pahroc se-

TABLE 1. MODAL PERCENT PHENOCRYSTS

Formation	Quartz	Plagioclase	Alkali Feldspar	Biotite	Pyroxene	Opaques	Other	Percent Crystals
Pahroc A	25	28	44	trace	—	3	—	29
Pahroc D	21	38	28	11	trace hbd	2	trace	25
Pahroc E	21	26	43	4	trace	5	trace zircon	18
Pahroc F	34	34	24	3	—	4	—	21
Pahroc G	5–25	30–67	5–25	—	7	19	—	7
Pahroc H	6–14	21–43	36–45	2–9	Tr–3	5–15	—	7
Pahroc I	—	95	—	5	trace	trace	trace hbd	12
Tuff of Hamilton Spring	—	73	—	—	19	19	—	38

hbd = hornblende; Tr = trace

quence is known to be exposed only in the North Pahroc Range. A few of the tuffs are exposed as thin units in the ranges immediately surrounding the North Pahroc Range. The vents for the Pahroc sequence units have not been identified, except for that of the Shingle Pass Tuff in the Quinn Canyon Range (Fig. 1; Sargent and Houser, 1970; J. M. Bartley, personal communication). Until vent areas and regional distributions are better known, it seems unnecessary to give formal names to the Pahroc sequence tuffs. The modal phenocryst percentages presented in Table 1 are based on point count data done to a more than 90 percent confidence interval.

Pahroc A. A lightly to highly welded ash-flow tuff with numerous gray fiamme, sparse gray volcanic clasts, and 30 percent phenocrysts. The phenocrysts in this unit are 25 percent quartz (some smoky), 44 percent sanidine, 28 percent plagioclase, trace to 5 percent biotite (<1.5 mm maximum diameter), 3 percent opaques, and trace hornblende near the base of the unit. Welding and compaction decrease upward in the unit, and more of the quartz is smoky upward. This tuff pinches out to the north and west within the study area.

Pahroc B. A columnar-jointed, moderately welded ash-flow tuff with gray pumice and fiamme. The tuff contains a moderate amount of phenocrysts, which consist of 30 percent gray and colorless quartz, 15 to 25 percent plagioclase, 30 to 40 percent colorless to gray sanidine, 10 to 15 percent biotite, and 1 to 5 percent hornblende. All phenocrysts are about 2 to 3 mm across except for the biotite, which is smaller. Two zones in the upper part of the tuff are richer in biotite than the rest. This tuff pinches out toward the north within the study area.

Shingle Pass Tuff. The Shingle Pass Tuff was named by Cook (1965) for exposures north of the study area in the Egan Range (Fig. 1). In contrast with some other workers (e.g., Ekren and others, 1977), I have mapped only tuffs that contain trace or no quartz as part of the Shingle Pass Tuff because the tuffs at the Shingle Pass type section contain only trace or no quartz. This is consistent with the lack of quartz in the vent area (J. M. Bartley, personal communication, 1987). In addition, inclusion of quartz-

rich units within the formation would increase the formation age range, the number of possible stratigraphic positions for the unit, and the chances of confusing units from different vents.

The Shingle Pass Tuff varies in thickness in the study area but generally is thin. Two cooling units are present and are recognizable from the mapped area south to the end of the North Pahroc Range. They correlate with the cooling units exposed near the vent in the Quinn Canyon Range.

The lower cooling unit is a moderately to lightly welded ash-flow tuff with a black vitrophyre; pink, purple, and gray pumice; and about 15 percent phenocrysts. The modal percent of phenocrysts is 0 to trace quartz, 70 to 75 percent plagioclase, 25 to 30 percent sanidine, and 3 percent biotite. Pumice clasts are less than 1 cm across, and the fiamme are up to several centimeters long in the upper, moderately welded part of the tuff. The tuff becomes less welded downward and near the base turns pinkish gray.

The upper cooling unit is a crumbly tan- to brown-weathering ash flow tuff with a black basal vitrophyre, volcanic clasts, and 15 percent phenocrysts. The phenocryst population is similar to the lower cooling unit except that the upper cooling unit contains fayalite and larger sanidine crystals. Welding and compaction decrease upward in this cooling unit. Just above the vitrophyre the tuff contains gray fiamme, and in the higher, less welded part it contains gray pumice lapilli. A sample of this fayalite-bearing cooling unit from the Quinn Canyon Range (Fig. 1) yielded identical $^{40}Ar/^{39}Ar$ dates of 26.2 ± 0.5 Ma on biotite and sanidine (Taylor and others, 1989).

Locally, the upper Shingle Pass is overlain by mafic lava flows. They are brown, purple, and black glassy flows with vesicular bases, plagioclase phenocrysts, and local autobrecciation.

Pahroc D. This Pahroc sequence unit generally forms a small cliff overlain by a slope. It is a lightly welded ash flow tuff with basal vitrophyre, 25 percent phenocrysts, and many pink and gray pumice clasts. The center of the cooling unit is most welded. The hornblende and large pale purple quartz phenocrysts are particularly diagnostic. The modal percent phenocrysts is trace pyroxene, trace to 5 percent hornblende, 11 percent biotite, 2 percent opaques, 38 percent plagioclase, 28 percent alkali feldspar, and 21 percent large pale purple quartz.

This tuff is overlain by a distinctive brick-red tuff that is only a few meters thick and too thin to map separately at a scale of 1:24,000. The brick-red tuff, which locally has a black basal vitrophyre, is moderately welded and contains orange-pink and black volcanic fragments and phenocrysts that are approximately 15 percent plagioclase, 75 percent sanidine, 5 percent horn-blende, and 5 percent biotite.

Pahroc E. This ash-flow tuff contains about 20 percent phenocrysts and white pumice. The crystals consist of 26 percent plagioclase, 21 percent smoky quartz, 4 percent biotite, 5 percent opaques, trace pyroxene, trace sphene, and 43 percent sanidine. This tuff is exposed over a limited area because of a combination of faulting and erosion. The only known exposures are near the range crest in the central North Pahroc Range.

Pahroc F. This unit is a columnar-jointed, brownish-weathering ash-flow tuff that contains gray pumice; red, cream, and brown volcanic clasts; and about 21 percent crystals. The phenocrysts are 34 percent plagioclase, 3 percent biotite, 4 per-cent opaques, 24 percent alkali feldspar, and 34 percent quartz. Sphene can be found in hand sample near the base of the unit. The lightly welded base of the unit is overlain by a vitrophyre, which in turn, is overlain by densely welded tuff that decreases in degree of welding upward.

Pahroc G. Based on phenocryst and pumice content as well as position in the section, this tuff is correlated with a tuff at Pahroc Spring (Fig. 1) dated at 24.6 Ma by Armstrong (1970; new constants). The Pahroc sequence underlies the Leach Can-yon Tuff, which has yielded K/Ar dates between 27 and 23 Ma (Armstrong, 1970) but is generally considered to be between 24 and 22 Ma (Ekren and others, 1977). In conjunction with dates of about 27 Ma on the Monotony Tuff and the tuff of Hamilton Spring (Taylor and others, 1989), this date suggests the restricted Pahroc sequence is about 27 to 24 Ma.

The tuff is moderately to lightly welded and contains gray to white pumice and 10 to 20 percent phenocrysts. Modal percent phenocrysts are 7 percent pyroxene, 30 to 67 percent plagioclase, 5 to 25 percent quartz, 5 to 25 percent alkali feldspar, and 19 percent opaques. Locally a lithic sandstone overlies the tuff. Lo-cally, vesicular black to dark gray olivine and plagioclase mafic lava flows underlie this tuff.

Pahroc H. This ash flow tuff is lightly to densely welded and contains tan and gray pumice (commonly flattened), volcanic clasts, and 10 percent crystals. The phenocrysts are 21 to 43 percent plagioclase, 36 to 45 percent sanidine, 6 to 14 percent quartz, 2 to 9 percent biotite, 5 to 15 percent opaques, and trace to 3 percent pyroxene. The clasts are black, salt-and-pepper, red-brown, purple, and gray volcanic fragments that include pieces of vitrophyre, older Pahroc sequence units, Petroglyph Cliff tuff, and plagioclase-bearing lava. The phenocrysts are generally less than 4 mm.

Pahroc I. This unit is a 2- to 3-m-thick, brick-red, frothy- to sandy-textured glassy tuff with a black basal vitrophyre, <10 percent crystals, and volcanic lithic fragments. The crystals are plagioclase with trace hornblende, biotite, and pyroxene. Most of the unit is black or black-brown vitrophyre.

This tuff is the uppermost unit in the Pahroc sequence. Tuffs of similar lithology appear elsewhere in the section but are too thin to map as separate units at a scale of 1:24,000.

STRUCTURES

The dominant structures of the North Pahroc and Seaman ranges are normal faults that formed during four separate periods of extension (Taylor and others, 1987, 1989): (1) prior to volcanism, pre–30.6 Ma; (2) synvolcanic, 30 to 27 Ma; (3) immediately postvolcanic, post–Hiko Tuff (post–18.8 Ma), but pre-Quaternary; and (4) Pliocene to Quaternary. Crosscutting relations were observed between some structures of the post–Hiko Tuff but pre-Quaternary period, but few structures of the different extensional periods crosscut each other. However, the four periods of extension can be distinguished because struc-tures of different ages cut through and are lapped by different stratigraphic units. Based on this information, it appears that ex-tension occurred in discrete periods of a few to several million years duration. The extensional periods have no consistent timing relation to volcanic activity (Fig. 3). The structures are described in reverse chronological order because removal of the effects of younger structures is critical to understanding the older structures.

In order to obtain sufficient detail to characterize the struc-tures, the area of the central North Pahroc Range and the south-eastern Seaman Range was mapped at a scale of 1:24,000 (Taylor and DiGuiseppi, in preparation). The essential informa-tion from that mapping is presented at a smaller scale on Plate 1.

Pliocene to Quaternary extension

Pliocene to Quaternary extension in the area is represented by two high-angle faults: the Pahroc fault (named by Tschanz and Pampeyan, 1970) and the Dry Lake Valley fault. These two faults are subparallel and lie 20 to 30 km apart (Fig. 1).

The Pahroc fault bounds the eastern side of the Seaman Range and continues south into the North Pahroc Range (Plate 1). The fault trends north-northwest and dips 60 to 70°E. Al-though no Quaternary scarp occurs along the Pahroc fault, it probably was active in the Pliocene(?) to Quaternary because it cuts strata believed to be of early Late Pliocene to Holocene age and is lapped by younger Holocene deposits (DiGuiseppi, 1988). The Pahroc fault has about 250 m of dip separation and 60 m of heave near White River Narrows. All motion along the fault probably occurred during the Pliocene(?) to Quaternary period, because south of the area covered by Plate 1, both the Miocene and Quaternary strata are offset the same amount. A maximum of –5 to –10 milligal Bouguer gravity anomaly is associated with

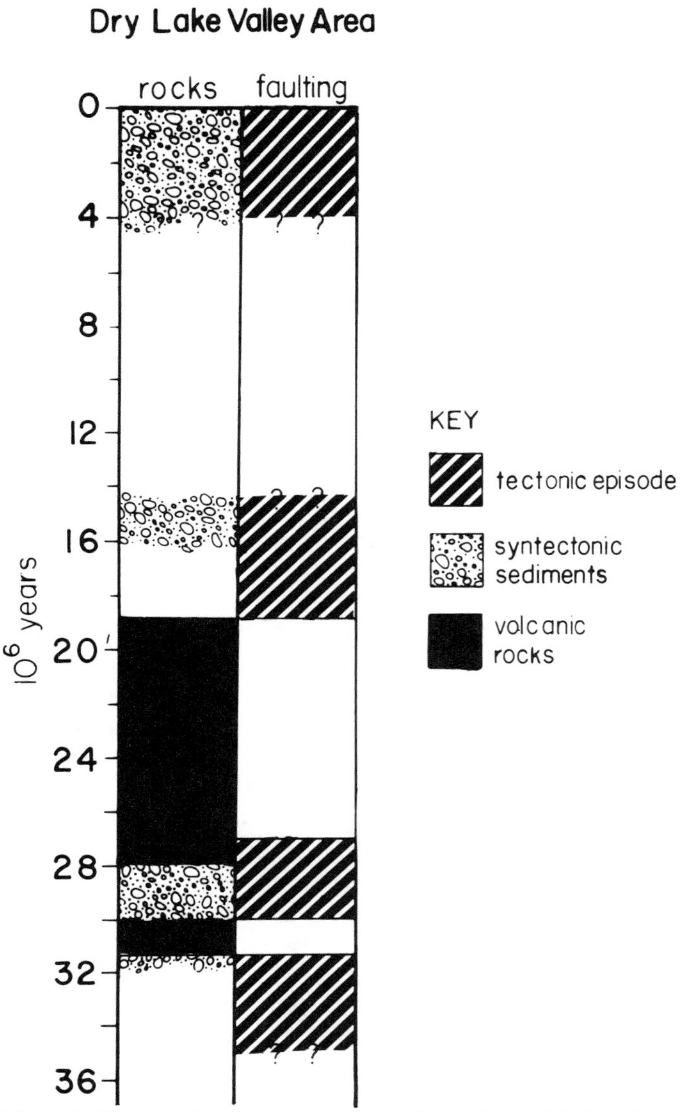

Dry Lake Valley Area

Figure 3. Columns showing periods of rock deposition and fault activity in the central North Pahroc and southeastern Seaman Ranges. Note that normal faulting occurred before, during, and after volcanism. Age data bracketing periods of extension are from Taylor and others (1989).

the basin-fill deposits east of the fault (Healey and others, 1981). Applying the gravity formula for a buried cylinder and using sediment densities ranging between 2,200 and 2,800 kg m^{-3} yields a maximum basin-fill thickness between 86 m and 216 m increasing toward the north.

A north-northeast trending, west-dipping fault in eastern Dry Lake Valley is marked by a Quaternary fault scarp about 40 km long (Fig. 1; Tschanz and Pampeyan, 1970). Small antithetic faults are represented by small, laterally discontinuous, east-facing Quaternary scarps located just west of the Dry Lake Valley fault. This fault may have been active in the Pliocene because a great thickness of basin-fill deposits is offset. The Dry

Lake Valley basin-fill deposits are associated with a −30 to −35 milligal Bouguer gravity anomaly (Healey and others, 1981). The gravity formula for a buried cylinder with the rock densities ranging between 2,200 and 2,800 kg m^{-3} yields a maximum basin-fill thickness between 600 m and 760 m. This thickness may include the middle Miocene conglomeratic McCullough Formation (Axen and others, 1988) because it is similar in lithology and density to the basin fill.

The North Pahroc Range sits in a graben formed by the Pahroc and Dry Lake Valley faults. The thickness of basin-fill deposits estimated from Bouguer gravity is much greater in Dry Lake Valley than in southern White River Valley. This suggests that the Dry Lake Valley fault may have greater offset than the Pahroc fault. Consequently, the graben is asymmetrical and probably tilted toward the Dry Lake Valley fault on the east.

Miocene extension

Postvolcanic Miocene faults cut units as young as the Hiko Tuff (18.8 Ma; D. R. Lux, personal communication, 1988) and are lapped by Pliocene(?) and Quaternary basin-fill sediments. This period of faulting includes four distinct structures that are (from youngest to oldest) (1) the west-dipping White River fault (Plate 1; Tschanz and Pampeyan, 1970) and related faults, (2) a west-dipping low-angle normal fault and related faults that internally deform its hanging wall, (3) east-dipping normal faults that probably are listric, and (4) a fold and a downward-steepening fault or group of faults that together accommodate the formation of an anticline but little extension. The chronologic order was determined from cross-cutting relations. Of these structures the oldest are located farthest east in the North Pahroc Range, and the youngest is located farthest west, except where the White River fault displaces the low-angle normal fault (Plate 1; Plate 2). These faults together with other high-angle normal faults that formed in the North Pahroc Range at this time accommodate about 4 km of extension measured east-west. Those faults with large separation or with a geometry that is generally unexpected in extensional terranes are discussed below.

White River fault. The White River fault, exposed on the west side of the North Pahroc Range, accommodated about 2 km of extension and dips between 18 and 37°WNW based on three-point solutions. The fault trace appears fairly straight on the map (Plate 1) because the local topographic relief along much of the fault exposure is less than 46 m. Near the central part of the map area (Plate 1), the White River fault splays to form a fault zone with several strands rather than a single fault surface. The White River fault places Miocene rocks on Oligocene rocks, which are the basal part of the Tertiary section, in the central part of the area, and Miocene rocks on Pennsylvanian or Permian rocks in the north and south. Apparent dip separation increases to the north and south because the White River fault cut out an older normal fault.

Some of the irregularity in the White River fault surface may result from its cutting across an older low-angle normal fault at a low angle. A complex zone of closely spaced normal faults (shown by pattern on Plate 1 and faults south of patterned area) occurs near and west of the locations where the White River fault cuts the older low-angle normal fault. The truncation is about 2 km south of cross section line B-B′ (Plate 1). The complex zone probably comprises both older faults in the upper plate of the low-angle normal fault and younger faults related to the White River fault. The White River fault is a new surface along much of its length, but it may have reactivated part of the older low-angle normal fault (see below) in this central region.

Low-angle normal fault. The low-angle normal fault truncated by the White River fault is exposed on the west side of the North Pahroc Range in the southern part of the area. The low-angle normal fault is discontinuously exposed for about 5.5 km just west of the White River fault in the vicinity of cross section line B-B′ (Plate 1). The low-angle fault places Hiko and Harmony Hills tuffs over the Candor Canyon Formation. Observed dips on the low-angle normal fault are about 8°NW.

The low-angle normal fault accommodated about 2.5 km of extension calculated in an east-west direction, based in part on correlation of offset segments of older, listric faults of this Miocene extension period. These fault segments in the upper plate of the low-angle normal fault are correlated with the older listric faults because (1) they juxtapose the correct units for the level at which the low-angle normal fault would have cut the listric faults when projected (Plate 2), (2) the upper plate faults and the listric faults have similar strikes and dips, and (3) the bedding to fault angle on the upper plate faults is the angle expected for the level at which the low-angle normal fault would have cut the listric faults. On section B-B′ the correlated upper-plate faults are more closely spaced than the listric faults. The listric faults are not parallel and converge south of the section line. If slip on the low-angle normal fault was west-northwest or northwest, directly down dip, then the closer spaced parts of the listric faults would have moved into the line of the cross-section.

Miocene strata exposed in the vicinity of the low-angle normal fault presently dip about 20 to 25°W. Since the low-angle normal fault presently dips about 8°W, rotating the strata back to horizontal suggests the possibility that the fault originally might have dipped 10 or 15°E, even though no structures are present along which such a rotation is indicated. If the low-angle normal fault originally dipped ⩽15°E and formed either before or after any or all normal faults exposed to the east, it should be exposed elsewhere in the North Pahroc Range. However, no fault of the correct orientation, correct juxtaposition of units, or bedding to fault angle is exposed at any of the possible locations. Therefore, the original dip direction of the low-angle normal fault was westerly, and it formed when the strata were horizontal or gently west dipping.

Two arguments suggest that the fault formed at a low dip. First, the bedding-fault angle is low, which suggests the strata and the fault had similar dips at the beginning of faulting. Restored cross sections suggest the involved strata dipped less than 30°W at the time this fault was active (Plate 2). Therefore, the fault would have dipped less than 30°W. Second, the low-angle normal fault probably cuts the older, steeply east-dipping listric faults at a high angle. Consequently, (1) the low-angle normal fault had an original gentle dip and the up-dip parts of the listric faults had a steep dip, or (2) the up-dip parts of the listric faults had an original gentle dip and the present low-angle normal fault formed with a steep dip. There is no evidence for the latter possibility. Maintaining the fault-fault cutoff angle and rotating the low-angle normal fault to a high-angle west dip would reduce the dip of the listric faults and could rotate them through the horizontal to an apparent reverse geometry. Westward rotation of 35° rotates the less steeply dipping parts of the faults to an apparent reverse geometry, and rotation of 70° or more would rotate the now steeply dipping parts of the listric faults through the horizontal (Plate 2). No structures are known that could explain such an orientation of the listric faults at any time. Therefore, the simplest interpretation that is consistent with all the data is that the low-angle normal fault originally formed at a low dip.

Due to the level of exposure, only one mapped normal fault can be observed to sole into the low-angle normal fault. This fault is too close to the low-angle normal fault to be shown on a map the scale of Plate 1. Two faults that may end at the low-angle normal fault appear to be displaced segments of the listric faults discussed below.

Strike-slip fault. A north-northwest–striking and steeply west-dipping fault is inferred on Plate 2 to sole into the low-angle normal fault. The steeply dipping fault cuts the stratigraphic pinch-out of the Pahranagat Lakes tuff. This fault may equally well sole into the White River Fault or cut both the low-angle normal fault and the White River fault. The stratigraphic pinch-out (Plate 1) forms a piercing point that is offset about 125 m in a left-slip sense and about 65 m in a normal sense. The precise amount of slip is uncertain because the pinch-out is not a straight line and the fault is not planar. Even though strike-slip movement cannot be documented on other north-northwest striking faults that cut the Hiko Tuff, the similar strike of all of these faults suggests that left-normal oblique slip may be possible across any of them. If the amount of left slip is large, the extension accommodated by these faults or any fault into which they sole was not perpendicular to strike of the fault (i.e., essentially east-west) but rather is oriented more northeast-southwest.

Listric postvolcanic faults. These faults have similar attitudes (approximately north-south strikes and steep east dips) and lie in the central North Pahroc Range (Plate 1). They are shown on the east side of cross section B-B′ (Plate 2) and the west end of cross section C-C′ (Fig. 4). They are inferred to be listric because they accommodate 15 to 25° of stratal rotation of the hanging-wall rocks with respect to the footwall rocks, and the footwall rocks were observed to be relatively planar and not folded by drag. Together they accommodate less than 400 m of extension.

Wheatgrass fault and fold. The Tertiary rocks in the North Pahroc and Seaman Ranges form a broad anticline, apparently related to a combination of folding and faulting. In the southeastern part of the map area, the anticlinal form is related to

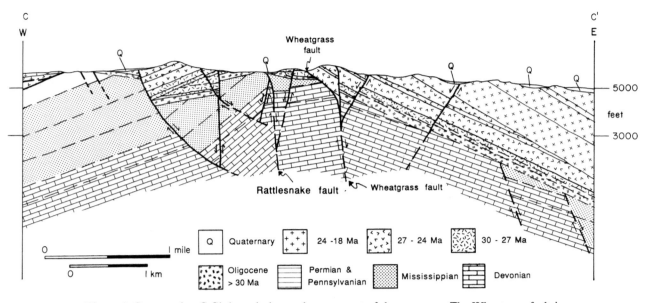

Figure 4. Cross section C-C′ through the southeastern part of the map area. The Wheatgrass fault is the downward-steepening fault near the center of the cross section. Cross section location is shown on Plate 1.

two east-dipping downward-steepening normal faults: the Wheatgrass fault and the Rattlesnake fault (Plate 1; Fig. 4). These faults can be seen to steepen downward, and three-point solutions on the Wheatgrass fault confirm this geometry. Space problems associated with the downward-steepening shape of the Wheatgrass fault are alleviated by a reverse fault located just above the sharpest part of the curve in the Wheatgrass fault (Fig. 4).

Northward the Wheatgrass and Rattlesnake faults become a northwest-trending, southeast-plunging anticline, here called the Wheatgrass fold (Plate 1). The fold becomes more open to the northwest. The Wheatgrass fold continues north-northwest from the Wheatgrass and Rattlesnake faults across the North Pahroc Range crest, west of which it is cut by a number of younger normal faults. Offsets on these faults cause the fold to appear rather discontinuous in the western North Pahroc Range. The White River fault displaces the Wheatgrass fold crest such that it is now concealed under southern White River Valley near the northern part of the mapped area.

The temporal relation between the Wheatgrass fault and fold and the listric normal faults is not well established. The listric faults appear to cut the western limb of the Wheatgrass anticline, but it is possible that the listric faults partially accommodated the folding and are of the same age.

The Wheatgrass fault and fold probably are the oldest of the post–Hiko Tuff pre-Quaternary structures because (1) the bedding to fault angles on other post–Hiko Tuff faults in the North Pahroc Range suggest the strata were tilted prior to faulting, (2) the tilting was in opposite directions on opposite sides of the range prior to the last stages of post–Hiko Tuff faulting, and (3) the Wheatgrass fold is cut by the White River fault and other normal faults (Plate 1).

Miocene unconformity

An unconformity exists beneath the Leach Canyon Formation throughout the area (Fig. 2). In the map area, all faults that cut units immediately below the Leach Canyon Tuff also cut the Leach Canyon and younger units. However, faults that are lapped by the Leach Canyon Tuff may be present in the Condor Canyon area (Axen and others, 1988). In the eastern North Pahroc Range and southeastern Seaman Range, there is a 5 to 10° difference in dip across the unconformity.

In the Seaman Range the unconformity apparently was caused by volcanic constructional and erosional topography, such as the edge of a lava flow exposed in the southeastern Seaman Range (Plate 1), and by the northwestward stratigraphic pinch-out of most of the underlying Pahroc sequence units. This sequence is very thin in the Seaman Range in the northern part of the study area (Plate 1). Some erosional topography clearly was present because the lava flow immediately below the Leach Canyon Tuff in the Seaman Range flowed down a 5° slope, as evidenced by the truncation of several tuffs by the lava flow. The erosional slope cuts across the strike of the tuffs at nearly 90°.

Synvolcanic extension and unconformity

In the North Pahroc Range, two late Oligocene unconformities resulted from episodes of movement on moderately to steeply dipping synvolcanic faults separated by 1 to 3 m.y. The oldest synvolcanic faults cut units as young as the tuff of Red Top (about 30 Ma; Taylor and others, 1989). The oldest strata that overlap the youngest synvolcanic faults are the Monotony Tuff and the tuff of Hamilton Spring, which yielded $^{40}Ar/^{39}Ar$ ages of about 27 Ma (Taylor and others, 1989). Therefore, these faults were active between about 30 and 27 Ma and probably record a single period of extension. An angular unconformity of less than 10° between 27- and 30-Ma units is regionally extensive (Bartley and others, 1988), but mapped synvolcanic normal faults extend the area considerably less than 1 km.

Only relatively short segments of the synvolcanic faults are exposed in the North Pahroc Range. Three of these faults are exposed between the Rattlesnake fault and the Wheatgrass fault near the southern end of the mapped area in the North Pahroc Range (Plate 1). Another synvolcanic fault is exposed both north and south of Deadman Spring in the northern end of the area mapped in the North Pahroc Range. Other synvolcanic faults were found in the east-central North Pahroc Range, where the conglomerate of Black Rock Spring (part of Tb on Plate 1) was deposited against some fault surfaces. In these places the contact was mapped as depositional because the conglomerate does not appear faulted.

Not all synvolcanic faults strike the same direction, but all generally trend north-northeast and dip both east and west. Estimated stratigraphic separations vary between a few meters and 300 m.

These faults are not clearly related to a basal detachment fault, primarily because no detachment of this age is known in the area. The Needles Range Group calderas were active between 30.6 Ma and 27.9 Ma (Best and Grant, 1987), similar to the time of activity on the synvolcanic faults. Removal of displacements on the Pliocene-Quaternary faults and the postvolcanic Miocene faults places the synvolcanic faults less than 25 km away from the southwest side of the Needles Range Group calderas. Therefore it is possible, but not required, that these faults are related to that volcanic activity or to caldera collapse.

Prevolcanic faults

No faults that cut Paleozoic rocks and are unequivocally lapped by Tertiary rocks are exposed in the North Pahroc and Seaman Ranges, but field evidence strongly indicates their presence. Some faults that cut only Paleozoic rocks and are cut by Tertiary normal faults were interpreted as prevolcanic faults. It is extremely difficult to explain the locations of present outcrops of Paleozoic rocks or to balance cross sections without postulating prevolcanic normal faults buried under Tertiary or Quaternary deposits within the North Pahroc Range and southern White River Valley. Extraordinarily large thicknesses (more than double the regional thickness in some cases) of the Paleozoic formations are required to balance sections without such faults. Prevolcanic normal faults that downdrop the Chainman Shale to the east on the east side of the North Pahroc Range (Plate 3) may explain the lack of exposed Chainman Shale.

In the North Pahroc Range Tertiary rocks as old as the Cottonwood Wash Tuff (30.6 Ma; Best and Grant, 1987) dip 20 to 30° E, and Paleozoic units dip 30° W, a 50 to 60° discordance across the sub-Tertiary unconformity (Plate 3). In the Seaman Range, Tertiary units dip 10 to 25° W, and gently folded Paleozoic units dip between 20° W and 10° E, a small angular discordance across the sub-Tertiary unconformity. Permian through Devonian rocks are preserved under the unconformity in the North Pahroc Range, but only Devonian and Mississippian rocks are preserved under the unconformity in the Seaman Range.

Armstrong (1968) interpreted the differences across the sub-Tertiary unconformity between the Seaman and North Pahroc Ranges to be due to a Mesozoic syncline related to the Sevier orogenic belt. However, the proximity of the westernmost exposed Permian and Pennsylvanian rocks in the North Pahroc Range to the easternmost Devonian rocks in the Seaman Range (particularly when all syn- and postvolcanic faulting is removed) leaves insufficient space for such a fold, and a concealed fault is required (Plate 3). The eastern limit of the Devonian rocks in the Seaman Range is marked by the Pahroc fault, and the western limit of Permian and Pennsylvanian rocks in the North Pahroc Range is marked on Plate 3. The data permit a steeply west-dipping reverse fault with steeply west-dipping footwall rocks and nearly horizontal hanging-wall rocks. No similar reverse faults are exposed elsewhere in the region. However, prevolcanic normal faults have been mapped east of the North Pahroc Range in the Ely Springs Range (Axen, 1986; Axen and others, 1988). Therefore, this fault has been interpreted as a normal fault (Taylor and Bartley, 1988).

Considering the above, restoring syn- and postvolcanic faults, and returning the oldest continuous Tertiary unit, the 29.5-Ma Wah Wah Springs Formation, to horizontal requires that a major down-on-the-east fault is buried under the basin between the two ranges (Plate 3; Taylor and Bartley, 1988, in preparation). This fault is responsible for the difference in dip of the Paleozoic rocks under the sub-Tertiary unconformity and for the preservation of younger units under the sub-Tertiary unconformity east of the fault. Oligocene (>30.6 Ma) conglomerate and lacustrine limestone of the formation of Rattlesnake Spring (Fig. 2) sit on the hanging wall of the buried prevolcanic fault and corroborate the presence of a paleotopographic low in this position. The conglomerate may be a syntectonic deposit or an immediately posttectonic deposit. The formation of Rattlesnake Spring is exposed just east of the White River fault in the central and southern part of Plate 1. The prevolcanic location of the exposed sediments is shown projected onto cross section A-A' (Plate 3).

This fault must become flatter at depth to allow the Mississippian through Permian units in the North Pahroc Range to rotate 45 to 50° relative to the Devonian through Mississippian units in the Seaman Range. The fault was drawn on Plate 3 with an inferred geometry of 90° to footwall bedding near the surface and 90° to hanging-wall bedding at depth. This results in a kink geometry for the fault. The kink was positioned 305 m above the Permian-Pennsylvanian contact, measured perpendicular to the contact. There is an uncertainty of 1.7 km in east-west position of this fault. A north-south–striking fault with the inferred geometry shown in Plate 3 would have 4.3 to 2.1 km of throw and 2.0 to 1.6 km of heave across it, depending on the fault location. The maximum values correspond to placing the fault as far west as possible, and minimum values correspond to placing the fault as far east as possible. On Plate 3 the fault is located in the center of all possible locations. If the fold in the footwall (Plate 1, Plate 3) is related to the fault, it accommodated 0.8 km of additional throw.

The angle across the sub-Tertiary unconformity is about 50 to 60° in the eastern North Pahroc Range where Devonian and Mississippian units underlie the unconformity. Another fault shown at the east end of section A-A' is inferred to be prevolcanic and slightly listric because it rotates the Paleozoic section in its hanging wall about 10° westward relative to its footwall. This fault is the cause of the increase in angle across the sub-Tertiary unconformity between the western and eastern sides of North Pahroc Range.

DISCUSSION

Relation of post–Hiko Tuff pre-Quaternary faults to the Highland detachment

Some of the post–18.8 Ma, pre-Quaternary normal faults in the North Pahroc Range may be interpreted to be related to the Highland detachment (Fig. 1). The Highland detachment, exposed in the Highland and Bristol ranges (Fig. 1), is an originally west-dipping low-angle normal fault with more than 6 km of hanging-wall west-southwest displacement along it (Axen and others, 1988; Axen, personal communication, 1988). It cuts and tilts syntectonic sedimentary deposits and an intercalated tuff (Axen and others, 1988) dated at 15.3 ± 0.2 Ma (Taylor and others, 1989). The ages of the Highland detachment and Miocene faults in the North Pahroc Range are compatible. Similar slip-directions for the Highland detachment and the faults in the North Pahroc Range also support this relation; left-normal oblique slip on the post–Hiko Tuff strike-slip fault (discussed above) suggests southward and westward components to the extension direction associated with the Miocene faults in the North Pahroc Range. Because of its westward dip the Highland detachment projects under the North Pahroc Range. Consequently, the North Pahroc Range is in the upper plate of the Highland detachment. Thus, Miocene faults in the North Pahroc Range may be upper-plate faults to the Highland detachment.

The Wheatgrass fault and fold are the oldest structures in the post–18.8 Ma period of extension. This relation, combined with the fact that this easternmost major structure is an anticline, suggests that a change in geometry of the basal Highland detachment may occur under the North Pahroc Range. One possibility is that the Wheatgrass fault and fold could have formed above a downward step or ramp in the Highland detachment—an extensional ramp anticline. After the formation of this anticline, it appears that the major internal extension of the Highland allochthon stepped westward, and the low-angle normal fault and the

White River fault were active. The part of the Highland detachment east of the low-angle normal fault may have been abandoned, and the low-angle normal fault and later the White River fault may have acted as secondary breakaways for the extensional system. This scenario of a secondary breakaway and abandonment of the up-dip part of the basal detachment is similar to that suggested by Spencer (1984), except that in order to accommodate a fold in the hanging-wall rocks of the North Pahroc Range, it is suggested that the step in the detachment surface is primary. Spencer (1984) explained warping of the basal detachment by secondary flexure of the detachment surface. Similar scenarios were suggested by Buck (1988) and Wernicke and Axen (1988). Secondary flexure cannot be ruled out here, but the interpretation with a primary step is preferred because it explains the downward-steepening faults and the fold, which are slightly different from structures predicted by secondary flexure.

Miocene faulting at the latitude of the study area has been documented from the Highland Range to Railroad Valley (Fig. 1; Bartley and others, 1988; Taylor and others, 1989). Although some faulting is similar in age across this area, a direct structural link between the Highland detachment and the Railroad Valley area is not apparent.

Regional implications of the major prevolcanic fault

Prevolcanic normal faults are exposed east of southern White River Valley, such as in the Ely Springs Range (Axen, 1986), but few, if any, prevolcanic normal faults are known west of White River Valley. The prevolcanic dip of the Paleozoic rocks in the North Pahroc Range is 40 to 60°W and in the Seaman Rnage is negligible. Therefore, it is likely that the fault concealed under southern White River Valley represents the western limit of prevolcanic extension. Taylor and Bartley (1988; in preparation) hypothesize that the buried prevolcanic fault may be the breakaway, called the Seaman breakaway, for a major originally east-dipping prevolcanic detachment system. The amounts of throw and heave on the fault are about the same as those determined for the breakaway of the Chemehuevi-Whipple detachment in the Little Piute Mountains (Howard and John, 1987), suggesting that its size is consistent with a breakaway interpretation.

In the Ely Springs Range, prevolcanic normal faults cut Cambrian to Silurian rocks (Axen, 1986) and are overlapped by the oldest tuff in the area, which yielded a $^{40}Ar/^{39}Ar$ plateau age of 31.3 Ma (Taylor and others, 1989). Using restored cross sections, Axen and others (1988) suggest that these east-dipping normal faults correlate with east-dipping normal faults exposed in the Highland Range that sole into the Stampede detachment. The Stampede detachment is a décollement within Middle Cambrian strata that is present throughout the area east of Dry Lake Valley (Fig. 1; Axen and others, 1988). The originally east-dipping Stampede detachment may be the basal detachment associated with the Seaman breakaway.

The age of the Seaman breakaway and Stampede detachment is constrained to between Permian and 31 Ma. Miller and others (1983) bracketed the age of the Snake Range system between about 35 and 27 Ma, and Lee and others (1987) bracketed it between 35 Ma and less than 24 Ma. Based on compatible timing and structural similarities, Bartley and others (1988) proposed that this prevolcanic extensional system is tectonically equivalent to and coeval with the Snake Range décollement and related structures. The Seaman breakaway may be structurally connected to the breakaway of the Snake Range system (Taylor and Bartley, in preparation).

Extension before 31 Ma associated with the Seaman-Stampede extensional system and the 35- to 27-Ma extension in the Snake Range can be documented only east of White River Valley. This location is distinct from that in which Miocene extension occurred, at least from the Highland Range to Railroad Valley (Fig. 1).

The Snake Range extensional system appears to be synvolcanic. Correlation of the Snake Range system with the Seaman breakaway and the Stampede detachment suggests a change along strike from pre- to synvolcanic extension.

Episodic extension

The timing of faulting, which could not have been determined without the long and complete Tertiary stratigraphic record, suggests that extension occurred episodically rather than continuously. The four periods of extension each lasted perhaps a few million years and were separated by periods of tectonic quiescence that also lasted a few million years (Fig. 3). The most poorly established time of quiescence is that between the Miocene and Pliocene to Quaternary faulting because of a lack of exposed datable units.

At least two major extensional systems were active in this area at different times, defining two overlapping regions of significant crustal extension: the prevolcanic (pre–31 Ma) Seaman-Stampede system, and the postvolcanic (post–18.8 Ma), pre-Quaternary Highland detachment system. Faults from each of the extensional systems also are exposed east of Dry Lake Valley (Fig. 1; Axen, 1986; Axen and others, 1988). Each of these two periods of extension is regional in extent. The regions affected do not coincide but overlap in the area between the western Highland Range and southern White River Valley (Fig. 1). This spatial distinction further corroborates the evidence that different detachment systems were active during different periods of extension. More generally, it appears that each episode of extension represents the initiation, action along, and later deactivation of a distinct extensional system.

Faults exposed in the mapped area (Plate 1) from all four periods of extension accommodate a minimum of 8 km of horizontal extension calculated in an east-west direction. Extension was calculated as the amount of east-west horizontal movement because that direction is essentially perpendicular to the strike of all the faults, and except for one case, the amount of strike-slip motion cannot be determined. The 6- to 10-km minimum offset

along the Highland detachment and the unknown displacement along the Stampede detachment increase the total amount of regional extension.

Structural style

Late Cenozoic faults have been presumed to represent a different fault style from the older detachment or core-complex style (e.g., Coney, 1980; Coney and Harms, 1984). However, these high-angle faults may correspond to upper-plate faults of detachments and therefore sole into detachments at depth (Wright and Troxel, 1973). Such buried detachments have been observed; the Sevier Desert detachment is an example (Allmendinger and others, 1983).

One difference between the Quaternary faults and faults that sole into older detachments is that the Quaternary faults appear to be more widely spaced. Upper-plate faults above the very shallow Miocene low-angle normal faults are spaced less than 0.5 km apart, and the upper-plate faults above the somewhat deeper Highland detachment are spaced about 0.5 to 1.0 km apart. This greater spacing may indicate a greater depth to the detachment. Without more information, it cannot be demonstrated that the Pliocene-Quaternary faults sole into a basal detachment, but the possibility should be considered.

It has been suggested that the older faults were associated with the mid-Tertiary "ignimbrite flare-up," whereas the younger basin-and-range faults postdate it (e.g., Coney, 1980). However, relations in the North Pahroc and Seaman Ranges show that the older faults need not correlate in time or space with volcanic activity (Fig. 3).

The prevolcanic faults are inferred to be approximately north-south striking and east dipping. Some exposed high-angle normal faults are inferred to be prevolcanic. The synvolcanic faults vary widely in strike and dip but generally trend north-northeast. The post–Hiko Tuff, but pre-Quaternary structures are (1) downward steepening faults with an associated fold, (2) east-dipping normal faults inferred to be listric, (3) west-dipping, north-northeast striking low-angle normal faults, and (4) north-northeast– to north-northwest–striking high-angle faults with normal or normal-oblique slip. The Pliocene(?) to Quaternary faults are high-angle normal faults, but one dips east and one dips west. No consistent evolution of structural style through time is recognized in this array of structures. Each period of extension, related to a detachment fault or not, includes high-angle normal faults. At least two groups of faults—prevolcanic and Miocene faults—may be associated with detachment faulting even though the structural styles are different.

The post–Hiko Tuff, pre-Quaternary structures represent the most structurally complicated period of extension. The complication may be related to the position of these structures within the extending region rather than to their time of formation. The post-Hiko pre-Quaternary structures occupy an area that could be particularly complicated because it may lie above an irregularity in an underlying structure, where the underlying structure cut deeper over a short distance, or because it is near the edge of a region of older extension.

Correlation between extension and volcanism

The tectonic association of lithospheric extension with volcanism is clearly established by decades of geological studies, but the nature of the genetic relation between the two processes remains uncertain. Christiansen and Lipman (1972) suggested that predominantly calc-alkalic andesitic rocks were succeeded by fundamentally basaltic (or bimodal rhyolite-basalt) volcanism that accompanied regional normal and strike-slip faulting.

In the Seaman and North Pahroc Ranges, extension and volcanism in a region are synchronous at times, but at other times are mutually exclusive (Fig. 3). From this discordance it can be concluded that crustal magmatism neither controlled, nor was controlled by, the creation or evolution of extensional systems. No genetic model that links crustal magmatism directly to extension predicts a time-space pattern in which there is no consistent relation between volcanism and extension. This lack of a consistent relation leads to doubt that extensional and magmatic processes are connected by any general process acting within the crust (Bartley and others, 1988). Rather, the breakdown of time-space correlation of extension to magmatism in the Great Basin at time scales of less than ten million years and spatial scales of less than hundreds of square kilometers implies that the genetic link between the two must be at a scale larger than the crust (Bartley and others, 1988). Therefore, extension and volcanism are distinct and independent crustal processes, and any time-space relation is possible locally. However, both processes may be manifestations of the same large-scale, deep-seated processes in the mantle.

CONCLUSIONS

The data and interpretations from the North Pahroc and Seaman ranges lead to several conclusions. (1) The extension occurred in discrete episodes and not continuously. (2) The oldest extension inferred in the area is older than 31 Ma and prevolcanic. It is represented by the Seaman breakaway and by the Stampede detachment exposed east of the study area. The timing and kinematics of this extension, based on extrapolation from nearby areas, permissive evidence in the mapped area, and geometric constraints, resemble those of the Snake Range extensional system located to the north. (3) Synvolcanic faulting between 30 and 27 Ma in the area resulted in a late Oligocene unconformity but minor extension. (4) Some, and perhaps most, of the postvolcanic extension in the North Pahroc Range may reflect upper-plate extension above the Highland detachment. (5) At least two major extensional systems were active in this area at different times. They define two overlapping regions of major crustal extension: the east-dipping prevolcanic Seaman-Stampede system, and the west-dipping postvolcanic (post–18.8 Ma) and pre-Quaternary Highland detachment system. Faulting similar in age to the Seaman-Stampede system is known only east and northeast of southern White River Valley. Miocene extension has been documented from the Highland Range east to Railroad Valley. (6) The temporally distinct extensional episodes documented in this area are pre-, syn-, and postvolcanic. There is thus no consistent relation between time of extension and volcanic eruptions. This argues against a simple, direct genetic relation between crustal magmatism and tectonic extension.

REFERENCES CITED

Allmendinger, R. W., and 7 others, 1983, Cenozoic and Mesozoic structure of the eastern Basin and Range province, Utah, from COCORP seismic reflection data: Geology, v. 11, p. 532–536.

Armstrong, R. L., 1968, Sevier orogenic belt in Nevada and Utah: Geological Society of America Bulletin, v. 79, p. 429–458.

—— , 1970, Geochronology of Tertiary igneous rocks, eastern Basin and Range province, western Utah, eastern Nevada, and vicinity, U.S.A.: Geochimica et Cosmochimica Acta, v. 34, p. 203–232.

Axen, G. J., 1986, Superposed normal faults in the Ely Springs Range, Nevada; Estimates of extension: Journal of Structural Geology, v. 8, p. 711–713.

Axen, G. J., Lewis, P. R., Burke, K. J., Sleeper, K., and Fletcher, J. M., 1988, Tertiary extension in the Pioche area, Lincoln County, Nevada; Geological Society of America Cordilleran Section Field Trip Guidebook: Reno, University of Nevada at Las Vegas Department of Geoscience Special Publication 2, p. 3–5.

Bartley, J. M., Axen, G. J., Taylor, W. J., and Fryxell, J. E., 1988, Cenozoic tectonics of a transect through eastern Nevada near 38°N latitude; Geological Society of America Cordilleran Section Field Trip Guidebook: Reno, University of Nevada at Las Vegas Department of Geoscience Special Publication 2, p. 1–20.

Best, M. G., and Grant, S. K., 1987, Stratigraphy of the volcanic Oligocene Needles Range Group in southwestern Utah and eastern Nevada: U.S. Geological Survey Professional Paper 1433-A, 28 p.

Best, M. G., Shuey, R. T., Caskey, C. F., and Grant, S. K., 1973, Stratigraphic relations of members of the Needles Range Formation at type localities in southwestern Utah: Geological Society of America Bulletin, v. 84, p. 3269–3279.

Buck, W. R., 1988, Flexural rotation of normal faults: Tectonics, v. 7, p. 959–973.

Christiansen, R. L., and Lipman, P. W., 1972, Cenozoic volcanism and plate tectonic evolution of the western United States; 2, Late Cenozoic: Philosophical Transactions of the Royal Society of London, series A, v. 272, p. 249–285.

Coney, P. J., 1980, Cordilleran metamorphic core comples; An overview, in Crittenden, M. L., Coney, P. J., and Davis, G. H., eds., Cordilleran metamorphic core complexes: Geological Society of America Memoir 153, p. 7–34.

Coney, P. J., and Harms, T. A., 1984, Cordilleran metamorphic core complexes; Cenozoic extensional relics of Mesozoic compression: Geology, v. 12, p. 550–554.

Cook, E. F., 1965, Stratigraphy of Tertiary volcanic rocks in eastern Nevada: Nevada Bureau of Mines Report 11, 61 p.

DiGuiseppi, W. H., 1988, Geomorphic and tectonic significance of Quaternary sediments in southern White River Valley, Nevada [M.S. thesis]: Salt Lake City, University of Utah, 62 p.

Ekren, E. B., Anderson, R. E., Rogers, C. C., and Noble, D. C., 1971, Geology of the northern Nellis Air Force Base Bombing and Gunnery Range, Nye County, Nevada: U.S. Geological Survey Professional Paper 651, 91 p.

Ekren, E. B., Orkild, P. D., Sargent, K. A., and Dixon, G. L., 1977, Geologic map of Tertiary rocks, Lincoln County, Nevada: U.S. Geological Survey Map I-1041, scale 1:250,000.

Healey, D. L., Snyder, D. B., Wahl, R. R., and Currey, F. E., 1981, Bouguer gravity map of Nevada; Caliente sheet: Nevada Bureau of Mines Map M70.

Hildreth, W., and Mahood, G., 1985, Correlation of ash-flow tuffs: Geological Society of America Bulletin, v. 96, p. 968–974.

Howard, K. A., and John, B. E., 1987, Crustal extension along a rooted system of imbricate low-angle faults; Colorado River extensional corridor, California and Arizona, *in* Coward, M. P., Dewey, J. F., and Hancock, P. L., eds., Continental extensional tectonics: Geological Society of London Special Publication 28, p. 299–312.

Lawson, A. C., 1906, The copper deposits of the Robinson Mining district, Nevada: University of California Department of Geology Bulletin 4, p. 287–357.

Lee, J., Miller, E. L., and Sutter, J. F., 1987, Ductile strain and metamorphism in an extensional tectonic setting; A case study from the northern Snake Range, Nevada, U.S.A., *in* Coward, M. P., Dewey, J. F., and Hancock, P. L., eds., Continental extensional tectonics: Geological Society of London Special Publication 28, p. 267–298.

Mackin, J. H., 1960, Structural significance of Tertiary volcanic rocks in southwestern Utah: American Journal of Science, v. 258, p. 81–131.

Miller, E. L., Gans, P. B., and Garing, J., 1983, The Snake Range décollement; An exhumed mid-Tertiary ductile-brittle transition: Tectonics, v. 2, p. 239–263.

Nolan, T. B., 1935, The Gold Hill mining district, Utah: U.S. Geological Survey Professional Paper 177, 172 p.

Sargent, K. A., and Houser, F. N., 1970, The Shingle Pass tuff of central Nevada: Geological Society of America Abstracts with Programs, v. 2, p. 140–141.

Spencer, A. C., 1917, The geology and ore deposits of Ely, Nevada: U.S. Geological Survey Professional Paper 96, 189 p.

Spencer, J. E., 1984, Role of tectonic denudation in warping and uplift of low-angle normal faults: Geology, v. 12, p. 95–98.

Taylor, W. J., and Bartley, J. M., 1988, Prevolcanic extensional breakaway zone, east-central Nevada: Geological Society of America Abstracts with Programs, v. 20, p. 236.

Taylor, W. J., Bartley, J. M., and Lux, D. R., 1987, ^{39}Ar/^{40}Ar age constraints on volcanism and extension in east-central Nevada: Geological Society of America Abstracts with Programs, v. 19, p. 457.

Taylor, W. J., Bartley, J. M., Lux, D. R., and Axen, G. J., 1989, Timing of Tertiary extension in the Railroad Valley–Pioche Transect, Nevada; Constraints from ^{40}Ar/^{39}Ar ages of volcanic rocks: Journal of Geophysical Research, v. 94, p. 7757–7774.

Tschanz, C. M., and Pampeyan, E. H., 1970, Geology and mineral deposits of Lincoln County, Nevada: Nevada Bureau of Mines and Geology Bulletin 73, 188 p.

U.S. Geological Survey, 1970, Geological Survey research 1970: U.S. Geological Survey Professional Paper 700-A, p. A39–A40.

Wernicke, B. P., and Axen, G. J., 1988, On the role of isostasy in the evolution of normal fault systems: Geology, v. 16, p. 848–851.

Westgate, L. G., and Knopf, A., 1932, Geology and ore deposits of the Pioche district, Nevada: U.S. Geological Survey Professional Paper 171, 79 p.

Williams, P. L., 1967, Stratigraphy and petrography of the Quichipa Group, southwestern Utah and southeastern Nevada [Ph.D. thesis]: Seattle, University of Washington, 141 p.

Wright, L. A., and Troxel, B. W., 1973, Shallow-fault interpretation of Basin and Range structure, southwestern Great Basin, *in* DeJong, K. A., and Scholten, R., eds., Gravity and tectonics: New York, John Wiley and Sons, p. 397–403.

MANUSCRIPT ACCEPTED BY THE SOCIETY AUGUST 21, 1989

Geological Society of America
Memoir 176
1990

Chapter 9

Tertiary normal faults superimposed on Mesozoic thrusts, Quinn Canyon and Grant Ranges, Nye County, Nevada

John M. Bartley and Gayle Gleason*
Department of Geology and Geophysics, University of Utah, Salt Lake City, Utah 84112

ABSTRACT

The Grant and Quinn Canyon ranges lie in a part of the eastern Great Basin commonly designated as the hinterland of the Mesozoic Sevier thrust belt. Published mapping of the northern and central Grant Range indicates that virtually all of the low-angle faults in that area are Cenozoic normal faults. However, our recent mapping in the southern Grant and northern Quinn Canyon ranges confirms the presence of Mesozoic thrust faults that have been overprinted by normal faulting.

Four major north-striking faults are exposed in an east-west transect across the study area. Two faults are east-vergent thrusts of probable Cretaceous age. We name the structurally higher thrust the Sawmill thrust and the lower the Rimrock thrust. Each thrust emplaced unmetamorphosed to very weakly metamorphosed Upper Cambrian to Lower Ordovician miogeoclinal strata upon Devonian rocks. The thrusts have the ramp-flat geometries and internally shortened hanging walls typical of foreland thrust belts. Together the thrusts accommodated at least 10 km of horizontal shortening. The age of thrusting is not yet constrained precisely but is most likely Cretaceous.

The actual thrust contacts are preserved only locally because two major west-dipping Cenozoic normal fault systems, the Oligocene Wadsworth Ranch fault system and the Miocene Little Meadow fault system, commonly excise the thrusts. A consequence of thrust excision is that local older-on-younger relations occur across the normal faults. Both of the normal fault systems are complex networks of intersecting planar segments. Geometric relations of the Wadsworth Ranch fault system indicate hanging-wall transport toward the southwest. By contrast, slip along the Little Meadow fault system appears to have been directed mainly west to west-northwest. This suggests a clockwise rotation of the extension direction from one phase to the next.

The thrusts in the Grant and Quinn Canyon ranges probably correlate along strike northward with the Mesozoic Eureka belt of folds and thrusts, which lies to the west of the Sevier hinterland. This belt of thrusts is probably similar in age to the frontal Sevier belt and, when effects of Tertiary extension are restored, is located less than 200 km west of the Sevier thrust front. Based on these relations and the fact that Cordilleran-type foreland thrust belts in Canada and the Andes are both about 200 km wide, we suggest that much of the Sevier "hinterland" is actually a part of the Sevier foreland thrust belt that has been intensely extended in Cenozoic time. The intense Cenozoic

*Present address: Department of Geological Sciences, Brown University, Providence, Rhode Island 02912.

Bartley, J. M., and Gleason, G., 1990, Tertiary normal faults superimposed on Mesozoic thrusts, Quinn Canyon and Grant Ranges, Nye County, Nevada, *in* Wernicke, B. P., ed., Basin and Range extensional tectonics near the latitude of Las Vegas, Nevada: Boulder, Colorado, Geological Society of America Memoir 176.

extensional overprint that obscures the thrust-belt structures is responsible for most of the distinctive features of the Sevier hinterland. Therefore, to refer to this region as the "Sevier hinterland" is inaccurate and misleading, and we favor abandonment of the term.

INTRODUCTION

The structural style and Mesozoic-Cenozoic tectonic evolution of east-central Nevada have long been controversial (Misch, 1960; Moores and others, 1968; Armstrong, 1972; Hose and Danes, 1973; Miller and others, 1983; and many others). Armstrong (1968) referred to this part of the Great Basin, located east of the Robert Mountains thrust and west of the Cretaceous Sevier thrust belt in Utah and southern Nevada, as the hinterland of the Sevier orogenic belt. Distinctive features of the Sevier hinterland include (1) low structural relief beneath the sub-Tertiary unconformity, (2) younger-on-older low-angle faults that attenuate pre-Tertiary strata, that is, the late Precambrian-Paleozoic miogeoclinal sequence, and (3) exposures of metamorphic and granitoid rocks in the footwalls of some of the low-angle faults, defining metamorphic core complexes (Misch, 1960; Armstrong, 1968, 1982).

Views of the tectonic significance of the Sevier hinterland vary considerably. Controversy particularly has centered on the age, style(s), and tectonic significance of the low-angle faults and of the ductile deformation and metamorphism in the metamorphic core complexes. Misch (1960) proposed that the younger-on-older low-angle faults represented a regional Mesozoic décollement related to thrusting in the Sevier belt. Armstrong and Hansen (1966) proposed a model, updated and elaborated by Armstrong (1982), in which the hinterland in the Mesozoic was characterized by a rigid, weakly deformed upper-crustal suprastructure that overlay a ductile deep-crustal infrastructure along a midcrustal zone of decoupling. However, Armstrong (1972), following Young (1960) and Moores and others (1968), noted that many of the exposed low-angle faults were of Tertiary age and related to extensional tectonics. Hose and Danes (1973) and Roberts and Crittenden (1973) interpreted the hinterland to be the denuded source of gravity-driven thrust sheets that were emplaced eastward to form the Sevier thrust belt. Such gravity-sliding models have been abandoned by most authors because of incompatible timing of deformation in the Sevier thrust belt and the hinterland (for example, Armstrong, 1968, 1972). Jordan and others (1983) likened the Mesozoic tectonics of the hinterland to the Puna plateau of the central Andes, an area of thickened crust and mild upper-crustal shortening, under which thrusts of the adjacent foreland thrust belt are rooted, perhaps into an Armstrong and Hansen–type ductile infrastructure. Regardless of the details of each model, the consistent view has been that a major change in Mesozoic structural style occurs passing westward from the thin-skinned Sevier foreland thrust belts to the hinterland.

The Grant Range (Fig. 1) was an early focal point in the controversy about low-angle faulting in east-central Nevada.

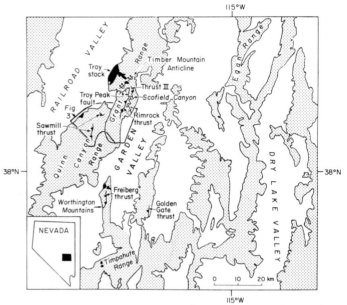

Figure 1. Location map of eastern Nevada near 38°N latitude. Black areas on main map are granitic stocks.

Low-angle, younger-on-older faults that cut Paleozoic strata in the Grant Range were interpreted by Moores and others (1968) to be late Cenozoic normal faults related to Basin and Range extension, whereas Cebull (1970) and Hyde and Huttrer (1970), following Misch (1960), interpreted these faults as thrusts related to Mesozoic crustal shortening. Fryxell (1984, 1988) remapped the Troy Canyon area of the central Grant Range and recognized structures related both to Mesozoic crustal shortening and to Cenozoic extension. Lund and Beard (1986) and Camilleri and others (1987) drew similar conclusions from remapping of the northern Grant Range. However, all of the major low-angle faults in these areas clearly are Cenozoic normal faults. Manifestations of Mesozoic crustal shortening are folds and cleavage formed during biotite-grade regional metamorphism, and very minor thrust faults.

This chapter reports the results of mapping structurally higher rocks exposed to the south in the southern Grant and northern Quinn Canyon ranges. Sainsbury and Kleinhampl (1969; also see Kleinhampl and Ziony, 1985) suggested the presence of Mesozoic thrust faults in the Quinn Canyon Range, but their mapping and structural data were not sufficiently detailed to resolve the complex overprinting of normal faults on the thrusts. In particular, we have found that excision of thrusts by normal faults has caused normal faults to be misinterpreted as thrusts. Our new mapping and structural analysis thus serve to delineate more clearly the complex structural geometries and to clarify the nature of the pre-Tertiary deformation in this area. Our results indicate that Mesozoic structures in the area are typical of foreland thrust belts.

STRATIGRAPHY

A detailed account of the stratigraphy of the area is beyond the scope of this chapter. Strata in the study area range in age from Cambrian to Tertiary (Fig. 2). The Paleozoic strata are typical of the miogeocline in this part of the western United States (Stewart and others, 1977) and include limestone, dolostone, quartz sandstone, and calcareous shale. Kellogg (1963) described a similar Paleozoic section that is exposed to the northeast of the study area in the Southern Egan Range (see Fig. 1 for location). Specific stratigraphic details of the Paleozoic section in the Grant and Quinn Canyon ranges were described by Cebull (1967, 1970), Murray (1985), and Gleason (1988). Nomenclature used here combines that used by Kellogg (1963) and by Fryxell (1988).

Differences between Upper Cambrian–Lower Ordovician stratigraphic sections in the southern Grant Range and the northern Quinn Canyon Range (Fig. 2) are germane to the study and therefore are discussed briefly here. The interval from the top of the Sidehill Spring Formation to the base of the Eureka Quartzite is about 315 m (24 percent) thicker in the Grant Range than in the Quinn Canyon Range. The Grant Range section contains a significant amount of dolostone in the upper Cambrian Little Meadow Formation, whereas the Little Meadow Formation is absent in the Quinn Canyon Range section, which indeed lacks any dolostone below the Eureka Quartzite. The Pogonip Group in the Grant Range is markedly more fossiliferous than in the Quinn Canyon section, which is dominated by micritic limestone that lacks recognizable macrofossils. All of these differences suggest that the Quinn Canyon section is a more distal shelf facies than the Grant Range section. Although this is the expected facies pattern, the change is abrupt. We interpret the abrupt change to reflect structural telescoping of the facies transition by movement of the Sawmill thrust fault.

Unconformably overlying the Paleozoic strata are Oligocene ash-flow tuffs, silicic lava flows, and subordinate mafic lava flows and sedimentary rocks. At or near the base of the Cenozoic section is the Windous Butte Formation, a rhyodacitic ash-flow tuff emplaced at about 32 Ma (Taylor and others, 1989, and references therein). Most of the overlying Tertiary section is composed of the Shingle Pass Tuff and related silicic volcanic and shallow intrusive rocks, formed in a major caldera system in the Quinn Canyon Range (Sargent and Houser, 1970; Ekren and others, 1977; Bartley, unpublished mapping) that was active at 26 to 27 Ma (Taylor and others, 1989).

Although strata as young as Devonian are exposed throughout the study area, the sub-Oligocene unconformity in the study area invariably is developed upon Ordovician rocks (Figs. 2 and 3). This relation is readily explained if the exposed Devonian rocks lie in the footwall of a pre-Oligocene thrust fault (specifically, the Sawmill thrust), whereas the Ordovician strata at the unconformity belong to the hanging wall. The hanging wall of the thrust was eroded down to Ordovician rocks by the time the Oligocene strata were deposited, but structurally underlying Devonian rocks were preserved from erosion.

THRUST FAULTS

Two Mesozoic thrust faults are exposed in the study area, as are minor imbrications related to each. Both thrusts strike north to northeast and verge toward the east. We name the structurally higher thrust the Sawmill thrust and the lower the Rimrock thrust. Figure 4 shows locations of thrust exposures and the distribution of the thrust plates thus defined.

Sawmill thrust

The Sawmill thrust is exposed in the northern Quinn Canyon Range in two windows, one at the head of Sawmill Canyon (whence the name) and the other on the east side of Hooper Canyon (Fig. 4). The Sawmill Canyon window was mapped by Murray (1985), who showed there the characteristic relation of Oligocene strata deposited upon Ordovician rocks above the Sawmill thrust, with strata as young as Devonian preserved beneath the thrust. However, thrust exposures at the Sawmill Canyon window are insufficient to constrain the thrust geometry tightly.

In this chapter we focus on relations around and to the west of the Hooper Canyon window (Fig. 5, in pocket). Along most of the perimeter of the window, the Sawmill thrust has been excised by Cenozoic normal faults and related strike-slip faults. However, along the southwest side of the window the actual thrust contact is preserved, based on recognition of typical thrust-fault geometries along it. At the west end of the window, the fault strikes northwest and dips southwest, subparallel to bedding in hanging-wall Cambrian rocks but sharply truncating southeast-dipping bedding in footwall Silurian-Devonian dolostones. The fault cuts up-section to the east on both sides of the contact, gently in the hanging wall but rapidly in the footwall. The Sawmill thrust therefore ramps upward toward the east or southeast in this area. That this ramp was tilted to the southeast in the Tertiary is confirmed by the consistent east and southeast dips of Tertiary strata in the vicinity (Figs. 3 and 5). At the east end of the preserved thrust trace (south-central side of the window), the Sawmill thrust and hanging-wall bedding together bend into parallel-with-footwall bedding. This bend defines a fault-bend anticline in the hanging wall, which we interpret to occur at the top of the ramp where the thrust enters a footwall flat in the lower Guilmette Formation (Figs. 5 and 6, in pocket).

The Sawmill thrust exposure in the Hooper Canyon window is interpreted to be a frontal ramp along an east-vergent thrust. Emplacement of Cambrian strata on Devonian at the top

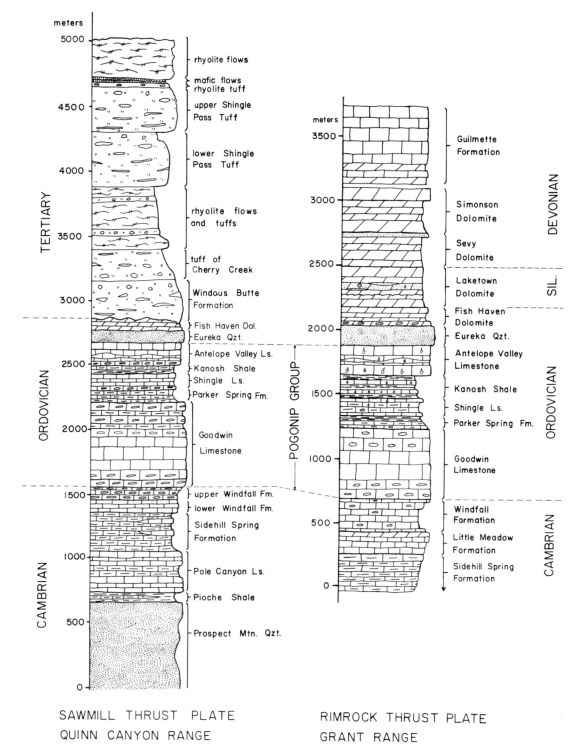

Figure 2. Stratigraphic columns for southern Grant Range (Rimrock thrust plate; modified from Cebull, 1967, and Gleason, 1988) and northern Quinn Canyon Range (Sawmill thrust plate). The Quinn Canyon Range stratigraphic section is composite: Paleozoic formations and thicknesses are pieced together from fault-bounded blocks in the area west and northwest of the Hooper Canyon window, and the Tertiary section is pieced together from sections exposed in various fault blocks in the Cherry Creek drainage (see Figs. 3 and 4 for locations). Lateral variations in the Tertiary section are extreme, mainly due to proximity of the Quinn Canyon Range caldera, and therefore thicknesses are only roughly representative. Note (1) differences in Upper Cambrian to Lower Ordovician sections, and (2) sub-Tertiary unconformity developed on Ordovician strata of the Sawmill thrust plate.

of the ramp requires a significant component of up-dip displacement, precluding a strict lateral-ramp geometry, but this alone does not exclude an oblique ramp. However, internal deformation of the upper plate records mild to intense layer-parallel shortening in an east-west direction. Thin-bedded Cambrian silty limestones (Sidehill Spring and Windfall formations) on the south side of the Hooper Canyon window contain abundant mesoscopic to small macroscopic kink and chevron folds, and rarely contain a tectonic cleavage. Poles to bedding in this area define a diffuse girdle with a best-fit axis plunging 20° toward S12E (found by the method described by Woodcock and Naylor, 1983), an orientation corroborated by orientations of minor-fold hinges (Fig. 7). To the west of Hooper Canyon, hanging-wall Cambrian strata are folded and imbricated by small thrusts, and silty and shaly units contain moderate to intense pressure-solution cleavage (S_1 in Fig. 7). The structure is noncylindrical, with thrust faults passing into folds along the strike. However, the faults, folds, and cleavage all consistently trend north-northeast, except at the northern foot of the range where folds and thrusts appear to

be dragged in a sinistral sense along the Cenozoic range-front fault (Fig. 5).

The folds and imbricate thrusts west of Hooper Canyon verge to the west (Figs. 5 and 6). This is interpreted to represent backthrusting above the frontal ramp exposed in the Hooper Canyon window. Backthrusts above ramps are common in foreland thrust belts. For example, more than half of the 47 cross sections of the Idaho-Wyoming thrust belt presented by Dixon (1982) show backthrusting or backfolding above ramps. It is noteworthy that, despite the eastward vergence of the main thrust, the west-vergent backthrust zone displays the most intense mesoscopic deformation observed in the Quinn Canyon Range. If the frontal ramp were not exposed in Hooper Canyon, one probably would draw the erroneous conclusion that the predominant vergence of Mesozoic structures in the area was westward. This fact highlights the dangers of inferring macroscopic shear sense in the region using only mesoscopic fabric elements.

In the eastern half of the Hooper Canyon window, Devonian dolostones of the footwall are folded into a macroscopic

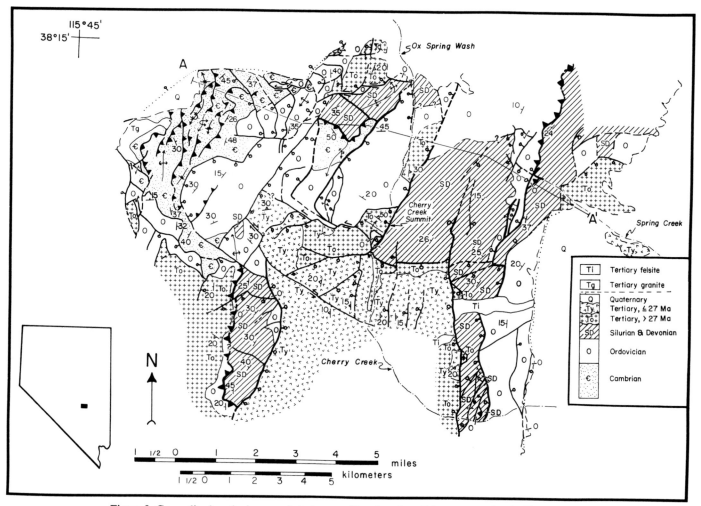

Figure 3. Generalized geologic map of study area. Note location of the cross section in Figure 6. The boundary between the Quinn Canyon Range to the southwest and the Grant Range to the northeast is drawn (rather arbitrarily) along Ox Spring Wash and Cherry Creek.

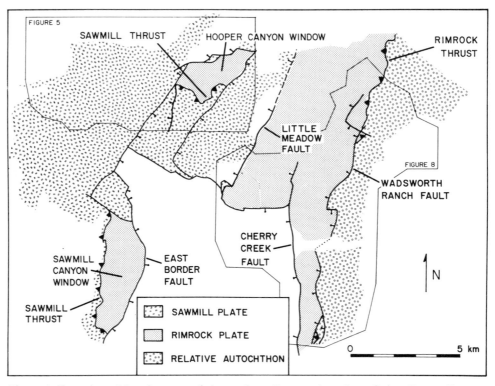

Figure 4. Tectonic and location map of the southern Grant and northern Quinn Canyon Ranges, showing distribution of Mesozoic thrust plates, windows through the Sawmill plate, and major Tertiary normal faults. Note locations of detailed maps of the Hooper Canyon (Fig. 5) and Spring Creek (Fig. 8) areas.

open anticline that trends northeast (Figs. 5 and 7). The anticline is separated from the footwall homocline in the western part of the window by a northwest-striking vertical fault (Fig. 5). Our preferred interpretation of this relation is that the vertical fault is a tear fault that separates folded from unfolded parts of the footwall of the Sawmill thrust. However, the axis of the anticline is discordant to most hanging-wall structures (Figs. 5 and 7). Therefore, if this interpretation is correct, displacements associated with the Sawmill thrust must have been complex.

The cross sections in Figure 6 illustrate the present-day structure and a restoration of Tertiary structures to Mesozoic thrust-belt geometry. The sections are based on surface data only, and therefore, many subsurface details are only plausible rather than definitive. The sections show 5 km of slip on the frontal Sawmill thrust and about 3 km of additional shortening within the hanging wall by backthrusting. These figures are minima based on the conservative assumption of no large bedding-parallel décollement along the Sawmill thrust as it ramped from Lower Cambrian Prospect Mountain Quartzite to Upper Devonian strata. A large décollement within this Cambrian to Devonian interval could increase substantially the estimated slip along the Sawmill thrust. However, no direct evidence exists for such a décollement, and the following observations considerably restrict the possibilities. The footwall ramp in Hooper Canyon cuts across bedding continuously from Silurian rocks to the base of Upper

Devonian strata and thus excludes detachment within that interval. Uppermost Cambrian rocks lie directly upon the Sawmill thrust in the Hooper Canyon window, yet Lower Cambrian rocks crop out in the hanging wall less than 5 km to the west. Therefore, the thrust also must ramp across the Cambrian section (which includes the only real shale in the range) without forming a significant bedding-parallel detachment. This leaves the Ordovician section as the only stratigraphic interval within which a décollement that would affect the slip estimate is geometrically possible. Such a décollement cannot be excluded. However, it would require fortuitous juxtaposition of a hanging-wall ramp through the Cambrian with a separate footwall ramp through Silurian-Devonian rocks. Without subsurface data, we choose the conservative interpretation of a single ramp that cuts upward directly from the Prospect Mountain Quartzite to the lower part of the Guilmette Formation.

Overprinting of the Sawmill thrust by Cenozoic normal faults

Immediately east of the fault-bend anticline on the south side of the Hooper Canyon window, a northeast-striking, southeast-dipping normal fault intersects the thrust. South of the fault intersection, the normal fault cuts only the Sawmill thrust plate and places Ordovician rocks upon Cambrian. North of the

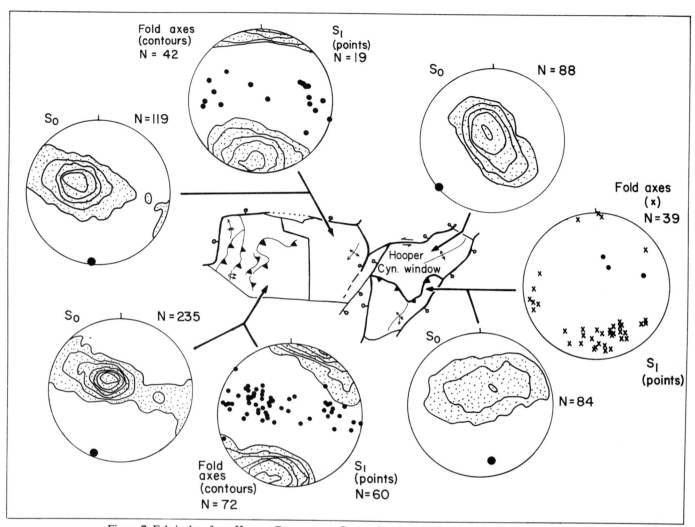

Figure 7. Fabric data from Hooper Canyon area. Contouring done by the Kamb method; contours are integral multiples of the expected concentration for randomly scattered data. Large solid dot on plots of poles to S_0 (bedding) is best-fit fold axis found by extracting eigenvectors of the orientation tensor (for example, Woodcock and Naylor, 1983). S_1 is pressure-solution cleavage in shale and silty limestone units.

intersection, the normal fault places Ordovician Goodwin Formation of the Sawmill thrust plate on Devonian Guilmette Formation of the underlying Rimrock plate. Because of this older-on-younger relation, this normal fault previously has been mapped as a thrust (Sainsbury and Kleinhampl, 1969; Kleinhampl and Ziony, 1985).

Pogonip Group rocks exposed on the north side of the window also belong to the Sawmill thrust plate. This interpretation is based on Pogonip Group stratigraphy and the fact that Oligocene rocks lie unconformably upon this Ordovician section (see above). From an upper-plate position, the Ordovician strata were emplaced beside Devonian rocks of the footwall of the Sawmill thrust along the west-trending Tertiary fault zone that now defines the northern margin of the window.

Discordances between some pre-Tertiary structures may reflect Tertiary vertical-axis rotations. The anticlinal axis in Devo-

nian strata in the Hooper Canyon window is refolded to a northwest trend in the northern part of the window, likely as a result of sinistral drag along the fault system that defines the window's northern boundary. Similarly, structures to the west in the backthrust zone above the Sawmill thrust show sinistral bending along the northern flank of the range. These observations raise the possibility that all Mesozoic structural elements have been reoriented to some degree by Tertiary rotations, so that present orientations cannot be assumed to be the orientations in which the structures formed.

Near the small granitic stock at the west edge of the study area (Figs. 3 and 5), mesoscopic folds in Cambrian strata become tighter and more sinuous, and bedding is transposed by a penetrative schistosity. These relations suggest that heat from the stock controlled the changes of deformation style. On the other hand, the stock itself is unfoliated and, at its east end, truncates the lowest exposed thrust of the backthrust zone. Field observations thus suggest that the stock may have been emplaced synkinematically with folding and thrusting. However, the stock recently yielded a preliminary U/Pb zircon age of 32 Ma (M. W. Martin and J. D. Walker, written communication, 1988), which makes its emplacement coeval with early stages of Cenozoic volcanism in the area and almost certainly much younger than the compressional structures. This apparent conflict may be resolved if the structural changes passing into the aureole of the stock are not related to formation of the folds but instead record modification of preexisting folds during diapiric emplacement of the stock. This interpretation is consistent with rare outcrops in which mesoscopic folds are transected by the schistosity.

Rimrock thrust

We name the Rimrock thrust for exposures in Rimrock Canyon, a few kilometers north of the study area on the east side of the Grant Range. The Rimrock thrust crops out for roughly 10 km along the strike; the southern part of this trace lies in the eastern part of our study area (Figs. 4 and 8; 8 is in pocket).

Relations of the Rimrock thrust differ substantially from earlier published descriptions of this fault. Cebull (1970) mapped it as part of his thrust V, but most of Cebull's thrust V corresponds to what we now call the Troy Peak fault, which clearly is a Tertiary normal fault (Fryxell, 1988). Unpublished mapping by S. U. Janecke (personal communication, 1986) shows that, at Scofield Canyon (see Fig. 1 for location), the Rimrock thrust is truncated by and carried in the hanging wall of the Troy Peak normal fault. The location of the remainder of the Rimrock thrust in the footwall of the Troy Peak fault is unknown.

Sainsbury and Kleinhampl (1969) and Kleinhampl and Ziony (1985) interpreted this thrust to continue southward through the study area beyond Cherry Canyon. This interpretation fails to explain a rapid southward change from older-on-younger to younger-on-older stratal juxtaposition across the fault (Figs. 3 and 8). New mapping (Fig. 8) shows that, from Spring Creek southward, the Rimrock thrust has been excised by the newly distinguished Wadsworth Ranch normal fault system. The only exposure of the thrust contact south of Spring Creek is within a horse in the Wadsworth Ranch fault zone, located where the Wadsworth Ranch fault zone crosses Cherry Creek (Fig. 8). The Wadsworth Ranch fault increases in displacement southward such that, near Cherry Creek, it places Devonian rocks from above the thrust upon Ordovician rocks from below the thrust.

Geometric data indicate that, like the Sawmill thrust, the Rimrock thrust verges to the east. Because fault-plane exposures are lacking and normal faults cut the thrust fault into short segments, the orientation of the thrust is not tightly constrained. The map pattern and three-point solutions, where possible, indicate that the thrust strikes north to northeast and dips gently to the west. Along most of its preserved trace the Rimrock thrust places Ordovician Shingle Limestone (middle Pogonip Group) on Devonian Sevy and Simonson Dolomites, a stratigraphic

duplication of at least 1,200 m. The thrust cuts up-section to the east in the footwall, truncating the Sevy/Simonson Dolomite contact. Based on the cutoff angle of hanging-wall bedding, the corresponding minimum horizontal shortening is about 2 km. Poles to bedding in the hanging wall of the thrust define a diffuse partial girdle on an equal-area plot with a gently south-southwest–plunging axis (Fig. 9a), a pattern broadly similar to that from above the Sawmill thrust (Fig. 7). Two minor anticlines exposed in the hanging wall corroborate southwest-plunging folding (Fig. 9a). The map pattern and orientation data suggest that the major hanging-wall structure is an open upright anticline (Fig. 10, Section C-C', in pocket). Bedding in the eastern limb of the fold is sharply truncated at an angle of about 40 to 50°, suggesting that this may be a fault-propagation fold rather than a fault-bend anticline (Suppe, 1983).

Relation between the Sawmill and Rimrock thrusts

At an early stage of our mapping, it seemed possible that the Sawmill and Rimrock thrusts were the same fault, repeated across the Little Meadow–Cherry Creek normal fault system. However, this correlation can be excluded for the following reasons. First, a "rule" of thrust belts (for example, Dahlstrom, 1969) is that thrusts cut up-section in the direction of transport. The strata directly beneath the Rimrock thrust (mainly Sevy Dolomite) are older than those exposed beneath the Sawmill thrust (Guilmette Formation), and therefore, correlation of the two thrusts would require the thrust to cut down-section in the footwall in the direction of transport. Second, everywhere in the study area that the base of the Oligocene section is exposed, it was deposited upon Ordovician rocks in the hanging wall of the Sawmill thrust. However, rocks as young as Upper Devonian Guilmette Formation are preserved above the Rimrock thrust. This is readily explained only if the Devonian rocks exposed in windows through the Sawmill thrust correspond to the Devonian rocks above the Rimrock thrust. Third, the facies difference in Cambro-Ordovician rocks noted above is between rocks that lie above the Sawmill thrust and those that lie above the Rimrock thrust. The abrupt facies change can be explained as telescoping by thrusting only if the Sawmill thrust separates the two stratigraphic sections, which requires the Rimrock thrust to be a separate, lower thrust. Finally, on the north side of the Hooper Canyon window a horse of Ordovician Pogonip Group rocks is faulted between Devonian strata of the window and Oligocene volcanic rocks to the north (Figs. 4 and 5). This occurrence of older rocks surrounded by younger rocks clearly resulted from normal-fault displacement of Ordovician rocks from above the Sawmill thrust to a position next to footwall Devonian rocks. A horse of Pogonip Group strata occurs in an identical situation at the southern terminus of the Little Meadow fault 1 km south of Cherry Creek Summit (Figs. 3 and 8), and there the underlying Devonian rocks belong to the hanging wall of the Rimrock thrust. This relation again requires the hanging wall of the Rimrock thrust to be the footwall of the Sawmill thrust.

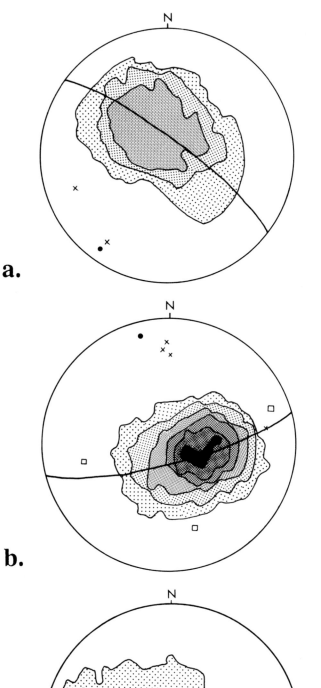

a.

Pole to Girdle: ●
Minor fold axes: ×
K = 0.95
C = 2.83
N = 46
Fraction of variation explained = 0.772

Figure 9. Lower-hemisphere equal-area plots from southern Grant Range. Contouring is as in Figure 7. K and C are statistical parameters defined by Woodcock and Naylor (1983). K > 1 indicates a cluster; K < 1 indicates a girdle; C > 3 indicates a strong preferred orientation. Contoured data are (a) poles to bedding in hanging wall of Rimrock thrust, (b) poles to bedding in footwall of Rimrock thrust, and (c) fault striae from Wadsworth Ranch fault system.

b.

Pole to Girdle: ●
Minor fold axes: ×
Poles to solution cleavage: □
K = 2.29
C = 2.39
N = 96
Fraction of variation explained = 0.635

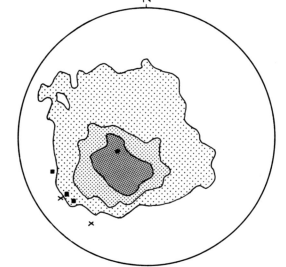

c.

Striae mean: ●
Intersection lines: Spring Creek: ■
                       Bruno Creek: ×
K = 3.78
C = 1.128
N = 100

Structures beneath the Rimrock thrust

Rocks beneath the Rimrock thrust are autochthonous with respect to Mesozoic thrusts exposed in the study area, but in a relative sense only. Basal Cambrian–upper Precambrian rocks lie above frontal Sevier thrusts to the south and east, demonstrating that the basal detachment of the Sevier belt was at or near the base of the Paleozoic section and projects underneath all of the rocks exposed in the study area. In fact, the entire Paleozoic miogeocline of the Great Basin was transported toward the foreland as part of the Sevier thrust belt (Armstrong, 1968; Royse and others, 1975).

The geometry of shortening in the relative autochthon resembles that above the overlying thrusts. Pogonip Group rocks exposed in the southeast corner of the study area are folded into a box-shaped anticline (Figs. 8, 10). Poles to bedding define a crude partial girdle with a north-plunging axis (Fig. 9b). Associated minor folds are concentric or kink folds that also plunge mainly northward. Some of these minor folds are cut by small east-vergent thrusts. Orientations of solution cleavage are inconsistent but loosely correspond with the fold axial-surface orientations. The general scatter of the orientation data may reflect either original geometric complexity or later deformation related to normal faulting.

Age of thrusting

The ages of the Sawmill and Rimrock thrusts presently are poorly constrained. The only firm maximum age constraint on thrusting is the lack of stratigraphic evidence for orogenic movements in this region in strata as young as Permian. The absolute minimum age is middle Oligocene, based on (1) unconformable overlap across the Sawmill thrust of the Oligocene section on the west side of the Sawmill Canyon window (Murray, 1985; this exposure is too small to distinguish at the scale of Figs. 3 and 4), and (2) truncation of the backthrust zone by the Oligocene granitic stock west of the Hooper Canyon window. A somewhat more restricted age is suggested by the presumably related east-vergent Timber Mountain Anticline in the central Grant Range, which is cut by the 70-Ma Troy stock (Fryxell, 1984; see Fig. 1 for location). These data restrict the age of the thrusts no more precisely than some time in the Mesozoic.

NORMAL FAULTS

Cherry Creek fault

We name the Cherry Creek fault for Cherry Creek, which this north-striking normal fault crosses about 3.3 km west of the mouth of Cherry Canyon (Figs. 4 and 8). Two segments are defined by intersection of the Cherry Creek fault with an east-trending, south-dipping normal (oblique?) slip fault within the hanging wall. The northern segment strikes north-northeast, dips 50 to 70° west, and places Devonian dolomite on Silurian and Devonian dolomite. Dip separation across this segment is small, amounting to about 30 m at the northern edge of the study area and increasing southward to about 300 m at Bruno Creek (Fig. 8). The southern segment of the fault strikes north-northwest, dips 36 to 51° west, and excises 300 to 500 m of Tertiary strata. Locally the southern segment cuts out an older fault in its footwall, which causes it to appear to have accommodated greater displacement, placing Oligocene volcanic and shallow-intrusive rocks on Paleozoic carbonate rocks.

The east-striking fault that defines the segments appears to have acted to transfer displacement from the Little Meadow fault (Fig. 4; see below) to the Cherry Creek fault, causing the apparent southward increase in displacement along the Cherry Creek fault. The lower fault dip and greater rotation of hanging-wall bedding south of this junction also are consistent with such a jump in displacement.

There also may be significant sinistral slip across the southern segment of the Cherry Creek fault. The fault cuts a large, subvertical, east-trending felsite dike in its footwall that probably correlates with a smaller felsite intrusion located to the south in the hanging wall (Fig. 8), giving sinistral slip of about 600 m. The Cherry Creek fault therefore appears to be a sinistral-normal oblique-slip fault, implying hanging-wall transport toward the southwest.

The age of slip along the Cherry Creek fault is not constrained tightly. The fault cuts the 26.2-Ma Shingle Pass Tuff and does not offset Quaternary deposits. However, its inferred relation to the Little Meadow fault (see below) suggests that it was active mainly during the Miocene.

Little Meadow fault

The Little Meadow fault (Fryxell, 1988) passes southward from Little Meadow Creek in the central Grant Range into the study area, terminating south of Cherry Creek Summit (Figs. 3 and 4). The fault is poorly exposed in the study area, but exposures are consistent with the moderate westward dip (30 to 40°) determined farther north by Fryxell. The Little Meadow fault and synthetic faults in its hanging wall cut the northern end of the Quinn Canyon Range into a series of domino-style tilted blocks that dip about 35° to the east (Figs. 5 and 6). The uniform dip of the domino blocks indicates that the synthetic faults are planar. It seems likely that the domino-style faults sole into a listric Little Meadow fault, as shown in Figure 6, but observations bearing on this possibility are ambiguous. Bedding dips more gently in the footwall than in the hanging wall (Fig. 6), which at least superficially favors a listric fault form. However, because the fault cuts through the Mesozoic fold and thrust structures described above, the difference in bedding attitude in Paleozoic strata need not necessarily be ascribed to Tertiary differential rotation.

The slip direction of the Little Meadow fault appears to be west-northwest, that is, more or less directly down dip, based on hanging-wall fault geometry north of the Hooper Canyon window. The faults that define the domino-block system north of the

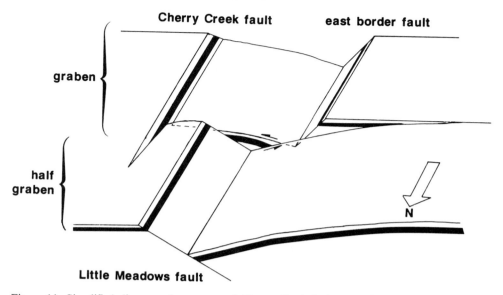

Figure 11. Simplified diagram of geometry of Cherry Creek fault, "east border fault," and Little Meadow fault. Note the asymmetric graben to south and half-graben to north. Synthetic, domino-style faults were omitted for clarity.

window compose a set of intersecting moderately west-dipping and steeply north-dipping faults. The geometry suggests overall west-northwest slip, with normal slip on the west-dipping faults and primarily sinistral slip on the steeper north-dipping faults. Sinistral slip along the latter faults is corroborated by sinistral bending of pre-Tertiary structures along the northern side of the Quinn Canyon Range (Fig. 5; see above). This discordance of the inferred slip directions of the related Little Meadow and Cherry Creek faults is unexplained but indicates that the kinematics of the fault system were not strictly two-dimensional.

In the central Grant Range, the Little Meadow fault cuts the Troy Peak fault, which is of late Oligocene or early Miocene age (Fryxell, 1988). A sequence of syntectonic clastic deposits is cut and tilted by the Little Meadow fault (Fryxell, 1988). Biotite from an air-fall tuff near the top of this clastic sequence yielded a $^{40}Ar/^{39}Ar$ total-gas age of 14.2 Ma (Taylor and others, 1989). Therefore, slip along the Little Meadow fault appears to have been mainly during the middle Miocene, although late Miocene or younger slip cannot be excluded.

At Little Meadow Creek, throw of the Little Meadow fault is estimated to be about 2 km (Fryxell, 1988). Based on the offset required to excise the Sawmill thrust, the throw appears to have decreased to about 1.5 km near Cherry Creek Summit (Fig. 6). However, only 1.5 km south of Cherry Creek Summit, the Little Meadow fault abruptly terminates. No fault with a throw of more than a few hundred meters is present within the Oligocene volcanic rocks south of this point. This relation cannot be explained by fault slip being older than the Oligocene rocks, because of the evidence that the fault is mainly of Miocene age. Instead, it appears that the displacement is transferred to two other normal faults, that is, eastward to the Cherry Creek fault and westward to the east-dipping normal fault that forms the eastern boundary of

the Sawmill Canyon window ("east border fault" of Murray, 1985; see Fig. 4). Murray (1985) estimated the "east border fault" to have accommodated 2,300 m of stratigraphic throw. Timing relations of the fault are similar to the Cherry Creek fault, in that it cuts the Shingle Pass Tuff and a swarm of east-west–striking felsite dikes.

The Little Meadow, Cherry Creek, and "east border" normal faults are interpreted to record a single extensional event that formed an asymmetric graben to the south and a half-graben, floored by synthetic domino-style faults, to the north (Fig. 11). Steep east-west– to west-northwest–striking faults acted as a transfer zone (Gibbs, 1984) that separates these two structural domains. In Figure 6, extension across the Little Meadows fault and hanging-wall domino faults is estimated to be about 2 km. Estimated extension across the combined Cherry Creek and the "east border" faults is 2 to 4 km, depending on the actual fault dips, which are not well known. These estimates are somewhat less than the 4.6-km horizontal extension estimated across the Little Meadow fault farther north in the Grant Range (Fryxell, 1988), but displacements along smaller faults between the Cherry Creek and "east border" faults may accommodate the remaining extension.

The transfer zone forms part of a regional tilt-domain boundary between eastward bedding dips to the north and westward bedding dips to the south (Stewart, 1980). Some authors have speculated that such transverse boundaries are strike-slip faults. However, strike slip only occurs locally along this boundary; to the west and east, strata are essentially continuous across the tilt-domain boundary, twisting along strike from west dips to east dips without significant fault offset. A similar situation exists at a major tilt-domain boundary in southern Nevada (Faulds and others, 1987). In these examples at least, no throughgoing fault is present at the tilt-domain boundary, and the mechanism of displacement transfer that causes the change of tilt direction must be more subtle.

Wadsworth Ranch Fault system

We name the Wadsworth Ranch fault system for Wadsworth Ranch, located in Cherry Canyon where a major strand of the fault system crosses the canyon (Figs. 4 and 8). The Wadsworth Ranch fault system is a complex network of intersecting normal and oblique-slip fault segments (Figs. 8 and 12) that form a zone of highly deformed rocks that divides two comparatively intact blocks of Paleozoic strata. Along most of its length, the Wadsworth Ranch fault cuts out the Rimrock thrust, placing the hanging wall of the thrust against the thrust footwall. This geometry results in an older-on-younger relation across the fault for about 3 km along its northern end (Figs. 3 and 8). However, farther south the throw of the Wadsworth Ranch fault exceeds the throw of the thrust, such that the fault places younger rocks on older but with an actual throw that exceeds the apparent stratigraphic throw by more than 1 km.

Net slip across the Wadsworth Ranch fault system is most likely sinistral-normal oblique, based on fault-segment intersection lines and orientations of fault striae (Fig. 9c). In order to avoid a space problem, slip across a highly segmented fault must be subparallel to the intersection lines of the segments. The Wadsworth Range fault system comprises east-striking segments that dip southward from 0 to 26°, and north-striking segments that are generally steeper and vary in dip from 22 to 70° west. Cross section D-D′ (Fig. 10) shows an example of the ramp-flat geometry typical of the low-angle south-dipping segments. Intersection lines of the fault segments at Bruno and Spring Creeks plunge southwest about 20° (Fig. 9c). Measured fault striae mainly are from minor fault surfaces above and below the main fault, because exposed striae are rare along the main fault. The data are scattered but cluster in the southwest quadrant with a mean plunge of 70° toward S65W. The steeper plunge of the striae compared to the fault-segment intersections reflects the steeper dip of the minor faults compared to the major faults.

The Wadsworth Ranch fault is older than the Cherry Creek fault based on cross-cutting relations, but the age of activity along the main strand is not tightly constrained. The fault cuts the Cretaceous(?) Rimrock thrust and therefore must be younger than it. Several strands of the fault system are cut by felsite dikes

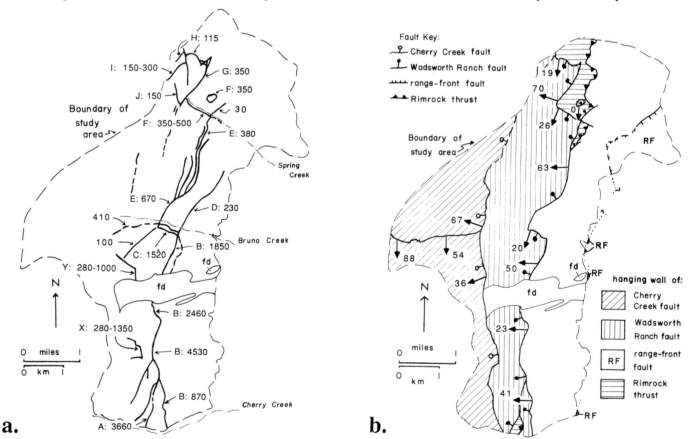

Figure 12. Tectonic maps of southern Grant Range (same area as Fig. 7). Felsite dike that cuts the Wadsworth Ranch fault but is cut by the Cherry Creek fault is labeled "fd." (A) Map of segments (identified by letters A to J, X, and Y) of the Wadsworth Ranch fault system, with separation estimate for each segment in meters. Note southward increase of separation. (B) Map of main fault blocks and dips of individual normal-fault segments.

that are probably related to the 26- to 27-Ma silicic caldera system in the Quinn Canyon Range. However, a more restricted age bracket can be inferred. Two faults located between the Cherry Creek and Wadsworth Ranch faults (segments X and Y in Fig. 12A) have similar orientations and geometries to the Wadsworth Ranch fault system, and one is cut by the large felsite dike that is offset by the Cherry Creek fault. Therefore, we consider these smaller faults to belong to the Wadsworth Ranch fault system. The faults cut the Windous Butte Formation (32 Ma); therefore, at least one of these faults is bracketed in age between about 32 and 26 Ma. We suggest that the Wadsworth Ranch fault system as a whole is largely, if not entirely, of this age.

Estimated separations across various segments of the Wadsworth Ranch fault system are summarized in Figure 12A. The values shown are the stratal thicknesses excised by the Wadsworth Ranch fault system plus the duplication across the Rimrock thrust where the thrust is cut out by the normal fault. Because the orientations of the stratigraphic units are different above and below the thrust fault and because the throw of the thrust probably varies along strike, these separation estimates are only approximate. However, it is obvious that separation increases southward, from hundreds of meters to more than 4 km.

Cross section E-E' (Fig. 10) was constructed parallel to the trend of Wadsworth Ranch fault-segment intersection lines and therefore to the inferred slip direction. Postkinematic Tertiary intrusions and the displacement across the Cherry Creek fault have been removed. Stratal thicknesses appear distorted because the cross section is not normal to the strike of bedding. The cross section yields an estimated 10 km of slip on the Wadsworth Ranch fault system. This is a conservative figure for two reasons: (1) the section was drawn near the north end of the Wadsworth Ranch fault, and separation increases southward; and (2) the high-angle hanging-wall fault near the center of the section (segment Y in Fig. 12a) is shown with the absolute minimum dip slip, about 400 m, but actually may have accommodated as much as 1 km of dip slip (Gleason, 1988).

Where exposed, the Wadsworth Ranch fault system cuts hanging-wall rocks of the Troy Peak fault, which is inferred to be a Tertiary extensional detachment (Fryxell, 1988). The slip direction of the Troy Peak fault is poorly known. Because the Wadsworth Ranch and Troy Peak faults do not intersect at the surface, the actual geometric relation between the faults cannot be demonstrated. However, the age of movement along the Wadsworth Ranch fault system is similar to that of the Troy Peak fault. We therefore suggest the interpretation that the Wadsworth Ranch fault system records internal extension within the hanging wall of the Troy Peak fault. If so, then displacement along the Troy Peak fault probably was in a northeast-southwest direction, although the sense of slip (that is, whether the hanging wall was displaced to the northwest or to the southeast) would remain in doubt.

Range-front faults

The faults that form the western boundary of the Grant and Quinn Canyon ranges in the study area are not exposed cutting bedrock. Degraded scarps in alluvium near the range front record Quaternary movement on the range-bounding faults in this area (Fig. 5). The range-front scarps define a segmented geometry closely similar to the geometries of the Miocene and Oligocene normal faults within the range. Various authors have inferred that a change of tectonic style occurred between mid-Tertiary "core complex" extension and late Cenozoic "Basin and Range" extension (for example, Coney and Harms, 1984; Snoke and Lush, 1984). Others have viewed core complexes and Basin and Range faults to represent the deeper and shallower components of a single structural style (for example, Wright and Troxel, 1973; Gans and others, 1985). Our observations favor the latter view, that is, that the style of normal faults in the Great Basin has not changed significantly from Oligocene to Recent.

The eastern range-front normal fault is exposed at the mouth of Cherry Canyon where its attitude is N4E, 70E. At the canyon mouth, the fault places Tertiary Windous Butte Formation in the hanging wall on Ordovician Eureka Quartzite in the footwall. Late slip along the fault is nearly pure dip-slip, as indicated by down-dip striae on the fault plane. The throw of the fault is not determinable because none of the same stratigraphic contacts are exposed on both sides of the fault, and there are no exposures of what underlies the Windous Butte Formation in the hanging wall. If the hanging-wall Windous Butte was deposited on the Sawmill thrust plate, as in the Quinn Canyon Range immediately to the west, then separation across the eastern range-front fault could be as much as 3,270 m. However, this may greatly overestimate the slip on the fault, because it does not take into account possible effects of other faults, such as the Wadsworth Ranch fault, that probably are older.

The eastern range-front fault continues as far north as Spring Creek. The exposure is poor, but outcrops show the fault strikes northeast from there and places Windous Butte Formation on Fish Haven Dolomite. Whether or not these two segments form a single nonplanar fault or are actually two faults, one of which cuts the other, is not clear. That they have nearly the same hanging-wall to footwall stratigraphic relations supports the idea that they are the same fault.

TERTIARY DIKES

Dikes in the study area are important tectonically for two reasons: (1) they constrain the ages of some of the structures, and (2) they provide constraints on the orientation of the local stress field at the time of injection.

Dikes of both mafic and felsic composition occur throughout the study area but are especially abundant in the southeastern part of the area. The largest felsite dike cuts the Wadsworth Ranch fault and intrudes the tuff of Cherry Creek. Smaller felsite dikes cut most of the strands of the Wadsworth Ranch fault. The Cherry Creek fault cuts dikes of both compositions. Contact relations therefore indicate that most or all of the dikes were intruded after slip along the Wadsworth Ranch fault but before slip along the Little Meadow–Cherry Creek faults. However, along the easternmost splay of the fault just north of Cherry Canyon, the dikes are cut by the splay (Fig. 8). This relation suggests that this splay is younger than other faults of the Wadsworth Ranch fault system or that it was reactivated after intrusion.

The predominant trend of Tertiary dikes in the study area, both mafic and felsic, is east-northeast (Fig. 13). Tensile fractures such as dikes usually form perpendicular to the least compressive stress direction (σ_3; Anderson, 1951). Therefore, an area in which

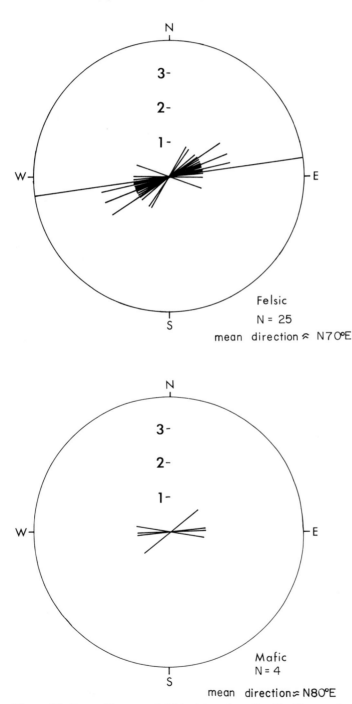

Figure 13. Rose diagrams of felsic (a) and mafic (b) dike trends. Numbers (1, 2, 3) indicate number observed in a given orientation.

the faults record east-west extension would be expected to contain north-trending dikes (such as the swarm of diabase dikes in the nearby Worthington Mountains; Martin, 1987). Instead, it appears that the least compressive stress in the study area at the time of dike injection trended north-northwest, discordant to extension directions indicated by faults both older and younger than the dikes.

This anomaly might be explained by the major volcanic vent nearby in the Quinn Canyon Range (Sargent and Houser, 1970; Ekren and others, 1977). Far-field stress trajectories may have been locally perturbed by forces related to buoyant rise of magma beneath the Quinn Canyon caldron complex (compare Odé, 1958). However, Best's (1988) regional compilation of mid-Tertiary dike trends in the Basin and Range shows that mid-Tertiary east-west dikes are typical across the region. The east-west dikes therefore may record a transient phase, regional in extent, of north-south tension. This stress-field reorientation is enigmatic, but it may be significant that Best's procedure in selecting dike sets tends to include only dikes that were emplaced during major crustal magmatism, which has long been known to sweep southward across the Great Basin in the Tertiary (Cook, 1965; Armstrong and others, 1969). This suggests that whatever tectonic process caused the southward-sweeping mid-Tertiary magmatism also may have caused the transient perturbation of the stress field.

DISCUSSION

Timing of Tertiary extension

Although it is obvious that the Great Basin as a whole underwent major crustal extension in the Tertiary, the detailed time-space relations of extension across the province are as yet uncertain. Recent detailed mapping and ^{40}Ar/^{39}Ar isotopic dating have documented four periods of extension in the Dry Lake Valley area, 70 km east of the Grant Range (see Fig. 1 for location): (1) pre–32 Ma, (2) 30.5 to 27 Ma, (3) about 16 to 14 Ma, and (4) latest Miocene to Quaternary (Bartley and others, 1988; Taylor, this volume; Taylor and others, 1989). The oldest period of extension in the Grant Range, during which the Wadsworth Ranch fault system and the Troy Peak fault formed, was more or less contemporaneous with the second period of extension at Dry Lake Valley. The next younger period of extension in the Grant Range, represented by the Little Meadow and related faults, apparently occurred contemporaneously with the third period of extension at Dry Lake Valley. Both areas also preserve evidence for late Miocene to Recent normal faulting (also see Nakata and others, 1982; Axen and others, 1988; DiGuiseppi, 1988).

Although timing data regionally are as yet less restrictive than we would like, it appears probable that extensional episodes in the middle to late Oligocene, the middle Miocene, and the Late Miocene to Recent affected on area presently at least 100 km wide at 38°N latitude in eastern Nevada. It is unclear whether there was a direct kinematic link between structures across the entire area, but this coincidence of timing suggests that a dynamic relation may have existed. We regard these episodes of extension to be a natural consequence of the shear-zone mechanism of crustal extension widely inferred in the Basin and Range province (Wernicke, 1981; Davis, 1983; Bartley and Wernicke, 1984; Davis and others, 1986; and many others). Each episode records the creation and subsequent deactivation of a particular crustal shear system. Upper-crustal extension within a single shear system would be expected to be spatially diachronous as the shear zone evolves (Spencer, 1984; Davis and Lister, 1988; Wernicke and Axen, 1988; Buck, 1988). However, periods of quiescence between extensional episodes, recognizable in at least some areas, suggest that the characteristic life span of an extensional shear system may be short enough that diachroneity within a single system need not obscure time-space distinctions between separate systems. We do not anticipate that these represent province-wide episodes. Instead, we hypothesize that, during periods of tectonic quiescence in a particular area, extension continued elsewhere in the province along other major shear zones.

Significance of thrusts in the Garden Valley area

Known thrusts in the Garden Valley area are shown in Figure 1. In addition to those described above, these include Thrust III of Cebull (1967, 1970), the Freiberg thrust in the Worthington Mountains (Tschanz and Pampeyan, 1970; Martin, 1987), and a thrust in the Golden Gate Range (Tschanz and Pampeyan, 1970) that we call the Golden Gate thrust. Thrusts in the Timpahute Range, mapped by Tschanz and Pampeyan (1970), are neglected here because present data do not permit us to distinguish confidently between thrusts and low-angle normal faults in that extremely complex area.

The Sawmill thrust is the structurally highest thrust we have recognized to date. The lower Rimrock thrust probably correlates southward with the Freiberg thrust. The two thrusts are on strike and appear to lie within the same major Cenozoic normal-fault block. Like the Rimrock thrust, the Freiberg thrust places middle Pogonip Group strata upon Sevy Dolomite (Martin, 1987), and the lithologies and fossil content of hanging-wall Pogonip Group strata resemble equivalent units above the Rimrock thrust (as opposed to the Pogonip strata above the Sawmill thrust; see Fig. 2 and earlier discussion). Both the Sawmill and Rimrock thrusts are in the hanging wall of the Troy Peak fault, whereas Cebull's thrust III lies in the footwall of that fault. This suggests that thrust III is structurally lower than the Rimrock thrust, although restoration of slip along the Troy Peak fault to yield an accurate picture of the relations between these thrusts is not yet possible. The Golden Gate thrust also is structurally lower than the Freiberg-Rimrock thrust, but because the Golden Gate thrust dies out northward into an anticline-syncline pair within the Golden Gate Range (P. A. Armstrong, personal communication, 1988), the Golden Gate thrust probably cannot be related directly to Cebull's thrust III.

The amount of displacement along each individual thrust appears to be relatively small. Minimum slip estimates along the Sawmill thrust, Rimrock-Freiberg thrust, and Cebull's thrust III are 8 km, 2 to 4 km, and 2.4 km, respectively (see above; Martin, 1987; Cebull, 1967). Nonetheless, the intensity of upper-crustal shortening in this area considerably exceeds that inferred immediately to the northeast in east-central Nevada (Armstrong, 1972; Gans and Miller, 1983). This raises the question of the existence and location of correlative structures to the north.

The Eureka belt (Speed, 1983; Speed and others, 1988) is a belte of broadly north-trending folds and thrusts located near 41°N latitude and directly west of the Sevier hinterland (Fig. 14). Some of the deformation in this belt is thought to reflect the Late Devonian/Early Mississippian Antler Orogeny (Roberts and others, 1958), but other folds and thrusts that affect Paleozoic strata in that area are demonstrably of Mesozoic age (Ketner and Smith, 1974; Smith and Ketner, 1977; Coats and Riva, 1983). The Cretaceous Newark Canyon Formation, exposed near Eureka, appears to represent syntectonic clastic sedimentation related to deformation and uplift in the Eureka belt, and Newark Canyon strata themselves are affected by east-vergent overturned folds (Schmitt and Vandervoort, 1987, and personal communication, 1988). It therefore seems probable to us that thrusts in the Garden Valley area and the Eureka belt are coeval and related. Although direct physical continuity along strike cannot be shown yet, we concur with Speed's (1983; Speed and others, 1988) suggestion that the Garden Valley thrust system and the Eureka belt are parts of a once-continuous belt of Cretaceous thrusts.

This proposed thrust belt would be broadly coeval with and subparallel to the Sevier thrust belt farther to the east (Fig. 14). Speed and others (1988) and Smith and Wright (1988a) interpreted the Sevier and Eureka belts to be distinct tectonic elements, separated by an area of minimal upper-crustal deformation corresponding to the Sevier hinterland. However, this view may not take sufficient account of the extreme Tertiary extension across the hinterland. The present distance from the Eureka belt to the Sevier thrust front is about 350 km. Gans (1987) estimated 141 km of Tertiary extension along a cross section that encompasses 323 km of this distance. Accepting this figure, it is then likely that the total Cenozoic extension between the Eureka belt and the Sevier thrust front exceeds 150 km. This places the Eureka belt in a pre-Tertiary position less than 200 km from the thrust front, with the hinterland at this latitude restoring to an even more external position (Fig. 14). By comparison, the Eastern Cordillera–Subandean thrust belt in the central Andes is about 200 km wide (Jordan and others, 1983, Fig. 11), as is the Rocky Mountain foreland thrust belt of southwestern Canada if one interprets the Purcell Anticlinorium to be thin skinned (Cook and others, 1988). Therefore, when Tertiary extension is restored in the eastern Great Basin, it is quite possible that thrusts now exposed as the Eureka belt formed as part of the Sevier foreland thrust system. This hypothesis complements Bartley and Wernicke's (1984) suggestion that the low structural relief beneath the sub-Tertiary unconformity in the Sevier hinterland reflects a broad flat (décollement on décollement) within the Sevier thrust belt. We therefore propose that the Garden Valley–Eureka thrust

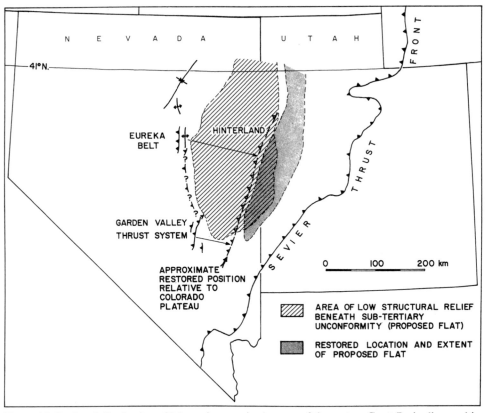

Figure 14. Regional distribution of Mesozoic tectonic elements of the eastern Great Basin discussed in the text.

belt may represent not a discrete belt of thrusting but the western part of the Sevier thrust belt that has been rifted away from the frontal Sevier belt by intense Tertiary extension.

Jordan and others (1983) proposed a similar but distinct interpretation in which thrusts exposed in the Sevier hinterland are analogous to the discontinuous and relatively small thrusts that characterize the upper crust of the Puna plateau in the central Andes, which lies behind the thin-skinned thrust belt of the eastern Cordillera and Subandean Belt. Such an interpretation may be accurate for the Sevier hinterland north of latitude 41°N, where much of the Sevier thrust belt lies outside of the Basin and Range. However, south of 41°N the tectonic equivalent of the Puna plateau may lie west of the "hinterland" in central Nevada, where the intensity of Mesozoic plutonism is much greater (for example, Smith and Wright, 1988a, b).

CONCLUSIONS

The structure of the Grant and Quinn Canyon ranges records overprinting of Mesozoic fold-and-thrust belt structure by multiple episodes of Cenozoic normal faulting. Recognition and analysis of the superposed faults has been complicated because (1) normal faults commonly emplace older rocks upon younger as they cut through the older thrust-belt structure, and (2) many of the normal faults have low dips, making distinction between

normal faults and thrusts particularly difficult. However, the normal faults consistently place younger strata on older where contained within a single thrust plate. The structural form of the normal faults also is distinctly different from the thrusts: the normal faults are divided into planar segments, hundreds of meters to a few kilometers long, that are commonly at a high angle to each other.

The ages of normal faults in the study area generally correlate with extensional episodes recognized farther east near Dry Lake Valley, suggesting that Basin and Range extension may be fundamentally episodic on a regional scale. We interpret these episodes to record the creation and deactivation of crustal-scale extensional shear zones. There appears to have been a clockwise rotation of extension direction, from southwest to west-southwest in the Oligocene extensional system to west or west-northwest in the Miocene system.

Age and regional relations suggest that Mesozoic structures in the Grant–Quinn Canyon range area correlate with Cretaceous folding, thrusting, and syntectonic sedimentation in the Eureka belt farther north. We interpret this thrust system to have been originally continuous along strike and to represent the internal part of the Sevier fold and thrust belt. This interpretation implies that what has been called the hinterland of the Sevier orogenic belt, at least south from 41°N latitude, actually lies *within* the Sevier thrust belt.

It has become increasingly clear in recent years that most of the characteristic features that were used to define the Sevier hinterland actually were formed in Cenozoic, not Mesozoic, time. This includes most of the major younger-on-older low-angle faults and the mylonitic rocks in the metamorphic core complexes. Combined with our suggestion that much of the "hinterland" lies within, rather than behind, the Sevier thrust belt, this implies that the "hinterland," at least south of 41°N, actually represents a part of the Sevier thrust belt that subsequently was disrupted by intense Cenozoic extension. The term *hinterland,* used in the Great Basin to imply a Mesozoic tectonic framework distinct from the Sevier thrust belt, therefore appears to be erroneous and misleading, and we recommend that it be abandoned.

ACKNOWLEDGMENTS

Major funding for this research came from the following grants to Bartley: 14455-AC2 from the Petroleum Research Fund, administered by the American Chemical Society, and EAR-8600518 from the National Science Foundation. Gleason received additional support from Sigma Xi and Cenex. Discussions with Gary Axen, Myron Best, Joan Fryxell, Suzanne Janecke, Mark Martin, Margie Murray, Jim Schmitt, and Wanda Taylor contributed to our thinking. Careful and constructive reviews by Teresa Jordan and Brian Wernicke significantly improved both the content and the presentation of the paper, although we remain responsible for its conclusions.

REFERENCES CITED

Anderson, E. M., 1951, The dynamics of faulting and dyke formation with applications to Britain: Edinburgh, Oliver and Boyd, 206 p.

Armstrong, R. L., 1968, Sevier orogenic belt in Nevada and Utah: Geological Society of America Bulletin, v. 79, p. 429–458.

——, 1972, Low-angle (denudation) faults, hinterland of the Sevier Orogenic belt, eastern Nevada and western Utah: Geological Society of America Bulletin, v. 83, p. 1729–1754.

——, 1982, Cordilleran metamorphic core complexes; From Arizona to southern Canada: Annual Reviews of Earth and Planetary Sciences, v. 10, p. 129–154.

Armstrong, R. L., and Hansen, E., 1966, Cordilleran infrastructure in the eastern Great Basin: American Journal of Science, v. 264, p. 112–127.

Armstrong, R. L., Ekren, E. B., McKee, E. H., and Noble, D. C., 1969, Space-time relations of Cenozoic silicic volcanism in the Great Basin of the western United States: American Journal of Science, v. 267, p. 478–490.

Axen, G. J., Lewis, P. R., Burke, K. J., Sleeper, K. G., and Fletcher, J. M., 1988, Tertiary extension in the Pioche area, Nevada, *in* Weide, D. L., and Faber, M. L., eds., This extended land; Geological journeys in the southern Basin and Range; Geological Society of America 1988 Cordilleran Section meeting Guidebook: University of Nevada at Las Vegas Department of Geoscience Special Publication 2, p. 3–5.

Bartley, J. M., and Wernicke, B. P., 1984, The Snake Range décollement interpreted as a major extensional shear zone: Tectonics, v. 3, p. 647–657.

Bartley, J. M., Axen, G. J., Taylor, W. J., and Fryxell, J. E., 1988, Cenozoic tectonics of a transect through eastern Nevada near 38°N latitude, *in* Weide, D. L., and Faber, M. L., eds., This extended land; Geological journeys in the southern Basin and Range; Geological Society of America 1988 Cordilleran Section Meeting Guidebook: University of Nevada at Las Vegas Department of Geosciences Special Publication 2, p. 1–3.

Best, M. G., 1988, Early Miocene change in direction of least principal stress, southwestern United States; Conflicting inferences from dikes and metamorphic core-detachment fault terranes: Tectonics, v. 7, p. 249–259.

Buck, W. R., 1988, Flexural rotation of normal faults: Tectonics, v. 7, p. 959–973.

Camilleri, P. A., Lund, K., and Beard, L. S., 1987, Superposed compressional and extensional strain in metamorphosed lower Paleozoic rocks of the northern Grant Range, east-central Nevada: Geological Society of America Abstracts with Programs, v. 19, p. 609.

Cebull, S. E., 1967, Bedrock geology of the southern Grant Range, Nye County, Nevada [Ph.D. thesis]: Seattle, University of Washington, 130 p.

——, 1970, Bedrock geology and orogenic succession in the southern Grant Range, Nye county, Nevada: American Association of Petroleum Geologists Bulletin, v. 54, p. 1828–1842.

Coats, R. R., and Riva, J. F., 1983, Overlapping overthrust belts of late Paleozoic and Mesozoic ages, northern Elko county, Nevada, *in* Miller, D. M., Todd, V. R., and Howard, K. A., eds., Tectonic and stratigraphic studies in the eastern Great Basin: Geological Society of America Memoir 157, p. 305–327.

Coney, P. J., and Harms, T. A., 1984, Cordilleran metamorphic core complexes; Cenozoic extensional relics of Mesozoic compression: Geology, v. 12, p. 550–554.

Cook, E. F., 1965, Stratigraphy of Tertiary volcanic rocks in eastern Nevada: Nevada Bureau of Mines Report 11, 61 p.

Cook, F. A., and 9 others, 1988, Lithoprobe seismic reflection structure of the southeastern Canadian Cordillera; Initial results: Tectonics, v. 7, p. 157–180.

Dahlstrom, C.D.A., 1969, Balanced cross sections: Canadian Journal of Earth Sciences, v. 6, p. 743–757.

Davis, G. A., and Lister, G. S., 1988, Detachment faulting in continental extension; Perspectives from the southwestern U.S. Cordillera, *in* Clark, S. P., Jr., Burchfiel, B. C., and Suppe, J., eds., Processes in continental lithospheric deformation: Geological Society of America Special Paper 218, p. 133–159.

Davis, G. A., Lister, G. S., and Reynolds, S. J., 1986, Structural evolution of the Whipple and South Mountains shear zones, southwestern United States: Geology, v. 14, p. 7–10.

Davis, G. H., 1983, Shear-zone model for the origin of metamorphic core complexes: Geology, v. 11, p. 342–347.

DiGuiseppi, W. H., 1988, Geomorphic and tectonic significance of Quaternary sediments in southern White River Valley, Nevada [M.S. thesis]: Salt Lake City, University of Utah, 62 p.

Dixon, J. S., 1982, Regional structural synthesis, Wyoming salient of Western Overthrust Belt: American Association of Petroleum Geologists Bulletin, v. 66, p. 1560–1580.

Ekren, E. B., Orkild, P. P., Sargent, K. A., and Dixon, G. L., 1977, Geologic map of Tertiary rocks, Lincoln County, Nevada: U.S. Geological Survey Miscellaneous Geologic Investigations Map I–1041, scale 1:250,000.

Faulds, J. E., Mawer, C. K., and Geissman, J. W., 1987, Possible modes of deformation along "accommodation zones" in rifted continental crust: Geological Society of America Abstracts with Programs, v. 19, p. 659.

Fryxell, J. E., 1984, Structural development of the west-central Grant Range, Nye county, Nevada [Ph.D. thesis]: Chapel Hill, University of North Carolina, 139 p.

——, 1988, Geologic map and descriptions of stratigraphy and structure of the west-central Grant Range, Nye County, Nevada: Geological Society of America Map and Chart Series MCH064, scale 1:12,000.

Gans, P. B., 1987, An open-system, two-layer crustal stretching model for the eastern Great Basin: Tectonics, v. 6, p. 1–12.

Gans, P. B., and Miller, E. L., 1983, Style of Mid-Tertiary extension in east-central Nevada, in Gurgel, K. D., ed., Geologic excursions in the overthrust belt and metamorphic core complexes of the Intermountain region: Utah Geological and Mineral Survey Special Studies 59, p. 107–160.

Gans, P. B., Miller, E. L., McCarthy, J., and Ouldcott, M. L., 1985, Tertiary extension faulting and evolving ductile-brittle transition zones in the northern Snake Range and vicinity; New insights from seismic data: Geology, v. 13, p. 189–193.

Gibbs, A. D., 1984, Structural evolution of extensional basin margins: Journal of the Geological Society of London, v. 141, p. 609–620.

Gleason, G. C., 1988, The structural geology of the east flank of the southern Grant Range, Nye County, Nevada [M.S. thesis]: Salt Lake City, University of Utah, 114 p.

Hose, R. K., and Danes, Z. F., 1973, Development of the late Mesozoic to early Cenozoic structures in the eastern Great Basin, in DeJong, K. A., and Scholten, R., eds., Gravity and tectonics: New York, John Wiley and Sons, p. 429–441.

Hyde, J. H., and Huttrer, G. W., 1970, Geology of the central Grant Range, Nevada: American Association of Petroleum Geologists Bulletin, v. 54, p. 503–521.

Jordan, T. E., and 5 others, 1983, Andean tectonics related to geometry of subducted Nazca plate: Geological Society of America Bulletin, v. 94, p. 341–361.

Kellogg, H. E., 1963, Paleozoic stratigraphy of the southern Egan Range, Nevada: Geological Society of America Bulletin, v. 74, p. 685–708.

Ketner, K. B., and Smith, J. F., Jr., 1974, Folds and overthrusts of Late Jurassic or Early Cretaceous age in northern Nevada: U.S. Geological Survey Journal of Research, v. 2, p. 417–419.

Kleinhampl, F. J., and Ziony, J. I., 1985, Geology of northern Nye County, Nevada: Nevada Bureau of Mines Bulletin 99A, 171 p.

Lund, K., and Beard, L. S., 1986, Structural history of the northern Grant Range, east-central Nevada; Overprinting of structural styles: Geological Society of America Abstracts with Programs, v. 18, p. 392.

Martin, M. W., 1987, The structural geology of the Worthington Mountains, Lincoln County, Nevada [M.S. thesis]: Chapel Hill, University of North Carolina, 112 p.

Miller, E. L., Gans, P. B., and Garing, J., 1983, The Snake Range décollement; An exhumed mid-Tertiary ductile-brittle transition: Tectonics, v. 2, p. 239–263.

Misch, P., 1960, Regional structural reconnaissance in central-northeast Nevada and some adjacent areas; Observations and interpretations, in Boettcher, J., and Sloan, W. W., Jr., eds., Guidebook to the geology of east-central Nevada: Intermountain Association of Petroleum Geologists 11th Annual Field Conference Guidebook, p. 17–42.

Moores, E. M., Scott, R. B., and Lumsden, W. W., 1968, Tertiary tectonics of the White Pine–Grant Range region, east-central Nevada, and some regional implications: Geological Society of America Bulletin, v. 79, p. 1703–1726.

Murray, M. E., 1985, Geology of the east-central Quinn Canyon Range, Nye County, Nevada [M.S. thesis]: Chapel Hill, University of North Carolina, 107 p.

Nakata, J. K., Wentworth, C. M., and Machette, M. N., 1982, Quaternary fault map of the Basin and Range and Rio Grande rift provinces, western United States: U.S. Geological Survey Open-File Report 82–579, scale 1:2,500,000.

Odé, H., 1958, Mechanical analysis of the dike pattern of the Spanish Peaks area, Colorado: Geological Society of America Bulletin, v. 68, p. 567–575.

Roberts, R. J., and Crittenden, M. D., Jr., 1973, Orogenic mechanisms, Sevier orogenic belt, Nevada and Utah, in De Jong, K. A., and Scholten, R., eds., Gravity and tectonics: New York, John Wiley and Sons, p. 409–428.

Roberts, R. J., Hotz, P. E., Gilluly, J., and Ferguson, H. G., 1958, Paleozoic rocks of north central Nevada: American Association of Petroleum Geologists Bulletin, v. 42, p. 2813–2857.

Royse, F., Warner, M. A., and Reese, D. L., 1975, Thrust belt structural geometry and related stratigraphic problems Wyoming-Idaho-Utah: Rocky Mountain Association of Geologists 1975 Symposium, p. 41–54.

Sainsbury, C. L., and Kleinhampl, F. J., 1969, Fluorite deposits of the Quinn Canyon Range, Nevada: U.S. Geological Survey Bulletin 1272–C, 22 p.

Sargent, K. A., and Houser, F. N., 1970, The Shingle Pass Tuff of central Nevada: Geological Society of America Abstracts with Programs, v. 2, p. 140–141.

Schmitt, J. G., and Vandervoort, D. S., 1987, Cretaceous through Eocene basin evolution in the hinterland of the Sevier orogenic belt, east-central Nevada: Geological Society of America Abstracts with Programs, v. 19, p. 833.

Smith, D. L., and Wright, J. E., 1988a, Mid- to Late-Cretaceous deformation and metamorphism in the hinterland of the Sevier orogenic belt, central Nevada: Geological Society of America Abstracts with Programs, v. 20, p. 233.

——— , 1988b, Late Cretaceous plutonism and associated deformation and metamorphism in central Nevada: Geological Society of America Abstracts with Programs, v. 20, p. A17.

Smith, J. F., and Ketner, K. B., 1977, Tectonic events since early Paleozoic in the Carlin–Pinon Range area, Nevada: U.S. Geological Survey Professional Paper 867–C, 18 p.

Snoke, A. W., Lush, A. P., 1984, Polyphase Mesozoic–Cenozoic deformational history of the northern Ruby Mountains–East Humbolt Range, Nevada, in Lintz, J., Jr., ed., Western geological excursions; Geological Society of America 1984 Annual Meeting Guidebook: Reno, University of Nevada Department of Geology, p. 232–260.

Speed, R. C., 1983, Evolution of the sialic margin in the central-western United States, in Watkins, J. S., and Drake, C. L., eds., Studies in continental margin geology: American Association of Petroleum Geologists Memoir 34, Hedburg Volume, p. 457–468.

Speed, R. C., Elison, M. W., and Heck, F. R., 1988, Phanerozoic history of the western Great Basin, in Ernst, W. G., ed., Metamorphism and crustal evolution, western United States; Rubey Volume 7: Englewood Cliffs, New Jersey, Prentice-Hall, p. 572–605.

Spencer, J. E., 1984, The role of tectonic denudation in the warping and uplift of low-angle normal faults: Geology, v. 12, p. 95–98.

Stewart, J. H., 1980, Regional tilt patterns of late Cenozoic basin-range fault blocks, western United States: Geological Society of America Bulletin, v. 91, p. 460–464.

Stewart, J. H., Stevens, C. H., and Fritsche, A. E., 1977, eds., Paleozoic paleogeography of the western United States: Los Angeles, California, Society of Economic Paleontologists and Mineralogists, Pacific Coast Paleogeography Symposium 1, 502 p.

Suppe, J., 1983, Geometry and kinematics of fault-bend folding: American Journal of Science, v. 283, p. 648–721.

Taylor, W. J., Bartley, J. M., Lux, D. R., and Axen, G. J., 1989, Timing of Tertiary extension in the Railroad Valley–Pioche Transect Nevada; Constraints from $^{40}Ar/^{39}Ar$ ages of volcanic rocks: Journal of Geophysical Research, M.A.L.E. special section (in press).

Tschanz, C. M., and Pampeyan, E. M., 1970, Geology and mineral deposits of Lincoln County, Nevada: Nevada Bureau of Mines Bulletin 73, 187 p.

Wernicke, B. P., 1981, Low-angle normal faults in the Basin and Range province; Nappe tectonics in an extending orogen: Nature, v. 291, p. 645–648.

Wernicke, B. P., and Axen, G. J., 1988, On the role of isostasy in the evolution of normal fault systems: Geology, v. 16, p. 848–851.

Woodcock, N. H., and Naylor, M. A., 1983, Randomness testing in three-dimensional orientation data: Journal of Structural Geology, v. 5, p. 539–548.

Wright, L. A., and Troxel, B., 1973, Shallow-fault interpretation of Basin and Range structure, southwestern Great Basin, in De Jong, K. A., and Scholten, R., eds., Gravity and tectonics: New York, John Wiley and Sons, p. 397–407.

Young, J. C., 1960, Structure and stratigraphy in the northern Schell Creek Range, in Boettcher, J., and Sloan, W. W., Jr., eds., Guidebook to the geology of east-central Nevada: Intermountain Association of Petroleum Geologists 11th Annual Field Conference Guidebook, p. 158–172.

MANUSCRIPT ACCEPTED BY THE SOCIETY AUGUST 21, 1989

Geological Society of America
Memoir 176
1990

Chapter 10

Shallow crustal deformation in the Pahranagat area, southern Nevada

A. S. Jayko
U.S. Geological Survey, MS 975, 345 Middlefield Road, Menlo Park, California 94025

ABSTRACT

The Pahranagat area lies in the Basin and Range Province of southern Nevada. Paleozoic rocks in the study area were folded and faulted during the Sevier orogeny and subsequently extended prior to deposition of Tertiary strata. Middle Oligocene strata overlie the Paleozoic rocks with pronounced angular unconformity and were deposited on rocks of Late Cambrian through Pennsylvanian age in the eastern part of the study area. Middle Oligocene and Miocene strata unconformably overlie lower Paleozoic and Precambrian strata in the western part of the study area.

In the eastern part of the study area, extension occurred prior to deposition of the middle Oligocene strata; the area was relatively stable between the middle Oligocene and latest Miocene, and there was renewed extension following the latest Miocene to present. There is a significant structural and stratigraphic break in Cenozoic rocks of the western part of the quadrangle where angular unconformities in the Tertiary section indicate extension continued intermittently during the late Oligocene and Miocene.

Faulting and folding that has formed the present Basin and Range topography of the study area is latest Miocene and/or younger in age. Fault scarps in alluvial deposits, active seismicity, and warm springs indicate the area is still tectonically active. The study area lies in a zone of northeast-southwest–trending structures characterized by structural, geophysical, and igneous trends that are referred to herein as the Escalante disrupted zone.

INTRODUCTION

Regional Setting

The study area (Fig. 1) lies within the Late Cretaceous and early Tertiary Sevier fold and thrust belt (Armstrong, 1968) and the Cenozoic Basin and Range Province (Gilbert, 1874, 1928). The area is underlain by a miogeoclinal section that ranges in age from Late Proterozoic to Pennsylvanian, a nonmarine clastic and volcanic section of middle Oligocene or older to late Miocene age, and alluvial deposits of Late Cenozoic age (Tschanz and Pampeyan, 1961, 1970; Ekren and others, 1977). Structures formed during at least three major tectonic events include folds and thrusts of Sevier age, pre- middle Oligocene normal faults and late Cenozoic—mainly latest Miocene to Holocene—normal faulting. The structures associated with the two earlier events are commonly obscured by the youngest extensional faulting. The Pahranagat area is seismically active, with numerous fault scarps in alluvial deposits.

The west half of the study area lies within the Nellis Air Force bombing and gunnery range. Most of the bombing range is presently inaccessible for geological investigations and can only be mapped in a reconnaissance fashion from aerial photographs. However, even this data base allows for refinement of previous, more regional studies.

This chapter summarizes the results of geological mapping and aerial photo interpretation (in restricted areas) of the Pahranagat 1° quadrangle, which will be published at 1:100,000 scale. Field studies were initiated in the spring of 1986, and work was carried out in the spring and fall of 1986 and 1987, and part of 1988. In addition, extensive aerial photo mapping in areas that have proved to be inaccessible due to military activities was

Jayko, A. S., 1990, Shallow crustal deformation in the Pahranagat area, southern Nevada, *in* Wernicke, B. P., ed., Basin and Range extensional tectonics near the latitude of Las Vegas, Nevada: Boulder, Colorado, Geological Society of America Memoir 176.

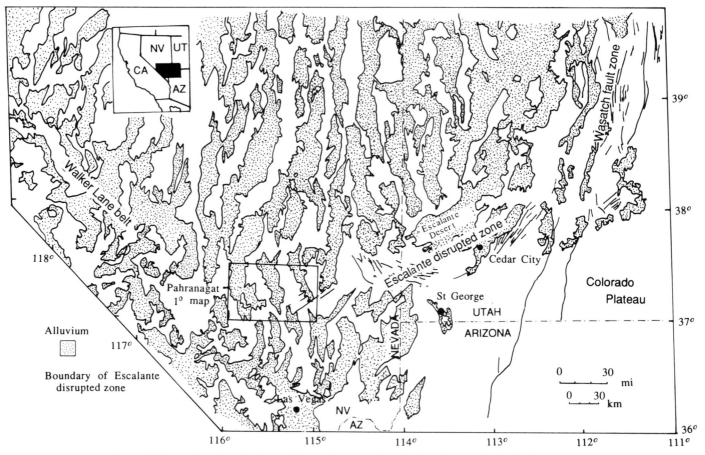

Figure 1. Map of southern Basin and Range Province showing distribution of alluvial deposits and bedrock and locations of Escalante disrupted zone, Walker Lane belt, and the Pahranagat ½ by 1° Quadrangle. Compiled from Stewart and Carlson, 1979; Hintze, 1980; Wilson and others, 1969.

conducted throughout the course of the study. The photo mapping was done on 1:31,680 scale natural color air photos and 1:,20,000, 1:40,000, and 1:60,000 black and white air photos.

Previous work

Previous studies within the Pahranagat area (Fig. 2) consisted of regional geological mapping at 1:250,000 and 1:200,000 and included the geology of Lincoln County (Tschanz and Pampeyan, 1961, 1970), the geology of southern Nye County (Cornwall, 1972), and geology of Tertiary rocks of Lincoln County (Ekren and others, 1977). Larger-scale mapping at 1:24,000 is restricted to the westernmost part of the quadrangle, which includes the eastern part of the Nevada Test site (Barnes and others, 1965; Byers and Barnes, 1967; Colton and Noble, 1967). Tertiary volcanic rocks within the northeast corner of the Pahranagat quadrangle have been mapped by Moring (1987).

The Paleozoic stratigraphy of the Upper Cambrian through Mississippian rock in the Pahranagat Range was studied by Reso (1963), and Late Proterozoic through Lower Ordovician strata in the Groom Range were studied by Barnes and Christiansen

(1967). The volcanic stratigraphy was studied by Dolgoff (1963); much of his stratigraphic nomenclature was revised by Ekren and others (1977) following earlier work by Cook (1965). Isotopic dating of volcanic rocks within the quadrangle is scant and consists of four determinations by Armstrong (1970) compiled in Ekren and others (1977). However, many other regionally extensive ash-flow tuff units that extend into the Pahranagat quadrangle have been dated (Marvin and others, 1970; Armstrong, 1972). Stratigraphic units used in this chapter are shown in Figure 3a and b.

TERTIARY STRATA

Tertiary clastic and volcanic rocks, principally ash-flow tuffs, unconformably overlie Paleozoic strata and are exposed in about a third of the Pahranagat Quadrangle (Fig. 4). Rocks of middle Oligocene and younger age in the eastern part of the quadrangle were relatively undisturbed until the latest Miocene, whereas those in the western part of the area were deposited synchronously with extensional deformation of Miocene and younger age.

Eastern section

The Tertiary section in the eastern part of the quadrangle is up to 1 km thick (Dolgoff, 1963). It includes a basal, red-weathering conglomerate that consists exclusively of clasts derived from the pre-Tertiary "basement" and lacks volcanic detritus. The conglomerate is locally overlain by limestone or by Oligocene to middle Miocene dacitic to rhyolitic ash-flow tuffs (Ekren and others, 1977). Basalt or basaltic andesite locally overlies the Harmony Hills, Hiko, and Kane Wash tuffs at various localities (general stratigraphic sequence and ages of units summarized in Fig. 3b).

The youngest basalt or basaltic andesite flows appear to have had a source area near the Kane Springs Wash caldera to the east (Novak, 1984), whereas the oldest may have flowed from the Bald Mountain volcanic center (Ekren and others, 1977) in the northwestern part of the quadrangle. Ekren and others (1977) suggested that extrusion of basalt or basaltic andesite flows was tectonically controlled by activity on the Pahranagat fault zone; however, the flows appear to be interlayered in a stratigraphic section that was not significantly disrupted along the Pahranagat fault zone until several million years after eruption of the flows—in the case of the oldest flows, about 10 m.y. following eruption. The youngest basaltic flows (unit Tb_3 of Figs. 3b and 9) at the southeastern edge of the quadrangle are faulted and openly folded, similar to the underlying volcanic strata, indicating that they were deposited prior to extension and lateral faulting in that area.

Several meter-thick deposits of reworked tuff, conglomerate, and very local lacustrine limestone are also interbedded within the volcanic section, recording erosion and sedimentation between eruptive events. The uppermost part of the Tertiary section is preserved only locally and consists of fine- to medium-grained alluvial deposits from thin (5 to 10 cm to 3 to 4 m) interbedded air-fall tuffs. Preliminary dating of tuffs from the upper part of this section suggests ages as young as 7.7 Ma (Jayko, Sarna-Wojcicki, and Meyers, unpublished data). The uppermost part of the Tertiary section is faulted out or covered. Although some tuff units pinch out locally within the section, it appears that there was no significant disruption of the section until after deposition of the 7.7-Ma tuff.

The distribution of Tertiary rocks in the eastern part of the quadrangle suggests low to moderate relief on the order of 1 km or less prior to deposition of the Tertiary section. The basal Tertiary(?) conglomerate and lacustrine limestone is broadly distributed in the southern part of the Pahranagat Range and northern part of the Sheep Range. The Tertiary(?) conglomerate is also present in large parts of the Jumbled Hills and Fallout Hills area (Tschanz and Pampeyan, 1970; Ekren and others, 1977). Successively younger ash-flow tuff units lap onto Paleozoic strata north

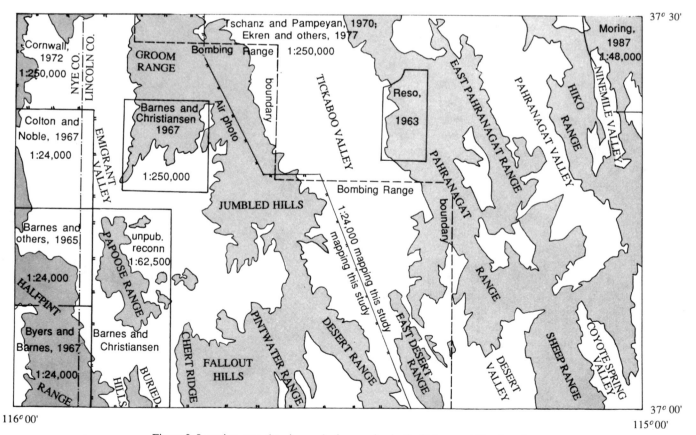

Figure 2. Location map showing geologic mapping in the Pahranagat Quadrangle.

and south of the present Pahranagat fault zone, suggesting that a localized, easterly trending basin occupied the area in the early Tertiary. East-west–trending early Tertiary paleovalleys that have a few hundred meters to a kilometer of relief have been reported farther east in eastern Nevada and southern Utah (Rowley and others, 1979; Best and others, 1987).

Western section

The Tertiary section in the western part of the quadrangle consists of a local basal conglomerate of probable middle Oligocene age, minor Monotony and Shingle Pass tuffs (see Fig. 3b for age of these units), that are overlain by middle Miocene and younger volcanic and clastic rocks (Barnes and others, 1965; Byers and Barnes, 1967; Marvin and others, 1970). The section includes the Monotony and Shingle Pass tuffs locally, the peralkaline Belted Range Tuff, which occurs very near the base of the section, the rhyolitic to latitic Paintbrush and Timber Mountain tuffs, which range in age from about 15 to 11 Ma (Marvin and others, 1970; Frizzel and Shulters, 1990), and basalt of late Tertiary age (Barnes and others, 1965; Byers and Barnes, 1967).

STRUCTURE

Features described in this section include structures that predate deposition of the Tertiary section, those that postdate deposition of most of the Tertiary section in the eastern part of the study area (Late Cenozoic structures), east-trending faults, and basins.

Structures that predate Tertiary strata

Structures that are unconformably overlain by Tertiary clastic and volcanic rocks (also referred to as sub-Tertiary structures) include thrust faults and folds that are probably related to the Late Cretaceous and early Tertiary Sevier orogeny (Tschanz and Pampeyan, 1970), as well as normal faults that are probably Tertiary in age.

Unambiguous compressional structures are present mainly in the eastern part of the quadrangle where they juxtapose Paleozoic strata. In the west-central part of the quadrangle (which is presently inaccessible due to military operations) unambiguous thrusts involve only the upper part of the Paleozoic section, principally Late Devonian and younger strata. Faults that juxtapose the older part of the section are permissibly either thrusts or normal faults and in some localities are more likely normal faults. In the western part of the quadrangle, low-angle faults previously mapped as thrust faults within the lower Paleozoic section (Barnes and others, 1965) are mainly normal faults.

Pahranagat and East Pahranagat Ranges. The four main sub-Tertiary structures in the Pahranagat and East Pahranagat Ranges are the East Pahranagat syncline, East Pahranagat fault, Badger Mountain fault, and Maynard Lake fault zone (Fig. 4). The East Pahranagat syncline is a compressional structure that probably formed during the Sevier orogeny.

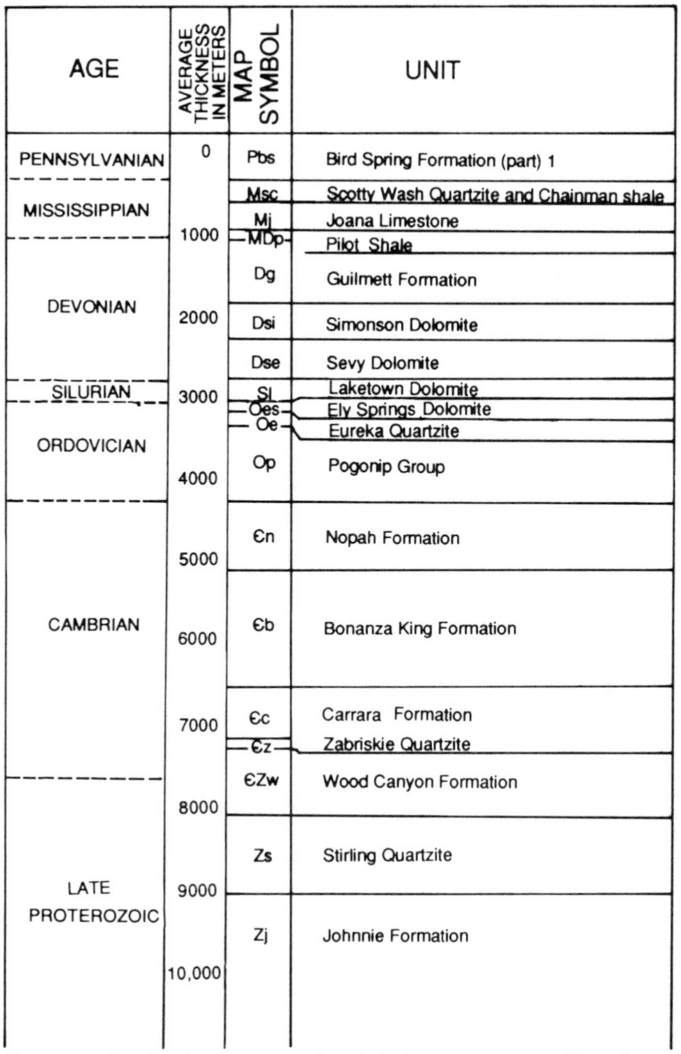

AGE	AVERAGE THICKNESS IN METERS	MAP SYMBOL	UNIT
PENNSYLVANIAN	0	Pbs	Bird Spring Formation (part) 1
MISSISSIPPIAN	1000	Msc	Scotty Wash Quartzite and Chainman shale
		Mj	Joana Limestone
		MDp	Pilot Shale
DEVONIAN	2000	Dg	Guilmett Formation
		Dsi	Simonson Dolomite
		Dse	Sevy Dolomite
SILURIAN	3000	Sl	Laketown Dolomite
		Oes	Ely Springs Dolomite
ORDOVICIAN		Oe	Eureka Quartzite
	4000	Op	Pogonip Group
	5000	Єn	Nopah Formation
CAMBRIAN	6000	Єb	Bonanza King Formation
	7000	Єc	Carrara Formation
		Єz	Zabriskie Quartzite
		ЄZw	Wood Canyon Formation
	8000	Zs	Stirling Quartzite
LATE PROTEROZOIC	9000	Zj	Johnnie Formation
	10,000		

Figure 3a. Pre-Tertiary stratigraphy of the Pahranagat area (from Reso, 1963; Barnes and Christiansen 1967; Tschanz and Pampeyan, 1970).

Both the East Pahranagat and Badger Mountain faults are interpreted as normal faults. The Maynard Lake fault zone is most likely a transfer fault or lateral ramp that was also active during Sevier time.

East Pahranagat syncline. The East Pahranagat syncline in the East Pahranagat Range was first mapped by Tschanz and Pampeyan (1970). It is a gently north-plunging, asymmetric fold with a gently west-dipping east limb and a steep to locally overturned west limb that involves rocks of Late Cambrian to Pennsylvanian age. The hinge of the fold is characterized by small-scale thrusts and east-verging overturned folds (Fig. 5a, b, and c); the Mississippian Joana Limestone is locally thrust over the Chainman Shale in the hinge. The youngest rocks exposed in the core of the fold belong to Pennsylvanian strata of the Bird Spring Formation, which are also the youngest exposed Paleozoic rocks in the Pahranagat Range (Fig. 4). Most of the east limb of

AGE		MAP SYMBOL	UNIT	APPROXIMATE TIME OF ERUPTION
QUATERNARY AND PLIOCENE		QTa	Alluvium	
MIOCENE	LATE	Ts	Sedimentary deposits	Alluvial deposits and interbedded tuffs
		Tb₃	Basalt or Basaltic Andesite	11 Ma (Novak; 1984)
	MIDDLE	Tk₃	Unit 3	
		Tk₂	Unit 2 Kane Wash Tuff	14 Ma (Novak, 1984)
		Tk₁	Unit 1	
	?	Tb₂	Basalt or Basaltic Andesite	
	EARLY	Th	Hiko Tuff	18-19 Ma (Armstrong, 1970; Noble and McKee, 1972)
		Tb₁	Basalt or Basaltic Andesite	
		Thh	Harmony Hills Tuff	20-21 Ma (Armstrong, 1970; Noble and McKee, 1972)
		Tpl	Pahranagat Lakes Tuff	22 Ma (Deino and Best, 1988)
		Tcc	Condor Canyon Tuff	22-23 Ma (Armstrong, 1970; Fleck and others, 1975
OLIGOCENE		Tlc	Leach Canyon Tuff	25 Ma (Armstrong, 1970)
		Tsp	Shingle Pass Tuff	26-27 Ma (Best, oral commun., 1988)
		Tm	Monotony Tuff	27 Ma (Armstrong, 1970; Marvin and others, 1970)
TERTIARY?		Tcl	Basal Conglomerate with limestone locally	

Figure 3b. Generalized Tertiary stratigraphy of the east half of the Pahranagat Quadrangle.

the fold is covered by Tertiary and Quaternary deposits. Three small areas of Paleozoic rocks exposed within the Pahranagat fault zone are inferred to lie along the east limb of the fold (Fig. 4). The west limb of the fold extends from the East Pahranagat Range to the Badger Mountain fault.

East Pahranagat fault. A major fault that truncates the west limb of the East Pahranagat syncline is inferred to underlie Tertiary and Quaternary cover in the East Pahranagat Range. This fault, the East Pahranagat fault, juxtaposes primarily Upper Devonian and Mississippian strata of the hinge area and east limb of the East Pahranagat syncline with Upper Cambrian through Mississippian strata of the west limb (Fig. 4). This fault is interpreted as an east-dipping normal fault, even though younger late Cenozoic west-dipping, down-to-the-west faults have reactivated this zone. Displacement along the East Pahranagat fault appears to die out to the north and increases to the south.

Badger Mountain fault. A prominent northwest-trending fault, here called the Badger Mountain fault, repeats the Upper Cambrian through Mississippian section in the central part of the Pahranagat Range (Fig. 6). This fault was interpreted as a thrust by Tschanz and Pampeyan (1970) and as a normal fault by Ekren and others (1977). Tertiary rocks are offset along the fault

zone; however, the Tertiary offset is minimal compared to the stratigraphic throw of the Paleozoic section. This sub-Tertiary structure is interpreted as a west-dipping normal fault for three reasons. First, the western block is characterized by numerous down-to-the-north normal faults that terminate at the Badger Mountain fault, a relation that results in a hanging wall broken by normal faults and a little-deformed footwall. Second, although a synclinal structure is present near Hancock Summit, the fold is cut by numerous normal faults. Small-scale folds and thrust ramps are not present, in contrast to the East Pahranagat Range area, suggesting the Hancock Summit syncline is a drag fold that formed by down-to-the-west displacement of the hanging wall (Fig. 6). Third, Burchfiel (1988) and Guth (1988) report that normal faults of the region to the south and west are characterized by prominent breccia zones, in contrast to thrust faults that commonly have sharper, cleaner contacts. The Badger Mountain fault is characterized by a major breccia zone, approximately 60 m wide. The larger normal fault zones in the Pahranagat area are also commonly accompanied by dolomitization of limestone in and near the faults.

In addition, the orientation of bedding in the footwall and hanging wall is not suggestive of a thrust fault. In a thrust inter-

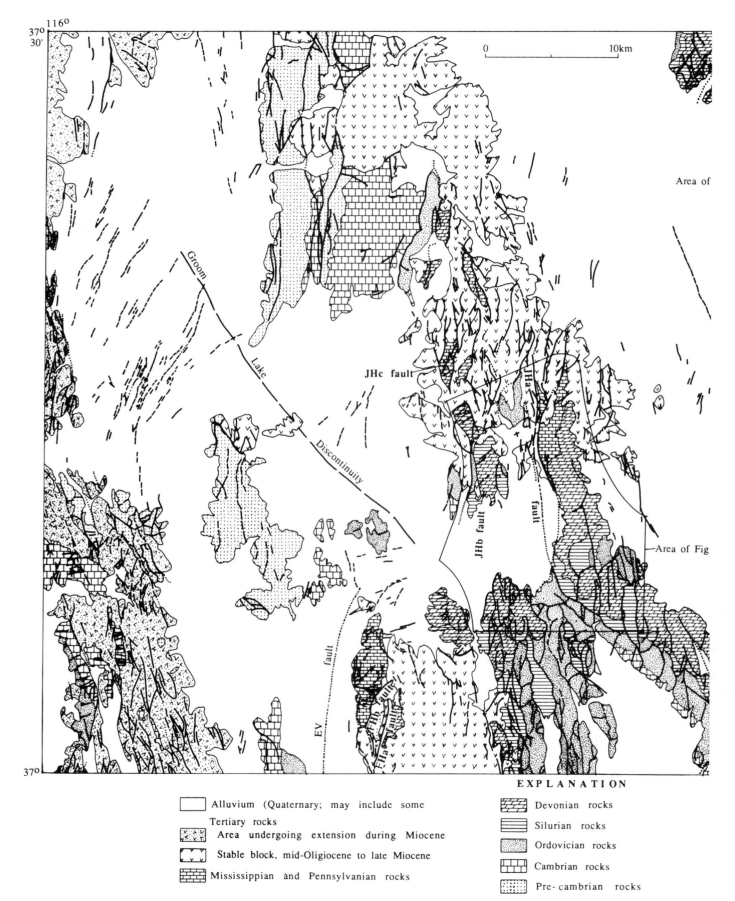

EXPLANATION

☐ Alluvium (Quaternary; may include some
   Tertiary rocks

▨ Area undergoing extension during Miocene

▨ Stable block, mid-Oligiocene to late Miocene

▨ Mississippian and Pennsylvanian rocks

▨ Devonian rocks

▤ Silurian rocks

▨ Ordovician rocks

▨ Cambrian rocks

▨ Pre-cambrian rocks

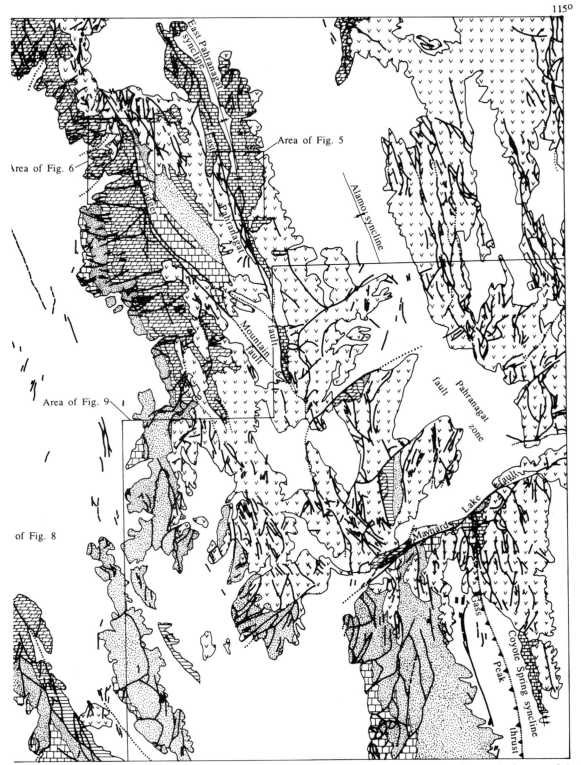

Figure 4. Generalized geologic map of the Pahranagat Quadrangle. Major sub-Tertiary structures in bold lines (1:24,000 scale mapping, this chapter, and modified from Tschanz and Pampeyan, 1970). Note abundant easterly trending faults north and west of the Pahranagat fault zone. Also shown is the general location of the Groom Lake Discontinuity between the different ages of the base of the Tertiary section, 30 Ma in the eastern part of the section and 14–16 Ma in the western part.

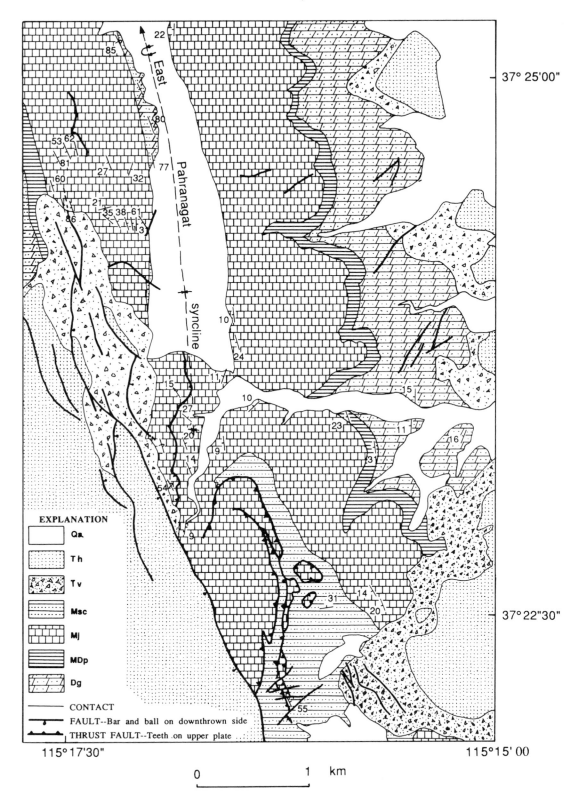

Figure 5. a. Geologic map of hinge of East Pahranagat syncline in East Pahranagat Range; 1:24,000 mapping this chapter, and after Reso (1963). See Figure 4 for location of map area. Qa = Alluvium (Quaternary); Th = Hiko Tuff (lower Miocene); Tv = Volcanic rocks (lower Miocene and upper Oligocene); MSc = Scotty Wash Quartzite and Chainman Shale undifferentiated (Mississippian; Mj = Joana Limestone (Mississippian); MD$_p$ = Pilot Shale (Mississippian and Devonian); Dg = Guilmette Formation (Devonian).

Figure 5c (above). Photograph of steep to overturned limb in the Joana Limestone from the hinge of the East Pahranagat syncline. View looking to south.

Figure 5b (left). Photograph of east-verging folds and related thrusts in the Joana Limestone from the hinge of the East Pahranagat syncline. View looking to south.

pretation the Paleozoic section in the hanging wall that is cut out toward the northwest would suggest a northwest-verging ramp emplaced on a footwall flat. An angular discordance of 40 to 60 degrees could be expected between hanging-wall and footwall strata where the ramp and flat are juxtaposed. In contrast, steronet plots of poles to bedding from the hanging wall and footwall are approximately concordant (Fig. 7).

The distribution of Tertiary strata also is generally consistent with a normal-fault interpretation. A basal Tertiary(?) conglomerate (discussed in the following section) is present on the west-southwest block (downthrown block with respect to a west-dipping normal fault) and not on the east block (which would be the upthrown block), suggesting a highland on the upthrown block during the time of conglomerate deposition.

Reso (1963), and subsequently Tschanz and Pampeyan (1970), described stratigraphic differences between the Paleozoic strata in the eastern and western parts of the Pahranagat Range, particularly with respect to the Pogonip Group and Pilot Shale. Reso (1963) noted that these differences could be ascribed to intervening normal faults. Layer-parallel normal faults and slickensides on bedding planes were observed in the Ordovician section on both sides of the Badger Mountain fault. Similarly, the Pilot Shale is reported to be considerably thicker in the east than on the west side of the Pahranagat Range. Structural thinning by normal faults was observed locally in the west near the Badger Mountain fault, whereas small-scale ramps and duplexes were observed in the Joana Limestone to the east and may occur

similarly within the Pilot. Therefore, the differences in stratigraphic thickness of some units do not necessarily require a thrust-fault interpretation for the Badger Mountain fault.

Maynard Lake fault zone. The Maynard Lake fault zone (Fig. 4) is the southernmost strand of the Pahranagat fault zone (Pahranagat shear system of Tschanz and Pampeyan, 1970), which is principally a zone of late Miocene to Holocene faulting; it is described more fully in the following section. The Maynard Lake fault zone is the only strand that appears to have some sub-Tertiary displacement. The basal Tertiary strata overlie the uppermost part of the Pogonip Group and erosional remnants of the Eureka Quartzite and very locally the Ely Springs Dolomite from the northeast corner of the Sheep Range and across the southwest part of the Pahranagat Range within the Pahranagat shear system (Fig. 4). Thus, similar Paleozoic strata were exposed north and south of the Maynard Lake fault zone in the southwestern part of the Pahranagat Range at the time of early Tertiary sedimentation. However, just a few kilometers to the east the basal Tertiary(?) conglomerate overlies Mississippian and upper Cambrian near the Gass Peak thrust south of the Maynard Lake fault zone and overlies late Ordovician through Devonian strata north of the Maynard Lake fault zone, suggesting there was a lateral ramp or possibly a transfer fault between the Gass Peak thrust and East Pahranagat syncline in this vicinity prior to Tertiary sedimentation.

Northern Sheep Range. The most prominent sub-Tertiary structure in the northern Sheep Range is the northern part of the

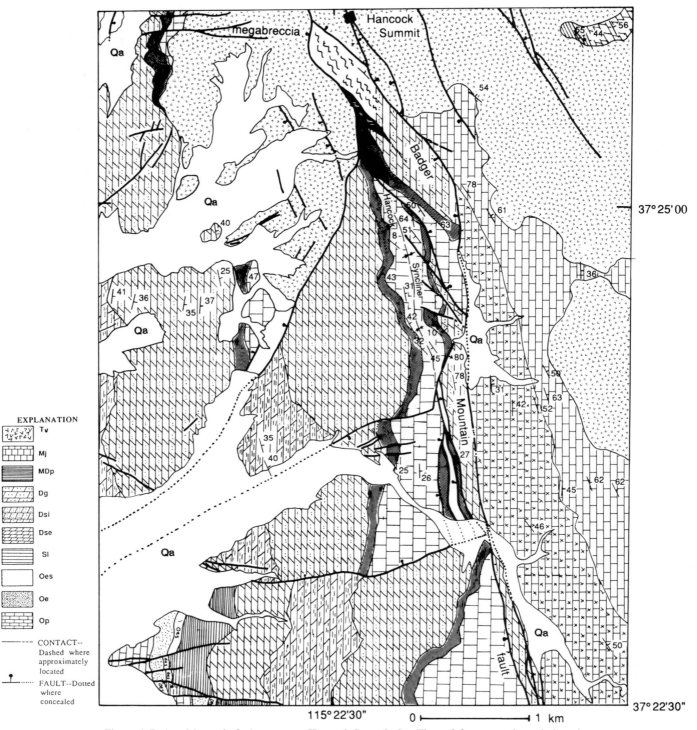

Figure 6. Badger Mountain fault zone near Hancock Summit. See Figure 3 for map-unit symbols and Figure 4 for location of map area. Other map-unit symbols used in this figure are: Qa, Quaternary alluvium; Tv, Tertiary volcanic rocks undifferentiated.

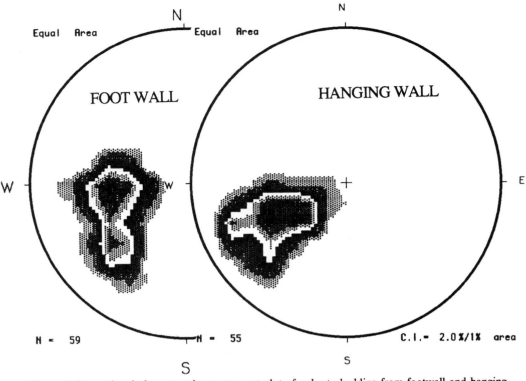

Figure 7. Lower hemisphere, equal area steronet plot of poles to bedding from footwall and hanging wall of the Badger Mountain fault. Contour interval 2 percent per 1 percent area.

Gass Peak thrust (Longwell, 1926), which is exposed in the hills just north of Coyote Spring Valley. An overturned syncline is present to the east (Tschanz and Pampeyan, 1970). A small-scale, east-directed thrust fault with west-facing ramps occurs within the upper part of the Bonanza King Formation on the west side of the Sheep Range but it is too small to show at the scale of Figure 4. These compressional structures probably formed during Sevier deformation.

Gass Peak thrust. The Gass Peak thrust (Longwell, 1926, 1945; Guth, 1981) is inferred to lie under alluvial cover along much of the northeast flank of the Sheep Range (Longwell and others, 1965; Tschanz and Pampeyan, 1970). The lowest stratigraphic unit exposed in the upper plate in this area is the upper part of the Banded Mountain Member of the Cambrian Bonanza King Formation, which is juxtaposed with lower-plate rocks consisting of the Pilot Shale, Mississippian limestone units, and the Bird Spring Formation. In the northernmost and topographically lowest part of the Sheep Range, the Gass Peak thrust is obscured by down-to-the-west, late Cenozoic normal faults, although very small, flat-lying klippen of dolomite and quartzite are preserved locally above the upper Paleozoic strata.

Coyote Spring syncline. An overturned, east-verging syncline, the Coyote Spring syncline, was mapped in Pennsylvanian strata on the northeastern flank of the northern Sheep Range by Tschanz and Pampeyan (1970). The axis of the fold plunges gently southward. Small-scale thrust faults are also present in the

upper Paleozoic strata. The east limb of the fold dips roughly 20° west, and the west limb dips moderately to steeply west.

Groom Range. Conjugate small-scale thrust faults and folds are present within the middle part of the Cambrian section, in particular within the Carrara Formation, in the south-central part of the Groom Range. These structures were observed on 1:36,180 scale air photos but are too small to show at the scale of Figure 4.

Jumbled Hills. At least three prominent sub-Tertiary structures are present in the Jumbled Hills area. They are here labeled, from east to west, JHa, JHb, and JHc (Fig. 8) due to the lack of geographic names in this area. Numerous late Cenozoic normal faults are present in the area; however, as in the Pahranagat area the displacement of Tertiary strata along the late Cenozoic faults is much less than the stratigraphic throw of the Paleozoic units. The sub-Tertiary faults are buried under middle Oligocene (or older) strata.

The Chainman Shale is juxtaposed against the Pogonip Group along the JHA fault. The JHa fault is interpreted as a normal fault with down-to-the-east-southeast displacement. The Ordovician rocks west of the fault presently dip 20 to 30° east (Tschanz and Pampeyan, 1970), and the Mississippian and older strata to the east of the fault dip gently west. Restoring 50 to 20° of late Cenozoic tilting of the Oligocene and Miocene rock decreases the dip of the inferred footwall strata, and the inferred hanging wall becomes steeply west-dipping, which is consistent

A. S. Jayko

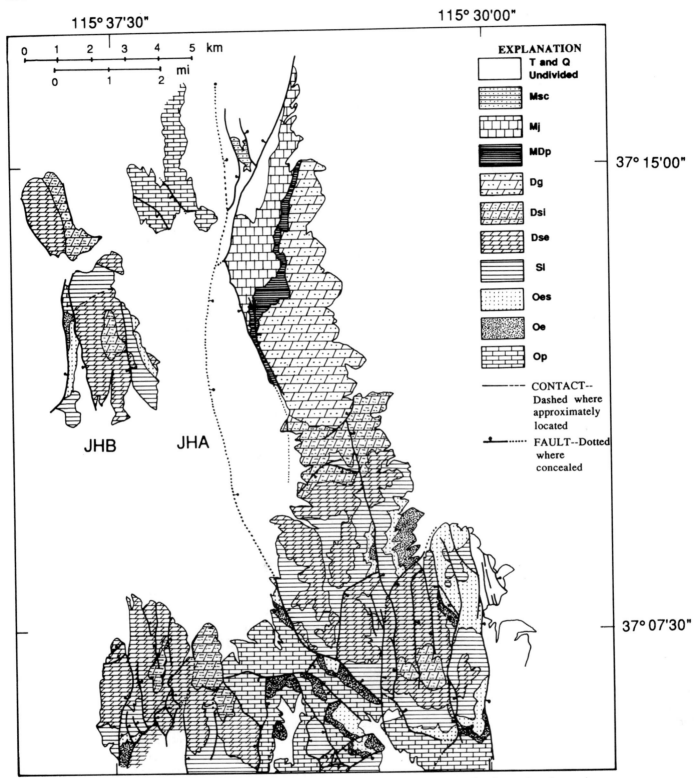

Figure 8. Map of the Jumbled Hills, northern Desert, and Pintwater ranges showing preferred tectonic interpretation of the JHA fault, an east-dipping normal fault that connects east-dipping normal faults in the Desert Range. See Figure 3b for map-unit symbols used in this figure; other map-unit symbol used here is T and Q, Tertiary cover rocks, undivided. Mapped from 1:36,180 color and 1:40,000 black and white air photos and modified from Tschanz and Pampeyan (1970).

with an east-dipping normal fault. The inferred hanging-wall rocks, where exposed near the footwall, are flat lying and lack any sign of folding or imbricate thrusting where observed on aerial photos. The hanging-wall rocks become highly extended toward the south. The JHa fault could conceivably connect with down-to-the-east faults of the northern Desert Range (Fig. 8).

About 4 km to the west of JHa, Tschanz and Pampeyan (1970) mapped a fault with apparent down-to-the-west displacement that is in most places covered by lower Tertiary deposits. A late Cenozoic down-to-the-west normal fault obscures the relations, but here again the stratigraphic throw of the Paleozoic section across the JHb fault suggests an older fault that is also a sub-Tertiary structure.

The fault labeled JHc (Fig. 4) appears to be a thrust fault that emplaces Devonian strata on Mississippian strata and is therefore probably of Sevier age (Tschanz and Pampeyan, 1970). Upper Devonian strata are thrust over Carboniferous and Permian strata elsewhere in the vicinity. For example, in the Timpahute Range to the north, the Guilmette Formation is thrust over the Chainman Shale and undivided Pennsylvanian and Permian strata, and in the northern part of the Spotted Range to the south, the Guilmette Formation is thrust over Mississippian limestone and the Chainman Shale (Tschanz and Pampeyan, 1970).

Fallout Hills. In Chert Ridge, along the western part of the Fallout Hills and adjacent Emigrant Valley area, Tschanz and Pampeyan (1970) mapped a block of east-dipping Proterozoic and Cambrian strata between east-dipping Mississippian strata on the west and west-dipping Upper Devonian strata on the east (Fig. 4). The faults that bound the Proterozoic and Cambrian block are labeled FHa and FHb (east to west). A fault labeled EV is inferred to lie west of the Mississippian and Upper Devonian strata.

East-dipping Cambrian and Precambrian rocks are juxtaposed against the west-dipping Guilmette Formation along the FHa fault. The structural significance of this block of Cambrian and Precambrian rocks is problematic. The strata could represent a down-thrown block from the upper plate of a thrust, an extensional window, or a slide block in the Tertiary clastic section that is faulted down against Mississippian and Devonian strata. The Cambrian and Precambrian rocks are on strike with remnants of the Spotted Range thrust plate that lies to the south (Guth, 1981), suggesting that these rocks have been down-dropped by normal faults against the Mississippian and Devonian from a structurally higher thrust plate. The basal Tertiary(?) conglomerate unconformably overlies the fault block or is only offset a minor amount along reactivated(?) normal faults near the margins of the block, indicating that most of the offset predates the late Cenozoic extensional activity.

The contact between the Cambrian and Ordovician strata of the Papoose Range and the Mississippian strata of the Chert Ridge area is buried beneath alluvium of the Emigrant Valley (Fig. 4). Limited exposures in this area suggest a series of down-to-the-east normal faults with a few hundred meters of offset. The block west of Chert Ridge includes Lower Cambrian through Lower Devonian strata (Tschanz and Pampeyan, 1970) that are attenuated by normal faults. Mississippian strata are faulted down against Devonian strata at the north end of Chert Ridge. It is conceivable that the structure here is analogous to the northernmost Desert Range (discussed below) and consists of horsts and grabens rather than a major thrust fault (for example, see Wernicke and others, 1988a, b). However, a lack of access and limited exposures preclude a more definitive interpretation.

Pintwater and Desert Ranges. The northernmost part of the Pintwater and Desert Ranges are characterized by numerous, northerly striking normal faults that juxtapose rocks primarily of Ordovician through Lower Devonian age. There is no evidence of thrust faulting in these ranges at this latitude. Tertiary strata are faulted down against the eastern and western flanks of this area on mainly late Cenozoic faults. Some of the faulting in this area may be sub-Tertiary if the correlation of the JHa fault is correct.

Halfpint Range. 1:24,000-scale map of the Halfpint Range (Barnes and others, 1965; Byers and Barnes, 1967) suggests that the lower Paleozoic strata were highly extended prior to deposition of the Miocene strata. However, the Tertiary section is only about 16 to 14 m.y. old or younger here (Marvin and others, 1970; Carr and others, 1986), in contrast to older strata in the eastern part of the Pahranagat Quadrangle. Barnes and others (1965) show west-dipping Precambrian and Lower Cambrian strata that are cut by flat-lying faults that place younger rocks on older. The low-angle faults restore to steeper, south-southeast-dipping normal faults after untilting late Cenozoic deformation. The older low-angle faults and Tertiary strata are cut by late Neogene and Quaternary high-angle normal faults.

Late Neogene and Quaternary structures

Late Cenozoic structures include abundant east- and west-dipping, north-striking, high-angle normal faults, northeast-striking normal and strike-slip faults, rollovers, monoclinal flexures, drag folds, and large basins. Northeast-trending, generally synclinal drag folds are prominent within the Pahranagat fault zone, a zone of dominantly left-lateral displacement (Tschanz and Pampeyan, 1970). Less obvious rollovers and monoclinal flexures occur along some of the north-trending high-angle faults (Figs. 9 and 10).

Pahranagat fault zone. The Pahranagat fault zone (Pahranagat shear system of Tschanz and Pampeyan, 1970) trends about N50°E and is about 12.5 km wide and 40 km long, extending east of the study area (Figs. 4 and 9). The fault zone generally forms the boundary between an actively extending area to the north and a previously extended area to the south. Liggett and Ehrenspeck (1974) and Wernicke and others (1984) first suggested that the Pahranagat fault zone is a tear fault that connects large-scale normal faults in the Dry Lake and Delamar valleys with the Desert Valley.

Three major N50°E-trending faults constitute the Pahranagat fault zone in the Pahranagat Quadrangle. From south to north they are the Maynard (Menard) Lake, Buckhorn, and Arrowhead

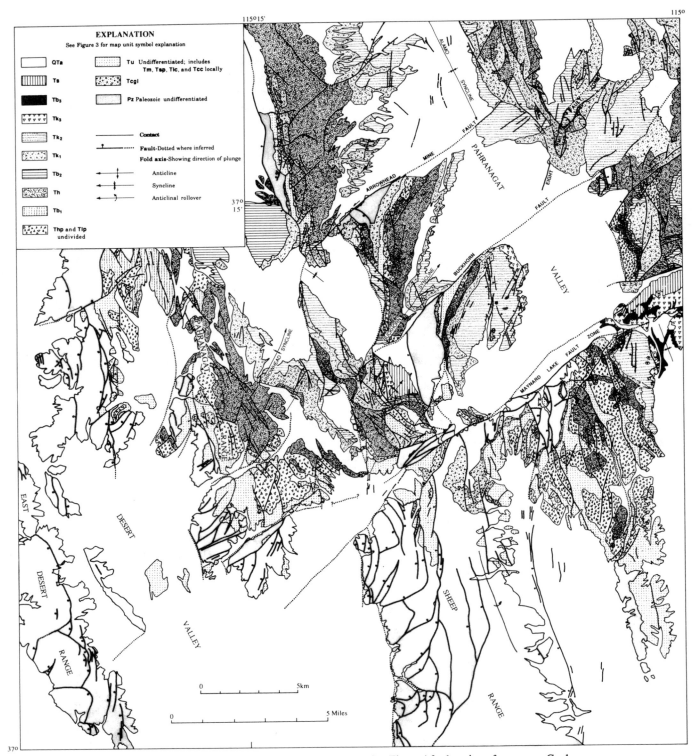

Figure 9. Generalized map of the Pahranagat fault zone. See Figure 4 for location of map area. Geology compiled from unpublished 1:100,000 scale mapping and this chapter and modified from Ekren and others (1977).

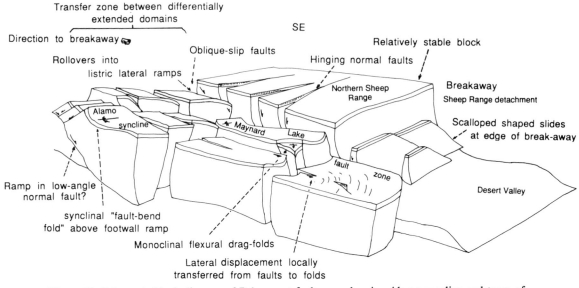

Figure 10. Schematic block diagram of Pahranagat fault zone showing Alamo syncline and types of structures, including left-lateral displacement, rollovers into north-dipping listric lateral faults, hinging normal faults, and monoclinal flexural drag folds.

Mine faults (Tschanz and Pampeyan, 1970, p. 83). These faults are generally steeply northwest-dipping, oblique-slip faults with a major component of dip-slip as well as left-lateral strike-slip displacement (Tschanz and Pampeyan, 1970; Ekren and others, 1977) (Fig. 9). Both Tschanz and Pampeyan (1970) and Liggett and Ehrenspeck (1974) estimated on the order of 9 to 16 km of displacement on the fault zone. South-southeast of the Pahranagat Valley, the Tertiary strata roll over gently toward the south into the major splays of the Pahranagat fault zone, suggesting that the faults are listric to the north.

The three major faults of the Pahranagat fault zone terminate just east of the Desert Range (Figs. 4 and 9). Although a few easterly trending faults are present in the East Desert Range, none have any significant lateral displacement. There is no evidence that the Arrowhead Mine, Buckhorn, or Maynard Lake faults continue to the west through the Paleozoic strata of the Desert Range or northern Pintwaters (see Fig. 4). The Spotted Range fold and thrust belt (Tschanz and Pampeyan, 1970), which involves Upper Devonian and Mississippian rocks, most likely continues to the north into the Chert Ridge area, where imbricate thrusting of the Upper Mississippian strata is evident on air photos, and into the Jumbled Hills area, where Devonian strata are thrust over the Mississippian, rather than correlating with the East Pahranagat syncline as previously suggested.

The middle Oligocene to upper Miocene strata that occur in the Pahranagat fault zone do not appear to have been significantly disrupted until after 7.7 Ma (Jayko, Sarna-Wojcicki, and Meyers, unpublished data), which is the youngest age obtained from interbedded tuffs and alluvial deposits that overlie the volcanic section. Fault scarps in alluvial deposits at the north end of the Sheep Range, as well as active seismicity (U.S. Geological Survey unpublished data) in the area, indicte Quaternary activity

of at least the Maynard Lake fault zone. Fault scarps also cut alluvial deposits north of the Arrowhead Mine fault.

Arrowhead Mine fault. The Arrowhead Mine fault is about 15 km long (Figs. 9 and 11). It appears to merge at its east end with east-dipping normal faults and die out toward the west in a syncline here referred to as the Arrowhead syncline. Down-dip displacement across the fault is greatest in the Pahranagat Valley area, with at least 0.5 km displacement inferred from offset Tertiary strata. Lateral displacement on the fault is on the order of 2 km, if the west-dipping normal faults that bound Paleozoic and Tertiary strata north and south of the Arrowhead Mine fault are correlative. A syncline in the Pahranagat Valley (described below) also appears to be offset across the Arrowhead Mine fault and is far less well defined south of the fault, suggesting synchronous development of the syncline and the Arrowhead Mine fault.

Nine Mile fault zone. A diffuse north 20 to 30° east-trending zone of faults splays off to the northeast from the Buckhorn fault. This fault zone forms the boundary between a structural domain dominated by east-dipping normal faults that lies north of the fault and east of the Pahranagat Valley and a structural domain dominated by west-dipping normal faults that lies south of the fault (Fig. 11).

Buckhorn fault. The Buckhorn fault is approximately 20 to 25 km long. Like the Arrowhead Mine fault, it also seems to have a hinge in the west with greater dip-slip displacement toward the axis of the Pahranagat Valley. The fault appears to merge into north-striking normal faults east of the Pahranagat Valley and it dies out into a complex zone of faults and gentle warps to the west. A pronounced faulted anticline-syncline pair occurs in Tertiary strata north and south of the fault in the Pahranagat Range. Tertiary strata in the blocks north and south of the fault generally

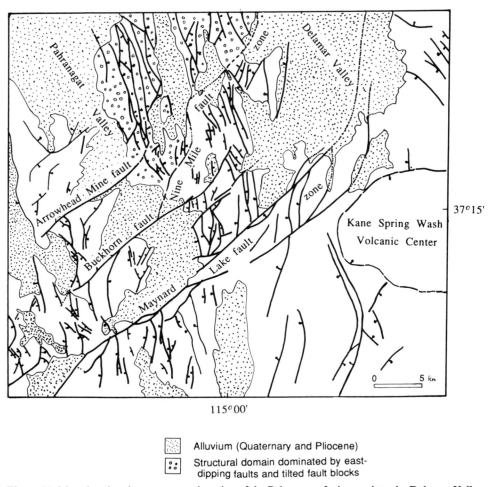

Figure 11. Map showing the eastern continuation of the Pahranagat fault zone into the Delamar Valley area. Also shown are domains of east- versus west-dipping faults. Compiled from Tschanz and Pampeyan (1970) and unpublished 1:100,000 scale mapping, this chapter.

dip southeast except in the hinge area of the folds. The folds probably initiated as monoclinal flexures that were simultaneously tilted and subsequently faulted. Additional tightening of the folds may have resulted from left-slip on the Buckhorn fault. In the Pahranagat Range, a minimum of 1 to 2 km of left-lateral displacement is suggested from offset faults, and as much as 2 to 5 km if most of the tilting of the Tertiary strata was prior to lateral displacement.

Maynard Lake fault zone. The Maynard Lake fault zone (Fig. 11) is the broadest and most continuous strand of the Pahranagat fault zone and is itself a fault zone that consists of multiple splays. It forms the structural boundary of the northern part of the Sheep Range and the southern part of the Pahranagat Valley and Pahranagat Range. It is approximately 40 km long and up to 4 km wide. Late Cenozoic displacement on the fault between the Pahranagat Range and northern Sheep Range can be inferred from the distribution of the Tertiary(?) conglomerate, which appears to pinch out stratigraphically in the western part of the Sheep Range. The conglomerate does not occur in the western part of the Pahranagat Range north of the Maynard Lake

fault zone, suggesting that the relative displacement across the fault in this area is not more than 5 to 6 km. Similarly, unit Tb3, the youngest basalt that overlies the Kane Wash Tuff in this area, may be offset a few kilometers within the Maynard Lake fault zone, but it does not occur to the west on the north of the fault. Instead, upper Miocene alluvial deposits that contain basalt clasts overlie the Kane Wash Tuff to the west. However, as the blocks both south and north of the fault are tectonically extended, the total displacement across the fault may be greater. Restoring the Paleozoic strata across the Maynard Lake fault zone is more difficult in light of earlier, probably Sevier-age, displacement.

Although left-lateral displacement appears to be the dominant lateral component, right-slip displacement probably also occurred during normal faulting and extension of the northern Sheep Range if the blocks are decoupled at depth (Fig. 12a). A small, relatively tight anticline occurs on the footwall of the Maynard Lake fault zone (see Figs. 9 and 14). The small hook occurs directly adjacent to the fault and at the end of a very broad open synclinal warp. This is interpreted as having formed in response to minor right-lateral slip following monoclinal folding

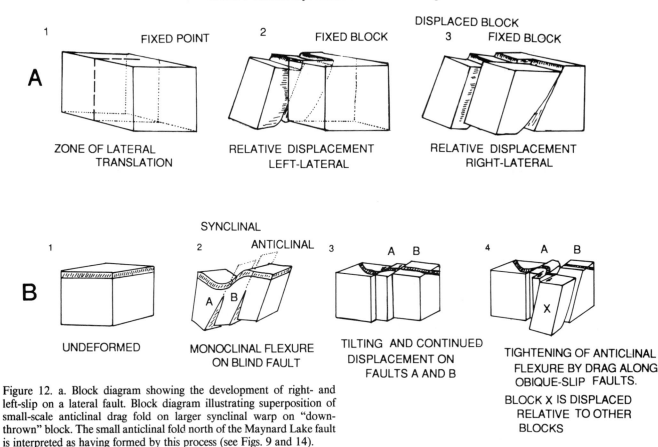

Figure 12. a. Block diagram showing the development of right- and left-slip on a lateral fault. Block diagram illustrating superposition of small-scale anticlinal drag fold on larger synclinal warp on "downthrown" block. The small anticlinal fold north of the Maynard Lake fault is interpreted as having formed by this process (see Figs. 9 and 14).

(Fig. 12b). Faulted monoclinal flexures are also present along the Maynard Lake fault zone, as is warping that is probably associated with drag due to lateral faulting. The monocline appears to be more steeply east tilted north of the Maynard Lake fault zone than south of it, indicating that some of the tilting was coincident with lateral faulting.

Fault-bend folds and blind normal faults. Most of the prominent folds within the Pahranagat fault zone are northeast plunging and trend roughly N35°E. A few monoclinal flexures also trend about N20° to 30°W, subparallel to the dominant trend of the normal faults. The folds probably were initiated as monoclinal flexures that formed over deeper-seated, blind normal faults and are a type of fault-bend fold or drag fold (Hamblin, 1965) (Fig. 13). As would be expected, synclinal flexures are typical of the footwall, and anticlinal flexures of the hanging wall, of fault-bend folds, whereas anticlinal rollovers occur in the footwalls of listric normal faults (Hamblin, 1965). These folds are probably subsequently tightened by drag folding associated with the lateral component of displacement within the Pahranagat fault zone.

Exhumed low-angle(?) normal fault. A prominent northwest-striking normal fault (fault X, Fig. 14) that is displaced across the Pahranagat fault zone may have been exhumed along

the southernmost extensional window of Paleozoic rocks exposed north of the Maynard Lake fault zone. Tertiary strata north of fault X dip as much as 50° to the north. Small-scale normal faults and lateral ramps in the Tertiary strata root into fault X. Paleozoic rocks south of (structurally below?) fault X consist of a megabreccia, within which Silurian and Devonian(?) strata are transported westward. The general stratigraphic succession within the megabreccia appears to be intact, though highly disrupted. Fault X is truncated by a high-angle normal fault (fault Y, Fig. 14). The basal Tertiary(?) conglomerate that unconformably overlies Paleozoic strata east of fault X^1 and south of fault X is cut out along fault X, although Tertiary(?) conglomerate in the wash that runs along the fault, near fault Y, suggests that there could have been a small sliver of conglomerate present in the fault zone. Fault X gradually cuts upsection to the east through the Tertiary strata from near the base of the Needles Range Group and interbedded limestone to the Kane Wash Tuff. Thus, X and X^1 are inferred to form the slide and end boundaries of a scoop-shaped fault. This low-angle(?) normal-fault interpretation of fault X is arguable; however, due to the proximity of the Maynard Lake fault zone, left-lateral displacement of Paleozoic strata within the extensional window would also transport younger Paleozoic strata westward.

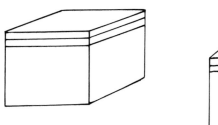

Figure 13. Block diagram illustrating development of a fault-bend fold above a blind normal fault.

East-trending faults

Faults that strike about N75°E occur north of the Pahranagat fault zone and are common in Paleozoic strata of the western Pahranagat Range and Halfpint Range; a few are present in the Jumbled Hills area (Fig. 4). In the Pahranagat Range the east-striking faults occur in the hanging wall of the Badger Mountain fault, a sub-Tertiary structure. In the Halfpint Range, east-trending faults are cut by northerly striking normal faults that displace Tertiary and younger strata and are at least locally overlain by middle Miocene and younger Tertiary strata (Barnes and others, 1965; Byers and Barnes, 1967). Reinterpretation of mapping by Barnes and others (1965) suggests that the Paleozoic strata were extended prior to deposition of upper Tertiary strata. In the Jumbled Hills area, the east-striking faults also appear to be older than and cut by north-striking faults. These relations suggest the east-trending faults formed earlier in the region, prior to initiation of the Pahranagat fault zone.

A few east-striking fault scarps were observed in alluvial deposits at the south end of Emigrant Valley, within a generally east-trending basin. Although these faults have the same strike as faults in the Pahranagat fault zone, they do not disrupt strata in the Desert Range.

Basins

The three main structural troughs in the area are the Pahranagat Valley, Tickaboo-Desert Valleys, and the Emigrant Valley–Papoose Lake trough. The Tertiary rocks in the central part of Pahranagat Valley are gently folded into a broad synclinal warp—the Alamo syncline—that is truncated by the Arrowhead Mine fault to the south, and is cut by a north-trending, west-dipping normal fault to the north. The axis of the syncline is also faulted. The fold probably formed in response to drag along a footwall ramp on a major west-dipping detachment fault that surfaces on the east side of the Delamar Valley (Figs. 10 and 11). Alluvial fill in the valley appears to be fairly shallow, as Tertiary rocks are nearly continuously exposed across parts of it. Normal faults in the Pahranagat Range to the west are dominantly down-to-the-east.

The Tickaboo-Desert Valley basin is a much broader feature that has a pronounced gravity low (Jachens and others, 1985).

Alluvial fill rests on a principally east-tilted block with a major range-front fault zone that runs down the east side of the valley. Tertiary strata in ranges both east and west of the valley are principally east-dipping. Fault scarps that cut alluvial deposits are scattered throughout the valley.

The Emigrant Valley–Papoose Lake trough is a broad feature that is more segmented than Tickaboo-Desert Valley. North- and northeast-trending scarps in alluvial deposits are abundant in the northern part of the valley. A few easterly trending scarps are present to the south. Tertiary strata west of the trough are nearly flat lying to very gently east dipping. East- and west-dipping faults are about equally represented in adjacent ranges.

Groom Lake discontinuity

A major structural and stratigraphic domain boundary of Tertiary age separates predominantly middle Miocene and younger strata of the Nevada Test site area to the west from the middle Oligocene and younger strata of the Pahranagat area to the east. The domain boundary passes northwesterly through the Emigrant Valley area and possibly part of the Jumbled Hills and is here referred to as the Groom Lake discontinuity (Fig. 4). West of the Groom Lake discontinuity, Tertiary volcanic and volcaniclastic rocks that date from 16 to 14 Ma and later rest unconformably on Paleozoic strata, whereas east of it the base of the Tertiary section is much older (approximately 30 Ma at a minimum). The Paleozoic strata in the Halfpint Range west of the discontinuity were disrupted by extensional faulting (reinterpreted from Barnes and others, 1965) prior to deposition of the middle Miocene strata.

DISCUSSION

Timing of deformation

Tertiary strata rest with pronounced angular unconformity on folded Paleozoic strata of Late Cambrian through Pennsylvanian age. Many sub-Tertiary structures, thrust faults, and folds, probably formed during the Sevier orogeny; however, several major faults that are overlain by Tertiary strata are interpreted as normal faults; these include the Badger Mountain, JHa, JHb, FHa, and FHb faults. Pre–middle Oligocene normal faulting had not previously been recognized in this area, although it recently has been reported to the north near Pioche (Bartley and others, 1988; Axen, 1988b).

A generally conformable Tertiary(?) and Tertiary section that consists primarily of a local basal Tertiary(?) conglomerate overlain by ash-flow tuffs, flows, and minor clastic rocks that range in age from approximately 30 to 8 Ma suggests that, following the middle Oligocene, there was only very little or no tectonic disruption in the east half of the study area until development of the present Basin-Range faulting. There are no major alluvial deposits or major angular unconformities in the Tertiary section from the eastern part of the study area that would suggest

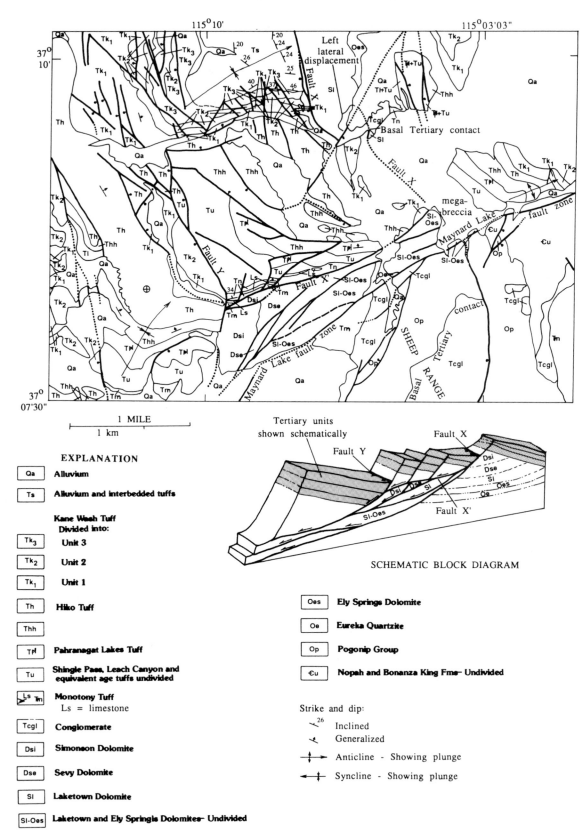

EXPLANATION

Qa	Alluvium
Ts	Alluvium and interbedded tuffs

Kane Wash Tuff
Divided into:

Tk₃	Unit 3
Tk₂	Unit 2
Tk₁	Unit 1
Th	Hiko Tuff
Thh	
Tpl	Pahranagat Lakes Tuff
Tu	Shingle Pass, Leach Canyon and equivalent age tuffs undivided
Ls Tm	Monotony Tuff Ls = limestone
Tcgl	Conglomerate
Dsi	Simonson Dolomite
Dse	Sevy Dolomite
Sl	Laketown Dolomite
Sl-Oes	Laketown and Ely Springs Dolomites- Undivided

Oes	Ely Springs Dolomite
Oe	Eureka Quartzite
Op	Pogonip Group
€u	Nopah and Bonanza King Fms- Undivided

Strike and dip:

- ⚲²⁶ Inclined
- ⚲ Generalized
- ＋→ Anticline - Showing plunge
- ←＋ Syncline - Showing plunge

SCHEMATIC BLOCK DIAGRAM

Figure 14. Map showing the locations of fault X, an exhumed low-angle(?) normal fault, fault X's, and fault Y and a schematic block diagram. See Figure 3a and 3b for description of map units. Geology from unpublished 1:24,000 mapping, this study.

that large-scale basins, on the order of magnitude of those forming today, developed in the Pahranagat area after the middle Oligocene and prior to the latest Miocene and/or Pliocene.

The time of initiation of extensional faulting within this relatively stable block is not precisely known, as the top of the conformable Tertiary section is not preserved or, if preserved, is not exposed. The uppermost part of the preserved Tertiary section consists of fine-grained sedimentary rocks that contain interbedded air-fall and water-worked tuffs that are tentatively correlated with tuffs that range from 9.9 to 7.7 Ma (Jayko, Sarna-Wojcicki, and Meyer, unpublished data). These alluvial deposits could have formed on the distal flanks of the large volcanic edifices associated with the nearby caldera complexes or at the distal edges of an incipient fault-bounded basin.

The Groom Lake discontinuity is interpreted as a boundary between structural domains that locally extended at different times in the eastern and western parts of the Pahranagat area. Within the Pahranagat area the western part was apparently deforming and developing basins in middle Miocene time, whereas the eastern part was relatively stable. Guth and others (1988) describe sedimentologic evidence for active extensional faulting south of the Pahranagat area during middle Miocene time, which is consistent with the timing of deformation-basin development from the western part of the Pahranagat Quadrangle (Barnes and others, 1965; Barnes and Christiansen, 1967). This discontinuity supports the contention that extensional deformation is domainal.

Bartley and others (1988) have reported that extensional deformation occurred prior to 32 Ma and episodically until the Quaternary north of the study area. In particular, they describe extension older than 31.3 Ma, between 30 and 25 Ma, between 18.8 and later than 14 Ma, and late Miocene(?) to Quaternary. Three of these extensional episodes are also represented in the Pahranagat area to one extent or another. Pre–middle Oligocene (30 Ma) extension is inferred from the Jumbled Hills, Fallout Hills, and northwestern Pahranagat Range, where Tertiary conglomerate and/or Monotony tuff unconformably overlie faults that are herein interpreted as normal faults. The 30- to 25-Ma extension that Bartley and others (1988) describe has not been recognized. Ash-flow tuffs of this age range seem to be conformable with the underlying section in the Pahranagat, Groom, and northern Sheep Ranges. The third episode that Bartley and others (1988) report (18.9 to younger than 14 Ma) may be expressed in the western part of the quadrangle, west of the Groom Lake discontinuity, as discussed above. However, this episode is not evident in the eastern part of the quadrangle where the 18- to 19-Ma Hiko tuff appears to be conformably overlain by the approximately 14-Ma Kane Wash tuff. The youngest episode, which in the Pahranagat area appears to be very latest Miocene or possible Pliocene to Quaternary, is also strongly expressed in the Pahranagat area. The youthful aspect of the most recent deformation is evident from prominent fault scarps in alluvial deposits in Tickaboo and Pahranagat Valleys and the northernmost part of the Desert Lake Valley.

The extensional history south of the Pahranagat area is reportedly largely of Miocene age (Guth and others, 1988); however, the "older basin deposits" of Guth and others (1988), which lie in the Spotted Range and Buried Hills, were previously mapped by Tschanz and Pampeyan (1970) as correlative with the basal Tertiary conglomerate that underlies Monotony tuff in the Groom Range area. These "older basin deposits" are lithologically similar to the basal mid-Oligocene or older conglomerate of the Jumbled Hills and northern Sheep Range in that they contain well-rounded clasts of Paleozoic and/or Precambrian detritus, lack volcanic detritus, and are dark red weathering. These conglomerates overlie structures with inferred normal displacement in the Fallout Hills area and also to the south in the Spotted Range (Guth and others, 1988), suggesting that the oldest mid-Oligocene or older episode of extension is also present to the south of the Pahranagat area (also see the section on correlation of thrusts).

The "younger basins" of Guth and others (1988), which are in part 14 to 16 m.y. old and younger, include 14- to 15-Ma megabreccia deposits that are interpreted as gravity-slide deposits, which suggests that the area was tectonically active at the time (Guth and others, 1988). This deformational episode is generally the same age as inferred for the area west of the Groom Lake discontinuity.

Late Cenozoic structures

The Alamo syncline is interpreted as overlying a footwall ramp and to have formed as a fault-bend fold above a detachment fault. The detachment fault may have a breakaway along the eastern edge of the Delamar and Dry Lake Valleys (Wernicke and others, 1984). Displacement appears to be transferred from this detachment to the Sheep Range detachment along the Pahranagat fault zone (Guth, 1981; Wernicke and others, 1984). East- and west-tilted domains of fault blocks occur within the Pahranagat fault zone and are bounded by strike-slip faults. Although left-slip displacement is the dominant sense of offset within the Pahranagat fault zone, some strike-slip faults have likely experienced both right and left sense of displacement as extension progressed step-wise across the area.

A major escarpment formed by a west-dipping normal fault bounds the east side of Tickaboo Valley, which like the Delamar and Dry Lake valleys, is characterized by a large negative gravity anomaly and Quaternary faulting. Depending on the model of preference, this escarpment could also be the breakaway to a detachment fault. The structure of Tickaboo Valley contrasts with the Pahranagat Valley to the east, which appears to have little alluvial fill and to have a general synclinal form.

East-trending structures

The study area lies near the intersection of two broadly diffuse zones of deformation: the Walker Lane belt (Stewart, 1980, 1988) and a zone, herein referred to as the Escalante zone, that extends southwestward from the Wasatch fault zone and is characterized by abundant easterly trending structures.

Easterly trending features of several types, including mineral belts (Butler and others, 1920; Hilpert and Roberts, 1964; Roberts, 1966; Shawe and Stewart, 1976), gravity anomalies (Cook and Montgomery, 1974), magnetic anomalies (Stewart and others, 1977; Ekren and others, 1977), topographic lineaments (Ekren and others, 1976), and igneous belts (Stewart and others, 1977; Rowley and others, 1978; Best and others, 1987; Best, 1988) have long been recognized within the Great Basin. Easterly trending features that have been described north and east of the Pahranagat area include the Pioche mineral belt (Roberts, 1966; Shawe and Stewart, 1976), the Timpahute lineament (Ekren and others, 1976, 1977), the Delamar mineral belt (Shawe and Stewart, 1976), the Blue Ribbon lineament (Rowley and others, 1978), and the Pioche-Marysvale igneous belt (Best and others, 1987). The location of many of these features, including seismic and magnetic lineaments, has previously been described for an area east and northeast of the Pahranagat Quadrangle (Rowley and others, 1987). Shawe and Stewart (1976) showed that the Pahranagat area lies within the general trend of the Pioche mineral belt. The term *Escalante zone* is used here for the broad zone of geographic, geologic, and geophysical features that trends southwest from the Wasatch fault zone into the Pahranagat area and probably terminates at the Walker Lane (Fig. 1). The disrupted zone is named after a large, prominent, easterly trending basin that lies in the eastern part of the zone (Fig. 1).

The Escalante zone generally parallels the northwest border of the Colorado Plateau but also extends well to the west of the western margin of the plateau, where it is characterized by a pronounced gravity gradient (Jachens and others, 1985), with a general gravity high south of the zone. Prominent structural features within the Escalante zone are generally localized, discontinuous, and domainal, similar to the blocky nature of the Walker Lane (Stewart, 1988). In addition to the linear fractures noted by earlier workers, the Escalante zone is characterized by the general southern termination of northerly trending basins and ranges of central Nevada, the easterly and westerly trending morphology and faults that are at an oblique angle to the basin and ranges to the north, and a zone of active seismicity previously referred to as part of the Intermountain seismic belt (Smith and Sbar, 1974).

Part of the Escalante zone generally parallels much older structural trends, including the eastern edge of the Sevier orogenic belt, which in turn appears to be structurally controlled by the Paleozoic shelf edge (Hunt, 1956; Gilluly, 1963; Hintze, 1973). On a regional scale, the zone also mimics the general northern limit of exposed Precambrian basement (Bennett and DePaolo, 1987). It is therefore likely, as has been speculated previously, that the Escalante zone reflects a fundamental, deep-seated crustal boundary (Stewart and others, 1977; Rowley and others, 1978).

The Pahranagat fault zone is a discontinuous, northeast-trending set of structures that lie within the Escalante zone. The Pahranagat fault zone appears to be a tear fault that in part relays displacement between the Dry Lake–Delamar and Desert valleys (Wernicke and others, 1984) (Fig. 11). The large escarpments along the east sides of the Delamar and Desert valleys have been interpreted as breakaway zones to major west-dipping detachment faults (Wernicke and others, 1984; Guth, 1988; Axen, 1988a, b).

Correlation of thrusts

Wernicke and others (1988a, b) infer that three Mesozoic structural levels bounded by major thrust faults occur within the Pahranagat Quadrangle (37°00″–37°30′ and 115°00″–116°00′ latitudes are mislabeled on their Fig. 5). These were referred to as: (m) rocks above the Marble Canyon thrust and west-vergent White Top Mountain backfold/thrust system, (c) rocks above the Clery thrust and below the Marble Canyon thrust, and (w) rocks above the Wheeler Pass system (Gass Peak thrust). Although the locations of the thrust faults/systems in the Pahranagat area are not critical to constraining the amount of extension inferred by Wernicke and others (1988a, b) from the Las Vegas–Death Valley area, the inferred location of thrusts and correlation of some structural levels are not well constrained and in some cases are mislocated, with the exception of part of the Wheeler Pass system (Gass Peak thrust).

Part of the (c) structural level of Wernicke and others (1988a, b) is shown as an isolated thrust plate in the central part of the Pahranagat Range; however, this plate continues eastward across the Pahranagat Range and is folded around the East Pahranagat syncline; thus, the central and eastern part of the Pahranagat Range are part of the same structural levels. Silurian strata that lie in the east limb of the Pahranagat syncline within the Pahranagat fault zone have thicknesses typical of the (w) plate. The bounding fault shown as a thrust in Wernicke and others (1988a, b) on the west side of the (c) plate in the Pahranagat Range (the Badger Mountain fault) is interpreted as a middle Oligocene or older normal fault, reactivated by late Tertiary or Quaternary normal faults.

A thrust fault that juxtaposes the (c) and (m) structural levels is inferred to pass through the Halfpint Range, between the Papoose Range and Chert Ridge, and between the northern part of the Pintwater Range and the Jumbled Hills. The geology does not strongly support such an interpretation. Thrust faults were originally mapped in the Halfpint Range by Barnes and others (1965); however, as their cross section implies, these low-angle faults all show a normal sense of offset and juxtapose mainly the lower member of the Bonanza King Formation with the underlying Carrara Formation. If the 15 to 20 degrees of Tertiary tilting is removed, the apparent thrust faults become generally south-southeast, shallow-dipping normal faults that are of pre–middle Miocene age.

Cambrian to Devonian rocks are exposed in the northern Pintwater Range, and Cambrian to Mississippian in the Jumbled Hills (Fig. 4). Structural relations in the Pintwater Range, which is well exposed relative to the Jumbled Hills, clearly indicates that Devonian strata are juxtaposed against Ordovician strata along normal faults (Fig. 7). Similar stratigraphic levels are also juxtaposed in the Jumbled Hills but in addition include rocks as young as Mississippian. Generally equivalent structural levels are exposed along strike in a north-south orientation between the Jumbled Hills and Pintwater Range, parallel to the strike of the normal faults exposed in the northern Pintwater and Desert Ranges (Tschanz and Pampeyan, 1970; Stewart and Carlson, 1979), suggesting that these faults continue under the alluvial cover into the Jumbled Hills. Some of these faults are overlain by middle Oligocene (or older(?) strata).

Similarly, a small block of Cambrian and Precambrian rock occurs in the eastern part of Chert Ridge and Cambrian and lower Ordovician rocks occur in the southwestern part of the Jumbled Hills. These early Paleozoic rocks are faulted against Mississippian and Silurian strata. The early Paleozoic rocks are on strike with a similar early Paleozoic block that occurs to the south in the Spotted Range (Tschanz and Pampeyan, 1970; Stewart and Carlson, 1979). Guth and others (1988) also recognize that extensional faulting occurred along the margins of an early Paleozoic block in the Spotted Range; however, they infer that the extensional faults are in part reactivated thrusts. If the early Cambrian rocks simply represent the basal part of the (c) structural level, then reactivated thrust is not required to bound these blocks. To summarize, most of the Paleozoic rocks of the Pahranagat Quadrangle belong to the (w) structural level as defined by Wernicke and others (1988a, b). Rocks that are lower plate with respect to the (w) level occur only in the southeasternmost part of the quadrangle below the Gass Peak thrust (Fig. 4). Rocks that are upper plate to the (w) structural level occur in the Chert Ridge area.

There is, however, a significant horizon of thrust faulting within Mississippian and Devonian strata of the study area that is also evident to the north in the Timpahute Range and to the south in the Spotted Range (see Tschanz and Pampeyan, 1970). This thrust fault (or faults) generally places the Devonian Guilmett Formation on top of Mississippian or younger strata. Mississippian strata are also locally imbricated by thrust faults in the Chert Ridge area (Jayko, unpublished data).

CONCLUSIONS

The Pahranagat area experienced a protracted history of extensional faulting during the Tertiary that continues today. There is evidence that extensional deformation began prior to the middle Oligocene, was active in the middle Miocene in the western part of the quadrangle, and active throughout the area from the latest Miocene or early Pliocene to the present. The apparent absence of middle Miocene deformation in the eastern part of the quadrangle suggests that the extension was domainal, with fairly large stable blocks preserved locally. The latest, shallow-level deformation is characterized by mainly high-angle normal faults (approximately 50° or more), whereas some of the older normal faults that are in part covered by Tertiary rocks are flatter lying (for example in the Halfpint Range), suggesting that the shallower fault dips could be related to rotation due to younger faulting and tilting as has been suggested elsewhere in the Basin and Range. Strike-slip faulting within the Pahranagat fault zone was also accompanied by folding of Tertiary strata. These folds are generally broad, open structures.

The Pahranagat fault zone did not become active until the latest Miocene or perhaps the early Pliocene (7.7 Ma or later), as suggested by the youngest deposits near the top of the conformable Tertiary section. The fault zone is interpreted as a transfer fault that accommodates extension (connects detachment faults) between the Delamare–Dry Lake Valleys and the Desert Valley, as suggested by previous workers (Liggett and Ehrenspeck, 1974; Wernicke and others, 1984). This fault is also part of the Death Valley normal-fault system described by Wernicke and others (1988 a, b).

The detachment that is inferred to lie on the east side of the Desert Valley, the Sheep Range detachment of Guth (1981), Wernicke and others (1984), and Guth and others (1988), has been interpreted as becoming active in the middle Miocene based on the age of small syntectonic basins to the south (Guth, 1981; Guth and others, 1988). If the younger timing of activity suggested from the Pahranagat fault zone also indicates timing of activity on the associated faults that it is accommodating, then the Sheep Range fault (or detachment) is probably also younger than 7.7 Ma. The basins that indicate middle Miocene deformation to the south are mainly bounded by the Wild Horse Pass fault (Guth, 1981; Guth and others, 1988). These relations suggest that deformation along the Sheep Range fault (detachment) may be younger than the middle Miocene extension along the Wild Horse Pass fault.

ACKNOWLEDGMENTS

I wish to thank Peter Guth, Dave Miller, Earl Pampeyan, Charles Tschanz, and Brian Wernicke for constructive comments on earlier versions of this paper. I also benefited from discussions with Mike D. Carr, Gary Dixon, Peter Guth, and Earl Pampeyan throughout the course of the field studies. Greg Eiche, Sue Culton, Paula Noble, and Leslie Ames ably assisted with fieldwork at various times.

REFERENCES CITED

Armstrong, R. L., 1968, Sevier orogenic belt in Nevada and Utah: Geological Society of America Bulletin, v. 79, p. 429–458.

—— , 1970, Geochronology of Tertiary igneous rocks, eastern Basin and Range province, western Utah, eastern Nevada, and vicinity, U.S.A.: Geochimica et Cosmochimica Acta, v. 34, p. 203–232.

—— , 1972, Low-angle (denudation) faults, hinterland of the Sevier orogenic belt, eastern Nevada and western Utah: Geological Society of America Bulletin, v. 83, p. 1729–1754.

Axen, G. J., 1988a, Tertiary detachment faulting in the Pioche area, Lincoln County, Nevada: Geological Society of America Abstracts with Programs, v. 20, p. 140.

—— , 1988b, Tertiary extensional and volcanic history of the Condor Canyon (CC) area: Geological Society of America Abstracts with Programs, v. 20, p. 140.

Barnes, H., and Christiansen, R. L., 1967, Cambrian and Precambrian rocks of the Groom district, Nevada, southern Great Basin: U.S. Geological Survey Bulletin 1244–G, p. G1–G34.

Barnes, H., Christiansen, R. L., and Byers, F. M., Jr., 1965, Geologic map of the Jangle Ridge Quadrangle, Nye and Lincoln Co., Nevada: U.S. Geological Survey Quadrangle Map GQ–363, scale 1:24,000.

Bartley, J. M., Axen, G. J., Taylor, W. J., and Fryxell, J. E., 1988, Cenozoic tectonics of a transect through eastern Nevada near 38°N latitude, *in* Weide, D. L., and Faber, M. L., eds., This extended land; Geological journey in the southern Basin and Range; Geological Society of America Cordilleran Section Field Trip Guidebook: University of Nevada Geoscience Department Special Publication 2, p. 1–20.

Bennett, V. C., and DePaolo, D. J., 1987, Proterozoic crustal history of the western United States as determined by Neodymium isotopic mapping: Geological Society of America Bulletin, v. 99, p. 647–685.

Best, M. G., 1988, Easterly trending Oligocene to Early Miocene (30–20 Ma) Paleotopography and other geologic features, southeastern Great Basin: Geological Society of America Abstracts with Programs, v. 20, p. 143.

Best, M. G., and Grant, K. S., 1987, Oligocene and Miocene volcanic rocks in the central Pioche–Marysvale igneous belt, western Utah and eastern Nevada: U.S. Geological Survey Professional Paper 1433–A, p. 3–28.

Best, M. G., Mehnert, H. H., Keith, J. D., and Naeser, C. W., 1987, Oligocene and Miocene volcanic rocks in the central Pioche–Marysvale igneous belt, western Utah and eastern Nevada: U.S. Geological Survey Professional Paper 1433–B, p. 29–47.

Burchfiel, B. C., 1988, Cenozoic extensional modification of the Mesozoic thrust belt, Clark Mountains, southeastern California and southern Spring Mountains, southern Nevada: Geological Society of America Abstracts with Programs, v. 20, p. 147.

Butler, B. S., Loughlin, G. F., Heikes, V. C., and others, 1920, The ore deposits of Utah: U.S. Geological Survey Professional Paper 111, 672 p.

Byers, F. M., Jr., and Barnes, H., 1967, Geologic map of the Paiute Ridge Quadrangle, Nye and Lincoln Counties, Nevada: U.S. Geological Survey Quadrangle Map GQ–577, scale 1:24,000.

Carr, W. J., Byers, F. M., and Orkild, P. P., 1986, Stratigraphic and volcanic-tectonic relations of Crater Flat Tuff and some older volcanic units; Nye County, Nevada: U.S. Geological Survey Professional Paper 1323, 28 p.

Christiansen, R. L., Lipman, P. W., Orkild, P. P., and Byers, F. M., Jr., 1965, Structure of the Timber Mountain caldera, southern Nevada, and its relation to range structure: U.S. Geological Survey Professional Paper 525–B, p. B43–B48.

Colton, R. B.,. and Noble, D. C., 1967, Geologic map of the Groom Mine Southwest Quadrangle, Nye and Lincoln Counties, Nevada: U.S. Geological Survey Quadrangle Map GQ–719, scale 1:24,000.

Cook, E. F., 1965, Stratigraphy of Tertiary volcanic rocks in eastern Nevada: Nevada Bureau of Mines Report 11, 69 p.

Cook, K. L., and Montgomery, J. R., 1974, Crustal structure and east-west

transverse structural trends in eastern Basin and Range province as indicated by gravity data: Geological Society of America Abstracts with Programs, v. 6, p. 158.

Cornwall, H. R., 1972, Geology and mineral deposits of southern Nye County, Nevada: Nevada Bureau of Mines and Geology Bulletin 77, 49 p.

Deino, A. L., and Best, M. G., 1988, Use of High-precision single-crystal $^{40}Ar/Ar^{39}$ ages and TRM data in correlation of an ash-flow deposit in the Great Basin: Geological Society of America Abstracts with Programs, v. 20, p. A397.

Dolgoff, A., 1963, Volcanic stratigraphy of the Pahranagat area, Lincoln County, southeastern Nevada: Geological Society of America Bulletin, v. 74, p. 875–900.

Ekren, E. B., Bucknam, R. C., Carr, W. J., Dixon, G. L., and Quinlivan, W. D., 1976, East-trending structural lineaments in central Nevada: U.S. Geological Survey Professional Paper 986, 16 p.

Ekren, E. B., Orkild, P. P., Sargent, K. A., and Dixon, G. L., 1977, Geologic map of Tertiary rocks, Lincoln County, Nevada: U.S. Geological Survey Miscellaneous Investigations Series, Map I–1041, scale 1:250,000.

Frizzell, V. A., and Shulters, J. C., 1990, Geologic Map of the Nevada Test Site: U.S. Geological Survey, scale 1:100,000 (in press).

Gilbert, G. K., 1874, 100th Meridian progress report 1872: U.S. Geographical and Geological Survey, 50 p.

—— , 1928, Studies of Basin-Range structure: U.S. Geological Survey Professional Paper 153, 92 p.

Gilluly, J., 1963, The tectonic evolution of the western United States: Quarterly Journal of the Geological Society of London, v. 119, p. 133–174.

Guth, P. L., 1981, Tertiary extension north of the Las Vegas Valley shear zone, Sheep and Desert Ranges, Clark County, Nevada: Geological Society of America Bulletin, v. 92, p. 763–771.

—— , 1988, Superposed Mesozoic thrusts and Tertiary extension, northwestern Clark County, Nevada: Geological Society of America Abstracts with Programs, v. 20, p. 165.

Guth, P. L., Schmidt, D. L., Deibert, J., and Yount, J. C., 1988, Tertiary extensional basins of northwestern Clark County, Nevada, *in* Weide, D. L., and Faber, M. L., eds., This extended land; Geological journeys in the southern Basin and Range; Geological Society of America Field Trip Guidebook Cordilleran Section Meeting: University of Nevada at Las Vegas Geoscience Department Special Publication 2, p. 239–254.

Hamblin, W. K., 1965, Origin of "reverse drag" on the downthrown side of normal faults: Geological Society of America Bulletin, v. 76, p. 1145–1164.

Hilpert, L. S., and Roberts, R. J., 1964, Economic geology, *in* U.S. Geological Survey, Mineral and water resources of Utah: Utah Geological and Mineralogical Survey Bulletin 73, p. 28–38.

Hintze, L. F., 1963, Geologic history of Utah: Provo, Utah, Brigham Young University Geology Studies, v. 29, pt. 3, p. 1–181.

—— , 1980, Geologic map of Utah: Utah Geological and Mineralogical Survey Map, scale 1:500,000.

Hunt, C. B., 1956, Cenozoic geology of the Colorado Plateau: U.S. Geological Survey Professional Paper 279, 99 p.

Jachens, R. C., Simpson, R. W., Blakely, R. J., and Saltus, R. W., 1985, Isostatic residual gravity map of the United States: National Geophysical Data Center Map, scale 1:2,500,000.

Liggett, M. A., and Ehrenspeck, H. E., 1974, Pahranagat Shear System, Lincoln County, Nevada: U.S. National Aeronautics and Space Administration Report CR–136388, 10 p.

Longwell, C. R., 1926, Structural studies in southern Nevada and western Arizona: Geological Society of America Bulletin, v. 37, p. 551–584.

—— , 1945 Low-angle normal faults in the Basin and Range province: EOS Transactions of the American Geophysical Union, v. 26, p. 107–118.

Longwell, C. R., Pampeyan, E. H., and Bowyer, B., 1965, Geology and mineral deposits of Clark County, Nevada: Nevada Bureau of Mines Bulletin 62.

Marvin, R. F., Byers, F. M., Mehnert, H. H., Orkild, P. P., and Stern, P. W., 1970, Radiometric ages and stratigraphic sequence of volcanic and plutonic rocks, southern Nye and western Lincoln Counties, Nevada: Geological Society of America Bulletin, v. 81, p. 2657–2676.

Moring, B. M., 1987, Geologic map of the south Pahroc Range, Lincoln County, Nevada: U.S. Geological Survey Miscellaneous Field Studies Map MF–1917, scale 1:48,000.

Noble, D. C., and McKee, E. H., 1972, Description and K-Ar ages of volcanic units of the Caliente volcanic field, Lincoln County, Nevada, and Washington County, Utah: Isochron-West, no. 5, p. 17–24.

Novak, S. W., 1984, Eruptive history of the rhyolitic Kane Springs Wash volcanic center, Nevada: Journal of Geophysical Research, v. 89, p. 8603–8615.

Reso, A., 1963, Composite columnar section of exposed Paleozoic and Cenozoic rocks in the Pahranagat Range, Lincoln County, Nevada: Geological Society of America Bulletin, v. 74, p. 901–918.

Roberts, R. J., 1966, Economic geology, in U.S. Geological Survey mineral and water resources of Nevada: U.S. 88th Congress, 2nd session, Senate Document 87, p. 39–48.

Rowley, P. D., Lipman, P. W., Mehnert, H. H., Lindsey, D. A., and Anderson, J. J., 1978, Blue Ribbon lineament, an east-trending structural zone within the Pioche mineral belt of southwestern Utah and eastern Nevada: U.S. Geological Survey Journal of Research, v. 6, p. 175–192.

Rowley, P. D., Steven, T. A., Anderson, J. J., and Cunningham, C. G., 1979, Cenozoic stratigraphic and structural framework of southwestern Utah: U.S. Geological Survey Professional Paper 1149, 22 p.

Shawe, D. R., and Stewart, J. H., 1976, Ore deposits as related to tectonics and magmatism, Nevada and Utah: American Institute of Mining, Metallurgia, and Petroleum Engineers Transactions, v. 260, p. 225–232.

Smith, R. B., and Sbar, M. C., 1974, Contemporary tectonics and seismicity of the western United States with emphasis on the Intermountain seismic belt: Geological Society of America Bulletin, v. 85, p. 1205–1218.

Stewart, J. H., 1980, Regional tilt patterns of late Cenozoic basin-range fault blocks, western United States: Geological Society of America Bulletin, v. 91, p. 460–464.

——, 1988, Tectonics of the Walker Lane belt, western Great Basin; Mesozoic and Cenozoic deformation in zone of shear, in Ernst, W. G., ed., Metamorphic and crustal evolution of the western United States, Rubey Volume 7: Englewood Cliffs, New Jersey, Prentice-Hall, Inc., p. 684–711.

Stewart, J. H., and Carlson, J. E., 1979, Geologic map of Nevada: U.S. Geological Survey State Geologic Map, scale 1:500,000.

Stewart, J. H., Moore, W. J., and Zietz, I., 1977, East-west patterns of Cenozoic igneous rocks, aeromagnetic anomalies, and mineral deposits, Nevada and Utah: Geological Society of America Bulletin, v. 77, p. 67–77.

Tschanz, C. M., and Pampeyan, E. H., 1961, Preliminary geologic map of Lincoln County, Nevada: U.S. Geological Survey Mineral Investigation Field Studies Map MF–206, scale 1:200,000.

——, 1970, Geology and mineral deposits of Lincoln County, Nevada: Nevada Bureau of Mines and Geology Bulletin 73, 187 p.

Wernicke, B., Guth, P. L., and Axen, G. J., 1984, Tertiary extensional tectonics in the Sevier thrust belt of southern Nevada: Geological Society of America Annual Meeting, Guidebook to Field Trips, v. 4, p. 473–510.

Wernicke, B., Axen, G. J., and Snow, J. K., 1988a, Basin and Range extensional tectonics at the latitude of Las Vegas, Nevada: Geological Society of America Bulletin, v. 100, p. 1738–1757.

Wernicke, B., Snow, J. K., and Walker, J. D., 1988b, Correlation of early Mesozoic thrusts in the southern Great Basin and their possible indication of 250–300 km of Neogene crustal extension, in Weide, D. L., and Faber, M. L., eds., This extended land; Geological journeys in the southern Basin and Range: University of Nevada at Las Vegas Geoscience Department Special Publication 2, p. 255–292.

Wilson, E. D., Moore, R. T., and Cooper, J. R., 1969, Geologic map of Arizona: Arizona Bureau of Mines Map, scale 1:500,000.

MANUSCRIPT ACCEPTED BY THE SOCIETY AUGUST 21, 1989

Geological Society of America
Memoir 176
1990

Chapter 11

Superposed Mesozoic and Cenozoic deformation, Indian Springs Quadrangle, southern Nevada

Peter L. Guth
Department of Oceanography, U.S. Naval Academy, Annapolis, Maryland 21402

ABSTRACT

Northwestern Clark County, Nevada, contains Tertiary extensional faults of the Sheep Range detachment that overprint the Mesozoic Sevier thrust belt. Three thrust faults occur: from west to east, the Spotted Range, Pintwater, and Gass Peak thrusts. The Spotted Range and Pintwater thrusts were minor imbrications in the thrust belt and have been excised by Tertiary extension. The Gass Peak thrust emplaced a major structural plate interpreted to have overridden a large ramp in the basal décollement of the Sevier belt, where the thrusts climb from the base of the Eocambrian clastic wedge to the middle Cambrian Bonanza King Formation.

Tertiary extension involved normal faults, steep at the surface but inferred to flatten into a deeper detachment; strike-slip faults that bound extensional blocks; and syntectonic sedimentary basins. The Spotted Range and Pintwater thrusts were largely excised by normal faults. The Dog Bone Lake fault is interpreted to have reactivated the basal thrust ramp, and other faults of the Sheep Range detachment may have reactivated the upper décollement in the Bonanza King Formation. Extensional faults are predominantly down to the west; they rotate bedding significantly in the eastern part of the region but much less to the west where the extensional allochthon was thicker and surficial extension less.

INTRODUCTION

This chapter summarizes results from compilation of a geologic map for the Indian Springs 1:100,000 quadrangle. This quadrangle (Fig. 1) forms the northwestern part of Clark County, Nevada, along with small portions of southwestern Lincoln and eastern Nye counties. The Indian Springs quadrangle contains portions of numerous mountain ranges north of Las Vegas Valley. Small bedrock outcrops occur south of Las Vegas Valley in the northwestern Spring Mountains in the southwestern corner of the quadrangle.

I mapped the southeastern part of the quadrangle during the period 1977 to 1979 (Guth, 1980). Mapping of the remainder of the quadrangle began in 1984 and continued until 1987. Detail of mapping varies with access restrictions imposed by the U.S. Air Force, which controls most of the area. The eastern half (Las Vegas, Sheep, and Desert ranges) has mostly been mapped in detail at a scale of 1:24,000 (Guth, 1980, 1986, and unpublished).

The western half has been mapped in reconnaissance, with selected areas mapped in detail at 1:24,000 and the remainder interpreted from aerial photographs. Three 1:24,000 quadrangles along the west edge of the Indian Springs quadrangle were mapped as part of detailed work in the Nevada Test Site (Barnes and others, 1982; Hinrichs and McKay, 1965; Poole, 1965).

Miogeosynclinal rocks exposed in northwestern Clark County range in age from Late Proterozoic to Permian, with a composite thickness of about 9 km (Fig. 2; stratigraphic nomenclature slightly modified from Barnes and others, 1982; Guth, 1980, 1986). Upper Proterozoic and Lower Cambrian clastic strata consist largely of sandstone, quartzite, and siltstone (Stewart, 1970). Middle Cambrian to middle Devonian rocks are mostly dolomite with some limestone and a few clastic units and are the most widely exposed rock units throughout the quadrangle. The upper Devonian and Mississippian rocks are mostly

Guth, P. L., 1990, Superposed Mesozoic and Cenozoic deformation, Indian Springs Quadrangle, southern Nevada, *in* Wernicke, B. P., ed., Basin and Range extensional tectonics near the latitude of Las Vegas, Nevada: Boulder, Colorado, Geological Society of America Memoir 176.

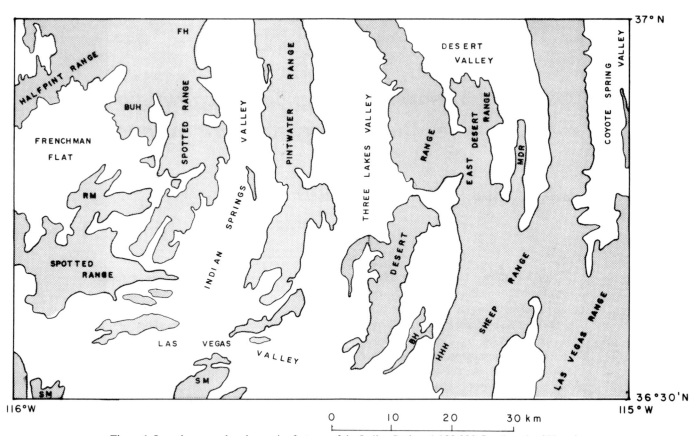

Figure 1. Location map showing major features of the Indian Springs 1:100,000 Quadrangle. Abbreviations used include BH, Black Hills; BUH, Buried Hills; FH, Fallout Hills; HHH, Hoodoo Hills Havoc; MDR, Mule Deer Ridge; RM, Ranger Mountains; SM, Spring Mountains.

limestone with a few clastic units and include the Mississippian (Chesterian) Chainman Shale, which is the highest preserved Paleozoic unit in most of the quadrangle. The Pennsylvanian and Permian Bird Spring Formation is preserved only in the Las Vegas Range beneath the Gass Peak thrust and south of the Las Vegas Valley shear zone. No Mesozoic units have been recognized within the quadrangle, although the older basinal deposits to be discussed below could be synthrust sediments.

The trace of the Sevier Gass Peak thrust runs along the eastern portion of the quadrangle (Fig. 3). Two additional thrusts were located in the Pintwater and Spotted Ranges, but those faults have been largely cut out during Tertiary extension. Because of extreme Tertiary overprinting of the Sevier thrust belt west of the Gass Peak thrust, detailed reconstruction of the Mesozoic belt remains difficult.

The Tertiary history of this region included extensional faulting on a detachment fault or faults (not well exposed at current erosion levels) involving normal faults that breached the surface with high-angle orientations, strike-slip faulting on the Las Vegas Valley shear zone along the southern boundary of the extensional terrane, syntectonic sedimentation in numerous basins that may once have been connected, landslides or gravity slides along fault scarps into the basins, and regional volcanism well removed from the surficial extension.

DESCRIPTIVE STRUCTURAL GEOLOGY

Gass Peak thrust

Rocks of the Gass Peak plate range in age from the Proterozoic Johnnie Formation to the Mississippian Chainman Shale. I interpret a ramp-flat-ramp geometry for the Gass Peak thrust with a décollement near the base of the Upper Proterozoic clastic wedge.

The upper ramp of the Gass Peak thrust is exposed in the Las Vegas Range (Ebanks, 1965; Guth, 1980). The lower plate contains an overturned syncline in the Pennsylvanian-Permian Bird Spring Formation. Structures within the lower plate of the Gass Peak thrust have not been mapped in detail, in part because of the lack of recognized mappable units within the thick Bird Spring Formation. The base of the Gass Peak thrust is a complex zone with small fault-bounded blocks of the Stirling and Wood Canyon Formations. Upper plate bedding dips moderately to steeply to the west along the thrust trace but shallows to gentle westward dips within 2 to 3 km from the thrust trace. Large north-trending open folds west of Quartzite Mountain along the southern boundary of the quadrangle are the only recognized major Mesozoic structures within the thrust plate. Cleavage and minor isoclinal folds developed within shales of the Carrara Formation in an outcrop band that parallels the trace of the thrust.

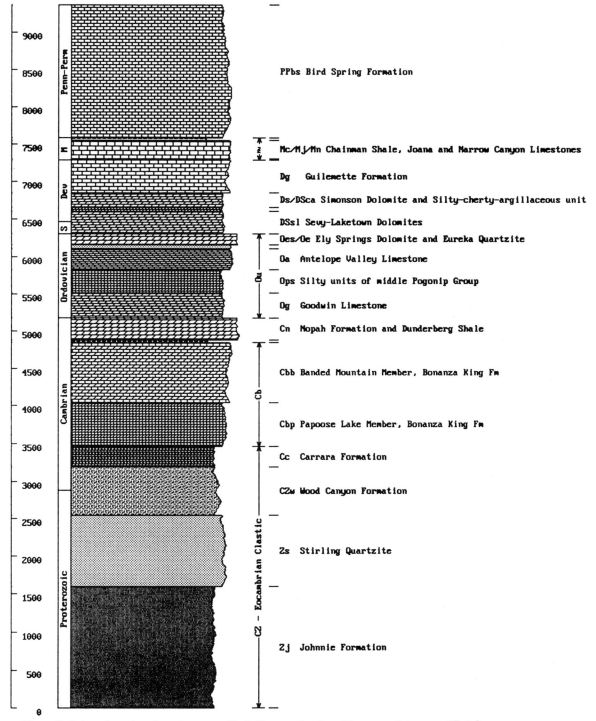

Figure 2. Paleozoic rocks of northwestern Clark County. Stratigraphic nomenclature modified from former usage.

Estimates of the combined thickness of the Stirling and Wood Canyon formations in the Las Vegas Range vary from 260 m (Guth, 1980) to 470 m (Ebanks, 1965) and 701 m (Stewart, 1970). These generally unresistant units form the base of the allochthon and are poorly exposed. Considering complex thrust slicing mapped along the trace of the thrust, the thicknesses may be original or tectonic. These thicknesses stand in marked contrast to the much thicker clastic section in the Desert Range currently 26 km to the west (more than 3,200 m of Johnnie Formation, Stirling Quartzite, and Wood Canyon Formation; Stewart, 1970). Tertiary extension has almost certainly extended the region between the present trace of the thrust and the section in the Desert Range (which now dips 50 to 60° to the east), so that originally the clastic section at the base of the thrust plate must have thickened rapidly from 300 to 700 m in the Las Vegas Range to 3,200 m in the Desert Range.

The Gass Peak thrust cannot be documented to have been reactivated where currently exposed in the Las Vegas Range. Mapping of the thrust ramp does not reveal major brecciation, characteristic of surficial levels of detachment faults, and the Mesozoic thrust surface appears unaffected by later deformation (Ebanks, 1965; Guth, 1980). Juxtaposition of the same stratigraphic levels along the exposed thrust ramp surface (Stirling Quartzite on Leonardian beds of the Bird Spring Formation) persists along strike in the Las Vegas Range and across Las Vegas Valley to the Wheeler Pass thrust in the Spring Mountains; this forms a piercing point for regional correlations and would not be expected to survive significant reactivation.

Away from the exposed ramp zone, however, the Gass Peak thrust may have been reactivated at depth. North of Wamp Spring, where the Gass Peak thrust disappears under alluvium, the thrust has probably been reactivated. Disappearance of the thrust, rotated dips in the Tertiary Wamp Spring basin (typically 20°E), and preservation of the basin overlying the thrust suggest reactivation. Down-to-the-west normal movement on the reacti-

vated Gass Peak thrust probably increases to the north and may be related to the major range-front fault on the west side of the Arrow Canyon Range (Langenheim, 1988), which also appears to gain displacement to the north. These normal faults could explain the northward disappearance of the Las Vegas Range and the appearance of the wide Coyote Spring Valley. Unmapped normal faults in this region could omit part of the late Precambrian–Lower Cambrian clastic wedge in the Las Vegas Range, accounting in part for the differences in estimated thickness between the northern Las Vegas Range (260 m; Guth, 1980) and the southern part of the Las Vegas Range (701 m; Stewart, 1970).

Pintwater thrust

Longwell and others (1965) reported a thrust in the Pintwater Range. A complex, steeply west-dipping fault zone occurs along the west side of the Pintwater Range for a distance of at least 25 km (Fig. 4). Near Pintwater Cave the fault currently juxtaposes deformed Bonanza King and Nopah Formations (with Dunderberg zone trilobites; A. R. Palmer, personal communication, 1984) in the hanging wall with the Ordovician section (uppermost Pogonip Group, Eureka Quartzite, and Ely Springs Dolomite) in the footwall (older on younger, about 1,000 m

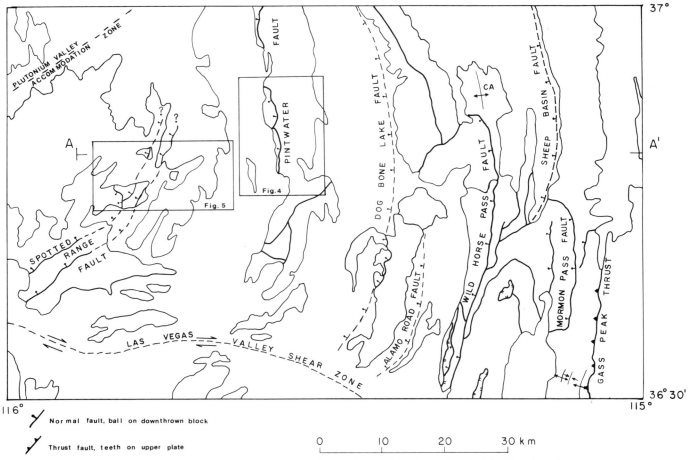

Figure 3. Major structural features of the Indian Springs 1:100,000 quadrangle. Note location of cross section A-A′ shown in Figure 7. CA denotes the Chowderhead Anticline in the East Desert Range.

stratigraphic duplication, with both blocks gently dipping). The fault cuts across the stratigraphic section, and farther to the north near Gravel Canyon and the northern edge of the quadrangle, Silurian-Devonian Laketown-Sevy formations form the hanging wall, and Ordovician Antelope Valley Limestone the footwall (younger on older, less than 1,000 m stratigraphic omission). At Gravel Canyon the footwall dips steeply to the west; otherwise, dips are gentle. This fault may be a Mesozoic thrust reactivated as a Tertiary normal fault, or it may be a new Tertiary structure that cuts out an older thrust.

Cleavage developed in Pogonip Group silty limestones in the footwall of the fault near Pintwater Cave provides additional evidence suggesting a Mesozoic thrust fault. Within this region, cleavage apparently did not develop during Tertiary tectonism; the only other cleavage developed along the Gass Peak thrust. The absence of such cleavage in adjacent ranges suggests cleavage development by a local structure and not the regional décollement, stratigraphically several kilometers below the Ordovician units.

Rocks on the west side of the Pintwater Range attributed to the upper plate of the Pintwater thrust range in age from the middle Cambrian Bonanza King Formation to the Silurian-Devonian Laketown-Sevy formations. Rocks in the Spotted Range to the west, in the upper plate of the thrust, include Ordovician through Mississippian units. The exposed lower plate is mostly Ordovician units, with some exposures of the Laketown-Sevy and Cambrian units (Bonanza King and Nopah Formations) in the southern Pintwater Range.

Spotted Range thrust

The Spotted Range thrust (Barnes and others, 1982; Longwell and others, 1965; Tschanz and Pampeyan, 1970) has been extensively modified by Tertiary extension. Exposed rocks of the Spotted Range plate range from Cambrian Carrara Formation to Mississippian Joana Limestone. The thrust is preserved primarily by normal fault juxtapositions, with part of the upper plate dropped down against the lower plate on Tertiary normal faults. The thrust occurs in two areas, with two exposures in the main block of the Spotted Range and eastern Ranger Mountains (see Fig. 5) and extensive exposures in the Mercury quadrangle (Barnes and others, 1982). The following discussion is based on the detailed mapping summarized in Figure 5, study of the map by Barnes and others (1982), and brief field checking of relations in the Mercury quadrangle. Relations in the northern Spotted Range are relatively simple, while those in the Mercury quadrangle are greatly complicated by strike-slip faulting (Barnes and others, 1982).

Two steeply west-dipping normal faults cut out the Mesozoic thrust; the eastern fault juxtaposes Cambrian rocks from the thrust's hanging wall with Mississippian rocks from the footwall, and the western fault juxtaposes Devonian and Mississippian rocks with Cambrian rocks. Cambrian rocks between the two

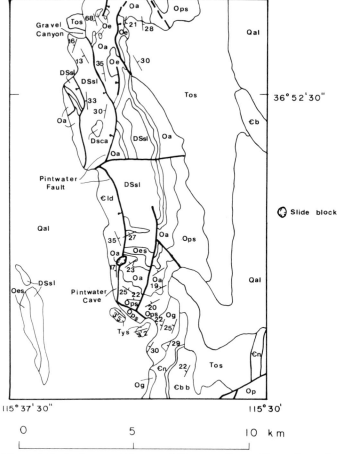

Figure 4. Geologic map of the central Pintwater Range. Formation units from Figure 2, with the following additions: €ld, Cambrian limestone and dolomite, Banded Mountain and Nopah formations; Tos, older Tertiary sediments; Tys, younger Tertiary sediments; Qal, Quaternary alluvium. Based upon 1:24,000 field mapping by Guth and Steve Garwin.

faults are the most resistant to erosion. Brecciation along the faults suggests Tertiary normal faulting rather than Mesozoic thrusting. Longwell and others (1965) did not identify the Cambrian block in the eastern Ranger Mountains; its identification demonstrates structural continuity of Cambrian rocks farther north in the Spotted Range with the Cambrian units in the Mercury klippe (Barnes and others, 1982). This fault zone may continue to the north to form the thrust mapped by Tschanz and Pampeyan (1970) on Chert Ridge.

In the Mercury quadrangle (southwest end of the Spotted Range), the two major normal faults occur on the north side of South Ridge and the south side of Mercury Ridge. The exposures on South Ridge expose an overturned syncline in Mississippian carbonates, so the normal fault may reactivate a thrust ramp. The Mercury Quadrangle has been extensively broken up by strike-slip faulting (Barnes and others, 1982) and unmapped gravity slide or landslide deposits (Guth, unpublished mapping).

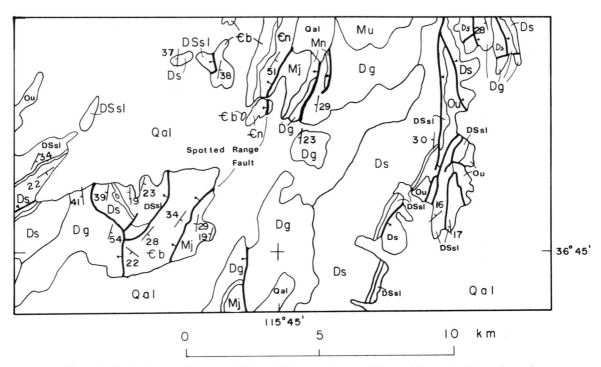

Figure 5. Geologic map of the central Spotted Range and eastern Ranger Mountains. Formation units from Figure 2; Qal is Quaternary alluvium. Based upon 1:24,000 field mapping by Guth.

Cenozoic normal faults

The Indian Springs quadrangle contains the surficial extension associated with an inferred major detachment system, the Sheep Range detachment. Current erosion levels do not expose the detachment, and subsurface geophysical evidence is not available. On a regional scale, the Sheep Range detachment belongs to a larger eastern Death Valley detachment system that includes faults on the west side of the Spring Mountains and the Kingston detachment (Burchfiel and others, 1983a; Burchfiel and Davis, 1988; Wernicke and others, 1988).

The Sheep Range detachment contains two distinct styles of Tertiary deformation. In the eastern part of the Indian Springs quadrangle, a series of closely spaced normal faults defines a number of discrete range blocks and progressively rotates bedding and greatly extends the section. Dips of bedding in the rotated blocks range from 20 to 60°. The major faults form scoops on the scale of individual mountain ranges. Faults broke to the surface without influence from Mesozoic thrusts. In the western part of the quadrangle, three major faults are more widely spaced and bedding rotations much less; each fault defines a single mountain range. The major faults in the western part of the Indian Springs quadrangle—the Dog Bone Lake fault, the Pintwater fault, and the Spotted Range fault—may have been localized by Mesozoic structures. Each fault occurs along the western edge of a range and defines a structural block that includes the next range to the west.

The Dog Bone Lake fault is not exposed, but a major fault is required between the Desert Range and the Pintwater Range, and

faults along the western edge of the southern Desert Range may be splays from this fault. This fault would require over 5 km of vertical motion to juxtapose Johnnie Formation on the east side of the valley in the Desert Range with Ordovician units on the west side in the Pintwater Range. Offset along the fault varies along strike. The Desert Range defines a structural culmination, with the oldest Eocambrian clastic rocks exposed at the highest topographic levels of the range west of Sheep Pass in the East Desert Range. Northward exposures of the late Precambrian clastic rocks disappear under cover, and 30 to 40 km to the north, where the Pintwater and Desert Ranges merge (within the Pahranagat quadrangle), offset on the fault must be minimal. I infer that this fault reactivated the ramp in the basal décollement for the Sevier thrusts and that the fault is probably on the eastern side of Three Lakes Valley.

Structural geology of the Pintwater Range cannot be easily categorized and consists of a number of individual domains along strike. These domains contain generally gently to moderately dipping bedrock, but dip directions vary considerably. Longwell (1945) defined the Pintwater anticline, which represents considerable simplification of complex geology. Detailed mapping in the Pintwater Range has not been completed because of restricted access for security reasons, limited roads, and extreme topographic ruggedness. Structural relations under the Pintwater Range must be complex. In the model presented here, the Dog Bone Lake fault reactivated the basal décollement of the Sevier thrusts and the ramp where the décollement cut from the base of the Eocambrian wedge to the Bonanza King Formation. The Pintwater Range originally sat above the upper flat of the thrust and has been dropped down the thrust ramp. This geometry would have created extensive fault slicing, not depicted on the cross section (see Fig. 7).

The Pintwater and Spotted Range faults reactivated or excised the Pintwater and Spotted Range thrusts, as discussed earlier. Exposed on the west side of the Pintwater Range, the Pintwater fault defines the structural block that makes up the Spotted Range. A number of east-dipping antithetic faults occur on the east side of the Spotted Range. The Spotted Range fault may extend beyond the Indian Springs quadrangle through the oroflexural bending in the Specter Range and continue toward the south (Burchfiel, 1965; Sargent and Stewart, 1971). The block defined by the Spotted Range fault is largely buried under Frenchman Flat and may be influenced by additional structures.

Sheep Range breakaway

Guth (1981) described the Sheep Range breakaway and named some of the major normal faults. Mapping of a larger region requires a more complex three-dimensional geometry of the breakaway zone (see Fig. 3). Three individual faults must be considered in defining the breakaway zone: the Sheep Basin fault, the Mormon Pass fault, and the Wildhorse Pass fault.

The Sheep Basin fault trends north-south in the alluvium on the west side of the Sheep Range and then bends into a northeast-southwest trend at the southern end of Sheep Basin. Longwell (1930) reported recent fault scarps along the trace of this fault. It forms the western boundary of the northern Sheep Range and the northwestern boundary of the main block of the Sheep Range. The northern Sheep Range east of this fault consists of essentially subhorizontal Cambrian and Ordovician rocks; the same rocks to the west, where exposed on Mule Deer Ridge, have been down-dropped and rotated and dip toward the east. The Sheep Basin fault extends to the north into the Pahranagat quadrangle. This fault merges with the Wildhorse Pass fault on the west side of the Sheep Range.

The Mormon Pass fault forms the eastern breakaway boundary of the southern part of the Sheep Range detachment and makes three abrupt scoop-boundary bends. The fault appears to be relatively high-angle, and the west side has been down-dropped. The northern bend separates the northern Sheep Range, composing a horizontal section of Cambrian and Ordovician rocks, from east-tilted rocks in the southern portion of the Sheep Range. At this bend the Mormon Pass fault joins the Sheep Basin fault. To the south, alluvium covers the fault until its next bend, where it cuts across a spur of the Las Vegas Range. The fault then returns to a north-south trace and forms the western margin of the Las Vegas Range. The region immediately south of the Indian Springs quadrangle probably contained another bend in the fault trace, but rotations along the Las Vegas Valley shear zone (Nelson and Jones, 1987) have obscured the original geometry. This analysis suggests that the Mormon Pass Fault contained three primary right-angle bends and relatively straight, north-south stretches 15 to 18 km long.

The Wildhorse Pass fault, which forms the eastern boundary of the Hoodoo Hills Havoc (Guth, 1981), continues along strike to the north as the western boundary of the main Sheep Range structural block and the eastern boundary of the Tertiary Black Hills Basin. Extension within the southern part of the Sheep Range on the Mormon Pass fault and other north-trending faults has been relatively minor, and the Wildhorse Pass fault marks the easternmost major normal fault of the Sheep Range detachment. Farther north, major extension is transferred to the east on the Sheep Basin fault. The Wildhorse Pass fault continues as the boundary of the Black Hills basin and then cuts through the East Desert Range where it breaks up the Chowderhead Tertiary basin.

Depositional basins

Tertiary sedimentary basins in northwestern Clark County record the extensional history of the region (Guth and others, 1988). Two sequences appear to be present: a poorly documented older sequence (Tos) (Tschanz and Pampeyan, 1970; Ekren and others, 1977) and a younger sequence (Tys) broadly correlative with the Horse Spring Formation of the Lake Mead region (Bohannon, 1984).

The older basin deposits appear to predate volcanism and present topography (Ekren and others, 1977). In the Spotted Range and Pintwater Range they include distinctive, reddish-colored, well-rounded conglomerates that contain cobble-sized (as much as 15-cm-long axes) clasts from the local late Precambrian clastic succession (brown to light purple clean quartzites) and reworked Eleana Formation chert pebble conglomerate (Tschanz and Pampeyan, 1970; Ekren and others, 1977; Guth, unpublished). The conglomerates are currently as far as 45 km east of the nearest exposures of the Eleana in the Nevada Test Site. Size and rounding of the cobbles require deposition by a major river. These deposits extend northward into the Pahranagat quadrangle, but access to the outcrops remains extremely difficult. Where exposed at the topographic crest of the Pintwater Range (Fig. 4), the older basin deposits dip 30° to the east. The Ordovician bedrock beneath the basin deposits dips 20 to 60° to the west. The contact between the basin and the Ordovician rocks appears conformable and not a major fault. Age of the basin deposits has been estimated as Cretaceous or Tertiary (Tschanz and Pampeyan, 1970; Ekren and others, 1977).

The younger Tertiary sequence previously has been lumped indiscriminately with the Horse Spring Formation. Bohannon (1984) redefined the Horse Spring Formation, restricting it to a single depositional basin and dating it between 20 and 12 Ma. Guth and others (1988) reviewed limited geochronologic work in the Tertiary basins of northwestern Clark County; three determinations of about 15 Ma agree with a median age of 15.1 Ma (11 samples) for the Thumb Member of the Horse Spring Formation in the Muddy Mountains (Bohannon, 1984). The younger deposits, consisting of conglomerate, sandstone, siltstone, claystone, lacustrine limestone, and subordinate tuff, occur in six different basins in the Spotted, Pintwater, East Desert, Sheep, and Las Vegas Ranges. Fill in all of the basins dips 20° or more toward the east.

Landslides/gravity slides

The Hoodoo Hills Havoc, lying on the west side of the Sheep Range, contains complexly deformed Paleozoic bedrock. In the southern portion of the Havoc, originally described by Guth (1981, 1986), brecciated Paleozoic rocks form the bulk of the exposure. Farther to the north, discrete lenses of brecciated Paleozoic rocks are interbedded with the Upper Tertiary sediments of the Black Hills basin. The Black Hills basin contains more than 1,500 m of lacustrine limestone, sandstone, conglomerate, and interbedded tuffs. Several masses of brecciated lower Paleozoic dolomite, ranging in outcrop size up to 400 by 2,400 m, slid into the basin. The landslide masses (or gravity slides) deformed the Tertiary limestones over which they slid, producing isoclinal folds. The brecciated dolomite was then unconformably overlapped by younger lacustrine limestone units.

The Wildhorse Pass fault forms the eastern boundary of the Hoodoo Hills Havoc and the Black Hills basin, without apparent structural discontinuity between the Havoc and the basin. The Black Hills basin and Hoodoo Hills Havoc developed in tandem along a depositional continuum: a major basin to the north, filled dominantly with sediments interspersed with episodic, thin gravity slides, that grades southward into a much more massive series of slides intercalated with only minor sediment fill.

Similar landslide deposits occur in the Heaven's Well basin on the west side of the Pintwater Range. The large slide mass on the east side of the Pintwater Range (Longwell and others, 1965; Tschanz and Pampeyan, 1970) probably formed in the same way.

Strike-slip faults

Strike-slip faults form the lateral boundaries of extensional domains in the Great Basin and in some ways resemble oceanic transform faults (Anderson, 1973; Davis and Burchfiel, 1973; Guth, 1981). These faults have recently been called "accommodation zones" (Bosworth, 1987) or "transfer zones" (Gibbs, 1984; Lister and others, 1986). Two major accommodation zones occur in the Indian Springs quadrangle: the Las Vegas Valley shear zone and the Plutonium Valley accommodation zone. The Las Vegas Valley shear zone forms the southern boundary of a large extensional terrane: the Sheep Range detachment (Guth, 1981; Wernicke and others, 1984). The Plutonium Valley accommodation zone is discussed below.

Fault-bend folding

Large-scale folds (5 to 10 km long) occur in conjunction with major normal faults in this region. The folds occur as footwall synclines and hanging-wall anticlines, are asymmetrical, and are usually severely brecciated. Major normal faults in this area dip west and cut east-dipping sedimentary rocks; the fault is probably propagating upward toward the surface from depth. Folds occur when faults do not propagate cleanly through the tilted section but leave a slab of rock along the fault plane. Rocks within the fault zone are dragged along the fault and rotated to westerly dips; if they maintain continuity with east-dipping units in the footwall they create the anticlinal structure; otherwise they form a syncline in the hanging wall.

The best example of a fault bend fold occurs in the Chowderhead anticline in the East Desert Range (Fig. 3) in southernmost Lincoln County, where the severely deformed rocks in the west limb of the structure puzzled Tschanz and Pampeyan (1970, p. 107). The east limb of the fold consists of a simple homocline, ranging in age from Cambrian Carrara Formation through the Ordovician Pogonip Group, and dipping moderately to the east. The west limb contains the same Cambrian and Ordovician units as the east limb, complexly brecciated, faulted, and dipping to the west. The western limb can probably best be depicted as a fault-zone breccia, but westward dips consistently define the anticlinal structure. The relation of the western limb of the fold to rocks in the Desert Range to the west is covered by alluvium, but it must be faulted because younger Ordovician and Silurian units occur across the alluvium.

A similar but smaller fold occurs at the south end of the East Desert Range. Other examples occur in neighboring areas of southern Nevada: Syncline Ridge in the Nevada Test Site (Orkild, 1963; Hoover and Morrison, 1980), where geophysical work identified a major fault with considerable vertical movement along the eastern side of the folded ridge (Hoover and others, 1982); and the Wheeler Syncline in the northwestern Spring Mountains (Burchfiel and others, 1974), which could not be readily related to Mesozoic structures.

DISCUSSION

Thrust model

From east to west, a transect through this portion of the Sevier belt includes the following thrusts: (1) Muddy Mountain–Glendale–Mormon–Tule Spring (Bohannon, 1983a, b; Skelly and Axen, 1988; Wernicke and others, 1985); (2) Dry Lake thrust (Longwell and others, 1965); (3) Gass Peak thrust (Ebanks, 1965; Guth, 1980); (4) Pintwater thrust (Longwell and others, 1965; this chapter); and (5) Spotted Range thrust (Barnes and others, 1982; this chapter). The two major faults are the Muddy Mountain and correlative thrusts, which place Middle Cambrian carbonates over Jurassic sandstone, and the Gass Peak thrust, which places uppermost Precambrian clastic sediments over Permian limestone.

I make the following assumptions:

1. The Dry Lake thrust shares, with the Muddy Mountain–Mormon thrust system, a décollement within the competent, carbonate Bonanza King Formation (Burchfiel and others, 1983b).

2. The Gass Peak thrust has a décollement near the base of the Johnnie Formation. The Noonday Dolomite regionally underlies the Johnnie but is not present within the immediate area. Noonday questionably reported from the Desert Range (Longwell and others, 1965, p. 13; Gillette and Van Alstine, 1982) is actually a fault block of Bonanza King Formation.

3. The Pintwater and Spotted Range thrusts were minor structures. Because of reactivation or excision along Tertiary normal faults, the original stratigraphic displacements can only be estimated: Bonanza King Formation on Laketown-Sevy Formations for the Pintwater thrust, Carrara Formation on Chainman Shale for the Spotted Range thrust.

A major ramp must offset the basal décollement of the Sevier thrusts from the base of the Eocambrian clastic wedge (allochthonous Johnnie Formation in the Desert Range, autochthonous Tapeats Sandstone in the Mormon Mountains) to the middle of the Bonanza King Formation. This interval is about 4,000 m thick in the Desert Range but only about 750 m thick in the Mormon Mountains. Except for structurally disrupted exposures in the Las Vegas Range along the Gass Peak thrust, there are no surface exposures of this interval between the Desert Range and the Mormon Mountains. Doubling of the Eocambrian clastic wedge and the lower Bonanza King Formation, equivalent to the amount of eastward overthrusting above the basal décollement, must occur east of the major ramp.

I place the major ramp under Three Lakes Valley. The associated ramp anticline may be preserved in the Pintwater anticline of Longwell (1945), and the ramp may have served as the locus for the Dog Bone Lake fault that created Three Lakes Valley. I infer that the upper-plate Eocambrian rocks in the Las Vegas Range originated along the ramp, and the complete section in the Desert Range originated west of that ramp.

The lack of highs in the gravity and aeromagnetic fields (Kane and others, 1979; Blank, 1988) indicates that crystalline basement is unlikely to directly underlie the Johnnie Formation in the Desert Range. Instead, a doubled Eocambrian section and Bonanza King Formation is inferred to underlie the Desert Range. Crystalline basement probably lies a relatively uniform 3 to 6 km below sea level.

Figure 6 details my interpretation of the major structure at the close of Mesozoic thrusting, based on the discussion above and typical thrust-belt behavior. The model generally resembles the eastern portion of the reconstruction of Wernicke and others (1988) but includes an undeformed autochthonous basement-sediment contact westward under the Dry Lake and Gass Peak plates. The model also assumes a wider extent for the Gass Peak allochthon than the 5 km inferred by Wernicke and others (1988).

The "space problem" at the base of the thrusts in the Spring Mountain and the Gass Peak thrust (Burchfiel and others, 1974; Guth, 1980) has been discussed in terms of the deeper décollement behavior of the thrusts. Burchfiel and others (1974, p. 1019) noted that the base of the Johnnie Formation in the Wheeler Pass thrust projects about 3,000 m above the same stratigraphic level

in the overridden Lee Canyon plate. This thickness and their section B-B′ show the base of the Johnnie at the level of the Bonanza King Formation. These problems disappear if the overridden plate (Lee Canyon/Dry Lake) never contained the Eocambrian wedge and if both thrusts (Wheeler Pass/Gass Peak and Lee Canyon/Dry Lake) ride on a common décollement within the Bonanza King Formation. Within reasonable uncertainties, this geometry holds for the Gass Peak thrust in the Las Vegas Range. Construction of cross sections through the Gass Peak ramp depends on the geometry of the thick Eocambrian wedge between the Las Vegas Range and the Desert Range, the geometry of the lower plate in the Las Vegas Range, and a possible duplex zone below the Gass Peak allochthon (suggested by open folds exposed west of Quartzite Mountain at the southern edge of the Indian Springs quadrangle).

Cross section through Indian Springs quadrangle

Figure 7 shows an interpretative cross section through the Indian Springs quadrangle. The section stops short of the western edge of the quadrangle and does not show the deepest portion of the Frenchman Flat basin (Miller and Healey, 1986); additional complexitities are likely under Frenchman Flat. The thick Tertiary basin inferred under Three Lakes Valley (west of the Dog Bone Lake Fault) is exposed on the east side of the Pintwater Range north of the line of section, where it extends to the crest of the Range (see Fig. 4).

Plutonium Valley accommodation zone

A major accommodation zone with northeasterly trend runs through the Plutonium Valley quadrangle (new interpretation of mapping by Hinrichs and McKay, 1965). Rocks north of the accommodation zone dip west, whereas those to the south dip east (Fig. 8). The accommodation zone runs through an area with only scattered Paleozoic outcrops, and published mapping in the Tertiary volcanics has few attitudes measured.

The Plutonium Valley accommodation zone appears to lack significant surficial strike-slip faults, instead forming a broad zone of tilted blocks within which the dominant dip direction reverses (Hinrichs and McKay, 1965), resembling the accommodation zone described by Faulds and others (1988) south of Lake Mead. Tertiary units drape across the accommodation zone, but Paleozoic units cannot be traced across the zone because of the inadequate exposure under the Tertiary cover.

The Plutonium Valley accommodation marks the southeastern boundary of a west-dipping domain, opposite to regional trends. This domain occurs around Yucca Flat at the junction of the Indian Springs, Pahranagat, Pahute Mesa, and Beatty 1:100,000 quadrangles. The eastern boundary of the west-dipping zone appears to lie between the Halfpint and Papoose Ranges; the western boundary is buried under the thick Tertiary volcanic pile from the Timber Mountain and related calderas.

Paleozoic rocks in the west-dipping domain include the

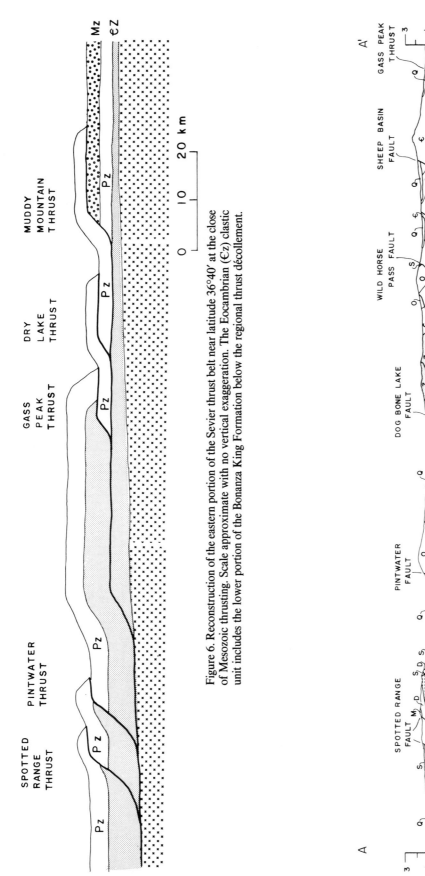
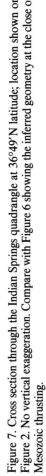

Figure 6. Reconstruction of the eastern portion of the Sevier thrust belt near latitude 36°40' at the close of Mesozoic thrusting. Scale approximate with no vertical exaggeration. The Eocambrian (€z) clastic unit includes the lower portion of the Bonanza King Formation below the regional thrust décollement.

Figure 7. Cross section through the Indian Springs quadrangle at 36°49'N latitude; location shown on Figure 2. No vertical exaggeration. Compare with Figure 6 showing the inferred geometry at the close of Mesozoic thrusting.

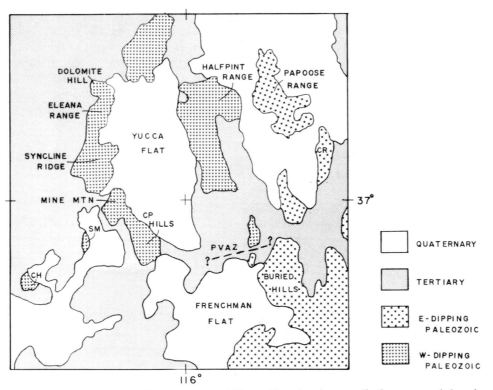

Figure 8. Bedrock geology of the area around Yucca Flat, showing east-dipping structural domain northwest of the Plutonium Valley accommodation zone. Based on U.S. Geological Survey 1:24,000 published quadrangle maps. Abbreviations used include CH, Calico Hills; CR, Chert Ridge; PVAZ, Plutonium Valley Accommodation Zone; SM, Shoshone Mountain.

Devonian sections at Dolomite Hill, Shoshone Mountain, Mine Mountain, and the Calico Hills; Ordovician rocks between the CP Hills and Mine Mountain; the Cambrian sections in the CP Hills, Smoky Hills (north end of Yucca Flat), and the Halfpint Range; and upper Proterozoic units in the Halfpint Range. These lower Paleozoic and Proterozoic rocks around Yucca flat dip consistently to the west, with a progression from the late Proterozoic rocks on the east side of the Halfpint Range to the Devonian sections farthest west. These west-dipping rocks appear to structurally overlie younger rocks of the Eleana and Bird Spring formations, which have highly variable dips but also dip dominantly to the west (CP Hills, Mine Mountain, Syncline Ridge, and Eleana Range).

Tertiary rocks within the domain in the Halfpint Range dip to the west but generally 10 to 20° less steeply than the underlying Paleozoic and Proterozoic rocks, which also dip to the west. This suggests that Tertiary rocks were deposited during extension, after underlying rocks had undergone some rotation, and that volcanic units underwent additional rotation with the Paleozoic bedrock. The Halfpint Range includes some older Miocene volcanic units (Indian Trail formation of former usage) (Barnes and others, 1965; Byers and Barnes, 1967), which implies an early age for the east-directed normal faulting. Relations at Mine Mountain (J. Cole, U.S. Geological Survey, and Guth, unpublished mapping) also suggest that east-directed extension was an early tectonic feature. This extension cannot now be related to structures in the Indian Springs quadrangle, and it greatly complicates deciphering the Mesozoic history of the region.

Mesozoic structure west of the Spotted Range thrust

Mesozoic structures west of the Spotted Range thrust (see Fig. 8) have undergone extreme extension (e.g., reconstruction of Wernicke and others, 1988) and were covered by the southwest Nevada volcanic field. The faults mapped as thrusts within the Nevada Test Site (Barnes and Poole, 1968) are here proposed to be at least in part Tertiary extensional features and normal fault repetitions. The upper plates of both the Mine Mountain and CP thrusts dip to the west, contain older rocks toward the east, and are repeated on north-trending normal faults (Orkild, 1963, 1968; McKeown and others, 1976). Both thrusts show a degree of brecciation and faulting style much more characteristic of Tertiary faulting than Mesozoic faults of the region. Carr (1984) interpreted the Mine Mountain thrust as a gravity slide block, and detailed mapping supports this view (J. Cole, U.S. Geological Survey, and Guth, unpublished mapping). In the CP Hills the Tertiary section is clearly involved in high-angle faulting: McKeown and others (1976) show five dips within Miocene tuffs ranging from 25 to 45° to the west and roughly similar to dips in the underlying lower Paleozoic rocks This requires deformation in the CP Hills after 12.6 to 13.4 Ma, the age of the tilted tuffs.

Although present relations at Mine Mountain and in the CP Hills resulted from Tertiary normal faulting, structural juxtapositions of lower Paleozoic rocks on the Mississippian Eleana Formation (Antler flysch) appear to require a major thrust fault. Mississippian paleogeography also suggests thrusting near Yucca Flat to telescope original depositional trends. Mississippian rocks in the Spotted Range south and east of Yucca Flat are dominantly limestone with minor shale, only 308 m thick (Barnes and others, 1982); they are currently 40 km from incomplete exposures of the correlative 2,350-m-thick Eleana Formation at Mine Mountain, the CP Hills, and the Calico Hills and 50 km from complete exposures of the Eleana Formation in the Eleana Range (Poole and others, 1961). This dramatic change in facies and thickness, oblique to depositional strike and extended during the Tertiary, suggests that Mesozoic thrusting telescoped Paleozoic trends.

CONCLUSION

The Sheep Range detachment system reactivated parts of the Mesozoic thrust belt, but the system also contains normal faults that broke through intact sections that had not been deformed during the Mesozoic and did not reactivate all Mesozoic structures. Tertiary extensional style varies, with imbricately extended blocks in the eastern half of the quadrangle having significant bedding rotations, and larger blocks with much smaller rotations in the western part of the quadrangle. This change in style probably reflects the depth to the Sheep Range detachment. Tertiary volcanism and plutonism did not occur within this quadrangle but were going on in the southwest Nevada volcanic field to the west simultaneously with upper crustal extension. Volcanism and detachment faulting may be genetically related but spatially offset components of continental extension.

ACKNOWLEDGMENTS

This chapter results from more than 10 year's work in southern Nevada and would not have been possible without discussions and collaboration with numerous coworkers at the Massachusetts Institute of Technology, the U.S. Military Academy, the University of Nevada Las Vegas, and the U.S. Geological Survey. Florian Maldonado mapped portions of the northern Sheep Range, and Steve Garwin assisted with field mapping in the summer of 1984. I thank Desert National Wildlife Range and Range Control Group, Nellis Air Force Base, for permission to enter land under their control. Thorough reviews by John Bartley and Will Carr greatly improved the manuscript.

REFERENCES CITED

Anderson, R. E., 1973, Large-magnitude late Tertiary strike-slip faulting north of Lake Mead, Nevada: U.S. Geological Survey Professional Paper 794, 18 p.

Barnes, H., and Poole, F. G., 1968, Regional thrust-fault system in Nevada Test Site and vicinity, *in* Eckel, E. B., ed., Nevada Test Site: Geological Society of America Memoir 110, p. 233–238.

Barnes, H., Christiansen, R. L., and Byers, F. M., Jr., 1965, Geologic map of the Jangle Ridge Quadrangle, Nye and Lincoln Counties, Nevada: U.S. Geological Survey Geologic Quadrangle Map GQ–363, scale 1:24,000.

Barnes, H., Ekren, E. B., Rodgers, C. L., and Hedlund, D. C., 1982, Geologic and tectonic maps of the Mercury Quadrangle, Nye and Clark Counties, Nevada: U.S. Geological Survey Miscellaneous Investigations Series Map I–1197, scale 1:24,000.

Blank, H. R., 1988, Basement structure in the Las Vegas region from potential-field data: Geological Society of America Abstracts with Programs, v. 20, p. 144.

Bohannon, R. G., 1983a, Mesozoic and Cenozoic tectonic development of the Muddy, North Muddy, and northern Black Mountains, Clark County, Nevada, *in* Miller, D. M., Todd, V. R., and Howard, K. A., eds., Tectonic and stratigraphic studies in the eastern Great Basin: Geological Society of America Memoir 157, p. 125–148.

———, 1983b, Geologic map, tectonic map, and structure sections of the Muddy and northern Black Mountains, Clark County, Nevada: U.S. Geological Survey Miscellaneous Investigations series Map I–1406, scale 1:62,500.

———, 1984, Nonmarine sedimentary rocks of Tertiary age in the Lake Mead region, southeastern Nevada and northwestern Arizona: U.S. Geological Survey Professional Paper 1259, 72 p.

Bosworth, W., 1987, Off-axis volcanism in the Gregory rift, east Africa; Implications for models of continental rifting: Geology, v. 15, p. 397–400.

Burchfiel, B. C., 1965, Structural geology of the Specter Range Quadrangle, Nevada, and its regional significance: Geological Society of America Bulletin, v. 76, p. 175–192.

———, 1988, Mesozoic thrust faults and Cenozoic low-angle normal faults, eastern Spring Mountains, Nevada, and Clark Mountains thrust complex, California, *in* Weide, D. L., and Faber, M. L., eds., This extended land; Geological journeys in the southern Basin and Range; Geological Society of America, Cordilleran Section Field Trip Guidebook: University of Nevada at Las Vegas Geoscience Department Special Publication 2, p. 87–106.

Burchfiel, B. C., Fleck, R. J., Secor, D. T., Vincelette, R. R., and Davis, G. A., 1974, Geology of the Spring Mountains, Nevada: Geological Society of America Bulletin, v. 85, p. 1013–1023.

Burchfiel, B. C., Walker, D., Davis, G. A., and Wernicke, B., 1983a, Kingston Range and related detachment faults; A major "breakaway" zone in the southern Great Basin: Geological Society of America Abstracts with Programs, v. 15, p. 536.

Burchfiel, B. C., Wernicke, B., Willemin, J. H., Axen, G. J., and Cameron, C. S., 1983b, A new type of décollement thrusting: Nature, v. 300, p. 512–515.

Byers, F. M., Jr., and Barnes, H., 1967, Geologic map of the Paiute Ridge Quadrangle, Nye and Lincoln Counties, Nevada: U.S. Geological Survey Geologic Quadrangle Map GQ–577, scale 1:24,000.

Carr, W. J., 1984, Regional structural setting of Yucca Mountain, southwestern Nevada, and Late Cenozoic rates of tectonics activity in part of the southwestern Great Basin, Nevada and California: U.S. Geological Survey Open-File Report 84–854, 109 p.

Davis, G. A., and Burchfiel, B. C., 1973, Garlock fault; An intracontinental transform structure, southern California: Geological Society of America Bulletin, v. 84, p. 1407–1422.

Ebanks, W. J., Jr., 1965, Structural geology of the Gass Peak area, Las Vegas Range, Nevada [M.A. thesis]: Houston, Texas, Rice University, 56 p.

Ekren, E. B., Orkild, P. P., Sargent, K. A., and Dixon, G. L., 1977, Geologic map of Tertiary rocks, Lincoln County, Nevada: U.S. Geological Survey Miscellaneous Investigations series Map I–1041, scale 1:250,000.

Faulds, J. E., Hillemeyer, F.L.B., and Smith, E. I., 1988, Geometry and kinematics of a Miocene "accommodation zone" in the central Black and southern Eldorado Mountains, Arizona and Nevada, *in* Weide, D. L., and Faber, M. L., eds., This extended land; Geological journeys in the southern Basin and Range; Geological Society of America Cordilleran Section Field Trip Guidebook: University of Nevada at Las Vegas Geoscience Department Special Publication 2, p. 293–310.

Gibbs, A. D., 1984, Structural evolution of extensional basin margins: Geological Society of London Journal, v. 141, p. 609–620.

Gillett, S. L., and Van Alstine, D. R., 1982, Remagnetization and tectonic rotation of upper Precambrian and Lower Paleozoic strata from the Desert Range, southern Nevada: Journal of Geophysical Research, v. 87, p. 10929–10953.

Guth, P. L., 1980, Geology of the Sheep Range, Clark County, Nevada [Ph.D. thesis]: Cambridge, Massachusetts Institute of Technology, 189 p.

—— , 1981, Tertiary extension north of the Las Vegas Valley shear zone, Sheep and Desert Ranges, Clark County, Nevada: Geological Society of America Bulletin, v. 92, p. 763–771.

—— , 1986, Bedrock geologic map of the Black Hill 1:24,000 Quadrangle, Nevada: U.S. Geological Survey Open-File Report 86–438, scale 1:24,000.

Guth, P. L., Schmidt, D. L., Deibert, J., and Yount, J., 1988, Tertiary extensional basins of northwestern Clark County, *in* Weide, D. L., and Faber, M. L., eds., This extended land; Geological journeys in the southern Basin and Range; Geological Society of America Cordilleran Section Field Trip Guidebook: University of Nevada at Las Vegas Geoscience Department Special Publication 2, p. 239–253.

Hinrichs, E. N., and McKay, E. J., 1965, Geologic map of the Plutonium Valley Quadrangle, Nye and Lincoln Counties, Nevada: U.S. Geological Survey Geologic Quadrangle Map GQ–384, scale 1:24,000.

Hoover, D. B., and Morrison, J. N., 1980, Geology of the Syncline Ridge area related to nuclear waste disposal, Nevada Test Site, Nye County, Nevada: U.S. Geological Survey Open-File Report 80–942, 55 p.

Hoover, D. B., Hanna, W. F., Anderson, L. A., Flanigan, V. J., and Pankratz, L. W., 1982, Geophysical studies of the Syncline Ridge area Nevada Test Site, Nye County, Nevada: U.S. Geological Survey Open-File Report 82–145, 55 p.

Kane, M. F., Healey, D. L., Peterson, D. L., Kaufmann, H. E., and Reidy, D., 1979, Bouguer gravity map of Nevada Las Vegas sheet: Nevada Bureau of Mines and Geology Map 61, scale 1:250,000.

Langenheim, R. L., Jr., 1988, Extensional and other structures in the Arrow Canyon and Las Vegas Ranges, Clark County, Nevada: Geological Society of America Abstracts with Programs, v. 20, p. 175.

Lister, G. S., Etheridge, M. A., and Symonds, P. A., 1986, Detachment faulting and the evolution of passive continental margins: Geology, v. 14, p. 246–250.

Longwell, C. R., 1930, Faulted fans west of the Sheep Range, southern Nevada: American Journal of Science, 5th series, v. 20, p. 1–13.

—— , 1945, Low-angle normal faults in the Basin and Range province: EOS Transactions of the American Geophysical Union, v. 26, p. 107–118.

Longwell, C. R., Pampeyan, E. H., Bowyer, B., and Roberts, R. J., 1965, Geology and mineral deposits of Clark County, Nevada: Nevada Bureau of Mines Bulletin 62, 218 p.

McKeown, F. A., Healey, D. L., and Miller, C. H., 1976, Geologic map of the Yucca Lake Quadrangle, Nye County, Nevada: U.S. Geological Survey Geologic Quadrangle Map GQ–1327, scale 1:24,000.

Miller, C. H., and Healey, D. L., 1986, Gravity interpretation of Frenchman Flat and vicinity, Nevada Test Site: U.S. Geological Survey Open-File Report 86–211, 36 p.

Nelson, M. R., and Jones, C. H., 1987, Paleomagnetism and crustal rotations along a shear zone, Las Vegas Range, southern Nevada: Tectonics, v. 6, p. 13–33.

Orkild, P. P., 1963, Geologic map of the Tippipah Spring Quadrangle, Nye County, Nevada: U.S. Geological Survey Geologic Quadrangle Map GQ–213, scale 1:24,000.

—— , 1968, Geologic map of the Mine Mountain Quadrangle, Nye County, Nevada: U.S. Geological Survey Geologic Quadrangle Map GQ–746, scale 1:24,000.

Poole, F. G., 1965, Geologic map of the Frenchman Flat Quadrangle, Nye, Lincoln, and Clark Counties, Nevada: U.S. Geological Survey Geologic Quadrangle Map GQ–456, scale 1:24,000.

Poole, F. G., Houser, F. N., and Orkild, P. P., 1961, Eleana Formation of Nevada Test Site and vicinity, Nye County, Nevada: U.S. Geological Survey Professional Paper 424–D, p. 104–110.

Sargent, K. A., and Stewart, J. H., 1971, Geologic map of the Specter Range NW Quadrangle, Nye County, Nevada: U.S. Geological Survey Geologic Quadrangle Map GQ–884, scale 1:24,000.

Skelly, M. F., and Axen, G. J., 1988, Thrust correlation and Tertiary disruption within the Sevier thrust belt, Muddy Mountains–Tule Springs Hills area, southern Nevada: Geological Society of America Abstracts with Programs, v. 20, p. 232.

Stewart, J. H., 1970, Upper Precambrian and Lower Cambrian strata in the southern Great Basin, California and Nevada: U.S. Geological Survey Professional Paper 620, 206 p.

Tschanz, C. M., and Pampeyan, E. H., 1970, Geology and mineral deposits of Lincoln County, Nevada: Nevada Bureau of Mines of Geology Bulletin 73, 187 p.

Wernicke, B., Guth, P. L., and Axen, G. J., 1984, Tertiary extensional tectonics in the Sevier belt of southern Nevada, *in* Lintz, J., Jr., ed., Western geological excursions: Reno, University of Nevada Department of Geological Sciences, Mackay School of Mines, v. 4, p. 473–510.

Wernicke, B., Walker, J. D., and Beaufait, M. S., 1985, Structural discordance between Neogene detachments and frontal Sevier thrusts, central Mormon Mountains, southern Nevada: Tectonics, v. 4, p. 213–246.

Wernicke, B., Axen, G. J., and Snow, J. K., 1988, Basin and range extensional tectonics at the latitude of Las Vegas: Geological Society of America Bulletin, v. 100, p. 1738–1757.

MANUSCRIPT ACCEPTED BY THE SOCIETY AUGUST 21, 1989

Geological Society of America
Memoir 176
1990

Chapter 12

Tectonic setting of Yucca Mountain, southwest Nevada

Robert B. Scott
U.S. Geological Survey, MS 913, Box 25046, Denver Federal Center, Denver, Colorado 80225

ABSTRACT

Yucca Mountain, in the south-central part of the Basin and Range Province, is characterized by structures typical of the Cenozoic extended terranes and oroclinal bending of the Walker Lane belt. The mountain consists of a series of ridges that bifurcate southward from a plateau-like remnant of a middle Miocene volcanic apron. The ridges are underlain by eastward tilted structural blocks and separated from one another by west-dipping, steep normal faults. Toward the south, the dips of normal faults decrease, but the number of normal faults, the amount of offset on individual faults, the amount of eastward tilt of the strata, and the degree of internal deformation within structural blocks all increase. Dips of major normal faults decrease southward. The northern end of the mountain has been extended about 10 percent, whereas the southern end has been extended about 60 percent. Progressive clockwise rotation about a vertical axis has produced a 30° oroclinal bend over a 25-km distance from north to south at Yucca Mountain.

Shallow exposure into the middle Miocene volcanic rocks beneath Yucca Mountain precludes observation of structural accommodation below the high-angle faults at the mountain. However, indirect evidence suggests the presence of an accommodation structure under the mountain, probably a low-angle normal fault at depths between 1 and 4 km. This evidence includes domino-style tilting of the blocks, probable listric faults, internal block deformation, closely spaced major normal faults, a probable decoupled stress field between Paleozoic and Tertiary rocks, and low-angle normal faults exposed in areas adjacent to Yucca Mountain. The presence of low-angle normal faults at several levels above a basal detachment fault to the east and west of Yucca Mountain suggests that an interconnected stack or tier of low-angle normal faults may exist under the mountain.

Rates of extensional deformation at Yucca Mountain reached an apparent maximum with geologic strain rates of nearly 10^{-14}/sec between 13 and 11.5 Ma and decreased to about 10^{-16}/sec afterward.

Clockwise oroclinal bending of rocks both at Yucca Mountain and at ranges affected by the Las Vegas Valley shear zone suggests that deformation is related. Except for small dextral strike-slip faults at the northern end of the mountain, the bending does not seem to be accommodated by the geometries of strike-slip faults. Oroclinal bending of rocks at the surface may reflect movement on deeper strike-slip zones or flexures that are partially decoupled along preexisting low-angle faults.

Scott, R. B., 1990, Tectonic setting of Yucca Mountain, southwest Nevada, *in* Wernicke, B. P., ed., Basin and Range extensional tectonics near the latitude of Las Vegas, Nevada: Boulder, Colorado, Geological Society of America Memoir 176.

INTRODUCTION

The purpose of this chapter is to (1) interpret the structural geometry and kinematic history of Yucca Mountain, including inferences drawn from structures exposed in the more deeply eroded regions to the east and west, and (2) to explain how Basin and Range extension may have interacted with oroclinal bending and strike-slip faulting in the area. To this end, I will use stratigraphic, structural, and kinematic constraints to predict how structures under Yucca Mountain may accommodate the extensional fault system at the mountain and how the rates of Cenozoic deformation have changed with time. Finally, I will suggest a regional tectonic setting consistent with the geologic relations at Yucca Mountain.

Geological interest in this area has intensified since Yucca Mountain was chosen in 1987 by the U.S. Congress as the primary site of investigation for an underground repository for commercial high-level nuclear waste. Suitability of this site is partly dependent on predictions of its future tectonic stability. Tectonic stability can be evaluated only after the structures at Yucca Mountain, particularly the Quaternary faults, are understood in terms of their displacement magnitudes, their rupture histories, and their role in the release of regional tectonic stresses.

The geology of Yucca Mountain has been mapped at a scale of 1:24,000 by Christiansen and Lipman (1965), Lipman and McKay (1965), and McKay and Sargent (1970) and at 1:48,000 by Swadley (1983). The geology of the eastern part of Yucca Mountain and Jackass Flats has been compiled by Maldonado (1985a). Several regional tectonic syntheses bearing on the geology of Yucca Mountain (W. J. Carr, 1974, 1984; U.S. Geological Survey, 1984; Hamilton, 1988; M. D. Carr and Monsen, 1988) have not adequately taken into account the geology of Yucca Mountain to describe the tectonic setting of the nuclear waste site. The geometric relations described in this chapter are based primarily on mapping by Scott and Bonk (1984) and on subsequent mapping by myself, all at a scale of 1:12,000.

Yucca Mountain lies in the central part of the southern Basin and Range Province, a region in which both normal and strike-slip faults have accommodated nearly 250 km of extension during the last 20 m.y. between the Colorado Plateau and the Sierra Nevada Mountains (Wernicke and others, 1988a). High ranges and broad basins characterize the Basin and Range structural province to the northeast; in contrast, relatively low ridges and narrow alluvial valleys characterize the Yucca Mountain area. The mountain lies directly south of a northwest-trending boundary separating north- to northeast-trending ranges in the north from generally northwest-trending ranges in the south (Fig. 1). Stewart (1988) considered this boundary to be the northeastern edge of the Walker Lane belt, a complex zone of right- and left-lateral faults, detachment faults, and northwest-trending Basin and Range structural blocks. The belt includes the southern part of the southwest Nevada volcanic field and the Las Vegas Valley shear zone, as originally postulated by Gianella and Callaghan (1934).

The repetition, eastward tilt, lateral offset, and rotation of strata at Yucca Mountain seen in Figure 2 are features found in areas extended by normal faulting and affected by strike-slip faulting and oroclinal bending. The volcanic strata are broken by high-angle, west-dipping Cenozoic normal faults, forming a series of north-trending and east-dipping structural blocks that underlie the ridges. These blocks are similar to tilted "dominoes" associated with upper plates of extensional allochthons (Wernicke and Burchfiel, 1982). Although erosion at Yucca Mountain exposes only a few hundred meters of middle Miocene volcanic strata and does not cut deep enough to expose structures below high-angle normal faults, low-angle normal or detachment faults are suggested at depth by indirect structural evidence at the mountain and by structures in deeper exposures in surrounding areas. (I will restrict the term *detachment fault* to those low-angle faults that emplace extended upper crustal rocks above mid-crustal rocks and the term *low-angle normal fault* to those low-angle faults that underlie extended upper crustal allochthons to avoid confusion found in the literature. Structures that accommodate overlying extended allochthons may be either discrete faults [simple shear] or pervasive coaxial deformation [pure shear] analogous to those recognized by Gans and others [1985]. In the absence of direct evidence of pure shear deformation in this study, only the presence of discrete faults will be proposed.)

STRATIGRAPHIC FRAMEWORK

The probable stratigraphic sequence of rocks beneath Yucca Mountain is summarized in Table 1 and discussed below. The pre-Cenozoic rocks were complexly faulted and folded by Mesozoic compressional tectonism before Cenozoic rocks were deposited.

The oldest rocks are gneiss and schist of an Early Proterozoic crystalline basement exposed in the Death Valley area; they date from 1.8 Ga (Wasserburg and others, 1959). The overlying upper Proterozoic clastic and carbonate metasedimentary rocks of the Late Proterozoic Pahrump Group and Noonday Dolomite are several kilometers thick in the Death Valley area and in the Funeral Mountains (Jennings, 1977; Wright and Troxel, 1984) but thin toward Yucca Mountain. Late Proterozoic to Middle Cambrian clastic strata are about 3 km thick in exposures at Bare Mountain and in the southern Specter Range, west and southeast of Yucca Mountain, respectively (Fig. 1). Middle Cambrian to Late Devonian carbonate strata are about 4.5 km thick in the region (U.S. Geological Survey, 1984).

Silurian carbonate rocks occur beneath the Tertiary cover in the east-central part of Yucca Mountain at drill hole UE-25p#1 (Fig. 3) (M. D. Carr and others, 1986). The geometry of the Paleozoic rocks under Yucca Mountain can be inferred by extrapolation of the geometry of Mesozoic structures from surrounding ranges (Robinson, 1985; Carr and Monsen, 1988; Burchfiel, 1965; Sargent and others, 1970; Sargent and Stewart, 1971; McKay and Williams, 1964). Thrusts generally consist of

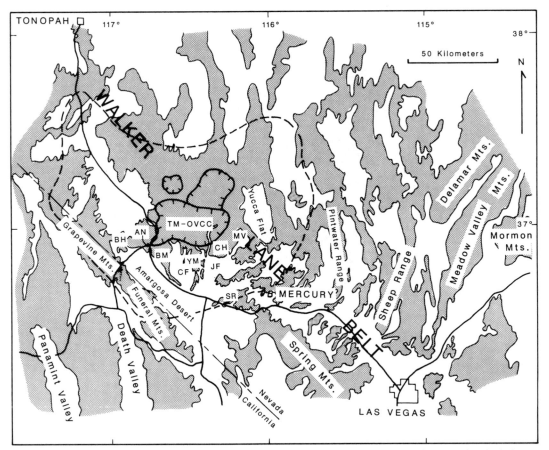

Figure 1. Location of regional geographic and specific geologic features. Bedrock is shown by shaded pattern. AN = Amargosa Narrows, BH = Bullfrog Hills, BM = Bare Mountain, CF = Crater Flat, CH = Calico Hills, JF = Jackass Flats, MV = Mid Valley, SR = Specter Range, TM-OVCC = Timber Mountain–Oasis Valley caldera complex, YM = Yucca Mountain. The dashed line encloses approximate limits of the Miocene southwest Nevada volcanic field. Bold hachured lines enclose calderas. Major highways are shown by bold lines. North- and north-northeast-trending mountain ranges are found northeast of the Walker Lane belt, whereas northwest-trending ranges are found generally southwest of the Walker Lane Belt (Stewart, 1988).

steep ramps that climb section toward the southeast; therefore, the upper and lower plates of the thrusts near the Specter Range and southern Bare Mountain consist of strata no younger than the upper part of the Devonian Nevada Fordmation of former usage. In contrast, in the northern part of Bare Mountain and in the Calico Hills, low-angle faults (either thrusts or low-angle normal faults) placed older Paleozoic rocks above Mississippian clastic rocks. These geometries suggest that under the northern part of Yucca Mountain, Mississippian clastic rocks are present within the Paleozoic sequence, whereas in the southern part of the mountain, older Paleozoic rocks are present (Robinson, 1985).

The Tertiary strata at Yucca Mountain consist of four major ash-flow tuff units that were erupted from the Timber Mountain–Oasis Valley caldera complex during the middle Miocene (Fig. 1; Byers and others, 1976b). From oldest to youngest these units include (1) several unexposed ash-flow tuffs, about 15 to 14 Ma, (2) the Crater Flat Tuff, about 14 Ma, (3) the Paintbrush Tuff, about 13.5 to 13 Ma, and (4) the Timber Mountain Tuff, about

11.5 Ma. Radiometric ages in this chapter (Byers and others, 1976a) are corrected for new K-Ar constants (Steiger and Jager, 1977). Study of cores from Yucca Mountain shows that the deeply buried, less welded tuffs are more pervasively altered to zeolites and clays than are the three younger units (Broxton and others, 1986). The rare exposures of the Crater Flat Tuff are shown as the volcanic rocks predating the Paintbrush Tuff in Figure 3. The mountain is capped by about 300 m of the Topopah Spring Member and 100 m of the overlying Tiva Canyon Member of the Paintbrush Tuff. The Rainier Mesa and Ammonia Tanks Members of the Timber Mountain Tuff erupted about 11.5 Ma and filled topographic lows between major fault blocks formed by block faulting between 13 and 11.5 Ma. Significantly, the Rainier Mesa Member is restricted to northern localities, whereas the younger Ammonia Tanks Member is restricted to southern localities north and northwest of the Quaternary basalt shown on Figure 3. No remnants of the Timber Mountain Tuff are present at the higher elevations on Yucca Mountain, even in

Figure 2. Oblique aerial photograph of Yucca Mountain. View to the northeast. Crater Flat forms the foreground; the northern end of Yucca Mountain (The Prow) is the triangular plateau on the left; the southern end of the mountain is in the lower right corner; and Fortymile Wash and Jackass Flats form the background east of Yucca Mountain. From north to south, Yucca Mountain is 25 km long. The dark features in the foreground, from left to right, are three basaltic cones (about 1.2 Ma), several irregular flows and basaltic vents (about 3.7 Ma), and an isolated cone at the southern end of Yucca Mountain (less than 250,000 B.P.).

the down-dropped blocks containing the nonwelded uppermost part of the Paintbrush Tuff.

The upper part of the Tertiary sequence has been studied by drilling at Yucca Mountain. The three deepest holes, USW G-1, G-2, and GU-3/G-3, were drilled in the central and northern part of the mountain to depths of 1.8 km in Miocene volcanic strata, but none reached Paleozoic rocks (Fig. 3) (Spengler and others, 1981; Maldonado and Koether, 1983; Scott and Castellanos, 1984). At drill hole UE-25p#1 on the east-central part of Yucca Mountain, a nonwelded ash-flow tuff is separated from underlying Paleozoic rocks by a fault of unknown attitude at a depth of 1.2 km (M. D. Carr and others, 1986). Geophysical data indicate that Tertiary rocks become significantly thicker to the west and northwest of Yucca Mountain; the gravity field decreases 16 mGal between the gravity high close to drill hole UE-25p#1 and the gravity low 6 km to the northwest (Snyder and Carr, 1984). Although Snyder and Carr (1984) suggest, on the basis of gravity and seismic reflection data, that Tertiary strata are thicker than 3 km, Ackermann and others (1988) use more recent seis-

mic reflection data to infer that the thickness of Tertiary strata in northwestern Yucca Mountain is 3 km or less.

Upper Miocene, Pliocene, and Quaternary rocks include basaltic lava, ash, and scoria erupted in Crater Flat and southern Yucca Mountain. The oldest basalts have been dated at 9 to 10 Ma (W. J. Carr, 1984). On the west side of Yucca Mountain, these old basalt flows are exposed only in southern Crater Flat, west of the areas shown in Figures 2 and 3; they were found in the subsurface of Crater Flat by drilling (Carr and Parrish, 1985). Basalt flows of similar age cap mesas east of Yucca Mountain (Fig. 2). Scattered basaltic dikes of this age in northern Yucca Mountain (Scott and Bonk, 1984) are too small to show at the scale of Figure 3. Pliocene basalts, erupted at 3.7 Ma, form an eroded complex of flows and vents in the southeast part of Crater Flat (Figs. 2 and 3; Vaniman and others, 1982). West and north of these Pliocene basalts, four basaltic cones were constructed at 1.2 Ma along an arcuate north-northeast alignment (Vaniman and others, 1982); Figure 2 shows the northern three cones. In the southern part of Yucca Mountain (Figs. 2 and 3), the youngest

TABLE 1. MAJOR STRATIGRAPHIC UNITS IN THE YUCCA MOUNTAIN REGION

Age	Stratigraphic Units	Major Lithology	Range of Thickness* (m)
Miocene	Volcanic rocks of southwest Nevada volcanic field	Silicic ash-flow tuffs and minor basalts	1,000 to 3,000
Permian and Pennsylvanian	Tippipah Limestone	Limestone	1,065 to 1,100
Mississippian and Devonian(?)	Eleana Formation	Shale, quartzite, conglomerate, limestone	2,345 to 2,400
Late Devonian to Middle Cambrian	Devils Gate Limestone, Nevada Formation[†], Ely Springs Dolomite, Eureka Quartzite, Pogonip Group, Nopah Formation, Dunderberg Shale, Bonanza King Formation, upper Carrara Formation	Limestone, dolomite, minor quartzite, shale, siltstone	4,310 to 4,830
Middle Cambrian to Late Proterozoic	Lower Carrara Formation, Zabriskie Quartzite, Wood Canyon Formation, Stirling Quartzite, Johnnie Formation[§]	Quartzite, siltstone, shale	2,765 to 3,090
Late Proterozoic	Noonday Dolomite, Pahrump Group**	Conglomerate, shale, limestone, dolomite	>3,000(?)
Early Proterozoic	Crystalline basement	Gneiss, schist	-----

*Ranges based on Robinson (1985), U.S. Geological Survey (1984), and Wright and Troxel (1984).
[†]Of former usage.
[§]Base not exposed in Yucca Mountain area.
**Isolated basins in crystalline basement prior to miogeoclinal accumulation between the Late Proterozoic and Permian. Although these basins are exposed in the Death Valley area, they may pinch out northward under the Yucca Mountain area (Wright and others, 1974).

basaltic center consists of an older platform of basaltic lava overlain by a younger cinder cone. The basaltic lava is less than 250,000 years old (Crowe and others, 1983), but the cone may have erupted as recently as the latest Pleistocene or early Holocene (Wells and others, 1988).

STRUCTURAL GEOMETRY

Yucca Mountain is the faulted, tilted, and eroded remnant of a middle Miocene volcanic apron on the south side of the Timber Mountain–Oasis Valley caldera complex. The northern, relatively unbroken end of the mountain forms a triangular plateau called The Prow (Figs. 2 and 3). West-dipping normal faults south of The Prow have broken that area into narrow, east-tilted blocks that extend 25 km southward (Figs. 3 and 4). Northwest-striking dextral and northeast-striking sinistral strike-slip faults are also present.

Dip-slip faults

Compared to major range-front faults, the offsets of 50 to 500 m on major dip-slip normal faults at Yucca Mountain are small; however, these normal faults play an important role in regional extension. Before discussing that role, the pattern and morphology of normal faults and the strain within intervening fault blocks are described.

A distinctive fan-shaped pattern of ridges at Yucca Mountain is formed where major normal faults bifurcate southward,

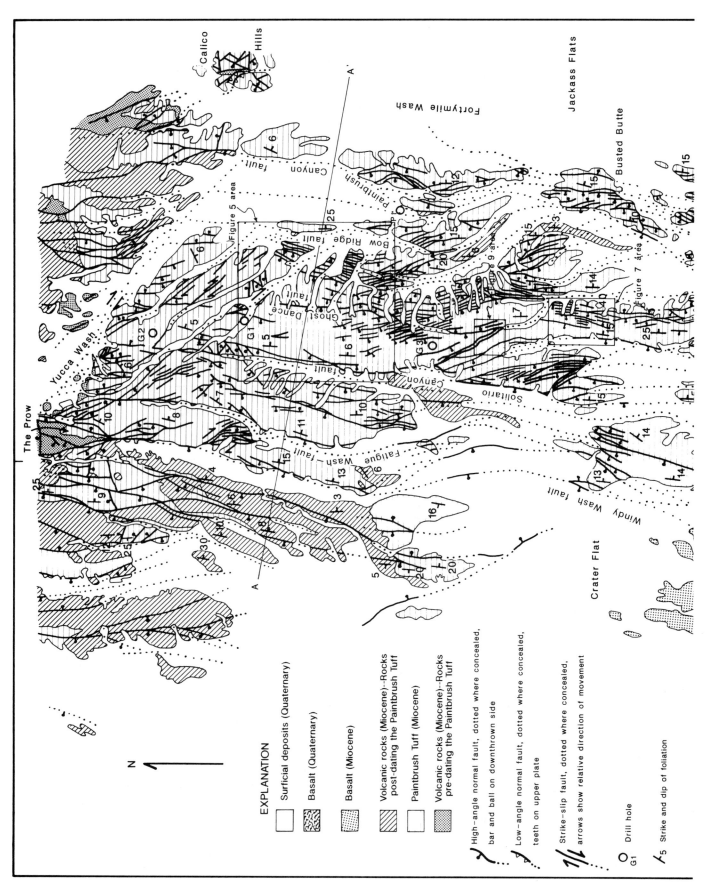

EXPLANATION

Surficial deposits (Quaternary)

Basalt (Quaternary)

Basalt (Miocene)

Volcanic rocks (Miocene)–Rocks post-dating the Paintbrush Tuff

Paintbrush Tuff (Miocene)

Volcanic rocks (Miocene)–Rocks pre-dating the Paintbrush Tuff

High-angle normal fault, dotted where concealed, bar and ball on downthrown side

Low-angle normal fault, dotted where concealed, teeth on upper plate

Strike-slip fault, dotted where concealed, arrows show relative direction of movement

Drill hole
G1

Strike and dip of foliation
5

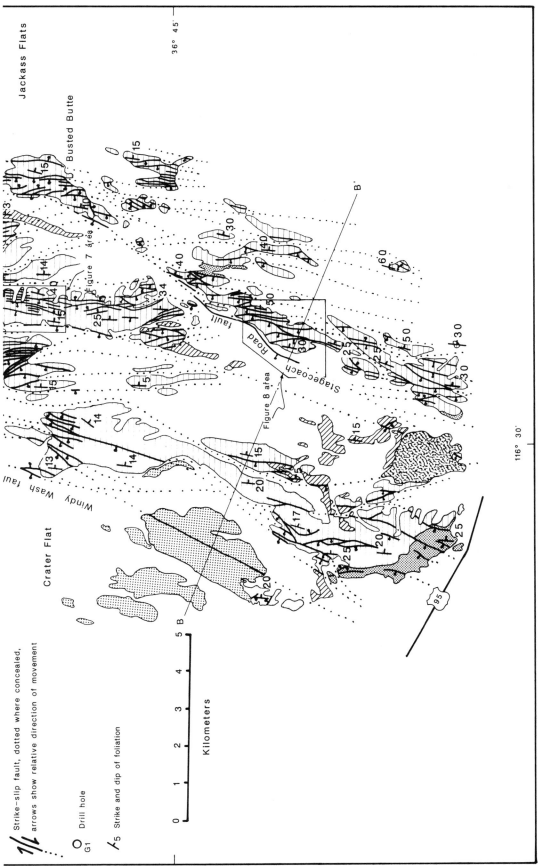

Figure 3. Generalized geologic map of Yucca Mountain. Geology from Scott and Bonk (1984) and current field mapping. Locations of the areas shown in Figures 5, 7, 8, and 9 are outlined. Drill holes USW G-1, USW G-2, USW G-3, and UE-25p#1 are shown by open circles (G1, G2, G3, and P1, respectively). Major normal faults are named in the northern part of Yucca Mountain. Both known and approximately located faults are illustrated with solid lines. A-A' and B-B' are lines of section shown in Figure 4.

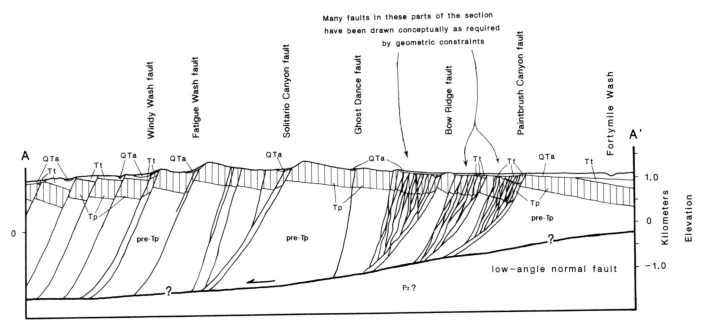

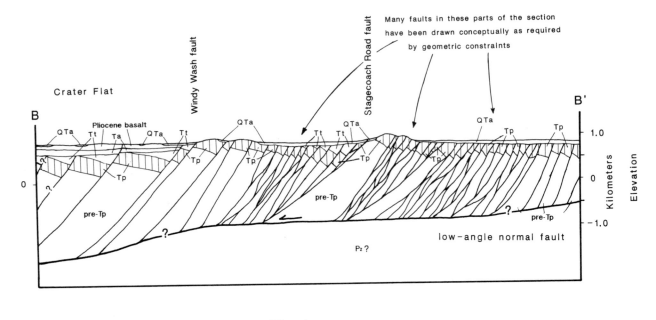

Figure 4. Generalized cross sections of Yucca Mountain. Locations of sections A-A′ and B-B′ are shown on Figure 3. The Paintbrush Tuff (Tp) is shown by the striped pattern; QTa = Quaternary and Tertiary alluvial deposits; Ta = Tertiary alluvial deposits; pre-Tp = Tertiary rocks predating the Paintbrush Tuff; and Tt = Timber Mountain Tuff (post–Paintbrush Tuff unit). Major normal faults are named in section A-A′; with the exception of the Stagecoach Road and Windy Wash faults, major faults in section B-B′ are unnamed. The depth to Paleozoic(?) rocks (Pz?) is estimated from gravity data (Snyder and Carr, 1984), seismic studies (Ackermann and others, 1988), and the drill hole UE-25p#1 (M. D. Carr and others, 1986). Zones of conceptualized faults are based on projection of exposed structures along strike and on the geometry of structural and stratigraphic constraints that are described in the text. An explanation for the low-angle fault at the base of the Tertiary rocks is also discussed in the text.

increasing the number of fault-controlled ridges. The offset on each normal fault and the eastward tilt on fault blocks between major normal faults generally increase southward (Figs. 3 and 4). For example, the Solitario Canyon fault branches into four separate major faults over a distance of 10 km as the cumulative offset increases from zero in the north to about 1 km at the southern end of the exposures. The eastward tilt of strata increases from less than 10° in the northern part to over 30° in the southern part of the mountain.

Three independent lines of evidence can be used to indicate that major normal faults are listric. First, the dip of the major west-dipping fault on the south slope of Busted Butte decreases from 85° to 73° over a decrease in elevation of about 275 m. Also, the dips of other major normal faults at Yucca Mountain are generally slightly lower at deeper stratigraphic levels than at higher ones.

Second, about 0.4 km east of drill hole USW GU-3/G-3, a southern extension of the Ghost Dance fault has more than 25 m of offset (Fig. 3). Scott and Castellanos (1984) assumed that the fault gouge intersected at a depth of about 1.3 km in the drill hole is the subsurface continuation of this fault because it is the closest fault with more than a few meters of offset east of the drill hole. The fault at the surface dips 77°W, and the gouge zone in the drill hole dips at 50°. This geometry indicates that the fault is listric with a decrease in dip of about 21°/km (Scott and Castellanos, 1984).

The third line of evidence is that on the eastern part of fault blocks at Yucca Mountain (the hanging-wall part of the blocks), strata dip eastward more steeply than in the western part of fault blocks (Fig. 5). The increase in stratal dip in the hanging wall above major normal faults is opposite in sense to that predicted by drag on the faults (Scott, 1984a); this relation has been recognized in brittle rocks by Hamblin (1965) and interpreted by him as analogous to "roll-over" structures found in ductile Gulf Coast sediments. If this structural analogy is applied to these structures at Yucca Mountain, then this geometry (Fig. 5) infers that the major normal faults at Yucca Mountain are listric.

Differences in degree and style of deformation exist within each structural block between bounding major normal faults (Fig. 5). In general, three structural zones can be recognized between and within the structural blocks bounded by major normal faults. (1) Between blocks, zones adjacent to the major normal faults are characterized by west-dipping strata, which contrasts with east-dipping strata within the blocks. The strata in these west-dipping zones are commonly intensely faulted and brecciated in part. Dips are generally less than the dips of the major normal faults, but in some localities stratal dips are steeper. (2) On the west sides (or leading edge) of most blocks, relatively unfaulted zones have uniform eastward dips that are more shallow than on the east sides. (3) The east sides (or trailing edges) of blocks have both distinctly steeper eastward dips and an imbricate pattern of closely spaced, steep, west-dipping faults with minor, down-to-the-west offsets of a few meters or less. These zones are herein referred to as imbricate fault zones. The exposed widths of imbricate fault zones relative to exposed widths of unfaulted zones generally increase southward where surficial deposits are more prevalent (Fig. 6). The southward increase in areas underlain by imbricate fault zones is probably even greater than shown in Figure 6, because imbricate fault zones are generally found in lower topographic areas than are unfaulted zones and therefore are more likely to be covered. Also, in general, the angle of eastward dip of strata in both unfaulted and imbricate fault zones increases southward.

Changes in the degree and style of deformation from north to south at Yucca Mountain can best be demonstrated by comparing selected areas representative of northern (Fig. 5), central (Fig. 7), and southern (Fig. 8) Yucca Mountain. A large-scale geologic map and section of a structural block typical of the northern part of Yucca Mountain show that strata dip eastward at 5° to 9°, and few faults occur in the unfaulted zone (Fig. 5). The adjacent imbricate fault zone has closely spaced faults that dip steeply westward and strata that dip eastward between 12 and 33°. The cross section in Figure 5 shows my concept of the anastomosing, interconnected, subparallel faults within the imbricate fault zone.

An important geometric relation exists between the attitude of the west-dipping faults and strata in the imbricate zones. The average dip of 40 west-dipping faults in the imbricate zones is 77°, and the dip varies between 58° and 88° in this northern area. These steep dips of imbricate faults contrast significantly with the shallower dips of the major faults. For example, the Windy Wash fault averages a dip of 59° (12 observations), the Fatigue Wash fault averages 74° (7), the Solitario Canyon fault averages 65° (31), the Bow Canyon fault averages 69° (3), and the Paintbrush Canyon fault averages 69° (14). The dip of strata in imbricate zones averages 20° and ranges between 3 and 80°. Angles between the tops of strata and imbricate faults on the footwall sides of the blocks average 97° and range between 80 and 155°, forming a slightly obtuse angle on an average. This geometry will be discussed in the interpretive section on internal block deformation.

In the central part of Yucca Mountain, strata dip eastward between 7 and 15° in the unfaulted zone and between 20 and 40° in the imbricate fault zone (Fig. 7). The closely spaced normal faults typical of the imbricate normal fault zone were mapped in the northeast and south-central parts of the area but could not be traced through the intervening area. Where mapped, swarms of normal faults cut sharp stratigraphic boundaries in bedded tuffs or margins of the cooling units. Individual faults have offsets of several meters at most and could not be traced through the massive, densely welded, highly fractured tuff of the intervening areas, although their presence is geometrically required.

Some excellent exposures show that faulting in the imbricate fault zones is so pervasive that it cannot be accurately depicted, even at the large scales shown on Figures 5, 7, and 8. But exposures are not good everywhere. Slopes are commonly covered by colluvium, and stratigraphic contacts between massive zones in ash-flow tuffs are gradational, making the recognition of small

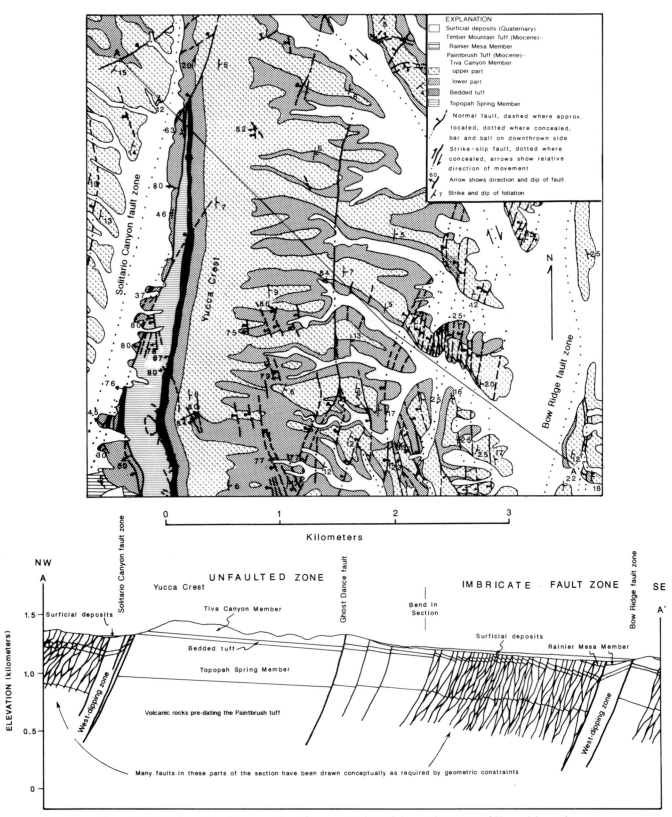

Figure 5. Geologic map and cross section of an area typical of the northern part of Yucca Mountain (Fig. 3). Geology from Scott and Bonk (1984). Line A-A′ locates cross section. Note that only a few of the faults in the imbricate fault zone shown in the cross section can be correlated with mapped faults. The faults shown are a conceptualized projection from fragmental evidence seen in small exposures.

faults difficult. Also, erosion over much of Yucca Mountain has restricted exposures to the massive parts of tuffs. There is thus an exposure-dependent lack of uniformity in mapping small faults. Because they can represent significant cumulative displacement, their omission can create important deficiencies in mapped total strain. The deficiency is commonly revealed in the construction of cross sections wherein faults must be added to meet the constraints of stratal dip and unit thickness. Addition of a few faults with large offsets would be geologically unreasonable because large offsets can be recognized even in poorly exposed massive tuffs. Therefore, geologically reasonable cross sections must include many faults with small offsets to account for the strain. Although these conceptual faults are shown in cross sections (Figs. 4, 5, 7, and 8), only those faults actually observed during mapping are shown on maps.

In the example of the southern part of Yucca Mountain (Fig. 8), strata in the unfaulted zone dip more steeply, 25° to 30° eastward, and the rocks in the imbricate fault zone dip between 20° and 59° eastward.

Dips on major block-bounding faults and on imbricate faults generally decrease southward. The average dip on block-bounding faults in the northern part of Yucca Mountain averages 66° (67 measurements) in contrast to an average of 51° (21 measurements) in the southern part. Observed dips in imbricate faults in the northern area average 77°, in contrast to those in the southern part of Yucca Mountain; in Figure 8 for example, observed dips on imbricate faults range from 33° to 61° and average 51°.

Faults cut surficial deposits more steeply than they cut underlying volcanic bedrock. For example, the Stagecoach Road fault bounding the west side of the ridge shown in Figure 8 dips only 29° to 45° where it cuts bedrock. Where the fault cuts alluvium, dips are between 75° and 77°. Presumably, the steeper dips of faults in alluvium result from the rotation of the stress field at the unconfined ground surface.

A distinctive type of small graben occurs in several of the unfaulted zones in the northern part of Yucca Mountain. Although grabens are commonly bounded by fault planes that dip toward one another and the downdropped block in an antithetic relation, most of the grabens at Yucca Mountain are bounded by fault planes that are nearly parallel to one another in a synthetic relation. The grabens and bounding faults were rotated after their formation, causing both bounding faults to dip westward. As demonstrated by the two examples of these grabens shown in Figure 9, the grabens vary from less than 0.1 to over 1 km long and from 10 to 30 m wide and are downdropped from a few to more than 10 m. Strata in the downdropped blocks are brecciated and chaotic. These grabens also occur in the imbricate fault zones but are very difficult to recognize in complexly faulted terranes.

Strike-slip faults

In addition to dip-slip faults, both dextral and sinistral strike-slip and oblique-slip faults cut Yucca Mountain. In the northeast-

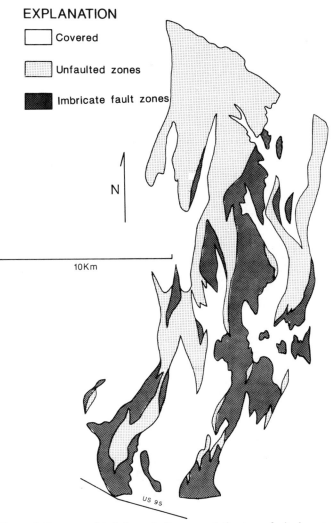

EXPLANATION

☐ Covered

▨ Unfaulted zones

■ Imbricate fault zones

Figure 6. Increase of imbricate fault zones relative to unfaulted zones from north to south.

ern part of the mountain, faults paralleling several northwest-trending washes show evidence for dextral offset (Scott and others, 1984; Scott and Bonk, 1984). The faults have steep dips and approximately horizontal fault-slip lineations. An aeromagnetic anomaly provided a basis for predicting the strike-slip fault in Yucca Wash, and strike-slip faults exposed in bedrock south of Yucca Wash were projected under alluvium based on resistivity surveys (Scott and others, 1984). Where projected toward the southeast, these strike-slip faults are inferred to end at the aeromagnetic anomalies related to the Paintbrush Canyon and the Bow Ridge faults (Fig. 3). Exposures east of the Paintbrush Canyon fault in bedrock in Yucca Wash contain no evidence of strike-slip faults (Scott and Bonk, 1984). Conversely, the aeromagnetic anomaly related to the Bow Ridge fault seems to terminate at the strike-slip fault in Yucca Wash, and other north-trending faults are not on strike with equivalent normal faults north of Yucca Wash. Although evidence for Quaternary

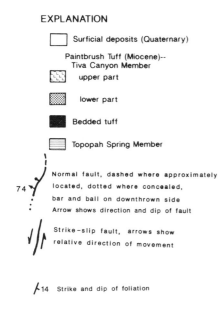

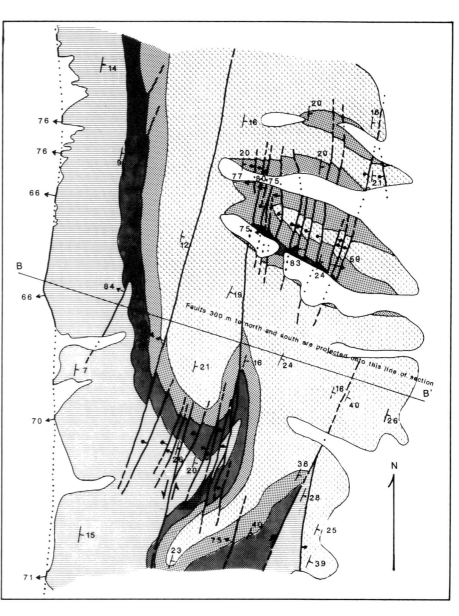

EXPLANATION

☐ Surficial deposits (Quaternary)

Paintbrush Tuff (Miocene)--
Tiva Canyon Member

▨ upper part

▨ lower part

◼ Bedded tuff

▤ Topopah Spring Member

Normal fault, dashed where approximately
located, dotted where concealed,
bar and ball on downthrown side
Arrow shows direction and dip of fault

Strike-slip fault, arrows show
relative direction of movement

⊢14 Strike and dip of foliation

Figure 7. Geologic map and cross section of an area typical of the central part of Yucca Mountain (Fig. 3). Geology from current field mapping. Line B-B′ locates cross section. Only three faults in the imbricate fault zone were traced across the line of section; others shown on the cross section were either projected from about 300 m onto the section or drawn conceptually as required by geometric constraints.

```
0    0.1   0.2   0.3   0.4   0.5

              KILOMETER
```

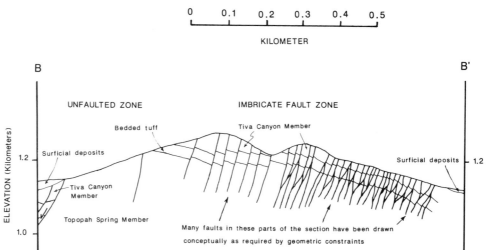

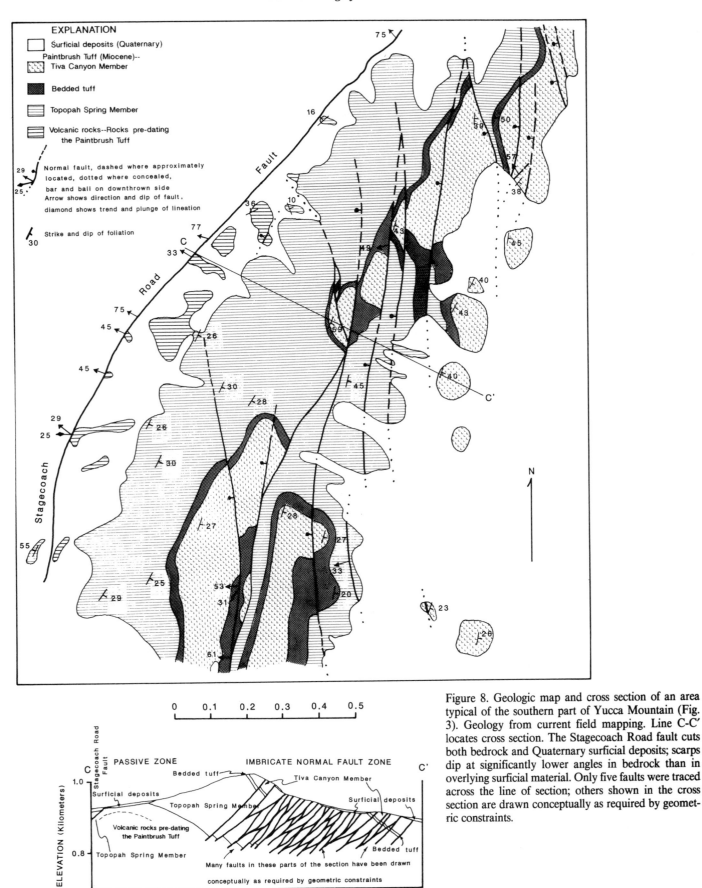

EXPLANATION

Surficial deposits (Quaternary)

Paintbrush Tuff (Miocene)--
Tiva Canyon Member

Bedded tuff

Topopah Spring Member

Volcanic rocks--Rocks pre-dating
the Paintbrush Tuff

Normal fault, dashed where approximately
located, dotted where concealed,
bar and ball on downthrown side.
Arrow shows direction and dip of fault,
diamond shows trend and plunge of lineation

Strike and dip of foliation

Figure 8. Geologic map and cross section of an area typical of the southern part of Yucca Mountain (Fig. 3). Geology from current field mapping. Line C-C' locates cross section. The Stagecoach Road fault cuts both bedrock and Quaternary surficial deposits; scarps dip at significantly lower angles in bedrock than in overlying surficial material. Only five faults were traced across the line of section; others shown in the cross section are drawn conceptually as required by geometric constraints.

EXPLANATION

☐ Surficial deposits (Quaternary)

Paintbrush Tuff (Miocene)
Tiva Canyon Member

▨ upper part--Caprock

▨ lower part

■ Bedded tuff

▨ Topopah Spring Member

78 ⌐ Normal fault, dashed where approximately located,
  • dotted where concealed, arrow shows direction and dip of fault,
  ⋮ bar and ball on downthrown side

⌐ 4 Strike and dip of foliation

Figure 9. Geologic map and cross section of synthetic grabens (Fig. 3). Geology from current field mapping and mapping by Scott and Bonk (1984). Line D-D' locates cross section. Strata within the grabens are coarsely brecciated and steeply dipping.

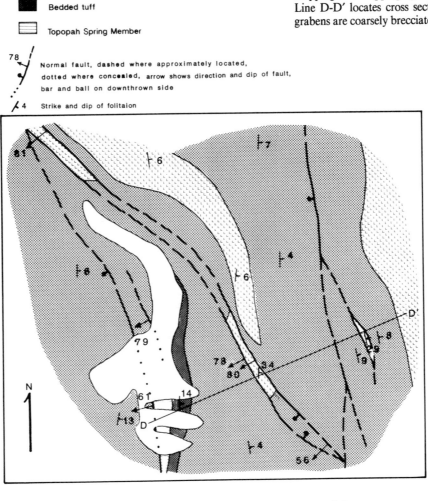

0   0.1   0.2   0.3   0.4   0.5

Kilometer

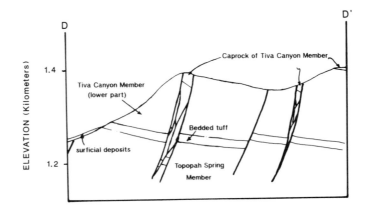

movement has been observed on the Bow Ridge and Paintbrush Canyon faults (Swadley and others, 1984), no Quaternary movement has been identified on any of the northwest-striking faults, including those in the vicinity of Yucca Wash. An interpretation of these seemingly contradictory relations will be presented below in the section on the model of plate-bounding faults.

Several sinistral, oblique-slip to horizontal-slip faults trend northeast in central and southern Yucca Mountain. The largest of these is the Stagecoach Road fault, which displays west-trending oblique slip (Fig. 8). J. W. Whitney found evidence for left-lateral offset on the Stagecoach Road fault to include (1) 5 to 7 m of left-lateral offset of washes in Quaternary fan deposits above a bedrock pediment; (2) steeply dipping caliche layers on the hanging-wall sides of the fault that project southward into washes, causing intermittent flow to be diverted around the more resistant caliche; and (3) oblique sinistral fault-slip striations on the relatively low-angle normal fault in the bedrock (Scott and Whitney, 1987).

North of the Stagecoach Road fault, nearly vertical devitrified veins in a vitrophyre have been offset about a meter in a left-lateral sense on minor northeast-striking faults. These structures occur just south of the area shown in Figure 7. Another fault, in the south-central part of Figure 7, requires left-lateral offset because the outcrop pattern in the northern part of the fault can fit either down-to-the-west or sinistral offset, but the southern part can fit either down-to-the-east or sinistral offset. Sinistral offset is chosen for consistency. Numerous minor, northeast-striking, steeply dipping faults in this area have almost horizontal fault-slip lineations, but no independent evidence indicates that these faults are sinistral.

In previous mapping and compilations, the Stagecoach Road fault was projected to the northeast, south of Busted Butte (Lipman and McKay, 1965; McKay and Sargent, 1970; Maldonado, 1985a). However, my more detailed mapping of the bedrock indicates that the fault probably projects east-northeast, west of Busted Butte, connecting with the Paintbrush Canyon fault. Also, no evidence of a fault cutting the Quaternary deposits in Fortymile Wash has been found. J. W. Whitney found the 0.74-Ma Bishop ash bed, buried in sand ramps west of Busted Butte, to be offset 4 m vertically along the Paintbrush Canyon fault (Scott and Whitney, 1987). This indicates that Quaternary movement has occurred not only on the Stagecoach Road part but also on the Paintbrush Canyon part of this fault system.

INDICATORS OF KINEMATIC HISTORY

Several features record deformational kinematics at Yucca Mountain. These include stratal tilt, vertical-axis rotation of paleomagnetic lineations, and direction and sense of fault slip.

Stratal tilt

Compaction foliation in ash-flow tuffs and bedding in bedded tuffs record the degree and direction of tilt. The assumption that compaction foliation and bedding were originally horizontal is based on two postulates. (1) Simple two-dimensional compaction is horizontal. Stratal tilt was not measured in rare cases of post-emplacement flow. Where ash-flow sheets are emplaced close to the margins of caldera complexes, slight original dips in ash-flow sheets may be inherited from slopes that dip radially away from the caldera or from resurgence of the caldera. Evidence of an original dip to compaction foliation related to the caldera is absent; therefore, I assume the original dip was horizontal. (2) I assume that rotation from the emplacement attitude to the present tilted state was made about a horizontal axis.

Vertical-axis rotation

Preliminary paleomagnetic evidence collected by J. G. Rosenbaum suggests that the Tiva Canyon Member of the Paintbrush Tuff at Yucca Mountain has been rotated clockwise about a vertical axis (Scott and Rosenbaum, 1986). Eleven sites in the Tiva Canyon Member were sampled from north to south at Yucca Mountain (Fig. 10a). After removing the dip of the strata, paleomagnetic pole positions of the samples form a 30° arc on a stereographic projection (Fig. 10b); the pole positions on the arc increase in a clockwise direction with sample distance from northern Yucca Mountain. Strikes of major normal faults at Yucca Mountain also swing in a clockwise direction from north to south (Figs. 2 and 3). These preliminary observations have been confirmed by further paleomagnetic studies at Yucca Mountain by Rosenbaum and Hudson (1988).

Fault-slip lineations

Eighty fault-slip lineations measured in the Paintbrush Tuff on normal faults and strike-slip faults in the northern part of Yucca Mountain were analyzed to quantify the kinematic transport direction and paleostress directions (Scott and Hofland, 1987). Fault-slip data used for this study were collected only in the northern area, where the effects of vertical- and horizontal-axis rotation are relatively small (Scott and Bonk, 1984). Valid corrections for structural rotations cannot be made to determine paleostress directions because the time of formation of fault-slip lineations relative to the time of rotation is not known. At Yucca Mountain, the age of the slip is poorly constrained; ages of movement on faults will be discussed below.

Striae on fault surfaces generally trend westward, as shown in Figure 11a. This relation is consistent with the general observation that southwest-dipping faults contain oblique striae that record a dextral sense of motion, whereas northwest-dipping faults contain oblique striae that record a sinistral sense of motion (Fig. 11a). Between fault strikes of N8°W and N6°E, a mixture of dextral and sinistral slips is observed. Of faults that strike west of N8°W, 29 have dextral slip and only 2 have sinistral slip. Of faults that strike east of N6°E, 14 have sinistral slip and only 1 has dextral slip.

The attitudes and relative magnitudes of principal stress axes

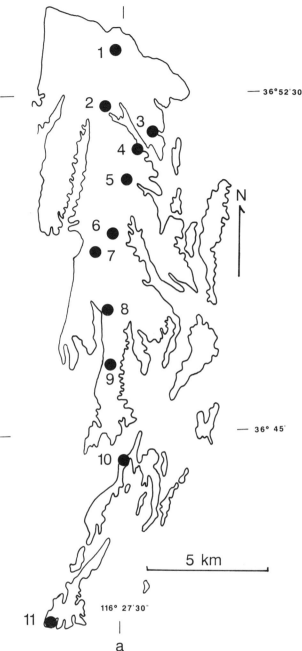

a

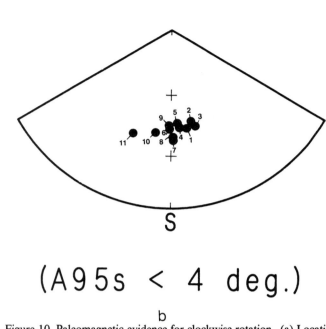

Tpc

(A95s < 4 deg.)

b

Figure 10. Paleomagnetic evidence for clockwise rotation. (a) Location of paleomagnetic samples of the Miocene Tiva Canyon Member of the Paintbrush Tuff at Yucca Mountain. (b) Lower hemisphere projection of paleomagnetic poles plotted after removal of stratal tilt about an assumed horizontal axis. Tpc = Tiva Canyon Member. Pole positions have a 95 percent confidence cone of less than 4° (from Scott and Rosenbaum, 1986).

were calculated from fault-slip data collected at Yucca Mountain using the iterative least-squares inversion technique of Angelier (1984). The results, shown in Figure 11b and c, indicate that the minimum horizontal stress axis trended nearly east-west (N89°E to N85°E) both for normal faults and for strike-slip faults at the time the striae were formed (Scott and Hofland, 1987). This direction is close to the middle Miocene minimum stress axis directions determined by Zoback and others (1981), which varied between about N45°E and N80°E for this part of the Basin and Range. Field evidence of an overprint of younger striae with a consistent change in attitude was not observed. Also, evidence to suggest that two populations of data exist was not found using a subroutine of the Angelier (1984) program. Given the large

variations in the small population of local minimum stress axis directions shown by Zoback and others (1981), the direction at Yucca Mountain is not considered significantly different from the regional middle Miocene minimum stress axis.

The present minimum horizontal stress direction at Yucca Mountain has been estimated to be about N65°W by hydraulic fracturing (Stock and others, 1985, 1986). This minimum axis direction compares with the N50°W direction determined for the region by W. J. Carr (1974) based on attitudes of fractures in Quaternary deposits, seismic evidence, and drill-hole ellipticity. Thus, at Yucca Mountain there appears to have been about 30° of clockwise rotation of the minimum stress axis between the time of formation of the fault-slip lineations and the present, comparable to the 45° of clockwise rotation that occurred regionally about 10 Ma according to Zoback and others (1981).

Stress orientations determined from the Hampel Wash area are consistent with this modern stress field (Frizzell and Zoback, 1987). The Hampel Wash area contains a seismically active sinistral strike-slip fault zone that strikes northeast about 20 km east of Fortymile Wash. Frizzell and Zoback found one set of faults with steep rakes (normal faults?) to have strikes clustered around

N35°E and another with low rakes (strike-slip faults?) to have strikes between N6°W and N80°E. Their paleostress analysis predicts a minimum least horizontal principal stress axis at N60°W. These results are similar to those determined by Stock and others (1986) using hydraulic fracturing at Yucca Mountain.

Calculations based on Yucca Mountain paleoslip data indicate that the relative differences between magnitudes of maximum and intermediate stresses for both normal and strike-slip faults are large. Values of ϕ, $(S_2\text{-}S_3)/(S_1\text{-}S_3)$, can express that difference and are provided by the least-squares inversion technique of Angelier (1984) (where S_1, S_2, and S_3 are the maximum, intermediate, and minimum stress axes, respectively). In the paleostress analysis of slip indicators at Yucca Mountain, ϕ values range from 0.1 to 0.4 (Scott and Hofland, 1987). In volcanic strata, Stock and others (1985, 1986) determined modern ϕ values of 0.22 (drill hole USW G-1), 0.59 and 0.39 (USW G-2), and 0.24, 0.35, and 0.36 (USW G-3) (average 0.34) from their hydraulic fracture studies, consistent with our paleostress ϕ. Yet in the single successful test in deeper Paleozoic strata (UE-25p#1), they found a significantly higher ϕ value, 0.7. Stock and others (1986, p. 36) state "In UE-25p1 . . . the stresses are near the transition between normal and strike-slip regimes." The significance of these relations will be interpreted below.

INTERPRETATION OF STRUCTURAL GEOMETRY AND KINEMATICS

The age and relative amounts of fault movement should be established before the structural geometry and kinematics at Yucca Mountain are interpreted.

Age and relative amounts of fault movement

Documentation of the age of movement on faults discussed in this chapter is based on the geologic map of Scott and Bonk (1984), on my subsequent mapping, and on the study of trenched faults (Swadley and others, 1984; Whitney and others, 1986; Taylor and Huckins, 1986).

Estimating the age and amount of movement on faults at Yucca Mountain is difficult for three principal reasons. (1) Although many members of the Crater Flat, Paintbrush, and Timber Mountain Tuffs have been dated, few rocks were deposited between 11.5 Ma and the beginning of the Quaternary, and few rocks from this period have been dated. (2) Differences in the amount of offset between older and younger units are difficult to measure in ash-flow tuffs. At many places, members of the Timber Mountain Tuff have been draped on preexisting fault scarps in the Tiva Canyon Member. Reactivation of faults has superimposed breccia and drag on the draped structures in the younger units. To make the distinction between drape and offset is very difficult; no localities at Yucca Mountain have been found where the difference in offset between the Timber Mountain and Paintbrush Tuffs can be unambiguously measured. (3) Comparisons of offsets in these two units measured at different localities along the same fault do not provide a measure of this difference because amounts of offsets change along strike.

A previous attempt to measure the timing and amounts of offsets on faults at Yucca Mountain was made by W. J. Carr, who stated, "Relatively minor displacement occurred on these faults after deposition of the Timber Mountain Tuff" (1984,

ALL FAULTS

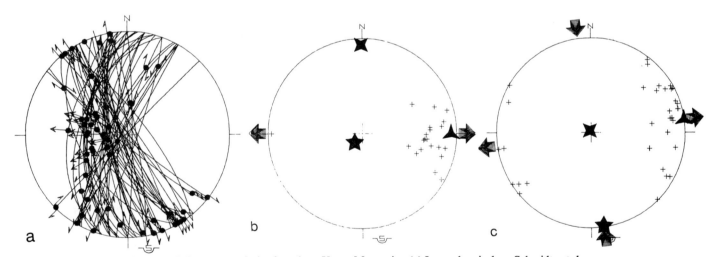

Figure 11. Paleostress analysis of northern Yucca Mountain. (a) Lower hemisphere Schmidt net showing projection of all fault strikes and fault striae. Single arrows show trends and plunges of normal faults, and double arrows show sense of shear on strike-slip faults. (b) Solution for normal faults on stereonet shows a nearly vertical maximum stress axis = 5-sided star (S_1 trends 220° and plunges 75°), a nearly horizontal intermediate stress axis = 4-sided star (S_2), and a nearly horizontal minimum stress axis = 3-state star (S_3 trends 89° and plunges 10°). The + symbols mark the poles to fault planes. Divergent arrows show extensional axes. (c) Solution for strike-slip faults shows a nearly horizontal S_1 that trends 175° and plunges 5°, a nearly vertical S_2, and a horizontal S_3 that trends 85° and plunges 0°. Divergent arrows show extensional axes, and convergent arrows show compressional axes.

p. 79). Most of his data compare the geographic distribution of faults in units of different age and do not provide comparisons of amounts of offset. In his Table 5, however, he reports three faults (faults A, H, and I, p. 94) at Yucca Mountain that offset the Paintbrush Tuff to a greater degree than volcanic units that postdate the Paintbrush (refer to his Figure 34A on p. 86 for locations). In all three cases, his estimates can be shown to be invalid or compromised by ambituities when they are compared with detailed mapping by Scott and Bonk (1984). His fault I (where the trace of the Solitario Canyon fault cuts bedrock north of the word *fault* in *Solitario Canyon fault* on my Figure 3) is a special case. The amount of offset of a 10-Ma basaltic dike cannot be established as less than 2 m, as claimed by Carr, because the exposures in a 2-m-deep trench at that locality do not provide enough vertical control on the nearly vertical dike.

Fault-movement ages fall into five periods: about 14 to 13.5 Ma, 13.5 to 13 Ma, 13 to 11.5 Ma, 11.5 to 1.7 Ma (beginning of the Quaternary), and 1.7 Ma to the present. Minor offsets of less than 1 m occurred on a few faults after emplacement of the 14-Ma Crater Flat Tuff, but the faults do not cut the 13.5-Ma Topopah Spring Member. These faults strike essentially east-west and offset units that predate the Paintbrush west of The Prow. They may be structurally related to caldera formation because they occur a few kilometers south of the edge of the Timber Mountain–Oasis Valley caldera complex (Fig. 1). The faults are too minor to show on Figure 3.

Two minor faults cut the older Topopah Spring Member (13.5 Ma) but do not offset the younger Tiva Canyon Member (13 Ma) of the Paintbrush Tuff. One of these faults shown in Figure 3 east of the word *fault* (in *Solitario Canyon fault*) is a northeast-striking fault east of the Solitario Canyon fault.

Several of the faults that cut the Paintbrush Tuff do not cut the overlying units that postdate the Paintbrush (Fig. 3). Areas north and west of Busted Butte, north of the Stagecoach Road fault, and west of Windy Wash fault show this relation. Also, many faults cut both the Paintbrush Tuff and younger units. The largest concentration of faults that cut both units is found west of the Windy Wash fault, but several faults in the northern, central, and southern parts of Yucca Mountain also cut the Rainier Mesa Member or Ammonia Tanks Member.

Because of the difficulty in comparing offset between the Paintbrush Tuff and younger units, I have assumed that progressive tilt of the strata is the best record of progressive fault movement and extension (Wernicke and Burchfiel, 1982). Thus, the relative degree of tilt is assumed to correlate directly with the relative amount of fault offset. This assumption greatly simplifies the estimation of relative amounts of offset because foliations in welded ash-flow tuffs are relatively easy to measure.

One of the best examples is in the northeast part of Yucca Mountain where the elongate exposure of the Rainier Mesa Member northwest of Busted Butte dips eastward at 6° to 9° (Fig. 3) and rests on an angular unconformity above the Tiva Canyon Member, which dips eastward at 20° to 29° (Scott and Bonk, 1984). At another elongate exposure of units that postdate

the Paintbrush west of Busted Butte, the Rainier Mesa Member dips eastward about 3°, and the underlying Tiva Canyon Member dips eastward at about 15°; however, the compaction foliation at this locality is poorly defined in the partially welded Rainier Mesa. Thus, at northeast Yucca Mountain, about 70 percent of the tilting occurred before 11.5 Ma. Where the Ammonia Tanks Member is faulted at the southern part of Yucca Mountain just north of the Quaternary basalt, the Ammonia Tanks dips one-third as much as the underlying Tiva Canyon; about two-thirds of the tilting occurred before 11.5 Ma. In the northwest part of Yucca Mountain, large variations in degrees of tilting occur; five examples of dips of the Rainier Mesa and Tiva Canyon are 5° and 9°, 17° and 20°, 5° and 8°, 9° and 12°, and 12° and 12°, respectively. An average of only about 25 percent of the tilting occurred before 11.5 Ma in the northwestern area.

The exclusion of the Rainier Mesa Member from areas where the Ammonia Tanks Member is found and vice versa has an important implication. The Ammonia Tanks Member (11.4 Ma) is restricted to the area 4 km north and west of the Quaternary basalt shown in Figure 3; the Rainier Mesa Member was not found beneath the Ammonia Tanks at this locality. Other exposures south of Yucca Wash of volcanic units that postdate the Paintbrush Tuff include only the Rainier Mesa Member (11.6 Ma). As discussed earlier, the Rainier Mesa Member probably puddled in topographic (and structural) lows after prior extension at Yucca Mountain. The distribution of the Ammonia Tanks Member indicates that it also puddled in structural lows formed during the 200,000 years between eruption of the two units.

Fault movement or relative dips of units between 11.5 Ma and the beginning of the Quaternary are difficult to quantify because, as stated above, few rocks were deposited at Yucca Mountain during this period. Several small 10-Ma basaltic dikes cut the Paintbrush Tuff at Yucca Mountain (Scott and Bonk, 1984; Carr, 1984). As discussed above, the Solitario Canyon fault has brecciated one of these dikes with an undetermined amount of offset.

North of Yucca Wash, the rhyolite flows of Fortymile Canyon were thought to have formed between 10 and 9 Ma based on stratigraphic relations, and faults cutting these units were therefore thought to be younger (Carr, 1984). However, recent remapping and dating (Warren and others, 1988) indicate that many of these rhyolites were erupted within the time spanned by the Paintbrush and Timber Mountain Tuffs (13.5 to 11.5 Ma). Therefore, the faults north of Yucca Wash are probably comparable in ages to the faults that cut units which postdate the Paintbrush at Yucca Mountain.

A layer of silicic pumice dated at 6 Ma by the fission track method (Swadley and Carr, 1987) occurs in the southwest part of Yucca Mountain on the downthrown side of a splinter of the Windy Wash fault east of the largest exposure of Pliocene basalt (Fig. 3). Lack of exposures leaves unsolved the relation between the fault and this layer. West of the Windy Wash fault, the Pliocene basalt (Crowe and others, 1983; Swadley and Carr, 1987) is offset a small but undetermined amount by the Windy

Wash fault. Tilting of these younger units cannot be measured because layering is indistinct.

At Yucca Mountain, at least 32 faults with evidence of Quaternary movement have been recognized from study of trenches and from field observations (Swadley and others, 1984). These faults include the Paintbrush Canyon, Bow Ridge, Solitario Canyon, Stagecoach Road, and Windy Wash faults. Study of the Windy Wash fault on the western side of Yucca Mountain has identified seven episodes of Quaternary faulting; the recurrence interval of the last four averages 75,000 years, and 40 cm of vertical offset occurred over 270,000 years (Whitney and others, 1986). Whitney and others used thermoluminescence methods to date the latest movement as having occurred between 6,500 and 3,000 years ago.

Low-angle normal fault under Yucca Mountain

Interpretation of the structural geometry and kinematics at Yucca Mountain should take into account the location of Yucca Mountain in a terrane affected by low-angle extensional faulting (Wernicke and others, 1988a) and in the Walker Lane belt affected by oroclinal bending (Stewart, 1988).

The structural geometry at Yucca Mountain indicates that a low-angle extensional fault underlies Yucca Mountain. Evidence to support this conclusion includes (1) domino fault-block geometry, (2) listric normal faults and internal deformation within fault blocks, (3) model of plate-bounding faults, (4) vertical-axis rotation of the southern end of Yucca Mountain, and (5) decoupled stress field. In my judgement, a convincing case for a low-angle normal fault under Yucca Mountain is made by the combination of this evidence, not necessarily by any one piece of evidence.

Domino fault-block geometry at Yucca Mountain. The major west-dipping normal faults repeat east-dipping strata, forming a series of structural blocks resembling tilted dominos. Although the amount of dip increases southward and the width of the blocks generally decreases southward, the overall pattern remains much the same. This pattern is similar to the structural pattern within allochthons that overlie low-angle normal faults or detachments (Wernicke and Burchfiel, 1982; Angelier and Colletta, 1983; Angelier and others, 1987).

In the previous section on the structural geometry, evidence was presented showing that the number of major normal faults, the amount of vertical offset on any one major fault, and the angle of eastward stratal tilt increase, whereas the angle of dip of major normal faults decreases, from north to south at Yucca Mountain. I interpret this geometric trend to indicate that the degree of extension above a low-angle normal fault increases southward at Yucca Mountain. By using Axen's (1988) synthetic model and the simplifying assumptions of planar faults and rigid blocks, the amount of extension can be calculated, given the amount of dip of the strata and major normal fault planes. In the northern area where major normal faults dip an average of 66° and strata dip between 5° and 15° in unfaulted parts of blocks,

between 4 and 8 percent extension, respectively, is calculated if the underlying low-angle fault is horizontal. Increasing the dip of the underlying low-angle fault as much as 15° in the direction of the major normal fault dips increases the extension only a few percent. In the southern area, where major faults dip an average of 51° and strata in unfaulted parts of blocks dip at about 25°, calculated extension is much more sensitive to the dip of the low-angle fault. A horizontal low-angle fault gives 27 percent extension, whereas a 15° dip to the fault gives 45 percent extension. In both cases, these calculations are minimal because the blocks are internally deformed, particularly in the southern part of the area. Using the sum of measured horizontal offsets, the northern area was extended about 10 percent (section A-A'), but the southern area was extended about 60 percent (section B-B') (Fig. 4).

Listric normal faults and internal block deformation. As discussed in the section on geometry, many of the major normal faults at Yucca Mountain are thought to be listric. If this inference is correct, a low-angle normal fault or some zone of accommodation is required under the mountain where the listric faults merge at depth.

The listric fault shapes may contribute to internal deformation of blocks by the formation of imbricate fault zones in the hanging wall above the major normal faults. Where the major normal fault east of each block does not have a constant radius of curvature, internal deformation of a block must occur to fill the void created by movement of the block over the curved fault surface (Fig. 12). The change in dip from a planar normal fault to a low-angle fault creates a similar geometric requirement. Experimental models of extension indicate that internal block deformation may account for as much as 50 to 60 percent of the strain, with only 40 to 50 percent accounted for on major normal faults (Kautz and Sclater, 1988). These values are consistent with the degree of internal deformation of blocks at Yucca Mountain. For example, about 50 percent of the extension between the Solitario Canyon and Bow Ridge faults occurred on the pervasive imbricate faults measured along section A-A' (Fig. 5).

The interpretation of the angular relation between east-dipping strata and west-dipping faults within the imbricate fault zones (Figs. 5, 7, and 8) has important implications for the sequence of structural events during internal block deformation. The upper surface of Yucca Mountain has always been close to the present surface of erosion; therefore, the faults would be expected to be steeper near the surface than at depth, approaching 90°, because of the rotation of the stress field at that unconfined boundary. The slightly obtuse angle between the top of the strata and the fault plane on the footwall side of the blocks, characteristic of the imbricate zones, disallows imbricate faulting of horizontal strata. I propose, therefore, that strata were tilted slightly before these faults propagated through the hanging-wall part of the blocks. Similar sequences of structural events have been found by Angelier and Colletta (1983) and Angelier and others (1987) but in areas more highly extended than Yucca Mountain.

Thus, at Yucca Mountain, I propose that block deformation

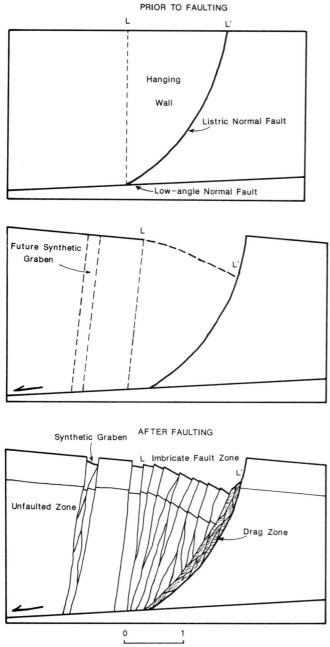

Figure 12. Conceptualization of internal block deformation. Upper diagram shows condition prior to faulting. Center diagram shows failure of hanging wall, analogous to Gulf Coast roll-over structures found in hanging walls of ductile material, after 0.4 km of extension; such a fold is not expected at Yucca Mountain without significant brittle failure in welded tuffs. Lower diagram shows final state after tilting of block, 0.4 km of extension on the low-angle fault, and brittle internal block deformation on steep normal faults to accommodate change of shape of hanging-wall part of block. Steep normal faults formed after some increase in dip related to failure of hanging wall. West-dipping zone is shown as chaotic drag. Area of deformed hanging wall increases less than 10 percent, as expected during dilation. Only 0.2 km of offset occurs on the major normal fault; the remainder, 50 percent of total extension, is accommodated by internal block deformation. L-L′ along stratum is constant in length.

evolved in the following way: (1) Movement occurred on listric normal faults and caused gentle tilting of the blocks. (2) As extension proceeded, the brittle equivalent of Gulf Coast roll-over structures formed in the hanging walls to fill gaps over the normal faults, thus creating steeper eastward dips (Scott, 1984a). (3) Concurrent with collapse of the hanging wall, nearly vertical faults propagated through the hanging walls of the blocks. (4) As extension and rotation continued, these small imbricate normal faults were in turn rotated to shallower dips and probably increased in offset. The result is shown conceptually in Figure 12. Based on this geometric model, the width of the imbricate zone is probably more or less a function of the lateral distance between the trace of the major normal fault on the surface of the mountain and the intersection of the fault with the low-angle accommodating structure under the mountain (Fig. 12).

The narrow, west-dipping synthetic grabens present at Yucca Mountain, discussed above, are compatible with the extensional environment there. The presence of steeply dipping, brecciated strata in their down-dropped central blocks (Fig. 9) indicates that blocks collapsed chaotically into gaps formed during extension. Prior to block tilting during early extension in the Paintbrush Tuff, nearly vertical grabens propagated from the low-angle fault under the mountain along preexisting vertical joints. Tilting of the block rotated the synthetic grabens along with the strata to the present attitudes (Fig. 9).

Between major normal faults, zones of west-dipping, highly deformed rocks commonly exist (Figs. 3, 4, and 5). The proximity of these zones to the bounding fault and the similarity of the dip directions of the strata and faults indicate that these are probably drag zones related to friction on the major bounding normal faults.

Model of plate-bounding faults. The interconnection of major normal, oblique-slip, and strike-slip faults (specifically, the Stagecoach Road fault, the southern extension of the Paintbrush Canyon fault west of Busted Butte, the northern part of the Paintbrush Canyon fault, and the Yucca Wash fault shown in Fig. 13) suggests that rocks bounded by those faults may have moved as a single entity (Scott and Whitney, 1987). Figure 13 is a conceptual map of this fault network. The trends of fault striae are compatible with a westward movement direction, and it is likely that these striae are relics of the middle Miocene stress environment. Probably the modern movement direction is about N65°W, similar to the direction of the minimum horizontal stress axis determined by Stock and others (1986) and by Frizzell and Zoback (1987). However, Quaternary movement has apparently not left a distinctive kinematic record in the bedrock here. The seemingly contradictory terminations of strike-slip and normal faults in the northeast part of Yucca Mountain (Fig. 13), discussed in the section on structural geometry, are consistent with the hypothesis that dip-slip and strike-slip faults accommodated different degrees of extension between this small allochthon and surrounding areas.

Vertical-axis rotation. Because the clockwise rotation of Yucca Mountain occurred progressively from north to south, and because no east-west–trending or northwest-trending strike-slip

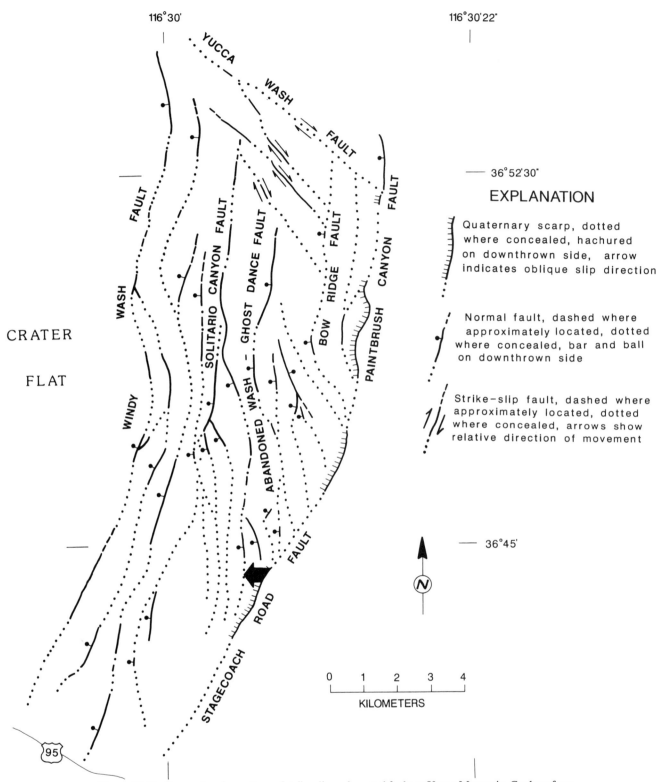

Figure 13. Fault map showing pattern of strike-slip and normal faults at Yucca Mountain. Geology from current field mapping, Scott and Bonk (1984), and Scott and Whitney (1987). The lineations on fault surfaces are probably related to the pre–10 Ma stress field. Modern movement should be in a N60°W direction.

faults occur south or west of the northeast part of the mountain, any one block must have followed an arcuate path during extension, pivoting about the northern end of the mountain not far from The Prow (Figs. 2 and 10). If Yucca Mountain is rotated 30° in a counterclockwise direction to remove vertical-axis rotation, the structural curvature of the mountain (Figs. 2 and 3) is straightened to a presumed original north-south alignment, and the southern end of the mountain is moved through a 5-km arcuate path. This distance is close to the 4.6-km lateral offset measured along section B-B' (Fig. 4).

This rotation and increased degree of extension may have an origin in dextral oroclinal bending, similar to that associated with the Las Vegas Valley shear zone and to the dextral strike-slip faults typical of the Walker Lane belt.

Clockwise rotation has occurred between the Pintwater Range and the west end of the Specter Range by the oroclinal bending of ranges to a nearly east-west alignment (Ekren, 1968). However, between the Specter Range and Tonopah, extensive cover by alluvium and Miocene volcanic rocks obscures structures, if any exist. W. J. Carr (1984) has summarized evidence relating to northwest-trending structures and aeromagnetic lineations in this region (see his Fig. 4), but apparently, with the exception of Yucca Mountain, none of the structures in the Yucca Mountain–Bare Mountain–Bullfrog Hills area is related to either clockwise oroclinal bending or to dextral strike-slip faults.

Studies in the Walker Lane belt have suggested that dextral shear deeper in the crust has partially decoupled mechanically from upper plates along low-angle faults. Burchfiel (1965) first suggested decoupling of an upper plate along thrusts in the Specter Range area from a lower plate containing strike-slip faults. More recently, Hardyman (1978) and Hardyman and others (1984) have proposed decoupling of strike-slip faults and overlying volcanic strata along low-angle normal faults 250 km northwest of Yucca Mountain in the Walker Lane belt. In the case interpreted by Hardyman, the low-angle faulting is attributed to motion on the underlying strike-slip faults. This decoupling mechanism may also operate by movement on strike-slip faults under a preexisting low-angle fault of an independent origin. The clockwise rotation about a vertical axis at the southern end of Yucca Mountain could have occurred in an upper plate above a pre-existing low-angle normal fault. In such a model, the upper plate decoupled sufficiently from a deeper zone of dextral strike-slip faults or ductile accommodation, producing clockwise rotation of the upper crust.

Because the degree of extension decreases toward the caldera complex north of Yucca Mountain, another explanation may involve calderas as a mechanical restraint or spot weld through a crust undergoing extension. The spot weld can be envisioned just north of The Prow at the caldera margin (Fig. 1), with Yucca Mountain pivoting about the spot weld in a clockwise direction as extension continues. Such pivoting, however, requires comparable vertical-axis rotations of paleomagnetic poles of ash-flow tuffs. The paleomagnetic study by Rosenbaum and others (1990) indicates that clockwise rotation increases southward at Yucca Mountain but does not increase westward, as required by the spot-weld model. Without more knowledge of the mechanical and kinematic processes that operate during extension, it is difficult to speculate how calderas might affect extension.

Decoupled stress field. Rogers and others (1987) have inferred from the study of focal mechanisms that the regional stress field is characterized by a gently west-northwest–plunging minimum stress axis and a gently north-northeast–plunging maximum stress axis. Although the direction of the minimum stress axis is consistent with the direction determined from hydraulic fracturing (N65°W) by Stock and others (1986), the maximum stress direction is generally perpendicular to that found by hydraulic fracturing. Focal mechanisms commonly indicate a mixture of normal and strike-slip faulting, rather than exclusive normal faulting as predicted by hydraulic fracturing in the volcanic rocks at Yucca Mountain. Rogers and others (1987) suggest that this mixture indicates that the magnitudes of intermediate and maximum stresses are relatively close to one another. This interpretation implies high ϕ values, near the transition between strike-slip and normal fault stress environments.

Rogers and others (1987, p. 50–52) suggested that a stress field decoupled along a low-angle (detachment) fault may explain the change from low ϕ values in Tertiary volcanic rocks (0.25 from paleostress calculations and 0.34 from an average of hydrofrac experiments) to a higher ϕ value of about 0.7 in Paleozoic rocks in drill hole UE-25p#1 at Yucca Mountain, as estimated by Stock and others (1986). The fault postulated by Rogers and others (1987) may correspond to the low-angle normal fault that detaches upper plate Tertiary rocks from lower plate Paleozoic rocks. Decoupled stress fields above and below low-angle normal faults are an attractive explanation for the apparent inconsistency between geological field observations of large normal faults and focal mechanism data that commonly are interpreted to indicate strike-slip faulting. However, in shallow excavations in volcanic bedrock at Yucca Mountain, I have observed that minute faults with subhorizontal slip lineations are common; these may be consistent with the abundance of small-magnitude seismic events with strike-slip focal mechanisms interpreted by Rogers and others (1987).

Depth to inferred low-angle normal fault. The depth to the inferred low-angle fault beneath Yucca Mountain can be estimated using several lines of evidence. These include (1) listric shape of major normal faults, (2) the width of internal block deformation exhibited in the imbricate fault zone, (3) lateral distance between major normal faults, (4) depth to apparent zone of decoupling of the stress field, and (5) extrapolation of structures exposed in areas surrounding Yucca Mountain.

The amount of curvature on the major faults can be used to estimate the depth of a low-angle fault under Yucca Mountain. Based on the data presented in the section on structural geometry (assuming that a curvature of 21°/km is typical of the major faults), the low-angle fault should be no deeper than 3 or 4 km. Higher curvatures, such as that at Busted Butte (where the curvature is 43°/km), would permit listric faults to intersect a low-angle fault at depths of about 1.5 km.

The widths of imbricate normal fault zones in major fault blocks at Yucca Mountain can be used to predict the depth of penetration of steep normal faults based on the model in Figure 12. If a dip of 60° is assumed for the simple case of a steep planar normal fault and a width of 2 km is assumed for an imbricate fault zone, then the depth to the low-angle normal fault should be no more than about 3.5 km.

The lateral distance between major block-bounding normal faults and the thickness of the plate above a low-angle extensional fault may be somewhat analogous to closely spaced fractures in thinly bedded rocks but widely spaced fractures in thickly bedded rocks (Hobbs, 1967). Normal faults in a thin extensional plate in Canyonlands National Park are spaced about 0.6 km apart, and the upper plate is 0.5 km thick above an accommodating gypsum layer (not a discrete fault) (McGill and Stromquist, 1979). At the other end of the scale are range-bounding normal faults in the Basin and Range of Utah and Nevada with a spacing of about 20 km and an assumed depth to the brittle-ductile transition of between 10 and 15 km, where extension of the upper plate was accommodated. Interestingly, the range of most fracture-spacing to bed-thickness ratios is similar to these fault block width-to-height ratios; the dimension ratios (width/thickness) seem to be between about 1 and 2 regardless of the scale. The major normal fault blocks at Yucca Mountain are between 1 and 4 km wide; therefore, if the dimension ratios are comparable to the examples given above, the depth to the low-angle normal fault under Yucca Mountain should be somewhere between about 0.5 and 4 km. The depths to Paleozoic rocks under Yucca Mountain (1.2 to about 3 km) fall into this range.

The change in relative magnitudes of stresses with depth, discussed above, has been interpreted by Rogers and others (1987) to be related to decoupling of the stress field across a low-angle normal fault: stresses are more conducive to normal faults above the detachment and more conducive to strike-slip faults below the low-angle fault. Since this change in stress magnitude occurs between Tertiary volcanic rocks and underlying Paleozoic rocks, this line of reasoning supports the presence of a low-angle normal fault at the contact between Paleozoic and Tertiary rocks.

At both Bare Mountain and Calico Hills, low-angle normal faults underlie Tertiary strata at or close to the contact between Paleozoic and Tertiary rocks. Therefore, the most logical location for the inferred low-angle fault under Yucca Mountain is close to the base of the Tertiary rocks. As mentioned above, a fault of unknown attitude was recognized at the contact between Paleozoic and Tertiary rocks (M. D. Carr and others, 1986) at a depth of 1.2 km in the eastern part of the mountain (Fig. 3).

Thus, these relations can all be used to infer that the steep normal faults at Yucca Mountain probably have a depth of penetration of between 1 and 4 km below Yucca Mountain to either a discrete low-angle fault plane or some zone of strain accommodation; they do not extend to the brittle-ductile transition. One or

more low-angle normal faults may occur within the volcanic rocks, along the boundary with the Paleozoic rocks, or within the Paleozoic rocks; but available data do not allow a precise depth or the nature of the accommodation structure to be predicted.

Rates of Cenozoic deformation

At Yucca Mountain, estimates of rates of Cenozoic deformation are functions of the periods during which extension is assumed to operate. Because of the gap in the rock record between 11.5 Ma and the present, two end-member rate models can be postulated. Late Cenozoic tectonic rates at Yucca Mountain can be determined only for the 13- to 11.5-Ma period and the middle to late Quaternary period during which rocks were deposited to record the events. One model, a stepwise decreasing rate model, assumes that rates sharply decreased about 11.5 Ma. As will be explained later, Bare Mountain rose along the Bare Mountain fault (Fig. 14) before 11.5 Ma and shed coarse debris beneath the Timber Mountain Tuff in central Crater Flat (Carr and Parrish, 1985). This uplift isolated the low-angle extensional fault system at Yucca Mountain from the more rapidly extending region west of Bare Mountain. A second model, an episodic model, is based on the assumption that a genetic link exists between crustal extension, fault movement, and volcanism in the Yucca Mountain area (K. F. Fox, written communication, 1988). Between 10 and 4 Ma there is a hiatus in volcanism in the vicinity of Yucca Mountain. This model assumes that a hiatus in fault movement coincides with the volcanic hiatus; following renewed volcanism at 3.7 Ma, fault movement also resumes. The decreasing rate and episodic models will be tested in part by the data discussed below and presented in Table 2.

The rate of deformation at Yucca Mountain during the period between 13 and 11.5 Ma can be expressed best by the relative degrees of tilt of the Paintbrush Tuff and overlying Timber Mountain Tuff, as discussed in the section on age of fault movement. Measurement of dip-slip offset on several major faults provides a maximum of about 0.4 km on the Solitario Canyon fault west of the area outlined for Figure 9 (Fig. 3). The Windy Wash fault has comparable estimates of maximum dip-slip offset. The Paintbrush Canyon fault, where measured in Figure 4, section A-A′, also has a comparable dip-slip offset. The dip-slip movement on the Stagecoach Road fault may be as much as 1 km (Fig. 4). Thus, between 13 and 11.5 Ma in northeast Yucca Mountain, 70 percent of this offset (using data from section on age of fault movement), or about 0.3 km, occurred in 1.5×10^6 years at a rate of 0.19 mm/yr for the Solitario Canyon and Paintbrush Canyon faults. The Windy Wash fault dip-slip rate during this period may be as much as 0.07 mm/yr. The Stagecoach Road fault had a dip-slip rate of about 0.45 mm/yr (Table 2A). These estimates are valid for either the stepwise or the episodic model.

Table 2B and C contains the estimates of rates on individual faults based on the stepwise model only. The rates for the period between 11.5 Ma and the present are based on the dip slip

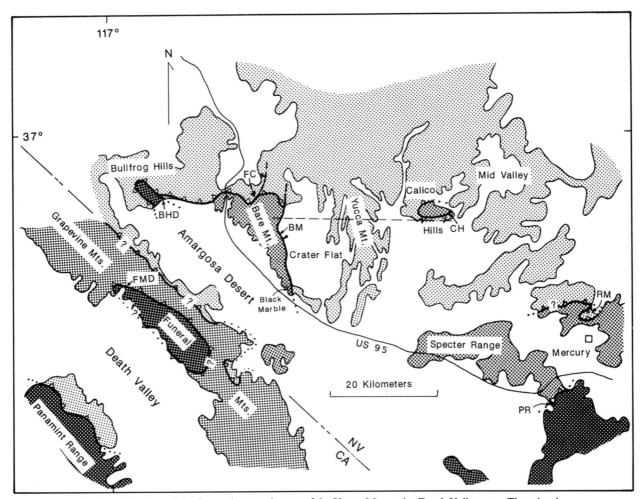

Figure 14. Generalized Cenozoic tectonic map of the Yucca Mountain–Death Valley area. Three levels of major low-angle normal faults as interpreted in this chapter are shown; the upper plate has the lightest shading, the middle plate has an intermediate shading, and the lowest plate has the darkest shading. Generalized low-angle normal fault locations are shown by bold lines with open teeth on the upper plate, by dotted lines where concealed, and by queries where uncertain. The fault shown in the Panamint Range actually consists of several low-angle normal faults and several levels of plates (Wernicke and others, 1988b). Several faults are named: BHD = Bullfrog Hills detachment fault; FMD = Funeral Mountains detachment fault; FC = Fluorspar Canyon fault; BM = Bare Mountain fault; CH = Calico Hills fault; RM = Red Mountain fault; and PR = Point of Rocks fault. Dashed line between Bare Mountain and Calico Hills shows the expected southern limit of the Eleana Formation.

remaining after the 13- to 11.5-Ma offset is subtracted from the total. Because rates measured by offset of Quaternary strata are even lower, correction for Quaternary offset was not included in this calculation. For the Windy Wash, Solitario Canyon, Paintbrush Canyon, and the Stagecoach Road faults the rates are 0.026, 0.010, 0.010, and 0.029 mm/yr, respectively, for the period from 11.5 Ma to the present. These values are about an order of magnitude less than for the 13- to 11.5-Ma period.

Rates of Quaternary movement have been calculated in several places where data are available on major faults (Table 2C). At the Paintbrush Canyon, Windy Wash, and Stagecoach Road faults the rates are >0.006, 0.0015, and >0.003 mm/yr, respectively. These rates are all considerably smaller than the rates calculated for the entire period between 11.5 Ma and the present.

Extrapolation of 13- to 11.5-Ma rates through the 11.5- to 10-Ma period, assumed by the episodic rate model, requires offsets greater than those observed on most faults. Only the Windy Wash fault has 200 m of offset remaining at 10 Ma. Also, the basic assumption of the episodic model—that crustal extension, fault movement, and volcanism have a close temporal and spatial relation in the Yucca Mountain area—seems doubtful because the area of greatest extension in the Basin and Range along the latitude of Las Vegas, Nevada, is almost free of volcanism (Wernicke and others, 1988a). I conclude from existing data that the stepwise model is the most reasonable.

TABLE 2. RATES OF MOVEMENT ON FAULTS AT YUCCA MOUNTAIN

Locality	Fault	Dip-slip Offset (mm)	Period (yr)	Rate (mm/yr)
A. BETWEEN 13 AND 11.5 MA				
Northwest Yucca Mountain	Windy Wash	0.14×10^6	1.5×10^6	0.07
Northeast Yucca Mountain	Solitario Canyon and Paintbrush Canyon	0.28×10^6	1.5×10^6	0.19
South Yucca Mountain	Stagecoach Road	0.67×10^6	1.5×10^6	0.45
B. BETWEEN 11.5 MA AND PRESENT				
Northwest Yucca Mountain	Windy Wash	0.26×10^6	11.5×10^6	0.026
Northeast Yucca Mountain	Solitario Canyon and Paintbrush Canyon	0.12×10^6	11.5×10^6	0.010
South Yucca Mountain	Stagecoach Road	0.33×10^6	11.5×10^6	0.029
C. QUATERNARY[*]				
Busted Butte[†]	Paintbrush Canyon	4.1×10^3	$<7.4 \times 10^5$	>0.006
Windy Wash Trench CF-2[§]	Windy Wash	4.0×10^2	2.7×10^5	0.0015
South Yucca Mountain[**]	Stagecoach Road	4.6×10^3	$<1.7 \times 10^6$	>0.003

[*]Only specific parts of Quaternary dated.
[†]Scott and Whitney (1987).
[§]Located east of word "Wash" on Windy Wash fault (Fig. 3); Whitney and others (1986).
[**]Located east of word "Road" on Stagecoach Road fault (Fig. 3).

An estimate of the rates of extension of the upper plate can be calculated for Yucca Mountain. If the amount of lateral offset on each normal fault is summed along section B-B′ (Fig. 4) for the southern part of Yucca Mountain, the total extension was about 4.6 km over an original distance of about 7.4 km (about 60 percent extension). During the period from 13 to 11.5 Ma, the geologic strain rate at this part of the mountain is about 8.7×10^{-15}/sec; this decreased to about 5.6×10^{-16}/sec between 11.5 Ma and the present. In the northern part of the mountain along section A-A′ (Fig. 4), about 10 percent extension occurred. Thus, for the northeastern part of the area, where about 70 percent of the deformation occurred between 13 and 11.5 Ma, a geologic strain rate of about 1.4×10^{-15}/sec compares with 8.3×10^{-17}/sec for that area in the last 11.5 m.y. The strain rates in the northwest part of the mountain along the same section decreased from about 5.3×10^{-16}/sec to 2.1×10^{-16}/sec for the same periods.

REGIONAL TECTONIC SETTING

Regional tectonic extension has been proposed by Wernicke and others (1988a) across an area of the southern Basin and Range Province that includes Yucca Mountain. West of Yucca Mountain, recent investigations have firmly established the presence of a system of low-angle extensional faults in the region between the east side of Bare Mountain, the Bulfrog Hills, and Death Valley (Troxel, 1988; Wernicke and others, 1988a, b; Hamilton, 1988; Carr and Monsen, 1988; Burchfiel and others, 1987; Maldonado, 1985b, 1990). Several recent studies have concentrated on the Bare Mountain–Bullfrog Hills area. The

Fluorspar Canyon fault at the northern end of Bare Mountain can be traced westward from the northeastern part of Bare Mountain (U.S. Geological Survey, 1984; Carr and Monsen, 1988) across the Amargosa Narrows into the Bullfrog Hills (Ransome and others, 1910) (Fig. 15). In the Bullfrog Hills the fault forms the gently domed Bullfrog Hills detachment (Maldonado, 1985b) above the metamorphic core complex in the Bullfrog Hills (McKee, 1983). Muscovite in the amphibolite-grade metamorphic rocks has a K-Ar age of about 11 Ma (McKee, 1983), but the age of the protolith is unknown. East and north of the metamorphic complex, but west of Bare Mountain, east-dipping volcanic strata as young as 8 Ma are truncated by the detachment (Maldonado, oral communication, 1989). At least 10 km of crustal attenuation in the Bullfrog Hills occurred, based on the thickness of missing upper Proterozoic and Paleozoic strata (Table 1); an estimate of 10 to 15 km of uplift is based on the amphibolite grade of metamorphism (Hamilton, 1988).

East of Yucca Mountain, Guth (1981), Wernicke and others (1984), and Wernicke and others (1988a) have described the geometry of extensional structures in the area west of a breakaway fault zone in the Sheep Range (Fig. 1). Between the Pintwater Range and Bare Mountain, evidence of the nature of extensional structures is less clear.

For the area of Yucca Mountain itself, several extensional tectonic settings have been suggested. These settings include (1) a volcano-tectonic origin (W. J. Carr and others, 1986; Carr, 1984; Snyder and Carr, 1984), (2) tilting of a detachment surface related to tectonic unloading in the Bare Mountain–Bullfrog Hills area (Hamilton, 1988), (3) an older period of extension, independent of extension in the Bare Mountain–Bullfrog Hills area (Carr and Monsen, 1988), and (4) a tiered normal fault system related to extension in the Bare Mountain–Bullfrog Hills area with superimposed dextral rotation possibly related to tectonism of the Walker Lane belt (this chapter). The detachment settings (2), (3), and (4) differ mostly in detail.

The evidence cited by W. J. Carr and others (1986) in support of a volcano-tectonic setting is equivocal. For example, the gravity low, interpreted by Snyder and Carr (1984) as evidence of a caldera beneath the southern end of Crater Flat, is as readily explained by low-density rocks in a structural depression with gently dipping sides. W. J. Carr and others (1986) state that the distribution and thicknesses of the members of the Crater Flat Tuff indicate the presence of a caldera under the southern end of Crater Flat. Yet the youngest member is only about half as thick in the proposed caldera as it is outside (Carr and Parrish, 1985; Scott and Castellanos, 1984). Petrographic evidence from Crater Flat (F. M. Byers, Jr., oral communication, 1985) indicates that thick, more mafic-rich, late-stage magmas expected within a caldera are not present (Lipman and others, 1966) and that members of the Crater Flat Tuff are not thicker than in surrounding areas.

Geologic evidence cited by W. J. Carr and others (1986) to support the proposed caldera is also equivocal. Rhyodacite dikes are parallel to the Bare Mountain fault rather than parallel to the proposed caldera in southern Crater Flat (compare Figs. 9 and 18 of W. J. Carr and others, 1986). The monolithologic breccias

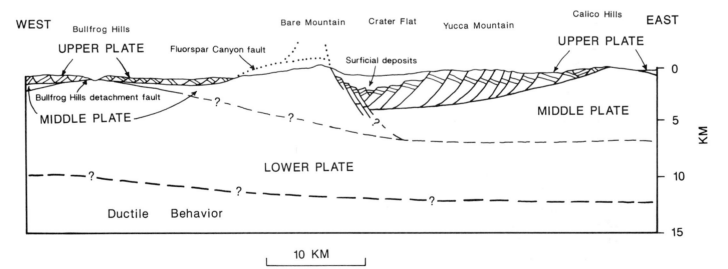

Figure 15. Conceptual cross section from Calico Hills to the metamorphic core complex in the Bullfrog Hills (McKee, 1983). No vertical exaggeration. Depths and configuration of detachment faults are speculative where dashed and queried. Generalized dips of strata are shown conceptually in the upper plate. Although listric faults under Yucca Mountain are shown to sole into the uppermost detachment, some may extend to a lower level. Steep normal faults, not shown here, probably translate extension from the lowest detachment upward to shallower low-angle faults and to the surface. The middle low-angle fault may surface near the metamorphic core complex in the Bullfrog Hills (Maldonado, 1985b), south of Mercury at Point of Rocks (Burchfiel, 1965) and possibly in the Funeral Mountains. The lowest detachment surface, between 10 and 15 km, is probably the modern shear between deeper, relatively ductile crust and shallower, relatively brittle crust.

near U.S. Highway 95 at the south end of Crater Flat, referred to by W. J. Carr and others (1986), could have been derived from nearby faulting related to regional tectonic events rather than from a local caldera. Northeast trends of faults in the southern part of Yucca Mountain are probably related to the clockwise rotation of normal faults and blocks about a vertical axis as discussed above (Scott and Rosenbaum, 1986).

Other evidence also suggests that a caldera does not exist in the southern part of Crater Flat. First, the Prow Pass Member of the Crater Flat Tuff is most readily recognized in the field by the presence of shale fragments derived from the Devonian(?) and Mississippian Eleana Formation, but the southernmost source of those lithic fragments is probably several kilometers north of the north edge of the proposed source of the Prow Pass Member (see dashed line in Fig. 14). The shales of the Eleana Formation are expected only under the northern part of Yucca Mountain. Second, petrologic studies using major- and trace-element data from the ash-flow tuffs of the southwest Nevada volcanic field show a chemical and petrological evolution consistent with close chemical communication between the sequence of eruptive products (Broxton and others, 1989; Scott, 1984b). Evidence of a continuous chemical evolution of magmas seems to preclude the possibility that one of the calderas might lie isolated 20 km south of the main cluster of calderas (Fig. 1). Third, the normal faults at the southern end of Yucca Mountain have several kilometers of cumulative offset that occurred after 13 Ma; therefore, fault control by a 14-Ma caldera proposed by W. J. Carr and others (1986) is a dubious explanation for these normal faults. I conclude that a volcano-tectonic origin of the structures in Yucca Mountain, as postulated by W. J. Carr and others (1986), is improbable.

Hamilton (1988) has proposed a detachment setting for the area between Yucca Mountain and the Bullfrog–Death Valley region; his setting is similar to Wernicke's (1985) simple shear model with minor additions. In brief, Hamilton proposes that both within the Funeral Range and in the Bare Mountain–Bullfrog Hills areas, detachment faults have sliced deep into the crust along surfaces that originally dipped northwest. Rocks in the middle and lowest plates (Fig. 14) in both the Bare Mountain–Bullfrog Hills area and in the Funeral Mountain area show an increase in metamorphic grade from low-greenschist to high-amphibolite in a northwest direction. In the Bare Mountain–Bullfrog Hills area, upper Proterozoic and Paleozoic rocks have been transported northwest to the Grapevine Mountains. Removal of these rocks has allowed the Bullfrog Hills–Bare Mountain area to rise isostatically, deforming the previously northwest-dipping detachment plane and exposing mid-crustal rocks in the Bullfrog Hills (Fig. 15). Hamilton further proposes that the time of cessation of movement on the detachment became younger toward the west. He suggests that extension on low-angle faults ceased after 11 Ma east of Bare Mountain and after 7 Ma in the Bullfrog Hills area and is still active in the Death Valley area.

As stated above, Hamilton gives evidence to support the existence of a detachment structure that originally dipped gently

through the crust from upper crustal levels at Yucca Mountain to mid-crustal levels at Bullfrog Hills. He considers that deformation at Yucca Mountain ceased as that sector of the detachment structure became inactivated by isostatic uplift about 11.5 Ma. The greater amount of tilt at southern Yucca Mountain is interpreted by Hamilton to indicate that the detachment surface under Yucca Mountain has been tilted eastward by an isostatic response to tectonic unloading in the Bare Mountain–Bullfrog Hills area. He envisions an unbroken detachment surface that rises out of Crater Flat to envelop Bare Mountain, from Black Marble at the southeast tip of Bare Mountain to the uppermost detachment surface at the north end of the mountain.

Although I endorse much of Hamilton's model, I disagree with several details. First, in contrast to the single detachment fault proposed by Hamilton (1988), I conclude that at least two, if not three, low-angle fault surfaces are present in the Funeral Mountains (highest crustal level, Swadley and Carr, 1987; intermediate level, Hamilton, 1988; and lowest, Troxel, 1988). Although Troxel did not specifically call for a lower detachment, the similarity in structures described by him above and below the detachment recognized by Hamilton suggests to me that another unexposed deeper detachment exists in the Funeral Range. The two low-angle fault surfaces at the Bullfrog Hills encapsulate slices of Paleozoic rocks between them (Maldonado, 1985b). Although these slices may be bits of debris left behind during tectonic denudation, similar perhaps to the origin of the Amargosa Chaos (Wright and Troxel, 1984), they may also be parts of an eastward-thickening intermediate plate above a lower detachment that I postulated to extend under Bare Mountain. Several younger-over-older low-angle faults occur below the uppermost low-angle normal fault at Bare Mountain (Carr and Monsen, 1988). These observations suggest that a stack or tier of low-angle normal faults exists.

Second, although Hamilton (1988) infers that extension at Yucca Mountain ceased after the middle Miocene, recurrent Quaternary movement on some normal faults shows that it continued at a much reduced rate. Farther east, Quaternary movement (Stewart and Carlson, 1978; Scott and others, 1988) on west-dipping normal faults along the breakaway fault zone along the western side of the Sheep Range and Delamar Range (Wernicke and others, 1988a) indicates that extensional processes are also active west of the Sheep Range.

Third, although Hamilton (1988) postulates that the detachment fault under Yucca Mountain has been tilted eastward and that the fault emerges from beneath Crater Flat along the east side of Bare Mountain, I support a different interpretation. His proposed detachment surface is exposed between Black Marble, a hill at the southeast tip of Bare Mountain (Fig. 14), and the rest of Bare Mountain. According to Hamilton, the detachment surface is not cut by a steeply dipping normal fault. Study of published maps in that area (Carr and Monsen, 1988; Cornwall and Kleinhampl, 1961; Swadley and Parrish, 1988; and Swadley and Carr, 1987), studies of the fault along the east side of Bare Mountain by Reheis (1986), and my own observations have led me to conclude that the detachment fault is not exposed at the locality postulated by Hamilton. I agree with Carr and Monsen (1988) that the low-angle fault under Black Marble is probably one of many low-angle normal faults within the lower plate at Bare Mountain.

Reheis (1986) documented Quaternary movement on the steeply dipping Bare Mountain fault along the eastern side of Bare Mountain (Fig. 14). East of Black Marble, this fault separates the Cambrian Zabriskie Quartzite and the 11-Ma Timber Mountain Tuff (Swadley and Carr, 1987). Although Hamilton cites the relatively gentle gravity gradient along the east side of Bare Mountain (Snyder and Carr, 1984) in support of his hypothesis of a low-angle fault along the eastern edge of Bare Mountain, the gradient can also be interpreted either as a series of steplike normal faults, as depicted by Swadley and Parrish (1988), or as a wedge of high-density Paleozoic clasts deposited against the steep Bare Mountain fault. Hence, I prefer to interpret the Bare Mountain fault as a steep normal fault that cuts the low-angle normal fault under Crater Flat.

Carr and Monsen (1988) propose a tectonic setting based on their mapping at Bare Mountain. They conclude that the Fluorspar Canyon fault, traced from the Bullfrog Hills into the northern part of Bare Mountain, reached the surface as a breakaway zone shown as the normal fault north of Bare Mountain in Figure 14. Carr and Monsen deduced that the fault moved between 10 and 8 Ma. They consider the normal faulting at Yucca Mountain to be an older and separate phase of extension related to a detachment at some unknown depth under Yucca Mountain. Carr and Monsen cite an assumed uniform eastward dip of strata at Yucca Mountain to conclude that planar normal faults, not listric faults, are present at Yucca Mountain.

For reasons enumerated above, I conclude that listric faults and a relatively shallow low-angle fault do exist under Yucca Mountain. Furthermore, evidence for the *maximum* age of low-angle normal faults at Bare Mountain (Carr and Monsen, 1988) is absent or equivocal. Therefore, older extension of an age similar to the 13- to 11.5-Ma pulse of extension at Yucca Mountain probably is present at Bare Mountain; the age of many of the low-angle faults within the Paleozoic rocks is unknown (Carr and Monsen, 1988). Thus, the breakaway and detachment documented by Carr and Monsen on the northwestern part of Bare Mountain is interpreted by me to be the youngest phase of extension at Bare Mountain. The continuation of the Fluorspar Canyon fault at the northeast part of Bare Mountain, east of the breakaway proposed by Carr and Monsen, may be part of the same low-angle extensional fault postulated at Yucca Mountain. Structural evidence (Carr and Monsen, 1988) suggests that relatively little extension has occurred above this part of the fault at Bare Mountain, comparable to the small amount of extension in the northern part of Yucca Mountain.

My preferred tectonic setting for the extensional structures at Yucca Mountain uses the basic model of Wernicke and others (1988a) and Hamilton (1988). However, I suggest several modifications (Fig. 15).

Complexly interconnected detachment system

Structures mapped at several isolated exposures between Bare Mountain and the Pintwater Range (Fig. 1) indicate that low-angle extensional faults occur at different crustal levels (Fig. 15). Myers (1987) reports a low-angle normal fault between nearly flat-lying Paleozoic strata and isoclinally folded Oligocene Horse Spring Formation (Hinrichs, 1968) at Red Mountain (Fig. 14). I concur with Myers' interpretation that this structure is related to regional extensional processes. At Point of Rocks, a few kilometers south of U.S. Highway 95 (Fig. 14), Burchfiel (1965) mapped three low-angle, younger-over-older faults in Late Proterozoic and Cambrian clastic strata; I interpret these to be an example of a stratigraphically deeper low-angle normal-fault complex. McArthur and Burkhard (1986) recognized a distinct flat-lying reflector at a depth of about 3 km in the Mid Valley region 30 km northwest of Mercury (Fig. 14). They proposed that this reflector might be part of a regional detachment system. Complexly anastomosing low-angle faults within Miocene volcanic strata and possibly within Paleozoic rocks in Calico Hills are considered part of the extensional system (Fig. 14) (Simonds and Scott, 1987). These subhorizontal faults commonly juxtapose steeply dipping Tertiary rocks above Paleozoic rocks. Several of these upper crustal low-angle normal faults in the Calico Hills dip gently toward Yucca Mountain. Abundant high-angle normal faults also cut Cenozoic strata in the area between the Pintwater Range and Yucca Mountain (Stewart and Carlson, 1978).

These isolated exposures of low-angle normal faults suggest to me that low-angle extensional structures occur at several upper crustal structural levels. Although only a conceptual diagram of the geometry of low-angle and high-angle normal faults between the Pintwater Range and Yucca Mountain can be proposed at this time (Fig. 15), I conclude that these low-angle normal faults overlie one or more detachment faults at depth and that all these faults together form a complexly interconnected detachment system.

Uniform distribution of strain

Extensional processes have been operating in the central part of the Basin and Range since about 20 Ma (Wernicke and others, 1988a). Between Bare Mountain and the Sheep Range, the extended terrane must be underlain by one or more detachment faults. Yet, mid-crustal rocks from this central part of the Basin and Range have not been exposed (Stewart and Carlson, 1978), and no major breakaway zones have been recognized west of the one recognized in the Sheep Range (Wernicke and others, 1984). Therefore, I conclude that attenuation of the crust between Bare Mountain and the Sheep Range must not have been as extreme as on the margins of the Basin and Range where mid-crustal rocks are relatively common. I conclude that a more uniform distribution of extensional strain (Buck and others, 1988) has probably affected the central Basin and Range and Yucca Mountain, rather than the simple shear model used for the margins of the Basin and Range (Wernicke, 1985).

Dextral bending

I propose that the extensional structures at Yucca Mountain have been affected by dextral bending within the Walker Lane belt. Compilations of the area southeast of Yucca Mountain (Carr, 1984; U.S. Geological Survey, 1984) show that northeast-trending structures are cut by east-northeast–trending sinistral-slip faults that offset rocks as young as late Pleistocene alluvial deposits (Yount and others, 1987). The increase in degree of extension, increase in eastward dip of strata, decrease in westward dip of faults, and progressive increase in rotation of faults and strata in a clockwise direction about a vertical axis toward the south end of Yucca Mountain may all be related, at least in part, to the effects of dextral strike-slip faulting or oroclinal bending beneath the detachment under the southern end of Yucca Mountain.

The postulated low-angle normal fault beneath Yucca Mountain is predicted to extend westward under Crater Flat (Scott, 1986, 1988) and to connect with the Fluorspar Canyon fault exposed at the northeast end of Bare Mountain (Figs. 14 and 15). I interpret this low-angle fault to have been cut by the Bare Mountain fault (Reheis, 1986) (or similar faults under alluvium along the east margin of Bare Mountain), probably during isostatic uplift of Bare Mountain, as a response to tectonic denudation farther west (Hamilton, 1988). The timing of this uplift and isolation of extension at Yucca Mountain is recorded in the Paleozoic debris drilled below and above the Timber Mountain Tuff from central Crater Flat (Carr and Parrish, 1985).

CONCLUSIONS

1. Steep normal faults at Yucca Mountain probably sole into a low-angle normal fault at relatively shallow depths (1 to 4 km).

2. A tier of low-angle faults probably interconnects to form an extensional system above a mid-crustal detachment at the brittle-ductile transition. Different high-angle normal faults probably extend to different depths; some cut upper low-angle faults, and others sole into low-angle faults above the basal detachment fault.

3. In detail, zones of low-angle faults may consist of several anastomosing individual faults similar to those mapped by Burchfiel (1965) near the Point of Rocks or those observed by Simonds and Scott (1987) in the Calico Hills. If the strain is sufficiently pervasive, it may approach pure shear accommodation rather than simple shear along a discrete fault.

4. Southern Yucca Mountain has been rotated 30° clockwise about a vertical axis relative to northern Yucca Mountain. This may reflect partial decoupling between an underlying dextral oroflexural bend or shear in the Walker Lane belt and an overlying preexisting system of low-angle normal faults below extended upper plate rocks.

5. The northern part of Yucca Mountain has been extended about 10 percent, whereas the southern part has been extended about 60 percent since 13 Ma. The geologic strain rate for the southern part of the mountain was about 8.7×10^{-15}/sec during the 13- to 11.5-Ma period and decreased to about 5.6×10^{-16}/sec after 11.5 Ma (a factor of 16 decrease). The rate in the northeastern area decreased from about 1.4×10^{-15}/sec to 8.3×10^{-17}/sec (a factor of 20 decrease), and that in the northwestern area decreased from about 5.3×10^{-16}/sec to about 2.1×10^{-16}/sec (a factor of 2.5 decrease), for the same periods. These decreases in rates probably were caused by the isostatic rise of Bare Mountain about 11.5 Ma, isolating Yucca Mountain from rapid regional extension.

6. The rate of dip-slip offset on individual major faults at Yucca Mountain is estimated to have been 0.1 to 0.5 mm/yr between 13 and 11.5 Ma; the rate appears to have decreased to 0.01 to 0.03 mm/yr between about 11.5 Ma and the beginning of the Quaternary. The rate decreased further to 0.006 to 0.0015 mm/yr during the Quaternary.

ACKNOWLEDGMENTS

Tectonic syntheses usually build on the detailed studies of many geologists and geophysicists; this synthesis is no exception. The input from many field trips and informal discussions with colleagues also contributed significantly; open exchanges of observations and concepts with R. E. Anderson, W. J. Carr, F. M. Byers, Jr., M. D. Carr, W. B. Hamilton, K. F. Fox, and W. B. Myers have been invaluable to my effort to extrapolate from my local geological observations at Yucca Mountain and Calico Hills to this regional synthesis. The fact that many of us have tectonic settings that diverge in detail has strengthened those contributions. The time and thought that went into constructive reviews of this manuscript and writing style by D. L. Schleicher, W. B. Hamilton, J. C. Cole, R. A. Schweickert, R. L. Bruhn, and particularly K. F. Fox are deeply appreciated.

This work was performed in cooperation with the U.S. Department of Energy, Yucca Mountain Project (Interagency Agreement DE-AI08-78ET44802).

REFERENCES CITED

Ackerman, H. D., Mooney, W. D., Snyder, D. B., and Sutton, V. D., 1988, Preliminary interpretation of seismic-refraction and gravity studies west of Yucca Mountain, Nevada and California, *in* Investigations of the geologic and hydrologic investigations of a potential nuclear waste disposal site at Yucca Mountain, southern Nevada: U.S. Geological Survey Bulletin 1790, p. 23–33.

Angelier, J., 1984, Tectonic analysis of fault slip data sets: Journal of Geophsical Research, v. 89, p. 5835–5848.

Angelier, J., and Colletta, B., 1983, Tension fractures and extensional tectonics: Nature, v. 301, p. 49–51.

Angelier, J., Faugère, E., Michel-Noël, G., and Anderson, R. E., 1987, Bassins en extension et tectonique synsedimentaire; Exemples dans les "Basin and Range" (U.S.A.): Notes et Memoires, no. 21, TOTAL Compagnie Francaise des Petrole, Paris, p. 51–72.

Axen, G. J., 1988, The geometry of planar domino-style normal faults above a dipping basal detachment: Journal of Structural Geology, v. 10, p. 405–411.

Broxton, D. E., Warren, R. G., Hagan, R. C., and Luedemann, G., 1986, Chemistry of diagenetically altered tuffs at a potential nuclear waste repository, Yucca Mountain, Nye County, Nevada: Los Alamos, New Mexico, Los Alamos National Laboratory Report LA–10802–MS, 160 p.

Broxton, D. E., Warren, R. G., Byers, F. M., and Scott, R. B., 1989, Chemical and mineralogical trends within the Timber Mountain–Oasis Valley caldera complex, Nevada; Evidence for multiple cycles of chemical evolution in a long-lived silicic magma system: Journal of Geophysical Research, v. 94, p. 5961–5985.

Buck, W. R., Martinez, F., Steckler, M. S., and Cochran, J. R., 1988, Thermal consequences of lithospheric extension; Pure and simple: Tectonics, v. 7, p. 213–234.

Burchfiel, B. C., 1965, Structural geology of the Specter Range Quadrangle, Nevada, and its regional significance: Geological Society of America Bulletin, v. 76, p. 175–192.

Burchfiel, B. C., Hodges, K. V., and Royden, L. H., 1987, Geology of Panamint Valley–Saline Valley pull-apart system, California; Palinspastic evidence for low-angle geometry of a Neogene range-bounding fault: Journal of Geophysical Research, v. 92, p. 10422–10426.

Byers, F. M., Jr., Carr, W. J., Orkild, P. P., Quinlivan, W. D., and Sargent, K. A., 1976a, Volcanic suites and related cauldrons of Timber Mountain–Oasis Valley caldera complex, southern Nevada: U.S. Geological Survey Professional Paper 919, 70 p.

Byers, F. M., Jr., Carr, W. J., Christiansen, R. L., Lipman, P. W., Orkild, P. P., and Quinlivan, W. D., 1976b, Geologic map of the Timber Mountain caldera area, Nye County, Nevada: U.S. Geological Survey Miscellaneous Investigations Series Map I–891, scale 1:48,000.

Carr, M. D., and Monsen, S. A., 1988, A field trip guide to the geology of Bare Mountain, *in* Weide, D. L., and Faber, M. L., eds., This extended land; Geological Society of America Cordilleran Section Meeting, Field Trip Guidebook: 1988: University of Nevada at Las Vegas Geoscience Department Special Publication 2, p. 50–57.

Carr, M. D., and 7 others, 1986, Geology of drill hole UE25p#1; A test hole into pre-Tertiary rocks near Yucca Mountain, southern Nevada: U.S. Geological Survey Open-File Report 86–175, 87 p.

Carr, W. J., 1974, Summary of tectonic and structural evidence for stress orientation at the Nevada Test Site: U.S. Geological Survey Open-File Report 74–176, 83 p.

——, 1984, Regional structural setting of Yucca Mountain, southwestern Nevada, and late Cenozoic rates of tectonic activity in part of the southwestern Great Basin, Nevada and California: U.S. Geological Survey Open-File Report 84–854, 109 p.

Carr, W. J., and Parrish, L. D., 1985, Geology of drill hole USW VH-2, and structure of Crater Flat, southwestern Nevada: U.S. Geological Survey Open-File Report 85–475, 41 p.

Carr, W. J., Byers, F. M., Jr., and Orkild, P. P., 1986, Stratigraphic and volcano-tectonic relations of Crater Flat Tuff and some older volcanic units, Nye County, Nevada: U.S. Geological Survey Professional Paper 1323, 28 p.

Christiansen, R. L., and Lipman, P. W., 1965, Geologic map of the Topopah Spring NW Quadrangle, Nye County, Nevada: U.S. Geological Survey Geologic Quadrangle Map GQ–444, scale 1:24,000.

Cornwall, H. R., and Kleinhampl, F. J., 1961, Geology of the Bare Mountain Quadrangle, Nevada: U.S. Geological Survey Geologic Quadrangle Map GQ–157, scale 1:62,500.

Crowe, B. M., Vaniman, D. T., and Carr, W. J., 1983, Status of volcanic hazard studies for the Nevada Nuclear Waste Storage Investigations: Los Alamos, New Mexico, Los Alamos National Laboratory Report LA–9325–MS, 47 p.

Ekren, E. B., 1968, Geologic setting of Nevada Test Site and Nellis Air Force Range, *in* Eckel, E. B., ed., Nevada Test Site: Geological Society of America Memoir 110, p. 11–19.

Frizzell, V. A., and Zoback, M. L., 1987, Stress orientation determined from fault slip data in Hampel Wash area, Nevada, and its relation to contemporary regional stress field: Tectonics, v. 6, p. 89–98.

Gans, P. B., Miller, E. L., McCarthy, J., and Ouldcutt, M. L., 1985, Tertiary extensional faulting and evolving ductile-brittle transition zones in the northern Snake River Range and vicinity; New insights from seismic data: Geology, v. 13, p. 189–193.

Gianella, V. P., and Callaghan, E., 1934, The earthquake of December 20, 1932, at Cedar Mountain, Nevada, and its bearing on the genesis of Basin Range structure: Journal of Geology, v. 42, p. 1–22.

Guth, P. L., 1981, Tertiary extension north of the Las Vegas shear zone, Sheep and Desert Ranges, Clark County, Nevada: Geological Society of America Bulletin, v. 92, p. 763–771.

Hamblin, W. K., 1965, Origin of "reverse drag" on downthrown side of normal faults: Geological Society of America Bulletin, v. 76, p. 1145–1164.

Hamilton, W. B., 1988, Detachment faulting in the Death Valley region, California and Nevada, *in* Investigations of the geologic and hydrologic characterization of a potential nuclear waste disposal site at Yucca Mountain, southern Nevada: U.S. Geological Survey Bulletin 1790, p. 51–85.

Hardyman, R. F., 1978, Volcanic stratigraphy and structural geology of the Gillis Range, Mineral County, Nevada [Ph.D. thesis]: Reno, University of Nevada, 248 p.

Hardyman, R. F., Ekren, E. B., Proffett, J. M., and Dilles, J. H., 1984, Tertiary tectonics of west-central Nevada; Yerington to Gabbs Valley, Field Trip 8, *in* Linz, J. P., ed., Western geological excursions, v. 4: Reno, Nevada, Mackay School of Mines, p. 160–231.

Hinrichs, E. N., 1968, Geologic map of the Camp Desert Rock Quadrangle: U.S. Geological Survey Geologic Quadrangle Map GQ–726, scale 1:24,000.

Hobbs, D. W., 1967, The formation of tension joints in sedimentary rocks; An explanation: Geological Magazine, v. 104, p. 550–556.

Jennings, C. W., 1977, Geologic map of California: California Division of Mines and Geology, California Geologic Data Map Series, scale 1:750,000.

Kautz, S. A., and Sclater, J. G., 1988, Internal deformation in clay models of extension by block faulting: Tectonics, v. 7, p. 823–832.

Lipman, P. W., and McKay, E. J., 1965, Geologic map of the Topopah Spring SW Quadrangle, Nye County, Nevada: U.S. Geological Survey Geologic Quadrangle Map GQ–439, scale 1:24,000.

Lipman, P. W., Christiansen, R. L., and O'Connor, J. T., 1966, A compositionally zoned ash-flow sheet in southern Nevada: U.S. Geological Survey Professional Paper 501-B, p. B74–B78.

Maldonado, F., 1985a, Geologic map of the Jackass Flats area, Nye County, Nevada: U.S. Geological Survey Miscellaneous Investigations Series Map I–1519, scale 1:48,000.

——, 1985b, Late Tertiary detachment faults in the Bullfrog Hills, southwestern Nevada: Geological Society of America Abstracts with Programs, v. 17, p. 651.

——, 1990, Geologic map of the northwest quarter of the Bullfrog 15-minute Quadrangle, Nye County, Nevada: U.S. Geological Survey Miscellaneous Investigations Series Map I-1985, scale 1:24,000.

Maldonado, F., and Koether, S. L., 1983, Stratigraphy, structure, and some petrographic features of Tertiary volcanic rocks at the USW G-2 drill hole, Yucca Mountain, Nye County, Nevada: U.S. Geological Survey Open-File Report 83–732, 83 p.

McArthur, R. D., and Burkhard, N. R., 1986, Geological and geophysical investigations of Mid Valley: Livermore, California, Lawrence Livermore National Laboratory Report UCID–20740, 92 p.

McGill, G. E., and Stromquist, A. W., 1979, The grabens of Canyonlands National Park, Utah; Geometry, mechanics, and kinematics: Journal of Geophysical Research, v. 84, p. 4547–4563.

McKay, E. J., and Sargent, K. A., 1970, Geologic map of the Lathrop Wells Quadrangle, Nye County, Nevada: U.S. Geological Survey Geologic Quadrangle Map GQ–883, scale 1:24,000.

McKay, E. J., and Williams, W. P., 1964, Geology of the Jackass Flats Quadrangle, Nye County, Nevada: U.S. Geological Survey Geologic Quadrangle Map GQ–368, scale 1:24,000.

McKee, E. H., 1983, Reset K-Ar ages; Evidence for three metamorphic core complexes, western Nevada: Isochron/West, no. 38, p. 17–20.

Myers, W. B., 1987, Detachment of Tertiary strata from their Paleozoic floor near Mercury, Nevada: Geological Society of America Abstracts with Programs, v. 19, p. 783.

Ransome, F. L., Emmons, W. H., and Garry, G. H., 1910, Geology and ore deposits of the Bullfrog district, Nevada: U.S. Geological Survey Bulletin 407, 130 p.

Reheis, M. C., 1986, Preliminary study of Quaternary faulting on the east side of Bare Mountain, Nye County, Nevada: U.S. Geological Survey Open-File Report 86–576, 13 p.

Robinson, G. D., 1985, Structure of pre-Cenozoic rocks in the vicinity of Yucca Mountain, Nye County, Nevada; A potential nuclear-waste disposal site: U.S. Geological Survey Bulletin 1647, 22 p.

Rogers, A. M., Harmsen, S. C., and Meremonte, M. E., 1987, Evaluation of the seismicity of the southern Great Basin and its relationship to the tectonic framework of the region: U.S. Geological Survey Open-File Report 87–408, 196 p.

Rosenbaum, J. G., and Hudson, M. R., 1988, Paleomagnetic investigation of Tertiary rotations, southwest Nevada; Yucca Mountain [abs.]: EOS Transactions of the American Geophysical Union, v. 69, p. 1164.

Rosenbaum, J. G., Hudson, M. R., and Scott, R. B., 1990, Paleomagnetic constraints on the geometry and timing of deformation at Yucca Mountain, Nevada: Journal of Geophysical Research (in press).

Sargent, K. A., and Stewart, J. H., 1971, Geologic map of the Specter Range NW Quadrangle, Nye County, Nevada: U.S. Geological Survey Geologic Quadrangle Map GQ–884, scale 1:24,000.

Sargent, K. A., McKay, E. J., and Burchfiel, B. C., 1970, Geologic map of the Striped Hills Quadrangle, Nye County, Nevada: U.S. Geological Survey Geologic Quadrangle Map GQ–882, scale 1:24,000.

Scott, R. B., 1984a, Internal deformation of blocks bounded by Basin-and-Range–style faults: Geological Society of America Abstracts with Programs, v. 16, p. 649.

——, 1984b, Evolution of magma below clustered calderas, southwestern Nevada volcanic field [abs.]: EOS Transactions of the American Geophysical Union, v. 65, p. 1126–1127.

——, 1986, Extensional tectonics at Yucca Mountains, southern Nevada: Geological Society of America Abstracts with Programs, v. 18, p. 411.

——, 1988, Tectonic setting of Yucca Mountain, southwest Nevada: Geological Society of America Abstracts with Programs, v. 20, p. 229.

Scott, R. B., and Bonk, J., 1984, Preliminary geologic map of Yucca Mountain, Nye County, Nevada, with geologic sections: U.S. Geological Survey Open-File Report 84–494, scale 1:12,000.

Scott, R. B., and Castellanos, M., 1984, Stratigraphic and structural relations of volcanic rocks in drill holes USW GU-3 and USW G-3, Yucca Mountain, Nye County, Nevada: U.S. Geological Survey Open-File Report 84–491, 94 p.

Scott, R. B., and Hofland, G. S., 1987, Fault-slip paleostress analysis of Yucca Mountain, Nevada [abs.]: EOS Transactions of the American Geophysical Union, v. 68, p. 1461.

Scott, R. B., and Rosenbaum, J. G., 1986, Evidence of rotation about a vertical axis during extension at Yucca Mountain, southern Nevada [abs.]: EOS Transactions of the American Geophysical Union, v. 67, p. 358.

Scott, R. B., and Whitney, J. W., 1987, The upper crustal detachment system at Yucca Mountain, SW Nevada: Geological Society of America Abstracts with Programs, v. 19, p. 332–333.

Scott, R. B., Bath, G. D., Flanigan, V. J., Hoover, D. B., Rosenbaum, J. G., and Spengler, R. W., 1984, Geological and geophysical evidence of structures in northwest-trending washes, Yucca Mountain, southern Nevada, and their possible significance to a nuclear waste repository in the unsaturated zone: U.S. Geological Survey Open-File Report 84–567, 23 p.

Scott, R. B., Swadley WC, and Novak, S. W., 1988, Preliminary geologic map of the Delamar Lake Quadrangle, Lincoln County, Nevada: U.S. Geological Survey Open-File Report 88–576, scale 1:24,000.

Simonds, F. W., and Scott, R. B., 1987, Detachment faulting and hydrothermal alteration in the Calico Hills, SW Nevada [abs.]: EOS Transactions of the American Geophysical Union, v. 68, p. 1475.

Snyder, D. B., and Carr, W. J., 1984, Interpretation of gravity data in a complex volcano-tectonic setting, southwestern Nevada: Journal of Geophysical Research, v. 89, p. 10193–10206.

Spengler, R. W., Byers, F. M., Jr., and Warner, J. B., 1981, Stratigraphy and structure of volcanic rocks in drill hole USWG-1, Yucca Mountain, Nye County, Nevada: U.S. Geological Survey Open-File Report 81–1349, 50 p.

Steiger, R. H., and Jager, E., 1977, Subcommission on geochronology; Convention on the use of decay constants in geo- and cosmochronology: Earth and Planetary Science Letters, v. 36, p. 359–362.

Stewart, J. H., 1988, Tectonics of the Walker Lane belt, western Great Basin; Mesozoic and Cenozoic deformation in a zone of shear, *in* Ernst, W. G., ed, Metamorphism and crustal evolution of the western United States, Rubey Volume 7: Englewood Cliffs, New Jersey, Prentice-Hall, p. 683–713.

Stewart, J. H., and Carlson, J. E., 1978, Geologic map of Nevada: U.S. Geological Survey and Nevada Bureau of Mines and Geology, scale 1:500,000.

Stock, J. M., Healy, J. H., Hickman, S. H., and Zoback, M. D., 1985, Hydraulic fracturing stress measurements at Yucca Mountain, Nevada, and relationships to the regional stress field: Journal of Geophysical Research, v. 90, p. 8691–8706.

Stock, J. M., Healy, J. H., Svitek, J., and Mastin, L., 1986, Report on televiewer log and stress measurements in holes USW G-3 and UE-25p1, Yucca Mountain, Nye County, Nevada: U.S. Geological Survey Open-File Report 86–369, 91 p.

Swadley, WC, 1983, Map showing surficial geology of the Lathrop Wells Quadrangle, Nye County, Nevada: U.S. Geological Survey Miscellaneous Investigations Series Map I–1361, scale 1:48,000.

Swadley, WC, and Carr, W. J., 1987, Geologic map of the Quaternary and Tertiary deposits of the Big Dune Quadrangle, Nye County, Nevada, and Inyo County, California: U.S. Geological Survey Miscellaneous Investigations Series Map I–1767, scale 1:48,000.

Swadley, WC, and Parrish, L. D., 1988, Surficial geologic map of the Bare Mountain Quadrangle, Nye County, Nevada: U.S. Geological Survey Miscellaneous Investigations Series Map I–1826, scale 1:48,000.

Swadley, WC, Hoover, D. L., and Rosholt, J. N., 1984, Preliminary report on late Cenozoic faulting and stratigraphy in the vicinity of Yucca Mountain, Nye County, Nevada: U.S. Geological Survey Open-File Report 84–788, 42 p.

Taylor, E. M., and Huckins, H. E., 1986, Carbonate and opaline silica fault-filling on the Bow Ridge fault, Yucca Mountain, Nevada; Deposition from pedogenic processes or upwelling ground water?: Geological Society of America Abstracts with Programs, v. 18, p. 418.

Troxel, B. W., 1988, A geologic traverse of the northern Funeral Mountains, Death Valley, California, *in* Weide, D. L. and Faber, M. L., eds., This extended land; Geological Society of America Cordilleran Section Meeting Field Trip Guidebook: University of Nevada at Las Vegas Geoscience Department Special Publication 2, p. 45–49.

U.S. Geological Survey, 1984, A summary of geologic studies through January 1, 1983, of a potential high-level radioactive waste repository site at Yucca Mountain, southern Nye County, Nevada: U.S. Geological Survey Open-File Report 84–792, 103 p.

Vaniman, D. T., Crowe, B. M., and Gladney, E. S., 1982, Petrology and geochemistry of hawaiite lavas from Crater Flat, Nevada: Contributions to Mineralogy and Petrology, v. 80, p. 341–357.

Warren, R. G., McDowell, F. W., Byers, F. M., Jr., Broxton, D. E., Carr, W. J., and Orkild, P. P., 1988, Episodic leaks from Timber Mountain caldera; New evidence from rhyolite lavas of Fortymile Canyon, SW Nevada volcanic field: Geological Society of America Abstracts with Programs, v. 20, p. 241.

Wasserburg, G. L., Wetherill, G. W., and Wright, L. A., 1959, Ages in Precambrian terrain of Death Valley, California: Journal of Geology, v. 57, p. 702–708.

Wells, S. G., McFadden, L. D., and Renault, C., 1988, A geomorphic assessment of Quaternary volcanism in the Yucca Mountain area, Nevada Test Site, southern Nevada: Geological Society of America Abstracts with Programs, v. 20, p. 242.

Wernicke, B., 1985, Uniform-sense normal simple shear of the continental lithosphere: Canadian Journal of Earth Sciences, v. 22, p. 108–125.

Wernicke, B., and Burchfiel, B. C., 1982, Modes of extensional tectonics: Journal of Structural Geology, v. 4, p. 105–115.

Wernicke, B., Guth, P. L., and Axen, G. J., 1984, Tertiary extensional tectonics in the Sevier thrust belt of southern Nevada, Field Trip 19, *in* Linz, J. P., ed., Western geological excursions, v. 4: Reno, Nevada, Mackay School of Mines, p. 473–510.

Wernicke, B., Axen, G. J., and Snow, J. K., 1988a, Basin and Range extensional tectonics at the latitude of Las Vegas, Nevada: Geological Society of America Bulletin, v. 100, p. 1738–1757.

Wernicke, B. P., Walker, J. D., and Hodges, K. V., 1988b, Field guide to the northern part of the Tucki Mountain Fault System, Death Valley region, California, *in* Weide, D. L., and Faber, M. L., eds., This extended land; Geological Society of America Cordilleran Section Meeting Field Trip Guidebook: University of Nevada at Las Vegas Geoscience Department Special Publication 2, p. 58–63.

Whitney, J. W., Shroba, R. R., Simonds, F. W., and Harding, S. T., 1986, Recurrent Quaternary movement on the Windy Wash fault, Nye County, Nevada: Geological Society of America Abstracts with Programs, v. 18, p. 787.

Wright, L. A., and Troxel, B. W., 1984, Geology of the northern half of the Confidence Hills 15-minute Quadrangle, Death Valley region, eastern California; The area of the Amargosa Chaos: California Division of Mines and Geology Map Sheet 34, 31 p., and map, scale 1:24,000.

Wright, L. A., Otton, J. K., and Troxel, B. W., 1974, Turtleback surfaces of Death Valley viewed as phenomena of extensional tectonics: Geology, v. 2, p. 53–54.

Yount, J. C., Shroba, R. R., McMaster, C. R., Huckins, H. E., and Rodriguez, E. A., 1987, Trench logs from a strand of the Rock Valley fault system, Nevada Test Site, Nye County, Nevada: U.S. Geological Survey Miscellaneous Field Studies Map MF–1824.

Zoback, M. L., Anderson, R. E., and Thompson, G. A., 1981, Cainozoic evolution of the state of stress and style of tectonism of the Basin and Range province of the United States: Philosophical Transactions of the Royal Society of London, v. A300, p. 407–434.

MANUSCRIPT ACCEPTED BY THE SOCIETY AUGUST 21, 1989

Chapter 13

Styles of extension in the Nevada Test Site region, southern Walker Lane Belt; An integration of volcano-tectonic and detachment fault models

W. J. Carr
11345 W. 38th Ave., Wheat Ridge, Colorado 80033

ABSTRACT

Detailed geological information, supported by geophysical data and drill holes, indicates that several deformational styles characterize the Walker Lane Belt of the south-central Great Basin and Nevada Test Site region.

The region is split by a north-trending major volcano-tectonic rift that includes several large calderas and is filled with more than 4 km of Miocene volcanic rocks. The rift lies in a large right-step in the Walker Lane Belt and separates areas to the west containing recognized detachment-style faults and metamorphic rocks from adjoining terrain on the east that contains no recognized major detachment faults or exposures of metamorphosed rocks.

The volcano-tectonic trough was most active from about 16 to 10 Ma. The style and timing of Cenozoic faulting is different east and west of the rift, and well-dated volcanic sequences show that the principal faulting events occurred at different times and rates within adjacent structural domains. This variability suggests that no single tectonic process produced the Cenozoic structure of the region. Normal faulting east of the rift may have been controlled in part by extension accommodated by Mesozoic thrust faults.

It is proposed that the volcanic rift represents a pull-apart at a right-step in the Walker Lane Belt and that the rift was the headwall or breakaway zone for detachment faulting to the west. In this model, extensional faults of Miocene age within and immediately east of the rift are largely gravitational responses to magmatism, rifting, and volcano-tectonic collapse.

INTRODUCTION

During the last two decades, large-magnitude crustal extension in the Basin and Range Province has been illustrated repeatedly by detailed geologic mapping in numerous areas. As geologists began to realize the geometric problems associated with large-scale extension, much attention was given to areas of steeply tilted Tertiary rocks. Extensive low-angle faults, many previously described as thrusts or gravity glide surfaces, were recognized as a way to accommodate extension of upper crustal rocks. These detachment surfaces, as they came to be known, had

been previously observed and mapped in regions such as Death Valley and the lower Colorado River Valley, but until about 20 years ago their significance and origin were not understood. Since the discovery of probable detachment faults in seismic profiles in the eastern Great Basin (e.g., Effimoff and Pinezich, 1986), it has become even more attractive for geoscientists to relate all basin-range–style faulting to underlying detachments. This chapter maintains that not only are there various kinds of low-angle faults in the south-central Great Basin, but some of the apparent

Carr, W. J., 1990, Styles of extension in the Nevada Test Site region, southern Walker Lane Belt; An integration of volcano-tectonic and detachment fault models, *in* Wernicke, B. P., ed., Basin and Range extensional tectonics near the latitude of Las Vegas, Nevada: Boulder, Colorado, Geological Society of America Memoir 176.

basin-range–style faulting may be volcano-tectonic in origin and not necessarily underlain by detachment faults. The model presented, however, attempts to relate detachment and volcano-tectonic processes in the area of an important volcanic rift that spans the Walker Lane Belt between Death Valley and the more traditional basin and range terrain to the northeast.

More than 30 years of detailed geological, geophysical, and hydrologic studies of the Nevada Test Site and surrounding region have provided an excellent perspective of the structural complexities of this part of the Great Basin. This work, largely supported by the U.S. Department of Energy, is continuing, and during the last 12 years or so has focused on an important national problem—that of radioactive waste disposal. Tuffs of Miocene age at Yucca Mountain (Fig. 1) are being studied as the site for an underground repository. Understanding the seismic and tectonic setting is important in evaluating the site's ability to safely contain the wastes for thousands of years.

REGIONAL SETTING

The southern Great Basin in the Nevada Test Site region (essentially the area of Fig. 1) exhibits diverse structural trends, styles, and tectonic activity and is divisible into three major structural-physiographic subsections (Carr, 1984a; Fig. 2): the Inyo-Mono, Walker Lane Belt, and Basin and Range. Most of the region discussed here is located within the Walker Lane Belt.

Compressional tectonism, most active in the Mesozoic, created a prominent structural grain of thrust faults and folds. Conjugate northwest- and northeast-striking strike-slip faults and right-lateral bending were formed within a thick section of Proterozoic and Paleozoic sedimentary rocks (Albers, 1967; Stewart and others, 1968). Granitic plutons are the only rocks of Mesozoic age in the region discussed here.

Much of the Mesozoic structure is buried beneath volcanic rocks, largely Miocene in age, that are more than 5 km thick in caldera areas (Snyder and Carr, 1984; Orkild and others, 1968; Hoffman and Mooney, 1983). Voluminous silicic tuff and lava eruptions occurred from about 16 Ma to 10 Ma, forming a complex of nested and overlapping calderas concentrated in a major volcano-tectonic rift (W. J. Carr and others, 1986). Volcanism and tectonism were closely related (Christiansen and others, 1965), and both began an abrupt decline about 10 Ma in all but the southwestern part of the region. This decline was accompanied by the first significant basaltic volcanism about 10 Ma; the last silicic eruptions in the region occurred about 5 Ma, but basaltic activity continued into the Quaternary (Vaniman and others, 1982).

The Walker Lane Belt is part of a megastructure or continental-scale lineament that crosses the Basin and Range Province from Texas to Oregon (Barosh, 1969; Carr, 1981). The Walker Lane Belt separates the northwest structural-physiographic trends in the southwestern Great Basin, east of the Sierra Nevada in California, from the predominantly north-south trends of the more typical basin and range structure of Nevada (Gianella

and Callaghan, 1934, p. 21). The belt is a zone of diversely oriented, relatively low-relief hills and valleys dominated by lateral rather than dip-slip faulting, and except for caldera structures, large vertical displacements are not characteristic. Gravity data (Healey and others, 1980a, b; Kane and others, 1979) show that most valleys are bordered by fairly gentle gravity gradients and have relatively thin Cenozoic deposits, generally less than 600 m. Shear zones of the southern Walker Lane Belt, particularly those of northwest strike, such as the Las Vegas Valley shear zone and Yucca-Frenchman shear zone (Carr, 1984a, Fig. 4), tend to be poorly exposed because most of them are inactive and the traces are largely buried beneath young volcanic rocks and alluvium. A few Quaternary faults of northwest strike are present in the alluvium of the Pahrump Valley area (Fig. 2), however.

As defined here, the Walker Lane Belt of the southern Great Basin is locally more than 100 km wide, and its boundaries are more definite than those in some previous descriptions (e.g., Stewart, 1980, p. 86). The southwestern boundary is the southern Death Valley–Furnace Creek–Fish Lake Valley fault system (Fig. 2). The northeastern limits, less well defined in some areas, are designated as the northeasternmost of a zone of partly en echelon, northwest-striking, right-lateral shear zones (Fig. 2).

Shear zones of the Walker Lane Belt are transform-like in the sense that they may display greater extension on one side than the other, and they have finite length, typically ending abruptly at north- to northeast-striking structural zones that appear to absorb the right-lateral component by extension on normal or oblique-slip faults (Anderson, 1973). Some authors (e.g., Burchfiel and others, 1987) have used the term *transfer fault* for this type of structure. In some areas, Paleozoic rocks are bent into large-scale oroflexes (Albers, 1967) along and within the belt.

Adding significantly to the tectonic diversity of the southern Walker Lane Belt are several northeast-trending structural zones (Fig. 2). In the Nevada Test Site area the most important of these is the Spotted Range–Mine Mountain structural zone of northeast-striking faults (Fig. 2) that spans the Walker Lane Belt. The locations of other important northeast-striking structural zones are shown on Figure 2. Many of these zones show evidence of left-lateral offset (e.g., Barnes and others, 1982), although in the Nevada Test Site region the amount of later offset in Tertiary rocks is small, generally less than 1 km on individual faults (Carr, 1974). The Spotted Range–Mine Mountain structural zone and several others of northeast trend are seismically active (Rogers and others, 1983) and contain a few faults that have had surface displacement in Quaternary time (Carr, 1974).

KAWICH-GREENWATER RIFT

Near the western edge of the Nevada Test Site, a series of major volcanic centers lies obliquely across the Walker Lane Belt (Fig. 1) in a north-trending structural trough here named the Kawich-Greenwater Rift. I suggest that the volcano-tectonic trough of the western Nevada Test Site region is structurally connected with the volcanic center of the Greenwater Range

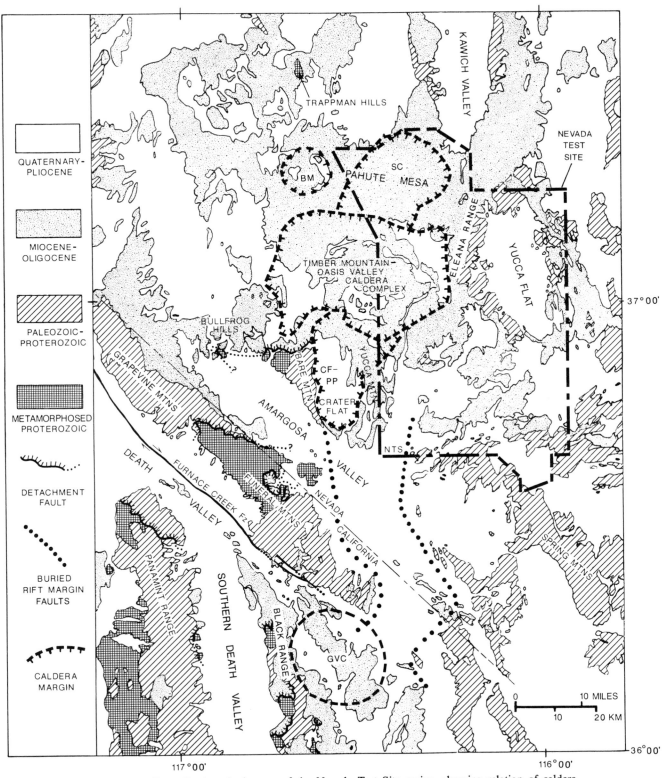

Figure 1. Generalized geologic map of the Nevada Test Site region, showing relation of caldera complexes, Greenwater volcanic center, and rift zone to metamorphic rocks and detachment structures. BM—Black Mountain caldera; SC—Silent Canyon caldera; CF-PP—Crater Flat-Prospector Pass caldera complex; GVC—Greenwater volcanic center. Buried rift margin faults shown are based on presence of steep, linear gravity gradients.

(Fig. 1) to the south. The continuity is supported by a southward continuation of the prominent linear gravity low (Fig. 3) that coincides with several large volcanic centers, including the Silent Canyon, Timber Mountain–Oasis Valley, and Crater Flat–Prospector Pass caldera complexes (Fig. 1). The gravity low is especially prominent from Crater Flat northward and reaches its maximum in the Pahute Mesa area, but the low also extends southward from Crater Flat across the Amargosa Valley at least to the Greenwater volcanic field in California near Death Valley (Fig. 1). The gravity low also extends northward into the Basin and Range subsection and central Nevada, where it is wider and more diffuse and consists of many subparallel, less continuous gravity lows.

The Kawich-Greenwater Rift obliquely spans the Walker Lane Belt and lies in a right-step in the belt boundaries (Fig. 2), which consist of several en echelon offsets from the northern end of the northwest-striking southern Death Valley fault (Fig. 2) to the southeastern end of the Furnace Creek fault. There are several right-steps of the northeastern boundary of the Walker Lane Belt, beginning with the northwest end (Carr, 1984b) of the Las Vegas Valley shear zone and continuing on several other northwest-striking fault zones (Carr, 1984b, p. 13) across the eastern part of the Nevada Test Site (Fig. 2). Wright (1971) originally noted an association of volcanism in the Greenwater area with the right-step between the southern Death Valley and Furnace Creek fault zones and suggested a genetic relation between the two features.

The Kawich-Greenwater Rift is structurally defined by north- to northeast-striking faults on the south and large-scale cauldron subsidence on the north. In most places, the west side of the rift is more abrupt than the east, resulting in an asymmetric

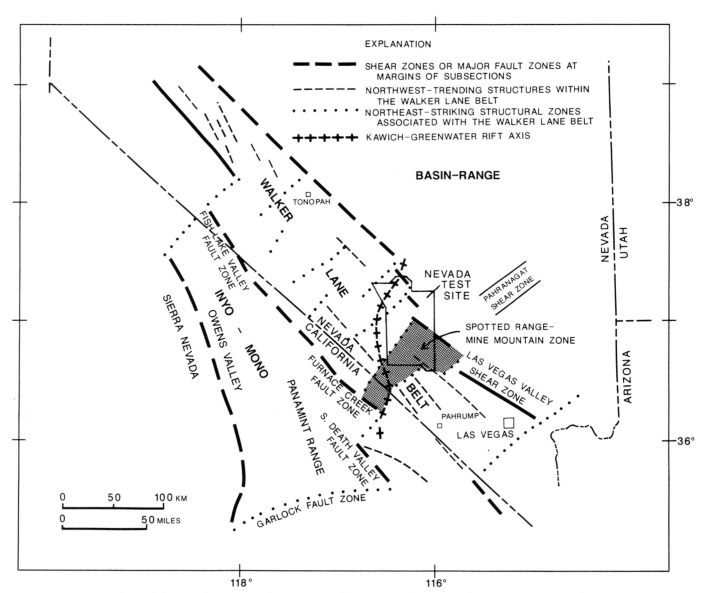

Figure 2. Structural-physiographic subsections of the southern Great Basin, important structures of the Walker Lane Belt, and location of volcano-tectonic rift.

graben. At Bare Mountain, and southward across the Amargosa Valley (Fig. 1), the west side of the rift is a relatively narrow fault zone of large displacement marked by a steep gravity gradient (Fig. 3) (Snyder and Carr, 1984). Beneath Pahute Mesa, the west floor of the Silent Canyon caldera appears to be deeper and the caldera wall more abrupt than on the east side (Orkild and others, 1969). Westward thickening of welded facies of the Ammonia Tanks Member of the Timber Mountain Tuff, exposed on the resurgent dome (Fig. 6) in the center of the Timber Mountain caldera, suggests that the west side of the Ammonia Tanks caldera collapsed more than the east (Carr and Quinlivan, 1968, p. 101). The facies change occurs along a line that trends N15°E, parallel to the faults along the east side of the Kawich-Greenwater Rift.

The east side of the rift is more diffuse than the west. On the north, the east margins of the Silent Canyon and Timber Mountain calderas approximate the boundary. In the Yucca Mountain area is a zone of faults that is strikingly similar in pattern to the one on eastern Pahute Mesa (see Fig. 6). Southeast of Yucca Mountain, the east margin of the rift continues southward into the Amargosa Valley as a buried fault scarp defined by gravity (Fig. 1).

The southern part of the rift, from the Amargosa Valley into California (Fig. 1), makes gentle bends to the southeast and then to the southwest to the area of the Greenwater volcanic center. Here also the western margin is fairly abrupt, based on the gravity contours (Fig. 3), and the eastern margin is more diffuse, just as it is farther north.

The northern part of the Kawich-Greenwater Rift contains volcanic rocks ranging in age from Miocene to Quaternary. The oldest widespread Tertiary unit identified in the rift with reasonable certainty is the tuff of Yucca Flat in the Yucca Mountain (M. D. Carr and others, 1986) and Pahute Mesa (W. J. Carr and others, 1986) areas; its age is approximately 14.5 to 15 Ma (W. J. Carr and others, 1986). Tertiary sedimentary and volcanic rocks probably underlie the tuff of Yucca Flat in the rift, but drill holes have not reached these units, with the exception of some older lavas beneath the western Pahute Mesa area (Orkild and others, 1969). The oldest tuff that probably originated from the rift, on the basis of its distribution and petrologic similarity with younger units from the Timber Mountain caldera magmatic center, is the Redrock Valley Tuff, whose age is about 16 Ma (W. J. Carr and others, 1986). This may approximately date the inception of rift formation in the northern part of the area.

A general absence of strong anomalies on aeromagnetic surveys (Kane and Bracken, 1983; U.S. Geological Survey, 1978) indicates that, except for scattered small areas of basalt, strongly magnetic volcanic rocks are thin or absent in the Amargosa Valley south of the southern boundary of the Nevada Test Site (Fig. 1). Relatively nonmagnetic Tertiary rocks of uncertain age crop out in a northwest-trending belt along the Nevada-California state line (Fig. 1). These rocks include tuffaceous sandstone, siltstone, limestone, and conglomerate and a few tuffs. In many places these rocks dip steeply, as much as 65° (Denny and

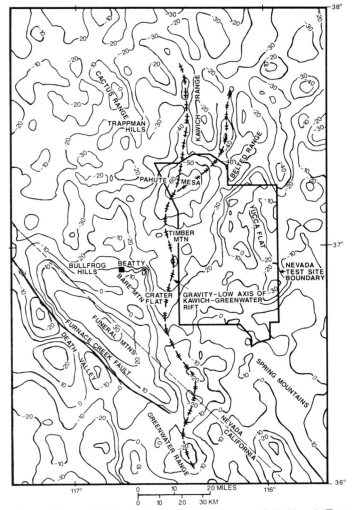

Figure 3. Generalized regional Bouguer gravity map of the Nevada Test Site region, showing the axis of the gravity low defining the Kawich-Greenwater rift. Contour interval 10 mgal. Adapted from gravity map by R. Saltus, U.S. Geological Survey.

Drewes, 1965) or more and are gently to sharply folded. Except for a K/Ar age of 13.2 Ma on a tuff near the southeastern end of these outcrops (L. A. Wright, written communication, 1989), the rocks apparently have not been radiometrically dated. Locally they are unconformably overlain by conglomerate similar to the Funeral Formation of the Furnace Creek Wash area, adjacent to the southeastern Funeral Mountains. The Funeral Formation is about 4 m.y. old (McAllister, 1973). The steeply dipping and folded sedimentary rocks along the state line are similar to rocks in the nearby Funeral Mountains and southern Nevada Test Site area. Cemen and others (1985) report ages of about 25 to 20 Ma for Tertiary rocks at the southeastern end of the Funeral Mountains. Similar rocks in the southern Nevada Test Site area called "older tuffs" and rocks of Pavits Spring are about 14 to 15 m.y. old (Carr and others, 1986). No volcanic rocks from the Nevada Test Site area have been recognized in the southern part of the rift. Large volume eruptions from the Test Site area essentially concluded with the Timber Mountain Tuff about 11 Ma. If the Tertiary rocks exposed sporadically in the northwest-trending belt along the state line are early or middle Miocene, as seems likely, this part of the rift may not have been very active since about 14 Ma.

The Greenwater volcanic center (Fig. 1) was the source of relatively young silicic and basaltic tuffs and lavas, which include the youngest silicic rocks of the region (McAllister, 1973; Fleck, 1970). Immediately northwest of the Greenwater volcanic center are thick tuffaceous sediments and tuffs of the Artist Drive and Furnace Creek Formations. The lower part of the Artist Drive is a temporal equivalent (14 to 10 Ma; Cemen and others, 1985) of the major ash-flow eruptions from the northern part of the Kawich-Greenwater Rift. The Artist Drive Formation has been correlated with the opening of the Furnace Creek basin (Cemen and others, 1985) near the southeast end of the Furnace Creek fault (Fig. 1). South and east of the Greenwater volcanic center are more thick silicic volcanic rocks, in part the "older volcanics" of Drewes (1963), which Haefner (1976) called the Shoshone volcanics. According to dates by Fleck (1970), some of these rocks are 6 to 8 m.y. old.

Thus, the southern end of the rift, as I envision it, was active at the same time as the northern part of the Nevada Test Site area, but to the south significant silicic volcanism continued until about 5 Ma. Cemen and others (1985) concluded that the complex tectonic framework of the area is incompletely understood, but attributed formation of the Furnace Creek basin in part to "subsidence marginal to a volcanic field and contemporaneous with the volcanism." They also attributed localization of volcanism southwest of the Furnace Creek fault to severe extension. This is a pattern I believe fits well with the rest of the Kawich-Greenwater Rift, but in the Greenwater area, late Cenozoic movements on the Furnace Creek fault zone and associated faults have interacted with, dismembered, and complicated the rift structure.

The Kawich-Greenwater Rift and gravity low lie near and parallel to the axis of a larger regional volcano-tectonic feature called the Death Valley–Pancake Range basalt belt (Carr, 1984a, p. 30). This zone of petrologically similar late Miocene, Pliocene, and Pleistocene basalts extends from the Lunar Crater basalt field in central Nevada, 150 km north of the Nevada Test Site, south-southwestward to southern Death Valley. Aeromagnetically detected buried basalts in the Amargosa Valley (U.S. Geological Survey, 1978) may also belong to this group. The Death Valley–Pancake Range basalt belt (Crowe and others, 1980) has been described (Carr, 1984a, p. 32) as a relatively youthful zone of slightly higher than regional tectonic flux (the sum of all elements of tectonism, including seismicity and volcanism, occurring in a region over a period of time). Compared to most adjacent areas, it displays a slight concentration of Quaternary faulting (Carr, 1974; 1984a) and seismicity (Rogers and others, 1983). No young basalts occur in large regions adjacent to the belt. It is interesting to note that, although the eastern part of

the basalt belt is seismically active, most of the Kawich-Greenwater Rift has a low level of natural seismicity (Rogers and others, 1983). The northern part of the rift, in the Pahute Mesa area, has been seismically active as a result of underground nuclear testing, and it is therefore difficult to assess the level of natural seismicity in that area.

Geophysical expression of the Death Valley–Pancake Range basalt belt includes the aforementioned gravity low, which roughly parallels and lies about 50 km west of the geophysical symmetry axis of the Great Basin described by Eaton and others (1978) near longitude 116° W. (Fig. 1). Coinciding with the north-south symmetry axis is a magnetic "quiet zone" 50 to 100 km wide (Mabey and others, 1978, Plate 4-1). Other anomalies, such as heat flow (Sass and Lachenbruch, 1982) and upper mantle velocity changes (Monfort and Evans, 1982), appear to parallel or lie within the basalt belt. More discussion of the belt and its significance can be found in Carr (1984a) and Crowe and others (1980). In general, the association of the basalt belt and its geophysical signatures underscores the importance of the Kawich-Greenwater Rift as a regional tectonic boundary.

METAMORPHIC ROCKS WEST OF KAWICH-GREENWATER RIFT

Strongly metamorphosed and ductilely deformed rocks are exposed in several areas west of the Kawich-Greenwater Rift. The principal areas of exposure of these rocks are shown on Figure 1. Gneissic rocks are present in the Trappman Hills (Ekren and others, 1971, p. 6), and a small exposure of gneiss occurs in the Bullfrog Hills (Cornwall and Kleinhampl, 1964, p. 1). Metamorphosed lower Paleozoic and Proterozoic rocks occur in the northwestern part of Bare Mountain (Monsen, 1983; Carr and Monsen, 1988). The area between the Trappman Hills and Bare Mountain (Fig. 1) is covered by thick volcanic rocks, but gravity data (Fig. 3) suggest that relatively dense metamorphic rocks could be locally present beneath the Tertiary cover just west of the rift. A short-wavelength gravity anomaly map (Hildenbrand and others, 1988, Fig. 2.10, p. 16) of the southern Great Basin shows that the high associated with the Funeral Mountains and Bare Mountain extends northward to the Cactus Range, parallel to the west side of the rift. A large area in the northern Funeral Mountains consists of mostly high-grade metamorphic Proterozoic and lower Paleozoic rocks (Labotka, 1980; Troxel, 1988). Farther south, several areas of highly metamorphosed sedimentary rocks, including gneiss, are exposed on the steep west flank of the Black Range (Fig. 1) facing Death Valley (Drewes, 1963). On the other side of Death Valley in the Panamint Range are extensive exposures of metamorphic rocks (Hunt and Mabey, 1966; Labotka and others, 1980), including gneiss and schist.

East of the Kawich-Greenwater Rift in the Nevada Test Site region, no rocks are present of metamorphic grade similar to those west of the rift. Relatively unmetamorphosed rocks as old as the upper Proterozoic Johnnie Formation are exposed in several areas, including the Halfpint Range (Barnes and others,

1965) northeast of Yucca Flat (Fig. 1), and in the northwest end of the Spring Mountains (Burchfiel, 1965; Stewart and Carlston, 1978).

The presence of extensive metamorphic rocks west of the Kawich-Greenwater Rift, and their absence to the east, indicates that the tectonic histories of the two areas have important differences and that rocks once deeper in the crust have been brought near the surface west of the rift.

DETACHMENT FAULTS OF THE NEVADA TEST SITE REGION

Low-angle faults of Tertiary age have been mapped and described in several areas of the south-central Great Basin region. In recent years, most of these faults have been interpreted as a mechanism for accommodation of tectonic extension in their upper plates. The term "detachment" is probably an unfortunate choice for many of these faults, particularly those that do not separate rock masses of distinctly different tectonic style. Furthermore, the assumption is commonly made that if basin-range faulting is present at the surface, a detachment fault must exist at depth.

Detachment faulting with many of the characteristics of the classic detachments of the Mojave-Sonoran region of California and Arizona (see report edited by Frost and Martin, 1982) is present in the area to the west of the Kawich-Greenwater Rift but not in the Nevada Test Site Region (Fig. 1) to the east. These characteristics include (1) a contrast in tectonic style between the allochthon and lower plate; (2) at appropriate crustal levels, a separation between ductilely deformed rocks below and brittle deformation above; (3) a fairly consistent pattern of faulting in the upper plate in harmony with its direction of transport; (4) downward flattening of upper plate faults as the low-angle fault is approached; and (5) considerable rotation of strata in the upper plate in geometric association with extensional faulting. Not all areas west of the rift display significant listric faults in combination with the other characteristics.

In my opinion, true detachment faulting, as outlined above, is not present in the Yucca Mountain area, or anywhere adjacent to the Kawich-Greenwater Rift on the east, although detachment faulting has been described (Guth, 1981) in the Sheep Range, 60 km southeast of the Nevada Test Site. I interpret low-angle faults in the Nevada Test Site area as reactivated Mesozoic thrust faults (Yucca Flat area), as gravitational sliding toward volcano-tectonic depressions in the rift, or as local horizontal sliding and folding of soft sediments by large earthquakes. Most of the area on the test site where low-angle faults are found is underlain by weak Mississippian clastic sedimentary rocks that provide an excellent slip surface. Carr and Monsen (1988) interpreted the faults at Yucca Mountain as related to the Crater Flat graben rather than to a detachment system. Scott and Hofland (1987), Scott (1988), and Simonds and Scott (1987) have reported a system of faults near Yucca Mountain that they call detachments. Scott and Hofland (1987) suggested that a west-dipping detachment lies

under Yucca Mountain. The faults they believe are associated with detachment are exposed mostly in the Calico Hills area 10 to 15 km northeast of Yucca Mountain and are described as low-angle normal faults along, above, and below the Tertiary-Paleozoic contact. At Yucca Mountain, Scott (1988) concluded that a detachment, which is not exposed, occurs between the Paleozoic and Tertiary rocks, and he believes it continues westward beneath Crater Flat to a connection with detachment faults at Bare Mountain.

Several detachment-style low-angle structures are present in the region west of the Kawich-Greenwater Rift (Fig. 1). Only small segments of these faults are well exposed, but in general they appear to have west- or northwest-displaced upper plates, tend to shoal eastward toward the rift, and contain mostly Tertiary rocks in their upper plates in areas adjacent to the rift (Fig. 1).

Low-angle structures at the north end of Bare Mountain and along the south edge of the Bullfrog Hills, though appearing to consist of a single continuous low-angle fault, may actually consist of several segments with slightly different ages of movement. These faults, including one called the Original Bullfrog, were recognized by Ransome and others (1910) in an early study of the Bullfrog mining district. Cornwall and Kleinhampl (1961, 1964) mapped the same structures as thrusts. Recent work by Maldonado (1988) identified the faults in the Bullfrog Hills as detachments. He mapped two closely spaced (within 150 vertical m) subparallel low-angle faults; the lower separates the gneissic rocks, exposed in only a small area, from an overlying middle plate composed of slivers of Paleozoic rocks, and the upper separates the slivered, attenuated Paleozoic rocks from a third and highest plate of highly faulted and rotated Tertiary volcanic strata. Carr and Monsen (1988, p. 50) described these faults as part of a "regional, low-angle extensional (detachment)" system and referred to the segment at Bare Mountain as the Fluorspar Canyon fault.

In the northern and central Funeral Mountains, 20 to 30 km south of the Bullfrog Hills, is another detachment called the Boundary Canyon fault (Labotka, 1980), which generally separates highly metamorphosed Proterozoic and Paleozoic rocks from unmetamorphosed Paleozoic and Tertiary rocks (Troxel, 1988). Carr and Monsen (1988) hypothesize that the Fluorspar Canyon and Original Bullfrog faults connect with the Boundary Canyon fault in the Funeral–Grapevine Mountains area. The trace would be buried beneath the Amargosa Valley (Fig. 1), and the geometry would require a gentle antiform and synform with northwest trend. I believe there is a good possibility that the Boundary Canyon fault also connects (Fig. 1) with some low-angle faults separating Tertiary and Paleozoic rocks (Swadley and Carr, 1986) farther south in the Funeral Mountains.

Other detachment-style faults occur in the Black Range (Fig. 1) west of the south end of the Kawich-Greenwater Rift. These are the "turtlebacks" (Curry, 1954; Drewes, 1959; Wright and others, 1974) at the west foot of the Black Range and the northern part of the Amargosa chaos (Noble, 1941). These faults are similar to those in the Funeral Mountain in having highly rotated and faulted unmetamorphosed Paleozoic and Tertiary rocks lying above a low-angle fault underlain by metamorphic rocks.

In the Panamint Range, on the west side of Death Valley, other low-angle, detachment-style faults are present. The complex Tucki Mountain fault system (Wernicke and others, 1988) consists of a basal detachment zone and structurally higher splays that generally cut across layering.

STRUCTURAL DOMAINS WITHIN AND ADJACENT TO THE KAWICH-GREENWATER RIFT

Small but significant differences in Tertiary structural style and timing occur in a 100-km transect across the Walker Lane Belt in the Nevada Test Site region (Fig. 4). A voluminous widespread ash-flow tuff sequence, the Timber Mountain Tuff, and related lavas, well dated at about 11.5 Ma (Marvin and others, 1970; Warren and others, 1988), provide an excellent structural datum in the northern half of the rift area. The source of the tuffs and lavas was the Timber Mountain–Oasis Valley caldera complex (Fig. 4) (Byers and others, 1976b). The region can be separated into two distinct zones or structural domains in which the Timber Mountain Tuff sequence is either distinctly discordant or paraconformable with the underlying rocks. These zones can be subdivided into areas that are slightly faulted or moderately faulted or that contain dips generally more or less than 30° (Fig. 4). The resultant zones or domains roughly parallel or coincide with the northern part of the Kawich-Greenwater Rift.

Zones 1 and 2 in the Kawich-Greenwater Rift

Throughout the general area of the rift, including much of Pahute Mesa, Crater Flat, and Yucca Mountain, the Timber Mountain Tuff is mildly to sharply discordant, and dips are low, generally 10° or less. In most of the rift the Timber Mountain Tuff is faulted but much less so than older rocks. On Pahute Mesa, the disconformity is not as well exposed or as striking as elsewhere, largely because structural relief on the underlying rocks was not great, especially within the Silent Canyon caldera (Orkild and others, 1969). In the Crater Flat–Yucca Mountain area, most exposures of Timber Mountain Tuff are sharply unconformable on fault blocks of older rocks (Fig. 5). The important point is that most of the fault displacement within the rift (but outside the Timber Mountain caldera) occurred prior to eruption of the Timber Mountain Tuff. The rift structure is attributed to several episodes of magmatic insurgence, doming, and caldera and sector graben collapse.

In addition to the timing of faulting, an east-west change occurs in the density and amount of displacement of faults offsetting the Timber Mountain Tuff (Figs. 4, 6, and 7; and see Fig. 8), not only in the Pahute Mesa area but especially to the south across Yucca Mountain and Crater Flat; on the west, in zone 1, very few faults displace the Timber Mountain Tuff. The east to

west decrease in the number and size of faults appears to reflect the "trap door" character of the caldera complexes; i.e., displacement along the eastern caldera wall is distributed over a wider zone than that at the west margin (Figs. 6 and 7). Gravity (Snyder and Carr, 1984) and aeromagnetic patterns (Kane and Bracken, 1983), as well as two drill holes (Carr, 1988) (Fig. 7), support these conclusions, as do geologic maps (Swadley and Carr, 1986; Byers and others, 1976a; Carr, 1988, Fig. 4.3).

A striking similarity (also noted by colleagues R. G. Warren and F. M. Byers, Jr., and P. P. Orkild [written communication, 1985]) exists between faults on Pahute Mesa and Yucca Mountain (Fig. 6). In addition to having similar patterns, the two fault groups have almost identical strike, spacing, and direction of displacement, strongly suggesting a genetic association.

On Pahute Mesa, no large post-Miocene vertical displacements have occurred because the volcanic plateau, capped by 11.5- and 7.5-Ma volcanic rocks (Orkild and others, 1969), is essentially intact, and only a few areas of very thin Quaternary deposits are present. Crater Flat, which superficially appears to be a typical basin-range graben, also has had little post-Miocene tectonic movement, based on the amount of burial of volcanic units younger than the Crater Flat Tuff in drill hole VH-2 (Fig. 7). The maximum rate of vertical tectonic adjustment determined for Crater Flat during the last 10 m.y. or so has been 0.03 m/1,000 years (Carr, 1984a, 1988, p. 46–48). This figure is based on the depth to a basalt dated at about 11 Ma (Carr and Parrish, 1985) in drill hole USW VH-2 in central Crater Flat (Fig. 7). This evidence, together with the fact that other younger basalts, also near the center of the valley, but essentially at the surface, are about 1.1 and 3.8 m.y. old, indicates that no large vertical tectonic movements have occurred in Pliocene or Pleistocene time. This is in sharp contrast with most typical basin-range grabens, which are generally considered to have formed mainly in the last 17 m.y.; however, present-day topographic basins probably formed in the last 10 m.y. and are still active (Carr, 1974; Stewart, 1978, p. 22). An example of such a basin is Yucca Flat, discussed in the next section of this chapter.

The presence of young basalts in Crater Flat and elsewhere in the rift, however, together with minor Quaternary faulting (Swadley and others, 1984), indicates that the process of rifting may be continuing but at a very much reduced rate and probably under a different stress regime than in the Miocene (Carr, 1974). A stress orientation model for the Nevada Test Site region that proposed (Carr, 1974) a late Cenozoic direction of minimum principal stress of about N50°W has received local and regional support from a number of investigations (e.g., Thompson and Burke, 1973; Wright, 1976; Zoback and Zoback, 1980; Frizzell and Zoback, 1987; Stock and others, 1985). The original model (Carr, 1974) was based mainly on the trend of Quaternary faults and fractures, the configuration of the basin beneath Yucca Flat, evidence from earthquakes, a few measurements of stress, and the preferential enlargement of drill holes. Dating of basalts in the Nevada Test Site region has since provided evidence of a regional clockwise rotation in the stress field, probably between about 6

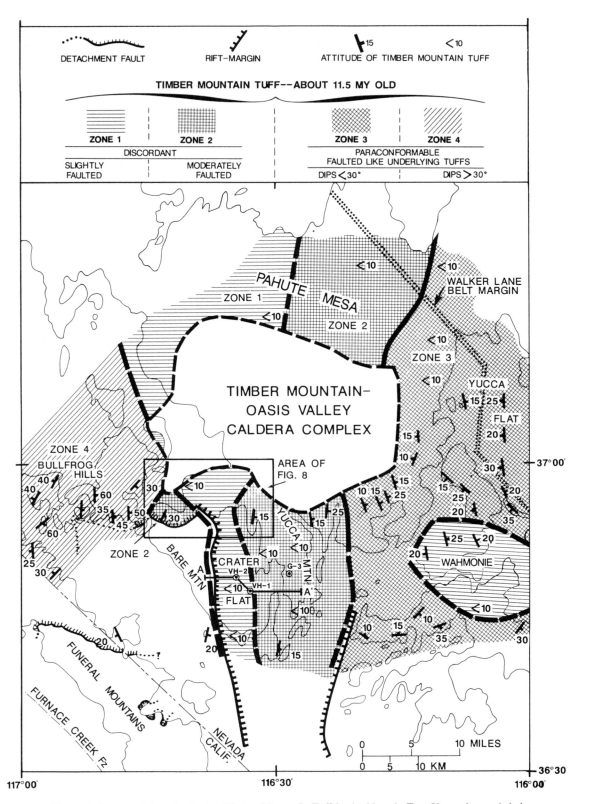

Figure 4. Structural domains in the Timber Mountain Tuff in the Nevada Test Site region and their relation to the Kawich-Greenwater Rift, showing location of cross section A-A' (Fig. 7) of Crater Flat and Yucca Mountain. Rift margins shown are fault zones well defined by gravity. To the north, rift is expressed by Timber Mountain, Silent Canyon, and Black Mountain calderas.

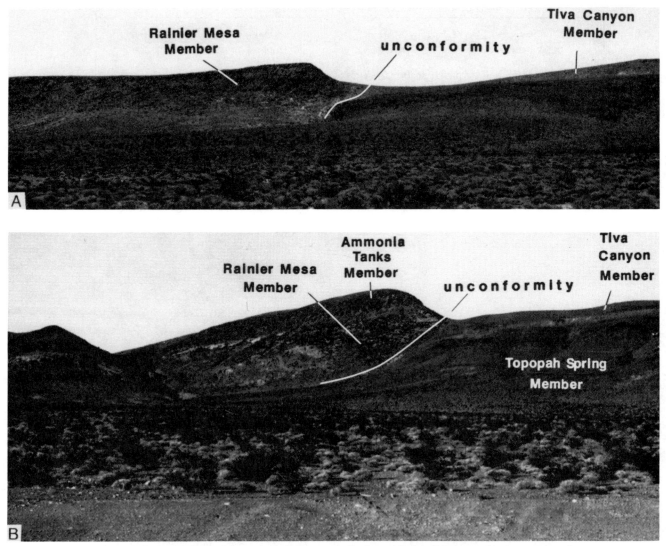

Figure 5. Onlap of Timber Mountain Tuff (Ammonia Tanks and Rainier Mesa members) on structural blocks of the Paintbrush Tuff (Tiva Canyon and Topopah Spring members) (A) on the east side of Yucca Mountain and (B) on the south end of Yucca Mountain.

and 4 Ma. Basalt dikes near the north edge of Pahute Mesa (Orkild and others, 1969), east of Yucca Flat in the Paiute Ridge (Byers and Barnes, 1967) and Plutonium Valley (Hinrichs and McKay, 1965) quadrangles, and at Yucca Mountain (Scott and Bonk, 1984) trend from N20°W to N20°E. The dikes and associated lavas range in age from 10.4 Ma to 6.3 Ma (Carr, 1984a, Figs. 14 and 25; R. F. Marvin, U.S. Geological Survey, written communications, 1979–1982). Although data are not complete, nearly all basalts in the region (Fig. 1) have been dated by radiometric or stratigraphic methods, and none fall in an apparent 2-m.y. hiatus between about 6.2 and 4.2 Ma (Carr, 1984a, Fig. 25). This hiatus in basaltic activity contains the last known significant silicic eruptions in the Nevada Test Site region—a 5.3-m.y.-old rhyolite on the northeast side of Stonewall Mountain (Foley and Sutter, 1978), about 50 km northwest of Black Mountain (Fig. 1), and 5.3- to 5.5-m.y.-old (Fleck, 1970) rhyolite at the

Greenwater volcanic center (Fig. 1). After this final episode of silicic volcanism, basalts erupted after about 4.2 Ma were confined to the Kawich-Greenwater Rift and were associated with preexisting calderas and/or northeast-striking faults at (1) Buckboard Mesa, in the moat of the Timber Mountain caldera (Byers and others, 1976a); (2) Sleeping Butte, near the northwest margin of the Timber Mountain–Oasis Valley caldera complex (Byers and others, 1976b); (3) Crater Flat–Lathrop Wells area (Vaniman and others 1982); and (4) Funeral–Furnace Creek Wash area (McAllister, 1973).

In the Crater Flat–southern Yucca Mountain area, the young basalts, which have been dated at approximately 3.7, 1.2, and 0.3 Ma (Vaniman and others, 1982), were erupted along structural trends of from N20° to 40°E. (Fig. 8). A strong negative aeromagnetic anomaly (Kane and Bracken, 1983) 2 km south of Lathrop Wells (Fig. 8) suggests a shallow, buried, re-

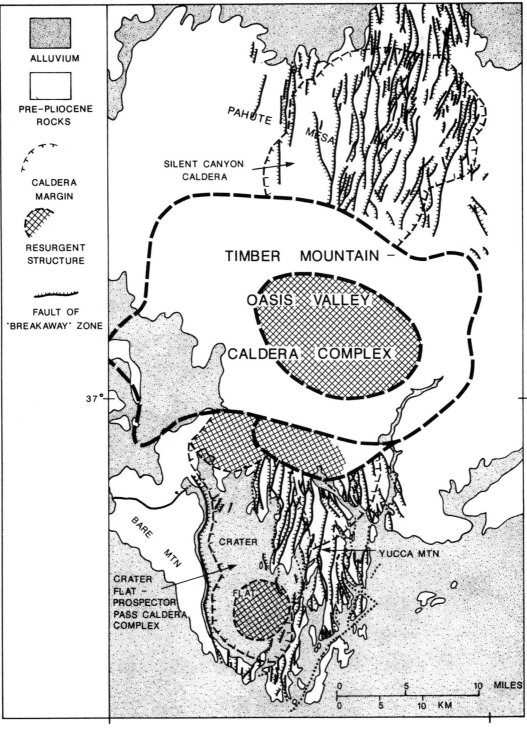

Figure 6. Fault system interpreted to be, in part, a "breakaway" zone along the eastern side of the Kawich-Greenwater Rift, showing the concentration of faults in the eastern part of the rift, within and adjacent to the Silent Canyon and Crater Flat–Prospector Pass calderas. Structure of resurgent domes is omitted, and faults outside the rift zone or within Timber Mountain caldera are not shown.

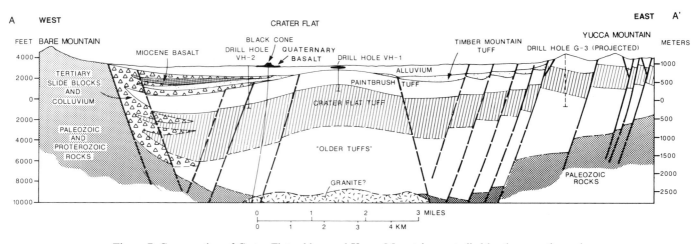

Figure 7. Cross section of Crater Flat caldera and Yucca Mountain, controlled by three continuously cored drill holes and interpreted with the aid of gravity and aeromagnetics. Location of section shown on Figure 4.

versely magnetized basalt. The reversed polarity of the body indicates it is probably older than 0.73 Ma, the end of the Matuyama reversed polarity zone. The shallow depth of burial, probably less than 60 m, and relatively small size (2 to 3 km across) of the anomaly-causing body suggest that it may be similar to the young basalt centers of the Crater Flat area, possibly those that are about 1.2 or 3.7 m.y. old. This reversely magnetized probable basalt was erupted near the edge of the rift and lies within a northeast-trending aeromagnetic anomaly (Fig. 8) that I interpret to be a buried fault-controlled graben filled with magnetic sediments derived from the volcanic terrain north of Jackass Flats.

The Big Dune basalt center, also called the Lathrop Wells cone (Vaniman and others, 1982), is situated at the southern end of a prominent northeast-striking aeromagnetic lineament (Fig. 8) (Kane and Bracken, 1983). Near the middle of the lineament is a coinciding fault that has had Quaternary movement (Swadley and others, 1984). The Big Dune basalt has been dated by K-Ar at roughly 0.3 Ma (Vaniman and others, 1982), but more recent studies suggest this age may be too old (Wells and others, 1988).

In Crater Flat, two groups of basalts have been dated at about 3.7 and 1.2 Ma. Both were erupted in the southern part of the Crater Flat–Prospector Pass caldera complex (Fig. 8) (W. J. Carr and others, 1986). The older group, in southeastern Crater Flat, was fed from dikes that trend north to northeast (Vaniman and others, 1982). The younger group of four centers is aligned along a curvilinear trend that strikes from about N20° to N40°E.

Thus, basalts younger than 4 Ma in the Crater Flat–Lathrop Wells area are associated with northeasterly trending structures, somewhat oblique to the overall rift trend; two of the groups are within the Crater Flat–Prospector Pass caldera complex. I infer that these latter basalts may have reached high crustal levels along the caldera ring fracture zone and followed northeast-striking tension fractures to the surface.

Zone 2—Area north of Bare Mountain

The area adjacent to the north side of Bare Mountain (Fig. 9) is of special structural importance. In terms of the zonation of Figure 4, it belongs in zone 2, in which Timber Mountain Tuff is moderately faulted and is discordant. Of particular interest is the fact that this domain is in the upper plate of the Fluorspar Canyon fault, previously mentioned as one of several detachment-style low-angle faults west of the Kawich-Greenwater Rift. Abrupt lateral changes in structure occur at the boundaries of the area, which lies in a wedge of terrain between a lobe of the Timber Mountain–Oasis Valley caldera complex to the north and the older Prospector Pass caldera segment (W. J. Carr and others, 1986) to the east. The boundary between zones 1 and 2 passes around the northeast corner of Bare Mountain and trends northwest to an intersection with the Timber Mountain caldera (Fig. 4). This boundary marks an abrupt change from nearly flat-lying and only slightly faulted Timber Mountain Tuff on the east to moderately faulted Timber Mountain Tuff on the west (Fig. 9). In zone 2, the Timber Mountain is sharply discordant on Paintbrush Tuff and older volcanic rocks that are standing vertical in some fault blocks (Fig. 9). Carr and Monsen (1988, p. 53) regarded the boundary between zones 1 and 2 as part of the breakaway for a large extensional allochthon northwest of Bare Mountain, and they did not recognize the important disconformity below the Timber Mountain Tuff.

The Fluorspar Canyon fault, which dips 25 to 35° to the north, separates Tertiary volcanic rocks from Paleozoic sedimentary rocks on the north side of Bare Mountain. As mapped (Fig. 9), the fault bends to the northeast and steepens to as much as 70°; at one point (near the 57° dip, Figure 9) slickensides indicate nearly pure dip-slip latest displacement on the northeast-striking segment. Recent mapping by M. D. Carr (U.S. Geological Survey, written communication, 1988) now suggests that the

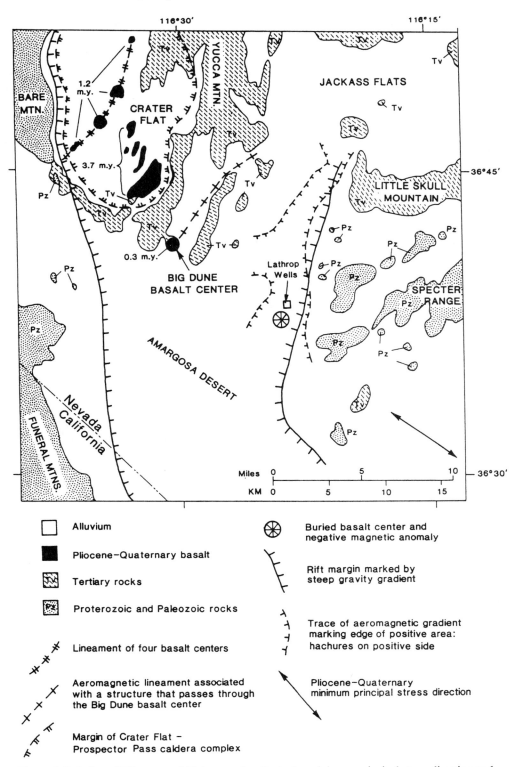

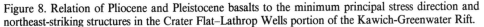

Figure 8. Relation of Pliocene and Pleistocene basalts to the minimum principal stress direction and northeast-striking structures in the Crater Flat–Lathrop Wells portion of the Kawich-Greenwater Rift.

northeast-striking, more steeply dipping segment does not connect with the main Fluorspar Canyon fault. More work is needed to understand the configuration and significance of faults in this area.

Important problems of continuity also exist at both ends of the Fluorspar Canyon fault, as mapped on Figure 8. On the east, the relatively steep dip of the fault virtually precludes a sharp right-angle bend that would be required to connect it with the large fault along the east side of Bare Mountain (Fig. 9) that has been interpreted as a caldera fault (W. J. Carr and others, 1986). Others (Carr and Monsen, 1988) have interpreted part of the Bare Mountain east frontal fault system as a low-angle normal fault, connecting steeper fault segments that are characteristic of range-bounding faults in the Great Basin. Gravity data (Snyder

and Carr, 1984) show clearly that the large gradient associated with the fault at the east foot of Bare Mountain continues north-northwest beneath the volcanic rocks, effectively terminating the Fluorspar Canyon fault. The lack of important structure in the Timber Mountain Tuff opposite the northeast-trending segment of the Fluorspar Canyon fault indicates little displacement has occurred on this part of the fault in the last 11.5 m.y., despite its northeast strike, which should have favored Quaternary movement with respect to the regional stress field (Carr, 1974). Sharp discordance of the Timber Mountain Tuff on steeply rotated blocks of older volcanic rocks (zone 2) persists westward from the northeastward bend in the Fluorspar Canyon fault to the vicinity of Beatty (Figs. 4 and 9). A large north-striking fault is required in the valley at Beatty (Ransome and others, 1910).

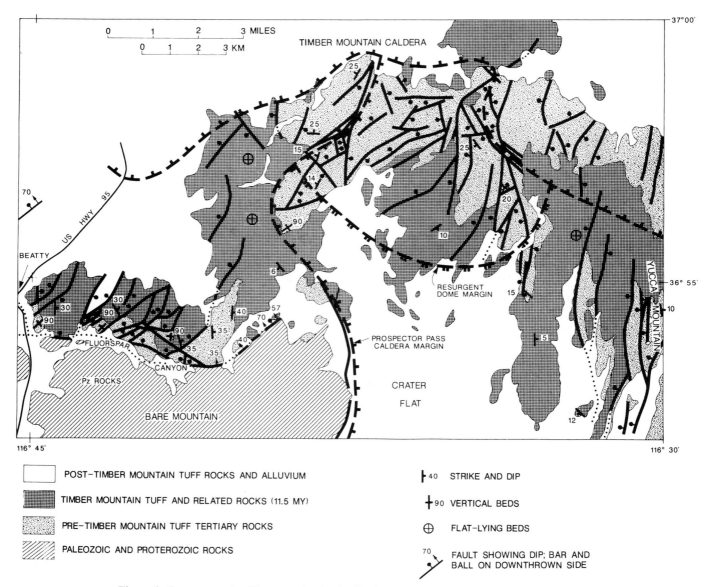

Figure 9. Structure and caldera margins in the Tertiary rocks north and east of Bare Mountain. Generalized from U.S. Geological Survey published (Byers and others, 1976a) and unpublished maps of the Bare Mountain 15-minute Quadrangle.

Even though the Fluorspar Canyon fault aligns across the narrow valley with a similar low-angle fault to the west (Figs. 4 and 9), timing of faulting in the upper plate Tertiary rocks west of Beatty is significantly different from that above the Fluorspar Canyon fault adjacent to the north edge of Bare Mountain. This problem will be further discussed in the section on zone 4.

Zone 3—Yucca Flat and the area east of the Kawich-Greenwater Rift

Yucca Flat lies mostly within the Basin and Range subsection, as defined here and elsewhere (Carr, 1984a) (Fig. 2), and in my view, has the only true basin-range structure in the transect discussed in this chapter. I define basin-range structure as that which has produced topographically well-expressed, north-trending, fault-bounded deep basins in the late Cenozoic. These basins have continued moderate to high tectonic activity in the Quaternary. Yucca Flat is underlain by a north-trending basin that gravity and drill holes (Carr, 1984a, Fig. 11; Ander and others, 1984) show consists of several depressions that are somewhat rhomboid in shape. The basin contains Miocene, Pliocene, and Quaternary deposits, but alluvium is as much as 1,200 m thick in one area (Carr, 1984a, Fig. 12). In zone 3, the Timber Mountain Tuff is paraconformable, and there is little or no thickening of the Timber Mountain Tuff in the basin (Fig. 10), indicating no deep depression was present at the time of eruption, so the main structural development of the Yucca Flat basin can be dated as after about 11.5 Ma. In southern Yucca Flat, near the deepest part of the basin, two drill holes intersected basalt dated at about 8 Ma (R. F. Marvin, U.S. Geological Survey, written communication, 1980), which is apparently offset about 750 m by major basin-controlling faults; thus, much of the faulting may have occurred after 8 Ma. Typical stratal dips in the basin are westward (Figs. 4 and 10), and the largest faults dip eastward, although on the east side of the valley the predominant fault dip is west. Westerly dips in the tuff continue west of Yucca Flat nearly to the rim of Timber Mountain caldera.

An exception to the paraconformity of the Timber Mountain Tuff east of the Kawich-Greenwater Rift is the Wahmonie area (Fig. 4), where the tuff is discordant on a prominent pile of lava flows.

The Mesozoic CP thrust (Barnes and Poole, 1968) is gently folded and dips eastward beneath Yucca Flat (Carr, 1974), as shown in cross sections (Fig. 10). It places a wedge of upper-plate, brittle carbonate rocks of middle and lower Paleozoic age over a thick, incompetent section of upper Paleozoic clastic rocks. The configuration of the CP thrust fault beneath and adjacent to Yucca Flat is based on drill holes and exposures at the northwest corner of the flat, near the Smoky Hills, where lower to middle Paleozoic carbonate rocks rest in low-angle fault contact on the Eleana Formation, largely of Mississippian age. This fault surface dips southeastward at 20 to 30° beneath the Smoky Hills and Yucca Flat; it was incorrectly mapped as a high-angle fault on the Oak Spring quadrangle (Barnes and others, 1963). Other evidence comes from several drill holes in western Yucca Flat,

where in the subsurface an eastward-thickening wedge of lower to middle Paleozoic carbonate rocks overlies the younger Eleana Formation. With less certainty, this same eastward-dipping low-angle fault relation appears to extend southward beneath the alluvium and tuff of Yucca Flat to the CP Hills at the southwest edge of Yucca Flat, where a similar thrust-fault relation has been mapped (McKeown and others, 1976). Based primarily on drill hole information, Barnes and Poole (1968) characterized the CP thrust as rooted beneath volcanic cover west of the Eleana Range (Fig. 1) (composed largely of the lower plate Eleana Formation). This geometry, combined with the later interpretation (Carr, 1974, 1984a, Fig. 23) in western Yucca Flat, resulted in a major fold of the CP thrust over the Eleana Range.

The CP thrust may have facilitated pull-apart of the Yucca Flat basin in late Cenozoic time. Some of the major faults on the cross sections are shown as somewhat listric, based partly on a suggestion that projection of surface fault dips to buried Paleozoic scarps defined by gravity requires either flattening of some faults with depth or an en echelon arrangement in cross sectional view. Elwood and others (1985) also give evidence, mostly drill hole and reflection seismic data, for listric faults in alluvium in Yucca Flat. In spite of suggestions of listric faults, however, detailed gravity data (D. L. Healey, U.S. Geological Survey, written communication, 1987) indicate that many linear buried scarps are present in the Paleozoic rocks, requiring considerable offset of the Paleozoic-Tertiary contact; the question of whether these faults also offset the CP thrust is not resolved, however.

In the western part of zone 3, adjacent to the Kawich-Greenwater Rift, the Timber Mountain Tuff is generally conformable, but structural attitudes are variable in domains on the order of 10 to 20 km across (Fig. 4). In the southern part of zone 3, attitudes of Timber Mountain Tuff are at least partially the result of a prominent northeast-striking fault system called the Spotted Range–Mine Mountain structural zone (Fig. 2) (Carr, 1984a, p. 30). Rotation of the volcanic rocks resulted in strikes that are roughly parallel to the northeast trend of this zone.

Zone 4—The Bullfrog Hills area

The complex structure between Bare Mountain and the Funeral Mountains is important, partly because it occurs in the only virtually continuous exposures of bedrock across this part of the Walker Lane Belt (Fig. 1). A detachment fault, or faults, called the Original Bullfrog fault (Ransome and others, 1910), is exposed at several points along the southern edge of the Bullfrog Hills as far east as Beatty. Throughout zone 4, Timber Mountain Tuff and some younger volcanic rocks just west of Beatty are paraconformable; the area is also distinguished by fairly consistent high angles of rotation of the Tertiary rocks—nearly everywhere over 30° and in some places over 60°. Although Timber Mountain Tuff or other tuff formations were not identified, the map by Cornwall and Kleinhampl (1964, Plate 1) shows the general structure and conformity of the volcanic units in the Bullfrog Hills.

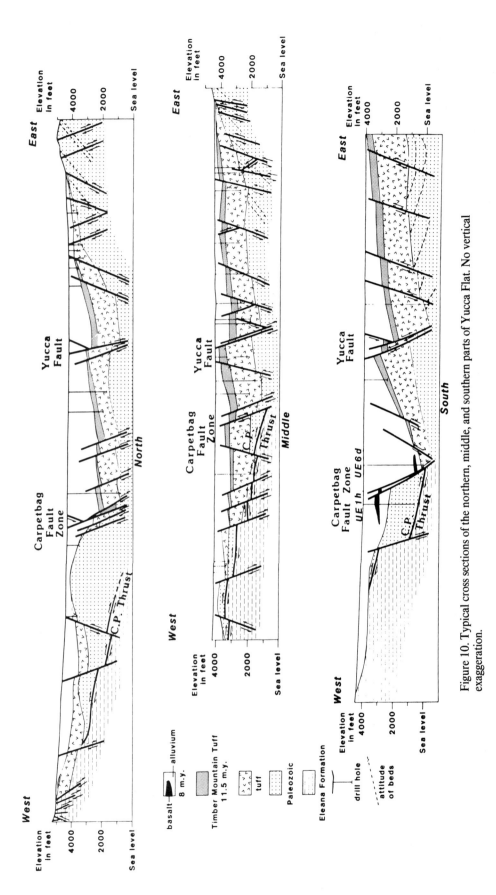

Figure 10. Typical cross sections of the northern, middle, and southern parts of Yucca Flat. No vertical exaggeration.

The structural attitude and fault pattern in the upper plate rocks in the eastern part of the Bullfrog Hills (Maldonado, 1988) are similar to those in zone 2 north of Bare Mountain, but structural involvement and paraconformity of the Timber Mountain Tuff and younger volcanic units indicate the main episode of faulting occurred somewhat later in the Bullfrog Hills.

Carr and Monsen (1988), who mapped the Bare Mountain area, believe that the Fluorspar Canyon fault connects with the Original Bullfrog fault—the detachment exposed south of Beatty and in the Bullfrog Hills. They correlate these faults with the Boundary Canyon fault in the Funeral Mountains; such a correlation suggests a gentle northwest-trending antiform and synform pair in the Amargosa Desert area south of the Bullfrog Hills (Fig. 1). The entire Fluorspar Canyon–Original Bullfrog–Boundary Canyon fault system is characterized (Carr and Monsen, 1988) as cutting deeper into the section to the west and shoaling eastward in the Bare Mountain area. The age of the oldest exposed Tertiary rocks in the upper plate at Bare Mountain (W. J. Carr and others, 1986, Fig. 11; Carr and Monsen, 1988) is, however, not significantly younger than Tertiary units of most of the Bullfrog Hills. As one goes farther west into the Funeral and Grapevine Mountains, however, distinctly older Tertiary rocks (Oligocene Titus Canyon Formation, for example, Reynolds, 1975) first become exposed in the allochthon near the Nevada-California border on the east flank of the Grapevine Mountains. In the western Bullfrog Hills, near the California-Nevada border, the volcanic section dips generally west-northwest at moderate angles (25 to 50° (Cornwall and Kleinhampl, 1964), instead of east-northeast as it does in the eastern Bullfrog Hills.

The just-described variability in timing and structural attitudes of the region between northern Bare Mountain and the Grapevine Mountains suggests that no simple model involving a single continuous detachment fault can account for the observed complexity.

INTEGRATION OF VOLCANO-TECTONIC AND DETACHMENT FAULT MODELS

The Kawich-Greenwater Rift provides a means for moderate extension across a portion of the Walker Lane Belt where comparatively little right-lateral offset has occurred. The distribution of detachment-style faults and metamorphosed rocks adjacent to the rift on the west and the styles and timing of faulting within and outside of the rift suggest that a combination of volcano-tectonic and detachment processes can account for the extension. The ideas presented here have been inspired in part by the models of Wernicke (1981), Wernicke and Burchfiel (1982), Stewart (1983), Howard and John (1987), and Wright and others (1974).

This model (Fig. 11) relates detachment-style faulting and pull-apart of the Kawich-Greenwater Rift, which is interpreted to have been localized within a right-step, or series of right-steps, in the Walker Lane Belt, in a style similar to that of "leaky transforms" (Weaver and Hill, 1979). In the model, the east side of the rift constitutes the headwall or footwall of the detachments to the west, and the faults of the rift zone (Fig. 6) are considered "breakaway" structures. Extensional structure of zone 3 east of the rift is not only somewhat younger than that of the rift itself but is also tectonically different in timing and probably in genesis, as discussed previously. Some of the zone 3 extension, particularly that of the Yucca Flat area, may have been accommodated by reactivation of the Mesozoic thrust system. The strike of the Tertiary normal faults east of the Rift generally parallels the strike of the thrust fault system (Carr, 1984a, Fig. 23); the variable dip direction (Fig. 4) in Tertiary rocks of this area could be attributed in part to stretching over gently folded thrust planes. The deeper parts of the Yucca Flat structural basin occur at the margins of the Basin and Range subsection where north-striking faults interact with northwest-striking shear zones, probably resulting in localized enhancement of a pull-apart mechanism (Carr, 1984a, p. 3). The configuration and age of thrust faults in the Nevada Test Site region need to be better known before the above suggestions can be validated. The main point here, however, is that the structure of the footwall of the detachment system area (zone 3) east of the Kawich-Greenwater Rift, as I see it, differs in some important ways from the hanging wall west of the rift. This is taken to be evidence of eastward termination at the Kawich-Greenwater Rift of the detachment system lying to the west.

The model (Fig. 11) is, of course, vastly oversimplified, but it illustrates the problem of placing continuous detachments beneath the rift and the terrain to the east and west. In order to explain the conflicts in chronology of faulting in the western part of this transect, a series of eastward-shoaling detachment lenses seems to be required, a scheme advocated by Hamilton (1988) as well. The changes in timing and structural style suggest several separate detachments—the Fluorspar Canyon, Original Bullfrog, and Boundary Canyon faults. The general upper plate structural pattern of the Fluorspar Canyon and Original Bullfrog faults is similar (Cornwall and Kleinhampl, 1964, Plate 4), but different in timing; the Boundary Canyon fault has a different structural pattern and involves older parts of the Tertiary section, but on the basis of degree of involvement of the Timber Mountain Tuff, its timing appears similar to that of the Original Bullfrog fault.

The small exposures of gneissic rocks beneath a major low-angle fault in the Bullfrog Hills (Fig. 1) suggest that a regional detachment or sole fault may underlie the region between the Kawich-Greenwater Rift and Death Valley. Such a structure would provide the ultimate basis for regional extension west of the rift and could accommodate the overlying lens-like detachments (Fig. 11). Because the sole fault in the model brings highly metamorphosed rocks relatively close to the surface, it is shown as being rooted to the west beneath Death Valley.

Movements on the higher, shallow detachments appear to have occurred in spurts, and it seems logical to relate their activity, especially that of the Fluorspar Canyon fault, to episodes of magmatism, large-scale ash-flow eruption, and caldera collapse. It may be significant that the trace of the Fluorspar Canyon fault is roughly parallel with the boundary of the nearby Timber

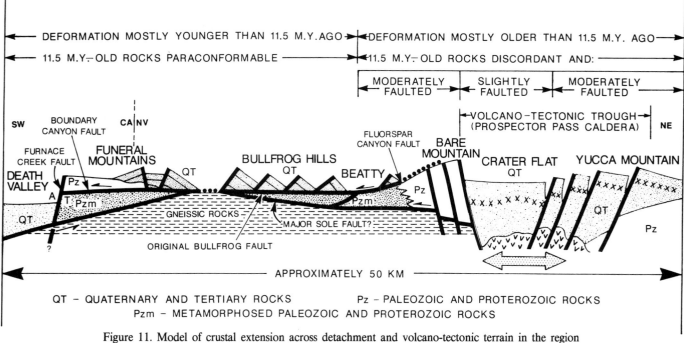

Figure 11. Model of crustal extension across detachment and volcano-tectonic terrain in the region between Death Valley and Yucca Mountain, showing lateral changes in style and fault chronology with respect to the Timber Mountain Tuff. The Crater Flat area is represented as a volcano-tectonic rift resulting from pull apart (arrow) and collapse at the headwall of the detachment system to the west.

Mountain–Oasis Valley caldera complex (Fig. 4). The scallop-like pattern of the Fluorspar Canyon fault and several low-angle faults on the north end of Bare Mountain (Carr and Monsen, 1988, Fig. 2) suggests large gravity-glide blocks that slid toward the caldera but at the same time were dragged off to the northwest on some deeper-seated structure. I suggest that, rather than continuity between the Original Bullfrog and Fluorspar Canyon faults, there is a series of northeast-striking scallop-like faults, beginning on the east with the one at the northeast corner of Bare Mountain, identified by M. D. Carr (written communication, 1988) as a fault separate from the Fluorspar Canyon. The low-angle fault on the hill south of Beatty would be one of this series, cutting off the Fluorspar Canyon fault and trending north-northeast beneath the alluvium at Beatty. This relation was suggested by Cornwall and Kleinhampl (1964, Plate 4) and could be the fault required to drop down the younger volcanic section just west of Beatty.

Westward and southwestward migration of the main pulses of detachment activity, from about 12 Ma in surface rocks within the northern Kawich-Greenwater Rift to about 7.5 Ma in the western Bullfrog Hills (Maldonado, 1988), and to younger still in and near Death Valley, agrees with the migration of silicic volcanism toward the west margin of the Great Basin (Luedke and Smith, 1981). Ductility and crustal weakness associated with magmatism and regional tumescence accompanied the rifting and detachments.

The structure within the Kawich-Greenwater Rift (Fig. 6) is related, I believe, to the presence of a major steep-sided deep trough in the basement rock. The en echelon fault system (Fig. 6) in the Paintbrush Tuff at Yucca Mountain could have formed by reactivation of properly oriented segments of buried caldera or sector graben structure (Carr, 1984a). The faults are interpreted as a response to weakening of lateral support by rapid withdrawal of magma during the major ash-flow eruptions. The tendency for the blocks to move laterally and downward toward the deep rift may help explain the fact that the least and greatest horizontal stresses reported (Stock and others, 1985) are less than the vertical stress in hydrofrac measurements in two drill holes on the crest of Yucca Mountain near the caldera or sector graben margin.

In the model proposed, therefore, the faults of the Yucca Mountain–Crater Flat area are essentially planar and need not be underlain by a regional detachment. These faults are here considered largely gravitational features of a breakaway zone within the Kawich-Greenwater Rift.

ACKNOWLEDGMENTS

Comments by M. D. Carr and an anonymous reviewer resulted in many improvements to the manuscript.

REFERENCES CITED

Albers, J. P., 1967, Belt of sigmoidal bending and right-lateral faulting in the western Great Basin: Geological Society of America Bulletin, v. 78, p. 143–156.

Ander, H. D., Byers, F. M., and Orkild, P. P., 1984, Geology of the Nevada Test Site, *in* Lintz, J., Jr., Western geological excursions, volume 2; Reno, University of Nevada Department of Geological Sciences, p. 1–35.

Anderson, R. E., 1973, Large-magnitude late Tertiary strike-slip faulting north of Lake Mead, Nevada: U.S. Geological Survey Professional Paper 794, 18 p.

Barnes, H., and Poole, F. G., 1968, Regional thrust-fault system in Nevada Test Site and vicinity *in* Eckel, E. B., ed., Nevada Test site: Geological Society of America Memoir 110, p. 233–238.

Barnes, H., Houser, F. N., and Poole, F. G., 1963, Geology of the Oak Spring Quadrangle, Nye County, Nevada: U.S. Geological Survey, Geologic Quadrangle Map GQ–214, scale 1:24,000.

Barnes, H., Christiansen, R. L., and Byers, F. M., Jr., 1965, Geologic map of the Jangle Ridge Quadrangle, Nye and Lincoln Counties, Nevada: U.S. Geological Survey Quadrangle Map GQ–363, scale 1:24,000.

Barnes, H., Ekren, E. B., Rogers, C. L., and Hedlund, D. C., 1982, Geologic and tectonic maps of the Mercury Quadrangle, Nye and Clark Counties, Nevada: U.S. Geological Survey Miscellaneous Investigations Series Map I–1197, scale 1:24,000.

Barosh, P. J., 1969, The Mojave lineament; A zone of possible wrench faulting of great length, *in* Abstracts for 1968: Geological Society of America Special Paper 121, p. 482.

Burchfield, B. C., 1965, Structural geology of the Specter Range Quadrangle, Nevada, and its regional significance: Geological Society of America Bulletin, v. 76, p. 175–192.

Burchfiel, B. C., Hodges, K. V., and Royden, L. H., 1987, Geology of Panamint Valley–Saline Valley pull-apart system, California; Palinspastic evidence for low-angle geometry of a Neogene range-bounding fault: Journal of Geophysical Research, v. 92, p. 10422–10426.

Byers, F. M., Jr., and Barnes, H., 1967, Geologic map of the Paiute Ridge Quadrangle, Nye and Lincoln Counties, Nevada: U.S. Geological Survey Geologic Quadrangle Map GQ–577, scale 1:24,000.

Byers, F. M., Jr., Carr, W. J., Christiansen, R. L., Lipman, P. W., Orkild, P. P., and Quinlivan, W. D., 1976a: U.S. Geological Survey Miscellaneous Investigations Series Map I–891, scale 1:48,000.

Byers, F. M., Jr., Carr, W. J., Orkild, P. P., Quinlivan, W. D., and Sargent, K. A., 1976b, Volcanic suites and related cauldrons of Timber Mountain–Oasis Valley caldera complex, southern Nevada: U.S. Geological Survey Professional Paper 919, 70 p.

Carr, M. D., and Monsen, S. A., 1988, A field trip guide to the geology of Bare Mountain, *in* Weide, D. L., and Faber, M. L., eds., This extended land; Geological Society of America Field Trip Guidebook, Cordilleran Section Meeting, Las Vegas, Nevada, 1988: University of Nevada at Las Vegas Geoscience Department Special Publication 2, p. 50–57.

Carr, M. D., Waddell, S. J., Vick, G. S., Stock, J. M., Monsen, S. A., Harris, A. G., Cork, B. W., and Byers, F. M., Jr., 1986: Geology of drill Hole Ue25p#1; A test hole into pre-Tertiary rocks near Yucca Mountain, southern Nevada: U.S. Geological Survey Open-File Report 86–175, 87 p.

Carr, W. J., 1974, Summary of tectonic and structural evidence for stress orientation at the Nevada Test Site: U.S. Geological Survey Open-File Report 74–176, 53 p.

Carr, W. J., 1981, Tectonic history of the Vidal–Parker region, California and Arizona [abs.], *in* Tectonic framework of the Mojave and Sonoran Deserts, California and Arizona: U.S. Geological Survey Open-File Report 81–503, p. 18–20.

—— , 1984a, Regional structural setting of Yucca Mountain, southwestern Nevada, and late Cenozoic rates of tectonic activity in part of the southwestern Great Basin, Nevada and California: U.S. Geological Survey Open-File Report 84–854, 109 p.

—— , 1984b, Timing and style of tectonism, and localization of volcanism in the Walker Lane belt of southwestern Nevada [abs.]: Geological Society of America Abstracts with Programs, v. 16, p. 464.

—— , 1988, Volcano-tectonic setting of Yucca Mountain and Crater Flat, southwestern Nevada, *in* Carr, M. D., and Yount, J. C., eds., Geologic and hydrologic investigations of a potential nuclear waste disposal site at Yucca Mountain, southern Nevada: U.S. Geological Survey Bulletin 1790, p. 35–49.

Carr, W. J., and Parrish, L. D., 1985, Geology of drill hole USW VH-2 and structure of Crater Flat, southwestern Nevada: U.S. Geological Survey Open-File Report 85–475, 41 p.

Carr, W. J., and Quinlivan, W. D., 1968, Structure of Timber Mountain resurgent dome, Nevada Test Site *in* Eckel, E. B., ed., Nevada Test site: Geological Society of America, Memoir 110, p. 99–108.

Carr, W. J., Byers, F. M., Jr., and Orkild, Paul P., 1986, Stratigraphic and volcano-tectonic relations of Crater Flat Tuff and some older volcanic units, Nye County, Nevada: U.S. Geological Survey Professional Paper 1323, 28 p.

Cemen, I., Wright, L. A., Drake, R. E., and Johnson, F. C., 1985, Cenozoic sedimentation and sequence of deformational events at the southeastern end of the Furnace Creek strike-slip fault zone, Death Valley region, California: The Society of Economic Paleontologists and Mineralogists Special Publication no. 37, p. 127–141.

Christiansen, R. L., Lipman, P. W., Orkild, P. P., and Byers, F. M., Jr., 1965, Structure of the Timber Mountain caldera, southern Nevada, and its relation to basin-range structure: U.S. Geological Survey Professional Paper 525B, p. B43–48.

Cornwall, H. R., and Kleinhampl, F. J., 1961, Geologic map of the Bare Mountain Quadrangle, Nevada: U.S. Geological Survey Geologic Quadrangle Map GQ–157, scale 1:62,500.

—— , 1964, Geology of Bullfrog Hills Quadrangle and ore deposits related to Bullfrog Hills caldera, Nye County, Nevada, and Inyo County, California: U.S. Geological Survey Professional Paper 454–J, 25 p.

Crowe, B. M., Vaniman, D. T., Carr, W. J., and Fleck, R. J., 1980, Geology and tectonic setting of a Neogene volcanic belt within the south-central Great Basin, Nevada and California: Geological Society of America Abstracts with Programs, v. 12, p. 409.

Curry, H. D., 1954, Turtlebacks in the central Black Mountains, Death Valley, California: California Division of Mines Bulletin, v. 170, p. 53–59.

Denny, C. S., and Drewes, H., 1965, Geology of the Ash Meadows Quadrangle Nevada–California: U.S. Geological Survey Bulletin 1181–L, 56 p.

Drewes, H., 1959, Turtleback faults of Death Valley, California; A reinterpretation: Geological Society of America Bulletin, v. 70, p. 1497–1508.

—— , 1963, Geology of the Funeral Peak Quadrangle, California, on the east flank of Death Valley: U.S. Geological Survey Professional Paper 413, 78 p.

Eaton, G. P., Wahl, R. R., Prostka, H. J., Mabey, D. R., and Kleinkopf, M. D., 1978, Regional gravity and tectonic patterns; Their relation to late Cenozoic epeirogeny and lateral spreading in the western Cordillera, *in* Smith, R. B., and Eaton, G. P., eds., Cenozoic tectonics and regional geophysics of the western Cordillera: Geological Society of America Memoir 152, p. 51–91.

Effimoff, I., and Pinezich, A. R., 1986, Tertiary structural development of selected basins; Basin and Range Province, northeastern Nevada, *in* Mayer, L., ed., Extensional tectonics of the southwestern United States: Geological Society of America Special Paper 208, p. 31–42.

Ekren, E. B., Anderson, R. E., Rogers, C. L., and Noble, D. C., 1971, Geology of northern Nellis Air Force Base bombing and gunnery range, Nye County, Nevada: U.S. Geological Survey Professional Paper 651, 91 p.

Elwood, R., McKague, H. L., and Wagoner, J., 1985, Evidence for listric faults in Yucca Flat alluvium, Nevada Test Site [abs.]: Geological Society of America Abstracts with Programs, v. 17, p. 217.

Fleck, R. J., 1970, Age and tectonic significance of volcanic rocks, Death Valley area, California: Geological Society of America Bulletin, v. 81,

p. 2807–2816.

Foley, D., and Sutter, J. F., 1978, Geology of the Stonewall Mountain volcanic center, Nye County, Nevada: Geological Society of America Abstracts with Programs, v. 10, p. 105.

Frizzell, V. A., Jr., and Zoback, M. L., 1987, Stress orientation determined from fault slip in Hampel Wash area, Nevada, and its relation to contemporary regional stress field: Tectonics, v. 6, p. 89–98.

Frost, E. G., and Martin, D. L., eds., 1982, Mesozoic–Cenozoic tectonic evolution of the Colorado River region, California, Arizona, and Nevada: San Diego, California, Cordilleran Publishers, 608 p.

Gianella, V. P., and Callaghan, E., 1934, The earthquake of December 20, 1932, at Cedar Mountain, Nevada, and its bearing on the genesis of Basin-Range structure: Journal of Geology, v. 42, p. 1–22.

Guth, P. L., 1981, Tertiary extension north of the Las Vegas Valley shear zone, Sheep and Desert Ranges, Clark County, Nevada: Geological Society of America Bulletin, v. 92, p. 771–783.

Haefner, R., 1976, Geology of Shoshone volcanics, Death Valley region, eastern California, *in* Geologic features, Death Valley, California: California Division of Mines and Geology Special Report 106, p. 67–72.

Hamilton, W. B., 1988, Detachment faulting in the Death Valley region, California and Nevada, *in* Carr, M. D., and Yount, J. C., eds., Geologic and hydrologic investigations of a potential nuclear waste disposal site at Yucca Mountain, southern Nevada: U.S. Geological Survey Bulletin 1790, p. 51–85.

Healey, D. L., Wahl, R. R., and Currey, F. E., 1980a, Bouguer gravity map of Nevada, Goldfield and Mariposa sheets: Nevada Bureau of Mines and Geology Map 68, scale 1:250,000.

Healey, D. L., Wahl, R. R., and Oliver, H. W., 1980b, Bouguer gravity map of Nevada, Death Valley sheet: Nevada Bureau of Mines and Geology Map 69, scale 1:250,000.

Hildenbrand, T. G., and 7 others, 1988, Regional geologic and geophysical maps of the southern Great Basin, *in* Carr, M. D., and Yount, J. C., eds., Geologic and hydrologic investigations of a potential nuclear waste disposal site at Yucca Mountain, southern Nevada: U.S. Geological Survey Bulletin 1790, p. 3–21.

Hinrichs, E. N., and McKay, E. J., 1965, Geologic map of the Plutonium Valley Quadrangle, Nye and Lincoln Counties, Nevada: U.S. Geological Survey Geologic Quadrangle Map GQ–384, scale 1:24,000.

Hoffman, L. R., and Mooney, W. D., 1983, A seismic study of Yucca Mountain and vicinity, southern Nevada; Data report and preliminary results: U.S. Geological Survey Open-File Report 83–588, 50 p., scale 1:250,000.

Howard, K. A., and John, B. E., 1987, Crustal extension along a rooted system of imbricate low-angle faults; Colorado River extensional corridor, California and Arizona, *in* Coward, M. P., Dewey, J. F., and Hancock, P. L., eds., Continental extensional tectonics: Geological Society of London Special Publication 28, p. 299–311.

Hunt, C. B., and Mabey, D. R., 1966, Stratigraphy and structure, Death Valley, California: U.S. Geological Survey Professional Paper 494–A, 162 p.

Kane, M. F., and Bracken, R. E., 1983, Aeromagnetic map of Yucca Mountain and surrounding regions, southwest Nevada: U.S. Geological Survey Open-File Report 83–616, 19 p.

Kane, M. F., Healey, D. L., Peterson, D. L., Kaufmann, H. E., and Reidy, D., 1979, Bouguer gravity map of Nevada, Las Vegas sheet: Nevada Bureau of Mines and Geology Map 61, scale 1:250,000.

Labotka, T. C., 1980, Petrology of a medium pressure, regional metamorphic terrane, Funeral Mountains, California: American Mineralogist, v. 65, p. 670–689.

Labotka, T. C., Albee, A. L., Lanphere, M. A., and McDowell, S. D., 1980, Stratigraphy, structure, and metamorphism in the central Panamint Mountains (Telescope Peak Quadrangle), Death Valley area, California; Summary: Geological Society of America Bulletin, Part 1, v. 91, p. 125–129.

Luedke, R. G., and Smith, R. L., 1981, Map showing distribution, composition, and age of late Cenozoic volcanic centers in California and Nevada: U.S.

Geological Survey Miscellaneous Investigations Series Map I–1091–C, scale 1:1,000,000.

Mabey, D. R., Zietz, I., Eaton, G. P., and Kleinkopf, M. D., 1978, Regional magnetic patterns in part of the Cordillera in the western United States, *in* Smith, R. B., and Eaton, G. P., eds., Cenozoic tectonic and regional geophysics of the western Cordillera: Geological Society of America Memoir 152, p. 93–106.

Maldonado, F., 1988, Geology of normal faults in the upper plate of a detachment fault zone, Bullfrog Hills, southern Nevada: Geological Society of America Abstracts with Programs, v. 20, p. 178.

Marvin, R. F., Byers, F. M., Jr., Mehnert, H. H., and Orkild, P. P., 1970, Radiometric ages and stratigraphic sequence of volcanic and plutonic rocks, southern Nye and western Lincoln Counties, Nevada: Geological Society of America Bulletin, v. 81, p. 2657–2676.

McAllister, J. F., 1973, Geologic map and sections of the Amargosa Valley borate area—southeast continuation of the Furnace Creek area—Inyo County, California: U.S. Geological Survey Miscellaneous Geologic Investigations Map I–782, scale 1:24,000.

McKeown, F. A., Healey, D. L., and Miller, C. H., 1976, Geologic map of the Yucca Lake Quadrangle, Nye County, Nevada: U.S. Geological Survey Geologic Quadrangle Map GQ–1327, scale 1:24,000.

Monfort, M. E., and Evans, J. R., 1982, Three-dimensional modeling of the Nevada Test Site and vicinity from teleseismic P-wave residuals: U.S. Geological Survey Open-File Report 82–409, 66 p.

Monsen, S. A., 1983, Structural evolution and metamorphic petrology of the Precambrian–Cambrian strata, northwestern Bare Mountain, Nevada [M.S. thesis]: Davis, University of California, 66 p.

Noble, L. F., 1941, Structural features of the Virgin Spring area, Death Valley, California: Geological Society of America Bulletin, v. 52, p. 941–999.

Orkild, P. P., Byers, F. M., Jr., Hoover, D. L., and Sargent, K. A., 1968, Subsurface geology of Silent Canyon caldera, Nevada Test Site, Nevada, *in* Eckel, E. B., ed., Nevada Test Site: Geological Society of America Memoir 110, p. 77–86.

Orkild, Paul P., Sargent, K. A., and Snyder, R. P., 1969, Geologic map of Pahute Mesa, Nevada Test Site and vicinity, Nye County, Nevada: U.S. Geological Survey Miscellaneous Geologic Investigations Map I–567, scale 1:48,000.

Ransome, F. L., Emmons, W. H., and Garrey, G. H., 1910, Geology and ore deposits of the Bullfrog District, Nevada: U.S. Geological Survey Bulletin 407, 130 p.

Reynolds, M. W., 1975, Geology of the Grapevine Mountains, Death Valley, California: California Division of Mines and Geology Special Report 106, p. 19–25.

Rogers, A. M., Harmsen, S. C., Carr, W. J., and Spence, W. J., 1983, Southern Great Basin seismological data report for 1981, and preliminary data analysis: U.S. Geological Survey Open-File Report 83–669, 240 p.

Sass, J. H., and Lachenbruch, A. H., 1982, Preliminary interpretation of thermal data from the Nevada Test Site: U.S. Geological Survey Open-File Report 82–973, 30 p.

Scott, R. B., 1988, Tectonic setting of Yucca Mountain, Nevada: Geological Society of America Abstracts with Programs, v. 20, p. 229.

Scott, R. B., and Bonk, J., 1984, Preliminary geologic map of Yucca Mountain, Nye County, Nevada: U.S. Geological Survey Open-File Report 84–494, scale 1:12,000.

Scott, R. B., and Hofland, G. S., 1987, Fault-slip paleostress analysis of Yucca Mountain, Nevada [abs.]: EOS Transactions of the American Geophysical Union, v. 68, no. 44, p. 1461.

Simonds, F. W., and Scott, R. B., 1987, Detachment faulting and hydrothermal alteration in the Calico Hills, S.W. Nevada [abs.]: EOS Transactions of the American Geophysical Union, v. 68, no. 44, p. 1475.

Snyder, D. B., and Carr, W. J., 1984, Interpretation of gravity data in a complex volcano-tectonic setting, southwestern Nevada: Journal of Geophysical Research, v. 89, no. B12, p. 10193–10206.

Stewart, J. H., 1978, Basin-range structure in western North America; A review, *in* Smith, R. B., and Eaton, G. P., eds., Cenozoic tectonics and regional geophysics of the western Cordillera: Geological Society of America Memoir 152, p. 1–31.

——— , 1980, Geology of Nevada: Nevada Bureau of Mines and Geology Special Publication 4, 136 p.

Stewart, J. H., 1983, Extensional tectonics in the Death Valley area, California: Transport of the Panamint structural block 80 km northwestward: Geology, v. 11, p. 153–157.

Stewart, J. H., and Carlson, J. E., 1978, Geologic map of Nevada: U.S. Geological Survey, scale 1:500,000.

Stewart, J. H., Albers, J. P., and Poole, F. G., 1968, Summary of regional evidence for right-lateral displacement in the western Great Basin: Geological Society of America Bulletin, v. 79, p. 1407–1413.

Stock, J. M., Healy, J. H., Hickman, S. H., and Zoback, M. D., 1985, Hydraulic fracturing stress measurements at Yucca Mountain, Nevada, and their relationship to the regional stress field: Journal of Geophysical Research, v. 90, no. B10, p. 8691–8706.

Swadley, W. C., and Carr, W. J., 1986, Geologic map of the surficial and Tertiary rocks of the Big Dune Quadrangle, California and Nevada: U.S. Geological Survey Miscellaneous Investigations Series Map I-1767, scale 1:48,000.

Swadley, W. C., Hoover, D. L., and Rosholt, J. N., 1984, Preliminary report on late Cenozoic faulting and stratigraphy in the vicinity of Yucca Mountain, Nye County, Nevada: U.S. Geological Survey Open-File Report 84–788, 42 p.

Thompson, G. A., and Burke, D. B., 1973, Rate and direction of spreading in Dixie Valley, Basin and Range province, Nevada: Geological Society of America Bulletin, v. 84, p. 627–632.

Troxel, B. W., 1988, A geologic traverse of the northern Funeral Mountains, Death Valley, California, *in* Weide, D. L., and Faber, M. L., eds., This extended land; Geological Society of America Cordilleran Section Meeting Field Trip Guidebook: University of Nevada at Las Vegas Geoscience Department Special Publication 2, p. 45–49.

U.S. Geological Survey, 1978, Aeromagnetic map of the Lathrop Wells area, Nevada: U.S. Geological Survey Open-File Report 78–1103, scale 1:62,500.

Vaniman, D. T., Crowe, B. M., and Gladney, E. S., 1982, Petrology and geochem-

istry of hawaiite lavas from Crater Flat, Nevada: Contributions to Mineralogy and Petrology, v. 80, p. 341–357.

Warren, R. G., McDowell, F. W., Byers, F. M., Jr., Broxton, D. E., Carr, W. J., and Orkild, P. P., 1988, Episodic leaks from Timber Mountain caldera; New evidence from rhyolite lavas of Fortymile Canyon, S.W. Nevada volcanic field: Geological Society of America Abstracts with Programs, v. 20, p. 241.

Weaver, C. S., and Hill, D. T., 1979, Earthquake swarms and local crustal spreading along major strike-slip faults in California: Pure and Applied Geophysics, v. 117, p. 51–64.

Wells, S. G., McFadden, L. D., Renault, C., Turrin, B. D., and Crowe, B. M., 1988, A geomorphic assessment of Quaternary volcanism in the Yucca Mountain area, Nevada Test Site, southern Nevada: Geological Society of America Abstracts with Programs, v. 20, p. 242.

Wernicke, B. P., 1981, Low-angle normal faults in the Basin and Range Province: Nature, v. 291, p. 645–648.

Wernicke, B. P., and Burchfiel, B. C., 1982, Modes of extensional tectonics: Journal of Structural Geology, v. 4, p. 105–115.

Wernicke, B. P., Walker, J. D., and Hodges, K. V., 1988, Field guide to the northern part of the Tucki Mountain fault system, Death Valley region, California, *in* Weide, D. L., and Faber, M. L., eds., This extended land; Geological Society of America Cordilleran Section Meeting: University of Nevada at Las Vegas Geoscience Department Special Publication 2, p. 58–63.

Wright, L. A., 1971, Evidence for tectonic control of volcanism, Death Valley: Geological Society of America Abstracts with Programs, v. 3, p. 221.

——— , 1976, Late Cenozoic fault patterns and stress fields in the Great Basin and westward displacement of the Sierra Nevada block: Geology, v. 4, p. 489–494.

Wright, L. A., Otton, J. K., and Troxel, B. W., 1974, Turtleback surfaces of Death Valley viewed as phenomena of extensional tectonics: Geology, v. 2, p. 53–54.

Zoback, M. L., and Zoback, M. D., 1980, State of stress in the conterminous United States: Journal of Geophysical Research, v. 85, p. 6113–6156.

MANUSCRIPT ACCEPTED BY THE SOCIETY AUGUST 21, 1989

Geological Society of America
Memoir 176
1990

Chapter 14

Effect of Cenozoic extension on Mesozoic thrust surfaces in the central and southern Funeral Mountains, Death Valley, California

Ibrahim Cemen
School of Geology, Oklahoma State University, Stillwater, Oklahoma 74078
Lauren A. Wright
Department of Geosciences, Pennsylvania State University, University Park, Pennsylvania 16802

ABSTRACT

The central and southern Funeral Mountains of the Death Valley region contain at least two structural relations that suggest reactivation of the Mesozoic thrust surfaces during Cenozoic extension. One is at the Bat Mountain area of the southern Funeral Mountains where the Bat Mountain fault, named by Denny and Drewes (1965), dips about 20° northwest and shows as much as 2,000 m normal dip-separation along its northern exposures. The fault loses this separation progressively southwestward and joins along its strike to the northwest-dipping Mesozoic Clery thrust, named by McAllister (1971). The thrust has as much as 1,600 m reverse dip-separation and dips about 30 to 40°. This geometry, together with a structural reconstruction through the Bat Mountain area, suggests that the Bat Mountain fault is a reactivated thrust surface. Since the Bat Mountain fault and the Clery thrust are essentially the same fault surface, we suggest that the name Clery–Bat Mountain fault be used for the entire length of the fault.

The other structural relation that suggests reactivation is in the Schwaub Peak area of the central Funeral Mountains where Schwaub Peak thrust and its associated faults extend across the Funeral Mountains. The northwest-trending Keane Wonder strike-slip fault divides the upper plate into an only slightly extended northeast part and a strongly extended southwest part, a geometry requiring reactivation along the thrust faults. An offset anticline in the area suggests a 5-km normal separation on the underlying Schwaub Peak thrust and associated faults.

INTRODUCTION

The reactivation of thrust faults during periods of later crustal extension has been recognized in various parts of the world since the 1950s. This phenomenon was first recognized in the North American Cordillera by Bally and others (1966), who observed evidence suggesting that some of the west-dipping Cenozoic normal faults have followed the older thrust surfaces in the foreland fold and thrust belt of Canada. Subsequently, reactivation has been proposed at various localities in the western United States. In several areas, the evidence is based on field-oriented geologic research (e.g., Platt, 1985; Guth, 1988). Reactivation also has been proposed based on geological research aided by the availability of data from seismic reflection profiling (e.g., Royse and others, 1975; Royse, 1983; Hauge and others, 1987). However, detailed geologic mapping (Wernicke and others, 1984, 1985) in southern Nevada suggests that extensional faults in the region tend to avoid preexisting zones of weakness, such as Mesozoic thrust faults.

The main purpose of this paper is to describe the geologic

Cemen, I., and Wright, L. A., 1990, Effect of Cenozoic extension on Mesozoic thrust surfaces in the central and southern Funeral Mountains, Death Valley, California, *in* Wernicke, B. P., ed., Basin and Range extensional tectonics near the latitude of Las Vegas, Nevada: Boulder, Colorado, Geological Society of America Memoir 176.

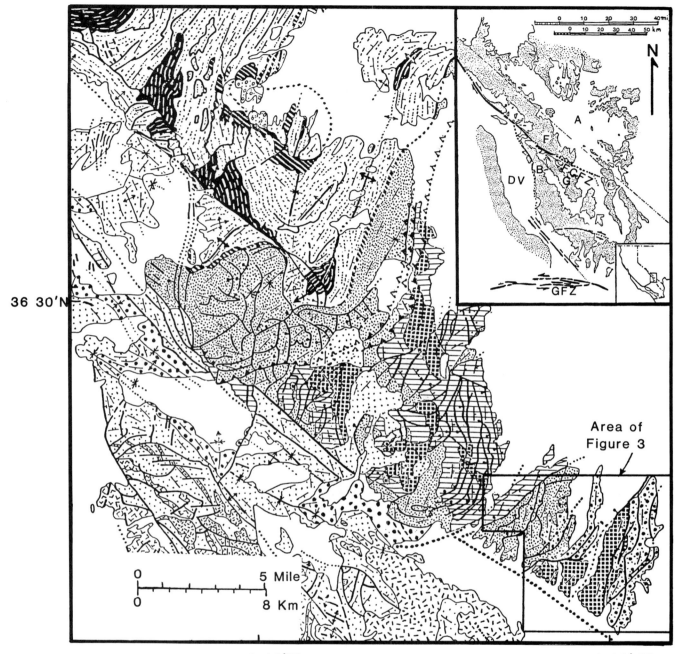

Figure 1. Generalized geological map of the central and southern Funeral Mountains of the Death Valley region, California and Nevada. The insert on the right corner is an index map of the region. Abbreviations on the index map are: A = Amargosa Valley; B = Black Mountains; DV = Death Valley; F = Funeral Mountains; FCFZ = Furnace Creek fault zone; G = Greenwater Range; GFZ = Garlock fault zone; RS = Resting Spring Range.

features at two locations in the central and southern Funeral Mountains of the Death Valley region where Cenozoic extension apparently followed Mesozoic thrust surfaces. The first location is in the Bat Mountain area at the southern end of the Funeral Mountains (Figs. 1, 3) where a northeast-trending, northwest-dipping fault with a sizable normal separation is connected along its trend with a northeast-trending and northwest-dipping Mesozoic thrust. The second location is in the Schwaub Peak area of the central Funeral Mountains where a zone of closely spaced northeast-trending thrust faults extends across the Funeral Mountains (Figs. 1, 7). The principal fault in this zone is here named the Schwaub Peak thrust (Fig. 7).

EXPLANATION

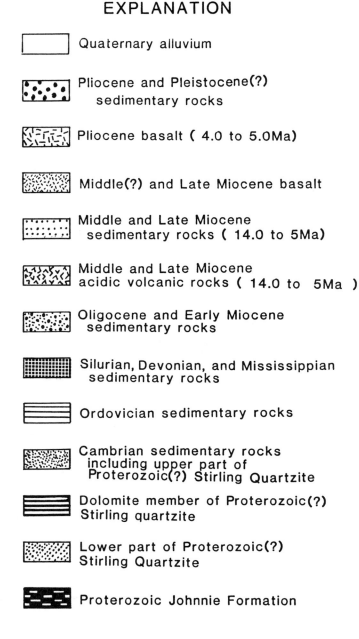

Quaternary alluvium

Pliocene and Pleistocene(?) sedimentary rocks

Pliocene basalt (4.0 to 5.0Ma)

Middle(?) and Late Miocene basalt

Middle and Late Miocene sedimentary rocks (14.0 to 5Ma)

Middle and Late Miocene acidic volcanic rocks (14.0 to 5Ma)

Oligocene and Early Miocene sedimentary rocks

Silurian, Devonian, and Mississippian sedimentary rocks

Ordovician sedimentary rocks

Cambrian sedimentary rocks including upper part of Proterozoic(?) Stirling Quartzite

Dolomite member of Proterozoic(?) Stirling quartzite

Lower part of Proterozoic(?) Stirling Quartzite

Proterozoic Johnnie Formation

BAT MOUNTAIN AREA

Geologic setting and previous investigations

In the Bat Mountain area, evidence for reactivation along a Mesozoic compressional fault is contained in geologic relations along and near a low-angle fault that separates two southeast-tilted blocks: the Bat Mountain block on the southeast and the Mine Camp block on the northwest (Fig. 3). The structural and stratigraphic features of the Bat Mountain area also clarify the mechanics and timing of Cenozoic extension in the area. Each of the two blocks consists of Paleozoic formations and remnants of a cover of Miocene sedimentary and volcanic rocks deposited within the 25- to 14-Ma interval (Cemen and others, 1982). Each

block also has been broken by normal faults of smaller displacements than that of the master fault that separates them.

The pre-Cenozoic rocks of the Mine Camp block consist mostly of Middle and Upper Cambrian strata, whereas the pre-Cenozoic rocks of the Bat Mountain block comprise strata of Silurian to Mississippian age. A columnar section (Fig. 2) shows, in a generalized form, dominant lithologies, ages, and reported thicknesses of the pre-Cenozoic and Cenozoic rock units of the two blocks. Both the Paleozoic and Miocene successions show prevailing dips of 35 to 45° southeastward and strikes northeastward (Fig. 3).

The Bat Mountain block lies within the Ash Meadows 15′ Quadrangle, the geology of which was mapped by Denny and Drewes (1965), whereas the geology of the Mine Camp block is included in a geologic map of the northeastern part of the Ryan 15′ Quadrangle by McAllister (1971). Denny and Drewes (1965) named the master fault separating the Bat Mountain block from the Mine Camp Mountain block as the Bat Mountain fault. A fault well exposed in the southeastern part of the Mine Camp Mountain block is designated the "Clery thrust" by McAllister (1971). Our observations indicate that these two faults are essentially the same fault surface. Therefore, we suggest the name Clery–Bat Mountain fault be used for the entire length of the fault (Fig. 3).

On Figure 3, the northeastern part of the Clery–Bat Mountain fault, which is exposed at two locations in the northern part of Bat Mountain, is the Bat Mountain fault of Denny and Drewes (1965). The fault trends northeastward and dips about 20° northwestward. It brings the sandstone member of the Bat Mountain Formation over the Red Sandstone unit at the more northeasterly of the two locations, and over the Silurian-Devonian Hidden Valley Dolomite (Figs. 3, 4a) at the more southwesterly site. Southwestward from the second locality, the Clery–Bat Mountain fault is covered by alluvium. In the southeastern part of the Mine Camp Mountain block to the northwest (Figs. 3, 6), the fault is continuously exposed for about 3 km and remains intact, with the exception of a small offset by a single fault. In the eastern part of this continuous exposure (Fig. 6) the fault dips about 20 to 25° northward. In the western part, the Clery thrust of McAllister (1971), the fault dips 35 to 40° northward, and separates the Cambrian formations in the hanging wall from the Ordovician, Silurian, and Devonian formations in the footwall (Fig. 6).

The southwestern part of the Bat Mountain block is separated from the Mine Camp block by a high-angle normal fault. The fault is not exposed at the surface but the stratigraphic relation along the line of cross section C-C′ (Figs. 3, 5) is best explained by a normal fault. The fault is inferred to extend along the western edge of the southern part of Bat Mountain block (Fig. 3).

The Miocene succession

The following is a brief description of the Miocene succession of the Bat Mountain area, mostly based on Cemen (1983),

Cemen and others (1982), and Cemen and others (1985). It is included here (a) to give a brief summary on the nature of the Cenozoic sedimentation in the area; and (b) to update one of the earlier stratigraphic correlations, namely that of the Horse Spring Formation.

The pre-Cenozoic strata are unconformably overlain by the Miocene succession, which is approximately 1,300 m thick and is divisible into three parts. Each is composed of mappable units and is separated from the other parts by minor unconformities

CENOZOIC	MIOCENE	Middle	Alluvium, Landslides		
		?	Bat Mountain Formation	Sandstone member	0-150
				Conglomerate member	0-350
		Early	Limestone		50-170
			Red Sandstone		100-350
	OLIGO.	Late	Playa Deposit		50-150
			Lower Conglomerate		0-200
PALEOZOIC	MIS.	L	Perdido Formation		150
		E	Tin Mountain Limestone		90
	DEVO.	L	Lost Burro Formation		760
		M			
		E			
	SIL		Hidden Valley Dolomite		430
	ORDO.	L	Ely Springs Dolomite		150
		M	Eureka Quartzite		120
		E	Pogonip Group		670
	CAMBRIAN	Late	Nopah Formation		520
		Middle	Bonanza King Formation		1100
			Carrara Formation		490
		Early	Zabriskie Quartzite		240
PRECAMBRIAN			Wood Canyon Formation		1220
			Stirling Quartzite		1460
			Johnnie Formation		300

Figure 2. Generalized columnar section of the rock units exposed in the central and southern Funeral Mountains (modified from Cemen and others, 1982). The column on the right shows approximate thicknesses of the rock units in meters. Thicknesses of the Precambrian and Paleozoic rock units are from McAllister (1974) and Stewart (1970).

(Fig. 3). The lower part consists, in upward succession, of (1) a locally derived lower conglomerate unit; (2) a siltstone, sandstone, limestone, and ash-fall-tuff–bearing playa deposit; and (3) a red sandstone unit. The middle part is composed of an algal limestone unit. The upper part is the Bat Mountain Formation, which contains a conglomerate and a sandstone member (Figs. 2, 3).

The lower conglomerate is a remnant of an alluvial fan whose source is to the south (Cemen and others, 1982). It is overlain by a playa deposit composed of interlayered limestone, siltstone, and sandstone. The unit contains a tuff layer, which yielded a K/Ar age of 25 Ma and is correlative, lithologically and chronologically, with the Horse Spring Formation of Anderson and others (1972) in southern Nevada. Therefore, Cemen and others (1982, 1985) correlated the unit with the Horse Spring Formation of southern Nevada. However, Bohannan (1984) reported that the fission-track age of zircon from the tuff beds in Horse Spring Formation is younger than the 23- to 25-Ma ages reported by Anderson and others (1972). The playa deposit of the Bat Mountain area is lithologically very similar but apparently older than the Horse Spring Formation in its type locality (Bohannan, personal communication, 1987). Therefore, the unit is referred to in this report as the playa deposit of the Bat Mountain area (Figs. 2, 3). A red sandstone unit that contains a tuff dated at 20 Ma (K/Ar) overlies the playa deposit. Unconformably overlying the lower part of the Miocene succession is an algal limestone unit that records an interval of tectonic quiescence. The conglomerate member of the Bat Mountain Formation records the presence of north-sloping alluvial fans that intertongue with flood-plain deposits of the sandstone member of the formation (Cemen and others, 1985).

Timing of the late Cenozoic extension

The two blocks of the Bat Mountain area were formed in response to the late Cenozoic extension of the Death Valley region. Detailed geologic mapping of the Miocene succession, together with radiometric age determination of the volcanic units, provided evidence that extension in the Bat Mountain area occurred at three times; one prior to 25 Ma, another about 20 Ma, and the third post–14 Ma. The latter period of extension produced the major fault-bounded blocks.

The evidence for the timing of the earliest Cenozoic extension is in the Mine Camp block where three of the normal faults that displace the lower Paleozoic rocks extend to the base of the Cenozoic lower conglomerate without offsetting it (Figs. 3, 4c). The conglomerate underlies the playa deposit, which contains a tuff bed dated radiometrically (K/Ar) at about 25 Ma (Cemen and others, 1985). These normal faults, first mapped by McAllister (1971), were field checked and remapped during this investigation.

The 20-Ma extension event is indicated by several normal faults in the Bat Mountain area. These bound horsts and grabens (Figs. 3, 4b) and preserve Miocene units in the grabens. In the

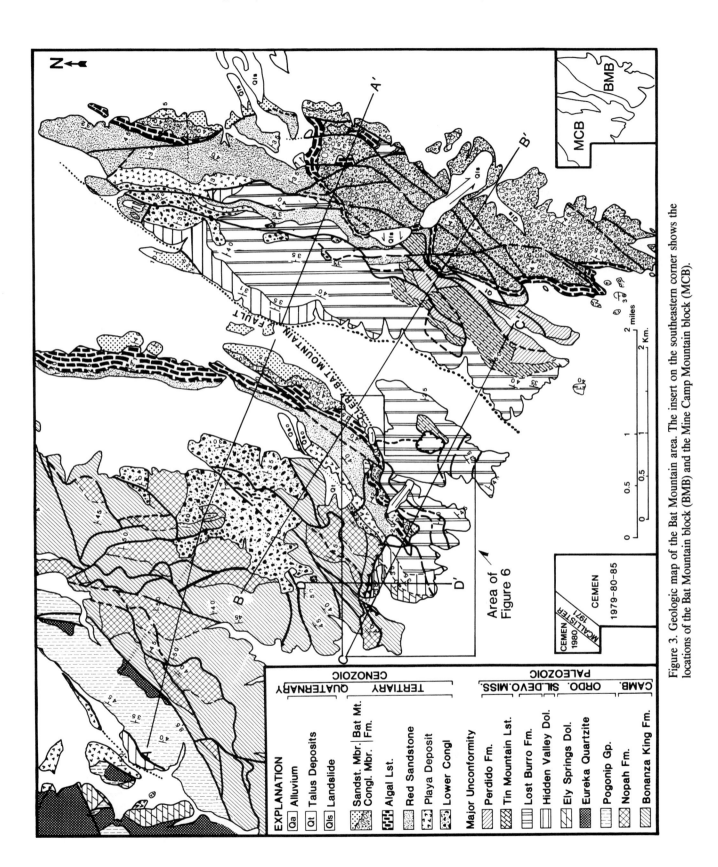

Figure 3. Geologic map of the Bat Mountain area. The insert on the southeastern corner shows the locations of the Bat Mountain block (BMB) and the Mine Camp Mountain block (MCB).

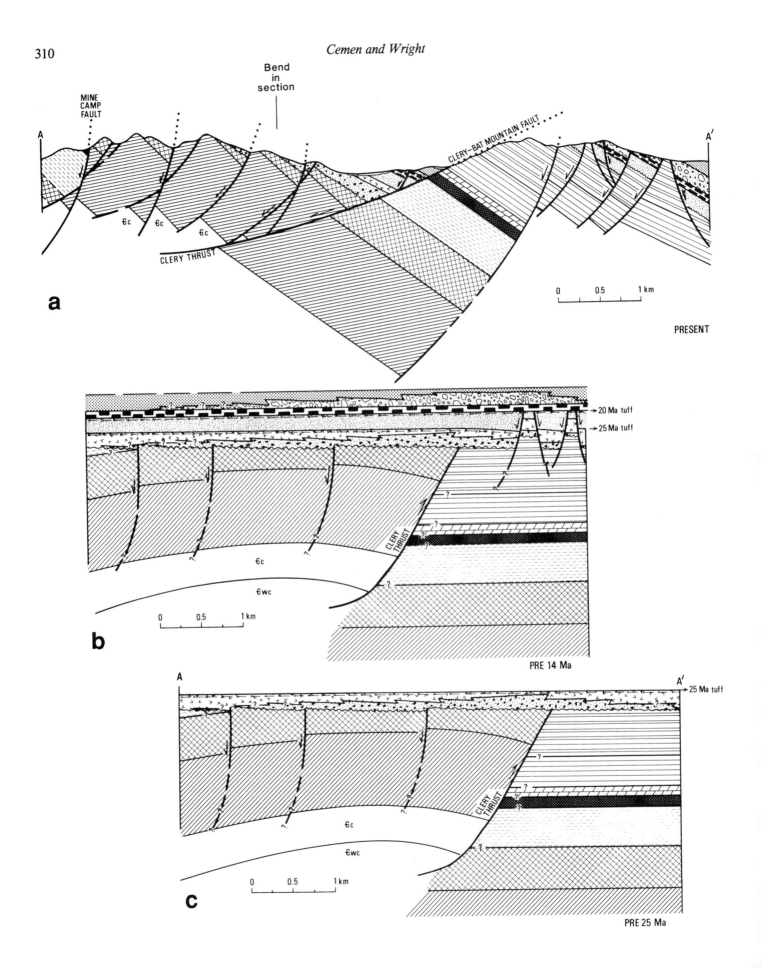

a   PRESENT

b   PRE 14 Ma

c   PRE 25 Ma

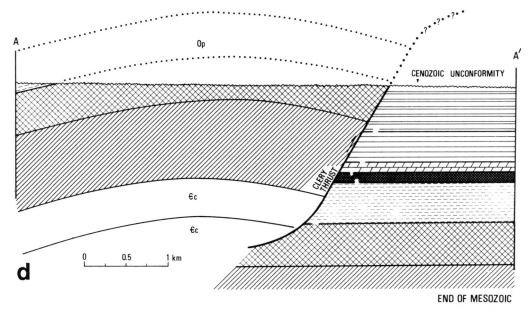

Figure 4. Cross section A-A' (a), and its reconstructions, prior to the major extension of the Bat Mountain area at 14 Ma (b); around the deposition of the tuff dated at 25 Ma (c); and at the end of Mesozoic (d). See Figure 3 for explanations of symbols.

northern part of the Bat Mountain block, they strike northward and join the Bat Mountain fault obliquely, but strike southwestward in the southern part (Fig. 3). Their arcuate shape suggests that they are spoon shaped in three dimensions. The time of faulting is evidenced by the observations that (1) from place to place and on opposite sides of a given fault the algal limestone above the unconformity rests on rock units of different ages, (2) the red sandstone unit shows marked thickness differences on both sides of a horst structure in the northern Bat Mountain, and (3) some faults that slightly offset the limestone separate the underlying rocks by much more (Fig. 3). Reconstruction of these faults, including rotation of the limestone to horizontal, show that they were once steeply dipping normal faults, and that the horsts and grabens they define predate the unconformity between the sandstone and the overlying algal limestone unit (Fig. 4b). Because the tuff layer exposed on the south side of Bat Mountain and stratigraphically immediately below the algal limestone dates to 20 Ma, we interpret these faults as essentially contemporaneous with the tuff (Cemen and others, 1985).

The Clery–Bat Mountain fault

The part of the Clery–Bat Mountain fault exposed at the southern part of the Mine Camp block (Figs. 3, 6) records the earliest detectable deformational event in the Bat Mountain area. It has brought the Cambrian Bonanza King and Nopah Formations in the hanging wall over the Ordovician Ely Springs, and the Silurian-Devonian Hidden Valley and the Devonian Lost Burro Formations in the footwall (Figs. 3, 6). The fault has three structural features typical of thrust environments. The first is its placement cutting rapidly upsection at a high angle to the bed-

ding. The second feature is a well-developed horse structure, which contains the Ordovician Eureka Quartzite and Pogonip Group rocks as a sliver between an upper and a lower strand. Third is a broad anticline (Figs. 5b, c, 6) in the lower block. The anticline is probably related to upper plate deformation of another thrust surface at depth. These features indicate that this part of the Clery–Bat Mountain fault exposed in the southern part of the Mine Camp block is a thrust fault as mapped by McAllister (1971).

The part of the Clery–Bat Mountain fault exposed in the northern part of the Bat Mountain, the Bat Mountain fault of Denny and Drewes (1965), shows normal dip-separation of as much as 2,000 m and a normal stratigraphic throw of 800 m along the northeastern flank of the Bat Mountain (Figs. 3, 4a). It shows as much as 1,500 m normal dip-separation along the line of cross section B-B' (Fig. 5a). Southwestward from there, the normal dip-separation along the fault decreases as it brings progressively older Cenozoic rocks over the Paleozoic rocks. In the area of Figure 6, the fault shows normal separation in the western part. However, as mentioned, the fault shows about 1,600 m reverse dip-separation along the line of cross section D-D'.

Evolution of the Clery–Bat Mountain thrust

Figure 4 shows our interpretation of the structural evolution of the Clery–Bat Mountain fault as reconstructed along cross section A-A' (Figs. 3, 4a). This reconstruction involves a rotation of the Cenozoic unconformity to its original position to remove the effects of Cenozoic extension. Although a southwestward onlap of the Cenozoic rocks against the Paleozoic basement suggests that the unconformity originally dipped about 5° northward

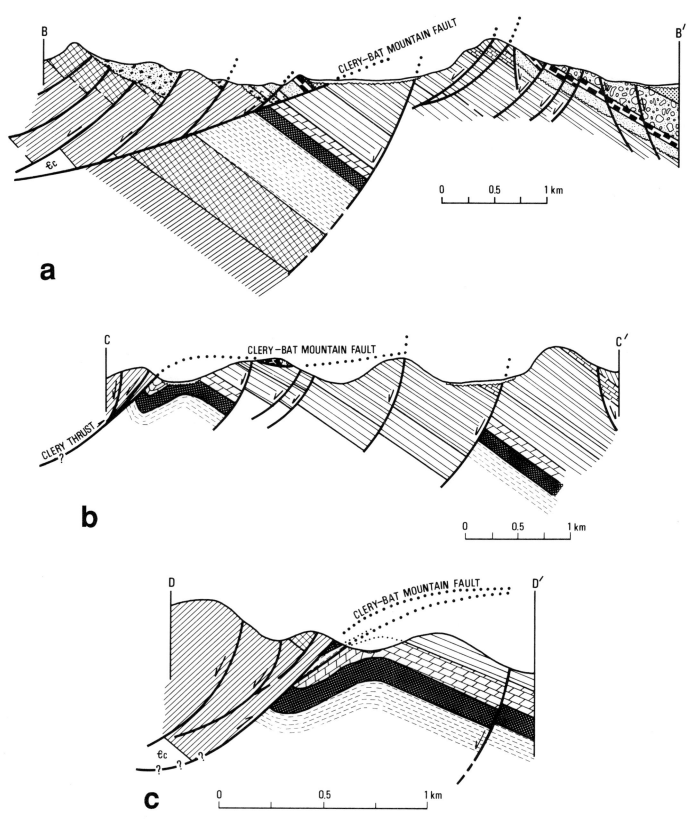

Figure 5. Cross sections B-B' (a), C-C' (b), and D-D' (c). See Figure 3 for explanation of symbols and location of cross sections.

(Cemen and others, 1982), the original position of the unconformity along the line A-A' can be shown as essentially horizontal. The extension along the major normal faults of the cross section is calculated to lie within the range of 20 to 30 percent, using the formulas of Wernicke and Burchfiel (1982). We assume an average 25 percent extension in our restoration of the crosssection A-A' to obtain the approximate pre-Cenozoic length (Fig. 4d). We detect no significant angular discordance between the Paleozoic and Cenozoic rock units in the lower block of the Clery–Bat Mountain fault along the plane of cross section A-A' (Figs. 3, 4). An approximately 10° difference in dip apparently commonly exists between the Paleozoic and Cenozoic rocks in the upper block, especially in the eastern part of the Mine Camp block (Fig. 3). This difference, shown in the reconstruction (Fig. 4d), is probably due mainly to a broad pre-Cenozoic anticline on the upper plate of the Clery thrust, the name maintained by us to refer to the pre-Cenozoic thrust nature of the fault plane. The pre–25 Ma normal faults (Fig. 4c) may have also contributed to the difference in dip. The pre-Cenozoic reconstruction (Fig. 4d), shows an initial dip of about 60° northwest and a reverse dip separation of about 2,100 m on the Clery thrust prior to the deposition of the Miocene succession.

A small percentage of total extension of the Bat Mountain area is accomplished by the pre–25 Ma normal faults (Fig. 4b), and by the 20-Ma horst and graben structures (Fig. 4c). When the cross section is reconstructed these normal faults become high-angle normal faults and the amount of extension along these faults could not be determined because of the uncertainties in determining the dip of the faults before and after each extensional

episode. Therefore, on Figures 4c and 4b, the pre–25 Ma and the 20-Ma normal faults are shown schematically as steeply dipping and as not affecting the pre-Cenozoic length of the cross-sectional area. In other words, we reconstructed the cross section as if all the extension was accomplished by the major post–14 Ma extension of the area. This major extension also produced the opening of the Furnace Creek basin (Cemen and others, 1985). Most, if not all, of the reversal of movement along the Clery–Bat Mountain fault occurred during this extension because the entire Miocene succession shows relatively uniform normal separation along the dip direction of the fault.

A well-exposed normal fault in the central part of the area of Figure 3 joins along its strike with the surface trace of the Clery–Bat Mountain fault whose surface trace is not displaced by other normal faults. Therefore we suspect other normal faults, too, may be projected as joining to the trace of the Clery–Bat Mountain fault underneath the alluvium. This geometry suggests to us that the normal faults in the upper plate of the Clery–Bat Mountain fault join to it in the subsurface (Figs. 4a, 5).

CENTRAL FUNERAL MOUNTAINS

At the locality in the central part of the Funeral Mountains, we detect evidence of reactivation along a segment of a narrow zone of closely spaced Mesozoic thrust faults that trend northeastward across the full width of the mountains, a distance of about 17 km (Fig. 1). We have designated the principal fault within this zone the Schwaub Peak thrust (Fig. 7). Its exposures lie mainly in the Ryan quadrangle where it was first recognized

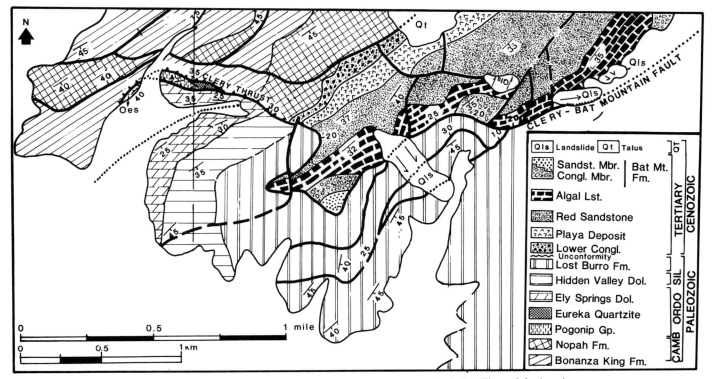

Figure 6. Geologic map of the southern part of the Mine Camp block. See Figure 3 for location.

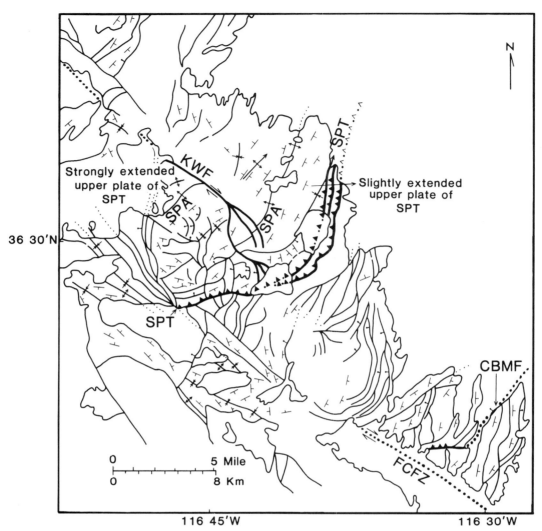

Figure 7. Simplified structure map of the central and southern Funeral Mountains showing location of several structural features discussed in the text. Abbreviations: CBMF = Clery-Bat Mountain fault; FCFZ = Furnace Creek fault zone; SPA = Schwaub Peak anticline; SPT = Schwaub Peak thrust.

and mapped by McAllister (1971). From there it extends north-eastward and northward into the Big Dune Quadrangle and part of the Funeral Mountains mapped by Troxel and Wright (1989).

The Schwaub Peak thrust and its associated faults display an arcuate trace, concave to the northwest, and dips ranging from 60 to 20° northwestward and westward. They consistently cause older rock units to overlie younger rock units, and define an upper plate which, within the area of Figure 1, consists entirely of late Proterozoic(?) and Cambrian Formations (Stirling Quartzite, Wood Canyon Formation, Zabriskie Quartzite, Carrara Formation, Bonanza King Formation). Along most of its trace the Schwaub Peak thrust has caused Cambrian formations to overlie Ordovician (Pogonip Group, Eureka Quartzite, and Ely Spring Dolomite) and Devonian (Hidden Valley Dolomite and Lost Burro Formation) formations. But from place to place along the thrust, various formations within these groups are juxtaposed.

Both the lower and upper plate of the Schwaub Peak thrust

contain normal faults. Although several of the normal faults extend to the Schwaub Peak and associated thrust faults, they do not offset the thrust surfaces (Figs. 1, 7). The thrusts surfaces apparently maintained their integrity during the Cenozoic extension.

Evidence for reactivation is contained in the pattern of Cenozoic coeval strike-slip and normal faults in the upper plate of the Schwaub Peak thrust and their relation to Mesozoic folds (Fig. 7). In brief, the upper plate has been divided into two parts by the northwest-trending Keane Wonder strike-slip fault zone, which terminates in the upper plate northwest of the surface trace of the Schwaub Peak thrust (Fig. 7). The part of the upper plate that lies northeast of the strike-slip fault (Fig. 7) is essentially intact, unbroken by normal faults and thus unextended. The part that lies southwest of the strike-slip fault contains numerous normal faults, which qualify as southward and southwestward splays of the Keane Wonder strike-slip fault zone and record extension in that part of the upper plate (Fig. 7). We interpret the normal faults as recording the southeastward termination of the Keane Wonder fault zone and as evidence for extension compatible with the right-lateral movement on the fault zone.

This pattern of Cenozoic faulting in the upper plate is compatible with other evidence for right-lateral movement on the Keane Wonder fault zone, principally a 5-km offset of a large Mesozoic anticline in the upper plate (Hunt and Mabey, 1966; Reynolds and others, 1986). This fold is informally named here as the Schwaub Peak anticline (Fig. 7). The anticline is recorded in exposures of the upper part of the Proterozoic Johnnie Formation and full thickness of the Stirling Quartzite and is discontinuously exposed and essentially unfaulted for a distance of 17 km northeast of the Keane Wonder fault zone (Fig. 1). It is strongly asymmetric (steepened on the southeast) and displays an estimated amplitude of 1 to 1.5 km. Only one fold of this type and with these dimensions has been observed within the Funeral Mountains. Together with a broad syncline on the northwest and a relatively tight syncline on the southeast, the Schwaub Peak anticline records an estimated shortening of about 2.6 km along a 17-km segment of the upper plate, a shortening of about 15 percent. This effect of Mesozoic compression underscores the significance of the bounding Schwaub Peak thrust and associated faults.

A southwest-plunging fold of similar amplitude, which also involves strata of the Stirling Quartzite, is exposed on the southwest side of the Keane Wonder fault zone. The traces of the two axial planes are separated by about 5 km in a right-lateral sense. We believe the similarity of the two, together with the pattern of Cenozoic faults associated with them, can be explained only if they are offset segments of the same fold. If so and if we have correctly interpreted the pattern of Cenozoic normal faults, the part of the anticline that lies southwest of the Keane Wonder fault zone records a 5-km normal separation on the underlying Schwaub Peak thrust and associated faults.

SUMMARY AND CONCLUSIONS

It has been long recognized that the Funeral Mountains of the Death Valley region of the Basin and Range Province contain numerous normal faults and several Mesozoic thrust surfaces (Noble and Wright, 1954; McAllister, 1971). Our observations in the central and southern parts of the Funeral Mountains suggest that Cenozoic extension in the area has caused reactivation of the Mesozoic thrust surfaces in at least two locations; one in the Bat Mountain area of the southern Funeral Mountains and the other in the Schwaub Peak area of the central Funeral Mountains (Fig. 1).

In the Bat Mountain area, the Clery–Bat Mountain fault separates the Cenozoic units exposed in the Bat Mountain block from the same Cenozoic units exposed in the Mine Camp Mountain block. The fault has about 2,000 m of normal dip separation in the northern part of Bat Mountain (Figs. 3, 4a) but shows about 1,500 m of normal dip separation along the line of cross section B–B' (Fig. 5a). It loses this normal separation progressively southwestward and shows about 1,600 m reverse dip separation along the line of cross section D–D' (Fig. 5c) in the southern part of the Mine Camp Mountain block (Figs. 3, 6) where it brings Cambrian units over the Devonian units.

A structural reconstruction along the line of cross section A–A' (Figs. 3, 4) shows that the Bat Mountain area has experienced about 25 percent extension in response to the Late Cenozoic extension. The reconstruction also shows that the Clery–Bat Mountain fault was dipping 55° northwest and had about 2,100 m reverse dip separation prior to the Cenozoic extension. Based on the reconstruction and field observations, we suggest that the Clery–Bat Mountain fault was a thrust fault prior to the Cenozoic extension. Since (a) our reconstruction shows an original reverse dip-separation of 2,100 m prior to the Cenozoic extension, and (b) the reverse separation measured along the line of cross section D–D' is about 1,600 m, the entire length of the fault has been reactivated during the late Cenozoic extension.

In the central part of the Funeral Mountains, the Schwaub Peak thrust and its associated faults display an arcuate trace and consistently cause older rock units in the hanging wall to overlie the younger rock units in the footwall. The Keane Wonder strike-slip fault zone divides the upper plate of the Schwaub Peak thrust into two parts. The northeastern part does not contain normal faults and thus is unextended. The southwestern part contains numerous normal faults and thus is extended. These normal faults record the southeastern termination of the Keane Wonder fault zone. The axial trace of the Schwaub Peak anticline in the northeastern part of the upper plate of the Schwaub Peak thrust is separated about 5 km in a right-lateral sense by the Keane Wonder fault from the same axial trace on the southwestern part. This records a 5-km normal separation along the underlying Schwaub Peak thrust and associated faults.

ACKNOWLEDGMENTS

We thank Bennie W. Troxel, Fred C. Johnson, Brian P. Wernicke, Peter Guth, and Mike Carr for helpful discussions during the various stages of this investigation. J. Kent Snow and Daniel K. Holm reviewed the manuscript. The project was supported by an American Chemical Society Petroleum Research Fund Grant, PRF # 18085-GB2, to Ibrahim Cemen and National Science Foundation Grants EAR 7927092 and EAR 8206627 to Lauren A. Wright.

REFERENCES CITED

Anderson, R. E., Longwell, C. R., Armostring, R. L., and Mervin, R. F., 1972, Significance of K-Ar ages of Tertiary rocks from the Lake Mead region, Nevada-Arizona: Geological Society of America Bulletin, v. 83, p. 273–288.

Bally, A. W., Gordy, P. L., and Stewart, G. A., 1966, Structure, seismic data, and orogenic evolution of the southern Canadian Rocky Mountains: Canadian Petroleum Geologists Bulletin, v. 14, p. 337–381.

Bohannan, R. G., 1984, Nonmarine sedimentary rocks of Tertiary age in the Lake Mead region, southeastern Nevada and northwestern Arizona: U.S. Geological Survey Professional Paper 1259, 72 p.

Cemen, I., 1983, Stratigraphy, geochronology, and structure of the selected areas of the northern Death Valley region, eastern California-western Nevada, and implications concerning Cenozoic tectonics of the region [Ph.D. thesis]: University Park, Pennsylvania State University, 235 p.

Cemen, I., Drake, R. E., and Wright, L. A., 1982, Stratigraphy and chronology of the Tertiary sedimentary and volcanic units at the southeastern end of the Funeral Mountains, Death Valley region, California, *in* Cooper, J. D., Troxel, B. W., and Wright, L. A., eds., Geology of selected areas in the San Bernardino Mountains, western Mojave Desert, and southern Great Basin, California: Shoshone, California, Death Valley Publishing Co., p. 77–88.

Cemen, I., Wright, L. A., Drake, R. E., and Johnson, F. C., 1985, Cenozoic sedimentation and sequence of deformational events at the southeastern end of the Furnace Creek strike-slip fault zone, Death Valley region, California, *in* Biddle, K. T., and Christie-Blick, N., eds., Strike-slip deformation and basin formation: Society of Economic Paleontologists and Mineralogists Special Publication 37, p. 127–141.

Denny, C. S., and Drewes, H., 1965, Geology of the Ash Meadows Quadrangle, Nevada-California: U.S. Geological Survey Bulletin 1181-L, p. L1–L56.

Guth, P. L., 1988, Superposed Mesozoic thrusts and Tertiary extension, northwestern Clark County, Nevada: Geological Society of America Abstracts with Programs, v. 20, p. 165.

Hauge, T. A., and others, 1987, Crustal structure of western Nevada from CO-CORP deep seismic-reflection data: Geological Society of America Bulletin, v. 98, p. 320–329.

Hunt, C. B., and Mabey, D. R., 1966, Stratigraphy and structure, Death Valley, California: U.S. Geological Survey Professional Paper 275, 172 p.

McAllister, J. F., 1971, Preliminary geologic map of the Funeral Mountains in the Ryan Quadrangle, Death Valley region, Inyo County, California: U.S. Geological Survey Open-File Report, scale 1:62,500.

—— , 1974, Silurian, Devonian, and Mississippian Formations of the Funeral Mountains in the Ryan Quadrangle, Death Valley region, California: U.S. Geological Survey Bulletin 1386, 35 p.

Noble, L. F., and Wright, L. A., 1954, Geology of the central and southern Death Valley region, California, *in* Jahns, R. H., ed., Geology of southern California: California Division of Mines and Geology Bulletin 170, p. 143–160.

Platt, L. B., 1985, Geologic map of the Hawkins Quadrangle, Bannock County, Idaho: U.S. Geological Survey Miscellaneous Field Studies Map MF-1812, scale 1:24,000.

Reynolds, M. W., Wright, L. A., and Troxel, B. W., 1986, Geometry and chronology of late Cenozoic detachment faulting, Funeral and Grapevine Mountains, Death Valley, California: Geological Society of America Abstracts with Programs, v. 18, p. 175.

Royse, F., 1983, Extensional faults and folds in the foreland thrust belt, Utah, Wyoming, Idaho: Geological Society of America Abstracts with Programs, v. 15, p. 295.

Royse, F., Warner, M. A., and Reese, D. L., 1975, Thrust belt structural geometry and related stratigraphic problems, Wyoming, Idaho, and northern Utah, *in* Bolyard, D. W., ed., Deep drilling frontiers in the Central Rocky Mountains: Denver, Colorado, Rocky Mountain Association of Geologists.

Stewart, H. J., 1970, Upper Precambrian and Lower Cambrian strata in the southern Great Basin, California and Nevada: U.S. Geological Survey Professional Paper 620, 206 p.

Troxel, B. W., and Wright, L. A., 1989, Geologic map of the central and northern Funeral Mountains, Death Valley region, southern California: U.S. Geological Survey Open-File Report 89-348, scale 1:48,000.

Wernicke, B., and Burchfiel, B. C., 1982, Modes of extensional tectonics: Journal of Structural Geologists, v. 104, p. 177–182.

Wernicke, B., Guth, P. L., and Axen, G. J., 1984, Tertiary extensional tectonics in the Sevier thrust belt of southern Nevada, *in* Lintz, J. P., Jr., ed., Western geological excursions, volume 4: Reno, University of Nevada Mackay School of Mines, p. 473–510.

Wernicke, B., Walker, D. J., and Baufait, M. S., 1985, Structural discordance between Neogene detachments and frontal Sevier thrusts, central Mormon Mountains, southern Nevada: Tectonics, v. 4, no. 2, p. 213–246.

Wright, L. A., and Troxel, B. W., 1970, Summary of regional evidence for right-lateral displacement in the western Great Basin; Discussion: Geological Society of America Bulletin, v. 81, p. 2167–2174.

—— , 1981, Geology of the northern half of the Confidence Hills 15-minute Quadrangle, Death Valley region, eastern California; The area of the Amargosa chaos: California Division of Mines and Geology Map Sheet 34, scale 1:24,000, 31 p.

MANUSCRIPT ACCEPTED BY THE SOCIETY AUGUST 21, 1989

Geological Society of America
Memoir 176
1990

Chapter 15

Late Cenozoic extensional and compressional tectonism in the southern and western Avawatz Mountains, southeastern California

Jon E. Spencer*
Department of Earth, Atmospheric, and Planetary Sciences, Massachusetts Institute of Technology, Cambridge, Massachusetts 02139

ABSTRACT

The late Cenozoic geologic history of the Avawatz Mountains reflects two successive tectonic settings. Middle Miocene high-angle normal faulting along the northwest-striking Arrastre Spring fault was associated with deposition of a thick clastic sequence that forms the lower part of the Avawatz Formation. Conglomerate and sedimentary breccia in the lower part of the Avawatz Formation were shed southwestward across the fault from a presently unrecognized terrane to the east of the Avawatz Mountains. Faulting and conglomerate deposition occurred largely between 21 and 12 Ma. This period of faulting and sedimentation is interpreted as reflecting the regional Miocene extensional tectonic setting of the southern Basin and Range Province and Mojave Desert region.

North-south shortening and associated folding and southward tilting of the largely Miocene Avawatz Formation occurred in late Miocene to Pliocene time. Interaction between the Garlock and Death Valley faults at their zone of intersection on the north flank of the Avawatz Mountains is the inferred cause of north-south compression and resultant folding and tilting of the Avawatz Formation. Continued movement on the two intersecting faults led to development of an increasingly arcuate reverse-fault system along the north and east flanks of the Avawatz Mountains. Quaternary deformation is characterized by northeast-directed reverse faulting, southwestward tilting, rapid uplift of the Avawatz Mountains, and probable counterclockwise rotation of faults and fault blocks in the northwestern Avawatz Mountains at the east end of the Garlock fault.

INTRODUCTION

The Avawatz Mountains are located at the eastern end of the active, left-slip Garlock fault in southeastern California. The Garlock fault separates the Sierra Nevada and an actively extending part of the Basin and Range Province to the north from the relatively inactive and topographically subdued Mojave block to the south (e.g., Davis and Burchfiel, 1973; Fig. 1). Part of the Garlock fault zone and the right-slip Death Valley fault zone

intersect on the north flank of the Avawatz Mountains where they merge to form a zone of northeast-vergent reverse faults. Uplift of the Avawatz Mountains due to movement on this reverse-fault system is largely responsible for the present morphology of the range.

The complex late Cenozoic geologic history of the Avawatz Mountains can be separated into two intervals: an earlier, largely middle Miocene period of high-angle normal faulting and associated sedimentation and a later period of shortening related to interaction of the Garlock and Death Valley fault zones. This study outlines and clarifies the nature and timing of these two periods of deformation and sedimentation.

---

*Present address: Arizona Geological Survey, 845 N. Park Avenue, Tucson, Arizona 85719.

Spencer, J. E., 1990, Late Cenozoic extensional and compressional tectonism in the southern and western Avawatz Mountains, southeastern California, *in* Wernicke, B. P., ed., Basin and Range extensional tectonics near the latitude of Las Vegas, Nevada: Boulder, Colorado, Geological Society of America Memoir 176.

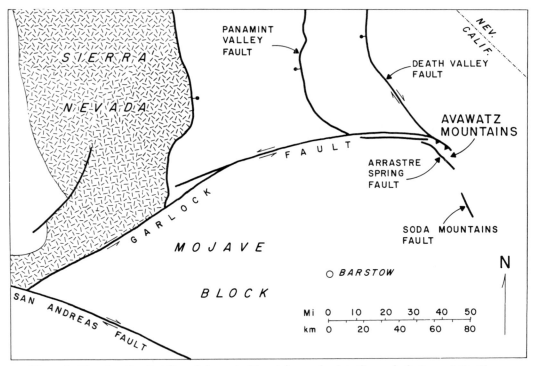

Figure 1. Map showing location of Avawatz Mountains, major late Cenozoic faults, and the Sierra Nevada. The topographically subdued Mojave block is bounded by the Garlock fault, the San Andreas fault, and a poorly defined eastern boundary that is commonly defined as extending southeastward from the Avawatz Mountains.

Middle Miocene extensional tectonism

The high-angle, northwest-striking Arrastre Spring fault in the southern and western Avawatz Mountains (Fig. 2) juxtaposes primarily Mesozoic plutonic rocks and older metamorphic rocks to the northeast with Mesozoic metavolcanic and Tertiary sedimentary rocks to the southwest. Coarse boulder conglomerate and sedimentary breccia, which now form much of the lower part of the Avawatz Formation, were shed southwestward across the fault and eventually buried it. The middle Miocene conglomerate was derived from a terrane that was buried by Quaternary deposits east of the Avawatz Mountains or displaced by faulting. K-Ar dates indicate that sedimentation directly west of the Arrastre Spring fault zone began at approximately 21 Ma and that faulting had largely ended by 13 to 12 Ma. Offset markers, fault dip, patterns of Miocene sediment dispersal, and differences in exposed structural level across the fault indicate that significant southwest-side-down displacement occurred on the Arrastre Spring fault zone during middle Miocene time. If there is any pre–middle Miocene strike slip, its magnitude is not well constrained but is probably less than about 15 km, as indicated by similar pink Mesozoic granites on both sides of the fault.

Late Miocene to Quaternary compressional tectonism

Late Cenozoic displacement on the Garlock fault is the result of extension on the north side of the fault and is of progres-

sively greater magnitude to the west. Approximately 50 to 60 km of displacement has occurred on the central Garlock fault (Smith, 1962; Smith and Ketner, 1970), and displacement of comparable magnitude is predicted to have occurred on the eastern Garlock fault near the Avawatz Mountains (Davis and Burchfiel, 1973). The northern part of the Garlock fault zone and the active, northwest-striking, right-slip Death Valley fault zone meet at the north flank of the Avawatz Mountains, where they merge to form an arcuate system of approximately northeast-vergent reverse faults (Fig. 2). This reverse-fault system consists primarily of two faults: the previously recognized eastern Mule Spring fault, which juxtaposes dissimilar rock types (Troxel and Butler, 1979; Brady and Troxel, 1981), and the Old Mormon Spring fault, which juxtaposes co-magmatic plutonic rocks. Displacement on the eastern Mule Spring fault reflects the combined displacements of the northern part of the Garlock fault zone and the Death Valley fault zone. Displacement on the Old Mormon Spring fault is probably much less than on the eastern Mule Spring fault and appears to be largely or entirely Quaternary in age.

The entire lower half of the Avawatz Formation is tilted 35 to 55 degrees to the south; underlying basement on both sides of the Arrastre Spring fault must be tilted as well. Sedimentary rocks in the upper part of the Avawatz Formation are broadly folded about east-trending axes. Tilting and folding of the Avawatz Formation, which occurred well after movement had ended on the Arrastre Spring fault, are interpreted as broadly synchronous phenomena that occurred during deposition of the uppermost part of the Avawatz Formation. The southwest dip of Quaternary strata along the southwest flank of the Avawatz Mountains, along with the physiography of the range and the form and nature of the Mule Spring and Old Mormon Spring faults, indicates that the Avawatz Mountains are undergoing uplift and southwestward tilting. The older period of southward tilting was probably related to north-vergent thrusting on an ancestral, more east-trending Mule Spring fault, and occurred before initiation of the Old Mormon Spring fault. The direction of tilting and inferred shortening appears to have rotated 30 to 40° clockwise during the late Cenozoic and is interpreted as reflecting interactions between the Garlock and Death Valley faults.

The northernmost part of the Arrastre Spring fault is undergoing Quaternary modification and reactivation, in part as a reverse fault, in response to shortening at the Garlock–Death Valley fault intersection. Inferred counterclockwise rotation of an adjacent fault block within the eastern Garlock fault zone appears to be a response to late Cenozoic shortening and left-lateral shearing.

STRUCTURES

Mule Spring and Old Mormon Spring faults

Several subparallel faults form the Garlock fault zone in the northwestern Avawatz Mountains. The Mule Spring fault in the northern part of this fault zone marks the northernmost limit of exposures of the Jurassic Avawatz Mountains Quartz Monzodiorite, which forms most of the exposed basement in the Avawatz Mountains. The Mule Spring fault truncates the multiple exposed traces of the Death Valley fault zone and changes eastward from a steeply dipping, high-angle, dominantly strike-slip fault to an arcuate reverse fault. The transition in fault geometry and kinematics occurs at the intersection area with the Death Valley fault zone. The reverse movement on the eastern part of the Mule Spring fault thus represents the combined movements of the northern part of the Garlock fault zone and the Death Valley fault zone (Troxel and Butler, 1979; Brady and others, 1980; Brady, 1986).

None of the various rock types north of the eastern part of the Mule Spring fault are correlative with any of the rock types to the south. Hanging-wall rocks consist almost entirely of Avawatz Mountains Quartz Monzodiorite, whereas footwall rocks are composed of a variety of rock types, including strata of the Proterozoic Pahrump Group and crystalline rocks of probable Proterozoic age (Troxel and Butler, 1979). This contrast in rock types suggests that total displacement on the eastern part of the Mule Spring fault is significant.

The Old Mormon Spring fault forms the southern continuation of the Mule Spring fault (Figs. 2, 3; Table 1). Quaternary reverse movement on the Old Mormon Spring fault and the eastern part of the Mule Spring fault is responsible for the rapid Quaternary uplift of the Avawatz Mountains and formation of

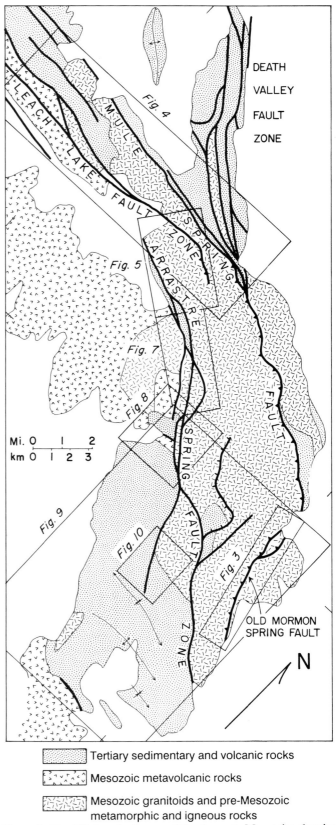

Figure 2. Simplified geologic map of the Avawatz Mountains showing major faults, rock types, and location of map figures.

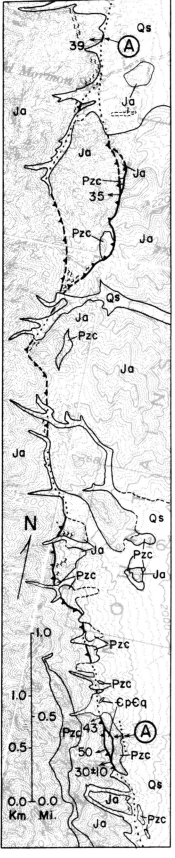

the steep, arcuate mountain face on the north and east flanks of the range. The Old Mormon Spring and Mule Spring faults have significant differences; the Old Mormon Spring fault strikes N5°W to N15°W and juxtaposes identical footwall and hanging-wall rock types, whereas the Mule Spring fault strikes N50°W to N60°W and juxtaposes completely dissimilar rock types. It therefore seems likely that the Mule Spring fault has larger displacement and a longer, more complex movement history than the Old Mormon Spring fault, which is probably largely or entirely Quaternary in age. An inactive, southeastward continuation of the Mule Spring fault, now entirely buried beneath Quaternary alluvium east of the southern Avawatz Mountains, is inferred to have accommodated most or all of the pre-Quaternary displacement on the eastern part of the Mule Spring fault. This now-inactive

TABLE 1. MAP UNITS AND SYMBOLS FOR FIGURES 3, 5, 7, 8, AND 10 AND MAP SYMBOLS FOR FIGURE 9

Qs	Surficial deposits (Quaternary)
QTs	Fanglomerate (Quaternary to upper Tertiary)
Tas	Avawatz Formation, sandstone and siltstone facies (Pliocene and Miocene)
Tac	Avawatz Formation, conglomerate facies (Miocene)
Tx	Sedimentary breccia (Miocene)
Ts	Sandstone and conglomerate, undivided (Miocene)
Tv	Volcanic rocks (Miocene)
Tsv	Sedimentary and volcanic rocks, undivided (Miocene)
Mzv	Metavolcanic rocks (Mesozoic)
Mzg	Granitic rocks, undivided (Mesozoic)
Ja	Avawatz Mountains Quartz Monzodiorite (Jurassic)
J℞qm	Quartz Monzonite (Jurassic or Triassic)
J℞g	Granites of Avawatz Peak (Jurassic or Triassic)
PℙPb	Bird Spring Formation (Permian and Pennsylvanian)
Pzc	Calcite and dolomite marble (Paleozoic)
€p€q	Quartzite (Cambrian or Proterozoic)

Faults--dashed where approximately located, dotted where buried and inferred. Arrow indicates dip

Reverse fault

Low-angle normal fault

Fault, sense of movement unspecified

Strike and dip of beds

30 Inclined

49 Overturned

Fold axes, showing plunge

Anticline

Syncline

Crushed rock and fault gouge

1877—ₓ K-Ar sample locality

Figure 3. Geologic map of the Old Mormon Spring fault. Quaternary alluvial fan deposits are clearly faulted at two locations, both designated "A." Map data are from Spencer (1990). See Table 1 for map units and Figure 2 for location.

segment of the Mule Spring fault possibly truncates or connects to one or both of two hypothetical, inactive, buried faults: the eastern extension of the Garlock fault (Davis and Burchfiel, 1973; see also Plescia and Henyey, 1982) or the southeastern extension of the Death Valley fault (Brady, 1984).

Denning Spring fault block

The Leach Lake fault zone consists of anastomosing, dominantly strike-slip faults that together form the southern part of the eastern Garlock fault zone (Figs. 2, 4). The most active faults within the Leach Lake fault zone converge eastward in the northwestern Avawatz Mountains into a single fault (Clark, 1973; Brady, 1986) that bends abruptly southeastward (location A on Fig. 5) and dies out into a wide zone of crushed rock and discontinuous reverse faults (Fig. 5). The Denning Spring fault block, composed primarily of Avawatz Mountains Quartz Monzodiorite, is bounded to the south by the Leach Lake fault zone and to the north by the western part of the Mule Spring fault. At the east end of the Denning Spring fault block is a 6.5-km-long

pendant of Paleozoic marble that extends eastward into the main fault block of the Avawatz Mountains (Fig. 4). Thus, the Denning Spring fault block is structurally connected to the Avawatz Mountains through a narrow strip of Paleozoic marble less than 1 km wide.

A strong crystalloblastic foliation of probable Late Cretaceous age (Spencer, 1987) is progressively more strongly developed westward within Avawatz Mountains Quartz Monzodiorite in the Denning Spring fault block (Fig. 4). The foliation strikes eastward, generally dips steeply to the south, and is locally folded about east-trending axes (Fig. 6). Biotite from foliated Avawatz Mountains Quartz Monzodiorite yielded an anomalously young K-Ar date of 46 Ma (Spencer, 1987), which suggests that the western end of the belt of exposed pre-Tertiary rocks in the Denning Spring fault block was at an anomalously great temperature and structural depth in early Tertiary time.

The foliation and the elongate, east-west trend of the Paleozoic marble pendant together define an east-trending structural grain in the Denning Spring fault block. This orientation contrasts with that of the main Avawatz Mountains fault block, in which

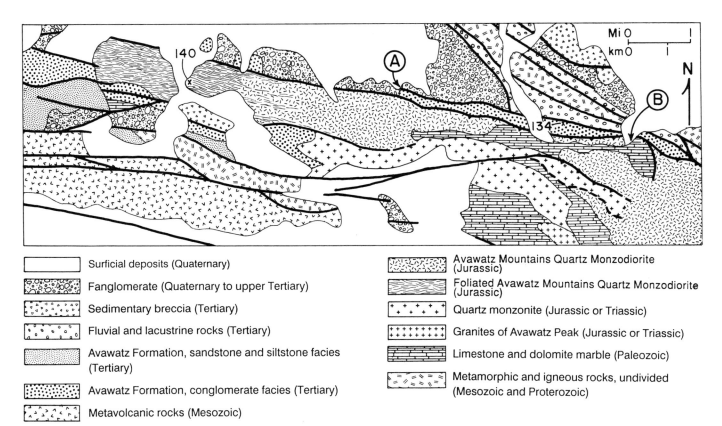

☐	Surficial deposits (Quaternary)	
▨	Fanglomerate (Quaternary to upper Tertiary)	
▨	Sedimentary breccia (Tertiary)	
▨	Fluvial and lacustrine rocks (Tertiary)	
▨	Avawatz Formation, sandstone and siltstone facies (Tertiary)	
▨	Avawatz Formation, conglomerate facies (Tertiary)	
▨	Metavolcanic rocks (Mesozoic)	

▨	Avawatz Mountains Quartz Monzodiorite (Jurassic)	
▨	Foliated Avawatz Mountains Quartz Monzodiorite (Jurassic)	
▨	Quartz monzonite (Jurassic or Triassic)	
▨	Granites of Avawatz Peak (Jurassic or Triassic)	
▨	Limestone and dolomite marble (Paleozoic)	
▨	Metamorphic and igneous rocks, undivided (Mesozoic and Proterozoic)	

Figure 4. Simplified geologic map of the eastern end of the Garlock fault zone. Fault at location A, which lies just north of the parallel Mule Spring fault, is the only fault in this part of the Garlock fault zone that can have the tens of kilometers of displacement proposed for the eastern Garlock fault by Davis and Burchfiel (1973). Location B is the eastern part of an elongate pendant of Paleozoic carbonate rock that extends westward from the main Avawatz Mountains fault block into the Denning Spring fault block and establishes a structural connection between the two. Two K-Ar sample localities (dates listed in Table 2) are also shown. Map data are from Spencer (1981 and unpublished) and Brady (1986). See Figure 2 for location.

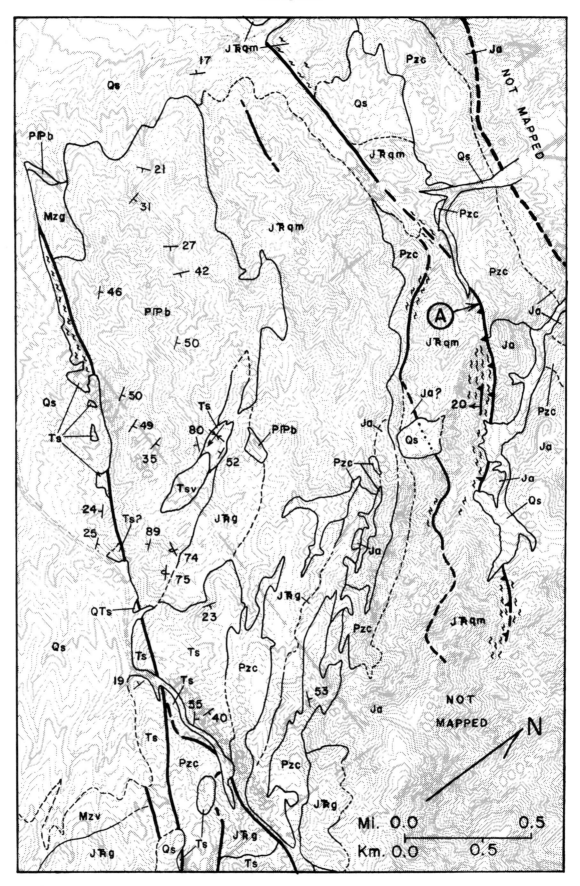

Paleozoic and upper Proterozoic metasedimentary rocks, forming roof pendants in the Mesozoic plutonic complex, are elongate in a northwest-southeast direction and contain bedding and foliation that commonly strike northwest. The contrast in the orientation of the structural grain between the Denning Spring fault block and the main fault block in the Avawatz Mountains suggests that the Denning Spring fault block has been rotated 30 to 50 degrees in a counterclockwise sense during left shear within the Garlock fault zone. Reconnaissance paleomagnetic data (Lisa Kanter, written communication, 1981) from an east-trending, 12-Ma dike within the Denning Spring fault block (Table 2; sample location 140 in Fig. 4) suggest that the fault block has been tilted northward and rotated in a counterclockwise direction.

Conglomerate containing a distinctive clast suite that includes abundant pink granitoid rocks and sparse hornblendite and ptygmatic-fold-bearing gneiss is exposed within and just north of the Denning Spring fault block (Avawatz Formation in Fig. 4). The conglomerate and overlying sandstone and siltstone were named the Military Canyon formation by Brady (1986). Conglomerate-clast compositions are very similar to those in the middle Miocene conglomerate facies of the Avawatz Formation in the southwestern Avawatz Mountains, and the two formations are probably correlative (see also Brady, 1984). Termination of the Leach Lake fault zone and the presence of the distinctive Avawatz Formation conglomerate on both sides of the western Mule Spring fault indicate that major post–middle Miocene displacement on the Garlock fault zone can only have occurred on the northernmost fault within the easternmost part of the Garlock fault zone (fault at location A in Fig. 4).

Arrastre Spring fault

Sense and amount of displacement. The Arrastre Spring fault forms a narrow anastomosing fault zone in the northwestern Avawatz Mountains (Figs. 5, 7, 8) that branches southeastward into east and west segments that bound a large fault block (Fig. 9), referred to here as the southern Avawatz fault block. Plutonic and metamorphic rocks that make up most of the Avawatz Mountains represent deeper structural levels than the Mesozoic metavolcanic rocks widely exposed west of the northern part of the Arrastre Spring fault (Fig. 2). The contrast in inferred structural levels represented by these different rock types suggests that southwest-side-down movement has occurred on the Arrastre Spring fault (see also Davis, 1977). The granites of Avawatz Peak form pendants and inclusions within the younger Avawatz Mountains Quartz Monzodiorite and are therefore better pre-

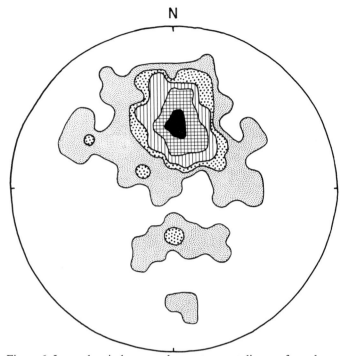

Figure 6. Lower-hemisphere equal-area stereonet diagram for poles to foliation in Avawatz Mountains Quartz Monzodiorite in eastern part of Denning Spring fault block (see Fig. 4). Foliation is east striking and is folded about east-trending axes. The foliation and the elongate carbonate pendant in the eastern part of the Denning Spring fault block define an east-trending, pre-Tertiary structural grain within the fault block. Contour intervals are 1, 3, 5, 10, and 15 points per 1 percent area (120 points represented).

served at higher structural levels. These granites are widely preserved within the southern Avawatz fault block and are juxtaposed across the east branch of the fault with structurally deeper Avawatz Mountains Quartz Monzodiorite, suggesting southwest-side-down movement on the east branch of the fault (Fig. 9). Miocene conglomerate forming most of the lower part of the Avawatz Formation is stratigraphically thicker on the southwest side of the west branch of the Arrastre Spring fault and onlaps eastward across the southern Avawatz fault block, further indicating southwest-side-down movement (Figs. 9, 10).

The east branch of the Arrastre Spring fault separates two northwest-striking, southwest-dipping homoclinal stratigraphic sequences extending from upper Proterozoic Stirling Quartzite to the Crystal Pass Member of the Devonian Sultan Limestone (Spencer, 1981). The two homoclines are approximately in alignment at present (Fig. 9). Due to the complex distribution of pre-Mesozoic rock types in detail, precise reconstruction does not seem possible. The general distribution of rock types indicates, however, that total strike slip (left or right) or dip slip on the east branch of the Arrastre Spring fault was not more than approximately 2 km.

The west branch of the Arrastre Spring fault extends southward into Miocene conglomerates of the Avawatz Formation. A

Figure 5. Geologic map of the northern part of the Arrastre Spring fault and the eastern end of the Leach Lake fault zone. Location A marks southward deflection of eastern Leach Lake fault and eastward transition from strike-slip to reverse fault. Map data are from Spencer (1981 and unpublished). See Table 1 for map units and Figure 2 for location.

TABLE 2. K-Ar GEOCHRONOLOGIC DATA, AVAWATZ MOUNTAINS, CALIFORNIA*

Sample Number	Latitude (N)	Longitude (W)	Material Dated	Rock type	$K_2O(1)$ (%)	$K_2O(2)$ (%)	$^{40}Ar_{rad}$ ($\times 10^{-11}$ mol/gm)	Ar_{rad} (%)	Date (Ma)
Avawatz Formation									
759C	35°26'46"	116°18'47"	biotite	tuff	6.11	6.14	51.4372	14.2	57.4 ± 0.8
759F	35°26'46"	116°18'47"	biotite	tuff	6.25	6.26	44.3526	8.3	48.6 ± 1.2
1877	35°30'16"	116°20'27"	biotite	tuff	6.82	6.88	20.9151	26.4	20.9 ± 0.2
Volcanic rocks west of Avawatz Peak									
1859	35°30'45"	116°29'09"	whole rock	tuff	3.24	3.36	5.7168	70.8	12.0 ± 0.1
1861	35°31'26"	116°20'45"	whole rock	flow	2.421	2.426	4.5948	68.3	13.1 ± 0.1
Clasts in Avawatz Formation									
134	35°36'12"	116°24'12"	biotite	gneiss	9.13	9.16	158.288	91.6	116.4 ± 0.7
738	35°27'51"	116°18'24"	hornblende	hornblendite	0.692	0.702	28.6098	89.5	264.7 ± 1.6
902	35°23'48"	116°18'20"	white mica	sedimentary breccia	9.08	9.11	200.217	82.7	146.7 ± 0.9
1209	35°26'45"	116°17'16"	hornblende	hornblendite	0.486	0.479	28.1797	57.8	365.9 ± 3.1
Intrusive rocks									
140	35°36'05"	116°30'45"	whole rock	dike	3.29	3.29	5.4514	27.5	11.9 ± 0.6
							5.8750	29.1	

*All samples are located on figures 4, 8, and 9. Can you find them?

Note: Date calculation based on decay and abundance constants given by Steiger and Jager (1977). Error in potassium analysis is either sample standard deviation of K_2O analysis or 0.5%, whichever is greater. Error in calculated ate for samples with a single argon extraction determined by method of Cox and Dalrymple (1967) assuming a standard deviation of 0.3% for tracer calibration. Error in calculated date for multiple argon extractions (samples 140 and 1877) is average analytical precision of individual analyses or is standard deviation of multiple dates, whichever is larger. Potassium was measured by flame photometry with a lithium internal standard, and was done by B. Lai, D. Vivit, and M. Taylor. Two analyses were done for each sample. Argon measurements were made using standard techniques of isotope dilution. Argon extractions and analyses done by J. Spencer and E. Sims at the U.S. Geological Survey, Menlo Park, California, in 1980 and 1981.

distinctive sequence of three south-dipping sedimentary breccia sheets within the conglomerate is offset by the fault and has a stratigraphic throw of 500 to 750 m (Fig. 10). The west branch of the Arrastre Spring fault dies out upward into conglomeratic sandstone in the upper part of the conglomerate facies, and the unfaulted, overlying sandstone, as well as underlying strata, are tilted 35 to 50 degrees to the south-southwest. Thus, the offset breccia sheets were approximately horizontal at the time of fault offset, and the stratigraphic throw of the breccia sheets represents original dip slip. The amount and sense of horizontal displacement on the west branch of the Arrastre Spring fault are poorly constrained. The pink, medium- to coarse-grained granites of Avawatz Peak, exposed on both sides of both branches of the Avawatz Spring fault, are probably correlative. The distribution of these granites suggests that total horizontal displacement on the west branch of the Arrastre Spring fault is less than approximately 15 km and could be negligible.

Fault dip. The dip of the west branch of the Arrastre Spring fault was determined at two locations where the fault is well exposed. At these locations the fault dips 65 to 75 degrees to the southwest, and beds in the Avawatz Formation dip 35 to 50

degrees to the south-southwest. Restoration of bedding to gently southwest to horizontal dips slightly decreases the dip of the fault.

In the northwestern Avawatz Mountains the Arrastre Spring fault is characterized by multiple anastomosing traces that curve westward toward the northwest where they project into the Garlock fault zone (Figs. 5, 7, 8). Outcrop patterns indicate that the faults are generally steep with both northeast and southwest dips. At one location, the southwesternmost fault in the fault zone is well exposed on a cliff face where it dips 26 degrees to the northeast (location A in Fig. 7). Footwall rocks include a small patch of conglomerate of probable Quaternary or late Tertiary age. The young reverse displacement at this location is probably the result of late Cenozoic, northeast-southwest compression associated with intersection of the Garlock and Death Valley fault zones.

Age of movement. Dominantly conglomeratic strata of the lower part of the Avawatz Formation were initially deposited on the southwest side of the Arrastre Spring fault and lap eastward across the west branch of the fault and onto the southern Avawatz fault block (Figs. 9, 10). Basal sandstone and local siltstone on the southwest side of the fault (Fig. 8) are interpreted to have

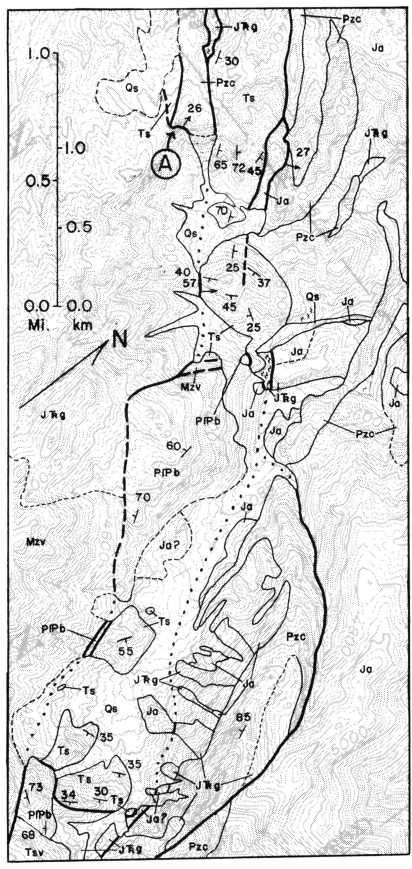

Figure 7. Geologic map of the Arrastre Spring fault zone in the vicinity of upper Sheep Creek. Paleozoic carbonate rocks are thrust southwestward over Quaternary or uppermost Tertiary fanglomerate (outcrop area too small to show on map) and underlying granite at location A. Map data are from Spencer (1981). See Table 1 for map units and Figure 2 for location.

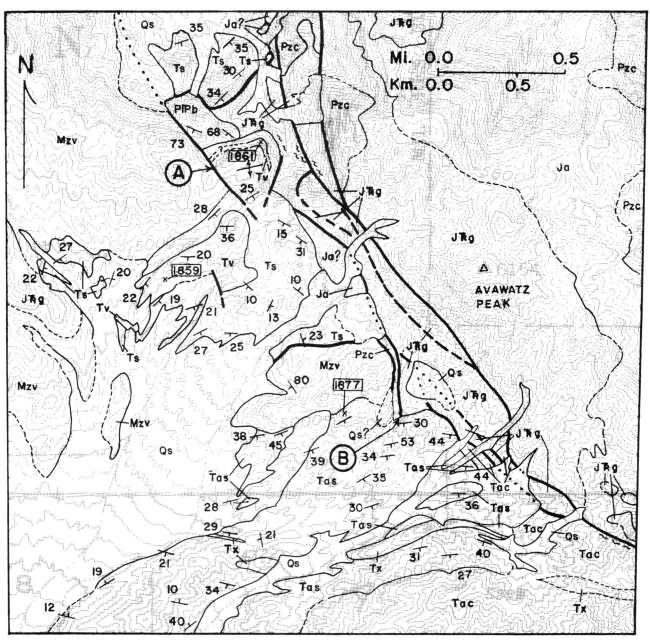

Figure 8. Geologic map of area west and south of Avawatz Peak. Localities A and B are explained in text. Map data are from Spencer (1981 and 1990). See Table 1 for map units and Figure 2 for location.

been deposited early during the movement history of the Arrastre Spring fault and associated sedimentary basin formation. A white, poorly consolidated tuff bed near the base of the section (sample location 1877 in Figs. 8, 9) yielded a biotite K-Ar date of 20.9 ± 0.2 Ma (Table 2). The basal strata overlap a splay of the Arrastre Spring fault (location B in Fig. 8), and thus some fault movement had occurred by this time. However, the great vertical relief that led to deposition of thousands of meters of coarse conglomerate and sedimentary breccia in the Avawatz Formation had not developed; most dip slip occurred after 21 Ma.

West of Avawatz Peak, the only trace of the Arrastre Spring fault that juxtaposes dissimilar rock types is overlapped by a sequence of Miocene sandstone, volcanic rocks, and sparse conglomerate that is only slightly offset by the fault (location A in Fig. 8). The sequence also overlaps crushed rocks adjacent to another fault trace. Two samples of the volcanic rocks yielded whole-rock K-Ar dates of 12.0 ± 0.1 and 13.1 ± 0.1 Ma (Table 2; Fig. 8), indicating that almost all fault movement on this trace had ended by this time.

Coarse conglomerate in the Avawatz Formation grades up-

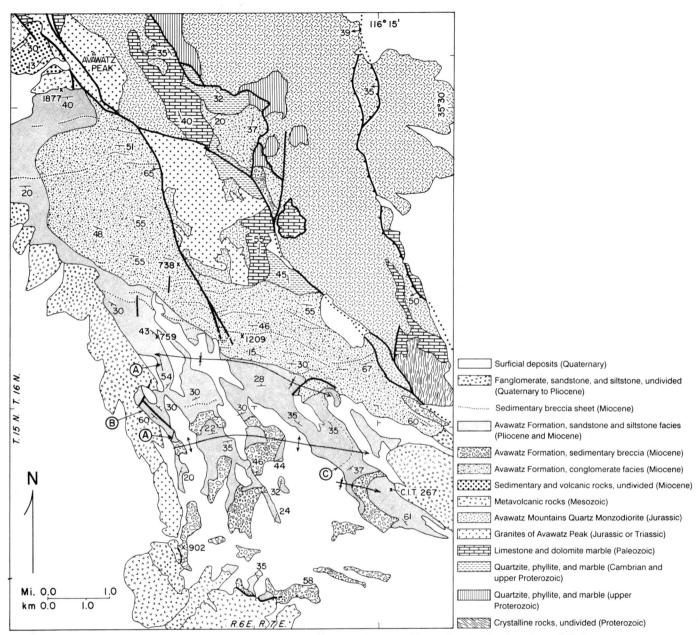

Figure 9. Simplified geologic map of the southern Avawatz Mountains showing locations of K-Ar samples listed in Table 2. Location of California Institute of Technology (C.I.T.) vertebrate fossil locality 267 from Henshaw (1939) is approximate tuff-sample location for 11-Ma K-Ar date reported by Evernden and others (1964). Map data are from Spencer (1990). Localities A, B, and C are explained in text.

ward into sandstone. The west branch of the Arrastre Spring fault dies out upsection just below this conglomerate-sandstone transition (Figs. 9, 10). Stratigraphically higher sandstone and siltstone contain sheets of sedimentary breccia derived from a source different than that for clasts and breccias in the underlying conglomerate. At the time these younger sandstones and breccias were deposited, topographic relief that developed during movement on the Arrastre Spring fault, and that exerted strong control over sediment dispersal patterns, was reduced sufficiently so that other

sediment sources had become dominant. A tuff bed within sandstone in the upper part of the Avawatz Formation yielded a sanidine K-Ar date of 11.0 Ma (Evernden and others, 1964; recalculated after Dalrymple, 1979). Movement on the west branch of the Arrastre Spring fault was over well before this time.

Quaternary fault movement along the northern part of the Arrastre Spring fault (Fig. 5, location A in Fig. 7) is almost certainly unrelated to earlier Miocene displacement. This young fault movement and reactivation are probably related to move-

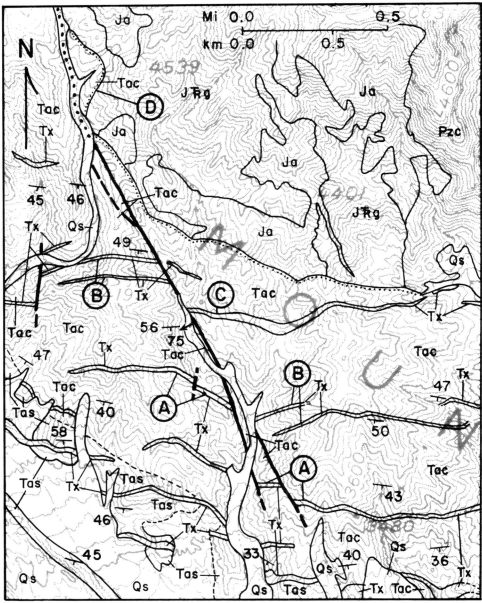

Figure 10. Geologic map of the southern termination of the west branch of the Arrastre Spring fault. A distinctive monolithologic sedimentary breccia sheet derived from white granite (designated A) and a pair of sedimentary breccia sheets derived from pink granitoid rocks (designated B) are displaced 500 to 750 m perpendicular to bedding and an unknown amount parallel to bedding. Displacement is greater for the stratigraphically lower breccia sheets, indicating that faulting and sedimentation were synchronous. Paired dotted and thin solid lines indicate depositional base of Avawatz Formation. Eastward-thinning wedge of conglomerate below breccia sheet C records onlapping of conglomerate onto upthrown footwall block. Exposure of conglomerate at location D is a filled paleocanyon in the footwall block. Map data are from Spencer (1990). See Table 1 for map units and Figure 2 for location.

ment on the active Garlock fault and compression generated at its intersection with the Death Valley fault zone. In addition, juxtaposition of Avawatz Formation strata on the east side of the east branch of the Arrastre Spring fault with pre-Tertiary rocks on the west side (Fig. 9) may be a result of possible Pliocene or Quaternary reverse faulting along this part of the Arrastre Spring fault. Reverse faulting also possibly displaced Paleozoic rocks north-

eastward over Avawatz Formation strata north of the east branch of the Arrastre Spring fault (this contact is not shown as a fault on Fig. 9 because its nature is not clear).

Low-angle faults

Segments of a low- to moderate-angle fault northeast of the east branch of the Arrastre Spring fault form a southwest-dipping fault zone with probable normal displacement. Along most of its trace, the fault, or basal fault in the fault zone, places Tertiary, Paleozoic, and uppermost Proterozoic metasedimentary rocks over Avawatz Mountains Quartz Monzodiorite and Proterozoic metasedimentary rocks generally of uncertain affinity (Fig. 9). The fault projects northwestward into the Mesozoic plutonic complex and has not been recognized in major canyons in the northern Avawatz Mountains. Because it places structurally higher rocks, including Miocene conglomerate, over structurally deeper plutonic rocks, it is interpreted to be a normal fault. The widespread presence of Avawatz Mountains Quartz Monzodiorite in both hanging-wall and footwall blocks, local juxtaposition of similar Proterozoic metasedimentary rocks, and apparent termination of the fault within the plutonic complex indicate that total displacement is not more than a few kilometers. The fault cuts conglomerates of the Avawatz Formation and is offset by the east branch of the Arrestre Spring fault; this suggests that fault movement occurred late during the Miocene movement history of the Arrastre Spring fault.

AVAWATZ FORMATION

The Avawatz Formation consists of thousands of meters of clastic sedimentary rocks in the southern Avawatz Mountains (Henshaw, 1939). Although previously broken into members by Henshaw (1939) and Spencer (1981), all member designations are dropped here because lateral facies changes and complex deformation obscure approximate time-stratigraphic contacts. The formation is here divided into a conglomerate and a sandstone and siltstone facies. The lowermost and uppermost parts of the formation are composed entirely of the sandstone and siltstone facies, whereas the middle part is composed of the conglomerate facies that grades laterally westward into the sandstone and siltstone facies (Fig. 9). For convenience, the Avawatz Formation is divided into lower and upper parts; the upper part includes all sandstone and siltstone-facies rocks that stratigraphically overlie conglomerate-facies rocks. Sedimentary breccias representing catastrophic debris avalanches (e.g., Shreve, 1968; Krieger, 1977) are common throughout the Avawatz Formation (e.g., Jahns and Engel, 1949).

Lower Avawatz Formation

Sandstone forms the lowermost part of the Avawatz Formation only in the area west of the Arrestre Spring fault (Figs. 8, 9). In this area, conglomerate is restricted to a small area adjacent to the Arrastre Spring fault. Conglomerate increases in abundance upsection and transgresses westward over the sandstone facies in the basal 1,000 m of the Avawatz Formation. The massive to poorly bedded, cobble to boulder conglomerate consistently grades westward into poorly sorted arkosic sandstone and silty sandstone. The conglomerate facies onlaps eastward across the southern Avawatz fault block (Fig. 10) and also rests disconformably on pre-Tertiary rocks northeast of the eastern branch of the Arrastre Spring fault (Fig. 9). The distribution of facies and

the thickness changes across the west branch of the Arrastre Spring fault indicate that southwest-side-down movement on the Arrestre Spring fault was at least in part responsible for topographic relief that controlled facies and thickness distributions during deposition of the lower part of the Avawatz Formation.

The composition of conglomerate clasts and rock fragments in sedimentary breccia sheets reflects the composition of the uplifted source area. Conglomerate clasts are typically subrounded to subangular and 4 to 80 cm in diameter, and are locally as large as 3 m. Cobble counts indicate that the clast composition of the uppermost part of the conglomerate is approximately as follows: 30 percent medium- to coarse-grained, equigranular, leucocratic, pink, biotite granitoid rocks, 25 percent medium-grained mafic granitoid rocks, some of which resemble Avawatz Mountains Quartz Monzodiorite; 15 percent other granitoid rocks; 10 percent Mesozoic metavolcanic rocks; 6 percent medium-grained biotite-quartz-feldspar gneiss; 3 percent metacarbonate and quartzite; 1 percent medium- to coarse-grained hornblendite; and 10 percent undivided, generally epidote-bearing metamorphic rocks. At lower stratigraphic levels, mafic granitoid and metavolcanic rocks are less abundant, and pink granitoid rocks are more abundant.

Clasts and breccia fragments in the Avawatz Formation do not generally resemble pre-Tertiary basement in the Avawatz Mountains. Clasts of Avawatz Mountains Quartz Monzodiorite, the dominant rock type in the Avawatz Mountains, are poorly represented in the Avawatz Formation. Most of the sedimentary breccias are composed of pink granitoid rocks. The granites of Avawatz Peak superficially resemble the abundant pink granitoid clasts and breccia fragments, but modal mineral analyses of basement and clast samples indicate that most clasts are dissimilar to local basement (Fig. 11). Distinctive hornblendite clasts, lo-

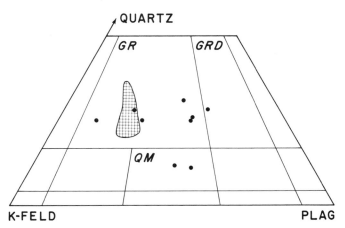

Figure 11. Modal mineralogy of conglomerate clasts and breccia fragments derived from pink granitoid rocks (dots) and field defined by 11 samples of the granites of Avawatz Peak (cross-hatch). Clasts and breccia fragments are dissimilar to exposed bedrock in the Avawatz Mountains. The clast source area has not been recognized. Each analysis represents at least 600 quartz and feldspar point counts from a stained rock slab. Estimated 2 sigma error for each sample is less than ±4 percent (Van der Plas and Tobi, 1965). GR = granite, GRD = granodiorite, QM = quartz monzonite (classification from Streckeisen, 1973).

cally as large as 1 m, resemble no known basement in the Avawatz Mountains. Two hornblendite clasts yielded hornblende K-Ar dates of 265 and 366 Ma (Table 1). In contrast, seven samples from widely spaced localities in the 175-Ma (DeWitt and others, 1984) Avawatz Mountains Quartz Monzodiorite yielded hornblende K-Ar dates of 77 to 176 Ma (Spencer, 1987). Distinctive clasts, also as large as 1 m, of complexly swirled and ptygmatically folded biotite gneiss slightly resemble weakly layered Proterozoic gneiss that locally contains ptygmatic folds at the southeastern tip of pre-Tertiary Avawatz basement exposures (Fig. 9). A K-Ar biotite date of 116 Ma from a gneiss clast (Table 1) is not greatly dissimilar to a 96-Ma K-Ar biotite date from the basement gneiss (Spencer, 1987).

In conclusion, clasts in the conglomerate facies and associated sedimentary breccias were primarily derived from basement different from that presently exposed in the Avawatz Mountains. The source area was probably directly east of the Avawatz Mountains and is now either buried, substantially displaced by faulting, or eroded away. Brady (1984) proposed that the crystalline basement of the Halloran Hills, located 15 to 20 km to the east of the southern Avawatz Mountains, was the source of the clasts. Considering the proximal character of the conglomerate facies, this is too distant to be a likely source area unless the two areas were originally adjacent and were later separated by movement on now-buried faults east of the Avawatz Mountains (Brady, 1984).

The conglomerate facies grades upsection into conglomeratic sandstone, sandstone, and in some areas, siltstone. This transition is transgressive from west to east. Transitional conglomeratic sandstone containing local channels up to 2 to 3 m deep, with lenticular, basal conglomerate beds having clasts commonly up to 50 cm in diameter, indicates a fluvial environment of deposition transitional between proximal alluvial-fan type environments and distal sand-flat and playa-fringing environments (see also Brady, 1984). The transition from conglomerate to sandstone deposition occurred during and after termination of movement on the west branch of the Arrastre Spring fault. The transition is broadly interpreted to reflect termination of movement on the Arrastre Spring fault and erosional destruction or tectonic displacement of a mountainous area to the east that had been the source of debris in the conglomerate facies.

Upper Avawatz Formation

The upper part of the Avawatz Formation is composed of sandstone and less abundant, locally gypsiferous siltstone, sedimentary breccia, conglomerate, and thin, unwelded tuff beds. Conglomerate-clast compositions change upsection to reflect increasingly significant contributions from Mesozoic metavolcanic and Paleozoic carbonate rocks (see also Lamey, 1945). Conglomeratic rocks in the uppermost Avawatz Formation are most abundant adjacent to the Red Pass Range at the southern margin of the area of Avawatz Formation exposures. The Red Pass Range is composed primarily of Mesozoic metavolcanic rocks and is the likely source for metavolcanic clasts in the adjacent upper part of the Avawatz Formation.

Areally extensive sedimentary breccia sheets—10 m to perhaps 100 m thick and composed of variably shattered metacarbonate rocks—form many of the hills and ridges in the southernmost Avawatz Mountains. Permian fusilinids within the carbonate, and the lithology, indicate that the breccias were derived primarily from the Pennsylvanian-Permian Bird Spring Formation (Lamey, 1945; Grose, 1959). Directly underlying some of the carbonate breccias are discontinuous breccia sheets and lenses of variably mixed metavolcanic rocks, argillite, local quartzite, and leucocratic, porphyritic granitoid rocks. Massive and brecciated magnetite is associated with the argillite and granitoid rocks and forms replacements and brecciated lenses within the limestone. Most of an estimated 6 million tons of high-grade magnetite iron ore is within the lower part of the limestone breccia (Lamey, 1945). Coarse white mica from within the iron ore yielded a K-Ar date of 147 Ma (Table 2), which is interpreted as a minimum age for iron mineralization.

A white, poorly consolidated tuff bed in the upper part of the Avawatz Formation yielded K-Ar dates of 57 and 49 Ma on coarse- and fine-grained biotite, respectively (Table 2). These dates are inconsistent with the 11-Ma sanidine K-Ar date obtained by Evernden and others (1964) from a tuff bed in the upper Avawatz Formation and are inconsistent with the 21-Ma date from a tuff bed at the base of the Avawatz Formation (Table 2). The anomalously old dates are interpreted to reflect contamination of the tuff by detrital biotite that is generally coarser than the volcanic biotite; the older date from the coarse fraction reflects a greater proportion of detrital biotite.

The upper part of the Avawatz Formation, unlike the lower part, is broadly folded and contains three east-trending folds with wavelengths of 1.5 to 2 km (Fig. 9). Numerous smaller folds and faults are especially abundant near the axes of larger folds (see also Henshaw, 1939). Two high-angle (up to 90°) unconformities (locations marked A in Fig. 9) within the Avawatz Formation near the axes of two of the large folds indicate that folding was followed by erosion, which was in turn followed by continued sedimentation. A gradational contact and progressively decreasing dip upsection into older Quaternary fanglomerate (location B in Fig. 9) and local faulting of Quaternary units (Spencer, 1990) indicate that deformation continued into Quaternary time and may still be active.

East-trending axes of the large folds in the upper part of the Avawatz Formation are parallel to the strike of moderately dipping (35 to 55 degrees) bedding in most of the lower part, suggesting that folding and tilting are related. In western exposures, sandstones of the upper part of the Avawatz Formation are tilted along with underlying transitional and conglomerate-facies rocks, indicating that tilting occurred after termination of conglomerate deposition in western exposures of the conglomerate facies. Thus, both tilting of the lower part of the Avawatz Formation and folding of the upper part occurred after the transition to sandstone-facies deposition in western exposures, and both are interpreted as broadly synchronous, related deformations.

In eastern exposures, transitional strata are much thinner or are absent, and sandstone, siltstone, and tuff appear to lap eastward onto the underlying conglomerate (note trace of tuff bed C on Fig. 9). This relation suggests that some erosion of the conglomerate occurred before deposition of most of the sandstone- and siltstone-facies rocks and well before deposition of the stratigraphically higher 11-Ma tuff (the tuff K-Ar locality is approximately at location C.I.T. 267 on Fig. 9).

INTERPRETATION OF GEOLOGIC RELATIONS IN THE SOUTHERN AVAWATZ MOUNTAINS

Southwest-side-down normal displacement on the high-angle, southwest-dipping Arrastre Spring fault began shortly before deposition of sandstone, siltstone, and a 21-Ma tuff within an incipient sedimentary basin. Continued displacement produced substantial surficial relief and was associated with deposition of a sequence of coarse conglomerate and sedimentary breccia that varies in thickness from one to several kilometers. Most clastic debris was derived from a terrane east of the Avawatz Mountains that is of uncertain present location. Termination of faulting and conglomerate deposition were approximately synchronous and ended substantially before deposition of an 11-Ma tuff. Most displacement occurred before deposition of 12- to 13-Ma volcanic and sedimentary rocks across the only strand of the Arrastre Spring fault in the area west of Avawatz Peak that juxtaposes dissimilar rock types. The sense and magnitude of strike slip on the Arrastre Spring fault are poorly constrained, and strike-slip displacement is possibly negligible. If significant strike slip occurred, it must have occurred on the west branch of the Arrastre Spring fault and must predate deposition of the upper part of the conglomerate facies, which is probably several million years older than the 11-Ma tuff.

Conglomerate deposition was followed by sandstone and siltstone deposition on the south flank of the Avawatz Mountains. Metavolcanic rock clasts in sparse conglomerates were probably derived from the south where Mesozoic metavolcanic rocks are exposed in the Red Pass Range (Grose, 1959). The carbonate breccias were possibly also derived from the south but from a source closer than areas where Paleozoic rocks are presently exposed. Folding about east-trending axes and southward tilting of underlying conglomerate and older crystalline rocks of the Avawatz Mountains occurred during sandstone and siltstone deposition in the upper part of the Avawatz Formation and largely or entirely after deposition of an 11-Ma tuff. Folding is interpreted as a consequence of shortening at shallow crustal levels, between the central Avawatz Mountains and the Red Pass Range, that occurred in the hinge zone of a large flexure produced by southward tilting of the Avawatz Mountains. Quaternary uplift, exhumation, and some of the deformation of sandstone-facies rocks in the southern Avawatz Mountains reflect uplift and southwest-

ward tilting of the Avawatz Mountains in response to northeast-directed reverse faulting along the Mule Spring and Old Mormon Spring faults.

IMPLICATIONS FOR THE GARLOCK AND DEATH VALLEY FAULTS

Evidence of middle to late Cenozoic compressional deformation is not common in the Basin and Range Province. Quaternary shortening in the Avawatz Mountains, which is most spectacularly expressed by displacement on the Mule Spring and Old Mormon Spring faults and uplift of the Avawatz Mountains, is clearly a local phenomenon related to intersection of two major strike-slip faults (Brady and Troxel, 1981). It seems unlikely that late Miocene to Pliocene southward tilting of much of the Avawatz Formation and of underlying rocks, and folding of the upper part of the Avawatz Formation, were related to a completely different type of local compressional phenomenon. Tilting and folding were certainly not related to movement on the Arrastre Spring fault, which had probably been inactive for millions of years. More likely, this deformation reflects local shortening also associated with intersection of the Garlock and Death Valley faults.

The north-south direction of pre-Quaternary shortening and southward tilting contrasts with the northeast-southwest direction of Quaternary shortening and southwestward tilting, which suggests that the orientation of maximum compressive stress in the Avawatz Mountains has rotated 30 to 40 degrees in a clockwise direction. The Old Mormon Spring fault can be viewed in this context as a Quaternary manifestation of a rotating compressive-stress vector that is producing an increasingly arcuate range-front reverse-fault system. If the Death Valley fault zone extended southeastward from the northeast flank of the Avawatz Mountains to the Silver Lake area between the Halloran Hills and Soda Mountains (Brady, 1984), then termination of movement on this southern extension may have coincided with initiation of movement on the Old Mormon Spring fault. This interpretation of the kinematic and geometric evolution of the Avawatz Mountains suggests that the Garlock–Death Valley fault intersection and associated shortening influenced the structural and stratigraphic evolution of the Avawatz Mountains since the beginning of probable late Miocene folding and southward tilting of the Avawatz Formation.

Tens of kilometers of left slip on the eastern Garlock fault are indicated by offset of several geologic features (Smith, 1962; Smith and Ketner, 1970; Davis and Burchfiel, 1973). Davis and Burchfiel (1973) considered the Panamint Valley fault (Smith and others, 1968; Fig. 1) to be a possible offset equivalent of the Arrastre Spring fault. However, the Panamint Valley fault is an active fault, whereas the Arrastre Spring fault was active largely or entirely in middle Miocene time. Until evidence for middle Miocene movement on the Panamint Valley fault is recognized, correlation of the two faults should be considered highly tentative.

The Arrastre Spring and Soda Mountains (Grose, 1959) fault zones (Fig. 1) both juxtapose dominantly Mesozoic plutonic and older metamorphic rocks to the east with regions containing large exposures of Mesozoic metavolcanic rocks to the west. In contrast, the Old Mormon Spring fault, which projects toward the Soda Mountains fault zone and was thought by Grose (1959) to be correlative, juxtaposes parts of the same co-magmatic plutonic complex. It is therefore probable that the Soda Mountains fault zone was originally correlative with the Arrastre Spring fault zone, and not with the Old Mormon Spring fault, a conclusion previously reached by Davis (1977). However, Pliocene to Quaternary deformation within the Soda Mountains fault zone probably reflects right-lateral displacement along the southern continuation of the Death Valley fault zone (Cregan and Brady, 1988). It thus appears that the Soda Mountains fault zone was initially correlative with the middle Miocene Arrastre Spring fault but underwent younger deformation as part of the southern continuation of the Death Valley fault system.

CONCLUSION

The late Cenozoic geologic history of the Avawatz Mountains was dominated by two distinct tectonic regimes. Middle Miocene, high-angle normal faulting along the Arrastre Spring fault resulted in formation of a sedimentary basin in which thousands of meters of clastic sedimentary rocks accumulated. Conglomerates and sedimentary breccias of the Avawatz Formation eventually buried the Arrastre Spring fault, which became largely inactive at about the time conglomerate deposition ended. The source area for the coarse clastic debris in the lower part of the Avawatz Formation has not been recognized; it could be displaced by faulting (Brady, 1984) or buried under younger alluvial deposits east of the Avawatz Mountains.

Folding of the upper part of the Avawatz Formation and tilting of underlying strata and pre-Cenozoic basement record a dramatic change in the tectonic setting of the Avawatz Mountains. Upper Miocene and Pliocene folding and tilting is the inferred consequence of shortening at the intersection of the Garlock and Death Valley fault zones. Continued interaction between these two faults has led to clockwise rotation of the direction of tilting and shortening and to reverse movement on the Old Mormon Spring fault. Counterclockwise rotation of the Denning Spring fault block in the northwestern Avawatz Mountains and local reverse reactivation of the Arrastre Spring fault appear to reflect complex shortening and shearing near the intersection of the Garlock and Death Valley fault zones.

ACKNOWLEDGMENTS

Most of this research was part of a Ph.D. dissertation done under the supervision of B. C. Burchfiel of the Massachusetts Institute of Technology, whom I especially thank for his guidance and interest and for financial support through NSF grant EAR 77-13637. I also thank Larry Smith, Martin Feeney, Jack Collender, and Henri Wathen for assistance in the field. Bob Fleck, Elliot Sims, Jerry Von Essen, and James Saburomura are gratefully acknowledged for their assistance and advice with K-Ar dating, which was done while I was a guest worker at the Laboratory of Isotope Geochronology, U.S. Geological Survey, Menlo Park, in 1979–1980. Additional field and geochronologic data were obtained while I was a National Research Council postdoctoral Research Associate at the U.S.G.S. in Menlo Park in 1981–1982, and I thank Keith Howard for field support at that time. Finally, Roland Brady and Bennie Troxel are gratefully acknowledged for many informative discussions in the field and elsewhere.

REFERENCES CITED

Brady, R. H., III, 1984, Neogene stratigraphy of the Avawatz Mountains between the Garlock and Death Valley fault zones, southern Death Valley, California; Implications as to late Cenozoic tectonism: Sedimentary Geology, v. 38, p. 127–157.

—— , 1986, Cenozoic geology of the northern Avawatz Mountains in relation to the intersection of the Garlock and Death Valley fault zones, San Bernardino County, California [Ph.D. thesis]: Davis, University of California, 292 p.

Brady, R. H. III, and Troxel, B. W., 1981, Eastern termination of the Garlock fault in the Avawatz Mountains, San Bernardino County, California: Geological Society of America Abstracts with Programs, v. 13, p. 46–47.

Brady, R. H. III, Troxel, B. W., and Butler, P. R., 1980, Tectonic and stratigraphic elements of the northern Avawatz Mountains, San Bernardino County, California, in Fife, D. L., and Brown, A. R., eds., Geology and mineral wealth of the California Desert (Dibblee Volume): South Coast Geological Society, p. 224–234.

Clark, M. M., 1973, Map showing recently active breaks along the Garlock and associated faults, California: U.S. Geological Survey miscellaneous Geologic Investigations Map I–741, scale 1:24,000, 3 sheets.

Cox, A., and Dalrymple, G. B., 1967, Statistical analysis of geomagnetic reversal data and the precision of potassium-argon dating: Journal of Geophysical Research, v. 72, p. 2603–2614.

Cregan, A., and Brady, R. H., III, 1988, Structure, style, and implications of the Soda-Avawatz fault zone, San Bernardino County, California: Geological Society of America Abstracts with Programs, v. 20, p. 152.

Dalrymple, G. B., 1979, Critical tables for conversion of K-Ar ages from old to new constants: Geology, v. 7, p. 558–560.

Davis, G. A., 1977, Limitations on displacement and southeastward extent of the Death Valley fault zone, California, in Short contributions to California geology: California Division of Mines and Geology Special Report 129, p. 27–33.

Davis, G. A., and Burchfiel, B. C., 1973, Garlock fault; An intracontinental transform structure, southern California: Geological Society of America Bulletin, v. 84, p. 1407–1422.

DeWitt, E., Armstrong, R. L., Sutter, J. F., and Zartman, R. E., 1984, U-Th-Pb, Rb-Sr, and Ar-Ar mineral and whole-rock isotopic systematics in a metamorphosed granitic terrane, southeastern California: Geological Society of America Bulletin, v. 95, p. 723–739.

Evernden, J. F., Savage, D. E., Curtis, G. H., and James, G. T., 1964, Potassium-argon dates and the Cenozoic mammalian chronology of North America: American Journal of Science, v. 262, p. 145–198.

Grose, L. T., 1959, Structure and petrology of the northeast part of the Soda Mountains, San Bernardino County, California: Geological Society of America Bulletin, v. 70, p. 1509–1547.

Henshaw, P. C., 1939, A Tertiary mammalian fauna from the Avawatz Mountains, San Bernardino County, California: Carnegie Institute of Washington Publication 514, p. 1–30.

Jahns, R. H., and Engel, A.E.J., 1949, Pliocene breccias in the Avawatz Mountains, San Bernardino County, California [abs.]: Geological Society of America Bulletin, v. 60, p. 1940.

Krieger, M. H., 1977, Large landslides, composed of megabreccia, interbedded in Miocene basin deposits, southeastern Arizona: U.S. Geological Survey Professional Paper 1008, 25 p.

Lamey, C. A., 1945, Iron Mountain and Iron King iron-ore deposits, Silver Lake District, San Bernardino County, California, *in* Iron resources of California: California Division of Mines Bulletin 129, part C, p. 39–58.

Plescia, J. B., and Henyey, T. L., 1982, Geophysical character of the proposed eastern extension of the Garlock fault and adjacent areas, eastern California: Geology, v. 10, p. 209–214.

Shreve, R. L., 1968, The Blackhawk landslide: Geological Society of America Special Paper 108, 47 p.

Smith, G. I., 1962, Large lateral displacement on Garlock fault, California, as measured from offset dike swarm: American Association of Petroleum Geologists Bulletin, v. 46, p. 85–104.

Smith, G. I., and Ketner, K. B., 1970, Lateral displacement on the Garlock fault, southeastern California, suggested by offset sections of similar metasedimentary rocks, *in* Geological Survey Research 1970: U.S. Geological Survey Professional Paper 700–D, p. D1–D9.

Smith, G. I., Troxel, B. W., Gray, C. H., and von Huene, R., 1968, Geologic reconnaissance of the Slate Range, San Bernardino and Inyo Counties, California: California Division of Mines and Geology Special Report 96, 33 p.

Spencer, J. E., 1981, Geology and geochronology of the Avawatz Mountains, San Bernardino County, California [Ph.D. thesis]: Cambridge, Massachusetts Institute of Technology, 183 p.

—— , 1987, K-Ar thermochronology of a Mesozoic plutonic complex, Avawatz Mountains, southeastern California: Isochron/West, no. 48, p. 3–7.

—— , 1990, Geologic map of the southern Avawatz Mountains, northeastern Mojave Desert region, San Bernardino County, California: U.S. Geological Survey Miscellaneous Field Studies Map MF-2117, scale 1:24,000.

Steiger, R. H., and Jager, E., 1977, Subcommission on geochronology; Convention on the use of decay constants in geo- and cosmochronology: Earth and Planetary Science Letters, v. 36, p. 359–362.

Streckeisen, A. L., 1973, Plutonic rocks; Classification and nomenclature recommended by IUGS Subcommission on Systematics of Igneous Rocks: Geotimes, v. 18, no. 10, p. 26–30.

Troxel, B. W., and Butler, P. R., 1979, Tertiary and Quaternary fault history of the intersection of the Garlock and Death Valley fault zones, southern Death Valley, California: unpublished report submitted to the U.S. Geological Survey, Menlo Park, California, 29 p.

Van der Plas, L., and Tobi, A. C., 1965, A chart for judging the reliability of point counting results: American Journal of Science, v. 263, p. 87–90.

Manuscript Accepted by the Society August 21, 1989

Geological Society of America
Memoir 176
1990

Chapter 16

Structural styles across an extensional orogen; Results from the COCORP Mojave and Death Valley seismic transects

Laura Serpa
Department of Geology and Geophysics, University of New Orleans, New Orleans, Louisiana 70148

ABSTRACT

Deep seismic reflection profiling in the Mojave and Death Valley regions of the southern Great Basin provides a basis for comparing the seismic reflection signatures of two adjacent, but distinct, extensional terranes. Those data show contrasting reflection characteristics that may indicate significant variation in upper crustal structure between the two areas. The Mojave data show predominantly low-angle (less than 20°) reflectors in the upper crust, with offsets indicative of a late stage of high-angle (more than 40°) faulting, whereas the Death Valley data show numerous moderately dipping reflectors above a subhorizontal, midcrust reflecting horizon. The Death Valley structures are interpreted to be extensional features related to the Pliocene to Recent tectonic activity in that area. The interpretation of the Mojave data includes identification of structures ranging in age from Mesozoic to Recent.

In contrast to the apparent record of faulting in the seismic data from the upper crust, the lower crustal reflectors appear to be similar throughout the two regions. In particular the reflection Moho is prominent at a depth of approximately 30 km in all of the seismic profiles. A midcrustal reflecting zone in Death Valley is interpreted to continue into the northern Mojave. That zone dips from the midcrust to the reflection Moho beneath the surface position of the Garlock fault zone and the Nopah Range, suggesting that the lower crust has the configuration of a flat-topped dome beneath the area of active upper crustal extension. That dome and the apparently continuous reflection Moho are here suggested to be primarily the product of magmatic activity in the extending lower crust and upper mantle.

INTRODUCTION

The southern Great Basin is divided into a variety of distinct extensional terranes that differ from one another in their times and modes of crustal deformation. Areas of active extension, such as the Salton Trough and the region bounded by the Garlock, Furnace Creek, and Owens Valley fault zones (referred to here as the California Basin and Range) (Fig. 1) are characterized by tilted strata, normal faults, high heat flow, and magmatic activity. Those extensional areas commonly are bounded by strike-slip fault systems that act as displacement transfer structures between the areas of active extension and adjacent areas of relative stabil-

ity, such as the Mojave Block in southern California and the Spring Mountains region of southwestern Nevada (e.g., Davis and Burchfiel, 1973). In this paper, the crustal structures that distinguish two such adjacent areas, the Mojave block and the California Basin and Range, are examined for evidence of deep-seated processes that may relate to their contrasting structural histories. The primary source of information used in this study is COCORP deep seismic reflection data (Cheadle and others, 1986; de Voogd and others, 1986; 1988; Serpa and others, 1988).

The COCORP Death Valley profiles provide continuous seismic coverage across the southwestern part of the California Basin and Range, from the northern side of the Garlock fault zone

Serpa, L., 1990, Structural styles across an extensional orogen; Results from the COCORP Mojave and Death Valley seismic transects, *in* Wernicke, B. P., ed., Basin and Range extensional tectonics near the latitude of Las Vegas, Nevada: Boulder, Colorado, Geological Society of America Memoir 176.

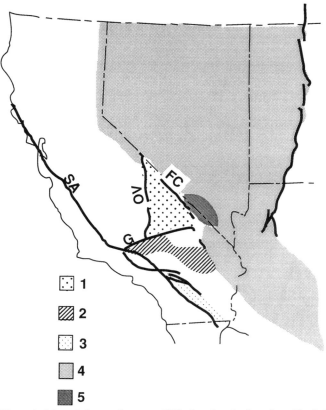

Figure 1. Map of the southwestern U.S. showing the locations (shaded) of some distinct extensional terranes. 1 = California Basin and Range, 2 = Mojave Extensional Terrane, 3 = Salton Trough, 4 = main Basin and Range region, 5 = Spring Mountain terrane, FC = Furnace Creek fault zone, OV = Owens Valley fault zone, G = Garlock fault zone, and SA = San Andreas fault zone.

to the eastern side of the Nopah Range (Fig. 2). The Mojave COCORP survey is separated from the Death Valley survey by a distance of approximately 50 km and provides continuous coverage from the southern edge of the California Basin and Range, across the northwestern part of the Mojave block, to the western side of the San Andreas fault zone. Thus, those two surveys provide seismic information on the crustal structures in two adjacent, but structurally distinct, regions.

LATE CENOZOIC HISTORY OF THE CALIFORNIA BASIN AND RANGE AND MOJAVE REGIONS

The late Cenozoic extensional history began in the Mojave during the early Miocene. Dokka (1986; 1989) provides a description of the Mojave extensional events. He notes that extension of the Mojave block began with an episode of volcanic activity at 26 to 23 Ma, and was followed by at least two episodes of extension faulting at 22 to 20 Ma and 20 to 17 Ma, respectively. The first episode of faulting produced low-angle detachment faults in the upper and middle crust of the Mojave block. Those detachments were uplifted along high-angle faults during

the second phase of extension and are now exposed in parts of the Mojave region. From 17 Ma to the present, the Mojave deformation has been dominated by right-lateral strike-slip faulting, related to movement along the San Andreas fault zone (Dibblee, 1961).

During the time of Mojave extension, the adjacent California Basin and Range appears to have been relatively stable. The main episode of volcanism and extension in the Death Valley portion of the California Basin and Range began approximately 14 Ma (Cemen and others, 1982; 1985), 3 m.y. after cessation of extension in the Mojave block. That extensional activity continued to modern times with the last known volcanic activity occurring approximately 690,000 years ago in the Death Valley region (Wright and Troxel, 1984; Fleck, 1970). During the time of extension in the California Basin and Range, faulted mountain blocks tilted as much as 60° down to the east (Wright, 1976). Based on that tilting, Wright estimates extension in the region to be in excess of 50 percent. Wernicke and others (1988) subsequently proposed that 160 km of extension have occurred within the Death Valley region since the mid-Miocene.

Throughout the late Cenozoic extension, the Garlock fault zone acted as a displacement transfer structure between adjacent areas of extension and nonextension. Davis and Burchfiel (1973) interpret the modern Garlock fault zone as an intracontinental transform boundary between the Sierra Nevada batholith and extending Basin and Range province to the north and the relatively stable Mojave block to the south. Similarly, Dokka (1989) suggests that the western half of the Garlock fault zone acted as a transfer structure separating the early Miocene Mojave extensional terrane from the then relatively stable Sierra Nevada and California Basin and Range terranes. Dokka further suggests that the eastern half of the Garlock did not form until the time of Basin and Range extension.

COCORP SEISMIC DATA

The divergent structural histories of the two regions separated by the Garlock fault zone appear to be recorded in the COCORP seismic reflection data (Fig. 3). In particular, the Mojave data (Cheadle and others, 1986) show a crust dominated by laterally continuous, subhorizontal reflecting zones, whereas the Death Valley data (Serpa and others, 1988) show predominantly dipping reflectors in the upper crust and subhorizontal reflectors in the lower crust. Those observations are discussed in more detail in the following sections.

To facilitate that discussion, the positions of features interpreted from the seismic data are given in terms of depth using the relatively simple assumption that unconsolidated sediments have a velocity of approximately 3 km/s and all other rocks have a velocity of 6 km/s. It is likely that the actual velocities are more complicated than those used in this chapter). As discussed below, however, the source of reflections is believed to be complex, and such complexity places severe limits on the accuracy of velocity measurements. Thus, the depths given in this chapter are only

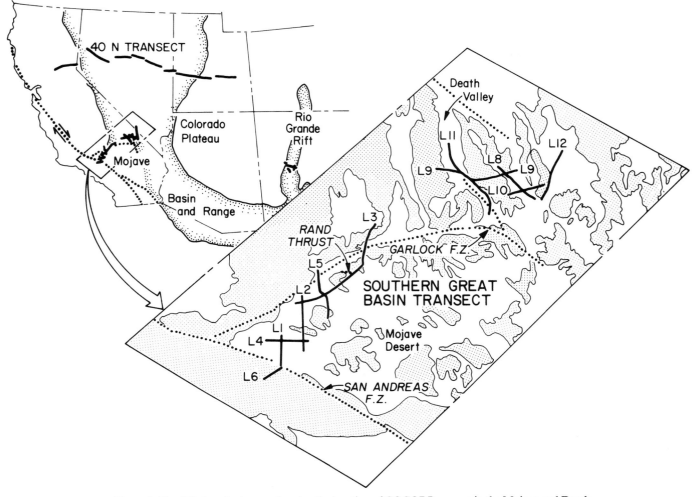

Figure 2. Simplified geologic map showing the location of COCORP surveys in the Mojave and Death Valley regions. Shaded areas represent areas of outcrop. Designations L1 through L6 and L8 through L12 indicate the line numbers of the seismic profiles.

approximations. The seismic sections also are shown unmigrated to minimize the effects of processing on the complex structural configurations. However, where appropriate or applicable, both Serpa and others (1988) and Cheadle and others (1986) show migrated seismic sections. In addition to the unmarked sections (Figs. 4a, 6a, 7a, 9a, 10a, and 11a), sections with the major trends highlighted (Figs. 4b, 6b, 7b, 9b, 10b, and 11b) are shown to draw the reader's attention to the areas discussed in the text.

The Mojave COCORP seismic reflection data

Figure 4a (on folded sheet in cover pocket) shows a typical example of the Mojave COCORP data (Line 3 in Fig. 2). The Mojave data initially were interpreted by Cheadle and others (1986), and much of the following is taken from that work. The interpretation included identification of a shallow, dipping reflector (E on Fig. 4b) between Vibrator Point (VP) 560 and 850 with travel times of 1 to 3 s (1.5 to 7.5 km, respectively) that projects

toward the surface position of the Mesozoic Rand Thrust. This inferred Rand Thrust reflector appears to be truncated by a sub-horizontal detachment (F on Fig. 4b) at a depth of approximately 7 km. That interpretation of Cheadle and others is further supported (Serpa and Dokka, in preparation) by the observation that the exposed Harper Lake detachment, located south of line 3, projects into the subsurface beneath line 3 at the approximate depth of the interpreted detachment imaged in the seismic data.

A second dipping event (G in Fig. 4b), located beneath event E, appears to continue to a depth of approximately 18 km (6 seconds) and has been interpreted by Cheadle and others to be a fault within the vertical plane of the seismic profile. Serpa and Dokka (in preparation), however, suggest that reflection is from out of the plane of the seismic section and represents seismic energy from a shallow portion of the Rand thrust.

The inferred second arrival from the Rand thrust terminates at a prominent reflecting horizon (D in Fig. 4b), which Cheadle and others suggest continues from the northeastern end of line 3

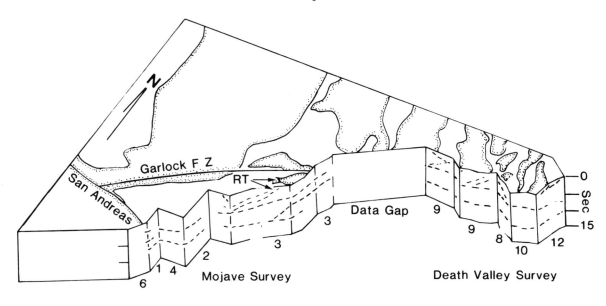

COCORP SOUTHERN GREAT BASIN TRANSECT

Figure 3. Schematic diagram showing the major features of the Death Valley and Mojave seismic profiles. Numbers refer to the line designations shown on Figure 2. RT = Rand Thrust.

in the California Basin and Range at a depth of 10 km, beneath the surface trace of the Garlock fault zone and across much of the Mojave block, lying at a depth of approximately 22 km at the southwestern end of line 3. Cheadle and others propose several possible interpretations for the source of this prominent event, ranging from a Mesozoic thrust to an extensional detachment. After reanalysis of Mojave line 3, however, Serpa (1987) suggested that event D does not continue beneath the Garlock fault zone but rather is a side reflection from the Garlock fault zone. That interpretation is based on the apparent existence of two reflections from the Rand thrust, discussed above, and on the velocity and amplitude characteristics of reflection D. This interpretation is further supported by the nature of the traveltime changes for that event as the profile moves toward and away from the Garlock fault zone (Serpa and Dokka, in preparation).

The yet unresolved differences in the two interpretations (i.e., Cheadle and others, 1986; Serpa, 1987; Serpa and Dokka, in preparation) of some upper crustal reflectors in the Mojave region (Fig. 5) make comparison of structural styles in the Death Valley regions somewhat difficult. However, the origins of some other upper crustal events recorded in the Mojave seismic data are not disputed. In particular, the existence of at least one zone of reflections from the Rand thrust (event E), a low-angle (less than 20°) fault detachment (event F), and a number of possible high-angle (40 or more degrees) shallow faults throughout much of the region are in general agreement in both interpretations. Thus, those events are emphasized for comparison with Death Valley.

Cheadle and others (1986) attribute offsets of their inferred Rand thrust reflector to be due to the presence of high-angle normal faults that do not penetrate below the inferred low-angle detachment (event F) at a depth of approximately 5 to 7 km.

Based on a detailed study of the shallow reflection data, Czuchra (1985) identified several high-angle faults within the young sedimentary basins of the Mojave. None of the inferred high-angle faults produces distinct reflections in the COCORP data, so their dip is assumed to exceed 40°. With the exception of a zone of diffractions at the intersection of Mojave lines 2 and 3, which Cheadle and others suggest may be related to a possible crustal-penetrating strike-slip fault, none of the inferred high-angle faults in the Mojave appear to penetrate to depths greater than 7 km.

Industry seismic data from the western Mojave (Lawson, 1987) show the presence of moderately dipping normal faults in the vicinity of some of the young basins, but those structures are interpreted to be related to the strike-slip and compressional history of the western Mojave rather than to the Mojave extensional events. The inferred fault geometries are generally consistent with the interpretation of Dokka (1989) that the early stage of Mojave extension produced the detachments, such as event F on Figure 4b, whereas the later extension produced predominantly high-angle faults. The existence of coherent reflections from the preextensional Rand Thrust further suggests that the extensional episodes did not significantly disrupt the older crustal structures.

Two prominent, deep reflecting horizons in the Mojave seismic data include the reflection Moho (following the definition of Klemperer and others, 1986) at a depth of approximately 30 km (Fig. 4b) and a lower crustal zone (event B on figure 4b) at a depth of approximately 16 km beneath the Garlock fault zone. Event B appears to continue into the California Basin and Range at the northeastern end of line 3 and curves into the reflection Moho within the Mojave region. Although the continuity of upper crustal structures between the two extensional terranes is in dispute (Cheadle and others, 1986; Serpa, 1987), the two deeper

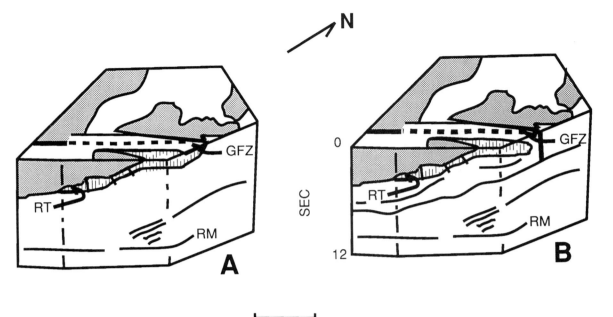

Figure 5. Two proposed interpretations of Mojave profile 3. (a) Serpa and Dokka, in preparation and (b) Cheadle and others, 1986. Shaded areas shown on tops of block diagrams denote the general location of exposed crystalline rocks. Shading is continued into the subsurface sections of the blocks in the area of the Rand Thrust (RT) to distinguish the inferred structure of that feature with dots indicating the upper plate and a line pattern indicating the lower plate of the Rand Thrust. GFZ denotes the position of the Garlock fault zone and RM the position of the reflection Moho.

events clearly are continuous across the Garlock fault zone and appear correlative with events in the Death Valley COCORP data. Thus, it appears likely that the active extension along the north side of the Garlock fault zone exerts some influence on the lower crust of the Mojave region in the area of the fault zone.

Death Valley COCORP data

Examples of the Death Valley data are shown in Figures 6, 7, 9, 10, and 11 (all on sheet in cover pocket). The geometries of the Death Valley reflections are similar to the Mojave reflections in that (1) subhorizontal events appear to dominate at travel times of 5 seconds or more, (2) high-angle shallow structures may exist (Geist and Brocher, 1987) but do not produce identifiable reflections in the seismic data, and (3) nearly all of the dipping reflections are inferred to have a source outside the vertical plane of the seismic section. The Death Valley data differ from the Mojave data in that the Death Valley reflections in the upper 5 seconds of the data commonly have dips of 25° to 40° and appear to come from structures that are exposed near the seismic lines. In contrast, the Mojave data show a preponderance of subhorizontal events at all traveltimes where reflections are present, and the nearby surface geology provides few clues as to the sources of the reflections.

The geometries and locations of reflectors in Death Valley bear a close resemblance to the extensional structure predicted by Wright and Troxel (1973) for the region. Thus, the seismic data have been interpreted (Serpa and others, 1988) in terms of the extensional deformation of the region. In particular, the seismic data indicate that moderate-angle (20° to 40°) faults are common in the upper 4 km of the crust and that there are several widely spaced faults that penetrate to a depth of approximately 15 km in the crust. Examples of all of the extensional structures interpreted to be the source of the shallow reflections are found in the surface geology of the region (Fig. 8) (e.g., Noble, 1941; Noble and Wright, 1954; Wright and Troxel, 1973, 1984; Wright, 1974). Indeed, the interpretation of many of the fault reflectors is based on their correlation with mapped faults.

The clearest examples of the fault reflectors in the CO-CORP data come from the central Death Valley basin because, in that area, the sediments are sufficiently thick (up to 3 km) and layered to provide an impedance contrast across the faults. That is also the area where two lines (lines 9 and 11) intersect to provide three-dimensional information on the geometry of the source region. As a result, the preliminary interpretation (Serpa and others, 1988) focused on the seismic profiles from that region.

Three distinct levels of faulting are identified near the area where lines 9 and 11 intersect (Serpa and others, 1988). Those are indicated on Figures 6b and 7b as reflectors A through D. Reflectors A represent the shallowest level of faults cutting through the basin fill from the surface to a depth of approximately 3 km, where they terminate against reflector B. Reflector

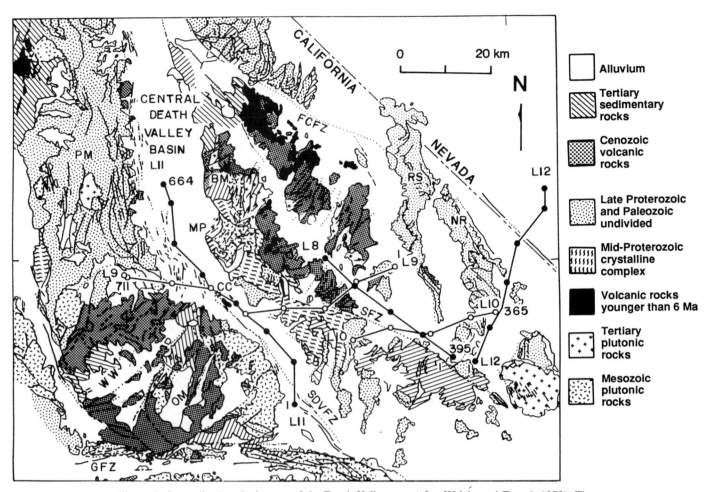

Figure 8. Generalized geologic map of the Death Valley area (after Wright and Troxel, 1973). The COCORP profiles (L8 through L12) are shown with circles indicating the vibrator locations; large letters and arrows indicate the inferred surface trace of events shown in Figures 6 and 7 and discussed in the text. SDVFZ = the southern Death Valley fault zone, FCFZ = the Furnace Creek fault zone, SFZ = the Sheephead fault zone, GFZ = the Garlock fault zone, WW = Wingate Wash, OM = Owlshead Mountains, PM = Panamint Mountains, BM = Black Mountains, RS = Resting Springs range, and NR = Nopah Range.

B appears to be a fault within the preextensional basement rocks that continues from a surface position in the Panamint Range to near the eastern side of the basin, where it terminates against D. Event D is also interpreted to be a zone of faults that is not exposed at the surface in the area of the seismic data but projects into mapped faults (Wagner, 1988) of Wingate Wash. Event C appears to be a subsurface expression of deep faults along the western front of the Black Mountains.

Events C and D appear to continue from near the surface to a depth of 15 km, where they terminate at or above a subhorizontal zone inferred to be part of a regionally continuous detachment and locally to include partially molten rock (de Voogd and others 1986; Serpa and others, 1988). Below 15 km depth, no significant dipping events are observed. Thus the subhorizontal reflector in the midcrust is interpreted to mark the base of the zone of brittle faulting.

The map traces of the inferred faults discussed above are shown in Figure 8 along with the surface features with which they appear to correlate. Those faults are typical of other inferred faults in the area (Figs. 9 through 11), in that multiple levels of faulting appear to be present. For example, a complex pattern of reflections is observed in the upper 2.5 seconds of COCORP line 12 (Fig. 9) where the seismic profile passes along the southern and eastern sides of the Nopah Range. Those reflectors have the greatest traveltimes when the line is oriented perpendicular to the strike of faults in the Nopah Range (Wright, 1974) (Fig. 2), and their dip appears to flatten as the seismic line moves into the strike direction of the Nopah Range faults. Those observations suggest that the complex pattern of reflections is related to the faulting in the Nopah Range. Despite the complexity of the apparent fault reflectors, they appear to be confined to the upper 4 km of the crust.

Elsewhere, such as within the Black Mountains (Fig. 6), minor variations in the upper approximately 0.8 seconds of the seismic data may be related to shallow faults. However, during the processing of the seismic data, most of the upper 0.5 seconds of data were muted (set to zero) to remove refracted energy. That muting left little or no information on the shallow faults mapped (e.g., Noble, 1941; Wright and Troxel, 1984) in the region. Because those faults commonly have low dips where exposed but are not clearly imaged in the seismic data, they are assumed to be confined to the uppermost levels of the subsurface as previously indicated by Noble (1941). That interpretation is consistent with observation (e.g., Noble and Wright, 1954; Wright and Troxel, 1973, 1984) that the top of the crystalline basement exposed in the Black Mountains acted as a lower boundary to many of the overlying sedimentary fault blocks.

Deep faults (i.e., those penetrating to approximately 15 km depth) appear to be more widely spaced in the Death Valley region than are shallow faults. Examples of such deep faults include the Wingate Wash fault zone and the frontal faults of the Black Mountains (events D and C, respectively, in Figures 6 and 7), discussed previously, as well as several other events observed on lines 8, 9, 10, and 11. Other west-dipping features that may be deep faults appear to be represented in COCORP line 9 as moderately dipping reflectors within the Black Mountains. However, those inferred faults are generally observed only between 2 and 5 seconds of traveltime and cannot be traced into the upper 2 seconds of the seismic data. Thus, their correlation with mapped faults is somewhat uncertain.

One set of dipping reflectors appears to be associated with the Sheephead fault zone (Wright and others, 1987), which formed as a detachment during an early stage of extension on the east side of the Black Mountains. Wright and others (1987; in preparation) recognized the early extensional event from surface geologic relations in the area. The seismic image of the Sheephead fault provides additional support for the interpreted early extensional event.

A detachment similar to that exposed in portions of the Mojave may now exist in the midcrust of Death Valley. The Death Valley data show a relatively continuous reflecting zone at a depth of approximately 15 km, which appears to truncate the upper crustal faults (de Voogd and others, 1988). Beneath the central Death Valley basin, that zone produces sufficiently high-amplitude reflections to suggest that it contains some molten material (de Voogd and others, 1986). Elsewhere the reflections from the midcrustal zone are strong but do not give the large amplitude variations observed within the basin region. Thus, the reflecting zone is interpreted to form a detachment that may locally include intrusive material at the base of the upper crustal faults (de Voogd and others, 1986, 1988; Serpa and others, 1988).

A reflection Moho similar to that observed in the Mojave data occurs throughout the Death Valley seismic data at a depth of approximately 30 km. Seismic refraction studies (Johnson, 1965; Prodehl, 1979; Roller and Healy, 1963) as well as other geophysical data (e.g., Mabey, 1960, 1963) show no evidence for a significant change in the depth of the Mohorovičić discontinuity across the Garlock fault zone. Therefore, the reflection Moho is assumed to be continuous and relatively flat throughout the two areas.

Correlation of reflections between the Mojave and Death Valley regions

Because the midcrustal zone appears to be continuous throughout the Death Valley region, it was considered possible that it also continued into the Mojave survey area. To examine that possibility, the Mojave seismic data were reprocessed (Serpa, 1987) in a manner similar to that of the Death Valley data to facilitate comparison of reflectors in the two data sets.

Initially, two reflecting horizons in the Mojave region were considered as possible continuations of the Death Valley midcrustal zone. The first of these, event C on Figure 4b, lies at a depth of 12 km in the northeastern part of line 3; the second, event B on Figure 4b, lies at a depth of approximately 18 km. As discussed previously, C is now inferred to be a side reflection from the Garlock fault zone (Serpa, 1987), and B appears to be correlative with the Death Valley midcrustal horizon. That correlation is based on the similarity of amplitude variations across the two events and the observation that they have similar widths (1 s) and often show three distinct reflecting bands, two near the top and one at the base of the zone, as shown in Figure 12. If that correlation is correct, it indicates that the lower crust of the California Basin and Range is bounded from above by a relatively flat reflecting zone that dips toward the Moho at the boundaries of the area of active extension: the Garlock fault zone and the Nopah range.

DISCUSSION

The comparison of the two sets of COCORP seismic profiles and their proposed interpretations (Serpa and others, 1988; Cheadle and others, 1986) show some fundamental differences in the styles of upper crustal deformation between the two areas, which may be due to differences in the amount of extension or the preextensional characteristics of the regions, or both. However, the most intriguing features of the combined data set come from an examination of the apparent relations between the deeper structures of the two regions. That examination suggests (1) that the Garlock fault zone penetrates to no more than 18 km and possibly as little as 7 km depth (Cheadle and others, 1986; Serpa and Dokka, in preparation), (2) the existence of a flat-topped, lower-crustal dome beneath the actively extending California Basin and Range (Serpa and de Voogd, 1987), and (3) a relatively flat, continuous reflection Moho that exists throughout the region. These observations are of particular interest because they give information about the manner in which extension is accommodated at different levels in the crust and upper mantle.

In particular, while the surface geology indicates that the

L. Serpa

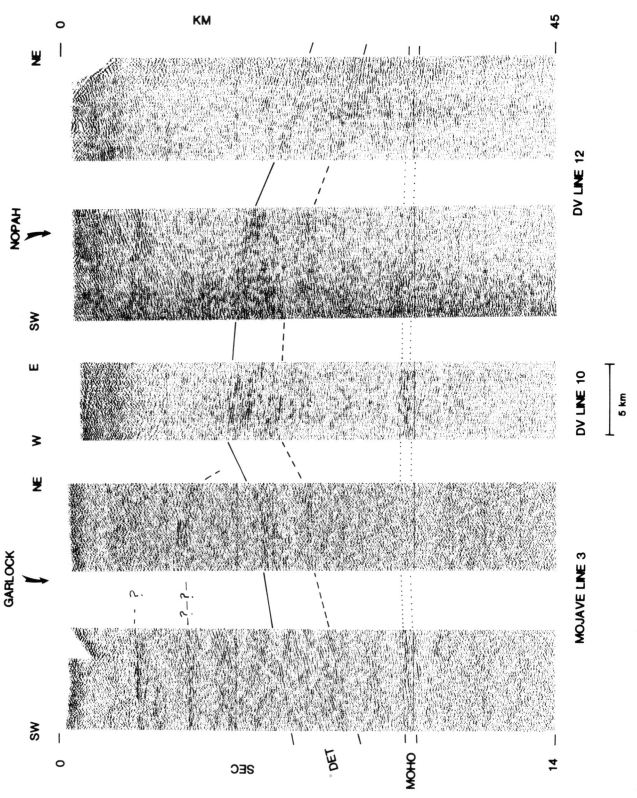

Figure 12. Sections of the seismic data showing the inferred correlation of the Death Valley midcrustal zone with event B on line 3.

amount and time of extension differ significantly between the California Basin and Range and the Mojave block (e.g., Dokka, 1989; Wernicke and others, 1988; Wright and Troxel, 1973), there is no significant change in crustal thickness between the two areas. Indeed, seismic reflection data indicate the crustal thickness is relatively uniform throughout the Great Basin (Allmendinger and others, 1987; Hauser and others, 1987; Klemperer and others, 1986), which raises a question regarding the relation between extension and crustal thickness. It has commonly been assumed, for example, that 100 percent extension would produce a crust half as thick as it was prior to extension. However, that model would suggest that the crustal thickness in the Basin and Range was highly variable prior to extension because of the differing rates of extension experienced in different regions of the province. It would seem quite fortuitous that the entire region would now have a uniform crustal thickness.

Alternatively, magmatic activity could play a role in maintaining a uniform crustal thickness in the Basin and Range province. Numerous workers (e.g., Wright and Troxel, 1973; Eaton, 1979; Miller and others, 1983; Smith and Bruhn, 1984; Furlong and Fountain, 1986; Serpa and de Voogd, 1987) have suggested that intrusive activity could have a significant effect on the rheology of the lower crust of extensional terranes.

A magmatic underplating model (e.g., Hertzberg and others, 1983; Furlong and Fountain, 1986) may provide an explanation for both the relative uniformity of crustal thickness throughout the Great Basin and the apparent flat-topped dome in the lower crust of Death Valley (Fig. 12). That model suggests that magmas rise to a level where their density and viscosity are essentially the same as that of the surrounding material. Fractionation may then produce a less dense magma than the parent magma, and that lighter magma may intrude to a shallower level. The crust-mantle boundary is generally considered (Hertzberg and others, 1983) to be a likely place for magma ponding and fractionation such that only those magmas that have densities similar to the existing lower crustal rocks will rise above the Moho. This is significant because the contrast between partially molten material and crystalline rocks would produce the strong reflections commonly associated with the reflection Moho in the Great Basin (e.g., Klemperer and others, 1986; de Voogd and others, 1988), and the lighter magma intruding into the crust would provide the mechanism for maintaining a relatively uniform crustal thickness by continually increasing the volume of crustal rocks in the extending region.

The magmatic model suggests that the midcrustal reflecting zone in the actively extending Death Valley region, combined with its inferred downward-dipping continuations near the boundaries of the region (the Garlock fault zone and the area between the Nopah Range and the Spring Mountains) (Fig. 12), represents the upper bounds of a highly intruded lower crust. That is, if we assume that magmatic activity has not increased the volume of upper crustal rocks in Death Valley, then the apparent 50 to 250 percent extension in that area (e.g., Wright, 1976; Wernicke and others, 1982, 1988) would place the now 15-km-

deep reflecting zone at a depth of 22 to 53 km prior to the onset of extension. The addition of magma to the upper crust would increase the depth estimate for this boundary. Thus, if that boundary existed prior to or formed early in the extensional history of Death Valley, then it has undergone significant uplift consistent with its apparent domed shape. Because the reflection Moho does not show similar doming, Serpa and de Voogd (1986) suggest that the doming has been accommodated by the addition of a large volume (as much as 100 percent) of magma to the lower crust.

In addition, the existence of a predominantly intrusive lower crust beneath the actively extending region could limit the depth of active faulting along the Garlock fault zone. Ductile flow or intrusive activity, or both, would accommodate changes in deformation between the lower crusts of the two areas, whereas brittle faulting should be confined to the upper crustal region. The continuity of deep reflections beneath the Garlock fault zone suggests the faulting is confined to the upper crust.

In summary, although many of the differences between the two areas remain poorly understood, the seismic data clearly indicate that the character of extensional structures and degree of disruption of preexisting structures can vary significantly over relatively short distances. Based on the existing data, a model for extension that includes a major role for magmatic activity and possibly ductile deformation in the lower crust appears most consistent with the observations in the California Basin and Range. Elsewhere, models for crust-penetrating (Wernicke, 1981) or anastomosing (Hamilton, 1982) shear zones may be more appropriate. However, it is reasonable to assume that the variations observed in the relatively small area discussed in this paper are similar to those in the other parts of the Great Basin. Therefore, it is likely that crustal thickness is not related to the amount of extension in any simple manner and that a single deformation model for the entire region does not exist.

REFERENCES CITED

Allmendinger, R. W., Hauge, T. A., Hauser, E. C., Potter, C. J., and Oliver, J., 1987, Tectonic heredity and the layered lower crust in the Basin and Range Province, western United States, *in* Coward, M. P., Dewey, J. F., and Hancock, P. L., eds., Continental extensional tectonics: Geological Society of London Special Publication 28, p. 223–246.

Cemen, I., Drake, R., and Wright, L. A., 1982, Stratigraphy and chronology of the Tertiary sedimentary and volcanic units at the southwestern end of the Funeral Mountains, Death Valley region, California, *in* Cooper, J. D., Troxel, B. W., and Wright, L. A., eds., Stratigraphy, structure, and geomorphology of selected areas in the San Bernadino Mountains, Mojave Desert and southwestern Great Basin, California: Shoshone, California, Death Valley Publishing Co., p. 77–88.

Cemen, I., Wright, L. A., Drake, R. E., and Johnson, F. C., 1985, Cenozoic sedimentation and sequence of deformational events at the southeastern end of the Furance Creek strike-slip fault zone, Death Valley region, California: Society of Economic Paleontologists and Mineralogists Special Paper 27, p. 127–141.

Cheadle, M. J., and 8 others, 1986, The deep crustal structure of the Mojave Desert, California, from COCORP seismic reflection data: Tectonics, v. 5, p. 293–320.

Czuchra, B. L., 1985, A study of the shallow structure of the Mojave desert, southern California, from COCORP seismic reflection data [M.S. thesis]: Ithaca, New York, Cornell University, 53 p.

Davis, G. A., and Burchfiel, B. C., 1973, Garlock fault; An intracontinental transform structure, southern California: Geological Society of America Bulletin, v. 84, p. 1407–1422.

de Voogd, B., and 8 others, 1986, The Death Valley bright spot; A midcrustal magma body in the southern Great Basin, California?: Geology, v. 14, p. 64–67.

de Voogd, B., Serpa, L., and Brown, L., 1988, Crustal extension and magmatic processes; COCORP profiles from Death Valley and the Rio Grande rift: Geological Society of America Bulletin, v. 100, p. 1550–1567.

Dibblee, T. W., Jr., 1961, Evidence of strike-slip movement on northwest-trending faults in the western Mojave Desert, California: U.S. Geological Survey Professional Paper 424-B, p. B197–B199.

Dokka, R. K., 1986, Patterns and modes of early Miocene crustal extension, central Mojave Desert, California, *in* Mayer, L., Extensional tectonics of the southwestern United States; A perspective on processes and kinematics: Geological Society of America Special Paper 208, p. 75–95.

—— , 1989, The Mojave extensional belt of southern California: Tectonics, v. 8, p. 363–390.

Eaton, G. P., 1979, Regional geophysics, Cenozoic tectonics, and geologic resources of the Basin and Range province and adjoining regions, *in* Newman, G. W., and Goode, H. D., eds., Basin and Range Symposium: Denver, Colorado, Rocky Mountain Association of Geologists, p. 11–39.

Fleck, L. J., 1970, Age and tectonic significance of volcanic rocks, Death Valley area, California: Geological Society of America Bulletin, v. 81, p. 2807–2816.

Furlong, K. P., and Fountain, D. M., 1986, Lithospheric evolution with underplating; Thermal-physical considerations: Journal of Geophysical Research, v. 91, p. 8285–8294.

Geist, E. L., and Brocher, T. M., 1987, Geometry and subsurface lithology of southern Death Valley basin, California, based on refraction analysis of multichannel seismic data: Geology, v. 15, p. 1159–1162.

Hamilton, W., 1982, Structural evolution of the Big Maria Mountains, northeastern Riverside County, southeastern California, *in* Frost, E. G., and Martin, D. L., eds., Mesozoic-Cenozoic tectonic evolution of the Colorado River region: San Diego, California, Cordilleran Publishers, p. 1–28.

Hauser, E. J., and 5 others, 1987, COCORP Arizona transect; Strong crustal reflections and offset Moho beneath the transition zone: Geology, v. 15, p. 1103–1106.

Herzberg, C. T., Fyfe, W. S., and Carr, M. J., 1983, Density constraints on the formation of the continental Moho and crust: Contributions to Mineralogy and Petrology, v. 84, p. 1–5.

Johnson, L. R., 1965, Crustal structure between Lake Mead, Nevada, and Mono Lake, California: Journal of Geophysical Research, v. 70, p. 2863–2872.

Klemperer, S. L., Hauge, T. A., Hauser, E. C., Oliver, J. E., and Potter, C. J., 1986, The Moho in the northern Basin and Range province, Nevada, along the COCORP 40°N seismic reflection transect: Geological Society of America Bulletin, v. 97, p. 603–618.

Lawson, H. R. III, 1987, Geophysical study of the western Mojave Desert [M.S. thesis]: Los Angeles, University of Southern California, 163 p.

Mabey, D. R., 1960, Gravity survey of the western Mojave Desert, California: U.S. Geological Survey Professional Paper 316-D, p. 51–73.

—— , 1963, Complete Bouguer anomaly map of the Death Valley region, California: U.S. Geological Survey Geophysical Investigations Map GP-305, scale 1:250,000.

Miller, E. L., Gans, P. B., and Garing, J., 1983, The Snake Range Décollement; An exhumed mid-Tertiary ductile-brittle transition: Tectonics, v. 2, p. 239–263.

Noble, L. F., 1941, Structural features of the Virgin Spring area, Death Valley, California: Geological Society of America Bulletin, v. 52, p. 941–1000.

Noble, L. F., and Wright, L. A., 1954, Geology of the central and southern Death Valley region, California: California Division of Mines Bulletin 170, p. 143–160.

Prodehl, C., 1979, Crustal structure of the western United States: U.S. Geological Survey Professional Paper 1034, 74 p.

Roller, J. C., and Healy, J. H., 1963, Seismic refraction measurements of crustal structure between Santa Monica Bay and Lake Mead: Journal of Geophysical Research, v. 68, p. 5837–5849.

Serpa, L., 1987, The three-dimensional geometry of the Garlock fault zone: Geological Society of America Abstracts with Programs, v. 19, p. 838.

Serpa, L., and de Voogd, B., 1987, Deep seismic reflection evidence for the role of extension in the evolution of continental crust: Geophysical Journal of the Royal Astronomical Society, v. 89, p. 55–60.

Serpa, L., and 6 others, 1988, Structure of the central Death Valley pull-apart basin and vicinity from COCORP profiles in the southern Great Basin: Geological Society of America Bulletin, v. 100, p. 1437–1450.

Smith, R. B., and Bruhn, R. L., 1984, Intraplate extensional tectonics of the eastern Basin-Range; Inferences on strauctural style from seismic reflection data, regional tectonics, and thermal mechanical models of brittle-ductile deformation: Journal of Geophysical Research, v. 89, p. 5733–5762.

Wagner, D. L., 1988, Evidence for late Cenozoic extension across Wingate Wash, southwestern Death Valley region, southeast California: Geological Society of America Abstracts with Programs, v. 20, p. 240.

Wernicke, B., 1981, Low-angle normal faults in the Basin and Range province; Nappe tectonics in an extending orogen: Nature, v. 291, p. 645–648.

Wernicke, B., Spencer, J. E., Burchfiel, B. C., and Guth, P. L., 1982, Magnitude of crustal extension in the southern Great Basin: Geology, v. 10, p. 499–502.

Wernicke, B., Axen, G. J., and Snow, J. K., 1988, Basin and Range extensional tectonics at the latitude of Las Vegas, Nevada: Geological Society of America Bulletin, v. 100, p. 1738–1757.

Wright, L. A., 1974, Geology of the southeast quarter of the Tecopa Quadrangle, Inyo County, California: California Division of Mines Map Sheet, p. 20.

—— , 1976, Late Cenozoic fault patterns and stress fields in the Great Basin and westward displacement of the Sierra Nevada block: Geology, v. 4, p. 489–494.

Wright, L. A., and Troxel, B. W., 1973, Shallow-fault interpretation of Basin and Range structure, southwestern Great Basin, *in* Dejong, K.A ., and Scholten, R., eds., Gravity and tectonics: New York, John Wiley and Sons, p. 397–407.

—— , 1984, Geology of the north ½ Confidence Hills 15′ Quadrangle, Inyo County, California: California Division of Mines and Geology Map Sheet 34, 31 p.

Wright, L. A., Serpa, L., and Troxel, B. W., 1987, Tectonic-chronologic model for wrench fault related crustal extension, Death Valley area, California: Geological Society of America Abstracts with Programs, v. 19, p. 898–899.

MANUSCRIPT ACCEPTED BY THE SOCIETY AUGUST 21, 1989

Geological Society of America
Memoir 176
1990

Chapter 17

Uplift and exposure of the Panamint metamorphic complex, California

Theodore C. Labotka
Department of Geological Sciences, University of Tennessee, Knoxville, Tennessee 37996-1410
Arden L. Albee
Division of Geological and Planetary Sciences, California Institute of Technology, Pasadena, California 91125

ABSTRACT

The central Panamint Mountains, Death Valley area, California, comprise three groups of rocks. The first consists of middle Proterozoic gneiss and upper Proterozoic sedimentary rocks that were regionally metamorphosed under low-pressure conditions during Middle Jurassic time, were intruded by the Late Cretaceous Hall Canyon granitic pluton, and were folded along NNW–trending axes during Late Cretaceous time. This group, called the Panamint metamorphic complex, makes up the core of the Panamint Mountains. The complex is cut by numerous west-dipping, low-angle normal faults that are locally intruded by the Miocene Little Chief stock. The second group consists of monolithologic breccias, called the Surprise breccia, derived from the local metamorphic rocks. The Surprise breccia forms the western slope of the Panamint Mountains north of Pleasant Canyon and forms the hanging wall of the west-dipping Surprise fault. Displacements along the fault, estimated from offset structures, are about 2,500 m down dip. The third group consists of the Nova Formation, which comprises fanglomerate, basalt, and minor breccia and which lies in the hanging wall of the west-dipping Emigrant fault. The fanglomerates contain abundant clasts of metamorphic and granitic rocks from the metamorphic complex. The three groups of rocks are separated from each other by intervening faults. The Panamint metamorphic complex is the structurally lowest group and is separated from the Surprise breccia by the Surprise fault. The breccia is separated from the structurally highest Nova Formation by the Emigrant fault. All these rocks lie above the regionally extensive Amargosa fault.

The difference in rock character among fanglomerates, breccias, and relatively intact metamorphic core rocks is readily visible in Thematic Mapper (TM) and Shuttle Imaging Radar (SIR-B) images. The TM image, which is sensitive to differences in mineralogic compositions of the rock types, distinguishes the metamorphic complex from the Surprise breccia because the breccias are more highly weathered than the metamorphic complex. The SIR-B image, which is sensitive to differences in surface roughness and topography, readily distinguishes between the breccia and the fanglomerate. The breccia is characterized by closely spaced, parallel drainages, whereas the fanglomerate contains a dense dentate drainage pattern. The combination of the images is a significant mapping aid in the central Panamint Mountains.

Most of the uplift of the Panamint metamorphic complex, from a Late Mesozoic depth of about 10 km to ~3 km, probably occurred during displacements along the Amargosa and related faults. Some of these faults were intruded by the late middle Miocene Little Chief stock. The maximum possible uplift rate at this time was 17 mm/yr;

Labotka, T. C., and Albee, A. L., 1990, Uplift and exposure of the Panamint metamorphic complex, California, *in* Wernicke, B. P., ed., Basin and Range extensional tectonics near the latitude of Las Vegas, Nevada: Boulder, Colorado, Geological Society of America Memoir 176.

the actual rate could have been lower if some uplift occurred prior to faulting. The metamorphic complex was largely unroofed by the time of deposition of the Nova Formation. Uplift of the range prior to, and partly contemporaneous with, Nova deposition resulted in formation of the Surprise breccia. The Emigrant fault formed late. The fanglomerates dip ~25° eastward against the Emigrant fault, but this tilting appears to have resulted from aggregate rotation along several fault surfaces rather than from uniform eastward tilting of the entire Panamint Mountain block. Isolated remnants of Surprise breccia on ridge crests indicate that the unroofing of the metamorphic complex south of Wildrose Canyon probably was not completed until after the breccia-mass development.

INTRODUCTION

The Panamint Mountains bound the western margin of central Death Valley, California, and contain a great areal exposure of the metamorphic complex that formed during the emplacement of Mesozoic batholith rocks. The mountains, forming the southern portion of the Panamint Range, consist largely of middle Proterozoic gneissic basement and upper Proterozoic supracrustal sedimentary rocks. These rocks have been broadly folded and cut by numerous faults, resulting in a mountain that crests at more than 3,400 m above the floor of Death Valley. The geology of the Panamint Mountains records several episodes of the history of the Cordillera, including the formation of continental crust before 1,400 Ma, the rifting of this crust at the beginning of the development of the Cordilleran continental margin during late Precambrian time, the folding and metamorphism accompanying emplacement of the Mesozoic batholith, and uplift and exposure of the metamorphic complex during Late Tertiary and Quaternary extension. The great relief and deeply incised canyons provide an excellent section through this geology.

The geology of the central part of the Panamint Mountains, near Telescope Peak, shows Late Tertiary extensional structures superimposed on Late Mesozoic folds and faults. The structure of the Telescope Peak area is dominated by a NNW–trending anticline and north-trending, steeply dipping faults that developed during Mesozoic time. The Mesozoic structures are cut by gentle, west-dipping normal faults and by the Miocene Little Chief granitic stock, which was emplaced at a shallow level in the crust. The extensional structures, although late, are at least partly responsible for the unroofing of the Panamint Metamorphic complex.

In this chapter the development of the extensional features and the exposure of the Panamint Metamorphic complex are described. Much of the discussion is based on the geology of the Telescope Peak quadrangle mapped by A. L. Albee, M. A. Lanphere, S. D. McDowell, and Labotka (Albee and others, 1981; Labotka and others, 1980a, 1980b; McDowell, 1974, 1978). Additional mapping in the Wildrose Canyon area in the Emigrant Canyon quadrangle was conducted in conjunction with a study of the application of space shuttle imaging radar (SIR-B) to geologic mapping. The geology of the Panamint Metamorphic complex is summarized first. Next, the Tertiary structures are

described, utilizing geologic maps and satellite imagery. Then the timing of the unroofing of the complex is discussed. The results of this study indicate that most of the uplift of the metamorphic complex occurred prior to the intrusion of the Little Chief stock. Extension occurred along west-dipping normal faults that cut the axis of the NNW–trending anticline. Monolithologic breccias developed along the western margin of the range late in the extension history, and the complex was exposed by the time of the deposition of the Plio-Pleistocene Nova Formation. The present level of exposure in the deeply incised canyons developed during Pleistocene to Recent uplift along the Panamint Valley fault zone.

GEOLOGY OF THE METAMORPHIC CORE OF THE PANAMINT MOUNTAINS

Introduction

The Panamint Mountains constitute a north-trending range composed largely of Precambrian rocks (Fig. 1). The range is a fault block bounded by Panamint Valley fault zone on the west and is locally faulted and tilted eastward toward Death Valley on the east. The Panamint Mountains occur at the eastern limit of extensive granitic intrusions associated with the Mesozoic batholith that forms the Sierra Nevada, the Argus Range, and the White and Inyo Mountains. The Panamint Valley fault zone and its northern extension, the Towne Pass fault of Hall (1971), separate the batholithic terrain and its middle to upper Paleozoic sedimentary host rocks from the lower Paleozoic to Precambrian rocks that form the metamorphic core of the middle to late Mesozoic Cordillera. The metamorphic rocks form the footwall of the Death Valley extended terrain.

The Panamint Mountains can be divided into three areas: Tucki Mountain, the Telescope peak area, and the Manly Peak area. The structure of Tucki Mountain at the northern end of the Panamint Mountains is documented by a dome cored by upper Precambrian sedimentary rocks, intruded by a granitic pluton near Skidoo, and cut by numerous normal faults containing either Paleozoic sedimentary rocks or Plio-Pleistocene fanglomerates on the hanging walls (Hunt and Mabey, 1966; Hodges and others, 1987; Wernicke and others, 1988a, c).

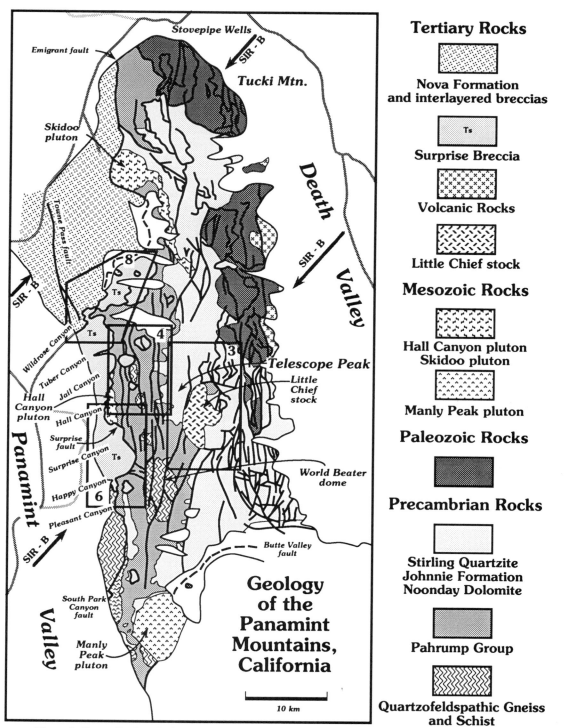

Figure 1. Generalized geologic map of the Panamint Mountains, California, simplified after Johnson (1957), Hunt and Mabey (1966), and Albee and others (1981). Locations of the detailed maps in Figures 3, 4, 6, and 8 are outlined. The shuttle imaging radar path is indicated by the arrows. The radar image is shown in Figure 10. Major structural features mentioned in the text and indicated on the map include the South Park Canyon fault, World Beater dome, Manly Peak pluton, Hall Canyon pluton, Little Chief stock, Skidoo pluton, Emigrant fault, and Towne Pass fault. Standard geologic map symbols are employed in this figure and in Figures 3, 4 6, and 8. Thin lines are geologic contacts; thick lines are faults. Dashed lines represent concealed contacts or faults. Some faults are decorated with hachures on the hanging-wall side. Shaded lines are roads, and dotted lines are ephemeral streams.

In the Telescope Peak area, in the central part of the Panamint Mountains, the Precambrian rocks form a NNW–plunging anticline that culminates in the World Beater dome. These rocks are intruded by the Cretaceous Hall Canyon pluton and by the Miocene Little Chief stock. The anticline is buried by monolithologic breccias and fanglomerates, which are in fault contact with the older rocks between Wildrose Canyon and Harrisburg Flats.

In the southern part of the Panamint Mountains, near Manly Peak, the Precambrian rocks that form the anticline were deformed by the intrusion of the Jurassic Manly Peak pluton. The South Park Canyon fault separates the metamorphic core of the Panamint Mountains from Proterozoic gneisses and schists along the western margin of the southern Panamint Mountains (Johnson, 1957; Miller, 1983). The metamorphic core of the Panamint Mountains is separated from upper Paleozoic and lower Mesozoic sedimentary and volcanic rocks by the Butte Valley fault, which is intruded by the Manly Peak pluton. This fault may be a thrust fault (Stevens and others, 1974), but where exposed, it is a steeply dipping, dip-slip fault (Johnson, 1957).

The following discussion concerns the geology of the central part of the Panamint Mountains, in the vicinity of Telescope Peak.

Stratigraphy

The oldest rocks in the central Panamint Mountains are gneiss, schist, and granite, which occur in the core of the NNW–trending anticline, in World Beater dome, and along the western margin of the Panamint Mountains south of Happy Canyon. Three rock groups make up the crystalline core of the Panamint Mountains. A sequence of metasedimentary micaceous schist and leucocratic, quartzofeldspathic gneiss is exposed along the western margin of the range south of Happy Canyon and occupies the breached core of the anticline in Surprise, Hall, and Jail Canyons. A gray, biotite-rich augen gneiss, having an age of ~1,750 Ma, and a gray porphyritic quartz monzonite, which intruded the augen gneiss at ~1,350 Ma, constitute World Beater dome (Murphy, 1932; Lanphere and others, 1964).

The middle Proterozoic gneisses and schists are unconformably overlain by upper Proterozoic metasedimentary rocks of the Pahrump Group. The Pahrump Group comprises three formations. The Crystal Spring Formation consists of basal quartzite and conglomerate, interbedded siliceous dolomite and argillaceous clastic rocks, and sills and dikes of diabase. The Beck Spring Dolomite consists of thick-bedded to massive dolomite. In some places, the upper part of the formation contains interbedded dolomitic breccias and argillaceous rocks. The Kingston Peak Formation contains a variety of lithologies, including locally thick sections of argillite and graywacke, conglomerate, and massive diamictite. These rocks were deposited in an ensialic basin that formed during the rifting of the continental margin at the beginning of the development of the Cordillera. The stratigraphy of the Pahrump Group and immediately overlying rocks is characterized by vertical and lateral lithologic heterogeneity, by local unconformities, and by substantial changes in thickness over distances on the scale of 100 m. These characteristics indicate substantial paleorelief during deposition and contemporaneous faulting. The detailed descriptions of the stratigraphy and depositional environment of the Pahrump Group and related rocks are given in Labotka and Albee (1977), Labotka and others (1980b), and Miller (1985, 1987).

The Pahrump Group is disconformably overlain by a package of sedimentary rocks of late Precambrian age consisting of Noonday Dolomite, Johnnie Formation, and Stirling Quartzite. Angular discordance between this group and the Pahrump Group is slight, and locally the groups may be conformable. The Noonday Dolomite consists of massive dolomite, interbedded argillaceous limestones and calcareous argillites, and quartzose and carbonate sandstone. The Johnnie Formation overlies the Noonday Dolomite and is predominantly composed of argillaceous and arenaceous rocks, although dolomitic rocks are abundant in the lower part. The Stirling Quartzite consists of medium- to coarse-grained feldspathic quartzite and conglomerate, minor argillaceous rocks, and abundant, crossbedded quartzite.

The Precambrian rocks are conformably overlain by the Cambrian Wood Canyon Formation and younger rocks. These rocks crop out northeast of the Telescope Peak area. The geology of that region is described by Hodges and others (this volume).

Structure

The structure of the relatively unextended core of the Panamint Mountains consists of broad, asymmetric folds; generally north-trending, steeply dipping faults; and the west-dipping South Park Canyon fault. These structures were intruded by the granitic Hall Canyon pluton, the Manly Peak pluton, and an unnamed granodiorite pluton in South Park Canyon.

The folded rocks consist of World Beater dome, a NNW–plunging anticline extending north from the dome, and a complementary syncline between the dome and the South Park Canyon fault. In the Manly Peak quadrangle, this broad anticline-syncline couple dominates the structure (Johnson, 1957). The domes and anticlines are asymmetric; east flanks dip gently east, but west flanks dip steeply west. The west flanks are overturned in some places near the Hall Canyon pluton.

World Beater dome is a persistent structure. It now is a structural dome, as the mantling rocks dip away from it in all directions. It was also a topographic mountain or island during deposition of the Pahrump Group; the Crystal Spring Formation and Beck Spring Dolomite appear to have shoaled against the dome, as evidenced by the abundance of locally derived sedimentary breccias, local unconformities, major differences in lithologic sequences over small distances, and absence of the lower parts of the Pahrump Group on the top, western, and southern flanks of the structure (Labotka and Albee, 1977). It may also have held substantial relief after the emplacement of the 1,400-m.y.-old quartz monzonite that forms the core of the complex, as rocks of the World Beater complex are found nowhere else among the exposures of middle Proterozoic gneiss and schist in the Panamint Mountains.

The anticline extending north-northwestward from the dome generally contains middle Proterozoic gneiss in the core, except in Tuber Canyon where the oldest exposed rocks are those of the Crystal Spring Formation. Although the Pahrump Group is folded across the axis of the anticline, much of the strain was assumed by displacement along north-trending, steeply dipping faults. The trend of the faults is oblique to that of the fold axis, indicating that the faults predated the folding.

Lineation is well developed along the west flank of the anticline. Cobbles within the lower Kingston Peak Formation are stretched and have lengths up to about 10 times the diameter. The long axes of cobbles generally plunge 20°/N10W. Mineral lineation is also well developed and is defined by the parallel alignment of hornblende grains and white mica pods. The plunge of the mineral lineation is similar to that of the stretched cobble lineation.

Folding appears to have been approximately contemporaneous with emplacement of the Hall Canyon pluton. The main body of the peraluminous granodiorite that makes up the pluton is concordant with the Kingston Peak Formation, and the granodiorite has a strong foliation near the walls of the main body. Other satellite plutons are unfoliated and crosscut the folded Kingston Peak Formation. Both the main body and its satellites have been dated by Labotka and others (1985) by the ^{39}Ar/^{40}Ar technique at 80 to 70 Ma.

At the south end of the Panamint Mountains, the folded rocks appear to have been deflected by the intrusion of the Manly Peak pluton, which has been dated by conventional K-Ar methods as Late Jurassic to Early Cretaceous (Armstrong and Suppe, 1973). Wright and others (1981) suggested that the Panamint anticlinorium developed during Jurassic time. Although it is possible that intrusion predated folding and that the Manly Peak pluton acted as a rigid body during Cretaceous deformation, the metamorphic rocks that make up the core of the Panamint Mountains were probably folded coaxially more than once during the Mesozoic Era.

The folded rocks are cut by an extensive network of generally north-trending, steeply dipping normal faults. There are some deviations in the trend, particularly near Little Chief stock, but some faults can be traced nearly continuously from near Manly Peak to Wildrose Canyon. The offset across the faults is mostly dip slip, but the displacement varies along individual faults from east-side up along the southern portion to west-side up along the northern portion. The westward step in the upthrown side of the fault occurs because the trend of the faults is oblique to that of the NNW–trending folds. This relation indicates that the faults predated folding and were used as surfaces of opportunity during folding.

The South Park Canyon fault is also a north-trending fault but has a much lower dip than the others and places middle Proterozoic gneiss over the Pahrump Group. This fault was intruded by metagranodiorite in the southern part of the Panamint

Mountains, and the Hall Canyon pluton was probably also emplaced along the fault. Displacement along the fault ceased prior to intrusion of the granodiorite and subsequent metamorphism. The fault may be a thrust of a similar age to that of the Last Chance system (Stewart and others, 1966; Dunne and others, 1978; Labotka and Albee, 1988; Wernicke and others, 1988a, b). Labotka and others (1980a, b) suggested that the down-dip steepening of the fault indicated that the fault originated similarly to the other north-trending faults but was subsequently folded to give the reverse geometry.

Metamorphism

The Pahrump Group and overlying rocks were regionally metamorphosed during Mesozoic time. The petrology of the metamorphic rocks is described by Labotka (1981, 1987) and Labotka and Albee (1988). The age of metamorphism has been determined by Lanphere and others (1964) and Labotka and others (1985). Metamorphism occurred in two episodes: a Jurassic prograde metamorphism and a Cretaceous retrograde metamorphism. The style of prograde metamorphism is characterized by the assemblages andalusite + staurolite + biotite and andalusite + cordierite + biotite in medium-grade pelitic schists. Where these assemblages are preserved, the host rocks possess weak or no secondary foliation. The textures are generally granoblastic. Temperature ranged from <415 to 650°C at a pressure of 2.4 to 3.0 kbar. Metamorphic grade increased westward, from incipiently metamorphosed rocks east of Telescope Peak to sillimanite-grade rocks near the mouths of Surprise, Hall, and Jail Canyons. Retrograde metamorphism strongly affected the rocks near the core of the anticline where sillimanite-grade rocks were recrystallized to garnet + chlorite-bearing assemblages at a temperature of ~450°C. The strong foliation and the mineral lineations on the western flank of the anticline formed during the retrograde metamorphism. Rb-Sr and K-Ar isotopic systematics indicate that prograde metamorphism occurred during Middle Jurassic time, in the period from 170 to 150 Ma, and that retrograde metamorphism occurred during Late Cretaceous time, between 80 and 70 Ma. Both periods correspond to the times of emplacement of granitic rocks in the nearby Argus, Inyo, and White Mountains and in the eastern Sierra Nevada.

TERTIARY STRUCTURES IN THE CENTRAL PANAMINT MOUNTAINS

Introduction

Extension of the central part of the Panamint Mountains is manifested in gently west-dipping normal faults that are extensively exposed on the east slope of the range, in isolated klippen of similarly oriented normal-fault blocks on the western slope of the range, in massive monolithologic breccias that form the western rampart of the range, and in fanglomerates that filled the proto–Panamint Valley north of Wildrose Canyon. The geology of four areas that illustrate these features are described. The locations of detailed maps of the four areas are shown in Figure 1, and a LANDSAT TM image of the Panamint Mountains is shown in Figure 2. The TM image illustrates most of the extensional features described here. Only the west-dipping normal faults on the east side of the range cannot be seen because of the lack in contrast between rock types affected by the faulting. The advantage of the TM image is that reflectivity of the infrared bands 4 and is sensitive to iron- and hydroxyl-bearing minerals, particularly clays that form by weathering of feldspar. The appearance of weathered rocks, especially those that have a desert varnish, is enhanced in this image. A disadvantage of this TM image is that many rock types are not discriminated; for example, brecciated granitic rocks have an appearance similar to that of weathered dolomite.

Little Chief Stock

Little Chief stock is a composite granite porphyry intrusion with an age of 10.6 Ma (McKenna, 1986), exposed at the crest of the Panamint Mountains near Telescope Peak (McDowell, 1974; Fig. 3) North of the stock, numerous west-dipping normal faults, with dips ranging from about 45° to 15°, cut east-dipping rocks of the Noonday Dolomite, Johnnie Formation, and Stirling Quartzite. Offsets are generally less than 200 m. These faults are similar in orientation and sense of displacement to the major normal fault at the east foot of the Panamint Mountains that Hunt and Mabey (1966) called the Amargosa thrust, after Noble (1941). South of the stock, similar west-dipping faults are uncommon, and steeply dipping normal faults occur instead. The stock itself has generally vertical walls, except on the eastern margin along the extension of a southeast-striking fault where the contact dips 35° inward. The stock apparently was emplaced along the intersection of the prominent north-trending fault system and the southeast-trending fault exposed on the eastern side of the stock. At the time of emplacement, a trap door formed between two east-trending vertical faults, with a hinge-line near a north-trending vertical fault.

McDowell (1974) determined that emplacement of the stock began with the intrusion of a felsic dike swarm east and north of the stock along the shallow, west-dipping normal faults. The southern part of the stock was emplaced first and formed the trap door, which cut the early dike swarm and the west-dipping faults. The northern part of the stock continued to rise, tearing the trapdoor along the southeast-trending fault. The presence of miarolitic cavities, micropegmatites, and a breccia zone indicates that the northern part of the stock vented to the surface. The groundmass composition and the compositional zoning patterns in the plagioclase phenocrysts led McDowell (1978) to conclude that the ground surface was about 1 km above the present position of the stock.

Extension in this part of the Panamint Mountains appears to have begun during the early stages of emplacement of the Little Chief stock (McDowell, 1974; Labotka and others, 1980a, b; McKenna, 1986) during Miocene time. By the time the stock was emplaced in its present position, the metamorphic complex was within a few kilometers of the surface.

Tuber and Jail Canyons

The geology of the western slope of the central Panamint Mountains centered around Jail Canyon is shown in Figure 4. This geology is typical of the crystalline core of the Panamint Mountains. The axis of the north-northwest-trending anticline traverses the center of the figure, oblique to the north-trending, steeply dipping faults. The characteristic reversals in the sense of displacement across the faults can be seen by tracing the fault that bounds the western side of the quartzofeldspathic gneiss in Hall Canyon northward to Jail Canyon where it bounds the eastern side of the gneiss. The northward plunge of the anticline can be seen in Tuber Canyon where marble, schist, and quartzite assigned to the Crystal Spring Formation form the core of the anticline rather than quartzofeldspathic gneiss. The highest metamorphic grade in the Panamint Mountains was attained in rocks exposed in the western part of this area.

On the west-trending ridges between the canyons are klippen with nearly flat or spoon-shaped bounding faults. The geometry and sense of displacement along these faults are similar to those of the west-dipping faults on the eastern slope of the range, but the character of the rocks in the hanging walls is more highly disrupted. This is better displayed by rocks in similar klippen north of Wildrose Canyon. Stratigraphic order within the klippen is preserved, but the rocks are fractured and locally brecciated. Numerous minor faults repeat or cut out section, as displayed by the klippe north of Tuber Canyon in Figure 4. Figure 5a is a photograph of this klippe showing that a thin, sheared layer of Noonday Dolomite forms the hanging wall, even where the klippe is composed mostly of Johnnie Formation rocks. The hanging walls of most klippen contain carbonate rocks, including Sourdough Limestone in the small klippen near South Park Canyon, and Noonday Dolomite in most klippen north of Wildrose Canyon. The brecciated and fractured nature of the hanging-wall rocks indicates that the klippen formed under less cover and later than the network of west-dipping faults on the eastern slope of the range.

The faults crosscut the older folded structures. Figure 5b shows the block composed of Kingston Peak Formation between Jail and Hall Canyons, cutting Beck Spring Dolomite on the west flank of the anticline. The clean, crosscutting relation can also be seen in Figure 2, the TM image, where dark Kingston Peak Formation in the block between Tuber and Jail Canyons truncates white Beck Spring Dolomite on the crest of the anticline.

Individual klippen shown in Figure 4 contain different rocks in the hanging walls from one another, and the elevations of the basal faults range considerably. These klippen probably are small, individual fault blocks, rather than remnants of a once-continuous normal fault block. The amount of displacement is difficult to determine accurately. The best estimate is obtained on the block between Jail and Tuber Canyons in which the Crystal

Figure 2. LANDSAT thematic mapper (TM) image of the central Panamint Mountains. The image covers an area similar to that shown in Figure 1. The location of Figure 1 is indicated by the tick marks. TM band 1 (450–520 nm) is blue, band 4 (780–910 nm) is green, and band 7 (2080–2350 nm) is red. The structure of the central Panamint Mountains can be discerned from the disposition of Beck Spring Dolomite, which shows as the white bedded layer halfway between the foot and the crest of the range. The normal fault block marked C in Figure 4 can be seen near the center of the image where dark Kingston Peak Formation cuts the white Beck Spring Dolomite on the west-trending ridge between Tuber and Jail canyons. The dark Surprise breccia mass can be seen at the center of the image, on the western edge of the range. Other portions of the breccia mass can be seen near the center and in the west-central part of the image near Wildrose Canyon. Fanglomerates of the Nova Formation can be seen as the gray area northwest of Wildrose Canyon. The Skidoo pluton can be discerned south of Tucki Mountain as the light gray, rounded area. Other features visible in the image are described in the text. The green-tinted region at the crest of the range is the sparsely forested Noonday Dolomite and Johnnie Formation. The bald upper Johnnie Formation near Telescope Peak is dark colored.

Spring Formation appears to have been displaced about 2 km west-northwest from a position on the east flank of the anticline in Jail Canyon. The sense of displacement is generally westward, with translation of the blocks across the axis of the anticline.

Surprise Canyon

The mouth of Surprise Canyon cuts through a mass of monolithologic breccia, called the Surprise breccia, composed largely of finely brecciated and pulverized Kingston Peak Formation, illustrated on the map in Figure 6. Breccia composed of Hall Canyon granodiorite occurs north of Surprise Canyon, and breccia composed of Noonday Dolomite crops out south of the canyon. The breccia rests on a surface, called the Surprise fault, that dips westward with moderate to shallow dip and cuts folded Kingston Peak Formation, the South Park Canyon fault, and the Hall Canyon pluton in the footwall. South of Happy Canyon,

isolated masses of breccia rest on surfaces that may be distinct from the Surprise fault. The Surprise fault is nearly continuously exposed northward to Wildrose Canyon. Near Jail Canyon the trace of the surface is covered by numerous landslides and may not be continuous. The northward extension of the fault can be seen in Figure 4.

Rocks making up the Surprise breccia mass are argillites and diamictites of the Kingston Peak Formation. The rocks are very finely pulverized and deeply weathered and resemble fault gouge. The breccia mass supports steep, smooth slopes with a moderately high density of gullies, as can be seen in the photograph in Figure 7 (taken from the vantage point labeled C in Fig. 6). Vestiges of shore lines from Pleistocene Panamint Lake can also be seen on the mass. Because most of the parent rocks of the breccia mass are diamictites, the mass has a distinct, dark appearance on the TM image, Figure 2.

The sense of displacement of the Surprise breccia mass can

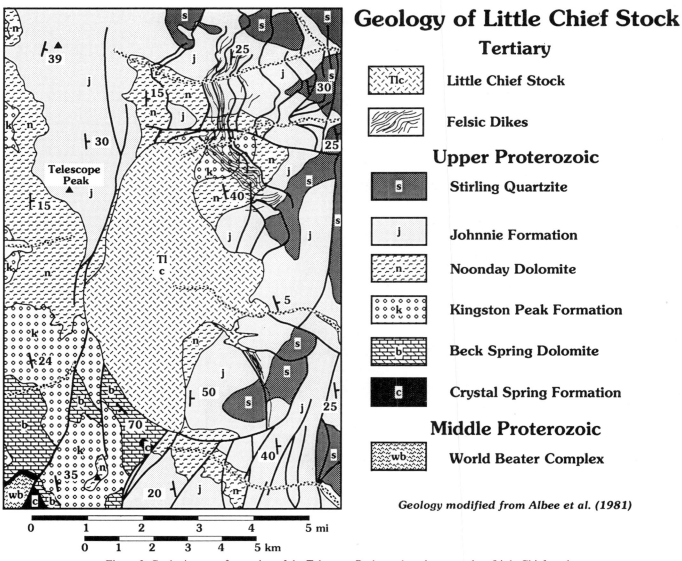

Figure 3. Geologic map of a portion of the Telescope Peak quadrangle centered on Little Chief stock.

be estimated from the offset of two structural features. The first, marked A in Figure 6, is the contact between Kingston Peak Formation and the Hall Canyon pluton. The equivalent contact in the footwall is marked A′. The second feature is the axis of the syncline with Noonday Dolomite in the core, marked B and B′ in Figure 6. Both indicate westward, down-dip displacement of about 2,500 to 2,800 m.

In many respects the Surprise breccia mass is similar to the hanging-wall rocks on the isolated klippen described in the previous section. Gross stratigraphic and structural disposition is preserved, even though the rocks are thoroughly fractured. The sense of displacement is also similar. The breccias also have the thoroughly brecciated character of landslides. The Surprise breccia appears to have formed at a time when the metamorphic complex was near the surface. The unconstrained upper surface allowed the rocks to become brecciated as the mass slid off the rising Panamint Mountains along the Surprise fault and related surfaces. Similarities between the breccia mass and the klippen indicate that both formed in response to the uplift of the Pana-

mint Mountains but that the breccias are younger, having formed under less cover.

Wildrose Canyon

The breccia mass can be mapped northward to Wildrose Canyon where the Plio-Pleistocene Nova Formation lies above it. Figure 8 shows the geology of the area near White Sage wash between Wildrose Canyon and Emigrant Pass, mapped by Lanphere (1962), Albee and others (1981), and Harding (1988), with some additional unpublished mapping by Labotka. The region is dominated by breccias derived from upper members of the Kingston Peak Formation, Noonday Dolomite, Johnnie Formation, and granitic rocks of the Skidoo pluton.

The breccias are bounded by numerous, generally flat to west-dipping fault surfaces and show a nearly continuous gradation in character from that of the isolated klippen to that of the breccia mass from east to west. The Surprise fault, which bounds the breccia mass against the core of the Panamint Mountains

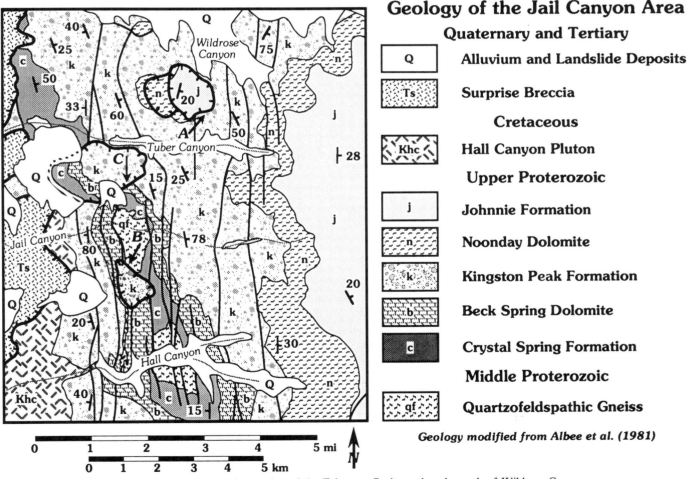

Figure 4. Geologic map of a portion of the Telescope Peak quadrangle south of Wildrose Canyon showing isolated klippen of normal-fault blocks cutting the Mesozoic anticline. A and B indicate the photographic views of the klippen shown in Figure 5. C marks the fault block that can be observed in the TM image, Figure 2.

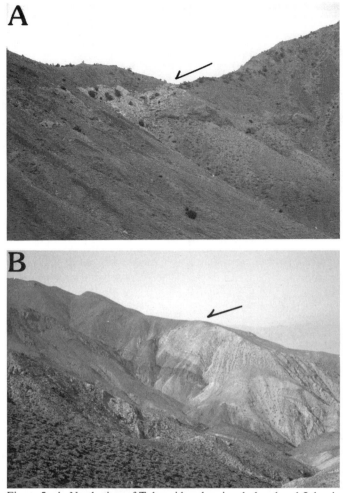

Figure 5. A. North view of Tuber ridge showing dark-colored Johnnie Formation in a normal fault block cutting across Sourdough Limestone and adjacent members of the Kingston Peak Formation. A light streak of Noonday Dolomite marks the position of the fault. B. Southwest view of a normal-fault block on the ridge between Jail and Hall canyons in which dark-colored Kingston Peak Formation cuts steeply dipping Crystal Spring Formation and Beck Spring Dolomite (white) on the west flank of the NNW-trending anticline.

south of Wildrose Canyon, can only be mapped with confidence to the north side of Wildrose Canyon. To the north, individual blocks of Noonday Dolomite and conglomeratic members of the Kingston Peak Formation rest on lower Kingston Peak Formation that appears to be part of the Surprise breccia mass. A continuous bounding surface between the breccia mass and relatively intact rocks cannot be mapped. To the east, the fault blocks contain relatively intact bits of Kingston Peak Formation, Noonday Dolomite, or Johnnie Formation. An eastern limit to the extended blocks can be seen north and south of Nemo Canyon in Figure 8 as a west-dipping fault.

The Nova Formation overlies the Surprise breccia mass, separated by a shallow, variably west-dipping fault that extends

northward toward Emigrant Canyon, where it is called the Emigrant fault (Wernicke and others, 1988c). The Nova Formation consists of medium- to coarse-grained sand and gravel deposited on alluvial fans. Common clasts include upper Kingston Peak Formation, Hall Canyon–type granite, Johnnie Formation, and Stirling Quartzite. Dacite clasts are also found locally. The fanglomerates generally dip eastward ~25° against the Emigrant fault, as shown in Figure 9. The Nova Formation has been divided into several units by Hall (1971), who recognized the presence of angular unconformities separating fanglomerate units within Hopper's (1947) Nova Formation. The fanglomerate contains interbedded basalt north and west of the area in Figure 8 and beds of monolithologic breccia near White Sage Wash and northwest of the mapped area.

The abundance of upper Proterozoic clasts in the Nova Formation indicates that the Nova fanglomerates began to accumulate after much of the metamorphic complex was unroofed. The presence of monolithologic breccia signifies that the initial accumulation of the fanglomerate probably occurred contemporaneously with development of the Surprise and associated breccia masses. Basalt interbedded with the fanglomerate has an age of 5 Ma (Hall, 1971), and basalt covers Noonday Dolomite breccia west of White Sage Wash, near the north edge of Figure 8.

The view from space

The extension in the Panamint Mountains resulted in displacement along west-dipping normal faults, in formation of monolithologic breccias along a west-dipping surface, and in deposition of fanglomerates in a basin prior to the opening of Panamint Valley. The breccias and fanglomerates are distinctive rock types that can be recognized in images produced by LANDSAT and space shuttle sensors. Both types of images have proved useful as aids in geologic mapping of these rock types, principally because the weathering and erosional characteristics distinguish them from the relatively intact rocks in the metamorphic complex.

The Landsat TM image, shown in Figure 2, displays marked contrasts in rock types, resulting from differences in mineralogy. The dark blue-gray rock mass near the center of the image, on the east flank of the Panamint Mountains south of Tucki Wash, is composed of Cambrian Bonanza King Formation and Nopah Formation. These formations contain abundant medium- to dark-gray dolomite layers. The pale tan to cream-colored rocks in Tucki Mountain are mostly middle to upper Paleozoic carbonate rocks, which occur in the hanging walls of detachment faults in the Tucki Mountain system, as described by Wernicke and others (1988c).

The structure of the metamorphic complex is outlined by the nearly white Beck Spring Dolomite. The dolomite defines the NNW–trending anticline and the northern flank of World Beater dome; Beck Spring Dolomite is absent south of Happy Canyon. The gneissic rocks in the cores of the folds are pale brown, and the Kingston Peak Formation in the limbs is dark brown. Noon-

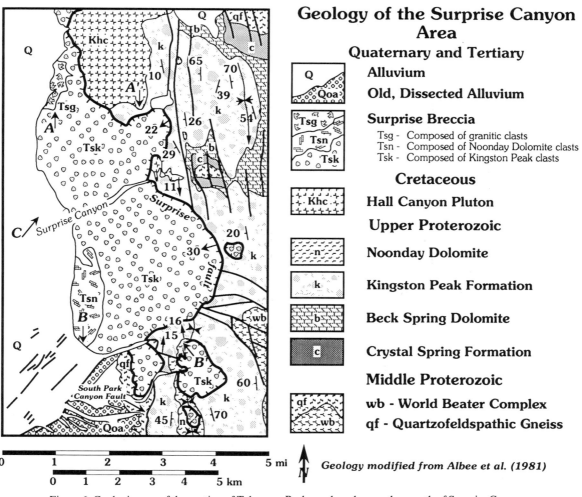

Geology of the Surprise Canyon Area

Quaternary and Tertiary

Q Alluvium

Qoa Old, Dissected Alluvium

Surprise Breccia

Tsg **Tsn** **Tsk**

Tsg - Composed of granitic clasts
Tsn - Composed of Noonday Dolomite clasts
Tsk - Composed of Kingston Peak clasts

Cretaceous

Khc Hall Canyon Pluton

Upper Proterozoic

n Noonday Dolomite

k Kingston Peak Formation

b Beck Spring Dolomite

c Crystal Spring Formation

Middle Proterozoic

wb - World Beater Complex

qf - Quartzofeldspathic Gneiss

0   1   2   3   4   5 mi

0   1   2   3   4   5 km

Geology modified from Albee et al. (1981)

Figure 6. Geologic map of the portion of Telescope Peak quadrangle near the mouth of Surprise Canyon showing the Surprise breccia mass. A-A′ and B-B′ mark structures offset by the breccia mass: Hall Canyon pluton–Kingston Peak contact and a syncline axis, respectively. C shows the photographic view of the breccia mass shown in Figure 7. The Surprise breccia mass can easily be seen in the TM image, Figure 2.

day Dolomite in the southwestern Panamint Mountains, where it is metamorphosed, appears white.

Some extensional structures in the central Panamint Mountains can be seen where the klippe composed of Kingston Peak Formation rest on the axis of the anticline. Compare the geology in Figure 4 with the image in Figure 2 to locate the klippe. The fault at the base of the klippe cuts the axis of the anticline, placing dark Kingston Peak Formation on white Beck Spring Dolomite.

Most west-dipping normal faults cannot be seen on the image because of the poor contrast between rock types on either side of the faults. The volcanic rocks that formed at the eastern foot of the Panamint Mountains along the trace of the Amargosa fault of Hunt and Mabey (1966) are seen in Figure 2 as the pink masses near Trail Canyon, where the dark-gray carbonate rocks occur, and elsewhere. In these places, middle Proterozoic gneisses were intruded by granite, felsic dikes, and sills. Individual sills,

pink in color, can be seen intruding the blue-gray carbonate near Trail Canyon.

The Surprise breccia shows a range in mottled colors on the TM image because the parent lithology consists of diamictite, quartzite, argillite, dolomite, and granite. Weathering of these parent rocks produces abundant oxidized-iron–bearing minerals and clay minerals, which generally appear with orange to brown colors on the combination of bands in Figure 2. Near Surprise Canyon, the breccia is composed of nearly black diamictites of the upper Kingston Peak Formation. Near Wildrose Canyon, the breccia mass consists of gray arenite and orange-brown amphibolite from the middle and lower Kingston Peak Formation. The breccia mass north of Wildrose Canyon has a mottled orange, brown, and white appearance because of the presence of Kingston Peak, weathered Noonday Dolomite, and granite clasts. On the ground, the breccia mass north of Wildrose Canyon is difficult to distinguish from unbrecciated rocks because the outcrop is

Figure 7. NNE view of the Surprise breccia mass from the floor of Panamint Valley. The finely brecciated Kingston Peak Formation supports steep slopes and narrow, closely spaced gullies. This particular composition of breccia mass appears very dark on the TM image, Figure 2.

poor. The spectral response on the TM image, however, is that of weathered rocks and is significantly different from that of the relatively intact parent rocks.

The fanglomerates that make up the Nova Formation appear as the gray mass near the west-central part of the image. The uniform gray appearance is interrupted by black basalt flows, which locally appear red where hydrothermally altered, and by dark gray Paleozoic rocks along the Towne Pass fault.

Although the TM sensor provides information about the mineralogical constitution of various rock types, a distinctive feature of the breccia masses and fanglomerates is their topographic expression. Figure 8 shows 400-ft contours on the Nova Formation and the breccia mass south of Wildrose Canyon. The fanglomerate has a highly dentate contour pattern, reflecting a high density of steep, sharp ridges and gullies arranged in a crudely radial pattern. The breccia mass is also drained by a relatively high density of narrow-sided washes, but the washes are generally parallel, have few tributaries, and are separated by rounded ridges. The intact core of the range is drained by west-flowing second- or third-order streams, spaced ~3 km apart, separated by sharp ridges with moderately steep slopes. The three types cannot be distinguished easily on Figure 2 because a moderately high sun angle illuminates the topography. Synthetic aperture radar, however, is sensitive to differences in surface textures of deposits and can characterize the deposits by complementing the compositional data from the TM image.

Figure 10 shows the radar image of the Panamint Mountains obtained from the second shuttle imaging radar (SIR-B) mission in October 1984, with a wavelength of 23.5 cm and a nominal incidence angle of 44°. A detailed description of the mission is given by Cimino and others (1986) and Elachi and others (1986).

The SIR-B image is used on conjunction with Landsat TM data to aid in distinguishing among relatively intact bedrock, breccia, and fanglomerate. The successful application of synthetic aperture radar (SAR) to geologic problems in arid terrains with low relief has been well documented. For example, McCauley and others (1986), using SIR-A and SIR-B, were able to identify paleodrainage systems that could not be recognized on the ground or by Landsat images. Daily and others (1979) coregistered Landsat multispectral scanner (MSS) data with airborne SAR to optimize the discrimination among alluvial deposits in fans in Death Valley. Schaber and others (1976) could readily distinguish the variety of surficial deposits in the central part of Death Valley, based on their surface roughnesses.

The backscatter, or brightness, of an object depends largely on its surface roughness if the object is relatively flat, but topography becomes the dominant source of brightness in mountainous terrains. Radar images in mountainous terrains take the appearance of sun-illuminated images. Use of radar images in mountainous terrains can be a significant aid, however, to geologic mapping, particularly when used in conjunction with other types of data, as illustrated by Fielding and others (1986).

The radar brightness of areas on this image having low relief depends on the surface roughness. Many geologic features of the floor of Death Valley described by Hunt and Mabey (1966) were identified on airborne radar images by Schaber and others (1976) and enhanced by coregistration of Landsat total intensity image with radar images by Daily and others (1979). Schaber and others (1976) discussed in detail the relation between the surface roughnesses of the salt, silt, and sand deposits and radar backscatter. Some of the same features on the floor of Death Valley can be seen in the SIR-B image in Figure 10. The brightest areas in the image represent rough, silty salt deposits, which surround the dark, flat flood plain deposits in the lowest parts of the playa. The radar image effectively discriminates among alluvial fan deposits of different ages because the old deposits have a smooth desert pavement developed on the surface. The smooth pavements tend to reflect the radar signal specularly and thus appear dark, whereas the active fans contain a rough accumulation of gravel and have a higher backscatter than do the older pavements. The dark band near the toe of the Tucki Wash fan, noted by Schaber and others (1976), is visible in Figure 10. The band corresponds to the silt facies of Hunt and Mabey (1966), and Schaber and others (1976) ascribed the dark appearance to the fine grain size and low surface relief of the silt, which combine to make the unit radar-smooth.

Faults that displace alluvial deposits are enhanced in the radar images, depending on the relative orientation of the fault with respect to the illumination angle. In Figure 10, faults can be seen on the Tucki Wash fan where old alluvial deposits, which appear dark, were uplifted relative to the actively accumulating deposits. In Panamint Valley, the Wildrose graben is clearly visible because the old alluvium on the uplifted sides is dark, whereas the alluvium in the graben is light. Other faults in the alluvium near the mouth of Wildrose Canyon can also be seen.

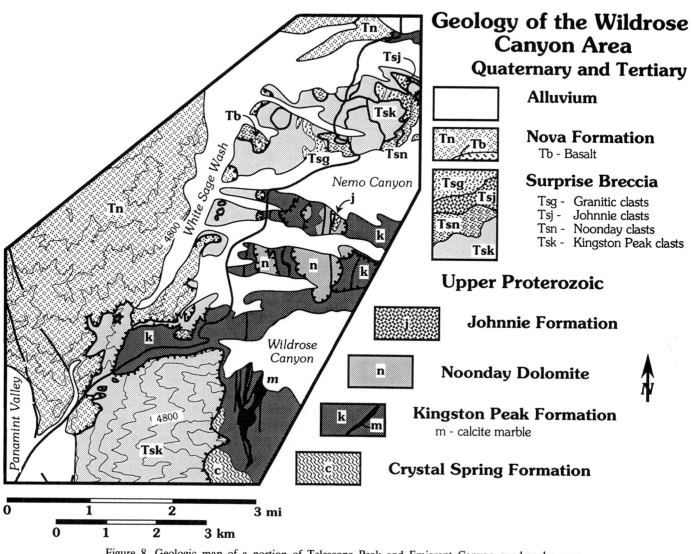

Geology of the Wildrose Canyon Area

Quaternary and Tertiary

Alluvium

Nova Formation
Tb - Basalt

Surprise Breccia
Tsg - Granitic clasts
Tsj - Johnnie clasts
Tsn - Noonday clasts
Tsk - Kingston Peak clasts

Upper Proterozoic

Johnnie Formation

Noonday Dolomite

Kingston Peak Formation
m - calcite marble

Crystal Spring Formation

Figure 8. Geologic map of a portion of Telescope Peak and Emigrant Canyon quadrangles near Wildrose Canyon and White Sage Wash. The geology of this region shows the three principal rock types associated with Tertiary extension. From east to west these are relatively intact metamorphic rocks of the core of the Panamint Mountains, highly disrupted and brecciated rocks of the Surprise breccia mass, and fanglomerates of the Nova Formation. The three types are separated by generally low-angle, west-dipping faults. Contours show the topography of the Nova Formation and Surprise breccia near the mouth of Wildrose Canyon.

In the mountainous terrain, the radar brightness is largely a function of the local incidence angle; the effect of the material roughness on the backscatter is secondary. The differences in erosional characteristics, however, are well displayed in this image. The fanglomerates of the Nova Formation have a highly reticulated pattern that presents a rough surface to the radar and results in a speckly image. The bright fanglomerate is interrupted by the Towne Pass fault, which juxtaposes smoother, darker rocks against the Nova Formation. The distribution of the Nova Formation can be seen easily, even in the northwestern part of the image where the radar signal was weak. The speckled slopes of the numerous gullies are evident.

The image clearly shows the closely spaced, elongate drainage pattern of the Surprise breccia, extending from Wildrose Canyon to Surprise Canyon. The drainages trend westerly, nearly at right angles to the illumination direction. The brecciated rocks north of Wildrose Canyon are not as well illuminated as those south of Wildrose Canyon. The elongate, closely spaced ridges, supported by breccia masses in the region around Nemo Canyon, show more clearly on the TM image (Fig. 2).

The relatively intact rocks that make up the core of the range are well displayed in the SIR-B image. These rocks support smooth slopes, in comparison with the breccias and Nova Formation. Ridges are widely and evenly spaced and are parallel. The

Figure 9. Photograph of the Emigrant fault near the mouth of Wildrose Canyon. The fault separates Nova fanglomerates in the hanging wall from highly brecciated, deeply weathered gouge of the Surprise breccia mass in the footwall.

drainage pattern on the east slope of the Panamint Mountains is dendritic rather than parallel. The slopes are held up by upper Proterozoic rocks near Telescope Peak and by Lower Paleozoic rocks south of Tucki Wash. The difference in drainage pattern probably reflects the dip-slope on quartzitic rocks near Telescope Peak and the thick section of carbonate rocks south of Tucki Wash.

Uplift of the Panamint Mountains has resulted in the development of three rock types. The first is the relatively intact metamorphic core of the range. Uplift of the core rocks was accompanied by displacements along west-dipping normal faults. The displacements, however, did not disrupt the integrity of the rocks. The primary mineralogic character of the rocks is evident in the TM image, and the erosional characteristics are seen in the SIR-B image. The second rock type is the breccia mass that formed from the core rocks during a late stage in the uplift. The breccias have mottled colors in the TM image, reflecting the weathered character of the clasts, and have narrow, parallel drainages in the SIR-B image. The third rock type is the fanglomerate of the Nova Formation. The fanglomerates have a uniform appearance on the TM image and a speckled appearance on the radar image because of the abundance of reticulated gullies.

EXPOSURE OF THE PANAMINT METAMORPHIC COMPLEX

The central Panamint Mountains show a progressive sequence of structures and rocks developed during the uplift and unroofing of the metamorphic complex that makes up the core of the range. During prograde metamorphism in Middle Jurassic time, upper Proterozoic rocks were buried to depths of 10 ± 1 km, corresponding to a pressure of $2,750 \pm 250$ kbar. This estimate is based on local stratigraphic thicknesses and does not

consider possible Jurassic volcanic rocks that may have been present. Although the pressure estimate is crudely based, it is consistent with the phase equilibria preserved in the metamorphic rocks (Labotka, 1981). These rocks underwent retrograde metamorphism during Late Cretaceous time, when the Hall Canyon pluton was intruded and the NNW–trending anticline was developed. The pressure during this time is not well known. The Hall Canyon pluton contains muscovite, which would indicate a pressure in excess of about 3 kbar; however, the muscovite contains abundant ferric iron (3 to 5 wt percent) in substitution for aluminum. Because muscovite is much more iron rich than sillimanite, the addition of Fe^{+3} stabilizes muscovite to higher temperatures than those for Fe-free muscovite. This effect reduces the minimum pressure necessary for muscovite-bearing granites (e.g., Zen, 1988). It seems likely, though, that the depth of emplacement of the pluton at 80 to 70 Ma was similar to that of the prograde metamorphism: ~ 10 km.

The west-dipping normal faults that crop out extensively on the east side of the range crest represent the earliest extension in the central Panamint Mountains. The faults cut the east-dipping limb of the anticline and are intruded by the ~ 11-Ma Little Chief stock. The faults are similar in attitude and sense of offset to the Amargosa fault at the east base of the Panamint Mountains. The footwall of the Amargosa fault contains Proterozoic gneiss, intruded by Miocene aplitic dikes (Hunt and Mabey, 1966), and may be the same rocks that form the turtlebacks in the Black Mountains (Hamilton, 1988). Stewart (1983) and Wernicke and others (1988a) argued that the central Panamint Mountains were displaced northwestward along this and related faults from a position near the Resting Springs Range.

When the Little Chief stock was emplaced, the core of the range was about 3 km from the surface. There is no direct evidence to indicate whether the uplift from a depth of 10 km to 3 km occurred gradually over the 60-m.y. period after emplacement of the Hall Canyon pluton or whether the uplift occurred by displacement along the system of normal faults, including those intruded by the Little Chief stock, during initial extension of the Death Valley region. Hodges (1988) indicated that at least half of the total uplift in other exposures of the Mesozoic metamorphic terrain occurred during extension. If extension in the Panamint Mountains began contemporaneously with that in the Bare Mountains and elsewhere in the Death Valley area, then much of the uplift of the Panamint Mountains occurred in a very short time interval. Detachment faulting appears to have begun at about 11 Ma (summaries by Hamilton, 1988; Carr and Monsen, 1988; and Wernicke and others, 1988a), and the Little Chief stock intruded some of the faults at 10.6 Ma (McKenna, 1986). If all the Miocene uplift occurred by displacement on the Amargosa and related faults, the uplift rate was about 17 mm/yr. Wernicke and others (1988a) indicated that at the same time, 10 to 15 Ma, the Sierra Nevada was moving westward at a rate of 20 to 30 mm/yr. The late middle Miocene seems to have been the time of most active extension here.

The formation of the monolithologic breccias and the low-

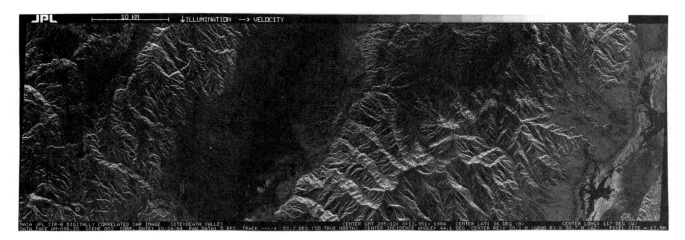

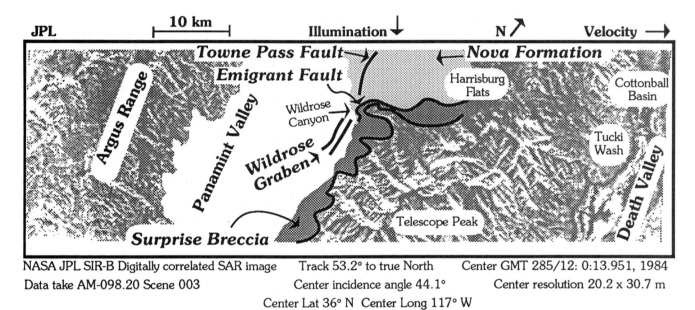

NASA JPL SIR-B Digitally correlated SAR image   Track 53.2° to true North   Center GMT 285/12: 0:13.951, 1984

Data take AM-098.20 Scene 003   Center incidence angle 44.1°   Center resolution 20.2 x 30.7 m

Center Lat 36° N Center Long 117° W

Figure 10. Shuttle Imaging Radar (SIR-B) view of the central part of the Panamint Mountains. The location of this image is shown in Figure 1. The image shows very clearly the different alluvial deposits in Death Valley and Panamint Valley. The deposits are distinct because of differences in the surface roughness of the composing material. The rough salt deposits are bright, fine-grained sands and desert pavements on old alluvium are dark. The physiography of the three principal rock types making up the extended terrain is easily seen in this image. Fanglomerate is speckled bright because of the high density of reticulated drainages developed on its surface. The breccia masses show the high density of elongate, closely spaced gullies. The metamorphic core rocks show widely spaced, knife-edge, west-trending ridges.

angle normal fault blocks on the west slope of the range constitutes the major expression of uplift in the central part of the Panamint Mountains. These structures formed later than the time of emplacement of the Little Chief stock, based on the presumption that the brecciated nature of the rocks reflects a shallow cover during displacement. The westward sense of displacement, across the axis of the anticline, indicates that the crest of the Panamint Mountains was in nearly the same position as it is now. Deposition of the Nova Formation occurred at least partly contemporaneously with breccia formation. The displacement of the breccia masses appears to have been accomplished by late Pliocene time when basalt flows covered them.

Tertiary volcanic rocks on the east side of the Panamint Mountains are tilted 20° or more eastward (Hunt and Mabey, 1966; Wernicke and others, 1988c), indicating eastward tilting of the Panamint block. The Nova Formation dips ~25° eastward. The profiles of the alluvial fans on the east side of the Panamint Mountains indicate eastward tilting of the mountain block by $\sim 1.8 \times 10^{-5}$ °/yr (Maxson, 1950; Hooke, 1965); at this rate, 20° rotation of the Panamint block would have been accumulated in little more than one million years. Hamilton (1988) argued that the rotation is occurring along an unexposed fault because dikes in the footwall of the Amargosa fault are also rotated by ~20° from the vertical. All the eastward rotation of the Panamint block appears to be very recent because indicators from mid-Miocene to present time are all rotated by about the same amount. If true, then displacement on the Amargosa fault system involved minor or negligible rotation of the hanging wall.

Late Tertiary rotation of the Panamint block would have affected the orientations of older structures in the core of the range. All the axial surfaces of the Mesozoic folds in the core of the Panamint metamorphic complex are nearly vertical. Labotka and Albee (1977) described the lithologic variations within the Pahrump Group and attributed to irregular topography during deposition the highly variable distribution of conglomerates, of locally derived clast types within the conglomerates, of local angular unconformities, of local gradational contacts, and of local absences of some lithologic units. The inferred topographic highs coincide with the crests of Mesozoic folds. It appears that Mesozoic deformation accentuated irregularities in the gneissic basement. The present orientation of the Mesozoic structures and the late Precambrian topographic features are consistent with only small amounts of Tertiary rotation of the core of the range. To be fair, the observations do not prove small amounts of rotation. If the entire block was rotated eastward, then the restored Mesozoic structures were strongly overturned westward, and the present orientation is coincidental.

Some evidence for the amount of rotation of the Panamint block can be obtained from the metamorphic rocks in the core of the range. If the entire block had been rotated 25° eastward, then the metamorphic rocks ought to preserve a lateral pressure gradient of about 133 bar/km. The total range in pressure in the exposed rocks, considering the topographic difference between the crest of the range and the deep canyons in the western margin, should be 2.3 kbar. This range requires a pressure of 4.5 to 5.0 kbar near the axis of the anticline. Although absolute quantitative values of pressure are difficult to obtain, the sequence of mineral assemblages in pelitic schists (Labotka, 1981) and in calcic schists (Labotka, 1987) is inconsistent with this large pressure range. Metamorphism appears to have occurred exclusively within a pressure range appropriate for andalusite stability at low temperatures, i.e., less than 3.7 kbar. The petrology seems to be consistent with eastward rotations of the metamorphic core of the range by no more than 15°. It seems likely, therefore, that the aggregate tilting of ~25° was distributed over smaller rotations along the late middle Miocene Amargosa fault, the Plio-Pleistocene Emigrant and Surprise faults, and the Recent Panamint Valley fault.

Although the Panamint metamorphic complex was essentially unroofed at the time of deposition of the Nova Formation, the current level of exposure is owed to recent uplift and deep incision of the west-flowing streams. Perched remnants of the Surprise breccia south of Happy Canyon attest to the recent uplift of the range. Present uplift is occurring along the Panamint Valley fault zone. The principal sense of displacement on the Panamint Valley fault zone at the north and south ends of Panamint Valley is right-lateral strike slip, with a thrust-fault component near Hunter Mountain at the north end of the valley (Smith, 1975). The central part of Panamint Valley is a pull-apart basin (Burchfiel and Stewart, 1966; Burchfiel and others, 1987). Most of the faults on the east side of the valley are discontinuous, and the west side is bounded by the Ash Hill fault, having principally normal displacement. Smith (1975) has documented Quaternary uplift of the Panamint Mountains of about 120 m relative to the valley floor by mapping a prominent high shoreline of pluvial Lake Panamint. The 120 m of uplift was attained since about 40,000 B.P. The imposing stature of the Panamint Mountains is all the more impressive considering that it has been a relative high throughout much of its recorded geologic history.

ACKNOWLEDGMENTS

The results presented here represent, in many ways, the culmination of geologic mapping in the Telescope Peak quadrangle begun in the early 1960s by Arden Albee. The work of Marvin Lanphere and Doug McDowell contributed greatly to this study. Tom Farr provided considerable assistance with the image processing, for which I am very grateful. This study was supported by grants from the National Science Foundation to Arden Albee and from the Geological Society of America and National Aeronautics and Space Administration to me. Reviews and critical comments by Warren Hamilton and Kip Hodges are greatly appreciated.

REFERENCES CITED

Albee, A. L., Labotka, T. C., Lanphere, M. A., and McDowell, S. D., 1981, Geologic map of the Telescope Peak 15' Quadrangle, California: U.S. Geological Survey Geologic Quadrangle Map GQ–1532, scale 1:62,500.

Armstrong, R. L., and Suppe, J., 1973, Potassium-argon geochronometry of Mesozoic igneous rocks in Nevada, Utah, and southeastern California: Geological Society of America Bulletin, v. 84, p. 1375–1392.

Burchfiel, B. C., and Stewart, J. H., 1966, "Pull apart" origin of the central segment of Death Valley, California: Geological Society of America Bulletin, v. 77, p. 439–442.

Burchfiel, B. C., Hodges, K. V., and Royden, L. H. 1987, Geology of Panamint Valley–Saline Valley pull-apart system, California; Palinspastic evidence for low-angle geometry of a Neogene range-bounding system: Journal of Geophysical Research, v. 92, p. 10422–10426.

Carr, M. D., and Monsen, S. A., 1988, A field trip guide to the geology of Bare Mountain, in Weide, D. L., and Faber, M. L., eds., This extended land; Geological journeys in the southern Basin and Range: University of Nevada at Las Vegas Geoscience Department Special Publication 2, p. 50–57.

Cimino, J. B., Elachi, C., and Settle, M., 1986, SIR-B; The second shuttle imaging radar experiment: Institute of Electrical and Electronics Engineers Transactions on Geoscience and Remote Sensing, v. GE–24, p. 445–452.

Daily, M. I., Farr, T., Elachi, C., and Schaber, G., 1979, Geologic interpretation from composited radar and LANDSAT imagery; Photogrammetric Engineering and Remote Sensing, v. 45, p. 1109–1116.

Dunne, G. C., Gulliver, R. M., and Sylvester, A. G., 1978, Mesozoic evolution of rocks of the White, Inyo, Argus, and Slate Ranges, eastern California, in Howell, D. G., and McDougall, K., eds., Mesozoic paleogeography of the western United States: Society of Economic Paleontologists and Mineralogists, Pacific Section, Pacific Coast Paleogeography Symposium 2, p. 189–207.

Elachi, C., Cimino, J., and Settle, M., 1986, Overview of the shuttle imaging radar; B, Preliminary scientific results: Science, v. 232, p. 1511–1516.

Fielding, E. J., Knox, W. J., Jr., and Bloom, A. L., 1986, SIR-B radar imagery of volcanic deposits in the Andes: Institute of Electrical and Electronics Engineers Transactions on Geoscience and Remote Sensing, v. G–24, p. 582–589.

Hall, W. E., 1971, Geology of the Panamint Butte Quadrangle, Inyo County, California: U.S. Geological Survey Bulletin 1299, p. 1–67.

Hamilton, W. B., 1988, Detachment faulting in the Death Valley region, California and Nevada: U.S. Geological Survey Bulletin 1790, p. 51–85.

Harding, M. B., 1988, Geology of the Wildrose Peak area, Panamint Mountains, southeastern California: Geological Society of America Abstracts with Programs, v. 20, p. 166.

Hodges, K. V., 1988, Metamorphic and geochronologic constraints on the uplift history of Cordilleran metamorphic core complexes: Geological Society of America Abstracts with Programs, v. 20, p. A18.

Hodges, K. V., Walker, J. D., and Wernicke, B. P., 1987, Footwall structural evolution of the Tucki Mountain detachment system, Death Valley region, southeastern California, in Coward, M. P., and others, Continental extensional tectonics: Geological Society of London Special Publication 28, p. 393–408.

Hooke, R. L., 1965, Alluvial fans [Ph.D. thesis]: Pasadena, California Institute of Technology, 192 p.

Hopper, R. H., 1947, Geologic section from the Sierra Nevada to Death Valley, California: Geological Society of America Bulletin, v. 58, p. 393–432.

Hunt, C. B., and Mabey, D. R., 1966, Stratigraphy and structure, Death Valley, California: U.S. Geological Survey Professional Paper 494–A, p. 1–162.

Johnson, B. K., 1957, Geology of a part of the Manly Peak Quadrangle, southern Panamint Range, California: University of California Publications in Geological Sciences, v. 30, p. 353–424.

Labotka, T. C., 1981, Petrology of an andalusite-type regional metamorphic terrane, Panamint Mountains, California: Journal of Petrology, v. 22, p. 261–296.

——, 1987, The garnet + hornblende isograd in calcic schists from an andalusite-type regional metamorphic terrain, Panamint Mountains, California: Journal of Petrology, v. 28, p. 323–354.

Labotka, T. C., and Albee, A. L., 1977, Late Precambrian depositional environment of the Pahrump Group, Panamint Mountains, California: California Division of Mines and Geology Special Paper 129, p. 93–100.

——, 1988, Metamorphism and tectonics of the Death Valley region, California and Nevada, in Ernst, W. G., ed., Metamorphism and crustal evolution of the western United States: New Jersey, Englewood Cliffs, New Jersey, Prentice-Hall, p. 714–736.

Labotka, T. C., Albee, A. L., Lanphere, M. A., and McDowell, S. D., 1980a, Stratigraphy, structure, and metamorphism in the central Panamint Mountains (Telescope Peak Quadrangle), Death Valley area, California: Geological Society of America Bulletin, v. 91, Part 1, p. 125–129.

——, 1980b, Stratigraphy, structure, and metamorphism in the central Panamint Mountains (Telescope Peak Quadrangle), Death Valley area, California: Geological Society of America Bulletin, v. 91, part 2, p. 843–933.

Labotka, T. C., Warasila, R. L., and Spangler, R. R., 1985, Polymetamorphism in the Panamint Mountains, California; A ^{39}Ar-^{40}Ar study: Journal of Geophysical Research, v. 90, p. 10359–10371.

Lanphere, M. A., 1962, I. Geology of the Wildrose area, Panamint Range, California; II. Geochronologic studies in the Death Valley–Mojave Desert region, California [Ph.D. thesis]: Pasadena, California Institute of Technology.

Lanphere, M. A., Wasserburg, G. J., Albee, A. L., and Tilton, G. R., 1964, Redistribution of strontium and rubidium isotopes during metamorphism, World Beater Complex, Panamint Range, California, in Craig, H., and others, eds., Isotopic and cosmic chemistry: Amsterdam, North Holland Publishing Company, p. 269–320.

Maxson, J. H., 1950, Physiographic features of the Panamint Range, California: Geological Society of America Bulletin, v. 61, p. 99–114.

McCauley, J. F., and 7 others, 1986, Paleodrainages of the eastern Sahara; The radar rivers revisited (SIR-A/B implications for a Mid-Tertiary trans-African drainage system): Institute of Electrical and Electronics Engineers Transactions on Geoscience and Remote Sensing, v. GE–24, p. 624–648.

McDowell, S. D., 1974, Emplacement of the Little Chief stock, Panamint Range, California: Geological Society of America Bulletin, v. 85, p. 1535–1546.

——, 1978, Little Chief granite porphyry; Feldspar crystallization history: Geological Society of America Bulletin, v. 89, p. 33–49.

McKenna, L., 1986, New Rb-Sr constraints on the age of detachment faulting in the Panamint Range, Death Valley, California: Geological Society of America Abstracts with Programs, v. 18, p. 156.

Miller, J. M., 1983, Stratigraphy and sedimentology of the Upper Proterozoic Kingston Peak Formation, Panamint Range, eastern California [Ph.D. thesis]: Santa Barbara, University of California, 355 p.

——, 1985, Glacial and syntectonic sedimentation; The upper Proterozoic Kingston Peak Formation, southern Panamint Range, eastern California: Geological Society of America Bulletin, v. 96, p. 1537–1553.

——, 1987, Tectonic evolution of the southern Panamint Range, Inyo and San Bernardino Counties: California Geology, v. 40, p. 212–222.

Murphy, F. M., 1932, Geology of a part of the Panamint Range, California: California Division of Mines, 28th Report State Mineralogist, p. 329–355.

Noble, L. F., 1941, Structural features of the Virgin Spring area, Death Valley, California: Geological Society of America Bulletin, v. 52, p. 941–1000.

Schaber, G. G., Berlin, G. L., and Brown, W. E., Jr., 1976, Variations in surface roughness within Death Valley, California; Geologic evaluation of 25-cm-wavelength radar images: Geological Society of America Bulletin, v. 87, p. 29–41.

Smith, R.S.U., 1975, Guide to selected examples of Quaternary tectonism in Panamint Valley, California: California Geology, v. 28, p. 112–115.

Stevens, C. H., Wrucke, C. T., and McKee, E. H., 1974, Directions and amount of movement on the Butte Valley thrust, southeastern California: Geological

Society of America Abstracts with Programs, v. 6, p. 261.

Stewart, J. H., 1983, Extensional tectonics in the Death Valley area, California; Transport of the Panamint Range structural block 80 kilometers northwestward: Geology, v. 11, p. 153–157.

Stewart, J. H., Ross, D. C., Nelson, C. A., and Burchfiel, B. C., 1966, Last Chance thrust; A major fault in the eastern part of Inyo County, California: U.S. Geological Survey Professional Paepr 550-D, p. 23–24.

Wernicke, B. P., Axen, G. J., and Snow, J. K., 1988a, Basin and Range extensional tectonics at the latitude of Las Vegas, Nevada: Geological Society of America Bulletin, v. 100, p. 1738–1757.

Wernicke, B. P., Snow, J. K., and Walker, J. D., 1988b, Correlation of early Mesozoic thrusts in the southern Great Basin and their possible indication of 250–300 km of Neogene crustal extension, *in* Weide, D. L., and Faber, M. L., eds., This extended land; Geological journeys in the southern Basin and Range: University of Nevada at Las Vegas Geoscience Department Special Publication 2, p. 255–267.

Wernicke, B. P., Walker, J. D., and Hodges, K. V., 1988c, Field guide to the northern part of the Tucki Mountain fault system, Death Valley region, California, *in* Weide, D. L., and Faber, M. L., eds., This extended land; Geological journeys in the southern Basin and Range: University of Nevada at Las Vegas Geoscience Department Special Publication 2, p. 58–63.

Wright, L. A., Troxel, B. W., Burchfiel, B. C., Chapman, R. H., and Labotka, T. C., 1981, Geologic cross section from the Sierra Nevada to the Las Vegas Valley, eastern California to southern Nevada: Geological Society of America Map and Chart Series MC-28M, scale 1:250,000.

Zen, E-an, 1988, Tectonic significance of high-pressure plutonic rocks in the western cordillera of North America, *in* Ernst, W. G., ed., Metamorphism and crustal evolution of the western United States: Englewood Cliffs, New Jersey, Prentice Hall, p. 714–736.

Manuscript Accepted by the Society August 21, 1989

Geological Society of America
Memoir 176
1990

Chapter 18

Constraints on the kinematics and timing of late Miocene–Recent extension between the Panamint and Black Mountains, southeastern California

L. W. McKenna and K. V. Hodges
Department of Earth, Planetary, and Atmospheric Sciences, Massachusetts Institute of Technology, Cambridge, Massachusetts 02139

ABSTRACT

Detailed mapping of extensional structures and synextensional volcanic rocks exposed in the eastern Panamint Mountains, southeastern California, place new constraints on the rates and geometry of late Miocene extension in the Death Valley area. At the eastern edge of the central Panamint Mountains, the Burro Trail and Amargosa "thrust" faults of Hunt and Mabey (1966) form subparallel roof and sole faults, respectively, of a kinematically related system of currently low-angle normal faults and subvertical strike-slip faults named here the Eastern Panamint fault system. The roof and sole faults initiated as 40 to 60°W–dipping normal faults in late Miocene time and were subsequently rotated to shallow dips by later, structurally lower, normal faults. Roughly 150 to 160 percent cumulative extension can be demonstrated for Eastern Panamint structures exposed in Trail Canyon.

Late Miocene tuffs and andesites exposed in the eastern Panamint Mountains are correlative with the Sheephead Andesite and Rhodes Tuff in the southern Black Mountains. Reconstruction of these sequences indicates 25 to 55 km of post–9 Ma extension between the eastern Panamint and southern Black Mountains along an azimuth of N55° ± 3 °W. This extension was dominantly accommodated by movement on the Amargosa fault system and late Neogene faults exposed along the western front of the Black Mountains. These data constrain the extension rate between the Black and Panamint Mountains to be between 6.4 and 2.7 mm/yr over the past 9 m.y.

Existing data on the direction and age of initiation and cessation of extension for faults in the Death Valley area show two periods of extension. The earlier period, from 15 to 10 Ma, appears to have widely varying extension directions; the later period, from 10 to 0 Ma, is characterized by consistently northwestern extension directions.

INTRODUCTION

The central portion of Death Valley, southeastern California, constitutes one of the world's greater topographic depressions: nearly 3.5 km of relief occur between the lowest point in the valley and Telescopic Peak, the highest point in the Panamint Mountains to the west (Fig. 1). There is little doubt that the central Death Valley graben developed as a consequence of "pull-apart" between the northwest-striking, right-lateral Furnace Creek and Southern Death Valley fault zones (Burchfiel and Stewart, 1966; Wright and Troxel, 1967), but there has been substantial debate regarding the age and amount of displacement on the normal fault systems that accommodated extension between the Panamint Mountains and the Black Mountains to the east. The fault systems involved include: (1) a group of northwest-plunging, domiform, normal faults (the Death Valley "turtlebacks" of Curry, 1938) that lie along the western foot of the Black Mountains and characterize the eastern margin of

McKenna, L. W., and Hodges, K. V., 1990, Constraints on the kinematics and timing of Late Miocene–Recent extension between the Panamint and Black Mountains, southeastern California, *in* Wernicke, B. P., ed., Basin and Range extensional tectonics near the latitude of Las Vegas, Nevada: Boulder, Colorado, Geological Society of America Memoir 176.

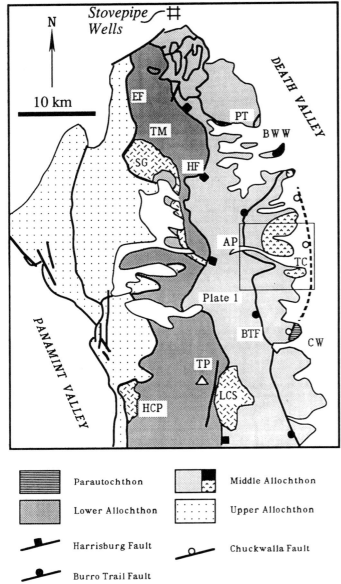

Figure 1. Tectonic map of the northern and central Panamint Range. See Figure 2 for location; structural packages (shown in key) are separated by normal faults shown by heavy black lines. Abbreviations are: AP, Aguereberry Point; BTF, Burro Trail fault; BWW, Blackwater Wash; CW, Chuckwalla Canyon; EF, Emigrant fault; HCP, Hall Canyon Pluton; HF, Harrisburg fault; LCS, Little Chief Stock; PT, location of Panamint Thrust; SG, Skidoo Granite; TC, Trail Canyon; TM, Tucki Mountain; TP, Telescope Peak. The study area is indicated by the box labeled "Plate 1."

the active central Death Valley basin (Otton, 1976; Wright and others, 1974; Troxel, 1986; Burchfiel and others, in preparation); (2) a complex of low-angle normal faults in the southern Black Mountains that corresponds to the Amargosa "chaos" of Noble (1941) and Wright and Troxel (1984); and (3) a similar normal fault complex along the eastern foot of the Panamint Mountains (Hunt and Mabey, 1966; Wright and Troxel, 1973). Although

the turtleback surfaces in the Black Mountains cut Holocene deposits and are therefore quite young (e.g., Troxel and Wright, 1987), most of the movement on the Amargosa system appears to have occurred in late Miocene to early Pliocene time (Wright and Troxel, 1984). Hunt and Mabey (1966) and Stewart (1983) interpreted the chaos structures in the Black Mountains and Panamint Mountains as part of a regionally extensive fault system, and Stewart (1983) inferred that it accommodated roughly 80 km of northwestward transport of the Panamint Mountains structural block relative to the Black Mountains block. In contrast, Wright and Troxel (1967) argued that the two systems were kinematically distinct and inferred substantially less relative displacement between the Panamint Mountains and the Black Mountains.

In this chapter, we present the results of our detailed study of the chaos structures along the eastern foot of the Panamint Mountains, herein referred to as the Eastern Panamint fault system. The Eastern Panamint system developed synchronously with eruption of a late Miocene volcanic sequence exposed along the foot of the range. Besides providing constraints on the paleohorizontal during movement on the Eastern Panamint system, these volcanic rocks place important constraints on regional reconstructions because they can be correlated confidently with volcanic sequences in the southern Black Mountains.

GEOLOGIC SETTING

The Panamint Mountains occupy a central position within the Death Valley extensional corridor (Fig. 1), a zone that experienced roughly 150 km of Neogene extension (Wernicke and others, 1988). The Panamint Mountains consist of four tectonic packages (Fig. 2; Hodges and others, this volume): (1) a Parautochthon, predominantly consisting of Precambrian basement gneisses; (2) a Lower Allochthon, containing upper Precambrian strata that were metamorphosed at greenschist to amphibolite facies conditions and intruded by granitoids in Mesozoic time; (3) a Middle Allochthon, including unmetamorphosed to greenschist-facies upper Precambrian to upper Paleozoic strata unconformably overlain by Neogene sedimentary and volcanic units; and (4) an Upper Allochthon, consisting of displaced fragments of the Lower and Middle Allochthons as well as latest Miocene to Pliocene extensional basin deposits. The Upper, Middle, and Lower Allochthons are separated by diachronous but uniformly top-to-the-northwest normal faults of Neogene age that collectively constitute the Tucky Mountain detachment system. Deformation on this system of faults initiated before 10.6 Ma with movement on the Harrisburg detachment, separating the Middle and Lower Allochthons, and continued until at least 3.7 Ma (Hodges and others, this volume).

The fault system that separates the Parautochthon from structurally higher tectonic packages is the focus of this paper. We will refer to it as the Eastern Panamint fault system because it is exposed along the eastern foot of the Panamint Mountains from Starvation Canyon to Blackwater Canyon (Fig. 2). Structures in

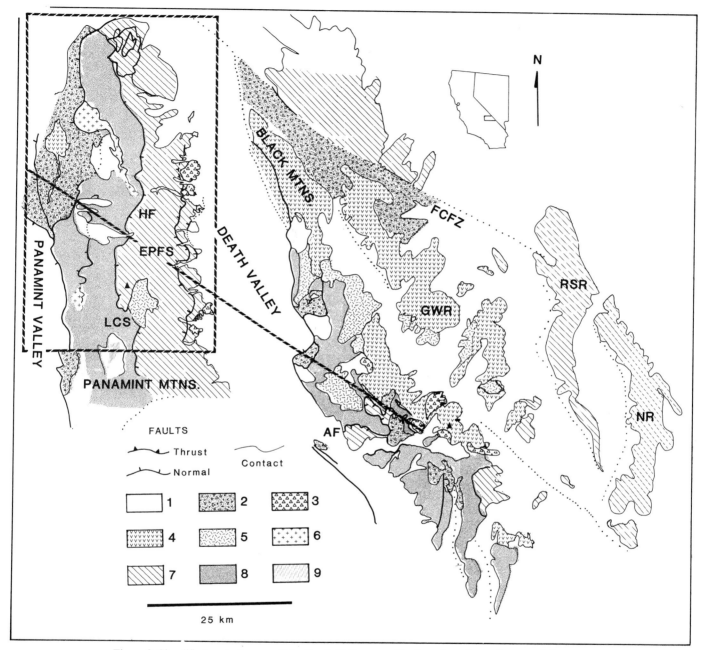

Figure 2. Simplified geologic map of the Death Valley area. The large box shows the area of Figure 1; line shows cross-section trace of Figure 8. Faults are shown by heavy lines (teeth on upper plate of thrust faults, barbs on upper plate of normal faults); contacts are shown by thinner lines. Rock types are identified by numbered key: 1, Recent alluvial fill; 2, older (generally Pliocene to recent) fanglomerate; 3, Trail Canyon Volcanic Sequence and correlative Rhodes Tuff and Sheephead Andesite; 4, Cenozoic volcanic rocks; 5, Cenozoic intrusive rocks; 6, Mesozoic intrusive rocks; 7, Miogeoclinal sedimentary rocks; 8, Miogeoclinal sedimentary rocks, metamorphosed; 9, Amphibolite grade metamorphic rocks and basement crystalline rocks. Abbreviations are: AF, Amargosa Fault; EPVS, Eastern Panamint Volcanic Sequence; FCFZ, Furnace Creek Fault Zone; HF, Harrisburg Fault; GWR, Greenwater Range; LCS, Little Chief Stock; NR, Nopah Range; RSR, Resting Spring Range.

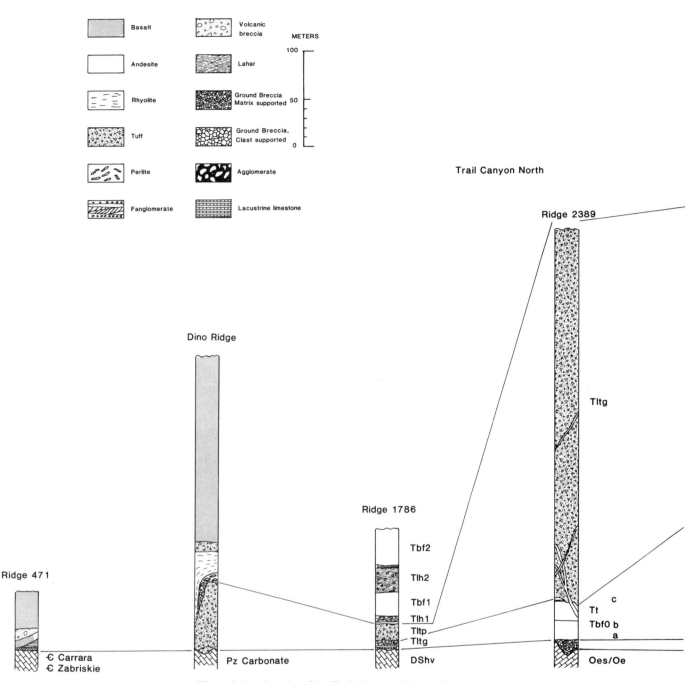

Figure 3. Stratigraphy of the Trail Canyon Volcanic Sequence.

this system were first mapped by Hunt and Mabey (1966), who correlated the structurally lowest exposed fault with the Amargosa thrust fault of Noble (1941). In the Panamint Mountains this fault places upper Proterozoic to middle Paleozoic miogeoclinal strata of the Middle Allochthon on Precambrian augen gneisses of the Parautochthon. Structurally above the fault, related structures deform the miogeoclinal strata and overlying Cenozoic volcanic rocks. Although the miogeoclinal strata of the Middle Allochthon and the Precambrian basement of the Parautochthon have been described elsewhere (Hunt and Mabey, 1966), the Cenozoic sequence had not been studied specifically prior to our investigation. Because these volcanic units are crucial for palinspastic reconstructions of the Death Valley area, we describe them in some detail below.

STRATIGRAPHY OF LATE MIOCENE VOLCANIC ROCKS

Lying above the miogeoclinal rocks of the Middle Allochthon along a regional unconformity is a sequence of Cenozoic

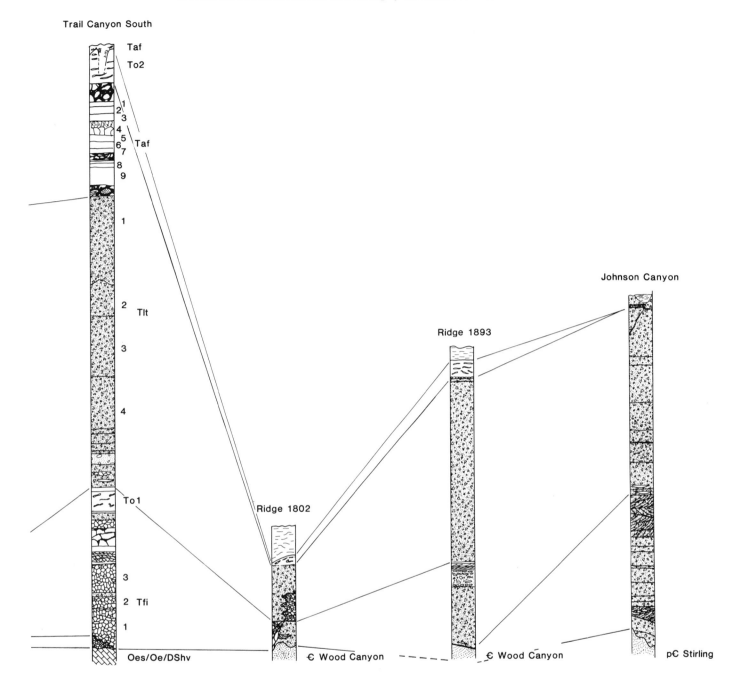

lapilli tuffs, agglomerates, and andesite flows. These units form a discontinuously exposed band along the eastern side of the Panamint Mountains and are referred to here as the Trail Canyon Volcanic Sequence. The stratigraphy of this sequence as exposed along the eastern Panamint Mountains is illustrated in Figure 3. Although this stratigraphy exhibits local variations along the exposed belt, each section includes a basal breccia unit, an overlying tuff unit, and an uppermost flow/agglomerate unit.

The basal units consist of generally clast-supported ground breccia, less than 50 m thick, lying unconformably on Precambrian to Silurian miogeoclinal rocks. Conformably overlying

these units are 100 to 300 m of pale green to white lapilli tuff. The tuff is poorly welded, contains approximately 10 to 30 percent of clasts of pumice, crystal fragments, and lithic fragments, and was deposited in at least four separate events. Locally interbedded in these tuffs are fanglomerates, finely bedded tuffaceous sandstones, and monolithologic breccias of Ordovician units (Ely Spring Dolomite and Eureka Quartzite); these clastic sequences are each less than 5 m thick.

On the ridges immediately south and north of Trail Canyon, the lapilli tuffs are conformably overlain by a sequence of basaltic-andesite flows and agglomerates with a total thickness of

110 m. The agglomerates contain clasts of intermediate volcanic rocks up to 2 m × 2 m × 1 m in size, surrounded by a fine-grained, locally altered matrix. At all other exposures of the volcanic sequence, the tuff is overlain by perlite and rhyolite flows. These flows are conformable on the tuff in the central Panamint Mountains (Fig. 3) but lie unconformably on the tuff at the extreme southern and northern exposures of the sequence. The three northern exposures of the sequence (see Fig. 1 for locations) are capped by basalt, which appears to be temporally equivalent to the basalts of the Funeral Formation (Cemen and others, 1985).

K-Ar ages for these volcanic units (Wes Hildreth, unpublished) indicate an age for the tuff and overlying basaltic andesites of 9.4 to 8.6 Ma and an age of 3.8 ± 0.1 Ma for basalts overlying the Trail Canyon sequence at Dinosaur Ridge. As noted by Wright and others (1984b), the Trail Canyon Volcanic Sequence is similar to the Rhodes Tuff and the Sheephead Andesite, exposed at Salsberry Pass and elsewhere in the southern Black Mountains (Fig. 2). Composite sections for the Rhodes Tuff, Sheephead Andesite (from Wright and others, 1984b), and the Trail Canyon Volcanic Sequence (this chapter) are shown in Figure 4, along with available geochronologic constraints. The correlation of these units is excellent: thicknesses, lithology, stratigraphy, and age of both the tuffs and the andesites are very similar. The ground breccias within the Trail Canyon Volcanic Sequence occur only locally, and their absence in the Salsberry Pass outcrops does not weaken the correlation. We conclude, as Wright and others (1984b) hypothesized, that the Trail Canyon Volcanic Sequence and the Rhodes Tuff and Sheephead Andesite are correlative units.

STRUCTURAL GEOLOGY OF THE TRAIL CANYON AREA

A geologic map and interpretive cross sections of the Trail Canyon area are shown on Plate 1 (in cover pocket) and Figure 5, respectively. The structural architecture of the area is dominated by the Eastern Panamint fault system. Faults within the system can be divided into three classes based on their orientation and structural relations: lower-angle faults, higher-angle faults, and E-W–striking faults.

The lower-angle faults are characterized by present-day dips of 5 to 30°W, bedding-fault angles of ~70°, brecciated contacts 0.1 to 10 m wide, and stratigraphic displacements of 300 to 1,400 m. These features are well illustrated on Figure 6, which shows the contact at Location A (Plate 1), looking north. Here the zone of fault gouge varies from 4 to over 8 m thick and consists of brecciated Ordovician Eureka Quartzite and Ely Spring Dolomite. Breccias of the two lithologies are separated by diffuse contacts (less than a few decimeters) and form lenses a few meters thick and 10 to 15 m wide (see right side of Fig. 6 photograph). At this outcrop, Ely Spring Dolomite and Eureka Quartzite overlie, along the brecciated contact, the older Pogonip Dolomite. This relation and the lensoidal morphology suggest normal displacement along this lower-angle fault. Similar younger-on-older

relations are seen on the other lower-angle faults, also suggesting normal displacement. Along the extreme eastern edge of the map area, lower-angle faults cut units of the Trail Canyon Volcanic Sequence, juxtaposing them with Cambrian Nopah and Bonanza King lithologies.

In contrast to the lower-angle faults, the higher-angle faults have steep present-day dips (60 to 75°E), low fault-to-bedding angles (0 to 10°), sharp, unbrecciated contacts, and stratigraphic displacements of less than a few hundred meters. These relations are well displayed at Location B on Plate 1, where a higher-angle fault at ~10° to bedding juxtaposes footwall Nopah Formation against hanging-wall Pogonip Limestone. The higher-angle faults cut units of the Trail Canyon Volcanic Sequence but both truncate and are truncated by the E-W–striking faults.

Subvertical E-W–striking faults with displacements of less than 100 to 200 m are the third type of faults exposed in the lower Trail Canyon area. These faults are nonplanar, displaying macroscopic warps with height to width ratios of ~1, as exhibited at Location C on Plate 1. E-W–striking faults can truncate (Location D) or splay out of (Location E) the lower-angle faults. In the latter case, the lower-angle faults form a continuous surface that is not offset by E-W–striking faults. Like the other fault types, the E-W–striking faults cut units of the Trail Canyon Volcanic Sequence.

STRUCTURAL INTERPRETATION

The structurally highest, lower-angle fault in the Eastern Panamint fault system corresponds to the Burro Trail fault of Hunt and Mabey (1966). The Burro Trail fault serves as an upper structural bound for the Eastern Panamint system (Plate 1). The base of the system is buried beneath the alluvium of Death Valley in the Trail Canyon area, but it is well exposed to the south in the vicinity of Chuckwalla Canyon (Fig. 1). Here the basal fault corresponds to the Amargosa "thrust" of Hunt and Mabey (1966); to avoid confusion with the Amargosa Chaos of the Black Mountains, we refer to the structure near Chuckwalla Canyon as the Chuckwalla fault. The Chuckwalla fault places Precambrian Stirling Quartzite on basement gneisses at Chuckwalla Canyon. Below the fault, the gneisses exhibit Type I S-C mylonitic fabrics (Lister and Snoke, 1984), indicating down-to-the-west (normal) displacement of the hanging wall. The degree of mylonitization increases toward the Chuckwalla fault, and we infer that the mylonitic fabric is related to displacement on the fault.

The geometry of the Eastern Panamint system can be considered an extensional duplex (cf., Gibbs, 1984; Burchfiel and others, in preparation). Following the original definition of duplex (Dahlstrom, 1970), we use the term extensional duplex in a purely geometric sense, without kinematic significance, because we can envision several distinct scenarios in which different fault-timing relations could lead to the same duplex geometry. The Eastern Panamint duplex contains four types of faults, shown schematically on Figure 7. Subparallel, *roof and sole normal*

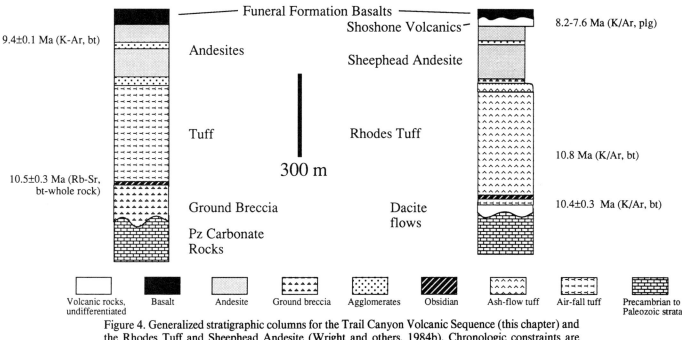

Figure 4. Generalized stratigraphic columns for the Trail Canyon Volcanic Sequence (this chapter) and the Rhodes Tuff and Sheephead Andesite (Wright and others, 1984b). Chronologic constraints are from: Wright and others (1984b, Rhodes Tuff and Sheephead Andesite); W. Hildreth (unpublished data, upper Trail Canyon Sequence), and McKenna (unpublished, lower Trail Canyon Sequence).

faults (the Burro Trail and Chuckwalla faults, respectively) form bounding surfaces, between which *roof-parallel* and *oblique normal faults* have extended the rocks within the duplex, and *transfer faults* separate differentially extended domains. Within the Trail Canyon area, the roof-parallel, oblique, and transfer faults appear as the lower-angle, higher-angle, and E-W–striking faults respectively.

AGE OF THE EASTERN PANAMINT FAULT SYSTEM

Many extensional fault systems in the Basin and Range Province exhibit tectonites that developed in a variety of deformational regimes, from high-temperature plasticity to cataclastic flow (e.g., Wernicke, 1981). In most cases, the oldest tectonites are mylonites developed at intermediate structural levels (e.g., Davis, 1983; Hodges and others, 1987). Consequently, we might expect the mylonitic fabrics developed below the Chuckwalla fault to be the oldest structural features of the Eastern Panamint system. Unfortunately, the age of this mylonitization is poorly constrained. Conventional K-Ar ages for biotites from the mylonitic gneiss of 14 ± 1.5 and 11 ± 1 Ma were reported by Stern and others (1966; recalculated using the decay constants of Steiger and Jäger, 1977), but these ages probably

reflect cooling of the gneiss through the biotite closure temperature after the intrusion of abundant felsic dikes (dated at 15 ± 1.5 Ma by Stern and others, 1966) rather than the age of mylonitization.

The most important constraint on the age of faults in the Eastern Panamint system is that they have cut and rotated some units of the Trail Canyon Volcanic Sequence. Older volcanic units in the sequence have been tilted to a greater extent than younger units, and the youngest units unconformably overlie some of the westernmost faults of the duplex. Consequently, we assign a late Miocene age to the Eastern Panamint system.

FAULT RECONSTRUCTION

Deformation along the Eastern Panamint fault system can be restored assuming an approximately horizontal original attitude of the basal units of the Trail Canyon Volcanic Sequence. The lowest units within the sequence (Fig. 3) include ground breccias, fluvially reworked tuffs, and monolithologic breccias of Ordovician Eureka Quartzite and Ely Spring Dolomite. All are subparallel with each other and the basal eruptive units. The fluvially reworked tuffs are laminated on scales of millimeters to centimeters, were deposited in a low-energy environment, and were arguably originally horizontal. Thus, we infer that the basal

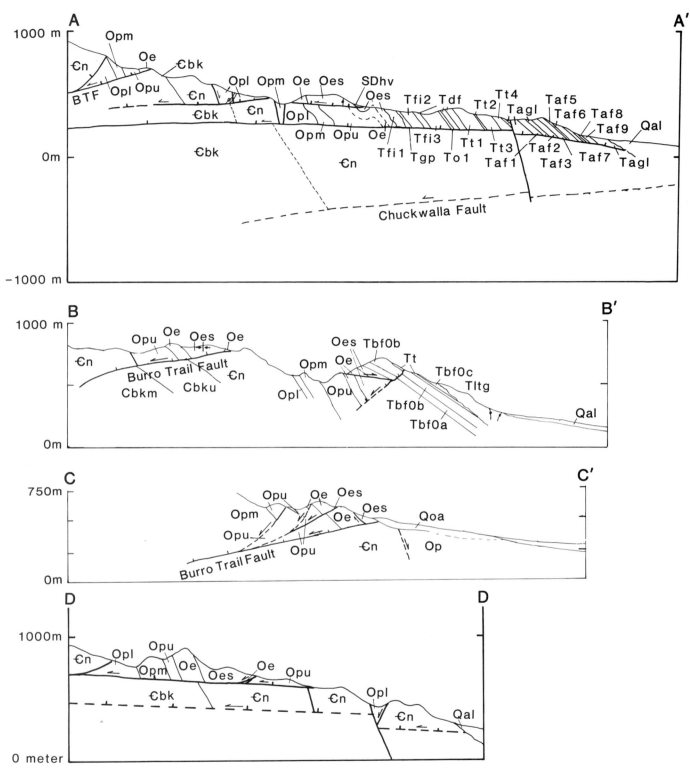

Figure 5. Cross section of the Trail Canyon Area; section lines are shown on Plate 1. A–D: Interpretive cross sections. E: Restored version of cross section AA′, rotated to paleohorizontal with control provided by volcanic units. Unit Tvu is undifferentiated volcanic rocks; individual units are omitted for clarity.

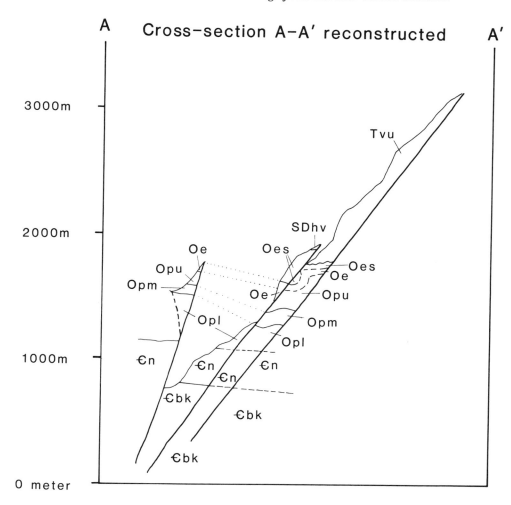

unconformity below the Trail Canyon Volcanic Sequence, and the basal units of the sequence itself, were originally subhorizontal.

With these constraints, a restored version of Section A-A' is shown on Figure 5e. Extension within the exposed portion of the Eastern Panamint fault system is approximately 150 to 160 percent, although this represents a minimum estimate for the total extension within the duplex. A maximum estimate for extension within the duplex can be made using the observation that the Eastern Panamint fault system juxtaposes Siluro-Devonian units with the basement gneisses exposed at Chuckwalla Canyon—the upper limit of extension would then be equivalent to the stratigraphic thicknesses of pre-Silurian units. This would indicate a displacement along the Eastern Panamint fault system of a minimum of 7 km. This estimate of stratigraphic thicknesses has an uncertainty of a few kilometers and should be viewed as an approximate limit only.

The reconstruction shown in Figure 5e also demonstrates that deformation in the Eastern Panamint fault system began at shallow depths, with moderate dips of 40 to 60°W. The present shallow dips of the roof and sole faults are due to syn- to postdeformational rotation of the entire duplex. This rotation is probably the same as that which folded the entire Panamint Mountains

into a shallowly NNW-plunging anticline (the F_6 deformation of Hodges and others, 1987; see Fig. 8a), with an axial trace that is approximately coincident with the crest of the range. The timing, cause, and nature of this folding are all somewhat controversial. Labotka and others (1980) concluded that the NNW-trending anticline formed between 80 Ma and the intrusion of the Little Chief Stock at 10.7 Ma, while Wright and others (1981) considered the Panamint Mountains to be a Mesozoic anticlinorium. On the contrary, we suggest that most of the folding associated with the NNW-trending anticline postdates middle Miocene intrusion of the Little Chief Stock for the following reasons. Units in all exposures of the Trail Canyon Volcanic Sequence along the eastern limb of the Panamint Mountains currently dip 20 to 40°E, suggesting that 20 to 40° of tilting along an approximately N-S-trending axis has occurred since deposition of the sequence at 9.0 ± 0.4 Ma. The Harrisburg fault (see Fig. 1), which formed prior to the intrusion of the Little Chief Stock, is also folded around this N-S axis. Near Telescope Peak, the Harrisburg fault dips approximately 10°E, whereas some 15 km northeast of Telescope Peak the fault dips 55°E, recording at least 45° of postfaulting folding. These data suggest that roughly 5 to 25° of rotation on the east side of the range occurred before 9.0 Ma and after formation of the Harrisburg fault. The amount of rotation increases eastward from the crest of the range, in a manner incompatible with simple block rotation of the range.

Labotka and others (1980) suggested that some of the deformation associated with the folding of the range is accommodated by north-south striking, subvertical faults common throughout the central Panamint Mountains. Both Labotka and others (1980) and Harding (1986) suggested that the deformation on some of these faults was Precambrian in age, but most apparently had Tertiary offset. Reconnaissance mapping in upper Trail Canyon (McKenna and Hodges, unpublished data) shows that these steeply east-dipping normal faults cut the Miocene Harrisburg fault. We interpret these faults to represent the brittle ac-

commodation of reverse drag along structurally lower, west-dipping listric normal faults (Hamblin, 1965). These conclusions do not exclude the possibility of Mesozoic folding within the Panamint Mountains but do indicate that the majority of folding took place after 10.7 Ma.

SIGNIFICANCE OF VOLCANIC CORRELATIONS

Correlation of the Trail Canyon Volcanic Sequence with the Rhodes Tuff and Sheephead Andesite allows constraints to be put on the timing and geometry of post-Oligocene extension between the Black and Panamint Mountains. The Rhodes Tuff and Sheep-

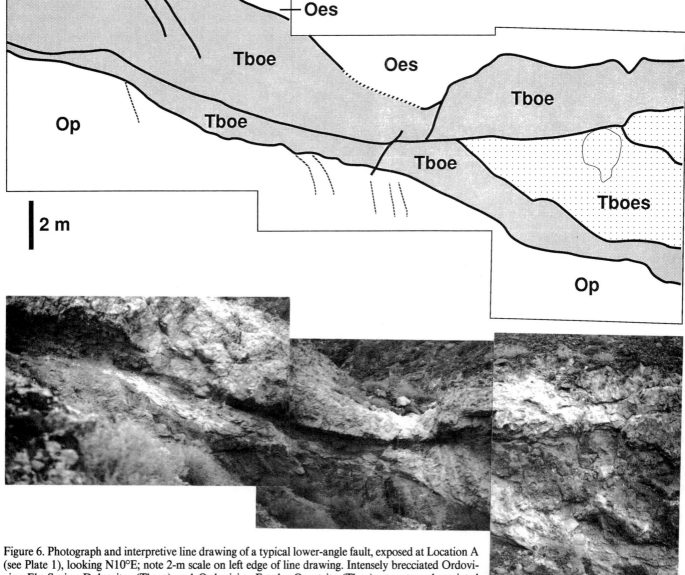

Figure 6. Photograph and interpretive line drawing of a typical lower-angle fault, exposed at Location A (see Plate 1), looking N10°E; note 2-m scale on left edge of line drawing. Intensely brecciated Ordovician Ely Spring Dolomitre (Tboes) and Ordovician Eureka Quartzite (Tboe) separate unbrecciated units of Ely Spring (Oes), Eureka Quartzite (in the hanging wall; the Eureka is out of view on the left), and Ordovician Pogonip Group (Op, footwall). The brecciated zone is 4 to 8 m thick and is formed by overlapping, lensoidal bodies of individual units with diffuse (decimeter-wide) contacts. Displacement along the fault zone was in a normal sense with the hanging wall to the west, or left; the displacement appears to be up dip due to postdisplacement rotation of the eastern Panamint Mountains.

head Andesite are exposed in a WNW-trending belt at the southern terminus of the Black Mountains, where they lie unconformably on the Johnnie and Stirling Formations (Wright and others, 1984b). Outcrops of the Sheephead Andesite, as shown on Figure 2, are preserved only along two narrow belts within a wider area underlain by the Rhodes Tuff. Similarly, the basaltic-andesite of the Trail Canyon Volcanic Sequence is restricted to an area 5 km wide astride Trail Canyon. Figure 8 shows a cross section of the palinspastically restored Death Valley area, with controls provided by matching outcrops of the Sheephead Andesite and its Trail Canyon Volcanic Sequence equivalent. The apparent azimuth of extension is 305°, in excellent agreement with the common assumption that Death Valley opened parallel to the N55°W strike of the Furnace Creek fault zone (e.g., Burchfiel and Stewart, 1966). A maximum estimate for the extension between the Panamint and Black Mountains after 9.0 Ma is approximately 45 km.

Our estimate of the amount of extension would be decreased by the presence of Trail Canyon Volcanic Sequence under the alluvium of Death Valley and would be increased by restoring the rotations and extension of the Rhodes Tuff within the Black Mountains. In the former case, a minimum estimate of approximately 25 km of post–9.0 Ma extension can be made by assuming that the entire width of Death Valley is underlain by units equivalent to the Trail Canyon Volcanic Sequence. Restoration of the extension within the Black Mountains is fraught with uncertainty, but we feel that at most only 10 km of extension could be added by this mechanism. Given these uncertainties, the total extension is 45 +10/−25 km, and the average rate of extension between the Black and Panamint Mountains is 6.4 to 2.7 mm/yr over the past 9 m.y.

LATE MIOCENE TO RECENT EXTENSION IN THE DEATH VALLEY AREA

Our interpretation of the post–late Miocene extensional development of the Death Valley area is shown by the cross sections in Figure 8. At present (Fig. 8a), the Trail Canyon and Rhodes Tuff–Sheephead Andesite sequences are separated by two major Neogene normal fault systems: the Amargosa fault system and the frontal faults of the Black Mountains (including the Death Valley "turtlebacks"). We infer that 25 to 55 km of extension between the correlative volcanic sequences was largely accommodated by movement on these fault systems. Removal of this deformation results in the geometry shown in Figure 8b for late Miocene time, subsequent to movement on the Eastern Panamint fault system. The reconstruction shown indicates that the Eastern Panamint system developed immediately west of the modern, western foot of the Black Mountains. We suggest that the Trail Canyon Volcanic Sequence in the footwall of the Amargosa system now lies buried beneath Death Valley. Restoration of displacement along the Eastern Panamint fault system is constrained by the presence of gneisses in its footwall and their inferred correlation to the gneisses exposed in the central Panamint Mountains (Labotka

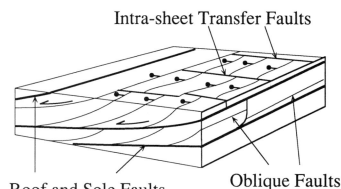

Figure 7. Block model for an extensional duplex, modified from an illustration by J. D. Walker, University of Kansas. The subparallel roof and sole faults bound a volume extended by additional normal faults (black lines with ball symbols). Intrasheet transfer faults (gray lines) separate domains of differential extension within the duplex. These two fault types are equivalent to the lower-angle and W-E striking faults within the Trail Canyon area.

and others, 1980). The implied middle Miocene reconstruction (Fig. 8c) restores the Harrisburg detachment and Panamint thrust such that they project above the present erosional level in the Black Mountains.

REGIONAL SIGNIFICANCE

Wernicke and others (1988) suggested that the likely correlation of the Panamint thrust fault in the Panamint Mountains with the Chicago Pass thrust in the Nopah Range (Fig. 2) implies roughly 90 km of extension over the past 15 m.y. They inferred, using the data of Wright and others (1984a), that extension rates over the past 10 m.y. were less than half the rates between 15 and 10 Ma. The reconstructions shown in Figure 8 suggest that at least 25 to 55 km of the extension occurred after 9.0 Ma, even if we assume no extension between the Black Mountains and the Nopah Range between 9.0 Ma and the present. A *minimum* estimate for the average extension rate for the last 9 m.y. between the Nopah Range and the Panamint Mountains is thus 6.4 to 2.7 mm/yr, while a *maximum* estimate for the extension rate between 15 to 9 Ma is 10.8 to 5.8 mm/yr. Within the precision of the available data, there is no clear distinction between extension rates in the Nopah-Panamint transect before and after 10 Ma.

Our results contribute to the growing quantitative database on extension in the Death Valley corridor. Figure 9 illustrates currently available constraints on the ages, movement directions, and displacement rates of major detachment systems within the corridor plotted as a function of approximate paleolongitude. Only two of the well-studied structures were initiated prior to late Miocene time, but the available data suggest that extension directions in the Death Valley corridor may have been variable prior to approximately 10 Ma, when an overall northwesterly extension direction became firmly established. Although there was a

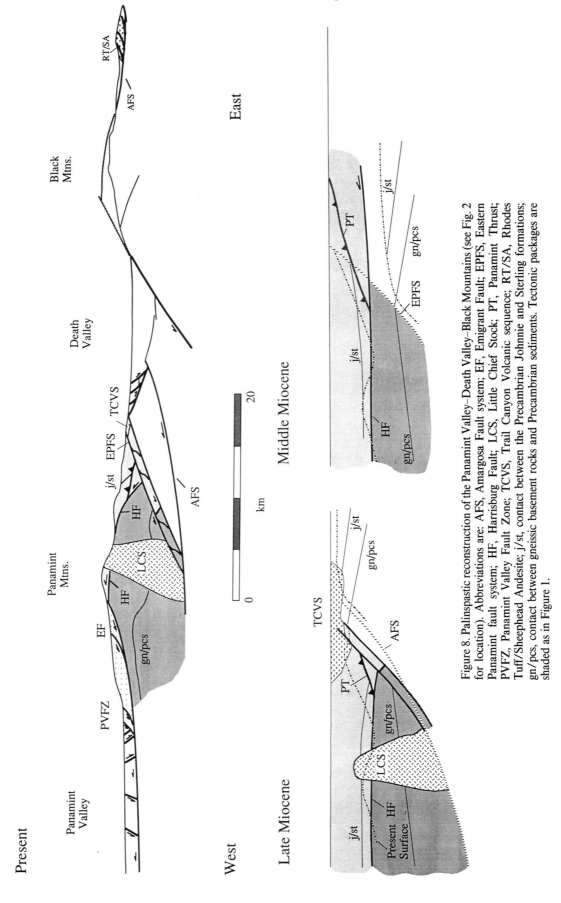

Figure 8. Palinspastic reconstruction of the Panamint Valley–Death Valley–Black Mountains (see Fig. 2 for location). Abbreviations are: AFS, Amargosa Fault system; EF, Emigrant Fault; EPFS, Eastern Panamint fault system; HF, Harrisburg Fault; LCS, Little Chief Stock; PT, Panamint Thrust; PVFZ, Panamint Valley Fault Zone; TCVS, Trail Canyon Volcanic sequence; RT/SA, Rhodes Tuff/Sheephead Andesite; j/st, contact between the Precambrian Johnnie and Sterling formations; gn/pcs, contact between gneissic basement rocks and Precambrian sediments. Tectonic packages are shaded as in Figure 1.

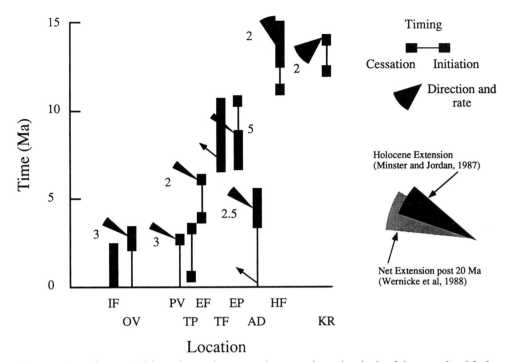

Figure 9. Synoptic graph of time of extension versus the approximate longitude of the extensional fault for the Death Valley Area. Only well-mapped faults are shown on the diagram. Location of faults are shown on Figure 2. Abbreviations used (and sources for data) are: AD, Amargosa and Death Valley faults (this chapter); EF, Emigrant fault (Hodges and others, 1987); EP, Eastern Panamint fault system (this report); HF, Harrisburg fault (Hodges and others, 1987); IF, Independence Fault; KR, Kingston Range Detachment (Burchfiel and others, in preparation); OV, Owens Valley and Independence faults (Bachman, 1978); PV, Panamint Valley; TF, Tucki Mountain Detachment system; TP, Towne Pass fault. Wedges give the direction (with its uncertainty) and the rate (mm/a, rates given adjacent to the wedges) of extension. The wedges are oriented with north to the top. Also given are the Holocene extension rate (Minster and Jordan, 1987) and a possible net extension vector for post–20 Ma extension (Wernicke and others, 1988). Although the age of initiation and cessation of extension generally youngs to the west (Wright and others, 1984a), two periods of extension can be discerned. The earlier period, from 15 to 10 Ma, has widely varying extension directions, whereas the later period, from 10 to 0 Ma, is characterized by consistently NW extension directions.

general tendency for extension to have begun and ceased westward with time across the corridor (Wright and others, 1984a), this generalization breaks down in the area between the Black Mountains and the Owens Valley over the late Miocene–Recent interval.

CONCLUSIONS

The Eastern Panamint fault system constitutes an extensional duplex that developed in late Miocene time. The initial dip of the system was moderately westward, and the total stratigraphic displacement across the system was between 3 and 7 km. Correlation of the Trail Canyon Volcanic Sequence with the Rhodes Tuff and Sheephead Andesite in the Black Mountains supports the hypothesis of Stewart (1983) that large-scale extension occurred between the Black Mountains and Panamint Mountains, but our results contradict Stewart's suggestion that this extension was accommodated by a detachment system that included the Amargosa Chaos in the Black Mountains and the

Eastern Panamint duplex. Specifically, the Eastern Panamint and Amargosa systems began with different geometries (moderate versus shallow westward dips) at different times (during versus after late Miocene eruption of the Trail Canyon–Sheephead–Rhodes volcanic sequence). The available data indicate that horizontal and vertical displacements of the Panamint Mountains relative to the Black Mountains were basically decoupled: most of the 25 to 55 km of horizontal displacement was accommodated by the Amargosa system and more recent faults along the western front of the Black Mountains, whereas most of the uplift of the Black Mountains relative to the Panamint Mountains (>5 km; Fig. 8c) occurred by movement on the Eastern Panamint system.

ACKNOWLEDGMENTS

Assistance in the field was provided by Jim Cureton and Elizabeth Spizman; Liz Schermer, Joan Fryxell, and Jim Knapp made useful observations and comments on the ideas presented herein. Lauren Wright and Terry Pavlis made thorough reviews of an earlier version of the manuscript; in addition, Wright made many excellent comments on the map and cross sections. Finally, thanks to Stan Hart for access to the geoalchemy labs. Support for this research was provided by National Science Foundation grants EAR-8319768 and EAR-8512283 to KVH.

REFERENCES CITED

Bachman, S. B., 1978, Pliocene-Pleistocene break-up of the Sierra Nevada—White–Inyo Mountains block and formation of Owens Valley: Geology, v. 6, p. 461–463.

Burchfiel, B. C., and Stewart, J. H., 1966, "Pull-apart" origin of the central segment of Death Valley, California, Geological Society of America Bulletin, v. 77, p. 439–442.

Cemen, I., Wright, L. A., and Drake, R. E., 1985, Cenozoic sedimentation and sequence of deformational events in the southeastern end of the Furnace Creek strike-slip fault zone, Death Valley region, California, *in* Biddle, K. T., and Cristie-Blick, N., eds., Strike-slip deformation, basin formation, and sedimentation: Society of Economic Paleontologists and Mineralogists Special Publication 37, p. 127–141.

Curry, H. D., 1938, "Turtleback" fault surfaces in Death Valley, California [abs.]: Geological Society of America Bulletin, v. 49, p. 1875.

Dahlstrom, C.D.A., 1970, Structural geology in the eastern margin of the Canadian Rocky Mountains, Bulletin of Canadian Petroleum Geology, v. 18, p. 332–406.

Davis, G. H., 1983, Shear-zone model of the origin of metamorphic core complexes, Geology, v. 11, p. 342–347.

Gibbs, A. D., 1984, Structural evolution of extensional basin margins, Journal of the Geological Society of London, v. 141, p. 609–620.

Hamblin, W. K., 1965, Origin of "reverse drag" on the downthrown side of normal faults, Geological Society of America Bulletin, v. 76, p. 1145–1164.

Harding, M., 1986, Structural evolution of the Wildrose Peak area, Death Valley, California [M.S. thesis]: Laramie, University of Wyoming.

Hodges, K. V., Walker, J. D., and Wernicke, B. P., 1987, Footwall structural evolution of the Tucki Mountain detachment system, Death Valley, California, *in* Dewey, J., and Coward, M., eds., Continental extension tectonics: Geological Society of London Special Publication 28, p. 393–408.

Hunt, C. B., and Mabey, D. R., 1966, Stratigraphy and structure, Death Valley, California: U.S. Geological Survey Professional Paper 494-A, 162 p.

Labotka, T. C., Albee, A. L., Lanphere, M. A., and McDowell, S. D., 1980, Stratigraphy, structure, and metamorphism in the central Panamint Mountains (Telescope Peak Quadrangle), Death Valley area, California, Geological Society of America Bulletin, v. 91, pt. 1, p. 125–129, pt. 2, p. 843–933.

Lister, G. S., and Snoke, A. W., 1984, S-C mylonites: Journal of Structural Geology, v. 6, p. 617–638.

Minster, J. B., and Jordan, T. H., 1987, Vector constraints on western U.S. deformation from space geodesy, neotectonics, and plate motions: Journal of Geophysical Research, v. 92, p. 4798–4804.

Noble, L. F., 1941, Structural features of the Virgin Springs area, Death Valley, California: Geological Society of America Bulletin, v. 52, p. 942–1000.

Otton, J. K., 1976, Geologic features of the Central Black Mountains, Death Valley, California, *in* Troxel, B. W., and Wright, L. A., eds., Geologic

features, Death Valley, California: California Division of Mines and Geology Special Report 106, p. 45–50.

Steiger, R. H., and Jäger, E., compilers, 1977, Subcommission on Geochronology; Convention on the use of decay constants in geo and cosmochronology: Earth and Planetary Science Letters, v. 36, p. 97–107.

Stern, T. W., Newall, M. F., and Hunt, C. B., 1966, Uranium-lead and potassium-argon ages of parts of the Amargosa Thrust complex, Death Valley, California, U.S. Geological Survey Professional Paper 550-B, p. B142–B147.

Stewart, J. H., 1983, Extensional tectonics in the Death Valley area, California; Transport of the Panamint Range structural block 80 km northwestward: Geology, v. 11, p. 153–157.

Troxel, B. W., 1986, Significance of Quaternary fault patterns, west side of the Mormon Point turtleback, southern Death Valley, California; A model of listric normal faults, *in* Troxel, B. W., ed., Quaternary tectonics of southern Death Valley, California, Field Trip Guide: Shoshone, California, Friends of the Pleistocene, Pacific Cell, p. 37–40.

Troxel, B. W., and Wright, L. A., 1987, Tertiary extensional features, Death Valley region, eastern California, *in* Hill, M. L., Cordilleran Section of the Geological Society of America: Boulder, Colorado, Geological Society of America, Centennial Field Guide, v. 1, p. 121–132.

Wernicke, B. P., 1981, Low-angle faults in the Basin and Range Province: Nappe tectonics in an extending orogen, Nature, v. 291, p. 645–648.

Wernicke, B. P., Snow, J. K., and Walker, J. D., 1988, Correlation of Early Mesozoic thrusts in the southern Great Basin and their possible indication of 250–300 km of Neogene crustal extension, *in* Weide, D. L., and Faber, M. L., eds., This extended land; Geological journeys in the southern Basin and Range: University of Nevada at Las Vegas Geoscience Department Special Publication 2, p. 255–268.

Wright, L. A., and Troxel, B. W., 1967, Limitations on right-lateral, strike-slip displacement, Death Valley and Furnace Creek fault zones, California, Geological Society of America Bulletin, v. 78, p. 933–958.

——, 1973, Shallow-fault interpretation of Basin and Range structure, southwestern Great Basin, *in* DeJong, K. A., and Scholten, R., eds., Gravity and tectonics: New York, John Wiley and Sons, p. 397–407.

——, 1984, Geology of the northern one-half Confidence Hills 15' Quadrangle, Inyo County, California: California Division of Mines and Geology, notes to accompany map sheet 34.

Wright, L. A., Otton, J. K., and Troxel, B. W., 1974, Turtleback surfaces of Death Valley viewed as phenomena of extension: Geology, v. 2, p. 53–54.

Wright, L. A., Troxel, B. W., Burchfiel, B. C., Chapman, R. H., and Labotka, T. C., 1981, Geologic cross section from the Sierra Nevada to the Las Vegas Valley, eastern California to southern Nevada, Geological Society of America Map and Chart Series, MC-28M.

Wright, L. A., Drake, R. E., and Troxel, B. W., 1984a, Evidence for the westward migration of Seiver Cenozoic extension, southeastern Great Basin, California: Geological Society of America Abstracts with Programs, v. 16, p. 701.

Wright, L. A., Kramer, J. H., Thoronton, C. P., and Troxell, B. W., 1984b, Type sections of two newly-named volcanic units of the central Death Valley volcanic field, eastern California: California Division of Mines and Geology, notes to accompany map sheet 34, p. 21–24.

MANUSCRIPT ACCEPTED BY THE SOCIETY AUGUST 21, 1989

Geological Society of America
Memoir 176
1990

Chapter 19

Structural unroofing of the central Panamint Mountains, Death Valley region, southeastern California

K. V. Hodges and L. W. McKenna
Department of Earth, Atmospheric, and Planetary Sciences, Massachusetts Institute of Technology, Cambridge, Massachusetts 02139
M. B. Harding
Union Exploration Partners Ltd., Lafayette, Louisiana 70501

ABSTRACT

Greenschist and amphibolite facies metamorphic rocks within the core of the Panamint Mountains of southeastern California were brought to the surface largely by movement on diachronous systems of west-dipping normal faults. Much of the unroofing can be attributed to displacement along the low-angle Harrisburg detachment, which placed weakly to unmetamorphosed upper Precambrian–Paleozoic strata on upper Precambrian metasedimentary rocks in Miocene time, prior to 10.6 ± 0.9 Ma intrusion of the Little Chief quartz monzonite porphyry. The Eastern Panamint normal fault system (late Miocene) initiated at a moderate angle (40 to 60°), juxtaposing amphibolite facies(?) Precambrian crystalline basement and upper Precambrian–Paleozoic sedimentary rocks. Range-scale anticlinal folding of the Harrisburg detachment and eastward tilting of the Eastern Panamint fault system are attributed to reverse-drag flexure induced by movement on the west-dipping Amargosa fault system (late Miocene?), which is exposed in the Black Mountains to the east of Death Valley and is inferred to dip beneath the Panamint Mountains. The low-angle Emigrant detachment (late Miocene to early Pliocene) incised the Harrisburg footwall and acted as the growth fault for the Neogene Nova Basin, which is dominated by material eroded from the metamorphic core.

INTRODUCTION

The Death Valley region of southeastern California (Fig. 1) has been the site of large-scale extension since at least early Miocene time (Cemen and others, 1982). This extension was accommodated by listric and low-angle planar normal faults and by northwest-trending, right-lateral strike-slip faults that served as transfer structures between normal fault systems. The interplay between normal and strike-slip fault systems led to the development of two spectacular examples of "pull-apart" (Burchfiel and Stewart, 1966) or rhombohedral basins: Panamint Valley and Death Valley itself. These valleys are separated by the Panamint Mountains, a metamorphic core complex that evolved over the Miocene-Recent interval.

Lower greenschist to amphibolite facies metamorphic rocks in the central Panamint Mountains were brought to the surface largely as a consequence of movement along three families of

normal faults. In this chapter, we describe in detail the geometry of these structures, geochronologic constraints on their development, and our interpretation of their kinematic evolution.

GEOLOGIC SETTING

The central and northern Panamint Mountains make up a northward-plunging anticlinal structure that involves (1) Proterozoic crystalline basement; (2) upper Proterozoic strata that represent the transition from rift-related sedimentation to miogeoclinal sedimentation (Fig. 2a); (3) uppermost Proterozoic-Permian clastic and carbonate strata characteristic of the Cordilleran miogeocline at this latitude; (4) Cretaceous muscovite-bearing monzogranites and middle Miocene quartz monzonite porphyries, which intrude the upper Precambrian section;

Hodges, K. V., McKenna, L. W., and Harding, M. B., 1990, Structural unroofing of the central Panamint Mountains, Death Valley region, southeastern California, *in* Wernicke, B. P., ed., Basin and Range extensional tectonics near the latitude of Las Vegas, Nevada: Boulder, Colorado, Geological Society of America Memoir 176.

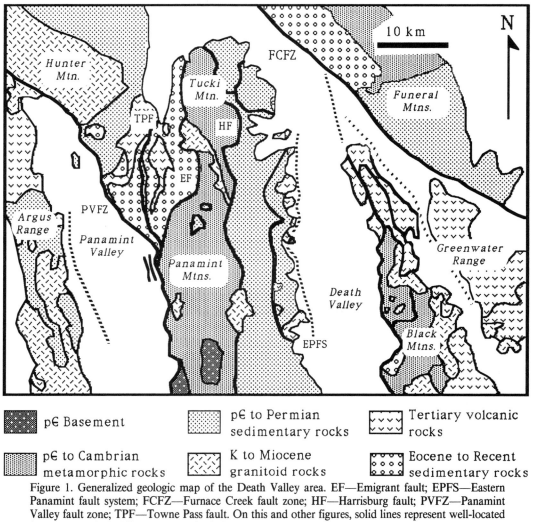

Figure 1. Generalized geologic map of the Death Valley area. EF—Emigrant fault; EPFS—Eastern Panamint fault system; FCFZ—Furnace Creek fault zone; HF—Harrisburg fault; PVFZ—Panamint Valley fault zone; TPF—Towne Pass fault. On this and other figures, solid lines represent well-located features, and dashed lines represent buried structures.

and (5) Miocene-Pliocene "fanglomerates" and intercalated volcanic rocks (Fig. 2b), which were deposited in extensional basins developed during uplift of the range (Hunt and Mabey, 1966; Hall, 1971; Labotka and others, 1980).

Although the structural relations between these lithologies are complex, it is convenient to think of the northern and central Panamint Mountains in terms of four tectonic packages distinguished by metamorphic grade and structural history (Fig. 3). The structurally lowest package (hereafter referred to as the "Parautochthon" because west-dipping detachment systems that crop out east of the Panamint Mountains probably root beneath this package) consists of Precambrian crystalline basement intruded by Miocene(?) granite porphyry dikes (Hunt and Mabey, 1966; Stern and others, 1966). The Parautochthon is overlain structurally by a "Lower Allochthon" composed of upper Precambrian Pahrump Group, Noonday Formation, and lower Johnnie Formation strata that were metamorphosed at greenschist to lower amphibolite facies conditions between middle Mesozoic and early Tertiary time (Labotka and others, 1985). The main sill-like

body of the Cretaceous Skidoo monzogranite and several smaller satellite bodies intrude these rocks in the Harrisburg Flats area. Several phases of ductile to brittle-ductile deformation affected the Lower Allochthon in Mesozoic-Cenozoic time (Hodges and others, 1987).

The "Middle Allochthon" contains lower greenschist facies to unmetamorphosed strata (upper Precambrian Johnnie Formation to Pennsylvanian-Permian Keeler Canyon Formation), which are unconformably overlain by upper Tertiary alluvial basin deposits and intercalated volcanic flows in the northeastern Panamint Mountains. Only the last two phases of brittle-ductile structures observed in the Lower Allochthon can be identified in the Middle Allochthon. The structurally highest "Upper Allochthon" includes some small (< 1 km^2) structural slices of Lower Allochthon and Middle Allochthon lithologies but consists primarily of Pliocene sedimentary and volcanic rocks of the Nova Formation (Hopper, 1947; Hall, 1971; Walker and Coleman, 1987).

The contacts between the four tectonic packages in the cen-

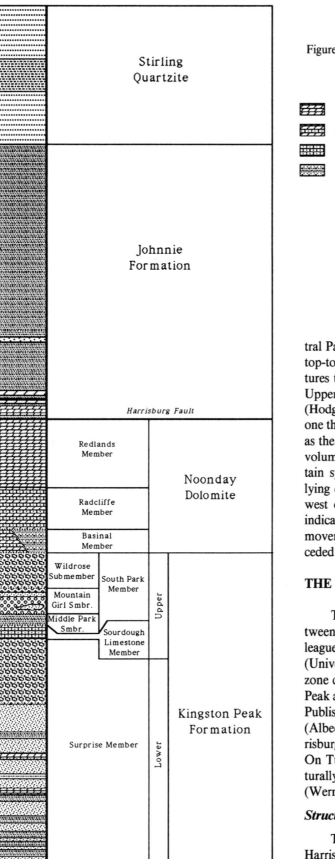

Figure 2. Upper Precambrian stratigraphy, central Panamint Mountains.

Dolomite marble
Sandy limestone/dolomite marble
Sandy limestone marble
Calcareous quartzite

Massive quartzite
Bedded quartzite
Metaconglomerate
Metadiamictite
Pelitic schist/phyllite

200 meters

tral Panamint Mountains are temporally distinct but consistently top-to-the-northwest normal faults. We define the family of structures that separates the Lower Allochthon from the Middle and Upper Allochthons as the Tucki Mountain detachment system (Hodges and others, 1987; Wernicke and others, 1988a) and the one that separates the Lower Allochthon from the Parautochthon as the Eastern Panamint fault system (McKenna and others, this volume). In the central Panamint Mountains, the Tucki Mountain system can be subdivided into the Harrisburg subsystem, lying east of the range crest, and the Emigrant subsystem, lying west of the range crest. Absolute and relative age constraints indicate that movement on the Harrisburg subsystem preceded movement on the Eastern Panamint system, which in turn preceded movement on the Emigrant subsystem.

THE HARRISBURG SUBSYSTEM

The Harrisburg subsystem (Fig. 3) marks the contact between the Lower and Middle allochthons. Along with our colleagues B. P. Wernicke (Harvard University) and J. D. Walker (University of Kansas), we have mapped the Harrisburg fault zone continuously over a distance of 35 km from the Telescope Peak area in the central Panamint Mountains to Tucki Mountain. Published geologic maps of the area south of Telescope Peak (Albee and others, 1981; Johnson, 1957) do not show the Harrisburg fault, and the southern extent of the system is unknown. On Tucki Mountain, the Harrisburg fault is truncated by structurally higher faults of the Tucki Mountain detachment system (Wernicke and others, 1988a; this volume).

Structural characteristics

The Harrisburg subsystem includes a basal detachment (the Harrisburg fault *sensu stricto*) as well as a variety of low- to

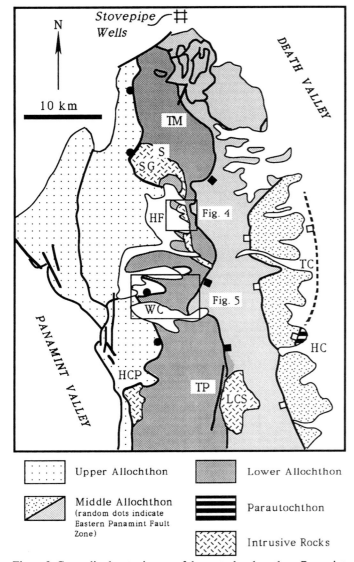

Figure 3. Generalized tectonic map of the central and northern Panamint Mountains. HC—Hanaupah Canyon; HCP—Hall Canyon pluton; HF—Harrisburg Flats; LCS—Little Chief stock; S—Skidoo townsite; SG—Skidoo monzogranite; TC—Trail Canyon; TM—Tucki Mountain; TP—Telescope Peak; TW—Tucki Wash; WC—Wildrose Canyon. Filled square ticks—Harrisburg detachment; open square ticks—roof and sole faults of the Eastern Panamint fault system; filled circles—Emigrant fault. Frames indicate areas shown in Figures 4 and 7.

high-angle hanging-wall splays and high-angle transfer faults. The Harrisburg detachment generally places greenschist facies rocks of the upper Johnnie Formation onto greenschist to amphibolite facies upper Precambrian strata (Kingston Peak Formation, Noonday Dolomite, and lower Johnnie Formation) or the Skidoo monzogranite. The fault lies subparallel to compositional layering in its hanging wall but transects footwall compositional layering at a variety of angles. This angular discordance arose because the fault cut across early (D_{1-2}) macroscopic fold structures that occur only in the Lower Allochthon (Hodges and others, 1987). This relation is demonstrated by the simplified geologic map and accompanying cross section of the Harrisburg Flats area (Fig. 4) that display a tight F_{1-2} fold beneath the Harrisburg detachment. Along most of its trace, the detachment dips eastward at low angles (<20°), but its dip increases to >50°E near the head of Trail Canyon and >70°E near the head of Tucki Wash. Because these structural culminations do not correspond to unusual angular relations between the fault and either hanging-wall or footwall strata, we believe that the steep dips indicate late modifications of the Harrisburg geometry as a consequence of movement on structurally lower detachments rather than original lateral ramps in the Harrisburg fault.

Like many other detachments in the North American Cordillera (e.g., the Whipple detachment; Davis and Lister, 1988), the Harrisburg fault is characterized by an early mylonitic fabric overprinted by younger brittle-ductile and brittle fabrics. Following general models proposed by Wernicke (1981, 1985) and by Davis and others (1986), Hodges and others (1987) interpreted the Harrisburg fabrics as having developed when the Lower Allochthon was transported from the middle crust toward the surface along the detachment. The early stages of movement (D_3) produced a pronounced stretching lineation (L_3) in footwall lithologies throughout the central and northern Panamint Mountains as well as S-C mylonitic fabrics immediately below the detachment surface. Fault rocks generated by later movement at higher structural levels include a thick sequence of fine-grained fault gouge at the head of Tucki Wash and fault breccia along most exposures of the fault. At Harrisburg Flats, the Harrisburg fault is characterized by discontinuous structural horses of highly brecciated Noonday Dolomite (Fig. 4).

Timing constraints

The structures of the Harrisburg subsystem cut the main body and satellite bodies of the Skidoo monzogranite in the Harrisburg Flats area (Fig. 4). Muscovite from one satellite body of the Skidoo monzogranite in Wildrose Canyon is commonly used as an interlaboratory standard for K-Ar (P207), yielding a K-Ar age of 83.3 ± 2.1 Ma (Lanphere and Dalrymple, 1967). Five whole-rock samples collected from the same body yield a Rb-Sr "errorchron" age of 100.6 ± 7.6 Ma (Table 1; Fig. 5). These data indicate an absolute upper bound for the development of the Harrisburg subsystem, but the style of faulting and the lack of evidence for substantial pre-Miocene extension in the Death Valley area (e.g., Cemen and others, 1982, 1985) suggest that the Harrisburg and related faults are probably much younger. Wernicke and others (1988a, 1988b) interpreted structures of Harrisburg age as having developed roughly synchronously with the deposition of probable middle Miocene fanglomerates exposed at the eastern foot of Tucki Mountain.

Detailed mapping in the Telescope Peak area reveals that the Harrisburg fault is offset by high-angle faults related to the intrusion of the Little Chief granite porphyry (Fig. 3; McKenna,

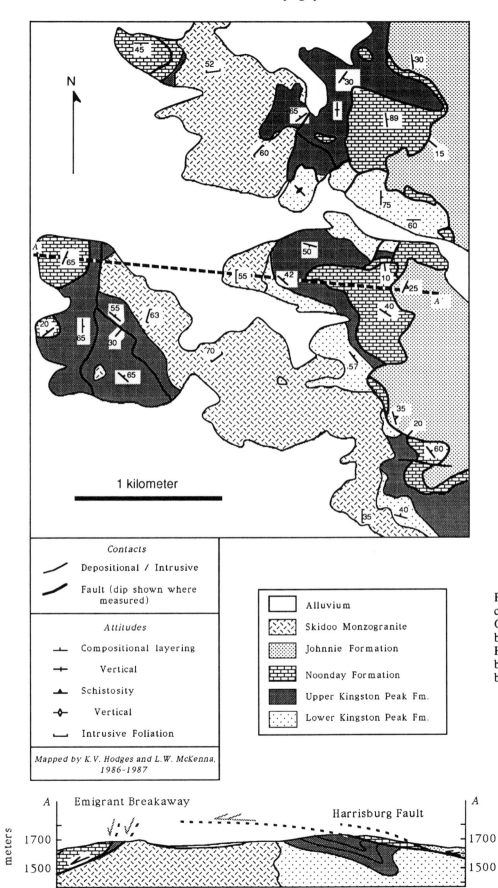

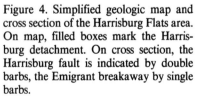

Figure 4. Simplified geologic map and cross section of the Harrisburg Flats area. On map, filled boxes mark the Harrisburg detachment. On cross section, the Harrisburg fault is indicated by double barbs, the Emigrant breakaway by single barbs.

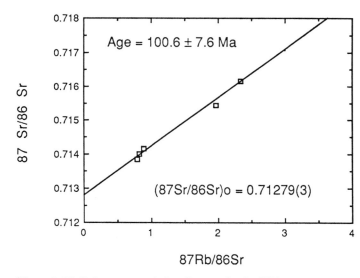

Figure 5. Rb-Sr isotope correlation diagram for the Skidoo monzogranite. Actual analytical errors for individual data points are smaller than the symbols shown.

TABLE 1. SKIDOO GRANITE Sr ISOTOPE DATA

	84-02	84-03	84-04	84-05	84-07
Rb	178	104	145	111	107
Sr	220	365	214	363	387
$^{87}Rb/^{86}Sr$	2.340(2)	0.8301(8)	1.962(2)	0.8892(9)	0.7980(8)
$^{87}Sr/^{86}Sr$	0.71615(3)	0.714014(3)	0.71544(3)	0.714164(4)	0.71383(3)

Notes: Analysis of whole-rock samples by M. S. Hubbard and L. W. McKenna, at MIT. All concentrations in ppm, $^{88}Sr/^{86}Sr$ normalized to 0.1194, all values reported relative to the E and A $SrCO_3$ standard $^{87}Sr/^{86}Sr$ of 0.708. Uncertainties (2s) in the last place given in ( ). The ^{87}Rb decay constant is $1.42 \times 10^{-11}y^{-1}$.

1986; McDowell, 1974). Hornblende, biotite, and plagioclase separates from the stock collectively yield a Rb-Sr internal isochron age of 10.6 ± 0.9 Ma (Table 2; Fig. 6), placing a minimum constraint on the Harrisburg event.

Kinematic evolution

Although the Harrisburg fault dips eastward along its entire trace, we believe this was not its original dip. Our interpretation is based principally on observations of the geometry of D_3 fabrics and of the composite detachment system that marks the contact between the Lower Allochthon and structurally higher packages. At Tucki Mountain, these elements are conspicuously folded in the NNW-plunging anticline that dominates the structure of the central and northern Panamint Mountains. Despite this geometry,

L_3 stretching lineations and D_3 S-C fabrics throughout the Lower Allochthon consistently indicate that the hanging wall of the composite detachment moved to the north-northwest (in present coordinates) relative to the footwall (Hodges and others, 1987). The uniformity of apparent extension direction, regardless of position on the anticline, suggests a more planar initial geometry (cf. Snoke and Lush, 1984; Davis and others, 1986; Davis and Lister, 1988). Given the fact that the Harrisburg detachment consistently places low-grade younger rocks on higher-grade older rocks (in typical normal fault fashion) and that various kinematic indicators suggest north-northwest movement of the hanging wall, we infer that the Harrisburg detachment initially dipped westward. Low-angle intersections between the Harrisburg detachment and Middle Allochthon strata suggest an initially low dip angle for the structure.

TABLE 2. LITTLE CHIEF STOCK Sr ISOTOPE DATA

	Plagioclase	Hornblende	Biotite
Rb	97.9	40.3	1120
Sr	212	16.8	15.8
$^{87}Rb/^{86}Sr$	1.336(1)	6.941(7)	205.8(2)
$^{87}Sr/^{86}Sr$	0.70787(3)	0.70990(3)	0.73917(3)

Notes: Analysis of mineral separates by L. W. McKenna, at the MIT Center for Geoalchemy. All concentrations in ppm, $^{88}Sr/^{86}Sr$ normalized to 0.1194, all values reported relative to the E and A $SrCO_3$ standard $^{87}Sr/^{86}Sr$ of 0.708. Uncertainties (2s) in the last place are given in ( ). The ^{87}Rb decay constant is $1.42 \times 10^{-11}y^{-1}$.

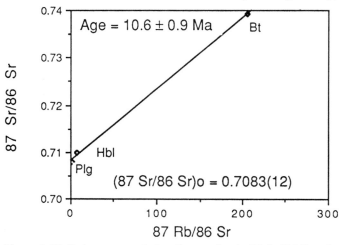

Figure 6. Rb-Sr isotope correlation diagram for the Little Chief stock. Actual analytical errors for individual data points are smaller than the symbols shown.

THE EASTERN PANAMINT FAULT SYSTEM

Hunt and Mabey (1966) were the first to map the complex fault system that occurs along the eastern foot of the central Panamint Mountains (Fig. 3). The structural evolution of the system is detailed elsewhere (McKenna and Hodges, this volume) and will be treated only briefly here.

Structural characteristics

The Eastern Panamint fault system occurs over a structural thickness of at least 3 km and carries upper Precambrian–Paleozoic strata of the Middle Allochthon over Proterozoic crystalline basement. It consists of a kinematically linked duplex system of imbricate normal faults that strike roughly north-south and dip shallowly to the west (McKenna and Hodges, 1988; McKenna and Hodges, this volume). These structures commonly transect bedding surfaces in structural horses of Paleozoic strata at angles in excess of 50°. Numerous roughly east-west–striking and steeply north- and south-dipping transfer faults occur within the duplex. Both high-angle transfer and low-angle normal faults are characterized by zones of fault breccia and gouge. Poorly exposed footwall gneiss exhibits S-C mylonitic fabrics that are interpreted as having developed during the early stages of movement on the system.

Timing constraints

The Trail Canyon volcanic sequence (McKenna and Hodges, this volume) crops out at the eastern foot of the range south of Trail Canyon (Fig. 3). Much of the sequence was involved in structures of the Eastern Panamint fault system; older volcanic units are tilted to a greater extent than progressively younger units, and the youngest units unconformably overlie some of the westernmost faults of the duplex system. There are no major angular unconformities and only local intercalations of fanglomerate within the sequence, indicating that all units were deposited over a relatively short interval. Thus, we infer that the Eastern Panamint system may have begun moving slightly prior to deposition of the Trail Canyon sequence but evolved principally during volcanism.

At present, there are few absolute age constraints for the Trail Canyon sequence. Wes Hildreth (unpublished data) obtained three conventional K-Ar ages of approximately 9 Ma for units from the lower part of the sequence. The Trail Canyon volcanostratigraphy seems similar to that of volcanic sequences in the Black Mountains and Greenwater Range (Fig. 1; Drewes, 1963, Haefner, 1976; Wright and others, 1984). In particular, portions of the Shoshone Volcanics of Haefner (1976) and the Rhodes Tuff of Wright and others (1984) could correlate with the tuff units within the Trail Canyon volcanic sequence of McKenna and Hodges (this volume). R. Drake (cited in Wright and others, 1984, and personal communication, 1989) obtained K-Ar ages that bracket the age of the Rhodes Tuff between 10.8

± 0.6 and 7.6 ± 0.4 Ma. Clearly, more precise dating of the eastern Panamint and Black Mountains volcanic sequences is necessary for firm regional correlations, but we tentatively assign a late Miocene age to both the Trail Canyon volcanism and development of the Eastern Panamint fault system.

Kinematic evolution

Despite the fact that the roof and sole faults of the Eastern Panamint system dip shallowly to the west, the angular discordance between these faults and the synextensional Trail Canyon volcanic rocks implies initially steeper dips. Parallel contacts between roughly tabular units within the volcanic sequence can be used to define paleohorizontal. Restoring the earliest volcanic units to horizontal rotates the roof and sole faults of the Eastern Panamint system to original dips of roughly 40 to 60°W.

Type I S-C mylonites (Lister and Snoke, 1984) are characteristic of exposures of Precambrian basement gneisses in the footwall. They consistently indicate a top-to-the-west sense of shear, but the paucity of well-developed stretching lineations in the coarse-grained basement rocks precludes more detailed kinematic analysis of the mylonitic fabrics.

EMIGRANT SUBSYSTEM

The Emigrant subsystem of the Tucki Mountain system includes (1) high-angle breakaway structures near the range crest, (2) a highly dissected assemblage of extensional fault blocks west of the range crest, and (3) the low-angle normal fault that marks the eastern limit of extensional basin deposits of the Nova Formation (the Emigrant Fault *sensu stricto*). We have mapped the breakaway structures and fault blocks in the greatest detail in the area between upper Wildrose Canyon and Harrisburg Flats (e.g., Harding, 1987), but similar structures run from Tucki Mountain (Wernicke and others, 1988a) at least as far south as the latitude of Telescope Peak (Albee and others, 1981), a distance of over 45 km. The Emigrant fault extends roughly 40 km from the northern end of Tucki Mountain to the mouth of Wildrose Canyon on the east side of Panamint Valley.

Structural characteristics

In the central Panamint Mountains, the breakaway zone consists of a discontinuous series of west-dipping listric normal faults that juxtapose a hanging wall of Upper Allochthon units against a footwall of equivalent Lower Allochthon and Middle Allochthon units. These structures are curviplanar in three dimensions and coalesce to form a scalloped basal detachment for the Emigrant subsystem (Figs. 7 and 8). Although the breakaway zone trends northerly, the strike of an individual segment commonly ranges from northwest through north to northeast. The dip of each segment ranges from 85°W to 60°W at the structurally highest exposures, to 30°W to 5°W at the structurally lowest exposures. Displacements across the breakaway zone range up to 500 m, with accompanying stratal tilting of up to 10°.

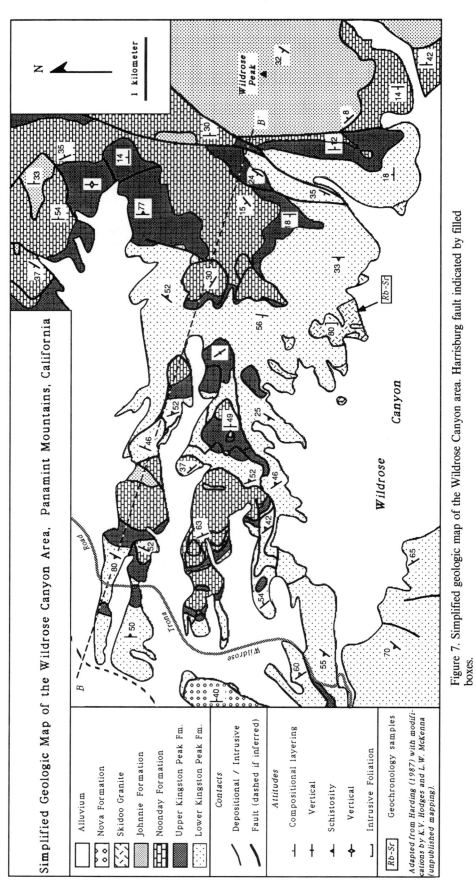

Figure 7. Simplified geologic map of the Wildrose Canyon area. Harrisburg fault indicated by filled boxes.

The Emigrant fault separates a structurally complex footwall of upper Precambrian strata and Mesozoic monzogranites from a structurally simpler hanging wall of Miocene-Pliocene Nova Formation strata. Unlike the basal detachment, the Emigrant fault defines a smooth, continuous surface along its trace. Its strike varies from NNW to NNE, and it consistently dips <20°W. The fault is generally marked by a 5- to 20-m-thick zone of fault breccia and variegated gouge.

A zone of tilted fault blocks or riders (Gibbs, 1984) occurs between the breakaway and the Emigrant fault trace. Excellent exposures on east-west ridges between upper Wildrose Canyon and Skidoo reveal that the faults bounding these blocks are curviplanar in three dimensions like the breakaway structures (Figs. 7 and 8). These faults strike northeast to northwest and dip up to 45°W. Up to 1.5 km of throw can be demonstrated for some of these structures. The riders consist of upper Precambrian strata of both Lower Allochthon and Middle Allochthon affinity, and several down-faulted segments of the Harrisburg detachment are preserved in individual fault blocks. Stratal tilts within the riders are consistently eastward, but the amount of tilting progresses from roughly 25° in the easternmost blocks to near 90° in the westernmost blocks.

Timing constraints

Because the breakaway zone cuts the Harrisburg detachment and because segments of the detachment occur within Emigrant riders, the Emigrant subsystem must be younger than the Harrisburg subsystem (middle to late Miocene). We have interpreted the Emigrant subsystem as the growth fault system for the basin in which the Nova Formation was deposited (Hodges and others, 1989). Reconnaissance K-Ar ages reported by Hall

(1971), Larsen (1979), and Wes Hildreth (unpublished data) for lower Nova volcanic rocks range from 5.3 ± 0.8 Ma to 4.0 ± 0.4 Ma (2σ uncertainties). Schweig (1984) argued that portions of the fanglomerate sequence in the northern Argus Range (Fig. 1), which he believed to be correlative with the lower Nova Formation, may have been deposited before 6.1 Ma. In the southern Harrisburg Flats area, a small, flat-lying exposure of olivine basalt lies in flow contact on steeply dipping late Precambrian strata within one of the Emigrant riders. Hodges and others (1989) reported whole-rock K-Ar data for two samples from this flow that yield ages of 3.63 ± 0.28 Ma and 3.80 ± 0.28 Ma. We interpret the existing data as indicative of a 6.1 to 3.7 Ma approximate age range for movement on the main segment of the Emigrant subsystem. Near the mouth of Wildrose Canyon, the Emigrant fault trace merges with that of the growth fault of Panamint Valley (Fig. 1), leading us to propose that some portions of the Emigrant fault were reactivated as part of the modern range-bounding fault zone (Hodges and others, 1989).

Kinematic interpretation

Figure 8 shows a typical cross section of the Emigrant subsystem in the Wildrose Canyon area. Field observations and palinspastic reconstructions indicate that the Emigrant riders are part of a westward-verging extensional duplex system. Listric faults of the breakaway zone merge to form a basal detachment dipping less than 15°W beneath the riders, and the Emigrant fault represents the roof fault of the duplex. Cross-cutting relations suggest that the progression of faulting in the duplex was from east to west. Restoration of the riders to their pre-Emigrant configuration (Fig. 8) requires a minimum cumulative displacement of roughly 4 km, implying about 180 percent local extension.

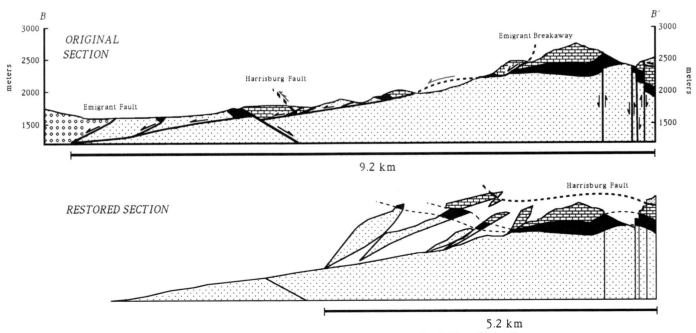

Figure 8. Geologic cross section and restoration for line B-B' on Figure 7.

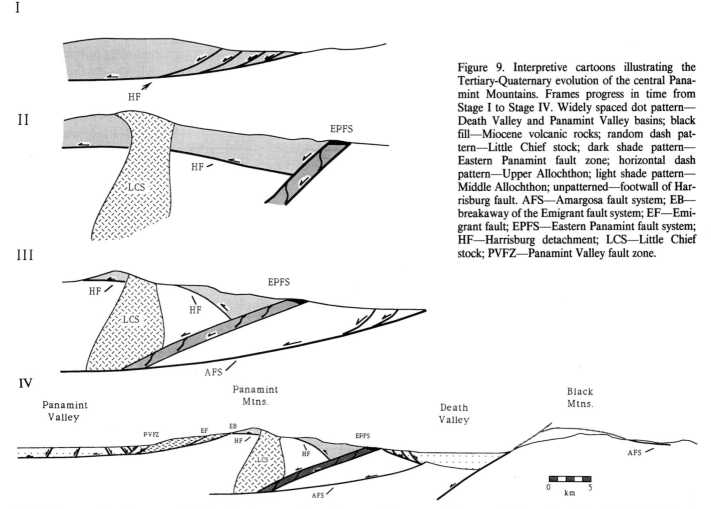

Figure 9. Interpretive cartoons illustrating the Tertiary-Quaternary evolution of the central Panamint Mountains. Frames progress in time from Stage I to Stage IV. Widely spaced dot pattern—Death Valley and Panamint Valley basins; black fill—Miocene volcanic rocks; random dash pattern—Little Chief stock; dark shade pattern—Eastern Panamint fault zone; horizontal dash pattern—Upper Allochthon; light shade pattern—Middle Allochthon; unpatterned—footwall of Harrisburg fault. AFS—Amargosa fault system; EB—breakaway of the Emigrant fault system; EF—Emigrant fault; EPFS—Eastern Panamint fault system; HF—Harrisburg detachment; LCS—Little Chief stock; PVFZ—Panamint Valley fault zone.

Total offset on the subsystem, including displacement along the Emigrant fault, must have been much greater; Hodges and others (1989) estimated >20 km of movement based on more regional reconstructions.

KINEMATIC MODEL FOR UNROOFING OF THE PANAMINT CORE COMPLEX

Structural relations suggest that greenschist to amphibolite facies metamorphic rocks in the core of the Panamint Mountains were brought to the surface as a consequence of movement along several temporally distinct normal fault systems. Our interpretation of the unroofing sequence is illustrated in Figure 9 as a series of cartoon cross sections. For ease of discussion, we arbitrarily subdivide the sequence into four stages.

Stage I: Development of the Harrisburg subsystem

Prior to intrusion of the middle Miocene Little Chief stock, the Harrisburg detachment and related structures juxtaposed greenschist to amphibolite facies rocks of the Lower Allochthon and greenschist facies rocks of the Middle Allochthon. Following

models proposed by several others (e.g., Wernicke, 1981; Davis and others, 1986), we believe that movement on this detachment was responsible for substantial upward transport of the footwall toward the surface. We have no real constraints on the magnitude of this transport because we cannot match hanging-wall and footwall cutoffs. Apparent stratigraphic throw across the fault commonly exceeds 1 km, but this must be considered an absolute minimum estimate of the true throw because it is insufficient to explain the observed metamorphic discontinuity across many segments of the detachment and the fact that synmetamorphic mesoscopic structures in the footwall (Hodges and others, 1987) have no clear correlatives in the hanging wall. Although pressures equivalent to 8 to 11 km depth were attained in the footwall during amphibolite-facies metamorphism (Labotka, 1981), no assemblages appropriate for quantitative thermobarometry occur in the hanging wall, and it is thus impossible to quantify the difference in Mesozoic paleopressures across the Harrisburg detachment. Even if it were possible to do so, the result probably would not accurately reflect throw on the detachment because of the likely differential uplift of hanging wall and footwall subsequent to Mesozoic metamorphism but prior to Harrisburg faulting.

Stage II: Development of the Eastern Panamint fault system

The Eastern Panamint fault system developed subsequent to intrusion of the Little Chief stock (10.6 Ma) and during late Miocene eruption of the Trail Canyon volcanic sequence. Near Hanaupah Canyon (Fig. 3), the sole fault of the system juxtaposes upper Precambrian Stirling Quartzite in the hanging wall and Proterozoic crystalline basement in the footwall. Stratigraphic throw across the sole fault here clearly exceeds 1.5 km (the approximate thickness of omitted Johnnie and Noonday strata). The cumulative throw on the entire Eastern Panamint system must have been close to the thickness of the entire upper Precambrian through lowest Silurian-Devonian section (McKenna and Hodges, this volume). Because the major unconformity developed beneath the Noonday Dolomite locally excised substantial Pahrump Group stratigraphy in the Death Valley region (Cloud and others, 1974; Wright and others, 1978), we cannot assume an omitted thickness of the Pahrump Group without qualification, but the total throw on the Eastern Panamint system is likely to have been in excess of 3 km and perhaps as much as 7 km. We infer that the most important consequence of movement on the Eastern Panamint system was the upward transport of the Parautochthon relative to the Lower and Middle Allochthons.

Stage III: Range-scale folding

The anticlinal geometry of the Panamint Mountains has been interpreted in a variety of ways. Hunt and Mabey (1966) suggested that the structure was in part related to doming over intrusions of plutons such as the Skidoo monzogranite but noted that some of the rotation of the range must have postdated eruption of the late Tertiary volcanic rocks on the eastern side of the range. Labotka and others (1980, 1985) also ascribed the folding to a late Cretaceous deformational event associated with plutonism. Wernicke and others (1986) and Hodges and others (1987) noted that late Tertiary structures of the Tucki Mountain detachment system are clearly involved in the anticlinal structure, and they attributed the folding to reverse-drag flexure above the Eastern Panamint fault system. We still believe that at least some reverse-drag might have occurred during Eastern Panamint movement; however, recent mapping of the Eastern Panamint system (McKenna and Hodges, this volume) reveals that these structures also have been rotated roughly 40° eastward during development of the range-scale anticline, and we must appeal to a different mechanism for the folding.

Recently, several workers have ascribed the domal form of metamorphic core complexes to isostatic rebound of a footwall denuded by movement along a detachment (e.g., Spencer, 1984; Buck and others, 1988; Davis and Lister, 1988). Although we concur that this mechanism probably was important in producing some of the broader domal morphologies of detachments in areas such as the Whipple Mountains, California, we are doubtful that it was the primary cause of the much tighter anticlinal structure of the Panamint Mountains. Block and Royden (1990) have shown that the wavelength/amplitude ratio of isostatically induced flex-

ures is a sensitive indicator of the effective elastic thickness of the lithosphere. For the Panamint Mountains, this ratio has an approximate value of 10.5, implying an effective elastic thickness of less than one-fourth of that permissible in other highly extended terrains like the Whipple Mountains. Even in a region of relatively high heat flow, such an elastic thickness seems unreasonably low.

A more plausible mechanism involves reverse-drag flexure above a detachment system lying below the Panamint Mountains that developed after movement on the Eastern Panamint system and before initiation on the undomed Emigrant subsystem. A likely candidate is the west-dipping, low-angle fault system that involves rocks ranging in age from Precambrian to Tertiary in the west-central Black Mountains (Fig. 1). Noble (1941) first described the complex geometric relations in this system, naming it the "Amargosa chaos." He believed that the Amargosa system was regionally extensive and included structures that we group as the Eastern Panamint system. Although Wright and Troxel (1973, 1984) abandoned the idea of a regionally extensive Amargosa system, Stewart (1983) postulated that the low-angle structures at the eastern foot of the Panamint Mountains and the western foot of the Black Mountains are part of a single detachment system that accommodated 80 km of northwest transport of the Panamint block relative to the Black Mountains.

Despite similarities between the Eastern Panamint structures and the type exposures of the Amargosa chaos in the Black Mountains, two lines of evidence suggest that the systems are not correlative. Reconstruction of Tertiary volcanic flow boundaries based on mapping by Noble (1941) and Wright and Troxel (1984) indicates that the Amargosa system initiated at a low angle; in contrast, mapping by McKenna and Hodges (this volume) demosntrated that the Eastern Panamint system must have initiated at a moderate angle. Furthermore, the upper Miocene Rhodes Tuff appears to have largely predated development of the Amargosa chaos (Wright and Troxel, 1984; Wright and others, 1984), whereas the apparently correlative tuffs within the Trail Canyon volcanic sequence were erupted synchronously with development of the Eastern Panamint system (McKenna and Hodges, this volume).

In Figure 9, we illustrate our bias that the Amargosa system dips westward beneath the Panamint Range and truncates the down-dip projection of the Eastern Panamint system. We infer that reverse-drag flexure as a consequence of movement on the Amargosa system was responsible for the modern eastward dip of the Harrisburg detachment and shallow westward dip of the Eastern Panamint system, as well as for the overall anticlinal structure of the range. Up to 1.2 km of uplift of the Lower Allochthon could have occurred during development of the flexure.

Stage IV: Development of the Emigrant subsystem and subsequent structures

Correspondence between the position of the Emigrant breakaway and the hinge zone of the range-scale anticline suggests that the high topography induced during Stage III flexure may have influenced initiation of the Emigrant subsystem. We believe that the Emigrant structures developed in order to minimize the thickness of the Amargosa hanging wall. Although the total displacement on the Emigrant subsystem could have been greater than 20 km (Hodges and others, 1989), palinspastic reconstructions of the breakaway zone in the Panamint Mountains (e.g., Fig. 8) indicate that Emigrant structures were responsible for no more than about 1.5 km of structural unroofing of the metamorphic core of the range. Substantial (but unquantified) erosion of the denuded core is recorded in the conglomerates of the Nova Formation.

After movement ceased on the Emigrant system in early Pliocene time, structures to the west, such as the Towne Pass fault and the Panamint Valley fault zone (Fig. 1), permitted further development of the Nova–Panamint Valley extensional basin (Burchfiel and others, 1987; Hodges and others, 1989). East of the range, the Death Valley basin continued to open as a consequence of pull-apart motion on the Southern Death Valley and Furnace Creek strike-slip fault zones (Burchfiel and Stewart, 1966) and movement on west-dipping faults that are now exposed as "turtleback" surfaces along the western front of the Black Mountains (Wright and others, 1974). Collectively, these structures have caused further eastward tilting and uplift of the Panamint Mountains relative to their surroundings.

CONCLUSIONS

The basic architecture of the central Panamint Mountains was developed during Tertiary extension. The resulting geometry of the range is characteristic of the Cordilleran metamorphic core complexes (e.g., Davis and Coney, 1979; Armstrong, 1982), but we stress the developmental complexity of this apparently simple geometry. We agree with Davis and Lister (1988) that many detachments in the Basin and Range are not single tectonic surfaces, and the Panamint Mountains provide an outstanding example of this phenomenon. The contact between the metamorphic core of the range and its unmetamorphosed structural cover (the Tucki Mountain detachment system) is diachronous, developing over more than 10 m.y. The youngest structures in the system (the Emigrant subsystem) cut and displace the oldest structures in the system (the Harrisburg subsystem), incising well over 1 km into the Harrisburg footwall.

The time-space sequence of the Panamint normal fault systems is contrary to simple models of extensional faulting, in which successive faults step consistently toward the undeformed footwall of the initial detachment (e.g., Gibbs, 1984). Harding (1987) demonstrated that the geometry of extensional riders within the Emigrant subsystem is best explained if the bounding faults developed sequentially from east to west, in the direction of tectonic transport. On a larger scale, it appears that out-of-sequence faulting was important: the Eastern Panamint system developed west of the Harrisburg breakaway, the Amargosa system breakaway developed east of the Eastern Panamint system, and the Emigrant breakaway occurred west of all previous structures (Fig. 9).

Structural and geochronological data from the central Panamint Mountains suggest that unroofing of the Panamint metamorphic core complex was largely accommodated by the movement on the Tucki Mountain, Eastern Panamint, and Amargosa detachment systems over the middle Miocene to Recent interval. The bulk of this unroofing occurred as a consequence of movement on the Harrisburg detachment, although movement on the Emigrant detachment and erosion were also important. The Eastern Panamint system was responsible for several kilometers of uplift of the Parautochthon relative to the Lower and Middle Allochthons. We infer that the modern elevation of the Panamint Mountains relative to Death Valley and Panamint Valley is the consequence of (1) reverse drag doming of the range as a consequence of movement on the Amargosa system and subsequent structures related to the opening of Death Valley, and (2) down-to-the-west movement on the Emigrant subsystem and subsequent structures related to the development of Panamint Valley.

ACKNOWLEDGMENTS

We would like to thank B. C. Burchfiel, B. W. Troxel, J. D. Walker, B. P. Wernicke, and L. A. Wright for fruitful discussions on Death Valley geology and extensional tectonics in general, and Leigh Royden for helping us to evaluate the potential role of isostatic uplift in development of the anticlinal form of the Panamint Mountains. We are grateful to Stan Hart for providing access to his isotope geochemistry facilities at MIT. Special thanks go to T. C. Labotka, M. A. Lanphere, and B. P. Wernicke for reviewing earlier versions of this chapter. Our work was supported by National Science Foundation grants EAR-8319768, EAR-8512283, and EAR-8816950.

REFERENCES CITED

Albee, A. L., Labotka, T. C., Lanphere, M. A., and McDowell, S. D., 1981, Geologic map of the Telescope Peak Quadrangle, California: U.S. Geological Survey Geologic Quadrangle Map GQ-1532, scale 1:62,500.

Armstrong, R. L., 1982, Cordilleran metamorphic core complexes; From Arizona to southern Canada: Annual Review of Earth and Planetary Science, v. 10, p. 129–154.

Block, M. A., and Royden, L. H., 1990, Core Complex geometry and large-scale flow of the lower crust: Tectonics (in press).

Buck, W. R., Martinez, F., Steckler, M. S., and Cochran, J. R., 1988, Thermal consequences of lithospheric extension: Pure and simple: Tectonics, v. 7, p. 213–234.

Burchfiel, B. C., and Stewart, J. H., 1966, "Pull-apart" origin of the central segment of Death Valley, California: Geological Society of America Bulletin, v. 77, p. 439–442.

Burchfiel, B. C., Hodges, K. V., and Royden, L. H., 1987, Geology of Panamint Valley–Saline Valley pull-apart system, California; Palinspastic evidence for low-angle geometry of a Neogene range-bounding fault: Journal of Geophysical Research, v. 92, p. 10422–19426.

Cemen, I., Drake, R. E., and Wright, L. A., 1982, Stratigraphy and chronology of the Tertiary sedimentary and volcanic units at the southeastern end of the Funeral Mountains, Death Valley region, California, *in* Cooper, J. D., Troxel, B. W., and Wright, L. A., eds., Geology of selected areas in the San Bernardino Mountains, western Mojave Desert, and southern Great Basin, California: Shoshone, California, Death Valley Publishing Co., p. 77–88.

Cemen, I., Wright, L. A., Drake, R. E., and Johnson, F. C., 1985, Cenozoic sedimentation and sequence of deformational events in the southeastern end of the Furnace Creek strike-slip fault zone, Death Valley region, California, *in* Biddle, K. T., and Christie-Blick, N., eds., Strike-slip deformation, basin formation, and sedimentation: Society of Economic Paleontologists and Mineralogists Special Publication 37, p. 127–141.

Cloud, P., Wright, L. A., Williams, E. G., Diehl, P., and Walter, M. R., 1974, Giant stromatolites and associated vertical tubes from the upper Proterozoic Noonday Dolomite, Death Valley region, eastern California: Geological Society of America Bulletin, v. 85, p. 1869–1882.

Davis, G. A., and Lister, G. S., 1988, Detachment faulting in continental extension; Perspectives from the southwestern U.S. Cordillera, *in* Clark, S. P., Jr., Burchfiel, B. C., and Suppe, J., eds., Processes in continental lithospheric deformation: Geological Society of America Special Paper 218, p. 133–160.

Davis, G. A., Lister, G. S., and Reynolds, S. J., 1986, Structural evolution of the Whipple and South Mountains shear zones, southwestern United States: Geology, v. 14, p. 7–10.

Davis, G. H., and Coney, P. J., 1979, Geological development of the Cordilleran metamorphic core complexes: Geology, v. 7, p. 120–124.

Drewes, H., 1963, Geology of the Funeral Peak Quadrangle, California, on the east flank of Death Valley: U.S. Geological Survey Professional Paper 413, 78 p.

Gibbs, A. D., 1984, Structural evolution of extensional basin margins: Journal of the Geological Society of London, v. 141, p. 609–620.

Haefner, R., 1976, Geology of the Shoshone Volcanics, Death Valley region, eastern California, *in* Troxel, B. W., and Wright, L. A., eds., Geologic features, Death Valley, California: California Division of Mines and Geology Special Report 106, p. 67–72.

Hall, W. E., 1971, Geology of the Panamint Butte Quadrangle, Inyo County, California: U.S. Geological Survey Bulletin 1299, 67 p.

Harding, M. B., 1987, Geology of the Wildrose Peak area, Death Valley region, California [M.S. thesis]: Laramie, University of Wyoming, 196 p.

Hodges, K. V., Walker, J. D., and Wernicke, B. P., 1987, Footwall structural evolution of the Tucki Mountain detachment system, Death Valley region, southeastern California, *in* Dewey, J., and Coward, M., eds., Continental extension tectonics: Geological Society of London Special Publication 28, p. 393–408.

Hodges, K., McKenna, L., Stock, J., Knapp, J., Page, L., Sternlof, K., Silverberg, D., Wüst, G., and Walker, J., 1989, Evolution of extensional basins and Basin and Range topography west of Death Valley, California: Tectonics, v. 8, p. XXX.

Hopper, R. H., 1947, Geologic section from the Sierra Nevada to Death Valley, California: Geological Society of America Bulletin, v. 58, p. 393–432.

Hunt, C. B., and Mabey, D. R., 1966, Stratigraphy and structure, Death Valley, California: U.S. Geological Survey Professional Paper 494-A, 162 p.

Johnson, B. K., 1957, Geology of a part of the Manly Peak Quadrangle, southern Panamint Range, California: University of California Publications in the Geological Sciences, v. 30, p. 353–423.

Labotka, T. C., 1981, Petrology of an andalusite-type regional metamorphic terrane, Panamint Mountains, California: Journal of Petrology, v. 22, p. 261–296.

Labotka, T. C., Albee, A. L., Lanphere, M. A., and McDowell, S. D., 1980, Stratigraphy, structure, and metamorphism in the central Panamint Mountains, Telescope Peak Quadrangle, Death Valley area, California: Geological Society of America Bulletin, v. 91, part 2, p. 843–933.

Labotka, T. C., Warasila, R. L., and Spangler, R. R., 1985, Polymetamorphism in the Panamint Mountains, California; A ^{39}Ar-^{40}Ar study: Journal of Geophysical Research, v. 90, p. 10359–10371.

Lanphere, M. A., and Dalrymple, G. B., 1967, K-Ar and Rb-Sr measurements on P-207, the U.S.G.S. interlaboratory standard muscovite: Geochimica et Cosmochimica Acta, v. 31, p. 1091–1094.

Larsen, R. W., 1979, Chronology of late Cenozoic basaltic volcanism; The tectonic implications along a segment of the Sierra Nevada and Basin and Range Province [Ph.D. thesis]: Provo, Utah, Brigham Young University, 95 p.

Lister, G. S., and Snoke, A. W., 1984, S-C mylonites: Journal of Structural Geology, v. 6, p. 617–638.

McDowell, S. D., 1974, Emplacement of the Little Chief Stock, Panamint Range, California: Geological Society of America Bulletin, v. 85, p. 1535–1546.

McKenna, L. W., 1986, New Rb-Sr constraints on the page of detachment faulting in the Panamint Range, Death Valley, California: Geological Society of America Abstracts with Programs, v. 18, p. 156.

McKenna, L. W., and Hodges, K. V., 1988, A late Miocene extensional duplex, east Panamint Range, Death Valley, California: Geological Society of America Abstracts with Programs, v. 20, p. 214.

Noble, L. F., 1941, Structural features of the Virgin Spring area, Death Valley, California: Geological Society of America Bulletin, v. 52, p. 941–1000.

Schweig, E. S., 1984, Neogene tectonics and paleogeography of the southwestern Great Basin, California [Ph.D. thesis]: Stanford, California, Stanford University, 207 p.

Snoke, A. W., and Lush, A. P., 1984, Polyphase Mesozoic-Cenozoic deformational history of the northern Rubey Mountains–East Humbolt Range, Nevada, *in* Lintz, J. P., Jr., ed., Western geological excursions, volume 4: Reno, University of Nevada Mackay School of Mines, p. 232–260.

Spencer, J., 1984, Role of tectonic denudation in uplift and warping of low-angle normal faults: Geology, v. 12, p. 95–98.

Stern, T. W., Newell, M. F., and Hunt, C. B., 1966, Uranium-lead and potassium-argon ages of parts of the Amargosa thrust complex, Death Valley, California: U.S. Geological Survey Professional Paper 550-B, p. B142–B147.

Stewart, J. H., 1983, Extensional tectonics in the Death Valley area, California: Transport of the Panamint Range structural block 80 km northwestward: Geology, v. 11, p. 153–157.

Walker, J. D., and Coleman, D. S., 1987, Correlation of Mio-Pliocene rocks of the northern Panamint Mountains and Darwin Plateau; Implications for normal-fault development and the opening of Panamint Valley: Geological Society of America Abstracts with Programs, v. 19, p. 879.

Wernicke, B. P., 1981, Low-angle faults in the Basin and Range Province; Nappe tectonics in an extending orogen: Nature, v. 291, p. 645–648.

——, 1985, Uniform-sense normal simple shear of the continental lithosphere: Canadian Journal of Earth Sciences, v. 22, p. 108–125.

Wernicke, B. P., Hodges, K. V., and Walker, J. D., 1986, Geological setting of the Tucki Mountain area, Death Valley National Monument, California, *in* Dunne, G. C., ed., Mesozoic and Cenozoic structural evolution of selected areas, east-central California: Geological Society of America Cordilleran Section Field Trip Guidebook: Geological Society of America Cordilleran Section, p. 67–80.

Wernicke, B. P., Walker, J. D., and Hodges, K. V., 1988a, Field guide to the northern part of the Tucki Mountain fault system, Death Valley region, California, *in* Weide, D. L., and Faber, M. L., eds., This extended land; Geological journeys in the southern Basin and Range; Geological Society of America Cordilleran Section Field Trip Guidebook: University of Nevada at Las Vegas Geosciences Department Special Publication 2, p. 58–63.

Wernicke, B. P., Snow, J. K., and Walker, J. D., 1988b, Correlation of early Mesozoic thrusts in the southern Great Basin and their possible indication of 250–300 km of Neogene crustal extension, *in* Weide, D. L., and Faber, M. L., eds., This extended land; Geological journeys in the southern Basin and Range; Geological Society of America Cordilleran Section Field Trip Guidebook: University of Nevada at Las Vegas Geosciences Department Special Publication 2, p. 255–267.

Wright, L. A., and Troxel, B. W., 1973, Shallow-fault interpretation of Basin and Range structure, *in* DeJong, K. A., and Scholten, R., eds., Gravity and tectonics: New York, John Wiley and Sons, p. 397–407.

——, 1984, Geology of the northern half of the Confidence Hills 15-minute Quadrangle, Death Valley region, eastern California: California Division of Mines and Geology Map Sheet 34 and accompanying notes, p. 1–20.

Wright, L. A., Otton, J. K., and Troxel, B. W., 1974, Turtleback surfaces of Death Valley viewed as a phenomenon of extensional tectonics: Geology, v. 2, p. 53–54.

Wright, L. A., Williams, E. G., and Cloud, P., 1978, Algal and cryptalgal structures and platform environments of the late pre-Phanerozoic Noonday Dolomite, eastern California: Geological Society of America Bulletin, v. 89, p. 321–333.

Wright, L. A., Kramer, J. H., Thronton, C. P., and Troxell, B. W., 1984, Type sections of two newly-named volcanic units of the central Death Valley volcanic field, eastern California: California Division of Mines and Geology Map Sheet 34 and accompanying notes, p. 21–24.

Manuscript Accepted by the Society August 21, 1989

Geological Society of America
Memoir 176
1990

Chapter 20

Geochemistry of Mio-Pliocene volcanic rocks from around Panamint Valley, Death Valley area, California

Drew S. Coleman and J. Douglas Walker
Department of Geology, University of Kansas, Lawrence, Kansas 66045-2124

ABSTRACT

Miocene-Pliocene volcanic rocks of the Nova Formation and Darwin Plateau near Death Valley, California, were erupted during extensional faulting and range in composition from basalt to rhyolite. Petrographic evidence, including sieved plagioclase, glass-bearing plagioclase, mafic and felsic xenoliths, and quartz, sanidine, and amphibole xenocrysts in samples of intermediate composition, suggest that they were derived through magma mixing or crustal assimilation. Chemical modeling indicates that rocks that show these disequilibrium textures can be derived through a combination of mixing between end-member basalt and rhyolite and fractionation of olivine, pyroxene, and plagioclase ± intergrown magnetite and ilmenite ± Cr-Al spinel. Pb and Sr isotopic data support these conclusions and may constrain the source of the contaminant to the lower crust.

The age (~4 Ma) and chemical similarity of rocks from Pinto Peak and Darwin Plateau and the apparent lack of vents and feeder dikes at Pinto Peak indicate that the lavas from these two areas probably shared a common source located at Darwin Plateau. This suggests that the two areas, now separated by Panamint Valley, were adjacent during the period of volcanic activity and that Panamint Valley has therefore opened in the last 4 m.y.

Volcanic activity in the study area progressed from exclusively basaltic to basaltic-andesitic-rhyolitic and shifted westward through time. These observations are consistent with a simple-shear mechanism for extension, because this mechanism better explains the "off-axis" nature of the volcanism and provides a more efficient means for crustal anatexis than a pure-shear mechanism.

INTRODUCTION AND GEOLOGIC SETTING

Essential to understanding the pure-shear (e.g., Thompson, 1960; Wright and Troxel, 1973) and simple-shear (Wernicke, 1981, 1985) models for crustal extension is an understanding of the role of magmatism during extension. The pure-shear model predicts both mantle and crustal magmas and, because the lithosphere behaves homogeneously across the extended region, laterally homogeneous volcanism. Furthermore, this model suggests that volcanic activity will be concentrated within the region of brittle, upper-crust deformation as igneous dilation partially accommodates extension directly below. The simple-shear model, however, suggests that magmatism will be heterogeneous across the extended region and offset from the axis of upper-crustal extension (Wernicke, 1985; Bosworth, 1987). Wernicke (1985) pointed out that extensional tectonics promotes adiabatic melting of the lithosphere and that, according to the simple-shear model, the product of this melting should vary with position in the extending region. In the lower plate of the extended region, the entire lithospheric column is able to melt as material above it is removed, whereas in the upper plate only the deep lithosphere is subject to adiabatic melting. Furthermore, volcanic activity should be concentrated in the region of maximum lithospheric thinning, which is "off axis" from upper-crustal brittle faulting (Wernicke, 1985; Bosworth, 1987). Investigation of the petrology and geochemistry of synextensional volcanic rocks will help

Coleman, D. S., and Walker, J. D., 1990, Geochemistry of Mio-Pliocene volcanic rocks from around Panamint Valley, Death Valley area, California, *in* Wernicke, B. P., ed., Basin and Range extensional tectonics near the latitude of Las Vegas, Nevada: Boulder, Colorado, Geological Society of America Memoir 176.

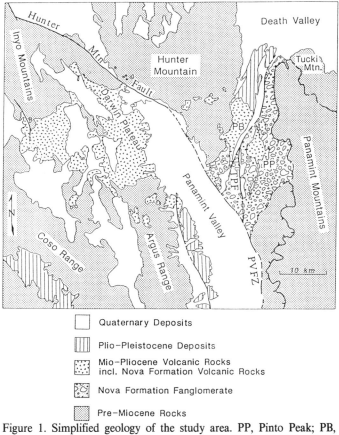

Quaternary Deposits

Plio-Pleistocene Deposits

Mio-Pliocene Volcanic Rocks
incl. Nova Formation Volcanic Rocks

Nova Formation Fanglomerate

Pre-Miocene Rocks

Figure 1. Simplified geology of the study area. PP, Pinto Peak; PB, Panamint Butte; TPF, Towne Pass Fault; PVFZ, Panamint Valley Fault Zone.

characterize their sources and determine the roles and interaction of the mantle and the crust during deformation. Understanding magmatic processes should, in turn, help constrain the tectonic processes in extensional systems.

The Great Basin of the southwestern United States was actively extending during middle and late Tertiary time, and extension was accompanied by voluminous mafic to felsic volcanism. In the Death Valley region of the Basin and Range Province, abundant sedimentary and volcanic rocks deposited during Tertiary extension are exposed, providing an excellent opportunity to study synextensional rocks. This study focuses on the Miocene volcanic rocks intercalated in the Nova Formation fanglomerate, exposed in the Panamint Mountains west of Death Valley, and on volcanic rocks of the same age on the Darwin Plateau (Fig. 1).

The best exposures of the Nova Formation are around Pinto Peak and the west slopes of Tucki Mountain in the northern Panamint Mountains (Fig. 1). This unit includes fanglomerate intercalated with mafic to intermediate volcanic flows, all deposited during Tertiary extension (Schweig, 1984; Wernicke and others, 1986; Walker and Coleman, 1987). The Nova Formation is at least 1,000 m thick and rests unconformably on Precambrian and Paleozoic basement rocks (Hooper, 1947). Intercalated volcanic units are up to 20 m thick, and field evidence suggests that

these units may be related to the extensive lavas of the adjacent Darwin Plateau (Schweig, 1984; Fig. 1).

Hall (1971) described two samples of quartz-olivine basalt from the Nova Formation near Towne Pass, and Larsen (1979) reported chemical analyses of two samples from Towne Pass. Larsen's analyses showed that the rocks are tholeiitic basalt and calc-alkaline, high-alumina andesite. Whole-rock, K-Ar dating by Hall (1971) and Larsen (1979) showed that the flows in the Nova Formation are 4 to 5 m.y. old.

Darwin Plateau lies at the north end of Panamint Valley, south of the Inyo Mountains (Fig. 1). The volcanic rocks of Darwin Plateau include olivine basalt flows and pyroclastic rocks interbedded with alluvial sediments (Schweig, 1984). These rocks rest unconformably on Permian and Triassic sedimentary rocks (Stevens, 1977) and Jurassic granites (Hall, 1971). Chemical analyses by Larsen (1979) show that the lavas include calc-alkaline, high-alumina basalt and K-rich, alkali olivine basalt. K-Ar ages of the lavas from Darwin Plateau range from 4 to 8 Ma (Larsen, 1979; Schweig, 1982).

Petrography

Miocene-Pliocene volcanic rocks are well exposed at both Pinto Peak and Darwin Plateau. Sample locations for this study are recorded in Coleman (1988). Flows are commonly gray to black and weather brown to red. Individual units are generally 1 to 10 m thick, but they are up to 20 m thick at Pinto Peak and up to 30 m thick on Darwin Plateau. The lavas are typically coarsely vesicular, with the vesicles being more abundant and rounder near the tops of individual flows. Units that are largely nonvesicular may be vesicular near their tops, and vesicles may be filled or lined with calcite and chalcedony. Some lavas show a distinct flow banding. The tops of the flows are commonly oxidized. Vents are common on Darwin Plateau (Schweig, 1982, 1984); however, no evidence of vents or feeder dikes was seen at Pinto Peak.

Table 1 contains a summary of the mineral assemblages of all the rocks examined in this study, and Table 2 shows preliminary microprobe analyses of most mineral phases. The volcanic rocks are generally fine- to medium-grained, porphyritic, aphanitic basalts and andesites. Common phenocryst, microphenocryst, and glomerocryst phases are plagioclase (2 to 5 mm), olivine (2 to 5 mm), augite (1 to 3 mm), and magnetite-ilmenite ± Cr-Al spinel. The lavas also commonly contain 1 to 4 mm quartz xenocrysts that variably show hexagonal, square, or embayed outlines and visible reaction rims. Several samples also contain mafic and felsic xenoliths and sanidine and amphibole xenocrysts. The groundmass of most samples consists of flow-aligned, intergranular, plagioclase microlites, pyroxene, and magnetite. The rocks rarely show significant alteration other than iddingsite rims on olivine phenocrysts.

Plagioclase. Plagioclase phenocrysts are commonly euhedral, twinned, and zoned. In many samples, the plagioclase exhibits sieved or spongy texture; it has a clear core, surrounded by a zone

TABLE 1. MINERAL ASSEMBLAGES OF SAMPLES FROM PINTO PEAK, DARWIN PLATEAU, AND THE SURROUNDING AREA*

Sample Number[†]	Olivine	Plagioclase	Pyroxene	Magnetite/ Ilmenite	Sieved Plagioclase	Glass-bearing Plagioclase	Xenoliths/ Xenocrysts
1 (bas)	P M	P M GM	GM	GM	----	----	----
2 (bas)	P M	P M GM	P M GM	GM	----	----	----
4 (bas)	P GL M GM	P GL GM	GL GM	M GM	----	----	----
5 (bas)	P	GL M GM	M GM	GM	(P)	----	----
6 (and)	P M	P M GM	GM	GM	P	P	S
7 (and)	P M	P M GM	M GM	M GM	P	P	Q S
8 (rhy)	----	----	P	----	----	----	----
9 (and)	P M	GM	GM	GM	P M (GL)	----	A
10 (bas)	P	M GL	P GM	GM	----	----	Q
11 (and)	P M GM	M GM	P GM	GM	P GL	----	Q A
12 (bas)	----	M GM	M GM	GM	P	----	----
13 (bas)	----	GM	GM	GM	----	----	----
14 (and)	P	M GM	P M GM	GM	----	----	----
15 (and)	----	GM	P M GM	GM	P	P	Q A
16 (and)	----	M GM	M GM	GM	P	----	Q
17 (and)	P GM	M GM	GM	GM	P	----	Q A
18 (and)	P GM	M GM	GM	GM	----	----	----
19 (bas)	P GM	GM	GM	GM	----	----	----
20 (bas)	P M GM	P M GM	(P) GM	M GM	----	----	----
21 (bas)	P M GM	P M GM	M GM	GM	P GL M	----	Q
22 (and)	P	P GM	P GM	M GM	----	----	----
23 (and)	P	GL M GM	P GL GM	GM	P GL	----	MX Q A
25 (bas)	P M GM	M GM	P M GM	GM	----	----	----
26 (bas)	P M	P M GM	P M GM	M GM	----	----	----
27 (bas)	P M GM	P M GM	P M GM	GM	----	----	----
28 (bas)	P M GM	P M GM	GM	M GM	(P)	----	----
29 (bas)	P M GM	M GM	GM	GM	P	----	Q
30 (bas)	P M GM	M GM	GM	GM	----	----	----
31 (bas)	P M GM	M GM	GM	M GM	----	----	----
32 (and)	----	GM	(P) GM	GM	P GL	----	FX Q
33 (bas)	P GM	M GM	----	GM	----	----	----
35 (and)	P M	P M GM	P GL M GM	GM	----	----	Q
36 (bas)	P	GM	GM	GM	P GL M	----	Q
37 (and)	P GM	P M GM	M GM	GM	P	----	MX Q
38 (and)	P	M	GL M GM	GM	P GL M	----	Q
39 (and)	P	M GM	P GM	GM	----	----	----
40 (and)	P M GM	M GM	GM	M GM	P	----	Q
41 (and)	P	GM	M GM	M GM	P M	----	Q
42 (bas)	P	P M GM	GL GM	GM	----	----	----
43 (bas)	P M GM	M GM	P M GM	M GM	----	----	----
44 (bas)	P	M GM	M GM	M GM	----	----	----
45 (bas)	P GM	M GM	M GM	M GM	----	----	----
46 (and)	P GM	M GM	M GM	GM	P	----	Q
48 (bas)	P GL GM	P M GM	M GM	GM	----	----	----
49 (and)	P	M GM	M GM	GM	P GL	P	----

*For primary phases, P = phenocryst; M = microphenocryst; GM = groundmass; GL = glomerocryst. For xenocrysts and xenoliths, Q = quartz; S = sanidine; A = amphibole; MX = mafic xenoliths; FX = felsic xenoliths. Parentheses indicate that phase is not abundant.

[†](bas) = basalt; (and) = andesite; (rhy) = rhyolite, according to the classification scheme of Irvine and Baragar (1971).

TABLE 2. MICROPROBE ANALYSES OF MINERALS*

Sample	SiO₂	TiO₂	Al₂O₃	Fe₂O₃	MnO	MgO	CaO	Na₂O	K₂O	Total	Cr	Ni	Ba
						OLIVINE							
11-core	38.97	0.01	0.03	14.67	0.22	45.58	0.19	....	....	99.68	29	180	....
11-rim	37.80	0.00	0.01	21.02	0.34	40.33	0.16	....	....	99.66	27	122	....
20-core	39.01	0.01	0.05	13.32	0.20	46.88	0.25	....	....	99.73	11	208	....
20-rim	36.80	0.00	0.04	23.20	0.41	39.02	0.32	....	....	99.80	8	149	....
20-GM	35.30	0.02	0.03	31.63	0.57	32.03	0.35	....	....	99.92	0	56	....
23-core	38.59	0.00	0.04	16.50	0.22	44.29	0.17	....	....	99.80	15	140	....
23-rim	38.62	0.01	0.02	16.54	0.20	44.12	0.22	....	....	99.72	19	211	....
29-core	37.56	0.03	0.06	23.90	0.31	37.59	0.38	....	....	99.83	15	125	....
29-rim	35.44	0.02	0.02	31.17	0.49	32.49	0.24	....	....	99.86	30	77	....
29-GM	33.66	0.05	0.01	40.11	0.58	25.24	0.26	....	....	99.90	16	61	....
						PYROXENE							
11-GM	51.91	0.70	1.11	15.48	0.43	19.93	10.36	....	....	99.92	29	40	....
23-GM	49.87	0.78	2.60	15.47	0.42	17.42	13.41	....	....	99.97	14	15	....
29-Ph	51.61	0.65	2.69	6.85	0.21	16.56	21.11	....	....	99.68	226	7	....
29-GM	50.56	1.26	2.56	10.16	0.28	14.93	20.18	....	....	99.93	55	0	....
						OXIDES							
11-Ph	0.53	19.80	1.51	76.23	0.28	1.08	....	....	....	99.43	184	....	....
20-GM	0.40	39.43	0.55	54.87	0.64	4.04	....	....	....	99.94	34	....	....
23-Ph	0.14	11.08	2.05	84.67	0.37	1.60	....	....	....	99.92	54	....	....
23-GM	0.09	14.05	1.56	82.14	0.37	1.72	....	....	....	99.92	54	....	....
29-Ph	2.02	30.38	0.94	63.94	0.51	2.15	....	....	....	99.93	22	....	....
11-Ph	0.10	0.89	28.30	30.14	0.25	11.72	....	....	....	99.32	27.93[†]	....	....
20-Ph	0.06	9.13	15.57	50.22	0.43	7.15	....	....	....	100.00	17.44[†]	....	....
						PLAGIOCLASE							
11-core	59.68	....	24.91	0.49	....	0.05	6.20	6.77	1.85	99.95	....	....	48
11-rim	61.56	....	24.28	0.15	....	0.05	5.19	7.11	1.68	100.02	....	....	23
20-core	50.22	....	31.64	0.48	....	0.06	13.82	3.63	0.16	100.01	....	....	0
20-rim	51.85	....	30.41	0.69	....	0.05	12.67	4.07	0.26	100.00	....	....	0
23-core	60.02	....	25.32	0.18	....	0.00	6.31	7.39	0.73	99.95	....	....	54
23-rim	61.11	....	24.61	0.23	....	0.01	5.39	7.42	1.20	99.97	....	....	47
23-GM	64.84	....	21.16	0.73	....	0.03	5.41	4.17	3.59	99.93	....	....	68
29-core	49.20	....	32.10	0.66	....	0.09	14.37	3.30	0.23	99.95	....	....	41
29-rim	49.71	....	31.68	0.60	....	0.11	14.09	3.49	0.26	99.94	....	....	45
29-GM	52.52	....	29.86	0.74	....	0.07	11.99	4.31	0.40	99.89	....	....	113

*Oxides are given in weight percent; Cr, Ni, and Ba are given in parts per million. GM = groundmass; Ph = average of at least two analyses of a phenocryst; .... = not analyzed.

[†]Cr given as weight percent Cr₂O₃ and added to total for Cr-Al spinel analyses.

of groundmass inclusions, surrounded by a clear rim (Fig. 2a). Sieved plagioclase is thought to be the result of mixing plagioclase, equilibrated with a felsic magma, into a mafic magma (Tsuchiyama, 1985; Tsuchiyama and Takahashi, 1983; Lofgren and Norris, 1981). A second population of plagioclase that contains irregular glass inclusions is also present (Fig. 2b) but is not as common as sieved plagioclase. This population is thought to have formed during rapid skeletal growth of plagioclase in equilibrium with a mafic magma when it was introduced into a cooler, felsic magma (Lofgren, 1978).

The results of microprobe analyses of plagioclase are given in Table 2. Unsieved plagioclase phenocrysts in mafic and intermediate rocks are distinctly different in composition. Phenocrysts in both mafic and intermediate samples are zoned normally, with compositions of cores and rims in the mafic samples averaging from An 80 to An 74, respectively, and cores and rims in the intermediate samples averaging from An 45 to An 40, respectively.

Microphenocrysts of plagioclase are subhedral to anhedral, up to 0.5 mm long, and twinned and zoned normally. Plagioclase microphenocrysts generally are not sieved and do not contain glass inclusions, suggesting that they grew after mixing, in equilibrium with the hydrid magma.

Groundmass plagioclase is distinctly different in the basalts and andesites. The composition of plagioclase in the groundmass of basalts is approximately An 72, whereas in andesites it is approximately An 54. An important observation is that the groundmass plagioclase of the andesite is more calcic than the phenocrysts. This is consistent with the argument that the andesite was derived by mixing of a basalt and a rhyolite. The phenocrysts were presumably formed in equilibrium with a more silicic magma, and the groundmass crystallized in equilibrium with the hybrid; thus, the groundmass plagioclase is more calcic than the phenocrysts. A similar scenario may explain why there is such a large gap between the compositions of the phenocrysts and the groundmass in the basalt.

Other trends observed in the plagioclase compositions are higher concentrations of K_2O, Fe_2O_3, and Ba in the groundmass plagioclase than in the phenocrysts.

Olivine. Olivine phenocrysts are euhedral and zoned, with cores being more forsteritic than rims (Fo 87 to 78 and Fo 78 to 64, respectively, Table 2). One phenocryst, which is in a basaltic inclusion in an andesite, shows no zoning, with core and rim compositions of Fo 84. Olivine may be partially or completely altered to iddingsite and serpentine and may contain inclusions of Cr-Al spinel and Fe-Ti oxides.

Microphenocrysts of olivine are as much as 0.5 mm long, subhedral, and unzoned and generally lack inclusions. Only one microphenocryst was analyzed: and its composition, Fo 70, falls within the range of composition of phenocryst rims. The groundmass olivine ranges from Fo 67 to Fo 55 and overlaps the composition range of phenocryst rims.

Olivine was also analyzed for CaO, TiO_2, MnO, Ni, and Cr. Of these elements, only MnO and Ni show clear trends. The Ni concentration decreases from core to rim in the phenocrysts, whereas the concentration of MnO increases from core to rim. Furthermore, the concentration of Ni in groundmass olivine is less than in the phenocrysts, and the concentrations of MnO is greater in the groundmass phase.

Augite. Phenocrysts of augite occur in some samples. Generally, they are anhedral and may contain inclusions of magnetite-ilmenite. Augite also occurs as fine-grained reaction rims around quartz and as granular aggregates completely replacing amphibole.

Microprobe analyses of augite were obtained from three samples (Table 2). In one sample, augite is present as a phenocrystic phase, whereas in the other two it occurs only in the groundmass. The phenocrystic augite is unzoned with respect to all elements except Cr, which is enriched toward the rim. Augite in all of the samples probed contains less than one weight-percent TiO_2 and has a range in Al_2O_3 from 0.7 to 6.1 percent.

Oxides. Microprobe analysis showed that the opaque phenocrysts are intergrown magnetite-ilmenite pairs (Table 2). The Fe-Ti oxides show a continuous range in composition from 46 to 93 percent Fe_2O_3 (total Fe as Fe_2O_3) and from 3 to 49 percent TiO_2. Al_2O_3 concentrations range from 0 to 2 percent, and MgO concentrations range from 0 to 4 percent. Cr concentrations are as high as 184 ppm but are commonly less than 50 ppm.

Euhedral Cr-Al spinel also occurs as a phenocryst phase in some of the mafic samples. Cr-Al spinel contains 15 to 30 percent Cr_2O_3 and is zoned; Cr_2O_3 concentrations in the core are 2 to 3 percent higher than in the rim. Phenocrysts are also zoned with respect to FeO, TiO_2, MgO, and Al_2O_3. FeO and TiO_2 have higher concentrations in the rim, whereas MgO and Al_2O_3 are concentrated in the core. Cr-Al spinel does not occur as a groundmass phase.

Xenoliths and xenocrysts. Small, mafic, lithic inclusions occur in several of the andesites. The inclusions usually contain phenocrysts of olivine and pyroxene in a glass-rich groundmass that is distinctly different from the groundmass of the host rock (Fig. 2c). Inclusions are less than 15 mm across and may have been crystal liquid or crystal glass. Olivine in one inclusion is approximately Fo 84 in composition and, as opposed to primary olivine phenocrysts in other samples, is not zoned.

Figure 2d shows a glomerocryst of plagiocalse. An important feature of these glomerocrysts is that the sieved zone occurs only on the outer rim of the glomerocryst rather than on the rim of each individual crystal. This suggests that it was introduced to the magma as a single glomerocryst from another magma or as a coherent xenolith by assimilation of older rocks.

Shattered quartz xenocrysts that appear in many of the samples are ubiquitously rimmed by pyroxene (Fig. 2e). Unfortunately, because they were shattered, whole xenocrysts rarely survived the thin-section–making process, and the thin sections show pieces of the crystal in a hole that is rimmed by pyroxene. However, where pieces are left, it is obvious that they are fragments of single quartz grains. Most quartz grains are anhedral and deeply embayed and may contain brown glass inclusions. Mies and Glazner (1987) suggest that quartz xenocrysts with these features were derived through assimilation of granite. A second population of quartz that is not embayed and that shows a sub-hexagonal outline is also present. The equant, hexagonal form of this quartz suggests that it was β-quartz that grew in a rhyolitic magma at depth. Thus, both assimilation of older crustal material and magma mixing are likely mechanisms for the introduction of felsic material into the basalts.

Other xenocrysts in the rocks include strongly resorbed, euhedral sanidine and amphibole (Figs. 2f, g). Amphibole is usually completely altered to a granular aggregate of pyroxene and opaque minerals and is only identifiable as amphibole by its euhedral outline. The presence of sanidine, a high temperature phase, and the euhedral form of both the sanidine and the amphibole suggest that they were derived from magma mixing rather than assimilation.

Chemistry

The methods used in preparing samples for major-, trace-, and rare-earth-element analysis and for isotopic analysis are given

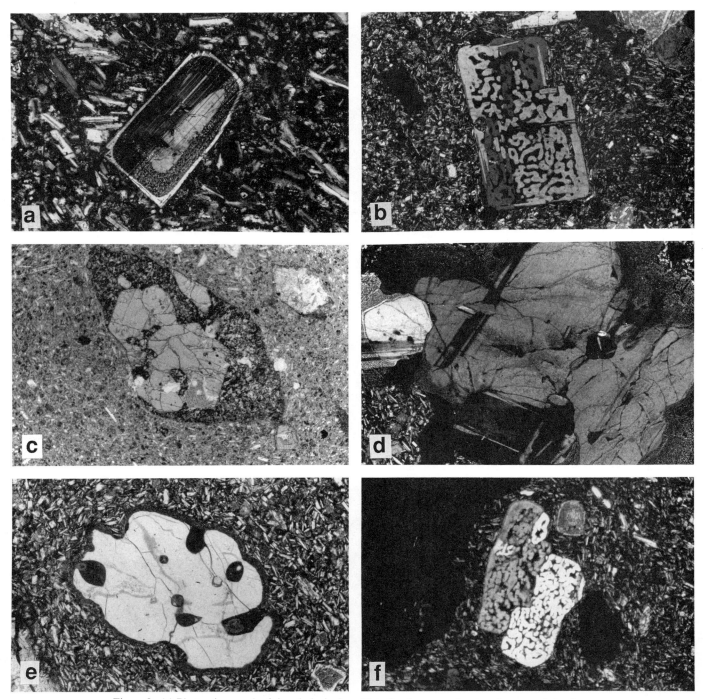

Figure 2. (a) Photomicrograph of sieved plagioclase. Note the clear core, the sieved zone, and the clear rim. Also note the resorbed outline of the core and the sieved zone cutting across twins in the core (crossed polars, 100×, field-of-view = 1.5 mm × 1.0 mm). (b) Photomicrograph of glass-bearing plagioclase (crossed polars, 25×, field-of-view = 3.6 mm × 2.2 mm). (c) Photomicrograph of a mafic inclusion in an andesite. Note that the groundmass of the inclusion is composed almost entirely of glass. The phenocrysts in the inclusion are pyroxene (uncrossed polars, 25×, field-of-view = 3.6 mm × 2.2 mm). (d) Photomicrograph of a plagioclase glomerocryst. Note that the sieved zone follows the outline of the glomerocryst rather than the individual grains (crossed polars, 25×, field-of-view = 3.6 mm × 2.2 mm). (e) Photomicrograph of a quartz xenocryst in a basalt. This xenocryst is resorbed, shattered, and surrounded by a thin rim of pyroxene (uncrossed polars, 25×, field-of-view = 3.6 mm × 2.2 mm). (f) Photomicrograph of a strongly resorbed sanidine xenocryst (crossed polars, 25×, field-of-view = 3.6 mm × 2.2 mm). (g) Photomicrograph of a euhedral amphibole xenocryst. The amphibole is completely altered to pyroxene and opaque minerals (uncrossed polars, 100×, field-of-view = 1.5 mm × 1.0 mm).

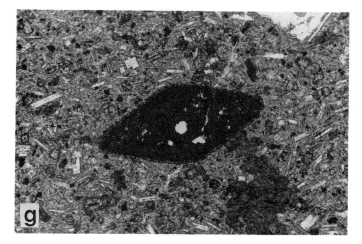

in Appendix 1. The results of x-ray fluorescence spectrometry and instrumental neutron activation analyses for major, trace, and rare-earth elements are given in Table 3, and the results of isotopic analyses are given in Table 4. The error in major-element analyses is ± 1 percent, and in trace-element analyses is ± 3 percent as determined by comparisons of U.S. Geological Survey standards. Error in instrumental neutron activation analysis data is ±4 percent. Error in Sr isotopic analyses is given with data for each sample and in Pb isotopic analyses is ± 0.1 percent, ± 0.15, and ± 0.2 for $^{206}Pb/^{204}Pb$, $^{207}Pb/^{204}Pb$, and $^{208}Pb/^{204}Pb$, respectively.

The samples range continuously in composition from 45 to 65 percent SiO_2 with the exception of sample 8, which is a late-stage ash flow with 73 percent SiO_2. The lavas all have high total alkalis ($Na_2O + K_2O > 4$ percent). According to the scheme of Irvine and Baragar (1971) the samples are classified as calc-alkaline basalts, andesites, and dacites. In general, the basalts are olivine- and hypersthene-normative. Several of the basalts have nepheline in the norm, and none of the basalts is quartz normative. The andesites have quartz and hypersthene in the norm and no olivine.

An AFM plot (Fig. 3) shows the distinct calc-alkaline trend of the rocks; it is important to note that samples from all of the areas studied plot along the same trend. The calc-alkaline trend suggests that if fractional crystallization was significant in causing the chemical variation in the lavas, the oxygen fugacity was high, as a low f_{O_2} would be expected to produce a tholeiitic trend.

Figure 4 shows the variation of the major oxides with SiO_2 concentration for samples from this study. With the exception of MgO, Al_2O_3, and Na_2O, all major oxides show linear variation with SiO_2. TiO_2, Fe_2O_3, and CaO decrease, whereas K_2O increases with increasing silica. Linear trends on these plots are consistent with a magma-mixing model, whereas kinks or bends would be expected in the trends as the assemblage of fractionating phases changed during fractional crystallization. The curved trend on the MgO plot may indicate that fractionation of a Mg-rich phase occurred, and the distinct bends in the Al_2O_3 and Na_2O trends are consistent with the combined effects of olivine frac-

tionation and addition of a felsic component (Glazner, 1990). It could be argued that samples from Pinto Peak and Darwin Plateau define two different trends on the Na_2O and Al_2O_3 plots; however, it is believed that the Darwin Plateau samples help define trends on these two plots because the Darwin Plateau samples plot on the same trends for all other major elements. It is an unfortunate coincidence that the only samples that fall in the 60 to 70 percent SiO_2 range, which is where the kink in the Na_2O trend is defined, happen to be from Darwin Plateau. In all the major-element plots, there is more scatter at the low-silica end than the high-silica end of the plots. This pattern may be the result of combined fractional crystallization of the mafic liquid and magma mixing, or of interaction with more than one contaminant, or may simply reflect the lack of data for felsic rocks.

Rb, Th, and Pb concentrations increase linearly with silica concentration, whereas Sr and Eu concentrations decrease (Fig. 5). Samples from Pinto Peak and Darwin Plateau plot along the same trends. The straight trace-element trends reemphasize that the compositional variation in the rocks is consistent with magma mixing. Plots of Cr and Ni versus SiO_2 (Fig. 5), however, show very poor curvilinear trends, which may indicate that fractional crystallization also occurred. All of the trace-element plots show significant scatter. This pattern may be due in part to mixing with different partial melts that have similar major-element chemistry

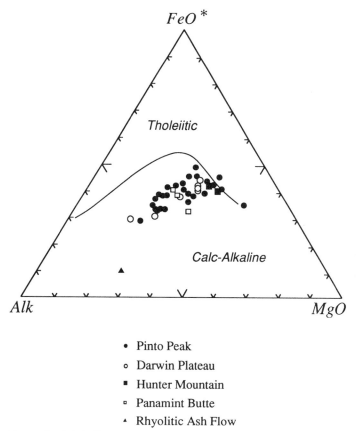

Figure 3. AFM diagram. Note the strong calc-alkaline trend of the samples.

- • Pinto Peak
- ∘ Darwin Plateau
- ▪ Hunter Mountain
- ▫ Panamint Butte
- ▲ Rhyolitic Ash Flow

TABLE 3. MAJOR-, TRACE-, AND RARE-EARTH-ELEMENT COMPOSITIONS OF SAMPLES FROM PINTO PEAK, THE DARWIN PLATEAU, AND THE SURROUNDING AREA*

Sample	1	2	4	5	6	7	8	9	10	11	12	13	14	15	16	17	18
SiO_2	46.50	45.64	47.44	51.62	57.99	58.33	73.35	58.39	48.28	57.75	51.58	49.00	54.69	57.21	56.54	57.76	52.99
TiO_2	1.49	1.53	1.28	1.33	1.06	1.05	0.15	1.02	1.35	1.02	1.23	1.47	1.20	1.01	1.02	0.96	1.27
Al_2O_3	17.09	15.71	16.14	16.08	15.90	16.16	15.56	16.72	17.51	16.51	17.39	17.87	18.37	16.45	16.47	16.14	15.51
Fe_2O_3	9.71	9.43	9.94	8.76	6.78	6.66	1.06	6.04	9.55	6.10	9.50	10.44	7.53	7.02	6.98	5.95	8.11
MgO	7.89	8.00	9.08	7.01	4.78	4.67	2.40	4.12	5.90	4.62	5.46	5.66	4.10	4.05	3.88	4.28	6.80
CaO	11.04	9.93	11.14	7.15	5.13	5.19	0.76	6.33	10.93	6.34	8.68	10.12	7.20	6.45	6.48	5.97	6.98
Na_2O	2.79	3.60	2.89	3.92	4.72	4.81	1.76	4.16	3.41	3.93	3.63	2.97	4.71	3.80	4.35	3.80	3.78
K_2O	1.07	1.38	0.82	1.64	2.64	2.68	4.14	2.61	0.78	2.50	1.04	1.11	1.90	2.23	2.27	2.62	2.21
P_2O_5	0.30	0.48	0.28	0.18	0.18	0.20	0.02	0.19	0.30	0.20	0.20	0.33	0.12	0.24	0.00	0.24	0.35
LOI	0.37	1.17	1.64	0.17	0.15	0.00	4.75	0.03	2.14	0.00	0.71	3.50	0.51	0.32	0.30	0.35	0.00
Total	98.25	96.87	100.65	97.86	99.33	99.75	103.95	99.61	100.15	98.97	99.02	102.47	100.33	98.78	98.26	98.07	98.00
Zr	138	148	133	170	198	198	88	168	147	180	142	137	173	159	157	175	180
Rb	15	29	6	23	50	51	105	41	5	46	12	11	28	50	54	57	40
Y	20	23	21	17	17	18	25	14	20	16	22	22	13	21	21	18	19
Th	3	5	4	12	4	2	19	5	5	4	5	2	3	4	8	9	3
Pb	2	7	0	7	10	13	34	15	11	16	9	6	6	9	8	14	11
Sr	772	981	701	461	439	462	94	707	590	728	446	810	840	493	487	491	769
Ba	339	575	423	364	816	797	56	892	355	884	391	419	1005	585	572	601	864
Cr	226	290	322	340	192	197	13	156	136	164	179	117	81	130	123	190	275
Ni	76	137	141	151	105	102	7	57	46	66	75	55	22	50	43	64	154
Ta	......	......	0.44	......	......	......	3.48	......	......	1.22	0.69	......	......	......	1.25	......	......
Co	......	......	37.4	......	......	......	0.5	......	......	21.7	33.0	......	......	......	21.9	......	......
Sc	......	......	30	......	......	......	3	......	......	17	22	......	......	......	16	......	......
Hf	......	......	0.0	......	......	......	4.1	......	......	3.6	2.7	......	......	......	3.3	......	......
La	......	......	19.8	......	......	......	28.7	......	......	25.3	13.7	......	......	......	22.0	......	......
Ce	......	......	44.8	......	......	......	67.3	......	......	54.6	28.9	......	......	......	43.9	......	......
Sm	......	......	4.0	......	......	......	3.7	......	......	4.1	3.3	......	......	......	3.8	......	......
Eu	......	......	1.40	......	......	......	0.15	......	......	1.21	1.17	......	......	......	1.12	......	......
Tb	......	......	0.67	......	......	......	0.92	......	......	0.60	0.66	......	......	......	0.61	......	......
Yb	......	......	1.79	......	......	......	2.85	......	......	1.76	2.07	......	......	......	2.01	......	......
Lu	......	......	0.29	......	......	......	0.35	......	......	0.27	0.31	......	......	......	0.30	......	......

TABLE 3. MAJOR-, TRACE-, AND RARE-EARTH-ELEMENT COMPOSITIONS OF SAMPLES FROM PINTO PEAK, THE DARWIN PLATEAU, AND THE SURROUNDING AREA*

(continued)

Sample	19	20	21	22	23	24	25	26	27	28	29	30	31	32	33	35	36
SiO_2	51.36	45.67	52.76	50.14	62.92	64.14	51.37	50.12	50.18	48.32	51.37	46.99	47.75	59.24	46.72	51.54	51.27
TiO_2	1.34	1.27	1.17	1.35	0.72	0.65	1.19	1.22	1.21	1.13	1.38	1.62	1.74	0.93	1.25	1.48	1.14
Al_2O_3	18.64	14.12	17.25	17.98	14.40	14.46	18.02	18.34	18.14	19.57	15.80	15.50	16.16	16.44	16.71	16.70	16.83
Fe_2O_3	7.92	10.31	8.13	8.20	5.35	4.64	7.40	8.73	8.66	8.83	9.09	10.18	10.15	6.06	9.64	8.01	8.06
MgO	4.22	13.65	5.38	4.65	4.06	2.70	5.31	6.25	6.34	5.96	7.05	9.32	8.14	3.59	8.00	6.43	5.98
CaO	8.13	8.20	8.18	8.49	4.15	3.71	8.47	8.97	8.83	10.12	8.09	9.31	9.44	5.76	10.67	8.32	8.23
Na_2O	4.00	2.67	3.70	3.94	3.60	3.66	3.94	3.38	3.36	3.13	3.31	2.93	3.17	3.87	2.66	3.86	3.69
K_2O	1.72	0.72	1.49	1.38	3.11	3.58	1.55	1.08	1.13	0.84	1.72	1.16	1.30	2.62	0.69	2.30	1.52
P_2O_5	0.52	0.36	0.17	0.29	0.16	0.18	0.24	0.12	0.20	0.19	0.23	0.34	0.44	0.26	0.25	0.43	0.30
LOI	1.65	0.64	0.00	0.74	0.32	0.59	0.05	0.00	0.00	0.05	0.00	0.40	0.79	0.74	1.20	1.77	0.03
Total	99.50	97.61	98.23	97.16	98.79	98.31	97.54	98.30	98.05	98.14	98.40	97.75	99.08	99.51	97.79	100.84	97.05
Zr	171	134	153	178	131	136	165	125	128	108	170	147	156	169	128	214	202
Rb	22	5	14	15	77	93	15	11	12	5	27	13	15	70	16	42	60
Y	20	21	15	21	17	19	16	16	18	16	20	20	24	20	25	23	20
Th	8	0	4	0	9	9	5	0	1	4	7	2	6	8	6	11	5
Pb	14	5	6	14	15	20	10	1	9	13	12	7	3	18	9	16	21
Sr	1063	549	584	784	402	383	1081	782	780	790	619	658	726	490	593	805	581
Ba	1332	382	660	574	759	773	803	649	683	717	549	397	403	634	.....	.....	974
Cr	91	663	177	63	172	128	93	112	109	102	276	477	337	84	.....	.....	103
Ni	47	379	56	21	100	70	37	47	49	49	119	193	135	38	.....	.....	72
Ta	.....	0.62	.....	1.07	1.57	.....	1.03	.....	.....	.....	1.28	1.48	.....	.....	.....	.....	.....
Co	.....	55.6	.....	39.4	22.7	.....	28.9	.....	.....	.....	37.0	47.9	.....	.....	.....	.....	.....
Sc	.....	24	.....	34	11	.....	23	.....	.....	.....	25	27	.....	.....	.....	.....	.....
Hf	.....	2.5	.....	5.3	3.7	.....	3.7	.....	.....	.....	4.0	3.3	.....	.....	.....	.....	.....
La	.....	18.1	.....	33.3	26.0	.....	25.6	.....	.....	.....	30.9	24.0	.....	.....	.....	.....	.....
Ce	.....	40.3	.....	72.8	53.6	.....	52.0	.....	.....	.....	66.4	52.0	.....	.....	.....	.....	.....
Sm	.....	3.8	.....	6.4	3.7	.....	4.5	.....	.....	.....	5.4	5.7	.....	.....	.....	.....	.....
Eu	.....	1.31	.....	2.18	1.05	.....	1.55	.....	.....	.....	1.71	1.89	.....	.....	.....	.....	.....
Tb	.....	0.63	.....	0.90	.....	.....	0.62	.....	.....	.....	0.71	0.85	.....	.....	.....	.....	.....
Yb	.....	1.85	.....	2.91	1.75	.....	1.74	.....	.....	.....	2.30	1.79	.....	.....	.....	.....	.....
Lu	.....	0.30	.....	0.42	0.27	.....	0.26	.....	.....	.....	0.31	0.28	.....	.....	.....	.....	.....

TABLE 3. MAJOR-, TRACE-, AND RARE-EARTH-ELEMENT COMPOSITIONS OF SAMPLES FROM PINTO PEAK, THE DARWIN PLATEAU, AND THE SURROUNDING AREA*

(continued)

Sample	37	38	39	40	41	42	43	44	45	46	48	49
SiO_2	60.00	52.87	53.57	53.88	52.56	54.90	46.55	49.07	47.03	55.58	50.98	57.00
TiO_2	0.83	1.19	1.37	1.36	1.39	1.10	1.70	1.66	1.89	1.10	1.46	1.13
Al_2O_3	16.27	18.05	15.55	15.39	16.79	16.80	15.95	16.39	15.68	16.55	16.42	16.53
Fe_2O_3	4.94	7.10	8.37	8.19	8.27	6.77	10.97	9.98	10.72	7.21	9.01	6.94
MgO	3.46	4.25	4.75	5.32	5.50	6.66	8.43	7.31	7.66	4.77	6.79	4.84
CaO	4.32	7.49	7.15	7.60	7.75	7.01	11.03	9.57	9.00	6.75	7.44	5.09
Na_2O	4.29	4.03	3.52	3.60	3.97	3.73	2.30	2.49	3.51	3.93	3.91	4.25
K_2O	3.10	1.84	2.49	2.41	2.20	2.19	1.04	1.60	1.46	2.07	1.70	2.57
P_2O_5	0.29	0.32	0.44	0.44	0.24	0.19	0.44	0.46	0.39	0.10	0.20	0.11
LOI	0.54	0.79	1.09	2.49	0.15	0.05	1.25	2.85	1.50	0.00	0.32	0.20
Total	98.04	97.93	98.30	100.68	98.92	99.40	99.96	101.38	98.84	98.06	98.23	98.66
Zr	159	163	176	183	206	165	176	177	.....	.....	167	197
Rb	17	26	42	54	28	31	17	23	.....	.....	33	43
Y	20	19	24	23	16	14	24	23	.....	.....	21	16
Th	5	7	2	9	8	5	1	1	.....	.....	4	8
Pb	15	12	13	16	13	14	12	11	.....	.....	10	18
Sr	746	840	683	663	881	776	716	1173	.....	.....	428	438
Ba	779	970	703	.....	911	771	438	670	.....	.....	.....	.....
Cr	184	61	212	.....	198	259	285	230	.....	.....	.....	.....
Ni	66	19	11	.....	83	126	113	92	.....	.....	.....	.....
Ta	1.08	.....	.....	.....	.....	.....	.....	.....	.....	.....	.....	.....
Co	11.5	.....	.....	.....	.....	.....	.....	.....	.....	.....	.....	.....
Sc	7	.....	.....	.....	.....	.....	.....	.....	.....	.....	.....	.....
Hf	3.4	.....	.....	.....	.....	.....	.....	.....	.....	.....	.....	.....
La	21.9	.....	.....	.....	.....	.....	.....	.....	.....	.....	.....	.....
Ce	42.5	.....	.....	.....	.....	.....	.....	.....	.....	.....	.....	.....
Sm	3.1	.....	.....	.....	.....	.....	.....	.....	.....	.....	.....	.....
Eu	0.90	.....	.....	.....	.....	.....	.....	.....	.....	.....	.....	.....
Tb	.....	.....	.....	.....	.....	.....	.....	.....	.....	.....	.....	.....
Yb	1.27	.....	.....	.....	.....	.....	.....	.....	.....	.....	.....	.....
Lu	0.19	.....	.....	.....	.....	.....	.....	.....	.....	.....	.....	.....

*Major elements are given as weight percent. Trace- and rare-earth-elements are given in parts per million.

(minimum melt granite?) but different trace-element characteristics. It may also be attributed to a combination of the effects of magma mixing and fractional crystallization.

Plots of Sc versus CaO (Fig. 6a) and Ni versus Cr (Fig. 6b) show linear, positive variation. The Sc-CaO trend suggests that pyroxene may have been a fractionating phase, whereas the Cr-Ni trend suggests that Cr-Al spinel, olivine, and pyroxene may have been fractionating. Fractionation of olivine and pyroxene is consistent with the curvilinear trends of MgO, Al_2O_3, and Na_2O versus SiO_2.

Figure 7 shows a condrite-normalized plot of rare-earth elements (REEs) in all of the samples analyzed. The rocks all show light rare-earth element (LREE) enrichment trends and lack a negative Eu anomaly, with the exception of the rhyolitic ash flow, which has a very large anomaly. Several basalts show a slightly positive Eu anomaly. This indicates that, with the exception of the rhyolite, plagioclase fractionation was probably not significant in producing the chemical variation in the lavas.

Pb and Sr isotopic compositions are given in Table 4. Correction for in situ decay of U, Th, or Rb was found to be unnecessary because the samples are so young. The variation in the isotopic compositions of the lavas is consistent with a three-component magma-mixing model (Walker and Coleman, 1989; Walker and Coleman, work in progress); however, some of the variation, particularly in the Sr data, may reflect inhomogeneities in the sources.

Figure 8 shows the variation in $^{208}Pb/^{204}Pb$ versus $^{206}Pb/^{204}Pb$ and therefore reflects the Th/U ratio of the source(s) and the contaminant(s). The samples define two parallel mixing trends on this plot, indicating that they may have interacted with two different contaminants. One of these may be represented by the rhyolitic ash flow. The high $^{208}Pb/^{204}Pb$, $^{206}Pb/^{204}Pb$, and $^{87}Sr/^{86}Sr$ ratios of this sample suggest that it was derived through melting of older (Precambrian) upper crust.

It is unlikely that the magmas that plot along the lower mixing line (Fig. 8) were contaminated by the upper crust, which would have drastically affected both their Pb and Sr isotopic compositions. The study area lies to the east of the 0.706 $^{87}Sr/^{86}Sr$ isopleth of Kistler and Peterman (1973) and in Pb province Ib of Zartman (1974). Zartman (1974) argues that the isotopic ratios of rocks in this area were affected primarily by interaction with granulitic lower crust that is depleted in Rb, U, and Th. Further evidence against upper-crustal contamination is the observation that, with the exception of two samples (and the ash flow, which is not shown on Fig. 9), the rocks with the highest $^{87}Sr/^{86}Sr$ ratios also have the highest concentrations of Sr (Fig. 9). Presumably, the samples with the least amount of Sr should show the most profound effects of contamination unless the isotopic composition of the contaminant was similar to that of the source, in which case the effects of contamination would be small. The isotopic composition of the lower crust *may* be similar to that of the mantle, but the isotopic character of the upper crust is significantly different.

TABLE 4. Pb AND Sr ISOTOPIC COMPOSITIONS OF SAMPLES FROM PINTO PEAK, DARWIN PLATEAU, AND THE SURROUNDING AREA

Sample	$^{87}Sr/^{86}Sr$	$^{206}Pb/^{204}Pb$	$^{207}Pb/^{204}Pb$	$^{208}Pb/^{204}Pb$
1	0.70633 ± 1	18.58	15.59	38.38
2	0.70623 ± 1	18.75	15.62	38.51
4	0.70521 ± 1	18.71	15.58	38.51
5	0.70387 ± 1	18.74	15.60	38.68
6	0.70470 ± 1	18.83	15.61	38.82
7	0.70479 ± 2	18.85	15.63	38.88
8	0.71653 ± 9	18.75	15.64	39.11
9	0.70565 ± 1	18.76	15.61	38.70
11	0.70572 ± 6	18.82	15.61	38.76
12	0.70449 ± 1	18.60	15.60	38.45
14	0.70567 ± 2	18.91	15.63	38.78
15	0.70518 ± 1	18.86	15.63	38.86
16	0.70511 ± 1	18.89	15.64	38.91
17	0.70499 ± 1	18.89	15.63	38.83
18	0.70596 ± 1	18.67	15.62	38.62
20	0.70509 ± 1	18.50	15.64	38.44
21	0.70540 ± 2	18.71	15.62	38.62
22	0.70513 ± 1	18.68	15.64	38.57
23	0.70638 ± 1	18.89	15.65	38.97
24	0.70642 ± 1	18.64	15.65	38.84
25	0.70595 ± 1	18.75	15.65	38.56
27	0.70568 ± 1	18.66	15.62	38.50
29	0.70602 ± 1	18.60	15.60	38.46
30	0.70520 ± 1	18.51	15.57	38.28
35	0.70646 ± 1	18.42	15.57	38.55
37	0.70611 ± 1	18.67	15.62	38.57
39	0.70651 ± 1	18.53	15.62	38.69
43	0.70611 ± 1	18.34	15.58	38.26
46	0.70518 ± 1	18.84	15.65	38.88

PETROGENETIC MODELING

Through use of the petrologic and chemical data presented above, it is possible to model the genesis of each of the different compositional types found in the study area. Although many different models can explain the derivation of the lavas, only those consistent with a majority of the data are presented.

Origin and variation of the basalts

The rocks discussed below include all of the samples that are classified as basalts according to the scheme of Irvine and Baragar (1971).

The basalts from Pinto Peak and Darwin Plateau were probably formed from mantle-derived melts. The LREE enrichment trends observed in the lavas are characteristic of mantle partial melts in which garnet is a residual phase (Henderson, 1984). The Pb and Sr isotopic compositions of some of the

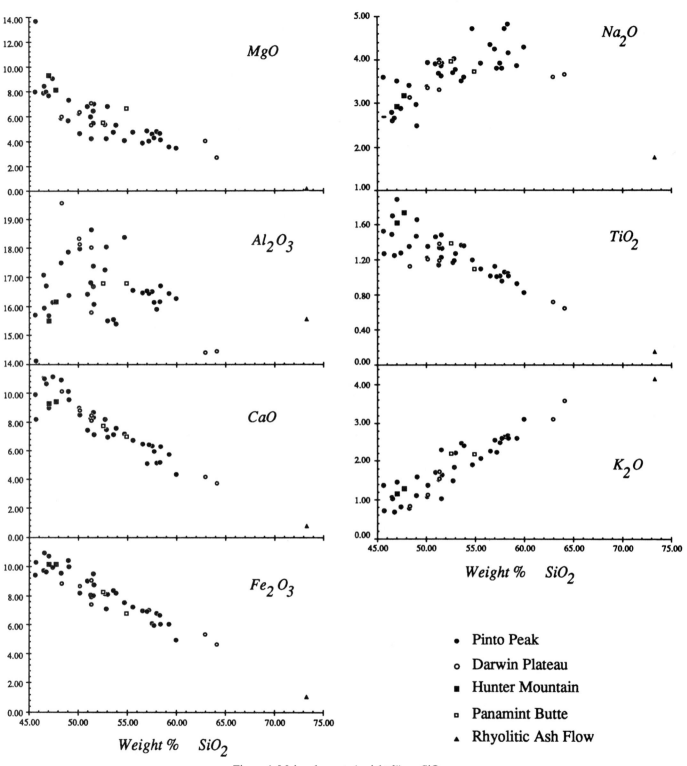

Figure 4. Major elements (weight %) vs. SiO$_2$.

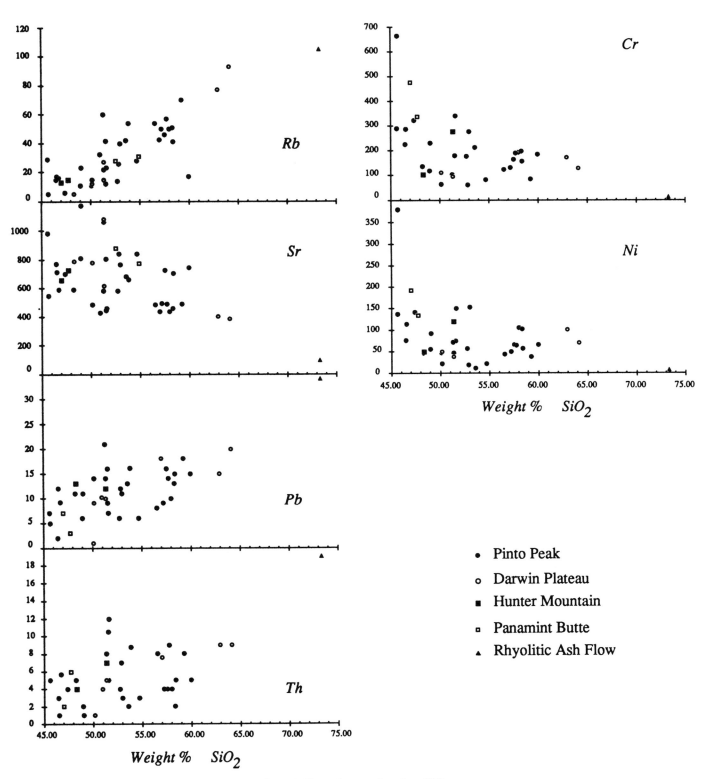

Figure 5. Trace elements (ppm) vs. SiO$_2$.

a)

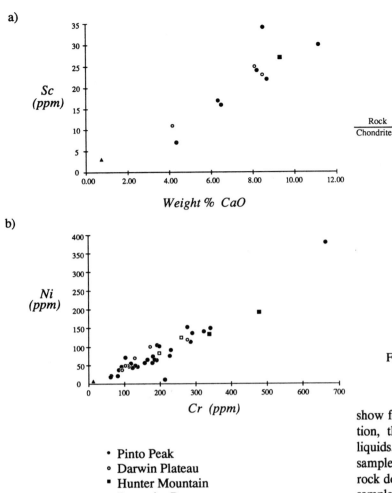

b)

Figure 6. (a) Sc vs. CaO. (b) Ni vs. Cr.

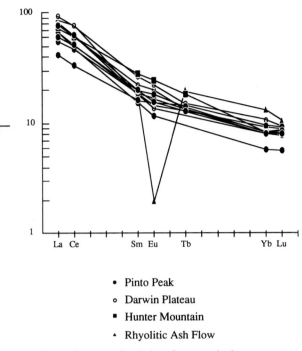

- Pinto Peak
- Darwin Plateau
- Hunter Mountain
- Rhyolitic Ash Flow

Figure 7. Chondrite normalized plot of rare earth elements.

basalts are also consistent with a mantle source. Some of the variation in both REE concentrations and isotopic compositions may be the result of mantle heterogeneities; however, the wide variation in the chemical and isotopic compositions cannot be wholly explained by mantle heterogeneity, and either magma mixing or fractional crystallization or a combination of both must be invoked to explain the differences. Furthermore, the presence of quartz xenocrysts and sieved plagioclase phenocrysts in basalts with as little as 48 percent SiO_2 indicates that magma mixing or assimilation must have occurred. Scatter in major- and trace-element variation trends of the basalts may also indicate that neither fractional crystallization nor magma mixing was acting alone but that some combination of these is responsible for the chemical variation.

The most primitive melts of the mantle, unaffected by assimilation, magma mixing, or fractional crystallization, should be characterized by the highest Mg and Cr concentrations and the lowest concentrations of K, Na, and other incompatible elements. Samples 4 and 20 both meet these criteria, and because they

show few or no effects of alteration and no signs of contamination, they are assumed to best represent the most primitive liquids. Therefore, microprobe data for phenocryst phases in sample 20 are used in the chemical modeling below. Because this rock does not contain pyroxene, the pyroxene composition from sample 29 is used.

Those basalts that do not have the chemical characteristics of primary mantle melts and that do not show any mixing features (no xenocrysts, xenoliths, or sieved plagioclase) are presumed to be affected by fractional crystallization. Table 5 shows representative results of modeling the development of "evolved" basalts from sample 20 by simple fractionation. Calculations show that any of the basalts can be derived satisfactorily from sample 20 by fractionation of varying amounts of olivine, pyroxene, and plagioclase ± magnetite and Cr-Al spinel.

The fractionation of significant amounts of plagioclase seemed to have been ruled out by the lack of a Eu anomaly in the REE data but is indicated by the chemical modeling. High oxygen fugacity in the magma chamber has the effect of lowering the distribution coefficient of Eu into plagioclase by increasing the ratio of Eu^{3+}/Eu^{2+}. Because Eu^{3+} does not fit into the plagioclase structure, the distribution coefficient decreases to almost zero at very high oxygen fugacities (Henderson, 1984). The distinct calc-alkaline trend of the rock suite (Fig. 3) is also indicative of high f_{O_2}. It is therefore possible that because the rocks exhibit a calc-alkaline trend, the lack of a Eu anomaly in samples that require plagioclase fractionation in modeling their derivation is due to high f_{O_2} in the fractionating magma chamber.

Several basalts contain quartz and plagioclase xenocrysts,

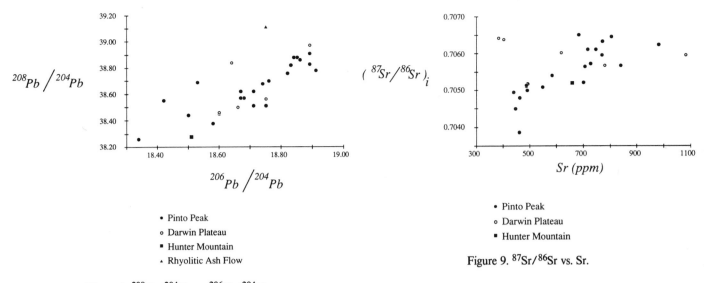

Figure 8. $^{208}Pb/^{204}Pb$ vs. $^{206}Pb/^{204}Pb$.

• Pinto Peak
○ Darwin Plateau
■ Hunter Mountain

Figure 9. $^{87}Sr/^{86}Sr$ vs. Sr.

indicating that their chemistry has been affected by magma mixing or assimilation. Whether the xenocrysts and xenoliths were introduced by mixing or assimilation is unimportant for the purpose of modeling the chemical evolution of these rocks. The xenocryst assemblage of the basalts, quartz, and plagioclase ± sanidine and amphibole suggests that the contaminant, whether through mixing or assimilation, was rhyolitic in composition. Sample 44 of Novak and Bacon (1986) was chosen as a representative rhyolitic composition and was used in modeling. The rhyolite in the Pinto Peak section (sample 8) was not used because its mineral assemblage and major-element and isotopic chemistry (Tables 1, 3, and 4) clearly show that it could not represent the contaminant.

Simple magma mixing between sample 20 and Coso-44 did not yield satisfactory results for the production of the xenocrystic basalts. Only by a combination of magma mixing and fractionation of olivine, pyroxene, and plagioclase ± Cr-Al spinel could the chemical variation be modeled closely. Table 5 shows the results of several representative mixing/fractionation calculations. In general, the amount of felsic material added to the basalt is small (less than 13 percent of the final liquid).

Origin and Variation of the Andesites

As for the basalts, the samples discussed in this section are those that plot as andesites according to the scheme of Irvine and Baragar (1971). In general, the andesites range in composition from 50 to 65 percent SiO$_2$. Nearly all the andesites show features characteristic of magma mixing, including quartz, sanidine, and amphibole xenocrysts; sieved plagioclase; and mafic and felsic inclusions. Therefore, they are presumed to be hybrid magmas, the result of mixing between basaltic and rhyolitic liquids. Although satisfactory results can be obtained for deriving the andesites from the basalts by simple fractional crystallization, the mixing features dismiss this possibility for their origin.

Modeling the variation of the andesites was done as it was with the basalts. Samples 20 and Coso-44 were used as end-member compositions, and as with the basalts, fractionation of significant amounts of olivine, pyroxene, and plagioclase ± Cr-Al spinel is required to model the variation closely. Table 5 shows the results of mixing calculations for some representative andesites.

Fractionation of significant amounts of plagioclase is required by the model, yet the samples show no negative Eu anomaly. The lack of a negative Eu anomaly in andesites thought to be derived by fractional crystallization of plagioclase and other phases is not uncommon and, in fact, appears to be the norm rather than the exception (e.g., Yajima and others, 1972; Dixon and Batiza, 1979). It seems likely that high oxygen fugacity explains the lack of a Eu anomaly in the andesites.

Unlike mixing calculations for the basalts, calculations for the andesites indicate that large percentages of felsic material (up to 50 percent of the final liquid) are required to produce some of the lavas. It is very unlikely that assimilation was the mechanism for addition of felsic material to these magmas, as too much heat presumably would have been required to accomplish this, and the basaltic magma would have frozen. Rather, those compositions that require a great deal of felsic material were probably derived through magma mixing. In fact, sample 23, which requires nearly a 1:1 mix of mafic and felsic end-members, contains euhedral xenocrysts of quartz and amphibole that most likely formed in a liquid, and has distinct mafic inclusions. Those samples that require only small amounts of felsic material may have formed by assimilation of older crust.

Origin of the rhyolite

Sample 8 is the only rhyolite in the Nova Formation volcanic sequence. The sample is an ash-flow tuff consisting of py-

TABLE 5. RESULTS OF LEAST-SQUARES CALCULATIONS FOR THE DERIVATION OF BASALTS AND ANDESITES BY FRACTIONATION OF OLIVINE (20-CORE), PYROXENE (29-PHENOCRYST), PLAGIOCLASE (20-CORE), MAGNETITE-ILMENITE (20-GROUNDMASS), AND Cr-Al SPINEL (20-PHENOCRYST, AND MAGMA MIXING*

	SiO_2	TiO_2	Al_2O_3	FeO	MgO	CaO	Na_2O	K_2O
20 (parent)	47.60	1.32	14.72	9.67	14.23	8.55	2.78	0.75
COSO-44 (contam)†	76.20	0.09	13.49	0.62	0.10	0.86	3.19	5.35

Sample No.	SiO_2	TiO_2	Al_2O_3	FeO	MgO	CaO	Na_2O	K_2O	Wt. Frac. Rhyolite in Liquid	Weight Fraction Phase Removed from Parent				
										Olivine	Pyroxene	Plagioclase	Magnetite-ilmenite	Cr
13 (bas.)														
Observed	50.04	1.50	18.25	9.59	5.78	10.33	3.03	1.13	......	0.74	0.05	0.20	0.01	......
Calc.	49.93	1.63	18.04	9.49	5.82	10.38	3.57	1.02						
Residual	0.04	-0.13	0.10	0.11	-0.04	-0.04	-0.54	0.12						
28 (bas.)														
Observed	49.71	1.16	20.13	8.18	6.13	10.41	3.22	0.86	......	0.81	0.13	......	0.06	......
Calc.	50.21	0.93	19.02	8.38	6.01	10.29	3.62	0.98						
Residual	-0.20	0.23	0.55	-0.20	0.12	0.12	-0.40	-0.11						
30 (bas.)														
Observed	48.78	1.68	16.09	9.51	9.67	9.66	3.04	1.20	......	0.72	......	0.26	......	0.02
Calc.	48.84	1.56	16.07	9.54	9.66	9.60	3.19	0.90						
Residual	-0.02	0.13	0.01	-0.03	0.02	0.06	-0.15	0.30						
5 (bas.)														
Observed	53.32	1.37	16.61	8.14	7.24	7.39	4.05	1.69	0.10	0.24	0.15	0.18	......	0.05
Calc.	53.38	1.38	16.66	8.14	7.23	7.37	3.89	1.63						
Residual	-0.02	-0.01	-0.02	0.00	0.01	0.02	0.16	0.07						
21 (bas.)														
Observed	54.16	1.20	17.71	7.51	5.52	8.40	3.80	1.53	0.13	0.23	0.07	0.06	......	0.02
Calc.	54.11	1.21	17.77	7.50	5.53	8.41	3.71	1.65						
Residual	0.02	-0.01	-0.03	0.01	-0.01	-0.01	0.08	-0.12						
29 (bas.)														
Observed	53.06	1.42	16.21	8.39	7.23	8.30	3.40	1.76	0.16	0.17	0.01	0.05	......	......
Calc.	53.15	1.43	16.21	8.39	7.22	8.27	3.30	1.63						
Residual	-0.03	-0.01	0.00	0.00	0.01	0.02	0.10	0.13						

TABLE 5. RESULTS OF LEAST-SQUARES CALCULATIONS FOR THE DERIVATION OF BASALTS AND ANDESITES BY FRACTIONATION OF OLIVINE (20-CORE), PYROXENE (29-PHENOCRYST), PLAGIOCLASE (20-CORE), MAGNETITE-ILMENITE (20-GROUNDMASS), AND Cr-Al SPINEL (20-PHENOCRYST), AND MAGMA MIXING*

Sample No.	SiO_2	TiO_2	Al_2O_3	FeO	MgO	CaO	Na_2O	K_2O	Wt. Frac. Rhyolite in Liquid	Weight Fraction Phase Removed from Parent				
										Olivine	Pyroxene	Plagioclase	Magnetite-ilmenite	Cr
11 (and.)														
Observed	58.71	1.04	16.79	5.58	4.70	6.45	4.00	2.54	0.28	0.21	0.12	0.11	......	0.05
Calc.	58.81	0.96	16.80	5.60	4.68	6.42	3.86	2.40						
Residual	-0.04	0.08	-0.01	-0.02	0.02	0.03	0.13	0.14						
23 (and.)														
Observed	64.25	0.74	14.70	4.92	4.15	4.24	3.68	3.18	0.50	0.15	0.09	0.16	......	0.03
Calc.	64.15	0.75	14.77	4.91	4.16	4.26	3.65	3.37						
Residual	0.04	-0.01	-0.03	0.01	-0.02	-0.03	0.03	-0.20						
42 (and.)														
Observed	55.64	1.11	17.03	6.17	6.75	7.10	3.78	2.22	0.21	0.15	0.10	0.04	......	0.04
Calc.	55.81	0.98	17.01	6.21	6.72	7.06	3.63	1.93						
Residual	-0.07	0.14	0.01	-0.04	0.03	0.05	0.15	0.29						

*All mineral compositions are given in Table 2. All oxides have been recalculated to 100%, on a water-free basis with Fe as FeO.
†Data for sample 44 from Novak and Bacon (1986).

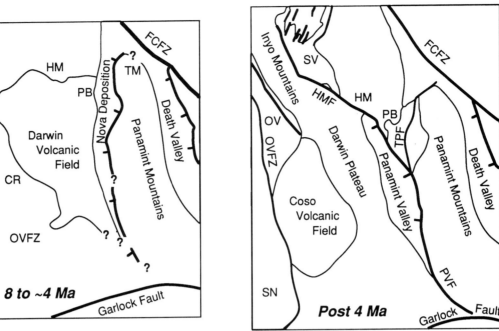

Figure 10. (a) Schematic drawing showing the Nova depositional trough adjacent to Darwin Plateau prior to motion along the Hunter Mountain Fault (HMF). (b) Schematic drawing showing the present configuration of Panamint and Saline Valleys. SV, Saline Valley; OV, Owens Valley; HM, Hunter Mountain, IM, Inyo Mountains; CR, Coso Range; SN, Sierra Nevada; PB, Panamint Butte; TM, Tucki Mountain; FCFZ, Furnace Creek Fault Zone; OVFZ, Owens Valley Fault Zone; PVF, Panamint Valley Fault; TPF, Towne Pass Fault.

roxene phenocrysts and pumice fragments in a glassy matrix. The ash flow occurs very high in the sequence, stratigraphically above an unconformity and all the basalt and andesite flows. Chemically, the sample is characterized by a very large, negative Eu anomaly and by unusually high Mg concentrations for a rhyolite.

The large Eu anomaly suggests two possible origins for this sample. The rhyolite may be the result of extreme fractionation of phases, including plagioclase, or it may represent a partial melt of the crust with plagioclase as a residual phase. Because pyroxene is the only phenocryst phase in the ash flow, it seems very unlikely that plagioclase could have been a fractionating phase. Efforts to model the derivation of the rhyolite by fractionation of pyroxene, or any other phenocryst assemblage, fail to yield satisfactory results. However, derivation of the rhyolite through partial melting of the crust with plagioclase as a residual phase would also yield a negative Eu anomaly and is supported by the isotopic data.

PALEOGEOGRAPHIC IMPLICATIONS

The fact that Miocene-Pliocene volcanic rocks from Pinto Peak and Darwin Plateau are petrographically, chemically, and isotopically the same is established by the data presented above. Furthermore, because the rocks are the same age and because apparently there are no vent areas or feeder dikes at Pinto Peak, it is reasonable to assume that the source area for both groups of

flows was the Darwin Plateau volcanic field. Therefore, during eruption of the 4 to 6 Ma lavas, the regions that are now Pinto Peak and Darwin Plateau were probably adjacent, indicating that Panamint Valley has opened in the last 4 m.y.

During late Miocene through Pliocene time, a volcanic center was apparently located on the Darwin Plateau. Lavas from this region probably flowed eastward, toward the proto–Panamint Mountains, which were shedding the Nova Formation fanglomerate (Fig. 10a). Basalt and andesite flows from Darwin Plateau were intercalated with the fanglomerate deposits. At the same time, volcanism was also starting in the Coso volcanic field, and Coso lavas may be present on Darwin Plateau and Pinto Peak. It is unclear whether at that time the Coso Range was adjacent to, and shared a magma chamber with, the Darwin Plateau. A more detailed investigation of the age and chemistry of the lavas on the Darwin Plateau may reveal the answer to this question.

As extension continued, normal faulting shifted into Panamint Valley and Saline Valley along the Hunter Mountain Fault (Burchfiel and others, 1987; Walker and Coleman, 1987; Fig. 10b), separating the Nova Formation depositional trough from Darwin Plateau. By 3.5 Ma, the center of volcanic activity had apparently shifted southwesterly away from the Darwin Plateau to the region of the Coso Range. There is no evidence for Coso volcanic rocks of this age on the Darwin Plateau. The Coso volcanic field is still active.

A MODEL FOR EXTENSIONAL VOLCANISM

Although the data in this study do not support unambiguously either a pure-shear or simple-shear model of extension, a model for volcanism consistent with simple-shear extension can be developed. Salient points to be explained in the model are (1) the progression of volcanism from basaltic to andesitic to rhyolitic, (2) the derivation of the rhyolitic magma through crustal anatexis, and (3) the shift of volcanic activity from Darwin Plateau westward to the Coso field through time.

At the onset of the extension that formed the Nova Formation depositional trough, and ultimately Panamint Valley, volcanism was exclusively basaltic. These original basalts seem to have passed through the crust relatively uncontaminated, implying that they moved quickly through a cold crust.

As extension progressed, younger basalts gained a greater crustal component, either by assimilation or magma mixing. By this time, parts of the crust were hot and melting. Presumably, as hot basaltic liquids pass through the crust or enter the lower crust to accommodate extension, they heat the crust significantly and induce melting. If simple shear is the mechanism for extension, this heating and melting might be enhanced in two ways. First, parts of the crust could begin to melt adiabatically as motion along the shear zone removes the rocks over them. Second, the simple-shear mechanism allows for regions of cold upper crust to be dragged down into contact with hotter lower crust over large areas. These two processes, combined with heating of the crust by injection of basalt, could produce voluminous felsic melts. These magmas could then mix with the basaltic magmas, giving rise to andesitic volcanism at the surface. Regardless of whether the mechanism for extension is pure-shear or simple-shear, the results of this study indicate the presence of rhyolitic magma mixing with basalt to create andesites. A simple-shear model of extension may provide a more efficient means of melting the crust to create this felsic liquid than a pure-shear model.

With increased extension, greater volumes of crust are melted, and rhyolites may finally reach the surface. However, volcanic activity will not necessarily become exclusively rhyolitic. As long as extension occurs, there should be an influx of new basalts that may reach the surface in relatively pristine form or may mix with the rhyolites to form andesites or contaminated basalts.

In addition to the compositional trends of volcanic rocks, spatial trends in this region are also significant. At the onset of extension in the Nova Formation depositional trough, the center of basaltic volcanism was located to the west of the depositional basin at the Darwin Plateau volcanic center and perhaps in the Coso volcanic field. Later, as faulting shifted into Panamint Valley along the Hunter Mountain transform, volcanic activity also shifted, out of the Darwin Plateau volcanic field and into the Coso Range. This "off axis" volcanism is to be expected if extension is accomplished by simple shear, because the region of maximum crustal thinning (and therefore melting) is offset from

upper-crustal brittle deformation (Wernicke, 1985; Bosworth, 1987). A pure-shear extension model predicts that volcanism and normal faulting would occur in the same basin.

SUMMARY AND CONCLUSIONS

The Miocene-Pliocene volcanic rocks of the Nova Formation range in composition from basalt to rhyolite. Chemical and isotopic data indicate that the source of the basaltic magmas was the mantle, and the felsic component of the basalts and andesites was probably derived through interaction with the lower crust. The rocks are calc-alkaline and show abundant petrographic and chemical evidence that lavas of intermediate composition were formed by fractional crystallization of the basalts and by magma mixing between basaltic and rhyolitic liquids. Chemical modeling shows that fractionating phases were probably olivine, pyroxene, and plagioclase $\pm$ magnetite-ilmenite and Cr-Al spinel and that both magma mixing and assimilation of older crust are possible mechanisms for introduction of felsic material into the basaltic magmas. The distinct calc-alkaline character of the suite and the lack of a Eu anomaly (despite apparent plagioclase fractionation) suggest that the oxygen fugacity in the magma chamber was high.

The petrologic and chemical similarity between rocks collected from Pinto Peak, Darwin Plateau, Hunter Mountain, Panamint Butte, and Black Point suggests that these lavas are all related. Furthermore, because no vents or feeder dikes were observed in any of the areas except Darwin Plateau, it is likely that the Darwin Plateau volcanic field was the source for all of the lavas. The presence of 4-Ma lavas from the Darwin Plateau volcanic field in the Nova Formation at Pinto Peak suggests that these two areas were adjacent prior to 4 Ma and that Panamint Valley has opened since that time.

On the basis of the chemical progression of the volcanic rocks and the "off-axis" nature of the volcanism, a model for extension consistent with the simple-shear mechanism of Wernicke (1981, 1985) can be developed. Simple shear provides more efficient means for crustal anatexis than pure shear, and pure-shear extension cannot explain "off-axis" volcanism. Simple-shear extension in the Panamint Valley area is consistent with the conclusions of the MIT Field Camp (MIT 1985 Field Geophysics Course and Biehler, 1987) and Burchfiel and others (1987), who showed that Panamint Valley is underlain by a low-angle normal fault.

Future studies of the Miocene-Pliocene volcanic rocks in the Death Valley region should concentrate on regional investigations. In particular, study of the volcanic rocks of Saline Mountain and Saline Valley is important because Saline Valley and Panamint Valley opened contemporaneously as paired pull-apart basins along the Hunter Mountain fault. A detailed investigation of the Sr, Pb, and Nd isotopic compositions of these rocks should also help further constrain the nature of the mantle below this region and the role of the crust during extension.

ACKNOWLEDGMENTS

This research was supported by a University of Kansas General Research Fund grant awarded to J. D. Walker and M. E. Bickford, a Shell Faculty Fellowship awarded to Walker, and NSF grant EAR 86-12283 awarded to K. V. Hodges. M. E. Bickford provided invaluable assistance in data collection and interpretation. Sample collection was permitted by Death Valley National Monument. Microprobe analysis was done at Washington University, St. Louis, and instrumental neutron activation analysis was performed by R. Cullers at Kansas State University. A. Glazner offered significant input on the subject of magma mixing. Helpful reviews were provided by R. L. Christiansen and L. C. Coleman.

APPENDIX

Methods

Whenever possible, approximately 5 kg of fresh sample with no weathered edges was collected in the field. After thin sections were cut, all saw marks and remaining weathered areas were removed with a hammer. The samples were milled in a jaw-crusher and cone-crusher, reducing them to pieces no larger than 1 cm across. All crushing equipment was precontaminated with a small amount of sample. The crushed sample was reduced to approximately 10 g with a quantitative mechanical splitter. The sample was then leached in 0.5 N HCl for one week. Weak acid was used in order to remove any calcite without also leaching out the iron. The samples were rinsed in distilled, deionized water and dried.

X-ray fluorescence spectrometry

Splits of the samples used for XRF analysis were ground to a fine powder in a tungsten-carbide ball mill. Major- and trace-element contamination by any of the crushing equipment was shown to be negligible by comparison with data from samples crushed by hand. Furthermore, comparison of results from leached and unleached samples showed that leaching did not affect the primary chemistry of the rocks.

For major-element analysis, the samples were dried in an oven overnight to remove any atmospheric water, then fused in a platinum/gold (95 percent/5 percent) crucible in lithium-tetraborate flux in a ratio of one part sample to about six parts flux, by weight, and cast into a disk. The glass disks were analyzed in a Rigaku S-max X-ray fluorescence spectrometer for nine major oxides: SiO_2, TiO_2, Al_2O_3, Fe_2O_3, MgO, CaO, Na_2O, K_2O, and P_2O_5. Data were reduced using the method of Norrish and Hutton (1969).

Samples for trace-element analysis were prepared by mixing five parts sample with one part cellulose binder, by weight, in a mixer mill and then pressing them into a cellulose pellet. The pressed powder pellets were analyzed by XRF spectrometry for nine trace elements: Zr, Rb, Y, Th, Pb, Sr, Ba, Cr, and Ni.

Instrumental neutron activation analysis

The fifteen samples chosen for instrumental neutron activation analysis were taken from a mechanical split of the material, which had been leached in 0.5 N HCl. The samples were ground to a fine powder with a ceramic mortar and pestle to avoid contamination by the tungsten-carbide ball mill. Approximately 450 mg of sample was placed in a plastic vial, which was then sealed with a heat gun and wrapped with 70 mg of iron wire to monitor the flux in the reactor. The samples were placed in the central thimble of the reactor at Kansas State University for four hours and counting was done after 5, 10, and 40 days. U.S. Geological Survey standard BCR-1 was used as a reference sample. Element peaks that were monitored include seven rare-earth elements (La, Ce, Sm, Eu, Tb, Yb, and Lu) and ten major elements and trace elements (Fe, Na, Rb, Ba, Th, Hf, Ta, Co, Sc, and Cr).

Isotopic analysis

Two hundred to six hundred milligrams of the powder prepared for major-element analysis were dissolved in a mixture of HF and HNO_3, and the liquid was split in half for separate Sr and Pb chemistry. Sr was separated using cation exchange chromatography; Pb was isolated using an anion exchange column. The isotopic compositions of both Sr and Pb were determined on a fully automated VG Sector mass spectrometer with a computer-controlled multicollector system. Sr was run on single Ta filaments in H_3PO_4, and Pb was run in silica gel on single Re filaments.

Electron microprobe analysis

Polished thin sections were analyzed for mineral compositions by electron microprobe at Washington University, St. Louis, Missouri. Unaltered grains of plagioclase, olivine, pyroxene, and oxides were analyzed for both major- and trace-element compositions in a suite of samples that spanned the range of whole-rock chemistry. The probe used was a JEOL 733 with three spectrometers and Tracor Northern TN 2000 automation. A 20 nanoamp beam current (measured above the sample) was used. Data correction was done by the Bence-Albee correction program.

REFERENCES CITED

Bosworth, W., 1987, Off-axis volcanism in the Gregory rift, east Africa; Implications for models of continental rifting: Geology, v. 15, p. 397–400.

Burchfiel, B. C., Hodges, K. V., and Royden, L. H., 1987, Geology of Panamint Valley–Saline Valley pull-apart system, California; Palinspastic evidence for low-angle geometry of a Neogene range-bounding fault: Journal of Geophysical Research, v. 92, no. B10, p. 10422–10426.

Coleman, D. S., 1988, Petrology and geochemistry of the volcanic rocks of the Nova Formation and Darwin Plateau, Death Valley, California; Implications for magmatic and tectonic processes in extensional orogens [M.S. thesis]: Lawrence, University of Kansas, 124 p.

Dixon, T. H., and Batiza, R., 1979, Petrology and chemistry of recent lavas in the northern Marianas; Implications for the origin of island arc basalts: Contributions to Mineralogy and Petrology, v. 70, p. 167–181.

Glazner, A. F., 1990, Recycling of continental crust in Miocene volcanic rocks from the Mojave block, Southern California, *in* Anderson, J. L., ed., The nature and origin of Cordilleran magmatism: Geological Society of America Memoir 174 (in press).

Hall, W. E., 1971, Geology of the Panamint Butte Quadrangle, Inyo County, California: U.S. Geological Survey Bulletin 1299, 67 p.

Henderson, P., 1984, General geochemical properties and abundances of the rare earth elements, *in* Henderson, P., ed., Rare earth element geochemistry: Amsterdam, Elsevier Scientific Publishers, p. 1–32.

Hooper, R. H., 1947, Geologic section from the Sierra Nevada to Death Valley, California: Geological Society of America Bulletin, v. 58, p. 393–423.

Irvine, T. N., and Baragar, W.R.A., 1971, A guide to the chemical classification of the common volcanic rocks: Canadian Journal of Earth Sciences, v. 8, p. 523–548.

Kistler, R. W., and Peterman, Z. E., 1973, Variations in Sr, Rb, K, Na, and initial $^{87}Sr/^{86}Sr$ in Mesozoic granitic rocks and intruded wall rocks in central California: Geological Society of America Bulletin, v. 84, p. 3489–3512.

Larsen, N. W., 1979, Chronology of late Cenozoic basaltic volcanism; The tectonic implications along a segment of the Sierra Nevada and Basin and Range Province boundary [Ph.D. thesis]: Provo, Utah, Brigham Young University, 94 p.

Lofgren, G. E., 1978, An experimental study of plagioclase crystal morphology; Isothermal crystallization: American Journal of Science, v. 274, p. 243–273.

Lofgren, G. E., and Norris, P. N., 1981, Experimental duplication of plagioclase sieve and overgrowth textures: Geological Society of America Abstracts with Programs, v. 13, p. 498.

Mies, J. W., and Glazner, A. F., 1987, Quartz xenocrysts with rhyolite glass inclusions in andesite as evidence of assimilated granite [abs.]: EOS Transactions of the American Geophysical Union, v. 68, p. 434–435.

MIT 1985 Field Geophysics Course and Biehler, S., 1987, A geophysical investigation of the northern Panamint Valley, Inyo County, California; Evidence for possible low-angle normal faulting at shallow depth in the crust: Journal of Geophysical Research, v. 92, no. B10, p. 10427–10441.

Norrish, K., and Hutton, J. T., 1969, An accurate x-ray spectrographic method for the analysis of a wide range of geological samples: Geochimica et Cosmochimica Acta, v. 33, p. 431–453.

Novak, S. W., and Bacon, C. R., 1986, Pliocene volcanic rocks of the Coso Range, Inyo County, California: U.S. Geological Survey Professional Paper 1383, 44 p.

Schweig, E. S., 1982, Late Cenozoic stratigraphy and tectonics of the Darwin Plateau, Inyo County, California [M.S. thesis]: Stanford, California, Stanford University, 85 p.

—— , 1984, Neogene tectonics and paleogeography of the southwestern Great Basin, California [Ph.D. thesis]: Stanford, California, Stanford University, 207 p.

Stevens, C. H., 1977, Permian depositional provinces and tectonics, western United States, *in* Stewart, J. H., Stevens, C. H., and Fritsche, A. E., eds., Paleozoic paleogeography of the western United States: Pacific Section, Society of Economic Paleontologists and Mineralogists, Paleogeography Symposium 1, p. 113–135.

Thompson, G. A., 1960, Problem of late Cenozoic structure of the Basin Ranges: 21st International Geologic Congress, Copenhagen, v. 17, p. 62–68.

Tsuchiyama, A., 1985, Dissolution kinetics of plagioclase in the melt of the system diopside-albite-anorthite, and the origin of dusty plagioclase in andesites: Contributions to Mineralogy and Petrology, v. 89, p. 1–16.

Tsuchiyama, A., and Takahashi, E., 1983, Melting kinetics of a plagioclase feldspar: Contributions to Mineralogy and Petrology, v. 84, p. 345–354.

Walker, J. D., and Coleman, D. S., 1987, Correlation of Mio-Pliocene rocks of the northern Panamint Mountains and Darwin Plateau; Implications for normal-fault development and the opening of Panamint Valley: Geological Society of America Abstracts with Programs, v. 19, p. 878.

—— , 1989, Crustal-scale kinematics of extensional deformation in the Death Valley extended area revealed by geochemistry of volcanic rocks: Geological Society of America Abstracts with Programs, v. 21, p. 154.

Wernicke, B., 1981, Low-angle normal faults in the Basin and Range Province; Nappe tectonics in an extending orogen: Nature, v. 291, p. 645–648.

—— , 1985, Uniform-sense normal simple shear of the continental lithosphere: Canadian Journal of Earth Sciences, v. 22, p. 108–125.

Wernicke, B., Hodges, K. V., and Walker, J. D., 1986, Geological setting of the Tucki Mountain area, Death Valley National Monument, California, *in* Dunne, G. C., ed., Mesozoic and Cenozoic structural evolution of selected areas, east-central California; Geological Society of America Cordilleran Section Guidebook: p. 67–80.

Wright, L. A., and Troxel, B. W., 1973, Shallow fault interpretation of Basin and Range structure, southeastern Great Basin, *in* de Jong, K. A., and Scholten, R., eds., Gravity and tectonics: New York, John Wiley and Sons, p. 397–407.

Yajima, T., Higuchi, H., and Nagasawa, H., 1972, Variation of rare earth concentrations in pigeonitic and hypersthenic rock series from Izu-Hakone region, Japan: Contributions to Mineralogy and Petrology, v. 35, p. 235–244.

Zartman, R. E., 1974, Lead isotopic provinces of the western United States and their geologic significance: Economic Geology, v. 69, p. 792–805.

MANUSCIPT ACCEPTED BY THE SOCIETY AUGUST 21, 1989

Geological Society of America
Memoir 176
1990

Chapter 21

Listric normal faulting and synorogenic sedimentation, northern Cottonwood Mountains, Death Valley region, California

J. Kent Snow and Carolyn White
Department of Earth and Planetary Sciences, Harvard University, Cambridge, Massachusetts 02138

ABSTRACT

The structure of the northern Cottonwood Mountains, located in the Death Valley region of southeastern California, is dominated by a faulted, east-facing, monoclinal flexure developed in Paleozoic strata of the Cordilleran miogeocline. We interpret this flexure as a *rollover* or fault-bend fold above a listric normal fault, probably the northward continuation of the Tucki Mountain normal fault system exposed about 45 km south of the study area. Synorogenic Tertiary sediments in the Ubehebe basin, overlying the rollover at the northern end of the Cottonwood Mountains, record the inception of normal faulting and eastward tilting around a horizontal axis trending about N25°W. Paleozoic strata in the Dry Mountain block to the west are subhorizontal. Racetrack Valley, a north-trending topographic depression between the Dry Mountain block and the northern Cottonwood Mountains, is interpreted as a major graben that accommodates differential stratal rotations within the rollover.

The juxtaposition of Mesozoic thrust plates by Tertiary normal faults has obscured the structural simplicity of the rollover. Structural and stratigraphic correlations indicate that strata exposed in the Dry Mountain block and northern Cottonwood Mountains are parts of a single Mesozoic thrust plate. This new evidence suggests that the Racetrack thrust of McAllister (1952) does not root in northern Racetrack Valley, contrary to previous interpretations. A previously unrecognized klippe and other parts of the Ubehebe thrust plate lie structurally above the northern Cottonwood Mountains. We suggest that normal faulting has downdropped a portion of the Ubehebe thrust plate into Racetrack Valley between strata of the Dry Mountain block and northern Cottonwood Mountains. Thus, the development of a major graben within the rollover has produced an apparent thrust relation along both sides of the Racetrack Valley block. We correlate the Racetrack Valley block and Ubehebe thrust plate with the Last Chance thrust plate of Stewart and others (1966).

Sequentially deformed, palinspastic reconstructions of the rollover indicate that conjugate faults formed symmetrical grabens during development of the rollover. The grabens accommodated bending within the rollover and probably nucleated above areas of maximum curvature on the basal listric fault. Thus, the nucleation of progressively younger grabens during extension apparently migrated toward the breakaway within the hanging-wall block while remaining fixed relative to the bend in the basal fault plane.

The pre–middle Pliocene(?) age and structural position of strata in the Ubehebe basin suggest that they are partially correlative with upper Miocene to lower Pliocene strata in the Nova basin, also located on the eastern margin of the Cottonwood Mountains structural block but adjacent to Tucki Mountain. The location of these basins in

Snow, J. K., and White, C., 1990, Listric normal faulting and synorogenic sedimentation, northern Cottonwood Mountains, Death Valley region, California, *in* Wernicke, B. P., ed., Basin and Range extensional tectonics near the latitude of Las Vegas, Nevada: Boulder, Colorado, Geological Society of America Memoir 176.

the hanging wall of the Tucki Mountain normal fault system suggests that they may be **allochthonous parts of an earlier basin. Distinctive cobbles with no known local source are abundant in a relatively thin stratigraphic zone within the Ubehebe basin. We interpret these cobbles as reworked clasts derived from the Oligocene Titus Canyon Formation. This is consistent with structural and stratigraphic correlations that indicate about 70 km northwest-directed transport of the Cottonwood Mountains block from a position adjacent to the Funeral Mountains (Snow and Wernicke, 1988, 1989; Snow, 1989; Snow and others, 1989).**

INTRODUCTION

Within the Basin and Range, differential stratal rotations across downward-flattening or listric normal faults are commonly observed (e.g., Anderson and others, 1983; Smith and Bruhn, 1984). Hamblin (1965) recognized that a monoclinal flexure or *rollover* ("reverse drag" of Hamblin, 1965; "roll-over" of Gibbs, 1983; "rollover structure" of McClay and Ellis, 1987a, b), along with associated antithetic faults, forms as a result of motion on a listric fault (Fig. 1). Recent work has discussed types of rotations possible in listric fault systems (e.g., Wernicke and Burchfiel, 1982); explored the relations among listric fault shape, rollover shape, and antithetic faulting that are required by balanced cross sections (e.g., Davison, 1986; Gibbs, 1983; White and others, 1986); and described the kinematic sequence of rollover development (e.g., Gibbs, 1984; McClay and Ellis, 1987a, b). Following previous studies, we describe a rollover (Fig. 1) in terms of differential stratal rotations, antithetic faults, synthetic faults, and symmetrical grabens ("crestal collapse grabens" of McClay and Ellis, 1987a, b) referred to here as *keystone grabens*.

In this chapter, we present data from field mapping and stratigraphic measurements in the northern Cottonwood Mountains that characterize a 10-km-scale rollover in the Death Valley region of southeastern California (Fig. 2). We show, with sequentially deformed, balanced cross sections, the importance of both antithetic faults and keystone grabens as accommodation structures during development of the rollover. The structural interpretations and Tertiary stratigraphic correlations we present, in the context of understanding the geometry and kinematics of the rollover, also form an essential part of regional reconstructions required to understand large-scale extensional tectonic processes within the Death Valley area (Snow and Wernicke, 1989; Wernicke and others, 1988).

The Cottonwood Mountains (Fig. 2) are characterized by relatively mild internal extension. There appears to be only modest extension between range-blocks west of the Cottonwood Mountains (Burchfiel, 1969; Burchfiel and others, 1987; Dunne, 1986; Ross, 1967), with the exception of the Saline Valley area (Fig. 2; Burchfiel and others, 1987). In contrast, the region southeast of the Cottonwood Mountains is highly extended, with estimates ranging from 30 to 40 percent (Wright and Troxel, 1973) to more than 1,000 percent (Wernicke and others, 1988a, 1989). The Cottonwood Mountains thus form the boundary between a relatively stable terrain and an area of great extension.

The Cottonwood Mountains block is bounded to the north-

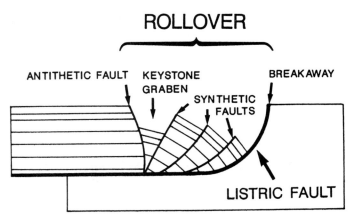

Figure 1. Conceptual model of a rollover developed above a listric normal fault showing major structural features.

east by the northern Death Valley fault zone (e.g., Stewart and others, 1968) and to the southwest by the Hunter Mountain fault zone (Fig. 2; Burchfiel and others, 1987). The Cottonwood Mountains block is separated from the Dry Mountain block to the west by Racetrack Valley and from structurally lower rocks to the southeast by a system of large-displacement, northwest-directed normal faults referred to as the Tucki Mountain normal fault system (e.g., Hodges and others, 1987). Normal faults within this system dip 20° to 30° northwest on the west flank of Tucki Mountain and project beneath the southern Cottonwood Mountains.

Palinspastic reconstructions of the Tucki Mountain area also indicate that the Tucki Mountain normal fault system underlies the Cottonwood Mountains block. The Tucki Wash fault, a structurally low fault within the normal fault system (Fig. 2), emplaces upper Paleozoic strata above Precambrian Z strata (Wernicke and others, 1988b, c; Hodges and others, 1989). Highly extended and steeply east-tilted upper Paleozoic strata exposed on Tucki Mountain, structurally above the Tucki Wash fault, restore to a thin sliver of rock adjacent to upper Paleozoic strata exposed along the eastern flank of the Cottonwood Mountains (Hunt and Mabey, 1966; Wernicke and others, 1986, 1988b, c; Hodges and others, 1987, 1989). Restoration of offset along the Tucki Wash and structurally higher faults of the Tucki Mountain normal fault system indicates that the entire Cottonwood Mountains block has moved northwest a minimum distance about equal to the 20 to 25 km width of Tucki Mountain relative to Precambrian Z strata below the Tucki Wash fault (Wernicke and others, 1988a).

The geology of the Cottonwood Mountains preserves evidence of movement on the underlying northward projection of the Tucki Mountain normal fault system. East-dipping Tertiary strata within the Ubehebe basin, at the northern end of the range (Figs. 2 and 3), provide evidence of tilting synchronous with normal faulting. The eastern flank of the range is pervasively extended by closely spaced, west-dipping normal faults with displacements typically less than 30 m. The west-dipping normal faults are cut by several east-dipping normal faults with displacements of 100 to 400 m (Fig. 3). These conjugate fault systems have accommodated a gradual decrease in the dip of strata from about 45° east on the eastern flank of the range to subhorizontal along the range-crest adjacent to Racetrack Valley. Simultaneously, the relative abundance of normal faults decreases from east to west across the range. Strata across Racetrack Valley in the Dry Mountain block are subhorizontal and unextended. We interpret this pattern of attitudes and faulting in the northern Cottonwood Mountains, Racetrack Valley, and Dry Mountain blocks as defining a rollover with a major keystone graben. We refer to this structure as the Tin Mountain rollover and attribute it to movement on the northward projection of the Tucki Mountain normal fault system.

TERTIARY STRATIGRAPHY

Detailed mapping and stratigraphic measurements in the northernmost Cottonwood Mountains (Figs. 2, 3, and 4) demonstrate rotation of the eastern flank of the Cottonwood Mountains block around a subhorizontal axis trending about N25°W, indicate that this rotation was synchronous with Tertiary sedimentation, provide age constraints on the inception of normal faulting, and constrain the movement history of the Ubehebe Crater fault. Detailed correlations of Tertiary strata in the Ubehebe basin with now-distant source terrains and other once-contiguous deposits may provide constraints on the movement history of the Cottonwood Mountains block within the Death Valley extensional system. A general description of the Tertiary stratigraphy of the Ubehebe basin is presented in this section (see also Fig. 5 and Plate 1). Detailed descriptions of measured stratigraphic sections are presented in Appendix 1.

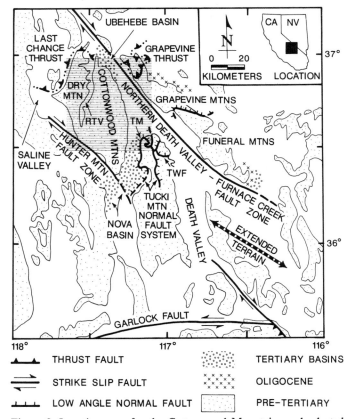

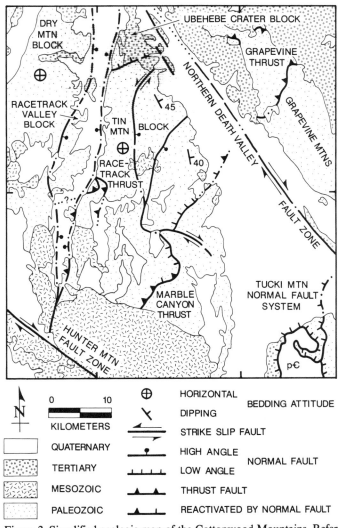

Figure 2. Location map for the Cottonwood Mountains and selected features of the Death Valley region, California and Nevada. Map symbols refer to: TM—Tucki Mountain, RTV—Racetrack Valley, TWF—Tucki Wash fault. Note the location of the Ubehebe and Nova basins, Tertiary sediments east of the Funeral Mountains, and Oligocene sediments east of the Grapevine and Funeral Mountains. The shaded area indicates the location of Figure 3.

Figure 3. Simplified geologic map of the Cottonwood Mountains. Refer to Figure 2 for the regional location of this map. The large shaded area indicates the location of Figure 4. The small shaded area indicates the location of Figure 13.

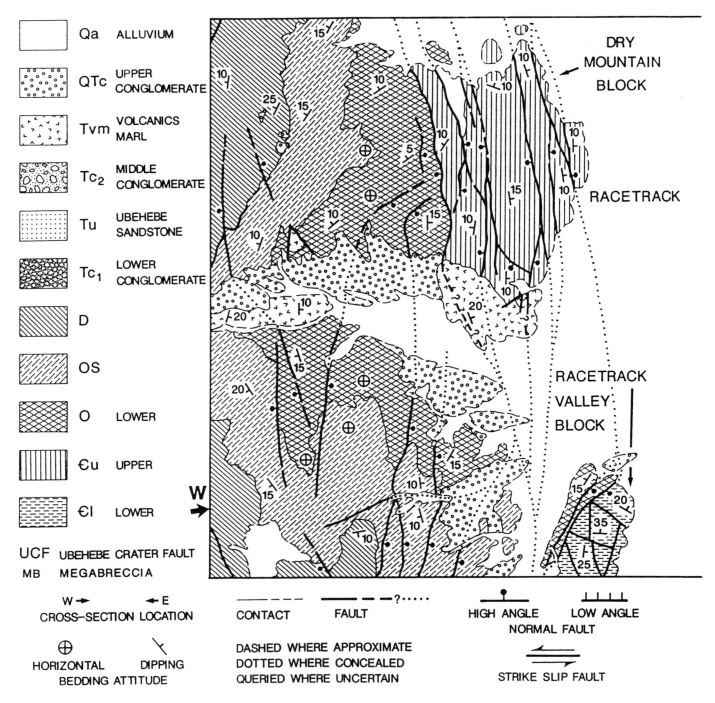

Qa   ALLUVIUM

QTc   UPPER CONGLOMERATE

Tvm   VOLCANICS MARL

Tc₂   MIDDLE CONGLOMERATE

Tu   UBEHEBE SANDSTONE

Tc₁   LOWER CONGLOMERATE

D

OS

O   LOWER

Єu   UPPER

Єl   LOWER

UCF   UBEHEBE CRATER FAULT
MB   MEGABRECCIA

W →   ← E
CROSS-SECTION LOCATION

⊕ HORIZONTAL   ⟍ DIPPING
BEDDING ATTITUDE

CONTACT   FAULT   — ? · · · · ·

DASHED WHERE APPROXIMATE
DOTTED WHERE CONCEALED
QUERIED WHERE UNCERTAIN

HIGH ANGLE   LOW ANGLE
NORMAL FAULT

STRIKE SLIP FAULT

DRY MOUNTAIN BLOCK

RACETRACK

RACETRACK VALLEY BLOCK

Tertiary strata of the northern Cottonwood Mountains area comprise five mappable units referred to as the lower conglomerate, Ubehebe sandstone, middle conglomerate, volcanics and marl, and upper conglomerate (Figs. 4 and 5). These five units lie above Paleozoic strata in two structural blocks, the Tin Mountain and Ubehebe Crater blocks, which are juxtaposed along the Ubehebe Crater fault (Figs. 3 and 4). The lower conglomerate, Ubehebe sandstone, and middle conglomerate are correlative, but not identical, across this fault. The volcanics and marl unit and upper conglomerate are also exposed to the west on the Dry Mountain block.

Lower conglomerate

The lower conglomerate (Tc₁) contains poorly sorted, subangular cobbles that appear to be locally derived from middle Paleozoic units. Lithologically distinct clasts were derived from the Ordovician Eureka Quartzite, basal part of the Silurian Hidden Valley Dolomite, and Lippencott Member of the Devonian Lost Burro Formation (see McAllister [1952] for descriptions of Paleozoic strata exposed within the Cottonwood Mountains area). Interbedded pebble-conglomerate and pebbly sandstone are common toward the top of the unit. The lower conglomerate

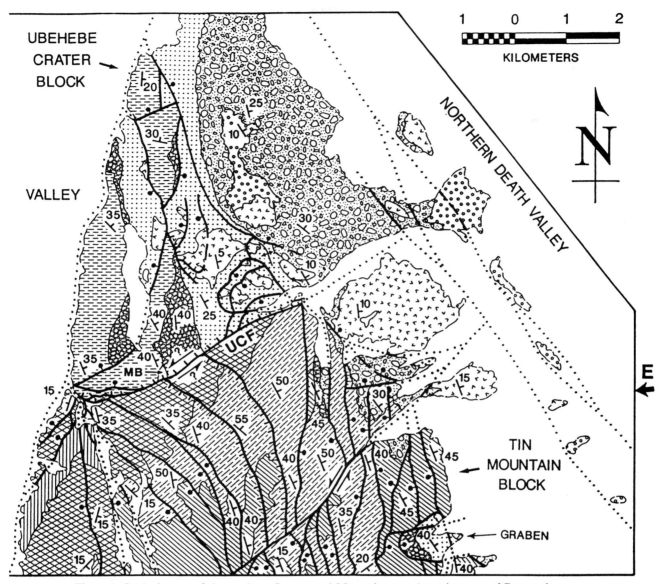

Figure 4. Geologic map of the northern Cottonwood Mountains area (mapping west of Racetrack Valley from Burchfiel [1969]). Arrows labeled E and W indicate the location of the cross sections shown on Figures 15 and 16. See Figures 2 and 3 for the regional location of this map.

is resistant and weathers pale reddish gray to light brown. Bedding is highly variable, ranging from massive to medium-bedded with erosional contacts. Where bedding can be discerned, the lower conglomerate unconformably overlies Paleozoic rocks with <5° angular discordance. The lower conglomerate measures at least 175 m thick on the Ubehebe Crater block. A structural thickness of 75 m is estimated on the Tin Mountain block at location 13 (Fig. 6).

Ubehebe Sandstone

The Ubehebe sandstone (Tu) is informally named for excellent exposures south of Ubehebe Crater on the Ubehebe Crater

structural block. A composite stratigraphic section was constructed by correlation of distinctive marker beds between measured sections (Figs. 4 and 6; Plate 1). The Ubehebe sandstone is predominantly a lithic wacke, composed of poorly sorted, subangular, medium-sized clasts, with subordinate silty mudstone, pebbly sandstone, cobble conglomerate, and tuff beds. With the exception of biotite, which is present throughout the unit, clasts appear to be derived from Paleozoic carbonate and clastic units. Interbedded, coarse-grained or pebbly, thin, resistant layers are common. The Ubehebe sandstone tends to erode easily and weathers pale red, pale brown, and pale olive. It is predominantly medium- to thick-bedded and conformably overlies the lower conglomerate on the Ubehebe Crater block. A maximum ex-

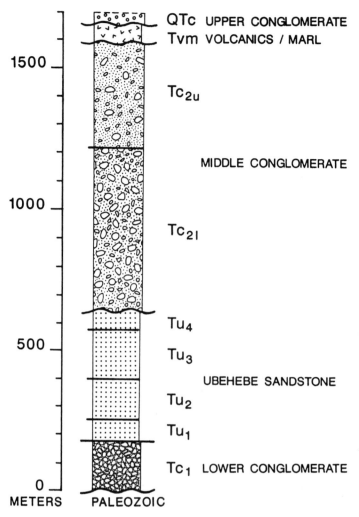

Figure 5. Composite stratigraphic section for Tertiary strata in the Ubehebe basin showing maximum measured thicknesses.

posed thickness of about 460 m is inferred from the composite section in this area.

Four mappable subunits are recognized (subunits 1–4 on Fig. 5; Plate 1). The lower two subunits, 1 and 2, do not contain tuff beds. The contact between them is drawn below the base of a thinly striped red and green zone (Plate 1 and Appendix 1). Three prominent white tuff beds are found in the upper half of the Ubehebe sandstone in subunits 3 and 4. These tuff beds contain biotite, quartz, and sanidine phenocrysts (see Appendix 1 for approximate proportions). In addition to these phenocrysts the uppermost tuff bed, located about 30 to 50 m above the base of subunit 4, contains abundant hornblende phenocrysts, and the lowermost tuff bed, which defines the base of subunit 3, contains mudstone rip-up clasts that impart a green hue. A noteworthy disconformity occurs at the base of subunit 4. The conglomerate (S on Plate 1) overlying this disconformity contains intraclasts of Ubehebe sandstone strata, which may be evidence of concurrent erosion on the Tin Mountain block.

The Ubehebe sandstone is only present on the Tin Mountain block within a small graben (Figs. 4 and 6; Plate 1). About half of the Ubehebe sandstone strata at this location are poorly sorted, pebbly, lithic wackes, composed of subangular, fine to medium-sized clasts, with subordinate conglomerate and silty mudstone layers. With the exception of distributed biotite, the clasts appear to be derived from Paleozoic carbonate and clastic units. The volcanic rocks forming the middle of the section (Plate 1) are massive tuff beds containing biotite, quartz, and sanidine phenocrysts (see Appendix 1 for approximate proportions). Strata within the Ubehebe sandstone tend to be easily eroded and weather pale yellowish green, light olive-brown, or moderate red. Well-developed medium-bedding is common. The Ubehebe sandstone unconformably overlies the lower conglomerate and is about 195 m thick on the Tin Mountain block.

Three subunits are recognized (subunits 2, 3, and 4 on Plate 1). The lowest, subunit 2, is a clastic unit exposed between the lower conglomerate and a volcanic sequence that forms most of subunit 3. The tuff beds in the lower part of subunit 3 are white and contain mudstone rip-up clasts. The lowest tuff bed is pale green. The massive tuff forming the upper part of the subunit weathers grayish orange-pink, is flow foliated, and contains minor hornblende in addition to phenocrysts found in the lower tuff beds. Several disconformities occur within the section, most notably below conglomerate G (Plate 1), which contains tuff intraclasts and forms the base of subunit 4.

Middle conglomerate

The middle conglomerate (Tc_2) can be divided into two subunits on the basis of average clast size and color. The lower subunit is dominantly a poorly sorted cobble conglomerate. Well-rounded to very well-rounded, moderately to highly spherical clasts in the basal part of the lower subunit were derived from the Precambrian Z to Cambrian Wood Canyon Formation, Cambrian Zabriskie Quartzite (see Stewart [1970] for descriptions of these units), Ordovician Eureka Quartzite, unknown mudstone units, and granitoids unlike any locally exposed intrusives. Subrounded to moderately rounded clasts representative of locally exposed middle Paleozoic units greatly increase in proportion upward to become the dominant clast type above the basal portion of the lower subunit. The matrix of the conglomerate is composed of moderately sorted coarse sand and granules. Moderately to well-sorted coarse sandstone with subrounded clasts is interbedded in increasing proportion upward within the lower subunit. The lower subunit weathers moderate reddish orange to reddish brown and is moderately resistant to erosion. Bedding is thick but poorly defined.

The upper subunit is dominantly interbedded cobble conglomerate with poorly sorted, subrounded clasts and poorly sorted, pebbly sandstone with coarse, subangular clasts. Clasts are similar to, but generally smaller than, those found in the upper part of the lower subunit. The upper subunit weathers dusky yellow, is moderately resistant to erosion, and is medium-bedded.

The middle conglomerate is at least 945 m thick and unconformably overlies the Ubehebe sandstone with about 5° angular discordance near location 6 on the Ubehebe Crater block (Figs. 4 and 6). The middle conglomerate unconformably overlies the Ubehebe sandstone at location 13. It overlies the lower conglomerate and upper Silurian to lower Devonian strata above an angular unconformity with at least 15° discordance at other locations on the Tin Mountain block. This major angular unconformity indicates a period of tectonism and erosion prior to deposition of the middle conglomerate.

Volcanics and marl

The volcanics and marl (Tvm) includes basalt, tuff, marl, caliche, and intercalated conglomerate layers with strong lateral variations in relative proportions. The lower part of the unit consists of basalt and/or marl with conglomerate that contains basalt boulders. The conglomerate is lithologically identical to the upper conglomerate. Tuff and/or tuffaceous marl forms the upper part of the unit.

Vesicular olivine basalt is exposed as flows or boulders in poorly sorted conglomerate at the base of the unit. Basalt flow thicknesses are highly variable, and chilled contacts are common. Syndepositional faulting appears to have controlled the location of some flows. Basalt flows exposed to the west on Dry Mountain (Fig. 4, unit Tvm dipping 10° to 20°E at the western margin of the map) appear to lie within an east-dipping channel trending toward basalt flows exposed in the northern Cottonwood Mountains (Burchfiel, 1969). Although the ages of these flows are unknown, a correlation seems likely between flows in the north-

ern Cottonwood Mountains area and other 4-Ma basalt flows exposed farther west in the Dry Mountain area (Elliott and others, 1984).

The marl consists of fine-grained muddy or tuffaceous limestone with wavy beds of thin to medium thickness. It forms resistant outcrops that weather grayish white to dark gray. The marl is typically porous and locally contains plant fossils. The stratigraphic relation between the marl and volcanic rocks is highly variable and incompletely defined. Thick caliche zones resembling the marl are locally exposed within conglomerate layers intercalated in the unit.

The Mesquite Spring tuff is informally named for prominent exposures of white tuff located west of Mesquite Spring campground in northern Death Valley. The tuff is composed largely of pumice lapilli and contains locally abundant lithic fragments and glass blebs (apache teardrops). It is poorly lithified and easily eroded. Some exposures appear to be reworked as volcanic-lithic sandstone but contain few clasts foreign to the tuff. At one location, spires of slightly more lithified tuff, interpreted as fossil gas-escape structures, indicate primary deposition. Tuffaceous marl overlies the tuff at some localities. At other localities, tuffaceous marl overlies basalt where it appears to have replaced the tuff. Marl that is associated with the tuff locally contains pumice lapilli and lithologically grades continuously from tuffaceous marl to altered tuff. This marl/tuff association appears to be a persistent stratigraphic marker within the Cottonwood Mountains.

The volcanics and marl unconformably overlie the middle conglomerate to the east and progressively older strata of the Ubehebe sandstone toward the west (Fig. 4; Plate 1). The unconformity below the middle conglomerate is truncated by the unconformity below the volcanics and marl with about 20° angular discordance. This relation, exposed near location 6 (Fig. 6) and evident on cross section 1 (Fig. 8), indicates a period of tectonism and erosion prior to deposition of the volcanics and marl.

Upper conglomerate

The upper conglomerate (QTc) contains poorly sorted, subangular to well-rounded cobbles in a poorly sorted matrix of subangular, coarse grains. Clasts are identical to those exposed in the lower and middle conglomerates except for angular basalt boulders. The upper conglomerate is well lithified and weathers grayish brown. It is poorly, medium to thickly bedded and unconformably overlies the volcanics and marl at some localities and the middle conglomerate at others. The presence of this unconformity, the similarity between clasts in the upper conglomerate and those in lower units, and the local absence of the volcanics and marl suggest that much of the upper conglomerate is reworked material locally derived from previous Ubehebe basin deposits. Similar Quaternary gravels, distinguished by their medium light gray color and less indurated state, overlie the upper conglomerate above an angular unconformity.

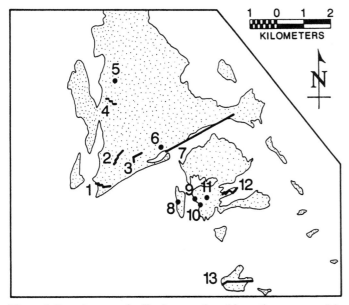

Figure 6. Location map for Tertiary stratigraphic sections measured in the Ubehebe basin. Shading indicates areas of Tertiary outcrop in the northern Cottonwood Mountains as shown on the right half of Figure 4. See Plate 1 and Appendix 1 for descriptions of measured sections.

Ubehebe basin

Sedimentation along the west flank of the Ubehebe basin was probably dominated by alluvial-fan processes. Interfingering stratigraphic relations within the volcanics and marl unit suggest a depositional environment transitional between a playa lake and an alluvial fan. Intercalated conglomerate layers in this unit may indicate the initial progradation of the upper conglomerate into the basin.

The distinctive, well-rounded cobbles that dominate the basal part of the middle conglomerate are an important marker within the Ubehebe basin. The maturity of these cobbles suggests transport over large distances and/or recycling of an older deposit. These factors, and the presence of cobbles of granitoids unlike any of the intrusives currently exposed in the range, indicate that the source of these cobbles is foreign to the Cottonwood Mountains. The cobbles resemble clasts from the Oligocene Titus Canyon Formation (Stock and Bode, 1935; Reynolds, 1969) exposed on the northeast side of the Grapevine Mountains (Fig. 2). Recent reconstructions of the Death Valley area prior to about 10 Ma (Wernicke and others, 1988a; Snow and Wernicke, 1989; Snow, 1989; Snow and others, 1989) place both the Cottonwood and Grapevine Mountains adjacent to the Funeral Mountains where Cemen and others (1985) document Oligocene deposits inferred to be correlative with the Titus Canyon Formation. We suggest that the basal part of the middle conglomerate was deposited in the Ubehebe basin prior to most translation of the Cottonwood Mountains and that the Titus Canyon Formation is the source of the distinctive cobbles. Isotopic age determinations from tuff beds within the Ubehebe sandstone (in progress) may test this hypothesis.

The middle conglomerate is correlated as a single lithostratigraphic unit based on the stratigraphic position of the distinctive cobbles immediately overlying the lower major angular unconformity. Additionally, the concentration of these cobbles within a relatively thin zone, as compared with the total thickness of strata in the Ubehebe basin, suggests that their influx into the basin was restricted to a relatively short time. Even though rapid facies changes are likely within an alluvial-fan–dominated environment, we infer that the well-rounded cobble zone is also a chronostratigraphic subunit along strike in the Ubehebe basin. In the following section, we present a test of this inference based on the pinchout of isochronous strata below the unconformities. The consistent occurrence of the lithologically distinctive Mesquite Springs tuff bed and associated basalt flows above the upper major angular unconformity indicates that the volcanics and marl is also a chronostratigraphic unit. Thus, we interpret the middle conglomerate as an approximately isochronous unit bounded by the two major angular unconformities.

Measured sections of the Ubehebe sandstone located within the Ubehebe Crater and Tin Mountain blocks are correlated as a single lithostratigraphic unit by (1) their relative positions between the lower and middle conglomerates, (2) their similar stratigraphic sequences, and (3) similarities between stratigraphi-

cally equivalent tuff beds (Plate 1). Lithological correlations between tuff beds suggest that at least subunit 3 of the Ubehebe sandstone is also a chronostratigraphic subunit. Geochronologic work in progress may provide better constraints on these correlations.

Ubehebe sandstone strata were probably continuous across the eastern flank of the Cottonwood Mountains prior to erosion along the lower major unconformity. The Ubehebe sandstone section at location 13 is located within a small graben (Figs. 4 and 6). The lack of any proximal fault-scarp facies at this location suggests that the graben developed after deposition of the Ubehebe sandstone. Thus, the Ubehebe sandstone was probably deposited in areas adjacent to the graben. The middle conglomerate is exposed as a relatively continuous band of outcrop unconformably overlying Ubehebe sandstone strata in the graben or lower conglomerate and Paleozoic strata in adjacent areas on the Tin Mountain block (Fig. 4). As will be discussed in the following section, Ubehebe sandstone strata located on the Ubehebe Crater block have also been downfaulted relative to the Tin Mountain block, largely prior to deposition of the middle conglomerate. The similar structural positions of correlative sections of the Ubehebe sandstone (Fig. 4; Plate 1) and probable age of normal faulting suggest that Ubehebe sandstone strata were removed by erosion along the lower major unconformity.

TERTIARY TECTONIC HISTORY

The Tertiary tectonic history of the northern Cottonwood Mountains is directly reflected in the deposits of the Ubehebe basin. Cross sections of the basin (Fig. 8, see also Figs. 4, 7) are

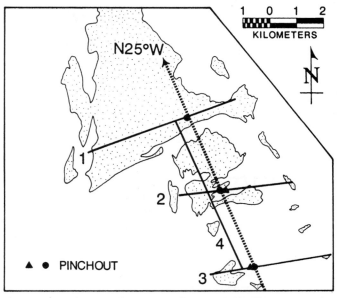

Figure 7. Location map for cross sections shown in Figure 8. Shading indicates areas of Tertiary outcrop in the northern Cottonwood Mountains as shown on the right half of Figure 4. Stratigraphic pinchouts, as defined on Figure 8, indicate that the northern Cottonwood Mountains tilt-axis trends N25°W, as shown by the dashed line.

based on measured stratigraphic data but assume that units can be projected to depth with roughly planar contacts. The lower conglomerate and Ubehebe sandstone are inferred to pinch in below the middle conglomerate east of the range front. These cross sections show the two major angular unconformities, discussed previously (cross sections 1, 2, and 3 on Fig. 8; see also Plate 1). The >30° angular discordance developed across these un-

conformities requires Tertiary rotation of Paleozoic strata forming the eastern flank of the range.

The attitudes of Paleozoic and Tertiary strata along the eastern flank of the range indicate a rotation or tilt-axis oriented roughly north-northwest. The pinchout of chronostratigraphic units below the two major angular unconformities (Fig. 8) can be used to further constrain the trend of the Cottonwood Mountains

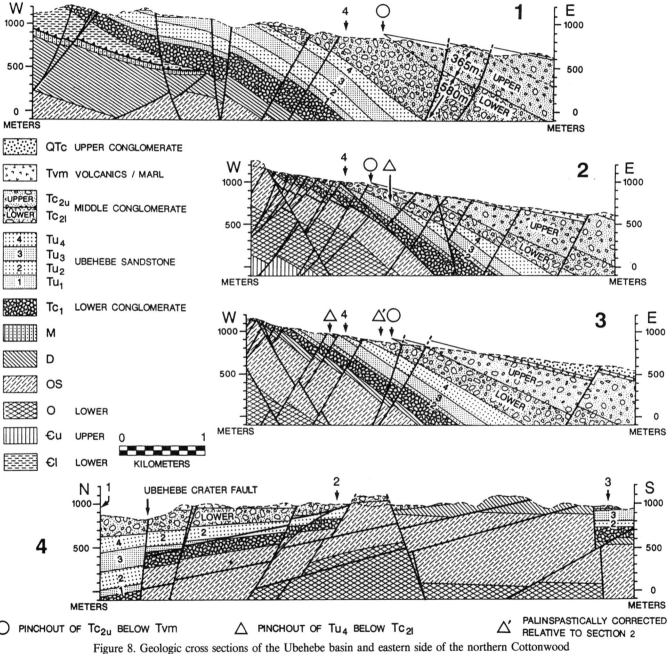

Figure 8. Geologic cross sections of the Ubehebe basin and eastern side of the northern Cottonwood Mountains. See Figure 7 for the locations of cross sections 1, 2, 3, and 4. Numbers above arrows indicate the location of cross-cutting section lines. Circles and triangles indicate the position of stratigraphic pinchouts, as discussed in the text. Note the inferred location of the Ubehebe thrust and a normal fault active prior to deposition of the lower conglomerate (cross section 1, located near the truncation of the thrust below the basal Tertiary unconformity). The throw and position of this fault are poorly constrained but reflect early normal slip on the Ubehebe Crater fault.

tilt-axis. However, if diachronous units are incorrectly correlated and inferred to be isochronous (perhaps because of lateral facies changes), then the tilt-axis trend indicated by the pinchout of such a unit will deviate from the true orientation. For example, the pinchout of successively older subunits of the Ubehebe sandstone below the lower unconformity (Fig. 8, cross section 2) occurs progressively farther toward the west so that a tilt-axis indicated by correlating the pinchout of subunit 1 with the pinchout of subunit 4 along strike will be skewed from the actual trend. Thus, the degree of parallelism among tilt-axis trends indicated by bedding attitudes and by the pinchout of different chronostratigraphic units serves as an internal check on inferred chronostratigraphic correlations.

Although the upper and lower subunits of the middle conglomerate (subunits Tc_{2u} and Tc_{2l}) are lithostratigraphic subunits, the contact between them is assumed to be relatively synchronous along the strike of the basin. The pinchout of subunit Tc_{2u} below the volcanics and marl is projected onto cross sections 1, 2, and 3 (circle on Fig. 8). Correlation of conglomerate S on the Ubehebe Crater block with conglomerate G on the Tin Mountain block (Plate 1) is used to infer the approximate subsurface position of the chronostratigraphic tuff bed U, located about 50 m above the base of subunit 4 of the Ubehebe sandstone (subunit Tu_4, Fig. 8). The pinchout of tuff bed U within subunit Tu_4 below the middle conglomerate is projected onto cross sections 2 and 3 (triangle on Fig. 8). The position of the Tu_4 pinchout on cross section 3 has been palinspastically corrected for faulting that occurred prior to deposition of the middle conglomerate and formed the small graben containing location 13 (Figs. 4, 6). The two sets of stratigraphic pinchouts define roughly parallel tilt-axis trends similar to the north-northwest oriented tilt-axis inferred from bedding attitudes (Figs. 4, 7). This parallelism of tilt-axis trends supports our chronostratigraphic correlations within the Ubehebe basin and collectively constrains the orientation of the syndepositional Tertiary tilt-axis of the northern Cottonwood Mountains to be about N25°W.

The trend of kinematic indicators from Tucki Mountain (Hodges and others, 1987) or map-scale features such as the Hunter Mountain fault zone, Furnace Creek fault zone, and turtleback surfaces of the Black Mountains are all roughly parallel to the regional west-northwest–oriented extension direction indicated by recent regional reconstructions (Wernicke and others, 1988a; Snow and Wernicke, 1989; Snow, 1989). The trend of the tilt-axis is oblique to this direction and apparently unrelated to the extension direction.

The Ubehebe Crater fault is a major, shallowly to moderately north-northwest–dipping normal fault in the northern Cottonwood Mountains (Fig. 4). The preservation of at least 600 m of additional Tertiary strata across the fault below the middle conglomerate suggests that the fault was active during Tertiary sedimentation. A megabreccia deposit exposed at the base of the lower conglomerate and adjacent to the fault suggests that the Ubehebe Crater fault was also active before deposition of the lower conglomerate. However, movement ceased before deposi-

tion of the upper subunit of the middle conglomerate (subunit Tc_{2u}). The pinchout of Tc_{2u} below the volcanics and marl on the Ubehebe Crater block (cross section 1, Fig. 8) is collinear with the same pinchout on the Tin Mountain block (Figs. 7, 8). This indicates that the Ubehebe Crater fault had locked and the Tin Mountain and Ubehebe Crater blocks were rotating as a unit during later Tertiary deposition.

Several lines of evidence indicate that motion on the Ubehebe Crater fault was dominantly normal dip-slip. Motion on the Ubehebe Crater fault occurred early during the rotation history of strata in the Ubehebe basin. Thus, large strike-slip offsets of shallowly dipping strata would be required to produce the observed left-separation of the basal Tertiary unconformity across the fault. Such a left-lateral offset would cause a space problem to the west in the Racetrack Valley during deformation or leave a void in the northern Cottonwood Mountains after reconstruction. Additionally, the Ubehebe Crater block is topographically low relative to the Tin Mountain block. Strike-slip offset prior to rotation would produce minimal topographic relief. Furthermore, in detail the Ubehebe Crater fault is not linear but rather is formed of generally east-west–trending, left-stepping fault segments that alternate with minor north-south–trending segments (Snow, unpublished mapping). This geometry indicates a slip vector oriented parallel to the intersection of these fault planes. Although the current trend of the slip vector relative to the Ubehebe Crater fault apparently indicates normal oblique-left slip in map view, the rake of the slip vector is roughly perpendicular when measured relative to bedding in the average plane of the Ubehebe Crater fault. Collectively, these observations suggest that motion on the Ubehebe Crater fault was dominantly normal dip-slip, even though the slip vector is not precisely constrained and some oblique-left slip is possible.

Tertiary strata preserved stratigraphically below the volcanics and marl unit record the onset of extensional faulting within the Tin Mountain block. The lower conglomerate lies on an apparently unfaulted surface of Paleozoic strata. With the exception of the Ubehebe Crater fault, detailed mapping in the area has revealed no normal faults demonstrably older than the lower conglomerate. The presence of intraclast conglomerates (S and G on Plate 1) at the base of subunit 4 of the Ubehebe sandstone is consistent with local tectonic activity between the time of deposition of subunits 3 and 4, but the absence of significant angular discordance between strata in subunits 3 and 4 or between strata of the Ubehebe sandstone and Tin Mountain block suggests that major extensional tectonism occurred later. Cemen and others (1985) document similar relations in the Funeral Mountains where minor high-angle normal faults are truncated by disconformably overlying mid-Miocene(?) strata that predate large-magnitude extension. The cross sections in Figure 8 show the middle conglomerate deposited with marked angular discordance on a faulted and eroded surface of Paleozoic and Tertiary strata. As disussed above, Ubehebe sandstone strata probably were continuously exposed across the Tin Mountain block. Thus, major normal faulting, tilting, and erosion of the Tin Mountain block apparently began after deposition of the Ubehebe sandstone but before deposition of the middle conglomerate. The great thickness of the middle conglomerate (Fig. 5) and its position between major angular unconformities (Fig. 8) suggest that deposition was synchronous with extensive normal faulting and formation of the Tin Mountain rollover during 70-km extensional translation of the Cottonwood Mountains block (Snow and Wernicke, 1989; Snow, 1989; Snow and others, 1989). This implied relation between tilting and extension will be discussed in subsequent sections.

PRE-EXTENSIONAL STRUCTURES

Prior to Tertiary extension, the northern Cottonwood Mountains area was part of a Mesozoic thrust belt (e.g., Dunne, 1986; Wernicke and others, 1988a). The recognition of pre-extensional structures is necessary before deformation attributed to formation of the rollover can be understood. Within the Cottonwood Mountains, the Tin Mountain block is bounded to the south by the structurally lower Marble Canyon thrust (Fig. 3; Johnson, 1971; Stadler, 1968; Snow, 1989, unpublished mapping; Snow and Wernicke, 1989). Detailed mapping indicates that no major thrusts exist within the Tin Mountain block (Snow, unpublished mapping). The west-vergent White Top Mountain backfold lies within the Tin Mountain block but is located south of the area considered herein (Snow, 1989; Snow and Wernicke, 1989; Wernicke and others, 1988a). Similarly, the Dry Mountain block is a single structural block containing no major Mesozoic structures (Burchfiel, 1969). It is bounded to the northwest by the structurally higher Last Chance thrust (Stewart and others, 1966). In this section we show that the Tin Mountain and Dry Mountain blocks are parts of a single Mesozoic thrust plate separated by a downdropped klippe of a structurally higher thrust plate (Fig. 3).

The Ubehebe Crater fault is a normal fault with an apparent thrust relation (Fig. 4). It has juxtaposed the hanging wall and footwall of a large thrust fault, referred to as the Ubehebe thrust (Snow, 1989; Snow and Wernicke, 1989). Restoration of the minimum slip on the Ubehebe Crater fault indicated by the offset basal Tertiary unconformity places lower Cambrian strata of the Ubehebe Crater block structurally above at least Silurian strata of the Tin Mountain block. Any normal slip that occurred on the fault prior to deposition of the lower conglomerate increases this estimate of throw. Concordant contacts between Lower Cambrian Wood Canyon Formation and Upper Devonian tectonite marble are exposed in megabreccia blocks found below the lower conglomerate adjacent to the Ubehebe Crater fault. They are probably remnants of the original Ubehebe thrust contact. Open to tight folds are common within structurally low Wood Canyon strata, consistent with the inferred presence of the Ubehebe thrust fault at shallow depth below these rocks. A brecciated klippe of Cambrian Zabriskie Quartzite, probably correlative with the Ubehebe thrust plate, lies in normal fault contact above Mississippian strata of the Tin Mountain block in the highest part of the

range about 7 km south of the Ubehebe Crater fault. These observations collectively suggest that Precambrian Z strata of the Ubehebe thrust plate were emplaced with a stratigraphic throw exceeding 4,700 m above Devonian and Mississippian strata of the Tin Mountain block.

The Racetrack thrust of McAllister (1952) is exposed in a complex duplex zone structurally above the Tin Mountain block about 13 km south of the Ubehebe Crater block (Fig. 3). Within the duplex zone, strata as old as the uppermost part of the Ordovician Pogonip Group overlie strata as young as the Mississippian Rest Spring Shale (McAllister, 1952; Snow, unpublished mapping), indicating a maximum stratigraphic throw of about 1,800 m for the Racetrack thrust at the type locality. Previous interpretations have projected the thrust under alluvium between the Cambrian through Silurian strata of the Racetrack Valley block and the generally younger strata of the Tin Mountain block (McAllister, 1956; Stewart and others, 1966; Burchfiel, 1969; Burchfiel and others, 1970). The Cambrian Nopah Formation, upper part of the Ordovician Pogonip Group, and lower part of the overlying Ordovician Eureka Quartzite exposed within the Racetract Valley block are stratigraphically different from equivalent strata exposed within the Tin Mountain block (Snow, unpublished data). Details of these same stratigraphic intervals do not show significant variation within the Tin Mountain block. These stratigraphic differences are consistent with interpreting these structural blocks as parts of different Mesozoic thrust plates.

The Racetrack thrust and duplex zone have been strongly modified by a large, down-to-the-west normal fault system forming the eastern boundary of Racetrack Valley (Fig. 3; McAllister, 1952; Snow, unpublished mapping). Steeply west-dipping faults with apparent thrust relations along the east side of southern Racetrack Valley have been previously correlated with the Racetrack thrust (McAllister, 1956). The down-to-the-west topographic step across these faults and their highly brecciated character suggest that they are normal faults that have excised the actual thrust contact and juxtaposed strata of different thrust plates. Although the Racetrack Valley block has been *correlated* with the Racetrack thrust plate exposed in the duplex zone, it is clear that strata within Racetrack Valley are only *constrained* to lie somewhere structurally above the Racetrack thrust fault and strata of the Tin Mountain block. Similarly, the fault between the Racetrack Valley block and Dry Mountain block dips 50° east, coincides with a down-to-the-east topographic step, and appears to be a normal fault with an apparent thrust relation (Burchfiel, 1969). Strata within the Racetrack Valley block are constrained to lie structurally above younger strata of the Dry Mountain block across this fault. We believe that interpretation of Racetrack Valley as a full graben bounded by these faults is the simplest way to explain the dips of these faults and the topographic depression. However, the geometry of structural blocks and their bounding faults in the northern Cottonwood Mountains area does not constrain the Mesozoic structural position of the Tin Mountain block relative to the Dry Mountain block.

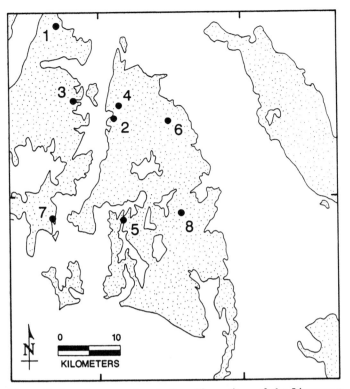

Figure 9. Location map for stratigraphic sections of the Lippencott Member of the Devonian Lost Burro Formation measured in the Cottonwood Mountains area. Shading indicates areas of Paleozoic outcrop as shown on Figure 3. See Figure 10 and Appendix 2 for descriptions.

The similarity of the Lippencott Member of the Devonian Lost Burro Formation (McAllister, 1952) across northern Racetrack Valley suggests that the Tin Mountain and Dry Mountain blocks are part of the same Mesozoic thrust plate. Measured stratigraphic sections in the Cottonwood Mountains area show a pair of distinctive marker beds (Figs. 9 and 10; Appendix 2). The upper marker is a massive bed of gray dolostone containing chert nodules that are contorted, commonly isoclinally folded, and randomly distributed. The marker bed appears to have been deformed as a soft sediment. A sandy dolostone bed containing sand-filled worm burrows (fuccoids of McAllister, 1952, 1974) is located 7.3 to 10.7 m below the cherty marker in the northern Racetrack Valley area. It is the first sandy bed exposed below the cherty marker. The existence and consistent spacing of these marker beds are not regionally persistent. The measured sections show general variability of stratigraphic details within the Cottonwood Mountains area. This close stratigraphic match across the northern Racetrack Valley does not support an interpretation of the Tin Mountain and Dry Mountain blocks as separated by a major Mesozoic thrust.

Paleozoic strata adjacent to the northern Racetrack Valley are roughly horizontal and coplanar with equivalent strata across the valley. The inferred presence of a Mesozoic thrust fault between the Dry Mountain and Tin Mountain blocks would require

a rather fortuitous relation between initial movement on the thrust and normal offset on the fault bounding the east side of Racetrack Valley. A correlation between the Racetrack and Ubehebe thrusts along the east side of the valley implied by such a thrust would require stratigraphic throw along the initial thrust to increase from 1,800 m to 4,700 m within 6 km along strike, remain at roughly 4,700 m for an additional 7 km along strike, and then be precisely reactivated by normal faults such that the structural relief between hanging wall and footwall are exactly erased. We suggest that these events are unlikely.

Based on the structural simplicity of the full graben interpretation of Racetrack Valley, the differences between Cambrian through Ordovician strata located in the Racetrack Valley and Tin Mountain blocks, the similarities of lower Devonian strata located in the Tin Mountain and Dry Mountain blocks, and the smooth contourability of stratigraphic horizons across Racetrack Valley, we conclude that the Tin Mountain and Dry Mountain blocks are parts of the same Mesozoic thrust plate.

Normal faulting has isolated the Racetrack Valley block, Ubehebe Crater block, and Zabriskie Quartzite klippe from the Tin Mountain block and superjacent Racetrack thrust plate, making regional tectonic correlations difficult. Lower Cambrian strata are exposed within the Ubehebe Crater block, Zabriskie klippe, and northern part of the Racetrack Valley block where they structurally overlie the Tin Mountain block with similar stratigraphic throws of about 5 km. The proximity among these structurally similar blocks suggests that all are parts of the Ubehebe thrust plate. The Racetrack thrust, exposed 6 km south of the Zabriskie klippe, also structurally overlies the Tin Mountain block. However, the significantly smaller stratigraphic throw of <2 km across the Racetrack thrust suggests that the Ubehebe thrust does not correlate with the Racetrack thrust. We correlate the Ubehebe thrust with the Last Chance thrust of Stewart and others (1966). Both thrusts emplace lower Cambrian above Mississippian strata with a large stratigraphic throw of about 5 km and occur as the first major thrust structurally above the Tin Mountain/Dry Mountain block. Although further work is necessary, folding within the Ubehebe thrust plate also seems consistent with the style of deformation documented within the Last Chance thrust plate elsewhere by Corbett and others (1988).

Available evidence suggests that the Tin Mountain and Dry Mountain blocks form parts of a single Mesozoic thrust plate. Thus, the Racetrack thrust does not root within northern Racetrack Valley but appears to be derived from an area west or south of the Dry Mountain block as an imbricate thrust structurally above the Tin Mountain/Dry Mountain block yet below the overlying Ubehebe/Last Chance thrust plate. The Last Chance thrust is correlated with the Grapevine thrust northeast of the northern Cottonwood Mountains area (Stewart and others, 1966; Burchfiel and others, 1970; Reynolds, 1974; Wernicke and others, 1988a; Snow, 1989; Snow and others, 1989; Snow and Wernicke, 1989). The Grapevine thrust emplaces upper-plate Cambrian strata above an intermediate thrust plate carrying Ordovician strata above lower-plate Mississippian strata (Reynolds,

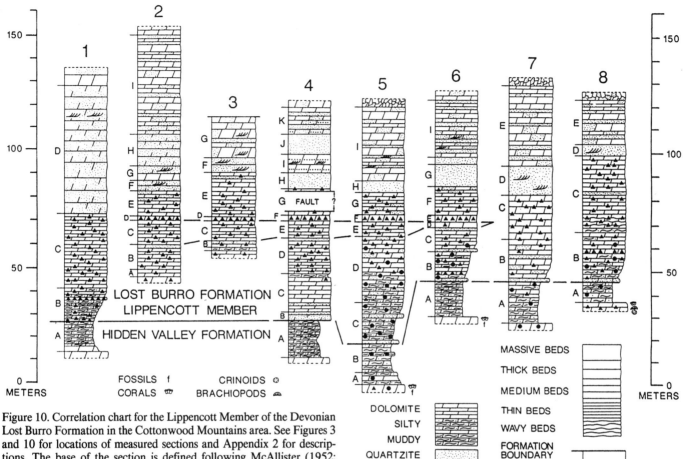

Figure 10. Correlation chart for the Lippencott Member of the Devonian Lost Burro Formation in the Cottonwood Mountains area. See Figures 3 and 10 for locations of measured sections and Appendix 2 for descriptions. The base of the section is defined following McAllister (1952; 1974). The interval between the cherty marker bed and the sandy dolomite marker bed is correlated between sections 2 through 6. Note the similarity of stratigraphic details in the Tin Mountain and Dry Mountain structural blocks across Racetrack Valley (sections 2, 3, and 4).

1974; personal communication, 1987), similar to our structural interpretation of the Ubehebe, Last Chance, and Racetrack thrusts in the northern Cottonwood Mountains area. We interpret Racetrack Valley to be a symmetrical full graben that has down-dropped strata assigned to the Ubehebe/Last Chance thrust plate between structurally lower rocks of the Tin Mountain/Dry Mountain block. We suggest that the Racetrack thrust is a minor duplex sliver that may be only locally exposed below the Last Chance allochthon.

TIN MOUNTAIN ROLLOVER

Formation of a rollover is a fundamental response to the space problem imposed by motion on a listric fault (Fig. 11; e.g., Hamblin, 1965). Rollovers are observable from the 10-cm scale in sandbox experiments (McClay and Ellis, 1987a, b) to the 10-km scale in seismic sections (e.g., White and others, 1986) as scale-independent products of the geometry of faulting. Two

well-defined examples from the northern Cottonwood Mountains are discussed in this section to illustrate the primary characteristics of a rollover.

A 100-m-scale rollover, displayed within a single outcrop, forms a natural cross section on a north-facing canyon wall located about 3 km northeast of Tin Mountain (Fig. 12). The change in dip of prominent marker beds shows the bending that forms the rollover. This bending of the hanging wall is geometrically accommodated by antithetic faults, closely spaced synthetic faults, and keystone grabens (Fig. 1). The keystone grabens and some closely spaced synthetic faults clearly end downward. They do not offset lower marker beds.

A geologic map of the outcrop-scale rollover forms an oblique projection of the natural cross section seen on the canyon wall (Fig. 13; compare with Fig. 12). The large, north-trending, east-dipping normal fault that bounds the rollover to the west (Fig. 13) projects under the rollover to the east. This dip-slip fault changes trend slightly north of the cross section to become a

LISTRIC FAULT

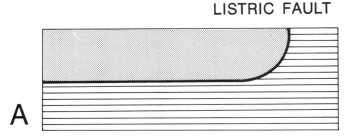

SPACE PROBLEM

SPACE PROBLEM

ROLLOVER

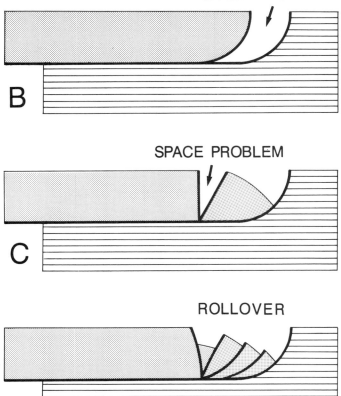

Figure 11. Conceptual model showing the space-problem caused by hanging wall motion along a listric fault above a rigid footwall block: A) initial geometry; B) space-problem caused by listric fault geometry; C) space-problem caused by hanging-wall rollover; D) space-problems solved by synthetic faults, an antithetic fault, and a keystone graben within the rollover.

steeply south-dipping, oblique-left-slip normal fault (Fig. 3). Although the fault is covered by alluvium near the rollover (Fig. 13), the fault probably dips at a moderate angle to the southeast below the rollover. Thus, the shallow dip inferred from the balanced cross section (Fig. 14) is probably an apparent dip. The northeast-oriented trend of the fault north of the rollover provides a constraint on the local extension direction. The balanced cross section (Fig. 14) is drawn through the rollover roughly parallel to the inferred, but imprecisely defined, extension

direction (between E and W on Fig. 13). Faults located within the hanging wall south of the cross section are generally subparallel. Thus, a roughly cylindrical fault geometry is present such that any potential motion of a fault block obliquely through the plane of the cross section would have a minimal effect on the area of the cross section. In spite of limitations imposed by an inferred extension direction and basal fault geometry, the balanced cross section reproduces well the natural cross sections displayed on the map and in outcrop.

Even though a balanced cross section is inherently non-unique, it forms a powerful constraint on the geometry of the rollover at depth. Deformation within the rollover was accommodated by mappable faults and limited penetrative strain by brecciation and probable bedding-parallel slip. Ductile deformation was not observed and is unlikely within the rollover at any shallow depth. The cross section is constrained to balance by bed length in fault-bounded blocks. Synthetic faults and keystone graben blocks that do not continue downward within the rollover (Figs. 12, 14) geometrically require differential stratal rotation between fault blocks as well as layer-parallel extension that decreases downward. A Tertiary age for the rollovers is indicated by many faults within the rollover and by the master fault bounding the rollover to the west that can be traced south to offset Tertiary strata. The eastern boundary of the rollover is a large, stable block that has experienced only simple normal motion with no differential rotation relative to footwall strata west of the rollover. With the exception of a small thrust fault (Figs. 12, 14) that has behaved as a passive marker during formation of the rollover, the only faults present in the rollover are normal faults. Thus, the initial geometry prior to formation of the rollover was simply parallel and roughly horizontal strata. With these constraints, the balanced cross section indicates that the basal fault below the outcrop-scale rollover is a listric fault. The balanced cross section demonstrates that the differential rotation of strata across the rollover is approximately equal to, and a direct result of, the attitude change along the basal listric fault, although in this case, motion is probably oblique to the true dip of the basal fault.

The outcrop-scale rollover, balanced cross section, and reconstruction (Figs. 12, 13, and 14) may be a good analogy for the 10-km-scale Tin Mountain rollover developed above the northward projection of the Tucki Mountain normal fault system. The pattern of faulting and differential stratal rotation across Tin Mountain, Racetrack Valley, and Dry Mountain is nearly identical (Fig. 4). Deformation in both cases is by brittle normal faulting with limited penetrative strain by brecciation and probable bedding-parallel slip. Tertiary strata in the northern Cottonwood Mountains area indicate the development of both rollovers near the surface, consistent with the observed lack of ductile deformation. In both cases, few faults are present other than Tertiary normal faults that are geometrically and kinematically related to the rollover. We have previously argued that the Tin Mountain and Dry Mountain blocks are parts of a single Mesozoic thrust plate and that, prior to Tertiary extension, they formed a single structural block. Mapping in the northern Cottonwood Moun-

Figure 12. Outcrop-scale rollover in the northern Cottonwood Mountains. See Figures 3 and 13 for the location of this view looking south. The cliff face measures approximately 350 m high and 1,000 m long. Symbols on the interpreted photo indicate the following: heavy lines—normal faults (plain) or thrust faults (teeth on hanging wall), dots—Devonian Lost Burro Formation subunit 2 (Dl$_2$) marker bed, crosses—boundary between Devonian Lost Burro Formation subunit 2 and subunit 1, and dash-dots— Devonian Lost Burro Formation subunit 1 (Dl$_1$) marker bed. Note the differential stratal rotation between fault blocks and that faults bounding the keystone graben and several synthetic faults die-out downward without offsetting lower strata. Compare with Figures 13 and 14.

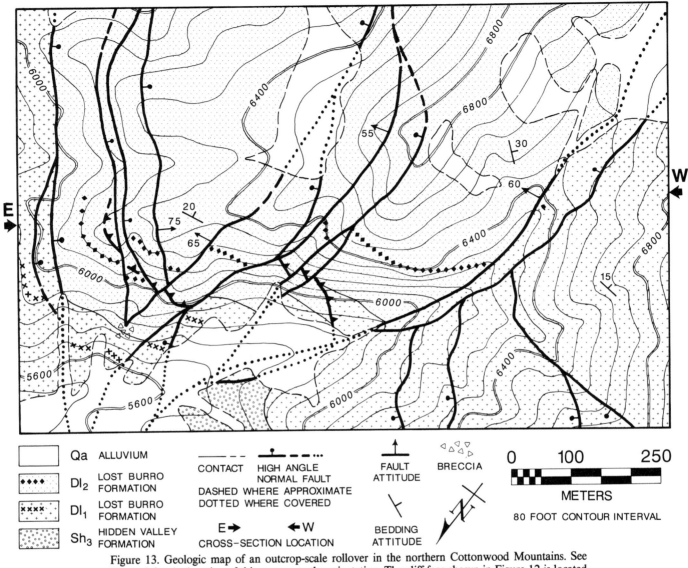

Figure 13. Geologic map of an outcrop-scale rollover in the northern Cottonwood Mountains. See Figure 3 for the location of this map; note the orientation. The cliff face shown in Figure 12 is located along the prominent drainage at the bottom of the map. Diamonds and crosses indicate marker beds within subunits Dl_2 and Dl_1, respectively, shown on Figure 12. EW arrows indicate the location of the cross section shown on Figure 14.

tains area (Burchfiel, 1969; Snow unpublished mapping) has revealed no evidence to suggest any pre-extensional structure other than roughly planar strata, although the precise initial geometry of the Tin Mountain rollover is not well constrained. Nonetheless, these considerations indicate that, in both cases, the geometry observed at the surface imposes severe constraints on the geometry of faulting at depth. If the initial geometry that we propose is at least approximately correct, then the cross section and reconstruction of the Tin Mountain rollover (Fig. 15) will be geometrically homologous to the outcrop-scale rollover to at least mid-crustal depth where redistribution of mass can be accommodated by ductile flow.

The structure of the Tin Mountain rollover is relatively simple in the northern Cottonwood Mountains, as illustrated by Figure 15. However, several factors limit the resolution of structural details. Closely spaced synthetic faults on the east flank of the range have been approximated by fewer faults of greater slip (compare Fig. 8, section 2, with Fig. 15). The cross section through the rollover is located to avoid unnecessary complication by a strike-slip fault (Fig. 4) but is probably oriented oblique to the local extension direction. The generally parallel arrangement of normal faults, which is similar to the outcrop-scale rollover example, justifies the assumption of a cylindrical fault geometry and greatly reduces problems associated with balancing an obliquely oriented cross section. The exact character and location of the basal fault below the rollover is unknown since it is not exposed in the northern Cottonwood Mountains area and must be projected about 45 km north from Tucki Mountain. As pre-

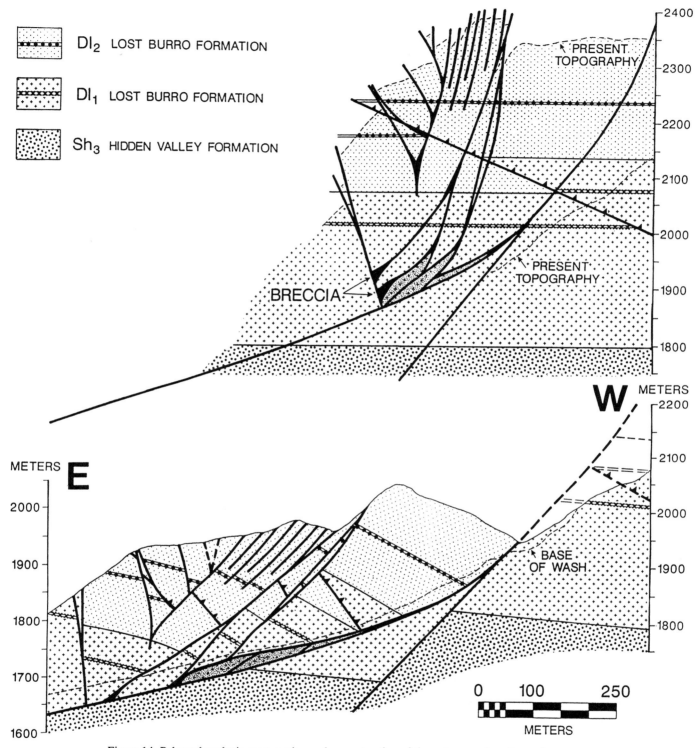

Figure 14. Balanced geologic cross section and reconstruction of the outcrop-scale rollover shown on Figure 12. Diamonds and crosses indicate marker beds within subunits Dl_2 and Dl_1, respectively, shown on Figure 12. The location of the cross-section line is between EW arrows on Figure 13.

viously discussed, however, a listric basal fault is suggested by the geometry of normal faults and fault-blocks within the northern Cottonwood Mountains area. Large-displacement normal faults at Tucki Mountain are listric, cutting strata at moderate to high angles but flattening to subparallel with bedding at structural levels deeper than about 6 to 7 km paleodepth (Wernicke and others, 1988c). The basal fault below the rollover is assumed to be planar at depth. Although some footwall deformation is probably likely (Wernicke and Axen, 1988; Wernicke and others, 1988c), it is poorly constrained at present. The resulting balanced

cross section suggests that the basal fault lies under roughly 1 to 2 km of basin fill in northern Death Valley (Fig. 15). Gravity data are interpreted as consistent with about 3 km basin fill about 20 to 30 km to the south where the valley is wider and presumably deeper (Hunt and Mabey, 1966). These limitations suggest that the balanced cross section and reconstruction of the Tin Mountain rollover (Fig. 15) are imprecise in detail but representative of the overall structure.

The balanced cross section demonstrates that the rollover model is a geometrically permissible explanation of the geology

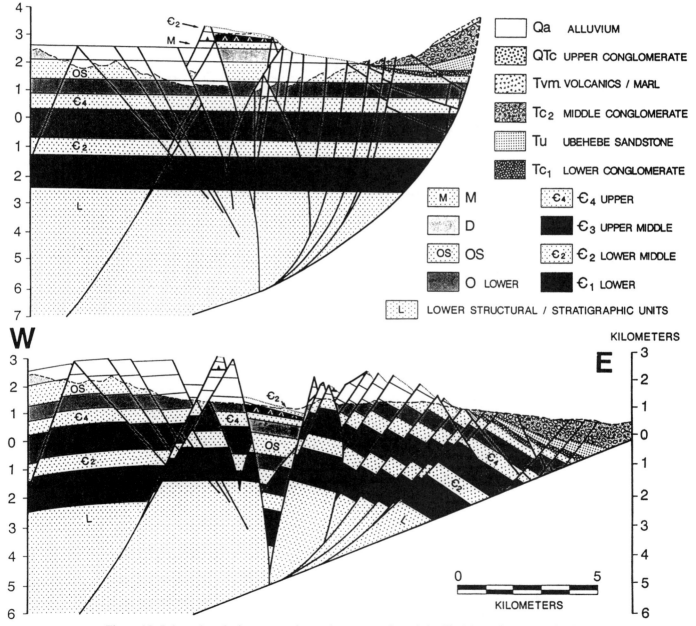

Figure 15. Balanced geologic cross section and reconstruction of the Tin Mountain rollover in the northern Cottonwood Mountains area. The cross-section line is between EW arrows on Figure 4. Compare with the outcrop-scale rollover shown on Figures 12 and 14. Note the structurally higher thrust plate (teeth on hanging wall) downdropped into the major keystone graben that forms Racetrack Valley.

exposed in the northern Cottonwood Mountains area. This model explains the morphology of the range, the geometry and distribution of faulting, the attitude of fault blocks, and the development of the Ubehebe basin. In particular, the rollover model is consistent with interepretation of Racetrack Valley as a major graben. Although Racetrack Valley can be modeled as a keystone graben above a more complex ramp-flat–style normal-fault geometry (e.g., Fig. 6 in McClay and Ellis, 1987b), the fundamental cause of this major graben appears to be an underlying bend in the basal fault. The rollover model provides a simple tectonic framework for interpreting many diverse observations in the northern Cottonwood Mountains area.

DISCUSSION

The space problem imposed by motion on a listric fault never actually occurs but is continuously accommodated within the hanging wall by the developing rollover, assuming minimal footwall deformation (Fig. 11). Sequential deformation of the reconstructed Tin Mountain rollover cross section (Fig. 16) demonstrates kinematic permissibility and provides insight into the development of the rollover. The hanging-wall flexure that defines the rollover is a direct result of a bend in the underlying basal fault, as indicated by the model cross sections. Irrespective of the precise basal fault geometry, the hanging-wall block sequentially moves over and away from the bend in the basal fault. Thus, the zone of active bending migrates through the hanging wall toward the breakaway (Fig. 1) as a continuous wave of deformation but remains fixed relative to the footwall. Antithetic faults and keystone grabens form as structures that accommodate hanging-wall bending. This results from the geometric constraint to balance deformation by bed length with minimal penetrative strain. As the zone of active bending migrates through the hanging wall, the zone of active accommodation structures also migrates toward the breakaway. Relative motion of accommodation structures during extension is away from the zone of active bending. Thus, during progressive extension, active accommodation structures are sequentially abandoned to new, mechanically more favorable accommodation structures located within the zone of active bending. This effect is illustrated on the sequentially deformed cross sections (Fig. 16) but is more complex in actuality. The curvature of the basal fault affects the width of the active bending zone, from a narrow zone above a sharp kink to a diffuse zone extending to the breakaway above a more gradual bend. Secondary faults that progressively step back from major faults (Gibbs, 1984; McClay and Ellis, 1987a, b) may obscure the dominant pattern. Nonetheless, the cessation of movement on major antithetic faults is progressively younger toward the breakaway within the rollover.

White and others (1986) modeled hanging-wall collapse by simple shear above a listric fault and concluded that, in general, planes of simple shear should be nonvertical and antithetic to the basal fault. The importance of this result is attested to by the Tin Mountain rollover, the outcrop-scale rollover, and the analog models of McClay and Ellis (1987a, b). However, the stratal

rotations that form a rollover are the product of synthetic faulting and are mitigated by antithetic faulting. Although both fault orientations have been recognized as essential parts of developing rollovers (e.g., Gibbs, 1984), McClay and Ellis (1987a, b) demonstrate with sand-box models the same relations between conjugate fault sets that are so prominantly displayed in the northern Cottonwood Mountains. Antithetic and synthetic faults are kinematically linked to form keystone grabens as the predominant mechanism to accommodate bending within a rollover. Both the Tin Mountain rollover cross sections (Fig. 16) and sand-box models (McClay and Ellis, 1987b) show the migration of keystone graben nucleation toward the breakaway with progressive extension. This migration may explain, in part, the tendency noticed by McClay and Ellis (1987a) for secondary faults to nucleate in the hanging wall of a primary fault. The striking similarities between the Tin Mountain rollover and sand-box models by no means imply that all rollovers behave analogously. The examples considered have in common an abundant supply of sediment to maintain a fairly constant load on the footwall block. An insufficient sediment supply may evoke an isostatic response from the footwall such that, in the extreme, the listric fault space problem is solved from below and a rollover never fully develops (Wernicke and Axen, 1988).

Differential rotation of strata is evident across the Tin Mountain rollover (Figs. 4, 15). However, superimposed uniform stratal tilting is probably also present. Sequentially deformed cross sections show that bending within the rollover occurs only during early motion of the hanging wall as it passes over the bend in the basal fault (cross sections a to d, Fig. 16). Differential stratal rotations within the Tin Mountain rollover end after only 5 to 10 km of extension as the hanging wall moves onto the planar part of the basal fault (cross sections e and f, Fig. 16). Even though this magnitude of offset depends on an assumed basal fault geometry, it is considerably less than the minimum offset of 20 km required of the Cottonwood Mountains block relative to Tucki Mountain. If the rollover model is correct, then faulting and tilting of younger Tertiary strata, such as the volcanics and marl or upper conglomerate (deposited during the time of cross section e, Fig. 16), is largely unrelated to development of the rollover. Basalt flows within the volcanics and marl on both the Tin Mountain and Dry Mountain blocks are faulted and show similar minor east dips, although their attitudes could be primary depositional features. The stratigraphic position of the basal Tertiary unconformity within the Cottonwood Mountains suggests that a pre-extensional 5 to 10°W dip of strata in the Dry Mountain block is permissible. Strata in the Dry Mountain block are generally flat lying at present. This may indicate minor east tilting of strata within the Dry Mountain block during extensional tectonism. However, the location of the Dry Mountain block west of the rollover and the main keystone graben precludes tilting associated with the rollover. These arguments point to roughly uniform east tilting of the entire northern Cottonwood Mountains area after development of the Tin Mountain rollover. East tilting of this magnitude could easily be accommodated by domino-style

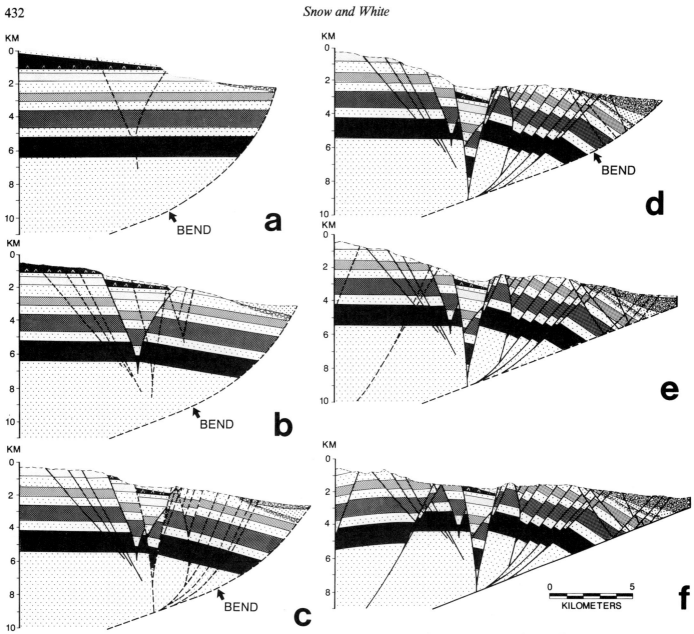

Figure 16. Sequential deformation of the reconstructed Tin Mountain rollover cross section on Figure 15. See Figure 15 for stratigraphic key. Dashed lines indicate active or incipient normal faults. Solid lines indicate inactive normal faults or thrust faults (teeth on hanging wall). Topographic profile on cross sections a–e is inferred. Note that keystone grabens tend to nucleate roughly above the bend in the basal listric fault.

extension (e.g., Wernicke and Burchfiel, 1982) of the rollover by planar normal faults (cross section e, Fig. 16), perhaps kinematically related to coeval extension west of Dry Mountain in the Saline Valley area (Burchfiel and others, 1987).

The age of the Tin Mountain rollover is difficult to determine at present. A pre–middle Pliocene age is suggested by the 4-Ma(?) age of basalt in the volcanics and marl and by arguments suggesting that basalt deposition occurred largely after formation of the rollover. Tuff beds in the upper part of the Ubehebe sandstone predate the beginning of major synthetic faulting of the Tin Mountain block (cross section b, Fig. 16) and thus provide a

lower bound on the age of the rollover. A large part of the pre–middle Pliocene Nova basin (Burchfiel and others, 1987; Hodges and others, 1989), located along the east side of the southern Cottonwood Mountains about 40 km south of the Ubehebe basin (Fig. 2), also rests structurally above the Cottonwood Mountains block in the hanging wall of the Tucki Mountain normal fault system. Within the southern Cottonwood Mountains, the pattern of normal faulting and the rollover of bedding attitudes from moderately to steeply east-dipping along the eastern flank of the range to subhorizontal along the range-crest to the west indicates that, although considerably more complicated than in the northern part of the range, the Tin Mountain rollover apparently continues to the south to dominate the structure of the entire range. The similar structural positions of the Ubehebe and Nova basins above a common basement block suggest that tuff beds in the Ubehebe sandstone may be correlative with upper Miocene volcanic units in the lower part of the Nova Formation (Burchfiel and others, 1987; Hopper, 1947). This is supported by the similarity of a distinctive 3.7±? Ma tuff (E. W. Hildreth, unpublished data), located in the middle part of the Nova Formation, with the post–4 Ma(?) Mesquite Spring tuff, located in the Ubehebe basin within the volcanics and marl. Thus, within the limits of available data, the Tin Mountain rollover appears to have formed largely during late Miocene to early Pliocene time. Although poorly constrained at present, these correlations can be tested with additional work on the geochronology of volcanic rocks in the Ubehebe and Nova basins.

SUMMARY

The Cottonwood Mountains form part of the boundary between a large, relatively stable terrain to the west and the highly extended Death Valley area to the east. We interpret the structure of the northern Cottonwood Mountains as a monoclinal flexure or rollover caused by motion above the northward projection of the northwest-directed Tucki Mountain normal fault system. This interpretation provides a simple tectonic framework for many diverse geological observations previously difficult to explain.

The juxtaposition of different Mesozoic thrust plates during Tertiary extension has disguised the structural simplicity of the rollover. Normal movement on the Ubehebe Crater fault has dropped the hanging wall of the Ubehebe thrust down against structurally lower strata. The large stratigraphic throw, regional structural position, and style of the Ubehebe thrust suggest that it is correlative with the Last Chance thrust. Stratigraphic and structural correlations across the northern Racetrack Valley indicate that the Racetrack thrust does not root in the northern Racetrack Valley. Normal faulting has produced an apparent thrust relation along both sides of the northern Racetrack Valley. We suggest that the Racetrack thrust is a minor duplex slice overlying parts of the Cottonwood Mountains but only locally exposed below the Last Chance allochthon. We interpret Racetrack Valley as a major keystone graben within the rollover and assign Lower Cambrian strata exposed within the northern Racetrack Valley to the Ubehebe/Last Chance thrust plate. Thus, we view the Tin Mountain and Dry Mountain blocks as parts of a single Mesozoic structural block that, together with Racetrack Valley, simply define the Tin Mountain rollover with a major keystone graben in the northern Cottonwood Mountains area.

Tertiary deposits of the Ubehebe basin, comprising lower conglomerate, Ubehebe sandstone, middle conglomerate, volcanics and marl, and upper conglomerate units, record the effects of extensional tectonism in the northern Cottonwood Mountains. Stratigraphic measurements and correlations of these strata constrain motion on the Ubehebe fault, indicate the inception of major synthetic normal faulting, and show progressive rotation of

the eastern flank of the range around a horizontal axis trending about N25°W. Palinspastic cross sections and unconformity relations indicate that the Tin Mountain rollover began forming after the deposition of tuff beds in the upper part of the Ubehebe sandstone. Differential stratal rotations within the rollover ceased largely prior to the deposition of middle Pliocene(?) basalt flows in the volcanics and marl, although extension of the area continued. The apparent age of the Ubehebe basin and its structural position above the eastern flank of the Cottonwood Mountains in the hanging wall of the northward projection of the Tucki Mountain fault system imply that deposits in the Ubehebe basin and Upper Miocene to Pliocene strata in the Nova basin are partially correlative. A first-order restoration of extension since late Miocene time in the Death Valley region places the northern Cottonwood Mountains proximal to exposures of Oligocene conglomerate in the southern Grapevine and Funeral Mountains. These conglomerates may be the source of distinctive, moderately to highly spherical cobbles found in the middle conglomerate of the Ubehebe basin that have no known local source. Correlations of Ubehebe basin strata, both internally and with strata in other areas, constitute important constraints on regional tectonic reconstructions.

The Tin Mountain rollover is a well-exposed example of a structure most often described from seismic data or analog models. Sequentially deformed, balanced, palinspastic cross sections, constrained by geologic mapping and stratigraphic data, suggest that antithetic faults and keystone grabens are the predominate means of accommodating bending within the rollover. Keystone grabens, formed by conjugate faults, appear to nucleate above areas of maximum curvature on the listric basal fault. The nucleation of progressively younger keystone grabens migrates toward the breakaway within the rollover during extension yet remains fixed relative to the footwall in the model cross sections. Once extension has progressed far enough, differential rotation of hanging-wall strata ceases as the rollover moves onto the planar part of the basal fault. We interpret tilting of younger Tertiary strata in the northern Cottonwood Mountains area as uniform tilting caused by domino-style extension on planar normal faults that were active after formation of the rollover. The cross sections suggest that the progressive development of the Tin Mountain rollover is a direct consequence of the initial listric geometry of the underlying Tucki Mountain normal fault system.

ACKNOWLEDGMENTS

This research was supported by National Science Foundation grants EAR-86-17869 and EAR-84-51181; grants from the Exxon Production Research Company, the Shell Foundation, and Texaco Incorporated awarded to Brian Wernicke; and by grants from the Harvard University Earth and Planetary Sciences Department awarded to Kent Snow. We have benefited from discussions with Gary Axen, Bryan Kriens, and Brian Wernicke and thank Dave Diamond, Ray Ingersoll, and Jack Stewart for careful and thought-provoking reviews. Their comments have helped us substantially improve this manuscript.

APPENDIX 1

TERTIARY STRATIGRAPHY of the northern Cottonwood Mountains: descriptions of measured sections. See also Figure 5, Figure 6, and Plate 1.

1. Tin Mountain 15′ Quadrangle; 6.36 km S, 4.15 km E of NW corner; 6/4/87-1.

Ubehebe sandstone, subunit 1:

A.

lithic wacke, grayish yellow-green (5GY 7/2), weathers olive-gray (5Y 4/1) and moderate reddish orange; fine grained, subangular, low sphericity clasts with coarse pebbly layers; moderately to poorly sorted; well cemented; poorly defined medium bedding; conformable basal contact; weathers to form slope.

lower conglomerate:

~575 ft
~175 m

conglomerate, red-brown to yellow-gray, weathers same; fine to coarse grained, subrounded to subangular, moderate sphericity matrix with cobble- to boulder-sized, subangular to angular, high sphericity clasts; poorly sorted; clast supported; clasts composed of dolomite (~40%), limestone (~10%), vitreous white quartzite from Ordovician Eureka Quartzite (~15%), black chert (~10%), mudstone (~5%), sandstone from Devonian Lost Burro Fm., Lippencott Member (~2%), and purple quartzite (~10%); clasts of chert, mudstone, and quartzite increase in proportion upward; well cemented; medium bedded contacts are conformable; weathers to form resistant hills; faulted section, thickness estimated.

Wood Canyon Formation

2. Tin Mountain 15′ Quadrangle; 4.8 km E, 5.75 km S of NW corner; 5/27/87.

volcanics and marl:

~200 ft
~61 m

basalt, thick desert varnished surface; slightly vesicular, chilled margin at base with pebbly texture, boulder-size blocks found above chilled zone; composed of plagioclase (~75%), clinopyroxene (~15%), and olivine (~10%) with interstitial texture.

Ubehebe sandstone, subunit 3:

K.
95 ft
29 m

lithic wacke, light brownish gray (5YR 6/1), weathers greenish gray (5GY 6/1); medium to coarse grained, subangular, low sphericity clasts with finer grained interbeds; moderately sorted, interbeds are well sorted; contains some biotite; moderately cemented, interbeds are well cemented and resistant; medium bedded, resistant ledges occur every 5 m and are up to 40 cm thick; resistant beds are not laterally continuous; contact with basalt is unconformable; unit weathers to form a slope.

J.
35 ft
10.6 m

tuff, white grading to pink at top, weathers same; fine grained matrix with phenocrysts of sanidine, biotite, and quartz and green mudstone rip-up clasts; well lithified; massive unit; sharp contact with overlying unit; weathers to form a resistant ledge.

Ubehebe sandstone, subunit 2:

I.
140 ft
42.6 m

lithic wacke, light brownish gray (5YR 6/1), weathers white (N9) at base, pale olive gray (5Y 6/1) throughout, with interbeds of pale red (10R 6/2), red-brown (5R 6/2) layer at top; medium grained, subangular to angular, low sphericity clasts with granular to coarse grained layer at base and coarser grained interbeds; moderately to poorly sorted; contains some biotite; moderately cemented with well cemented resistant interbeds; medium to very thickly bedded; sharp and conformable contact with tuff defined by a resistant ledge; weathers to slope with resistant ledges throughout.

Offset in section—overlying unit measured about 30 ft/9 m south of underlying units.

H.
150 ft
45.7 m

lithic sandstone, light brownish gray (5YR 6/1), weathers pale red (10R 6/2) to grayish brown-yellow (5Y 8/1), pale red (5R 6/2) at base; medium grained, angular to subangular, low sphericity clasts with coarse grained pebbly layers; moderately to poorly sorted; contains biotite and pebbles of carbonate, chert, quartzite, mudstone, and sandstone; well cemented interbeds in moderately cemented unit; medium bedded with thin interbeds, occasional planar cross bedding; conformable and sharp contact with overlying unit; weathers to form steep slope with resistant ledges.

G.
50 ft
15.2 m

lithic wacke, greenish gray (5GY 6/1), weathers grayish yellow-green (5GY 7/2) to light olive-gray (5Y 6/1); fine to coarse grained, subangular, low sphericity clasts; moderately to poorly sorted; contains some biotite; well cemented resistant bed at top of unit, poorly cemented at base; thickly bedded but poorly defined; sharp contact with overlying unit; weathers to form slope with resistant ledges.

Offset in section—overlying unit measured about 50 ft/15 m north of underlying unit.

F.
40 ft
12 m

lithic sandstone, pale red (10R 6/2), weathers pale red-gray (5R 6/2); medium to coarse grained, subangular, low sphericity clasts; moderately to poorly sorted; biotite rich; moderately cemented, well-cemented resistant ledge toward top; medium bedded; sharp and conformable contacts; weathers to form slope with resistant ledge.

E.
30 ft
9 m

lithic wacke, light olive-gray (5Y 5/2), weathers yellowish gray (5Y 7/2) to pale olive (5Y 6/2); fine to coarse grained, subangular, low sphericity clasts; well sorted at base, poorly sorted at top; biotite rich; moderately cemented; medium bedded; sharp and conformable contacts; weathers to form slope.

D.
35 ft
10.6 m

lithic wacke, white (N9), weathers pale red (5R 6/2); medium-coarse grained, subangular, low sphericity clasts; moderately sorted; biotite rich; moderately cemented with resistant, well-cemented layers at top; medium bedded; sharp and conformable contacts; weathers to form slope with ledges toward top.

Offset in section—overlying units measured about 20 ft/6 m south of underlying units.

C.
75 ft
23 m

lithic wacke, light brownish gray (5YR 6/1), weathers alternately pale red (5R 6/2) and pale olive-gray (5Y 6/2) to yellowish gray-green (5GY 7/2); silty to medium grained, subangular to rounded, low sphericity clasts with coarse pebbly beds at base; poorly sorted at base grading to moderately sorted at top; contains biotite and pebbles of mudstone, quartzite, and carbonates; well cemented with resistant interbeds containing cobbles of siltstone concretions; thinly to medium bedded; sharp and conformable contacts; weathers to form resistant slope.

Ubehebe sandstone, subunit 1:

B.
25 ft
7.6 m

lithic wacke, olive-gray (5Y 4/1), weathers pale green (10Y 6/2) to light olive-gray (5Y 5/2) to grayish yellow-green (5GY 7/2); fine grained, subangular, low sphericity clasts with coarse pebbly beds at base; poorly sorted; biotite rich with pebbles of quartzite, chert, mudstone, and carbonate; moderately cemented, resistant at base; medium bedded; sharp and conformable contacts; weathers to form a slope.

Offset in section—overlying units measured about 20 ft/6 m south of underlying units.

A.
215 ft
65.5 m

lithic wacke, grayish yellow-green (5GY 7/2), weathers olive-gray (5Y 4/1) and moderate reddish orange; fine grained, subangular, low sphericity clasts with coarse pebbly layers; moderately to poorly sorted; contains biotite and pebbles of carbonate, quartzite, and sandstone; well cemented; poorly defined medium bedding; conformable contacts; sharp contact with overlying unit, obscured basal contact; weathers to form slope and resistant ridge.

Offset in section—overlying units measured about 30 ft/9 m north of underlying units.

lower conglomerate:

conglomerate, moderate reddish orange (10R 6/10), weathers same; very fine to medium grained matrix with granule-to cobble-sized, subangular, low sphericity clasts; clast supported; poorly sorted; clasts composed of dolomite, limestone, sandstone, quartzite, chert, and mudstone; well cemented; poorly bedded; contact with upper unit is obscured but appears conformable; weathers to form a fairly resistant slope.

3. Tin Mountain 15′ Quadrangle; 5.65 km S, 5.53 km E of NW corner; 5/29/87-1.

Ubehebe sandstone, subunit 3:

Q.
>20 ft
>6 m

lithic wacke, light brownish gray (10YR 6/1), weathers pale olive (10YR 6/2) to light purple-gray (5RP 6/2); fine grained, subangular, low sphericity clasts grading to coarse and pebbly toward top; well sorted grading to poorly sorted at top; biotite rich with pebbles of shale, quartzite, chert, granitoids, mudstone, and carbonate; moderately cemented with well-cemented resistant ledges; medium bedded; fault at top of section; weathers to form slope with resistant ledges toward top.

P.
35 ft
10.6 m

siliceous lithic wacke, light gray to gray-brown at top, weathers pale gray-green (5GY 6/2) to pale red-brown and white; fine to coarse grained, subangular, low sphericity clasts; moderately sorted; contains biotite and concretions of altered tuff (?); moderately cemented with well-cemented, cherty and silty mudstone layers in middle of unit; medium bedded; contact at top is sharp and conformable, basal contact is gradational; weathers to form steep slope with resistant ledges.

O.
20 ft
6 m

lithic sandstone and conglomerate, light olive-gray (5Y 5/2) to grayish orange (10YR 7/4) at base, pale red (10R 5/4) at top, weathers same; fine to medium grained, subangular, low sphericity clasts at base grading to cobble-sized, subrounded, moderate sphericity clasts at top; moderately sorted; biotite rich with pebbles and cobbles of shale, quartzite, chert, white tuff, pink tuff, carbonate, and mudstone; conglomerate is clast supported; moderately cemented at base, conglomerate is poorly cemented; base is medium bedded, conglomerate is poorly bedded; top of unit grades into overlying unit, basal contact is sharp and conformable; weathers to form slope with resistant ledge of conglomerate.

Offset in section—overlying unit measured 30 ft/9 m south of underlying unit.

N.
40 ft
12.2 m

siliceous lithic sandstone, light brownish gray to grayish white, weathers light gray; fine to medium grained, subangular, low sphericity clasts; poorly sorted; biotite rich with tuffaceous bands and chert nodules, some quartz (sanidine?) phenocrysts; poorly cemented with ledges of resistant altered tuff; thinly bedded; basal contact is gradational, contact at top is sharp and conformable; weathers to form resistant slope with recessive interbeds.

M.
37 ft
11.3 m

lithic sandstone, gray green-brown (5Y 6/2), weathers light gray-green to grayish white; medium to coarse grained, subangular, low sphericity clasts; moderately sorted; biotite rich with abundant plant fragments at the top; resistant at base and top, recessive in middle; poorly bedded; gradual contacts to top and bottom; weathers to form slope.

L.
40 ft
12.2 m

tuff, white grading to pale pink, gray-green at top, weathers same; fine grained matrix with quartz, sanidine, and biotite phenocrysts and mudstone rip-up clasts; well lithified and resistant; massive but grades to thinly bedded at top; sharp contact with basal unit; weathers to form massive resistant ledge.

K.
80 ft
24.4 m

lithic wacke, grayish olive-brown (5Y 6/1), weathers same; medium to coarse grained, subangular, low sphericity clasts; biotite rich; recessive and poorly cemented with resistant interbeds; medium to thickly bedded; sharp contact at top and gradational contact at base; weathers to form a recessive slope.

J.
40 ft
12.2 m

tuff, white, weathers same; fine grained matrix with phenocrysts and green mudstone rip-up clasts; well-lithified; massive; sharp basal contact; weathers to form a resistant ledge; composed of glass shards (~90%) and phenocrysts of sanidine (~60%), plagioclase (~25%), biotite (~10%), and quartz (~5%).

Ubehebe sandstone, subunit 2:

I.
>120 ft
>36.6 m

lithic wacke, light gray-white to light olive-gray, weathers dusky gray (5YR 8/1); coarse grained, subangular, low sphericity clasts at base grade upward to medium grained; pebbly at base; contains biotite; poorly cemented with well-cemented interbeds; medium bedding; sharp contact at top; base of unit is covered; weathers to form a slope.

4. Tin Mountain 15′ Quadrangle; 4.55 km, E, 3.3 km S of NW corner; 6/2/87-1.

volcanics and marl:

marl, white to gray, weathers same; fine grained; porous texture; very well cemented; thickly bedded with wavy bedding planes; 15 ft/4.5 m of basalt pinches out below marl south of section; weathers to form a resistant ledge.

Ubehebe sandstone, subunit 3:

R.
40 ft
12.2 m

lithic wacke, gray to light gray-green, weathers pale olive to grayish yellow-green; fine to medium grained, subangular, low sphericity clasts; contains biotite; poorly cemented; medium bedded, upper contact defined by angular unconformity; weathers to form a recessive slope.

Q.
70 ft
21.3 m

lithic wacke, greenish gray, weathers pale olive; medium to coarse grained, rounded to subangular, low sphericity clasts with pebbly beds; contains biotite and pebbles of carbonate, mudstone, chert, quartzite, granitoids, tuff, and sandstone; base of unit is conglomerate with medium to coarse grained matrix and cobble-sized clasts; moderately cemented with well-cemented coarser beds; medium bedded with thin coarser interbeds; contacts are sharp and conformable; weathers to form a resistant slope.

Offset in section—overlying units measured about 50 ft/15.2 m south of underlying units.

P.
45 ft
13.7 m

lithic wacke, yellowish gray, weathers moderate brown and gray; medium grained, rounded to subangular, low sphericity clasts with coarser interbeds; contains biotite; moderately cemented with resistant interbeds; medium bedded; contacts are conformable and sharp; weathers to form a slope.

O.
40 ft
12.2 m

lithic sandstone, gray-white, weathers light brownish gray; medium to granule sized, rounded to subangular, low sphericity clasts; pebble conglomerate at top; contains biotite and clasts of tuff, granitoids, mudstone, sandstone, quartzite, chert, and carbonate; poorly cemented at base, resistant and well cemented at top; medium bedded; contacts are sharp and conformable; weathers to form slope with resistant ledges at top.

N.
35 ft
10.6 m

lithic sandstone, light gray, weathers light brownish gray; medium grained, subangular, low sphericity clasts; contains biotite, layers of altered tuff, and chert nodules; well cemented with resistant layers; medium bedded; contacts are sharp and conformable; weathers to form a resistant slope.

M.
35 ft
10.6 m

lithic wacke, white, weathers light gray; fine to medium grained; subangular, low sphericity clasts; contains biotite; poorly cemented; medium bedded; contacts are sharp and conformable; weathers to form recessive slope.

L.
~40 ft
~12.2 m

tuff, white grading to pink, weathers same; fine grained, slightly vesicular matrix with phenocrysts and mudstone rip-up clasts; well lithified; massive; contacts sharp and conformable at top, faulted at base; weathers to form a resistant ledge; composed of glass shards (~70%) and phenocrysts of sanidine (~50%), plagioclase (~25%), biotite (~15%), and quartz (~10%).

K.
>35 ft
>10.6 m

lithic wacke, yellowish gray, weathers pale olive-gray with pale brown interbeds; fine to coarse grained, subangular, low sphericity clasts; biotite rich; poorly cemented with resistant interbeds; medium bedded; contact at base is sharp and conformable, faulted at top; weathers to form a slope.

J.
30 ft
9.1 m

tuff, white, weathers same; fine grained, slightly vesicular matrix with phenocrysts and green mudstone rip-up clasts; well lithified; massive; sharp conformable contacts; weathers to form a resistant slope; composed of glass shards (~90%) and phenocrysts of sanidine (~60%), plagioclase (~25%), biotite (~10%), and quartz (~5%).

Offset in section—overlying unit measured about 20 ft/6 m south of underlying unit.

Ubehebe sandstone, subunit 2:

I.
140 ft
42.7 m

lithic wacke, light brownish gray, weathers pale olive and pale red; fine to medium grained, subangular, low sphericity clasts with coarse and pebbly interbeds; contains biotite and pebbles of black dolomite, quartzite, chert, granitoids, sandstone, and mudstone; poorly cemented with resistant coarser beds; medium to thickly bedded; contacts are sharp and conformable; weathers to form slope.

H.
135 ft
41 m

lithic wacke, light brownish gray, weathers pale red; fine to coarse grained, subangular to angular, low sphericity clasts with granule- to pebble-sized conglomerate interbeds; contains biotite and clasts of chert, quartzite, granitoid, sandstone, and mudstone; moderately cemented with resistant conglomerate layers; medium bedded; contacts are sharp and conformable; weathers to form a steep, slightly resistant, slope.

E.F.G.
100 ft
30.5 m

lithic wacke, yellowish gray, pale red, or light brownish gray, weathers light grayish brown, grayish orange-pink, and pale olive-gray; fine to medium grained, subangular, low sphericity clasts; contains biotite; moderately cemented; medium bedded; contacts are sharp and conformable; weathers to form a recessive slope.

D.
>45 ft
>13.7 m

lithic wacke, pale red to light grayish green, weathers light olive-gray, white at top; fine grained, subangular, low sphericity clasts grade upward to coarse grained; contains biotite; moderately cemented becoming more resistant toward top; medium to thickly bedded; contact at top is sharp and conformable; base of section is obscured.

5. Tin Mountain 15′ Quadrangle; 2.92 km S, 4.83 km E of NW corner; 6/2/87-2.

middle conglomerate

conglomerate, moderate reddish brown (10R 4/6), weathers same; coarse grained, subangular to rounded matrix with pebble- to cobble-sized, subrounded to well-rounded, moderate to high sphericity clasts; coarse grained, pebbly, sandstone at base; highly spherical cobbles more abundant above basal sandstone; clast supported; clasts composed of granitoids, quartzite, sandstone, mudstone, and carbonate; very well lithified; medium to thickly bedded; basal contact is an angular unconformity.

Ubehebe sandstone, subunit 4:

V.
~120 ft
~36.5 m
lithic wacke, light gray-brown, weathers gray-green; medium grained, subangular, low sphericity clasts; moderately well sorted; contains biotite; moderately cemented; poorly thick bedded; upper contact is unconformable, basal contact is conformable; weathers to form a slope.

U.
~120 ft
~36.5 m
tuff, white, weathers same; fine grained matrix with subangular, low sphericity lithic clasts and phenocrysts of biotite, hornblende, and sanidine; moderately lithified, slightly recessive; massive; contacts are obscured; weathers to form a slope.

T.
40 ft
12.2 m
lithic wacke, light gray-brown, weathers same; fine to medium grained, subangular, low sphericity clasts; moderately well sorted; contains biotite; poorly cemented; medium bedded; contacts are sharp and conformable; weathers to form recessive slope.

S.
~50 ft
~15.2 m
conglomerate and lithic wacke, light brownish gray, weathers same; conglomerate has a coarse- to granule-sized matrix with cobble-sized, round to subangular, moderately sphericity clasts; interbedded with pebbly wacke of medium to coarse, round to subangular, moderate sphericity clasts; poorly sorted; clasts composed of chert, black dolomite, granitoids, quartzite, mudstone, and sandstone; moderately well cemented; medium bedded; upper contact is conformable; lower contact is unconformable; weathers to form a resistant slope.

Ubehebe sandstone, subunit 3:

R.
115 ft
35 m
lithic wacke, gray to light gray-green, weathers pale olive to grayish yellow-green; fine to medium grained, subangular, low sphericity clasts; moderately sorted; contains biotite; poorly cemented; medium bedded but poorly defined; upper contact is disconformable, lower contact is conformable with underlying greenish gray, medium to coarse grained, pebbly sandstone; weathers to form recessive slope.

6. Tin Mountain 15′ Quadrangle; 5.15 km S, 6.5 km E of NW corner; 6/1/87.

volcanics and marl:

>80 ft
>24 m
limestone, white to gray to light brown, weathers same; fine grained; porous, vesicular texture; very well cemented; poorly bedded; contains plant fragments; basal contact is sharp and conformable; weathers to form a resistant cliff.

15 ft
4.5 m
basalt, desert varnished surface; slightly vesicular; boulder-size blocks.

middle conglomerate:

30 ft
9.1 m
sandstone and conglomerate, moderate reddish brown (10R 4/6), weathers same; coarse grained, pebbly sandstone in lower half; upper half is conglomerate with coarse grained, subangular to rounded matrix and pebble- to cobble-sized, subrounded to well-rounded, moderate to high sphericity clasts; clast supported; clasts composed of granitoids, quartzite, carbonate, siltstone, sandstone, and chert; very well lithified; medium to thickly bedded; contacts are unconformable; weathers to form resistant cliff.

Ubehebe sandstone, subunit 4:

X.
>30 ft
>9.1 m
lithic wacke, gray-green, weathers same; medium grained, subangular, low sphericity clasts; pebbly layer at base; moderately sorted; contains biotite; moderately cemented; thick bedded but poorly defined; upper contact is unconformable, lower contact is conformable; weathers to form a slightly recessive slope.

W.
45 ft
13.7 m
lithic sandstone, moderate reddish orange, gray at top, weathers same; fine to medium grained, subangular, low sphericity clasts; coarse and pebbly at top; moderately sorted; contains biotite; moderately cemented; medium bedded; contacts are conformable; weathers to form a slope with resistant ledge at top.

Offset in section—overlying unit measured 10 ft/3 m north of underlying unit.

V.
60 ft
18.3 m
lithic wacke, light gray-brown, weathers same; fine to medium grained, subangular, low sphericity clasts grading upward to coarse grained; cobble conglomerate at top; poorly sorted, clast supported; subrounded to subangular, low sphericity clasts; contains clasts of gray carbonate, chert, quartzite, mudstone, and granitoids; contains biotite; moderately cemented; medium bedded; sharp, conformable contacts; weathers to form slightly recessive slope with resistant ledge at top.

U.
30 ft
9.1 m
tuff, white, weathers same; fine grained matrix with subangular, low sphericity lithic clasts and phenocrysts; moderately lithified; poorly bedded; sharp and conformable contacts; weathers to form a slightly recessive slope; composed of glass shards (~40%) and phenocrysts of sanidine (~40%), plagioclase (~25%), biotite (~15%), and hornblende (~10%), with volcanic lithic clasts (~10%).

Offset in section—overlying unit measured 20 ft/6 m north of underlying unit.

T.
30 ft
9.1 m
lithic wacke, white to grayish green, weathers gray; fine to medium grained, subangular, low sphericity clasts; moderately sorted; contains biotite; moderately cemented with well-cemented coarse pebbly layer in middle; medium bedded; sharp and conformable contacts; weathers to form a recessive slope with resistant ledge in middle.

S.
130 ft
39.6 m

lithic sandstone and conglomerate, light gray-brown, weathers same; sandstone has medium to coarse grained, subrounded to subangular, moderate sphericity clasts; conglomerate; poorly sorted, clast supported; contains biotite and clasts of gray carbonate, chert, quartzite, mudstone, granitoids, biotite bearing sandstone, and black dolomite; well cemented; medium bedded; sharp conformable contact at top, unconformity at base; weathers to form slightly resistant slope.

7. Tin Mountain 15′ Quadrangle; 5.23 km S, 6.52 km E of NW corner; 5/28/87-2.

upper conglomerate:

conglomerate, pale yellowish brown (10YR 6/7), weathers same; coarse- to granule-sized matrix with cobble- to boulder-sized, subrounded to highly rounded, low to high sphericity clasts; very poorly sorted; clast supported; well cemented; clasts composed of quartzite, limestone, dolomite, basalt, and sandstone; massive; well cemented and resistant; basal contact is an unconformity, the underlying Mesquite Spring tuff pinches out to the north; weathers to form a resistant slope.

middle conglomerate, upper subunit:

1200 ft
365 m

conglomerate and sandstone, dusky yellow (5Y 6/4), weathers same; conglomerate has medium- to granule-sized, subangular to subrounded, moderate sphericity matrix with pebble- to cobble-sized, well-rounded, high sphericity clasts, some small boulders; interbedded sandstone has medium to coarse grained, subangular to subrounded, moderate sphericity clasts; poorly sorted; clast supported; clasts composed of granitoids, mudstone, quartzite, sandstone, biotite bearing wacke, carbonate, and chert; very well lithified with less resistant interbeds of sandstone; medium to thickly bedded; lower contact is gradational, upper contact is unconformity below upper conglomerate; weathers to form resistant hills; thickness approximate, palinspastically corrected for minor faulting (see Fig. 7).

middle conglomerate, lower subunit:

1905 ft
580 m

conglomerate, moderate reddish brown (10R 4/6), weathers same; coarse grained, subangular to rounded matrix with pebble- to cobble-sized, subrounded to well-rounded, moderate to high sphericity clasts; coarse- to granule-sized, pebbly sandstone at base and top; high sphericity cobbles more abundant in lower part; clast supported; clasts composed of granitoids (~20%), vitreous white quartzite derived from Ordovician Eureka Quartzite (~10%), purple quartzite derived (?) from Cambrian Wood Canyon Fm (~10%), carbonate (~30%), siltstone (~5%), sandstone (~5%), chert (~5%), tuff (~5%), and greenish quartzite (~5%); very well lithified; medium to thickly bedded; basal contact is an angular unconformity; contact at top is conformable and gradational; weathers to form resistant hills; thickness approximate, palinspastically corrected for minor faulting (see Fig. 7).

Ubehebe sandstone, subunit 4:

X.

lithic wacke, gray-green, weathers same; medium grained, subangular, low sphericity clasts; moderately sorted; con-

tains biotite; moderately cemented; thick bedded but poorly defined; upper contact is unconformable; weathers to form a slightly recessive slope.

8 and 9. Tin Mountain 15′ Quadrangle; 7.1 km S, 6.15 km E, and 7.1 km S, 6.45 km E of NW corner; 5/21/87-1 and 2, respectively.

lower conglomerate:

conglomerate, moderate reddish brown (10R 4/6), weathers light brown (5YR 5/6); medium grained, subangular, high sphericity matrix with pebble- to cobble-sized, subangular, low sphericity clasts; very poorly sorted becoming moderately sorted toward top, sandy interbeds found toward top; clast supported; clasts composed of quartzite, sandstone, dolomite, chert, and siltstone; well cemented and resistant; bedding is medium to massive, slight imbrication of clasts; weathers to form resistant hills.

10 and 11. Tin Mountain 15′ Quadrangle; 7.15 km S, 7.9 km E and 7.0 km S, 8.2 km E of NW corner, 5/21/87-3 and 4, respectively.

middle conglomerate:

conglomerate and interbedded sandstone, reddish orange (10R 6/6), weathers moderate reddish brown (10R 4/6); matrix and sandstone have coarse- to granule-size, subrounded grains; conglomerate clasts are pebble- to cobble-sized, subrounded, and have high sphericity; sandstone is moderately sorted, conglomerate is poorly sorted and clast supported; clasts composed of granitoids, shale, sandstone, limestone, dolomite, quartzite, and mudstone; well cemented; medium to thick bedded, sandstone is cross-bedded; erosional surfaces between conglomerate and sandstone are common; weathers to form resistant hills.

12-1. Tin Mountain 15′ Quadrangle; 6.7 km S, 9.3 km E of NW corner; 5/22/87-7 and 8.

volcanics and marl, Mesquite Spring tuff:

~25 ft
~7.6 m

tuff, white, weathers same; clasts are granule- to pebble-sized, angular, low sphericity pumice lapilli; poorly sorted; porous texture with large holes; well cemented but friable; massive but slightly bedded at base; contact with conglomerate at base is erosional; weathers to form a moderately resistant ledge; composed of >90% pumice lapilli with a randomly oriented foliation of stretched vesicles, lapilli are not flattened but some are bent against adjacent clasts, most show abraded edges; phenocrysts are sanidine (~40–90%), plagioclase (~5–40%), biotite (~5–10%), and hornblende (~0–5%) with volcanic (~0–5%) and sedimentary (~0–5%) lithic clasts; pumice lapilli and sanidine appear to increase upward; lithic clasts, hornblende, plagioclase, and glass shards appear to decrease upward.

Offset in section—overlying unit measured at: Tin Mountain 15′ Quadrangle; 6.52 km S, 9.4 km E of NW corner.

volcanics and marl:

37 ft
11.2 m

conglomerate, pale yellowish brown (10YR 6/7), weathers same; coarse- to granule-sized matrix with cobble- to boulder-sized, subrounded to highly rounded, low to high sphericity clasts; very poorly sorted; clast supported; well cemented; clasts composed of quartzite, limestone, dolomite, basalt, and sandstone; massive; intercalated with beds of caliche; base is 2 ft/0.6 m caliche bed, white, weathers same; fine grained; well cemented and resistant; basal contact covered, upper contact is conformable; weathers to form a resistant slope.

12.2. Tin Mountain 15′ Quadrangle; 6.7 km S, 8.6 km E of NW corner; 5/22/87-1.

volcanics and marl:
    basalt, thick desert varnished surface; slightly vesicular, chilled margin at base with pebbly texture, boulder-size blocks found above chilled zone.

10 ft
3 m
    caliche and marl, white to gray, weathers same; fine grained, chalky; fossilized plant fragments at top; porous texture; very well cemented; thickly bedded with wavy bedding planes; contacts with upper and lower unit are sharp and conformable; weathers to form a resistant ledge.

~2.5 ft
~0.7 m
    conglomerate, light brown (5YR 6/4); weathers same; fine to coarse, subrounded to subangular, low sphericity matrix with pebble- to cobble-sized, subangular to subrounded, low sphericity clasts; poorly to moderately sorted; clast supported; well cemented; clasts composed of quartzite, granitoids, dolomite, sandstone, limestone, and chert; medium bedded; upper contact is conformable, basal contact is angular unconformity.

middle conglomerate:
    lithic sandstone, light brown (5YR 6/4), weathers same; fine grained, subangular, low sphericity clasts; moderately sorted; moderately cemented; medium bedded; upper contact is angular unconformity, basal contact is covered; weathers to form recessive slope.

12-3. Tin Mountain 15′ Quadrangle; 6.75 km S, 8.85 km E of NW corner; 5/22/87-2 and 3.

volcanics and marl:
>44 ft
>13.3 m
    conglomerate, pale yellowish brown (10YR 6/7), weathers same; coarse- to granule-sized matrix with cobble- to boulder-sized, subrounded to rounded, low to high sphericity clasts; very poorly sorted; clast supported; well cemented; clasts composed of quartzite, limestone, dolomite, and sandstone, intercalated lenses of basalt boulders toward top; massive; basal contact is angular unconformity with sandstone; weathers to form a slope.

Offset in section—overlying unit measured at: Tin Mountain 15′ Quadrangle; 6.55 km S, 9.0 km E of NW corner.

middle conglomerate:
>90 ft
>27.5 m
    sandstone, light brown (5YR 6/4) to pale yellowish orange (10YR 8/6), weathers same; fine grained, subangular to rounded, moderate sphericity clasts with some rounded, moderate sphericity, pebbly layers; moderately sorted, poorly sorted pebbly layers; moderately well cemented; contains biotite and pebbles composed of siltstone, quartzite,

dolomite, and tuff; thinly bedded with large scale cross beds; contact with overlying conglomerate is angular unconformity, base not exposed; weathers to form a slightly recessive slope.

13. Tin Mountain 15′ Quadrangle; 9.95 km S, 9.0 km E of NW corner; 4/30/87.

middle conglomerate:
>200 ft
>61 m
    conglomerate, grading upward to sandstone, moderate reddish brown (10R 4/6), weathers same; coarse- to granule-sized matrix with cobble- to boulder-sized, rounded, high sphericity clasts; sandstone has fine, rounded, moderate sphericity clasts; spherical cobbles decrease in abundance upward; clast supported; moderately well cemented becoming friable at top; poorly sorted; clasts composed of granitoids, quartzite, and carbonates; massive to thickly bedded; lower contact is unconformable, upper limit of unit is eroded; weathers to form slightly resistant hills.

Ubehebe sandstone, subunit 3:
H.
140 ft
42.7 m
    lithic wacke, gray-green to moderate red, weathers light gray-green to moderate red; scattered pebbles and medium- to granule-sized, subangular, low sphericity clasts; poorly sorted; contains biotite and pebbles of dolomite, quartzite, and tuff; moderately cemented; medium bedded with high angle cross beds; lower contact is sharp and conformable; upper contact is defined by an unconformity with the cobble conglomerate; unit weathers to form a slightly recessive slope.

G.
35 ft
10.7 m
    conglomerate, grading upward to lithic sandstone, dusky red to pale red, weathers same; medium- to granule-sized, subangular, low sphericity matrix with cobble-sized, similar shaped clasts; grades upward to sandstone with coarse grained, similar shaped clasts; very poorly sorted; clast supported; clasts composed of tuff, quartzite, dolomite, and sandstone; well cemented and resistant; medium to thick bedded with high angle cross beds toward top; upper contact is sharp and conformable, lower contact is unconformable; weathers to form a resistant ledge.

F.
55 ft
16.7 m
    lithic wacke, pale yellowish green to grayish pink, weathers same; silty, grading upward to medium grained, subangular, low sphericity clasts; moderately sorted; contains some biotite; well cemented; medium bedded; contacts are sharp and conformable; weathers to form a resistant slope.

E.
200 ft
61 m
    tuff, grayish orange-pink (10R 8/2), weathers moderate reddish orange (10R 6/6); very fine grained matrix with medium to coarse sized phenocrysts; welded, conchoidal fracture; zenolith agglomerate bed (?) toward base of unit; massive; contact with overlying unit is conformable, basal contact is unconformable; weathers to form a resistant ledge; composed of moderately flattened glass shards (~80%) and phenocrysts of sanidine (~50%), quartz (~25%), and biotite (~15%) with glass blebs (~10%).

D.
60 ft
18.3 m
    tuff, pale pink (5RP 8/2), weathers fine; fine grained matrix with phenocrysts and mudstone rip-up clasts; moderately to well lithified; massive; unconformable with overlying unit,

basal contact is conformable and sharp; weathers to form a slightly resistant slope; composed of glass shards (~90%) and phenocrysts of sanidine (~55%), plagioclase (~30%), biotite (~10%), and quartz (~5%).

C.
40 ft
12.2 m

tuff, white grading upward to grayish pink (5R 8/2), weathers moderate pink (5R 7/4); fine grained, slightly vesicular matrix with phenocrysts and mudstone rip-up clasts; cobbles of vitreous, pale olive-gray tuff are found toward top of unit; moderately lithified; massive; contacts are sharp and conformable; weathers to form a slightly resistant ledge; composed of glass shards (~90%) and phenocrysts of sanidine (~55%), plagioclase (~30%), biotite (~10%), and quartz (~5%).

B.
20 ft
6 m

tuff, white, weathers pale green (10Y 8/2); fine grained matrix with phenocrysts of biotite, sanidine, and quartz and green mudstone rip-up clasts; moderately lithified; massive; contact with upper unit is sharp and conformable, basal contact is unconformable; weathers to form a slightly resistant ledge.

Ubehebe sandstone, subunit 2:

A.
100 ft
30.5 m

lithic sandstone, light olive-gray (5Y 6/1), weathers pale red (10R 6/2); fine grained, subangular, low sphericity clasts, very fine grained and silty at top; pebbly interbeds; moderately well sorted at base grading upward to poorly sorted; contains some biotite; moderately well cemented, some friable, interbeds, strongly cemented at top; thin to medium bedded, low angle cross bedding at base; contacts are defined by unconformities; weathers to form slopes with some prominent layers at base and top.

lower conglomerate:

>140 ft
>42.6 m

conglomerate, moderate reddish brown (10R 4/6), weathers to pale reddish brown (10R 5/4); fine to coarse grained matrix with cobble-sized, subangular to rounded, low sphericity clasts; very poorly sorted; clast supported; clasts composed of gray carbonates, quartzite, and sandstone; well cemented and resistant; base of unit is massive, grading to medium bedded toward top; contact at base is faulted; upper contact is unconformable; weathers to form resistant hills.

APPENDIX 2

DEVONIAN LOST BURRO FORMATION, LIPPENCOTT MEMBER: descriptions of stratigraphic sections measured in the Cottonwood Mountains area. See also Figures 9 and 10.

1. Last Chance Range 15′ Quadrangle; 0.2 km N, 5.72 km W of SE corner, 8/25/85.

Devonian Lost Burro Formation, Lippencott Member:

dolomite, medium dark gray, weathers same, medium light gray, and light brown; fine grained; quartzite, weathers light to moderate yellowish brown (10YR 5/2); medium grained; thickly interbedded.

D.
180 ft
55 m

calcareous quartzite, medium light gray to light gray, weathers grayish orange (10YR 7/4) to rusty; thick bedded to massive, cross-bedded at 135 ft/41 m.

C.
105 ft
32 m

dolomite, medium dark gray, weathers medium gray to brownish gray (5YR 4/1) fading to medium light gray toward top; chert, medium dark gray to dark yellowish brown (10YR 4/2); thinly interbedded dolomite with chert nodules, lenses, and beds.

B.
46 ft
14 m

dolomite, medium light gray, weathers light brownish gray (5YR 6/1) to yellowish gray (5Y 7/2) to grayish orange (10YR 7/4); fine grained and silty; chert, medium gray and brownish gray (5YR 4/1); silt decreases upward toward yellowish orange (10YR 7/6) weathering bed of chert at 34.5 ft/10.5 m; very thinly bedded dolomite interbedded with chert nodules.

Silurian Hidden Valley Formation:

A.
45 ft
14 m

dolomite, medium gray at base grading to medium brownish gray (5YR 5/1) upward, weathers yellowish gray (5YR 8/1) at base grading to grayish orange (10YR 7/4) upward; fine grained and silty; medium bedded at base grading to thinly bedded upward; weathers to form rubble-covered recessive slope.

dolomite, medium to medium dark gray, weathers medium light gray; fine grained; massive.

2. Tin Mountain 15′ Quadrangle; 14.4 km S, 1.13 km E of NW corner; 8/29/85.

Devonian Lost Burro Formation, Lippencott Member:

dolomite, medium gray, weathers medium light gray; fine grained to sandy; interbedded sandy beds decrease upward; thinly to thickly bedded.

I.
140 ft
43 m

dolomite, medium gray, weathers medium light gray; fine grained to sandy; quartzite interbeds weather rusty brown; quartzite and sandy lenses decrease upward, sand becomes less mixed with dolomite toward top; top of unit has several 3–5 ft/1–1.5 m white quartzite beds; thinly to thickly bedded.

H.
45 ft
14 m

quartzite, vitreous white; poorly medium bedded.

G.
20 ft
6 m
dolomite, medium gray, weathers same and grades to brown at top; fine grained grading upward to medium grained and sandy; quartzite at top; cross-bedded.

F.
15 ft
4.6 m
calcareous quartzite, brownish gray (5YR 4/1), weathers grayish orange (10YR 7/4) to rusty; fine grained; interbeds of dolomite, medium gray, weathers medium light gray; fine grained and sandy; cross-bedded.

E.
35 ft
10.6 m
dolomite, medium dark gray, weathers medium light gray; fine grained; thinly interbedded with chert, dark gray; top has interbeds of quartzite, brownish gray, weathers grayish orange; fine grained.

D.
5 ft
1.5 m
dolomite, medium dark gray, weathers medium light gray; fine grained; disrupted, massive bed; contains contorted, elongate, chert nodules; cherty marker bed.

C.
35 ft
10.6 m
dolomite, medium dark gray, weathers medium gray; fine grained; irregular chert nodules; contorted beds; very thin interbeds of fine quartzite at top of unit.

B.
35 ft
10.6 m
dolomite, medium dark gray, weathers medium light gray; fine grained; thinly interbedded with chert, dark gray; top of unit has bed of sandy fuccoids.

A.
10 ft
3 m
dolomite, medium dark gray, weathers medium light gray; fine grained; thinly bedded with chert nodules.

dolomite, medium dark gray, weathers medium light gray; fine grained; medium bedded with interbeds of chert, dark gray.

3. Dry Mountain 15′ Quadrangle; 11.36 km S, 4.8 km W of NE corner; 8/30/88-2.

Devonian Lost Burro Formation, Lippencott Member:

G.
60 ft
18 m
dolomite, medium gray, weathers medium light gray; fine grained; interbedded with dolomite medium dark gray; weathers medium gray; fine grained; scattered quartzite, medium light gray; medium grained; medium to thick beds, cross-bedded or sandy lenses; rusty banded appearance; faulted at top of unit.

F.
20 ft
6 m
quartzite, medium light gray, weathers pale yellowish brown (10YR 6/2); fine to medium grained; medium bedded, cross-bedded; rusty streaks.

E.
62 ft
19 m
dolomite, medium dark gray, weathers medium light gray; fine grained; thinly to medium bedded; interbedded with chert, medium light brownish gray (5YR 5/1), weathers same to grayish orange (10YR 7/4); bedded and nodular; quartzite found near top, medium light gray.

D.
7 ft
2.1 m
dolomite, medium dark gray, weathers medium light gray; disrupted massive bed; contains contorted elongate chert nodules; cherty marker bed.

C.
30 ft
9.1 m
dolomite, medium dark gray, weathers medium light gray; fine grained; thinly to medium bedded; abundant chert, pale red purple (5RP 6/2) at base to medium gray upward; bedded and nodular.

B.
7 ft
2.1 m
dolomite, dark gray, weathers medium light gray; fine grained; thinly to medium bedded; base has chert nodules, medium light gray to pale red-purple (5RP 6/2); top has sandy fuccoids.

A.
5 ft
1.5 m
dolomite, medium dark gray, weathers light brownish gray (5YR 6/1) to grayish orange (10YR 7/4); fine grained to silty; massive.

dolomite, medium dark gray, weathers medium light gray to yellowish gray (5Y 8/1); fine grained; thinly interbedded with chert, dark brownish gray (5YR 3/1); nodular and bedded.

4. Tin Mountain 15′ Quadrangle; 12.74 km, 2.57 km E of NW corner; 8/17/85.

Devonian Lost Burro Formation, Lippencott Member:
dolomite, medium gray, weathers medium to medium light gray; coarse grained; sandy; medium to thickly bedded.

K.
40 ft
12.2 m
dolomite, dark gray grading to medium light gray, weathers same; fine grained; moderately sandy; medium to thickly bedded; interbedded quartzite, decreases upward; dolomite has light brown sand lenses and wisps.

J.
28 ft
8.5 m
quartzite, pinkish white and vitreous; thinly to medium bedded but massive appearing outcrop.

I.
27 ft
8.2 m
dolomite, light gray to very light brownish gray (5YR 7/1), weathers same; fine grained; sandy; thickly bedded; scattered sand layers, rusty brown; medium grained; some streaks and laminae of sand, light brownish gray (5YR 6/1); good cross beds at mid-unit.

H.
20 ft
6 m
quartzite, white; weathers same; fine grained; massive; streaks of sand, very pale brown (5YR 6/2).

faulted section—thickness of unit G estimated from section 2.

G.
35 ft
10.6 m
dolomite, dark gray to slightly purplish dark gray, weathers light gray to yellowish gray (5Y 8/1); fine grained; medium to thinly bedded; abundant layers of chert nodules, black to medium brownish gray (5YR 5/1); dolomite at base is rusty brown and silty.

F.
10 ft
3 m
dolomite, dark gray to slightly purplish dark gray, weathers light gray to yellowish gray; fine grained; massive bed, disrupted with elongate chert nodules, chert is chocolate brown to grayish red-purple (5RP 4/2); cherty marker bed.

E.
20 ft
6 m
dolomite, dark gray to slightly purplish dark gray, weathers light gray to yellowish gray; fine grained; thinly to medium bedded; abundant chert nodule layers, black to medium light gray to grayish red-purple.

D.
50 ft
15.2 m
dolomite, dark gray to purplish gray, weathers light gray to yellowish gray; fine grained; thinly to medium bedded; layers of chert nodules, black, lighter in color toward top; top is sandy bed, light brown, with fuccoids.

C.
48 ft
14.6 m
dolomite, dark gray to slightly purplish dark gray, weathers yellowish gray (5Y 8/1); fine grained; thinly to medium bedded; scattered thin layers of chert, black; near base there is sandy dolomite bed, dark brownish gray (5YR 5/1), weathers yellowish gray; contains rusty sand-filled worm tubes; top of unit is thinly interbedded light gray dolomite and black chert with pale red (5R 6/2) muddy dolomite partings.

B.
14 ft
4.2 m
calcareous quartzite, medium to dark brownish gray (5YR 5/1 to 3/1), weathers light gray; fine grained; medium to thickly bedded grading upward to thinly bedded.

Silurian Hidden Valley Formation:

A.
52 ft
15.8 m
dolomite, medium to medium dark gray, weathers light gray to yellowish gray; fine grained and silty; thinly bedded; midunit is dolomite, dark gray, weathers dark yellowish orange (10YR 6/6); fine grained and silty; top 1 ft/0.3 m of unit is muddy dolomite, medium brownish gray (5YR 5/1), weathers yellowish gray (5Y 8/1) to pale red (10R 6/2); poorly laminated.

dolomite, medium gray, weathers medium light gray; fine grained; thickly bedded; very thin rusty silty layer at top.

5. Marble Canyon Quadrangle; 3.72 km S, 2.5 km E of NW corner 8/20/85.

Devonian Lost Burro Formation, Lippencott Member:
sedimentary breccia, medium to dark gray; composed of fine grained dolomite and quartzite clasts; sand decreases above breccia bed.

I.
105 ft
32 m
dolomite, medium dark gray, weathers medium gray to rusty streaked; fine to coarse grained and sandy; thinly to thickly interbedded with quartzite, light gray, weathers light gray to brownish gray (5YR 4/1) to rusty; medium grained; quartzite has scattered, cross beds in lower half, decreasing upward; sand mixes into dolomite as lenses, laminae, and thin beds, decreasing upward.

H.
15 ft
4.5 m
quartzite, medium light gray, weathers light brownish gray (5YR 6/1) to rusty; fine to medium grained; massive.

G.
30 ft
9 m
dolomite, medium to medium light gray, weathers medium light gray; fine grained; thinly interbedded with black chert nodules and beds; lower half has scattered rusty fuccoids in dolomite.

F.
10 ft
3 m
dolomite, medium gray to medium light gray, weathers medium light gray to yellowish orange-gray (10YR 7/4); fine grained; massive bed, disrupted with contorted chert nodules, black to medium gray; cherty marker bed.

E.
20 ft
6 m
dolomite, medium gray to medium light gray, weathers medium light gray to medium grayish orange (10YR 6/4); fine grained; thinly interbedded with beds and lenses of chert, black to medium gray, weathers rusty.

D.
95 ft
29 m
dolomite, dark brownish gray (5YR 3/1) grading upward to medium dark gray, weathers pale yellowish brown (10YR 6/2) to grayish orange (10YR 7/4) grading upward to yellowish gray (5Y 7/2) to grayish orange; silty at base grading upward to fine grained; thinly to medium bedded; rusty silty/sandy lenses, nodules, and fuccoids decrease upward; dark gray to dark olive-gray (5Y 3/1) chert lenses increase upward to become interbedded; scattered quartzite.

C.
60 ft
18.2 m
dolomite, dark brownish gray, weathers pale yellowish brown to grayish orange; silty; thinly to medium bedded; abundant rusty silty/sandy lenses, nodules and fuccoids at base and mid-unit.

Silurian Hidden Valley Formation:

B.
40 ft
12.2 m
dolomite, dark gray to brownish gray (5YR 4/1), weathers light olive-gray (5Y 6/1) to medium yellowish gray (5Y 6/2) grading upward to dark yellowish orange (10YR 6/6); fine grained and silty; medium bedded; rusty silty streaks and lenses at mid-unit.

A.
15 ft
4.6 m
dolomite, interbedded dark gray and dark brownish gray (5YR 3/1), weathers mottled medium gray and grayish orange (10YR 7/4) to light olive-gray (5Y 6/1); thinly to thickly interbedded fine grained and silty fine grained dolomite; scattered rusty silty lenses.

dolomite, dark gray, weathers medium dark gray; fine grained; medium to thickly bedded; rusty chert and silt nodules; silicified fossils, corals, horn corals, and favosites.

6. Tin Mountain 15′ Quadrangle; 14.23 km S, 10.12 km E of NW corner; 9/2/85.

Devonian Lost Burro Formation, Lippencott Member:
dolomite, medium dark gray, weathers medium gray; fine grained; medium to thickly bedded; scattered sandy dolomite decreases upward.

I.
80 ft
24 m
interbedded calcareous quartzite, medium gray, weathers rusty; medium to fine grained; laminated, cross-bedded; dolomite, medium dark gray, weathers medium light gray; fine grained, sandy; dolomite, medium dark gray, weathers medium gray; medium to fine grained; thinly and thickly interbedded; and quartzite, vitreous white; sand and quartzite decrease in proportion upward but become more segregated as prominent beds; last prominent quartzite bed at top.

H.
10 ft
3 m
quartzite, vitreous white; massive.

fault—section offset to: Tin Mountain 15′ Quadrangle; 14.5 km S, 10.23 km E of NW corner.

G.
30 ft
9 m
quartzite, medium gray, weathers light brown to rusty; medium to fine grained; medium bedded, some laminae.

F.
37 ft
11.3 m
dolomite, medium dark gray, weathers medium light gray to light gray to yellowish gray (5Y 8/1); fine grained; thinly bedded; interbedded with chert, medium gray; top has quartzite interbeds, medium dark gray, weathers light brown.

E.
10 ft
3 m
dolomite, medium dark gray, weathers medium light gray; fine grained; massive disrupted bed; contains distorted elongate chert nodules, dark gray; cherty marker bed.

D.
10 ft
3 m
dolomite, medium dark gray, weathers medium light gray to yellowish gray; fine grained; thinly to medium bedded; chert, dark gray; weathers rusty to light gray; base is calcareous quartzite bed, weathers light brown; fine grained; contains fuccoids and some silty nodules.

C.
32 ft
9.7 m
dolomite, medium dark gray, weathers medium light to yellowish gray (5Y 8/1); base is calcareous quartzite, medium light gray, weathers light brown; contains chert nodules.

B.
43 ft
13 m
dolomite, medium gray, weathers yellowish gray (5Y 7/2) to dark yellowish orange (10YR 6/6); fine grained and silty; silt decreases upward; thinly to medium bedded; rusty silty nodules; chert nodules, dark gray, weather rusty; base has sandy fuccoids and bedded chert.

Silurian Hidden Valley Formation:

A.
50 ft
15 m
dolomite, medium brownish gray, weathers yellowish gray to pale yellowish brown (10YR 6/2) in lower half or dark yellowish orange in upper half; fine grained and silty; thinly bedded; top of unit is very thinly bedded pale red (5R 6/2) calcareous shale; weathers to form recessive slope.

dolomite, dark gray, weathers medium dark gray; fine grained; medium bedded; silicified fossils, favosites, horn corals.

7. Ubehebe Peak 15′ Quadrangle; 7.45 km W, 2.42 km S of NE corner; 8/26/85.

Devonian Lost Burro Formation, Lippencott Member:
sedimentary breccia, dark gray to medium gray dolomite with brown quartzite clasts; poorly developed.

E.
115 ft
35 m
dolomite, medium gray, weathers medium light to light brownish gray (5YR 6/1 to 7/1), medium dark gray at top; fine to medium grained and sandy; thinly and thickly interbedded with quartzite, light brownish gray (5YR 6/1);

abundant sandy streaks and lenses; sand and quartzite decrease upward from 40 ft/12 m; 5 ft/1.5 bed of quartzite at 40 ft/12 m.

D.
40 ft
12.2 m
quartzite, very light gray, weathers light brown with rusty streaks; fine to medium grained; massive with some laminae and cross beds.

C.
60 ft
18.2 m
dolomite, medium dark gray, weathers medium gray; fine grained; medium bedded; abundant chert nodules, olive-gray (5Y 4/1), weathers olive-brown (5Y 4/4) to rusty.

B.
60 ft
18.2 m
dolomite, medium gray, weathers same; fine grained; scattered interbeds of pinkish white quartzite; abundant rusty weathering silty layers; medium bedded; base and mid-unit have beds of abundant sandy fuccoids, weather rusty; scattered chert nodules.

Silurian Hidden Valley Formation:

A.
60 ft
18.2 m
dolomite, dark brownish gray (5YR 3/1) grading upward to medium dark gray, weathers light brown (5YR 6/4) to yellowish gray (5Y 7/2) grading upward to medium brownish gray (5YR 4/1); fine grained and silty to fine grained; medium to thinly bedded; rusty silty streaks; contains quartzite/silty nodules, grayish red purple (5RP 4/2), weather rusty light brown; scattered chert nodules.

dolomite, medium gray, weathers same; fine grained; scattered rusty silty nodules; medium to thickly bedded.

8. Marble Canyon 15′ Quadrangle; 0.5 km S, 10.55 km W of NE corner; 8/28/85.

Devonian Lost Burro Formation, Lippencott Member:
sedimentary breccia, composed of dolomite, medium light and medium dark gray; fine grained; and quartzite, rusty; sandy matrix.

F.
65 ft
20 m
dolomite, medium dark to medium light gray, weathers same; fine grained and sandy; sandy wisps and lenses weather rusty; thinly interbedded with quartzite, light gray, weathers rusty; sand and quartzite decrease upward.

E.
15 ft
4.6 m.
quartzite, light gray, weathers rusty; fine to medium grained; thickly bedded, cross-bedded.

D.
55 ft
17 m
dolomite, dark gray, weathers yellowish gray (5Y 8/1) to light gray; fine grained; base has pale red (5R 6/2) silty dolomite and bedded chert followed by wavy, lumpy bedded, dolomite and chert; mid-unit is interbedded sandy dolomite and quartzite; medium bedded.

C.
50 ft
15.2 m
dolomite, dark gray, weathers grayish orange (10YR 7/4) to yellowish gray (5Y 7/2) to light gray; fine grained and silty; silt decreases upward; rusty silt nodules are gradually replaced by chert upward; abundant chert nodules at base; poorly medium bedded.

B.	dolomite, grayish orange, weathers dark yellowish orange
70 ft	(10YR 6/6); fine grained; sandy fuccoids at base, weather
21 m	rusty; chert nodules, medium gray to medium brownish gray
	(5YR 5/1), weather rusty.

Silurian Hidden Valley Formation:

A.	dolomite, dark brownish gray (5YR 2/1), weathers yellow-
30 ft	ish gray (5Y 8/1) to dark yellowish orange (10YR 6/6)
9 m	near top; fine grained and silty; scattered silty lenses and
	nodules weather rusty; poorly medium bedded.

dolomite, medium dark gray, weathers same; fine grained; rusty chert nodules; silicified favosites, crinoids, brachiopods; medium bedded.

REFERENCES CITED

Anderson, R. A., Zoback, M. L., and Thompson, G. A., 1983, Implications of selected subsurface data on the form and evolution of some basins in the northern Basin and Range province, Nevada and Utah: Geological Society of America Bulletin, v. 94, p. 1055–1072.

Burchfiel, B. C., 1969, Geology of the Dry Mountain Quadrangle, Inyo County, California: California Division of Mines and Geology Special Report 99, 19 p.

Burchfiel, B. C., Pelton, P. J., and Sutter, J., 1970, An early Mesozoic deformation belt in south-central Nevada–southeastern California: Geological Society of America Bulletin, v. 81, p. 211–215.

Burchfiel, B. C., Hodges, K. V., and Royden, L. H., 1987, Geology of Panamint Valley–Saline Valley pull-apart system, California; Palinspastic evidence for low-angle geometry of a Neogene range-bounding fault: Journal of Geophysical Research, v. 92, p. 10422–10426.

Cemen, I., Wright, L. A., Drake, R. E., and Johnson, F. C., 1985, Cenozoic sedimentation and sequence of deformational events at the southeastern end of the Furnace Creek strike-slip fault zone, Death Valley region, California, *in* Biddle, K. T., and Christie-Blick, N., eds., Strike-slip deformation, basin formation, and sedimentation: Society of Economic Paleontologists and Mineralogists Special Publication 37, p. 127–141.

Corbett, K., Wrucke, C. T., and Nelson, C. A., 1988, Structure and tectonic history of the Last Chance thrust system, Inyo Mountains and Last Chance Range, California, *in* Weide, D. L., and Faber, M. L., eds., This extended land; Geological journeys in the southern Basin and Range; Geological Society of America Cordilleran Section Field Trip Guide: University of Nevada at Las Vegas Geoscience Department Special Publication 2, p. 269–292.

Davison, I., 1986, Listric normal fault profiles; Calculation using bed-length balance and fault displacement: Journal of Structural Geology, v. 8, p. 209–210.

Dunne, G. C., 1986, Mesozoic evolution of southern Inyo, Argus, and Slate ranges, *in* Dunne, G. C., ed., Mesozoic–Cenozoic structural evolution of selected areas, east-central California; Geological Society of America Cordilleran Section Field Trip 2: Los Angeles, Department of Geology, California State University at Los Angeles, p. 3–21.

Elliott, G. S., Wrucke, C. T., and Nedel, S. S., 1984, K-Ar ages of Late Cenozoic volcanic rocks from the northern Death Valley region: Isochron/West, no. 40, p. 3–7.

Gibbs, A. D., 1983, Balanced cross section construction from seismic sections in areas of extensional tectonics: Journal of Structural Geology, v. 5, p. 153–160.

——, 1984, Structural evolution of extensional basin margins: Journal of the Geological Society of London, v. 141, p. 609–620.

Hamblin, W. K., 1965, Origin of "reverse drag" on the downthrown side of normal faults: Geological Society of America Bulletin, v. 76, p. 1145–1164.

Hodges, K. V., Walker, J. D., and Wernicke, B. P., 1987, Footwall structural evolution of the Tucki Mountain detachment system, Death Valley region, southeastern California, *in* Coward, M. P., Dewey, J. F., and Hancock, P. L., eds., Continental extensional tectonics: Geological Society of London Special Publication 28, p. 393–408.

Hodges, K. V., Wernicke, B. P., and Walker, J. D., 1989, Day 6; Middle Miocene(?) through Quaternary extension, northern Panamint Mountains area, California, *in* Wernicke, B. P., and 6 others, Extensional tectonics in the Basin and Range Province between the southern Sierra Nevada and the Colorado plateau: 28th International Geological Congress Field Trip Guide T-138, p. 45–55.

Hopper, R. H., 1947, Geologic section from the Sierra Nevada to Death Valley, California: Geological Society of America Bulletin, v. 58, p. 393–432.

Hunt, C. B., and Mabey, D. R., 1966, Stratigraphy and structure, Death Valley, California: U.S. Geological Survey Professional Paper 494–A, 162 p.

Johnson, E. A., 1971, Geology of a part of the southeastern side of the Cottonwood Mountains, Death Valley, California [Ph.D. thesis]: Houston, Texas, Rice University, 81 p.

McAllister, J. F., 1952, Rocks and structure of the Quartz Spring area, northern Panamint range, California: California Division of Mines Special Report 25, 37 p.

——, 1956, Geology of the Ubehebe Peak (15-minute) Quadrangle, California: U.S. Geological Survey Geologic Quadrangle Map GQ–95, scale 1:62,500.

——, 1974, Silurian, Devonian, and Mississippian strata of the Funeral Mountains in the Ryan Quadrangle, Death Valley region, California: U.S. Geological Survey Bulletin 1386, 35 p.

McClay, K. R., and Ellis, P. G., 1987a, Analogue models of extensional fault geometries, *in* Coward, M. P., Dewey, J. F., and Hancock, P. L., eds., Continental extensional tectonics: Geological Society of London Special Publication 28, p. 109–125.

——, 1987b, Geometries of extensional fault systems developed in model experiments: Geology, v. 15, p. 341–344.

Reynolds, M. W., 1969, Stratigraphy and structural geology of the Titus and Titanothere Canyons area, Death Valley, California [Ph.D. thesis]: Berkeley, University of California, 310 p.

——, 1974, Geology of the Grapevine Mountains, Death Valley, California; A summary, *in* Guidebook; Death Valley region, California and Nevada; Geological Society of America Cordilleran Section Field Trip 1: Shoshone, California, Death Valley Publishing Company, p. 92–97.

Ross, D. C., 1967, Geologic map of the Waucoba Wash (15-minute) Quadrangle, Inyo County, California: U.S. Geological Survey Geologic Quadrangle Map GQ–612, scale 1:62,500.

Smith, R. B., and Bruhn, R. L., 1984, Intraplate extensional tectonics of the eastern Basin-Range; Inferences on structural style from seismic reflection data, regional tectonics, and thermal-mechanical models of brittle-ductile deformation: Journal of Geophysical Research, v. 89, p. 5733–5762.

Snow, J. K., 1989, Day 7; Neogene dextral translation of the Cottonwood Mountains area, California, *in* Wernicke, B. P., and 6 others, Extensional tectonics in the Basin and Range Province between the southern Sierra Nevada and the Colorado plateau: 28th International Geological Congress Field Trip Guide T-138, p. 56–67.

Snow, J. K., and Wernicke, B., 1988, Mesozoic backfold in the Death Valley extended terrane; New constraints on offset of the northern Death Valley–Furnace Creek fault zone; California and Nevada: Geological Society of America Abstracts with Programs, v. 20, p. A272.

——, 1989, Mesozoic backfold in the Death Valley extended terrain; New constraints on offset of the northern Death Valley–Furnace Creek fault zone, California and Nevada: Geological Society of America Bulletin, v. 101, p. 1351–1362.

Snow, J. K., Wernicke, B. P., Burchfiel, B. C., and Hodges, K. V., 1989, Day 8; Neogene extension between the Grapevine Mountains and Spring Mountains, California and Nevada, *in* Wernicke, B. P., and 6 others, eds., Extensional tectonics in the Basin and Range Province between the southern Sierra Nevada and the Colorado plateau: 28th International Geological Congress Field Trip Guide T-138, p. 67–75.

Stadler, C. A., 1968, The geology of the Goldbelt Spring area, northern Panamint Range, Inyo County, California [M.S. thesis]: Eugene, University of Oregon, 78 p.

Stewart, J. H., 1970, Upper Precambrian and Lower Cambrian strata in the southern Great Basin, California and Nevada: U.S. Geological Survey Professional Paper 620, 206 p.

Stewart, J. H., Ross, D. C., Nelson, C. A., and Burchfiel, B. C., 1966, Last Chance thrust; A major fault in the eastern part of Inyo County, California: U.S. Geological Survey Professional Paper 550-D, p. D23-D34.

Stewart, J. H., Albers, J. P., and Poole, F. G., 1968, Summary of regional evidence for right-lateral displacement in the western Great Basin: Geological Society of America Bulletin, v. 79, p. 1407-1414.

Stock, C., and Bode, F. D., 1935, Occurrence of lower Oligocene mammal-bearing beds near Death Valley, California: National Academy of Science Proceedings, v. 21, p. 571-579.

Wernicke, B. P., and Axen, G. J., 1988, On the role of isostasy in the evolution of normal fault systems: Geology, v. 16, p. 848-861.

Wernicke, B., and Burchfiel, B. C., 1982, Modes of extensional tectonics: Journal of Structural Geology, v. 4, p. 105-115.

Wernicke, B., Hodges, K., and Walker, D., 1986, Geologic evolution of Tucki Mountain and vicinity, central Panamint Range, *in* Dunne, G. C., ed., Mesozoic–Cenozoic structural evolution of selected areas, east-central California; Geological Society of America Cordilleran Section Field Trip 2: Los Angeles, Department of Geology, California State University at Los Angeles, p. 67-80.

Wernicke, B., Axen, G. J., and Snow, J. K., 1988a, Basin and Range extensional tectonics at the latitude of Las Vegas, Nevada: Geological Society of America Bulletin, v. 100, p. 1738-1757.

Wernicke, B., Snow, J. K., and Walker, J. D., 1988b, Correlation of Early Mesozoic thrusts in the southern Great Basin and their possible indication of 250-300 km of Neogene crustal extension, *in* Weide, D. L., and Faber, M. L., eds., This extended land; Geological journeys in southern Basin and Range; Geological Society of America Cordilleran Section Field Trip Guide: University of Nevada at Las Vegas Geoscience Department Special Publication 2, p. 255-268.

Wernicke, B., Walker, J. D., and Hodges, K. V., 1988c, Field guide to the northern part of the Tucki Mountain fault system, Death Valley region, California, *in* Weide, D. L., and Faber, M. L., eds., This extended land; Geological journeys in southern Basin and Range; Geological Society of America Cordilleran Section Field Trip Guide: University of Nevada at Las Vegas Geosciences Department Special Publication 2, p. 58-63.

Wernicke, B. P., and 6 others, 1989, Extensional tectonics in the Basin and Range Province between the southern Sierra Nevada and the Colorado plateau: 28th International Geological Congress Field Trip Guide T-138, 80 p.

White, N. J., Jackson, J. A., and McKenzie, D. P., 1986, The relationship between the geometry of normal faults and that of the sedimentary layers in their hanging walls: Journal of Structural Geology, v. 8, p. 897-909.

Wright, L. A., and Troxel, B. W., 1973, Shallow-fault interpretation of Basin and Range structure, southwestern Great Basin, *in* DeJong, R., and Scholtern, R., eds., Gravity and tectonics: New York, John Wiley and Sons, p. 397-407.

MANUSCRIPT ACCEPTED BY THE SOCIETY AUGUST 21, 1989

Geological Society of America
Memoir 176
1990

Chapter 22

Changing patterns of extensional tectonics; Overprinting of the basin of the middle and upper Miocene Esmeralda Formation in western Nevada by younger structural basins

John H. Stewart
U.S. Geological Survey, 345 Middlefield Road, Menlo Park, California 94025
David S. Diamond
Department of Earth and Space Sciences, University of California, Los Angeles, California 90024

ABSTRACT

The middle and upper Miocene Esmeralda Formation of western Nevada was deposited in a continental basin that crops out over an area of about 2,000 km^2. The formation consists of thin, westerly derived sedimentary rocks in the western three-quarters of the outcrop area and of thick (3+ km) easterly derived sedimentary rocks in the eastern quarter. Megabreccias along the eastern margin of the basin are interpreted as landslide deposits derived from fault scarps. The basin was probably a half-graben with a major fault or faults on the east side. The position of the basin, its size, and the inferred major syndepositional faults on its east side are all unrelated to present-day topography and the distribution of major faults in the area and indicate a change in paleogeography and structural pattern since the late Miocene. In the eastern part of the basin, this change was accompanied by deformation that includes low-angle-fault detachment of the Esmeralda Formation from underlying amphibolite-grade Late Proterozoic and lower Paleozoic rocks in the Mineral Ridge–Weepah Hills area and uplift, folding, faulting, tilting, and surface exposure of the entire 3+ km thickness of the formation. Middle and upper Miocene basins in the northern part of the Basin and Range province commonly have been attributed to the onset of basin-range tectonism. The tectonic history of the Esmeralda Formation, however, indicates that some of these basins do not occupy the same area, nor are they related to the same syndepositional faults, as present basins. The extensional basin of the Esmeralda Formation can be viewed either as an early structure in an evolving, but kinematically related, extensional terrane in which the distribution of basins and faults changed gradually with time, or as the product of an extensional event kinematically different from that which produced present structures in the same area. The latter hypothesis is favored because of the marked contrasts in the paleogeography and structures associated with the Esmeralda basin compared with modern basins.

Stewart, J. H., and Diamond, D. S., 1990, Changing patterns of extensional tectonics; Overprinting of the basin of the middle and upper Miocene Esmeralda Formation in western Nevada by younger structural basins, *in* Wernicke, B. P., ed., Basin and Range extensional tectonics near the latitude of Las Vegas, Nevada: Boulder, Colorado, Geological Society of America Memoir 176.

INTRODUCTION

Miocene sedimentary rocks are widespread in Nevada and provide an important record of late Cenozoic tectonic events. Some present subsurface basins of the Basin and Range province apparently contain Miocene sedimentary rocks, suggesting that in these locations the present pattern of basins and ranges has been in place since the Miocene (e.g., Hastings, 1979; Anderson and others, 1983; Effimoff and Pinezich, 1986). However, basin-range fragmentation has in other places overprinted Miocene basins that were of great areal extent compared to present basins (Gilbert and Reynolds, 1973; Golia and Stewart, 1984). Differentiating between these two basin types may provide critical information on the kinematics, timing, and regional variability of late Cenozoic extension in the Basin and Range province.

The purpose of this chapter is to describe the Esmeralda Formation and its structural setting. The Esmeralda Formation is particularly useful in unraveling structural history because it is relatively well exposed and contains rocks that present a fairly clear picture of structure during deposition. The analysis presented here shows that the Esmeralda Formation was deposited in an extensional basin, but an extensional basin that is much more widespread than present basins and bounded by faults that have a much different distribution than present faults. These observations lead to the hypothesis that the Esmeralda basin may have been related to an extensional regime kinematically different than that of today.

The present study builds on many previous investigations that have outlined the general stratigraphic and structural setting of the region. The Esmeralda Formation was named by Turner (Turner, 1900a, b) for outcrops in the Coaldale and Alum areas (Fig. 1), and the formation has subsequently been studied in greater detail by Moiola (1963, 1964, 1969, 1970), Robinson (1964), Suthard (1966), Robinson and others (1968), Davis (1981), Moore (1981), and Stewart (1989). Information on the general geology of the region is included in a study of Esmeralda County by Albers and Stewart (1972). Much of the region has been mapped at 1:62,500 or 1:24,000 (Robinson and Crowder, 1973; Robinson and others, 1976; Crowder and others, 1972; Stewart and others, 1974; Stewart, 1979, 1981a, b, 1989). The fauna and flora in the Esmeralda Formation have been extensively studied, and the formation has been radiometrically dated at several localities.

STRATIGRAPHY AND STRUCTURE

The Esmeralda Formation is exposed in scattered outcrops within an area of about 2,000 km^2. The name has also been applied to sedimentary rocks exposed outside this area, but we propose that the name be restricted to the depositional basin (Esmeralda basin) outlined here. The formation is described separately in each of the major areas where it crops out, namely the Alum, Silver Peak, Blanco Mine, Coaldale, and northern Fish Lake Valley–Volcanic Hills–Basalt areas.

Alum area

Stratigraphy. The Esmeralda Formation is extensively exposed in the Alum area (Figs. 1, 2). Moiola (1969; also *in* Robinson and others, 1968) divided the formation in the Alum area into seven units: units A through F, and the Weepah unit (also called unit G). His nomenclature is used here, except that we restrict the Esmeralda to only units A through F. In addition, a tuff unit (here called the tuff unit of Big Smoky Valley) between units C and D is recognized. Two other units, the Alum and Twin Peaks units, are also recognized in the Alum area but cannot be correlated with other units in the formation.

The stratigraphic and structural relations presented here differ in two major respects from those described by Moiola (1969). First, most of the gravel deposits that Moiola (1969) considered to be older alluvial deposits of Quaternary age are here included in the Miocene Esmeralda Formation. These gravel deposits interfinger with the finer grained, generally tuffaceous sedimentary rocks of the Esmeralda Formation. Second, Moiola (1969) mapped these gravels as lying depositionally on pre-Tertiary rocks, whereas later mapping (Stewart, 1989) shows that they are separated from pre-Tertiary rocks by a major low-angle normal fault (Weepah detachment fault). This low-angle fault is critically important in evaluating the tectonic setting of the Esmeralda Formation.

The Esmeralda Formation in the Alum area consists of two contrasting facies (Fig. 3). One consists of conglomerate, sedimentary breccia, and monolithologic breccia and blocks and contains easterly derived detritus composed largely of Cambrian and Ordovician sedimentary rocks. This facies is referred to here as the conglomerate facies. The other facies consists of largely westerly derived volcaniclastic siltstone, sandstone, and minor amounts of claystone and conglomerate. It is referred to here as the siltstone-sandstone facies.

The conglomerate facies forms most of units A, E, and F and the Alum unit. On Figures 2 and 3, the conglomerate facies of units E and F are shown as E_c and F_c, respectively. The name "Alum unit" designates rocks that are separated by a low-angle fault from the rest of the Esmeralda Formation and cannot be correlated with assurance with any other unit in the Esmeralda. The conglomerate facies consists mostly of greenish-gray, and rarely grayish-red, poorly stratified, pebble to boulder conglomerate and sedimentary breccia. These rocks intertongue in a complex manner with rocks of the siltstone-sandstone facies (Fig. 4). Both clast- and matrix-supported conglomerate and sedimentary breccia occur in the conglomerate facies. The clasts consist of limestone, phyllitic siltstone, very fine to fine-grained quartzite, and sparse dolomite, chert, quartz, and porphyritic mafic igneous rocks. Clasts average 1 to 10 cm in size and are as large as 2 m. Most of the clasts were derived from Lower Cambrian strata that are widely exposed in the Weepah, Silver Peak, and Fish Lake Valley region (Fig. 5). Some limestone clasts contain oncoliths (so-called *Girvanella*) and were derived from the Lower Cambrian Mule Spring Formation (Fig. 5), which is the only forma-

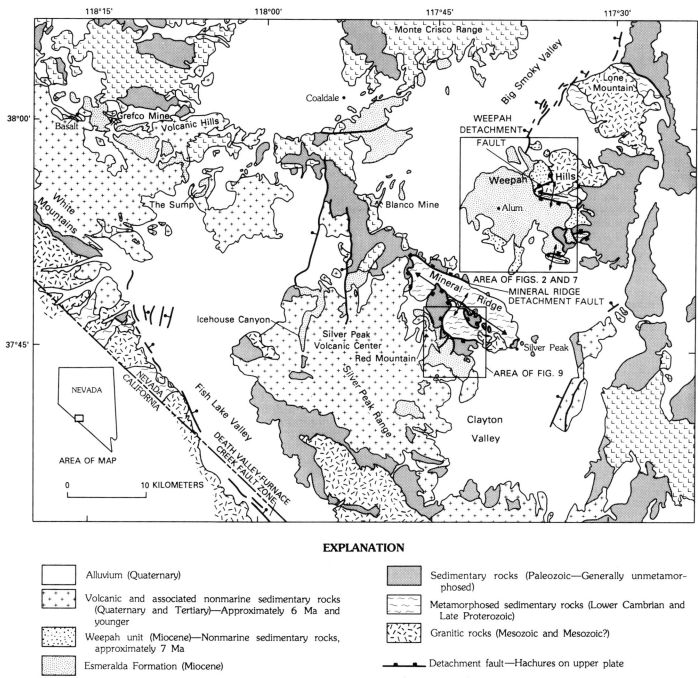

EXPLANATION

Alluvium (Quaternary)

Volcanic and associated nonmarine sedimentary rocks (Quaternary and Tertiary)—Approximately 6 Ma and younger

Weepah unit (Miocene)—Nonmarine sedimentary rocks, approximately 7 Ma

Esmeralda Formation (Miocene)

Andesitic rocks, rhyolite tuff, and associated sedimentary rocks (Tertiary)—Approximately 15 Ma to 26 Ma

Sedimentary rocks (Paleozoic—Generally unmetamorphosed)

Metamorphosed sedimentary rocks (Lower Cambrian and Late Proterozoic)

Granitic rocks (Mesozoic and Mesozoic?)

Detachment fault—Hachures on upper plate

Normal fault—Bar and ball on downthrown side

Anticlinal axis

Figure 1. Generalized geologic map of west-central Esmeralda County and southernmost Mineral County, Nevada, and eastern Mono County, California. Modified from Albers and Stewart (1972), Stewart and others (1982), and Strand (1967).

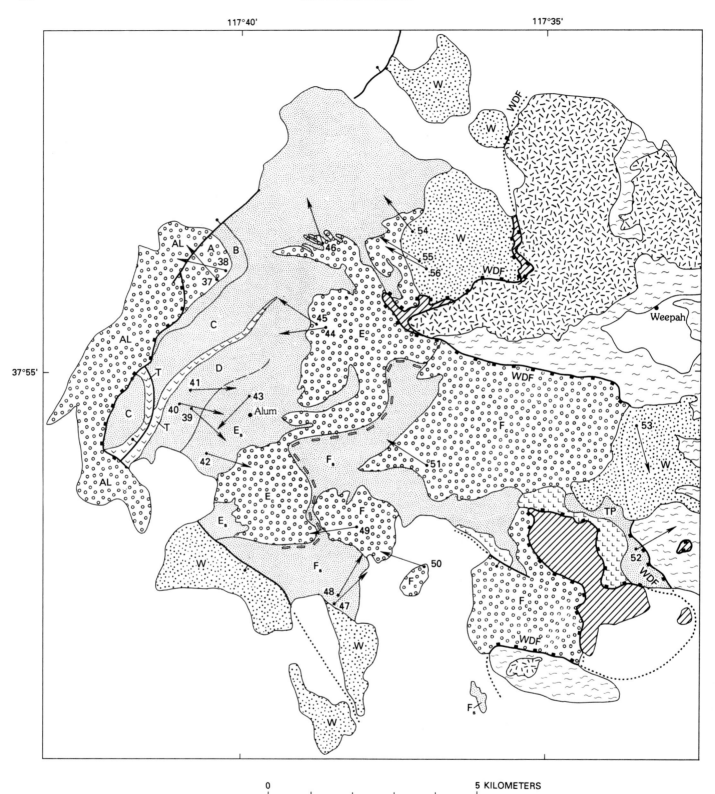

Figure 2. Generalized geologic map of the Alum area and paleocurrent directions. In Esmeralda Formation, light stipple is siltstone-sandstone facies and small circle pattern is conglomerate facies.

EXPLANATION

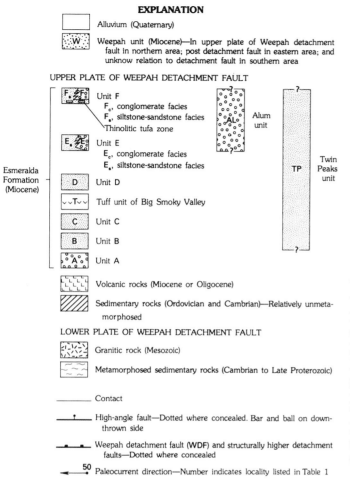

Alluvium (Quaternary)

Weepah unit (Miocene)—In upper plate of Weepah detachment fault in northern area; post detachment fault in eastern area; and unknow relation to detachment fault in southern area

UPPER PLATE OF WEEPAH DETACHMENT FAULT

Unit F
  F_c, conglomerate facies
  F_s, siltstone-sandstone facies
  Thinolitic tufa zone

Unit E
  E_c, conglomerate facies
  E_s, siltstone-sandstone facies

Unit D

Tuff unit of Big Smoky Valley

Unit C

Unit B

Unit A

Alum unit

TP   Twin Peaks unit

Esmeralda Formation (Miocene)

Volcanic rocks (Miocene or Oligocene)

Sedimentary rocks (Ordovician and Cambrian)—Relatively unmetamorphosed

LOWER PLATE OF WEEPAH DETACHMENT FAULT

Granitic rock (Mesozoic)

Metamorphosed sedimentary rocks (Cambrian to Late Proterozoic)

Contact

High-angle fault—Dotted where concealed. Bar and ball on downthrown side

Weepah detachment fault (WDF) and structurally higher detachment faults—Dotted where concealed

50 Paleocurrent direction—Number indicates locality listed in Table 1

tion that contains these algal structures in the region near Alum. Archeocyathids also occur rarely in the limestone clasts, and these fossils are common in the Lower Cambrian Poleta Formation and lower part of the Lower Cambrian Harkless Formation. Clasts of phyllitic siltstone and very fine to fine-grained quartzite apparently were derived from the Lower Cambrian Harkless Formation or the Lower Cambrian Campito Formation (age after Mount and others, 1983), which are composed dominantly of these rock types. Clasts of porphyritic mafic igneous rocks most likely were derived from igneous dikes that cut the pre-Tertiary rocks in the Alum area. A few clasts of welded tuff occur in unit F_c and in the Alum unit, but none were noted in unit E_c. Serpentinite clasts occur in unit F_c at several exposures of conglomerate 2.5 km south-southwest of Weepah. No granitic clasts were noted anywhere in the conglomerate facies.

The conglomerate facies also contain large masses of monolithologic breccia of either limestone, phyllitic siltstone, and quartzite or isolated blocks of these same rock types. These rock types are all common in the Lower Cambrian section exposed in nearby areas. Individual intact blocks are as large as 10 m, and masses of breccia are as thick as 200 m. One breccia mass can be traced nearly continuously for 1.5 km along the outcrop.

Transport directions in the conglomerate facies are generally

westward, based on measurements of clast imbrication at seven localities (Fig. 2; Table 1).

The siltstone-sandstone facies constitutes all of units B, C, and D, most of the Twin Peaks unit, and parts of units A, E, and F. On Figures 2 and 3, the siltstone-sandstone facies of units E and F are shown as E_s and F_s, respectively. The siltstone-sandstone facies consist generally of very pale orange, yellow-gray, and light-gray, evenly laminated to thin-bedded claystone and siltstone. Siltstone in the lower 80 to 250 m of unit F_s contains interstratified 0.5- to 2-m-thick lenses of thinolitic tufa. This tufa-bearing sequence can be traced for 5.5 km along outcrops and forms a well-defined marker unit in the Esmeralda Formation (Fig. 2). Sandstone occurs in minor amounts in the siltstone-sandstone facies and forms a conspicuous part of unit D, which also contains conglomerate. The sandstone consists mostly of quartz, feldspar, and aphanitic volcanic fragments (Moiola, 1969) as well as tuffaceous material and is cross stratified or thin bedded. The conglomerate in unit D contains granules and pebbles of rhyolitic welded tuff, flow-banded rhyolite, sparse vesicular basalt, and sparse chert. The maximum clast size is 6 cm. The sandstone and conglomerate constitute about 25 percent of unit D in the southern part of the Alum area, but as first noted by Robinson and others (1968) and Moiola (1969), the sandstone grades out northward along the outcrops so that in the northern part of the Alum area, unit D and unit E_s are indistinguishable. The tuff unit (tuff unit of Big Smoky Valley) between units C and D also grades, or pinches out, northward, and north of the limit of this tuff, units C through unit E_s cannot be mapped as separate units.

The Twin Peaks unit (originally called the Twin Peaks sequence by Moiola, 1969) contains a mixture of rocks of the siltstone-sandstone and the conglomerate facies that crops out in a relatively small area 4.5 to 7 km south of Weepah (Fig. 2). This unit is at least 200 m thick and consists of yellow-brown, very thin bedded and cross-stratified, fine- to coarse-grained, locally conglomeratic sandstone and yellow-gray, very thin-bedded siltstone. The conglomeratic sandstone contains granules and pebbles of rhyolitic tuff and occurs primarily in the basal part of the unit, where it apparently lies unconformably on welded tuff of probable late Oligocene or early Miocene age. The Twin Peaks unit also contains some coarse matrix-supported conglomerate layers composed of subangular clasts, as large as 0.5 m, of greenish-gray phyllitic siltstone, medium-gray limestone, and sparse chert and rhyolitic welded tuff in a silt matrix. These coarse conglomerate layers are lithologically similar to rocks in the conglomerate facies of units E and F (E_c and F_c). Although the exact relations are poorly understood, the Twin Peaks unit apparently lies at the base of the Esmeralda Formation and may be overlain by unit F_c, although this latter relation is difficult to evaluate because exposures of contacts are poor.

Paleocurrent studies in cross-stratified sandstone of the siltstone-sandstone facies indicate eastward transport directions in unit D, east and southwest in unit E_s, northeast in unit F_s, and northeast in the Twin Peaks unit. The southwest current direction in sandstone of unit E_s (Fig. 2, Table 1) is probably in a distal sandstone of the conglomerate facies and reflects the generally westerly flow directions in that facies rather than the generally easterly flow in the siltstone-sandstone facies.

A tuff unit (tuff unit of Big Smoky Valley) is mapped between units C and D (Fig. 2). This tuff forms a narrow 5.5-km-long outcrop band in the western part of the Alum area. It is yellow gray and crystal poor (feldspar, quartz, and a trace of biotite and hornblende; Table 2) and contains 10 percent reddish-purple flow-banded rhyolite clasts and 10 percent or more round pumice. This tuff is lithologically similar to, and is correlated with, a tuff mapped as unit Tst by Robinson and others (1976) as much as 13 km west of Alum in the central part of Big Smoky Valley. The same tuff also occurs in a very small outcrop on the north side of an isolated hill at 37°57′05″N. and 117°45′13″W. The tuff unit of Big Smoky Valley is distinctly different (Table 2) from the tuff unit of Jacks Springs that crops out in the Blanco

Mine area and areas farther west. The tuff unit of Jacks Spring, in contrast to the tuff unit of Big Smoky Valley, is crystal rich and contains abundant clasts of brown andesitic lava.

Thickness. Estimates of the total thickness of the Esmeralda Formation in the Alum area have varied greatly. Turner (1900b) originally indicated that the total thickness of the Esmeralda in the Alum area, excluding the Weepah unit, is 4,084 m. Moiola (1969) indicated 2,612 m for the same stratigraphic succession, and Davis (1981), 2,075 m. We here suggest that the thickness may be 4,400 or even 5,400 m. The variations in estimates of thickness are the result mainly of different interpretations of structural relations in an area of poor exposure. The estimate presented here is based on field mapping that suggests continuity (Fig. 2) of units across the exposure area. Marker units such as unit B, the tuff unit, unit D, and the thinolitic tufa zone at the base of unit F apparently are not repeated by faults, except for the tuff unit in the western part of the area (Fig. 2). A much thinner

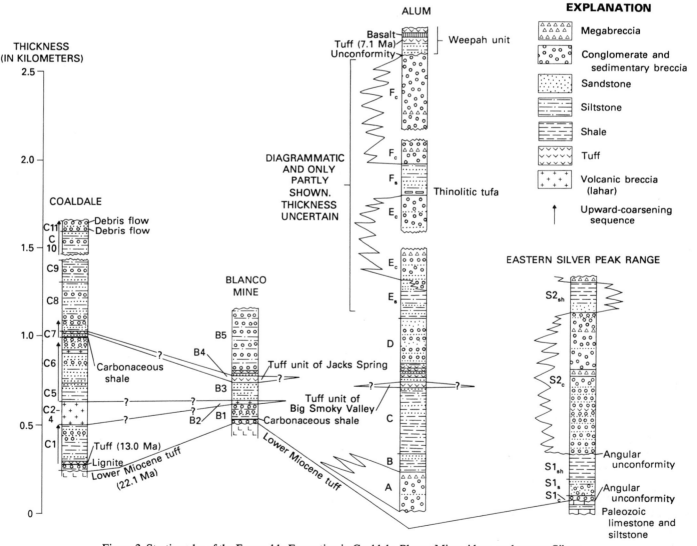

Figure 3. Stratigraphy of the Esmeralda Formation in Coaldale, Blanco Mine, Alum, and eastern Silver Peak Range. See Figure 1 for localities. Letters to left of columns are units described in text.

succession is possible if any part of the section is duplicated by faults, but the continuity of units suggests that such faulting is unlikely. Considerable differences in estimates of the thickness of units E and F are possible because poor exposures could conceal faults. However, if relatively unfaulted, the units could be 1 to 2 km thick on the basis of the width of the outcrop and the moderately steep dip of the beds. The uncertain thicknesses of units E and F, combined with fairly certain thicknesses of units A to D, indicates that the Esmeralda must be several kilometers thick, probably in the range of 3 to 5 km.

Age. Fossils of fresh-water mollusks, ostracods, fish, and plants occur in the Esmeralda Formation in the Alum area (Turner, 1900b; Robinson and others, 1968; Moiola, 1969). Of these, only the mollusks and ostracods indicated a specific age for the formation (Fig. 6). James Firby (*in* Robinson and others, 1968; Moiola, 1969) assigned a Barstovian age (middle Miocene) for mollusks in the lower part of unit E and a Clarendonian age (middle and late Miocene) for mollusks in the lower part of unit F. Ostracods identified by R. M. Forester (written communication, 1981) in undifferentiated units E to C (sample 782-38J at 37°56′14″N, 117°38′51″W) are *Heterocypris* new species and *Limnocythere* new species. Forester indicates that *Heterocypris* sp. is a long-ranging form that may be as old as middle Miocene and that *Limnocythere* sp. probably is restricted to the upper Miocene. In summary, paleontologic information indicates a middle and late Miocene age for the Esmeralda Formation in the Alum area.

Relation to overlying rocks. The Esmeralda Formation is unconformably overlain by the Weepah unit (also called unit G),

which was named by Robinson and others (1968) and Moiola (1969). These authors included the Weepah unit in the Esmeralda Formation, but it is here excluded because of its unconformable relation with the Esmeralda and its young age (Fig. 6). The Weepah unit is significant because it locally contains abundant coarse clasts of granitic and metamorphic rocks derived from deep structural levels, suggesting significant tectonic denudation and/or erosion between the time the Esmeralda Formation and the Weepah unit were deposited.

The Weepah unit crops out in the northern, eastern, and southern parts of the Alum area and has a somewhat different lithology in each of these areas. These differences may indicate that the unit is not strictly correlative, or of exactly the same age, from area to area. In the northern part of the Alum area the Weepah unit consists of lapilli tuff, tuff, tuffaceous sandstone, and minor layers of conglomerate, and the upper part consists mostly of conglomerate. The conglomerate contains clasts as large as 1.5 m of phyllitic siltstone, spotted hornfels, limestone, chert, quartz, mafic dike rock, andesite, diorite, and granitic rocks. The spotted hornfels, diorite, and granitic rocks probably all were derived from nearby sources. The diorite clasts are lithologically similar to diorite mapped by Moiola (1969) 1 km north of Weepah. The Weepah unit in the eastern part of the Alum area consists of a lower and upper sequence of conglomerate and a middle sequence of tuff and interstratified conglomerate. The conglomerate contains clasts as large as 1 m of phyllitic siltstone, limestone, quartz, quartzite, dolomite, mafic dike rocks, granitic rock, and, at one locality, serpentinite. The Weepah unit in the southern part of the Alum area consists of a lower part of tuff, lapilli tuff, and

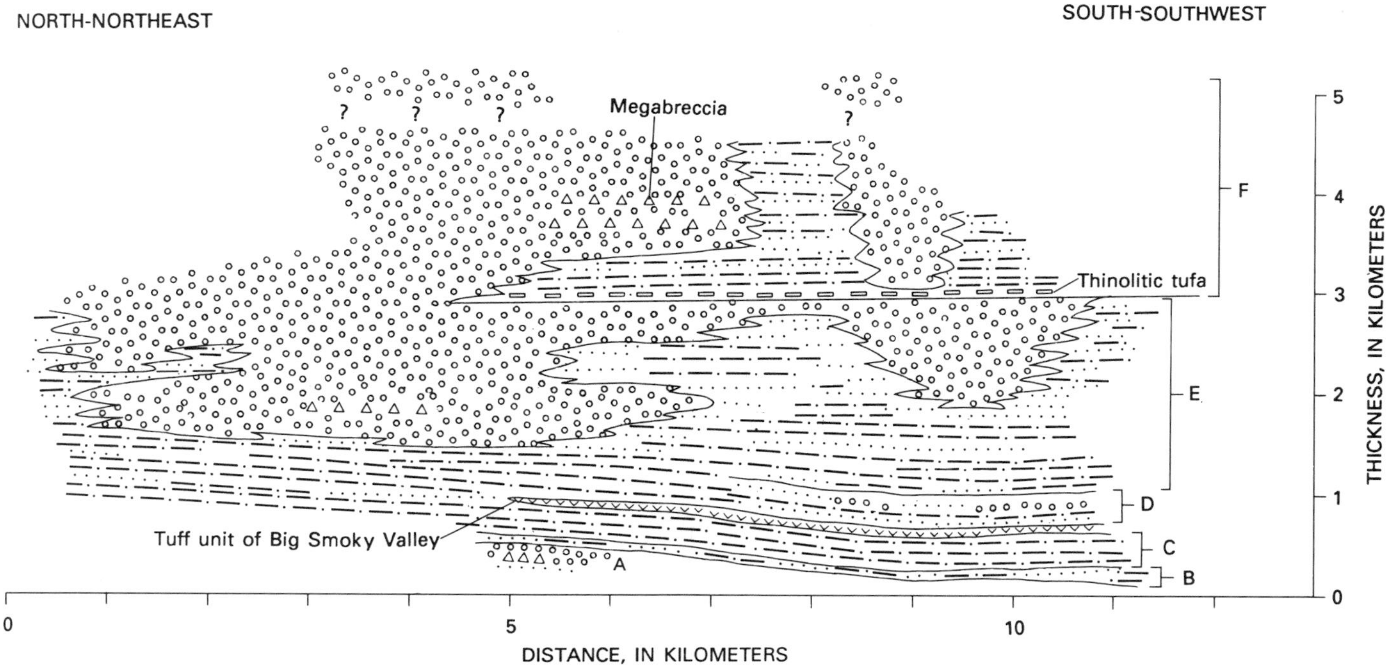

Figure 4. Diagrammatic cross section trending north-northeast across the Alum area showing stratigraphic units in the Esmeralda Formation approximately at right angles to flow directions in conglomeratic units. Palinspastically restored for folding. See Figure 3 for explanation. Letters indicate units described in text.

TABLE 1. PALEOCURRENT DIRECTIONS IN LATE CENOZOIC SEDIMENTARY ROCKS, WESTERN NEVADA*

Locality number in this chapter	Field Number	Latitude (N)	Longitude (W)	Number of readings	Mean azimuth	Consistency ratio	Type of study, description of unit, comments
1	1-115-38J	37°59'53"	118°15'01"	2	144	0.99	c; ES; Tc of Crowder and others, 1972
2	1-115-25J	38°00'35"	118°14'40"	29	141	0.68	c; ES; Tc of Stewart (1979); <12.0 Ma
3	1-115-22J	38°00'32"	118°14'09"	21	141	0.61	c; ES; Tc of Stewart (1979); <12.0 Ma
4	1-115-22J	38°00'32"	118°14'09"	22	30	0.59	i; ES; Tc of Stewart (1979) 12 to 13 m stratigraphically above study at locality 3
5	1-115-22J	38°00'32"	118°14'09"	12	68	0.96	i; ES; Tc of Stewart (1979) 48 to 75 m stratigraphically above study at locality 3
6	1-159-1J	37°57'54"	118°08'03"	21	102	0.92	c; ES; Ts of Robinson and Crowder (1973)
7	....	37°55'54"	118°06'01"	14	121	54	c; ES; Ts of Robinson and Crowder (1973)
8	....	37°55'35"	118°04'50"	10	109	10	c; ES; Ts of Robinson and Crowder (1973)
9	....	37°56'07"	118°04'21"	31	56	39	c; ES; Ts of Robinson and Crowder (1973)
10	SP88-7B	37°45'27"	117°56'39"	1	166	....	i; ES; unit S2$_S$, Ts3 of Robinson and others (1976)
11	SP88-7A	37°45'27"	117°56'39"	1	51	....	i; ES; unit S2$_S$, Ts3 of Robinson and others (1976)
12	1232-2J	37°49'37"	117°52'27"	41	109	0.12	c, ch; ES; Ts3 of Robinson and others (1976)
13	1232-2J	27°49'37"	117°52'27"	10	149	0.91	i; ES; Ts3 of Robinson and others (1976)
14	1234-2J - 3J	37°55'10" - 37°55'20"	117°49'54" - 117°49'51"	26	75	0.43	c; ES, unit B5
15	1236-2J	37°59'10"	117°49'40"	6	37	0.85	c; ES, unit C6
16	1236-1J	37°59'32"	117°49'42"	15	47	0.78	c; ES, unit C8
17	P88-1-25	37°42'38"	117°46'15"	5	117	0.78	c; ES, unit S2$_S$
18	P88-2-1	37°42'24"	117°46'01"	8	59	0.90	c; ES, unit S2$_S$
19	SP-88-M	37°46'31"	117°45'32"	2	349	0.97	c; ES, unit S2$_S$
20	SP-88-24	37°44'04"	117°44'59"	1	89	....	c; ES, unit S2$_S$
21	P-88-2-9	37°43'52"	117°44'50"	4	89	0.68	c; ES, unit S2$_S$
22	SP87-42	37°42'59"	117°44'52"	1	335	....	i; ES, unit S2$_C$
23	SP87-45	37°42'48"	117°44'55"	1	21	....	i; ES, unit S2$_C$
24	3-46-11J	37°44'55"	117°43'56"	19	114	0.61	c; ES, unit S2$_S$
25	3-46-10J	37°45'08"	117°43'34"	20	114	0.77	c; ES, unit S2$_S$
26	SP-88-T82	37°45'36"	117°43'42"	1	7	....	i; ES, unit S1$_C$
27	G128m	37°44'10"	117°44'29"	4	119	0.95	c; ES, unit S2$_S$
28	P88-1-21	37°43'51"	117°44'04"	1	239	....	i; ES, unit S2$_C$
29	B83m	37°43'47"	117°43'50"	1	267	....	i; ES, unit S2$_C$
30	SP88-E	37°43'59"	117°43'37"	1	358	....	i; ES, unit S2$_C$
31	B400m	37°43'44"	117°43'26"	1	297	....	i; ES, unit S2$_C$
32	P87-2-14	37°44'04"	117°42'55"	1	320	....	i; ES, unit S2$_C$
33	SP87-63	37°43'46"	117°42'51"	1	8	....	i; ES, unit S2$_C$
34	SP87-75	37°43'38"	117°42'02"	1	279	....	i; ES, unit S2$_C$
35	SP87-76	37°43'39"	117°42'04"	1	273	....	i; ES, unit S2$_C$
36	SP87-16	37°43'02"	117°42'41"	1	272	....	i; ES, unit S2$_C$
37	782-87J	37°56'11"	117°40'26"	1	315	....	i; ES, unit A
38	782-85JA	37°56'19"	117°40'18"	1	282	....	i; ES, unit A
39	782-1J	37°54'34"	117°40'52"	28	132	0.79	c; ES, unit D
40	782-3J	37°54'36"	117°41'05"	14	106	0.58	c; ES, unit D
41	782-2J	37°54'48"	117°40'53"	8	89	0.59	c; ES, unit D
42	782-58J	37°53'58"	117°40'36"	11	110	0.59	c; ES, unit E$_S$
43	782-5J	37°54'42"	117°39'49"	20	222	0.61	c; ES, unit E$_S$
44	782-34J	37°55'33"	117°38'39"	1	259	....	i; ES, unit E$_C$
45	782-173J	37°55'36"	117°38'48"	1	302	....	i; ES, unit E$_C$
46	782-40J	37°56'38"	117°38'43"	1	340	....	i; ES, unit E$_C$
47	782-47J	37°51'52"	117°38'30"	11	45	0.99	c; ES, unit F$_S$
48	782-48J	37°52'04"	117°38'25"	16	30	0.51	c; ES, unit F$_S$
49	782-114J	37°52'56"	117°38'07"	1	260	....	i; ES, unit F$_C$
50	772-20J	37°52'26"	117°37'03"	1	292	....	i; ES, unit F$_C$
51	782-120J	37°53'47"	117°36'59"	1	303	....	i; ES, unit F$_C$
52	772-63J	37°52'39"	117°33'31"	2	61	0.86	c; ES, Twin Peaks unit
53	772-53J	37°54'18"	117°33'33"	1	165	....	i; ES, Weepah unit
54	782-81J	37°56'48"	117°37'14"	1	320	....	i; ES, Weepah unit

TABLE 1. PALEOCURRENT DIRECTIONS IN LATE CENOZOIC SEDIMENTARY ROCKS, WESTERN NEVADA* (continued)

Locality number in this chapter	Field Number	Latitude (N)	Longitude (W)	Number of readings	Mean azimuth	Consistency ratio	Type of study, description of unit, comments
55	782-76J	37°56'25"	117°37'08"	1	300	....	i; ES, Weepha unit
56	782-75J	37°56'19"	117°36'59"	1	300	....	i; ES, Weepah unit
57	2695-10J	38°29'30"	118°55'40"	27	302	0.37	c; CV
58	2695-12J	38°30'11"	118°54'18"	8	300	0.77	c; CV
59	2695-13J	38°29'59"	118°54'18"	5	332	0.19	c; CV
60	2695-14J	38°29'55"	118°54'07"	9	261	0.93	c; CV
61	2351-35J	38°57'52"	119°30'42"	10	348	0.60	c; Ts of Stewart and Noble (1979)
62	2351-36J	38°58'30"	119°31'35"	10	234	0.89	c; Ts of Stewart and Noble (1979)
63	2351-37J	38°58'38"	119°32'04"	7	256	0.77	c; Ts of Stewart and Noble (1979)
64	1-94-16J	38°58'34"	119°32'15"	10	247	0.95	c; Ts of Stewart and Noble (1979)
65	3481-2J	38°27'21"	119°09'22"	23	77	0.42	c; unnamed unit, lower? Miocene
66	2577-16J	38°45'02"	119°11'50"	31	354	0.42	c; CV
67	7241-2J	38°19'35"	118°36'48"	43	164	0.47	c; CV?
68	2575-4J	38°44'37"	119°24'54"	10	294	0.62	c; QTs of Stewart and others (1989) <7.8 Ma
69	2577-18J	38°42'54"	119°14'00"	31	299	0.45	c; CV
70	2577-23J	38°44'56"	119°10'28"	7	284	0.56	c; CV, 60 to 90 m above base
71	2577-24J	38°44'57"	119°10'39"	9	305	0.70	c; CV, 150 to 200 m above base
72	2577-25J	38°45'00"	119°10'13"	16	299	0.48	c; CV
73	2577-26J	38°44'56"	119°11'08"	21	292	0.56	c; CV
74	2577-27J	38°45'00"	119°11'08"	16	305	0.75	c; CV
75	2577-28J	38°44'58"	119°12'07"	22	312	0.38	c; CV
76	2579-18J	38°42'30"	119°05'33"	7	337	0.96	ch; CV
77	3298-1J	38°48'15"	119°13'20"	26	324	0.42	c; CV
78	3-74-11J	38°39'20"	119°25'00"	18	268	0.51	c; QTs of Stewart and others (1989); Pliocene?
79	3-74-13J	38°39'21"	119°23'01"	14	298	0.84	c; QTs of Stewart and others (1989); Pliocene?
80	3-72-9JA	38°38'18"	119°25'18"	4	342	0.95	c; QTs of Stewart and others (1989); Pliocene?
81	3-72-8J	38°37'35"	119°24'35"	4	252	0.83	c; QTs of Stewart and others (1989); Pliocene?
82	3-72-9JB	38°38'18"	119°25'15"	12	307	0.88	c; QTs of Stewart and others (1989); Pliocene?
83	4-22-14J	38°43'31"	119°22'10"	36	264	0.37	c; Tsl of Stewart and others (1989); <18.4 Ma, >7.8 Ma
84	4-22-6J	38°42'50"	119°21'33"	6	322	0.61	c, ch; Tsl of Stewart and others (1989); <18.4 Ma, >7.8 Ma
85	1-116-16J	39°01'56"	119°33'43"	7	199	0.59	c; equivalent to Ts of Stewart and Noble (1979), some deltaic cross-strata
86	2577-41J	38°43'57"	119°10'35"	9	320	0.27	c; AS
87	2696-54J	38°29'25"	118°53'38"	18	283	0.59	c; AS. Some deltaic cross-strata
88	3298-2J	38°49'10"	119°13'50"	29	248	0.50	c; CV
89	2689-5J	38°34'25"	119°12'28"	38	57	0.33	c; Ts unit of Stewart and Reynolds (1987); probably intertongues with lower Miocene andesitic lahars and flows
90	2696-60J	38°33'02"	118°54'18"	40	283	0.59	c; CV
91	7247-1J	38°22'21"	118°56'20"	46	356	0.57	c; CV?
92	7247-2J	38°20'48"	118°56'28"	28	341	0.59	c; CV?
93	7247-4J	38°21'50"	118°56'28"	4	148	0.98	c; Eolian cross-strata; CV
94	7247-6J	38°25'25"	119°01'20"	21	265	0.62	c; CV?
95	7247-7J - 8J	38°25'35"	119°59'37"	7	245	0.79	c; CV?
96	11923-1J	38°30'48"	117°45'12"	18	312	0.68	c; unnamed unit
97	15158-21J	38°17'41"	117°50'35"	5	50	0.32	c; unnamed unit
98	15154-48J	38°16'10"	117°37'59"	10	214	0.51	c
99	15154-49J	38°16'06"	117°38'11"	1	176	....	c
100	15154-54J	38°17'04"	117°39'29"	3	182	0.67	c

*Reading in middle or upper Miocene rocks unless otherwise indicated; c = cross-strata; i = imbrication; ch = channels; AS = Aldrich Station Formation; CV = Coal Valley Formation; ES = Esmeralda Formation.

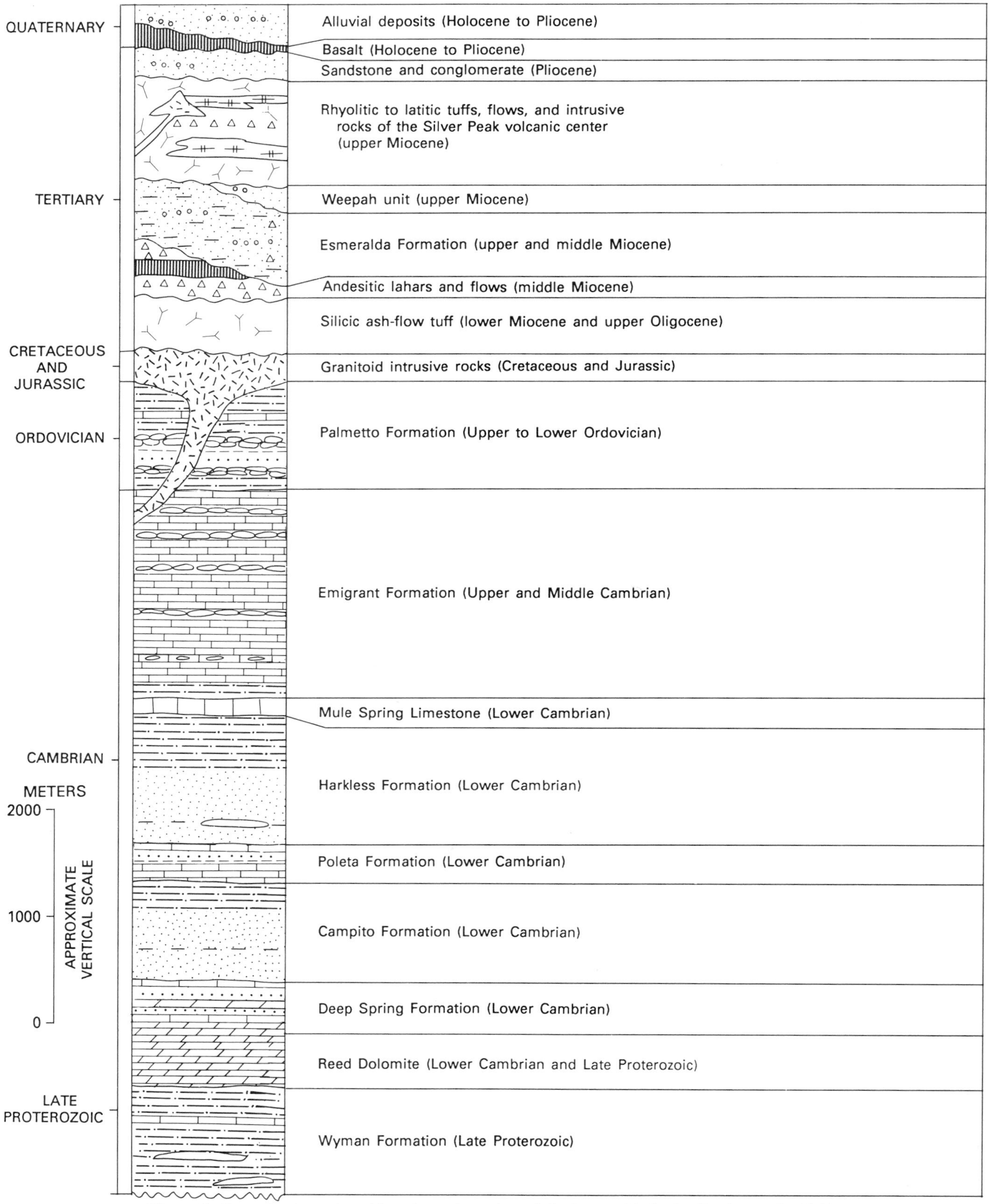

Figure 5. Generalized stratigraphic column in region of the Esmeralda basin. Tertiary units highly variable from area to area. Ages of Late Proterozoic and Cambrian formations after Mount and others (1983).

TABLE 2. MODAL ANALYSES OF TUFFS IN ESMERALDA FORMATION*

Sample No.	Tuff of Jacks Spring												
	1	2	3	4	5	6	7	8	9	10	11	12	13
Groundmass	80.2	71.3	78.2	75.3	66.3	72.3	73.7	67.0	74.2	60.8	81.6	86.3	58.9
Plagioclase	10.9	12.0	9.8	10.1	11.9	8.8	12.8	10.6	12.5	6.0	7.8	7.7	13.4
Sanidine	6.1	10.2	9.0	12.1	20.0	14.1	9.5	16.6	8.2	5.3	9.3	4.3	19.5
Quartz	....	....	....	....	....	....	....	....	....	....	....	....	....
Biotite	0.4	tr	0.4	0.5	1.2	0.6	0.7	tr	0.4	0.6	0.5	0.8	tr
Hornblende	tr	2.0	0.6	0.4	0.2	0.6	tr	tr	tr	0.4	0.3	0.2	....
Augite	....	....	....	....	....	....	....	....	....	....	....	....	....
Opaques	0.4	0.7	1.1	0.4	0.2	....	0.3	0.5	0.6	0.2	0.2	0.2	0.4
Rock fragments	1.7	3.5	0.7	1.2	0.2	3.5	2.8	5.1	3.9	26.7	0.2	0.4	7.8
Other	0.4	0.2	0.2	....	....	....	....	....	0.2	....	....	0.2	....

Sample No.	Tuff of Jacks Spring						Tuff of Big Smoky Valley				Other tuffs	
	14	15	16	17	18	19	20	21	22	23	24	25
Groundmass	61.7	43.7	77.5	83.2	91.3	72.8	95.9	85.9	80.6	94.8	85.0	85.2
Plagioclase	9.3	8.9	7.7	6.4	3.6	10.4	0.4	1.2	0.4	0.8	10.3	9.4
Sanidine	10.0	6.2	5.1	6.1	3.0	11.6	1.7	0.6	3.0	1.8	1.9	0.6?
Quartz	0.2	....	....	....	....	....	1.5	0.8	0.2	0.2	0.6	tr
Biotite	0.2	0.2	tr	tr	tr	0.6	tr	....	tr	....	1.0	....
Hornblende	....	....	tr	0.4	....	tr	tr	tr	tr?	tr?	....	....
Augite	....	0.2	0.4?	....	....	....	....	....	....	....	....	....
Opaques	0.9	0.2	1.3	0.7	0.8	1.2	....	....	....	....	0.2	0.2
Rock fragments	17.8	40.7	7.9	3.1	1.3	3.5	0.6	11.2	15.8	2.3	0.4	4.3
Other	....	....	0.2	....	....	....	....	0.4	....	....	0.6	0.4

*tr = trace.
1–4, ½ km northeast of Jacks Spring (20 km west northwest of Basalt); 5, 1 km southwest of Basalt; 6–7, Lower cooling unit, 3 km west of Grefco diatomite mine; 8–9, Upper cooling unit, 3 km west of Grefco diatomite mine; 10, 4 km southeast of Grefco diatomite mine; 11, South of Volcanic Hills, 8 km southeast of Grefco diatomite mine; 12, The Sump (or The Bowl), northern part of Fish Lake Valley; 13, Lower cooling unit, Icehouse Canyon, Silver Peak Range; 14–15, Upper cooling unit, Icehouse Canyon, Silver Peak Range; 16–17, Blanco Mine section; 18–19, Upper tuff, unit C7, Coaldale section; 20–21, 5 km northeast of Blanco Mine, Big Smoky Valley; 22–23, Alum area; 24, Unit C1, Coaldale section; 25, Tuff near base of unit C7, Coaldale section.

tuffaceous sandstone; a middle olivine basalt; and an upper part of tuff and sandstone. Transport direction, based on four studies of the imbrication of clasts (Fig. 2), is northwest in the northern outcrop of the Weepah unit and south in the eastern outcrop. A K-Ar age on biotite in an air-fall tuff in the Weepah unit in the southern part of the Alum area (Robinson and others, 1968; Table 1, No. 13) is 7.1 ± 0.3 Ma (recalculated using new constants, Dalrymple, 1979).

In the northern outcrop, the Weepah unit apparently is underlain by the same low-angle fault that underlies the Esmeralda Formation. This relation is suggested by the strike of the Weepah unit locally at a high angle to the strike of the presumed fault and the moderate to high dip of strata eastward toward the presumed gently west-dipping fault (Fig. 7). Thus the Weepah unit in this area is structurally attached to the Esmeralda Formation and has moved with it relative to pre-Tertiary autochthonous rocks. In the eastern outcrop area, however, the Weepah unit lies depositionally on pre-Tertiary autochthonous rocks. This relation can be

seen in a small outcrop 2.5 km S. 5°W. of Weepah. The structural setting of the Weepah unit is quite different in the northern area than in the eastern area, indicating that these two sections are most likely not exactly equivalent. The Weepah unit in the southern area unconformably overlies the Esmeralda Formation and its structural relation to pre-Tertiary rocks cannot be determined.

Structure. Three structural units are recognized in the Alum area (Fig. 7). (1) The lower unit, below the Weepah detachment fault, consists of metamorphosed sedimentary rocks of the Wyman, Reed, Deep Spring, and Campito formations intruded by Mesozoic granitic rocks. (2) The middle unit consists of relatively unmetamorphosed Cambrian and Ordovician sedimentary rocks that occur in three moderately intact to highly faulted and brecciated lenses above the Weepah detachment fault. (3) The upper unit consists of the Esmeralda Formation, which is in low-angle fault contact with the lower structural unit or with the middle structural unit where it is present. In the eastern part of the Alum area, Tertiary volcanic rocks that occur in apparent unconformable contact below the Esmeralda Formation are shown on Figures 2 and 7 as separated by a detachment fault from underlying Cambrian and Ordovician sedimentary rocks of the middle plate. This fault relation is unclear, however, and conceivably the Tertiary volcanic rocks are locally in unconformable contact with the Cambrian and Ordovician rocks. If so, the middle structural unit, which clearly was highly deformed prior to deposition of the Tertiary volcanic unit, was subsequently deformed along with the Esmeralda Formation during extension above the Weepah detachment fault.

The Esmeralda Formation and unconformably underlying Tertiary rocks in the Alum area dip generally 20 to 40° SE (Fig. 7). The rocks are folded in open southeast-plunging anticlines and synclines spaced about 1 to 2 km apart and dip into low-angle detachment faults that separate the Tertiary rocks from the underlying rocks of the lower and middle structural units. The anticlines and synclines are on line with antiforms and synforms, respectively, on the surface of the detachment fault (Figs. 7, 8).

Previous workers in the Alum area (Turner, 1900b; Moiola, 1969) mapped the contact between the Esmeralda Formation and underlying pre-Tertiary rocks as a depositional contact and believed that the Esmeralda onlapped the pre-Tertiary surface. However, the Esmeralda Formation in many areas strikes at a high angle to the trace of the contact between the Esmeralda and the pre-Tertiary rocks and dips at a high angle into this contact. In addition, pre-Tertiary rocks in much of the Alum area adjacent to the Esmeralda Formation consist of the Late Proterozoic Wyman Formation, the Late Proterozoic and Lower Cambrian Reed Dolomite (age after Mount and others, 1983), and Mesozoic granitic rocks, yet clasts in the Esmeralda Formation are derived mainly from the Lower Cambrian Campito, Poleta, and Mule Spring formations. The lack of Wyman, Reed, and granitic clasts clearly indicates that the Esmeralda Formation did not onlap these pre-Tertiary rocks.

Silver Peak Range

Stratigraphy. Sedimentary rocks assigned to the Esmeralda Formation underlie volcanic and volcaniclastic strata of the approximately 6-Ma Silver Peak volcanic center and crop out south and west of Mineral Ridge in the eastern part of the Silver Peak Range (Figs. 1, 9) (Robinson, 1964; Robinson and others, 1968,

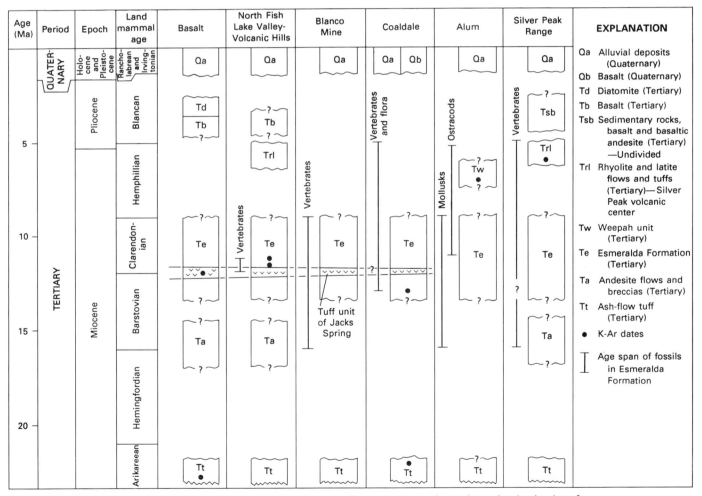

Figure 6. Diagram showing age information on the Esmeralda Formation and associated units. Ages for Tertiary subdivisions after Berggren and others (1985).

1976; Stewart and others, 1974; Keith, 1977; Davis, 1981). Robinson (1964) divided these rocks into a sequence of thirteen informal units, although many of these units are severely restricted in their distribution. Robinson and others (1968) further refined and summarized this stratigraphy in two partly correlative sections on the east and west flanks of the range. Several units included in the Esmeralda Formation by Turner (1900b) and clearly younger than volcanics of the Silver Peak volcanic center (Robinson, 1964; Robinson and others, 1968; Stewart and others, 1974; Robinson and others, 1976) are excluded from the Esmeralda Formation as defined in this chapter.

Stratigraphic and structural relations described here differ in three major respects from those described by Robinson (1964) and Robinson and others (1968). (1) Outcrops mapped as "sedimentary unit 1" on the basis of lithology by Robinson (1964), Robinson and others (1976), and Stewart and others (1974) on the western flank of the range lie below either rhyolite tuffs or younger andesite breccias. The tuffs, for which K-Ar ages of 22.0 ± 1.0 Ma and 23.4 ± 1.0 Ma have been reported (Robinson and others, 1968; recalculated using new constants, Dalrymple, 1979), are part of a widespread sequence of 22- to 26-Ma tuffs interpreted to have been erupted onto a surface of low relief in western Nevada (Robinson and Stewart, 1984). Robinson (1964), Stewart and others (1974), and Robinson and others (1976) considered "sedimentary unit 1" on the western flank of the range to be correlative with rocks mapped as sedimentary unit 1 on the eastern flank of the range. However, a Clarendonian, Hemphillian, or possibly Barstovian fossil (approximately 5 to 16.6 Ma) collected from the lowermost part of sedimentary unit 1 on the eastern flank indicates a considerably younger age for this supposed correlative unit. Thus, correlation of "sedimentary unit 1" between the western and eastern flanks of the range appears to be invalid. We here exclude "sedimentary unit 1" of the western flank from the Esmeralda Formation. (2) Robinson (1964), Robinson and others (1968), and Kirsch (1968, 1971) assumed that contacts between the Esmeralda Formation and the Wyman Formation and Reed Dolomite were depositional. Our mapping shows that, as in the Alum area, these contacts are exposures of an extensive low-angle normal fault, referred to here as the Mineral Ridge detachment fault. (3) The mapped units of Robinson (1964), Robinson and others (1968), Keith (1977), and Stewart and others (1974), although distinguished largely on the basis of lithology, have generally been considered time-stratigraphic units. Our mapping indicates that these units are in large part lateral facies equivalents and should therefore be described as lithostratigraphic units.

Two unconformity-bounded sequences make up the Esmeralda Formation in the Silver Peak Range (Fig. 10). The older of these two sequences (sequence 1) crops out only on the eastern flank of the range (Fig. 10), whereas the younger sequence (sequence 2) crops out widely within and on both flanks of the range. Each of these sequences is composed of rocks of three major lithofacies: (1) an easterly derived conglomerate facies similar to that in the Alum area and composed principally of conglomerate, breccia, and sandstone with detritus derived mainly from Late Proterozoic and Cambrian sedimentary rocks; (2) a westerly derived volcaniclastic facies composed of sandstone, siltstone, conglomerate, and shale, similar to the siltstone-sandstone facies of the Alum area and referred to here by the same name; and (3) a facies composed of shale, mudstone, and sandstone, referred to here as the "shaly facies."

Conglomerate Facies (S1$_c$, S2$_c$). The conglomerate facies consist of crudely bedded, poorly sorted, greenish to purplish-gray conglomerate and breccia derived almost entirely from Late Proterozoic and Cambrian sedimentary rocks. The conglomerate contains clasts ranging from granules to clasts as much as about 3 m in size, although clasts ranging from 1 to 20 cm are most common. Matrix material is generally silty to sandy and both matrix-supported and clast-supported conglomerates occur. Clasts are generally angular to subangular and are composed almost entirely of greenish-gray phyllitic siltstone, blue-gray or yellowish-gray limestone, brown to gray quartzite, yellow-gray dolomite, and significantly less black chert and siliceous to intermediate volcanics. Oncoliths (so-called *Girvanella*) are fairly common in limestone clasts, indicating derivation from the Lower Cambrian Mule Spring Formation, whereas sparse archeocyathid-bearing limestone clasts are derived from the Lower Cambrian Poleta or Harkless Formations. The phyllitic siltstone and quartzite are probably derived from the Lower Cambrian Harkless and Campito Formations, which are largely made up of these lithologies, whereas yellowish-gray dolomite is similar to that found in the Late Proterozoic and Lower Cambrian Reed Dolomite and Deep Spring Formation. Paleocurrent data, determined from pebble imbrications and orientations of breccia-filled debris-flow channels, indicate consistently westward flow directions (Table 1).

Numerous lenses of monolithologic breccia, as much as 50 m thick and traceable as much as 0.75 km along strike, are intercalated with the conglomerate. These are composed of clasts derived from the same Late Proterozoic and Paleozoic formations present as clasts in the conglomerate. The breccias are generally structureless masses having essentially no matrix, although some of the lenses, especially those higher in the section, have a mosaic-like texture in which individual blocks appear to have moved or rotated only slightly in relation to neighboring blocks. The maximum dimension of individual blocks is 20 m.

Provenance of the breccia lenses defines a crude inverted stratigraphy in that lenses lower in the section are composed primarily of lithologies most common in the Middle and Upper Cambrian Emigrant Formation and the Lower Cambrian Mule Spring Formation, whereas lenses near the top of the section reflect derivation most likely from the Lower Cambrian Harkless, Poleta, and Campito Formations and the Late Proterozoic and Lower Cambrian Reed Dolomite and the Late Proterozoic Wyman Formation.

Siltstone-sandstone facies (S1$_s$, S2$_s$). These strata consist of tuffaceous sandstone, vitric tuff, and nontuffaceous volcaniclastic siltstone, sandstone, and conglomerate. Outcrops in the eastern

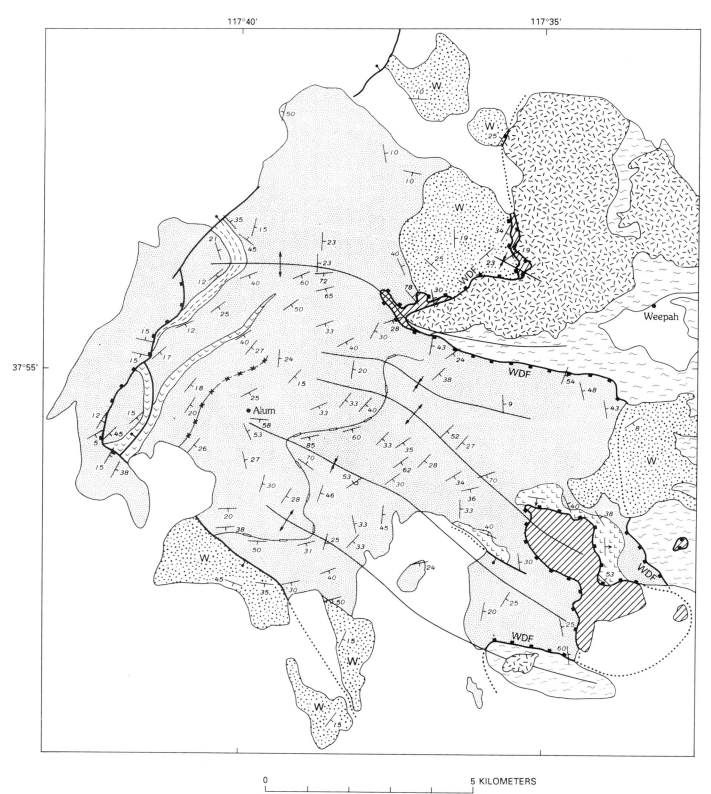

Figure 7. Generalized structure map of the Alum area.

EXPLANATION

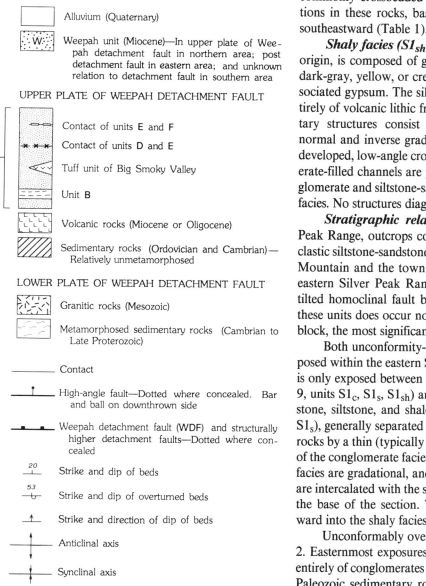

Alluvium (Quaternary)

Weepah unit (Miocene)—In upper plate of Weepah detachment fault in northern area; post detachment fault in eastern area; and unknown relation to detachment fault in southern area

UPPER PLATE OF WEEPAH DETACHMENT FAULT

Esmeralda Formation (Miocene)

Contact of units E and F

Contact of units D and E

Tuff unit of Big Smoky Valley

Unit B

Volcanic rocks (Miocene or Oligocene)

Sedimentary rocks (Ordovician and Cambrian)—Relatively unmetamorphosed

LOWER PLATE OF WEEPAH DETACHMENT FAULT

Granitic rocks (Mesozoic)

Metamorphosed sedimentary rocks (Cambrian to Late Proterozoic)

Contact

High-angle fault—Dotted where concealed. Bar and ball on downthrown side

Weepah detachment fault (WDF) and structurally higher detachment faults—Dotted where concealed

20 Strike and dip of beds

53 Strike and dip of overturned beds

Strike and direction of dip of beds

Anticlinal axis

Synclinal axis

part of the range are largely nontuffaceous; the tuffaceous sandstone and vitric tuff are restricted to the central and western parts of the range. The sandstone and siltstone are composed largely of intermediate to silicic volcanic rocks and feldspar crystals. Clasts in the conglomerate are rounded to subrounded, have maximum clast sizes of up to 20 cm, and consist of andesite, rhyolite, silicic tuff, pumice, and minor chert and siltstone derived from Paleozoic rocks. In the eastern part of the range, strata of the siltstone-sandstone facies show gradational contacts with strata of the shaly facies. In sequence 1, the sandstone-siltstone facies fines upward into the shaly facies, whereas in sequence 2, the sandstone-siltstone facies coarsens upward from the underlying shaly facies. Above its basal contact, unit $S2_s$ consists of several 10- to 50-m-thick upward-fining and thinning sequences of conglomerate, sandstone, and siltstone. The nontuffaceous rocks are commonly crossbedded and ripple marked. Paleocurrent directions in these rocks, based on cross-bed orientations, are east-southeastward (Table 1).

Shaly facies ($S1_{sh}$, $S2_{sh}$). This facies, mainly of lacustrine origin, is composed of gray to buff siltstone and sandstone and dark-gray, yellow, or cream laminated shale commonly with associated gypsum. The siltstone and sandstone consist almost entirely of volcanic lithic fragments and feldspar crystals. Sedimentary structures consist of parallel bedding and laminations, normal and inverse grading, massive bedding, and some poorly developed, low-angle cross stratification. Some scoured conglomerate-filled channels are present where conglomerate of the conglomerate and siltstone-sandstone facies are intercalated with this facies. No structures diagnostic of paleoflow were observed.

Stratigraphic relations. Throughout the western Silver Peak Range, outcrops consist primarily of strata of the volcaniclastic siltstone-sandstone facies (unit $S2_s$), whereas between Red Mountain and the town of Silver Peak (Figs. 9, 10, 11) in the eastern Silver Peak Range, all three facies crop out in several tilted homoclinal fault blocks. Although some interfingering of these units does occur north-south along strike within each fault block, the most significant facies changes occur normal to strike.

Both unconformity-bounded sequences (S1 and S2) are exposed within the eastern Silver Peak Range (Fig. 10). Sequence 1 is only exposed between Red Mountain and Coyote Spring (Fig. 9, units $S1_c$, $S1_s$, $S1_{sh}$) and is composed almost entirely of sandstone, siltstone, and shale of the siltstone-sandstone facies (unit $S1_s$), generally separated from underlying Paleozoic sedimentary rocks by a thin (typically less than 30 m) section of conglomerate of the conglomerate facies ($S1_c$). The contacts between these two facies are gradational, and numerous thin layers of conglomerate are intercalated with the siltstone-sandstone facies, especially near the base of the section. The siltstone-sandstone facies fines upward into the shaly facies ($S1_{sh}$).

Unconformably overlying sequence 1 are strata of sequence 2. Easternmost exposures of this sequence are composed almost entirely of conglomerates and breccias ($S2_c$), which lie directly on Paleozoic sedimentary rock. Significantly, the breccia lenses in unit $S2_c$ are most extensive and thickest and contain the largest intact blocks in easternmost outcrops.

Unit $S2_c$ intertongues complexly (shown schematically on Fig. 10) with lacustrine shale, siltstone, and sandstone of unit $S2_{sh}$. This repetition results on the map in alternating outcrops of $S2_c$ and $S2_{sh}$ in what is essentially a homoclinal section (Fig. 9).

Robinson (1964) and Robinson and others (1968) reported that rocks mapped here as units $S2_c$ and $S2_{sh}$ were overlain unconformably by unit $S2_s$. However, our mapping shows that lacustrine strata of unit $S2_{sh}$ interfinger westward with volcaniclastic sandstones and conglomerates of unit $S2_s$, just as they interfinger eastward with conglomerate and breccia of unit $S2_c$.

Thickness. Thickness of the Esmeralda Formation in the eastern Silver Peak Range (Robinson, 1964; Robinson and others, 1968) has been significantly overestimated as a result of nonrecognition of faults that duplicate the section and of the

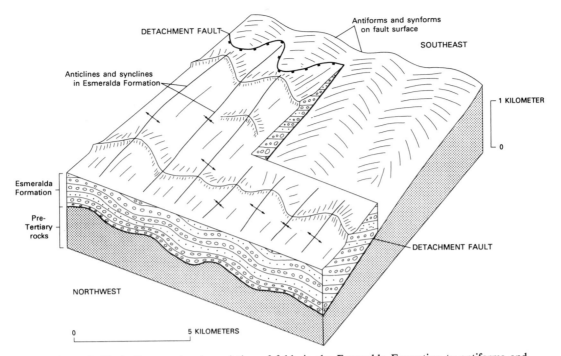

Figure 8. Block diagram showing relation of folds in the Esmeralda Formation to antiforms and synforms on detachment surface.

erroneous assumption that mapped units were time-stratigraphic units. In a measured section between Red Mountain and Silver Peak, sequence 1 has a maximum thickness of 262 m. In this same area, the thickest section of sequence 2, which is composed primarily of conglomerate and breccia of the conglomerate facies, is 963 m. However, this represents a minimum because the base of this section is not exposed, and the upper contact is a fault. This thickness contrasts greatly with the approximately 1,700 m reported by Robinson (1964) for sequence 2 at this location, probably because he did not recognize faults that duplicate the section. It is possible that the section is actually thinner than reported here, as a result of unrecognized faulting in areas of poor exposure. However, we feel that this is unlikely because mapped faults have generally consistent strikes, and in areas where unrecognized faults might occur, Paleozoic strata, which are apparently in depositional contact with underlying Tertiary rocks, are clearly not faulted along the presumed strike of these faults. Robinson (1964) reports nearly 615 m of section on the western flank of the range, equivalent to unit $S2_s$ on the eastern flank.

Age. A single camel bone collected from near the base of unit $S1_c$ has an age range from Clarendonian to Hemphillian but may be as old as Barstovian (S. D. Webb *in* Robinson, 1964; Robinson and others, 1968) (Fig. 6). Robinson (1964) noted poorly preserved plant fossils in unit $S1_{sh}$ and poorly preserved plant remains, mollusks, gastropods, and mastodon bone fragments in unit $S2_s$, but none of these was sufficiently well preserved to indicate specific age.

Robinson and others (1968) reported several K-Ar ages from rocks of the Silver Peak volcanic center that unconformably overlie, and thus place an upper limit on the age of, the Esmeralda Formation in the Silver Peak Range. These ages (recalculated using new constants, Dalrymple, 1979) are 6.2 ± 0.5 Ma on a rhyolite tuff, 6.1 ± 0.2 Ma on a trachyandesite flow, 6.3 ± 0.3 Ma on trachyandesite welded tuff overlying the rhyolite, and 4.9 ± 0.6 Ma on a basalt flow overlying the trachyandesite.

Thus, the age of the Esmeralda Formation in the Silver Peak Range can be constrained as middle and late Miocene between about 16.6 Ma (absolute age of basal Barstovian mammal age) and approximately 6 Ma (K-Ar age of lowermost volcanic rocks associated with the Silver Peak volcanic center).

Structure. The Esmeralda Formation between Red Mountain and Silver Peak crops out along the southern flank of the Mineral Ridge detachment fault, a dome-shaped fault surface elongated approximately N60° to 70°W. (Albers and Stewart, 1972; Kirsch, 1971). The detachment fault makes up the upper boundary for a distinct lower-plate assemblage of the metamorphosed Late Proterozoic Wyman Formation and the Late Proterozoic to Lower Cambrian Reed Dolomite intruded by Mesozoic (?) granitoids. Remnants of relatively unmetamorphosed Late Proterozoic to Upper Cambrian strata (Campito, Poleta, Harkless, Mule Spring, and Emigrant formations) and Ordovician cherts and shales (Palmetto Formation) lie structurally above, and form several klippen atop the Mineral Ridge detachment. This upper-plate assemblage has been severely disrupted and slivered by pervasive low-angle faults, which in almost all cases place younger strata on older and grossly attenuate upper-plate section.

As in the Alum area, previous workers assumed that the

Esmeralda Formation unconformably overlapped the aforementioned pre-Tertiary rocks and Mineral Ridge detachment fault (Robinson, 1964; Robinson and others, 1968; Kirsch, 1971), thus postdating all movement on the fault. At several places where the Esmeralda Formation lies on upper-plate pre-Tertiary rocks, the contact is demonstrably depositional, although local shearing and folding are common, and a lag of pebbles and cobbles derived from immediately underlying lithologies commonly makes up the basal part of the Esmeralda Formation. Deposition of the Esmeralda Formation postdates movement on the aforementioned pervasive younger-on-older faults. However, numerous generally 15 to 16° west-dipping, low-angle normal faults, which either merge with or are cut at low angles by the Mineral Ridge detachment fault, cut both the Esmeralda Formation and upper-plate pre-Tertiary rocks. These faults bring the Esmeralda Formation into fault contact with both upper- and lower-plate pre-Tertiary rocks and at several locations have left klippen of the Esmeralda Formation stranded above the Mineral Ridge detachment fault (Fig. 9). Strata of the Esmeralda Formation generally dip moderately to steeply eastward into the Mineral Ridge detachment fault and in all cases are highly fractured or have well-developed gouge zones along the contact with the lower-plate assemblage. Nowhere in the Silver Peak Mountains does the Esmeralda Formation lie depositionally on rocks of the lower-plate assemblage.

Several lines of evidence suggest that movement along the west-dipping normal faults was at least in part coeval with deposition of the Esmeralda Formation. In the vicinity of Coyote Spring, several of these faults bring unit $S1_{sh}$ into contact with upper-plate pre-Tertiary rocks but are clearly truncated by the unconformity underlying relatively untilted outcrops of sequence 2 (Fig. 9). Where faults of similar orientation cut both older and younger sequences, offset of the base of sequence 1 is greater than that of sequence 2, suggesting a growth fault relation.

Two of the faults near Coyote Spring clearly shallow with depth where the fault planes are exposed. Also, unit $S1_{sh}$ dips significantly more steeply to the east than unit $S2_s$ near the Coyote Spring fault, and dips in unit $S2_s$ clearly decrease markedly within several hundred meters west of the fault. We interpret these relations to show that tilting here is due to reverse-drag flexure of beds along a listric fault plane rather than being due to a regional tilting event.

Blanco Mine area

About 630 m of the Esmeralda Formation is exposed in the Blanco Mine area (Vanderbilt area of Robinson and others, 1968; Moiola, 1969) on the east side of the Silver Peak Range about 10 km north of Mineral Ridge (Figs. 1, 12). The formation appears to rest unconformably on upper Oligocene or lower Miocene welded tuff, although the coarsest material at the base of the formation is granules and pebbles in claystone in the basal 30 cm of the formation. The formation is divided into five units (Stewart, 1989), designated B1 through B5. Units B1, B3, and B5

consist mostly of dusky-yellow, yellowish-gray, and pale-olive clayey sandstone and siltstone and minor conglomerate (Fig. 3). The sandstone is locally cross-stratified; current directions in unit B5, based on 26 measurements of cross-strata (Fig. 12; Table 1), are east-northeast. The conglomerate contains clasts with an average size of less than 3 cm and a maximum size of about 6 cm. The clasts include chert, siltstone, rhyolite, silicic welded tuff, andesite, and vesicular mafic lava. A 9-m-thick grayish-red volcanic breccia (unit B2) occurs from 111 to 120 m above the base of the formation. It is composed of angular clasts of hornblende andesite, related rocks of intermediate composition, and sparse silicic welded tuff. These clasts range in size from less than a centimeter to about 1 m and are set in a poorly sorted, silt to very coarse grained sand matrix. The volcanic breccia is probably a volcanic debris flow (lahar) and may correlate with volcanic breccia (units C2 and C4) in the Coaldale area (Fig. 3). Tuff, tuffaceous sandstone, and interstratified clayey sandstone and conglomeratic sandstone form unit B4, which occurs from 218 to 279 m above the base of the formation. The tuff is composed of 12 to 13 percent crystals (plagioclase, sanidine), trace amounts of biotite and hornblende, 3 percent clasts of andesitic lava, 10 percent round pumice, and an ashy matrix. On the basis of crystal content and type of lithic clasts, this tuff is considered an eastern distal part of the tuff unit of Jacks Spring, which is widespread in areas to the west.

Vertebrate remains in the middle of the Esmeralda Formation in the Blanco Mine area are Barstovian (middle Miocene) or Clarendonian (middle and late Miocene) in age (Robinson and others, 1968; Moiola, 1969).

Coaldale area

Stratigraphy. The stratigraphy of the Esmeralda Formation in the Coaldale area, about 10 km north of the Blanco Mine area (Figs. 1, 12), has been described by Turner (1900a, b), Hance (1913), Robinson and others (1968), Moiola (1969), Moore (1981), and Stewart (1989). Robinson and others (1968, 1976) and Moiola (1969) indicate a thickness of 930 m for the Esmeralda Formation in the Coaldale area; they did not make detailed subdivisions. Moore (1981) divided the Esmeralda into four members in the Coaldale area and considered the formation to be about 646 m thick. Stewart (1989), on the basis of detailed studies in a larger area than that studied by Moore (1981), divided the formation into eleven units (C1 through C11) and indicated that the formation is 1,327 m thick.

The Esmeralda Formation in the Coaldale area contains several upward-coarsening sequences (Fig. 3) that characteristically contain very pale orange, laminated to very thin bedded siltstone and porcelaneous siltstone in the lower part; dusky-yellow, indistinctly to massive bedded, very fine to fine-grained sandstone in the middle part; and interstratified siltstone, fine-grained sandstone, and medium- to very coarse-grained sandstone and conglomerate in the upper part. Carbonaceous shale and lignite occur near the base of these two upward-coarsening se-

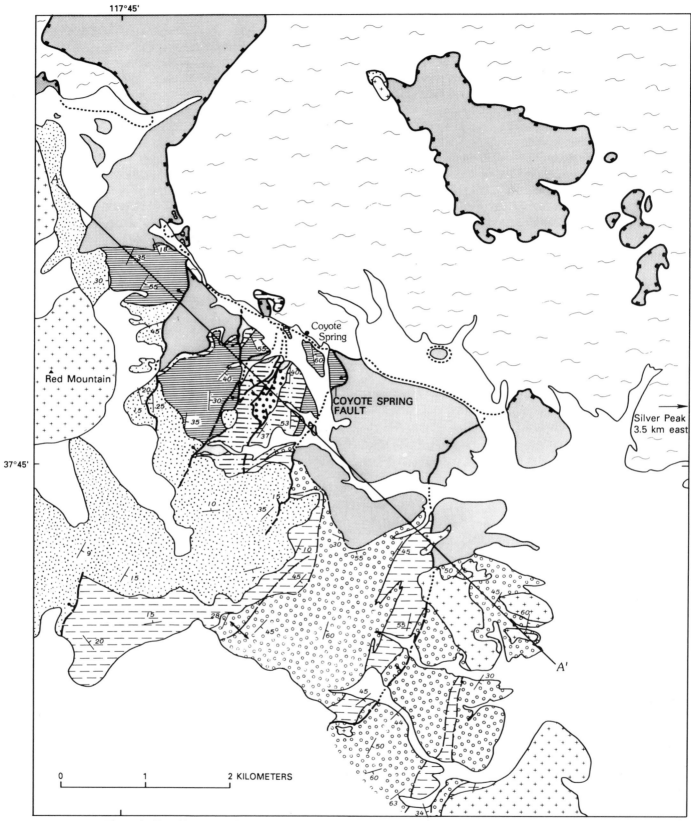

Figure 9. Simplified geologic map of the eastern Silver Peak Range. See Figure 11 for cross section A-A'.

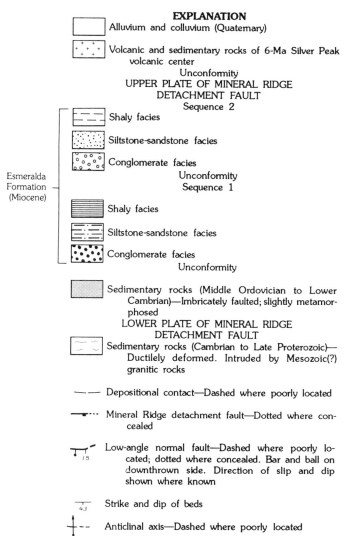

EXPLANATION

Alluvium and colluvium (Quatemary)

Volcanic and sedimentary rocks of 6-Ma Silver Peak volcanic center

Unconformity

UPPER PLATE OF MINERAL RIDGE DETACHMENT FAULT

Sequence 2

Shaly facies

Siltstone-sandstone facies

Conglomerate facies

Unconformity

Sequence 1

Shaly facies

Siltstone-sandstone facies

Conglomerate facies

Unconformity

Esmeralda Formation (Miocene)

Sedimentary rocks (Middle Ordovician to Lower Cambrian)—Imbricately faulted; slightly metamorphosed

LOWER PLATE OF MINERAL RIDGE DETACHMENT FAULT

Sedimentary rocks (Cambrian to Late Proterozoic)—Ductilely deformed. Intruded by Mesozoic(?) granitic rocks

Depositional contact—Dashed where poorly located

Mineral Ridge detachment fault—Dotted where concealed

Low-angle normal fault—Dashed where poorly located; dotted where concealed. Bar and ball on downthrown side. Direction of slip and dip shown where known

Strike and dip of beds

Anticlinal axis—Dashed where poorly located

quences. The conglomerate in the upper parts of these sequences contains granules and pebbles of Tertiary volcanic rocks and, locally, Paleozoic chert. The upper part of the lowest upward-coarsening sequence, unit C1, contains distinctive brown-weathering limestone layers containing abundant pelecypods and gastropods. Near the top of the highest upward-coarsening sequence (units C10 and C11) are several layers of matrix-supported conglomerate with angular to subround clasts of rhyolitic welded tuff and minor chert and argillite set in a silty to coarse sand matrix. Coarse volcanic breccia, locally 181 m thick, composes units C2 and C4. These two units are separated in the eastern part of the Coaldale area by siltstone, porcelaneous siltstone, conglomerate, and silty limestone of unit C3. The volcanic breccia is composed of angular grains to boulder-sized clasts of aphanitic to porphyritic andesite, pale-red rhyolitic ash-flow tuff, and sparse chert set in a fine sand to mud matrix. Locally the clasts of rhyolitic ash-flow tuff are as large as 30 m in maximum diameter. The volcanic breccia probably formed as volcanic debris flows (lahars). Unit C6 also contains a volcanic breccia, which is only 6 m thick.

Tuff occurs as a 15-m-thick layer near the base of unit C1 and as two thin layers, one near the base and one near the top, of unit C7. The tuff in unit C1 (Table 2) contains about 14 percent crystals (plagioclase, sanidine, quartz, and biotite), set in an ashy matrix, and sparse flattened pumice. No lithic clasts were noted. The lower tuff in unit C7 (Table 2) contains about 10 percent crystals (plagioclase, sanidine, and quartz) and 15 percent rounded pumice in an ashy matrix. The upper tuff in unit C7 (Table 2) contains from 7 to 22 percent crystals (plagioclase, sanidine), trace amounts of biotite and hornblende, very sparse clasts of black chert and brown andesitic lava, and a variable amount of flattened pumice. The upper tuff in unit C7 is similar to, and is tentatively correlated with, the tuff unit of Jacks Spring that occurs in the Blanco Mine area and areas in, and to the west of, northern Fish Creek Valley. The tuff in unit C1 and near the base of unit C7 cannot be correlated with tuffs elsewhere in the Esmeralda basin.

Paleocurrent directions in the Esmeralda Formation in the Coaldale area are northeast, based on studies of cross-strata in units C6 and C8 (Fig. 12; Table 1).

The Esmeralda Formation in the Coaldale area rests unconformably on upper Oligocene and lower Miocene tuffs, one of which has a K-Ar date of 22.1 ± 1.0 Ma (Robinson and others, 1968; revised using new constants, Dalrymple, 1979). The lowermost meter of the formation above the tuffs contains silicified tree logs as large as 2 m in diameter lying parallel to the unconformable contact. The Esmeralda Formation is overlain in the Coaldale area by Quaternary alluvial deposits and locally by Quaternary basalt (Robinson and others, 1976).

Age. The Esmeralda Formation in the Coaldale area contains a fairly abundant flora consisting of carbonized plant remains, pollen, silicified wood (Knowlton, 1900; Axelrod, 1940; J. P. Bradbury *in* Moore, 1981), and fauna of mollusks, ostracods, fish, and vertebrates (Lucas, 1900; Stirton, 1936; J. R. Kirby *in* Robinson and others, 1968; J. R. Kirby, R. M. Forester, G. R. Smith, and C. A. Repenning *in* Moore, 1981). These fossils indicate a late Barstovian (middle Miocene) to Hemphillian age (late Miocene) (Robinson and others, 1968; Moore, 1981). A 13.0 ± 0.2 Ma K-Ar date (recalculated using new constants, Dalrymple, 1979) has been obtained (Evernden and James, 1964) on a tuff, probably the one in the lower part of unit C1. Thus, paleontological and radiometric dating indicates a middle and late Miocene age for the Esmeralda Formation in the Coaldale area.

Northern Fish Lake Valley, Volcanic Hills, and Basalt areas

Stratigraphy. The Esmeralda Formation is exposed in a series of outcrops trending northwest in the western areas of exposure of the formation in northern Fish Lake Valley, on the south side of the Volcanic Hills, and near the abandoned settlement of Basalt (Figs. 1, 12). These rocks are shown as unit Ts on the geologic map of the Davis Mountain quadrangle (Robinson

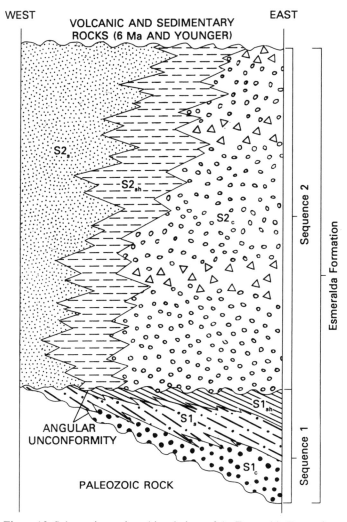

Figure 10. Schematic stratigraphic relations of the Esmeralda Formation in Silver Peak Range. See Figure 9 for explanation. Triangle pattern indicates megabreccia. S1$_c$ and S2$_c$ indicate conglomerate facies, S1$_s$ and S2$_s$ indicate siltstone-sandstone facies, and S1$_{sh}$ and S2$_{sh}$ indicate shaly facies.

and Crowder, 1973) and as unit Tc on the Benton (Crowder and others, 1972), Basalt (Stewart, 1981a), and Miller Mountain quadrangles (Stewart, 1979). They have been studied extensively by Suthard (1966) in northern Fish Lake Valley.

Rocks exposed in the northern Fish Lake Valley and on the south side of the Volcanic Hills are at least 621 m thick (Suthard, 1966) and consist primarily of yellow-gray, blue-gray, and yellow-brown, fine- to medium-grained, locally coarse-grained sandstone with well-defined small-scale trough cross-strata. Silt-stone, tuff, conglomerate, and andesite breccias ((Robinson and Crowder, 1973) are locally present. Near locality 9 (Fig. 12), a 1- to 2-m thick conglomerate in the upper part of the sequence contains clasts as large as 30 cm of andesite, tuff, and black chert. Some of the tuff clasts are derived from the Candelaria Junction Tuff (Speed and Cogbill, 1979) that is widely distributed in west central Nevada (Robinson and Stewart, 1984).

Four studies of cross-stratified sandstone in the northern Fish Lake Valley indicate easterly current directions (Fig. 12; Table 1). Previous studies in northern Fish Lake Valley by Suthard (1966) indicated generally westerly current directions, the opposite of that obtained here. Suthard measured the trend of clearly defined troughs but misinterpreted the shape of the trough cross-strata to indicate westerly, rather than easterly, flow.

Strata exposed in the Basalt area consist mostly of conglomerate with minor amounts of sandstone, diatomite, and tuff. These rocks are best seen in road cuts along an abandoned part of U.S. Highway 6 about 3.2 km east of Basalt and are widely exposed in low hills extending from 1.5 to 3.5 km southeast of Basalt. In places, the conglomerate is not indurated and is better called a gravel. It is characteristically composed of rounded to sub-rounded pebbles and cobbles, and locally boulders as large as 50 cm, set in a coarse to very coarse sand matrix. Clasts are Tertiary andesite, rhyolite, basalt, and welded tuff and Paleozoic chert, schist, and phyllite. In places, the conglomerate, and locally sedimentary breccia, is composed entirely of clasts of the Candelaria Junction Tuff (Speed and Cogbill, 1979; Robinson and Stewart, 1984). Fine- to very coarse-grained sandstone and local sedimen-

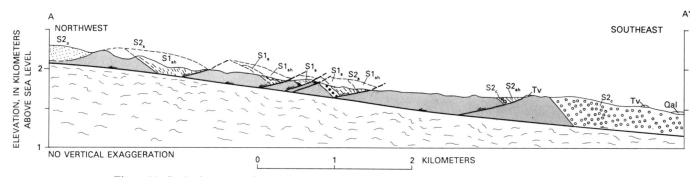

Figure 11. Geologic cross section of the eastern Silver Peak Range. Relations above and below surface projected from south and north of section. Note that the westward rise in elevation of detachment fault is due primarily to orientation of section line oblique to axis of domed detachment fault. See Figure 9 for location of section and Figures 9 and 10 for explanation. Arrows show slip direction along low angle normal faults. Tv indicates volcanic and sedimentary rocks at 6-Ma Silver Peak volcanic center. Qal indicates Quaternary alluvium and colluvium.

tary tuff, air-fall and ash-flow tuff, and diatomite occur interstratified with the conglomerate. The main diatomite mined from 0.5 to 6 km east of Basalt at the Grefco mine, however, appears to be younger than that in the conglomeratic sequence (Stewart, 1979, 1981a). The thickness of the sedimentary sequence in the Basalt area is poorly known but appears to be at least 180 m. Based on five studies (Fig. 12; Table 1) of the imbrication in conglomerate and direction of dip of cross-strata in associated sandstone and sedimentary tuff, current directions in the conglomeratic sequence in the Basalt area are northeast to southeast.

A distinctive ash-flow tuff occurs interlayered with the lower or middle part of the Esmeralda Formation in the northern Fish Lake Valley, Volcanic Hills, and Basalt areas. This tuff was called unit B of the Esmeralda Formation by Suthard (1966); it forms unit Twt of Stewart (1979) and most of what Robinson and Crowder (1973) mapped as unit Tt. It is here correlated with the tuff unit of Jacks Spring that crops out extensively to the west of Basalt (Stewart, 1981a, 1981b). In the northern Fish Lake Valley, Volcanic Hills, and Basalt areas, the tuff unit of Jacks Spring is about 30 to 50 m thick, poorly welded, and locally at least, composed of two cooling units. It contains (Table 2) about 10 to 20 percent crystals of feldspar (plagioclase and sanidine); less than 1 percent biotite, hornblende, and opaque minerals; 2 to 15 percent brown andesite clasts; and 5 to 20 percent round pumice. The size of the andesite clasts varies from 5 to 35 cm, and

the pumice from 1 to 25 cm. The coarsest andesite clasts and pumice are near Basalt, suggesting that the source area may be nearby, perhaps from a caldera underlying an area of widespread rhyolite flows and domes mapped by Robinson and Crowder (1973) and Crowder and others (1972) in the northern part of the White Mountains.

The Esmeralda Formation in the northern Fish Lake Valley, Volcanic Hills, and Basalt areas rests unconformably on various units (Robinson and Crowder, 1973; Crowder and others, 1972; and Stewart, 1979), including the Ordovician Palmetto Formation, upper Oligocene and lower Miocene ash-flow tuffs, and Miocene andesitic lavas and breccias. It is overlain in these same areas by Pliocene rhyolite tuff or younger basalt.

Age. A fairly extensive fauna (see summary by Suthard, 1966; Evernden and others, 1964) indicates an early Clarendonian age (middle and late Miocene) for the Esmeralda Formation in the northern Fish Lake Valley and southeastern part of the Volcanic Hills. Tuff beds stratigraphically near the faunal beds give K-Ar dages of 11.4 ± 0.2 and 11.7 ± 0.2 Ma (Evernden and others, 1964; recalculated using new constants, Dalrymple, 1979). A K-Ar age of 12.0 ± 0.6 Ma (McKee and Klock, 1984) was obtained on the tuff unit of Jacks Spring 3.2 km east of Basalt. Thus, paleontologic and radiometric dating indicate a middle and late Miocene age for the Esmeralda Formation in the northern Fish Lake Valley, Volcanic hills, and Basalt areas.

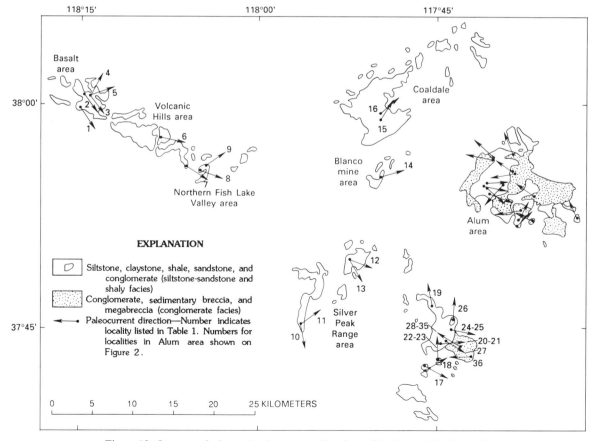

Figure 12. Outcrops, facies, and paleocurrent directions of the Esmeralda Formation.

ESMERALDA BASIN

The depositional setting of the rocks described here is highly variable because of rapid facies changes within, as well as between, individual outcrops. Except for the tuff unit of Jacks Spring that forms a marker from area to area (Figs. 3, 13) and for a volcanic breccia (lahar) that may correlate between the Coaldale area and the Blanco Mine area (Fig. 3), specific units have not been recognized or correlated from area to area. In fact, each area has a somewhat different lithologic character, and conceivably each area could represent an individual isolated basin. However, we interpret the Esmeralda as having been deposited in a single basin (Fig. 13), based on (1) the continuity of the tuff unit of Jacks Spring throughout much of the proposed basin, (2) the similarity in ages of the strata in the various areas (Fig. 6), (3) the generally short distances between outcrops (Fig. 12), (4) geologic mapping that indicates that the Esmeralda is bounded by the same or similar units from area to area (Fig. 6), and (5) paleocurrent directions that suggest a uniform drainage pattern over a large area (Fig. 12).

DEPOSITIONAL ENVIRONMENTS, PALEOGEOGRAPHY, AND STRUCTURAL SETTING OF ESMERALDA BASIN

The fauna, flora, and sedimentary assemblages of the Esmeralda Formation indicate deposition in shallow-water lacustrine, marginal-lacustrine, paludal, fluvial, and alluvial-fan environments and deposition by volcanic processes (Turner, 1900a, b; Axelrod, 1940; Suthard, 1966; Robinson and others, 1968; Moiola, 1969; Moore, 1981). The most abundant deposits are lacustrine. They are characterized by laminated to thin-bedded claystone, shale, siltstone, fine-grained sandstone, and local limestone containing ostracods, pelecypods, and gastropods. Marginal-lacustrine and paludal deposits consist of carbonaceous shale and lignite that crop out in the Coaldale area. Cross-stratified, fine- to medium-grained sandstone associated with the lacustrine deposits is interpreted as braided stream deposits. Coarse conglomerate with rounded clasts, which is characteristic of the Esmeralda Formation in the Basalt area, indicates high-energy streams and moderate to large distances of transport. The coarse matrix-supported conglomerate and sedimentary breccia in the Alum and Silver Peak areas indicates rapid deposition in debris flows and braided streams in a near-source environment, most likely on alluvial fans. Megabreccia deposits and blocks of pre-Tertiary rocks associated with the alluvial-fan deposits in the Alum and Silver Peak areas are considered landslide deposits derived from nearby escarpments, most likely fault scarps.

Volcanic deposits consist of air-fall and ash-flow tuff and volcanic breccia. Transported tuffaceous material and local air-fall tuff are characteristic of much of the deposition in the Esmeralda basin. In addition, the tuff unit of Jacks Spring and the tuff unit of Big Smoky Valley are widespread ash-flow sheets. Coarse volcanic breccia composed mostly of angular andesitic lava frag-

ments in a silt and sand matrix occurs in the Coaldale, Blanco Mine, northern Fish Lake Valley, and Volcanic Hills area. These breccias appear to be volcanic debris flows (lahars) from volcanoes adjacent to the Esmeralda basin.

The Esmeralda Formation was deposited in an asymmetrical basin (Figs. 13, 14) with coarse, near-source alluvial-fan and landslide deposits in the eastern part and generally finer-grained, westerly derived deposits in the western part. This interpretation is supported by the abundance of thick, easterly derived, coarse alluvial-fan and landslide deposits in the Alum and Silver Peak areas (Figs. 12, 13) and by the dominance in the central and western parts of the basin of thinner, finer grained, westerly derived sediments (Figs. 12, 13). The coarse conglomerate in the Basalt area indicates that this area was fairly close to a source region, but still far enough away to allow for significant rounding of clasts. Other coarse conglomerate occurs locally in the Esmeralda basin, suggesting multiple minor source regions peripheral to the basin in addition to major source regions to the east and west.

The asymmetrical shape of the basin and the presence along the east side of the basin of landslide blocks and megabreccia suggests a half-graben with a master syndepositional normal fault or faults on the east side (Figs. 13, 14). No major fault escarpment now exists along the east side of the basin, and the presumed fault is in part buried under Clayton Valley. In the Alum area, the Weepah detachment fault may be the downdip, flatter part of a listric fault that originally bounded the eastern side of the basin (Fig. 14). The present low dip of the fault may also be due in part to tilting above a listric fault that rotated the detachment fault along with overlying sediments (Fig. 14) and/or to tilting associated with isostatic uplift of the denuded footwall (Spencer, 1984; Wernicke and Axen, 1988).

The master fault on the east side of the basin probably originally trended approximately north-northeast, based on the distribution of near-source coarse conglomerate and megabreccia along a NNE trend from the eastern Silver Peak Range to the Alum area (Fig. 12). This trend is also suggested by the previously described syndepositional NNE-trending faults in the Esmeralda Formation in the eastern Silver Peak Range and by the tilt directions in strata of the Esmeralda Formation orthogonal to this trend in both the Silver Peak and Alum areas.

STRUCTURAL DEVELOPMENT

A critical element in the structural development of the Esmeralda basin is extension on the Mineral Ridge and Weepah detachment faults. These faults occur in a complex setting that includes three structural units. (1) Amphibolite-grade, penetratively deformed metasedimentary rocks (Kirsch, 1968, 1971) and associated granitoids form the lowest of the three units and are restricted to the lower plates of the Mineral Ridge and Weepah detachment faults. The metasedimentary rocks in this package consist of calc-silicate schist, mica schist, marble, and quartzite and have been correlated on the basis of lithology with the Late Proterozoic Wyman Formation and the Late Proterozoic and

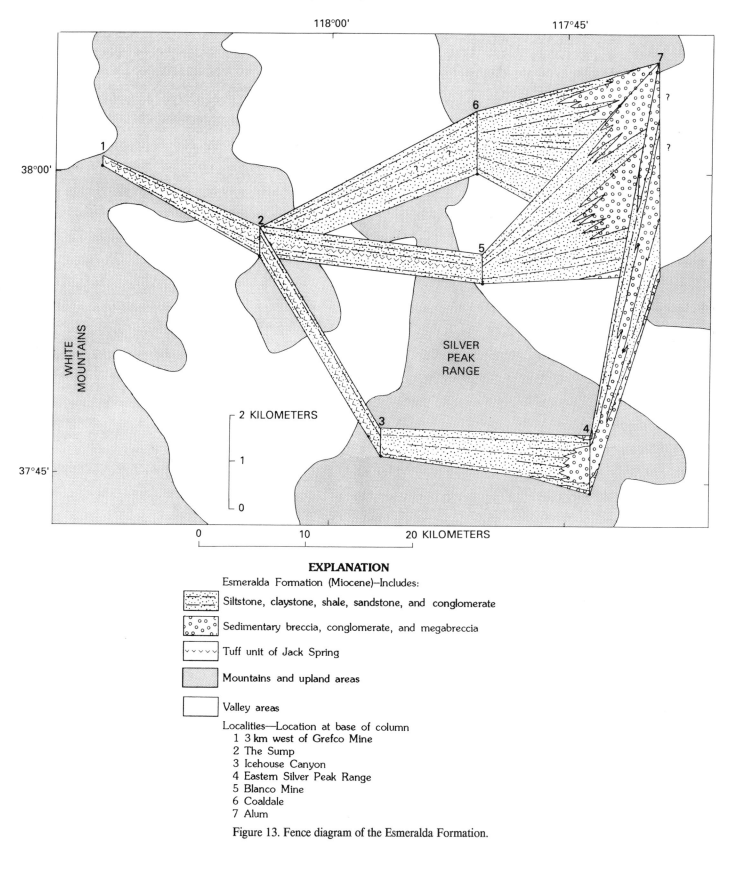

118°00' 117°45'

38°00'

37°45'

7

6

1

2

5

WHITE
MOUNTAINS

SILVER
PEAK
RANGE

3

4

2 KILOMETERS

1

0

0   10   20 KILOMETERS

EXPLANATION

Esmeralda Formation (Miocene)—Includes:

Siltstone, claystone, shale, sandstone, and conglomerate

Sedimentary breccia, conglomerate, and megabreccia

Tuff unit of Jack Spring

Mountains and upland areas

Valley areas

Localities—Location at base of column
  1 3 km west of Grefco Mine
  2 The Sump
  3 Icehouse Canyon
  4 Eastern Silver Peak Range
  5 Blanco Mine
  6 Coaldale
  7 Alum

Figure 13. Fence diagram of the Esmeralda Formation.

Lower Cambrian Reed Dolomite (Albers and Stewart, 1972). (2) Relatively unmetamorphosed sedimentary rocks of Late Proterozoic to Middle Ordovician age form the middle structural unit. These rocks are restricted to the upper plates of detachment faults and have been severely attenuated or chaotically slivered by imbricate low-angle faults. On Mineral Ridge, the detachment fault is in most places overlain by this unit, but in the Alum area the detachment fault is overlain by the second structural unit at only three locations. (3) The highest of the three structural units is the less deformed Esmeralda Formation. In the Silver Peak area, south of Mineral Ridge, the Esmeralda Formation appears to rest depositionally on rocks of the second structural unit, and the second and third units are both cut by broadly spaced listric faults that sole in, or are cut at low angles by, the Mineral Ridge

WEST NORTHWEST   EAST SOUTHEAST

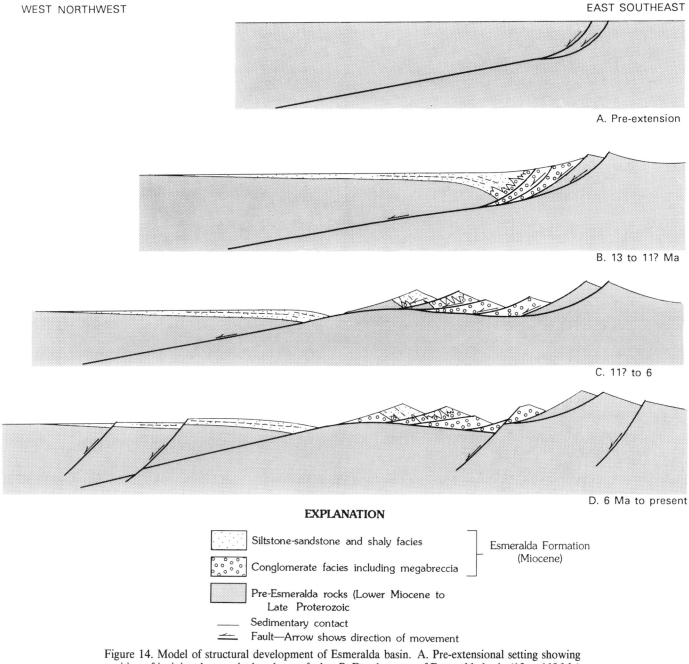

A. Pre-extension

B. 13 to 11? Ma

C. 11? to 6

D. 6 Ma to present

EXPLANATION

⣿ Siltstone-sandstone and shaly facies	Esmeralda Formation
⣿ Conglomerate facies including megabreccia	(Miocene)

Pre-Esmeralda rocks (Lower Miocene to Late Proterozoic

—— Sedimentary contact

⚡ Fault—Arrow shows direction of movement

Figure 14. Model of structural development of Esmeralda basin. A. Pre-extensional setting showing position of incipient low-angle detachment faults. B. Development of Esmeralda basin (13 to 11? Ma) as a result of extension related to movement of major block westward on detachment faults. C. Further extension, dismemberment of Esmeralda basin, and uplift (11? to 6 Ma). D. Cessation of detachment faulting prior to development of 6-Ma Silver Peak volcanic center (not shown). Development of high-angle basin-range faults.

detachment fault (Fig. 9). Owing to this faulting, or to movement on the Mineral Ridge detachment fault, the Esmeralda Formation rests in a few places in fault contact directly on metamorphic core rocks of Mineral Ridge. In much of the Alum area, rocks of the Esmeralda Formation are in fault contact along the Weepah detachment fault (a presumed continuation of the Mineral Ridge detachment fault) with metamorphic rocks of the lowest structural unit.

Initiation of extension, and presumably detachment faulting, preceded the deposition of the Esmeralda Formation, because unmetamorphosed sedimentary rocks of the second structural unit were highly deformed and attenuated in the Mineral Ridge area before deposition of the Esmeralda Formation. The extensional half graben of the Esmeralda Formation may have been initiated by this early attenuation above the detachment, presumably shortly before the start of deposition of the Esmeralda Formation about 13 Ma (Figs. 6, 14). Continued movement on the Mineral Ridge and Weepah detachment faults may have caused further subsidence of the basin during deposition of the Esmeralda Formation. However, extension on these detachment faults did not stop after deposition of the Esmeralda Formation because (1) the Esmeralda Formation is cut by the detachment fault in the Silver Peak and Alum areas, and (2) sediments above the detachment fault that contain clasts derived from unmetamorphosed Cambrian and Ordovician sedimentary rocks are juxtaposed against rocks below (Late Proterozoic metasedimentary and Mesozoic granitic rocks) that could not have supplied these clasts. Dismemberment of the Esmeralda basin by these detachment faults (Fig. 14), although poorly constrained in time, may have started near the end of deposition of the Esmeralda Formation (11? Ma or perhaps as late as 9 Ma, Fig. 6) and have terminated by 6 Ma when the relatively undeformed rocks of the Silver Peak volcanic center were deposited.

In addition to detachment of the Esmeralda Formation from underlying rocks, the Esmeralda Formation in the Alum area is folded. These folds trend northwest and consist of open anticlines and synclines spaced 1 to 2 km apart. The anticlines and synclines are on line with antiforms and synforms on the detachment fault (Fig. 8). Similar undulations or corrugations on detachment faults in southeastern California (John, 1987; Davis and Lister, 1988) have been interpreted as primary fault-surface irregularities that are elongate in the direction of extension. Such an interpretation may apply to the Alum area; if so, the folds in the Esmeralda Formation may have been produced by deformation as strata of the Esmeralda Formation moved down dip along this irregular surface. Alternately, the detachment surface and the overlying Esmeralda Formation were folded together after movement on the fault ceased. Such an interpretation is supported by the presence of anticlines in pre-Tertiary rocks that correspond locally to antiforms in the detachment surface. With present information, however, no clear decision can be made as to whether the undulations in the fault surface are original irregularities or whether they are later folds. The antiformal shape of Mineral Ridge (Kirsch, 1968, 1971) suggests that it, too, is an undulation or fold with the

same trend as those in the Alum area, but of a much larger size. However, no evidence exists in the Mineral Ridge area for folding of the Esmeralda Formation, which strikes into the detachment fault with little or no deviation in strike.

The post-Esmeralda structural development (Fig. 1) of the Weepah, Silver Peak, and northern Fish Lake Valley areas includes (1) uplift that exposed the metamorphic core rocks of the Mineral Ridge and Weepah areas, (2) related uplift that exposed the entire 3+ km thickness of the Esmeralda Formation in the Alum area, (3) NE- and NNE-trending, high-angle normal faulting (Fig. 1) in the Clayton Valley, Big Smoky Valley, and Silver Peak Range (Davis, 1981; Robinson and others, 1976; Albers and Stewart, 1972), (4) right-lateral faulting near the northern termination of the northwest-trending Furnace Creek fault zone in northern Fish Lake Valley (Stewart, 1988), and (5) possible strike-slip faulting (either right- or left-lateral) along the east-trending Coaldale fault zone in the Coaldale area (Stewart, 1985).

COMPARISON OF ESMERALDA AND PRESENT BASINS

The Esmeralda basin lies within the northwest-trending Walker Lane belt (Stewart, 1988), a subprovince of the actively extending Great Basin portion of the Basin and Range province. Strike-slip and normal faults characteristic of this subprovince show abundant evidence of Quaternary slip, including historic faulting, and exert a strong control on both physiography and the location and geometry of present depocenters. Several of these depocenters, specifically the Fish Lake Valley, Clayton Valley, and Big Smoky Valley basins, occur within the outcrop belt of the Esmeralda Formation and have basin-bounding fault systems that truncate outcrops of the Esmeralda Formation (Fig. 1), thus dismembering the once continuous Esmeralda basin. These relations reveal that the Esmeralda basin differs in size and shape from present basins and is related to a different set of syndepositional faults and mountain source areas than present basins.

The contrast in size and shape of the Esmeralda basin and present basins is marked. The Esmeralda basin is exposed in an approximately 60-km by 40-km swath across uplands of the Silver Peak Range, Weepah Hills, and White Mountains as well as in several major intervening valleys. Attenuation of the Esmeralda Formation by imbricate normal faulting, as observed in the eastern Silver Peak Range, has undoubtedly increased the original northwest-southeast dimension of the Esmeralda basin to its present 60 km. However, from Basalt eastward to the Blanco Mine area, a distance of over 40 km (Fig. 1), outcrops of the Esmeralda Formation or immediately underlying volcanic rocks are fairly continuous and show relatively low dips and relatively minor structural complication (Robinson and Crowder, 1973; Robinson and others, 1976), and attenuation of these outcrops is minimal. Therefore, even allowing for considerable attenuation east of Blanco Mine, the minimum width of the Esmeralda basin is about 40 km.

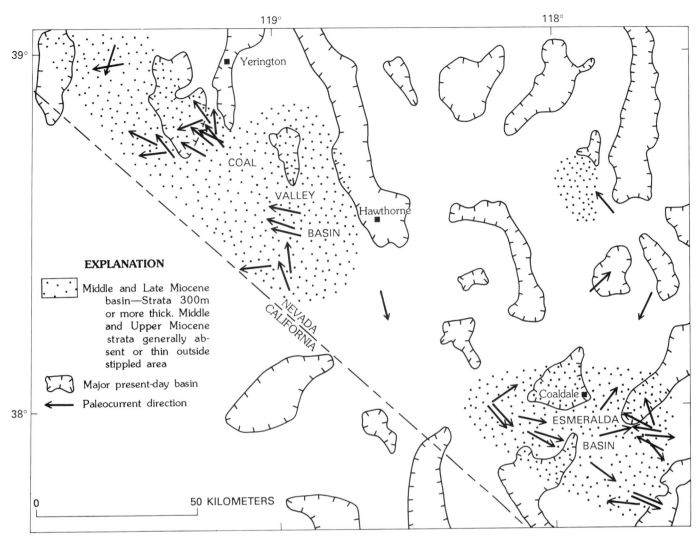

Figure 15. Distribution of middle and upper Miocene sedimentary basins, generalized paleocurrent directions in middle and upper Miocene fluvial units, and distribution of major present basins, eastern California and western Nevada. Modified from Stewart (1983b). Detailed information on paleocurrents shown in Figures 2 and 12 and in Table 1.

In contrast, present basins in western Nevada (Fig. 15) are irregular, but commonly north-trending, elongate troughs that parallel their fault-bounded margins (e.g., Link and others, 1985). These elongate basins typically have widths of 10 to 20 km and lengths in excess of 50 km, as is true of Quaternary basins throughout the Great Basin (e.g., Stewart, 1971; Fletcher and Hallett, 1983).

The distribution of syndepositional faults and mountain source areas is distinctly different for the Esmeralda basin than for present basins in the same area. Coarse alluvial-fan deposits and associated landslide deposits indicate a major fault escarpment on the east side of the Esmeralda basin; yet, as described above, no present-day major highland or fault escarpment exists there now. In addition, the Esmeralda Formation lacks coarse detrital debris that could have been derived from what are now the Silver Peak Range and the White Mountains, and we infer that these moun-

tains did not exist during deposition of the Esmeralda Formation. These upland areas are now flanked by major Quaternary alluvial-fan deposits and are major source areas for present-day basinal deposits. A further indication of a change in physiography since the Miocene is the presence of outcrops of the Esmeralda at elevations as high as 2,240 m in mountains and as low as 1,460 m in valleys, a relief of 780 m. The original relief on the depositional surface of the Esmeralda basin must have been fairly low, and the present-day variation of elevation of the outcrops must be due primarily to structural deformation after final deposition in the basin.

The Miocene Coal Valley basin, 140 km to the northwest of the Esmeralda basin, has several similarities to the Esmeralda basin, including large size (Fig. 15), consistent paleocurrent directions over a broad region, and overprinting by younger basins and structures (Gilbert and Reynolds, 1973). Development of this basin may be related to the same extensional event that produced the shallowly dipping Miocene extensional faults in the Yerington area (Proffett, 1977).

DISCUSSION

A relation between large-scale extension and basin development has been noted in many parts of the Basin and Range Province (e.g., Coney, 1980, p. 15; Cemen and others, 1985; Guth, 1981; Teel and Frost, 1982; Stewart, 1983a; Bohannon, 1984; Wernicke, 1985). In the case of the Esmeralda Formation, this extension may be related to movement on the Mineral Ridge and Weepah detachment faults (Fig. 14) that caused large-scale attenuation of pre-Esmeralda rocks above the detachment and resulted in structural subsidence and basin development.

The development of the Miocene Esmeralda basin as a consequence of extension on low-angle faults, and its subsequent overprinting by structures clearly related to current Basin and Range physiography, is a common relation reported in many detachment fault terranes of the Basin and Range province (Miller and others, 1983; Coney, 1987; Reynolds and Rehrig, 1980). Two distinctly different interpretations of such relations are possible.

The first is that detachment faulting and basin-range faulting represent kinematically related and simultaneously active processes, the surficial expression of which varies in time and space. This variation occurs because surface structure varies with the depth of a shallowly dipping detachment that underlies an upper crustal wedge of extended material (e.g., Wernicke, 1981, 1985; Wernicke and others, 1985). The locations of active detachment faults and of associated high-angle faults in the overlying allochthonous plate change with time as detachments are warped and isostatically uplifted (Hamilton, 1987; Wernicke and Axen, 1988). This allows overprinting relations, as described above, to develop within a continuously evolving extensional allochthon.

In the other interpretation, extensional basin-range faulting is kinematically different from, and largely postdates, extensional low-angle faulting in detachment terranes (e.g., Eaton, 1982; Zoback and others, 1981; Reynolds and Rehrig, 1980; Coney, 1987; Jackson, 1987).

We favor the second interpretation because the Esmeralda basin contrasts distinctly in size, distribution, and position of syndepositional faults with present basins in the same area. In addition, an evolution of basin and structural styles was not noted between the Esmeralda and present basins, as would be expected by the first interpretation. Corollary arguments are based on analysis of the Coal Valley basin, which is also fragmented by modern basin-range faults (Gilbert and Reynolds, 1973). In the Coal Valley region, a contrast in structural style is indicated by Miocene extension that is characterized by tilted normal faults (Proffett, 1977) spaced 0.5 to 1.5 km apart measured normal to fault surfaces. This compares to present major basin-range faults spaced about 20 to 40 km apart (Gilbert and Reynolds, 1973). The large width of the Esmeralda and Coal Valley basins is considered the result of extension due to slip on shallowly dipping detachment faults, whereas the relatively narrow width of present basins may indicate steep dips of basin-bounding fault systems, a conclusion that is supported by the steep dips of present faults determined by earthquake focal mechanisms in the western Great Basin (e.g., Vetter and Ryall, 1983; Okaya and Thompson, 1985; Jackson, 1987). Eaton (1982) and Kusznir and Park (1987) have suggested models in which regionally restricted areas of closely spaced normal faults and large-scale extension occur during times of fast strain rates, and more widely spaced faults and regional extension occur in times of slow strain rates. These models may have application to the apparent change in character of extension with time in the Great Basin.

ACKNOWLEDGMENTS

We thank J. P. Calzia, J. C. Dohrenwend, D. I. Axelrod, R. V. Ingersoll, T. A. Hauge, and an anonymous reviewer for their helpful reviews of the manuscript. We benefited from discussions and field trips with C. A. Nelson, R. V. Ingersoll, B. J. Bilodeau, and T. Riksheim. Acknowledgment is made by Diamond to the Geological Society of America, White Mountain Research Station, Wilbur Sherman Fellowship Fund, the University of California at Los Angeles Department of Earth and Space Sciences, and the Donors of The Petroleum Research Fund administered by the American Chemical Society, for partial support of this research.

REFERENCES CITED

Albers, J. P., and Stewart, J. H., 1972, Geology and mineral deposits of Esmeralda County, Nevada: Nevada Bureau of Mines and Geology Bulletin 78, 75 p.

Anderson, R. E., Zoback, M. L., and Thompson, G. A., 1983, Implications of selected subsurface data on the structural form and evolution of some basins in the northern Basin and Range province, Nevada and Utah: Geological Society of America Bulletin, v. 94, p. 1055–1072.

Axelrod, D. I., 1940, The Pliocene Esmeralda flora of west-central Nevada: Washington Academy of Science Journal, v. 30, p. 163–174.

Berggren, W. A., Kent, D. V., Flynn, J. J., and Van Couvering, J. A., 1985, Cenozoic geochronology: Geological Society of America Bulletin, v. 96, p. 1407–1418.

Bohannon, R. G., 1984, Nonmarine sedimentary rocks of Tertiary age in the Lake Mead region, southeastern Nevada and northwestern Arizona: U.S. Geological Survey Professional Paper 1259, 72 p.

Cemen, I., Wright, L. A., Drake, R. E., and Johnson, F. C., 1985, Cenozoic sedimentation and sequence of deformational events at the southeastern end of the Furnace Creek strike-slip fault zone, Death Valley region, California, *in* Biddle, K. T., and Christie-Blick, N., eds., Strike-slip deformation, basin formation, and sedimentation: Society of Economic Paleontologists and Mineralogist Special Publication 37, p. 127–141.

Coney, P. J., 1980, Cordilleran metamorphic core complexes; An overview, *in* Crittenden, M. D., Jr., Coney, P. J., and Davis, G. H., Cordilleran metamorphic core complexes: Geological Society of Memoir 153, p. 7–31.

——, 1987, The regional tectonic setting and possible causes of Cenozoic extension in the North American Cordillera, *in* Coward, M. P., Dewey, J. F., and Hancock, P. L., eds., Continental extensional tectonics: Geological Society of London Special Publication 28, p. 177–186.

Crowder, D. F., Robinson, P. T., and Harris, D. L., 1972, Geologic map of the Benton Quadrangle, Mono County, California, and Esmeralda and Mineral Counties, Nevada: U.S. Geological Survey Geologic Quadrangle Map GQ–1013, scale 1:62,500.

Dalrymple, G. B., 1979, Critical tables for conversion of K-Ar ages from old to new constants: Geology, v. 7, p. 558–560.

Davis, G. A., and Lister, G. S., 1988, Detachment faulting in continental extension; Perspectives from the southwestern U.S. Cordillera, *in* Clark, S. P., Jr., Burchfiel, B. C., and Suppe, J., eds., Processes in continental lithospheric deformation: Geological Society of America Special Paper 218, p. 133–159.

Davis, J. R., 1981, Late Cenozoic geology of Clayton Valley, Nevada, and the genesis of a lithium enriched brine [Ph.D. thesis]: University of Texas at Austin, 234 p.

Eaton, G. P., 1982, The Basin and Range province; Origin and tectonic significance: Annual Review of Earth and Planetary Sciences, v. 10, p. 409–440.

Effimoff, I., and Pinezich, A. R., 1986, Tertiary structural development of selected basins; Basin and Range Province, northeastern Nevada, *in* Mayer, L., ed., Extensional tectonics of the southwestern United States; A perspective on processes and kinematics: Geological Society of America Special Paper 208, p. 31–42.

Evernden, J. F., and James, G. T., 1964, Potassium-argon dates and the Tertiary floras of North America: American Journal of Science, v. 262, p. 945–974.

Evernden, J. F., Savage, D. E., Curtis, G. H., and James, G. T., 1964, Potassium-argon dates and the Cenozoic mammalian chronology of North America: American Journal of Science, v. 262, p. 145–198.

Fletcher, R. C., and Hallet, B., 1983, Unstable extension of the lithosphere; A mechanical model for Basin and Range structure: Journal of Geophysical Research, v. 88, p. 7457–7466.

Gilbert, C. M., and Reynolds, M. W., 1973, Character and chronology of basin development, western margin of the Basin and Range province: Geological Society of America Bulletin, v. 84, p. 2489–2510.

Golia, R. T., and Stewart, J. H., 1984, Depositional environments and paleogeography of the upper Miocene Wassuk Group, west-central Nevada: Sedimentary Geology, v. 38, p. 159–180.

Guth, P. L., 1981, Tertiary extension north of the Las Vegas Valley shear zone, Sheep and Desert Ranges, Clark County, Nevada: Geological Society of America Bulletin, v. 92, p. 763–771.

Hamilton, W., 1987, Crustal extension in the Basin and Range Province, southwestern United States, *in* Coward, M. P., Dewey, J. F., and Hancock, P. L., eds., Continental extensional tectonics: Geological Society of London Special Publication 28, p. 155–176.

Hance, J. H., 1913, The Coaldale coal field, Esmeralda County, Nevada: U.S. Geological Survey Bulletin 531–K, p. 313–322.

Hastings, D. D., 1979, Results of exploratory drilling northern Fallon Basin, western Nevada, *in* Newman, G. W., and Goode, H. D., eds., Basin and Range Symposium: Denver, Colorado, Rocky Mountain Association of Geologists, and Salt Lake City, Utah, Utah Geological Association, p. 515–522.

Jackson, J. A., 1987, Active normal faulting and crustal extension, *in* Coward, M. P., Dewey, J. F., and Hancock, P. L., eds., Continental extensional tectonics: Geological Society of London Special Publication 28, p. 3–17.

John, B. E., 1987, Geometry and evolution of a mid-crustal extensional fault system; Chemehuevi Mountains, southeastern California, *in* Coward, M. P., Dewey, J. F., and Hancock, P. L., eds., Continental extensional tectonics: Geological Society of London Special Publication 28, p. 313–335.

Keith, W. J., 1977, Geology of the Red Mountain mining district, Esmeralda County, Nevada: U.S. Geological Survey Bulletin 1423, 45 p.

Kirsch, S. A., 1968, Structure of the metamorphic and sedimentary rocks of Mineral Ridge, Esmeralda County, Nevada [Ph.D. thesis]: Berkeley, University of California, 79 p.

——, 1971, Chaos structure and turtleback dome, Mineral Ridge, Esmeralda County, Nevada: Geological Society of America Bulletin, v. 82, p. 3169–3176.

Knowlton, F. H., 1900, Fossil plants of the Esmeralda Formation: U.S. Geological Survey 21st Annual Report, part 2, p. 209–227.

Kusznir, N. J., and Park, R. G., 1987, The extensional strength of the continental lithosphere; Its dependence on geothermal gradient and crustal composition and thickness, *in* Coward, M. P., Dewey, J. F., and Hancock, P. L., eds., Continental extension tectonics: Geological Society of London Special Publication 28, p. 35–52.

Link, M. H., Roberts, M. T., and Newton, M. S., 1985, Walker Lake basin, Nevada; An example of Late Tertiary(?) to Recent sedimentation in a basin adjacent to an active strike-slip fault, *in* Biddle, K. T., and Christie-Blick, N., eds., Strike-slip deformation, basin formation, and sedimentation: Society of Economic Paleontologists and Mineralogists Special Publication 37, p. 105–125.

Lucas, F. A., 1900, Description of a new species of fossil fish from the Esmeralda Formation: U.S. Geological Survey 21st Annual Report, part 2, p. 223–226.

McKee, E. H., and Klock, P. R., 1984, K-Ar ages of Cenozoic volcanic rocks; Walker Lake 1° by 2° Quadrangle, eastern California and western Nevada: Isochron/West, no. 40, p. 9–11.

Miller, E. L., Gans, P. B., and Garing, J., 1983, The Snake Range décollement; An exhumed mid-Tertiary ductile-brittle transition: Tectonics, v. 2, p. 239–263.

Moiola, R. J., 1963, Origin of authigenic silicate minerals in the Esmeralda Formation of western Nevada [abs.]: Geological Society of America Special Paper 76, p. 116–117.

——, 1964, Authigenic mordenite in the Esmeralda Formation, Nevada: American Mineralogist, v. 48, p. 1472–1474.

——, 1969, Late Cenozoic geology of the northern Silver Peak region, Esmeralda County, Nevada [Ph.D. thesis]: Berkeley, University of California, 139 p.

——, 1970, Authigenic zeolites and K-feldspar in the Esmeralda Formation, Nevada: American Mineralogist, v. 55, p. 1681–1691.

Moore, S. W., 1981, Geology of a part of the southern Monte Cristo Range, Esmeralda County, Nevada [M.S. thesis]: San Jose, California, San Jose State University, 157 p.

Mount, J. F., Gevirtzman, D. A., and Signor, P. W. III, 1983, Precambrian–Cambrian transition problem in western North America; Part 1, Tommotian fauna in the southwestern Great Basin and its implications for the base of the Cambrian System: Geology, v. 11, p. 224–226.

Okaya, D. A., and Thompson, G. A., 1985, Geometry of Cenozoic extensional faulting; Dixie Valley, Nevada: Tectonics, v. 4, p. 107–125.

Proffett, J. M., Jr., 1977, Cenozoic geology of the Yerington district, Nevada, and implications for the nature and origin of Basin and Range faulting: Geological Society of America Bulletin, v. 88, p. 247–266.

Reynolds, S. J., and Rehrig, W. A., 1980, Mid-Tertiary plutonism and mylonitization, South Mountain, central Arizona, *in* Crittenden, M. D., Jr., Coney, P. J., and Davis, G. H., Cordilleran metamorphic core complexes: Geological Society of America Memoir 153, p. 159–175.

Robinson, P. T., 1964, The Cenozoic stratigraphy and structure of the central part of the Silver Peak Range, Esmeralda County, Nevada [Ph.D. thesis]: Berkeley, University of California, 107 p.

Robinson, P. T., and Crowder, D. F., 1973, Geologic map of the Davis Mountain Quadrangle, Esmeralda and Mineral Counties, Nevada, and Mono County, California: U.S. Geological Survey Geological Quadrangle Map GQ–1078, scale 1:62,500.

Robinson, P. T., and Stewart, J. H., 1984, Uppermost Oligocene and lowermost Miocene ash-flow tuffs of western Nevada: U.S. Geological Survey Bulletin 1557, 53 p.

Robinson, P. T., McKee, E. H., and Moiola, R. J., 1968, Cenozoic volcanism and sedimentation, Silver Peak region, western Nevada and adjacent California, *in* Coats, R. R., Hay, R. L., and Anderson, C. A., eds., Studies in volcanology; A memoir in honor of Howel Williams: Geological Society of America Memoir 116, p. 577–611.

Robinson, P. T., Stewart, J. H., Moiola, R. J., and Albers, J. P., 1976, Geologic map of the Rhyolite Ridge Quadrangle, Esmeralda County, Nevada: U.S. Geological Survey Geologic Quadrangle Map GQ–1325, scale 1:62,500.

Speed, R. C., and Cogbill, A. H., 1979, Cenozoic volcanism of the Candelaria region, Nevada: Geological Society of America Bulletin, v. 90, Part 2, p. 456–493.

Spencer, J. E., 1984, Role of tectonic denudation in warping and uplift of low-angle faults: Geology, v. 12, p. 95–98.

Stewart, J. H., 1971, Basin and Range structure; A system of horsts and grabens produced by deep-seated extension: Geological Society of America Bulletin, v. 82, p. 1019–1044.

—— , 1979, Geologic map of Miller Mountain and Columbus Quadrangles, Mineral and Esmeralda Counties, Nevada: U.S. Geological Survey Open-File Report 79–1145, scale 1:24,000.

—— , 1981a, Geologic map of the Basalt Quadrangle, Mineral County, Nevada: U.S. Geological Survey Open-File report 81–369, 1:24,000 scale.

—— , 1981b, Geology of the Jacks Spring Quadrangle, Mineral County, Nevada: U.S. Geological Survey Open-File report 81–368, 1:24,000 scale.

—— , 1983a, Extension tectonics in the Death Valley area, California; Transport of the Panamint Range block 80 km northwestward: Geology, v. 11, p. 153–157.

—— , 1983b, Cenozoic structure and tectonics of the northern Basin and Range province, California, Nevada, and Utah, *in* The role of heat in the development of energy and mineral resources in the northern Basin and Range province: Davis, California, Geothermal Resource Council Special Report 13, p. 25–40.

—— , 1985, East-trending dextral faults in the western Great Basin; An explanation for anomalous trends of pre-Cenozoic strata and Cenozoic faults: Tectonics, v. 4, p. 547–564.

—— , 1988, Tectonics of the Walker Lane belt, western Great Basin; Mesozoic and Cenozoic deformation in a zone of shear, *in* Ernst, W. G., ed., Metamorphism and crustal evolution of the Western United States, Rubey Volume 7: Englewood Cliffs, New Jersey, Prentice-Hall, Inc., p. 683–713.

—— , 1989, Description, stratigraphic sections and maps of middle and upper Miocene Esmeralda Formation in the Alum, Blanco Mine, and Coaldale areas, Esmeralda County, Nevada: U.S. Geological Survey Open-File Report 89–324.

Stewart, J. H., and Noble, D. C., 1979, Preliminary geologic map of the Mount Siegel Quadrangle, Nevada–California: U.S. Geological Survey Open-File Report 79–225, scale 1:62,500.

Stewart, J. H., and Reynolds, M. W., 1987, Geologic map of the Pine Grove Hills Quadrangle, Lyon County, Nevada: U.S. Geological Survey Open-File Report 87–658, scale 1:62,000.

Stewart, J. H., Robinson, P. T., Albers, J. P., and Crowder, D. F., 1974, Geologic map of the Piper Peak Quadrangle, Nevada–California: U.S. Geological Survey Geologic Quadrangle Map GQ–1186, scale 1:62,000.

Stewart, J. H., Carlson, J. E., and Johannesen, D. C., 1982, Geologic map of the Walker Lake 1° × 2° degree quadrangle, California and Nevada: U.S. Geological Survey Miscellaneous Field Studies Map MF–1382–A, scale 1:250,000.

Stewart, J. H., Brem, G. F., and Dohrenwend, J. C., 1989, Geologic map of the Desert Creek Peak Quadrangle, Nevada and California: U.S. Geological Survey Miscellaneous Field Studies Map MF–2050, scale 1:62,500.

Stirton, R. A., 1936, Succession of North American continental Pliocene mammalian faunas: American Journal of Science, 5th series, v. 32, p. 161–206.

Strand, R. G., 1967, Mariposa Sheet: California Division of Mines and Geology, Geologic map of California, Marioposa Sheet, scale 1:250,000.

Suthard, J. A., 1966, Stratigraphy and paleontology in Fish Lake Valley, Esmeralda County, Nevada [M.A. thesis]: Riverside, University of California, 103 p.

Teel, D. B., and Frost, E. G., 1982, Synorogenic evolution of the Copper Basin Formation in the eastern Whipple Mountains, San Bernardino County, California, *in* Frost, E. G., and Martin, D. L., eds., Mesozoic–Cenozoic tectonic evolution of the Colorado River region, California, Arizona, and Nevada: San Diego, California, Cordilleran Publishers, p. 275–285.

Turner, H. W., 1900a, The Esmeralda Formation: The American Geologist, v. 25, p. 168–170.

—— , 1900b, The Esmeralda Formation, a fresh-water lake deposit: U.S. Geological Survey 21st Annual Report, part 2, p. 191–208.

Vetter, U. R., and Ryall, A. S., 1983, Systematic change of focal mechanisms with depth in the western Great Basin: Journal of Geophysical Research, v. 88, p. 8237–8250.

Wernicke, B., 1981, Low-angle normal faults in the Basin and Range province; Nappe tectonics in an extending orogen: Nature, v. 291, p. 645–648.

—— , 1985, Uniform-sense normal simple shear of the continental lithosphere: Canadian Journal of Earth Sciences, v. 22, p. 108–125.

Wernicke, B., and Axen, G. J., 1988, On the role of isostasy in the evolution of normal fault systems: Geology, v. 16, p. 848–851.

Wernicke, B., Walker, J. D., and Beaufait, M. S., 1985, Structural discordance between Neogene detachment and frontal Sevier thrusts, central Mormon Mountains, southern Nevada: Tectonics, v. 4, p. 213–246.

Zoback, M. L., Anderson, R. E., and Thompson, G. A., 1981, Cainozoic evolution of the state of stress and style of tectonism of the Basin and Range province of the western United States: Philosophical Transactions of the Royal Society of London, series A300, p. 407–434.

MANUSCRIPT ACCEPTED BY THE SOCIETY AUGUST 21, 1989

Geological Society of America
Memoir 176
1990

Chapter 23

Reconstruction of extensionally dismembered early Mesozoic sedimentary basins; Southwestern Colorado Plateau to the eastern Mojave Desert

John E. Marzolf
Department of Geology, Southern Illinois University, Carbondale, Illinois 62901

ABSTRACT

On the Colorado Plateau of southwestern Utah, the Lower Jurassic Glen Canyon Group comprises, in ascending order, the Moenave and Kayenta Formations and the Navajo Sandstone. In southern Nevada and southeastern California, the lithostratigraphic equivalent of the Navajo Sandstone is the Aztec Sandstone. In southern Nevada, the Aztec Sandstone is conformably underlain by four informally recognized stratigraphic units (A–D) of the undifferentiated Moenave and Kayenta Formations. The Glen Canyon Group unconformably overlies the Upper Triassic Chinle Formation above a regional unconformity. In addition to the Petrified Forest and Shinarump Members, the Chinle Formation contains a distinctive limestone-pebble conglomerate at its base.

Using the Aztec Sandstone as a distinctive reference unit, the Glen Canyon Group and its relation to underlying and overlying lower Mesozoic depositional sequences are traced southwestward from the Las Vegas extensional domain, along the eastern edge of the relatively unextended Las Vegas Range–Spring Mountains block, into the Jurassic arc terrane of the eastern Mojave Desert. Southwestward, the regional unconformity at the base of the Glen Canyon Group truncates progressively older strata into the arc terrane. Although Middle Jurassic strata have been erosionally or tectonically removed from the Las Vegas extensional basin, volcanic-clast–bearing marginal marine facies of the Middle Jurassic Carmel Formation are tentatively correlated with silicic volcanic, volcaniclastic, and epiclastic rocks of the southern end of the Spring Mountains extensional domain.

Stratigraphic and facies boundaries in lower Mesozoic strata potentially serve as important strain markers to test models of Cenozoic extension. Restoration of structural blocks containing lower Mesozoic outcrops to their pre-Tertiary positions is based on restoration of the Las Vegas Range–Spring Mountains block to its preextension position. The reconstruction reveals that (1) the limestone-pebble conglomerate at the base of the Chinle Formation is truncated on the east by the north-south–trending Vermilion Cliffs paleovalley; (2) the undifferentiated Moenave and Kayenta Formations were deposited in a north-south–trending, incipient foreland basin that deepened to the north; (3) alluvial fans were shed northeastward, at right angles to the Triassic paleoslope, into this basin from the arc terrane; and (4) volcanic centers lying east of the present Colorado River served as the source of volcanic clasts in the Carmel Formation.

Marzolf, J. E., 1990, Reconstruction of extensionally dismembered early Mesozoic sedimentary basins; Southwestern Colorado Plateau to the eastern Mojave Desert, *in* Wernicke, B. P., ed., Basin and Range extensional tectonics near the latitude of Las Vegas, Nevada: Boulder, Colorado, Geological Society of America Memoir 176.

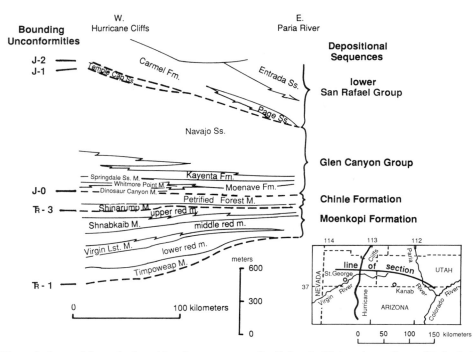

Figure 1. Lower Mesozoic depositional sequences on the Colorado Plateau in southwest Utah, their bounding unconformities, and stratigraphic subdivision (modified from Pipiringos and O'Sullivan, 1978; Peterson and Pipiringos, 1979; Blakey and Middleton, 1983).

INTRODUCTION

The existence of an early Mesozoic Andean-type volcanic arc in the southern Basin and Range and Mojave Desert has been well documented (Burchfiel and Davis, 1975, 1981; Hamilton, 1978; Dickinson, 1981). Because of late Mesozoic deformation and metamorphism and Cenozoic extension, the relation of volcanic and sedimentary rocks of the arc terrane to back-arc stratigraphy of the Colorado Plateau is not well understood. On the Colorado Plateau, the lower Mesozoic stratigraphic section has been subdivided into five unconformity-bounded depositional sequences (Pipiringos and O'Sullivan, 1978; Peterson and Pipiringos, 1979). The term *depositional sequence* is here used as defined by Mitchum and others (1977). From bottom to top, the five depositional sequences and their bounding unconformities include the Ŧ-1 unconformity, the Lower Triassic Moenkopi Formation, the Ŧ-3 unconformity, the Upper Triassic Chinle Formation, the J-O unconformity, the Lower Jurassic Glen Canyon Group, the J-1 unconformity, the Middle(?) Jurassic Temple Cap Sandstone, the J-2 unconformity, and the Middle Jurassic Carmel Formation and Entrada Sandstone. In southwestern Utah, the Glen Canyon Group comprises three conformable, genetically related formations, which are, in ascending order, the Moenave and Kayenta Formations and the Navajo Sandstone. In southern Nevada and southeastern California, the lithostratigraphic equivalent of the Navajo Sandstone is the Aztec Sandstone. The Temple Cap Sandstone, the Carmel Formation, and the Entrada Sandstone compose the lower part of the San Rafael Group (Peterson, 1986). Depositional sequences, their

bounding unconformities, and stratigraphic subdivisions are illustrated in Figure 1.

The Lower Triassic Moenkopi Formation and the Lower Jurassic Navajo Sandstone are the only two lower Mesozoic formations on the Colorado Plateau of which the chronostratigraphic and lithostratigraphic equivalents, respectively, have consistently been recognized within the arc terrane. Intervening strata between the Moenkopi Formation and the Navajo Sandstone, including the Upper Triassic Chinle Formation and the Lower Jurassic Moenave and Kayenta Formations, are either absent or have not been identified within the arc terrane.

Because of its homogeneity in texture, composition, and large-scale cross-stratification, the Navajo or Aztec Sandstone serves as an important lower Mesozoic stratigraphic marker throughout the Colorado Plateau and across the Basin and Range of southern Nevada into the arc terrane of the eastern Mojave Desert. This marker permits reliable correlation of Glen Canyon Group lithofacies below the Aztec Sandstone as well as the bounding unconformities of the Glen Canyon Group. Correlation of these bounding unconformities into the arc terrane establishes important stratigraphic relations between lower Mesozoic depositional sequences described here and elsewhere (Marzolf, in preparation).

The homogeneity that makes the Navajo and the Aztec Sandstones important stratigraphic markers masks the effects of subsequent extensional deformation. Stratigraphic and facies relations within pre- and post-Navajo and Aztec lower Mesozoic strata are recognizable because of the position of the Navajo and Aztec Sandstones. These relations provide important insight into early Mesozoic tectonic setting and paleogeography and subsequent deformation.

The stratigraphy documenting the transition from back-arc to arc is preserved in virtually unmetamorphosed Upper Triassic and Lower Jurassic sedimentary and volcanic rocks in a narrow corridor extending from the southwest corner of the Colorado Plateau to the eastern Mojave Desert. Although rocks correlative with Middle Jurassic strata of the lower part of the San Rafael Group depositional sequence are not present in southern Nevada, unmetamorphosed volcanic and sedimentary rocks of known or probable Middle Jurassic age are present within the arc terrane of southeastern California.

From east to west, the corridor of lower Mesozoic rocks can be divided into three extensional domains based on the amount and timing of extension (Wernicke and others, 1988). On the east lies the Las Vegas extensional basin, in which large-scale extension began approximately 15 Ma and ended 6 to 10 Ma. On the west, north of the Garlock fault, lies the Death Valley extensional basin, in which large-scale extension began at approximately the same time as in the Las Vegas basin and continues to the present. Between these two low-lying basins lies the high-standing, relatively unextended Spring Mountains–Las Vegas Range block referred to hereafter as the Spring Mountains block. Within the extended basins, lower Mesozoic rocks are exposed over relatively small areas within isolated mountain ranges separated by broad valleys filled with Cenozoic rocks. Within the unextended Spring Mountains block, relatively small outcrops of lower Mesozoic rocks are aligned in a north-south direction below thrust sheets of the Late Cretaceous Sevier belt. The distribution of lower Mesozoic strata within the corridor is shown in Figure 2.

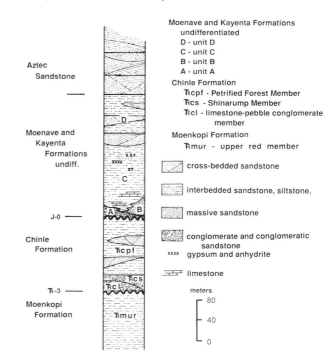

Figure 3. Representative composite stratigraphic section illustrating Upper Triassic and Lower Jurassic depositional sequences below the Aztec Sandstone, their bounding unconformities, and stratigraphic subdivision.

In southern Nevada, lower Mesozoic rocks within the Las Vegas extensional basin and along the eastern edge of the Spring Mountains block lie east of the late Mesozoic Sevier belt and, therefore, are autochthonous or parautochthonous relative to Mesozoic compressional deformation. A representative composite section of Upper Triassic and Lower Jurassic stratigraphic units present in southern Nevada is illustrated in Figure 3. The outcrops in the Clark and Mescal Ranges near the Nevada-California state line also lie east of the Sevier belt, restored for Cenozoic right-slip on the State Line fault (Burchfiel and others, 1982). Other lower Mesozoic outcrops in the eastern Mojave Desert south of the Death Valley extensional basin also are believed to be autochthonous.

Analysis of measured sections documenting lithofacies variability within Upper Traissic and pre-Aztec Lower Jurassic strata from each of these autochthonous and parautochthonous outcrops has led to the following conclusions: (1) facies relations in lower Mesozoic strata cannot be understood without palinspastic reconstruction of Cenozoic extensional deformation, and (2) better understanding of early Mesozoic depositional environments, paleogeography, and tectonic setting places important constraints on models of Cenozoic extension.

The purpose of this chapter is to (1) describe lithofacies within Upper Traissic and Lower and Middle Jurassic depositional sequences in southwestern Utah and southern Nevada, (2) correlate Upper Triassic and Lower and Middle Jurassic depositional sequences from the southwestern Colorado Plateau

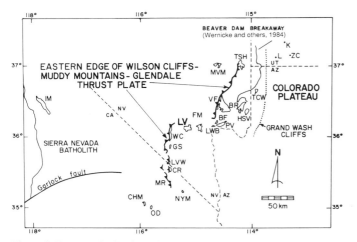

Figure 2. Present distribution of lower Mesozoic outcrops and localities mentioned in the text relative to the Colorado Plateau, eastern edge of the Sevier Orogenic belt, and Sierra Nevada batholith. ZC, Zion Canyon; K, Kanarraville; L, Leeds: TCW, Tom and Cull Wash; TSH, Tule Spring Hills; MVM, Meadow Valley Mountains; VF, Valley of Fire; BR, Bitter Ridge; HSV, Horse Spring Valley; PV, Pinto Valley; BF, Bowl of Fire; LWB, Lovell Wash block; WC, Wilson Cliffs; GS, Goodsprings; LVW, Lavinia Wash; CR, Clark Range; MR, Mescal Range; NYM, New York Mountains; OD, Old Dad Mountain; CHM, Cowhole Mountains; and IM, Inyo Mountains.

into the eastern Mojave Desert, (3) palinspastically restore Upper Triassic and Lower and Middle Jurassic outcrops to their preextension positions, (4) establish facies and stratigraphic patterns within the palinspastically restored Late Triassic and Early and Middle Jurassic basins, and (5) interpret Late Triassic and Early and Middle Jurassic depositional environments, paleogeography, and paleotectonic setting.

Because Mesozoic outcrops compose only a small percent of the total area over which they are presently distributed, the initial phase of my ongoing research has emphasized between out-crop variability. For most outcrops, only a single section has been measured; however, meaningful patterns have emerged that not only have important implications for early Mesozoic sedimentary basins but may also serve as important strain markers to more tightly constrain Cenozoic extension. The Mesozoic outcrops studied are autochthonous with respect to late Mesozoic compression and therefore are presumed to have suffered little compressional deformation. Crustal shortening resulting from the Bird Spring thrust, which separates lower Mesozoic rocks in the Spring Mountains from equivalent strata in the Las Vegas extensional domain, is considered to be small relative to rather large uncertainties in the amount of extension between the Spring Mountains and the Colorado Plateau and has not been considered in this first approximation. Because stratigraphic throw on the Bird Spring thrust increases from north to south, orientation of the line of outcrops at the eastern edge of the Sevier belt will have to be rotated slightly clockwise in future reconstructions. Late Mesozoic strike-slip deformation (Burchfiel and Davis, 1981) is potentially more significant but has not been evaluated in this chapter.

STRATIGRAPHY

Chinle Formation

The Chinle Formation is a widespread, lithologically heterogeneous lithostratigraphic unit recognizable throughout the Colorado Plateau and in southern Nevada. It consists predominantly of claystone, mudstone, siltstone, sandstone, conglomeratic sandstone, and conglomerate. A minimum of six formally named members and several informally named members have been recognized in southeastern Utah and northeastern Arizona (Stewart and others, 1972). From stratigraphically lowest to highest, the formally named members are the Shinarump, Monitor Butte, Moss Back, Petrified Forest, Owl Rock, and Church Rock. The lower four members contain abundant siliceous volcaniclastic detritus. Blakey and Gubitosa (1983) recognize six depositional phases represented in three fining-upward cycles of fluvial, paludal, and fluvio-lacustrine deposition. Coarse fluvial deposits initiating each cycle were deposited in broad alluvial valleys cut in underlying strata. The Shinarump Member was deposited in three north- and northwest-trending paleovalleys cut in the underlying Moenkopi Formation. Cross-bed orientation in Shinarump sandstones indicates streams flowed to the north, northwest, and west.

Clasts within conglomeratic strata are predominantly quartz, quartzite, and chert and lesser amounts of siliceous volcanics at more southerly localities. Maximum clast size decreases from south to north.

The Chinle Formation rests unconformably on the Moenkopi Formation above the Ŧr-3 unconformity. It is overlain, above the J-O unconformity, by the Glen Canyon Group. Westward from southeastern Utah and northeastern Arizona to southwestern Utah, the J-O unconformity bevels across older parts of the Chinle Formation so that only the Shinarump and Petrified Forest Members are present in southwestern Utah.

In southern Nevada, Wilson and Stewart (1967) redefined the Chinle Formation of earlier stratigraphers (Longwell, 1928; Glock, 1929; Hewett, 1931), assigning the upper part to the Moenave and Kayenta Formations undivided. As in southwestern Utah, only the Shinarump and Petrified Forest Members of the Chinle Formation as redefined are present (Stewart and others, 1972). A limestone-pebble conglomerate and interbedded ripple-laminated siltstone and associated shale assigned to the Moenkopi Formation by Stewart and others (1972) and to the Chinle Formation by Bohannon (1983) and Riley (1987) is here recognized as an informal member of the Chinle Formation underlying the Shinarump Member (Figs. 3, 4). Although either my students or I have measured the thickness of the Petrified Forest Member at all localities discussed in the following pages, sedimentological emphasis has been on the Shinarump Member and underlying limestone-pebble conglomerate member.

Limestone-pebble conglomerate member. The limestone-pebble conglomerate has been described in detail by Riley (1987) from which the following summary has been taken. The limestone-pebble conglomerate is composed of weakly stratified, grayish-green, clast- to matrix-supported limestone-pebble conglomerate interbedded with ripple-laminated calcareous siltstones and fine-grained sandstones, cross-bedded calcareous sandstones, and calcareous mudstones. Typically, limestone-pebble conglomerate occurs in repeated fining-upward sequences each capped by ripple-laminated siltstone. Fining-upward sequences commonly have erosional bases. From place to place within stratigraphic sequences, the limestone-pebble conglomerate is cross-stratified in trough and tabular-planar sets. Petrified wood fragments and concave-down pelecypod valves are less common components.

Limestone clasts range in size from medium sand to coarse pebbles except at the southern end of the Wilson Cliffs, where well-laminated carbonate clasts as large as 10 cm in diameter are common. Typical clasts contain subconcentric laminations composed predominantly of microspar. Commonly, laminations have formed around a nucleus, which is typically of quartz but may also be anhydrite, chalcedony, shell fragments, and other limestone fragments. Limestone clasts are enclosed in a sandy matrix.

Friable, green, fine-grained sandstone interfingers with the limestone-pebble conglomerate. The sandstone is ripple laminated in sets 1 to 5 cm thick. Ripple laminations are typically of climbing-ripple and trough type. The calcite-cemented sandstone

Figure 4. Limestone-pebble conglomerate member, Ŧcl, and Shinarump Member, Ŧcs, of the Chinle Formation above the Ŧ-3 unconformity in Pinto Valley. Ŧmur and Ŧcpf are the upper red member of the Moenkopi Formation and Petrified Forest Member of the Chinle Formation, respectively. The limestone-pebble conglomerate member in the foreground is 19 m thick.

is composed predominantly of quartz but also contains minor feldspar and sedimentary rock fragments of chert and limestone, ostracod specimens of a single type, and poorly preserved gastropods. Sandstone bodies are lenticular and range in thickness from a few decimeters to 1 m.

Cross-bedded sandstones are rare except at the Valley of Fire, where tabular-planar cross-bed sets have a maximum thickness of 0.5 m. Other sedimentary structures include recumbent cross-stratification, low-angle trough cross-stratification, and straight- and sinuous-crested ripples. Sandstone bodies appear to be lenticular and to interfinger with limestone-pebble conglomerate and laterally discontinuous mottled red, green, and yellow calcareous mudstones. At Horse Spring Valley, the Valley of Fire, and the Wilson Cliffs, where mudstones have more lateral continuity, they contain resistant mottled zones of carbonate nodules, glaebules, and root tubes.

Shinarump Member. At all localities examined in southern Nevada except the Tule Spring Hills, the Shinarump Member overlies the limestone-pebble conglomerate member (Figs. 3, 4). The contact is interpreted as unconformable. Typically, the Shinarump consists of yellow to reddish-brown conglomerate, conglomeratic sandstone, and sandstone (Becker, 1986). Becker recognized two distinct lithofacies within the Shinarump: lithofacies A—unstratified to crudely stratified, clast-supported conglomerate; and lithofacies B—planar and trough cross-stratified, conglomeratic sandstone and sandstone.

Lithofacies A typically is shades of yellowish brown and dark reddish brown, including grayish yellow to purplish gray. Beds of clast-supported conglomerate alternate with matrix-supported conglomerate, producing a crude horizontal stratification with weak imbrication in places. Clasts are subround to round. Exclusive of the Wilson Cliffs, the most abundant clast types include quartzite (63 to 68 percent), chert (15 to 33 percent), and vein quartz (4 to 17 percent). At the Wilson Cliffs, the conglomerate is notably chert rich; chert makes up 73 percent of the dominant clast types. Less abundant clast types include sedimentary, metamorphic, and volcanic rock fragments. Quartzite clasts are light yellowish brown; chert clasts are green, gray, red, and black. Clasts range in size from granules up to 10.0 cm. The matrix consists of angular to round, very fine to medium sand-sized quartz arenite. From place to place, lenses of sandstone are enclosed within the conglomerate.

Lithofacies A grades upward and is interbedded with conglomeratic sandstone and sandstone of lithofacies B, which typically is shades of yellowish brown to yellowish orange, including greenish yellow, light yellowish brown, and purplish gray. The sandstone typically is poorly to moderately well sorted, angular to subangular sublitharenite. The predominantly monocrystalline quartz sandstone contains sedimentary, volcanic, and low-rank metamorphic rock fragments. The sandstones are calcite cemented and contain pervasive hematite staining. Abundant kaolinite, kaolinized feldspars, and weathering rinds on chert clasts are common.

The Shinarump Member reaches its maximum thickness in southern Nevada at the Wilson Cliffs, where it forms prominent lenses of yellowish-brown conglomerate and conglomeratic sandstone. Clast-supported conglomerate (lithofacies A) is particularly well developed, reaching a maximum thickness of 7 m at Spring Mountain Ranch.

Glen Canyon Group

Moenave Formation. In southwestern Utah, the Moenave Formation is separated from the underlying Chinle Formation by the J-O unconformity. Criteria for the recognition of this contact have been discussed by Wilson and Stewart (1967). The Moenave Formation is divided into three members. From bottom to top, they are the Dinosaur Canyon, the Whitmore Point, and the Springdale Sandtone Members. The Dinosaur Canyon Member consists of red to orange siltstone, very fine-grained sandstone, and minor claystone enclosing lenticular cross-stratified sandstones and siltstones (Wilson, 1958; Blakey and Middleton, 1983). The Whitmore Point Member is of limited areal extent and thickness. It consists of gray and red siltstone, claystone, and minor carbonate. The Springdale Sandstone Member contains small- to large-scale cross-stratification developed in red, yellow, and gray fine- to medium-grained sandstone (Blakey and Middleton, 1983). It forms a prominent sandstone ledge, the top of which serves as a distinct marker defining the top of the Moenave Formation. The Springdale Sandstone Member pinches out southwestward toward the western edge of the Colorado Plateau. Harshbarger and others (1957) considered the Uncompahgre Highlands the dominant source of Moenave sediments.

Kayenta Formation. The base of the Kayenta Formation is marked by the abrupt transition from sandstones of the Springdale Sandstone to siltstones and shales. Harshbarger and others (1957) divided the Kayenta Formation into two facies, a sandy facies in southeastern Utah and northeastern Arizona and a silty facies in southwestern Utah. The silty facies is typified by lenticular sandstone bodies, cross-stratified on a large scale, enclosed in horizontally stratified siltstone and shale. The upper contact is conformable and gradational, marked by extensive intertonguing of fluvial facies with eolian facies of the Navajo Sandstone. Based on paleocurrent and petrographic analysis, Luttrell (1986) concluded that the bulk of Kayenta sediment was transported southwestward from a source in the Uncompahgre Highlands. In the southern part of the depositional basin, paleocurrent data and rhyolitic to andesitic rock fragments suggest a southern source area.

Moenave and Kayenta Formations undifferentiated. Because of the southwestward pinchout of the Springdale Sandstone Member, Wilson and Stewart (1967) were unable to differentiate the Moenave and Kayenta Formations in southern Nevada. The contact between the undivided Moenave and Kayenta Formations and Chinle Formation, as restricted by Wilson and Stewart, is implicitly the J-O unconformity of the Colorado Plateau. In southern Nevada, four informal stratigraphic units have been recognized in strata equivalent to the Moenave and Kayenta Formations (Zaengle, 1984; Potochnik, 1985;

Figure 5. Basal conglomerate (unit A) of the undivided Moenave and Kayenta Formations, Jm/k, resting on the J-O unconformity in the Bowl of Fire. Ja and Ŧcpf are the Aztec Sandstone and Petrified Forest Member of the Chinle Formation, respectively. The conglomerate is approximately 5 m thick.

Burdette, 1986) (Figs. 3, 5, and 6). In the following discussion, these stratigraphic units are referred to as A through D stratigraphically upward. Their characteristics are as follows: unit A—cross-stratified conglomeratic sandstone and conglomerate; unit B—laminated and structureless sandstone; unit C—calcite- and anhydrite-cemented rhythmically interbedded mudstone, siltstone, and very fine-grained sandstone; and unit D—horizontally stratified siltstone and shale and lenticular cross-stratified sandstone.

Unit A. Unit A is predominantly trough cross-stratified sandy conglomerate (Fig. 5). Where it is thick—Wilson Cliffs, Lovell Wash block, Bowl of Fire, Pinto Valley, and Horse Spring Valley—sets of cross-strata have amplitudes of 1 to 2 m; where thin—Frenchman Mountain and the Valley of Fire—set amplitudes are less than 1 m. Set amplitude, like maximum clast size, decreases upward. Unit A is composed of texturally submature to mature but compositionally immature volcanic and sedimentary litharenite and lithrudite. These conglomerates and conglomeratic sandstones pass upward from limestone and chert lithrudite to volcanic lithrudite. Petrified wood notably is absent. At the Wilson Cliffs and Horse Spring Valley, the basal 1 to 2 m is silicified with pervasive fibrous chalcedony cement.

Unit A is present at all but one locality where Moenave-Kayenta sections were measured in southern Nevada. The unit is absent in the Tule Spring Hills. It also is absent at Tom and Cull Wash in the transition zone in northwestern Arizona. Thickness of unit A varies from 0 to 24 m from one mountain block to another. Within localities in which the lower Mesozoic outcrop pattern trends north-south—Wilson Cliffs, Frenchman Mountain, and Horse Spring Valley—changes in thickness of unit A along the outcrop are gradual; whereas in east-west–oriented outcrop belts—Pinto Valley, Bowl of Fire, and the Lovell Wash

Figure 6. Stratigraphic subdivisions of the undivided Moenave and Kayenta Formations, Jm/k, at the Bowl of Fire: gyp, conglomeratic gypsum; C, interbedded mudstone, siltstone, and sandstone of unit C; lst, limestone-bearing interval of unit C; D, interbedded lenticular, cross-bedded sandstone and horizontally stratified siltstone and mudstone of unit D. The dashed line marks the top of the limestone-bearing interval of unit C. Ja is the Aztec Sandstone. The portion of the undivided Moenave and Kayenta Formations (Jm/k) visible in the photograph is approximately 230 m thick.

block—unit A thickens and thins markedly in relatively short distances.

At all localities in southern Nevada, unit A overlies sandstones, siltstones, and mudstones of the Petrified Forest Member of the Chinle Formation. The contact is abrupt. The basal 0.5 m of unit A contains rip-up clasts of siltstone and sandstone from the underlying Petrified Forest Member. The upper contact of unit A is gradational. At most localities, conglomeratic sandstone at the top of unit A grades upward to calcareous siltstone and sandstone of unit C. Everywhere that unit A was observed at the Bowl of Fire, and in places at Pinto Valley, unit A grades upward into evaporitic conglomerate and conglomeratic evaporite, which grades upward into mudstones and siltstones of unit C. At the Valley of Fire and Horse Spring Valley, unit A grades upward to the well-sorted sandstone of unit B.

Because of the potential for confusion in distinguishing the Shinarump Member of the Chinle Formation and the basal conglomerate (unit A) of the undivided Moenave and Kayenta Formations as these units are traced into the arc terrane, criteria for their discrimination are given here. The color of the Shinarump typically is yellowish brown, whereas the Moenave-Kayenta conglomerate is shades of dark reddish-brown. The Shinarump Member exhibits higher proportions of both clast-supported conglomerate and nonconglomeratic, cross-stratified sandstone. Although both stratigraphic units are lithrudites and litharenites, the Shinarump Member conglomerates and sandstones are more mature; the conglomerates contain higher proportions of chert and quartzite relative to a greater abundance of Paleozoic limestone and volcanic rock fragments in the Moenave-Kayenta basal con-

glomerate. Shinarump sandstones tend to be light-colored sublitharenites, whereas unit A sandstones typically are dark reddish-brown volcanic litharenites. Petrified wood can almost always be found within the Shinarump. Petrified wood has not been observed in unit A. Everywhere the Shinarump Member has been observed in southern Nevada, it overlies the distinctive limestone-pebble conglomerate.

Unit B. Unit B is present at the Valley of Fire, Horse Spring Valley, and Tom and Cull Wash. At the Valley of Fire, it is 45 m thick and consists of well-sorted, fine to medium sandstone. Both its upper and lower contacts are conformable. In places, the basal 25 m is unstratified sandstone containing very abundant twig-like iron concretions a few centimeters long and 1 to 3 mm thick. From place to place, sandstone outcrops contain irregularly shaped patches of cross-stratified sandstone, giving evidence of previously more pervasive cross-stratification.

The unstratified sandstone is overlain by 20 m of evenly laminated, well-sorted, medium sandstone. Although some laminae are thicker, most are 1 cm thick or slightly thinner. Heavy mineral concentrations on the soles of some laminae preserve rill marks. At other outcrops in the Valley of Fire, unit B consists entirely of sandstone, slightly more poorly sorted. Bedding is irregular, suggesting syndepositional water expulsion or bioturbation. Bedding-plane parting ranges from slabby to blocky and, in places, massive. In the lower half of the sandstone, extensive bedding surfaces are marked by straight-crested, symmetrical ripples having wavelengths of 10 to 20 cm.

Unit C. Unit C makes up the greatest thickness of undivided Moenave and Kayenta strata at all localities. It also is the most lithologically variable, comprising mudstone, siltstone, sandstone, and silty limestone and limestone (Fig. 6). The clastic strata consist of texturally immature but compositionally mature subfeldslutite and subfeldsarenite and quartz arenite. Finer-grained clastics of unit C—reddish-brown and dark reddish-brown shales, siltstones, and very fine sandstones—are subfeldslutites and subfeldsarenites. Their lower textural maturity is a function of their finer grain size. Very fine grained to fine-grained "purple sandstone beds" present throughout unit C range from plagioclase feldsarenite to feldspathic volcanic litharenite. These sandstone beds are thin and few in number, composing only a few percent of the total thickness of unit C. At Spring Mountain Ranch, a single conglomerate bed, approximately 4 m thick, is present at the base of the upper of two tongues of the Aztec Sandstone. The conglomerate is composed of cobbles and boulders of flow banded, porphyritic volcanic rocks up to 1.5 m in diameter, supported in a matrix composed of volcanic pebbles and reddish-brown quartzose siltstone (Fig. 7).

At all places where unit A is present and unit B is thin or absent, one or more limestone beds, interbedded with mudstone, shale, siltstone, and sandstone, are present a few meters above unit A. The transition strata between the top of unit A and the lowest limestone of unit C consist of thin-bedded calcareous siltstone and sandstone. The thickness of the limestone-bearing interval in the Las Vegas extensional basin ranges from 26 m at

Figure 7. Flow-banded volcanic boulders in volcanic-pebble and quartzose siltstone matrix in debris flow at the base of the upper tongue of Aztec Sandstone in the Wilson Cliffs, Spring Mountain Ranch. The scale is 15 cm long.

Horse Spring Valley and the Lovell Wash block to zero at the Valley of Fire. Limestones are unstratified micrite having bedding-plane parting from 2 to 12 cm thick. Neomorphosed but recognizable ostracods are common. At the Wilson Cliffs, the stratigraphic interval in which limestone beds are present reaches a maximum thickness of 30 m near the Pahrump–Blue Diamond Highway, where at least six limestone beds, which commonly are oncolitic, are present.

Above the limestone-bearing interval, very thin, discontinuous beds of gypsum and anhydrite are interbedded with mudstone, shale, siltstone, and sandstone. Whether calcite or evaporite cemented, unit C is characterized by rhythmic interbedding of slightly differing lithologies and colors. Although probably of primary origin, differences in the rhythmically bedded sediments are subtle, resulting from differences in color, induration, and cement as much as in texture. Pedogenic features are common in the siltstone beds.

At the Wilson Cliffs, the rhythmic bedding of unit C is developed in sets of dark reddish brown siltstone having flaggy to slabby parting and lacking in internal stratification alternating with dark reddish-brown shale. Sandstone beds, rare at the base, increase in thickness and abundance upward. Mudstone is rare, and evaporites are absent.

Unit D. Unit D is best developed at the Valley of Fire where it is 105 m thick. It is also present at Pinto Valley and the Bowl of Fire. Where well developed, unit D consists of lenses of reddish-brown sandstone up to 150 m wide and 10 m thick (Fig. 8). Both the bottom and top of the lenses are marked by secondary bands of light greenish-gray sandstone. The sandstone lenses are cross-stratified in tabular-planar sets 0.3 to 1 m thick. Typically, the sandstone lenses are capped by 0.5 to 1.5 m of climbing-ripple stratification. Sandstone lenses are enclosed in horizontally stratified dark reddish-brown siltstone and shale.

Unit D is similar in character at Pinto Valley where it is 90 m thick, and the Bowl of Fire where it is 77 m thick. At both of these localities, cross-stratified sandstones are thinner and laterally more continuous. Notably at the Valley of Fire and at Pinto Valley, where unit D is best developed, anhydrite and gypsum are absent. At the Bowl of Fire, evaporites are not present within cross-stratified sandstone lenses but are present in the horizontally stratified siltstones and shales.

The Navajo and Aztec Sandstones. Various aspects of the eolian transition from back-arc basin to arc terrane have been discussed recently by Marzolf (1983 a, b), Porter (1986), and Bilodeau and Keith (1986). The Navajo and Aztec Sandstones form a westward-thickening wedge of fine-grained, texturally mature, subarkose characterized by large-scale cross-stratification. The sandstones are extremely uniform in texture and composition over very large areas. In southwestern Utah, the basal Navajo Sandstone intertongues with the underlying Kayenta Formation on a large scale. In southern Nevada, two or more units of cross-bedded eolian sandstone, separated from the main body of the Aztec Sandstone by a few meters to a few tens of meters of lithologies of the undifferentiated Moenave and Kayenta Formations, are known or presumed to merge laterally with the base of the Aztec Sandstone. Large-scale intertonguing of this type is present at the Valley of Fire, Tom and Cull Wash, and the Wilson Cliffs.

Although cross-stratified sandstone is the dominant lithology in the Navajo and Aztec Sandstones, non-cross-stratified sandstone and minor proportions of other lithologies are present. In southwestern Utah and southern Nevada, non-cross-stratified lithologies are restricted to the basal tongues and basal 100 m of the Navajo and Aztec Sandstones. Non-cross-stratified lithologies are interpreted as the result of sand deposition under the influence of a shallow groundwater table (Marzolf, 1983a).

In southwestern Utah and southern Nevada, cross-bed orientation in the Navajo and Aztec Sandstones has been shown to change in vertical sections (Marzolf, 1983a). At Zion Canyon,

Figure 8. Cross-stratified lenticular sandstone enclosed in horizontally stratified sandy siltstone and siltshale of unit D, upper part of the undivided Moenave and Kayenta Formations, Valley of Fire.

the Valley of Fire, and Wilson Cliffs, dip direction of cross-beds in basal tongues and approximately the basal 100 m of the Navajo and Aztec Sandstones is to the southeast. Cross-bed dip direction rotates clockwise approximately 45° vertically through the section to southwesterly at the top of the sandstone at these localities. Comparison of cross-bed orientation between Zion Canyon and the Wilson Cliffs indicates little or no rotation of the Spring Mountains about a vertical axis relative to the Colorado Plateau since deposition of the Navajo and Aztec Sandstones. Although only the lower part of the Aztec Sandstone is present in the Lovell Wash block, comparison of cross-bed orientation data from this section with the regional pattern indicates 130° of rotation about a vertical axis if measured clockwise (Burdette and Marzolf, 1986). Both conclusions are consistent with unpublished paleomagnetic data (E. Shoemaker, personal communication, 1985). Because of ambiguities arising where incomplete sections of the Aztec Sandstone are not present, up to but no more than 45° of rotation about a vertical axis is permitted by cross-bed orientation data obtained from the lower part of the Aztec Sandstone at Pinto Valley and Horse Spring Valley.

Figure 9. Rhyolite-tuff boulder in massive sandstone of the upper member of the Middle Jurassic Carmel Formation, White House Ruin trail head, Paria Wilderness area, Utah.

San Rafael Group

In southwestern Utah, the Navajo Sandtone is separated from the overlying Temple Cap Sandstone by the J-1 unconformity. The Temple Cap Sandstone is separated from the overlying Carmel Formation by the J-2 unconformity. Eastward, the J-2 unconformity truncates the J-1 unconformity, and the Carmel Formation lies directly on the Navajo Sandstone.

Temple Cap Sandstone. The Temple Cap Sandstone (Peterson and Pipiringos, 1979) has been recognized only in southwestern Utah, where it comprises the Sinawava and White Throne Members. From the eastern limit of the formation, the Sinawava Member underlies the light-colored, cross-bedded sandstone of the White Throne Member westward to the Hurricane Cliffs. The Sinawava Member, consisting predominantly of reddish-brown interbedded siltstone, silty sandstone, and mudstone, maintains a nearly constant thickness, not exceeding 6.5 m. It contains well-rounded very coarse sand grains or fine pebbles of chert, which increase in abundance westward. West of the Hurricane Cliffs, where the Sinawava Member laterally replaces the White Throne Member, the Sinawava contains as many as eight thin beds of bentonite.

Carmel Formation. In southwestern Utah, Peterson and Pipiringos (1979) have divided the Carmel Formation into four members; from oldest to youngest, these are the limestone member, banded member, gypsiferous member, and Winsor Member. West of Mount Carmel Junction, the banded member contains a conglomerate bed 3 m thick, composed of chert and quartzite pebbles as large as 2.5 cm in diameter. Elsewhere, the banded member contains scattered pebbles of chert, quartzite, tuffaceous sandstone, and microcrystalline and porphyritic igneous rocks.

In south-central Utah and north-central Arizona, east of the truncation of the Temple Cap Sandstone, the Carmel Formation undergoes a rapid facies change eastward. The limestone, banded, and gypsiferous members are replaced eastward by the Page Sandstone. The lateral equivalent of the Winsor Member, the upper member, overlies the Page. The basal strata of the upper member consist of reddish-brown, poorly sorted volcanic litharenite. Massive silty sandstones display abundant evidence of liquefaction and fluidization, including remnants of contorted stratification, foundered conglomerate beds, and spectacular elutriation pipes (Marzolf, 1988). Rhyolite-tuff boulders as large as 2.5 m in diameter are widely disseminated within these once liquefied sandstones (Fig. 9). The massive sandstone beds are interbedded with thinner, medium-bedded pebble to cobble conglomerate. Conglomerate clasts are predominantly of siliceous pyroclastic and volcanic rocks, which along with the rhyolite-tuff boulders, were derived from a source area that lay to the southwest (Chapman, 1987).

In southern Nevada, the upper boundary of the Aztec Sandstone is either a thrust fault overlain by lower Paleozoic rocks or an unconformity overlain by Cretaceous or Tertiary rocks. Middle Jurassic rocks lithostratigraphically equivalent to the Temple Cap Sandstone, Carmel Formation, or overlying formations of the San Rafael Group are not known in southern Nevada.

AGE OF DEPOSITIONAL SEQUENCES

Evidence bearing on the age of the Chinle Formation has been reviewed by Stewart and others (1972) and more recently by Lupe and Silberling (1985). Most recently, Ash (1986) and Litwin (1986) have concluded that the Carnian-Norian boundary lies within the Petrified Forest Member. The age of the Glen Canyon Group has been reviewed by Pipiringos and O'Sullivan (1978), Peterson and Pipiringos (1979), and Marzolf (1983a).

Palynomorphs in the Whitmore Point Member of the Moenave Formation indicate a Sinemurian to Pliensbachian age (Cornet in Peterson and Pipiringos, 1979). Most recently, Litwin (1986) has identified Hettangian to Sinemurian polynomorphs in the Dinosaur Canyon Member of the Moenave Formation. Because the Navajo and Aztec Sandstones prograde into the arc terrane, the base of these sandstones presumably becomes younger to the southwest (Marzolf, 1983a).

Marine invertebrates obtained from the limestone member of the Carmel Formation overlying the J-2 unconformity indicate a late middle Bajocian age (Peterson and Pipiringos, 1979). Marvin and others (1965) interpreted Rb/Sr and K/Ar ages on biotite obtained from bentonites in the Carmel Formation in southwestern Utah to indicate a minimum age of 163 Ma. From their stratigraphic description of the occurrence of the bentonites, the single sample from Gunlock, Utah, is interpreted to have come from the Temple Cap Sandstone; the three samples at Mt. Carmel Junction, Utah, from the Carmel. When their K/Ar ages are corrected for the new decay constants (Dalrymple, 1979), a minimum age of 169 Ma is suggested for the Temple Cap Sandstone and 166 Ma for the Carmel Formation (Table 1).

The J-1 unconformity cannot be more tightly constrained than the constraints on the underlying Glen Canyon Group and the overlying Carmel Formation. On the basis of stratigraphic position, Peterson and Pipiringos (1979) correlate the unfossiliferous Temple Cap Sandstone with the Gypsum Spring Formation of western Wyoming. Based on this lithostratigraphic correlation, they suggest an early and early middle Bajocian age for the Temple Cap Sandstone.

Reynolds and Spencer (1987) interpreted U-Th-Pb isotope data obtained from silicic volcanics overlying rocks that they tentatively correlate with the Glen Canyon Group as indicating a minimum age of 160 to 155 Ma. They concluded that the emplacement age of the volcanic rocks cannot be more than 165 to 160 Ma. Busby-Spera (1988) has summarized additional data on the absolute ages of lower Mesozoic volcanics interbedded with cross-bedded quartz arenites and other epiclastic rocks at other localities within the arc terrane. In southern Arizona, the quartz arenites are interbedded with volcanic rocks yielding U-Pb zircon ages of 205 to 210 Ma (Riggs and others, 1986) and 190 Ma (Wright and others, 1981). In the eastern Mojave Desert, volcanic rocks interbedded with cross-bedded quartzose sandstones in the Cowhole Mountains have yielded U-Pb zircon ages of 172 Ma (Busby-Spera, 1988). Overlying silicic volcanic rocks have been dated at 167 Ma (Busby-Spera, 1988).

In summary, available data suggest that the lacuna represented by the J-0 unconformity may include part of latest Triassic (late Norian) and earliest Jurassic (early Hettangian) time. Although the consensus is that the entire Glen Canyon Group is Early Jurassic in age, the possibility that the uppermost Glen Canyon Group and, therefore, the uppermost part of the Navajo Sandstone are earliest Bajocian in age cannot be ruled out. Available data permit a liberal estimate for the age of the Navajo Sandstone of Pliensbachian to Bajocian in southwestern

TABLE 1. Rb/Sr AND K/Ar BIOTITE AGES ON BENTONITES FROM THE TEMPLE CAP SANDSTONE AND CARMEL FORMATION

Sample No.	Rb/Sr*	K/Ar*	K/Ar corrected†
	Ages in Ma		
Gunlock, Utah			
1.	85 ± 50	165	169
Mt. Carmel Junction, Utah			
2.	163 ± 10	162	166
3.	163 ± 15	151	155
4.	148 ± 15	151	155

*Data from Marvin and others (1965).
†Corrected value using conversion tables of Dalrymple (1979).

Utah. The Navajo may be older in southeastern Utah (Marzolf, 1983a). Sedimentary and volcanic rocks within the arc terrane probably equivalent to the Glen Canyon Group and lower part of the San Rafael Group accumulated over a period of 40 m.y. (Busby-Spera, 1988), but correlation of sequences in the arc terrane with specific formations on the Colorado Plateau remains uncertain.

It is well to remember that calibration of absolute ages to series and stage boundaries is very poorly constrained for the Lower and Middle Jurassic. In addition, the ages of strata within the Chinle Formation and the Glen Canyon and San Rafael Groups are based on a variety of nonmarine and marine faunal and floral data. In addition to uncertainty in calibrating the absolute with the relative time scale in this part of the stratigraphic column, the varied types of biostratigraphic data themselves may not be internally consistent.

CORRELATION OF DEPOSITIONAL SEQUENCES INTO THE ARC TERRANE

Spring Mountains block

Wilson Cliffs. The lower Mesozoic outcrop in the Wilson Cliffs is the northernmost outcrop in the Spring Mountains block that preserves a nearly complete Upper Triassic and Lower Jurassic section. In addition to forming an important tie between the Las Vegas extensional basin and the Spring Mountains block, this outcrop of Upper Triassic and Lower Jurassic strata provides an important reference section from which the Glen Canyon Group and its relation to underlying depositional sequences can be traced southward within the Spring Mountains block.

Wilson Cliffs to Mescal Range. The Spring Mountains block maintains its structural coherence as an unextended block, in which frontal thrusts of the Sevier belt can be identified, southward from the Wilson Cliffs through the Clark Range and Clark Mountains to the Mescal and Ivanpah Ranges. Keys to correlation of lower Mesozoic depositional sequences southward from the Wilson Cliffs into the arc terrane are recognition of the Aztec Sandstone and conformably underlying red beds, correct identification of red beds at intervening localities where the Aztec Sandstone is not present, and recognition that the J-O unconformity cuts progressively down section from the Wilson Cliffs to the Cowhole Mountains (Marzolf, 1987; in preparation).

The most southerly exposure of the Aztec Sandstone within the Spring Mountains lies in the footwall of the Contact thrust approximately 45 km north of Goodsprings (Burchfiel and Davis, 1988). Texturally mature, large-scale, cross-bedded subarkose to quartz arenite of the Aztec Sandstone conformably overlies dark reddish-brown siltstones and sandstones of the undivided Moenave and Kayenta Formations. Neither the base nor the top of the Glen Canyon Group is exposed. To the south, the next locality where texturally mature cross-bedded sandstone correlated with the Aztec Sandstone is exposed is beneath the Mollusk Mine thrust (Burchfiel and Davis, 1988) at the eastern end of the Mescal Range.

In the Mescal Range, the Aztec Sandstone is only 137 m thick. Preliminary observations indicate that from place to place the texturally mature cross-bedded sandstone is interbedded with thick lenses of dark reddish-brown siltstone containing pebbles and cobbles of volcanic rocks. At the western end of Mesozoic outcrop, in the vertical to overturned limb of the Kokoweef syncline, dark reddish-brown sandstones and siltstones conformably underlying the Aztec Sandstone rest unconformably on yellowish-brown sandy limestones and calcareous sandstones at the top of the Virgin Limestone Member of the Moenkopi Formation. Although Hewett (1956) assigned the strata underlying the Aztec Sandstone to the Chinle Formation, these strata, which bear little resemblance to either the Petrified Forest or Shinarump Members, are here correlated with unit C of the undivided Moenave and Kayenta Formations of southern Nevada.

Between the outcrops of the Glen Canyon Group near Goodsprings and the Mescal Range, two additional localities further document the progressive downcutting of the J-O unconformity. At Lavinia Wash, a silica-cemented conglomerate assigned by Carr (1980) to the Shinarump Member of the Chinle Formation is here tentatively correlated with the basal chalcedony-cemented part of Unit A of the undivided Moenave and Kayenta Formations at the Wilson Cliffs. The conglomerate (unit A) overlies reddish-brown siltstones and mudstones of the upper red member of the Moenkopi Formation. The J-O unconformity has truncated the Upper Triassic Chinle formation between the Wilson Cliffs and Lavinia Wash. Unit A and an overlying covered interval are unconformably overlain by cobble- to boulder-conglomerate of the Upper Cretaceous Lavinia Wash sequence, which truncates the undivided Moenave and Kayenta strata southwestward.

Approximately halfway between Lavinia Wash and the Mescal Range, Walker and others (1983) described a clast-supported, cobble conglomerate, which they included in the upper part of the Shnabkaib Member of the Moenkopi Forma-

tion. The lower Mesozoic rocks crop out beneath the Mesquite Pass thrust in the Clark Range. This conglomerate also is here tentatively correlated with the Moenave-Kayenta conglomerate. The stratigraphic position of the conglomerate at the top of the Shnabkaib Member of the Moenkopi Formation is to be expected at this locality midway between Lavinia Wash and the Mescal Range as the J-O unconformity cuts down section from the upper red member, to the Shnabkaib Member, to the top of the Virgin Limestone Member. Paleocurrent data obtained from clast imbrication in the Clark Range (Walker and others, 1983) are nearly identical to those obtained from cross-stratification in unit A at the Wilson Cliffs (see Fig. 12e). Unfortunately, the upper part of the undivided Moenave and Kayenta section is not exposed because of truncation by the Mesquite Pass thrust.

Within the Spring Mountains block, rocks of probable Middle Jurassic age overlying the Aztec Sandtone are known only in the Mescal Range. In the Mescal Range, in addition to the anomalous thickness of the Aztec Sandstone, cross-beds dip consistently to the southeast from bottom to top of the section. These relations suggest that approximately 600 m of Aztec Sandstone were removed by erosion prior to deposition of an unmeasured thickness of poorly exposed epiclastic, volcaniclastic, and volcanic rocks. This poorly exposed sequence is overlain by over 400 m of green, purple, and red porphyritic rhyolite flows and ash-flow tuffs of the Mountain Pass Rhyolite (Evans, 1971). The unconformity at the top of the Aztec Sandstone is believed correlative with either the J-1 or J-2 unconformities. If the J-1 unconformity, the J-2 may lie within the overlying Mountain Pass Rhyolite; if the J-2 unconformity, the J-1 has been truncated by the J-2.

Cowhole Mountains and Old Dad Mountain

In the Cowhole Mountains and Old Dad Mountain, fine-grained, mature subarkose to quartz arenite, cross-bedded on a large scale and interbedded with intermediate to silicic volcanic and volcaniclastic rocks, has been considered lithostratigraphically equivalent to the Aztec Sandstone (Novitsky-Evans, 1978; Marzolf, 1983 a, b, 1988; Marzolf and Cole, 1987). In the Cowhole Mountains, the Aztec Sandstone overlies and is interbedded at its base with dark reddish-brown volcanic-clast–bearing quartzose siltstones similar to those underlying the Aztec Sandstone in the Mescal Range. At Old Dad Mountain, the dark reddish-brown siltstone unit is not present. In both the Cowhole Mountains and Old Dad Mountain, the base of the conformable sedimentary and volcanic sequence in which the Aztec Sandstone occurs is marked by a limestone breccia composed of angular blocks of Paleozoic limestone derived predominantly from the Pennsylvanian and Permian Bird Spring Formation. The entire sequence was deposited on a surface of moderate relief (at least 200 m) developed on deformed Paleozoic carbonates. Andesitic volcanics fill paleotopographic lows eroded in the Paleozoic carbonate terrane (Marzolf, 1983b). The limestone breccia overlies the volcanic rocks or lies directly on Paleozoic carbonates over paleotopographic highs. In places at Old Dad Mountain, the limestone breccia is intruded by mafic hypabyssal rocks. Where the contact has not been obscured by hypabyssal rocks, the Aztec Sandstone and basal breccia rest unconformably on Paleozoic carbonates.

In the Cowhole Mountains, the Aztec Sandstone is overlain concordantly by over 550 m of red and purple porphyritic rhyolite flows and rhyolitic tuffs. In a few places, volcanic-clast–bearing sandstone lenses are intercalated within the volcanic rocks. At the north end of the mountains, the Aztec Sandstone and overlying volcanics are intruded by flow-banded rhyolite, which in turn is intruded by a brecciated plug and associated radial dikes (Marzolf and Cole, 1987). At Old Dad Mountain, a thin unit of silicic volcanics overlies the Aztec Sandstone below the Playground thrust.

Busby-Spera (1988) has challenged correlation of the cross-bedded sandstone in the Cowhole Mountains with the Aztec Sandstone. On the basis of U/Pb ages of 172 Ma and 167 Ma on zircons obtained from volcanic rocks interbedded with and overlying the cross-bedded sandstone, respectively, she suggests correlation of the cross-bedded sandstone with the upper Bajocian and Bathonian Carmel Formation or the Callovian Entrada Sandstone.

The stratigraphic data presented here support correlation of the cross-bedded sandstone and overlying volcanics in the Cowhole Mountains with the Glen Canyon and San Rafael Groups, respectively. Evidence supporting this correlation includes (1) the progressive southwestward overstep of the Glen Canyon Group onto progressively older Triassic strata from the Wilson Cliffs to the Mescal Range, (2) the striking similarity between lower Mesozoic sedimentary and volcanic sequences in the Cowhole Mountains and the Mescal Range, (3) the reasonably well-established correlation of the lower Mesozoic rocks in the Mescal Range with the Glen Canyon Group at the Wilson Cliffs, (4) lack of documentation of a western eolian facies of the Carmel in southeastern California, southern Nevada, or on the Colorado Plateau, and (5) the 169- to 166-Ma minimum K/Ar ages on biotite in bentonites in the Temple Cap Sandstone and Carmel Formation, respectively, in southwestern Utah. Although the groundwater-altered bentonites yielded anomalous results, the 169- and 166-Ma ages interpreted from the data of Marvin and others (1965) as the best estimate of the minimum age of the bentonites is remarkably close to the 167 Ma obtained by Busby-Spera from volcanics overlying the cross-bedded sandstone in the Cowhole Mountains and the 165 to 160 Ma interpreted as the emplacement age of silicic volcanic rocks overlying rocks that Reynolds and Spencer (1987) tentatively correlate with the Glen Canyon Group.

If, as Busby-Spera implies, the entire Mesozoic sequence in the Cowhole Mountains is chronostratigraphically equivalent to the lower part of the San Rafael Group, erosional removal of the Moenkopi and Chinle Formations and the Glen Canyon Group prior to deposition of a sedimentary and volcanic sequence nearly identical to the Glen Canyon Group and overlying volcanic rocks

in the Mescal Range is required. This is particularly unlikely in the absence of evidence for southwestward overstep of the San Rafael Group into the arc terrane. Correlation of the sandstone in the Cowhole Mountains with the Entrada Sandstone suffers similar but greater difficulties.

Previous correlation of the cross-bedded sandstone in the Cowhole Mountains with the Aztec Sandstone appears justified. The unconformity at the base of the sequence is interpreted as the J-O unconformity, which has cut down section from the Virgin Limestone Member of the Moenkopi Formation in the Mescal Range to deformed Paleozoic rocks. The dark reddish-brown siltstones below the cross-bedded sandstone are tentatively correlated with unit C of the undivided Moenave and Kayenta Formations. The limestone breccia, overlying the J-O unconformity, occupies a stratigraphic position similar to that of unit A of the undivided Moenave and Kayenta Formations at the Wilson Cliffs and elsewhere in the Las Vegas extensional domain. Similar polylithologic breccias and conglomerates occupying approximately the same stratigraphic position are known in southwestern Arizona (Reynolds and Spencer, 1987), southeastern California (Burchfiel and Davis, 1977; Hamilton, 1987), eastern California (Oborne and others, 1983; Stone and Stevens, 1986), and western Nevada (Speed and Jones, 1969; Stanley, 1971; Oldow and Bartel, 1987). As in the Mescal Range, the concordant contact between Aztec Sandstone and overlying volcanics is interpreted as a disconformity and correlated with either the J-1 or J-2 unconformity.

The present problem in correlation of absolute ages with lithostratigraphic units is more one of limited relative age constraints on the Lower and Middle Jurassic of the Colorado Plateau and poorly constrained calibration of absolute and relative ages for the Early and Middle Jurassic than a problem of lithostratigraphic correlation. In the absence of direct stratigraphic evidence linking cross-bedded quartz arenites in southern and southwestern Arizona and southeastern California to the Colorado Plateau, correlation of individual Jurassic sequences in the arc terrane with specific formations in the Glen Canyon and San Rafael Groups must remain uncertain. As Busby-Spera (1988) suggests, the 205 to 210 Ma sequence in southern Arizona may be chronostratigraphically equivalent to the Wingate Sandstone, the basal formation of the Glen Canyon Group in southeastern Utah and northeastern Arizona. Although Busby-Spera correlates the younger (190 Ma) sequence with the Navajo Sandstone, chronostratigraphic equivalence with the Kayenta Formation or even the upper part of the Wingate Sandstone cannot be ruled out.

PALINSPASTIC RECONSTRUCTION

Relation of Cowhole Mountains–Old Dad Mountain block to the Las Vegas Range–Spring Mountains block

Southward from the Ivanpah Range, the structural coherence of the Spring Mountains block and the Sevier Orogenic belt, which it carries, is not maintained because of intrusion by Mesozoic plutons, Tertiary volcanic cover, and Cenozoic alluvium (Burchfiel and Davis, 1988). Similarity of structural and stratigraphic relations between the Cowhole Mountains and Old Dad Mountain, Clark Mountain and the Mescal Range, and the New York Mountains suggests that the Cowhole Mountains and Old Dad Mountain form a single block displaced westward by Tertiary extension from the southern end of the Sevier belt. This interpretation is based on the following relations:

1. Early Mesozoic thrust faults of probable latest Triassic or earliest Jurassic age are present in both areas.

2. The J-O unconformity oversteps progressively older strata into the arc terrane and is overlain by a limestone- and volcanic-clast conglomerate derived from a deformed Paleozoic carbonate terrane.

3. Late Mesozoic east-vergent thrust faults of demonstrated or probable Late Cretaceous age are present in both areas.

4. Late Mesozoic thrusts in both areas place Paleozoic carbonates on autochthonous Mesozoic volcanics and volcaniclastics.

5. Autochthonous rocks in both areas are cut by high-angle faults of probable Cretaceous age with a significant component of left slip. These faults place Precambrian crystalline rocks against Paleozoic and Mesozoic sedimentary rocks.

Burchfiel and Davis (1972, 1975, 1981) maintain that an early Mesozoic fold and thrust belt converges in southern Nevada and southeastern California with the Cretaceous Sevier belt. At Clark Mountain and the Mescal Range and in the New York Mountains, early Mesozoic thrusts are believed to be older than 200 Ma (Sinemurian) (Burchfiel and Davis, 1977, 1988). Within the Cowhole Mountains–Old Dad Mountain block, a low-angle, younger-on-older fault cuts folded Paleozoic rocks and is depositionally crosscut by the Glen Canyon Group, thus constraining its age as post–Early Permian to Early or Middle Jurassic (258 Ma to 172 Ma). Novitsky and Burchfiel (1973) interpreted this fault as a thrust.

The basal Lower Jurassic Glen Canyon Group in its western exposures contains limestone-clast breccia or conglomerate derived from a Paleozoic carbonate terrane. In the New York Mountains, Mesozoic volcanics rest unconformably on calc-silicate rocks correlated with the Moenkopi Formation. At the base of the volcanic rocks, limestone- and volcanic-clast conglomerate overlies the unconformity. In places, the contact has been intruded by hypabyssal rocks. This relation has similarities to both the Cowhole Mountains–Old Dad Mountain block, where the basal limestone- and volcanic-clast breccia of the Glen Canyon Group also is intruded by mafic hypabyssal rocks, and localities in the southern Spring Mountains block where the basal Glen Canyon Group, with or without basal limestone- and volcanic-clast conglomerate, rests on the Moenkopi Formation. These relations suggest that the basal limestone breccias and conglomerates were derived from a narrow early Mesozoic fold and thrust belt of probable latest Triassic or earliest Jurassic age, segments of which are preserved in the Clark Mountain–Mescal

Range, New York Mountains, and Cowhole Mountains–Old Dad Mountain areas.

In all three areas, the early Mesozoic thrusts are overprinted by Late Cretaceous thrusts. In the Mescal Range, lower Paleozoic rocks in the upper plate of the Late Cretaceous Mollusk Mine thrust have been thrust eastward over silicic volcanics unconformably overlying the Aztec Sandstone (Burchfiel and Davis, 1988). At Old Dad Mountain, the Late Cretaceous Playground thrust places the Bird Spring Formation on silicic volcanics overlying the Aztec Sandstone (Dunne, 1977). In the New York Mountains, rocks ranging in age from Precambrian to Mesozoic, including the Bird Spring Formation, have been thrust eastward over autochthonous Mesozoic epiclastic and volcaniclastic rocks of the Slaughterhouse Canyon sequence (Burchfiel and Davis, 1977). The Slaughterhouse Canyon sequence unconformably overlies the volcanic rocks that contain limestone-clast conglomerate at their base. Although these lower volcanic rocks contain metasiltstones, lithologies identifiable as Aztec Sandstone are not present.

In both the Mescal Range–Clark Mountain area and the New York Mountains, a high-angle fault placing Precambrian crystalline rocks against Paleozoic and Mesozoic autochthonous strata is left lateral and of probable Cretaceous age. At Old Dad Mountain, the Late Cretaceous Playground thrust crosscuts a high-angle fault that also places Precambrian crystalline rocks against Paleozoic rocks. This high-angle fault has a significant component of left slip (Dunne, 1977).

The remarkable similarity in structural and stratigraphic relations between the Cowhole Mountains–Old Dad Mountain block and the Clark Mountain–Mescal Range–New York Mountains segment of the Sevier belt is too striking to be mere coincidence. The Playground thrust at Old Dad Mountain occupies the same structural position as the Mollusk Mine thrust in the Mescal Range. The pre–Glen Canyon Group thrust in the Cowhole Mountains is interpreted as part of the early Mesozoic thrust system of probable Late Triassic or Early Jurassic age intimately associated with the Sevier belt in the southern Cordillera.

Reconstruction of early Mesozoic sedimentary basins

Recognition that lower Mesozoic strata considered here are autochthonous with respect to the Late Cretaceous Sevier thrust belt implies that little or no palinspastic correction need be made for Mesozoic compression. For the purpose of palinspastic reconstruction of Cenozoic extension, the lower Mesozoic outcrops are divided into three categories. The first is that of outcrops within the Las Vegas extensional basin and transition zone not far traveled from the edge of the Colorado Plateau so that their preextension positions can be easily ascertained. These localities include Horse Spring Valley, Tom and Cull Wash, and Bitter Ridge. The second category consists of outcrops within the Spring Mountains block, the present position of which relative to the easternmost thrusts of the Sevier belt is known or can easily be determined. In addition to the Cowhole Mountains and Old Dad Mountain, these localities include the Tule Spring Hills, Valley of Fire, Frenchman Mountain, Wilson Cliffs, Lavinia Wash, Clark Range, and Mescal Range. The third category includes the remaining outcrops lying within the Las Vegas extensional basin, the positions of which cannot easily be related to the Colorado Plateau nor the Sevier belt. The restored positions of these outcrops must be determined on a combination of structural, stratigraphic, and sedimentological grounds. These localities include the Bowl of Fire, Pinto Valley, and the Lovell Wash block.

Horse Spring Valley and Bitter Ridge have been transported west southwestward by left lateral displacement along the Gold Butte and Lime Ridge faults, respectively (Fig. 10). The preextension position of Bitter Ridge was approximately halfway to the Grand Wash fault from its present position (R. Bohannon, personal communication, 1988). The Gold Butte fault turns northward in Cottonwood Wash (Bohannon, 1984). The bend in the fault establishes the approximate easternmost position of the Horse Spring Valley Mesozoic rocks. The amount of northward displacement along the north-south trending segment is uncertain. Tom and Cull Wash lies immediately west of the Grand Wash Cliffs and appears to have been transported only a short distance from its original position by high-angle, down-to-the-west normal faults. Although data from Tom and Cull Wash are very preliminary, anomalous thicknesses suggest that this outcrop, like Horse Spring Valley, has been transported southward by left slip on one or more faults between the wash and the Grand Wash fault.

Placing the Cowhole Mountains–Old Dad Mountain block at the southern end of the Sevier belt, a first approximation of the size, shape, and position of the basin in which the lower Mesozoic rocks were deposited can be obtained by restoring the Sevier belt to its preextension position relative to the Colorado Plateau. The preextension configuration of the Sevier belt is obtained by restoring 62 km of right slip on the Las Vegas Valley shear zone and 12 km of right slip on the State Line fault (Stewart and others, 1968; Burchfiel and others, 1982). Reconstruction of the Sevier belt, with the Old Dad Mountain–Cowhole Mountains block at its southern end, fixes the positions of the Cowhole Mountains, Mescal Range, Clark Range, Lavinia Wash, and Wilson Cliffs relative to each other along the western margin of the Early Jurassic depositional basin (Fig. 11a).

The progressive separation of the Sevier belt from the Colorado Plateau during extension requires that the Sevier belt could not have lain farther from the Plateau than it does at present. Thus, the present easternmost location of the Sevier belt, in southern Nevada, can be taken as the maximum possible distance of the belt from the Plateau prior to extension. The easternmost position thus established is the position of the Glendale thrust in the Mormon Mountains. Pinning the reconstruction of Burchfiel and others (1982) in the Mormon Mountains at its northern end and maintaining the same north-south alignment of the Sevier belt places the Wilson Cliffs adjacent to the present western end of Lake Mead; Lavinia Wash, the Clark Range, and Mescal

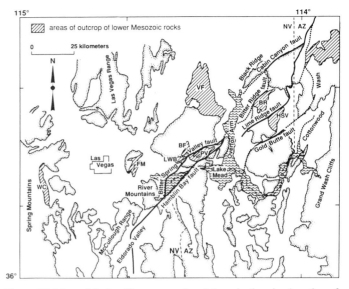

Figure 10. Map of the Las Vegas extensional domain showing location of faults of the Lake Mead fault system and the present locations of Upper Triassic and Lower Jurassic outcrops (outcrop abbreviations as in Fig. 2).

Range, along the present Colorado River, in southeastern Nevada; and the Cowhole Mountains and Old Dad Mountain at the present intersection of the Nevada, Arizona, and California state lines. By restoring 10 km of right-lateral offset between the Mormon Mountains and the Northern Muddy Mountains and restoring the Mormon Mountain allochthon to its pre-Miocene position above the Tule Spring Hills allochthon (Wernicke and others, 1984), the relative positions of the Valley of Fire and Tule Spring Hills Mesozoic outcrops also become fixed relative to the Sevier belt. These relations are shown in Figure 11b.

Restoring 55 km of crustal extension in a S70°W direction (Anderson, 1973; Bohannon, 1984) places the Wilson Cliffs at the present location of the Overton Arm of Lake Mead in southeastern Nevada, and Lavinia Wash, the Clark Range, Mescal Range, Cowhole Mountains, and Old Dad Mountain east of the present Colorado River in northwestern Arizona in the locations shown in Figure 11c. The Mormon Mountains and Tule Spring Hills accordingly are restored to the Beaver Dam Mountain breakaway along the Nevada-Utah state line (Wernicke and others, 1984). Frenchman Mountain lies at the western end of Black Ridge of the Virgin Mountains, as suggested by Bohannon (1984). As previously stated, crustal shortening along the Bird Spring thrust has not been considered in this reconstruction.

The restored position of the Wilson Cliffs in the southern Spring Mountains presented here contradicts the interpretation of Bohannon (1984), who concluded that the preextension position of the southern Spring Mountains lay to the northwest of the restored positions of the Valley of Fire and Frenchman Mountain northeast of the present location of Las Vegas. Bohannon arrived at this interpretation by concluding that the southern Spring

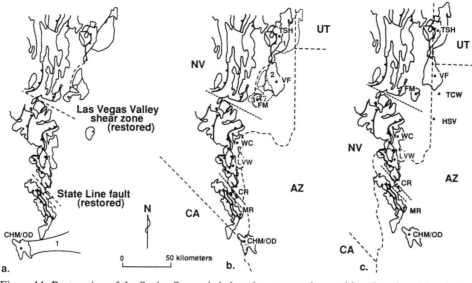

Figure 11. Restoration of the Sevier Orogenic belt to its preextension position (location abbreviations same as in Fig. 2). In these and subsequent maps of Figure 12, unrestored state boundaries, the Beaver Dam breakaway (Wernicke and others, 1984), and the Grand Wash Cliffs are shown as a frame of reference fixed relative to the Colorado Plateau. a. Removal of right slip on the Las Vegas shear zone and State Line fault (after Burchfiel and others, 1982) and (1) the postulated location of the Cowhole Mountains–Old Dad Mountain block at the southern end of the orogenic belt. b. The location of the straightened Sevier belt with its northern end positioned in the Mormon Mountains and north-south alignment maintained. (1) Position of the Tule Spring Hills relative to the Mormon Mountains after removal of extension on the Mormon thrust (Wernicke and others, 1984). (2) Position of the Valley of Fire after removal of 10 km of dextral folding at the northern end of the Weiser syncline (Wernicke and others, 1984). (3) Position of Frenchman Mountain required by the reconstruction of the River Mountains (Weber and Smith, 1987). c. Preextension position of the Sevier Orogenic belt obtained by removing 55 km of west-southwest extension (Anderson, 1973; Bohannon, 1979).

Mountains have been translated to their present position along the Hamblin Bay fault, which he concluded extends into Eldorado Valley as a left-slip fault (Fig. 10). Weber and Smith (1987) have shown that the left slip on the Hamblin Bay fault north of Lake Mead was taken up by normal displacement on the fault trending north-south in Eldorado Valley. Assuming the McCullough Range and the Spring Mountains are not separated by major Cenozoic extensional faults, the reconstruction of Weber and Smith is consistent with the reconstruction of the Wilson Cliffs Mesozoic outcrops shown in Figure 11b.

In addition to closing Eldorado Valley in their palinspastic reconstruction, Weber and Smith restored the River Mountains eastward along the Hamblin Bay fault by matching Tertiary extrusive rocks in the River Mountains with their intrusive equivalents south of the fault. According to E. I. Smith (personal communication, 1987), Frenchman Mountain and the River Mountains form a structurally coherent block. The restoration of the River Mountains established by Weber and Smith (1987) thus requires Frenchman Mountain to occupy the approximate position shown in Figure 11b. This location of Frenchman Mountain is consistent with sedimentological and stratigraphic data obtained from Upper Triassic and Lower Jurassic strata. In particular, paleocurrent and thickness data obtained from unit A of the undivided Moenave and Kayenta Formations imply that

Frenchman Mountain occupied a position intermediate between the Wilson Cliffs outcrop on the southwest and the Valley of Fire on the northeast. These data appear to preclude the Wilson Cliffs outcrop from having lain northwest of Frenchman Mountain as suggested by Bohannon (1984).

The reconstruction of the Sevier belt defines a narrow belt presently occupied by Precambrian and Paleozoic rocks along the upturned and eroded western edge of the Colorado Plateau. Into this belt the remaining Mesozoic outcrops of the Las Vegas extensional basin must be fitted. Positions of these three remaining Mesozoic localities—Pinto Valley, the Bowl of Fire, and Lovell Wash block—are suggested by sedimentological, stratigraphic, and structural data.

If the palinspastic restoration presented in Figure 11c is valid, geologically meaningful facies patterns must result for *all* facies. Thus, if sufficient data are available from measured sections whose preextension locations are known, a measured section, the location of which cannot be determined directly from structural data, can be restored to its correct preextension position by resorting to isopach maps drawn for each stratigraphic unit in the measured section. The section must be located such that the thickness of each stratigraphic unit within the section is consistent with the corresponding isopach map of the unit. As the number of measured sections constraining the isopachous contours and the

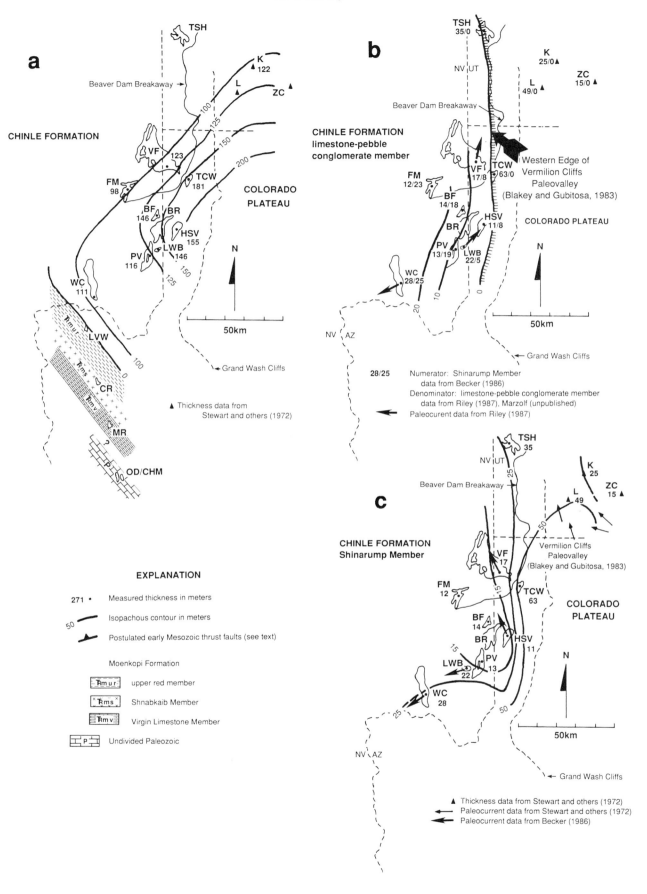

a

CHINLE FORMATION

Beaver Dam Breakaway →

COLORADO PLATEAU

TSH
K ▲ 122
L ▲
ZC ▲
VF • 123
FM 98
TCW • 181
BF ▲ 146
BR
HSV • 155
PV 116
LWB • 146
WC • 111
LVW
CR
MR
OD/CHM

N

50km

b

CHINLE FORMATION
limestone-pebble
conglomerate member

COLORADO PLATEAU

Beaver Dam Breakaway

TSH 35/0
NV|UT
K ▲ 25/0
L 49/0 ▲
ZC 15/0 ▲
VF 17/8
TCW 63/0
Western Edge of
Vermilion Cliffs
Paleovalley
(Blakey and Gubitosa, 1983)
FM 12/23
BF 14/18
BR
HSV • 11/8
PV 13/19
LWB 22/5
WC • 28/25
NV\AZ

N

50km

← Grand Wash Cliffs

28/25   Numerator: Shinarump Member
         data from Becker (1986)
         Denominator: limestone-pebble conglomerate member
         data from Riley (1987), Marzolf (unpublished)
←   Paleocurent data from Riley (1987)

c

CHINLE FORMATION
Shinarump Member

COLORADO PLATEAU

Beaver Dam Breakaway

TSH 35
NV|UT
K 25
L ▲ 49
ZC 15 ▲
Vermilion Cliffs
Paleovalley
(Blakey and Gubitosa, 1983)
VF 17
FM 12
TCW 63
BF 14
BR
HSV 11
PV 13
LWB 22
WC 28
NV\AZ

N

50km

← Grand Wash Cliffs

▲ Thickness data from Stewart and others (1972)
← Paleocurrent data from Stewart and others (1972)
← Paleocurrent data from Becker (1986)

EXPLANATION

271 •   Measured thickness in meters

50 ——   Isopachous contour in meters

⊾——   Postulated early Mesozoic thrust faults (see text)

Moenkopi Formation

ℝmur   upper red member

ℝms   Shnabkaib Member

ℝmv   Virgin Limestone Member

P   Undivided Paleozoic

▲ Thickness data from
  Stewart and others (1972)

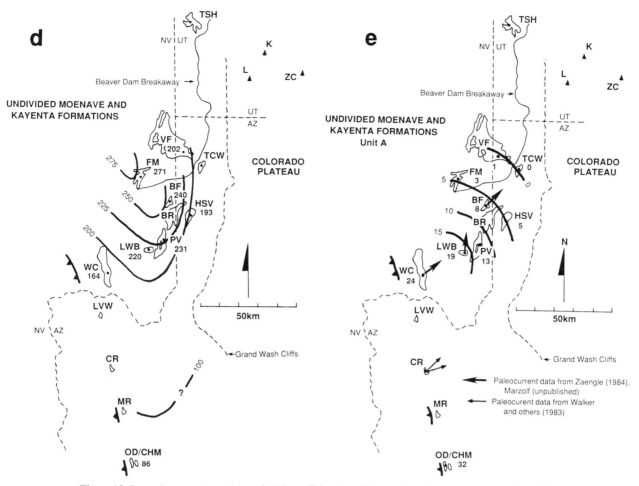

Figure 12. Isopachous contours drawn for Upper Triassic and Lower Jurassic outcrops restored to their preextension positions (location abbreviations same as in Fig. 2). Positions of the Bowl of Fire, Lovell Wash block, and Pinto Valley were determined based on stratigraphic and sedimentological criteria. a. Isopachous contour map of the Upper Triassic Chinle Formation and southwestward truncation of progressively older strata beneath the J-O unconformity. Contours in Utah after Stewart and others (1972). The location of the zero contour for the Chinle Formation is uncertain but must lie between the southern end of the Wilson Cliffs and Lavinia Wash and have an orientation similar to that shown. Lithologic symbols for the upper red, Shnabkaib, and Virgin Limestone members of the Moenkopi Formation indicate approximate bands of uncertainty for truncation of each of these stratigraphic units. Relationship of the lower part of the Moenkopi Formation to deformed Paleozoic rocks in the Old Dad Mountain–Cowhole Mountain block is problematic. b. Isopachous contours drawn on the limestone-pebble conglomerate member of the Chinle Formation. The zero isopach indicates the position of the western edge of the Vermilion Cliffs paleovalley (Blakey and Gubitosa, 1983). c. Paleocurrents and isopachous contours drawn for the Shinarump Member of the Chinle Formation. Contours indicate the location of the Vermilion Cliffs paleovalley in southwest Utah and northwest Arizona (Blakey and Gubitosa, 1983). d. Paleotectonic and isopachous contour map for the Lower Jurassic undivided Moenave and Kayenta Formations. e. Paleotectonic and isopachous contour map and paleocurrents for unit A of the undivided Moenave and Kayenta Formations.

number of stratigraphic units generating the isopach maps increases, the precision of the "best fit" increases. In the present study, the small number of measured sections provides limited but adequate precision for the drawing of isopachous contours.

The restored positions of all Mesozoic localities studied except the Pinto Valley, the Bowl of Fire, and Lovell Wash block are shown in Figure 11c. Isopach maps (not shown) were drawn for five Upper Triassic and Lower Jurassic stratigraphic units

based on the restored positions of these localities. The final positions of the Pinto Valley, the Bowl of Fire, and Lovell Wash block were obtained by requiring the thickness of each stratigraphic unit for each measured section to be consistent with each of these isopach maps (Figs. 12a–e). These preliminary data suggest that the Bowl of Fire lay north of Bitter Ridge (east of the Overton Arm of Lake Mead). Pinto Valley must have lain to the south or southwest of Bitter Ridge along the Bitter Ridge or Lime

Ridge fault (Fig. 10). The position of the Lovell Wash block is ambiguous, lying east of Pinto Valley in Figures 12a and b, and west of Pinto Valley in Figures 12c, d, and e. This ambiguity cannot be resolved with presently available data.

The reconstruction based on thickness data is supported by sedimentological data. At Bitter Ridge, the Chinle Formation and the lower part of the undivided Moenave and Kayenta Formations are overturned beneath local transpression developed along the Bitter Ridge fault (R. Bohannon, personal communication, 1988). These strata lie in the overturned limb of a southeast-vergent recumbent syncline whose axial surface lies within the undivided Moenave and Kayenta Formations. Unit A is well exposed and bears a striking similarity to unit A outcrops at Pinto Valley, the Bowl of Fire, and the Lovell Wash block, thus placing Pinto Valley, the Bowl of Fire, and the Lovell Wash block in close proximity to Bitter Ridge as shown in Figures 12a–e. Facies relations within unit A indicate that Pinto Valley and the Bowl of Fire occupied similar positions on the margin of an alluvial fan as it spread across sabkha mud flats. Although the position of the Lovell Wash block is ambiguous when all Upper Triassic and Lower Jurassic stratigraphic units are considered, data from unit A suggest it occupied a more proximal-fan position to the west of Pinto Valley (Fig. 12e). Similarities between the Bowl of Fire and Pinto Valley outcrops, along with north-northeasterly paleocurrents in the Lovell Wash block and the Bowl of Fire, suggest that all three localities occupied a position in the northeastern quadrant of a fan having its apex in the vicinity of the northern Wilson Cliffs. Clast size and thickness of the alluvial fan facies indicate that these three localities lay south of Frenchman Mountain and the Valley of Fire and east of Horse Spring Valley. Although, in detail, this interpretation is difficult to reconcile with the reconstruction of Bohannon (1984), in general, preextension close proximity of these localities east of Lake Mead with Frenchman Mountain to the northwest, is common to both interpretations. In the Tertiary, these blocks have been displaced southwestward along a combination of the Gold Butte, Lime Ridge, Bitter Ridge, Hamblin Bay, and Bitter Spring Valley faults.

SEDIMENTARY BASINS AND DEPOSITIONAL ENVIRONMENTS

Although the number of data points provided by localities considered in this study is small, isopachous contours of Moenave-Kayenta lithofacies can be drawn that are geologically reasonable for *all* stratigraphic units without resorting to artificially complex curves (Figs. 12a–e). In addition, geologically significant relations can be discerned for the Chinle Formation and the limestone-pebble conglomerate and Shinarump Member that are not at all apparent with Mesozoic localities in their present positions. These results are shown in Figures 12a–c.

Chinle Formation

Figure 12a illustrates the distribution and thickness of the Chinle Formation. West-southwest-trending isopachous con-

tours in southwestern Utah (Stewart and others, 1972) continue into southern Nevada, where they turn abruptly southeastward, indicating abrupt thinning of the Chinle Formation beneath the J-O unconformity. From the Wilson Cliffs to the Mescal Range to the Cowhole Mountains, the J-O unconformity is interpreted to have cut down section from the Petrified Forest Member of the Chinle Formation to the Virgin Limestone Member of the Moenkopi Formation, to deformed Paleozoic carbonates, respectively. Although the exact location and trend of the truncated edge of the Chinle is uncertain, it must lie between the southern end of the Wilson Cliffs and Lavinia Wash and have a northwest-southeast trend as indicated in Figure 12a. Lithologic symbols for the upper red, Shnabkaib, and Virgin Limestone members of the Moenkopi Formation in Figure 12a indicate the approximate bands of uncertainty for truncation of these stratigraphic units below the J-O unconformity. The relation of the lower part of the Moenkopi Formation to deformed Paleozoic rocks in Old Dad Mountain and the Cowhole Mountains is more problematic and is indicated by a question mark in Figure 12a.

Limestone-pebble conglomerate member. Figure 12b illustrates the distribution, thickness, and paleocurrent directions of the limestone-pebble conglomerate beneath the Shinarump Member. Thickness of the limestone-pebble conglomerate is indicated by the denominator of fractions at each data point; the numerator indicates thickness of the Shinarump Member. Also shown is the western edge of the north-trending Vermilion Cliffs paleovalley. Limestone-pebble–conglomerate paleocurrents are approximately parallel to those for the Shinarump except in the Lovell Wash block, where they are in direct opposition. A geologically significant pattern in the thickness of the limestone-pebble conglomerate is not immediately apparent; however, where the Shinarump is thickest, the limestone-pebble conglomerate is absent. The points where the Shinarump is thickest lie along the western edge of the paleovalley where the valley has been cut through the underlying limestone-pebble conglomerate.

Shinarump Member. Figure 12c shows the distribution and thickness of the Shinarump Member of the Chinle Formation. The zero isopachous contour delineates the western edge of the Vermilion Cliffs paleovalley (Blakey and Gubitosa, 1983). The Shinarump Member thins westward into southern Nevada from the western edge of the paleovalley. Paleocurrents for the Shinarump Member (Becker, 1986; Stewart and others, 1972) are to the northwest, west, and southwest. The increased thickness of the Shinarump Member in the Wilson Cliffs and Lovell Wash block is interpreted as a tributary to the Vermilion Cliffs paleovalley, but the alternative interpretation—that the palinspastic reconstruction has placed the Wilson Cliffs too far to the west—cannot be ruled out on stratigraphic and sedimentological evidence.

Moenave and Kayenta Formations undivided

Maps for the undivided Moenave and Kayenta stratigraphic units are shown in Figure 12d and e. Figure 12d is a paleotectonic and isopach map for the entire Moenave-Kayenta interval. The position of the volcanic arc and the eastern edge of the Early Jurassic thrust belt delineates the western edge of a trough deepening to the north. The shallow basin in which the Lower Jurassic strata accumulated was supplied with both arc- and craton-derived sediment.

Figure 12e illustrates the distribution, thickness, and presently available paleocurrent data for unit A. Unit A is interpreted as the result of deposition by braided streams on an alluvial fan. Paleocurrent data and isopachous contours define an alluvial fan with a source on the southwest side of the basin. Sediment was transported down-fan toward the north and northeast. This interpretation is consistent with the petrofacies data, which indicate a volcanic and Paleozoic-limestone source. Predominance of cross-stratified sandy conglomerate and conglomeratic sandstone suggests mid-fan deposition for the Wilson Cliffs, Pinto Valley, and Lovell Wash block, whereas distal-fan sedimentation is suggested by finer grain-size, reduced thickness of cross-bed sets, and attenuated thickness at Horse Spring Valley, Frenchman Mountain, and the Valley of Fire.

CONCLUSIONS

At the onset of Cenozoic extension, the eastern limit of Mesozoic compression approximately coincided with the eastern limit of Cenozoic extension (Wernicke and others, 1988). All of the early Mesozoic sedimentary strata described in the foregoing originally lay within a narrow north-south–trending zone between the subsequently developed Sevier thrust belt and the western and southwestern edge of the Colorado Plateau. Although lower Mesozoic outcrops compose but a small percentage of the total surface area over which they are now distributed, when restored to their early Mesozoic positions they are seen to preserve a much more significant proportion of the original sedimentary basins. Facies changes that now appear gradual become very rapid. Within-outcrop variability assumes much greater importance.

Although reconstruction of early Mesozoic sedimentary basins presented here must be viewed as preliminary because of limited data, geologically meaningful patterns have been obtained for all Upper Triassic and Lower and Middle Jurassic stratigraphic units investigated. This result strengthens the belief that interpretations presented are a good first approximation.

After deposition of the Moenkopi Formation during the mid-Triassic hiatus, a calcic soil was developed on the Moenkopi surface over a broad area extending from Colorado to southern Nevada (Stewart and others, 1972; Blakey and Gubitosa, 1983; Lupe and Silberling, 1985). In southern Nevada and along the western edge of the Colorado Plateau, the Chinle depositional sequence was initiated by headward erosion reworking and redepositing the Moenkopi soils to form the limestone-pebble conglomerate (Riley and Marzolf, 1986). Subsequent fluvial degradation cut the Vermilion Cliffs paleovalley through the

limestone-pebble conglomerate into the upper Moenkopi Formation, leaving the limestone-pebble conglomerate along its western margin. Three phases of fluvial erosion and deposition (Blakey and Gubitosa, 1983) transported voluminous fine clastics into a marine basin now preserved in western Nevada (Lupe and Silberling, 1985). In southern Nevada, volcanic clasts in the Shinarump Member of the Chinle Formation were derived from the south and southeast and give no hint of a volcanic arc terrane to the west.

The discordant stratigraphic relation and radical change in paleoslope between the Upper Triassic Chinle Formation and the Lower Jurassic Glen Canyon Group indicate a major change in tectonic setting in Late Triassic to Early Jurassic time. Speculations of an extensional setting (Busby-Spera, 1988) and interpretation of transtensional basins (Oldow and Bartel, 1987) not withstanding, the data presented here argue for initiation of a foreland basin in response to east-vergent thrusting. The age of initiation is constrained as post-Chinle and pre-Moenave (Norian to Hettangian). This age assignment is consistent with radiometric ages of arc volcanics, which indicate Early to Middle Jurassic ages (210 to 167 Ma) (Wright and others, 1981; Riggs and others, 1986; Busby-Spera, 1988). Arc-derived and cratonally derived clastics were shed into a newly created basin from the southwest and northeast, respectively. Arc-derived coarse clastics were shed at right angles or directly opposite to the Late Triassic paleoslope.

Figures 13a–d illustrate successive stages in development of the Glen Canyon depositional sequence. Deformation initiated erosion. The Moenkopi Formation and possibly the Chinle Formation were stripped from the uplifted terrane along with an unknown thickness of Paleozoic strata. Paleozoic-carbonate clasts and volcanic clasts derived from syntectonic volcanism were shed as alluvial fans prograding northeastward into an elongate trough that deepened northward across a marine shelf (Fig. 13a). During the erly stages of trough sedimentation, the southern end of the trough was occupied by a freshwater marsh; northward, more saline conditions prevailed adjacent to the marine shoreline in the vicinity of Valley of Fire. As the arc continued to develop, saline conditions prevailed throughout the trough. In the late stages of trough sedimentation, the Kayenta delta prograded into the trough from the east (Fig. 13b). With continued emergence of the volcanic arc, the sea retreated northward. Wind direction shifted from northwest (Fig. 13c) to northeast (Fig. 13d) (present coordinates), blowing eolian sand into the arc terrane to interfinger with volcanics. Evidence of a falling water table during deposition of the Navajo-Aztec sand sea is consistent with northward retreat of marine environments and increasing elevation of the surface of sand accumulation as the sand sea prograded into the volcanic arc.

The Glen Canyon depositional sequence was terminated by renewed tectonic activity and volcanism in the arc terrane. Renewed subsidence in response to widespread, voluminous silicic volcanism created a deep trough invaded by the Carmel Sea (Blakey and others, 1983). Braided streams and quartz-rich debris

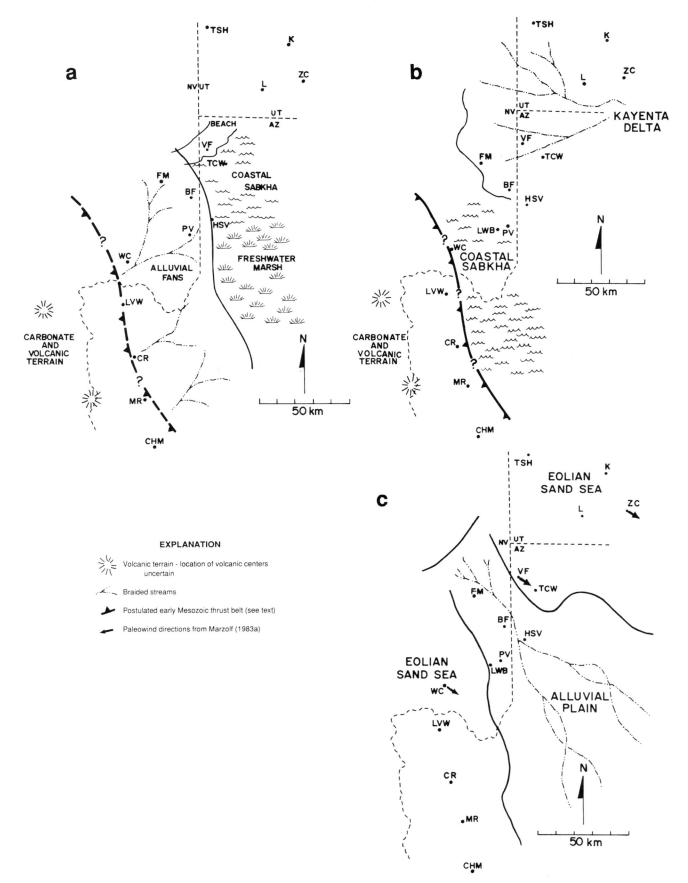

EXPLANATION

☀ Volcanic terrain - location of volcanic centers
uncertain

⋰⋱ Braided streams

◄ Postulated early Mesozoic thrust belt (see text)

← Paleowind directions from Marzolf (1983a)

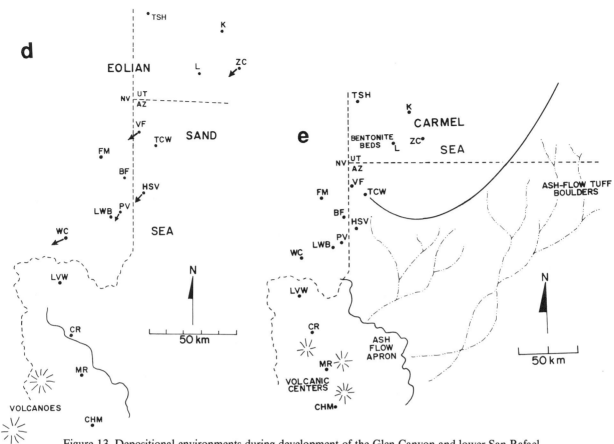

Figure 13. Depositional environments during development of the Glen Canyon and lower San Rafael depositional sequences (location abbreviations same as in Fig. 2). a. Depositional environments during deposition of units A and B and lower part of unit C of the undivided Moenave and Kayenta Formations. b. Depositional environments during deposition of the upper part of unit C and unit D of the undivided Moenave and Kayenta Formations. c. Depositional environments during deposition of the upper part of units C and D of the undivided Moenave and Kayenta Formations and the lower Navajo and Aztec Sandstones. d. Eolian sands spread southwestward into the arc terrane (paleowind directions from Marzolf, 1983a, and unpublished data). e. Depositional environments during deposition of the upper member of the Middle Jurassic Carmel Formation (modified from Blakey and others, 1983; Chapman, 1987).

flows transported volcanic clasts, including boulders of rhyolite tuff, to the southern shore of the sea (Fig. 13e).

Stratigraphic relations between, and facies relations within, lower Mesozoic depositional sequences provide potentially useful strain markers for the palinspastic reconstruction of Cenozoic extension. Most notable is the progressive southwestward truncation of progressively older Triassic strata beneath the basal conglomerate of the undivided Moenave and Kayenta Formations (Fig. 12a). In this regard, the possibility that the limestone- and volcanic-clast conglomerate overlying Lower Triassic strata in the southern Inyo Mountains (Oborne and others, 1983; Stone and Stevens, 1986) may be lithostratigraphically equivalent to the Lower Jurassic basal conglomerate should be considered. The lower Mesozoic rocks of the southern Inyo Mountains lie west of the truncation of the Chinle Formation but sufficiently far east that the uppermost Lower Triassic basinal facies, equivalent to the upper Moenkopi Formation, lie beneath the J-O unconform-

ity. If these speculations prove to be true, they suggest that the Inyo Mountains presently lie far to the west of their preextension position as suggested by Wernicke and others (1988). In similar fashion, conglomerate overlying the upper red member of the Moenkopi Formation in the Meadow Valley Mountains, assigned to the Shinarump Member by Shorb (1983), requires reexamination.

Other stratigraphic horizons that provide potentially useful strain markers include (1) the limestone-pebble conglomerate, not only because it is useful in correct identification of the Shinarump Member but also because its presence or absence indicates the preextension position of Chinle outcrops relative to the Vermilion Cliffs paleovalley; and (2) the basal conglomerate of the Glen Canyon Grup, which because of distinctive lithology and rapid thickness and facies change, has great potential in testing extensional models. Corroboration of the correlation offered here between the rhyolite-tuff–bearing facies of the

Carmel Formation and rhyolite tuffs overlying the Aztec Sandstone in the Mescal Range and the Cowhole Mountains will support the interpretation that the preextension position of the arc terrane lay east of the Colorado River. This interpretation not only largely solves the problem of a source for the rhyolite boulders in the Carmel Formation but also implies that facies change from marginal marine and marine sedimentary strata to pyroclastic and volcanic rocks is rapid. The latter has broader implications for the nature and position of the western boundary of the Twin Creek–Carmel deep marine trough from southern Utah to western Wyoming and southeastern Idaho.

The palinspastic reconstruction offered here generally is in agreement with that of Bohannon (1984). A significant point of departure is the placement of the southern Spring Mountains Mesozoic rocks. Bohannon's (1984) reconstruction is difficult to reconcile with any geologically reasonable interpretation of the basal conglomerate of the Glen Canyon Group. In addition, Bohannon's interpretation requires that either the Spring Mountains block be cut from northeast to southwest by a left-lateral fault for which there is presently no evidence or that the entire Spring Mountains block be translated northward to place the Mescal Range in southeastern Nevada near the present position of Horse Spring Valley. As the entire region east of the Mescal Range all the way to the Colorado Plateau is a Precambrian terrane, return of this terrane almost directly eastward beneath the Colorado Plateau offers a more plausible alternative and is the reconstruction presented here.

Considering the profound effect of Cenozoic extension, all previous paleogeographic and paleotectonic interpretations of the southern Basin and Range that have not taken this effect into account must be viewed with skepticism. Extension not only has greatly expanded cross-sectional geometries and lateral facies changes but also changed the angular relations of stratigraphic or facies boundaries relative to the Colorado Plateau. Such boundaries that now depart from the western edge of the Plateau at a high angle, prior to extension, nearly paralleled the Plateau margin. In the future, stratigraphers must maintain a disciplined freedom to place their measured sections in positions that make good stratigraphic and sedimentologic sense. In a stratigraphic sense, the southern Basin and Range must be treated as a giant three-dimensional puzzle in which fitting a single piece of the puzzle in the correct position for one stratigraphic horizon must, of necessity, be the correct position for all stratigraphic horizons.

ACKNOWLEDGMENTS

An earlier version of this manuscript was reviewed by J. H. Stewart and J. D. Walker. Their helpful criticisms greatly improved this final version. Additional helpful suggestions were made by M. L. Porter, S. R. Rowland, E. T. Walin, and E. I. Smith. Responsibility for any errors or misinterpretations is mine. Assistance of N. Stout and W. Gilmore in preparation of illustrations is gratefully acknowledged. The field research was supported by the Office of Research Development and Administration and the Geology Department at Southern Illinois University at Carbondale.

REFERENCES CITED

Anderson, R. E., 1973, Large-magnitude Late Tertiary strike-slip faulting north of Lake Mead, Nevada: U.S. Geological Survey Professional Paper 794, 18 p.

Ash, S., 1986, Biostratigraphic correlation of the Chinle Formation (Late Triassic) on the Colorado Plateau; A progress report: Geological Society of America Abstracts with Programs, v. 18, p. 338–339.

Becker, J. E., 1986, Sedimentology of the Upper Triassic Shinarump Member of the Chinle Formation, southern Nevada [M.S. thesis]: Carbondale, Southern Illinois University, 121 p.

Bilodeau, W. L., and Keith, S. B., 1986, Lower Jurassic Navajo-Aztec-equivalent sandstones in southern Arizona and their paleogeographic significance: American Association of Petroleum Geologists Bulletin, v. 70, p. 690–701.

Blakey, R. C., and Gubitosa, R., 1983, Late Triassic paleogeography and depositional history of the Chinle Formation, southern Utah and northern Arizona, *in* Reynolds, M. W., and Dolly, E. D., eds., Mesozoic paleogeography of the west-central United States: Rocky Mountain Section, Society of Economic Paleontologists and Mineralogists Rocky Mountain Paleogeography Symposium 2, p. 57–76.

Blakey, R. C., and Middleton, L. T., 1983, Lower Mesozoic stratigraphy and depositional systems, southwest Colorado Plateau, *in* Marzolf, J. E., and Dunne, G. C., eds., Evolution of Early Mesozoic tectonostratigraphic environments; Southwestern Utah to southern Inyo Mountains: Utah Geological and Mineral Survey Special Studies 60, Guidebook Part 2, p. 33–39.

Blakey, R. C., Peterson, F., Caputo, M. B., Geesman, R. C., and Voorhees, B. J., 1983, Paleogeography of Middle Jurassic continental shoreline and shallow marine sedimentation, southern Utah, *in* Reynolds, M. W., and Dolly, E. D.,

eds., Mesozoic paleogeography of the west-central United States: Rocky Mountain Section, Society of Economic Paleontologists and Mineralogists Rocky Mountain Paleogeography Symposium 2, p. 57–76.

Bohannon, R. G., 1979, Strike-slip faults of the Lake Mead region of southern Nevada, *in* Armentrout, J. M., Cole, M. R., and TerBest, H., Jr., eds., Cenozoid paleogeography of the western United States: Pacific Section, Society of Economic Paleontologists and Mineralogists Pacific Coast Paleogeography Symposium 3, p. 129–139.

—— , 1983, Geologic map, tectonic map, and structure sections of the Muddy and northern Black Mountains, Clark County, Nevada: U.S. Geological Survey Miscellaneous Investigations Map I-1406, scale 1:62,500.

—— , 1984, Nonmarine sedimentary rocks of Tertiary age in the Lake Mead region, southeastern Nevada and northwestern Arizona: U.S. Geological Survey Professional Paper 1259, 72 p.

Burchfiel, B. C., and Davis, G. A., 1972, Structural framework and evolution of the southern part of the Cordilleran orogen, western United States: American Journal of Science, v. 272, p. 97–118.

—— , 1975, Nature and controls of Cordilleran orogenesis, western United States: Extensions of an earlier synthesis: American Journal of Science, v. 275-A, p. 363–396.

—— , 1977, Geology of the Sagamore Canyon–Slaughterhouse Spring area, New York Mountains, California: Geological Society of America Bulletin, v. 88, p. 1623–1640.

—— , 1981, Mojave Desert and environs, *in* Ernst, W. G., ed., The geotectonic development of California, Rubey Volume 1: Englewood Cliffs, New Jersey, Prentice-Hall, Inc., p. 217–252.

—— , 1988, Mesozoic thrust faults and Cenozoic low-angle normal faults, eastern Spring Mountains, Nevada, and Clark Mountain thrust complex, California, *in* Weide, D. L., and Faber, M. L., eds., This extended land; Geological journeys in the southern Basin and Range; Geological Society of America Cordilleran Section Field Trip Guidebook: University of Nevada at Las Vegas Geoscience Department Special Publication 2, p. 87–106.

Burchfiel, B. C., Wernicke, B., Willemin, J. H., Axen, G. J., and Cameron, C. S., 1982, A new type of décollement thrusting: Nature, v. 300, p. 513–515.

Burdette, D. J., 1986, Sedimentology of Moenave-Kayenta equivalent strata in the northern Black Mountains, southern Nevada; Early Mesozoic depositional environments and implications for Cenozoic tectonics [M.S. thesis]: Carbondale, Southern Illinois University, 102 p.

Burdette, D. J., and Marzolf, J. E., 1986, Sedimentology of Moenave/Kayenta strata in southern Nevada; Early Mesozoic depositional environments and implications for Cenozoic tectonics: Geological Society of America Abstracts with Programs, v. 18, p. 344.

Busby-Spera, C. J., 1988, Speculative tectonic model for the early Mesozoic arc of the southwest Cordilleran United States: Geology, v. 16, p. 1121–1125.

Carr, M. D., 1980, Upper Jurassic to Lower Cretaceous(?) synorogenic sedimentary rocks in the southern Spring Mountains, Nevada: Geology, v. 8, p. 385–389.

Chapman, M. G., 1987, Depositional and compositional aspects of volcanogenic clasts in the upper member of the Carmel Formation, southern Utah [M.S. thesis]: Flagstaff, Northern Arizona University, 93 p.

Dalrymple, G. B., 1979, Critical tables for conversion of K-Ar ages from old to new constants: Geology, v. 7, p. 558–560.

Dickinson, W. R., 1981, Plate tectonic evolution of the southern Cordillera: Arizona Geological Society Digest, v. 14, p. 113–135.

Dunne, G. C., 1977, Geology and structural evolution of Old Dad Mountain, Mojave Desert, California: Geological Society of America Bulletin, v. 88, p. 737–748.

Evans, J. R., 1971, Geology and mineral deposits of the Mescal Range Quadrangle, San Bernardino County, California: Sacramento, California Department of Conservation Division of Mines and Geology Map Sheet 17, scale 1:62,500.

Glock, W. S., 1929, Geology of the east-central part of the Spring Mountain Range, Nevada: American Journal of Science, v. 17, p. 326–341.

Hamilton, W., 1978, Mesozoic tectonics of the western United States, *in* Howell, D. G., and McDougall, K. A., eds., Mesozoic paleogeography of the western United States: Pacific Section, Society of Economic Paleontologists and Mineralogists Pacific Coast Paleogeography Symposium 2, p. 33–61.

—— , 1987, Mesozoic geology and tectonics of the Big Maria Mountains region, southeastern California, *in* Dickinson, W. R., and Klute, M. A., eds., Mesozoic rocks of southern Arizona and adjacent areas: Arizona Geological Digest, v. 18, p. 33–47.

Harshbarger, J. W., Repenning, C. A., and Irwin, J. W., 1957, Stratigraphy of the uppermost Triassic and the Jurassic rocks of the Navajo Country: U.S. Geological Survey Professional Paper 291, 74 p.

Hewett, D. F., 1931, Geology and ore deposits of the Goodsprings Quadrangle, Nevada: U.S. Geological Survey Professional paper 162, 172 p.

—— , 1956, Geology and mineral resources of the Ivanpah Quadrangle, Nevada and California: U.S. Geological Survey Professional Paper 275, 172 p.

Litwin, R. J., 1986, The palynostratigraphy and age of the Chinle and Moenave Formations, southwestern U.S.A. [Ph.D. thesis]: University Park, Pennsylvania State University, 265 p.

Longwell, C. R., 1928, Geology of the Muddy Mountains, Nevada: U.S. Geological Survey Bulletin 798, 152 p.

Lupe, R., and Silberling, N. J., 1985, Genetic relationship between lower Mesozoic continental strata of the Colorado Plateau and marine strata of the western Great Basin; Significance for accretionary history of Cordilleran lithotectonic terranes, *in* Howell, D. G., ed., Tectonostratigraphic terranes of the Circum-Pacific region: Circum-Pacific Council for Energy and Mineral Resources Earth Science Series 1, p. 263–271.

Luttrell, P. R., 1986, Provenance and basin analysis of the Kayenta Formation (Early Jurassic); central Portion Colorado Plateau: Geological Society of America Abstracts with Programs, v. 18, p. 392.

Marvin, R. F., Wright, J. C., and Walthall, F. G., 1965, K-Ar and Rb-Sr ages of biotite from the Middle Jurassic part of the Carmel Formation, Utah: U.S. Geological Survey Professional Paper 525-B, p. B104–107.

Marzolf, J. E., 1983a, Changing wind and hydrologic regimes during deposition of the Navajo and Aztec Sandstones, Jurassic (?), southwestern United States, *in* Brookfield, M. E., and Ahlbrandt, T. S., eds., Eolian sediments and processes; Developments in sedimentology, v. 38: Amsterdam, Elsevier, p. 635–660.

—— , 1983b, Early Mesozoic eolian transition from cratonal margin to orogenic volcanic arc, *in* Marzolf, J. E., and Dunne, G. C., eds., Evolution of Early Mesozoic tectonostratigraphic environments; Southwestern Utah to southern Inyo Mountains: Utah Geological and Mineral Survey Special Studies 60, Guidebook Part 2, p. 39–46.

—— , 1987, Lower Jurassic overstep of Triassic depositional sequences; Implications for timing of Cordilleran arc development: Geological Society of America Abstracts with Programs, v. 19, p. 762.

—— , 1988, Reconstruction of Late Triassic and Early and Middle Jurassic sedimentary basins; Southwestern Colorado Plateau to the eastern Mojave Desert, *in* Weide, D. L., and Faber, M. L., eds., This extended land; Geological journeys in the southern Basin and Range; Geological Society of America Cordilleran Section Field Trip Guidebook: University of Nevada at Las Vegas Geosciences Department Special Publication 2, p. 177–200.

Marzolf, J. E., and Cole, R. D., 1987, Relationship of the Jurassic volcanic arc to backarc stratigraphy, Cowhole Mountains, San Bernardino County, California, *in* Hill, M. L., ed., Cordilleran Section of the Geological Society of America: Boulder, Colorado, Geological Society of America, The Geology of North America, Centennial Field Guide, v. 1, p. 115–120.

Mitchum, R. M., Jr., Vail, P. R., and Thompson, S. III, 1977, Seismic stratigraphy and global changes of sea level; Part 2, The depositional sequence as a basic unit for stratigraphic analysis, *in* Payton, C. E., ed., Seismic stratigraphy; Applications to hydrocarbon exploration: American Association of Petroleum Geologists Memoir 26, p. 53–62.

Novitsky, J. M., and Burchfiel, B. C., 1973, Pre-Aztec (Upper Triassic(?)–Lower Jurassic) thrusting, Cowhole Mountains, southeastern California: Geological Society of America Abstracts with Programs, v. 5, p. 855.

Novitsky-Evans, J. M., 1978, Geology of the Cowhole Mountains, southern California; Structural, stratigraphic, and geochemical studies [Ph.D. thesis]: Houston, Texas, Rice University, 95 p.

Oborne, M., Fritzche, A. E., and Dunne, G. C., 1983, Stratigraphic analysis of Middle(?) Triassic marine to continental rocks, southern Inyo Mountains, east-central California, *in* Marzolf, J. E., and Dunne, G. C., eds., Evolution of early Mesozoic tectonostratigraphic environments; Southwestern Utah to southern Inyo Mountains: Utah Geological and Mineral Survey Special Studies 60, Guidebook Part 2, p. 54–59.

Oldow, J. S., and Bartel, R. L., 1987, Early to Middle(?) Jurassic extensional tectonism in the western Great Basin; Growth faulting and synorogenic deposition of the Dunlap Formation: Geology, v. 15, p. 740–743.

Peterson, F., 1986, Jurassic paleotectonics in the west-central part of the Colorado Plateau, Utah and Arizona, *in* Peterson, J. A., ed., Paleotectonics and sedimentation in the Rocky Mountain region, United States: American Association of Petroleum Geologists Memoir 41, p. 563–596.

Peterson, F., and Pipiringos, G. N., 1979, Stratigraphic relations of the Navajo Sandstone to Middle Jurassic formations, southern Utah and northern Arizona: U.S. Geological Survey Professional Paper 1035-B, 43 p.

Pipiringos, G. N., and O'Sullivan, R. B., 1978, Principal unconformities in Triassic and Jurassic rocks, western interior United States; A preliminary survey: U.S. Geological Survey Professional Paper 1035-A, 29 p.

Porter, M. L., 1986, Sedimentary record of erg migration: Geology, v. 14, p. 497–500.

Potochnik, M., 1985, Petrology and depositional environment of the Lower

Jurassic Moenave/Kayenta-equivalent strata, southeastern Spring Mountains, southern Nevada [M.S. thesis]: Carbondale, Southern Illinois University, 101 p.

Reynolds, S. J., and Spencer, J. E., 1987, Stratigraphy and U-Th-Pb geochronology of Triassic and Jurassic rocks in west-central Arizona, *in* Dickinson, W. R., and Klute, M. A., eds., Mesozoic rocks of southern Arizona and adjacent areas: Arizona Geological Disgest, v. 18, p. 65–80.

Riggs, N., Mattinson, J. M., and Busby-Spera, C. J., 1986, U-Pb ages of the Mount Wrightson Formation, southern Arizona, and possible correlation with the Navajo Sandstone: EOS Transactions of the American Geophysical Union, v. 64, p. 1249.

Riley, G. W., 1987, Sedimentology and stratigraphy of a limestone-pebble conglomerate at the base of the Late Triassic Chinle Formation, southern Nevada [M.S. thesis]: Carbondale, Southern Illinois University, 180 p.

Riley, G. W., and Marzolf, 1986, A trasported caliche at the top of the Moenkopi Formation; A pre-Chinle event: Geological Society of America Abstracts with Programs, v. 18, 406 p.

Shorb, W. M., 1983, Stratigraphy, facies analysis, and depositional environments of the Moenkopi Formation (Lower Triassic), Washington County, Utah, and Clark and Lincoln Counties, Nevada [M.S. thesis]: Durham, North Carolina, Duke University, 205 p.

Speed, R., and Jones, T. A., 1969, Synorogenic quartz sandstone in the Jurassic mobile belt of western Nevada; Boyer Ranch Formation: Geological Society of America Bulletin, v. 80, p. 2551–2584.

Stanley, K. O., 1971, Tectonic and sedimentologic history of Lower Jurassic Sunrise and Dunlap Formations, west-central Nevada: American Association of Petroleum Geologists Bulletin, v. 55, p. 454–477.

Stewart, J. H., Albers, J. P., and Poole, F. G., 1968, Summary of regional evidence for right-lateral displacement in the western Great Basin: Geological Society of America Bulletin, v. 79, p. 1407–1414.

Stewart, J. H., Poole, F. G., and Wilson, R. F., 1972, Stratigraphy and origin of the Chinle Formation and related Upper Triassic strata in the Colorado Plateau region: U.S. Geological Survey Professional Paper 690, 336 p.

Stone, P. A., and Stevens, C. H., 1986, Triassic marine section at Union Wash, Inyo Mountains, California, *in* Dunne, G. C., compiler, Mesozoic and Cenozoic structural evolutio of selected areas, east-central California, Guidebook for Field Trip 2: Los Angeles, California, Geological Society of America Cordilleran Section Meeting, p. 45–51.

Walker, J. D., Burchfiel, B. C., and Royden, L. H., 1983, Westward-derived conglomerates in the Moenkopi Formation of southeastern California, and their probable significance: American Association of Petroleum Geologists Bulletin, v. 67, p. 320–322.

Weber, M. E., and Smith, E. I., 1987, Structural and geochemical constraints on the reassembly of disrupted mid-Miocene volcanics in the Lake Mead–Eldorado Valley area of southern Nevada: Geology, v. 15, p. 553–556.

Wernicke, B., Guth, P. L., and Axen, G. J., 1984, Tertiary extensional tectonics in the Sevier thrust belt of southern Nevada, *in* Lintz, J., ed., Western geological excursions, v. 4: Reno, University of Nevada Mackay School of Mines, p. 473–510.

Wernicke, B., Axen, G. J., and Snow, J. K., 1988, Basin and Range extensional tectonics at the latitude of Las Vegas, Nevada: Geological Society of America Bulletin, v. 100, p. 1738–1757.

Wilson, R. F., 1958, The stratigraphy and sedimentology of the Kayenta and Moenave Formations, Vermilion Cliffs region, Utah and Arizona [Ph.D. thesis]: Stanford, California, Stanford University, 337 p.

Wilson, R. F., and Stewart, J. H., 1967, Correlation of Upper Triassic(?) formations between southwestern Utah and southern Nevada: U.S. Geological Survey Bulletin 1244-D, 20 p.

Wright, J. E., Haxel, G., and May, D. J., 1981, Early Jurassic uranium-lead isotopic ages for Mesozoic supracrustal sequences, Papago Indian Reservation, southern Arizona: Geological Society of America Abstracts with Programs, v. 13, p. 115.

Zaengle, D. G., 1984, Provenance and depositional environment of the basal conglomerate of the Moenave-Kayenta equivalent strata, Spring Mountains, southern Nevada [M.S. thesis]: Carbondale, Southern Illinois University, 121 p.

MANUSCRIPT ACCEPTED BY THE SOCIETY AUGUST 21, 1989

Index

[Italic page numbers indicate major references]

Typeset by WESType Publishing Services, Inc., Boulder, Colorado
Printed in U.S.A. by Malloy Lithographing, Inc., Ann Arbor, Michigan